COLLEGE ADMINISTRATION
A HANDBOOK

Editor: Ian Waitt

Published by
THE NATIONAL ASSOCIATION OF TEACHERS IN
FURTHER AND HIGHER EDUCATION
Hamilton House, Mabledon Place, London WC1H 9BH

Printed by Victoria House Printing Co (TU), 25 Cowcross Street, London EC1

First Published May 1980

ISBN 0 901390 30 5

CONTENTS

INTRODUCTION

1. This book is primarily a work of reference. It is concerned with the administration of public sector further and higher education in England and Wales. It is intended for the use of educational administrators, elected representatives, teachers, students, and all who have an interest in the operation of the further and higher education system. It is offered to readers in other countries since it both effectively describes our system and offers our experiences and practices for consideration.

2. Although this is a reference book, it is proper to consider its context. The discussion in paragraphs 3-11 below should be appreciated in that light, and not be taken to detract from the practical value which this publication is intended to have.

3. As education is experienced by every citizen, there are many opinions as to what it is, and should be about. It can be all too easily assumed that there are defined national educational objectives. This is not the case. There exist only two governmental sources which state such objectives, and both are severely limited.

4. Initiating the "great debate" about education, the then prime minister stated in 1976:
"The goals of our education, from nursery school through to adult education, are clear enough. They are to equip children to the best of their ability for a lively, constructive place in society and also to do a job of work. Not one or the other, but both... There is a challenge to us all in these days [of scarce resources] and a challenge in education is to examine its priorities and to secure as high efficiency as possible by the skilful use of existing resources."[1]

5. Three statements of further and higher education objectives are to be found in the White Paper of 1972, *Education: A Framework for Expansion*. These are:

   (i) that education must expand if it "is to make its full contribution to the vitality of our society and our economy";
   (ii) that "The further education system has a vital contribution to make in ensuring that the country has a work force capable of meeting – at all levels – the changing demands of industry and commerce"; and
   (iii) that recurrent education, *inter alia*, is "to make good for individuals the absence or loss of earlier opportunities and to encourage the renewal of knowledge and skills made obsolete by the explosion of knowledge and the impact of technology on a rapidly changing environment."[2].

---

1 Speech by the The Rt. Hon. James Callaghan, MP at a foundation stone-laying ceremony at Ruskin College, Oxford. 18 October 1976.

2 *Education: A Framework for Expansion*, Cmnd. 5174, HMSO, 1972, paras. 1, 101. 105.

6. It is a matter of belief whether these goals, in Mr Callaghan's words, are "clear enough"; but they have certainty not been formally defined in a coherent sense. Moreover, the expansionist intent of the 1972 White Paper was frustrated by economic crises and restraints in public expenditure. The issue to be faced therefore, and however regrettably, is the one of administration. Administration here is taken to mean the sum of legislation and practice which determines the operation of the further education service.

7. Such legislation and practice, either by commission or omission, implies the implementation of a philosophy. As we have no written constitution in this country, it is scarcely surprising that we have no coherent, fully stated educational policy: for good or ill we do not possess defined national goals which form a basis for the defining of our educational objectives. Therefore, our actual educational philosophy has to be inferred from our administrative framework – and that framework includes the operation of the law of the land as it affects every individual. However, elements of the framework can be contradictory, be open to different interpretations, and contain significant discretionary areas which may be affected by considerations which have little to do with education.

8. It is necessary to draw attention to a philosophy which does have a certain current acceptance, itself based on an historical growth. The education service is often represented as a partnership between national and local government. While this partnership may at times be strained, and even perhaps more apparent than real, its existence may make inappropriate the search for national policy, or at least qualify the nature of the goals to be achieved. It remains a matter for debate.

9. National educational debate can be inspired by events, and almost casually by a prime minister or secretary of state. There is no national forum for educational debate. There are indeed philosophies which obtain, hold sway, and actually determine how the service is operated but these may be bred in the darkness of governmental process: overall government and local authority spending policies in fact largely decide the nature of education. To argue in isolation for purely educational objectives, therefore, is to make the cardinal error of ignoring that education is part of the political process. It is for such reasons that the title of *College Administration* rather than "College Management" has been chosen for this book.

10. There is a view of a certain currency that administration is some sort of bureaucratic process to be undertaken after management roles, structures and organization have been determined. Management, therefore, becomes the important, dynamic activity; and administration the subservient tool. Such a view may be succinctly described in the context of the education system of this country as a misunderstanding. The constraints upon "management" – in the sense of the term representing the conceptual and actual processes as applied in industry and commerce, especially in the United States of America – are such that as applied to education here, management becomes the means by which limited goals might be achieved.

Much can be achieved by effective and efficient management, and that is an object which this work seeks to promote. The point remains, however, that administrative constaints determine much of the process.

11. This introductory discussion is not intended to imply that the editor, contributors and publisher do not possess opinions as to the aims of education, and the goals to be achieved. NATFHE policy is indicated, usually in appendices or footnotes, where it is considered that issues are acute. However, the essential purpose of the book is to provide the information which will allow for an understanding and appreciation of the processes which determine the nature of public sector post-school education. The complexity of the society in which we live is such that, in most areas of life, the individual has little opportunity ever to understand "the system". Teachers and students are largely unaware, and could scarely be expected to be aware, of all the processes by which their lives in education are governed. It is unreasonable to suppose that educational administrators themselves are constantly aware of every aspect of law, educational provision, and developmental process; and equally unreasonable to expect or require that such persons become polymaths. As a former student of history, I offer the observation that human organizations collapse when they are no longer able to control, or at least effectively ameliorate, the complexity of the society in which they function. Thus, the Roman Empire fell essentially because it could not contain, in any sense, a population explosion in Central Asia; and the regime in Tsarist Russia collapsed because it was not equipped to encounter the problems facing that country in 1917. This is not to argue any grand purpose for this book; it is intended to be of service in its particular area. It can be used as the reader thinks fit: to serve individual or institutional needs, to stimulate discussion, or to serve collective processes. Its intended purpose is to provide information on the operation of a complex system. In the wider sense, it is only with access to such information that there can be informed appreciation and participation in the processes which determine the allocation and use of national educational resources.

12. It is recognised and intended that the book should also be a working manual whereby explanation of particular discrete issues can be readily obtained. It is for this reason that the subtitle, *a handbook*, has been employed. Indeed, this will be of one of the main uses of the book. Information is provided therefore with little comment: it is only in this introduction, perhaps, that axes are being intentionally ground. Where an issue which has provoked comment is discussed, it has been the intention that the arguments or processes should be fairly presented. Where issues involve discretion, in presenting the cases it is the intention to leave the drawing of conclusions to the reader. Further, while the nature of our educational system is such that it is at times necessary to offer advice, the advice extended in the text sometimes represents the advocacy of good practice: it is not obligatory, and the status of the advice is made clear.

13. As this work has been required to provide legal guidance, to be descriptive, and also to present issues for debate, its style varies according to topic. For example, the sub-section on staff development is largely occupied with

discussion, and the sub-section concerning employment law is a summary of legal provision. Thus, the nature of the writing varies. No apology is made for the precision of language employed where legal matters are discussed for it is vital to safeguard against misunderstandings. **It must also be stated that the legal guidance is no more than that: while every attempt has been made to ensure accuracy, an individual contemplating legal action must seek professional advice and not act solely on an assumed understanding of the information provided here. All information contained in this book, as far as could be ascertained, was correct at the time of going to press.** Where topics are largely those for debate, an essay style has been adopted. Where possible, comment has been separated from fact. The usual pattern in the book is for discussion, where it is employed, to follow the provision of factual information.

14. There are occasions where comment is offered, and where certain practices are criticised. This criticism is intended to be constructive. We are justified in having a certain pride in elements of our education system, but that is not to say that it is not capable of significant improvement.

15. In order to provide internal cross-referencing – essential in the description of a system which overlaps and intertwines – while also allowing for the study in depth of particular topics, the book is arranged in numbered Sections and paragraphs. Sections are divided into numbered sub-sections. For example, a textual reference to Section **1.2.**40 refers to Section **1**, sub-section **2**, paragraph 40. Where Sections are complete in themselves and have no sub-sections, the second number in bold type is omitted. Thus a reference to Section **9.**12 refers to paragraph 12 of Section **9.** The arrangement of the book into Sections which, for ease of reference, are largely discrete has entailed in some instances a certain repetition. However where information has been given in outline for a certain purpose – for example, in detailing the legal structure of further and higher education – a fuller treatment of the topic will generally be found under the relevant Section. In order to prevent confusion with statute, section numbers of Acts of Parliament are abbreviated throughout to s.

16. The diversity of the types of institution which form establishments of further and higher education is such that the only convenient word which can be used to describe them is "colleges". Thus, except where a particular type of institution is discussed, the word "college" is used throughout.

17. References, as sources and for further reading, are supplied at the end of each sub-section. Annotation appears at the foot of pages. The notes are numbered consecutively within sub-sections. A list of abbreviations used both in the text and in the context of the educational system forms Section **1.4.**

18. The names of the contributors to the book are given under their contribution title in the table of contents. Where a name is not given, the Section or sub-section has been written by the editor, except in the cases of Sections **2.2.**54, **10.2** and **11.10.**78 where a joint or separate authorship is indicated in

annotation or in the text. Where the editor has been given significant assistance in the preparation of a sub-section, the persons providing the assistance are given full acknowledgement in paragraph 27 below.

19. The book is published by the National Association of Teachers in Further and Higher Education (NATFHE) with assistance from an Editorial Advisory Board. The Board consists of persons of expertise who have a professional interest in educational administration at national levels. The membership of the Board is:

G M Lee (Chairman); J C N Baillie; W A G Easton; John Farrow; Jean Finlayson; A G Gronow; Peter Knight; Paula Lanning; R G Morris; Keith Scribbins; L K Street; and C A Thompson.

20. The Board has offered advice and comment at each stage in the drafting of the book. I am greatly indebted for the advice and help which I have received. Every attempt has been made to incorporate the views expressed by Board members. Where, in very few cases as it happens, there have been disagreements I have been guided in making editorial decisions by the balance of opinion. Any errors of fact or judgement, however, are my own.

21. Contributors have also been able to comment, at each stage of drafting. I thank them for their considerable help and concern, and also wish to express my appreciation to them for their prompt delivery of copy, and co-operation in completing this undertaking. In particular I would like to thank those contributors who undertook at unavoidably short notice what have been considerable tasks.

22. Various experts have assisted me in the preparation of the book by offering advice and commenting on drafts. I would like to express my thanks to: W.L. Browne (Director, Colleges of Education Redeployment Bureau); John Mockford (ILEA); Beryl Sowerbutts (Central Register and Clearing House); Brian A. McAndrew, Chief Personnel Officer of the City of Bradford Metropolitan Council, and his staff; Denis Coe, Diana Barr and James Allen (National Bureau for Handicapped Students): Phil Barnett, Steven Bryson, Sue Edwards and Michael A. Jacoby (National Union of Students); Val Benson (Divisional Careers Officer, ILEA); John Huitson (former Principal, Darlington College of Education); K.P. Jones (County Architect, Gwent); J.R.M. Davies (Director of Education, The Publishers Association/Educational Publishing Council); W.F. Dennison and J.C. Tyson (School of Education, University of Newcastle upon Tyne); Graham Clayton (Solicitor, NATFHE); F.C.A. Cammaerts (Principal, Rolle College); W.A.C. Kendall (The College, Swindon); R.P. Grace (Newcastle Polytechnic); J.W.P. Taylor (Redland College, Bristol); Nanette Whitbread (Leicester Polytechnic), Isla Evans (Central Bureau for Educational Visits and Exchanges); Colin J. Marsh; John Bagshaw and Eric Hardy (Newcastle College of Arts and Technology); Geoffrey Lyons and Vernon Trafford (Anglian Regional Management Centre); D.L. Parkes (Coombe Lodge); Tom Driver (former General Secretary, NATFHE); S.J. Tarling (Principal

Education Officer, Oxfordshire County Council); and the County Treasurer's Department, Lancashire County Council.

23. Lynton Gray, a major contributor to the book, wishes to acknowledge the help which he has received from Jo Aitken (Finance Officer, North East London Polytechnic), Dereck Thomas (Treasurer, Surrey County Council); Dr Peter Dixon (Education Officer, EEC), Norman Stone (Director of Information, MSC) and John McKelvie (Information Officer, MSC). Keith Scribbins, another major contributor, wishes to acknowledge the assistance given by Lesley Edwards and Joan Gordon (Administrative Assistants, NATFHE) for the work they have done over several years on the Colleges of Education (Compensation) Regulations without which the book's sub-section on this topic could not have been written; he is indebted to Frank Walton (Deputy Secretary, LACSAB) for the discussions which they have had on the vagaries of these regulations. He wishes also to acknowledge the assistance he has received from Roy Bayliss (Dacorum College), John Jones (HM Detention Centre, Usk, Gwent) and Lesley Edwards in the preparation of Section **11.14**. Peter Dawson wishes to acknowledge assistance received from Peter Coles (Association of County Councils) and the Association of Agricultural Education Staffs. Paula Lanning wishes to acknowledge the generous help given by Rodney Bickerstaffe and Harold Wilde (NUPE) and Alison Mitchell (NALGO) in the preparation of Sections **11.8** and **9** and also, in respect of the latter, Charles Donnett (GMWU), John Jones (ATPE), Lucia Jones (AACE), Mick Martin (TGWU), John Parrett (AAES) and Tom Robb (NSAE).

24. The publishers are grateful to HMSO, the DES, CIPFA, and the AAES for permission to quote from copyright material, and the NFER for permission to quote from *Head's Tasks* by Geoffrey Lyons.

25. In making my particular acknowledgements, I wish to thank Paul Smith, Juliet S. Newone, and all those who have rendered into typescript my invariably untidy manuscript; Dianne Howard (NATFHE Assistant Librarian) for greatly facilitating the tasks of research; Maureen Smith and Janet Johnson (NATFHE print staff) for greatly aiding speed of production; and Peter Dawson and the headquarters staff and officials of NATFHE for their patient help and encouragement.

26. I am especially grateful to John Baillie, Paul Bennett, Jean Bocock, Alun Gronow and Peter Knight for their careful, precise and always stimulating comments. To Bob Morris I owe a large debt, and I wish to thank him for his generous assistance and always perceptive, challenging and rigorous comment. I wish to thank Jack Hendy for commenting so helpfully, and for his incisive, illuminating advice and guidance delivered always with wit and precision; and also Tom Driver and Bill Easton for their kind and painstaking assistance at a time when it was most needed. John Baillie and Paula Lanning have shared with me the task of proof reading.

27. There are three people whom I wish thank above all. Paula Lanning has assisted me immeasurably by her patience, kindness and unfailing help and

encouragement. Section **2.2** could not have been written without the great assistance given by Lyn Gray; and nor could Sections **11.1** and **11.3** have ever been completed without formidable help from Keith Scribbins. Indeed, without the personal generosity, friendship, dedication and wealth of experience so freely given by Keith and Lyn, I could not have completed my task. I hope that the publication of this book will in some measure reward their efforts, for I shall remain personally forever in their debt.

28. Finally, I wish to express my sincere thanks and gratitude to Malcolm Lee and the NATFHE members of the Editorial Advisory Board for inviting me to undertake what has been an arduous but immensely exciting and invigorating task, and for sustaining and supporting me during its progress. I am deeply grateful for the opportunity which I have been afforded and it is my hope that this book, the result of their confidence, will be of service to NATFHE, and to further and higher education.

Ian Waitt
March 1980

Section 1

INSTITUTIONS OF FURTHER AND HIGHER EDUCATION: THEIR FUNCTION AND STATUS

1 INTRODUCTORY NOTE

1. This Section is largely concerned with the current function and status of further and higher education. In order to offer an explanation of any coherence, it is necessary to duplicate some of the information contained elsewhere in this book; but even then, many complex issues have to be compressed. Indication is given in the text, therefore, where particular issues can be more fully pursued.

2. Although it is the usual practice in this publication to provide annotation at the foot of the page wherever a source is referred to in the text, in the case of sub-section **2**, below, the amount of annotation required would be excessive. In this case only, therefore, official reports are not referred to in annotation in full wherever they are quoted but a list of selected reports is included instead as sub-section **5.** Similarly, further education, like so many services, makes use of a wide variety of abbreviations and acronyms, and while it is the usual practice to give the full title of an abbreviated term followed by the abbreviation in the rest of the text, it is appropriate here to offer a general glossary. An abbreviations list, therefore, forms sub-section **4.**

2 FURTHER AND HIGHER EDUCATION – ITS DEVELOPMENT FROM 1944 AND CURRENT FUNCTION

1. The Education Act, 1944 requires every local education authority to provide "adequate facilities" for further education in its area. Further education is defined as being full or part-time education and leisure time occupation for persons over compulsory school-leaving age. This education could and did vary from courses of an advanced and specialised nature to courses intended simply to provide training for leisure. As the system developed it became common to distinguish between "technical, commercial, and art" education and "other" further education and, later, between further and higher education. Especially since the establishment and growth of the polytechnics, the terminology "further and higher education" has implied a distinction between the types of post school education which are provided under the maintained sector of the binary system. The "binary system" is the term used to describe the twin methods of educational provision for persons over the compulsory school leaving age: there are the universities which are funded mainly by central government through the University Grants Committee (UGC) and are largely autonomous; and there are the colleges which are maintained by local education authorities (whose finances are supported by government funds : see Sections **3, 4** and **8**). Maintained institutions can indeed be distinguished on occasion, by reference to the types of courses which they provide, as places of further or higher education; but in the matter of the statutes to which they are subject – and hence for all administrative purposes – they are correctly termed establishments of further education. The same observation applies to voluntary and direct grant institutions. These institutions exist in parallel to the maintained sector.

2. Although the statutory framework of further education is investigated under sub-section **3**, below, it is important to note here that there is now an administrative coherence obtaining in the maintained further education system which makes for an easier understanding than obtained formerly. Teacher education has been integrated within the system after two centuries of varying status. In appreciating that since The Further Education Regulations 1975, as amended 1976 and 1977, govern the system under and in conjunction with various statutes, it is proper to refer to "further education" for administrative purposes, it remains now by discussing the system's growth to attempt to demonstrate how the current position developed.

3. The County Colleges which the Education Act, 1944 sought to have established were not, in fact, created. Many local authorities had made provision for what was then largely known as technical education before 1944, but such provision was discretionary only. This provision was made obligatory by the 1944 Act and in consequence was greatly increased in the immediate post war years, but without any particular coherence: although local education authorities were required to submit their "schemes of further education" to the Ministry and consult with other authorities in their region,

they tended to act unilaterally. This resulted in course overlap, a problem compounded by restrictions on new buildings: further education suffered from a similarity in appearance to a patchwork quilt. Moreover, the 1944 Act imposed a duty to provide only "adequate facilities" for further education, a phrase capable of varying interpretation. However, regional collaboration among LEAs has strengthened over the years since 1944.

4. The Percy Report of 1945 made important recommendations for higher technological education. Most of the recommendations were implemented. Regional Advisory Councils (RACs) were set up (where not already in being) to co-ordinate technical studies on a regional basis, and to ensure consultation with industry concerning the provision of necessary courses. The National Advisory Council on Education for Industry and Commerce was set up to advise the Minister for Education and the UGC. Limited numbers of specialised colleges were created to develop technological courses comparable in standard to those leading to university degrees.

5. By 1956 a discernible pattern had emerged. Regional colleges offered courses which included advanced full-time and sandwich courses of university first degree and postgraduate standard. Area colleges offered a variety of courses, some of which were advanced, on a mainly part-time basis. Local colleges offered mainly non-advanced part-time vocational courses. The evening institutes provided mainly recreational courses, although in some cases this was supplemented by vocational courses, some of a fairly advanced nature.

6. Government acceptance of the 1956 White Paper, *Technical Education,* led to the expansion of further education. Certain of the regional colleges were designated as Colleges of Advanced Technology (CATs). These colleges were to engage in advanced level work and be controlled by independent governing bodies. By 1961 the CATs had been taken out of the local authority framework and had become national, direct grant institutions funded by the Ministry of Education and independently governed. During the subsequent decade all the CATs obtained university status (see paragraph 9, below).

7. The Diploma in Technology suggested by the Percy Report was implemented by the National Council for Technological Awards. This Council was created in 1955 and made its first award in 1958. It was superseded by the Council for National Academic Awards (CNAA) in 1964. This body validates degree courses and awards degrees to students in maintained institutions and certain voluntary and direct grant institutions.

8. Development of further education was greatly influenced by the publication of the Carr Report in 1958, and the Crowther Report in 1959. The Carr Report, *Training for skill : recruitment and training of young workers in industry,* recommended that industrial training should remain the responsibility of industry. The Industrial Training Council was set up in 1958. The Crowther Report, *15 to 18,* was highly influential in the development of further education. It suggested that the service be expanded to provide an alternative route for continuing education for all young people. The

alternative would consist of an education which had breadth and humanity as well as a "practical" bias, and offer a choice to the route of grammar school and higher education. The Crowther Report gave rise to the 1961 White Paper, *Better Opportunities in Technical Education,* which recommended the creation of courses for the training of junior technicians, craftsmen and operatives. Crowther had emphasised the importance of day release and the closer integration of further with secondary education. Most local colleges soon acted upon the White Paper recommendations and as the evening institutes largely concentrated their efforts on the operation of recreational classes and some non-advanced vocational courses, so the current pattern began to emerge.

9. The Robbins Report of 1963, *Higher Education,* led to the establishment of the CNAA and the completion of the transition of the CATs into universities. The White Paper of 1966, *A Plan for Polytechnics and Other Colleges,* led to the creation of the polytechnics. The polytechnics were formed from among those regional colleges which had not become CATs. Often this was done by the amalgmation of several institutions. Many art colleges merged with polytechnics. The setting up of polytechnics, the first of which was given conditional approval in 1968, was intended to meet the demand for higher education within the further education system whilst not prejudicing the opportunities of students following non-advanced courses. Concentration of full-time advanced courses in polytechnics was intended to promote efficiency and economy. Opportunities were to be created for part-time students and students from the local community. Although the Committee of Directors of Polytechnics (CDP) has recommended that polytechnics should, like universities, be granted Royal Charters to make them independent of local authorities, the Secretary of State for Education and Science rejected this proposition in December 1979, stating also that polytechnics should concentrate on fulfilling vocational objectives.

10. The Henniker-Heaton Report of 1964, *Day Release,* recommended by 1969 that there should be a doubling in the number of young employees released to attend day classes, and that in the first instance day release should be tailored to the types of education supplied by the further education service. This Report was widely criticised for its omissions and did not produce any real expansion of release. However, the Industrial Training Act 1964 recognised that for training to be effective it could not be left to the voluntary provision of industry. The Act empowered the creation of Industrial Training Boards (ITBs) which ary responsible for ensuring that the training provided is adequate to meet industrial needs. The lack of strength of the Henniker-Heaton Report has been attributed to the anticipation at the time that the Industrial Training Act would be firmer, ensuring that day-release was associated with training for workers of all levels. Whilst the quality of training improved as a result of the activities of the ITBs, the numbers of those following further education day and block release courses declined. Between 1971 and 1977 there was a decline of 20% in the numbers of day and block release enrolments.

11. The Employment and Training Act 1973 amended certain of the provisions

of the 1964 Act. Certain companies were exempted from the levy raised by the ITBs. This levy is raised from companies for the purposes of approved training. The approved training is conducted partially in colleges and partially in industry. The 1973 Act also created the Manpower Services Commission (MSC) which took over the responsibilities for training of the Department of Employment.

12. The MSC operates by way of divisions such as the Employment Service Division (ESD) and the Training Services Division (TSD). Various schemes administered by the MSC entailed colleges having to make provision for increased numbers of students undertaking training courses. Some MSC funded courses occur in government skillcentres. These courses and the topics mentioned in paragraph 11, above, are referred to in more detail in Section **4,** below, but it is important here to note that the further education service has had to expand its training capacity and provision in order to service them, although current restrictions on expenditure may result in a reduction in the numbers of MSC sponsored students and courses.

13. To return to the theme of further education development, the Haslegrave Report of 1969 recommended the establishment of bodies which would validate courses and certification on a national basis in the fields of technician and business education. This is being achieved by way of the Technician Education Council (TEC) and Business Education Council (BEC). These councils were set up in 1973 and 1974 respectively and resulted from the Haslegrave Report. The aims expressed by Haslegrave were being catered for at the time by City and Guilds of London Institute and other courses (see Section **10.2**). The Russell Report of 1973 was concerned with the planned development of adult education. Partly as a result of this report there has been an increase in the provision of courses of various kinds for those groups of people who may be described as disadvantaged. Russell noted the concern for these groups, and pressed for further course development. The Russell Committee was asked to assess needs and make recommendations to obtain "the most economical development of available resources to enable adult education to make its proper contribution to the national system of education conceived of as a process continuing through life." Russell suggested that there should be a stage of education which was identifiably adult, and that the needs of certain groups must be taken into account in future planning. Examples of these groups are the disadvantaged, the retired, and those, such as elected representatives, undertaking new responsibilities. Russell's recommendations for a Development Council for Adult Education and local councils and sub-committees have not yet been fully implemented, although the Development Council proposal has been partially met by the setting up of ACACE (but see paragraph 20 (vi)). Although the varieties of further education remain diverse, and while the courses taught vary immensely, there has been a continuing movement towards administrative coherence. Also, there has been a movement in further education away from purely "training" schemes to what may be described as schemes of further education. This has led on occasions to an inappropriate split between education and training (cf Sections **4** and **6.2**-**6.3**).

14. The growth of teacher education had begun with a voluntary provision supplemented by maintained institutions only during the current century. There were thus separate funding and administrative arrangements. The McNair Report of 1944 contained recommendations which led to the establishment of Area Training Organizations (see Section **8.**66) in the form of university institutes and schools of education. The Robbins Report of 1963 led to the Secretary of State approving the new title of colleges of education, and the closer academic connection of the colleges with the universities (including the arrangement for the validation of degrees whereby a college student could gain the degree of a university). College administration however, unlike the arrangements for CATs, was left within the hands of the existing maintaining bodies. Thus local authorities continued to have responsibility for their colleges, and the various voluntary bodies (such as the Church of England, and the Catholic Church: see Section **2.2,** Appendix 5) for theirs. The voluntary bodies received a direct grant from the Department of Education and Science.

15. The 1971 James Report, *Teacher Education and Training,* offered avenues for development – some of which, especially where the universities were affected, were acted upon, particularly in-service provision – but did not at the time receive the entire attention it deserved since not all of the evidence on which its recommendations were made was released to the public. The Secretary of State outlined the proposals for the Diploma in Higher Education (DipHE) and the integration into the further education system of the colleges of education in the 1972 White Paper, *Education: A Framework for Expansion.* The Further Education Regulations 1975 brought teacher education into the further education system. Administrative coherence was however accompanied by drastic change.

16. "College reorganization" has entailed the closure of many of the colleges of education, the amalgamation of some, and the merger of others with polytechnics and universities. In many cases merger has meant disguised closure. The basic problems of a falling birth rate, existing over provision, and the monotechnic base of teacher education, required change. The Department of Education and Science took that opportunity to effect much larger changes, some of which have been subject to cogent criticism. Where colleges of education survived or amalgamated they have been largely required to diversify. This has generally meant the provision of degree and DipHE courses. Relatively few "monotechnics", that is, colleges providing solely teacher education courses, continue in existence. The colleges which have survived, diversified and amalgamated have often adopted the designation of "institutes" or "colleges of higher education". These terms label the colleges fairly accurately, but they are not legally precise.

17. The status of the colleges of higher education therefore remains in doubt especially since in January 1980, the DES was planning a far-reaching rationalization of higher education courses (the purposes being to eliminate duplication, save money and allow new initiatives). The status of the colleges of higher education however is not merely one of having achieved current

survival. The diversification of colleges and institutes of higher education has been primarily into liberal arts courses, thereby providing a complementary function to certain areas of polytechnic work, which have a more vocational base. Cuts in teacher training provision and changes of policy have made planning difficult, as well as leaving staff with feelings of insecurity. Diversification in the colleges of higher education has been achieved at the cost of great effort, and often with arguably inadequate resources. Patterns of diversification are discussed in Section **10.2.**52 but the problem relates to all colleges rather than just those of higher education. As is demonstrated in paragraphs 28, 30 and 37, below, there will be a decline in the numbers of the age group which most usually undertakes advanced level courses in the late 1980s. It may well be that changes in the further education service as a whole will compensate for this fall in numbers. It must be said that in any event, and quite apart from the expenditure cuts afflicting education, that further education must prepare itself once again for considerable changes in its function and status.

18. The 1978 Oakes Report was concerned with the management of higher education in the maintained sector. It recommended the creation of a National Body to be concerned with demand (and by inference, standards) and costing for higher education whilst nonetheless recommending that individual maintaining and governing bodies should retain overall management control. The establishment of nine new regional councils was also recommended. The Oakes Committee regarded its recommendation that individual maintaining and governing bodies should directly meet part of the cost of higher education which they provide to be essential to the welfare of the maintained system, since this was a vital safeguard to both prudent management and freedom from absolute central control.

19. Although not the subject of a recommendation since it was outside the terms of reference, the Oakes Report records its belief that direct grant institutions should continue, and not be isolated by any management changes from the maintained sector. It is not likely that the Oakes Report will be implemented in the near future; and the Government has not thus far established machinery for consultation about the national planning of advanced further education. Certainly, any implementation of Oakes, however partial, will have consequences for the whole further education service. With the caveats in mind of diversification, future changes in the numbers and types of student, and possible changes in the education structure, arising from the policies of the Government elected in May 1979, it is now appropriate to investigate the current situation.

20. Current further education provision may be categorised in institutional terms thus:
    (i) *Polytechnics.* The 30 polytechnics in England and Wales complement the universities and cater for full-time, sandwich and part-time study at all levels of higher education. Various colleges of education have been amalgamated with the polytechnics.
    (ii) *Other maintained and assisted major establishments.* This somewhat unwieldy title, usually shortened to "other major establishments"

embraces the former area and local colleges, encompasses establishments with names such as "college of technology", "technical college", and "college of further education", and also includes the new "colleges of higher education." A "major establishment" is one with daytime as well as evening courses but may be defined in practice as an establishment of further education, other than a polytechnic, maintained or assisted by a local education authority and providing courses in teacher training, art, agricultural, commercial, technical and other subjects. Reference is still commonly made to "local colleges," however. There were 563 major establishments in England and Wales in November 1976. A decline in this number has occurred because of teacher education reorganization, and a further decline is possible.

(iii) *Direct-grant establishments.* This designation is used to describe major establishments which receive direct grant aid from the DES. Music colleges are examples of such establishments. The designation also includes certain agricultural establishments run by governing bodies on behalf of charitable trusts in receipt of grant on a deficiency basis from the DES, and also various national and local colleges which provide further education courses and receive a DES direct grant.

(iv) *Voluntary Colleges.* This term refers to institutions, often colleges of education (which may therefore have become "colleges of higher education") which were established by educational foundations rather than local authorities. They are often denominational, and are maintained by grant aid from the DES (see also Section **2.2** Appendix 5).

(v) *Independent Colleges.* This term is used in certain circumstances to embrace categories iii and iv: see also the distinction made in sub-paragraph vii, and paragraph 22, below. There were 61 such establishments in England and Wales in November 1976.

(vi) *Adult education centres.* These are establishments maintained by local authorities which provide a wide range of courses, usually non-advanced. Many of these courses are of a recreational nature and are mainly provided for evening students. The centres have a variety of names, and the old established term "evening institute" remains in use in some places. Adult education centres are frequently accommodated in premises which are used by the day for similar or other educational purposes: the buildings occupied are often those of schools and colleges. The term "adult education centre" is used to include all maintained, non-residential institutes of adult education, community centres, village halls, and youth and other clubs which operate classes or courses which are supervised by paid instructors. There were 6,242 adult education centres in England and Wales in November 1976. Adult education centres are subject to local administrative differences. Distinctions are often made between the administration of urban and rural centres. They may be administered and financed by way of secondary school allowances, or they can be dealt with as an annexe of a local education authority's further education provision. Although the centres are often physically based in schools, most local authorities are attempting to establish close links and liaison between the adult education institutions and the local further education college. The courses offered in adult education represent a significant service to the community. The provision includes education for leisure, leisure facilities, remedial education, the opportunity to develop skills, courses designed to allow consideration of the problems facing society, and courses and facilities for the disadvantaged and physically and mentally handicapped. There has been a large growth in the provision of adult literacy programmes. The Advisory Council for Adult and Continuing Education (ACACE) was established to facilitate policy development throughout adult education but, as a result of the recommendations of the White Paper, *Report on Non-Departmental Public Bodies*, Cmnd. 7797, HMSO, 1980 will not be reappointed after its current three year term. Certain adult education courses are provided by "responsible bodies". These bodies are the Workers' Educational Association, the Welsh National Council of Young Men's Christian Association, and university extra mural departments; and the provision made may be described as complementary to that of the maintained further education system. Full-time courses lasting one or two years are provided in six long term residential colleges. Short-term residential colleges provide residential courses lasting a few days. Some voluntary institutions, such as the National Federation of Women's Institutes and Young Men's Christian Association also provide adult education in their specialist fields of interest.

(vii) *Independent establishments recognised as efficient.* The DES operates a procedure whereby independent institutions may be given an approved status by being recognised as efficient. Often these institutions engage in the teaching of English to foreign students; and their courses are at the non-advanced level. In November 1976 there were 108 independent establishments recognised as efficient. Although the DES and LEAs have no statutory powers to control or monitor the provision offered (which is broadly comparable to parts of the FE system) in independent establishments, many such institutions apply for recognition. The DES encourages LEAs to take an interest in independent establishments and draw attention to the significance of efficiency recognition. After recognition, establishments are open to inspection by HMI. The Council for Accreditation of Correspondence Colleges (CACC) and the Association of Recognised English Language Schools (ARELS) establish and monitor standards for their colleges. These standards are closely related to those of the DES.

21. As it is a partnership between voluntary youth organizations, LEAs and central government, it is inappropriate to include the youth service in the summary above. However, there is co-operation and liaison between the various bodies making provision for youth. There are approximately 3,000 full-time youth and community workers, and many paid and voluntary part-time youth workers. Urdd Gobaith Cymru (Welsh League of Youth) has the function of encouraging the young in Wales to participate in Welsh cultural activities. The National Youth Bureau, a body funded largely by the DES,

provides information, training and research services to both statutory and voluntary bodies.

22. The total number of maintained, assisted and grant aided establishments in England and Wales in November 1976 was 6,896. This figure includes certain independent colleges. There are 40 independent colleges which operate as limited companies or charitable trusts but may receive a central government grant. The grant may be of up to 100% of the colleges' capital and running costs. These institutions in 1975/76 had over 47,000 full-time and sandwich course students. The types of such institutions are: former voluntary colleges of education, which may have amalgamated; mixed institutions created by the merger of a voluntary college with an LEA college; five polytechnics which are assisted by the Inner London Education Authority; and ten direct grant further education institutions which are grant-aided by the DES.

23. **Higher education: advanced further education**

The DES often uses the term advanced further education (AFE) to refer to the higher education component of the further education system, i.e. excluding the universities. Advanced courses are defined, for the purposes of DES statistical analyses, as courses followed by students undertaking postgraduate, post-diploma or research work; courses in preparation for university first and higher degrees; CNAA first and higher degrees (including the former Diploma in Art and Design and the Higher Diploma in Art and Design); Higher Diplomas and Certificates of TEC and BEC; the Higher National Diploma or Certificate; the Diploma in Management Studies; or a final professional examination or college Diploma or Associateship if above the standard of instruction required for the Ordinary National Certificate, or General Certificate of Education (advanced level), or any course of study of an equivalent standard. In the case of certain courses, the later year or years are treated as advanced and the earlier year(s) as non-advanced.

24. As it takes considerable time before statistics can be processed and published, many of the figures quoted below refer to the period 1975/76. Where projected figures are quoted, it has to be remembered that these are estimates only and may not always accurately foreshadow the actual result. The numbers of full-time and sandwich students undertaking courses of higher education in England and Wales during the last two decades are:[1]

---

1 Tables and statistics quoted below are drawn from: *The Management of Non-University Higher Education,* DES Report on Education No.90 May 1977; *Report of the Working Group on the Management of Higher Education in the Maintained Sector,* Cmnd. 7130, HMSO; *Further Education,* DES Statistics of Education 1976 Vol.3, HMSO; *Teachers,* DES Statistics of Education 1976 Vol.4, HMSO; *Non-advanced Further Education* DES Report on Education Number 94, December 1978; and *Future Trends in Higher Education,* DES March 1979. The statistics quoted do not all refer to the same year. This inconsistency results from the availability of sources at the time of writing. Uniformity of information can be obtained from the most recent DES *Statistics of Education* publications.

Table 1

Public sector higher education student numbers

1954/55	1962/63	1969/70	1974/75	1978/79 (Estimated Dec. 1978)
34,400	85,750	190,200	210,230	219,000

These figures include CATs up to the time at which they became universities, and also include the colleges of education. During 1974/75, public sector student numbers reached parity with those at universities but since that time they have fallen below university numbers. There were some 7,000 more students following university courses in 1975/76, and the DES anticipates that there will be 60,000 more students following such courses in 1982/83 (cf also paragraph 37, below).

Table 2

AFE enrolments November 1976, at maintained, assisted and grant aided establishments

A: ENROLMENT ACCORDING TO TYPE & INSTITUTION

	Polytechnics	*Other maintained major establishments*	*Direct grant*	*Total major establishments*	*Adult education centres*	*Total grant-aided*
Full-time	74,282	64,114	32,902	171,298	—	171,298
Short full-time	832	935	—	1,767	—	1,767
Sandwich	32,885	7,924	648	41,457	—	41,457
Total full-time and sandwich	107,999	72,973	33,550	214,522	—	214,522
Block release	1,360	1,717	14	3,091	—	3,091
Day release	32,604	45,610	49	78,263	—	78,263
Total released	33,964	47,327	63	81,354	—	81,354
Other part-time day	4,351	2,552	206	7,109	97	7,206
Total part-time day	38,315	49,879	269	88,463	97	88,560
Evening only	16,164	20,236	203	36,603	359	36,962
Total all modes	162,478	143,088	34,022	339,588	456	340,044

NB: Table 2A includes evening courses at adult education centres; these courses are not shown in table 2B

B: ENROLMENT ACCORDING TO QUALIFICATION AIM

AFE (Full-time and sandwich)	
Higher degree, postgraduate and research	3,913
Postgraduate teacher training	4,972
University first degree	4,449
CNAA first degree	66,522
Initial teacher training	79,169
HND/HNC	14,758
TEC/BEC higher certificate/ diploma	7,948
Dip HE	1,952
Professional qualifications	19,219
College diploma/certificate	10,501
Other advanced	1,119
Total advanced	214,522
AFE (Part-time day)	
Higher degree, postgraduate and research	5,891
University first degree	265
CNAA first degree	3,925
HND/HNC	26,749
TEC/BEC higher certificate/ diploma	7,456
Dip HE	79
Professional qualifications	36,846
College diploma/certificate	2,506
Other advanced	4,746
Total advanced	88,463
AFE (Evening only)	
Higher degree, postgraduate and research	2,138
University first degree	1,055
CNAA first degree	1,432
HND/HNC	1,704
TEC/BEC higher certificate/ diploma	2,669
Dip HE	5
Professional qualifications	23,651
College diploma/certificate	698
Other advanced	3,251
Total advanced	36,603

25. Table 2 illustrates AFE enrolments at maintained, assisted and grant aided establishments at November 1976. 112,165 men and 102,357 women undertook full-time and sandwich courses. In total, 216,290 men and 123,298 women undertook AFE courses.

26. The cost of public sector further and higher education is referred to in Section **3.**1. Staffing costs for 1979 are referred to in Section **8.**45, unit costs in Section **8.**52 and 64, and staff:student ratios in Sections **3.**50 and **11.2.**

27. In 1978 there were 143,983 full-time equivalent polytechnic students; and 41,914 full-time equivalent students pursuing advanced courses at other institutions.

28. The DES document, *Future Trends in Higher Education,* March 1979, contains student numbers projections. These planning figures are set for 1982/83 (a proposition adopted for the White Paper, Cmnd. 7437, January 1979). The planning figures propose 310,000 university places and 250,000 public sector higher education places (although there is a lower possible total figure quoted in the document of 540,000 places for university and public sector institutions combined). Future public sector numbers based on the set planning figures are: 229,000 in 1980/81; 236,000 in 1981/82; and 250,000 in 1982/83. However, it must be remembered that these figures represent hypotheses and that the most recent estimates (see pagraph 37) suggest even lower figures for 1983/84.

29. **Non-advanced further education**

The range of courses in non-advanced further education (NAFE) is immense. Investigation of courses will be found in Section **10.2**. As NAFE is often thought of as an alternative to school sixth forms, it is worth noting that only 16% of all students pursue GCE courses. In November 1976 287,000 students were enrolled on full-time day NAFE courses: and 682,000 enrolled on NAFE evening courses. These figures include students enrolled only, and do not include enrolments on more than one course or enrolments on courses at adult education centres. Nearly half of the students on full-time and sandwich courses are women. About 90% of the part-time day and evening only students were enrolled on non-examined courses, although there are now increasing numbers of students studying at these times on vocational preparation courses. 445,000 students were undertaking advanced further education courses. 9.7% of the population over the minimum school leaving age was in full-time non-advanced further education in 1976/77, and 2.3% in advanced further education. Recurrent institutional expenditure per full-time student in NAFE, calculated by the DES at net cost to public funds, amounted to £1,240 in polytechnics and £890 in other major establishments of further education.

30. Since 1966/67, the numbers of full-time and sandwich students in non-advanced further education have almost doubled. This rate of expansion is partially accounted for by the activities of the MSC. Given the current restrictions on the Commission's operations and the overall increases in fee levels, the rate of expansion may slacken. However, the decrease in employment opportunities also currently being suffered may act as a stimulant to further enrolments. Demographic predictions show that the numbers of the total population aged 16-18 will peak in 1981/82 and decline by about 25% by 1991/92. If there is not to be a decline in the numbers of

full-time and sandwich non-advanced further education students after 1986/87, there will have to be an increased participation rate.

31. In 1975/76, adult education centres provided for about 1,797,257 students. In 1977/78 the figure was 1,710,000. The decline in numbers has been attributed to increased fees and other consequences of cuts in local authority spending. It has been demonstrated that about 6% of the adult population is likely at any particular time to be following a course of adult education, and that at some time over 40% of adults will participate in such education.

32. Course enrolments in non-advanced further education according to qualification aim (including only once those students enrolled for more than one qualification course, and excluding adult education centre courses) at November 1976: are given in Table 3, overleaf.

33. The pattern of non-advanced further education enrolments during the period 1966/67-1976/77 is illustrated in Table 4, overleaf. It will be appreciated that a hiatus occurred in 1973 because of the raising of the school leaving age. Enrolment figures are expressed in thousands.

34. **All further education establishments**

Excluding independent establishments both recognised and not recognised as efficient, residential colleges of adult education and adult education provided by responsible bodies, in England and Wales at November 1976 the total course enrolments for all types of course (including full and part-time, sandwich, evening, and block and day release) were:

Polytechnics	:	192,697
Other maintained major establishments	:	1,693,230
Direct grant, including voluntary colleges	:	36,047
Adult education centres	:	1,797,257

The total enrolment at major establishments (including polytechnics) was thus 1,921,974, and the total grant aided enrolment 3,719,231.

35. At 31 March 1976, the number of teachers in establishments of further education in England and Wales working full-time was 76,403. Of this number 61,068 were men and 15,335 women. There were 14,009 polytechnic teachers; 57,867 teachers in other maintained major establishments; 3,808 in direct grant establishments; and 719 full-time or divided service adult education centre teachers. There are, of course, especially in adult education centres, many part-time teachers. The grades of full-time teachers in maintained, assisted and grant aided further education establishments, including former colleges of education, at 31 March 1976 (provisionally) are shown in Table 5, overleaf.

36. In 1977/78 of those young people reaching school leaving age in 1976/77, 213,000 (108,000 male and 105,000 female) were at school; 109,000 (45,000

Table 3

NAFE enrolments 1976 according to qualification aims

(Students following courses with more than one qualification aim are shown only once in the main table; the final column shows the total number of students studying for each qualification.)

	AGE AT 31 DECEMBER 1976 (all student numbers expressed in thousands)												
	AGED 16-18			AGED 19 or 20			AGED 21 OR OVER			ALL AGES			QUAGIFI-CATIONS AIMS
	Men	*Women*	*Total*	*Men*	*Women*	*Total*	*Men*	*Women*	*Total*	*Men*	*Women*	*Total*	
NAFE (Full-time and sandwich)													
GCE A	15	15	30	7	3	10	5	2	7	27	20	47	53
GCE O and CSE	13	18	30	2	1	3	1	2	3	16	20	36	36
OND/ONC	8	2	10	4	0	4	3	0	3	15	3	18	18
TEC/BEC	5	8	13	1	1	2	1	1	2	7	9	16	17
Professional Qualifications	1	18	19	1	2	3	3	3	6	6	22	28	29
College Certificates and Diplomas	2	2	4	1	1	2	2	1	3	5	5	10	11
City and Guilds	25	14	39	2	1	3	3	2	5	30	17	47	57
Other	15	31	46	3	5	8	12	18	29	30	54	84	89
TOTAL	84	107	192	21	14	35	31	29	60	136	150	287	310
NAFE (Part-time day)													
GCE A	2	2	4	1	1	2	2	6	8	5	9	14	14
GCE O and CSE	4	5	9	1	1	2	2	7	9	6	13	19	20
OND/ONC	10	1	11	6	1	8	5	1	6	22	3	25	25
TEC/BEC	13	12	24	7	3	10	5	3	9	25	18	43	43
Professional Qualifications	3	2	5	2	1		9	4	13	14	7	21	21
College Certificates						3							
and Diplomas	0	0	0	0	0	0	0	1	1	1	1	2	2
City and Guilds	172	18	190	81	3	84	35	15	50	288	36	324	330
Other	10	16	26	4	6	10	30	102	132	44	123	167	168
TOTAL	213	55	268	103	16	119	89	138	227	405	209	614	622
NAFE (Evening only)													
GCE A	6	6	11	5	4	9	14	16	30	24	26	51	51
GCE and CS.	15	14	29	5	5	10	19	29	49	39	49	88	88
OND/ONC	0	0	0	0	0	0	1	0	1	1	0	1	1
TEC/BEC	1	0	1	1	0	1	3	1	3	4	1	6	6
Professional Qualifications	1	1	2	1	1	2	12	5	16	14	7	21	21
College Certificates and Diplomas	0	0	0	0	0	0	1	0	1	1	1	1	1
City and Guilds	4	2	6	5	1	6	21	7	27	30	9	39	40
Other	14	44	58	7	20	27	122	268	390	144	332	475	477
TOTAL	41	68	108	25	31	56	191	326	518	256	425	682	685

Table 4

NAFE enrolments 1966-1977 (thousands)

ENROLMENTS IN NOVEMBER OF FIRST YEAR SHOWN	FULL-TIME AND SANDWICH			PART-TIME DAY			EVENINGS ONLY			ALL MODES OF STUDY		
	Men	*Women*	*Total*	*Men*	*Women*	*Total*	*Men*	*Women*	*Total*	*Men*	*Women*	*Total*
1966/67	82	66	148	498	152	651	343	413	756	923	632	1,555
1967/68	86	69	156	507	165	672	344	421	765	937	656	1,593
1968/69	93	75	168	515	168	681	318	396	714	926	636	1,562
1969/70	99	79	178	512	172	684	295	376	671	906	627	1,532
1970/71	103	83	187	494	185	680	299	397	696	896	666	1,562
1971/72	105	90	195	464	186	648	295	413	708	865	687	1,551
1972/73	110	98	208	443	197	639	300	431	730	852	725	1,577
1973/74	104	100	204	424	204	628	294	453	748	823	757	1,579
1974/75	115	114	230	420	226	647	285	465	749	820	805	1,625
1975/76	132	139	417	417	241	658	287	477	764	837	856	1,693
1976/77	136	150	287	405	209	614	256	425	682	798	785	1,582
% change 1966/67 to 1976/77	+ 67.0	+ 126.7	+ 93.6	– 18.7	+ 37.4	– 5.6	– 25.3	+ 3.0	– 9.8	– 13.6	+ 24.3	+ 18

Table 5

Grades of full-time teachers, 31 March 1976

Type of institution	*Principals*	*Vice-Principals (including vice principqals who were heads of department)*	*Other Heads of depart-ments*	*Readers*	*Principal Lecturers*	*Senior Lecturers*	*Lecturers Grade 2*	*Lecturers Grade 1*
Polytechnics	30	87	598	43	2,454	6,620	3,927	249
Other Major Establishments	672	546	2,487	4	3,954	11,897	18,643	23,473
Adult education centres and divided service	107	54	74	1	9	27	244	203
Total:-	809	687	3,159	48	6,417	18,544	22,814	23,925

male and 64,000 female) were in full-time further education; 109,000 (85,000 male and 24,000 female) were employed with part-time day further education; 278,000 (126,000 male and 152,000 female) were employed without part-time day further education; and, at January 1978, 65,000 were unemployed (32,000 male and 33,00 female).

37. **Projected numbers in higher education: possible consequences**

During the last two years the DES issued two consultative documents concerning projected student numbers in higher education.[2] However, these numbers have since been revised downwards. At the time of writing the DES had not published its current run of estimates, but they show that the total higher education student numbers in 1983-84 will reach only 545,000. Of this number, 313,000 are expected to be at universities, and 232,000 in the public higher education sector. These estimates must also be regarded as no more than tentative, for the expenditure cuts of the current government may well result in a further drop in numbers. For example, the announced intention to remove the subsidy to overseas students from September 1980 may have a serious effect on student numbers, and not just in higher education but throughout the further education sector. In November 1976, there was a total of 47,646 full-time and sandwich students from overseas enrolled at maintained, assisted and grant-aided establishments. Of this total, 20,514 students were undertaking advanced courses, and 27,132 undertaking non-advanced courses. It should be remembered, however, that many overseas students undertake non-advanced courses in order subsequently to gain admittance to advanced courses.

38. The consultative document *Higher Education into the 1990s* contained a scheme, Model E, which won general acceptance from colleges. This scheme, rather than being based on the assumption of a sharp decline of the traditional client groups for demographic reasons took as its main assumption that social and economic requirements might cause significant changes in the pattern and types of student requiring higher education. Thus, groups which currently did not use, or fully utilize, higher education opportunities but who might avail themselves of such opportunities were identified, and suggestions offered for action:
(i) that the children of manual workers should be encouraged to attain the higher education participation levels of the children of non-manual workers;
(ii) in the climate created by the reorganization of secondary education and health, housing and social policies generally, higher education could be made a more attractive prospect – a necessary achievement since evidence suggests that young people take their decisions concerning higher education entrance well before the age of 18; and
(iii) more resources might be devoted to those already in employment to provide systematic opportunities for recurrent education for mature

2 *Higher Education into the 1990s A Discussion Document,* DES/Scottish Education Department, February 1978: often referred to as the "Brown Paper". *Future Trends in Higher Education,* DES, March 1979. This document is often referred to as the "Blue Paper".

students (with priority possibly given to those without higher education experience), but that this could also involve developments such as schemes for continuing education at an advanced level, and also at non-advanced level.

39. The Labour Government which lost office in 1979 had made it clear that it approved of Model E. However, the document, *Future Trends in Higher Education,* ("the Blue Paper"), contained revisions of student numbers projections. It stated that the numbers had fallen, and that target enrolments had to be revised. Parity in student numbers with the universities could not at present be achieved. Model E appeared less likely to achieve implementation.

40. However, despite the projected fall in numbers there remain many routes for creative expansion, both for individual institutions and for further education as a whole. There are obvious consequences for non-advanced further education of any changes occurring in the advanced sector. Consequences of the decline in demand for higher education from its traditional users because of demographic factors ought not necessarily to be seen as leading to a decline of the further education service. A paper, also entitled *Future Trends in Higher Education,*[3] presented to the same conference as the DES Blue Paper,outlined policies of positive discrimination which were estimated to be able to create a pool of students which would more than offset the predicted decline. Such policies involved greater encouragement of potential students, course developments, the evident increasing demand for career development and retraining programmes, an increase in part-time and short courses, and measures taken to lessen the student "wastage" rate. These proposals have been criticised as over optimistic but nonetheless represent a possible strategy. It now remains to give some summary of two current issues. The topics discussed refer to present debates, and are included here as they highlight an area of particular concern in further education, other recent developments affecting the function of colleges are referred to in Section **10.2.**

41. Possible developments in further education and training for 16-18 year olds: discussion of some current issues

The eventual aim outlined in the consultative document *16-18,*[4] is a universal scheme of education and training opportunities for the entire 16-18 age group. The document emphasised that because the periods between 16 and 18 represent turning points at or between which crucial decisions are made, a very careful examination of provision was necessary. In attaining progress, the paper stated that a requirement was a measure of agreement among local authorities, teachers, voluntary bodies, employers, trade unions, and young people and their parents. The paper instanced challenges as

---

3 *Future Trends in Higher Education,* Background paper by R.M.W. Rickett presented to the THES/DES Conference, 5 March 1979.

4 *16-18, Education and training for 16-18 year olds,* A consultative paper presented by the Secretaries of State for Education and Science, for Employment and for Wales, DE/DES, 1979.

being: the growing demand for places in education and training; the need to maintain and enhance quality, to adapt to changing employment needs, and to provide adaptability and training necessary because of the pace of technological and economic change; the need to meet and understand employers' needs; the equipping of teachers to meet the challenges; and the special needs of the various disadvantaged groups. Because of limited resources, however, objectives had to be set in some order of priority.

42. The paper offered items upon which debate was needed: the varied educational and training needs of young people; employers' requirements; the best use of available resources; arrangements for curriculum development and coherence; careers education, guidance and help; provision for progression from one learning opportunity to another; distribution of educational responsibility (such as between the MSC and further education system); co-operation and co-ordination at all levels; the vocational needs of young employees and the extension of day release; the pattern of local educational provision; and the implications of demographic trends.

43. A further consultative paper, *A Better Start in Working Life*,[5] referred to vocational preparation for employed young people. The proposals for expanding such provision included the development of "traineeships" formally recognised in the same way as apprenticeships for young people in their early months at work. Traineeships, to be provided in a joint enterprise between the training and the education service, would be work-based. They would last several months and would provide an integrated programme of education and training, both on and off the job, combining elements of induction, basic job skills and knowledge, and personal skills required at work and in adult life. The proposals are aimed at assisting the large numbers of young people who take jobs which do not provide for education and training, and are intended to build on the practical experience gained from the pilot Unified Vocational Preparation (UVP) programme and the Youth Opportunities Programme (YOP). Subject to consultations and resource availability, the paper envisaged a voluntary approach whereby employers initially would be helped with grants covering the main costs of participating in the programme. In proposing the setting of a target, the paper gave the example of one third of new entrants to employment receiving vocational preparation three years after the start of the programme. The document also suggested that the target be reviewed, and that statutory enforcement might subsequently be necessary.

44. **Conclusion**

Conclusions cannot be more than general. The proposals outlined in paragraphs 38-43 were made during the term of office of the Government which lost office in 1979. It may be that few of the proposals will be implemented, and that the education service will undergo a period of contraction. At the same time as the ACACE published its discussion paper, *Towards Continuing Education* – a document arguing for expansion of this

---

5 *A Better Start in Working Life*, A consultative paper presented by the Secretaries of State for Employment, for Education and Science, for Industry, for Scotland and for Wales, DE/DES, 1979.

provision and stating that the mere filling of gaps in the present arrangements would be an inadequate measure – several local authorities reacted to government expenditure restraint by suspending their adult education provision. The Secretary of State has indicated that adult education will be severely curtailed, although greater provision would be made for the 16-18 age group: "It is that section of the school population which is expanding and there is a greater, more urgent need for qualified technicians."[6] Although increased opportunities for the 16-18 age group will have consequences for the education service – leading, perhaps, to an increased participation in higher education – it seems likely that the opportunities for expansion are, for some time at least, not to be made available. It is worth noting a recent statement by a former Permanent Secretary of the Department of Education and Science: "The disappointment about non-advanced further education is ... that ... A systematic nationwide scheme of part-time attendance at colleges for all those under 18 who are not in school is the only major objective of the 1944 Act that has proved unattainable. Any compulsory system was, and in the new period of restraint is likely to remain, too costly."[7]

45. The White Paper of November 1979, *The Government's Expenditure Plans 1980-81,* stated that "some modest expansion of non-advanced further education, especially vocational courses" should be possible to meet the needs of the rising numbers of students aged 16 to 18. Provision for capital expenditure on further and higher education building programmes was to be reduced "by about half".[8]

REFERENCE

A Better Start in Working Life, A consultative paper presented by the Secretaries of State for Employment, for Education and Science, for Industry, for Scotland and for Wales, DE/DES, 1979.

Advanced Further Education In Polytechnics and Colleges of Further Education (Including Colleges of Art), Pooling Committee Report On Monitoring of Student/Staff Ratios in 1978.

Further Education, DES Statistics of Education 1976 Vol 3, England and Wales, HMSO 1979.

Future Trends in Higher Education, A follow up report on "Higher Education into the 1990s" presented to the THES/DES Conference of 5 March 1979, DES, March 1979.

Higher Education into the 1990s A Discussion Document, DES/SED, February 1978.

Non-advanced Further Education, DES Report on Education, Number 94, December 1978.

Report of the Working Group on the Management of Higher Education in the Maintained Sector, Cmnd. 7180, HMSO, 1978.

Further information relevant to this report will be found in the following papers of the Working Group on the Management of Higher Education:

---

6 Speech by the Rt. Hon. Mark Carlisle, MP to the TUC education committee, 25 September 1979.

7 Sir William Pile, *The Department of Education and Science,* George Allen and Unwin, 1979, p.231.

8 *The Government's Expenditure Plans 1980-81,* Cmnd. 7746, HMSO, p.6.

Background Paper (MHE(77)2), DES; *Background Paper – Statistical Addendum,* (MHE(77)2) Addendum); and *Evidence Submitted by the National Association of Teachers in Further and Higher Education,* (MHE (77)12). In June 1978, NATFHE issued its *Response to the Oakes Report: A Discussion Paper.*
16-18, Education and training for 16-18 year olds, A consultative paper presented by the Secretaries of State for Education and Science, for Employment and for Wales, DE/DES, 1979.
Teachers, DES Statistics of Education 1976 Vol.4, England and Wales, HMSO, 1979.
The Educational system of England and Wales, DES, 1978.
The Government's Expenditure Plans 1980-81, Cmnd.7746, HMSO, 1979.
The Management of Non-University Higher Education, DES Report on Education No.90 May 1977.

D.F. Bratchell, *The Aims and Organization of Further Education,* Pergamon 1968.
Adrian Bristow, *Inside the Colleges of Further Education,* 2nd Edition, HMSO, 1976.
L. Cantor and I.F. Roberts, *Further Education in England and Wales,* Routledge and Kegan Paul, 1969.
L. Cantor and I.F. Roberts, *Further Education Today: A Critical Review,* Routledge and Kegan Paul, 1979.
Peter Clyne, *The disadvantaged adult,* Longman, 1972.
S.J. Curtis, *History of Education in Great Britain,* 7th Edition, University Tutorial Press, 1967.
J. Dean, *et al., The Sixth Form and Its Alternatives,* NFER, 1979.
David Hencke, *Colleges in Crisis,* Penguin, 1978.
ed. E.M. Hutchinson, *Aims and action in adult education 1921-71,* NIAE, 1971.
Maurice Kogan, *Educational Policy-Making,* Allen and Unwin, 1975.
John Lello, *The Official View of Education,* Pergamon, 1964.
Michael Newman, *The Poor Cousin, a Study of Adult Education,* George Allen and Unwin 1979.
A.J. Peters, *British Further Education,* Pergamon, 1967.
Sir William Pile, *The Department of Education and Science,* George Allen and Unwin, 1979.
John Pratt and Tyrrell Burgess, *Polytechnics: A report,* Pitman, 1974.
A strategy for the Basic Education of Adults, ACACE, 1979.
Education for Adults, NATFHE, 1979.
Future Trends in Higher Education, Background paper by RMW Rickett, presented to the THES/DES Conference, 5 March 1979.
Towards Continuing Education, ACACE, 1979.

3 THE LEGAL STRUCTURE OF FURTHER AND HIGHER EDUCATION

1. Education is often described as a national service locally administered. The same description may be applied to most other local government services. The relationship between local authorities and central government is traditionally described as one of partnership whereby the authorities do not enjoy total freedom of action but are more than the agents of the Secretary of State. Thus, although recommending the creation of a National Body for higher education, the Oakes Report [1] was careful to state its belief that freedom from complete central control was "essential to the welfare of the maintained system." Local authorities' freedom, however, can be severely curtailed by the exercise of governmental control of expenditure. The legal structure of further education creates and allows both freedom and constraint.

2. It is necessary to distinguish between the types of statute which govern further education. There are few Acts of Parliament which have direct application. More common are statutory instruments which are made by Secretaries of State under one or more Acts. These instruments have legal force. Colleges are further subject to the general law of the land: no reference will be made however in this sub-section to the requirements of, for example, employment law and health and safety legislation which are dealt with elsewhere in this book, except where specific issues arise from the way in which education is administered.

3. The legal structure of further education may be summarised thus:

   (i) Educational provision is made mainly by the Education Act, 1944, the Education (No.2) Act 1968, and The Further Education Regulations 1975.
   (ii) Financial provision is made by the Local Government Acts and by statutory instruments which govern, for example, matters such as pooling and student grants.
   (iii) Training provision is made by the Industrial Training Act 1964 and the Employment and Training Act 1973.
   (iv) Teachers' pay arrangements are made under the Remuneration of Teachers Act 1965, and teachers are also subject to instruments made under The Superannuation Acts. The Colleges of Education (Compensation) Regulations 1975 made compensation provision for staff in colleges of education who have lost their posts as a result of a direction of the Secretary of State.

4. This summary has the advantage of clarity but it must be appreciated that one set of provisions impinges on another, and that the legislation enmeshes and intertwines to produce the overall structure. The Further Education

---

1 *Report of the Working Group on the Management of Higher Education in the Maintained Sector*, Cmnd.7130, HMSO, 1978.

Regulations, for example, are made under four Acts of Parliament and govern matters as diverse as premises and the discontinuance of courses of teacher training. As stated above, the legal structure of further education does not stand independently. A member of staff may lose her or his post as a result of a direction of the Secretary of State made under The Further Education Regulations but compensation for that loss may be determined by either or both of the provisions of compensation regulations and employment law: the Secretary of State's direction may cause the loss but the local authority as employer has a duty under other legal provision to provide suitable alternative employment where it is possible to do so.

5. Even within the concept of a legal structure for further education there are areas of doubt and discretion. Local authorities are not bound to follow the advice of the DES or Welsh Office Education Department: the consequences of ignoring advice depend entirely upon the circumstances. The DES communicates with authorities by means of administrative memoranda and circulars. Advice may also be extended to colleges by means of circular letters or by way of HMI. Administrative memoranda are the most frequent form of communication, and while they refer often to routine and procedural matters may on occasion impart advice of moment. Circulars have a varying function: they may give advice, suggest action, request information or invite discussion. However, both circulars and memoranda are not issued lightly and they carry the weight of the authority of the DES. Local authorities and voluntary bodies are expected to observe the DES guidance, although they may argue against it or the precise form of its implementation. Guidance is also given in Ministerial speeches and in White Papers. Changes recently adopted concerning AMs and circulars are discussed in paragaph 46, below.

6. It is often stated that circulars and memoranda present guidance and do not have the force of law. This is generally true but there are circumstances in which this may not be the case. Three instances will serve to illustrate this point. Failure to comply with a circular may involve an authority in incurring a legal penalty from another source. For example, an authority may disregard DES advice on overseas students but in doing so will have relinquished the legal protection which the Secretary of State has obtained from the Race Relations Act and incorporated in advice, and may therefore become liable to proceedings under that Act. Failure to comply with constructional standards contained in administrative memoranda, because much of educational building is exempt from the Building Regulations and provision to obtain uniformity with those regulations is made via memoranda and other advice, may again render an authority liable to proceedings. The guidance offered by the DES on matters relating to welfare provision under the Health and Safety at Work etc. Act may be found only in any specific sense in memoranda, circulars and other advisory material yet these may be held by a court to be admissible in evidence in cases arising under that Act. Thus, while DES advice does not carry the clear force of law, as obtains for statutory instruments, there are occasions where it may have a legal relevance, especially where the advice is concerned with the implementation of statute.

7. It is perhaps regrettable that any explanation of advisory procedures seems to raise more problems. However, the observations in the previous paragraph must be qualified by the nature of the relationship between local and central government, although the generality of that relationship cannot be held to apply without exception. Local authorities certainly act in accordance with DES guidance on most occasions. The usual reasons for this are not only the traditional relationship of partnership but also because the Department can have recourse to sanctions which are available under other regulations. For example, the Government by reason of the Local Government Act 1972 has sanction over the borrowing of capital by local authorities and, further, the Act empowers the district auditor to apply to a court for a declaration that an item of local authority expenditure is contrary to law; and the court is empowered to order repayment of unlawful expenditure from those persons responsible. Yet there remain limits to the Secretary of State's powers of intervention. The difficulties suffered by Labour Governments in enforcing the reorganization of schools along comprehensive lines are well known. Existing legislation enabled comprehensive school policies to be enforced only where new school building had to be approved, and it was argued that it would be too damaging to relationships with the local authorities to legislate in such a way as directly to enforce local authority compliance with government wishes. It should also be considered that there are occasions when the weight of publicity and public opinion are such that either the Department or LEAs may find themselves deciding to resist particular policies. A further example can be given concerning the overseas students' quota system (see Section **12.10.**18): no one ever succeeded in clarifying how numerically strict was to be its interpretation, whether it would have been lawful to restrict pooling in respect of students in excess of the quota, the extent to which the quota could be enforced upon individual colleges, or how many students were likely to be exempted.

8. Issues for colleges may be rather simpler than those outlined above, but it is necessary to appreciate how the further education structure can operate. The clearest example in recent times refers to the reorganization of teacher education. It took several years for the reorganization envisaged in Circular 7/73 to be achieved and during that period there were several changes of course, some colleges were able successfully to sustain campaigns against closure, and some authorities to defy Ministerial wishes.[2] Confusion seemed to obtain at the highest levels:
"Minister : I have decided to give Brighton College of Education to the university.
"Adviser : But Minister, it is not yours to give."[3]

9. It now remains to investigate the components of the legal structure. Only brief mention will be made of provisions such as finance and the remuneration of teachers which are dealt with in detail elsewhere in this book.

10. **Education Act, 1944**
This Act established the present relationship between the local authorities

and the Secretary of State for Education and Science (the then Minister of Education). S.1.(1) of the Act gives to the Secretary of State the "duty... to promote the education of the people of England and Wales and the progressive development of institutions devoted to that purpose, and to secure the effective execution by local authorities, under his control and direction, of the national policy for providing a varied and comprehensive educational service in every area". This duty to promote, secure, control and direct is clearly very wide but the powers of the Secretary of State remain limited to those which the Act allows, and to those of subsequent enactments and regulations.

11. The Act allows the Secretary of State the power of intervention in certain circumstances. Under s.68 there is the power if "satisfied, either on complaint by any person or otherwise" that any local education authority or college governors have used or intend to use their powers unreasonably, for the Secretary of State to direct that their functions be exercised reasonably. S.99 allows the Secretary of State powers where local education authorities, managers or governors are in default: the Secretary can give directions for the relevant duty to be discharged, the directions being enforceable by

---

2 Interesting examples are to be found in the North East of England. Darlington College of Education, a voluntary college, convinced the Minister that it ought not to be closed. The Minister recommended that it should continue but in a different form as an annexe of a local authority college. The local authority refused to accept the arrangement and the college closed. Middleton St George College of Education was recommended by the DES to be transferred to a polytechnic in a nearby authority. The college's providing authority refused to agree to the transfer and so the college was directed to cease its function, interestingly enough during the term of office of the Minister who had less than a decade before performed the opening ceremony. These examples serve to illustrate the mechanics of the type of consultation which often obtained in teacher education reorganization. The criteria of Circular 7/73 and the actual criteria used have been said to be confusing and contradictory: the defence to these charges is that difficult problems required the resolution of considerations which were conflicting. It has been argued that the processes of decision were carried out secretly and therefore without the colleges being able to contribute to the whole debate: instead, they were picked off singly. The defence is that delicate matters ought not to be widely broadcast – and yet, in the case of the voluntary colleges, "the lists of proposed changes and closures ... were more or less agreed in advance," and in one instance only challenged because "the local reaction was, however, so violent and awe inspiring that compensating reductions were volunteered elsewhere." (Hugh Harding, writing in *Education,* 29 December 1978). However the Department might defend its procedures, the determining issue ultimately remained one of power. The Churches were powerful enough to defend their position, within certain limits; the British and Foreign School Society was not. Issues were largely decided by the DES and LEAs, not necessarily by agreement; for there were instances where the one was able successfully to combat the other, and in some cases (for example in Hereford and Worcester) where the Department returned the choice of which institution to close to the LEA. The point is that whatever the legal structure, its operation in areas of discretion largely depends on how power is wielded and operated; and that for individual institutions it is difficult to fight in a fog. To anticipate such crises, therefore, it is necessary to have developed strong relationships with the providing and maintaining body, the Department, the local community, the Inspectorate, and by means such as involvement with the teachers' associations to ensure that issues are considered as a whole.

3 Anecdote quoted in David Hencke, *Colleges in Crisis,* p.85.

mandamus,[4] and in determining whether default has occurred the Secretary of State is the sole judge. The Act gives the Secretary of State powers to inspect education establishments; it is accepted that HMI advice in selection of teacher training colleges for closure was vital.

12. These powers of oversight and intervention give the Secretary of State the means to ensure an efficient education service without allowing the authority for him, or the Government, to enforce specific policies without consent, except where enabled by other statute and regulation and the kinds of sanction referred to above.

13. The partnership in the operation of the education service is largely determined by the local authorities having been given specific duties in its operation (see also Section **8.**13). Under s.41 of the Act, the local education authorities are charged with certain general duties with respect to further education. Further education is defined as:

> "(a) full-time and part-time education for persons over compulsory school age; and
>
> "(b) Leisure time occupation, in such organized cultural training and recreative activities as are suited to their requirements, for any persons over compulsory school age who are able and willing to profit by the facilities provided for that purpose."

Ss 41 and 42 continue to describe and stipulate the preparation and approval procedures for schemes of further education but part of the original format envisaged (county colleges) did not come into operation, and the schemes have not been updated. The power remains, however, and under the London Government Act 1963, the relevant authorities were required to reproduce statements of their further education schemes for approval. The 1944 Act empowers the Secretary of State to make such modification as he thinks fit after consultation with the local education authority.

14. The duties imposed on the local authorities and the powers of the Secretary of State combine to allow a simple interpretation: the authorities are expected to manage their own affairs subject to the approval of the Secretary of State. Thus the partnership of the national service locally administered is in theory established. However, what is not established for further education are the facilities to be afforded, other than in a general sense. S 41 states merely that:
"It shall be the duty of every local education authority to secure the provision for their area of adequate facilities for further education."

15. Whereas further education is defined by the Act, adequate facilities are not. Given the need for the further education service to be flexible and responsive to change, and its consumers being over school leaving age, this lack of prescription is both necessary and understandable. However, it also

---

4 Judicial writ issued from the Queen's Bench Division as a command to an inferior court.

allows local authorities considerable discretion in the facilities which they provide, a situation perpetuated by The Further Education Regulations 1975. Hence, on the matter of accommodation standards, for example, there is a discretion which does not apply in the case of schools where, as a mandatory service, facilities are subject to regulations. This discretion and flexibility form a virtue in many instances but allow for potential difficulty in others (see Sections **5.3.** and **5.5.**). A local authority's discretion, moreover, is limited by obligations other than to the Secretary of State. These limits are investigated below and in Sections **3** and **8**.

16. The DES has a grant making power under the 1944 Act which extends beyond local authorities. This power has been consolidated in subsequent enactments and represents the means whereby voluntary colleges have been financed largely by direct grant from the Department. Direct grant is not, of course, restricted to voluntary colleges: other voluntary education bodies receive grants from the DES.

17. **Education (No.2)Act 1968**
This Act applies only to England and Wales and is concerned with provision for the government and conduct of colleges. The Act arose from the Weaver recommendations[5] concerning colleges of education but it extended the Weaver principles to institutions of further education.

18. As local authorities accepted, for colleges of education, the Secretary of State's requirements concerning the approval of the instruments and articles of government which the Act demanded, its provisions were quickly introduced for those colleges. However, in the instance of further education, the authorities found themselves unable to accept the Department's proposals for the enforcement of the Act. It was only after lengthy consultation that guidance on implementation could be made under Circular 7/70. Implementation was further delayed in some instances by the reorganization of local government.

19. The Act requires that for every maintained institution of teacher training, or institution providing full-time education pursuant to an approved scheme of further education, that there shall be an instrument of government which provides for the constitution of a body of governors; and that every institution shall be conducted in accordance with articles of government.

20. Instruments of government are to be made for colleges of education by order of the authority with the approval of the Secretary of State, and in any other case by order of the LEA. The constitution of the governing body is to be determined by the LEA, or for colleges of education by the LEA with the approval of the Secretary of State. The articles of government determine the functions of the LEA, governing body, principal and academic board, if any. The articles are to be made by order of the LEA with the Secretary of State's approval.

---

5 See Sections **1.5** and **2.1**; cf Section **8.**17.

21. Subject to the approval of the Secretary of State, a local education authority may constitute a single governing body for two or more institutions providing full-time education pursuant to a scheme of further education (excluding colleges of education). Such arrangements may be terminated at any time by the local education authority by which they were made.

22. Under the 1944 Act, where there is a dispute between a local education authority and the governing body, the issue may be referred to the Secretary of State, who will determine the matter. The implementation of the Education (No.2) Act is discussed fully in Section **2.1**, and the legal consequences of certain delegated autonomous powers conferred on governing bodies are outlined below.

23. **The Local Government Acts and related statute and advice**
Although Section **8** of this book (particularly paragraphs 13-23) deals in detail with local authorities and the law, it is appropriate here to give an outline of their place in the legal structure of further education.

24. Local authorities may incur expenditure only in accordance with their legal powers, whether their monies result from central or local sources. Under s 161 of the Local Government Act 1972, the court may order that the accounts be rectified, or disqualify an individual from membership of the local authority where the expenditure exceeds £2,000. Under the Local Government Act 1978, authorities have the power to incur expenditure in order to remedy injustices caused by maladministration.

25. As the accounts of an institution which it maintains are part of those of an authority, college finances are subject to the Act's provisions. In practice this means that the authority draws up the financial regulations for its colleges; there is, however, no statutory duty for the authority to maintain a review of spending item by item. Moreover, among the advice extended by the DES in Circular 7/70 concerning the implementation of the Education (No.2) Act 1968 was the recommendation for colleges to enjoy within certain prescriptions a measure of freedom in determining expenditure (see Section **3.**63;74).

26. To attempt to provide a simple picture of the FE structure, it is perhaps better to think less of the partnership between central and local government but instead to consider a circular relationship where a college stands between the DES and its maintaining authority. In one segment of the circle there is the DES – LEA partnership, which has obvious consequences for colleges. In another there is the relationship between the DES and the college, whereby the Department operates statutory controls via its powers over courses and less direct control by way of advice: whilst also, by way of the protection it affords through its interest in college government, and through its other legal powers, guaranteeing the college a measure of independence from the local education authority. The third segment is the relationship between the college and its LEA. The local authority acts as the employer of college staff and therefore carries the duties imposed by employment law. It also has legal duties and liabilities as the provider and

occupier of premises. This relationship can be the subject of unease: authorities may have little control over areas of a college's business but remain responsible in law for certain of the consequences. Colleges, however, can experience similar unease where their business is affected by policy decisions of the authority.

27. Although provision for governmental financial support of education is made by the Education Act, 1944, authorities currently receive monies for education (along with other services) by way of the rate support grant under the Local Government Act 1966. This is investigated in Section **3.**18 below, The point to be noted is that which refers to the national and local partnership: whereas the local authorities' and the Secretary of State for Education's forecasts may be accepted by the Government in determining the relevant expenditure on which the rate support grant is then payable, and although this assumes expenditure on component items, the allocation of finance is for the LEA to make at its discretion (within the constraints of its statutory duties). Therefore, no Minister has the power to require local authorities to allot their monies, and certainly not to ensure that finance is given for any particular educational provision or is spent on that purpose.

28. The Local Government Act 1972 allows for governmental control of local authorities' borrowing of capital. For education, capital expenditure invariably involves building, a topic investigated in Section **3.**10 and **5.2**, below. It is worth noting here however that capital building programmes for education fall normally under "key sector" schemes, in terms of the Department of the Environment Circular 2/70, which require specific approval.

29. Other financial arrangements (see Section **3.**44; 72; 74) are made by way of the pooling regulations, and individual college and authority practices vary concerning budgeting and spending according to how discretion is operated within statutory requirements and guidance advice. The Capps Report (a "Pilkington Report") was commended by the DES in Administrative Memorandum 1/69. This report referred to the use of costing and other financial techniques in technical colleges.

30. **The Further Education Regulations**

The Further Education Regulations 1975, Statutory Instruments 1975 No. 1054, are made under four Acts of Parliament. These regulations allowed for the grouping under one heading of establishments of further education, amended the regulations relating to the training of teachers (see Section **12.3.**), enabled the Secretary of State to effect the reorganization of the colleges of education, and also make provision concerning premises, courses and other matters. Again, the regulations do not stand alone, and it will be necessary to make reference to other law.

31. The regulations empower the Secretary of State for the purposes of facilitating reorganization of teacher training to direct an authority, or the governing body of a voluntary establishment, after consultation, to discontinue such courses or effect alteration in the numbers and categories of student and to cease the payment of any grant. Staff affected by such a

direction may become eligible for the application of The Colleges of Education (Compensation) Regulations, and may receive compensation if they satisfy the provisions of those latter regulations (see Section **11.5.**). The providing bodies of voluntary institutions grant aided by the DES whose establishments discontinue as a result of a direction are required to repay to the Secretary of State "so much as is determined by him to be just" of the grant by means of the disposal of premises and equipment.

32. The grant making power conferred on the Secretary of State is consolidated in the FE Regulations. This refers to voluntary establishments and organizations. In certain cases for voluntary establishments the amount of capital grant is restricted to 85% of the expenditure incurred. Such grants are subject to such conditions as the Secretary of State may impose. The Secretary of State may also make grants to other voluntary institutions and organizations, subject to various conditions as well as constraints concerning amounts. Grants may be made to responsible bodies (see Section **1.2.**20) towards the cost of providing tuition in any course of liberal adult education in an approved programme; to national associations providing certain educational services; and for village halls and community centres, the training of youth leaders, and for recreation and leisure time activities. Under The Further Education (Amendment) Regulations 1976, the Secretary of State was empowered to pay grants to the TUC and independent trade unions in respect of courses in trade union studies. Under The Further Education (Amendment) Regulations 1977, the Secretary of State was enabled to pay grants to district committees of the Workers' Educational Association.

33. The 1975 regulations make provision concerning fees (see Section **3.**69). The requirements are that fees should not differ substantially from the corresponding fees charged by neighbouring authorities; and that, after consultation, authorities must comply with the direction given by the Secretary of State as to the fees which may be charged for certain designated courses which fall into the category of advanced level work (see Appendix 1). Except in the case of overseas students up to the academic year 1979/80, the Secretary of State does not make recommendations for fees for non-advanced courses. Fee levels for advanced non-designated courses, non-advanced courses, and from the academic year 1979/80, overseas students are recommended by CLEA. By reason of The Education (Miscellaneous Provisions) Act 1953 and subsequent statutory instruments, there are arrangements which allow local authorities to charge the home authorities of students the fees for courses undertaken, where the students were not resident in the course providing authority area. In the case of certain part-time and vocational courses, some authorities operate a standard permit scheme. A permit is issued by the home authority to a student when the home authority's colleges do not offer the desired course. The home authority accepts responsibility for paying recoupment for the student on a particular course at a particular college. Except where particularly allowed, for example under the London Government Act (although the relevant section is proposed for repeal under the Education (No.2) Bill 1979), it appears that "free trade" arrangements between authorities are passing out

of existence since District Auditors are insisting on full recoupment, and since individual LEAs are generally responding to expenditure restraint by looking harder than hitherto at extra-district arrangements.

34. While the stipulation of the 1944 Act concerning "adequate facilities" extends to courses, it is only under The Further Education Regulations that there is a more direct statutory provision. The regulations require that the provision of advanced courses is subject to the approval of the Secretary of State. This approval, however, is qualified by other factors. Circular 7/70, where it is implemented, provides for colleges to determine the content of academic courses but that freedom is also subject to the requirements of the various examining bodies (see paragraph 42, below, and Section **10.2.**18).

35. In the matter of premises, The Further Education Regulations are more specific than the "adequate facilities" requirement of the 1944 Act but are not sufficiently full to enable full guidance to be given on health and safety matters (see Section **5.3.** and **5.5.**). However, the requirements of the regulations concerning effective and suitable provision being made, and especially with regard to equipment, fire, accident prevention, maintenance and environmental factors, do have an effect on premises provision. The approval of the Secretary of State is required in the provision of new premises and the alteration of existing premises. That approval power gives the DES a control over local authority educational building (see Sections **3.**10 and **5.2.**) and also extends to voluntary institutions. The voluntary bodies to which the DES and local authorities may pay grants must also conform to the facilities standards which the regulations require. While the status in law of DES circulars and other advice may at times be dubious, it is safe to assume that, unless there were good grounds to the contrary, where advice concerning facilities was not taken, it would be held to be a breach of the facilities provisions of The Further Education Regulations, and also the 1944 Act.

36. The Further Education Regulations place a limit on equipment expenditure (but see para. 47, below): "no installation or article of equipment costing £2,500 or more shall be provided for teaching or research without the approval of the Secretary of State." Governors are empowered under the model articles of government in Circular 7/70 to spend up to £500 on maintenance and minor alterations, (although actual sums will depend upon particular articles approved for a college). The regulations also require that the Secretary of State's approval be given for instruction involving the use of radioactive materials.

37. On the matter of teaching staff, the regulations require that: "The teachers shall be sufficient in number and have the qualifications necessary for the adequate instruction of the students in the courses provided." Again, it is necessary to go beyond statute to discover the criteria relevant to the word "sufficient", and to the designation of necessary qualifications.

38. To consider determination of sufficiency in number, with the rider that sufficiency will be dependent on the type of course taught, it is necessary to

reverse the concept and discuss the numbers of students who require tuition. While the ratios of staff to students will vary according both to circumstance and to recruitment patterns, a basis of guidance can be found in the first Pilkington report, *Report on the Size of Classes and Approval of Courses*, NACEIC, 1966. The recommendations of the report were accepted by the Secretary of State in Circular 11/66, and thus were intended to form a basis for DES approval of courses where statutorily empowered to do so. The Report states: "The following should be normal minimum requirements for initial enrolments before a course is approved:

(i)	Full-time (including sandwich) courses	24
(ii)	Part-time day courses involving a large element of workshop practice	15
(iii)	Other part time courses	20

"A minimum enrolment of say 50 in the relevant field should be required before courses are approved at new centres in subjects for which there is already provision accessible to the new prospective students." In practice, however, the major influence on college staff: student ratios has been the Pooling Committee's attempt to establish "norms" for such ratios (see Section **3.**51). There are also a variety of practices involving staff:student ratios. These are referred to in the matter of staffing establishment in Section **11.2.**

39. Local authorities, too, may generally accept such criteria in their course approval as a way of providing "adequate facilities". The Secretary of State has power to determine the numbers of students undertaking initial teacher training, and therefore indirectly the sufficient numbers of staff required. Otherwise, staff numbers may be determined by the college establishment under arrangements made under The Remuneration of Teachers Act 1965 and according to course. However, The Further Education Regulations' requirement concerning qualifications requires some explanation. The "qualifications necessary" will again depend on the course to be taught. In some subjects and courses it is possible for a teacher to have few formal qualifications: the appointment could be made on the basis that the qualifications were those represented by an individual's experience and expertise in industry. It is also possible for the necessary qualifications to be determined effectively by the requirements of the examining body for the course which is to be taught: the CNAA has refused in some cases to validate a course because staff who were to teach on it were insufficiently qualified.

40. The arrangements for the negotiation of teachers' pay are made by The Remuneration of Teachers Act, conditions of service arrangements are made within a national framework agreed between the teachers' associations and the Council of Local Education Authorities (CLEA), being superseded at the time of going to press by the National Joint Council for Further Education Teachers in England and Wales. Articles of government usually describe appointments and dismissals procedures. These matters are discussed in Sections **2, 9, 11.6, 11.7**, and **11.9**, below. The appointments

provisions of The Further Education Regulations do not conflict with those of employment law, but it is worth drawing attention to the regulations which restrict the employment of teachers on medical grounds and grounds of misconduct (see Section **11.6**, appendices 4 and 6). Wherever a teacher's employment is terminated by dismissal or resignation because of misconduct or conviction of a criminal offence, the regulations require that the facts shall be reported to the Secretary of State. These regulations apply to youth club leaders, youth workers, community centre wardens, and youth and community workers as well as teachers.

41. **Training Acts**

The further education system has had to make provision for industrial and other training by reason of the Industrial Training Act 1964 and the Employment and Training Act 1973. The first Act established industrial training boards charged with ensuring that there were adequate facilities for training. Some of the training is conducted in industry, and some in colleges. The 1973 Act relaxed certain of its predecessor's provisions and also established the Manpower Services Commission. The Commission is charged with the duty "to make such arrangements as it considers appropriate for the purpose of assisting persons to select, train for, obtain and retain employment suitable for their ages and capacities and to obtain suitable employees (including partners and various business associates)". Courses and placement on courses operated by colleges have resulted from the arrangements made by the MSC through its Divisions and various programmes (see Sections **4, 10.2.**81, and **12.11.**24).

42. **Other bodies**

Examining bodies may have a statutory base: the CNAA, for example, is established by charter but there are other examining bodies which have grown from a voluntary basis. Regional Advisory Councils (see Section **8.**65 and **10.2.**26) have only limited statutory power but their advisory function allows them considerable power of influence. The RACs consider proposed advanced courses before they are submitted to the DES for approval, and have an advisory power concerning non-advanced courses. There are also non-statutory bodies, such as the various regional associations of education authorities which possess in some areas a "power of influence" comparable to that of an RAC.

43. **Conclusion**

The complexity of the legal structure of further education will have been appreciated. While it is a simple enough matter to detail relevant Acts of Parliament and certain statutory instruments, it must be appreciated that educational law alone is sufficient to fill a large volume;[6] and that educational institutions are also subject to general law. While the grey and discretionary areas in educational law may be annoying for those who wish to obtain a detailed legal code applicable in all circumstances, it must be remembered that the legal educational structure reflects both the necessity

---

6 cf G. Taylor and J.B. Saunders, *The Law of Education*, 8th Edition, Butterworths, 1976.

for further education quickly to adapt to new circumstance and the policy of partial decentralisation which allows the admittedly circumscribed partnership between central and local government. While the operation of this partnership may cause both sides, and colleges too, to indulge in a manoeuvring bordering on the unseemly, the system does allow for some initiative and discretion. This is not to argue that there is no need for reform. The influence of civil servants has been heavily criticised, and the criticism as stringently answered[7], but without doubt the consultative machinery does not always operate as effectively as it might. Both the local authorities' and the teachers' associations are seeking the repeal of The Remuneration of Teachers Act. With all its faults however, our somewhat loose system may be preferable to that operated by at least one European country where the permission of central government is necessary before a college can use its minibus to facilitate an educational excursion by foreign visitors, and where the curriculum is rigidly prescribed.

44. Whereas the legal structure of our system is incomplete and does not define all the actions which a local authority might take – and indeed, allows authorities to disregard central government's intentions over important items such as financial allocation and the payment of discretionary grants to students – there remain ultimate boundaries which both local and central government cannot overreach. Regulations allow both prescription and discretion and as a body provide a working national framework. DES advice is of varying status and may on occasion provoke considerable disagreement. The partnership between the DES and the LEAs may be compared to a non-aggression pact based on the recognition that the Department's powers can be almost overwhelming and the local authorities' capacity for guerrilla resistance daunting; and that the practice of consultation means that generally acceptable solutions are often amicably reached.

45. An important rider must be added to this description, however. Little mention has been made of colleges since the areas of their discretion will become apparent in the reading of this book: determination of the college establishment is an obvious example, as are certain staff development policies. No mention has been made of the role of the teachers' associations. Consultations do occur – both in negotiations arising from the legal structure, in the composition of committees of inquiry, and over proposed legislation. The teachers' associations on occasion seek to ensure both by negotiation and legal processes that the DES and LEAs observe their obligations (for example, see Section **11.5**). Thus while the partnership between central and local government is often amicable, it too is subject to the checks and balances provided by teachers' associations and other interested parties. It should be noted also that the legal structure as it affects both educational provision and employment is subject to changes arising from judicial interpretations. It may be consolidated or modified as a result of actions at law undertaken by any of the parties involved.

---

7 cf Hencke, *op. cit,* pp 106-116; a reply to the criticisms is contained in *Education*, 29 December 1978 and 5 January 1979.

46. At the time of writing, the Government was engaged in the alteration of education law. The alterations were included in an Education Bill which had its second reading on 5 November 1979. The items which would directly affect colleges if the whole bill is enacted are:
   (i) alterations to the system of designating courses: the power is to be given to the Secretary of State to extend the designation of advanced courses as "mandatory" for awards purposes, and to give industrial scholarships;
   (ii) powers for the Secretary of State to limit advanced further education pooled expenditure; and
   (iii) the rectification of anomalies which prevented the pooling of certain categories of compensation payable as a result of the reorganization of the colleges of education.

47. Parts of the proposals contained in the White Paper, *Central Government Controls over Local Authorities,* Cmnd. 7634, have been taken up in the Education Bill. It is expected that action will be taken on more of the proposals – for example, the amendment of The Further Education Regulations 1975 to remove the DES oversight of FE equipment expenditure.[8] There is an exercise currently in progress whereby local authorities' duties, and restrictions on their abilities to levy charges, are being reviewed. It is intended that every major local authority obligation should be reviewed by March 1980. Changes which may affect the legal structure of further education arising from the successor to the withdrawn Local Government, Planning and Land Bill 1979 are investigated in Sections **3** and **8,** below.

48. Following the general election of 1979, the new Government announced, as a matter of principle, that it would be issuing fewer circulars than its predecessors. As a result, advice and information which previously would have appeared in circulars and administrative memoranda has been given in Ministerial statements (as reported in Hansard and the public media) or has been passed on to local authorities through their associations. This has resulted already in the local authority associations providing their member LEAs with a substantial amount of information.[9] Local authority associations' circulars, unlike those of the DES and Welsh Office, go only to member local authorities, with courtesy copies to a restricted number of interested parties. This will inevitably restrict access to what may be crucial information.

---

8 The Secretary of State has the power to effect this change by the amendment of the regulations. At the time of writing it seemed possible that the regulations would be amended early in 1980.

9 Since the local authority associations are financed by the subscriptions of member LEAs and other local authorities,the cost of distributing the material ironically still represents a charge on public expenditure.

APPENDIX 1

COURSES SUBJECT TO THE APPROVAL OF THE SECRETARY OF STATE

Schedule 1 of The Further Education Regulations defines the courses for which the approval of the Secretary of State is necessary as being any full-time course of more than one month's duration, and any part-time course occuping more than forty hours, which are:

"(a) a course of post-graduate or post-diploma instruction;

(b) a course of study in preparation for a degree, a Diploma of Higher Education, a Higher National Diploma, a Higher National Certificate, a Diploma in Management Studies, or a final professional examination of a standard above that of the examination for the Ordinary National Certificate or General Certificate of Education (advanced level);

(c) a course of study of at least two years' duration if part-time other than block release or of equivalent length if full-time or block release, following an initial course of not less than one year's duration or equivalent length respectively, in preparation for an Advanced or Final Certificate at full Technological Certificate of the City and Guilds of London Institute or other course for which the possession of such an Advanced or Final Certificate is a minimum qualification for entry;

(d) any other course in preparation for an examination of a standard above that of the examination for the Ordinary National Certificate or General Certificate of Education (advanced level) for which the normal age of entry is not less than 18 years and the normal minimum qualification for entry is, or is of a standard not below, one of the following:-

   (i) an Ordinary National Certificate;

   (ii) five passes in examinations for Certificates of Education being passes at the ordinary level in the examination for the General Certificate of Education or at the grade 1 level in the examination for the Certificate of Secondary Education;

   (iii) two passes in the examination for the General Certificate of Education, one of which is at the advanced level."

NB: The higher diploma and certificate courses of BEC and TEC will replace several of those instanced above but will remain subject to the Regulations.

REFERENCE

Education Act, 1944, Chapter 31, HMSO.
The Education (Miscellaneous Provisions) Act 1953, Chapter 33, HMSO.
Education (No.2) Act 1968, Chapter 37, HMSO.
Industrial Training Act 1964, Chapter 16, HMSO.
Employment and Training Act 1973, Chapter 50, HMSO.
Local Government Act 1933, Chapter 51, HMSO.
Local Government Act 1966, Chapter 42, HMSO.
Local Government Act 1972, Chapter 70, HMSO.
Local Government Act 1974, Chapter 7, HMSO.
Local Government Act 1978, Chapter 39, HMSO.
The Remuneration of Teachers Act 1965, Chapter 3, HMSO.
The Colleges of Education (Compensation) Regulations 1975, Statutory Instruments 1975, No. 1092, HMSO.
The Further Education Regulations 1975, Statutory Instruments 1975, No. 1054, HMSO.
The Further Education (Amendment) Regulations 1976, Statutory Instruments 1976, No. 1191, HMSO.
The Further Education (Amendment) Regulations 1977, Statutory Instruments 1977, No. 887, HMSO.
Education (No. 2) Bill, HMSO, 1979.
Local Government, Planning and Land Bill, HMSO, 1979.
Central Government Controls over Local Authorities, Cmnd. 7634, HMSO, 1979.

Report on the Size of Classes and Approval of Further Education Courses, NACEIC, 1966.
Report of the Working Group on the Management of Higher Education in the Maintained Sector, Cmnd. 7130, HMSO.
Report on the Use of Costing and other Financial Techniques in Technical Colleges, Committee on the more effective use of Technical College Resources, 1969.
Technical College Resources: Size of Classes and Approval of Further Education Courses, DES Circular 11/66, 12 April 1966.
Technical College Resources, the Use of Costing and Other Financial Techniques, DES Administrative Memorandum 1/69, 6 January 1969.
Government and Conduct of Establishments of Further Education, DES Circular 7/70, 14 April, 1970.
Development of Higher Education in The Non-University Sector, DES Circular 7/73, 26 March 1973.
The Reorganisation of Higher Education in The Non-University Sector: The Further Education Regulations 1975, DES Circular 5/75, 18 July 1975.

Hugh Harding, "Harding replies to Hencke over college closures," *Education,* 29 December 1978.
Hugh Harding, "Dull truth transmuted to fool's gold," *Education,* 5 January 1979.
David Hencke, *Colleges in Crisis,* Penguin, 1978.
John Lello, *Accountability in Education,* Ward Lock, 1979.
Michael Locke, *The Statutory Framework of Further Education,* Coombe Lodge Report Vol.9, No.8, 1976.
G. Taylor and J.B. Saunders, *The Law of Education,* 8th Edition, Butterworths, 1976.

4 TERMS AND ABBREVIATIONS

1. Any area of human activity quickly develops its own specialist language. Education is no exception to this rule and acronyms, abbreviations and special terms are always present in its literature.

2. This sub-section dealing with terms and abbreviations is presented with the specific intention of providing a reference to those acronyms that are in common usage in further education. While it has proved impossible to include every entry that one would have wished, abbreviations have been included if they satisfy any of the following criteria.

   (i) They occur elsewhere in this book.
   (ii) They refer to a union or association involved in the education sector and listed in Appendix 1 of the 1978 *Report of the Certification Officer* (see Section **11.6**, Appendix 1).
   (iii) They are an abbreviated form of the major educational qualifications. It has not been possible to refer to all the associateships, memberships and fellowships of professional institutions. An excellent reference to these can be found in ed. Barbara Priestley, *British Qualifications*, 9th Edition, Kogan Page.
   (iv) They refer to societies or associations whose work has a particular relevance to the further education sector.

Finally, while every effort has been made to ensure the accuracy of this list, it has to be accepted that further education is not static. New societies are created, and old associations fragment. With the passage of time, the accuracy of the list will fall. Consequently, any suggestions for additions to the list or amendments to existing entries should be sent to the editor so that the necessary changes can be made in subsequent editions.

AACE – Association for Adult and Continuing Education.
A teachers' association formed on 1 January 1978 by the amalgamation of the Association for Adult Education, the National Federation of Continuative Teachers' Associations, and the Association of Principals in Short Term Residential Colleges. Affiliated to NATFHE. See Section **9**, Appendix 2.

AAE – Association for Adult Education.
A teachers' association, now part of AACE.

AAES – Association of Agricultural Education Staffs.
A teachers' association in agricultural and horticultural education. A member of the Burnham Further Education Committee. Affiliated to NATFHE. See Section **9.**30.

AAI – Association of Art Institutions.
The association provides a forum for the discussion of matters affecting art education.

ABRC – Advisory Board for the Research Councils.

ACACE – Advisory Council on Adult and Continuing Education.
A body established by the DES to advise the Secretary of State on matters relating to adult and continuing education.

ACACHE – Association of Careers Advisers in Colleges of Higher Education.
An organization of careers advisers formed to carry out functions similar to AGCAS in colleges and institutes of higher education which may not be members of AGCAS.

ACAS – Advisory Conciliation and Arbitration Service (see Section **11.6**).

ACC – Association of County Councils.
The Association of County Councils, the Association of District Councils (ADC), and the Association of Metropolitan Authorities (AMA) are the three major associations of local authorities in England and Wales. The ACC and AMA include all the 104 Local Education Authorities (LEAs) and represent them in negotiations with government and on the Burnham Committees; they jointly form the Council of Local Education Authorities (CLEA).

ACE – Advisory Centre for Education.
A private body established to advise consumers of education; active mainly in the schools sector.

ACFHE – Association of Colleges for Further and Higher Education.
Previously the Association of Technical Institutions (ATI), ACFHE consists of colleges in membership, each college having three representatives: the principal, the chairman of governors (or alternative governor) and the chief education officer or alternative officer).

ACID – Association of Colleges implementing DipHE.

ACL – Awards Circular Letter.
See Circular letters.

ACRA – Association of College Registrars and Administrators.
A professional association of chief administrative officers, registrars and other first line administrators reporting directly to them.

ACSCC – Association of Community Schools, Colleges and Centres.

ACSTT/ACSET – Advisory Council for the Supply and Training of Teachers.
A body established by the Department of Education and Science to advise the Secretary of State on aspects of teacher

training and supply. Reconstituted in 1979 as the Advisory Committee on the Supply and Education of Teachers.

ACSTT(FE) – The further education sub-committee of ACSTT. This sub-committee will shortly be reconstituted as a consequence of the changes in ACSTT/ACSET.

ACT – Association of Career Teachers.

ACTS – Administrative, Clerical, Technical, and Supervisory section ("white collar") of the TGWU.

ACU – Association of Commonwealth Universities.

ACUCHE – Association of Computer Units in Colleges of Higher Education.

ACUA – Association of Cambridge University Assistants.

ADC – Association of District Councils.
See ACC

AE – Adult Education.
A general term usually applied to non-vocational part-time education for mature students.

AEB – Associated Examining Board.
One of the GCE examining boards. This board has specialised in the examination of mature students and students in further education generally.

AEC – Association of Education Committees.
A body that was established to represent the interests of education committees. It ceased to exist after local government reorganization. Now replaced, in many respects, by CLEA.

aegrotat – A degree classification that may be awarded when a candidate was unable to sit a final examination due to illness.

AEO – Assistant Education Officer.
A grade in local authority education offices.

AEO – Association of Education Officers
A professional association for education officers in local authorities. See SEO.

AFE – Advanced Further Education. Usually refers to the work of further education that leads to a degree or a degree equivalent qualification. In many respects, it is synonymous with the term higher education (HE), except that this may be used to include the universities. Consequently, AFE should refer specifically to the local authority and voluntary college sector.

AGCAS	– Association of Graduate Careers Advisory Services. Used to be called Standing Conference of University Appointments Services (SCUAS). An organization of careers advisors to co-ordinate careers advice to graduates in universities and polytechnics.
ALCES	– Association of Lecturers in Colleges of Education in Scotland. A teachers' association. Affiliated to the STUC. A constituent member of FACLS.
ALE	– Association for Liberal Education.
ALRA	– Adult Literacy Resource Agency. See Section **10.2.**9.
ALSCI	– Association of Lecturers in Scottish Central Institutions. A teachers' association affiliated to the STUC. A constituent member of FACLS.
ALSSF	– Adult Literacy Support Services Fund. See Section **10.2.**97 n 45.
ALU	– Adult Literacy Unit. A non-statutory body set up by the DES.
AM	– Administrative Memorandum. A communication from a government department such as the DES or Welsh Office Education Department to local authorities on an administrative matter. See Section **1.3.**5.
AMA	– Association of Metropolitan Authorities. See ACC
AMMA	– Assistant Masters and Mistresses Association. A teachers' organization recruiting in the schools sector. A member of the Burnham Primary and Secondary Committee.
APC	– Association of Principals of Colleges. A teachers' organization in further education. A member of the Burnham Further Education Committee: see Section **9.**34.
APEX	– Association of Professional, Executive, Clerical and Computer Staff. A union affiliated to the TUC.
APSTRC	– Association of Principals of Short Term Residential Colleges. Now part of AACE.
APT	– Association of Polytechnic Teachers.
APT&C	– Administrative, Professional, Technical and Clerical Grades. A term used to describe one of the three main national

negotiating groups that affect further education. The trade unions involved in representing this group of employees are NALGO, GMWU, NUPE, and TGWU. See Section **9.**45.

APU – Assessment of Performance Unit.
A unit established in 1974 within the DES (see Section **7.**39) mainly concerned with primary and secondary education.

ARC – Agricultural Research Council.

ARE – Association for Recurrent Education.

ARELS – Association of Recognised English Language Schools.

ASC – Association for Student Counsellors.
The association has now affiliated as a division of the British Association of Counselling (BAC).

ASE – Association for Science Education.

ASLIB – Association of Special Libraries and Information Services.
An association to promote the development of libraries and information services in industry, academic institutions and the government.

ASTMS – Association of Scientific, Technical and Managerial Staffs.
A TUC affiliated union with a wide membership including the technical staff in some local authority colleges. It is also a union for teaching staff in some Scottish Central Institutions.

ATC – Adult Training Centre.

ATCDE – Association of Teachers in Colleges and Departments of Education.
A teachers' association. Now part of NATFHE.

ATD/C – Art Teachers Diploma/Certificate.

ATDS – Association of Teachers of Domestic Science.
A teachers' organization affiliated to NATFHE and NUT.

ATI – Association of Technical Institutions.
Now ACFHE.

ATO – Area Training Organization.
Prior to 1975 there were twenty three Area Training Organizations which were responsible for the academic oversight of the colleges of education and for the co-ordination of teacher training facilities in their area. Normally based on universities, their membership included representatives of LEAs, teachers and institutions.

ATPE – Association of Teachers in Penal Establishments.
A teachers' association affiliated to NATFHE: see Section **9.**37.

ATTI	–	Association of Teachers in Technical Institutions. A teachers' association. Now part of NATFHE.
AUCAS	–	Association of University Clinical Academic Staff. Now Medical Academic Staffs Committee, a section of the British Medical Association.
AUT	–	Association of University Teachers. A teachers' association affiliated to the TUC.
AVPC	–	Association of Vice Principals of Colleges. A teachers' association.
BA	–	Bachelor of Arts.
BA (often BAAS)	–	British Association for the Advancement of Science.
BAC	–	British Association of Counselling. An organization which includes a number of specialist divisions such as the Association for Student Counselling (ASC).
BACIE	–	British Association for Commercial and Industrial Education. A private body established by commerce and industry to act as a pressure group and a professional association for training officers.
BAS	–	British Association of Settlements. See Section **10.2.**96.
BCS	–	Bachelor of Combined Studies.
BEAS	–	British Educational Administration Society.
BEC	–	Business Education Council. Established by the DES in 1974 to plan a structured set of certificates and diplomas other than degrees and to devise and approve courses leading to such awards: see Section **10.2.**33.
BEEA	–	British Educational Equipment Association.
BEd	–	Bachelor of Education.
B Hum	–	Bachelor of Humanities.
BIM	–	British Institute of Management.
BLL	–	British Lending Library.
BC	–	British Council. An organization designed to promote educational and cultural relations between the United Kingdom and the rest of the world. See Section **2.2.**11.

B Mus	– Bachelor of Music.
BNL	– Background Noise Level. An acoustic measurement relevant in building standards. See Section **5.3.**6.
"Bridlington"	– A name given to a series of resolutions governing the membership and recruitment procedures of unions affiliated to the TUC. The main purpose was to prevent the competitive recruitment of members of one union by another union (poaching), but also covers other matters such as ensuring that union dues are paid up on transfer between unions. Procedures were revised in 1979, and are published in *Disputes Principles and Procedures*, TUC, 1980.
B.Sc.	– Bachelor of Science.
B.Soc Sc.	– Bachelor of Social Science.
B Th.	– Bachelor of Theology.
Burnham	– The name given to the Committees now constituted under the Remuneration of Teachers Act to advise the Secretary of State on the rates of pay of teachers in England and Wales.
CAC	– Central Arbitration Committee. See Section **11.6.**16
CACC	– Council for the Accreditation of Correspondence Colleges.
CAFAD	– Council for Academic Freedom and Democracy.
CAO/SAO	– Chief Administrative Officer/Senior Administrative Officer. The senior administrative post in many colleges. The holder of the post may also act as clerk to the governing body of the college. Some polytechnics use the title Polytechnic Secretary to describe this type of post.
CAPITB	– Chemical and Allied Products Industry Training Board.
CAPES	– Certificate d'Aptitude Pédagogique a l'Enseignement Secondaire. A certificate obtained (France) for a one year course of teacher training and practice carried out at a regional centre following a three year teacher training course (as opposed to the two year course for university students undertaken after one year at university). See Section **6.2.** table one.
CAPS	– Cooperative Awards in Pure Science. An SRC research student award. Now replaced by CASE.
CASE	– Cooperative Awards in Science and Engineering. An award for funding an SRC research student on a project in cooperation with industry.
CASE	– Cooperative Awards in the Sciences of the Environment.

Similar to the SRC scheme above, but operated by NERC.

CASE – Confederation for the Advancement of State Education.
A private confederation of local associations of parents, teachers and other interested parties which acts as a pressure group for the interests of the state education system. Mainly active in the primary and secondary sector.

CAT – College of Advanced Technology.
These colleges were established as a result of a proposal in the 1956 White Paper on Technical Education (Cmnd. 9703). In 1961 the nine maintained CATs transferred from the local authority sector to become direct grant institutions and following a recommendation of the Robbins Report (Cmnd. 2154) became universities in 1966.

CBEVE – The Central Bureau for Educational Visits and Exchanges. See Section **2.6.**2.

CBI – Confederation of British Industries.

CCETSW – Central Council for Education and Training in Social Work.
An independent body financed by government which, through the Health and Social Work (Training) Act 1962, has statutory authority throughout the United Kingdom to promote education and training for social work and for certain other work in the personal social services.

CD – Council Decision (of the EEC).

CDP – Committee of Directors of Polytechnics.

CEA – Council for Educational Advance.
A national body working for the improvement and expansion of the education system. Bodies affiliated to the Council include: teachers' associations, parents' organizations, trade unions and professional bodies.

CED – Centre for Information and Advice on Educational Disadvantage.
A body established by the DES (which announced its intention to withdraw support in November 1979).

CEDEFOP – European Centre for the Development of Vocational Training. See Section **6.2.**15.

CEE – Certificate of Extended Education.
A proposed advanced form of the Certificate of Secondary Education (CSE). See Section **10.2.**11.

CEI – Council of Engineering Institutions.
A federal body of fifteen chartered engineering institutions. It was established by Royal Charter in 1965 and sets standards for the award of Chartered Engineer (C Eng) and professional engineering qualifications through recognition of other awards and its own examinations.

Cert Ed – Certificate in Education.
A qualification obtained after a three year course of teacher training. The Certificate is now being phased out and with the exception of a limited number of one year non-graduate courses in shortage subjects, the last entry to the course was in 1979/80.

CEO – Chief Education Officer.

CERB – Colleges of Education Redeployment Bureau.
See Section **11.7.**15.

CET – Council for Educational Technology.

C Eng – Chartered Engineer.
A qualification awarded by the Council of Engineering Institutions.

CFE – Certificate of Further Education
See Section **10.2.**24 n 11.

CFE – College of further education.

CHE – College of higher education.

CHE – Community Homes with Education on the premises.

"Crombie" – The popular name for the regulations by which staff in teacher training who lose their post as a result of a direction from the Secretary of State receive compensation. See Section **11.5**.

CGLI – City and Guilds of London Institute.
The CGLI awards certificates for studies, mainly part-time and primarily at craft, operative and technician level. See Section **10.2.**18.

CI – Central Institution.
Colleges in Scotland teaching advanced work and funded directly by the Scottish Education Department.

CI – Chief Inspector.
A grade in Her Majesty's Inspectorate of Schools and Colleges.

CI – Community Industry.
A Manpower Services Commission (MSC) employment preparation service especially relevant to the disadvantaged. See Section **4.**14.

CII – Chartered Insurance Institute.
A professional body responsible for insurance examinations.

Circular Letters – An informal and public means of communication from the Department of Education and Science. Designation is now usually FECL (Further Education College Letter) but reference may be made to CL (College Letter), VCL (Voluntary College Letter), ACL (Awards Circular Letter), and TTCL (Teacher Training Circular Letter). See Section **7**, appendices 1-3.

Circulars – Guidance from government departments to local authorities and other bodies. See Section **1.3.**5.

CIPFA – Chartered Institute of Public Finance and Accountancy.

CIPFA FIS – CIPFA Financial Information Service. See Section **3.**75

CITB – Construction Industry Training Board.

CL – College Letter. See Circular Letters.

CLEA – Council of Local Education Authorities. See ACC, AMA, and AEC. The former negotiating forum for matters other than pay for further education lecturers is CLEA/FE. It has been succeeded by a National Joint Council for Further Education (NJC/FE). See also FEAT and FEJWP.

"Clegg" – The popular name for the Standing Commission on Pay Comparability (Clegg Commission) chaired by Professor Clegg of Warwick University. As a result of the 1979 Burnham Agreement the question of teachers' pay was referred to the Commission for investigation.

CLSA – Corporation of London Staff Association.

CNAA – Council for National Academic Awards. See Section **10.2.**42.

COIC – Careers and Occupational Information Centre. A service operated by the Manpower Services Commission.

Coombe Lodge – The Further Education Staff College. See Section **11.13**.

COPOL – Council of Polytechnic Librarians. See Section **5.10.**6.

COPS – Conference of Polytechnic Secretaries. See Section **11.11.**5.

COSLA – Convention of Scottish Local Authorities. The association for Scottish Authorities. Comparable to the ACC and AMA in England and Wales.

COSMOS – Committee on Organisation, Staffing and Management of Schools. See Section **2.2.**52.

CQSW – Certificate of Qualification in Social Work.

CRAC – Careers Research and Advisory Centre.
An independent body, registered as an educational charity whose objectives include the improvement of careers information.

CRC – Community Relations Commission.
Now replaced by the Commission for Racial Equality (CRE).

CRE – Commission for Racial Equality.
A statutory body obliged to discharge certain duties under the Race Relations Act 1976.

CRITE – Committee for Research into Teacher Education.

CSE – Certificate of Secondary Education.
See Section **10.2.**10.

CSU – Central Services Unit.
A unit established to provide assistance and information for university and polytechnic careers and appointment services.

CSU – Civil Service Union.
A TUC affiliated union whose membership includes instructor grades in MSC Skillcentres.

CTC – Central Training Council.
An obsolete body, superseded by the Manpower Services Commission. See Section **10.2.**76.

CTEB – Council of Technical Examining Bodies.
See Section **10.2.**22.

CVCP – Committee of Vice Chancellors and Principals.

CYSA – Community and Youth Services Association.
A professional association for workers in this area. A central association of the NUT.

DATEC – The art and design committee of TEC. See Section **10.2.**70.

DE – Department of Employment.

DES – Department of Education and Science.
See Section **7**.

DGs – Directorates General.
See Section **6.1.**2.

DHSS – Department of Health and Social Security.

Dip AD – Diploma in Art and Design.
A degree equivalent qualification now replaced by a Bachelor of Arts.

Dip HE	– Diploma in Higher Education. A qualification awarded by the CNAA after two years full-time study at advanced level. See Section **10.2.**57.
District Auditor	– A generic term which encompasses the officials appointed on a regional basis by the Department of the Environment. See Section **3.**76.
DITB	– Distributive Industries Training Board.
DMS	– Diploma in Management Studies.
DoE	– Department of the Environment.
DOG	– Directory of Opportunities for Graduates. A directory published annually by Haymarket Press Ltd.
D.Phil	– Doctor of Philosophy.
EAT	– Employment Appeals Tribunal. The "superior court" to industrial tribunals.
ECO	– Entry Certificate Office. See Section **12.10.**8.
EDU	– Educational Disadvantage Unit See Section **7.**39.
EEC	– European Economic Community.
EFL	– English as a Foreign Language.
EFMD	– European Foundation for Management Development. See Section **2.2.**57.
EFVA	– Educational Foundation for Visual Aids.
EIS	– Educational Institute of Scotland. The largest teachers' association in Scotland covering primary, secondary and further education. A TUC and STUC affiliate. See entry for FELNS.
EITB	– Engineering Industry Training Board.
EMA	– Educational Maintenance Allowance. Discretionary grants payable by LEAs to assist students continuing full-time education after 16 in school or further education. Some authorities call FE EMAs "minor awards".
EMAS	– Employment Medical Advisory Service.
EMEU	– East Midlands Educational Union. An examining body. See REB.
EOC	– Equal Opportunities Commission. A statutory body charged with certain duties under the Sex Discrimination Act 1975.

EPA	– Employment Protection Act 1975.
EP(C)A	– Employment Protection (Consolidation) Act 1978.
ERC	– Employment Rehabilitation Centre. A service of the MSC extended to the disabled to assist in overcoming handicaps to employment.
ESD/ESA	– Employment Services Division/Agency. A section of the MSC. The former agency is now termed a division and is responsible for Job Centres.
ESF	– European Social Fund.
ESGE	– Expenditure Steering Group for Education See Section **3.**19.
ESL	– English as a Second Language.
ESN	– Educationally Sub Normal. Currently sub-divided between ESN(M): "mild": and ESN(S): "severe".
ETTUC	– Council of European Teachers' Trade Unions. A joint body of IFFTU and WCT, but exclusive to their European affiliates. Designed specifically for negotiation with the EEC.
ETUC	– European Trades Union Confederation. See Section **6.1.**6.
EUA	– European Unit of Account. See Sections **6.2** and **6.3.**
FACLS	– Federation of Associations of College Lecturers in Scotland. A loose Federation consisting of SFEA, ALCES and ALSCI. The FELNS and ASTMS are not members.
FDTITB	– Food, Drink and Tobacco Industrial Training Board.
FE	– Further Education. The correct administrative term to mean all post-school education excluding the universities, but sometimes used to describe vocational education, as distinct from non-vocational and advanced further education.
FEAT	– Further Education Advisory Team. Officers in the employment of CLEA who advise local authorities and their colleges on expenditure, organization and management of advanced further education.
FECRDU	– Further Education Curriculum Research and Development Unit. See FEU.
FEIS	– Further Education Information Service. See Section **12.1.**8.

FEIS	– Fellow of the Educational Institute of Scotland.
FEJWP	– Further Education Joint Working Party. A group of employer and employee representatives which services both the Burnham Further Education and the NJC/FE committee by considering technical and detailed matters; colloquially pronounced "fudge-up".
FELNS	– Further Education Lecturers National Section (of the Educational Institute of Scotland). A semi independent section of the EIS representing lecturers in further education in Scotland. The section is affiliated to NATFHE.
FERA	– Further Education Research Association. A body of affiliated colleges concerned with the development of research into and within FE. See Section **10.2.**121.
FESC	– Further Education Staff College. (Coombe Lodge) See Section **11.13**.
FESR	– Further Education Statistical Record.
FEU	– Further Education Unit. A shorter version of the full title of FECRDU. Set up by the DES, the unit is responsible for investigating alternatives to and innovation in the FE curriculum. See Section **10.2.**15.
FHE	– Further and higher education.
FISE	– Fédération International Syndicat de l'Enseignement. The largest of the four world teachers' internationals with about 13 million members. Recruits mainly in countries of the socialist bloc.
FITC	– Foundry Industries Training Committee.
"F" level	– A proposed substitute for GCE "A" level examinations. See Section **10.2.**7
FSSU	– Federated Superannuation Scheme for Universities. The pension scheme for university teachers now superseded by a new scheme called the Universities Superannuation Scheme (USS).
FTEs	– Full-time Equivalent students. A measure for costing, accommodation and other purposes where a number of part-time students are held to be equivalent to one full-time student. See Section **8.**52.
GCE	– General Certificate of Education. See Section **10.2.**6.
GET	– Graduate Employment and Training. A directory published annually by Careers Research

	Advisory Centre (CRAC).
GLCSA	– Greater London Council Staff Association. A TUC affiliated union.
GMWU	– National Union of General and Municipal Workers. A TUC affiliated union. See Section **9.**48.
GO	– Graduate Opportunities. A directory published annually by New Opportunities Press.
GPTD	– Guild of Professional Teachers of Dancing.
GSO	– Guild of Senior Officers of the Greater London Council and Inner London Education Authority.
GTC	– General Teaching Council.
GTTR	– Graduate Teacher Training Register Application for Post graduate Certificate in Education courses are made through the GTTR which acts as a clearing house. See Section **12.2**.
"Handbook"	– Abbreviated title for The Handbook of Degree and Advanced Courses in Institutes/Colleges of Higher Education/Colleges of Education, Polytechnics, University Departments of Education. Compiled by the Central Clearing House Ltd and published annually by NATFHE.
HASWA	– Health and Safety at Work etc. Act 1974. A term of convenience rather than delicacy.
HC	– Headmasters' Conference.
HCITB	– Hotel and Catering Industry Training Board.
HE	– Higher Education. A term usually referring to studies of degree or degree equivalent level that require two "A" levels or equivalent as an entry qualification.
HGTA	– Honours Graduate Teachers' Association.
HMI	– Her Majesty's Inspector of Schools. Despite the title HMI also serve colleges. They are answerable to the Secretary of State but are intended to preserve an independence from DES advice. See Section **7.**42.
HMSO	– Her Majesty's Stationery Office.
HNC/D	– Higher National Certificate/Diploma See National Certificates and Diplomas.
HoD	– Head of Department.

Holland Programme	– Named after G. Holland, Director of the Special Programmes Division of the Manpower Services Commission. Holland was chairman of a working party whose report, *Young People at Work*, 1977, led to the creation of the Youth Opportunities Programme.
Hons	– Honours Degree.
Houghton	– The popular name for the report of the Committee of Inquiry into the Pay of Non University Teachers. Chaired by Lord Houghton of Sowerby, the Committee reported in December 1974.
HSC	– Health and Safety Commission. See Section **11.10.**16.
HSE	– Health and Safety Executive. See Section **11.10.**18.
IB	– International Baccalaureate. See Section **10.2.**9.
IBE	– International Bureau of Education. An organ of UNESCO.
ICET	– International Council on Education for Teaching.
ICO	– Institute of Careers Officers.
IDS	– Incomes Data Services.
IES	– Illuminating Engineering Society.
IFFTU	– International Federation of Free Teachers' Unions. One of the four teachers' international organizations; membership of 2,000,000. Mainly European and Social Democrat. The only United Kingdom affiliate is NAS/UWT.
ILEA	– Inner London Education Authority.
IoP	– Institute of Physics.
ITB	– Industrial Training Board. See Sections **4** and **10.2.**75
IRLR	– *Industrial Relations Law Reports.*
ISTC	– International Student Travel Conference. See Section **2.6.**13.
JCC	– Joint Consultative Committee. This can take many forms but often refers to the meeting between representatives of the teachers' associations and officers and members of the education committee within an authority.

JCG	– Joint Consultative Group
JCP	– Job Creation Programme. Now obsolete. The programme was introduced by the MSC in 1975 to provide temporary employment for unemployed people. See STEP.
JEC	– Joint Education Committee. A body constituted to be responsible for a polytechnic or other large institution that is the responsibility of more than one local authority.
JMB	– Joint Matriculation Board. An examining body.
JNC/NJC	– Joint National Council (or Committee)/National Joint Council. A committee of representatives of employers and employees convened to negotiate and to conclude agreements on terms and conditions of service (cf Section **9.**44). SeeNJC.
Joint Committee.	– The term usually applied for the committee of industry and the professions charged with determining the standard of National Certificates and Diplomas.
Joint Secretaries	– There are many bodies which have Joint Secretaries. A particular example is the Burnham FE Committee where the Joint Secretaries are a representative of the Management Panel, an official of LACSAB; and a representative of the Teachers' Panel, the General Secretary of NATFHE.
JUC	– Joint Union Committee. A committee of unions organizing within a particular institution or workplace.
LI; LII	– Lecturer Grade I; Lecturer Grade II. The latter is the more senior of these lecturing grades established under the Burnham Committee.
LACSAB	– Local Authorities' Conditions of Service Advisory Board. This body provides the management side secretariat of Burnham and many other negotiating bodies in local government.
LAMSAC	– Local Authorities' Management Services and Computer Committee. See Section **8.**70.
LCC	– London Chamber of Commerce and Industry. This body offers examinations in secretarial and commercial subjects.
LEA	– Local Education Authority. The local authority responsible under the Education Acts for the provision of education within that area. In England and

Wales (except Inner London) the responsible authorities are non-metropolitan county councils and metropolitan district councils.

LGTB – Local Government Training Board.

MA – Master of Arts.

"Manual" – A loose term used to describe a group of local government workers employed under terms and conditions negotiated in the manual workers' JNC.

MATSA – Managerial, Administrative, and Technical Staff Association. The "white collar" section of the GMWU.

MbO – Management by Objectives. See Section **2.2.**16.

M Ed – Master of Education.

"Milk round" – The practice whereby major employers tour polytechnics, universities and other colleges seeking to recruit graduates and other students.

"Minor Awards" – Discretionary awards to students from local authorities. Each authority will determine its own policy and attitudes. See EMAs.

MMFPITB – Man Made Fibres Producers Industrial Training Board.

Modular – A term used to describe a course of study made up of a number of distinct components. A student may have some choice as to the components to be studied.

M Phil – Master of Philosophy.

MRC – Medical Research Council.

MSC – Manpower Services Commission. A body established under the Employment and Training Act 1973 to undertake the Department of Employment's responsibilities for training and employment exchanges. See Section **4**.

MSc – Master of Science.

NACAE – National Advisory Council for Art Education.

NACE – National Association of Counsellors in Education. An association for counsellors working in the schools sector.

NACEIC – National Advisory Council on Education for Industry and Commerce. Now Defunct.

NACRO – National Association for the Care and Resettlement of

Offenders.
See Sections **10.2.**98 n 49.

NAFE – Non-Advanced Further Education.
A section of the further education system. It may be defined as having an entry requirement of less than two "A" levels.

NAHMAC – National Association of Heads and Matrons of Assessment Centres.

NAHT – National Association of Head Teachers.
A union for head teachers. A member of the Burnham Primary and Secondary Committee.

NAIEA – National Association of Inspectors and Educational Advisers. See Section **8.**37.

NALGO – National and Local Government Officers Association.
A TUC affiliated union. See Sections **8.**39 and **9.**57.

NAME – National Association for Multi Racial Education.

NAS/UWT – National Association of Schoolmasters and Union of Women Teachers.
A union recruiting in primary and secondary edution, a member of the Burnham Primary and Secondary Committee, and TUC affiliated.

NATFHE – National Association of Teachers in Further and Higher Education.
The largest association in further and higher education. It has members in England, Wales and Northern Ireland, and in Scotland though an agreement with the FELNS. It was formed on 1 January 1976 by the merger of the ATCDE and the ATTI; a TUC affiliated union; and the majority member of the Teachers' Panel of the Burnham Further Education Committee. See Section **9.**6.

National Certificates and Diplomas – A structure of courses administered by a Joint Committee comprising representatives of industry, commerce, professional institutions, teachers and other educationalists (and including DES representation). Now being phased out. See Section **10.2.**25.

NATMH – National Association of Teachers of the Mentally Handicapped.

NAYC – National Association of Youth Clubs.
See Section **10.2.**88.

NAYCEO – National Association of Youth and Community Education Officers.
An autonomous national association that has the status of a Central Association of the NUT.

NCTEC	– Northern Counties Technical Examinations Council. A regional examining body. See REB.
NEBSS	– National Examination Board in Supervisory Studies.
NERC	– Natural Environment Research Council.
NES	– National Engineering Scholarships. A scholarship that provides an award in addition to the normal student grant for students on first degree courses in engineering which will form a sound basis for a career in manufacturing. Administered by the DES.
NFER	– National Foundation for Educational Research.
NFPW	– National Federation of Professional Workers.
NIAE	– National Institute for Adult Education. See Section **10.2.**93 n 41.
NFCTA	– National Federation of Continuative Teachers' Associations. Now incorporated in the Association for Adult and Continuing Education (AACE).
NGO	– Non Governmental Organization. A term usually used in international affairs to describe a pressure or interest group which is multi national. As an example, the teachers' internationals, particularly WCOTP and FISE, are recognised by UNESCO as NGOs.
NJC	– National Joint Council. A committee of representatives of employers and employees convened to negotiate and to conclude agreements on terms and conditions of service.
NJC APT&C	– National Joint Council for Administrative, Professional Technical and Clerical Services. The negotiating body for non-manual local government staff.
NNEB	– National Nursery Examining Board.
N+W	– New Opportunities for Women. Manpower Services Commission access courses for women.
NSAE	– National Society for Art Education. A professional association for art teachers with membership in primary, secondary and further education. See Section **9.**41.
NUGMW	– National Union of General and Municipal Workers. See GMWU.
NUPE	– National Union of Public Employees. A TUC affiliated union. See Section **9.**50.
NUS	– National Union of Students.

NUT – National Union of Teachers.
The largest of all teachers' associations. It is a TUC affiliate and recruits in primary and secondary education. It has the majority membership of the Teachers' Panel of the Burnham Primary and Secondary Committee. The NUT and NATFHE have a joint membership scheme.

OECD – Organisation for Economic Co-operation and Development.

OJ – Official Journal of the European Communities.
See Sections **6.2** and **6.3.**

ONC/D – Ordinary National Certificate/Diploma.
See Section **10.**2.25 *et seq.*

ORSP Act – Offices, Shops and Railway Premises Act 1963.

OU – The Open University.

PAR – Programme Analysis and Review.
A central government mechanism for evaluating spending programmes. See Section **3.**7.

PARG – Polytechnic Academic Registrars' Group.
See Section **11.11.**5.

PARVO – Professional and Academic Regional Visits Organisation.
An organization catering for individuals (of postgraduate age) intending to make cultural visits to Britain. See Section **2.6.**4.

"Partnership" Schemes – Programmes designed to revitalise inner city areas under the Inner Urban Areas Act 1978.

PAT – Professional Association of Teachers.

PCET – Polytechnic Council for the Education of Teachers.
A forum for considering the problems of teacher training as they affect the polytechnics.

PEL – Paid Educational Leave.
See Section **10.2.**94.

Pelham – The name given to the committee of teachers and employers which determined the pay of teachers in colleges of education. The resonsibilities of the Pelham Committee were taken over by the Burnham FE Committee following recommendations in the Houghton Report.

PER – Professional and Executive Recruitment.
Operated by the MSC through its Employment Services Division, the PER is desgned to find jobs for people seeking the types of post within its remit.

PESC – Public Expenditure Survey Committee.
See Section **3.**6.

PFOG – Polytechnic Finance Officers' Group. See Sections **3.**73 and **11.11.**5.

PGCE – Postgraduate Certificate of Education. A one year course for graduates to confer qualified teacher status.

PhD – Doctor of Philosophy.

PL – Principal Lecturer.

Polytechnics – Thirty polytechnics were created in England and Wales to become the major institutions in the public sector offering higher education. The initiating White Paper was *A Plan for Polytechnics and Other Colleges: Higher Education in the Further Education System*, Cmnd. 3006.

PPBS – Planned Programme Budgeting System Also known as Output Budgeting or Programme Budgeting.

PPITB – Printing and Publishing Industry Training Board.

Public Sector – A phrase usually used to distinguish local authority and voluntary colleges from the universities: a misleading expression as the universities are heavily dependant on public as distinct from private funds. The universities are referred to by the contrasting expression "the autonomous sector".

"Purple Book" – The common name for the collection of agreements covering administrative, technical and clerical staff in colleges. The abbreviated title is *The Scheme of Conditions of Service* issued by National Joint Council for Local Authorities Administrative, Professional, Technical and Clerical Staffs. See also Section **11.8**.

PWLB – Public Works Loan Board. See Section **3.**34.

QUANGO – Quasi Autonomous Non Governmental Organization. A term, becoming pejorative, which can be used to describe any public body that has any responsibility for advising or determining any matter. Almost every educational body is a quango, but examples might include the CNAA, ACSET and BEC.

RAC – Regional Advisory Council. These were established in 1946 to ensure co-operation between authorities and co-ordinate the provision of both non-advanced and advanced further education. See Sections **8.**65 and **10.2.**23.

RADAR – The Royal Association for Disability and Rehabilitation.

RCCO – Revenue Consequences of Capital Outlay.

REB	– Regional Examining Bodies. The six associations – East Midlands Education Union; Union of Lancashire and Cheshire Institutes; Northern Counties Technical Examinations Council: Union of Educational Institutions: Welsh Joint Education Committee: Yorkshire and Humberside Council for Further Education – which offer various courses at craft and technician level. See Section **10.1.**21.
RMC	– Regional Management Centre. (also known as RCME: Regional Centre for Management Education). A unit designed to concentrate management expertise and advise on the provision of courses, primarily at an advanced level, in management studies within the region.
RNIB	– Royal National Institute for the Blind.
RNID	– Royal National Institute for the Deaf.
RSG	– Rate Support Grant. See Section **3.**18.
RSA	– Royal Society of Arts. See Section **10.2.**20.
RSI	– Regional Staff Inspector. A grade in Her Majesty's Inspectorate of Schools and Colleges.
S	– Section (of an Act of Parliament) : pl. ss.
SAGSET	– Society for Academic Gaming and Simulations in Education and Training.
Sandwich Courses	– Courses designed to include a period of training in industry or commerce.
SAO	– See CAO.
SASSA	– Scottish Approved Schools Staff Association.
SCATO	– Standing Conference of Area Training Organisations.
SCEDSIP	– Standing Conference of Educational Development Services in Polytechnics. See Section **11.11**, reference.
SCOEG	– Standing Conference of Employers of Graduates.
SCONUL	– Standing Conference of National and University Libraries. See Section **5.10.**6.
SCOPADOC	– Standing Conference of Principals and Directors of Colleges.

SCOPE	– Standing Conference on Overseas Placements and Exchanges. See Section **2.6.**4.
SCOTBEC	– Scottish Business Education Council. See BEC.
SCOTEC	– Scottish Technician Education Council. See TEC.
SCRAC	– Standing Conference of Regional Advisory Councils.
SCRE	– Scottish Council for Research in Education.
SCUAS	– Standing Conference of University Appointments Services. See AGCAS.
SED	– Scottish Education Deparmtent.
SEO	– Society of Education Officers. Very closely connected to the affairs of the Association of Education Officers, but the Society acts as a trade union for this group. See Section **8.**37.
SFEA	– Scottish Further Education Association. A union for lecturers in further education in Scotland. A STUC affiliate. A constituent member of FACLS.
SHA	– Secondary Heads Association. A union for head teachers in secondary education. A member of the Burnham Primary and Secondary Committee.
SI	– Statutory Instrument. These usually contain detailed regulations, have legal force, and are made by Secretaries of State under Acts of Parliament.
SL	– Senior Lecturer.
SPD	– Special Programmes Division (of the MSC). The division is responsible for the Youth Opportunities Programme (YOP) and the Special Temporary Employment Programme (STEP). See Section **4.**
SRC	– Science Research Council.
SRHE	– Society for Research into Higher Education.
SSR	– Student: Staff Ratio. See Section **3.**52 and **11.5**.
SSRC	– Social Science Research Council.
SSTA	– Scottish Secondary Teachers' Association.

STEP – Special Temporary Employment Programme.
An MSC programme which has replaced the Job Creation Programme for adults. It seeks to provide adults with temporary employment, particularly in areas of high unemployment. See Section **4.**14 and **10.2.**83.

STSCC – Scottish Teachers Service Conditions Committee.

STUC – ScottishTrades Union Congress.

TEC – Technician Education Council.
See Section **10.2.**27.

Tertiary College – A term normally used for a college run under FE regulations and encompassing both sixth form and FE curricula. Often distinguished from a sixth form college, the latter being run under school regulations and almost exclusively for full-time students.

TES – *Times Educational Supplement.*

TETOC – Technical Education and Training Organisation for Overseas Countries.
See Section **2.6.**14.

TGWU – Transport and General Workers Union.
A TUC affiliated union. See Section **9.**52.

THES – *Times Higher Education Supplement.*

TOPS – Training Opportunities Scheme.
An MSC scheme for adults who require retraining in order to gain employment. The training courses are under the Training Services Division and are related to specific skills and qualifications for which there is a demand. See Sections **4.**7, **10.2.**80 and **12.1.**7.

TPL – Teachers' Pension Letter.

TRADEC – Trade-Education.
See Section **10.2.**24.

Training and FE Consultative Group – A body set up by the MSC and the DES to provide a national forum for the discussion of training and educational matters.

TTCL – Teacher Training Circular Letter.
See Circular Letters.

TSC – Teachers' Service Card.

TSD/TSA – Training Services Division/Agency.
A department of the MSC. The former agency is now called a division. See Section **4.**

TSS – Teachers' Superannuation Scheme.
The pension scheme that applies to teachers, other than in

universities, in the United Kingdom.

TUC – Trades Union Congress.

UCAABAU – Undeb Cenedlaethol Athrawon Addysg Bellach Ag Uwch. (National Association of Teachers in Further and Higher Education.)

UCAC (Pron. ick-ack) – Undeb Cenedlaethol Athrawon Cymru. (National Association of Teachers of Wales).

UCCA – Universities Central Council on Admissions.

UDE – University Department of Education.

UEI – Union of Educational Institutions. This is a regional examining body which offers a wide range of examinations in engineering and commercial subjects; see REB.

UCET – Universities Council for the Education of Teachers.

UGC – University Grants Committee.

UKCOSA – United Kingdom Council for Overseas Student Affairs. An independent body with a membership drawn predominantly from interested organizations rather than individuals. A pressure group for overseas student affairs. See Section **2.6.**15.

ULCI – Union of Lancashire and Cheshire Institutes. An examining body; see REB.

UNESCO – United Nations Educational, Scientific and Cultural Organization.

USS – Universities Superannuation Scheme.

UTMU – University of London Teaching Methods Unit.

UVP – Unified Vocational Preparation. This is a scheme operated jointly by the DES and TSD and is intended to develop forms of vocational preparation that will benefit young people in jobs in which systematic further education and training have not normally been available. See Section **10.2.**73.

VCL – Voluntary College Letter. See Circular Letters.

Virement – The process whereby funds may be transferred from the purpose for which they were originally approved in estimates to another purpose. See Sections **3.**65 n 49.

Voluntary College – An institution with corporate status usually owned by a church or trust and receiving a grant in aid from the DES.

WCOTP – World Council of Organizations of the Teaching Profession. The second largest teachers' international body; recruits mainly in the Western and Third World. Its membership includes NATFHE, NUT, EIS, AMMA. Membership is six million. See Section **9**, Appendix 3.

WCT – World Council of Teachers. The smallest of the four teachers' international bodies; recruits predominately from teachers' associations in catholic schools; largely European. Total membership, 500,000.

WEA – Workers' Educational Association.

WEEP – Work Experience on Employers' Premises. An MSC scheme. See Section **10.2.**85.

WEP – Work Experience Programme. This was an MSC scheme whereby an employer may offer an unemployed young person an opportunity to gain work experience for up to six months. Now absorbed into YOP. See Section **10.2.**83.

WJEC – Welsh Joint Education Committee. Part II of Schedule I of the Education Act, 1944 provides that the WJEC shall be comprised of representatives of teachers in schools and colleges, the University of Wales, the Chief Education Officers and industrial interests in Wales. The WJEC serves as an association of LEAs, a Regional Advisory Council, and an examining body. It has no counterpart in England. See Section **8.**67.

WOED – Welsh Office Education Department.

WOW – Wider Opportunities for Women. MSC access courses for women.

YCHFE – Yorkshire and Humberside Council for Further Education. A regional examining body.

YES – Youth Employment Subsidy. An MSC scheme designed to assist long term unemployed young people into regular employment.

YOP – Youth Opportunities Programme. An MSC scheme directed to those aged 19 and under who have been unemployed for six weeks or more. The range of opportunities covers work experience, work preparation, and includes some special courses in FE colleges. See Sections **4.**12 and **10.2.**84.

YSA – Youth Services Association.

YSF – Youth Services Forum. This is a central body concerned with youth services. One of the quangos abolished in 1979/80.

5 REPORTS AND OFFICIAL PUBLICATIONS

It is a common practice to refer to reports by the name of the chairman of the committee which investigated the subject, and to other official publications by their number. This convenient and sensible mode of reference is not always recognised in library catalogues. To aid further reference therefore a list of reports and official publications relevant to further education since 1944 is given below. The list is not intended to be exhaustive and refers mainly to documents which have either a current significance or are of significant historical note. Short descriptions of the documents are given where appropriate. Because they are the most recent reports, those of Finniston and Mansell have been given more space.

Administrative Memorandum 8/67	*Polytechnics.* The DES issued guidance on the government of polytechnics in this document.
Alexander Report	*The Public Relations of Further Education,* A report by a Sub-Committee of NACEIC, DES and Central Office of Information, 1964.
Bains Report	The introduction of corporate management in local authorities (whereby the chief officers and others work as a team under a chief executive, rather than as separate pinnacles of their own services) was encouraged by a working group of the Study Group on Local Authority Management Structures. The working group chairman was M.A. Bains, Clerk of Kent CC. The Bains Report was intended to make local authority management more effective following the reorganization of local government in 1974; *The New Local Authorities : Management and Structure,* HMSO, 1972.
Bullock Report	*A Language for Life,* the report of the committee of inquiry appointed by the Secretary of State into reading, writing and literacy, HMSO, 1975.
Capps Report	See Pilkington Reports.
Carr Report	*Training for skill : recruitement and training of young workers in industry,* Ministry of Labour and National Service, 1958.
Circular 7/70	*Government and conduct of establishments of further education.* The Circular contains detailed guidance concerning the form and

wording of instruments and articles of government for institutions of further education established according to the Education (No. 2) Act, 1968.

Circular 7/73

Development of higher education in the non-university sector. This Circular followed the White Paper of 1972 and announced the processes and criteria the DES intended to implement in the reorganization of the colleges of education.

Crowther Report

15 to 18, Central Advisory Council for Education (England), 1959.

Dadd Report

See Pilkington Reports.

Delaney "Report"

This is a misnomer. It is not strictly a report, but a set of recommended bands of student:staff ratios for groups of subjects in advanced further education, and was first issued by the Pooling Committee in 1972. The "Delaney norms" are so called after Mr V.J. Delaney (now Director of Financial Services, DES) who produced the original material for the Pooling Committee and who has updated the work annually.

Finniston Report

Engineering Our Future, Report of the Committee of Inquiry into the engineering profession, Cmnd. 7794, HMSO, January 1980. The Committee, under the chairmanship of Sir Monty Finniston, recommended that an Engineering Authority be set up with Parliamentary powers to advance the cause of engineering throughout the economy and the manufacturing industry. An executive of between 15 and 20 members, mostly engineers, would implement the remaining proposals. These proposals are: the creation of a three-tiered system of engineering titles (Registered Engineering Diplomate; Registered Engineer; Associate Engineer), the quality of those gaining the qualifications to be controlled by the new authority; degrees of BEng and M Eng to replace existing BSc, BA and MSc engineering degrees, the new degrees to be more practical and contain more training elements; a minimum of two years' training following graduation and before registration, company training schemes to be monitored; the new university courses to be monitored and accredited by the Engineering Authority and those below standard not to be allowed to award B Eng or M Eng titles; the introduction of a recognition system for engineering teachers with strong industrial experience (and accreditation of courses then to depend on the number of "recognized" staff in a department); polytechnics to be given complete autonomy to set up strong engineering courses and education independent of local authorities' control; the Engineering Authority to advise the Government on proposals for a scheme to license consultant engineers; in certain health and safety matters (e.g. mining and maritime work) regulations should require the employment of a "suitably qualified person who is a registered engineer"; the Government and public sector to set a lead in recruiting engineers on the new register and to encourage industry to do the same; the Engineering Authority to draw up a code of professional conduct; and M Eng and B Eng students to receive bursaries (of £250) on top of grants. The proposed three tier organization of engineering education would entail the first level (Associate Engineer) being based on the new TEC qualifications of higher certificates and higher diploma in engineering subjects (to be done mainly part-time and accumulate considerable practical experience). The other two levels (REng and REng Dip) are proposed to be based on the proposed new engineering degrees (BEng and MEng). The most significant element of the Finniston document is the establishment of the Engineering Authority. In its proposed functions of reviewing standards, qualifications, courses, research and development, technology, and industrial and employment practices, and also in establishing national engineering manpower audits, encouraging the use of registered engineers, and finding means of attracting more women into engineering, it may well, if established, change dramatically the nature of engineering and engineering education. The Report envisages industry helping by way of joint initiatives in the planning of courses. Its essential purpose is the production of more practically and industrially motivated engineers.

Haslegrave Report

Report of the Committee on Technician Courses and Examinations, HMSO, 1969. This report recommended the establishment of the Business Education Council and the Technician Education Council.

Haycocks Report

The Haycocks Report of 1975 which was not published until 1977 is commonly referred to as "Haycocks 1." As the other two documents have not yet been endorsed by ACSET, though some RACs have begun to implement their proposals, their formal status is currently that of documents sent out to interested bodies for comment. Hence it is technically correct to refer to the 1975/77 report as the Haycocks Report, but the successor documents are commonly termed "Haycocks 2" and "Haycocks 3". The documents are:
The Training of Teachers for Further Education: a report by the Sub-Committee on the Training of Teachers for Further Education relating to the training of full-time teachers in Further Education, ACSTT, June 1975 (DES, November 1977);
The Training of Adult Education and Part-Time Education Teachers: a report by the Sub-Committee on the Training of Teachers for Further Education, ACSTT.
Training Teachers for Education Management in Further and Adult Education: a report by the Sub-Committee on the Supply and Training of Teachers, ACSTT, August 1978.

Henniker-Heaton Report

Day Release: the report of a committee set up by the Minister of Education, DES, 1964.

Houghton Report

Report of the Committee of Inquiry into the Pay of Non-University Teachers, Cmnd. 5848, HMSO, 1974. This major review of teachers' salaries resulted in substantial reform.

Hudson Report

This 1973 report concerning education for agriculture and allied subjects has not yet had any action taken upon it.

Hunt Report

See Pilkington Reports.

James Report

Teacher Education and Training, HMSO, 1972. This report proposed the reorganization of teacher training in three cycles : periods of general education, professional training, and induction. ACSTT (now reconstituted as ACSET: see Section **1.4**) was set up as a result of the report. The 1972 White Paper was based on the report's recommendations as well as the debate which it provoked.

Keohane Report

Proposals for a Certificate of Extended Education, Cmnd. 7755, HMSO, 1979. This report recommended the national introduction of the CEE. The examination is proposed to have a vocational and personal developmental content. It is intended to cater for those whose examination achievements at 16 plus were in the range covered by CSE grades 2-4 who have no clear career intentions, wish to continue their education for a further year, and do not aspire to "A" levels. The Report stresses that the Keohane Committee considers the preparation of young people for employment crucial (see also Section **10.2.**11).

Layfield Report

Local Government Finance, Report of the Committee of Enquiry, Cmnd. 6453, HMSO, 1976.

Longden Report

See Pilkington Reports.

Mansell Report

A Basis for Choice, Further Education Curriculum Review and Development Unit, 1979. A report concerned with 16 year olds on pre-employment courses. It advocates a common core curriculum laid down in checklists of skills and experiences a young person should possess, the core to occupy 60% of a one year course. The remaining time would be divided equally between learning about a broad vocational sector and learning some specific job skills. The core proposed is based on 12 major aims, each aim being expressed through specific objectives. The report suggests that the objectives should be assessed in the form of a profile. Although the report is concerned directly only with the 16-19 age range on pre-employment courses, the Mansell Committee states that it is based on education for all young people and takes into account the demands of adult and working life.

Newsom Report

Half our Future. A report of the Central Advisory Council for Education, (England), Ministry of Education, HMSO, 1963. This report considered the education of average and below average 13-16 year old pupils. Its main recommendations included the raising of the school leaving age to 16 and a more outward looking curriculum.

Oakes Report

Report of the Working Group on the Management of Higher Education in the Maintained Sector, Cmnd. 7130, HMSO, 1978. This report recommended the creation of a National Body which would be concerned with the planning and costing of advanced further education although individual maintaining and governing bodies would retain overall institutional management control. The establishment of nine new regional councils was recommended.

Percy Report

Higher Technological Education, Ministry of Education, 1945.

Pilkington Reports

This common name has been used for the reports of a committee of NACEIC concerning the more effective use of college resources, which was under the chairmanship of Lord Pilkington until December 1966 and Sir Joseph Hunt from January 1967. The first report, which contains recommendations concerning minimum student numbers is the best known. The reports are: *The Sizes of Classes and Approval of Further Education Courses,* NACEIC/HMSO, 1966 (Pilkington Report). *Report of the Advisory Committee on Agricultural Education;* NACEIC/HMSO, 1955 (Dadd Report). *A Report on the Use of Buildings and Equipment,* NACEIC/HMSO, 1967 (Longden Report). *A Report on the Use of Costing and other Financial Techniques in Technical Colleges,* NACEIC/HMSO, 1969 (Capps Report). *An Inquiry into the Pattern and Organisation of the College Year,* NACEIC/HMSO, 1970 (Hunt Report).

Plowden Report	*Children and their Primary Schools,* A report of the Central Advisory Council for Education (England), 2 vols, HMSO, 1967. This report had considerable influence in primary school development and in the nature of teacher education.
Robbins Report	*Higher Education,* Cmnd. 2154, HMSO, 1963. This report provided the rationale for the expansion of higher education in the 1960s.
Russell Report (1)	*The Supply and Training of Teachers for Further Education,* Report of the Standing Sub-Committee on Teachers of the National Advisory Council on the Training and Supply of Teachers, 1966, HMSO.
Russell Report (2)	*Adult Education : A Plan for Development,* HMSO, 1973.
Taylor Report	*A New Partnership for our Schools,* Report of a Committee of Enquiry, DES, 1977. This report refers to the government and management of schools but has been held in some quarters to indicate possible developments which could affect FE : this view does not have universal acceptance.
Warnock Report	*Special Educational Needs,* Report of the Committee of Enquiry into the Education of Handicapped Children and Young People, Cmnd. 7212, HMSO, 1978.
Weaver Report	*Report of the study group on the government of colleges of education,* HMSO, 1966.
White Paper 1956	*Technical Education,* Cmnd. 9703, HMSO. This document proposed the expansion of FE, particularly in advanced work, and the creation of the CATs.
White Paper 1961	*Better Opportunities in Technical Education,* Cmnd. 1254, HMSO. This White Paper led to the implementation of the Crowther Report.
White Paper 1966	*A Plan for Polytechnics and Other Colleges,* Cmnd. 3006, HMSO. This document proposed the expansion of polytechnics.

White Paper 1972

Education A Framework for Expansion Cmnd. 5174, HMSO, 1972. Referred to by the disaffected as a framework for contraction or confusion, the White Paper proposed the expansion of nursery education, the creation of the DipHE and the reorganization of the colleges of education (see Circular 7/73).

Willis Jackson Report

The Supply and Training of Teachers for Technical Colleges, Ministry of Education, 1957. Suggested the creation of a residential college to provide management training for senior college lecturers and administrators, resulting in the creation of The Further Education Staff College. Also suggested compulsory teacher training for further education teachers, a recommendation rejected simultaneously with its publication by the then Secretary of State.

Section 2

COLLEGE GOVERNMENT AND MANAGEMENT

1 COLLEGE GOVERNMENT

1. The document which carries the recommendations of the DES on the implementation of the Education (No.2) Act 1968, is *Government and Conduct of Establishments of Further Education,* Circular 7/70. The purpose here is to outline provisions arising from the Act and Circular 7/70, to give some explanation of their growth, to discuss their implementation, and to give indications of the debate concerning revision. Inevitably, the issue of college government is closely linked to that of college management and it is presumed that this sub-section will be considered in conjunction with its successor.

2. Many of the features of the governing bodies recommended by Circular 7/70 had been sought both officially and unofficially for some considerable time. Circular 98 of 1946, the White Paper of 1956 on *Technical Education,* the 1959 Further Education Regulations and Circular 7/59, and the Robbins Report of 1963, *Higher Education,* all contained recommendations and guidance concerning the government of colleges. The issues may be summarised broadly as those of control, and by whom: it was urged that governing bodies should be strong and adequately represent industrial, commercial, professional, university and local authority interests.

3. It followed that if there were to be strong governing bodies which would secure better educational provision, then they should enjoy a certain freedom of action. The issue of freedom of action was not confined to governing bodies but, especially during the 1960s, was of concern to academic staff and to students : many staff believed that in order that they might better carry out their academic functions there should be less local authority control of colleges; and students, as consumers, maintained that they had a right to participate in decisions concerning their education. It was against this background of long held central recommendations, current debate and the expansionist policies and beliefs of the time that the Weaver Committee was constituted.

4. The Weaver Committee's brief was originally narrow, relating only to the colleges of education. However, the issue of how far academic freedom and student participation was compatible with local authority responsibility and public control was clearly relevant to all colleges. The recommendations of the 1966 Weaver Report, *Report of the study group on the government of colleges of education,* were partially applied to the further education system, an action encouraged by the establishment of the polytechnics. A condition of the designation of a polytechnic imposed by the DES was the making of approved instruments and articles of government based on the Weaver model. (Administrative Memorandum 8/67 contains the DES recommendations for the government of polytechnics, but as they do not differ significantly from those of Group A colleges under Circular 7/70 they are not here usually discussed separately). Weaver had recommended that governing bodies should have a legal status.

This status would be both a safeguard against interference, and allow the government of colleges to be of an approved form and nature. This was effected by the Education (No.2) Act 1968. The Act stated that there should be an instrument of government which provided for the constitution of a body of governors of an institution. The institution had to be conducted in accordance with articles of government. However, it took some two years of consultations by the DES with authorities and staff and student organizations – against a backcloth of political unrest on the issues of academic freedom and student participation – before Circular 7/70 was issued to give recommendations on the implementation of the Act. While the Circular was quickly implemented for the colleges of education, there was considerable delay for other colleges (see Section **1.3.**18) and it was not until September 1972 that the 1968 Act was brought into force for maintained establishments of further education.

5. Circular 7/70 may be seen as the Department's wish in reforming college government to provide for a circumscribed institutional freedom accompanied by student representation and reduction of local authority representation on the governing body. Some legal implications of the 1968 Act and Circular 7/70 are discussed in Sections **1.3** and **12.6.**25; other implications and the subsequent debate are discussed below.

6. Circular 7/70 relates to all establishments of further education under the 1968 Act (except polytechnics, but as noted above the advice contained in Administrative Memorandum 8/67 is sufficiently similar to allow parallel consideration here); and although instruments of government for establishments of further education did not require the approval of the Secretary of State, it was considered "helpful to the authorities if he offers some general advice" concerning the composition of governing bodies. Colleges of education under the 1968 Act were treated separately, their instruments of government requiring the Secretary of State's approval. However, after reorganization, despite being a part of the further education system, those colleges which offer teaching training courses continue to be regarded as "colleges of education" for the purpose of college government; the Secretary of State's approval remains necessary here for instruments of government. Articles of government of all institutions engaged in the provision of full-time and sandwich FE courses have to be submitted to the Secretary of State for approval.

7. Circular 7/70 considered that if major establishments of further education were to function effectively, then their governing bodies would need to include "substantial representation of industrial, commercial and other appropriate interests from the areas they serve." This advice was supplemented by other criteria:

   (i) There should normally be 20-25 governors: exceptions could be made to allow for representation of an unusually wide range of interests; but more than one interest might be represented by a single individual.

   (ii) LEA representatives should account usually for one third, or even one quarter, of the governing body; and in any event be less than half of the total composition. Included in providing LEA representation should be, where appropriate, representatives of other LEAs.

(iii) While the governing body should consist largely of persons with current industrial, commercial and other relevant experience who have an active interest in further education, there should also be "substantial provision" for representation of employers, unions and senior industrial and commercial personnel with training responsibilities (such as industrial training board representatives). One third of the governing body should consist of direct representation of commercial and industrial interests.

(iv) Specialist colleges should have governing bodies which reflect their activities: art colleges should have strong relevant industrial and commercial representation and the participation of distinguished artists and designers; professional institutions, polytechnics and universities should be represented where colleges undertake a substantial proportion of advanced work, and representation here (in the person of the principal) of a feeder college supplying preparatory non-advanced courses would also be appropriate. A head teacher from a school providing a college with students is also considered often to be appropriate as a governing body member.

(v) Although the exact number of staff members of the governing body are to be determined according to the levels of work and other circumstances of the college, Circular 7/70 recommends that staff representation should consist of at least the principal and two other teaching staff members. The academic board, where it exists, should appoint one or more staff governors; and, in addition, at least one staff governor should be elected by the whole teaching staff.

(vi) The Circular advises that where colleges have a substantial number of students aged over 18, or a substantial number of advanced courses, "consideration should be given to the inclusion of students [in the governing body] appointed through the students' union", and that while such representation is offered for consideration in other cases, that the general power of co-option is available to governing bodies. (See also Section **12.7**.11).

(vii) Powers of co-option can, and should, be used to obtain the services of further representatives as instanced in the categories above. While it would not be appropriate for the person chairing the governing body to be the principal or a staff or student governor, the Circular specifies that the person need not be an LEA representative but could usefully be drawn from industrial, commercial or professional representatives, whether a co-opted member or not.

(viii) In the case of residential colleges of adult education and agricultural colleges, while the composition of the governing body should still reflect the interests and activities of the college, the Circular states that there will be variations according to the circumstances of the institution.

8. The Circular contains advice on the making of instruments of government and grouping arrangements. As this issue now largely relates to revision rather than original constitution, it can be summarised briefly; the DES welcomes consultation concerning the preparation of instruments, and draws

attention to the need to consult with appropriate local interests, the present governing body, teaching staff, and students' union or similar body: such DES consultation can include the composition of the governing body and matters related to the appointment and terms of office of governors, meetings and proceedings, election of officers, and the right of the chief education officer or his representative (where not appointed clerk to the governors) to receive papers and attend meetings. Where a single body governs more than one college (see Section **1.3.**21) the approval of the Secretary of State is necessary and most of the recommendations concerning the composition of the governing body will apply, subject to necessary adjustments because of the involvement of several institutions. Where a college is jointly maintained, it is for the maintaining authorities to decide whether they themselves or the joint education committee should make the instrument and articles of government.

9. Although 7/70 observes that all the characteristics of a college will have to be taken into account in the drafting of articles of government, it itemises three major determining criteria, the first of which it states to be the most significant and the second of considerable importance. The criteria are: the proportion and volume of advanced work (see Sections **1.2.**23, **1.3**, Appendix 1, and **11.2**) undertaken in the college; the overall size of the college; and the number of students aged over 18 engaged on all categories of work. For the purposes *only* of drafting articles of government, 7/70 defined three broad categories of institution, the definitions intended to be no more than general guides:

Group A : colleges with a substantial proportion of advanced work;
Group B : other colleges with a significant amount of advanced work; and
Group C : colleges with little or no advanced work.

This classification is not directly relevant to the position of students. The criteria recommended here to LEAs are the age composition of the students, particularly those aged 18 or over; and the numbers of full-time or sandwich students and evening or part-time day students.

10. The Annex to Circular 7/70 contains notes and model articles of government. The model articles are recommended as being appropriate to Group A colleges, are not intended to be comprehensive, but in the matter of the headings of interpretation, conduct of the college, and committees, are advised as applicable to all colleges. In the case of the headings: academic organization, staff appointments, and finance, Groups B and C college articles will require to be considered according to their circumstances. The provisions of the model articles are summarised in paragraphs 11-29 below, except in the cases of finance and students, of which brief mention only is made since these topics are investigated thoroughly under Sections **3.**63; **12.7.**11; and **12.6.**25.

11. *Interpretation.* The terms "college", "governors", "authority" and "Secretary of State" require to be defined, and a clause is inserted concerning the application of The Interpretation Act 1889 to apply as it does for Acts of Parliament. (There is now an Interpretation Act 1978).

12. *Conduct of the college.* The model articles here state that the college is to be conducted in accordance with the current and any subsequent Education Acts and statutory instruments "and, subject thereto, with the provision of these Articles."

13. The general educational character of the college and its place within the local system is the responsibility of "The Authority, in consultation with the Governors," although the governors are responsible "for the general direction of the college." The principal is to be responsible to the governors for the internal organization, management and discipline of the college, and the chief administrative officer of the college is recommended to act as clerk to the governors. A note to the Annex observes that while it will usually be appropriate for a CAO to act as Clerk for Group A and some Group B colleges, in other cases such designation will depend upon college circumstance and "no doubt often be considered appropriate" for this function to be exercised by the chief education officer of the authority.

14. *Committees.* It is recommended that governors establish such committees as they think fit, and determine their membership and functions. Where appropriate, committee membership should include student representation, and any committee might establish sub-committees and determine their membership and function.

15. *Academic organization.* The notes recommend the model article concerning academic boards as appropriate for Group A colleges, and refer to the desirability of student representation or attendance with observer status, adding the reminder of the power of co-option. While provision for an academic board in other cases will depend on circumstance, for Group B colleges this is stated to be "usually ... desirable": membership here would consist of the principal, vice-principal where such a post exists, and such other members of the teaching staff appointed to the board according to the arrangements which the governors may make. In the case of Group C colleges where a substantial number of students are aged over 18 and following full-time courses, the notes state that LEAs "may wish to include specific provision for an Academic Board", and that where this action is not taken the articles of government should require the governors regularly to consult the teaching staff concerning the regulation and organization of the academic work of the college.

16. The model article provides for there to be a college academic board which comprises: the principal (who will take the chair); the vice-principal, if any, all heads of department and other teaching staff with comparable responsibilities; the college CAO; the college librarian; and not less than six teaching staff members – the exact number being determined by the governors – elected from their own number according to arrangements devised and approved by the academic board. The model provides for co-option, the numbers to be determined.

17. The academic board is to be "responsible for the planning, co-ordination, development and oversight of the academic work of the college", subject to

the governors' overall responsibilities but including arrangements for student admissions and examinations. As for the governing body, the academic board is to establish committees as it thinks fit, determine membership and function, and the committees may establish and determine the membership and function of sub-committees. Where appropriate, committees shall include student representatives. The academic board is given the power of delegation: this allows delegation to departments where issues do not affect other departments or the college as a whole.

18. *Appointment, promotion and dismissal of staff.* (NB: the provisions of the model articles summarised below should be considered in conjunction with the provisions of employment law and conditions of service agreements: see Sections **11.6-9**, below).

19. The model article makes reference to seven topics. Where a vacancy arises in the posts of principal, vice-principal (if any), or chief administrative officer, it is to be advertised and a short list of candidates selected for interview by a committee. The committee is to consist of whatever number of governors decided upon by the governing body and one or two persons appointed by the LEA. Unless the committee elects to re-advertise the post, it is to interview the candidates and make an appointment subject to LEA confirmation.

20. The principal is to have general responsibility for the appointment of other teaching staff members, subject to arrangements made by the governors after consultation with the academic board; but with the exception that where a head of department is to be appointed, there is to be representation of the governing body on the selection committee and the appointment subject to its confirmation.

21. Apart from the post of chief administrative officer, in accordance with arrangements approved by the governors after taking the principal's advice, the responsibility for the appointment of non-teaching staff within the approved establishment is to be delegated to the principal.

22. The model states that all staff shall be appointed to specified posts in the college in the service of the LEA, such appointments to be subject to "such conditions of service as the Authority may determine."

23. The governors, or their chairman, have the power to suspend the principal, vice-principal or chief administrative officer, provided such actions are reported at once to the govenors. With the similar proviso of immediate report to the govenors, the principal is empowered to suspend any member of staff other than the vice-principal or CAO. Any instance of suspension is to be notified at once to the LEA.

24. Governors are empowered in the model articles to recommend to the LEA that the principal, vice-principal or CAO should be dismissed, and to dismiss any other staff member, subject to the LEA's confirmation. A staff member is entitled to a personal hearing of his or her case, accompanied by a friend if

so desired, at any meeting of the governors, LEA or their committees or sub-committees at which the dismissal is to be considered.

25. The notes to this model state that such procedures are appropriate for Group A colleges and that while the general pattern will be suitable for other colleges, LEAs will wish to consider variations according to college circumstance; for example, the extent of the governors' involvement in the appointment of different grades of teaching staff.

26. *Finance, premises and supplies* As this model article is considered in detail in Section **3.**65, only a general summary is given here. The proposed powers for governors are: an entitlement to incur expenditure approved in estimates (which have been submitted to the LEA) without reference back, including powers to execute repairs, maintenance and alterations up to a determined figure (the sum of £500 is suggested); to order supplies, services and equipment up to a determined figure without there being a requirement to use the authority's central purchasing arrangements; to exercise virement within accounts headings; and to determine the numbers and grades of teaching staff, subject to the provisions of the Burnham salaries documents.

27. *Students.* A summary of the model provisions relating to students will be found under Sections **12.6.**26, and **12.7.**11.

28. *Consultative committees.* The model provides for governing bodies to make consultative arrangements allowing for the expression of commercial, industrial, professional, and art and design interests.

29. *Copies of articles.* A copy of the articles is to be given on appointment to every governor, every member of the full-time teaching staff and the CAO. A copy is to be available on request to all part-time teachers, students and members of the non-teaching staff. The date is to be given on which the articles come into force.

30. **Discussion of college government**

No matter to what extent the model articles contained in Circular 7/70 have been adopted, it is vital to understand the legal implications of instruments and articles. Articles are made under an instrument of government of a body which has legal status (although it should be added that there is a view that this status could be challenged in a court of law). However, articles may be held to constitute what may be termed for the purposes of any further education institution, a codified domestic law. This domestic law has to have regard to matters of employment law, and the law of the land. For example, the procedures of employment law relating to dismissal of staff will have to be observed. The crucial employment law issue for maintained colleges is that the LEA is the employer (see paragraph 38, below). However, college articles form part of the contract with the college of both staff and students.

It is essential for this reason, especially in the case of students, that the provisions of the college domestic law are well understood by all whom they govern, and by all responsible for their implementation.

31. It is now appropriate to consider in turn the components of college government, and to indicate to what extent DES advice has been implemented.

32. **Governing bodies**
Although the Education (No.2) Act 1968 did not require the Secretary of State's approval of the instruments of government of the then further education colleges, the DES nonetheless considered these instruments and commented on them. It will have been noted that it took some time before Circular 7/70 was generally implemented, and since then there have been subsequent revisions in many institutions of the instruments and articles of government. However, certain general conclusions can be drawn.

33. In the composition of the governing body, it appeared in 1976 that local authority representation accounted for between a quarter and half of the total membership, [1] but this total could include local authority representatives who were *ex officio* members. It is often the case that local authority representatives are specified as being education committee members, elected members, or council members who are members of the education committee. According to Locke a variety of arrangements apply for commercial, industrial, professional and other representatives: the most common appear to be co-option or nomination by the governing body; or appointment according to the nomination of the particular relevant interests; or appointment according to imprecise methods. Locke states that numbers of such persons vary from four to 13. Staff representation appears to go no further than that suggested in 7/70 but that of students is more than might have been expected from the terms of the Circular. Special categories of membership, such as life membership, obtain in some cases. Most governing bodies appear to have a membership of between 20 and 30.

34. It appears usual now for instruments in metropolitan district authorities to

1 This information, and other estimates contained in paragraphs 33-36 are drawn largely from information provided by Lynton Gray and the survey published by Michael Locke in *The Instruments and Articles of Government of FE Colleges*, Coombe Lodge Report, Vol. 9 No. 2, 1976. The survey sample, it should be noted, was small. Present conclusions can be no more than general. For example, an FE college governing body not surveyed by Locke has five LEA representatives; two neighbouring LEA representatives; two external teacher representatives; and 16 industrial and commercial representatives.

insist on the person occupying the chair of the governing body being an authority representative. This stipulation is less common in the counties. However, students, staff and principals are generally excluded from holding such office. The post of clerk to the governors appears to be held more often by the chief education officer (or the borough treasurer) than the college CAO but there are cases where this provision was made in the first instance only: as a college developed, it was accepted that the post could be taken over by the CAO. Most authorities insist that the CEO or his representative shall have the right to attend meetings and to speak.

35. Academic board representation on the governing body is occasionally restricted to heads of department. Locke suggests that elected staff representation follows 7/70 in that there is a common practice of the election of representatives by the whole teaching staff. Student representatives are either union officers *ex officio* or else elected to the governing body. Locke's survey shows that powers of co-option are used. Some authorities have adopted a method of staff representation which follows this pattern: two teachers elected by the academic board; two teachers elected by the full-time teaching staff; and two representatives elected by the non-teaching staff.

36. The three groups of colleges established for the purpose of Circular 7/70 allowed those colleges with greater proportions of advanced work to have greater independence. This independence gave more power to governing bodies, especially in financial matters, and also to academic boards. However, the groups of colleges were never distinctly categorised in practice, and this has resulted in the modification of stated arrangement by practice. There has been a loss of distinction in many instances between Groups B and C; whereas the DES exerted its influence to ensure a general adherence of Group A colleges to model procedures, this was less so in the case of the other groups, with the result that in some authorities there is similarity between all college instruments and articles, and in others group distinctions or modifications are maintained. Some authorities make no distinctions and have identical instruments and articles for all their colleges. In other places, distinctions made in government – and in the staffing establishment – can be severe: for example, it can be the practice that a Group B college is prevented in any significant way from approaching the status of a Group A institution. However, the 7/70 model article statement that "The governors shall be responsible for the general direction of the college" is common to many institutions. While this duty is modified both by 7/70 and according to the circumstances of institutions, and limited by the responsibilities allocated to the authority, principal and academic board, governing bodies retain considerable powers and duties. Those powers for individual institutions depend on particular instruments and articles but may be generally ascertained from the summary of 7/70, above and paragraphs 38-41 below. It is necessary however, to indicate areas of difference and discretion which may occur in practice.

37. Articles of government frequently specify the functions of the governing

body. These functions may be seen as the means of ensuring a balance between a college's degree of independence and the various responsibilities of the LEA. The major headings in this respect are usually summarised as: estimate preparation; buildings maintenance; supplies and equipment; expenditure and virement; staff; and student discipline. In each case, however, the governing body's power is hedged by other considerations, such as the allocated (or real, whether officially allocated or not) power of the academic board, principal, local authority, NATFHE branch, non-teaching staff union branches, and the student union. Much therefore depends on individuals, and circumstance. The governors retain considerable real powers: for example, the power of dismissal subject to LEA approval; and articles of government frequently allocate responsibility for matters which can be of consequence, such as the arrangement of lettings (see Section **5.10.**5) or the fixing of vacations. The essential consideration is that while instruments and articles of government allow for the formal allocation of powers and responsibilities, it is difficult if not impossible for a formal constitution wholly to determine how powers are exercised.

38. Nonetheless, governing bodies are responsible for "the general direction of the college", however that is defined and implemented in practice, and can have recourse to law. They may sue and be sued, seek a court order to uphold their powers, and in extremity might appeal to the Secretary of State or to the local ombudsman. Yet by contrast the LEA has wider legal functions: the LEA is the employer of staff, responsible for the premises, and has a duty under the Education Act, 1944 to provide "adequate facilities" for further education. It is difficult therefore to draw clear distinctions in any practical sense, between an LEA and a governing body where conflicts might arise, especially since Circular 7/70 gives LEAs responsibility for the "general educational character" of a college. An illustration of function difference and overlap may be seen under 7/70 model articles where governors' appointments functions below the grade of head of department are delegated to the principal, but in the case of dismissal, the governors make the decision, subject to the LEA's confirmation. Thus, the LEA here retains a control and responsibility as the employer but is removed from decisions until the latest possible stage, which while although consonant with college independence makes difficult the fulfilling of a principle of the Employment Protection Acts which insist that the employer has a responsibility toward the person whom he or she has employed. In the employment market the principle of *caveat emptor* may be said to apply, but here the buyer is a delegate of the governors, and the body with ultimate responsibility for the purchase, the LEA. This perhaps unpleasant analogy is not intended to argue for change or limitation in college freedom, and especially in this example since colleges are more qualified to make academic appointments than LEAs; rather, it is to demonstrate both possible confusions and the need for consultation and liaison between all those with college governmental responsibilities. But to return to the governors' powers, although the cost and disruption might be considerable, it is possible

for them to insist to a large extent on their policies being implemented.

39. At one extreme a governing body might act as no more than a rubber stamp to decisions taken elsewhere; at another, the governors might dominate an institution (as might a principal). Governors themselves may be professional persons, unwilling to criticise or act against staff or a principal since those persons are fellow professionals, and are in consequence to be allowed their professional discretion. However, the most powerful governors can often be the LEA members. There are also simple practicalities which inhibit action: the office of clerk to the governors is crucial, for the composition of agenda and the recording of minutes can determine action; and whatever decisions a governing body might take depend for their effectiveness upon how and by whom they are executed. Trite and unhelpful though it may seem, all which can really be said with any certainty is that while governors have considerable powers under the instruments and articles of college government, whatever the degree of implementation of Circular 7/70, the determinant in any issue remains that of circumstance: governing bodies may generally be said in theory to have a function which is both one of watchfulness as a monitoring body and allowing of action in an emergency; but often in practice they are fairly passive entities and only brought into action, as an emergency service, in times of need. However, an important rider must be added, for it is in the sub-committees of the governing body that real power can be wielded. Sub-committees such as Finance and General Purposes (especially in estimates preparation) and Establishment can determine much college policy.

40. In practical terms, governing bodies are limited in their actions. Whatever financial arrangements they make or may wish to make, they have to respect the financial policies and available resources of the LEA; the actual competence of the governing body to provide the college with a general direction may not be achieved; and it can be argued that such is the force of circumstance that governors are, in reality, almost powerless to exercise any real function. This raises the question of the necessity for the existence of governing bodies. In supplying one answer, Michael Locke puts forward six arguments[2]:

(i) whereas governors in the role of watchdog may go to sleep, and in the role of fire brigade may act neither wisely nor with experience, there is a need for bodies in emergencies which can act in "a more public or more muscular" way than can formal bureaucracy;

(ii) governors can reconcile the interests of the public, LEA, teaching and non-teaching staff, and students;

(iii) the governing body can act as the forum in which educational issues are debated;

---

2 *Handbook for College Governors*, Coombe Lodge Report Vol.11, No.10, 1978, pp 374-76. There has been a tendency of late to increase the proportion of elected teachers serving on governing bodies, and also to include more non-teaching staff and student representatives: see Keith Ebbutt and Roger Brown, "The Structure of Power in the FE College", *Journal of Further and Higher Education*, Vol.2, No.3, Autumn, 1978, p.15.

(iv) governors can monitor developments, and be sufficiently above the heat of college activities to exercise independent judgement;

(v) even if acting merely as a rubber stamp, governing bodies by their decisions facilitate action and also then open those decisions to public comment and debate; and

(vi) that the existence of a governing body will allow for a portion at least of its membership to offer a wise and improving counsel compatible with the processes of democracy.

41. Locke's arguments presume other factors. Acceptable in themselves they may be, but the issue is bound up with other facets of college management: an LEA is as responsible for a good working relationship as a governing body (as indeed is a principal), and it is argued by many that the use of corporate management within local authorities (see Section **8**.9) inhibits the development of institutional autonomy. The reverse can also be argued. Participatory democracy within a college need not be seen as a management problem (not, in fairness, a view Locke puts forward but one which does have a certain currency) or an addendum to the discussion but instead a natural development (stemming from at least 1946 and inspired by university models). This opinion relates to a premise that academic institutions are impoverished and failing if the talents they contain are not utilized, and are not instrumental in the process of determining progress, development and policy. It may also be the case that college government is not a subject which matters greatly to many teachers. However, it is a matter of great importance to the teachers' representatives. It is worth reflecting that the governmental power which the "withdrawal" (i.e. their choice not to exercise their powers) of governing bodies gives to principals and academic boards is unique to this country.

42. The function of the governing body is part of the larger debate with which the rest of this sub-section is concerned, but it is relevant here to investigate the implications of the Taylor Report.[3] It has been argued that this report which refers to schools has implications for further education, and that certain of its recommendations could be effected in that latter system to allow for the better government, management and conduct of colleges.[4] The recommendations cited as relevant are: that there be more delegation of LEA power to governors; that there should be a changed balance in the composition of governing bodies to allow for greater staff, and community, representation; that governors should receive from relevant staff, by way of a full consultative process, the necessary documentation required to exercise responsibility for aims, methods and assessments; that there should be four-yearly evaluations by the governors of progress made; that governors should have responsibility for staff appointments; and that governors undertaking such new responsibilities should receive training. It can be seen from these recommendations that, if they were extended to further education in only a slightly amended form, the governing body might begin to assume the role of

3 *A New Partnership for our Schools*, Report of a Committee of Enquiry, HMSO, 1977.
4 This view is expressed in an interesting manner by David Parkes in *A Handbook For College Governors*, Coombe Lodge Report, Vol.11, No.10, 1978, pp. 347-358.

the academic board. Certainly, there would appear to be opportunity for a move towards greater staff and academic board accountability.

43. Certain of Taylor's recommendations will be argued to have no relevance to colleges, and there is also the counter argument that Circular 7/70 admits many of these possibilities which are therefore attainable by the revision of existing instruments and articles. The issue of the Taylor Report does not stand alone. It has to be considered within the context of the whole government and management issue. A qualification might be added here, however, in that governing bodies may be required by the changes which take place in society to alter the manner in which they function, even though the written and legal formulations of their functions do not change.

44. The Oakes Report made recommendations which, if implemented, would involve changes in college government in the advanced work sector. However, the present Government has no commitment to this report, and implementation is not likely in the near future. Oakes recommended that in matters relating to the appointment of all grades of staff, including non-teaching staff, and purchases and contracts, "institutions and their governing bodies should be accorded the greatest practicable degree of operational freedom." [5] The retention of detailed establishment control by the LEA was considered to be unreasonable, and possibly uneconomic. Therefore, Oakes stated that governing bodies should have "prime responsibility" for the determination of the establishment and grading of all college staff within a budget and total numbers ceiling; and that the LEA would not lay down any actual establishment for the institution. Governing bodies, before the proposed management changes are effected, "must know clearly the extent of their discretion." Oakes emphasised that, however much responsibility may be delegated in an institution, "the governing body is ultimately responsible to the LEA ... It may be that to make the relationship between governing body and academic board clearer than it may have been in the past, articles should in future be fuller than hitherto."

45. Oakes sought to assist governing bodies to acquire a sense of corporate identity and have a full responsibility for the running of their college. Attention was drawn to three issues: appointments procedures for non-staff governors should ensure sufficient continuity of membership; governors should, by means of joint sub-committees and other methods, be involved with staff in specific areas of college work, including planning; and that the composition of the governing body should provide "a reasonable balance". To enable common procedures to continue and to obtain for all colleges, no matter what level of work is engaged in, Oakes recommended that the formulation of guidance and approval of articles of government should be the responsibility of the Secretary of State who would, however, look to the proposed National Body for advice.

---

5 *Report of the Working Group on the Management of Higher Education in the Maintained Sector*, Cmnd. 7130, HMSO, 1978, p.34 (**See** also Sections **1.2.**18; **1.5**; **3.**53; and **11.2**).

46. **Academic boards**

It will have been noted that the Weaver Report was of considerable importance in the framing of Circular 7/70. Weaver stated that: "Academic freedom is a necessary condition of the highest efficiency and of the proper progress of academic institutions ... The academic affairs of a college are primarily for academic people to deal with, and we have concluded ... that every college [of education] should have an academic board."[6] The arguments of the 1960s for academic boards were drawn from a parallel with universities; from the consideration that as they were the practitioners of their craft, academics ought also to have responsibility; from the need to have external control pressures relaxed in order the better to initiate curriculum development and respond to changing demands; and from the need for teachers and students to develop their studies, thus allowing the pursuit of excellence. Weaver stated that it was essential for every college to possess a properly constituted academic board and, witnin the general college framework and subject to consultation, that the board should be responsible for the academic work of the college and the selection of students. Further, Weaver stated that the board: "should recommend to the governing body how the total number of teaching staff of different grades should be apportioned to departments and subjects. There will be other functions which follow from those set out above. For example, the academic board will be concerned with reviewing methods of teaching; with the assessment of work and the evaluation of students' progress; and with consideration of the estimates, particularly where they bear on such items as library facilities, equipment and educational excursions and visits. Finally, we have suggested that the academic board should elect the members of the teaching staff, other than the principal, who will serve on the governing body."[7]

47. In the year after the publication of the Weaver Report, the DES emphasised the importance of the academic board by requiring that polytechnics must possess systems of government which would attract the essential highly qualified staff and enable them to participate fully in the government of their academic community: "these objectives can only be achieved by delegating the main responsibilities for conducting the affairs of Polytechnics to suitably constituted governing bodies with a large measure of autonomy, and, under the general direction of the governing body, to the Director and academic board."[8]

48. Although Circular 7/70 followed Weaver's recommendations in some instances, it did not extend Weaver's purpose "to enable the colleges to take full academic responsibility and to exercise it in an atmosphere of freedom, unhindered by unnecessary restrictions" to all colleges. What Circular 7/70 did was to extend to the Group A colleges the same sort of provision as had been made under AM 8/67 for the polytechnics: academic boards were given powers of decision, instead of powers of a consultative or advisory nature. For this reason, and because where academic boards have advisory powers

6 *Report of the study group on the government of colleges of education*, HMSO, 1966, p.3.
7 *Ibid*, p.21.
8 *Polytechnics*, Administrative Memorandum 8/67.

only (see paragraphs 52 and 55) there is little which can be said concerning their function since issues are detemined by the principal (and management committee) and governors, significant attention will be given here only to academic boards which have a decision making role. This statement must be qualified immediately, for academic boards are not standard entities: there are variations according to individual articles of government; there are instances of conflict between boards and principals and governors; and there are a variety of external factors, such as cuts in public expenditure, which can limit and inhibit board action. Whatever system obtains, and whatever powers are actually designated under the articles of government, the academic board has still possibly to determine and certainly to function within the college's management system; and this entails at least the formal and informal circumscriptions arising from its relationship with faculties, departments, the principal and governing body. [9]

49. Although Circular 7/70 recommended a model academic board composition, there are variations in practice. There are instances where board membership is determined by the governing body; but it is usual for boards always to include the principal, vice-principal, and all heads of department. The number of academic staff representatives appears usually to vary from three to ten [10] in colleges other than polytechnics and total membership from ten to the mid-twenties. Election processes for staff representatives vary from being from the whole college, from departments, and from a mixture of both. Librarians and CAOs are usually, but not always, board members. Locke states that only in a minority of colleges outside the polytechnics and colleges of higher education do students sit on the board.

50. Where academic boards have powers of decision, the articles of government generally follow closely the wording of 7/70 concerning their function. However those functions of planning, co-ordination, development and oversight of the academic work of the college may be further specified. For example, there may be a consultative function in the appointment of staff below the grades of principal and vice-principal; the suggestion in the Weaver Report, not included in 7/70, that academic boards should participate in the allocation of staff to departments (within the global establishment – see Section **11.2** – agreed between the governors and the LEA) has been adopted in many articles of government. While academic

9 A summary of NATFHE policy concerning college government is given in Appendix 1. It is NATFHE policy that all college boards and committees should be decision making bodies.

10 Michael Locke, *The Instruments and Articles of FE Colleges,* Coombe Lodge Report. Vol.9, No.2, 1976, p.58. In polytechnics in 1972 the figures were one to twelve. Locke's study of polytechnics which gives these latter figures, *The Instruments and Articles of Polytechnics,* Coombe Lodge Report, Vol.5, No.15, 1972, has not been quoted significantly here as there has been development since its publication. To give an example of the current composition of a polytechnic academic board, at Middlesex Polytechnic the board consists of fourteen *ex officio* members (the director, assistant directors, deans, secretary, academic registrar, librarian and student union president); six elected course leaders; six elected subject chairpersons; six teachers elected by faculty board area; three teachers elected from the polytechnic as a whole; and six elected students, one from each faculty board area.

boards have not often been given responsibility in the drawing up of estimates (because, although recommended by Weaver, LEAs have not usually found it possible to devolve such responsibilities) there are "college boards which have such a function, and rather more commonly in the polytechnics where the boards of about half such institutions exercise decision making powers in estimate preparation."[11]

51. Academic boards appear always to be consulted by governors in the preparation of student discipline procedures but there are differences concerning suspension: some boards may suspend students, and others are able only to recommend suspension.

52. Board functions show variation according to circumstance – for example, where certain subject areas are removed from the board because they fall into other joint college or LEA arrangements – but the main variations occur in those institutions where the board has only an advisory or consultative role. This variation arises from the imprecision of Circular 7/70 which allowed wide discretion in the framing of articles. Therefore, such boards exhibit a variety of terminology, and may advise the principal or the governors. Similarly, the functions of advisory boards differ, and there are differences in how they are established: they may have a formal establishment implemented by action of the governors, or only be convened for the purpose of regular consultation. Crucial to the function of any advisory academic board, for its reason for existence may require continuing proof, is not only its designated responsibility but both its accountability and record of recommendations as shown by its minutes: it appears often to be the case that there are specific minuting requirements made of advisory boards.

53. Where the articles of government allow, the control of academic policy may be said to be vested in the academic board but this appearance of power is subject to several restrictions. What may be debated is determined by the agenda; decisions taken remain to be implemented; the powers of the board cannot be precisely determined except by practice – which even then can be altered – for the terminology of 7/70 concerning academic board responsibilities does not, and nor could it have been expected to, ultimately determine what is and what is not "the academic work of the college."

54. The procedure for construction of the agenda varies widely. The agenda may be determined solely by the principal, or by an elected or principal-appointed standing committee, or simply by the inclusion on request of any item brought forward by a board member. There may also be restricted business which necessitates the withdrawal of certain board members, usually students. It appears that there has recently been a change from informal to formal agenda procedures.[12]

55. The matter of permissible business remains one of conflict. The issue is not

11 Locke, *Instruments and Articles of FE Colleges,* pp. 56-57.
12 Ebbutt and Brown, *op.cit,* p.15.

only one of power but relates to the consideration that what may be regarded as an administrative issue can nonetheless have important academic consequences. A recent survey suggests that boards which confine themselves strictly to academic issues are the more influential, and that while boards have increasingly acquired executive functions "in practice little difference could be detected between those which were executive and those which were advisory", although increased student and non-teaching staff representation in conjunction with NATFHE board members appears to have resulted in the outvoting on occasion of the principal and heads of department.[13]

56. The Oakes report considered that the tension inherent in the relationship between governors, principal and academic board could be beneficial but also lead to conflict. The recommendation of joint planning committees was designed to minimise this conflict but Oakes also recommended that:
"the academic board should have sufficient access to relevant financial information to ensure that its recommendations on academic matters are always taken in full knowledge of their financial implications and of the general state of the institution's finances. The corollary would be that the governing body should not take decisions on matters relating solely to expenditure without also considering, on the basis of advice from the academic board, their academic implications."[14]

57. This recommendation has to be considered in the light of Oakes' concern for the delegation of management functions throughout a college: "Our recommendations for the carrying forward of savings are put forward not only as an incentive to prudent management but because we believe that initiative and responsibility at any level can only be fostered if there is some source of funds, however small, within the control of management at that level."[15]

58. **The principal**

It will have been seen from Circular 7/70 that the principal's powers and responsibilities are wide. He or she is responsible to the governing body, under 7/70 is designated to chair the academic board, and may be described in summary as the chief academic and administrative officer of the institution. The role of the principal is discussed under sub-section **3**, below, but it is important to note here that there are great differences in the extent to which principals act under articles of government: the behaviour may be autocratic, benevolently dictatorial, or according to a pattern whereby the principal mediates, co-ordinates, and acts within the advice and guidance of the governors and academic board, both initiating development and responding to the guidance and decisions of the academic board.

59. Oakes notes that the principal has a "major responsibility" for harmonious relationships between governing body and academic board, and ensuring

13 *Ibid.*
14 *Report of the Working Group on the Management of Higher Education in the Maintained Sector,* p.40.
15 *Ibid,* p.54.

that the one did not encroach upon the other. Further implications of the "clear line of authority" which Oakes recommended should exist between governing body, principal and subordinate staff are investigated below.

60. **The chief administrative officer**

It is the policy of the Association of College Registrars that the CAO should act as clerk to the governors and be responsible to them for the implementing of their decisions. However, Circular 7/70 gives the principal the status of an institution's chief academic and administrative officer. This clearly has consequences for the CAO. Where that person acts as clerk to the governors, the post of CAO can carry substantial power and responsibility. Where that is not the case, the CAO can often have the status of head of department (although salary and conditions of service will not necessarily be determined in that context), be a member of the academic board, but have a managerial role as only one member of a corporate managerial team. The CAO may be, for example, a member of a Management Committee which has responsibilities both to the governors and the academic boards, but within which the principal functions as *primus inter pares.*

61. **Heads of department**

Responsibilities in college government for senior staff such as heads of department (the term is adopted here for convenience to include deans, faculty board leaders and other titles which denote senior staff) have generally to be inferred from Circular 7/70, but may well form part of the contract of employment. Obviously senior staff will exercise responsibility, and 7/70 offers advice on one issue: so far as is practicable, the academic board is to delegate its functions to departments in matters which do not affect other departments of the college as a whole. Again this raises a larger question: presuming that the delineation can be made, the internal practices of one department – for example, in matters such as timetabling – may well affect the college as a whole, if for no other reason than by enabling comparisons to be drawn. 7/70 appears by inference to give heads of department a significant responsibility in the planning of academic developments, for maintaining and improving teaching standards, and playing a significant governmental role. However, except for the issues discussed below, since the functions of heads of department are better considered under the heading of college management, they are examined in Section **2.2**.39).

62. The Oakes Report stated that the articles of government "should provide for strong representation of departmental and faculty heads and of others involved in management, so that they may be able to make a contribution not only as prominent members in their own fields but also as persons with senior management responsibility within the institution."[16] Oakes also recommended that the possibility of extending an institution's right to hold funds and carry over savings to faculties and departments ought to be examined. This recommendation is intended to provide an incentive to greater financial responsibility and efficiency.

16 *Ibid,* p.41.

63. A survey suggests that the academic board functions in a way which modifies the relations between a principal and the heads of department, although it seems to do so at the expense of the heads of department. On the other hand, there are wide differences in practices concerning the internal government of departments. While there is a general trend towards greater consultation between the head of department and his or her staff, there are a great variety of practices, and heads vary widely in their approach from that of consensus to the authoritarian; and some are said to have little effective control. Departments appear to function better where consultation is part of the normal procedures. Heads of departments, however, have been found to be the group least adaptable to change, and the more disturbed by the introduction of academic boards; and friction in a college tends to be at its greatest within departments.[17]

64. **The college government debate**

It is not the intention here to be prescriptive. Rather, the purpose is to identify significant areas of the current debate in order to promote further discussion. Issues which have already formed part of the above survey will not be referred to again, except where emphasis is required. There have been requests from many quarters for a revision of Circular 7/70. The document is often described as being out of date. Any revision of 7/70 will have to take account of a large number of factors such as financial stringencies and a wish for greater participation and democracy – and in consequence, especially where priorities and interests conflict, may therefore be long delayed.

65. **Departmental democracy**

Ebbutt and Brown contend that further education colleges (i.e. excluding the polytechnics) are historically hierarchic institutions which have undergone an imposed form of change at the top of their structure by means of Circular 7/70. However, they maintain that the reform has not been fully effective because it has not reached sufficiently within the departmental structure. Thus they state that because colleges are strongly departmentalised, "only the introduction of academic board equivalents at this level can change the college to participative rather than a hierarchical organization". Moreover, while stating that some power decentralization has occured, they warn that there is a growing tension and that unless there is a departmental representative structure, "conflict may be hard to avoid."[18]

66. **The local authority**

It can be said that, given legal and financial responsibilities, authorities at the very least will require their colleges to demonstrate their eligibility for the further power which they seek. It is possible that the central controls which do allow current college freedom from LEAs will be removed, thus restricting academic democracy. The local authority associations anticipate that the White Paper, *Central Government Controls over Local Authorities*, Cmnd. 7634, is only a preliminary step in the dismantling of Government

---

17 Ebbutt and Brown, *op.cit*, pp.13-16.
18 *Ibid.* p.16.

requirements, and have included the powers over the terms of college articles in their list of undesirable central controls.[19] The local authority associations' particular objections are to the exercise of the employer's functions without responsibility, and what is represented as an arguably excessive delegation of spending powers. A basic LEA argument rests on the premise that the most accountable body is the directly elected local authority, and that "Weaverism" may thus derogate from the most democratic body to bodies that are part elected, but also part appointed and part nominated. It is also argued by some LEAs that the DES power of approval interferes in the relationship between authorities and colleges, loosening LEA controls.

67. **The critical view of academic democracy**

There is a view that there is no point in colleges managing their own affairs unless they possess adequate resources, that such resources require development, and that current systems are open to criticism.[20] The criticisms are:

(i) Academic democracy can become a time wasting device since it might allow: over indulgence in consultation; the identification of authority as a barrier to progress and thus lead to the creation of conflict; too much time can be devoted to the discussion of administrative matters; committees and working parties over-proliferate; and policy decisions can be delayed too long, or else be unsatisfactory compromises.

(ii) Democracy, it is argued, works only where it is manipulated and this involves principals and senior staff in attaining Machiavellian talents, or at least an administrative competence, which they may be unwilling or unable to acquire. (This argument may be used in a variety of ways: a case can be made out for the necessity of training senior staff to exercise managerial functions, or for maintaining that appointments to senior positions are made on other than academic grounds).

(iii) Administration should be left to administrators; greater resources should be devoted to administration, enthusiastic amateurs cause only damage, and those judged incompetent should be easily removed by an appointments procedure which for senior posts adopts only the fixed term contract, and for more junior staff ensures by means of secondments and staff development that exposure to new ideas prevents the limitations of horizons.

68. **The extension of academic democracy**

The argument for greater democracy rests on the Weaver Report statement of purpose "to enable the colleges to take full academic responsibility and to exercise it in an atmosphere of freedom, unhindered by unnecessary restrictions" and is influenced by considerations arising from, *inter alia,* the Oakes and Taylor Reports. The arguments presented here are drawn from a NATFHE policy document.[21]

---

19 *Review of Central Government Controls over Local Authorities,* ACC, ADC, AMA, LBA, GLC, 1979.

20 cf Derek Severn, "Professionals and Benevolent Dictators," *Guardian,* 29 May, 1979, p.11.

21 *The Future Development of College Government,*NATFHE, 1979. cf K. Thomas and K. Levine, "What progress towards college democracy", *NATFHE Journal,* Vol.4, No.7, October 1979, pp.10-11.

(i) For there to be the kind of community control outlined in the Oakes and Taylor Reports, governing bodies require more power, and in consequence there should be greater college staff and student representation on the governing body; governing body structures should allow for the full representation of interests – which means that all members are eligible for election to the chair – and that all members may participate fully. Oversight of the institution, however, is here regarded as one of monitoring; the academic board is to make staffing and financial recommendation to the governors although determination of academic policy remains the main power of the board.

(ii) Academic boards should have a reduction in the numbers of *ex officio* members and an increase in the numbers of elected representatives in order to allow for a decision making process which is more democratic. Academic board offices should be elective. Other staff may be requested to attend board meetings to advise on areas in which they have expertise. Information relating to committees should be available to all college staff members. Sub-committee procedures should, as far as possible, be the same as those for the academic board.

(iii) Again to allow for greater participation, academic boards should be involved, subject to the responsibilities of the principal and governors, in shortlisting, appointments and (within the authorised establishment) have control over the allocation of posts to departments, such functions to be delegated as appropriate.

(iv) It is argued that the principles outlined in (i)-(iii) above, should cover all further education establishments, and that responsibility for the approval of new instruments and articles embodying such principles should rest with the Secretary of State.

69. **The issue of power**

The debate concerning college government is concerned ultimately with power. Ebbutt and Brown suggest that real power does not lie with the governing body, or with the academic board as such for it is "a battleground for competing interests rather than a power centre in its own right." Ebbutt and Brown argue that, excluding the LEA, power is shared between the principal and heads of department, and that where other teaching staff have acquired influence it has been at the expense of heads of department rather than the principal. The NATFHE branch, according to circumstances, can also be a significant centre of power and the balance, it is argued, depends largely upon the particular issues, considerably upon personalities, and the geographical location and history of the college.[22]

70. This view can be extended further. Governmental issues have been said to depend, albeit in an unfortunate phrase, on "the ecology of the situation" : the sum of personality and environment. Thus neither governors not academic boards have the powers which they anticipated holding a decade ago, and mainly because of simple practicalities. This revolves not only around practical institutional issues such as the writing of minutes and the

22 Ebbutt and Brown, *op.cit*, p.16.

consideration that not all departments are vulnerable to interference, but also in the wider sense that decisions may often be taken elsewhere and on other than academic grounds.

71. Academic democracy in further education developed at a time of expansion. It can be argued that, in a climate of cuts and contraction, it is not equipped to cope with the current realities. Further, it has been contended that the value placed on education by society, or at least by its elected representatives, is now less than at the time of the Weaver Report (and even the Houghton Report). If that is so, and education is less valued, then academic democracy has less status too. Power structures – whatever the constitutional structure on paper – are argued also now not to allow academics to possess real influence. One reason adduced for this is an alleged tendency to financial prodigality. Hence the decisions in education which are now required relate to what is represented to be the real, rather than the former relative priorities, and academics are not in a position to make the choices: priorities are being sought to satisfy externally imposed criteria rather than internal academic criteria.

72. This argument challenges the entire concept of the academic board. To use historical terminology, the concept of the "moot" continues to be advocated but it is the tight group of three or four "wise men" which is actually making decisions. In emergencies, it is argued, power is always concentrated in the hands of a few. This view is supported by a substantial body of research concerning university resource allocation in the United States: in periods of expansion, resources are allocated according to universalistic criteria but, in periods of stringency, political and coalitional processes determine priorities.

73. This approach may be described as being that of crisis administration. It may well be the case, but it is not the whole case, and nor is it as enclosed as it seems. If the presumption exists that academic boards are not competent to take decisions related to real priorities, it then remains to the board to demonstrate its competence in such matters. Crisis administration may well mean the wielding of power by a few, but power continues to depend on consent. While it is true that many an historical argument can be adduced for caucus administration during a crisis, it ought also to be pointed out that those propelled into such administration are not always those usually involved in, or usually qualified for, such office. The point can be made by a study, for example, of the personnel appointed to – and dismissed from – the war-time cabinets of 1914-18 and 1939-45.

74. It is at this point however, that discussion of college government develops into discussion of management and properly belongs to the following sub-section. Whatever governmental procedures colleges may possess, they remain vulnerable to decisions taken elsewhere, and within their constitutions they depend not just upon the instruments and articles of government but also upon how and by whom power is wielded. Nonetheless, it must be remembered that the academic freedom debate is concerned essentially with the means to secure the best possible educational provision.

APPENDIX 1

NATFHE CONFERENCE MOTIONS CONCERNING COLLEGE GOVERNMENT

1. The text of the 1976 motion is:-
"Conference calls upon the National Executive Committee to enter into negotiations with the Secretary of State for Education and Science for a revision of Circular 7/70 to embody the following:-
   - (i) The changing of all college boards and committees into decision making bodies.
   - (ii) A majority of elected staff representatives on the Academic Boards or their equivalent and Sub-Committees of all colleges with adequate opportunity for consultation with those represented.
   - (iii) The Academic Board to be elected and the Chairman should also be elected.
   - (iv) Representation of organized labour affiliated to the TUC on Governing and Advisory bodies equal to that of industry, commerce and the professions.
   - (v) The setting up of appointments procedures and committees to ensure elected staff representation on panels for internal and external appointments, this procedure to ensure that no discrimination takes place on the grounds of sex, sexuality, age, family status, race, nationality, creed, political belief or record.
   - (vi) College Governing Bodies to include a minimum of one quarter of the members elected by and from the full-time teaching staff as a whole."

3. The text of the 1978 motion is:-
"Conference resolves that Association policy on college democracy should embody the following:
   - (i) College governing bodies to include a minimum of one quarter of the members elected by and from the full-time teaching staff as a whole;
   - (ii) Teacher governors to be eligible for election as Chairman;
   - (iii) The members of the Academic Board to be elected except that the Principal be an *ex-officio* member;
   - (iv) The Academic Board Chairman to be elected;
   - (v) The setting up of democratic appointments procedures and committees with adequate elected representation of the teaching staff;
   - (vi) Information relating to all committees and sub-committees within the college to be freely available to all NATFHE members."

REFERENCE

A New Partnership for our Schools, Report of a Committee of Enquiry. DES. 1977.
A Plan for Polytechnics and other Colleges, Cmnd. 3006, HMSO, 1966.
Government and Conduct of Establishments of Further Education, DES Circular 7/70, 14 April 1970.
Polytechnics, DES Administrative Memorandum 8/67.
Report of the study group on the government of colleges of education, HMSO, 1966.
Report of the Working Group on the Management of Higher Education in the Maintained Sector, Cmnd. 7130, HMSO, 1978.

A Handbook for College Governors, Coombe Lodge Report, Vol. 11, No.10 1978.
Anthony Arblaster, *Academic Freedom,* Penguin, 1974.
D. Charlton, W.Gent, and B. Scammells, *The Administration of Technical Colleges,* Manchester University Press, 1971.
Keith Ebbutt and Roger Brown, "The Structure of Power in the FE College". *Journal of Further and Higher Education,* Vol.2, No.3, .Autumn 1978.
Michael Locke, *The Instruments and Articles of Government of Polytechnics,* Coombe Lodge Report, Vol.5, No.15, 1972.
Michael Locke, *The Instruments and Articles of FE Colleges,* Coombe Lodge Report, Vol.9, No.2, 1976.
Derek Severn, "Professionals and Benevolent Dictators", *Guardian,* 29 May, 1979, p.11.
B.F. Tipton, *Conflict and Change in a Technical College,* Hutchinson, 1973.
The Duties and Status of a College Registrar, The Association of College Registrars, 1974.
The Future Development of College Government, NATFHE, 1979.

2 COLLEGE MANAGEMENT

1. As this book is concerned throughout with managerial or administrative issues, the purpose of this sub-section is briefly to discuss the context in which those matters occur. Management theories, structures and some particular issues will be discussed in turn. It is neither intended nor possible to give a complete guide to theories of education management, or indeed to the many and various forms of structure which may obtain. Rather, it is hoped that the reader will be able sufficiently to draw from the summary material here to facilitate further independent investigation.

2. For some time colleges have been offered a considerable canon of literature and ideas concerning management. Ideas drawn from the social science disciplines, science and philosophy, and some practices which have found acceptance in industry and public undertakings, are argued to have relevance to education. Some approach to education whereby its resources – especially in a climate of financial stringency – can be best deployed is clearly necessary. Colleges can hardly be exempt, either, from the expectation to achieve the sort of management efficiency which may be taught in courses such as business studies or education management, and which may be more readily sought in industry and commerce. The dilemma facing college management is acute: inspired amateurism arising from past personal experience would not be accepted by many as being the most appropriate way to the best management of an institution; the theoretical models may be inappropriate; the pressure of administrative and social circumstance can well inhibit managerial action; and, most important, management has now to adapt itself to the problems – in some areas at least – of contraction. Given the historically rooted system of often appointing persons to managerial college posts whose previous experience has been largely academic, there remains a real need for guidance, information and assistance to be available to the new manager. Education management programmes are discussed in paragraphs 54-59, below.

3. As a preface to the discussion of management theory, it is necessary to indicate the restrictions in operation on education. The service is affected by events over which it has little control. National and local government actions, and change in the nature of local industry can both fundamentally alter a college's existence, whatever its planning might have been. Within colleges, changing student needs, staff expectations, and the behaviour of managers and staff, similarly affect the operation of management. Any theory or structure adopted therefore will need to be flexible, and, some would argue, be of necessity of a restricted value. A task of the manager is the ability ot select appropriately from a repertoire of management and organizational theories and structures those which most effectively fulfil specific needs.

4. One goal can perhaps be identified. The purpose of college management may be said to be the attempt to ensure that the institution operates as efficiently and effectively as possible. Effective management is usually defined as that

which secures identified objectives; and efficient management that which attains those objectives with the greatest economy in the use of resources. The division of the adjectives is an aid to thought, but issues arising from the one can seriously affect the other: a technical efficiency which prevents, for example, staff influence in policy-making, will scarcely be effective since it may provoke serious resistance.

5. Approaches to management theory are influenced usually by the discipline which forms the point of departure and the circumstances of application. Outlined below is a brief summary which reflects the historical development of management theory, and approaches designed for different management tasks or functions. Indication is given in footnotes and in references as to where issues might be more fully pursued.

6. **Scientific management**

Scientific management represents perhaps the earliest attempt to develop theories designed to make management more effective. Its major application has been in industrial management. Attempts to apply these approaches in education, involving the detailed specification of individuals' tasks and work norms have been singularly unsuccessful. Modern variants of this have all in common a mechanistic view which seeks to some extent to establish educational institutions as organizations capable of responding to methodology in a quantifiable sense. Thus, the production approach is concerned with deriving activity standards by analysis, or else using performance analysis in order to set targets for higher standards. The economic approach to education would place managerial emphasis on the best attainable performance subject to cost restraints, or else the diminution of costs according to output requirements. Fundamental and intractable problems relating to the management of – and even the definition of – educational output now suggest that some approaches are chimeric.

7. **Decision theory**

The decision-making approach is concerned with the methodology of decision making, seeking by way of quantitative and qualitative models which act as aids in illustration and evaluation, the means to rational action. Choices for action are presented to the manager, the consequences are evaluated (in terms, for example, of "certainty", "risk", and "uncertainty") and the appropriate "rational" decision is then taken. Other mathematically based management science or operations research approaches attempt to discover quantitative bases for management decisions by expressing the nature of an organization in terms of systems and models.[1] Modelling approaches to timetabling are examples of these. Operational research is a particularly influential technique in this sphere.

8. **Systems theory**

More generally, systems theory, which has powerfully influenced the sciences, technology and social sciences, has been argued to have a particular

1 cf Colin Morgan, *Management in Education – Dissimilar or Congruent?* Educational Studies A Third Level Course, E321, Unit 1, Open University Press, 1976, pp.16-19.

virtue in the study of management by showing how parts of an organization relate to each other, and how relationships between objects and ideas can be illustrated. The central tenet of open systems theory is that systems exist within an environment of which they are an inseparable part. This theory allows for varieties of factors affecting organizations. Thus, educational organizations may be perceived as part of an open system which includes central and local government structures and provides insights into economic, social and political processes. It can allow, for example, the demonstration of the relationship between an LEA and a college. In simple terms, systems illustrations can show how the inputs, such as money, materials and students, into a college system then undergo conversion or process into a product or output – better educated students. Output in theory can then be monitored in order to discover changes necessary in input or process. Since no educational institution can be regarded as a closed system, boundaries to the system have to be established, and an open form of analysis maintained. Effective systems approaches require considerable information, and continual monitoring of all college – and contributory – activities and results. Within the overall system, various sub-systems operate. Many, if not most, systems approaches inevitably concentrate upon inputs because of the difficulty of evaluating processes and outputs. Analysis may be quantitative, qualitative, or both.[2]

9. **Human relations approach**

This approach differs from, and developed in reaction to, scientific management and related theories in that it focuses upon the individual in organizations rather than the task. Drawing heavily on the behavioural sciences, it lays emphasis on interpersonal relationships and is concerned with aspects such as motivation and job satisfaction. This school of thought has produced particular tools for managers.[3] The key words often employed are self explanatory of the ideas: conflict resolution; harmony; the hierarchy of needs: motivation and participation. The human relations approach has influenced quite strongly ways of thinking about the education manager's tasks. One manifestation is that of Organization Development whereby the manager focuses intensively with subordinates upon the processes which expedite group cohesion. Processes such as communication thereby assume a dominant role.[4]

10. **Theories of policy-making**

Rather different approaches focus upon the policy-making process within and affecting organizations. One approach usefully distinguishes between three distinguishable but overlapping stages of policy-making: formulation,

2 Digby Davies, *Schools as Organisations*, Educational Studies: A Third Level Course, E321, Unit 3, Open University Press, 1976, pp. 46-49, gives a useful introduction to the systems approach. J. Latcham and R. Cuthbert in "A Systems Approach to College Management". *College Administration*, Coombe Lodge Report, Vol.11, No.14, 1979, pp. 689-93, offer a qualified advocacy.

3 cf Colin M. Turner, *Inter-Personal Skills in Further Education*, Coombe Lodge, 1978.

4 cf Davies, *op.cit*, pp. 43-44; Morgan, *op.cit*, p.17; R.A. Schmuck and P.J. Runkel, *Handbook of Organization Development in Schools*, National Press Books, 1972.

determination and implementation.[5] Another approach which has been applied to educational organizations sees them as anarchies in which choices are made in conditions of uncertainty and ambiguity, and where policies are shaped in spite of unclear goals, conflicting groups and participants with other things on their minds. In contrast, policy science perspectives focus upon the development of information systems[6] which enable strategic future planning, using predictive models to achieve identified operational objectives.

11. **Bureaucracies**

Some sociological perspectives of organizations follow Max Weber in perceiving them as bureaucracies characterised by a hierarchy of control and authority, by specified rules which circumscribe the powers of officials, themselves appointed for their technical competence, and by a written information system. While some elements might be applicable to educational organizations, this mechanistic view has been much criticised for its inflexibility and for its inability to cope with the concept of professionalism (see paragraph 33, below). Contrasted "organistic" views of organizations have been developed which encompass a network, rather than a hierarchy of control and authority, and professional commitment which extends outside the organization.[7]

12. **The phenomenological approach : a method of understanding**

This inelegantly named theory may be described as a philosophy of experience, thus rejecting theory which is beyond the possibilities of experience. Phenomenology represents a recent and radical departure in management theory. It contends, for example, that organizations are unreal, and that any attempt to understand them from single standpoints will fail; any organizational theory assuming universality is suspect; and that, fundamentally, there are no fixed ways in which the world can be construed.[8] The abstraction termed organization is rejected, being replaced by "the varied perceptions by individuals of what they can, should, or must do in dealing with others within the circumstances in which they find themselves." Thus, while not creating the world, people making it – and respond to this self manufactured reality: ultimate goals therefore retreat the more they are approached since new "realities" are always interposed. Phenomenology requires that theory and practice must be closely associated: "Theory must arise out of the process of inquiry itself and be intimately connected with the data under investigation ... [research should aim] ... at dealing with the direct experience of people in specific situations."[9] Instead of adopting the view of organizations always in chaos and perpetuated by the

---

5 cf T.R. Weaver, "Comparisons between types of institution in an LEA", published in ed. P. Andrews and D.L. Parks, *Participation, Accountability and Decision-Making at Institutional Level,* proceedings of the Third Annual Conference of the BEAS, BEAS, 1975.

6 See paragraph 44, below.

7 cf T. Burns and G.M. Stalker, *The Management of Innovation,* Tavistock, 1961.

8 The phenomenological approach is represented by T. Barr Greenfield, "Theory about Organization: A New Perspective and its Implications for Schools", ed. Houghton *et al.,' Management in Education Reader 1,* Ward Lock/OU Press, 1975, pp 59- 84.

9 *Ibid,* p. 65; pp. 70-71.

institutionalization of conflict, the phenomenological approach is to determine who maintains order, how, and with what consequences. Conflict in organizations arises from conflicting beliefs held by individuals; and so objectives which differ within organizations and their relative success should be related to power differences or access to resources.

13. **Parenthetical man (the end of traditional organization?)**
A view which might be described as a revelationist iconoclasm challenges the whole of existing organizational theory.[10] The existence of a new type of individual, "parenthetical man" – who reflects and reacts to the new social circumstances facing the world – is argued to have rendered present managerial theory and practice irrelevant. Inputs and outputs, as presently defined, are described as naive. Since, increasingly, there are those who can rise above their circumstances and challenge theories with a critical eye, not only has current theory and practice become outdated, but it can also no longer be regarded as legitimate. Hence, the conclusion is "that it is not enough today to manage organizations ... [for] ... it is necessary to manage the whole society."[11] A view which argues that all managers need to perceive the broader societal implications of their managerial functions would seem to be of particular significance to education managers.

14. **Summary**
The outline sketch above must not be regarded as more than the briefest of introductions intended for the reader searching for points of departure. Nonetheless, certain points of summary can be made. The degree to which the management of society rather than its organizations is necessary is a fascinating topic, but beyond the scope of this book. The various scientific approaches have been criticised for their inhumanity; and the redressing human relations approaches have also been attacked for the opportunities afforded for manipulation. For example, a manager might encourage employee participation in order to secure a higher motivation, and also to place the employee in the kind of position which subverts individuality: critics, or "trouble makers", depending upon the point of view, can thereby be kept quiescent. By stressing the need for theories derived from practices, and allowing human need and nature more expression, the phenomenological approach indicates a way to a form of synthesis which may find acceptance, while the insights of parenthetical man suggest a realistic reappraisal of those needs and natures within and beyond organizations.

15. If it is the case that many of the theories have, at least in part, a relevance to education, it is necessary for college managers to make pragmatic syntheses. The following propositions may aid choice: total application of one theory may be inappropriate for, since it is unlikely to meet all requirements, overall management efficiency may be reduced; choice of an approach should only be made after careful consideration of the varieties of option; definition of goals, and the means to their measurement, is essential before choice of approach is made; and that managerial theory and practice in education has

10 Alberto Guerreiro Ramos, "Models of Man and Administrative Theory", ed. Houghton *et al, op.cit,* pp 46-55.
11 *Ibid,* p 52.

to be justifiable to students, staff, authority and public. Total solutions are illusory, consent is necessary for whichever managerial approaches are adopted, and, as in the rest of existence, there is no golden key or magic solution.

16. A discourse on management theory, however fascinating, will suffer – at least from the phenomenologists' point of view – if it does not address itself to the practical. Illustrations may serve to demonstrate how apparently minor items can affect severely the operation of a college. It has been argued that since colleges exist to educate students, the overriding necessity is for principals to provide effective leadership of high quality; and that management and administration should be relegated to secondary positions in order that principals might pursue the goals of the attainment of educational excellence.[12] Such an aspiration may be an ideal to some, but significant problems may arise in an institution as a result. However, this wish demonstrates the impossibility of any individual fully to master all the information necessary for the successful operation of a college. It is in such circumstances that some management concepts might achieve an easy acceptance. For example, one technique designed to make organizations more effective, management by objectives (MbO)[13] was taken from an American industrial context, gaining some adherents and indeed a significant short-term success in some areas of education until fundamental weaknesses involving the formulation of educational objectives and the measurement of their attainment were exposed.[14] Finally, and especially in a climate of contraction, it should be stressed that the educational manager cannot depend upon any one set of concepts or theories. A broad understanding of available theory and of appropriate techniques drawn from such theory is necessary, along with the commonsense to know when and where such concepts and techniques can effectively be applied – and, most important of all, might not be appropriately applied.

17. **Management structures**

The management structures devised for an institution may represent the practical application of theories of management. Overall structures vary, but all reflect the values and political intentions of those who established and now operate them. The illustration below may be taken to represent the basic hierarchical pattern.[15] In larger institutions, such as polytechnics, principal (director), vice-principals (assistant directors) and other senior

---

12 cf. Sir Norman Lindop, "Sustaining Educational Leadership", *College Administration, op.cit,* pp 557-559. Such a view in isolation is as sadly a failure to recognise that change has occurred as a current prime minister wishing to emulate Sir Robert Peel and oversee in detail the work of every department of government.

13 cf. B. Baron, *The Managerial Approach to Tertiary Education,* Studies in Education No.7, University of London Institute of Education, 1978, MbO specifies detailed objectives and then attempts to measure the extent to which they have been met.

14 cf. J.L. Davies, "A Discussion of the Use of PPBS and MBO in Educational Planning and Administration", ed. L. Dobson, *et al., Management in Education Reader 2; Some Techniques and Systems,* Ward Lock Educational/Open University Press, 1975, pp 339-356. Davies discusses the problems of introducing MbO in English educational institutions.

15 cf. *Submission to the Standing Commission on Pay Comparability,* Teachers' Panel of the Burnham Further Education Committee, October 1979, p 82.

staff form "the directorate". In some institutions, principal, vice-principal, and certain senior staff (often elected from and by the heads of department) form the "management committee." The chief administrative officer may (usually) be a member of this committee. Non-teaching staff may be classified further than appears in Figure 1. Administrative staffs include: the CAO, senior administrative officers, registrars, bursars, finance officers, and examinations officers; catering staff: domestic bursars, cooks, kitchen and restaurant assistants, and cashiers; caretaking staff: cleaning, maintenance,

Figure 1:

Basic management structure

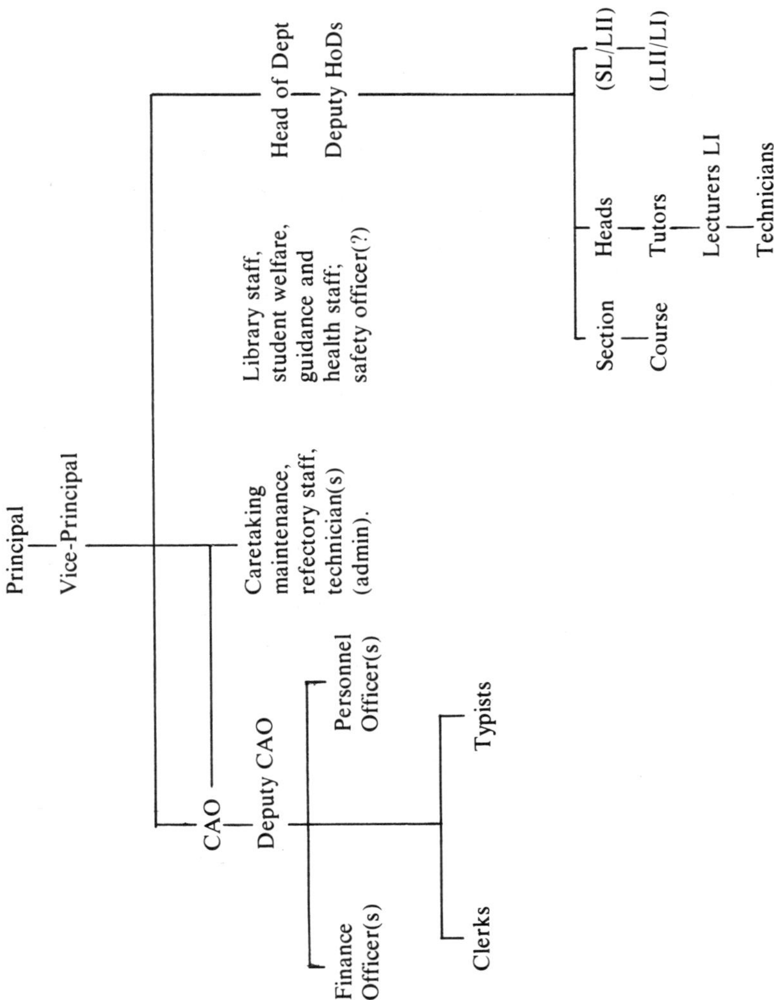

security, and general services – led by staff such as head caretakers, senior services superintendents and school keepers (London); garden staff; technicians and technical assistants: workshop, maintenance, academic, and general services; clerical staff: secretaries, typists, and clerks. Whether librarians are members of the non-teaching or teaching staff depends upon their contracts; assistant librarians and library clerical staff will usually be members of the non-teaching staff. This overall structure has to be considered in conjunction with the academic structure and also the informal power structure, and in many cases only the latter will identify the foci of decision making. In figures 1 and 2 it will be appreciated that the structure

Figure 2:

Basic academic structure

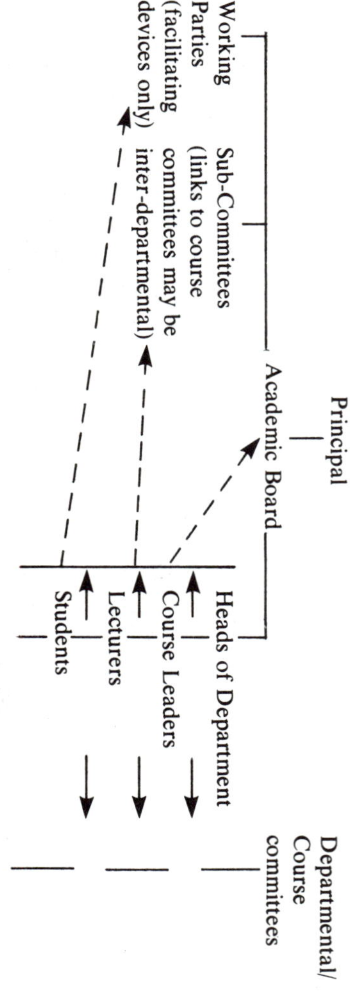

extends upwards to the governing body and the LEA. In Figure 2, short broken lines illustrate elective routes/channels of communication. Since functions vary, the vice-principal(s) and CAO are not shown in Figure 2. They will, however, usually be members of the academic board.

18. Both illustrations are somewhat simplified. Under Circular 7/70, the principal has control over non-teaching staff. The CAO can be seen as the head of a "service" department, although the particular role depends on the responsibilities allocated. Generally, the CAO will have responsibility for all administrative and maintenance staff,[16] representing their views where appropriate; and while the salaries and conditions of service of academic technicians will be dealt with usually by the CAO, in other matters the technicians are responsible to heads of department in some institutions. The informal power structure is often a better indicator of the involvement of non-teaching staff in policy and decision making than is the formal structure. An example of its dynamic nature can be found in the changes, in some colleges, consequent upon industrial action by some non-teaching staff in 1979.

19. A variety of factors influencing the operation of the academic structure has been identified.[17] The main issues put forward for consideration are: how far the academic board dominates departments; the degree to which consultation and policy making occur within departments, and how far are departmental decisions represented at higher levels; whether the principal's responsibilities for internal organization override the structure, and whether the academic board limits action, or expands its responsibilities; whether students, if they encounter resistance at departmental level, are able effectively to represent their interests by appeal to the governing body or academic board; whether staff, where their departments are not represented effectively at board or board sub-committee levels, have a recourse to compensatory action; and how far a principal might become a prisoner of the board. The creation of academic boards certainly affected college management in many instances by redistributing responsibilities for policy and decision making, by altering the degree of participation, and by reshaping the power structure. Although the change was an imposed one, of its nature perpetuating hierarchical structures, and although it provides for checks and balances, it is still one in which numerical majorities have usually to react rather than initiate. Management has certainly assumed a more corporate nature;[18] its freedom to manage, given the increased pressures of

---

16 The complaint is sometimes made by CAOs that administrative staff should be increased in proportion to increases in college activities. They may argue that where this does not occur, understaffing inhibits the provision of adequate service.

17 cf. Colin Morgan and David Parkes, *Management and the Academic Board in Further Education Colleges,* Educational Studies: A Third Level Course, E 321, Unit 12, Open University Press, 1977, pp 25-26; *passim.*

18 One example drawn from a medium sized college will serve to make the point. Following the creation of an (advisory) academic board, a management committee was established. The committee consisted of the principal, vice-principal, CAO and heads of department. It met weekly. This proved to be unsatisfactory since the heads of department considered that this was occupying too much of their time. The committee now meets on a monthly basis. Interim action is taken by an executive committee consisting of the principal, vice-principal and two heads of department (who function as a "research and development unit"). Academic board reports are sent to the governors. Necessary action is implemented by the executive and management committees.

change upon it, has possibly lessened. College academic structures are said to enshrine a perpetual power struggle, resulting in informal behaviour and organizational patterns. However, since the principal's role remains crucial, a new appointment to the post usually disturbs the overall pattern even though the formal structure remains unchanged.

20. **Course structure and management structure**
In some colleges the basic hierarchical pattern illustrated in paragraph 17, Figure 1, can be extended to courses. Courses are allocated to departments; the departments arrange their operation, including timetabling; ranges of courses are the responsibility of section heads; and particular courses the responsibility of course tutors. Departmental committees make representations to the academic board, and are often supplemented by advisory committees which consist of the head of department, senior departmental staff, and representatives from commerce and industry.

21. During the last decade, course structures in some institutions have allowed students to build their own courses by choosing to study from a range of course units. This practice has also allowed timetabling to occur on a college rather than departmental basis, enabling wider access to the college's educational resources (see Section **5.8.**12-13). Structural change resulting from the Houghton Report, staffing establishment requirements (see Section **11.2**), and variable levels of student recruitment, has required flexibility. Obvious instances can be found in the colleges of higher education which were required rapidly to transform themselves. In many colleges there is perpetual flux in course provision: courses developed in one department may subsequently be better conducted in another; courses which service other courses may more effectively be placed (for educational, or administrative reasons, or both) under other control.

22. One result has been the creation of "modular grids" and the unified integrated timetable.[19] The modular grid is a timetabling device containing the total number of course units and allowing movement between options without loss of teaching time. "Unit" here refers both to a unit of knowledge and a unit of time. Within the timetable pattern, the unit of knowledge may occupy several weeks or months, and the unit of time the specific periods at which teaching occurs.

23. While students might operate some freedom of course choice, it is necessary for total study programmes to be approved. Thus academic, and administrative, responsibilities of teaching staff have had to be revised. Course units require design and approval; students have to be advised and their progress monitored; and the whole course may cross traditional subject and departmental boundaries. This development has brought with it a wider use of team teaching, and greater college integration. It also upset previous hierarchical relationships: a course leader responsible for academic content, co-ordination, student discipline and monitoring might have as a course contributor a teacher of greater seniority in salary and status, but who

19 Examples are contained in ed. D.L. Parkes, *College Management, Readings and Cases*, Vol.5, Coombe Lodge, 1976.

consequently had to fulfil requirements instanced by a theoretical junior. In some cases, therefore, individual teachers have enjoyed wider responsibility and freedom.

24. Course, timetable, and managerial developments have entailed in some colleges the adoption of "matrix structures," replacing the kind of academic structure illustrated in paragraph 17, Figure 2. Matrix structures are often said to allow: the stressing of the importance of curricula; teacher participation; a theoretical separation of administrative and academic functions which allow heads of department primarily to organize, administer and develop courses whilst retaining responsibilities for general discipline and progress; the organization of academic staff in teams, allowing greater academic freedom and also the development on a college basis of the pursuit of particular individual disciplines; academic leadership and co-ordination may be provided by heads of studies (who are not necessarily heads of department), and study teams may become academic board sub-committees; and that matters such as curriculum development, staff development, educational technology and resource provision, and student and welfare services might be integrated within, or cross between, the various areas. There are many varieties of approach and implementation. Advantages and dangers are readily apparent.

25. The traditional management of non-teaching staff may be altered where a college operates on an integrated basis. Roles of heads of department, heads of studies, and course teachers require identification, and may moreover be modified by practice. Whatever the structure, former hierarchies may prevail. Particular initiatives may require encouragement, or not occur because of the bureaucratic weight of the structure. In terms of power, the practice of divide and rule may well operate. What is intended to be progress may result in many persons being deflected from their immediate responsibilities, and further, being too occupied with minutiae to be able to adopt an overall view. The most common criticism of matrix structures is that they tend to spawn interminable committees, and the disaffected would claim that more time is consumed in attending inter-staff meetings than is used for the actual teaching of students. There is also the consideration that a structure involving devolved control also must provide the necessary resources: it follows that finance may be allocated to academic teams as well as heads of department.

26. Perhaps the commonest manner in which matrix systems are operated is where departments have been brought together into faculties (although there are possibly almost as many matrix systems as there are colleges which operate them). The general justification is to ease movement of staff for whatever purpose, and to facilitate communications across departmental boundaries, the better to utilize resources. Heads of department often undertake certain functions across the faculty (for example, responsibility for finance or accommodation) but generally retain some academic responsibilities. Staff may work in administrative or educational task groups which may be formal or informal, and linked to subjects or courses. Actual roles may change, as may group composition; lecturers or senior lecturers

may undertake some of the former functions of heads of department. Evaluation, co-ordination and development responsibilities may be retained at senior levels, or be part of a continual monitoring process carried out through faculty and academic board committees. For administrative purposes, across or as a part of each faculty, there can be various directors or deans (of vice-principal, principal lecturer or head of department salary grade) with responsibilities for matters such as staffing, resource, finance, and student affairs. General academic management may be undertaken by principal or senior lecturers, and particular courses and subjects can be the responsibility of a lecturer Grade I or II. Particular responsibility may be given, for example, to almost any grade of staff for matters such as counselling or welfare.

27. Where faculties obtain, a danger is for there to be little communication between them. The faculty may be defined as an area of study, and its head may have the title of dean, itself a post which may occur by election, selection, or rotation; and the dean may also continue to function as a head of department where departments continue to exist within the faculty system. Faculties can have their boards or committees which may or may not be sub-committees of the academic board. Where they are not, academic boards generally create committees which provide a link with the faculties. A faculty system does not necessarily entail the accompaniment of the matrix approach, and may in reality be no more than a strictly departmental system refined into the creation of super-departments.

28. Another management structure method is for operation according to particular functions. Staff may be grouped into divisions. Divisions will be concerned with particular subject areas, but may also have wider functions; heads of divisions may form a committee responsible for considering the whole work of the college, particularly in a strategic sense.

29. One more example, drawn from a particular institution, illustrates further possibilities concerning matrices and faculties. Academic work can be organized around a two-sided matrix. On one side of the matrix are the subject areas which provide staff and facilities. These subject areas are broadly based. On the other side of the matrix are courses and groups of courses. The subject area matrix serves the course matrix. Courses are the responsibility of the faculty boards. These boards are representative bodies, each responsible in turn to the academic board. Policy and academic direction for each course (or groups of courses) is the function of boards of study. The boards of study are responsible to the faculty board. This structure is illustrated in Figure 3, opposite. This system (as might the previous examples) involves considerable devolution of power, with the consequence that the full academic board, while meeting regularly, does so less often.

30. Matrix operation is illustrated opposite. The example is simple. No attempt has been made to present all a college's activities and channels of communication in diagrammatic form since such an exercise, while

Figure 3:

Courses/resources matrix system: outline representation

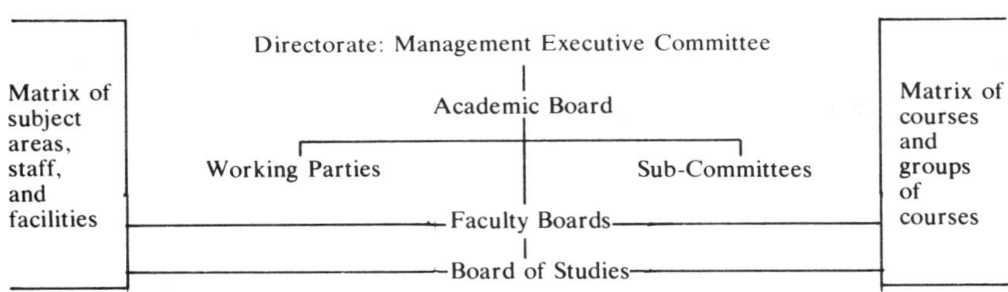

fascinating to the compiler, is not always of significantt use to the reader.[20] The diagram can be explained thus. Subject area contributions to particular courses are marked x. Course tutors are board of studies members (often chair meetings), and have an administrative function to advertise courses, and ensure that they are taught. The board of studies is responsible partly to the academic board, partly to validating bodies, and partly to the governors. The role of the board of studies is to: monitor student admissions and certifications; undertake curriculum responsibilities delegated by the validating body; exercise power delegated from the governors regarding how course procedures are administered, and possibly, in some institutions, to

Figure 4:

Basic Matrix Structure

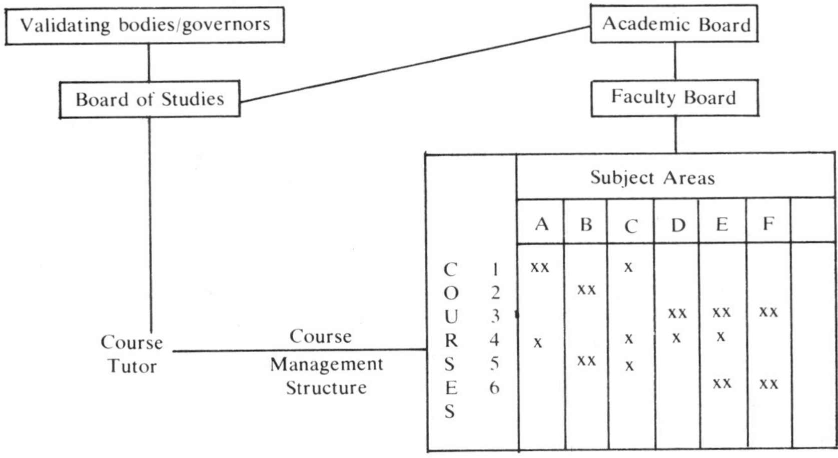

20 Diagrammatic expressions are quite plentiful. Examples can be found in J. O'Neill, *College Management Structures,* Coombe Lodge Working Paper, Information Bank Number 756. C.T. Ferguson, *Alternative Organisational Structures in Higher and Further Education,* Coombe Lodge Working Paper, Information Bank Number 1197, p.27, presents a three dimensional model.

undertake the role, delegated from the academic board, to monitor and determine the size, nature and balance of courses. The faculty board is responsible to the academic board. It is responsible for: the servicing of courses by academic disciplines; maintenance and research and other departmental activities within the subject areas (and here makes recommendations to the academic board); making recommendations directly to the governors regarding resource needs (such as staffing, finance, and space). Within the faculty board structure there are subject boards which have particular responsibilities for areas such as contributions to courses by their particular discipline, the maintenance of research, general subject area updating, and liaison with course tutors to ensure adequate servicing of courses.

31. Course design depends upon the nature of the curriculum (see Section **10**), institutional organizational structure, and the initiative of individuals and groups within and without the college. In most establishments with conventional departmental (and possibly faculty) structures, the head of department usually assumes curriculum leadership. The head organizes meetings with appropriate staff, agrees the general overall design, delegates specific subject responsibilities, and acts as a co-ordinator. The academic board or a faculty committee may wish to discuss the overall design. Where the curriculum is cross disciplinary, the departmental approach may not always be suitable and some inter-departmental co-ordinating function necessary. This often entails either a special committee or a senior staff member acting as a co-ordinator. With short courses, this is invariably a departmental operation but the initiative could come from a staff member, from an employer, or result from enquiries to the institution. Course design within matrix structures has the same roots and its expression will be apparent from the discussion of matrices above.

32. **Management issues**

The issues selected for discussion below relate to theoretical and practical problems. Selection has been on the basis of potential or actual problems stemming from theoretical approaches and practical concerns. The list is not exhaustive; appendices 2-4 provide some supplement; and much of this book is concerned in some way with managerial issues. Some personnel aspects of management are considered first: the issues of professionalism, collegiality and the role of the head of department. Resource issues, information systems and timetabling, are considered next. Finally, the relationship between theory and practice is examined in the context of the management of change, and a brief guide is presented to available management education activities wherein other themes may be studied at length.

33. **Professionalism, collegiality, committees**

The expressions professionalism and collegiality[21] may be used with reference to the term: "dynamic interplay of sub-systems". The essential points to be discussed are the professional ethic, and collegiality as

---

21 cf. T. Noble and B. Pym, "Collegial authority and the receding locus of power". *British Journal of Sociology,* Vol.21, December 1970; Morgan and Parkes, *op. cit,* pp. 48-9; Morgan *op.cit,* p.22.

expressed in committee activity: implicit in both questions is the teacher's managerial role.

34. A definition of the professional person could include the individual's espousal of an ethic entailing the independent exercise of trained judgement. Commitment to this ethic may be stronger than to the employing organization, and may also be seen by the individual as establishing social status. If this is the case, it can be argued that although an educational institution may possess a hierarchic structure, professional personnel make difficult the establishment or maintenance of bureaucratic authority. However, this concept of a professional ethic cannot be assumed always to be obstructive to management: it could be manifested in one sense by a refusal to accept a quasi-cabinet responsibility for the decisions and policy of an academic board of which the professional is a member; and in another sense by working in reverse so that an excessive confidentiality is maintained (especially with regard to the communication of information to students). An issue for the manager, therefore, is the development of the most appropriate structure and organizational ethos which takes account of the organization's professional membership.

35. To concentrate on a professional ethic is restrictive. More discomfort to management may be caused by political ethics. Moreover, professionalism presumes a term not evidenced in contracts of employment. The teacher is employed according to a contract. Once the contractual obligation is fulfilled, there can be no further requirement. In one sense, as the Haycocks Reports suggest (see Sections **1.5**, **11.12**, Appendix 1, and para 58 below), teachers are managers since they are required to manage the resources necessary for their teaching, and they are also required to participate to some degree in course planning, operation and assessment. However, it remains the function of those appointed to managerial posts to exercise management responsibilities; employee interests are represented by trade unions. Where managers and the managed are members of the same trade union or professional association, the union or professional association will probably have some procedure for determining the nature of the representation available (for example, See Sections **2.4.**8 and **9.**66.

36. Matrix structures, and some course developments, have involved teachers in more managerial processes (which has in turn created pressure for relevant staff development policies). However, if the education service is to contract, issues will change rapidly. Policies of redeployment and training will be necessary; staff welfare will require attention, and the professional ethic, which may be acceptable in times of expansion, is unlikely to exist unchanged when not all of the community of equals may retain employment. The role of the professional associations is also unlikely to remain unchanged, and their involvement in the management process seems likely to become more clearly defined.

37. Collegiality is concerned with the operation of democracy, especially in the separation of institutional powers, and in representative and collective policy making. Its achievement raises issues of considerable sensitivity for all

educational institutions whose aims include the preparation of their students for life in a democratic society, but who find difficulties in translating such an aim into particular management structures. The term is applied usually to formal power structures – such as college committees – but may be extended in considering trade union operations, and informal interest and social groups (possibly including non-teaching staff). The democratic/managerial dilemma is at its most acute when considering the place of students within such structures.

38. Committees represent important arenas of college power. Ironically, in a governmental system designed with a democratic appearance, college committees have been described as constituting a ruling oligarchy: the frequent right of the principal to sit on all committees and sub-committees, and the usual presence of heads of department on academic boards is said to have maintained hierarchical structures. (Oligarchy is used as a term in this argument only loosely: to adopt a historical perspective, committee management is hardly baronial rule, and while overmighty subjects may exist, actual usurpation seems rare). Much of an institution's management may be said to have the appearance of being vested in committees. Effective institutional policy-making can depend on the ability of any committee to restrict the choices open to superior or subordinate committees. In many institutions, the same sets of individuals tend to serve on committees: a result of their seniority, resource control power, diligent application, and membership of other committees or groups. The system would seem to work least effectively when operated by those who have not developed the distinctive skills and attitudes required for the effective manifestation of collegiality. Power is consolidated by the ability to confer patronage on subordinate bodies. Collegial processes, which can be slow and cumbersome, can be circumvented when quick action is necessary by the oligarchic group, or a power group within it, as represented by recurrent committee members. This circumvention, as well as committee, collegial, professional and governmental processes, can exert pressure at the point of middle management as represented by the head of department. Such pressures have been expressed in requests for special conditions of service agreements for managers. Whatever the merits of that case, it is proper now to consider the management area where problems appear to be most acute: at departmental level or its equivalent, that which most immediately affects both staff and students.

39. **The head of department**

Although Circular 7/70 appears to take away power from the head of department by creating greater democracy, in its provision for departmental autonomy within college freedom the head of department has an opportunity to exercise control over departmental planning, the nature and quality of its work, and its relation to college developments. Oligarchic grouping of heads of department has been represented as a fount of wisdom: restraint is exercised on an autocratic principal, and wise counsel extended to the academic board. Such liberal enlightenment presupposes a considered adoption of thought patterns, and allows little scope for the impact of events requiring immediate reaction.

40. Where responsibilties of the head of department have been increased (for committee membership involves more than attendance) some growth of academic leadership by subordinate staff has occurred. *Submission to the Standing Commission, op.cit,* identifies the general management role of the head of department which has increased as departments have become fewer but larger. Responsibilities which can be for 50 or more academic, clerical and technical staff are equivalent to those of a head teacher in a substantial school. This circumstance entails, in turn, a political growth since if committees allocate resources, representation of departmental interest is essential. Issues arise where changing roles are not accepted, which may in turn create problems for individuals, groups or the whole institution. Among the reasons offered for some heads of department failing to accept such changes are a reluctance or inability to delegate, and the lack of effective guidance. Refuge may be sought by the head in a morass of routine administration, and the real or imagined excuse used of impotence to influence or effect change. Employment of such means to retain departmental control indicates, at least, an unsureness of function. The head may also feel sandwiched by pressures from above and below. Research into such matters is made difficult in that, apart from general responsibilities, there are no particular defined problems common to all departments. All departments will have some common problems, albeit differing in acuteness and longevity. Even where responsibilities are defined there is little evidence to illustrate exactly what, and how effectively, heads of department do: job analysis (i.e. defined individual responsibilities, tasks, and consequent demands) in education is not well developed.[22] A recent survey[23] indicates the nature of the problem. Oxtoby found that whereas most applicants for head of department posts ought to be able to gain a reasonable idea of the necessary qualities, duties and responsibilities, job details were insufficient for selection committees readily to match applicants to requirements. Nor was the information sufficient to allow a basis for the monitoring and assessment of the successful applicant. Oxtoby suggests the need for job analyses to determine whether the tasks actually performed are relevant to departmental and college objectives. However, although a number of colleges have adopted methods of job analysis, while some advantages are apparent, there are many associated problems.

41. Using as a method of analysis the identification of "critical incidents" – that is, the most difficult tasks or situations with which during a two to three day span a head of department was required to deal – Oxtoby concludes that heads seemed "to be preoccupied with day to day problems that are more closely allied to checking and routine maintenance functions than to monitoring and future planning", [24] and that the majority of these problems were probably raised by students and subordinate staff. If the most urgent task of heads of department is to review their own use of time and redeploy

---

22 Examples of inquiry are contained in J. Latcham *et al., Ways of Looking at a Department,* Coombe Lodge Information Bank Number 1348, 1979; and Ferguson, *op.cit,* pp 15.16. An example of general responsibilities is contained in *Submission to the Standing Commission on Pay Comparability, op.cit,* pp.85-86.

23 Bob Oxtoby, "Problems Facing Heads of Department", *Journal of Further and Higher Education,* Vol.3, No.1, Spring 1979, pp.46-59.

24 *Ibid,* p.55.

it effectively, the consequence of inability to perform such tasks is likely to be an inefficient resource control and use. Oxtoby concedes that his survey does not provide information on whether heads are pursuing the tasks with which they ought to be engaged; or whether they are "over-busy rather than over-worked."[25]

42. The head of department may be seen as the person best placed to provide the link between theory and practice in college management; or on the other hand, an example of the difficulties afflicting middle management. The ambiguity of the position in the managerial sandwich is compounded where the role becomes more managerial but the head is required, because of validating body pressure, still to maintain academic leadership and authority. There is a strong case for clear role definition.

43. In practice, many colleges still appear to be highly departmentalised. The head of department may often be identified as the "boss", in effect the person with the employer image, who determines working conditions by means of timetables and teaching policies. Ebbutt and Brown discovered that heads saw themselves in a paternalistic role, concerned about staff and ready to deal with complaints; and yet their staff often complained that this did not occur, and that their interests were neither considered not defended. It was also found, however, that where consultations regularly occurred and where all staff had some administrative responsibility, there was total loyalty to the head of department: "To most teachers, the degree of participation within the department is more crucial than at college level".[26] Although unhelpfully ambiguous, Ebbutt and Brown conclude realistically that heads of department tend to be more authoritarian than principals; and whereas weaker heads seem not to run their departments at all (the departments being said "to just occur"), authoritarian heads elicit two kinds of response: co-operation, or strong antagonism. This can be related to suggestions that departmental issues refer more to personalities than to the lack of provision of staff meetings; and that while departments are discrete, the sections within them are even more so. Certainly, within larger colleges with few departments there is often little communication between sections, especially where the subjects taught are largely discrete (for instance, within one department there may be courses taught on public health, joinery, building, and technician subjects). Perhaps the issues and problems relating to college management can be more starkly identified in the head of department role than in that of any other individual within the college system.

44. **Information systems and resource use**

For resource use to be effective, an efficient information system is necessary. Information gathering, and resource and activity monitoring, will presumably both be part of a college's information system. There will be a need to process external information arising from new legislation, conditions of service agreements, government policy changes, local industrial and commercial developments, and the varieties of information put forward by

---

25 *Ibid,* quoting G. Tolley, "The Managerial Role of a Head of Department," *Technical Journal,* Vol.10, No.3, 1972, p.16.
26 Ebbutt and Brown, *op.cit.,* p.14.

local government departments and specialist bodies.[27] Internal information systems [28] will usually have regard to the resource areas of: courses and students; staff; costing; and accommodation use. The information within them may be used to appraise the operation of the government and management structure, and even to encompass most college activities, including student progress, staffing establishment, and building use. For example, in the case of course and student information, data will usually be compiled concerning student numbers, the number of weekly study hours at college, the modes of study, and course gradings. Much of the information is collected not only for internal uses but to meet the requirements of central and local government agencies (see Section **8**, Appendix 2). This may be taken to represent an input, but the desired output is not readily identifiable, and therefore the necessary resource allocation is not readily measurable.

45. It is at the point of the application of information that debate becomes acute: by what criteria are resources to be allocated? On the one hand there are the kinds of criteria which exist as management tools: performance indicators [29], activity accounting [30]; monitoring of staff use by way of ratios [31]; staff appraisal; and effective and efficient accommodation use.[32] On the other there are the limits of individual college circumstance; practices in one institution may be wholly inappropriate to another; and the balance of educational and human factors may at least seriously qualify the use of any such devices. Introduction of information processes will require careful presentation, and implementation based on consent.

46. **Timetabling**

Timetabling is an important function of college management which can reflect the organizational complexity of the institution. It raises issues of planning, participation, resource deployment, the use of information systems, *et cetera.* The usual timetabling method in some colleges is for senior lecturers in a department (or section/division of a department), after consulting their colleagues, to draw up a timetable. This is ratified or amended by the head of department. In other colleges, timetabling is undertaken by the vice-principal. The timetable may be drawn up manually or with the help of a computer, sometimes displayed on peg board, and is often publicly displayed. This basic process may be subject to change: there may be reasons for timetabling to be based on a college rather than a

---

27 for example, CIPFA in its *Manual of Guidance for a Financial Information System for Institutions of Higher Education and Further Education;* the MSC; professional associations; and the Educational Publishers' Council.

28 cf. Derek Birch, "An Overview of Management Information Systems", *Use of Resources in College Management,* Coombe Lodge Report, Vol.11, No.11, 1978. pp 412-419; D.W. Birch and J.R. Calvert, *A proposal for a management information system for further education colleges,* Coombe Lodge Information Paper (IBN 1195), August 1976; C.M. Turner, *College Information Systems,* Coombe Lodge Information Paper (IBN 1180) January 1977 (revised); Latcham *et.al., op.cit.,* pp 3; 6-7.

29 cf John Sizer, "Developing Performance Indicators for Institutions of Higher Education", *Use of Resources, op.cit,* pp 404-419.

30 cf M.A. Sims, "Accounting Information in Universities," *Higher Education Review,* Vol.5, No.3, 1973, pp 3-23.

31 cf Section **11.2** and **3.**51; Norma Whittaker, "The Allocation of Resources and The Monitoring of Their Use," *Use of Resources, op.cit,* pp 395-403.

32 see Section **11.11** and **5.8** below.

departmental basis (see Section **5.8.** 12-13) and there are advocates of a full staff participation in timetabling (see paragraph 47). Since it has a large influence on staff and student life, timetabling can be a cause of discontent (and, equally, a process often made complex). Timetables may be issued dictatorially: they may be discussed in draft at staff or faculty or departmental level, and the resultant horsetrading and bargaining, confused or illuminated by educational, salary (bar transfer) and personal issues, may result in reasonable content. Staff aspirations and the process of staff development may form a part of the timetabling criteria; the meek and the willing may be exploited; and there may be some staff who consider that they suffer the imposition of a disproportionate amount of low level work. It has been argued that where bargaining and horsetrading are applied without a coherent guiding philosophy, the results may not always be the best, in institutional terms; or the fairest, in personal terms; or even educationally desirable.

47. It has been argued that motivation is strongest when each individual can be given freedom in making factual judgements, and that only value judgements involving the wider working environment should be referred to the appropriate person at a high level. The management technique known as "management by exception" expresses this view in practical terms: functions regarded as factual judgements are delegated to individuals, thus leading to high motivation, and the manager retains only the exceptional functions which are defined as involving value judgements.

48. From this technique there springs the suggestion that staff should write their own timetables. The argument runs thus: as a professional, the teacher will be fully aware of personal abilities and shortcomings, research interests and avenues for their development, and the kinds of irritation which can be accepted and those which present a deterrent to achievement.[33]

49. Timetabling which has its origins in the idea of motivation can also be seen as part of the human relations approach to management. It may satisfy desires for staff participation. The reverse of the case involves arguments such as motivation and participation being forms of manipulation whereby staff do more work, relieving the manager of tedious responsibilities, believing that they are enjoying participation, and being kept too busy properly to be able to express their views. At root, therefore, is the nature of the employer/employee relationship. Thus there may be a staff response which insists that managerial functions should be left to those with contractual responsibilities.[34]

50 Where timetabling is college based, and especially where computer

---

33 D.D. Simmons and J.M. Gibb, "Timetabling Without Tears", ADM 06-010, p.4, in *College Management Readings and Cases*, Vol.1, Coombe Lodge, 1971.

34 During the course of the preparation of this book, one commentator expressed an opinion thus: "I firmly adopt the view expressed in the aphorism of the late George Woodcock, former general secretary of the TUC, that 'you can be as broad-based as you like but you cannot sit on both sides of the same table at the same time.' Hence I would never agree with the startling suggestion ... that staff should write their own timetables. One can only wonder who will write the pay slips."

techniques are used (see Section **5.8.**12-14), there will need to be staff participation in some form if all interests are to be represented but this may still usually be achieveable at department level (and with the draft timetable still being constructed by a senior lecturer). Matrix forms of management structure can present particular timetabling problems where staff have to be deployed across several departments and courses. Similar problems can occur where inter-departmental programmes are established for bodies such as the MSC.

51. **The management of change**

The volatile nature of further and higher education has meant that colleges have had to respond rapidly to change, whether inspired by central or local government decisions, the initiatives of external organizations such as the MSC, new legislation, or from student/employer decisions concerning the desirability or otherwise of particular courses. In consequence, colleges must recognise that they are in a process of continuous change, and need to develop strategies for dealing with it, whether these have been designed to facilitate or to check its implementation. In some cases colleges have been only reactive, responding to external initiatives. In other cases college managements have dealt with change more successfully by being proactive, and thereby contributing to the processes of change management. Whatever strategies are adopted, colleges have had to face up to the problems of the irreversibility of those strategies, in that failed strategies generally also produce undesirable changes. It is incumbent upon the educational manager to understand change processes before implementing strategies. Management and organization theory have provided insights into change processes. Some of these are discussed below, in an attempt to illustrate possible relationships between theory and management practice which might facilitate the management of change.

52. It has been suggested that there are at least four different types of strategies for effecting change, which may be related to the differing management approaches discussed in paragraphs 6 to 13, above. Three broad classes have been labelled "empirical-rational", wherein it is assumed that behaviour is rational and that people will follow their rational self-interest when the reasonableness of planned change is demonstrated: "normative-re-educative" strategies make assumptions that group activities, attitudes and values can be aligned to match norms which will facilitate change; "power-coercive" strategies demand compliance with those holding power and authority.[35] A further strategy, labelled "political-manipulative", assumes strategies which persuade others to accept change through negotiation and bargaining. As with management theories generally, a prime task of the college manager is the recognition of the most appropriate strategy in any given context, and its application by means of an adequate repertoire of skills and techniques.

53. Thus, in the areas discussed above, it would seem likely that normative re-

35 cf ed. W.G. Bennis, K.D. Benne, and R. Chin, *The Planning of Change,* Holt. Rinehart, and Winston, 1969; Per Dalin, *Limits to Educational Change,* Macmillan, 1978.

educative and political-manipulative strategies might in many circumstances cope better with changes related to issues of professionalism and collegiality than power-coercive strategies. These latter strategies might, however, have their place in resolving some resource issues arising from the use of information systems. The management of change requires quite fundamental analysis by those with managerial responsibilities. Among issues to be considered are the analysis of the discontinuities between the existing situation, the recognition of the "dynamic interplay of sub-systems" which can alter, facilitate, or assist planned change in any organization, and the boundaries of management itself. This all argues for quite remarkable qualities in those undertaking managerial responsibilities in colleges of further and higher education, even where such responsibilities are only a part of their broader academic and administrative tasks. This would, therefore, seem to be an appropriate juncture at which to discuss the education of such managers.

54. **Education management programmes**[36]

In comparison with other public services in England and Wales, and with education services in English speaking countries such as the USA, Canada and Australia, our education services have been slow to realise that there is a need and demand for formal managerial preparation and training. A tradition of apprenticeship still persists. The criteria leading to promotion appear to be academic qualification, teaching competence, length of service, and extra-curricular enthusiasm. Experience for managerial and administrative posts seems to have been acquired often by observing and working for experienced managers and administrators (whose own preparation has been similarly informal and in-post).

55. Changes in the nature of educational institutions and in society have entailed the incurring of greatly increased risks when managerial experience is gained by learning from mistakes. In the past decade therefore, there has been demand for and some provision of mid-career in-service programmes for teachers, lecturers and administrators. Such programmes attempt to offer formal and systematised training for managerial and administrative positions in the education service. In 1967 the Secretary of State for Education and Science asked HMI to give high priority to such programmes. This led to the major series of short "COSMOS" (Committee on the Organization, Staffing and Management of Schools) courses for head teachers and other secondary school staff. Local authorities began to organize management training programmes for teachers, a development which increased after local government reorganization when larger authorities, themselves equipped with new management structures and more resources, offered both directly and indirectly a diverse range of long and short programmes.

56. This provision is augmented by a varied group of organizations, including regional consortia of LEAs, local teachers' groups, the Advisory Centre for Education, teachers' unions and professional associations, and institutions of

36 Paragraphs 54-59 were written in conjunction with Lynton Gray, and much of the information is drawn from his unpublished paper, *Education Management Programmes in England and Wales.*

further and higher education. A distinction may be drawn between such entrepreneurial programmes, offered speculatively by organizations or institutions which determine the structure, content, duration and location of the programmes, and programmes sponsored by employers, whether LEAs or institutions. Employer programmes entail the employers determining courses' membership and aspects of the content and structure of the programme along with the providing body. Increasingly, employers are providing internal programmes where they determine course membership, location, structure and curriculum, and also provide at least part of the tutorial staff. This process makes sensible use of employer resources, but some concern has been expressed that such programmes might be used by employers for purposes of both training and selection.

57. Major programmes of education management training leading to postgraduate equivalent qualifications are relatively recent innovations. There are a small number of full-time residential programmes, which recruit both nationally and internationally, leading to a diploma or Master's degree. Part-time, day-release or block release programmes, usually of 18 months' duration, can lead to a diploma (in education management or in management studies) or a Master's degree. Structures and curricula vary considerably. Addresses of the providing institutions form Appendix 1 of this sub-section.

58. The special needs of further education were considered by the Haycocks Committee. The Haycocks Report,[37] "Haycocks 3", after examining present provision, including that of the universities, the regional management centres, the Further Education Staff College (see Section **11.13**), the Regional Advisory Councils, the Local Government Training Board, the City and Guilds of London Institute, the College of Preceptors and institutions specializing in the professional education of further education teachers, argued that there is a need to improve both the quality and quantity of present provision. Among the Report's recommendations were suggestions that education management training should be given special emphasis in programmes of post-initial training for further education teachers; individual staff training should be related to present and likely future managerial responsibilities; institutions should designate a senior member of staff who should ensure coherent training for staff; and that staff should receive appropriate training just prior to, or soon after, major changes take place or new responsibilities are undertaken. Recommendations were also made concerning the structure and content of appropriate programmes. An advisory and consultative group to consider the content and quality of such programmes was deemed necessary (an issue taken up by at least one RAC).

59. International interest in education management is growing. The OECD Education Committee funds a research and training programme in institutional management in higher education. In its study of management education in the EEC, the European Foundation for Management

---

37 *Training Teachers for Education Management in Further and Adult Education:* a report by the Sub-Committee on the Supply and Training of Teachers, ACSTT, August 1978. See also Sections **1.5.** and **11.12.**

Development made significant recommendations.[38] The study distinguished management schools as having "a whole nexus of teaching, research, consulting and information activities" which determined two crucial future developments. The study stated that:[39]

> Management education establishments would be no longer able just to teach what they knew. As their "somewhat arrogant previous approach – in instructing managers what they should do – declines", the establishments should not move away from the realities of life.
>
> Linked with the need to cope with uncertainty is the demand that establishments "*should involve themselves even more with the real, messy world where managers operate,*[40] where the ideal solution is a theoretical luxury, where the important thing is to make decisions which are right enough (and right often enough) to get effective results. In the coming decade sophistication is required less in management techniques themselves than in the effective transfer to users of current best practices."

60. **Conclusion**

This sub-section has attempted to reflect certain management provisions and practices in England and Wales, and to give an introduction to some management theories. There are no agreed comprehensive guidelines for education managers, and nor is there a unified education management system. All principals and heads of department have problems to face and to solve. While these will vary, it can at least be said that the government of a college determines much of its management; and the academic board, too, will have to encounter the various issues upon which this sub-section has touched. Each management system has its merits and demerits. Selection of, and from, the appropriate methodologies, approaches and systems is vital.

---

38 EFMD, *Management education in the European Community,* Commission of The European Communities, Studies Collection, Education series No.4, Brussels, 1978.
39 *Ibid,* paras 45-46, p.62.
40. Editor's italics.

APPENDIX 1

QUALIFICATION – BEARING PROGRAMMES IN EDUCATION MANAGEMENT, 1980-81

Centre	*Qualification*	*Validating body*	*Type of study*	*Period of study*	*Application*
Anglian Regional Management Centre/North East London Polytechnic in association with Essex County Council	Diploma in Management Studies MSC in Education Management (1981)	CNAA	pt pt	2 years 1 year	Registrar, ARMC, Asta House, Romford, Essex, RM6 6LX.
University of Bath	MEd in Educational Management	University	ft	1 year	School of Education Claverdon Down, Bath, BA2 7AY.
University of Birmingham	MEd in Educational Admin. BPhil (Ed) in School Organization and Management and in Educational Policy and Planning.	University	ft or pt ft + pt	1 year 2 or 3 yrs 1 year + 6 months	Faculty of Education, PO Box 363, Birmingham B15 2TT.
Bolton College of Education (Technical)	Diploma in Advanced Study in Technical Education.	University of Manchester	pt	2 years	Secretary to Faculty of Education Studies, Chadwick Street, Bolton, BL2 1JW.
Brunel University	MA in Public and Social Administration (with specialization in Educational Policy)	University	ft or pt	1 year 2 years	School of Social Science, Department of Government Uxbridge, Middx. UP8 3PH.
Derby Lonsdale College of Higher Education	Diploma in Education Management	East Midlands Regional Management Centre	pt	2 years	Admissions Office, School of Management & Business Studies Kedleston Road, Derby, DE3 1GB.

Centre	*Qualification*	*Validating body*	*Type of study*	*Period of study*	*Application*
Garnett College	Diploma in Further Education	University of London	ft or pt	1 year 3 years	Downshire House, Roehampton Lane, London SW15 4HR
	Diploma in Education Management		pt	2 years	
University of Hull	MA in Educational Organisation, Administration & Management. MA in the Organization & Management of Post-Secondary Education.	University	ft or pt	1 year 3 years	Institute of Education, 173 Cottingham Road, Hull, HU5 2EH
University of Lancaster	Post-Graduate Diploma in Management Learning	University	pt	2 years	Director, CDMTT Gillow House, Lancaster LA1 4YX.
La Sainte Union College of Higher Education	Diploma in Advanced Educational Studies: Educational Management	University of Southampton	pt	2 years	The Avenue, Southampton, SO9 5BH
London University Institute of Education	MA in Educational Administration	University	ft or pt	2 years	Institute of Education, Bedford Way, London WC1H 0AL.
	Diploma in Educational Administration		pt	2 years	
Manchester Polytechnic	Diploma in Management in Education	Manchester Polytechnic	pt	2 years	Tutor for Admissions, Dept of Management, Hilton House, Hilton Street, Manchester M1 2FE.

Centre	*Qualification*	*Validating body*	*Type of study*	*Period of study*	*Application*
University of Manchester	MEd in the Organization and Planning of Education	University	ft or pt	1 year 2 or 3 yrs	Faculty of Education, Manchester M13 9PL.
Mid-Kent College of Higher & Further Education	Diploma in Management Studies (Education)	CNAA	pt	2 years	Dept of Management & Social Studies, Maidstone Road, Chatham, Kent ME5 9UQ.
University of Newcastle	MEd (Management & Administration in Education)	University	ft or pt	1 year 2 years	School of Education, Joseph Cowen House, St Thomas' Street, Newcastle NE1 7RU
	Diploma in Advanced Educational Studies (Management and Administration)		pt	2 years	
North East Wales Institute of Higher Education	Diploma in Education Management	CNAA	ft pt	1 year 2 years	Head of Continuing Education, Cartrefle College, Cefn Road, Wrexham, LW3 9NL
Oxford Polytechnic	Diploma in Educational Studies (Organization and Administration)	CNAA	pt	2 years	Academic Secretary, Lady Spencer-Churchill College, Wheatley, Oxford OX9 1HX
Oxford University	MSc in Educational Studies (the Governance of Education)	University	ft	1 year	Dept of Educational Studies, 15 Norham Gardens, Oxford, OX2 6PY.
	Special Diploma in Educational Studies (Educational Administration)		ft	1 year	

Centre	*Qualification*	*Validating body*	*Type of study*	*Period of study*	*Application*
Sheffield City Polytechnic	MSc in Education Management Diploma in Education Management	CNAA	ft or pt ft or pt	1 year 3 years 1 year 2 years	Dept of Management and In-Service Education, Pond Street, Sheffield S1 1WB.
Sunderland Polytechnic	Diploma in Education Management	CNAA	pt	2 years	In-Service Training Unit, Faculty of Education, Hammerton Hall, Gray Row, Sunderland, SR2 7EE.
Trent Polytechnic	Diploma in Education Management	CNAA	pt	2 years	School of Education, Burton Street, Nottingham NG1 4BU
Thames Valley Regional Management Centre	MEd in School Administration Diploma in Management Studies (Education)	CNAA	pt pt	3 years 2 years	Registrar, Bulmershe College of Higher Education, Woodlands Avenue, Earley, Reading R96 1HY
Wolverhampton Polytechnic	Diploma in Management Studies MEd in School Administration	CNAA	pt	2 years	Co-ordinator, In-Service Education, Wulfruna Street, Wolverhampton, WV1 1LY.

APPENDIX 2

TEACHING ON NON-COLLEGE PREMISES

1. Many of the developments in further education which have required teaching to take place outside colleges have been welcomed by the teachers' associations. In order to obviate difficulties which can occur in such circumstances, NATFHE has outlined procedures which it advises should be applied. These procedures are summarised below.

2. When it is not practicable for teaching to occur in college, when it is educationally desirable and when adequate teaching aids are provided, then teaching may take place in the premises of a private firm or organization.

3. In some cases firms and organizations operate courses solely for their employees. It is not unreasonable here for teachers to co-operate in assisting with these courses. However, where this is not a requirement every effort should be made to ensure that courses operated on non-college premises are as open to any student as they would be if they were offered as part of the normal college programme.

4. The premises on which the teaching is to take place must be satisfactory and approved by the LEA as suitable for teaching purposes. Particular attention should be given to the requirements of the Health and Safety at Work etc. Act. Premises which might reasonably be regarded as safe in relation to the performance of the usual functions for which they are used, may not be suitable as premises for teaching.

5. In every case where staff are asked to teach on non-college premises the conditions of service must be regarded as a matter for negotiation with the branch and liaison committee concerned. The conditions should be no less favourable than those laid down in the recommendations of the national agreement which have been agreed in the particular authority: participation in schemes of teaching on non-college premises should not be expected unless agreed college conditions have been applied by negotiation to these schemes. Work outside the normal college year must be subject to the Conditions of Service Agreement and particular attention should be paid to the following:

   (i) the services of the teachers should not be required outside normal teaching hours, nor at times when the college is closed;
   (ii) staff level courtesies and facilities should be extended by the firm or organization;
   (iii) the teacher should be appointed to the college;
   (iv) the assessment of travelling time and cost should be made as if the journey started from the college, and entitle the teacher to a reduction of class contact hours;
   (v) as the teacher should not be responsible for providing transport since the possession of a car should not be a condition of appointment, where the teacher's own car is used the travelling allowances should be paid at least at the nationally negotiated local authority rate for casual users. Where public transport is used, the teacher should be reimbursed to the extent of the whole cost of the fares; and
   (vi) the LEA should ensure that the teacher is insured to cover the same risks as at college and also any additional risks resulting from teaching outside the college. The teacher should be informed by the authority of his or her obligations under the Health and Safety at Work etc. Act and any other relevant legislation.

6. Teachers on non-college premises should have the same professional responsibility for teaching methods, the allocation of time between different parts of the course, and the other matters appropriate to the teachers' professional skill as they would have if they were teaching in the college. The college should retain the same responsibility for the course content that it would have were the courses to be held at the college. Classes held on non-college premises should be the responsibility of the teacher at all times that they are being taught.

7. Whilst it will be necessary for the teachers to liaise with representatives of the firm or organization on whose premises they are to teach, they should remain primarily responsible to the principal of the college. Where teachers are required to teach on school premises, it is recognised that they will be responsible also to the head teacher. Similarly, where teachers are involved in teaching on Home Office Premises, such as Police Training, College and Penal Establishments, they will have a responsibility to the head of the organization concerned.

APPENDIX 3

STAFF HANDBOOKS

1. One method in which the problems of communication in colleges can be addressed is by the provision of a staff handbook.[1] A handbook would supplement other communications exercises such as induction courses for new staff (and also social gatherings). The handbook should be of service to teaching and non-teaching staff.

2. The handbook should enable staff quickly to assimilate and have reference to the nature of college organization. An amended edition for part-time staff will be appropriate. Loose leaf presentation, or else separate publications (possibly in the form of a combined diary), will allow for easy updating. While preparation of the handbook will be a managerial function, staff consultation will be necessary.

3. Contents may include the following:

   (i) a general information section providing, *inter alia,* an index, term dates, internal telephone directory, facilities and room booking arrangements, stationery issue, and some guide to community activities;
   (ii) emergency, accident and first aid arrangements and procedures;
   (iii) conditions of service information, especially locally negotiated matters;
   (iv) college government and management arrangements, including brief job descriptions as appropriate (a useful way for staff to identify those with special managerial responsibilities);
   (v) financial arrangements, including procedures for the ordering of goods and materials, and the use of petty cash;
   (vi) college services: details concerning educational technology, library organization and provision;
   (vii) welfare matters: details may include information necessary under the Health and Safety at Work etc.Act; and
   (viii) students: information can be given concerning visits, services, regulations and discipline.

   The handbook may be supplemented by departmental information.

---

1 NATFHE policy is contained in the document *Staff Handbooks,* 6/77. The policy document contains useful practical guidance. A good example of a staff handbook/diary is produced by Middlesex Polytechnic.

APPENDIX 4

RACIALIST ACTIVITY IN COLLEGES

1. This potentially difficult problem requires a prepared management policy. Lettings policy is discussed in Section **5.10**. The problem may not arise through a letting, however. The law concerning racialist activity may be summarised thus:

   (i) it is a criminal offence to publish or distribute written matter, or use in any public place or at any public meeting language which is threatening, abusive, insulting or likely, having regard to all the circumstances, to stir up hatred against any racial group (except in the reporting of judicial and parliamentary proceedings); and

   (ii) it is a defence for an accused person to demonstrate unawareness of the content of written matter, and neither to have suspected nor had reason to suspect that it was threatening, abusive or insulting.

2. Where union members are aware of racialist propaganda being circulated within a college, they are advised both to bring the matter to the attention of college management and to act through their union. Management therefore can expect to be informed of the activity, be provided with a copy of the alleged offensive material, and be requested to notify the LEA and to prohibit the further dissemination of the material. Where a member of the public seeks to disseminate such material, that person should be asked to desist and leave the premises; and in the case of a refusal the principal should contact the LEA and consider calling the police. Where a student seeks to disseminate racialist propaganda, it may be appropriate initially to undertake an informal approach, to implement the appropriate established college procedures and to inform the student union of the circumstances. In the case of a staff member being engaged in racialist practices, staff will usually seek the assistance of their unions, and will usually make representation to management. The principal here should usually first undertake an informal approach to the staff member concerned (where the matter has not been already settled), implement the relevant procedures, and take further advice. Close consultation with LEA and unions will be essential. Persons wishing to complain of a contravention of the law have a right to inform the police.[1]

---

1 NATFHE recommends that contact with the police should be made at Branch or Liaison Committee level, and that requests for referral to the Commission for Racial Equality and the Director of Public Prosecutions should be made via head office.

APPENDIX 5

PROVIDING BODIES FOR VOLUNTARY COLLEGES

1. The management and government of voluntary colleges may vary according to the composition of the providing bodies concerned, some of which take a greater direct interest and involvement than others. The various church foundations in particular are part of a network of colleges and other educational institutions, and the churches have established a formal structure of committees or boards to oversee their development. The major providing interests are as follows.

2. *The Church of England*
While the Church is actually the overall providing body, each college is established under a trust, which will specify, *inter alia,* that the college must have regard to the principles of the Church of England. There are two organizations within the Church which have special interests in a number of colleges and frequently appoint the Foundation Governors of the college. These are the National Society for Promoting Religious Education and the Church of England Board of Education. Frequently local diocesan interests will also be represented on the governing body and representation from the universities or other sectors of education will often be selected with some regard for religious commitment, as well as a contribution to education.

3. *The Catholic Church*
Originally the major providing bodies were the religious orders and they still act severally as providing bodies for a number of Catholic colleges. In most cases they are responsible for a single institution but some providing bodies, such as the Society of the Sacred Heart, are responsible for more than one. The Catholic Education Council is a providing body in its own right as well as being the representative body for Catholic educational interests at a national level. It has sole responsibility for two colleges and has a joint responsibility with certain religious orders for two further colleges.

4. *The Methodist Church*
The Methodist Church Board of Education and Youth is the providing body for two colleges, both established under a trust and for whom the Board provides or nominates a number of governors.

5. There are some colleges which are voluntary institutions whose providing bodies do not come under the categories provided above, for example, Froebel Institute College (part of the Roehampton Institute of Higher Education) whose providing body is the Froebel Educational Institute Inc. Such colleges are however very few in number: the overwhelming proportion of voluntary institutions are maintained by the religious authorities.

REFERENCE

ed P. Andrews and D.L. Parkes, *Participation, Accountability and Decision-Making a*ₜ *Institutional Level,* proceedings of the Third Annual Conference of the BEAS, BEAS, 1975.

ed W.G. Bennis, K.D. Benne, R. Chin, *The Planning of Change,* Holt, Rinehart and Winston, 1969.

B. Baron, *The Managerial Approach to Tertiary Education,* Studies in Education No 7, University of London Institute of Education, 1978.

D.W. Birch and J.R. Calvert, *A proposal for a management information system for further education colleges,* Coombe Lodge Information Paper IBN 1195, August 1976.

T. Burns and G.M. Stalker, *The Management of Innovation,* Tavistock, 1976.

College Administration, Coombe Lodge Report, Vol.11, No.14, 1978.

College Management, Coombe Lodge Report, Vol.10, No.10, 1977.

Per Dalin, *Limits to Educational Change,* Macmillan, 1978.

Digby Davies, *Management: Some Cultural Perspectives,* Educational Studies: A Third Level Course, E 321, Unit 13, Open University Press, 1976.

N.H. Davies, "Managing a further education college", *Education and Training,* October 1975.

ed. Lance Dobson *et al., Management in Education Reader 2,* Ward Lock Educational/Open University Press, 1975.

Keith Ebbutt and Roger Brown, "The Structure of Power in the FE College", *Journal of Further and Higher Education,* Vol.2, No.3, Autumn 1978.

EFMD, *Management Education in the European Community,* Commission of the European Communities, Studies Collection, Education Series No. 4, Brussels, 1978.

C.T. Ferguson, *Alternative Organisational Structures in Higher and Further Education,* Coombe Lodge Working Paper, IBN 1197, revised, February 1979.

J. Fielden and G. Lockwood, *Planning and Management in Universities,* Chatto and Windus, 1973.

Lynton Gray, *Education Management Programmes in England and Wales,* unpublished paper, 1979.

Charles Handy, *Understanding Organizations,* Penguin. 1976.

ed. Vincent Houghton *et al., Management in Education Reader I,* Ward Lock Educational/Open University Press, 1975.

D.A. Howell, *A bibliography of educational administration in the United Kingdom,* NFER, 1978.

E.F. Huse and J. Bowditch, *Behaviour in Organizations – A Systems Approach to Management,* Addison Wesley, 2nd Edition, 1977.

ed J. Karabel and A.M. Maisey, *Power and Ideology in Education,* Oxford, 1977.

J. Latcham, *et al., Ways of Looking at a Department,* Coombe Lodge Exercise, IBN 1348, revised, February 1979.

J. March and J. Oslen, *Ambiguity and Choice in Organizations,* Universitaat forlaget, Bergen, 1976.

Colin Morgan, *Management in Education – Dissimilar or Congruent?* Education Studies: A Third Level Course, E 321, Unit 1, Open University Press, 1976.

Colin Morgan and David Parkes, *Management and the Academic Board in Further Education Colleges,* Educational Studies: A Third Level Course, E321, Unit 12, Open University Press, 1977.

Colin Morgan and Colin Turner, *Role, the Educational Manager and the Individual in the Organization; The Manager and Groups in the Organization,* Education Studies: A Third Level Course, Units 14 and 15, Open University Press, 1976.

T. Noble and B. Pym, "Collegial authority and the receding locus of power", *British Journal of Sociology,* Vol.21, December 1970.

J. O'Neill, *College Management Structures,* Coombe Lodge Working Paper, IBN 756, April 1973.

Bob Oxtoby, "Problems Facing Heads of Departments". *Journal of Further and Higher Education,* Vol 3, No.1, Spring 1979, pp 46-59.

ed. D.L. Parkes and D.D. Simmons, *College Management Readings and Cases,* Vols 1-5, Coombe Lodge 1971-75.

R.A. Schmuck and P.J. Runkel, *Handbook of Organization Development in Schools,* National Press Books, 1972.

Submission to the Standing Commission on Pay Comparability, Teachers' Panel of the Burnham Further Education Committee, October 1979.

M.A. Sims, "Accounting Information in Universities", *Higher Education Review,* Vol. 5, No.3, 1973.

B.F. Tipton, *Conflict and Change in a Technical College,* Hutchinson, 1973.

Training Teachers for Education Management in Further and Adult Education: A report by the Sub-Committee on the Supply and Training of Teachers, ACSTT, August 1978.

C.M. Turner, *College Information Systems,* Coombe Lodge Information Paper, IBN 1180, revised January 1977.

Use of Resources in College Management, Coombe Lodge Report, Vol.11, No.11, 1978.

3 THE ROLE OF THE PRINCIPAL

1. This subsection is written not as a prescription of one single way in which principals and directors should exercise their responsibilities, but rather as a discussion of the different ways in which they may act, in different colleges and in the same college at different times and in different situations. It will be appreciated that there is a considerable difference in role and responsibility between, for example, the principal of a small college and a polytechnic director.

2. The prime responsibilities of a principal are specified in the annex to Circular 7/70, which recommends that the articles of government should include certain specific requirements. Particularly in paragraph 2(d): "The Principal shall be responsible to the Governors for the internal organization, management and discipline of the college". In addition, paragraphs 5(a), (b) and (c) suggest that the principal shall have responsibility for the preparation of estimates and the appointment of teaching and non-teaching staff as delegated by the governing body (see Sections **2.1.**13, 20, 21, 57, and **3.**63).

3. The principal is generally the chief academic and administrative officer of the college, a role specified by Circular 7/70. Normally his or her chief lieutenants in these functions will be the vice-principal and chief administrative officer respectively. Additionally, he or she may be seen as the senior executive in the college ensuring that the regulations of the local education authority are observed, as the senior public relations officer for the college, and perhaps as the equivalent of a "managing director" in a large industrial firm.

4. As the chief academic in the college, the principal is usually chairman of the academic board, which may be either consultative only or have full responsibility for "the planning, co-ordination, development and oversight of the academic work". (see Section **2.1.**15). This can sometimes lead to difficulties between the principal and the academic board. If the board has been given a full responsibility by the articles of government, then the principal is the chief executive of the academic board. Thus, the board may require the principal to account for his or her actions (or perhaps lack of action) where a course of action has been decided by the board. However, it must be remembered that decisions of the board must be within the regulations of the LEA and also within the financial estimates. If there are difficulties in that the board has taken decisions outside its competence in these matters, the principal would have no alternative but to take the issue to the governing body, or the Chief Education Officer, in order to safeguard himself in the position of being the chief executive of the LEA in the college. In the event of a conflict between the principal and the academic board, the matter can only be referred to the governing body for final decision.

5. Clearly, within the college, the principal has responsibility for being an educational initiator, either by introducing ideas, or encouraging others to bring forward ideas for the consideration of either particular departments or

the academic board. Such initiatives may take the form of encouraging educational development, or increasing motivation. The introduction of microelectronics into colleges may be taken as a current example. If the heads of departments involved are concerned directly with the introduction of appropriate courses, then the principal may have to ask for action to be taken. In a more general sense, the academic board may have to decide on how instruction concerning the effect of microelectronics on the individual and on society may be given to students. Above all, the board will need to consider the allocation, or at the present time re-allocation, of college resources to allow the introduction of a new topic in the curriculum.

6. As a member of the governing body the principal will need to present such matters as new courses, and resource allocation to both the governors and departmental advisory committees, where the latter exist. It is one of the principal's duties to keep all those connected with the college informed of college affairs. Any college spends considerable sums of public monies; the principal has a duty to inform not only local authority members but also the general public as to the use to which these monies are being put. The college has a duty to issue an annual report, either connected with a college prize-giving or similar function, or an open day when the public, including parents and prospective students, can visit the college and gain an appreciation of its activities.

7. Within the governing body, the principal has a special responsibility to ensure that all governors are aware of the work of the college, its policies and principles, the physical environment and resources, and its aspirations. There are many ways in which governors can be involved with the college, for example: invitations to college functions, plays, musical and other entertainments; lunch with the principal, vice-principal and heads of departments in which the governor has a particular interest or expertise. Most governors wish to be involved and know the college, beyond merely attending meetings. Governors should also be encouraged to attend courses (for example at Coombe Lodge, and those increasingly offered by local authorities and other agencies). Within a governing body there will be three main groups. Local authority representation will normally constitute the minority; there will be college staff and students; and others representing industry, commerce, the professions, and other interests. Particularly at times of scarcity, when the principal is pressing through the governing body, with the support of the college and other members, for increased resources of finance, staffing and accommodation, there may be real danger of the governing body dividing sharply, even irreconcilably, between the authority representatives and the rest, to the college's detriment. To avoid this, it is essential that the authority representatives should convince the rest that they are indeed pressing the college's needs, and that the rest, having been so convinced, should exercise responsibly their majority in the governing body. Securing such an understanding will depend mainly on the chairman and principal.

8. As an administrator the principal has a responsibility to see that the college operates smoothly; that staff and students know the rules and regulations of

the college and the LEA; and are aware of the academic regulations of the various courses and validating bodies. Many colleges now have staff and student handbooks to assist in such matters, and induction courses for both staff and students (see Sections **2.2**, Appendix 2 and **11.11**). Should a member of the college transgress against the regulations, normally only the principal (or in his or her absence the vice-principal acting as the principal) has the power to take action against an individual. Such procedures must be clearly laid down so that all participants know precisely what is involved and the procedure to be followed. It should be noted that where matters are sufficiently serious for legal processes to commence, the courts are strict in their insistence that procedures should be, and should have been observed.

9. While many incidents which occur are spontaneous, some disputes can or should be anticipated, and action taken to avoid the issue coming to a head. Many minor problems in colleges become major disputes merely because no one informs senior staff, particularly the principal, of what is causing dissent or friction. Frequently a principal could take action to prevent problems developing but is unable to because no one has informed him or her of the difficulty. Should a grievance occur then the principal may have a duty to act as mediator under the code for grievance procedures. This usually involves one individual complaining about another but occasionally may involve a group (such as a class of students) complaining against an individual (perhaps a member of staff or even another student): see Section **12.6.**41.

10. The principal clearly has a responsibility to deal with the trade unions in the college, most commonly NATFHE, NALGO and NUPE, although other unions may be involved, as well as the student union and perhaps the NUS (see Sections **2.4**; **9**; **11.7-9**; **12.7**). Differences and disagreements within and between the diverse parties to college government and management are of course natural and desirable; it would be a strange college if all, from authority to students, thought alike. The different views will, quite properly, be strongly held, with the concomitant danger that the disagreements may widen into gulfs. If, then, there is one role and responsibility for principals, common to widely differing institutions and situations, it is constructively to manage these differences, to prevent them from widening into unbridgeable gulfs, and to lead the parties forward in broad agreement. Many principals are also members of a union, and often of NATFHE. Occasionally, conflict may arise for a principal as an individual between a decision of the NATFHE Branch and his or her responsibility to the LEA for the care and security of the college. In such instances the principal should seek the advice of a Regional Official of NATFHE or an official at Headquarters. In general, the principal should not see himself as an LEA "negotiator" in dealings with unions in the college, but rather as an interpreter of agreements reached between unions and the LEA (see Section **2.4**).

11. As has been indicated, in administrative matters the principal may be regarded as a manager acting on behalf of the LEA. This may lead to difficulties at times due to the dichotomy between his or her position as an academic member of staff and as an administrator. For example, the Health and Safety at Work etc. Act has introduced many anomalies for senior staff in colleges (cf Section **11.10.** 33).

12. Apart from the obvious responsibilities undertaken by all principals, some find themselves with additional duties arising from specialist facilities within the college. For example, in colleges with advanced catering facilities, the principal may well find her or himself holding the alcohol licence on behalf of the college. If the college has a public theatre, the principal may also hold the licence and be responsible whenever public performances are held. (See also Sections **12.7**.23, and **5.10**; if the principal is within the GLC area, there are 28 pages of closely printed regulations to be followed!).

13. The principal maintains contact with many external bodies associated with the college. In the development and sponsoring of courses, the principal's relations with employers and other agencies can be crucial. As far as the local authority is concerned the principal has to deal with many departments in addition to Education: perhaps the Chief Executive on legal matters, the Borough Treasurer, Architect and Engineer, and often the Parks Superintendant if the college grounds are maintained by the authority. The principal is in contact with HMI, the Regional Advisory Council, external examining boards – a normal FE College will deal with between ten to 20 – local industries and, frequently, professional and trade associations, and many local bodies and associations. Many colleges act as a centre for the local community and the principal will frequently be invited to attend local functions as the representative of the college, and often to speak to local assemblies.

14. It can be seen that a principal must be a person of many parts. It is obvious that he or she must have the ability to get on with people, the capacity to give leadership, act as mediator, take action when required, be "a good committee man" and possess a strong academic background as well as having administrative flair and expertise.

REFERENCE

E. Briault. "The Role of the Principal", *Education Administration*, 4 (2), 35-40. 1976.

D. Charlton *et al.*, *The Administration of Technical Colleges*, Manchester University Press, 1971.

Coombe Lodge, *Reports* (many reports are appropriate to principals).

W.A.G. Easton, "Analysis of a (FE) College," *Technical Journal*, 1969:
I 7 (1) Feb. 1969, pp. 9-10; II 7 (2) March 1969, pp.10-11; III 7 (3) April 1969, pp.7-9; IV 7 (4) May 1969, pp.15-16; V 7 (5) June 1969, pp.21-22.

J. Hicks, "College principals and vice principals: roles and functions" *Education Administration*, (1) pp.48-59, 1975.

B.F.A. Tipton, "Some organizational characteristics of a technical college", *Res. Ed.*, 7 pp.11-27, 1972.

G.E. Wheeler, "The Management of Colleges," *Technical Journal*, (4-4), pp.8-11, 1966.

J. Porter, "The new role of the college principal", *London Education Review*, pp.29-33, 1972.

Some ACFHE publications are also appropriate.

4 RELATIONS WITH TRADE UNIONS

1. It is not the purpose of this sub-section to attempt guidance on how to proceed in a dispute at college level between management and trade union(s). In such a situation, recourse will be advisable to the advice of one's trade union and/or the local authority. This sub-section concerns itself with the establishment of a regular procedural framework designed to avoid disputes before they arise.

2. Relations between management and trade unions at college level should be viewed in the context of industrial relations at national and local education authority level. Their purpose and nature have ben defined by LACSAB as follows: "Industrial relations are about the relationships between employers and the people they employ – their aspirations, expectations, achievements, successes and failures. The satisfaction of the employee in doing a good job contributes to the successful implementation of the policies of the employer and the effectiveness of his undertaking. Conversely, the anxieties, frustrations and failures of employees in their working environment can diminish the effectiveness of the organization. Employers and employees therefore have a mutual interest in maintaining and developing good industrial relations."[1]

3. Industrial relations are thus essentially the transactions occurring between employer and employee. Employer responsibilities for maintained establishments of further, higher and adult education attach to individual local education authorities, and the essential nexus is therefore between the local education authority and the trade union's organizational unit responsible for the LEA area – for teachers, the NATFHE Liaison Committee, and for other occupations, the union branch and Joint Works Committee. In the case of certain establishments of higher education maintained jointly by two or more LEAs, employer responsibilities attach to a joint education committee drawing its membership from the constitutent authorities. Voluntary or grant-aided establishments are usually constituted as employers in their own right; it is often, and appropriately, a condition of grant that employee's terms and conditions of employment are comparable with those in maintained establishments.

4. Conventional wisdom, however, continues to describe education as "a national service locally administered". The local authority associations and the trade unions concerned have found it helpful to establish national negotiating and consultative machinery, in order to conclude agreements binding at least in honour upon all local education authorities and upon the trade unions concerned at all levels of organization (see Section **11.7**). In respect of teachers, such agreements may leave scope for determination of certain matters at local authority level; both national and local authority level agreements may leave scope for discussion as to implementation at

1 *Employee Relations: Reference Guide for Chief Officers and Managers in Local Authorities,* Local Authorities' Conditions of Service Advisory Board and Local Government Training Board, 1978, p.2.

college level. In respect of non-teaching staff, variations will also occur at Provincial Council and local authority level. What is crucial for all concerned in such discussions is a realisation that both the college management (however constituted: for example, principal and chief administrative officer) and the college union membership are constrained by agreements made elsewhere. For the college management, there is also the overriding constraint that the level of financial resources (whether for accommodation, staffing, or equipment and materials) is determined outside the college, so that while discussions at college level may influence the deployment of resources already allocated, such discussion cannot increase the resource allocation without reference to the authority.

5. An intermediate stage of discussion may involve the college governing body, whose powers are determined by the articles (and instrument) of government for the college concerned. If the local education authority has expressly delegated some of its powers and responsibilities as an employer to the governing body, any local discussions must have regard to the fact: on the whole, however, industrial relations are better handled through other channels. Similarly, the academic board is not normally a satisfactory vehicle for the ventilation of industrial relations issues as such.

6. In the previous paragraphs, the term "discussion" has been used to describe exchanges of view at college level. A great deal of heat has been expended on the question of whether such discussions constitute "consultation" or "negotiation", and it may be helpful to attempt working definitions of the two. Consultation concerns matters which are regarded by the management as responsibilities which it cannot or will not share, but on which it is prepared to inform the trade union(s) concerned of actions intended or envisaged, and to receive representations thereon before acting. The intended actions are sometimes modified or abandoned in the light of representations made, and sometimes not: the decision is with the management. Occasionally consultation may be statutorily prescribed, for example, where there are impending redundancies. Negotiation concerns matters which are mutually accepted by employer and union(s) as suitable for collective bargaining, the outcome of which is expected to be a collective agreement freely entered into by the parties concerned, which then becomes binding at least in honour upon them. Both consultation and negotiation can take place at college level, so long as a negotiated agreement restricts itself to matters where the college management has power to decide: if not such an agreement would need confirmation or repudiation at local authority level. In the event of a continuing difference of opinion over intended action which has been the subject of consultation, or over a matter which has been the subject of unsuccessful negotiation, the situation may become serious enough to describe as a dispute: the negotiated procedure for dealing with disputes involving teachers' unions which may arise at college level is to be found in Section **11.7.9**. Grievance and disputes procedure governing non-teaching staff are covered by the national agreements. The college principal may be called upon by staff in the college and by the local authority to act as the agent of the employer in initial discussions on any matter; such discussions will often resolve the problem without the need to refer beyond the college.

7. Examples of issues for discussion at college level include the following:-
   (i) *Manning levels*
      (a) current establishments of full-time and part-time staff, their deployment within the college and between departments;
      (b) future estimates of manning requirements for submission to the local education authority; and
      (c) departmental and other staffing patterns (it is helpful for any changes to have been discussed before they are implemented).
   (ii) *Staff selection and development*
      (a) procedures within the college for the appointment of staff;
      (b) procedures within the college for the promotion of staff; and
      (c) staff development procedures within the college.

      Note: Any such college procedures will naturally have to satisfy the requirements of procedures at authority level, but these usually incorporate scope for variation.
   (iii) *Timetabling*

      The teachers' conditions of service agreement (see Section **11.7.**6) requires access to timetables on request for representatives of the recognised trade unions.
   (iv) *Working conditions*
      (a) variations to daily starting times for classes;
      (b) (for technicians) the timetabling of laboratory use to permit access for preparatory work; and
      (c) provision of working space outside teaching areas.

      Note: There may well be "welfare" issues more suitably considered by a college Safety Committee established within the purview of the Health and Safety at Work etc. Act 1974 (see Sections **11.10**; **5.3**; and **5.5**).

8. It would be possible to multiply the examples in the previous paragraph almost indefinitely: a college union branch or group of members could well carry a resolution on almost any matter of concern within the college for presentation to the college management. A major concern, however, is almost certain to be the position of individual union members in multifarious contexts – the situation familiarly described by the teaching unions as "casework". Much of this casework arises from misunderstanding at some level; by the union member or representative on the one hand or by a senior member of staff on the other. A recent NFER survey[2] has found that most teachers regard the head of department as their "boss", a view shared by some heads of department! It is important that any delegation by the principal or chief administrative officer of managerial responsibility for industrial relations should be clearly defined. In particular, the power to "hire and fire" part-time staff should be explicitly assigned, if assigned at all (at least one large LEA forbids the termination of part-time teachers' contracts by staff other than the principal). Teachers and principals should avoid coming into conflict. Where conflict seems likely to arise, either party should seek advice from the LEA or its relevant officers, or from their professional association or its full-time officials.

---

2 Judy Bradley and Jane Silverleaf, *Making The Grade*, NFER, 1979; cf Sections **2.1.**61; **2.2.**39; and **11.11.**9.

9. Consideration should be given at college level to the procedure for management-trade union discussions. Casework is often urgent, and may require access to a designated member of the college management team by a union representative without undue formality. Other matters merit pre-arranged meetings with defined agenda and a proper record of proceedings available to the representatives of both parties. A reliance on meetings arranged *ad hoc* is seldom satisfactory, and a regular calendar of meetings (which can always be cancelled in the absence of business to consider) is both mutually beneficial in itself and facilitiates adjustments to the timetables of the teachers concerned to avoid adverse consequences to students.

10. The three main negotiating groups of trade unions recognised nationally are as follows:-
Teachers – NATFHE (including AACE), NSAE, APC, AAES.
APT&C – NALGO, GMWU, NUPE, TGWU, COHSE. (Administrative, Professional, Technical, and Clerical grades).
Manual – GMWU, NUPE, TGWU. (School meals staff, caretakers and cleaners, residential employees).
At college level, the three groups may have formed a Joint Union Committee (JUC) to co-ordinate policies and action on matters of common concern, and it may be appropriate on occasion for JUC representatives to meet college management. This may be particularly suitable in the context of health and safety matters. For most issues, however, separate meetings will probably be more helpful. All the unions mentioned above favour local consultation and negotiation (except of course in respect of matters which can only be determined elsewhere in the bargaining structure) and believe that problems should be resolved at local level wherever possible. The manual workers' unions' particularly encourage the development of shop steward or workplace representative systems and most unions provide some access to industrial relations training for their workplace representatives. The NATFHE Rules give specific authority for a college Branch or Co-ordinating Committee to discuss with the college principal and governing body all matters domestic to the institution. The involvement in discussions of a full-time official from the union concerned may be arranged; the union(s) will more usually be represented by elected lay members, on most occasions drawn from the college staff.

11. Good industrial relations at college level can thus be seen not just as a one-way process involving a management decision followed by its willing and successful implementation; to paraphase LACSAB,[3] good industrial relations involve give and take, with the staff, through their unions, influencing the decisions that have to be taken and their subsequent implementation. With good industrial relations, this influence is of benefit to the college, and thus to the authority. With indifferent or bad industrial relations, important decisions may be deferred or, if taken, may be impossible adequately to implement.

---

3 LACSAB, *op.cit, ibid.*

2.4

REFERENCE

Employee Relations: Reference Guide for Chief Officers and Managers in Local Authorities, LACSAB, 1978.
The LACSAB Employee Relations Handbook, revised edition, LACSAB, 1978.

5 PUBLIC RELATIONS

1. As colleges exist to meet the needs of students and the educational and manpower needs of the country, so they have effectively to advertise the opportunities which they offer. Courses have to be brought to the attention of intending and potential students, and be known by employers, parents and careers advisers. Equally, a college must have the means of communication with its clients and local community to ensure that their needs are met. Whatever the vagaries of our political system, and the stringencies imposed by national expenditure restraint, colleges must continue to bring before their public the service which they offer. In stating the value of education, and the educational provision which is made, the approach must not be defensive.

2. In the apparently hierarchic public relations chain which leads from the Department of Education and Science to the Regional Advisory Councils on to the local authority and thence to the college, there may be an inclination unthinkingly to accept that fourth place. In many instances this will occur: colleges are not policy making bodies in a formal sense. However, locally, the broad policy statements emanating from Government or civil servants often take second place to the educational attitudes and activities that relate to the local community. Where a college identifies an educational need, it is failing in its duty to the community which it serves if it does not do its utmost to fulfil that demand. Public relations for colleges involves not just reaching out to clients and sponsors but entails also the process of representing those interests wherever it can.

3. Before discussing public relations methods and direction, it is appropriate first to consider the institutional structure. It was the conclusion of a sub-committee of the NACEIC in making a report on the public relations of further education that the way to improvement lay: "in the establishment of systematic arrangements whereby the responsibility for co-ordinating and overseeing public relations activities, including the dissemination of information, should be assigned to specific individuals."[1] The report also stated that the individuals' responsibilities should be fully known through the institution.

4. Although the NACEIC sub-committee report recommended that there should be an appointment at senior level of a person responsible for public relations, it was recognised that circumstance would dictate whether the post was full- or part-time. In some instances the public relations officer could be an existing senior staff member whose contract was altered by agreement to accommodate the new duties. It is essential in all cases that the officer has the time properly to perform the necessary duties. The officer will naturally be under the direction of the governors, principal, and academic board and as well as co-operating in close and co-ordinated liaison, those persons and

---

1 *The Public Relations of Further Education*, a report by a Sub-Committee of the National Advisory Council on Education for Industry and Commerce, DES and Central Office of Information, 1964.

bodies will need to be mindful too of their public relations functions. While it is not intended here to provide a job description for an information officer, the importance of the post must be recognised. The officer will have to be seen to occupy an important position in a college; and must possess the necessary personal qualities and specific communication skills. However, apart from the polytechnics, very few colleges have full-time information officers. There is therefore a need to provide training where a member or members of staff have a public relations role. Any public relations exercise will deservedly fail if it is presented in a manner which is ridden with jargon or other instances of linguistic inaccessibility. This is not always a simple task: the language of the curriculum often requires translation before it can become widely intelligble. On occasion, staff will address themselves directly to the public; on any major issue the information officers should always be consulted.

5. The means of public relations communication are determined by a college's function, the opportunities it affords, and the needs of the community it serves. In investigating those means, therefore, the types of education which colleges supply have to be considered. While it is assumed that the careers services in conjunction with colleges are providing information in the schools, that of itself is not enough. Nor will the provision of link and experience courses betwween school and college – vital though that development is and should be – be sufficient without the implementation of a comprehensive system of involving potential students in the appreciation of what a college can offer. There will need to be a co-ordinated approach which involves the school, the college, and the careers service, supplemented by the participation of employers, students from the college, and specialists able to extend particular expertise. It is vital that the intending or potential student should have full information about the college, its structures and its courses, and that the college too should be aware of the demands which could be made upon it. For example, extra provision for the handicapped may be required; or special arrangements made for the young unemployed. The essential issue however remains one of knowledge of opportunity: a public relations purpose is to ensure full awareness.

6. If colleges are to achieve their purposes, there must be full knowledge available to their students' employers and prospective employers of what they offer, can offer, and how they can adapt. To this end there needs to be a clear system of industrial and commercial liäison. By whatever method this is achieved, there should be no weakening of existing individual and college departmental links with employers. A formal system which informs employers of current practices, particular developments in course and funding provision, and also allows employers to give colleges leads to which they can respond, is vital. It will also be necessary to inform employers of practices and liabilities (for example, in the case of employers of day release students, the means by which they can fulfil their duties under the Health and Safety at Work etc. Act to those persons while they are at college (see Section **11.10.**72-74).

7. Probably partially attributable to its status and the diversity of its activities,

the further education service does not always receive the attention it deserves from the general public. It will be useful here to make distinctions between the parents of young students or potential students; those to whom course provision may be appropriate and whose interest requires awakening; and those who may never have had the need for the system's services but should be made aware of the college's functions if it is to have the support of its community.

8. Apart from general publicity which is discussed below, parents can be reached via the co-operation of schools and parent-teacher associations. There are other methods of achieving parent involvement, for example: by means such as open days or by way of the student services department where there is a clear information or counselling need, especially when monitoring the progress of courses designed to meet particular social needs.

9. Recruitment by direct publicity requires a college to have a clear aim. It is pointless to provide a special course for a particular group if that group is left largely unaware of it. Notices posted in the locality at enrolment time are useful but not in themselves enough. Placement of information with specific bodies such as advisory committees, trade unions, community associations, citizens' advice bureaux and community groups is an essential activity, as is full response to their needs. The overall target should be still greater. Newsheets and newsletters issued to the communtiy are effective. The local newspapers, radio and television can provide significant assistance. The placing of advertisements demands care. Television advertising is undertaken by the DES and certain local authorities. This should be followed up and used. Although television advertising is generally too expensive for a single institution, the co-operation of several colleges to promote common courses may well be worthwhile. Advertisements in the national press can be effective although larger institutions which use the national press will need to take decisions concerning the types of publication in which they advertise. Local commercial radio may well allow free advertising in certain circumstances and all local radio stations, as well as regional television services to a lesser extent, have a duty to provide information of local interest to the areas which they serve.

10. In the wider sense of informing the public of college activities, there exist many opportunities for using broadcasting and the press. Each medium seeks to inform its public: there may be media coverage of significant college events such as open days, exhibitions, awards ceremonies and musical, dramatic and sporting activities. However, the media also require stories of general interest. Colleges might provide such stories, and so establish good relationships with the media. Even so, the media are unlikely regularly to approach the college: the college will often have to instigate the process by providing items of news. The college information officer in liaising with news editors and reporters can ensure that the college is contacted by the media whenever items of relevance occur.

11. The issuing of information by the college in written form is not only an aid to accuracy but also allows the stressing of significant issues. It should be brief,

clear, and indicate avenues for further exploration. Timing is important: there is no point in issuing information too late for its proper use. Where staff are likely to be interviewed it will be useful if they have been given some instruction in interview technique. Any media exercise, and indeed any significant development affecting the college, should be brought by internal news means to the attention of staff and students. This allows the exercise not only to be supplemented by the college as a whole but also ensures that any public announcement has been first the subject of college knowledge, if not always prior comment. College internal communications processes may be linked to the public relations function. A full media campaign is advisable wherever the college is engaged in educational initiative. Courses designed for special groups require full publicity to attract recruitment and inform the public of the college's progress.

12. A college's initial means of presentation is by its prospectus. College prospectuses (see also Sections **12.1** and **12.6.**14), vary according to the nature and policy of the institution. However, information concerning courses, facilities, costs, administration, personnel and procedural structures should be readily available and accompanied by such statements of intent as are appropriate. Whether this results in a single publication or guide supplemented by separate booklets and pamphlets an essential consideration is that the information should be clearly presented and be such as to stimulate and satisfy initial enquiry. The Careers Service Advisory Council has advised that odd shapes and sizes should be avoided in designing prospectuses; and that A5 paper size is preferable. Prospectus information should always begin with courses, for that is the prime interest of the readership. The prospectus should also provide careers guidance information, including routes to further courses and qualifications. Short explanations of courses are advisable.

13. While a college prospectus is one of the most immediate forms of advertising, the presentation of the college should be matched by the college itself. Its buildings, appearance, services and overall image should be attractive. Care should be taken to establish good relationships with residents near the college, and to minimise the disruption which can be caused by noise, car parking, and also damage to property. There are instances where the college might provide its services free or at reduced rates to community groups (cf. Section **5.10.**5). The consequences of successful public relations will be the better and fuller use of the college by the community. A college may therefore expect to become a source of public information. In many cases this will mean being able to advise enquirers where it cannot fulfil their course requirements of the institution to which they should have recourse. Often, however, a college may need to give the location of many diverse sources of advice.

14. There will need to be close involvement with the local education authority. The authority may make special funds available. It may co-operate closely in publicity activities, and it will have its own public relations policies and publications. In any event the college will require the authority's support if it is to be fully effective. A usual objection to any development of a college's

activities is cost. The NACEIC report stated: "More important however in the long term is the contribution which better public relations will make to the more effective use of capital and other resources."[2] College effectiveness can itself be raised by public appreciation of its achievements.

REFERENCE

The Public Relations of Further Education, A report by a Sub-Committee of the National Advisory Council on Education for Industry and Commerce, DES and Central Office of Information, 1964.
How To Handle The Media, TUC, 1979.
Denis MacShane, *Using The Media,* Pluto Press, 1979.
Press and Public Relations Guide, NATFHE.

2 *Ibid,* p.22.

6 INTERNATIONAL RELATIONS

This sub-section should be read in conjunction with Section **12.10**. International teachers' organizations are referred to in Section **1.4** and **9**, Appendix 3.

1. Many colleges incorporate into their curricula contacts with countries abroad. Such contacts are used to reinforce a very wide number of teaching disciplines and to provide opportunities for students and staff to gain a wider perspective as a base for their studies. The contacts are developed by exchange of information, documentation and bibliographies, and by the exchange of staff and students for periods of study, recreation and work. The whole area of contact spreads around the world, and many organizations are involved in providing contacts and information. The most important of these bodies are discussed below. Exchange visit facilities are first considered, and then some information is given concerning bodies with international educational functions. Some useful addresses are contained in Appendix 1.

2. **The Central Bureau for Educational Visits and Exchanges**
This bureau's administrative budget is provided by the Department of Education and Science, Welsh Office Education Department[1], Scottish Education Department and Department of Education for Northern Ireland. It works under the auspices of these departments and has the status of a governmental agency in the educational sphere. Its status approximates to that of the Arts Council and the British Council: it is an independent foundation but is governed by a board of trustees appointed on a personal basis by the Secretary of State. The Bureau's task is to enrich UK education provision through international work. The Bureau works in consultation and co-operation with the education departments and HM Inspectorate. Budget is established on a triennial "rolling grant" basis by way of the education departments, which also exercise overall policy control to prevent overlap with other government departments and agencies. Although not an officially aiding organization, the Bureau's work assists developing countries in establishing links, training placements, in-service training, study abroad and other areas.

3. Much of the Bureau's work involves schools. However, as well as the facilities afforded to local authorities concerning matters such as transport, accommodation, study abroad and foreign agencies and institutions, the Bureau affords considerable service to further and higher education. It assists colleges in identifying potential foreign partners both for permanent links – which may be institutional or departmental – and for individual and group study visits, field work, courses, practical training and jobs abroad. Advice and facilities are offered to individual students.Foreign institutions are assisted in finding exchange partners.

---

1 At the time of writing the contribution of WOED had still to be determined. However, it is anticipated that by the time of publication this department will be one of the CBEVE's providing bodies.

4. The Bureau administers a Standing Conference on Overseas Placements and Exchanges (SCOPE), which brings together representatives of colleges, government departments, industry, and other organizations involved in overseas placements. A forum at international level is provided for action and discussion. The Bureau provides headquarters and certain services for a variety of bodies. Among such bodies are the Joint Advisory Committee on Teacher Exchange[2], the Professional and Academic Regional Visits Organization (PARVO) and various bodies concerned with travel facilities for the handicapped. This latter work has led to the foundation of Mobility International, which brings together over 40 countries in co-operation in affording travel and exchange schemes for the disabled.

5. Senior students and young teachers are placed as assistants in English language teaching for an academic year in schools and colleges in Europe. Foreign assistants are allocated to UK educational institutions (mostly schools). Official teacher exchange schemes in Europe are administered and interchanges are negotiated elsewhere in Europe. The UK/US Teacher Exchange Scheme is administered by the Bureau. Teacher exchange schemes are supplemented by the Intensive Study Visits Scheme for senior teaching and advisory staff.

6. The Bureau advises and assists young people engaged in the performing arts who wish to arrange exchange visits and tours. The Community Education Abroad scheme offers placement services – mainly in social work agencies and hospitals (lasting a year) in France and Germany – to young people who have left school and are awaiting college entry. A similar placement service exists for those with a good knowledge of French and German to gain experience as senior language assistants. Students and teachers aged between 18 and 30 are recruited to assist at organized camps in certain European countries. International meetings, tours and study courses are also arranged.

7. **League for the Exchange of Commonwealth Teachers**
This body exists to promote education links between commonwealth countries. It does this mainly by arranging teacher exchanges. The annual average of such exchanges is currently 300. Each country participating in the scheme is subject to an annual quota. It is a condition of exchange that UK teachers must become members of the League; teachers from Commonwealth countries receive full benefit from the League but membership is not at present obligatory. There are Exchange Teachers' Clubs affiliated to the League. They arrange their own programmes, and entertain colleagues currently on exchange in their area. The League wishes to promote more exchanges throughout the Commonwealth. It arranges short-term exchanges for senior teaching staff and local authority officials. The League is independent, non-political and non-sectarian.

8. **Exchange schemes: tenure and maintenance**
Arrangements for teachers from overseas are outlined in Section **11.6**,

---

2 A body functioning as a national forum for the discussion of teacher exchange and in-service training abroad.

Appendix 5. UK teachers on approved exchange schemes continue to be employed by their home authorities who grant leave of absence and pay salaries; security of tenure is maintained. Where teachers are located in countries with higher living costs than the UK, they receive government grants subject to a maximum figure (currently £2,000) according to country. Grants are also available for accompanying dependent children, and for half the cost of return air fare. In the case of students, it is permissible for an institution which has enrolled a student and has undertaken to arrange for the provision of tutition against the normal fee then to arrange for the tuition to be provided elsewhere on a reciprocal basis. Where the course for which the student has enrolled is not designated for a mandatory award (see Sections **12.5**.2 *et seq.;* **1.3**, Appendix 1; **3.**32 and **8.**53), the UK institution needs only to assure itself that the arrangements made with the institution abroad are on a fully reciprocal basis.

9. However, where exchange arrangements are introduced into a designated course, certain rules apply: as long as the whole course is demonstrably organized and supervised by the UK institution, a three year course containing periods abroad of in total not more than one year would satisfy regulations. A course organized jointly by two institutions, one of which was outside the UK, and involving periods abroad of a much as half the total course could not be regarded at present as UK based. This position may change in mid 1980 when the Education Bill 1979 becomes law. The Bill provides for mandatory grant arrangements to be made for courses provided in conjunction with overseas institutions.

10. Student maintenance grants are paid directly to the holder. Therefore, any contribution to be made by a mandatory award holder towards the maintenance of an overseas student coming to the United Kingdom is a matter for voluntary arrangement between the student and the institution. Maintenance grant paid to a UK student at the lower rate because of provision of board and lodging by the academic authority may be only voluntarily reassigned. Where parental contributions to such grants are to the degree that they contribute to board and lodging costs, parents should continue to make this contribution: the college should ensure that the student is provided with board and lodging free of charge by the overseas institution.

11. **The British Council**

The British Council was founded in 1940 to promote a wider knowledge of the UK and the English language abroad, and the development of closer cultural relations with other countries – the developing countries in particular. The Centre for Educational Development Overseas was merged with the Council in 1974. This extended the Council's work in curriculum development. The Council is responsible for a variety of educational schemes: the Aid for Commonwealth English Scheme; the Aid for Commonwealth Teaching of Science Scheme; and also schemes under the Expanded Programme of Books Aid. Officers of the Council also work in technical education, industrial training, and management development in conjunction with two bodies: the Technical Education and Training

Organization for Overseas countries (TETOC) – part of the functions of which it is to assume in 1981 – and the Inter-University Council for Higher Education Overseas. The former body is discussed in paragraph 14 below. The Council is financed almost entirely by Government grants, but it retains a considerable degree of independence. The Council's main functions – to foster cultural relations and administer educational aid – are exercised throughout the world, but about two thirds of its services are devoted to developing countries. One third of the Council's annual income of c. £19m is allocated to educational activities; over £2m are spent on specific projects administered by the Ministry of Overseas Development. The Council's main activities are concerned with the teaching of English abroad (generally in direct co-operation with ministries of education in overseas countries); educational aid; the conducting of British examinations abroad; provision in Britain for scholars, trainees and visitors from overseas; the development of professional scientific collaboration; promotion of personal contacts; the promotion and use of books written in English; and the assistance or promotion of the arts overseas. The Council is normally the Government's agent in the carrying out of bilateral cultural agreements. It aims to promote the better understanding of Britain overseas, and of overseas countries in Britain. The English Teaching Information Centre (a study centre and clearing house for information and advice about all aspects of teaching English) provides specialist support from British Council headquarters to its representatives overseas.

12. **The English Speaking Union of the Commonwealth**

The Union, which is incorporated by Royal Charter, aims to foster mutual understanding and trust and friendship between the peoples of the Commonwealth and the United States by way of programmes of information and education. The Union also administers certain awards for students and teachers. It enables more than 500 persons annually to further their education in either the Commonwealth or United States. The Union offers some fellowships – in the physical sciences, and other subjects – and arranges visits by students and teachers.

13. **The International Student Travel Conference (ISTC)**

This body is the association of the National Student Travel Bureau and other organizations concerned with student travel. Members of the Conference organizing student charter flights form the Student Air Travel Association. Conference arranges transport facilities for students' holiday centres, work camps, educational visits, study tours, insurance schemes and other related matters. The aim of the ISTC is the furthering of international understanding and friendship among students. This is carried out by providing individual students with cheap means of travel in order to allow them to meet their counterparts in other countries.

14. **Technical Education and Training Organization for Overseas Countries (TETOC)**

TETOC was formed in 1962. It is a specialist agency of the Ministry of Overseas Development, and is used by that ministry as its first source of professional advice on overseas aid in technical education, agricultural education and training, industrial training, public administration and management development. TETOC is under the direction of a Board of Governors which consists of officials appointed by the Minister. It helps to diagnose overseas needs, identifies appropriate British resources to meet those needs, matches the two and monitors the results. TETOC plans, develops and monitors programmes and projects, recruits staff, facilitates institutional links, and arranges courses and training both overseas and in the UK. Close collaboration is maintained with the British Council and with British diplomatic posts overseas. During 1978/79, 19 British educational institutions participated in TETOC overseas assignments. The types of assignment undertaken[3] demonstrate TETOC's concentration upon the practical application of management and training techniques (see Section **2.2.**54-59). It was announced in January 1980 that TETOC is to be disbanded in 1981 and its functions taken by Overseas Development Administration and the British Council. This action results from the Government's policy of expenditure restraint.

15. **United Kingdom Council for Overseas Student Affairs**
UKCOSA was established in 1968. It is an independent national body which serves overseas students, organizations and people concerned in overseas student affairs. The Council provides a forum for ideas, as well as a medium for consultation with government and other authorities. It works in conjunction with other bodies with interests in the same field.

16. **Voluntary Service Overseas**
There are a number of agencies co-ordinated by VSO providing opportunities for recently graduated students to work as volunteers, mostly in Third World countries. The openings are in teaching, youth work, agricultural and rural development and in many other areas of work.

3 see *Annual Report 1978-79*, TETOC, Appendix F, pp. 24-34.

APPENDIX 1

USEFUL ADDRESSES

British Council,
10 Spring Gardens,
London SW1
01-930 8466

British National Committee for Cultural
Co-operation in Europe,
c/o Shell Centre,
London SE1 7NA
01-934 6555

Central Bureau for Educational Visits and Exchanges,
43 Dorset Street,
London W1H 3FN
01-486 5101
(general enquiries and publications: 01-487 5961)

Commonwealth Secretariat,
Education Division,
Marlborough House,
Pall Mall,
London SW1Y 5HX
01-838 3411

English Speaking Union of the Commonwealth,
Dartmouth House,
37 Charles Street,
London W1X 8AB
01-629 0104

National Union of Students,
International Department,
3 Endsleigh Street,
London WC1H 0DU
01-387 1277

Technical Education and Training Organization
for Overseas Countries,
Dacre House,
17-19 Dacre Street,
London SW1H 0DJ
01-222 8133

United Kingdom Council for Overseas Student Affairs,
60 Westbourne Grove,
London W2
01-229 9268

Voluntary Service Overseas,
9 Belgrave Square,
London SW1
01-253 5347

REFERENCE

Student Exchange Schemes: Arrangements for Tuition Fees and Maintenance, DES FECL 3/79, 26 March 1979.

Annual Report and Accounts, UKCOSA, 1979.
Annual Report 1978-79, TETOC.
Annual Report of the British Council, HMSO, 1979.
Educational Exchange, Central Bureau for Educational Visits and Exchanges, termly.
Exchange Teachers, Annual Report of the League for the Exchange of Commonwealth Teachers, 1979.
Guide to Adventure and Discovery, Central Bureau for Educational Visits and Exchanges, 1980.
Higher Education Exchange, Central Bureau for Educational Visits and Exchanges, bi-annual.
Higher Education in the United Kingdom: a handbook for overseas students and their advisers, British Council/Association of Commonwealth Universities.
Intercommunity, Central Bureau for Educational Visits and Exchanges, three times per year.
School Travel and Exchange 1980/81, Central Bureau for Educational Visits and Exchanges, 1979.
Sports Exchange World, Central Bureau/Centre for International Sports Studies, three times per year.
The First Thirty Years, Central Bureau for Educational Visits and Exchanges, 1978.
The Story of the League for the Exchange of Commonwealth Teachers, Christopher Bell, 1979.
Volunteer Work Abroad, Central Bureau for Educational Visits and Exchanges, 3rd edition, 1978.
What is the British Council? British Council, 1979.
Working Holidays 1980, Central Bureau for Educational Visits and Exchanges, 1979.
Young Visitors to Britain, Central Bureau for Educational Visits and Exchanges, 1979.

Section 3

EDUCATION FINANCE

1. The public education system, from nursery through to higher and adult education, absorbed something over £8,000 millions in 1978-9, amounting to about 12% of total public expenditure.[1] Of this, further and higher education, excluding the university sector, took some 20%, or about £1,600 millions.[2]

2. Control of the volume and disposition of these funds occurs at three broad levels. Within central government, decisions are made concerning the global allocation of financial resources. At local authority level the detailed deployment of these and other resources takes place. Within educational institutions, detailed apportionment of resources to departments and programmes occurs within the constraints laid down at the other two levels. Relationships between and within the three levels are both complex and dynamic. It is not possible here to do more than outline some of the features of significance for the management of further and higher education.

3. The provision and maintenance of the major part of the further and higher education sector is the responsibility of the local authorities, who, therefore, provide by far the largest part of that sector's resources. The Department of Education and Science[3] makes only a relatively small direct contribution to further education finances, although central government funds from other sources – most notably the Manpower Services Commission – have increased considerably in recent years, and local authorities themselves obtain a large part of their funds from central government. A small but significant proportion of further and higher education finance is derived from students, their employers, or their families in the form of fees. Table 1 summarises the main sources of further and higher education funds in 1977-78.

Table 1

Sources of further and higher education finance, 1977-78[4]

	£ millions
Local authorities	1,070
Department of Education & Science	151
Other central government sources (inc MSC)	58
Households & industry	149
Total	1428

1 *The Government's Public Expenditure Plans, 1979-80 to 1982-3*, Cmnd. 7439, HMSO, 1979.

2 This figure includes student support costs.

3 Throughout this Section the DES is taken to include the educational functions of the Welsh Office.

4 *Education Statistics 1977-8 Actuals*, CIPFA, 1979; *Statistics of Education 1977. Vol 3 Further Education HMSO, 1979* and Cmnd. 7439, *op.cit.* The figures are provisional. Over 60% of local government finance was obtained from central government.

4. **Central government**
Table 1 does not indicate the full significance of central government's control over educational expenditure, a control which is maintained through three major mechanisms involving three government departments – the Treasury, the DES and the Department of the Environment (DoE). The mechanisms are the control of capital expenditure through loan sanctions, the control of local authority total recurrent expenditure through the provision of the annual rate support grant and associated cash limits, and the manpower controls exercised directly only in initial teacher training, but operating indirectly and often unintentionally through the need for Treasury approval of the global sums available for annual pay settlements. All these control mechanisms operate within the over-riding constraints of relevant legislation and supportive circulars, administrative memoranda and regulations (see also Section **1.3.**5 & **1.3.**46).

5. Constitutional control over central government expenditure rests with the House of Commons. However, this is restricted by a number of Parliamentary conventions governing the Financial Resolutions which authorise government spending. These Resolutions cannot be submitted by individual MPs, but must be initiated by a Treasury Minister. The powers of the Treasury have been reinforced by a series of reforms of the system of public expenditure management and control in the wake of the 1961 Plowden Report.[5]

6. A major reform was the establishment of an inter-departmental Public Expenditure Survey Committee (PESC) comprising civil servants who consider each spending department's expenditure estimates and anticipated local authority expenditure over the next five years. Negotiations between the departments represented on PESC result in five-year rolling programmes for each department. After Cabinet discussion and approval a White Paper is published annually, usually between November and February, which outlines the Government's public expenditure proposals for the next four years. Each year's proposed budget is then re-considered by PESC and is revised in the light of changed governmental priorities and policies. The 1979 White Paper[6] was unusual in that it indicated relatively few changes from the 1978 proposals,[7] but major changes of policy are outlined in the proposals for 1980-81 onwards, arising from the change of government in May 1979.[8]

7. A rather different control mechanism is provided by the system for programme analysis and review (PAR). Individual programmes or groups of programmes within departments are scrutinised in terms of their objectives, activities, achievements and required resources. Alternative means of

---

5 *The control of public expenditure.* Report of the Committee chaired by Lord Plowden, Cmnd. 1432, HMSO, 1961.

6 *The Government's Public Expenditure Plans, 1979-80 to 1982-83, op.cit.*

7 White Paper: *The Government's Public Expenditure Plans, 1978-79 to 1981-82,* Cmnd. 7049, HMSO, 1978.

8 *The Government's Expenditure Plans 1980-81,* Cmnd. 7746, HMSO, 1979.

achieving the objectives are also considered, and the final report – to an inter-departmental co-ordinating committee of civil servants – could well influence the programme's re-consideration by PESC.

8. Central government finances for education along with the other public services are authorised by a House of Commons vote after the annual debate on the Public Expenditure White Paper. However, direct central government control of educational expenditure is relatively slight. The direct authorisation, the DES "Vote", covers only a small part of the educational expenditure envisaged in the White Paper. This part is used to fund mandatory student awards (see below, para. 32), the Open University and some other directly funded institutions,[9] educational research and a number of associated activities. The forecast revenue expenditure on education and other services by local authorities is aggregated in the White Paper, and an agreed proportion added to the Department of the Environment's Vote for the rate support grant (RSG). This is the largest grant paid to local authorities, and is intended to finance a major but unspecified part of each local authority's educational expenditure. RSG is explained further in paragraphs 18 to 27. Central control of both capital and revenue finance depends upon a variety of complex mechanisms.

9. **Capital expenditure**

The distinction between capital and revenue transactions is not precise. Capital expenditure can be defined as that which is incurred on assets with a life of more than one year, while revenue expenditure is incurred on items whose benefits are used up within the year. In practice, revenue expenditure also includes the cost of relatively inexpensive items with a life of more than one year. Capital expenditure by local authorities is included in the Public Expenditure White Paper figures, although it is neither incurred directly by central government, nor included in the RSG negotiations. However, the DES exercises detailed control over capital expenditure by legislative, administrative and financial means. Regulation 11 of the FE Regulations 1975 requires that the provision of new premises and the alteration of existing premises need the approval of the Secretary of State, as does the provision of equipment costing more than £2,500. DES Circular 13/77 raised this to £10,000 for items given Key Sector approval (see para. 13 below), but the present government proposes, in Cmnd. 7634, *Central Government Controls over Local Authorities,* to remove entirely this requirement. See Section **1.3**.44.

10. DES Circulars 13/74 and 16/76 outline the procedures for educational building programmes. They maintain a distinction between major and minor works, with the former costing more than, and the latter less than a

9 Establishments funded directly by the DES include the remaining voluntary colleges (see paras. 79 & 80), The Royal College of Art, Cranfield Institute of Technology, the Open University and 10 institutions under further education regulations – 3 agricultural colleges (Harper-Adams, Seale-Hayne and Shuttleworth), 3 colleges of music (the Royal Academy, the Royal College and Trinity College of Music), the Royal College of Nursing, Rolls Royce Technical College, the College of the Sea and the National Sea Training Trust.

prescribed fixed limit (at present £120,000)[10] which is reviewed occasionally. For major works, procedures intended to facilitate long-term planning by local authorities have not been operated effectively.[11] In general the procedures whereby local authorities have to submit proposals to the DES for new capital building projects at least two or three years ahead of the date that building is due to start have been subject to Treasury interference, resulting in disruptions and cancellations to planned projects. Local authorities are permitted to start building schemes selected by the DES, within Treasury constraints and after the DES has considered the most recent cost estimates, in the light of current government policies on public expenditure. The detailed scrutiny by the DES involves its Architects and Buildings Branch, its territorial officers and the relevant HMI. It ensures not only that cost limits are adhered to, but that departmental priorities are stressed. This level of detailed control of individual projects is no longer maintained in the schools sector, where it has been replaced by block loan sanction allocations (but see paragraph 16 below).

11. Local authorities have greater freedom in undertaking minor works. Each authority is allowed to seek funds within its share of the total annual block allocation for education, including minor works in the FE and schools sector, and major works in schools. The allocation is calculated proportionally in accordance with the numbers of students in each authority's maintained institutions. The authority can then decide what part of the allocation it wishes to spend, and the proportion it wishes to devote to FE minor works.

12. Polytechnic building programmes are subject to a further control, established by DES *Notes on Procedure for the Approval of Polytechnic Projects,* 1971. This requires that all polytechnic building projects must be related to the institution's long-term development plan. The DES is thus able to ensure that each polytechnic establishes such a plan, and that the DES maintains some degree of control of that plan. (See also Section **5.3**).

13. **Loan sanctions**

DES approval of capital expenditure on building and related programmes does not involve central government funding for such expenditure. It merely permits the local authority to spend money in order to carry out the capital programme. Authorities also have to comply with the regulations governing all local authority capital expenditure, which requires DoE approval. The current system was established by DoE Circular 2/70[12] which distinguished between three types of capital expenditure. Key Sector programmes are those which require specific departmental approval, where departments hold specified national responsibilities. They include most DES major works, and DES approval ensures automatic Key Sector inclusion. However, although further and higher education schemes carry Key Sector approval, youth clubs and community schemes are excluded.

---

10 DES Letter AB/13/12/010, dated 31/7/79.

11 The procedures may well soon be substantially changed or abolished. They are described in detail in Section **5.2.**1-10.

12 DoE Circular 66/76 codified alterations since Circular 2/70 was introduced.

14. Subsidiary Sector programmes are those, associated with Key Sector schemes, which do not require such detailed government control. They include the purchase of land for educational purposes. Authorities have automatic consent to purchase sites for school and college building, without reference to any government department. Acquisition of land for future development is, therefore, subject only to the constraint that the authority must find the consequential interest and loan repayment costs.

15. Subsidiary Sector loan sanctions do not count against the amount allowed for local authority borrowing in the third, Locally Determined Sector. Here each authority is given an annual block loan sanction, within which it can determine its own priorities. This Sector includes not only youth and community schemes, but also furniture and equipment, and it can include schemes which have failed to gain inclusion in the Key Sector programmes, although it was never the Government's intention that Key Sector controls should be avoided in this way. Education projects have, of course, to compete with those of other local authority departments for a place in the Locally Determined Sector. Further, there is no obligation on local authorities to make full use of their allowances in any of these Sectors, although only 10% of each year's approved allowance can be carried forward to the following year, and regular under-spending results in reduced future approval levels.

16. The intention of Circular 2/70 was to establish a system of local authority capital development whereby central government maintained overall control of the level of local authority spending, while permitting maximum local authority freedom within these constraints. In practice a series of economic crises and consequent emergency measures throughout the 1970s have combined with a rigid interpretation of the distinctions between Key Sector and Locally Determined Sector allocations to frustrate the achievement of the flexible long-term planning machinery initially envisaged. In consequence there are mounting pressures to replace the existing system with a block allocation within which local authorities make their own apportionment. The proposals of the Local Government, Planning and Land Bill 1979 (withdrawn; re-issued 1980) go some way towards such a system. If implemented, the present system will be replaced by a centrally established capital expenditure ceiling for each local authority, within which authorities would have considerable freedom in the determination of allocations between major expenditure headings and between authorities.

17. None of the procedures described above for controlling capital expenditure in itself provides funds. Once building projects have been approved and loan sanction obtained, local authorities must then seek the necessary finance, as described below (paragraphs 34-40).

18. **Revenue expenditure: the rate support grant**

The procedures whereby central government departments control capital expenditure through loan sanctions and building approvals are quite separate from central government controls over revenue expenditure, except where both are considered in the PESC system. However, capital approvals have considerable revenue implications, not only through long term debt charges, but also through the maintenance and staffing costs implicit in capital schemes. As with capital expenditure, central government controls over the recurrent expenditure are neither simple nor direct. The major mechanism is the annually negotiated rate support grant. This was established by the Local Government Act 1966. Its purpose is to provide from central government funds a substantial proportion of local authority recurrent expenditure and, in so doing, take account of the varying needs and resources of different authorities, while maintaining some overall control of the level of local authority spending.

19. Annual negotiations take place between central government, represented by the DoE, and local authorities, represented by the local authority associations, in the Consultative Council on Local Government Finance. The Council is chaired by the Secretary of State for the Environment, and contains other Ministers or their representatives. It is served by a number of RSG Committees, including the Expenditure Steering Group on Education. These committees, comprising both central and local government officers, establish first the likely total local authority expenditure for the coming year – the Estimated Relevant Expenditure. This includes all expenditure eligible for grant-aid, but excludes local authority housing and trading activities. Once the Estimated Relevant Expenditure is decided, that proportion to be met from central government funds is negotiated. This is fixed as a percentage of the Estimated Relevant Expenditure – the Aggregate Exchequer Grant. Central government grants which are specified for particular purposes such as the police force, slum clearance, housing improvement grants and transport subsidies are then subtracted – these are the Specific and Supplementary Grants.

20. The remaining sum comprises the rate support grant (RSG). It must then be allocated to the individual local authorities according to a complex formula determined by the Government, after consultation with the local authority associations, in accordance with PESC directives and current government priorities. The formula has three elements, each related to a different objective of the RSG – the Domestic, Resources and Needs Elements.

21. The Domestic Element comprises a subsidy for the domestic rate payer, designed to compensate for rising rate burdens, as householders are not eligible for the tax relief against profits available to industrial rate payers. It is currently 18.5p in the £ per domestic rate payer, except in Wales where, because water services are included in rate charges, it amounts to 36p in the £. The Resources Element is an equalising device, designed to raise the grant income of the poorer authorities up to a minimum rateable value level, without penalising the wealthier authorities.[13] In the 1979-80 settlement the threshold was £175 per head of population.

22. The largest, most complex and most controversial part of the RSG is the

13 Wealthy authorities do argue that they are penalised indirectly, as the Resources Element reduces the size of the remaining Needs Element, which they share.

Needs Element. Its purpose is to relate each authority's grants to its perceived needs, and as different needs are identified from year to year the formula varies accordingly. Thus the 1979-80 formula utilizes 23 different factors (26 in Outer London boroughs), weighted by means of a multiple regression analysis of authorities' past expenditure; while different factors with different weightings or "multipliers" apply to Outer London boroughs, Inner London boroughs, the City of London, and metropolitan districts and non-metropolitan counties. These factors include the authority's population, its rate of growth, its acreage per head, numbers of new dwellings, and social need factors including numbers of pensioners, one-parent families and overcrowded households. Education factors are also significant, with full-time or full-time equivalent FE students yielding the largest "per capita" return for most local authorities, as table 2 indicates. Advanced FHE students are not considered in the RSG calculations as their costs are pooled between local authorities.[14]

Table 2

Additional "education factors" used in calculating 1979-80 Rate Support Grant [15]

	Non-metropolitan county or metropolitan district	*Outer London Borough* [16]
FE students, full-time or FTE, living in their area, in excess of 0.6 per 100 of population (0.5 in Outer London)	x £672	x £298.2
Secondary school pupils over 16 years, in excess of 0.3 per 100 (0.25 in Outer London)	x £604.8	x £268.3
Secondary school pupils under 16 years in excess of 6 per 100 (5.4 in Outer London)	x £670.4	x £531.8
Primary school pupils in excess of 7 per 100 (6 per 100 in Outer London)	x £512.8	x £461.8

14 The costs of advanced FE students are taken into account when fixing the Estimated Relevant Expenditure.

15 *Rate Support Grant Order 1978,* Statutory Instrument 1967, HMSO, 1978.

16 All London totals to be multiplied by an adjustment coefficient which takes account of each borough's rateable income.

23. The Needs Element comprises the largest part of the RSG, although its proportion has declined from over 80% when the RSG was first established in 1967-8. Table 3 summarises the 1979/80 RSG proportions and totals.

Table 3

The 1979-80 Rate Support Grant Settlement

		£ million	
1.	Estimated Relevant Expenditure	14,111	
2.	Aggregated Exchequer Grant	8,607	61% of 1
3.	Supplementary & Specific Grants	1,349	
4.	Rate Support Grant	7,258	84.3% of 2
	Needs Element	4,434	61% of 4
	Resources Element	2,137	29.5% of 4
	Domestic Element	687	9.5% of 4

The Needs Element formula has been adjusted in recent years to meet the needs at different times of rural counties and inner urban areas. To prevent these adjustments producing marked variations in the sums received by individual authorities a damping procedure has been introduced whereby the Needs Element formula for the current and four preceding years each provides one-fifth of that part of the RSG to each authority. Furthermore, a safety-net has been added to prevent any authority losing more than the equivalent of a 2p. rate in any one year. Until 1979-80 the Needs Element was paid only to London boroughs, metropolitan districts and non-metropolitan counties. Henceforth parts of the Needs Element will be paid directly to non-metropolitan districts, who have no educational responsibilities. In consequence, education will feature as an even larger proportion of the total budget in non-metropolitan counties, and it may be difficult for some counties to increase their precepts on district councils in line with their Needs Element losses. (Precepts are orders from one authority to another for collection or payment of money under a rate).

24. Estimated Relevant Expenditure is assessed at a known price base, usually in the November preceding the year to which the grant applies. This, combined with high levels of inflation, requires the allocation of a mid year supplementary RSG to authorities. Thus, an Increase Order has been necessitated when expenditure unforeseen at the time of RSG negotiations has been incurred as a result of central government policies, particularly where pay settlements for teachers and other local government workers have exceeded initial government expectations.

25. The RSG is a complex and cumbersome instrument. Its weaknesses have led to its becoming even more complex, but it remains based upon the increasingly difficult estimate of future expenditure levels. However, from the central government's perspective it has proved a useful means of curbing and steering local government expenditure, while the local authorities have preserved their independence as to how they actually spend the RSG because, although expenditure guidelines are produced by PESC and in the RSG Order, these can only be advisory. The RSG is a block grant, which

authorities can apportion as they please within legislative constraints. The education service, as the largest area of local government expenditure, is particularly vulnerable, and there are some indications that, in recent years, education has not been receiving as large a proportion of the local government budget as the RSG settlement envisaged.[17] Thus there have been criticisms that funds intended for in-service education and training in the RSG settlement have not been so deployed by some authorities,[18] although attempts by central government to specify the uses to be made of parts of the RSG run counter to the principles underlying the block grant system.[19] Most fundamentally, there is increasing confusion as to whether the level of estimated relevant expenditure upon which the RSG is based represents a forecast of expected local authority spending, or is rather a framework whereby central government outlines the levels and patterns of local authority expenditure it requires. The establishment of the Consultative Council on Local Government finance, while meeting some local authority criticisms, has not yet resolved these difficulties. Demands for a specific grant for education, as is the case with the police force, are resisted by local authorities as, if met, they would reduce local discretion considerably, and the recent experience of the National Health Service would suggest that central financing offers no protection against expenditure cuts.

26. The Local Government, Planning and Land Bill, 1979, proposed to alter the rate support grant system substantially from 1981-2, but in a way which would seem to resolve few of the problems discussed above. The needs and resources elements are to be replaced by a single block grant, to be calculated by procedures at least as complex as those followed at present. Domestic rate relief will comprise a separate grant. Other proposals in the bill suggest a possible significant increase in the extent of central government control. The Secretary of State for the Environment is seeking powers to enable him to penalise any authority whose expenditure significantly exceeds agreed relevant expenditure, by reducing the authority's grant. Such powers would be operable even before the introduction of the new grant system. Other major financial controls are being acquired by the DES through the "capping" of the Advanced FE Pool (see para. 54).

27. **Cash limits**

As the RSG system is based upon the detailed estimation of future levels of public expenditure it is hardly surprising that its weaknesses have been most apparent during periods of rapid inflation, when, although the volume of expenditure might remain as forecast, price changes require upward adjustments which can run counter to the government's economic policy. The search for mechanisms which would indicate to local authorities the

---

17 See A. Pollock "Rate Support Grant and the Education Service". *Educational Administration*, Vol. 6, No. 1, Winter, 1977-8.

18 For example, the Rt. Hon. Mrs. Shirley Williams' speech as Secretary of State for Education and Science to CASE Conference, 9.9.1977. This view is disputed by local authority associations both for its misunderstanding of the purpose of the RSG and for its too narrow an interpretation of in-service education by the DES.

19 Specific grants to education are considered below (para.32).

level of inflation beyond which compensatory reductions in the volume of expenditure would be required led to the introduction of a system of "cash limits", first applicable in 1976-7. A financial limit is set to both capital and revenue public expenditure by local authorities and other public bodies. Should these limits be exceeded, central government finance will not be available to supplement existing grants.[20] The operation of cash limits seems to have fulfilled the government's intentions of restraining local authority expenditure. In attempting to ensure that budgets do not exceed cash limits, many local authorities have curbed expenditure more strictly than before. In order to achieve this in a period of rapid inflation the level of some local authority services has been significantly reduced. Thus in 1977-8 public expenditure was over 2½% less than had been planned for. Inevitably the education service has suffered at least proportionately. As with the RSG, cash limits depend upon the accurate estimation of future levels of inflation, both nationally and in the public sector. Where such estimates have been inaccurate an understandable over-reaction by some local authorities has ensued, in order to avoid being penalised should wages and prices rise substantially faster than had been estimated. Such problems are compounded when, as in June 1979, the Government refuses to increase cash limits to take full account of expenditure incurred as a result of central government policies.[21]

28. **Manpower controls and staff costs**

Indirect, but very important controls over educational finance are exercised by the DES through its powers under the Remuneration of Teachers Act 1965. The Act provides that the Secretary of State determines representation on the Management Panel of the Burnham Committee, and for the right of Parliament to set aside even arbitration decisions.[22] Thus the DES has a major influence upon the size of the largest single element in the education service budget, the salaries of teachers. Furthermore, as well as having the major voice in establishing the global sum available for teachers' salaries, the DES also influences the apportionment of that sum, through its representation on the Management Panel (see Section **11.1.**3).

29. The DES controls the number of students entering teacher education programmes in the non-university sector of higher education, through powers under the Training of Teachers Regulations 1967. It thus controls quite closely the level of expenditure on teacher education. Indeed, the remaining voluntary colleges of education and higher education are amongst the few institutions to negotiate directly their funding from the DES. More indirectly, the DES thus maintains some control over the total numbers of qualified teachers available for employment, although this has been vitiated by the increasing proportion of trained teachers provided by the university

---

20 Specific grants have so far been excluded and adjustments are possible should interest rates rise.

21 In consequence, expenditure cuts not anticipated at the time of the RSG settlement were required in order to finance national pay settlements agreed by the Government.

22 Since the passage of the 1965 Act no Secretary of State has as yet sought to set aside the Committees' findings or the findings of arbitrators to whom disputes from the Committees have been referred.

sector, over which the DES has no such control.[23]

30. Another control exercised by the DES with indirect financial implications arises from the requirement that under Regulation 8 of The Further Education Regulations 1975 a very wide range of courses of further and higher education are subject to the approval of the Secretary of State, who can impose conditions or discontinue such courses. Such approvals are normally dealt with by Regional Staff Inspectors, after considering advice from Regional Advisory Councils.

31. The DES's powers under Regulation 6 of The Further Education Regulations 1975 to control tuition fees for degree-level and equivalent courses provides another indirect financial control. More directly, recent government policy of restricting the numbers of overseas students studying in institutions of further and higher education by means of establishing "quotas" (see Sections **1.3.**7 and **12.10.**18), while intended to reduce public expenditure, has resulted in the loss of substantial fee income for some colleges and local authorities where places formerly taken by overseas students are now unfilled. The recent change of government policy, requiring charging fully economic fees to overseas students, could have considerable financial implications for a number of institutions, some of whom seem likely to benefit by attracting overseas students paying full-cost fees, although others, by losing their remaining overseas students, may well lose courses and suffer resultant diseconomies.

32. **Specific grants**

The major specific grant for education is that for mandatory student awards, described in detail in Section **12.5.** 90% of the grants which local authorities must pay to students on "designated" courses is recoverable from the DES.[24] Other grants, for specified institutions and for research, come directly from the DES and are referred to above (para 8). Few of the other central government grants which must be used for specified purposes are of relevance to the education service. Exceptions are the grants for the Urban Programme and for Commonwealth immigrants, both administered through the Home Office. The Urban Programme was established to assist local authority expenditure in urban areas of acute social need, and under the Local Government Grants (Social Need) Act 1969, specific grants of 75% of the cost of approved capital and revenue projects are obtainable. Such projects might include youth and community facilities, additional educational materials and equipment, short-stay hostels and intermediate treatment schemes, and nursery places. Other further education, youth and community schemes have been established under the Inner Urban Areas Act 1978 which made available grants for capital and revenue projects to revive certain inner city areas through partnerships of local authorities and other governmental organizations. Specific grants at 75% of the costs of employing staff in order to make special provision for substantial numbers of Commonwealth

---

23 Controls in the university sector are exercised by the University Grants Committee.

24 "Designated" courses are outlined below (para 57). All fees up to £595 per year for such courses are paid by LEA on behalf of home students.

immigrants whose customs and languages are different from the rest of the community are obtainable under s 11 of the Local Government Act 1966. And the full cost of removing or demolishing air raid shelters is payable under the Removal of Defence Works Grant Regulations 1971, although current proposals, if enacted, seem likely to terminate such grants.

33. **Local authorities**

The above paragraphs might imply that a considerable system of central government financial controls is used to regulate further and higher education. In practice, in spite of the comprehensive array of available controls, it would seem that it is not employed in any co-ordinated way in order to support and maintain a coherent strategy for the development of further and higher education in England and Wales. The powerful localist tradition in the education service would, furthermore, seem to render the emergence of such a centrally-controlled strategy at least unlikely in the near future. As a consequence, the local authorities have a considerable degree of discretion in the financial management of their establishments of further and higher education.

34. **Capital finance**

Education comprises the largest area of local authority revenue expenditure, and the second largest area – after housing – of capital expenditure by local authorities. Capital expenditure on further and higher education has in recent years amounted to about 13% of the total capital expenditure on education. Local authorities make use of four main sources of finance for their capital programmes. The major source is from loans, raised under powers conveyed by Schedule 13 of the Local Government Act 1972 and with central government approval through the system of loan sanctions. The private money market is normally the chief venue for local authority borrowing. Long-term borrowing usually takes the form of mortgages or bonds, whereby the loan is tied for at least a year; or by the issue of local authority stock, involving complex and expensive mechanisms including the employment of a stockbroker, and requiring Bank of England approval.[25] Difficulties in obtaining funds from the private market have led authorities to resort increasingly to borrowing from the Government Public Works Loan Board (PWLB). A basic allocation for PWLB borrowing is made to each authority based upon its existing outstanding debts and its capital outgoings. Beyond this quota, loans from PWLB incur higher interest rates than those prevailing on the private market. PWLB finance amounts to about one third of local authority borrowing, usually for a minimum of 10 years at fixed interest rates.

35. Maximum repayment periods are specified under the loans sanction system according to the notional life of the asset. Thus loans for land can be for as long as 60 years; for school and college buildings up to 40 years; for furniture and machinery 20 years, and for books and office equipment only 10 years. Interest rates have fluctuated wildly in recent years, from below 10% up to 20%. Debt charges, comprising interest, capital repayments and the costs of

25 Under Local Authority (Stocks & Bonds) Regulations, 1974.

servicing the loans are, consequently, a significant part of local authority annual outgoings. In 1979-80 they are estimated at nearly 9% of local authorities' total relevant expenditure.[26]

36. Short-term loans are raised by local authorities from City brokers and from their own superannuation funds. A good deal of six month, seven day and even one day money is borrowed to meet immediate outgoings. A bank overdraft is another common source of short-term funds, although the former freedom for local authorities to negotiate overdraft facilities has now been considerably curtailed.

37. Loans account for about three-quarters of local authority capital expenditure. Rising interest rates have, in recent years, encouraged authorities to establish capital or reserve funds from their own revenues or from capital receipts.[27] Capital receipts from the sale of the authority's assets such as land or buildings provide about 10% of capital expenditure, although the amounts vary considerably from time to time and between authorities. As they are free from the constraints applicable to loans, these funds can be used to finance schemes which have not received loan sanction. However, they cannot be used to finance revenue expenditure.

38. Revenue expenditure provides a further 10% of local authority capital expenditure. It is usually confined to the purpose of relatively small capital items, but increasingly such income is not used directly for capital schemes, but is used to augment the Capital Fund.

39. Government grants provide the fourth source of capital finance for local authorities. They normally amount to no more than about 5% of the total, and are of little relevance to educational capital expenditure, except for those obtained from the Urban Programme and for Commonwealth immigrants (discussed above in para 32). Of marginal, but increasing signficance are the grants available from various EEC funds and institutions. The current education budget is very small, but the Social Fund is a significant source of education finance. Requirements and procedures for dealing with EEC administration are discussed in Section **6.3**.

40. Reference should also be made to the practice of leasing as an alternative, if usually expensive, source of capital finance. Vehicles, furniture, plant and equipment can be leased through finance companies, and in this way local authorities can circumvent controls on Locally Determined Sector borrowing. Although ownership normally remains with the finance company, purchasing arrangements and discounts are usually negotiated directly between the local authority and the supplier. Local authorities can also lease buildings by arrangement with financial and property institutions, thereby avoiding controls over capital expenditure. Some college and polytechnic

---

26 DoE Circular 15/79, *The Government's Expenditure Plans: Implications for Local Authority Expenditure 1979-83,* HMSO, 1979.
27 Under powers conveyed by the Local Government (Miscellaneous Provisions) Act 1976.

developments are currently being financed in this way. At the time of writing it seems possible that leasing might be brought within the ambit of central government controls over local authority capital finance.

41. **Revenue expenditure**

The rate support grant (see above, paras 18-27) is the major source of local government revenue expenditure. Although fixed as a proportion – 61% in 1979-80 – of total local authority relevant expenditure, this varies considerably between authorities, from 40% to about 70%. Authorities are not permitted to raise loans to cover revenue expenditure. The other major sources of revenue funds are the rates, income from services or trading activities, and income from other authorities through recoupment or pooling procedures.

42. Rates provide between 20% and 30% of most authorities' income. About half comes from domestic ratepayers. Rates are the only direct taxes collected by and for the local government system. They suffer from the inflexibility of only occasional and irregular revaluations of property, and plans for revaluations in 1978 and in 1982 have subsequently been cancelled. Hence, with a fixed rateable value base, established in 1973, local authorities respond to rising costs by annual adjustments of the rate levied per £ of rateable value. The Layfield Report [28] considered that the advantages of the rating system, and in particular its predictability and its ease of collection, exceeded its disadvantages, and a subsequent Green Paper [29] agreed with this. Its major disadvantages are its lack of buoyancy in periods of inflation, its inequity when not regularly revised, and its regressiveness, falling more heavily upon those with low incomes, although this has to some extent been countered by the system of rate rebates. The rate yield for an authority depends in part on the rateable value of that authority's property, bearing in mind that certain types of property, most notably agricultural land and buildings, are exempted from paying rates. Charitable organizations, including voluntary colleges, receive 50% mandatory rate relief, with further relief at the discretion of the local authority. Full rates are payable on local authority colleges. The other factors influencing an authority's rate yield are the differential rates fixed for industrial and domestic properties, and any constraints which might be imposed by central government on the extent to which rates might be increased in any one financial year. [30]

43. A third source of local authority revenue is the income derived from charges made for local government services and from profits from trading enterprises. These can range from under 20% to over 40% of an authority's revenue. Important sources of income include rents from local authority housing, school and college meals charges, and fees paid by students attending establishments of further, higher and adult education. Fees obtained from the letting of authority premises, including schools and

---

28 *Local Government Finance.* Report of the Committee of Enquiry chaired by Frank Layfield, Cmnd. 6453, HMSO, 1976.

29 *Local Government Finance,* Cmnd. 6813, HMSO, 1977.

30 Central government has no statutory control over rate levels at present, although the present administration has indicated that it may seek such powers.

colleges, are further sources of income. Local authorities are also permitted, under the Lotteries and Amusements Act 1976, to raise income from lotteries, the proceeds of which can be used for educational purposes and any other purposes for which they are empowered to raise money. The object of the lottery must be specified by the local authority, a separate fund has to be maintained for each lottery, lotteries may not be promoted more frequently than weekly, and the maximum ticket price is 25p. Maximum amounts which may be raised depend upon the frequency of the lotteries. Short-term lotteries, occurring more frequently than monthly, cannot raise more than £10,000, with a maximum prize of £1,000. Medium-term lotteries, occurring between one and three months after the previous lottery, can raise up to £20,000, with a maximum prize of £1,500. Other lotteries can raise up to £40,000, with maximum prize £2,000, and must be at least three months apart. Authorities which have espoused lotteries have usually done so for schemes, such as arts and recreation projects, which would not otherwise have been undertaken. Thus the public is invited to contribute to readily identifiable and attractive activities which are not likely to make regular, substantial demands on local authority resources once undertaken.

44. Recoupment and pooling

Recoupment and pooling procedures for educational services provide substantial revenue for some authorities, although, unlike the source of income referred to above, they are distributive mechanisms whereby one authority's income comes from other authorities' payments. Recoupment is a procedure whereby, under the Education (Miscellaneous Provisions) Act 1953, an authority can recover from another, usually neighbouring, authority part or all of the costs of providing further educational facilities for the latter authority's students.[31] The Local Education Authorities' Advisory Committee on Inter-Authority Payments advises authorities on the financial basis and procedures of recoupment, in order to avoid the necessity of regular bargaining between individual authorities over the cash involved. It recommends standard rates of payment based on actual average costs at primary, secondary and further education levels, and its recommendations are accepted by all authorities. The 1979-80 rates of payment for further education students are:-

Burnham Category	*Pence Per Hour*[32]
I	196
II	188
III	231
IV	115
V	103

---

31 The Local Education Authorities Recoupment (Further Education) Regulations 1954 prescribe the conditions governing recoupment. A similar system for primary and secondary school pupils had been established in 1948.

32 Rates are calculated on "imputed" student hours irrespective of actual attendance. For full-time students "imputed" hours are 95% of course hours, for sandwich course students 110% and for part-time students actual registered hours. Burnham categories are explained in Sections **11.1** and **11.2.**

Standard weekly boarding charges of £26.50 in the London area and £20.50 elsewhere (1979-80) are the basis whereby student charges are fixed, the actual residual costs then being recouped, or pooled. The 1978-9 recoupments in the further and higher education sector amounted to over £80 millions. Some authorities have made "free-trade" arrangements with neighbours whereby students from one authority can attend the other's colleges with the former automatically meeting recoupment charges. In other cases quite complex "permit" systems have evolved. (See also Section **1.3.**33).[33]

45. The pooling system is the means whereby local authorities pay and receive payment for those activities and responsibilities which are considered national rather than local concerns. There are a number of different pools, but the operating principle is similar for each of them. Providing authorities claim allowable costs and the total bill is then divided amongst all authorities, who contribute according to an agreed formula.

46. **The "no-area" pool**

Students who are not located in any local authority are financed, when undertaking further education, under the Local Education Authorities Recoupment (Further Education) Regulations 1954, revised in 1965 and 1971. Categories of students funded in this way include those whose parents are employed abroad, although normally resident in this country; those resident in charitable institutions; those resident and receiving further education in hospital; and those temporarily resident having accompanied a member of a visiting military force. All authorities contribute to the "no area" pool in proportion to their school populations as the pool includes school pupils. In 1979-80 "no area" payments for further education students are estimated at over £24m.[34] Authorities claim 45% of the appropriate recoupment rate and 100% of actual residual boarding costs above the standing boarding charge (see above para. 44).[35] Similar pooling arrangements apportion the costs of the training of educational psychologists and the Hereward College of Further Education for the physically handicapped.

47. **The Advanced Further Education Pool**

By far the largest pool is that which shares the costs of advanced further education in the maintained sector. This was established in 1959 by the General Grants (Pooling Arrangements) Regulations, in order to ease the financial burden for the then relatively few authorities with institutions engaged in higher education, and to safeguard the expansion of advanced technology courses. In 1975 the AFE Pool was merged with the previously separate teacher training pooling system. The present statutory basis is

---

33 The London Government Act 1963 guaranteed a "free trade" system throughout the London area, but the Education (No.2) Bill, 1979 proposes to terminate this, and to introduce a standard national system whereby the consent of the student's home authority is required before attending another authority's institution.

34 CIPFA, *Education Statistics 1979-80 Estimates,* 1979.

35 Boarding charges cannot be claimed for students from outside England and Wales, who should be charged the full economic rate. See Section **12.10.**21.

Schedule 2 (3) of the Local Government Act 1974, and the subsequent Rate Support Grant (Adjustment of Needs Element) Regulations of 1976 (as amended). Each authority is required to contribute to the AFE Pool according to its school population and its non-domestic rateable value. At present 69% of the total pool is charged proportionately according to each authority's school population, thus taking into account the notional demand from school leavers. The remaining 31% is based upon each authority's non-domestic rateable value, thus attempting to relate costs to the notional needs of industry and commerce. No authority's contributions are in any way related to the actual numbers of its students undertaking poolable courses. Such courses are defined as:

(i) post graduate, first degree and comparable courses and other advanced courses defined in the regulations; [36]
(ii) facilities provided in connection with any such course; and
(iii) facilities for research. [37]

In general terms they are courses and other activities which are perceived as meeting a national rather than a local need.

48. In order that they might obtain reimbursement from the pool, authorities must submit to the DES annual statements of actual relevant expenditure in the past financial year, as well as estimated relevant expenditure in the current and following year. They must first obtain from each institution details of teaching staff class contact time on advanced and non-advanced work. The authority's treasurer then normally completes further calculations, and figures of teaching costs for advanced and non-advanced work are then computed by reference to salary, national insurance and superannuation costs of the staff concerned. The pooling formula then assumes that the cost of advanced work is:

$$\frac{\text{teaching cost advanced}}{\text{teaching costs advanced + non-advanced}} \times \begin{array}{c}\text{net college expenditure}\\\text{(including administration)}\end{array}$$

Costs of each institution are then aggregated and, after verification by the District Auditor, claims are submitted to the DES. The total size of the pool is determined solely by the demands made upon it by those authorities whose institutions provide relevant courses. Reimbursement takes place only when all claims for a particular year have been received, each authority's gross contribution then calculated, and this subtracted from its claim on the pool. Net receipts or contributions are achieved by adjusting upwards or downwards the authority's share of the rate support grant Needs Element, on an estimated basis, with relatively few subsequent final marginal adjustments. In practice all authorities have some receipts from the pool, but these are likely to vary in 1979-80 from under £30,000 to nearly £60 million. [38] The AFE Pool in 1979-80 is estimated as over £400m. This

36 Schedule 1 of The Further Education Regulations 1975 defines such courses. These are listed in Section **1.3,** Appendix 1.
37 Rate Support Grants (Pooling Arrangements) Regulations 1967.
38 CIPFA. *op.cit.*

includes all teacher education, including as much compensation for lecturers made redundant from colleges of education as is poolable (the Education (No.2) Bill, 1979 proposes to make all such expenditure poolable), and the costs of training youth leaders and community centre wardens.

49. The size of the pool has grown rapidly with the expansion of higher education in the maintained sector since the mid-1960s. Not surprisingly, the system has been criticised by contributing authorities, whose costs have increased tenfold in little more than a decade, but who have no control over the uses made of those contributions. Providing authorities have been accused of extravagance because they do not have to bear the full costs of their expenditure. Conversely, the providing authorities complain of the administrative burden of maintaining institutions with national rather than local functions, although some central administrative costs are poolable.

50. Attempts have been made to meet some of these criticisms. The Pooling Committee was set up in its present form in 1968, chaired and serviced by the DES. Its terms of reference are to consider and keep under review the arrangements for pooling educational expenditure and to make recommendations to the Secretary of State or to the local authority associations, as may be appropriate. Thus it is an advisory body, with no powers of compulsion. A large part of its work is in advising whether or not specific courses or other activities should be poolable, although it is not involved in course approval. However, another important activity has been its attempt to provide means for standardising and controlling expenditure, through the development, recommendation and monitoring of staff: student ratios. In that the numbers of teaching hours spent proportionately on advanced and non-advanced work determines the total size of the pool, it makes sense to seek some measure of the efficient deployment of such hours. In this way the Pooling Committee's activities have influenced the whole of the further education sector, and not just that part engaged in higher education.

51. The Pooling Committee's recommendations were for two types of student:staff ratio (SSR), distinguished by the nature of the academic activity carried out in the department or faculty.[39] Group I faculties, with a recommended student:staff ratio of between 7.5 and 8.5 are: technology, engineering, science, applied science, health, art and design (including drama and music), and vocational studies (architecture and town planning only). Group II faculties, with a recommended SSR of 9.2-10.2 are: social, administrative and business studies, education, languages, arts and vocational studies (except architecture and town planning). Recommendations were made for weighting students according to type of course and whether part-time or sandwich students, to produce full-time equivalent (FTE) student numbers. These are considered in Section **8.**52. Similarly, methods for calculating staff numbers were recommended. They excluded directors, principals and deputies, and proposed weightings for part-time staff, for academic staff with non-teaching duties, and for staff

39 *Memorandum by the Pooling Committee on Student/Staff ratios for Advanced Level Work in Polytechnics and Colleges of Further Education,* 1972.

teaching in part non-advanced work.

52. Later Pooling Committee recommendations [40] included a formula for calculating student:staff ratios:

$$\text{SSR} = \frac{\text{Average class size}^{41} \times \text{average lecturer teaching hours}}{\text{average student taught hours}}$$

In this way the Committee considered that levels of expected performance might be set, which could become "norms". These, along with methods suggested for calculating the variance from such recommendations, have been adopted by a majority of local authorities and institutions providing advanced work. They have become known, after the DES cost accountant on the Pooling Committee, as "Delaney norms". It was initially intended that SSRs should be used as a means of allocating the pool, with those institutions not achieving the bands getting only a proportion of their claims, but these proposals have since been abandoned as impracticable. There is at present no national policy on SSRs although the Pooling Committee conducts annual national surveys of SSRs.

53. Various proposals to change the pooling system have been made, most notably by the Oakes Committee,[42] which recommended that a National Body replace the AFE Pool in order to estimate annual needs, fix the global requirements, feed it into the rate support grant negotiations, and then distribute the major part of AFE needs to the providing authorities, who, however, should contribute initially 5% and later 15% of the total finance. The Report further suggested that the Pooling Committee should examine and advise upon alternative formulae for assessing authorities' contributions. More recent proposals have been for the enforcement of student:staff ratios by the District Auditor, in order to restrain and equalise expenditure, as part of a search for alternative means for closing the open-ended nature of the pool.

54. The present government has indicated that it intends to control the pooling system, in order to restrain public expenditure, in three stages. The first stage, from 1980-81, will "cap" the pool. The Secretary of State,under powers being sought in the Education (No.2) Bill, 1979, will fix the total size of the annual pool, and this will then be allocated by means of a rough and ready formula.[43] The second stage would be a subject related resource allocation

40 *Assessment of Curricular Activity and Utilization of Staff Resources in Polytechnics and Further Education Colleges,* Councils & Education Press, 1972.

41 Average class size is calculated by dividing the number of student taught hours by the number of staff teaching hours. This overcomes the problems of classes meeting for different lengths of time.

42. *Report of the Working Group on the Management of Higher Education in the Maintained Sector,* Cmnd. 7130, HMSO, 1978.

43 This will entail, for 1980-81 (and probably 1981-2) the averaging of 1978-9 expenditure and 1980-81 estimated expenditure for each authority, to produce a notional sum. The percentage of all local authorities' notional sums which this figure represents will comprise an authority's percentage entitlement of whatever total sum available is determined by the Secretary of State. Certain types of unavoidable expenditure such as debt charges, rents and leases, will be excluded from this system and met in full. Although not yet law (March 1980) the impact of these proposals is already dramatic, involving plans for massive retrenchment, course closure and staff redundancies.

system based upon established unit costs per subject. A third stage would examine the need for a central advisory body. Although at the time of writing this has not become law and no details are as yet available as to how it might operate, its implications for establishments undertaking significant amounts of advanced further education are, if implemented, likely to be considerable. Local authority pressures to contain expenditure levels within the allocated financial limits are likely to be intense, as presumably, any excess expenditure will have to be met entirely by the maintaining authority. Furthermore, the proposed resource allocation system could well provide central government with unprecedented course and manpower planning controls by fixing recommended levels of support for particular types of courses.

55. **Local authority financial management**

Of the funds received by local authorities, only specific government grants are earmarked for defined educational purposes, although the receipts from pooling and recoupment are in respect of previous specified expenditure. For the rest, allocative decisions have to be made within the structure of local authority government. Two broadly different systems of financial management have emerged in the 1970s. One is the traditional pattern of spending committees, including the Education Committee being allocated funds by the council, and then making decisions as to the deployment of those funds. The other has been termed "corporate management". Here, at least in theory, the needs, problems and objectives of the authority are first identified, then corporate policies are devised to meet those needs and objectives. Individual departments, including the Education Department, are then allotted resources with which to implement those policies. The crucial decisions concerning policies, including educational priorities and the consequential allocation of resources, may be taken, not in the Education Committee, but in what is termed a Management Committee or a Policy and Resources Committee (see Section **8**.9-12). The major financial difference between the two approaches is that, in a corporate management system, decisions concerning the allocation of resources to the various sectors of the education service – in other words the relative priorities accorded to those sectors – may be determined outside the Education Committee, in the light of perceived objectives wherein educational needs and priorities could be of relatively minor importance.

56. However, the education service makes by far the largest demands upon the local authority budget, and the major part of those demands is pre-determined by existing commitments. Employees have to be paid, debts have to be repaid. Whatever system of local government is employed, authorities have to meet their statutory duties. It is, therefore, extremely difficult for authorities to make abrupt shifts in the patterns of allocation to the education service or to its component sectors.

57. The financial requirements on local authorities for the provision of further and higher education are surprisingly few. S 41 of the Education Act, 1944 merely required that local authorities should secure the provision of adequate facilities for further education. It neither specified these facilities, nor did it require that they should be established by the local authority itself

(see Section **1.3.** 13-14). The Education Act 1962 made it a duty that local authorities should provide grants for resident students with the relevant academic qualifications who are admitted to first degree or comparable courses in Great Britain. The Education Act 1975 extended this duty to include courses of teacher education, and those leading to the Diploma in Higher Education and the Higher National Diploma. 90% of such expenditure is recoverable in the form of a specific grant from the DES.[44]

58. In contrast to these rather limited duties, the discretionary powers of local authorities are very extensive. The vaguely defined ss 41 and 53 of the Education Act, 1944 have permitted authorities to provide a remarkably diverse range of facilities for further, higher and adult education. Subject only to the constraints of central government on capital expenditure, establishments for further, higher and adult education, as well as the youth and community services, have been set up by most local authorities, who in so doing have taken advantage of their powers enabling the compulsory purchase of land for educational purposes. Within the broad guidelines established through the Burnham and Soulbury Committees authorities have enjoyed considerable discretion concerning staffing structures, and their consequent levels of expenditure.[45] The employment and deployment of part-time staff is an area of particularly wide variation between authorities, as are staffing levels for non-teaching staff. Authorities may further determine the financial support other than staffing for their colleges; the arrangements whereby such support is deployed; and the institutions' degree of freedom in managing their own financial affairs.

59. In spite of a stream of advice from the DES in the form of administrative memoranda, circulars and circular letters, authorities have the power to accept as much or as little of this advice as they choose, as for example in the spheres of student:staff ratios, class sizes, and the levels of course fees. They also have the power to spend moneys on research activities and conferences which might improve the area's educational facilities, under ss 82 and 83 of the Education Act, 1944,[46] and this can include substantial support for in-service education and training facilities. Of particular significance are the powers under s2 of the Education Act 1962 to bestow awards on students of post compulsory school leaving age attending any courses for which grants are not mandatory. This has enabled authorities to offer discretionary grants for attendance at a vast array of courses in the maintained, voluntary and (very occasionally) private sectors of further and adult education, including the payment of travelling and other out-of-pocket expenses, and, in a few cases, of maintenance allowances (see Section **12.5.** 11-13).

60. There are striking variations in the extent to which local authorities have taken advantage of these powers. Similarly, contrasts abound between different authorities' decisions as to what constitutes eligible courses,

---

44 Local Government Act 1974; s.8 See above para. 32.

45 These are described in detail in Section **11.2**, and resultant diversity in Section **8.**43-53.

46 The Education (No.2) Bill proposes to repeal the Secretary of State's reserve powers in these sections, thereby increasing local authority discretion.

eligible categories of student or permissible levels of support. Some contrasts in levels of provision are discussed further in Section **8**.43-53. During the current period of retrenchment in public sector finance, these discretionary powers of local authorities offer the most obvious areas for reducing the authority's financial commitment. Course fees are being raised, discretionary grants reduced or abolished, and part-time staff dismissed. Furthermore, the effects of rate support grant restrictions and the rigid adherence to cash limits are causing some local authorities to look carefully at their statutory educational requirements. Proposals are being canvassed for legislation to withdraw some of the relatively few statutory obligations with financial implications, which would permit still further reductions in local authorities' commitments.

61. **Maintained institutions**

Recurrent financial expenditure by local authorities on further and higher education takes two main forms, apart from the contributions to pooling and recoupment procedures. Direct payments are made to, or on behalf of, students attending establishments of further and higher education in the form of discretionary or mandatory grants. But the major form of local authority expenditure is through the payment of annual allowances to meet the costs of the institutions. The largest part of such payments comprises salaries, for both teaching and non-teaching staff. For 1979-80 teaching staff costs were estimated to amount to almost 50% of authorities' gross expenditure on further and higher education (excluding debt charges), and salaries and wages amounted altogether to about 70% of total estimated expenditure.[47]

62. The major areas of local authority recurrent expenditure on institutions of further and higher education are summarised in table 4. They exclude debt charges and any revenue contributions to capital expenditure, which amount to about 10% of recurrent expenditure, and any boarding or catering costs.

Table 4

Estimated categories of expenditure 1979-80[48]

	Polytechnics (%)	*Other F.E. (%)*
Teaching staff	50	49
Other employees	24	14
Premises	10	7
Supplies and Services	10	7
Transport	1	1
Establishment Expenses	3	2
Agency Services[49]	1	10
Miscellaneous Expenses[50]	1	10

The table excluded central government expenditure on mandatory student awards.

---

47 CIPFA, *op.cit.*

48 CIPFA, *op.cit.*

49 These comprise the costs to local authorities of their resident students attending other LEAs' colleges, ie recoupment.

50 These include discretionary awards to students.

63. **Institutional estimates**
The system of financial management for establishments of further and higher education is governed by the Education (No.2) Act 1968 and the subsequent DES Circular 7/70, except for polytechnics, whose similar system was established in 1967.[51] The 1968 Act specifies that every maintained institution with full-time students should be conducted according to articles of government made by the local education authority and approved by the Secretary of State. The articles should specify the functions of the local education authority, the governing body, the principal and the academic board, if any.

64. Circular 7/70 appended model articles of government considered appropriate for colleges with a substantial proportion of advanced work. The requirement of Secretary of State approval ensured some degree of uniformity in the articles of government for such colleges. However, colleges with less than a substantial proportion of advanced work were permitted to have articles appropriate to the college's individual characteristics and circumstances. In consequence there is considerably more diversity in the articles approved for such colleges.

65. Model article 6 in Circular 7/70 specified the management of finance, premises and supplies, and is appended (Appendix 1). It outlines broadly the structure operative for most maintained establishments of further and higher education, although the detailed procedures are extremely varied. Institutions draw up cost estimates annually, normally in relation to projected student numbers, and in a manner prescribed by the authority. The task of assembling the estimates is formally that of the principal, although in practice it is commonly the responsibility of the finance officer or chief administrative officer. The estimates are then submitted to the governing body, although commonly after prior scrutiny by a finance committee of the governors. Thereafter the governing body submits the estimates to the local education authority for approval by the Education Committee. After such approval the governors can then incur expenditure involving the ordering of supplies and equipment, undertaking minor repairs and maintenance, and exercising virement[52] within approved headings. However, they are not permitted, without consent from the authority, to undertake expenditure with financial implications beyond the end of the financial year.

66. In practice considerable informal discussion, advice and negotiation supplements this formal machinery. The influence of the local authority on the process is particularly strong where, as occurs in some authorities, an officer of the local authority acts as college finance officer. Negotiations are likely to centre around the overall level of resources available to the college, and the data base from which the estimates are constructed, in particular relating to projections of student numbers.

---

51 *Polytechnics*, DES Administrative Memorandum 8/67.
52 Virement is the facility to transfer funds from one budget heading to another, and so finance over-spending in one area from savings or under-spending elsewhere. See Appendix 2.

67. In consequence an extremely diverse variety of approaches to financial management has emerged in further and higher education. Considerably different approaches can be found not only between authorities but also between different establishments within the same authority. Two broadly different styles of management can, however, be distinguished. A traditional, incremental or "open-ended" style involves colleges making estimates of future needs based upon existing resources with something added to cover inflation and projected developments. Such estimates are then commonly pared by the local authority, either by the removal of specific items of expenditure, or by an overall downwards adjustment, the implementation of which is left to the college. Dissatisfaction with this incremental approach has led to the increasing use of a "close-ended" style, argued to be better suited to a period of financial stringency. Here the local authority specifies its cost limits at an early stage in the budgetary process. The institution then prepares its estimates within these limits and in close consultation with the authority, allocating resources internally according to constraints established by the authority.

68. A third approach to institutional financial management is found mainly in the polytechnics at present, although its adoption by other establishments is being strongly advocated. The limitations of the annual budgetary process have led some authorities to establish longer-term planning machinery. Thus four or five year development plans are revised annually, and the annual budget is shaped by the requirements of the rolling programme. However, as long as the national and local authority financial systems are dominated by the annual adjustments inherent in the rate support grant system, such attempts at longer term planning are not likely to be widely adopted. The Oakes Committee[53] recommended that the autonomy of institutions providing higher education in the maintained sector should be more clearly specified, and that they should operate at least three-year rolling programmes for financial planning and control. It further sought regulations which would clarify the financial relationships between institutions and local authorities and within institutions, with reference to estimates, accounting and auditing procedures, virement and both capital and revenue finance.

69. **College revenues**

The major source of income for an institution of further and higher education is the local authority, although a proportion related to the amount of advanced level work is in turn recouped from the AFE Pool. In many authorities, however, colleges have a number of other sources of revenue.[54] The largest of these normally is income from student fees, which amounts to about 20% of polytechnic revenue, and just over 10% of the income of other institutions. Although fee levels for full-time designated courses are fixed nationally,[55] other fees are fixed by the local authority after

53 Cmnd. 7130, *op.cit.*

54 In some authorities all income goes direct to the authority, from whom colleges receive all their funds.

55 Administrative Memorandum 9/66. Regulation 6, Further Education Regulations 1975, gives the Secretary of State powers to direct tuition fees and boarding costs for prescribed courses.

recommendations by regional advisory councils or regional local education authority associations. (See Section **1.3.**33). Although local authority regulations vary, many authorities allow colleges to retain all or part of the fee income received in excess of that allowed for in the annual estimates, while not penalising those whose fee income does not reach estimated levels. Other authorities take the view that, as they provide the college, they should benefit from any fee incomes which may accrue. However, some institutions are able to fix fee levels for a variety of courses in such a way as to provide valuable additional college revenues. Such self-financing courses can be either open to all and advertised, or tailor-made for a specific group. They are financed either by individual students paying full economic rates or, most usually, by employers or other sponsors. When budgeting for such programmes, as for related consultancy activities by an institution, it is important that full costs of materials, equipment and accommodation should be calculated, and that staff time, normally the course's most expensive resource, should be fully and accurately costed. As an incentive to seek such revenues many institutions, including most polytechnics, have established separate net budget accounts within the local authority's financial system.

70. Colleges also undertake a wide range of non-LEA financed courses for the Manpower Services Commission and Industrial Training Boards. These are discussed in detail in Section **4**. Fees are negotiated annually with local authorities represented by the Council of Local Education Authorities (CLEA). Rates are based on information obtained from a DES survey of selected colleges' costs, so that fees represent as far as is possible actual costs including some central (i.e. LEA) administrative costs. Similarly courses expressly laid on for overseas students should be costed at full economic rates, which include allowance for overheads and capital costs. DES Circulars 2/78 and 8/78 advise local authorities on tuition fees for full cost courses. Although tuition fees commonly go to the colleges, they are then offset in part or in total from local authority payments to the college.

71. Other revenue is obtained from sales, although this heading amounts to only about 2% of total income. Grants are obtainable from public and private sources, commonly for research and development activities within the college, including Industrial Training Board activities. Rents and hire charges also provide income for many institutions, in return for letting accommodation, equipment or other facilities, although in some areas such revenues revert directly to the local authority. The articles of government normally specify the degree of financial control exercised by a local authority over its colleges and their governing bodies. Informal negotiations can sometimes extend the area of a college's financial discretion. Many institutions have established contingency or reserve funds, to be employed at the discretion of the governing body. These have enabled colleges to cope with unexpected fluctuations of income and unbudgeted cost increases. Separate college funds are used to handle non-local authority revenues. These can be deployed at the discretion of the principal or the governing body, and can be used to provide facilities, equipment, materials or staffing that the local authority is unable or unwilling to provide.

72. **Internal resource allocation**
Very little is known about the ways in which financial resources are allocated to and within college and polytechnic faculties and departments. There would seem to be almost as many systems as there are establishments. The current situation is particularly confused as, in the wake of the reorganization of college government following Circular 7/70, opportunities for establishing some degree of financial control within institutions were provided to a wide range of groups and individuals, including the principal or director, the governing body or its finance committee, the chief administrative officer or finance officer, the departmental or faculty heads, local authority officials, and a bewildering array of committees and working parties.

73. Traditional incremental approaches to budgeting are still employed in many colleges, whereby departments or faculties submit estimates of future needs usually somewhat in excess of expectations, to be trimmed internally before completion of the annual college estimate. Other institutions have developed internal allocation systems which are "close-ended", allocating the total college income according to capitation or other formulae. An increasing number of institutions have established "cost centres", comprising groups of activities and facilities which can be managed discretely by the allocation of specific expenditure and income. The absence of any uniformity between colleges makes any comparative study of such resource allocation procedures, whether at local, regional or national levels, virtually impossible. Although the Polytechnic Finance Officers Group now publishes annually comparative polytechnic expenditure statements, these do not provide comparative data on faculties or departments.[56]

74. A further area of considerable diversity between establishments is that of virement. Circular 7/70 recommended that all colleges should employ the budget headings for virement purposes recommended in the 1966 Weaver Report on the government of colleges of education,[57] and laid down for FE colleges in the 1969 Capps Report [58] as part of its recommendations for a standardised financial management structure. However, not all establishments have adopted these headings for virement purposes. Even where they have been adopted there are very considerable variations in the degree of virement permitted within these headings, and similar variations in permitted virement between some or all of these headings.

75. The Chartered Institute of Public Finance and Accountancy (CIPFA) has been concerned at the lack of any uniformity in the system of financial management for colleges of further education. In an attempt to establish a standard accounting system with standard cost centres it has produced a Manual of Guidance,[59] which, if accepted by authorities and institutions,

---

56 *Polytechnic Expenditure Statements.* Polytechnic Finance Officers Group, Sheffield City Polytechnic. Annual.
57 *Report of the Study Group on the Government of Colleges of Education,* HMSO, 1966.
58 *Report on the Use of Costing and other Financial Techniques in the Technical Colleges,* HMSO, 1969. The headings are listed in Appendix 2.
59 *Financial Information System for Institutions of Higher & Further Education in the Maintained Sector.* Manual of Guidance, CIPFA, 1979.

should provide financial information which would enable analysis of course costs and comparative studies by means of a system of accounting information which is compatible at institutional, local authority and national levels. Furthermore, a CIPFA working party has been examining the planning procedures in and for further education institutions. When it reports, probably early in 1980, it hopes to identify some problems associated with the financial planning and control systems, and to point to some possible solutions, including a recommended code of good practice.

76. **Accounting and auditing**

Further and higher education expenditure must, like all public expenditure, be audited annually, as required by s154 of the Local Government Act 1972 and the Accounts and Audit Regulations 1974. A complex and comprehensive administrative structure exists within institutions and local authorities, designed to ensure that accounting systems balance, that spending is efficient, that revenues are appropriately handled and that fraud is prevented or detected. District auditors are appointed by the Secretary of State for the Environment in order to audit local authority accounts, including those of its institutions of further and higher education, according to the DoE Code of Practice 1972. They are required to ensure that proper accounting procedures have been observed, that accounts, income and expenditure all comply with statutory requirements, that tests are conducted to detect fraud, and that the accounts do not reveal losses due to waste, extravagance or inefficiency. District auditors have considerable powers in order to undertake such investigations. They report on further education institutions to the Education Committee, but are not expected to pass comment on authority policies. Where it is considered that the local authority has acted illegally, or that losses have occurred through wilful misconduct, the district auditor may ask the court to declare resultant expenses or losses contrary to the law. The court may then require restitution and, if the expenditure or loss exceeds £2000 and the offenders are members of a local authority, it may disqualify from membership for a specified period. However. in recent years district auditors would seem to have become less involved with the details of institutional accounting systems, and rather more concerned to ensure that authority policies are being efficiently pursued. Comments on a particular institution are normally incorporated in the annual report to the Council, which is usually considered in the first instance by the Policy or Finance Committee.

77. **The internal audit**

The Accounts and Audit Regulations 1974 require that each local authority's chief financial officer maintains a system of internal auditing. Internal auditors undertake a more detailed and continuous survey of local authority spending, including college accounts. Their task is to ensure that the financial management system is operating soundly and complying with any regulations the authority may have made, with books and records balanced and up-to-date, clearly specified administrative responsibilities, with no staff member handling any financial transaction from beginning to end, and with payments made only when properly authorised. Checking arrangements, as between treasurer's department, education department and college, should prevent or detect fraud. Stocks should tally with records, and consumption of supplies should be at an acceptable level. The internal auditor reports to the authority's chief finance officer, and liaises with the district auditor. In smaller colleges, where the local authority chief finance officer is also the finance officer for the authority's colleges, the internal auditor provides the principal system of financial control. However, in larger colleges and polytechnics this role can overlap with that of the college finance officer.

78. The auditing system has been criticised for being so concerned with the prevention of fraud that it is not geared to promote efficiency. By checking only on existing accounting and invoicing procedures it is not capable of identifying more efficient alternatives which have not been selected, of seeking means of reducing costs for a given output, or of increasing output without increasing expenditure. However, the highly specialised nature of many activities in further and higher education makes it very difficult for auditors to recognise whether or not expenditure and consequent activities are efficient, while more fundamentally, there are no generally acceptable ways of evaluating any college's output.

79. **Voluntary institutions**

The financial arrangements for voluntary institutions differ in some significant ways from those for maintained establishments. They are funded for both capital and revenue expenditure for the most part by direct grant from the DES. Proposals for capital expenditure are submitted by the governing bodies of such colleges to the DES, which approves, rejects or amends them in the light of its perceived needs and priorities. If the college's governing body has a majority appointed to represent the interests of a particular religious denomination the maximum grant towards such expenditure is 85% of the total, although a loan to cover the outstanding 15% is available from the DES.[60] Some colleges have established building funds, drawing upon private incomes, donations and fund-raising activities, to meet the difference between DES grants and total expenditure, or to provide facilities which have not been approved for expenditure by the DES. However, the terms and conditions of such funds, if drawn too tightly, have been found to inhibit desired activities, particularly if the building fund, designed in a period of college expansion, is required to ease the problems of retrenchment.

80. The current expenditure of voluntary colleges is obtained on submission of estimates from the governing body to the DES, in a form prescribed by the Department. Negotiations between college and DES officials result usually in revised, then approved, estimates. Staged payments are then made by the DES through the financial year, and the college must operate within the approved limits, although supplementary grant is normally available to cover unforeseen additional costs, such as salary increases. Voluntary colleges normally have greater freedom than maintained colleges in their acquisition and expenditure of supplementary income from sales, rents and hire charges, grants, donations and special course fees. Such activities are subject only to

60 The Further Education Regulations 1975; Regulation 19.

the approval of the governing body. Vacation lettings and conferences have become substantial sources of income for some establishments.

81. One final, distinctive form of institutional financial management should be referred to. The Inner London Education Authority's five polytechnics are registered as limited companies,[61] as are a number of the independent establishments of further education recognised as efficient by the DES. They are, therefore, subject to company law, with shareholders (the governing bodies for the ILEA polytechnics) receiving the reports of commercial auditors who check the financial management system.

61 The five ILEA polytechnics are in receipt of a block grant, and are exempt from district auditor control. However, in practice ILEA's own scrutiny of their finances indicates that they do not seem to enjoy significantly greater financial discretion than other polytechnics.

APPENDIX 1

EXTRACT FROM ANNEX TO CIRCULAR 7/70
MODEL ARTICLES OF GOVERNMENT AND NOTES

"FINANCE, PREMISES AND SUPPLIES

6. a. The annual financial estimates of the College shall be prepared under the direction of the Principal and in the form laid down by the Authority for submission by the Governors to the Authority by such a date and with such supporting data as the Authority may require.

b. Within the estimates as approved by the Authority, the Governors shall be entitled to incur expenditure without further reference to the Authority and shall be empowered:

(i) To exercise virement within the headings shown in the Appendix to these articles.

(ii) To determine, subject to the provisions of the Burnham Further Education Report, the numbers and grades of teaching staff.

(iii) To carry out repairs, maintenance and minor alterations up to a figure of £500 per job (or such higher figure as the Authority may determine) by what they judge, having regard to economical management, as the best means.

(iv) To place orders for supplies (including equipment) and services at their discretion, subject in the case of items costing more than £100 each (or such higher figure as the Authority may determine) to their making use of any central purchasing arrangements of the Authority where this would be more economical.

Provided that the Governors shall not, without the consent of the Authority, undertake in any financial year any commitment which would involve the Authority in continuing expenditure after the end of that year.

c. Subject to the provisions of these Articles, the financial administration of the College shall be conducted in accordance with financial rules to be made by the Authority after consultation with the Governors.

NOTES:

(i) This article will be appropriate for most colleges in Group A. A suggested list of headings for virement purposes is to be found in Appendix B of the Report of the Study Group on the Government of Colleges of Education.

(ii) In the case of other colleges, the aim should be to give the Governors the maximum responsibility for incurring expenditure within approved estimates which is reasonable and appropriate in relation to the particular circumstances of the college. Special consideration will be necessary in the case of agricultural colleges with trading departments."

APPENDIX 2

VIREMENT: TWO RECOMMENDED LISTS OF HEADINGS

EXTRACT FROM REPORT OF THE STUDY GROUP ON THE GOVERNMENT OF COLLEGES OF EDUCATION, HMSO, 1966

"The five groups for virement purposes used by the Department of Education and Science for voluntary colleges.

GROUP A
EMPLOYEES (incl. salaries, wages etc. for all college employees other than those included in Head IV (a) and (c)).

I Salaries and wages:
- (a) teaching staff – (i) contributory service
  (ii) other service
- (b) domestic bursars, catering officers, cooks, kitchen and dining assistants, etc.
- (c) caretakers and cleaners
  technical assistants (library and laboratory)
- (e) administrative staff
- (f) others (specify)

II National insurance (employer's contributions etc.)

III Superannuation charges (employer's contributions etc.)
- (a) under the Teachers (Superannuation) Acts
- (b) under the Local Government Superannuation Acts, or other approved pension schemes.

GROUP B
RUNNING EXPENSES

IV Premises:
- (a) repair and maintenance of buildings (incl. staff wages etc.)
- (b) alterations to buildings
- (c) maintenance of grounds (incl. staff wages etc.)
- (d) fuel, light, cleaning materials and water
- (e) rents
- (f) rates

GROUP C

V Provisions

GROUP D

VI (a) Lodgings for students.
- (b) School practice (incl. transport, travelling, subsistence and/or school meals of students and staff)

GROUP E

VII (a) books – library (incl. text books)
- (b) books for resale
- (c) equipment, stationery and materials (incl. provisions for instructional purposes)
- (d) furniture and fittings
- (f) laundry

(g) other hired and contracted services (incl. examination fees and medical fees)
(h) repairs, petrol, oil, tyres, licences, etc.
(i) purchase of replacement vehicles

VIII Establishment expenses:
(a) printing, stationery, advertising, postage, telephones and general office expenses
(b) travelling and subsistence expenses of staff (excluding amounts chargeable to school practice)
(c) insurances
(d) other establishment expenses (specify)

IX Miscellaneous expenses:
(a) educational excursions and visits
(b) fees and other payments to universities or other institutions for the instruction of students
(c) other items (specify)

FIFTEEN HEADINGS FOR VIREMENT PURPOSES SUGGESTED FOR MAINTAINED COLLEGES

Employees

1. Salaries and wages (including superannuation and national insurance) of teaching staff
2. Salaries and wages (incluing superannuation and national insurance) of non-teaching staff
3. All other employees' expenses

Premises

4. Repair, maintenance and alteration of buildings and grounds
5. Fuel, light, cleaning materials and water
6. Rent and rates
7. Other

Supplies and services

8. Books, educational equipment, furniture, fittings, stationery, consumable materials, and educational visits and excursions
9. Cleaning, domestic and administrative equipment
10. Provisions
11. Other

Transport

12. New vehicles
13. Other

Establishment

14. All establishment expenses

Miscellaneous

15. All other expenses"

APPENDIX 3

THE FINANCIAL CALENDAR

The chart below is a very approximate summary of some of the stages of financial decision-making at national, local authority and institutional levels. They are subject to quite drastic modifications, usually resulting from delays or sharp changes in central government policy procedures.[1]

	CENTRAL GOVT.	*LOCAL GOVT.*	*COLLEGE*
MAR	Revenue-raising decisions – Budget & Finance Act		Department & faculty estimates submitted
APR MAY	Analyses of past and present spending: initial forecasts of future spending level, based on current year's budget	Effects of salary and other cost increases assessed. Fees etc. adjusted. Policies and future policies, including capital and revenue programmes, discussed.	College budget prepared. Initial discussions with LEA.
JUN			
JLY			
AUG			
SEPT	Rate Support Grant negotiations Forecasts obtained from previous year's out-turn figures.		
OCT	Capital allocations announced	Capital programmes fixed	Budget submitted to governors
NOV	Final PESC Report prepared and considered internally.		
DEC	Rate Support Grant Order	RSG allocation fixed	Budget considered by FE Sub-Committee
JAN	Public Expenditure White Paper	Final adjustments	Budget considered by Education Committee
FEB		Rate fixed and budgets approved	Budget approved by Council[2]

1. At least one authority (ILEA) has aligned the college financial year with the academic year (August to July); requiring book-keeping across two financial years at authority level.
2. When reductions in local authority expenditure are made at this stage delays can occur while they are related to specific institutions at Committee and Sub-committee levels.

REFERENCE

Education Act, 1944, Chapter 31, HMSO.
Education (Miscellaneous Provisions) Act 1953, Chapter 33, HMSO.
Education Act 1962, Chapter 12. HMSO.
Education (No. 2) Act 1968, Chapter 37, HMSO.
Education Act 1975, Chapter 2, HMSO.
Local Government Grants (Social Need) Act 1969, Chapter 2, HMSO.
Local Government Act 1966, Chapter 42, HMSO.
Local Government Act 1972, Chapter 70, HMSO.
Local Government Act 1974, Chapter 7, HMSO.
Local Government (Miscellaneous Provisions) Act 1976, Chapter 47, HMSO.
London Government Act 1963, Chapter 33, HMSO.
General Grants (Pooling Arrangements) Regulations, 1967, HMSO.
Accounts and Audit Regulations, 1974, HMSO.
Local Education Authority Recoupment (Further Education) Regulations, 1954, S.I. 815, HMSO.
Rate Support Grants (Pooling Arrangements) Regulations, 1967, S.I. 467, HMSO.
The Further Education Regulations, 1975, s.1. 1054, HMSO.
Removal of Defence Works Grant Regulations, 1971, HMSO.
Local Authority (Stocks and Bonds) Regulations, 1974, HMSO.
DES Administrative Memorandum 8/67, *Polytechnics.*
DES Circular 2/70, *The Chance to Share,* 1970.
DES Circular 7/70, *Government and Conduct of Establishments of Further Education,* 1970.
DES Circular 13/74, *Educational Building after 1974-5,* 1974.
DES Circular 16/76, *Educational Building in 1976-77 and 1977-78,* 1976.
DES Circular 5/75, *The reorganisation of Higher Education in the Non-University Sector: The Further Education Regulations 1975,* 1975.
DES Circular 13/77. *Approval of Equipment Purchases at Establishments of Further Education,* 1977.
DES Circular 2/78, *Tuition Fees in Further Education,* 1978.
DES Circular 8/78, *Tuition Fees in Further Education (overseas students).*
Report on the Use of Costing and other Financial Techniques in Technical Colleges (the Capps Report), HMSO, 1976.
Report of the Study Group on the Government of Colleges of Education (the Weaver Report) HMSO, 1966.
Report of the Working Group on the Management of Higher Education in the Maintained Sector, (the Oakes Report) Cmnd. 7130, HMSO, 1978.
Local Government Finance, Report of the Committee of Enquiry chaired by Frank Layfield. Cmnd. 6453, HMSO, 1976.
Green Paper: *Local Government Finance,* Cmnd. 6813, HMSO, 1977.
White Paper: *The Government's Public Expenditure Plans 1979-80 to 1982-83.* Cmnd. 7439, HMSO, 1979.
Rate Support Grant Order, 1978. S.I. 1867, HMSO.

DES, *Statistics of Education* : Vol 3, 1977 Further Education, HMSO, 1979.
Memorandum by the Pooling Committee on Staff-Student Ratios for Advanced Level Work in Polytechnics and Colleges of Further Education. August 1972.
Assessment of Curricular Activities and Utilisation of Staff Resources in Polytechnics and Further Education Colleges. Councils and Education Press, 1972.
DoE, *Local Government Financial Statistics England and Wales, 1977-78,* HMSO, 1979.
DoE Circular 2/70, *Capital Programmes,* HMSO, 1970.
DoE Circular 15/79, *The Government's Expenditure Plans: Implications for Local Authority Expenditure 1979-83,* HMSO, 1979.

CIPFA, *Financial Information System for Institutions of Higher and Further Education in the Maintained Sector* : Manual of Guidance, 1979.

CIPFA, *Educational Statistics, 1979-80, Estimates,* 1979.

Polytechnic Expenditure Statements, Polytechnic Finance Officers Group, Sheffield City Polytechnic, Annual.

N.P. Hepworth, *The Finance of Local Government* (4th Edition) George Allen and Unwin, 1978.

J. Mann, *Education,* Pitman, 1979.

Open University, *The Finance of Education,* Block IV, ED322, Economics and Education Policy, Open University Press, 1977.

J. Pratt, T. Travers, and T. Burgess *Costs and Control in Further Education,* NFER, 1978.

Section 4

THE MANPOWER SERVICES COMMISSION

1. The distinction between education and training has never been very clear in the further education service, and the developments of the last decade have done little to clarify a complex and confused situation. The establishment and growth of a major source of post-school training which is independent of the local education authorities, the Department of Education and Science, and, indeed, any direct ministerial control has considerable implications for the further education service. This Section examines these developments and some of their implications. It must be stressed that this is an area of unprecedentedly rapid change, and it would be surprising if events did not rapidly overtake some of the aspects described herein.

2. The rationalisation of industrial training in England and Wales was not attempted until 1964, when the Industrial Training Act established Industrial Training Boards, responsible to the Secretary of State for Employment and Productivity. The Act, however, reiterated that, under s. 41 of the Education Act, 1944, local education authorities held responsibilities for vocational and industrial training.[1] 29 Industrial Training Boards and a Central Training Council were established by this Act, financed initially by levies upon employers. This system was drastically revised by the Employment and Training Act 1973. The Manpower Services Commission was established, subsuming the powers of the Central Training Council. A remarkable expansion of activities has followed, fuelled by the extensive autonomy of the Manpower Services Commission (MSC), and by its expanding annual budget which, by 1978-9, had reached £643 millions.[2]

3. This growth has resulted primarily from governmental concern at the high levels of unemployment in the 1970s and related problems of redundancy, the rapid rates at which traditional skills were becoming obsolete; and a growing disenchantment expressed by employers and others with the performance of the primary and secondary sectors of the education system in preparing young people for working life. Concern for the large numbers of 16-18 year olds who were unable to find work on leaving school caused the MSC to set up a working party whose Report[3] led to a further expansion of MSC activities, producing a wide range of special programmes for school leavers and the young unemployed (see paras. 11-14 below).

4. **MSC: organization**

The Manpower Services Commission is a quasi-autonomous national governmental organization, controlled by a Board of ten members representing the interests of employers and trade unions, local authorities and the education service.[4] There are separate boards for Wales and

---

1 Industrial Training Act, 1964; s.16.

2 *Annual Report 1978-79,* Manpower Services Commission, 1979. This provisional figure includes £134m spent on behalf of the Department of Employment.

3 *Young People and Work* ("The Holland Report"), MSC, 1977.

4 Three are appointed after consultation with the TUC, one the CBI, one the Local Authorities of England and Wales, one the Scottish Local Authorities, and professional educational interests (currently R.L. Helmore, Principal, Cambridgeshire College of Arts & Technology). They serve for a term of three years.

Scotland. The Boards are accountable to the Secretary of State for Employment and the Secretaries of State for Wales and Scotland. Seven Regional Manpower Service Boards, comprising the managers of MSC's local operations are chaired by the Regional Manpower Director and serviced by his staff. Their tasks are to integrate MSC activities at local and regional levels. There are currently (1979) 26,000 employees of whom about 15,000 are in the Jobcentres and employment offices and another 9,000 in the Skillcentres, while approximately 1,400 civil servants administer the MSC's services in Great Britain.

5. The MSC has set itself five main tasks.[5] They are to contribute to efforts to reduce unemployment and raise employment, to develop the country's manpower resources so that they make a fuller contribution to the nation's economic health, to help secure for each worker the opportunities needed to achieve a satisfactory working life, to improve the quality of decisions affecting manpower, and to improve the effectiveness of the MSC itself. At present the MSC is organized in three major operating divisions, for Employment Service, Training Services and Special Programmes, and two support divisions (Corporate Services and Manpower Intelligence & Planning). The Employment Service Division (ESD) deals with the search for employment and provision of workers to employers and is responsible for recruitment to TOPS. It operates over 600 Jobcentres, which are replacing the former employment exchanges, and has aimed to remove the latter establishments' rather unsavoury image, and thereby offer a more comprehensive and successful service to employers and to those seeking and changing jobs. With more, better trained and younger staff the Jobcentres have been more cost effective than the employment offices.[6] In offering help to the young unemployed they provide a service which overlaps with many of the activities of the Careers Service.[7] This Division also operates a variety of special employment services, including the self-financing Professional and Executive Recruitment, whose consultants attempt to meet the specialist needs of a wide range of technical and managerial staff. ESD also provides a careers information service – the Careers and Occupational Information Centre – a number of services facilitating geographical mobility, resettlement and rehabilitation for disabled persons, and experimental "joblibraries". It also provides a network of Employment Rehabilitation Centres, offering courses for those wishing to re-enter employment after periods of illness, injury or unemployment, and gives financial assistance to approved rehabilitation courses run by local authorities and voluntary bodies. The Sheltered Employment Scheme, mainly funded by the Department of Employment, and operated by local authorities, voluntary bodies and Remploy, provides work under sheltered conditions for the severely handicapped.

---

5 *Review and Plan, 1977,* Manpower Services Commission, 1977.

6 *Jobcentres: An Evaluation,* MSC, 1978. This view has been challenged recently. R. Layard, "Do Jobcentres cause Unemployment?". *Guardian,* 5th November, 1979.

7 The importance of the client's right to choose Careers Service or Jobcentre assistance was stressed in *The Careers Service, Guidance to LEAs in England and Wales,* Dept of Employment 1975, which also emphasised the need for co-operation and the exchange of information between the two services. See Section **12.9**.

6. The Training Services Division (TSD) aims to develop an efficient national training system which will improve both the quality and quantity of available training, with programmes to meet the needs of industry, of individuals and of national priorities. It attempts to achieve these objectives by liaison with the Industrial Training Boards, and the further education service, through voluntary providers of appropriate programmes and in part through its own direct provision in "Skillcentres". There are now 69 Skillcentres plus their 32 annexes (although the MSC proposes to close nine centres and eleven annexes as part of current cuts in public expenditure). In general the centres run vocational courses largely in engineering and construction skills for adults though with increasing numbers of young people. Courses operate in industrial conditions with normal working hours. They are staffed by instructors, employed as civil servants, whose practical experience has been supplemented by short periods of training in instructional skills. Training is undertaken at two Instructor Training Colleges and at units attached to Skillcentres. In some cases centres have been established without consultation with local education authorities, and there have been complaints of unnecessary duplication of facilities. Further, comparative cost studies at Skillcentres and further education colleges have indicated that Skillcentres are in some circumstances an expensive means of providing training.[8] Concern has also been expressed at the substantial differences between salary scales and conditions of service from those applicable at further education establishments, with Skillcentre instructors on average paid less than further education lecturers for a longer working week with more contact hours.

7. The provision of TSD-funded activities in colleges of further education has increased from 21,692 places in 1974 to 37,136 in 1979. Many are on programmes sponsored by Industrial Training Boards and individual employers, designed to help avoid any future shortfall of trained people at technician and craft levels and below. A large part of TSD finance is expended in the form of grants to colleges and to students under the Training Opportunities Scheme (TOPS). The scheme is designed for adults who, for whatever reason, need retraining in order to seek new employment in Britain or the EEC. This may be because they failed to acquire training early in their working life, made a wrong choice of career, have skills which have become outdated, want a better job than their existing qualifications allow, or, like married women, have spent some time out of the labour market and need some training before returning to work. The scheme caters for those who voluntarily give up their jobs to acquire new skills, as well as those made redundant, and for the disabled. TOPS also fulfils economic as well as social needs by helping to meet specific shortages of skilled manpower. Courses are held in colleges of further education, Skillcentres, private colleges, employers' establishments and in residential training centres and other special establishments for disabled people. Courses are administered through the 9 regional and 46 district offices according to

8 An unpublished MSC study for a new Skillcentre at Ashford, Kent, found that provision could be made most economically at the local further education college. *The Coventry Report,* MSC 1977, recommended experimental liaison between Skillcentres and FE Colleges in terms of course provision and the exchange of tutorial specialisms.

identified demands for specific skills or qualifications. Clerical and commercial and engineering and automotive skills are the major TOPS training fields, but special priority has been given to technician training, especially for computing operations, and to the needs of the hotel and catering industry. Management training, including the management of small businesses, is also sponsored under TOPS. Just over half of TOPS trainees are in further education colleges. The remainder are in Skillcentres (one-third) and on employers' premises.[9] Trainees receive allowances which ensure that they are at least no worse off than if they were in receipt of unemployment benefit. They also receive a free mid-day meal or an allowance in lieu and travelling expenses if their journey to the training centre is over two miles and, if eligible, an Earnings Related Supplement. Similarly, employers who agree to the use of their spare training capacity by the TSD for TOPS training purposes receive appropriate fees. In 1979 over 70,000 people undertook TOPS courses, of whom 55% were women. Some colleges have established "pre-TOPS" courses for those without the minimal entry requirements needed for TOPS programmes, in order to provide the necessary basic skills required for entry.[10] Some concern has been expressed at the extent to which newly acquired or updated skills are being employed as a consequence of TOPS courses, with less than half of those trained in colleges of further education in 1977-8 (largely in clerical and commercial courses) using what had been learned in their subsequent employment, and another third still unemployed three months later. A subsequent review of TOPS activities recommended that provision should be more closely related to employers' needs, and that TOPS management should have much closer contact with the further education service and with Industrial Training Boards.[11] The cost of the 600 TOPS courses in 1978-9 amounted to over £200m, but £22m was reimbursed from the EEC Social Fund, and the gross figure does not take into account significant savings in state benefits to participants. Recent reductions in MSC activities have cut back the TOPS budget by £22 millions per year. Technician and computer-related training has been little affected by these cuts. Further education colleges could well be affected by substantial reductions in commercial and clerical courses, as it seems possible that TOPS programmes will in future concentrate upon the acquisition and revision of those skills seen as necessary to ensure the modernisation and restructuring of industry.

8. TSD offers employers direct training services for training their employees. Training in craft and related operative skills takes place at Skillcentres and on employers' premises, using mobile instructors. Training of supervisors, instructors and training officers, and training in trade procedures is offered in-company or on TSD premises. Training for instructors is also carried out at the Instructor Training Colleges at Letchworth and Glasgow. Charges are made for such services. TSD also finances the National Centre for Industrial Language Training, and the local language training units operated, and

9 In Wales half are in Skillcentres, and just over 1/3 in further education colleges.
10 J. Marshall, "Pre-TOPS in Practice", *NATFHE Journal*, April, 1979.
11 *TOPS Review 1978*, Manpower Services Commission, 1978.

previously part-financed, by local education authorities.[12] TSD's Directorate of Training plays an important co-ordinating role in the national training network. Its overall aim is to help improve the efficiency (output per unit cost) and effectiveness (resources devoted to worthwhile ends) of training nationally. It provides assessors and members for a number of major education and training bodies; gives advice and puts key people in touch with each other: and undertakes research and development projects, including research along with ILEA into innovative training based on the identification and use of the common or generic skills. It also has commissioned a number of research and allied activities from universities, regional management centres and other organizations, including the YMCA. Advisory units promote action learning and in-company training. It has also to give approval to training recommendations from Industrial Training Boards.

9. Industrial Training Boards

The Training Services Division now undertakes the responsibilities for the Industrial Training Boards which formerly rested with the Department of Employment. It funds the boards' operational expenses and makes grants for training programmes both to the boards and to individual employers through the boards. As well as making the boards accountable to the MSC the Employment and Training Act 1973 removed the requirement that boards should levy employers. Boards are now empowered to levy employers for training purposes but most exempt small firms, and those employers with acceptable internal training arrangements. Recent studies indicate that the majority of major employers in several industries are so exempted. The levies raised by the boards are used for training activities organized on employers' premises, in colleges of further education and in the boards' own training centres. One common training pattern is for initial training to be undertaken in craft and technical skills at a further education college possibly in conjunction with a training centre, followed by industrial placement and day-release training. Boards assist employers in paying course fees and students' out-of-pocket expenses, and some offer scholarships to students. Industrial Training Boards have developed distinct and different patterns of activity according to the industry they serve and the assertiveness of their governing bodies. In general, however, most have concentrated upon the development of technical and craft skills, and, to a lesser extent, supervisory skills. Much of the training is specified in precise detail and instructors are expected to follow closely the board training manuals and approved training recommendations. As yet, the Boards have not as a rule been extensively involved in the training of operatives and unskilled workers. Nor have they been much concerned until recently with professional and managerial training. Finally, mention should be made of the Exchequer funded incentive training grants available through the 1975-78 Special Measures programme to meet anticipated manpower needs at the higher skill levels. Employers', further education colleges' and Industrial

12 The units provide English language training for those in need of basic instruction. Training is also provided for supervisors responsible for workers whose command of English is not yet adequate.

Training Boards' premises provided the courses arranged through ITBs and individual employers. (see also Section **10.2.**75-8).

10. TSD support for ITBs and other training organizations, including those in the nationalised industries, now comes largely through the "Training for Skills" programme which commenced in the autumn of 1979. Its aims are to make long-term improvements in the quality and quantity of training by eliminating persistent skill bottlenecks, and initiating non-traditional approaches to craft and technician training. The ITBs and other training bodies are expected to identify their industries' needs, and to ensure that they will be met efficiently. TSD funds are available where skill imbalances affect several industries, and when it becomes clear that the efforts of employers and ITBs will be insufficient to meet required needs.

11. **Special Programmes Division**
The third and most recent area of MSC activities has arisen out of the Holland Report's recommendations for a major series of integrated programmes to cope with the problems of very high unemployment rates among young people aged 16-18. Most severely affected are those leaving school with few or no qualifications, girls, and those from ethnic minorities. High unemployment rates are expected to persist for at least several years, and problems are likely to be exacerbated by the increasing numbers of school-leavers entering the labour market until 1982. The problem was seen as too urgent to risk experimenting with entirely new approaches, and the Report recommended that existing schemes should be extended and supplemented by new schemes to provide an integrated range of opportunities.

12. The government of the day accepted the Holland recommendations. A Special Programmes Board and 28 Area Boards and 31 Area Offices were established from April 1978, to operate the Youth Opportunities Programme (YOP). Its immediate objectives were twofold: first that no school-leaver should remain unemployed by the next Easter without the offer of a place on a YOP course: and secondly that 187,000 places should be established during the first full calendar year. The first objective was very largely achieved in YOP's first year of action, with only about 1,600 eligible young people mainly in areas of very high youth unemployment not having taken up one of the available schemes, and the second target was completely met. In 1979-80 YOP aims to repeat the Easter undertaking to school leavers and to offer a suitable place on the programme to every young person unemployed for over 12 months by Easter 1980. The planning of local provision under the programme is the responsibility of the Area Board, comprising representatives of local employers and trade unions, voluntary organizations, the education service and other interested bodies, supported by the Area Offices. The Special Programmes Board, which includes representatives of the CBI, the TUC, the NUS, voluntary organizations and the education service, exercises general oversight of the programme. However, there is normally no specific representation for the further education service. Young people are eligible for YOP after a minimum of 6 weeks' registered

unemployment. The selection is shared by the Employment Service Division and the Careers Service. Once accepted, participants are paid a standard flat-rate tax-free allowance, currently £23.50 per week (1979). Two major types of provision are available, courses preparing young people for work and schemes offering work experience in a variety of settings. Their curricula are considered in Section **10.2.**83-9. The work preparation programmes are of three types. Assessment and employment induction courses are designed to improve course members' employability by identifying the kinds of work they are best suited for and interested in, by improving their knowledge of the world of work, and by providing them with some basic social skills. Courses of normally between 2 and 13 weeks are held at Skillcentres, further education colleges, and particularly on employers' premises. Short industrial courses are designed to provide specific training in a broad occupational area at semi-skilled levels. They last 13 weeks normally, at Skillcentres and further education colleges, as well as at employers' premises. Some lead to further, more specific, training at further education colleges. More usually, they lead to employment or a work experience scheme. The third type of work preparation course comprises the remedial and preparatory courses designed to help members reach the basic levels of numeracy and literacy necessary before they might benefit from other available opportunities. They last for as long as individuals need them, are held at further education colleges, Skillcentres, special schools and some residential training colleges; and they normally lead to other YOP programmes.

13. The second type of opportunity under YOP is work experience. Four kinds of schemes are available. Schemes offering work experience on employers' premises are designed to give first hand experience of different kinds of work, and usually last for 6 months. To date those have proved by far the most popular part of the YOP programme. Project-based activities are provided by sponsors, including local authorities and voluntary bodies, and are designed through projects to provide first hand experience of a number of different kinds of work. Similar activities, also lasting up to 12 months, are training workshops established in vacant factories and similar sites, which provide opportunities for first hand experience of producing goods and/or services in a work group. Community service activities are organized through the Social Services and voluntary organizations. They again can last up to 12 months and provide first hand experience of different kinds of work, by means of local community activities, in schools, hospitals, youth clubs, and services such as community health services to the housebound. All work experience programmes include the opportunity for young people to obtain day-release to pursue general vocational training, remedial or further education or training, and development in life and social skills. The majority of these activities are provided by colleges of further education and are funded directly by MSC. Work experience programmes are designed to lead participants to normal employment, although some go on to work preparation courses or to further education. Four-fifths of the 113,000 YOP places (taken up by 162,000 participants) were on work experience in 1978-9. Of these one quarter (23,000 places) were sponsored by

local authorities and local education authorities.[13] It is intended that places be found for over 200,000 young people in 1979-80. One result of this rapidly expanding range of training activities has been the acceptance by further education colleges of a substantial group of students for which most colleges had not previously provided. The group contains students with fewer than the minimal entry qualifications normally required for further education programmes, whose previous experiences of education, in schools, had been marked by failure, apathy and, in many cases, long periods of absence including truancy. It is as yet too early to judge whether such activities mark the begining of more comprehensive role for the further education service in catering across the whole ability range for young people between 16 and 19. However only 30% of MSC funds of £2.5m for capital developments in colleges providing YOP courses was in fact taken up, suggesting some reluctance on the part of many colleges or LEAs to become involved.

14. Two other related schemes are the Community Industry Scheme and the Special Temporary Employment Programme. The former is financed through the MSC but has a separate management board and is staffed by the National Association of Youth Clubs. It is designed to assist young people who are either seriously handicapped or disadvantaged in other ways, or who experience particular difficulties in finding and holding down jobs. Working with local authorities, sponsored projects last for up to 12 months. The Special Temporary Employment Programme (STEP) replaced the Job Creation Programme in 1978, and in 1978-9 provided about 20,000 temporary jobs for those aged 19 to 24, unemployed for at least 6 months, and for those over 24 unemployed for 12 months. Participants are employed by sponsors, normally for a maximum of 12 months, on projects of benefit to the community. The scheme is now confined to inner urban areas as designated in the Inner Urban Areas Act 1978, Special Development and Development Areas, and will cater more specifically for the long-term unemployed. Planned expenditure has been halved, and the number of available places reduced to between 12,000 and 14,000.[14]

15. **MSC and the further education service**

MSC programmes are likely in 1979 to involve over 370,000 students, of whom about 90,000 students are in colleges of further education and polytechnics. Provisional expenditure in 1978-9 included approximately £400m on training activities of which £40m went to the further education sector in the form of fees and other charges. In a period when other curricular developments have been curtailed by local authority financial stringency they represent the major area of growth and change in the further education sector in the late 1970s. Persistently high levels of unemployment seem likely to last into the early 1980s, and to require the maintenance of a form of educational and training provision which, unlike other forms of post-school education and training, is directly responsive to central government requirements. Whereas central government cannot guarantee

---

13 *Review of the first year of Special Programmes*, MSC Special Programmes Division, 1979.

14 *Ibid.*

that funds proposed for further education in the annual rate support grant are so deployed by individual authorities, the moneys voted to the MSC are deployed in broad accordance with the MSC's medium term strategy as endorsed by the Secretary of State for Employment. In view of this, it is a cause of considerable concern to some in the education world that the Commission should be ultimately responsible for its training functions to the Secretary of State for Employment rather than the Secretary of State for Education and Science.[15] Relationships with the Department of Education and Science and with local education authorities are more harmonious than they were in the early days of the MSC. The Training and Further Education Consultative Group, established in 1976, provides a link between MSC and the DES, intended as a national forum for discussing matters of common interest to the training and further education services. Members are drawn from further education colleges, local education authorities and Regional Advisory Councils as well as from MSC, DES, and the ITBs. The Group has considered MSC initiatives, areas of dispute between training and educational interests, and joint DES/MSC involvement in vocational preparation. This latter has taken the form of the Unified Vocational Preparation (UVP) experimental programme which has recently been expanded, with over 150 schemes in operation in late 1979, based in colleges and in industry. UVP is considered further in Section **10.2**.

16. In 1977 the DES published recommendations for improving links between training and further education at all levels.[16] These included the need for liaison between the TSD and Regional Advisory Councils before major changes of policy by either side, and for involvement at the outset of all relevant interests, including examination boards, in initiatives by Industrial Training Boards and others. To improve liaison a senior HMI has been attached to MSC as adviser on educational matters. The DES is also using MSC facilities to finance some desired objectives, such as the one-year training for mathematics, craft and other shortage-subject teachers in order to meet urgent and (hopefully) short-term national needs, in a way not possible from the ordinary resources of individual LEAs.[17]

17. However, major and continuing anomalies persist. One is that young people on YOP courses receive allowances of £23.50 per week (1979), considerably more than the discretionary and minor awards paid by most authorities to students under the age of 19 on non-advanced courses. While some students receive no grants at all, others attend specially designed part-

---

15 A discussion paper, *Education & Training for the 16-19's*, NATFHE, 1979 has suggested a single Department of Education & Training as a long-term prospect with a National Council "The Manpower, Training & Further Education Commission" for the planning, co-ordination and monitoring of post-school education as a more immediate solution.

16 DES Administrative Memorandum 12/77.

17 Although DES Circular 10/77, *Unemployed Young People – The Contribution of the Education Service*, announced the Government's intention that rate support grant settlements would take account of YOP places in colleges, but it is not possible for the DES to ensure that rate support grant funds are used for such specified purposes. LEAs were, however, asked to keep the Secretary of State informed as to the outcome of their schemes in response to this Circular.

time programmes which enable them to receive supplementary or unemployment benefits of between £11 and £32 per week. Proposals in the abortive Education Bill 1978, for paying maintenance allowances for all students under the age of 19 would have gone some way towards rationalising this area, but they seem unlikely to be revived in the near future, and only a handful of local authorites are paying discretionary and means-tested maintenance allowances (of currently about £7 per week).

18. Another area of contention is the incompatibility between the MSC's budgetary system and that of the education service. The Commission has been careful to employ as few administrators as possible and to maintain advisory boards at small sizes. As a result, with a budgetary system which gives considerable autonomy to MSC local offices and to MSC officials who may, individually, be responsible for allocating substantial budgets, the decision-making powers of these officials is not matched by officials in the education service, making close liaison between the two systems sometimes rather difficult. Furthermore, the areas of MSC boards are not coterminous with those of LEAs. From the education officer's point of view, MSC decisions can seem hasty and unconsidered, without heed to a host of implications when establishing programmes. The MSC officials in turn may find the education service's system of discussion, consultation and reporting back between departments and institutions tedious and unnecessarily time-consuming. Certainly, the speed with which MSC programmes can be mounted makes them attractive to many in further education. But concern has been expressed that this rapid expansion might well be followed by as rapid a contraction—or by a shift of resources which could create very severe problems for some educational institutions. Problems have occurred where Skillcentres have seemed to duplicate the provision by further education colleges. They also arise where local authority and further education colleges come into conflict over the ultimate responsibility for MSC funds. Fee rates paid by MSC to LEAs are negotiated annually.[18] The income accrues to the LEA as provider of the college, but some LEAs make equivalent payments to colleges in respect of MSC courses; others retain this income.

19. As a result of MSC activities, England and Wales probably have a more comprehensive programme of provision for the young unemployed than any other major industrialised nation. However, the development of a separate organization, funded directly from central government, is a sharp break with the long established, devolved and locally autonomous system of education and training which has characterised post-school provision until recently. The advent of the MSC has ensured that a substantial amount of national resources have been devoted to the 16-19 age group, which would not have accrued to this group had provision been left to the Department of Education and Science – whose White Paper; *Education: A Framework for*

18 Negotiations are between the MSC and the local authority associations (with DES assistance). Rates are based on average actual costs in the previous year, adjusted to take account of inflation: they are, therefore, a proxy for full costs incurred by LEAs in individual colleges. As they are averages, it follows that in some colleges payments will appear inadequate, while in others apparently profitable.

Expansion (1972) proposed the major features of the next decade's education service without reference to non-advanced further education. Thus MSC resources have benefited the further education sector in ways that the DES has been neither willing nor able to do (cf. Section **10.2.**90). The future of these developments is at present uncertain.[19] The advent of co-operation between educational and training agencies in the Unified Vocational Preparation programmes might well develop until, together with continuing YOP and other further education programmes, they form the initial stage of a comprehensive national system of education and training for the 16 to 19 year old age group. Conversely, future financial difficulties in both educational and training sectors may mean that the further education service's involvement with a much broader clientèle is but a temporary phenomenon.

19 At the time ot writing, unconfirmed reports suggest that cuts of between £100 and £150 million in planned MSC expenditure are being considered. One possible option under review is reported to be the abolition of STEP and a major reduction in TOPS. *Guardian*, 29.7.1979.

APPENDIX 1

COLLEGES OF FURTHER EDUCATION AND THE MSC

1. Initiatives for college-based activities which might be funded wholly or in part by the MSC can come from a number of sources. These can include Industrial Training Boards, TSD regional boards, TSD district and regional offices, SPD area boards and offices, MSC Head Offices, local authorities and, of course, the colleges themselves. The distinction between TSD-funded and SPD-funded schemes has become increasingly clear in recent months, in that TSD supports schemes for the post-18 age group. Only the truncated STEP programme supports schemes for adults with SPD funding.

2. The procedures for obtaining approval from TSD for TOPS schemes are normally that suggested schemes are considered first at the local TSD district office. However, all schemes now have to be considered further and finally authorised by one of the nine regional offices. A few schemes – usually those requiring high technology – require approval from TSD's head office.

3. SPD support for possible YOP and STEP schemes should be sought from the local SPD area office. SPD-funded capital developments in colleges normally require headquarters approval, as well as that of the maintaining local authority.

REFERENCE

Industrial Training Act 1964, Chapter 16, HMSO.
Employment and Training Act 1973, Chapter 50, HMSO.
Links between the Training and Further Education Services, DES AM 12/77.
Education: A Framework for Expansion, DES Circular 4/72, 1972.
Unemployed Young People – The Contribution of the Education Service, DES Circular 10/77.
Training and Further Education Consultative Group *Bulletins* 1-5, DES, 1977-79.
16-18: Education and training for 16-18 year olds. A consultative paper, Departments of Education and Science and Employment, 1979.
Providing educational opportunities for 16-18 year olds, A consultative paper, Departments of Education and Science and Employment, 1979.
A Better Start in Working Life. A consultative paper, Departments of Education & Science, Industry, Employment, Scotland & Wales, 1979.

These latter three consultative papers are available, free of charge, from Publications Despatch Centre, Department of Education & Science, Honeypot Lane, Canons Park, Stanmore, Middlesex HA7 1AZ.

The Careers Service, Guidance to LEAs in England and Wales, Dept. of Employment, 1975.

Annual Report 1978-79, Manpower Services Commission, 1979.
MSC Review and Plan 1977, Manpower Services Commission, 1977.
MSC Review and Plan 1978, Manpower Services Commission, 1978.
Young People and Work, Manpower Services Commission, 1977.
The Employment Service in the 1980s, Manpower Services Commission, 1979.
Improving the Effectiveness and Efficiency of Training, The Directorate of Training, Training Services Division, MSC, 1979.
Review of the first year of Special Programmes, Special Programmes Division, MSC, 1979.
Jobcentres: An Evaluation, Employment Service Division, MSC, 1978.
A Programme for Action: Training for Skills, Manpower Services Commission, 1977.
Training in Industry: Industrial Training Boards and the Manpower Services Commission, Training Services Division, MSC, 1979.
Manpower Services Publications can be obtained from the Manpower Services Commission, Selkirk House, 166 High Holborn, London WC1V 6PF.

Education and Training for the 16-19s: a discussion paper, NATFHE, 1979.
M. Farley, "YOP needs you too", *NATFHE Journal*, Oct 1979.
S. Maclure, "Financial Support for the 16-18s", *Education Policy Bulletin*, vol. 7, no. 1, Spring 1979.
Patricia Santinelli, "The Manpower Services Commission", *Times Higher Education Supplement*, 9.6.1978.
J. Marshall, "Pre-TOPS in Practice", *NATFHE Journal*, April 1979.

Section 5

BUILDINGS

1 INTRODUCTORY NOTE

1. This Section is concerned with buildings. It has to do with their design and operation. It has been necessary in places to go into particular detail because such is the operation of the law, that is the only way in which areas of concern can be illuminated. At the very outset, therefore, three qualifications must be made. They relate to design, the law, and the everyday practicalities of buildings use.

2. There is a need for the building user to be familiar with regulations and guidance set down for the design of buildings. In the case of new building, it is the function of the architect to produce the design in co-operation with the client. In practice, this will usually involve the college, the local authority's buildings department, HMI and other representatives of the DES or Welsh Office Education Department. The partnership between architect and client is crucial. Normally the LEA is the client in design and building work, which means that formal instruction to the architect must come only from the LEA. College staff ought, however, to be fully involved in the consultative process. Ideas for development should be considered together from the outset of the enterprise. The architect can give expression to the required educational thought only if he or she is involved from the time at which the educational need is first conceived. Partnership between college, LEA and architect therefore is crucial. College staff are not here being encouraged to design their own buildings. It is hoped that the knowledge which they might acquire from reading this Section will assist them in design consultations, and not be used in an attempt to dictate a design. The users, providers, and designers of buildings will be extremely unwise if they do not work in partnership. Principals need to develop good, unambiguous professional relationships with clerks of works, LEA buildings officers, specialist engineering staffs of LEAs, and also to be scrupulous about channels of communication.

3. It can generally be said that as regards health and safety, it is the LEA's responsibility to ensure that the basic facilities of a building meet an adequate standard. The college has a responsibility to ensure that once facilities are provided they are not subject to abuse. An LEA must provide a college with smoke stop doors, but a college must ensure that they are not left propped open. However, the detailed health, safety and welfare investigation contained in this Section (and also in Section **11.10**) remains highly necessary since the law surrounding its provision is remarkably complex. There is arguably an urgent need for regulations specifically for education to be made under the Health and Safety at Work etc. Act. The answers to simple questions concerning welfare provision are not always easily answered. Detailed investigation has therefore been necessary – and even then there are questions which cannot be clearly resolved. There is a tendency at times for individuals to wish to establish absolute standards: to have laws which will provide an answer. In a largely discretionary system, such as that of further education premises provision, this is unattainable, and, given the need of the service to be flexible and responsive to change,

not always wholly desirable. If provision is demonstrably inadequate, there are routes to legal recourse, or to a requirement that conditions are improved.

4. Many of the standards cited below relate to new buildings, and to buildings extensions. In existing buildings – many of which will have been converted from other purposes as a college expanded – it is almost certain that provision will not match all current standards. Standards will have risen since the building was designed, or been affected by *ad hoc* alterations. In other instances, standards themselves are out of date. In either event the route to improvement is not easy. Legal questions concerning reasonable practicability (the balance of cost against the likelihood of injury) have to be encountered. In a time of public expenditure cuts, finance for buildings is inevitably affected. However, there are two items which must be given prominence. They can be expressed in simple terms: more students require more facilities – as a college's intake rises, it will have to provide more lavatories and cloakrooms. The matter of energy conservation is urgent and vital (see Section **5.4**). An energy conservation programme in a college will very probably require alterations being made to existing buildings, and therefore regard will have to be paid to the relevant standards.

5. There is a grey area, which requires some discussion, even though little immediate comfort might be drawn. Some further education provision, particularly adult education, requires the use of premises which are not always those of a college. Many adult education classes are held in school buildings. Such classes are held under The Further Education Regulations. (The Standards for School Premises Regulations are unspecific about practically everything that might affect dual or multiple use). However, simple practical problems highlight the difficulties: a school's heating system may be operated on a time cycle set to supply no heat after 3.30pm. By 8pm in winter, the adult class may have to be abandoned. Further, in rural areas, for example, adult classes may have to be held on primary school premises – and may therefore may be subject to the inconveniences, for their purposes, of small desks and tables, or open plan learning areas. Resolution may or may not be simple, requiring at least liaison between college, adult institute, school and LEA. The same principle applies, however, in the use of a building. The problems encountered in daily use are often capable of easy resolution, but as they may involve considerations of cost and welfare, it is important that procedures are known to all involved.

2 PROCEDURES FOR EDUCATIONAL BUILDING[1]

NB: This sub-section should be read in conjunction with Section **3.**10-11.

1. Although it is the wish and policy of the DES and Welsh Office to leave many decisions concerning the use of their building allocation sums to the local authorities, restrictions have also to be operated in order to satisfy the wish of government to control and regulate public expenditure and public capital investment. National capital allocations (ie normally, permissions to raise loans) are made for building programmes undertaken at colleges. Within this allocation, authorisation is necessary for individual projects. Each year local authorities are asked to submit proposals for the addition of new capital building projects.

2. Building projects are divided into major and minor. A major project is one costing £120,000 or more, and a minor project is one costing less than that amount. This figure is subject to review. All major projects have to be submitted to the DES or Welsh Office Education Department at the stage of tender, and by that stage will have already had to have found a place within an approved programme. No other formal approval is required but it is expected that there will be consultation with an authority throughout the planning stages. The Departments' role is to approve LEA projects, not to fund them directly. Resources are not allocated separately for minor works except in Wales. Within their lump sum allocations, authorities have discretion to carry out such minor works at they think fit. In the case of voluntary colleges the minor works limit continues to apply but there are circumstances in which, because of the more direct financial involvement of the DES, approval is required for expenditure below this limit. In Wales, a regional allocation (based on the total number of students in further education institutions) is made and distributed annually for specific projects by the Welsh Office Education Department: bids for minor works allocations are invited from local education authorities and voluntary bodies.

3. Both the DES and Welsh Office have the right to disallow an individual project at tender stage on cost grounds in cases where their consent is necessary. However, it is the aim of both bodies to ensure that formal approval processes can be operated easily and efficiently by means of close liaison with authorities and providing bodies during the preparatory stages.

4. The planning of building is subject to a three stage "rolling programme." This programme has been subject to "a degree of flexibility" in previous

---

1 At the time of writing the Government had indicated a wish to make alterations in the procedures. The alterations suggested were the removal of equipment controls, and some streamlining of approvals for the design of individual building projects.

years but it is the wish of the DES to revert more strictly to the procedures.[2] The programme stages for major projects are: Provisional, Planning and Final. Allocations are made (either as lump sums or for specific projects) and may be adjusted at each stage. Final allocations represent the totals within which the cost of building work must be contained, and are not then subject to further increase because of a rise in costs. Such cost rises have to be taken account of in the final allocation. Allowances are added for abnormal building costs, however, within allocations.

5. The Provisional List is a register open to the admission of new major projects at any time. It is not related to a commencement in any particular year. New and revised projects are normally requested for provisional listing some two to three years ahead. The Provisional List consists of projects put forward by authorities and voluntary bodies agreed by the Department as suitable to start in about five years. As soon as the project is given sufficient definition, a provisional financial allocation is decided should the project be admitted to the list.

6. The Planning List is established each autumn and consists of projects which authorities wish to start in the financial year beginning some 18 months ahead. Provisional List projects sufficiently advanced in planning are eligible to transfer, according to resource availability, to the Planning List. The DES asks bodies with provisionally listed projects whether they wish them to be considered for Planning List inclusion. After priorities have been discussed, the DES makes a final selection. The Planning List is finalised by the year in which the projects are intended to commence.

7. The Final List of "starts" from Planning List projects is drawn up from projects ready to commence and which can be accommodated within governmental financial allocation. The drawing up of the Final List takes place in consultation with authorities and providing bodies six months before the beginning of the year in which a start is to be made. To facilitate early decisions and enable allocations to be fully used, it is then necessary for detailed planning to be well advanced and for the DES to be informed of changes in cost estimates.

8. In the case of minor works in England, authorities are informed of the total figure allocated. The sum is then distributed as part of the lump sum authorisations with regard to the numbers of students in their maintained establishments of further education. The authority decides what proportion of the allocation it wishes to devote to FE minor works. Although authorities are free to spend within these authorised allocations, minor works are monitored as a check on the size of the national allocation.

---

2 The "flexibility" has been caused by stop-go government financial policies. The capital programme can be used as a particularly blunt fiscal instrument, resulting in either sudden, savage cuts, or unexpected generosity. Under circumstances suitable to itself, the Treasury appears at times to commit the error of accounting capital along with recurrent expenditure. The result has been an uneven operation of the rolling programme. The information above, therefore, represents what the DES *intends* now to occur. If this should not obtain, it is likely that the stages will operate thus: Provisional; Final; and actual starts.

9. Special arrangements may be made whereby, because a cost threshold is only marginally exceeded, a low cost major work may be given an accelerated passage through the rolling programme. The DES and Welsh Office will offer assistance and guidance on this and other matters relating to building progammes. In some circumstances the regulations concerning building allocations can be circumvented by authorities or institutions who enter into leasing arrangements with a property or financial institution (see also Section **3.**40).

10. It is important to note that within the further education arrangements, allocations are given for higher education on specific notification of work. In October 1979, the Government issued a consultative document proposing some quite radical changes in its control of local authority capital expenditure on education and most other services. The proposals, which were the subject of lively debate as this book went to press, would produce block allocations except for some higher education projects and would, at least in theory, give LEAs more discretion over the use of capital resources. The expenditure control would be based on an assessment of actual expenditure incurred and not on, as now, the rather misleading records of "starts".

11. Buildings are designed by architects from a brief given to them by local authority education departments, or providing bodies, and colleges. Because most new buildings both now and in the foreseeable future consists of extensions rather than whole new colleges, there exist real opportunities for design improvement since the clients are fully available for consultation. A great deal of design consideration will be given to teaching demands. Understandably, the teaching profession is not widely acquainted with items such as space provision. The sub-section below dealing with construction standards and environmental and welfare provision may well be of some assistance in this respect. It may be useful here, however, to give an indication of areas in which experience has demonstrated that difficulties can arise.

12. In the matter of extensions, it is important to consider time scales. Whatever the nature of the project, whether major or minor, it can be assumed that there will be a queue at either or both the Department or local authority. There has been an inclination by some colleges to keep their plans to themselves for too long. To expedite matters, it is better to avoid delays at any of the formal approval stages. Therefore, the project should be considered some time well ahead. College and LEA should together determine requirements. This is especially relevant for cost and design considerations. It will then be appropriate to commence discussions with the college HMI (since that person in the first instance advises the DES or Welsh Office) where the expenditure is to be large. It should be noted that HMI advice concerning approval and priorities is often crucial. In the matter of liaison, it is vital for there to be close contact with whichever bodies control the building programme. The list here can be long, and will include: architects, local authority technical services departments, the assistant director for buildings, and the education committee. In some cases, there may be a need to consult the Department of the Environment. Normally, the

LEA officers will undertake the necessary consultation, but colleges need to be aware of the multiplicity of time lags which occur at each stage.

13. It can be generally stated that authorities tend to alter facilities or extend them where there is a demand. This observation is especially relevant to such matters as the provision of facilities for the disabled. Any extension of premises to cope with increasing demand will require increased cloakroom and lavatory provision.

14. Great danger can be caused by unauthorised extensions. The temptation exists to provide facilities where, because of a lack of money, official approval cannot be gained. Such action, however, renders the college liable to a variety of penalties if the facilities are unsafe or contravene regulations or advice. In the same way, it has been found in some cases that dangers and hazards in buildings arise more often from abuse and unauthorised alterations than from design faults. Even though a college may possess personnel with high qualifications and expertise in a particular area, it will be a fortunate institution indeed which possesses specialists capable of encompassing all aspects of any structural and use problem. And even where college staff are better qualified than their LEA counterparts, which they may well be, it remains improper for teaching staff to carry out adaptations without permission. This observation extends to unauthorised use of student labour.

15. In general, therefore, colleges must seek the assistance of their local authority and their HMI. There is one problem, however, to which it is appropriate to draw attention. The advent of tertiary colleges in some areas presents difficulties: it will have to be determined exactly whether they fall under The Standards for School Premises Regulations or whether they fall under the looser further education arrangements. For schools, the standards are relatively detailed, but in FE there are no specific regulations. It will be necessary to ensure that where *ad hoc* arrangements are made, close attention is paid to the possible consequences. In general, however, tertiary colleges are set up under The Further Education Regulations, the reason being that whereas all maintained school teachers are qualified to teach in FE, not all further education teachers are qualified to teach in schools.

16. Details concerning costing and certain of the Departments' requirements will be found in *Notes on Procedure For The Approval of Further Education Projects (Other than Polytechnics)* DES/Welsh Education Office, 1972 and *Notes on Procedure For The Approval of Polytechnic Projects,* DES. However both these publications are out of print and are expected to be revised shortly. A guide to certain of their provisions is contained in Section **5.3** below.

17. The White Paper, *The Government's Expenditure Plans, 1980-81,* stated that building programmes for further and higher education would be reduced by about half.

REFERENCE

Educational Building After 1975-75, DES Circular 13/74; Welsh Office Circular 281/74, 31 December 1974.
Education Building in 1976-77 and 1977-78, DES Circular 16/76; Welsh Office Circular 193/76, 23 December 1976.
Notes on Procedure For The Approval of Further Education Projects (Other than Polytechnics), DES/Welsh Education Office, 1972.
Notes on Procedure For The Approval of Polytechnic Projects, DES.
The Government's Expenditure Plans 1980-81, Cmnd. 7746, HMSO.

3 CONSTRUCTION, ACCOMMODATION AND DESIGN STANDARDS: ENVIRONMENTAL AND WELFARE PROVISION

NB: This sub-section should be read in conjunction with Sections **5.5** and **11.10.**

1. It is regrettable that a legalistic approach has to be adopted in this sub-section. The main purpose in the designing of educational buildings is to provide efficient and agreeable environments for teaching and learning. The discussion below is not intended to undervalue that essential purpose. However, concerns and possible interpretations relating to health and safety legislation demand a significant degree of legalistic discussion. As might perhaps be expected, the issue of construction and design provision is not simple. Although most new buildings in England and Wales are subject to building regulations, college buildings are not; because constructions for Crown purposes, including maintained institutions of education, and undertakings required by statute are exempt. This situation will apply until the provisions of the Health and Safety at Work etc. Act concerning the extension of the building regulations to education are brought into force by statutory instrument. The Standards for School Premises Regulations do not apply to colleges. Construction and design standards for all colleges are recommended by the DES via administrative memoranda, procedural notes, building bulletins and design notes. Among these standards are those intended to achieve at least uniformity with all new building subject to building regulations. The Building (First Amendment) Regulations 1978 came into force on 1 June 1979. The latest DES advice aims to achieve at least conformity with these regulations.

2. The legal position is complex. Colleges are subject in the matter of buildings to a variety of statutory provisions, among which are the Public Health Acts, Gas Act, and the Offices, Shops and Railway Premises Act. Each of these Acts, *inter alia,* has a direct application in certain circumstances. Such relevant law is discussed elsewhere in this Section of the book. Detailed examination of the Health and Safety at Work etc. Act is found under Section **11.10.** Reference to that Section ought to be made, but in summary it can be stated that, for college purposes, where statutory regulations do not exist reference must then be made to relevant codes of practice and other advice. Although it is a matter for the courts ultimately to determine, it may be generally held that good cause would have to be shown why relevant advice was not followed where it is considered that duties under the Health and Safety at Work etc. Act were not fulfilled. This would involve the question of reasonable practicability where the determinant is that of cost balanced against the likelihood of injury. It is unfortunate therefore that whereas DES recommended standards have risen, and in many instances are higher than statute, cost provision has not for building programme allocations have been subject to governmental restraint on public expenditure.

3. General statutory provision concerning college premises is made by The Further Education Regulations 1975. However, all that the regulations require is that "effective and suitable provision" should be made, particularly regarding: lighting, heating, sanitation and ventilation; the safeguarding against danger from fire and accident; the maintaining of the premises in good repair and their cleanliness; and the equipment of the premises. The approval of the Secretary of State is necessary for the provision of new premises and the alteration of existing premises, as well as the purchase of equipment costing above a certain amount. The reason for this general statutory requirement only is that whereas authorities have a duty to make arrangements for schools, provision of further and higher education is largely discretionary. The burden, therefore, of ensuring satisfactory standards in premises which are provided by discretion falls on the provider. That education has been included in the scope of the Health and Safety at Work etc. Act means that further education is subject to general duties, and to such standards as are relevant; but it is difficult in many cases to state what those standards are, except where imposed by other statute, such as the Factories Act. DES advice on standards, therefore, ought not to be lightly ignored, although this norm will in practice be varied according to the circumstance of a college, its use, and the nature of the courses which it operates.

4. As it is hardly likely that the Standards for School Premises Regulations would be held by a court to apply under the Health and Safety at Work etc. Act, the only recourse in certain instances is to turn to DES documents originally provided for other purposes, such as costing, to obtain what a court may hold to be "standards" or "codes". This sub-section therefore has to deal with design and environmental matters in two ways: in giving general guidance on certain design matters, it is also necessary to provide – in default of any other published guidance on the matter – information in some detail where design and costing criteria have a health, safety, and welfare importance. It is only by such investigation that any meaning can be given to the duty imposed on employers by the Act to ensure the health, safety and welfare of their employees.

5. The Department requests in its Administrative Memorandum 2/79 that certain standards are applied by local authorities to all educational projects commencing on or after 1 June 1979.[1] These standards do not apply to the Inner London Education Authority because it is subject to certain Acts concerning the government of London. The DES is monitoring compliance with its standards so that it may consider the implications of bringing educational building within comprehensive national standards. The DES constructional standards for educational buildings which are identical with the Building Regulations are in: materials, preparation of site and resistance to moisture, structural stability, chimneys and flues, heat-producing

1 *Constructional Standards for Maintained and Direct Grant Educational Building in England.* DES Administrative Memorandum 2/79, 9 February 1979. Constructional standards in Wales are outlined in Welsh Office Administrative Memorandum 3/79 and do not differ significantly from the English arrangements.

appliances and incinerators, drainage, and sanitary conveniences. Some environmental provision – which may be construed as being relevant to welfare under the Health and Safety at Work etc. Act – is made by Design Note 17, *Guidelines for Environmental Design and Fuel Conservation in Educational Buildings.* This publication deals with acoustics, lighting, and the thermal environment, and contains examples of energy consumption and costs. The main recommendations are summarised below. The recommendations constitute standards to be achieved and while intended for new buildings are suggested as providing a framework for the improvement of existing buildings, subject to considerations of cost.

6. **Acoustics**

The acoustics of a building should be such that clear audibility is achieved where required, and that noise emanating from other parts of the building ought not to obtrude. It is necessary to plan to avoid noise interference: noise creation activities should be separated in a college where possible from areas requiring quiet. The DES recommends that consideration be given to noise control within a college and to the reduction of external noise by ensuring that noises from all sources in each unoccupied space should not be greater than specified Background Noise Levels (BNL). The maximum Background Noise Levels recommended are:- [2]

Type of Space	*BNL*
Music and Drama	25
Teaching groups of more than 35 persons with a communication distance of over 8m	
Large lecture rooms	
Language Laboratories	30
Teaching groups of between 15 and 35 persons with a communication distance of not more than 8m	
Small lecture rooms	
Presentation rooms	
Offices	
Medical inspection rooms	
Seminar rooms	35
Teaching groups of less than 15 people with a communication distance of not more than 4m	

2 This table is taken from *Guidelines For Environmental Design and Fuel Conservation in Educational Buildings,* DES Architects and Buildings Branch Design Note 17, DES, 1979, p.3. BNLs are the desirable levels which the octave band decibel – level values of noise measurement should come as close as possible to meeting, ± 2.5 decibels.

Sports Halls (subject to the requirements of multiple use)

Resource areas

Libraries

Individual study areas (where a large area contains a number of small groups)

Practical areas

Workshops where equipment is not in use 45

7. There are also standards concerning room volume and optimum reverberation time. A detailed explanation of both calculation methods and criteria will be found in *Acoustics in Educational Buildings*, Building Bulletin 51, HMSO. 1975.

8. **Lighting**
Wherever appropriate maximum use should be made of daylight. All teaching spaces should possess a window area of at least 20% of the internal elevation of the external wall. The window should give a satisfactory external view and allow minimal use of electric light by giving maximum uniformity and penetration of daylight. The DES recommends that the lowest illumination level on a working surface should not be less than 150 lux (and if fluorescent lighting is used, not less than 300 lux). The Glare Index for electric lighting in teaching spaces should not be more than 19. These lighting standards refer to those of the Illuminating Engineering Society (IES).[3] IES standards are generally used because statutory lighting standards are out of date. It is appropriate here therefore to refer in greater detail to IES standards but it must be remembered that while these standards represent a code relevant, if so determined by a court, under the Health and Safety at Work etc. Act that the test of reasonable practicability will apply. IES standards in four situations perhaps relevant to colleges but not quoted by the DES Design Note are:

Machine shops :	rough work and assembly	300 lux
	medium bench and machine work	500 lux
	fine bench and machine work	1000 lux
Office work :	general	500 lux
	more detailed work	750 lux
	very fine work	1000 lux
Stores and warehouses :	rough work	150 lux
	medium work	300 lux
Entrance halls		200 lux

3 *Code of Interior Lighting Design*, Illuminating Engineering Society, 1977.

9. To give an indication of measured light strength, the amount of light outside on a day in the middle of winter may be up to 10,000 lux, and on a dull day in summer between roughly 30,000 and 40,000 lux. In some cases reference may be made to "lumens". These metric terms are used instead of the former foot candles.
1 lux = 1 lumen/m^2.

10. In general, the DES recommends for college purposes that the level of lighting should not be less than 300 lux, and that where lighting schemes combine the use of daylight and electric light, the lowest level should be not less than 350 lux. As electric lighting may account for up to between 30% and 40% of a college's annual fuel consumption, it is worth noting that fluorescent lighting is more economical than tungsten.

11. **Thermal environment**
The DES recommends various resultant temperatures in the following situations,[4] subject to a maximum temperature swing of within 2°C:

(i) where persons are lightly clad and inactive, for example in medical inspection rooms. 21°C

(ii) where clothing and activity are average, such as in classrooms 18°C

(iii) in dormitory accommodation 15°C

(iv) where persons are lightly clad and engaged in vigorous activity 14°C

12. The heating system should be such as to be able to heat a minimum of 10m^3 of fresh air per hour whilst the above circumstances and activities occur. The ventilation rate is that of 30m^3 of fresh air per hour for each person normally so engaged, although it may be higher to ensure comfortable conditions.

13. The DES also recommends that when dealing with ventilation there should be adequate measures taken for the prevention of condensation and removal of noxious fumes from every kitchen and other rooms where such conditions might prevail. At least six changes of air per hour should be achieved.

14. Guards or screens should be provided where an accessible metal surface is likely to have a temperature greater than 43°C.

15. Subject to a swing of not more than 4°C at the high level, resultant temperatures in all spaces should be 23°C during the summer. A temperature in excess of 27°C for a ten day period in the summer is considered by the DES in design matters to be a reasonable predictive (ie, acceptable) risk.

---

4 These temperatures are to be maintained at a height of 0.5m above floor level during normal occupation hours where the normal external design temperature is – 1°C. This "normal" temperature will be subject to modification according to the conditions prevailing in different parts of the country.

16. **Accommodation provision**

The DES advice concerning accommodation provision for colleges other than as instanced above is contained in four publications: *Notes On Procedure For The Approval Of Further Education Projects (Other Than Polytechnics); Notes On Procedure For The Approval of Polytechnic Projects; Designing For Further Education,* Design Note 9; and *Polytechnics: Planning For Development,* Design Note 8. In the case of the procedural *Notes,* they are currently out of print and are expected to be fully revised shortly. The Design Notes are largely general. Both sets of publications predate The Further Education Regulations 1975, which required only that "effective and suitable provision" should be made. It is thus impossible to give up-to-date advice, or to suggest remedial legal measures except where the accommodation provision constitutes a danger to health or a serious injury risk. While it may be safest to assume that local authority architects are well aware of their business and are not in the habit of providing accommodation which is not effective or suitable, in the case of teaching and teaching-related accommodation in older buildings or where there has been a change of use, suitability tests will ultimately depend upon circumstance. To provide assistance in determining that circumstance, some guidance to the DES publications already quoted is given below, *although it must be noted that most provisions are intended to apply to new buildings and extensions.* Significant features only are identified. Colleges will normally ask the LEA architect, surveyor, or director of works to inspect newly acquired old properties, and to certify their suitability for use. The college will need to be clear about the kinds of use it requires.

17. In the matter of accommodation area recommendations, the figures are drawn from DES recommendations for the costing of major projects. The purpose of including them here, apart from the costing relevance, is that in default of any other precise recommendations concerning dimensions and therefore the facilities which can be provided, they could be held to have a welfare relevance at law.

18. *Teaching area: further education other than polytechnics*

In assessing teaching area, it is assumed that colleges are open for 40 hours a week for day-time use and that utilization levels (see Section **5.8.**4) will be at optima 80% and 70% for non-specialised and specialised accommodation respectively. Therefore, spatial accommodation should be according to the correct utilization rate, and not related to actual student numbers as represented by FTEs (full-time equivalent students). The accommodation is then grouped into non-specialised and specialised and workshop accommodation areas. The 1971 recommended usable areas were:

Accommodation Type	*Usable area (m^2/Working space)*
Non-specialised	
Teaching/tutorial rooms with informal seating	1.85
Teaching rooms with tables/desks	2.3
Teaching rooms with demonstration facilities	2.5
Lecture theatres and rooms with close seating	1.0
Drawing offices using A1 and smaller boards	3.7
Drawing offices using A0 and larger boards	4.6

Area so calculated includes space for the teacher and demonstration facilities.

Specialised and Workshop

Laboratories	: advanced science and engineering	5.6
	: non-advanced science and engineering	4.6
Management and business studies :	work study	4.6
	typewriting	3.2
	accountancy	2.8
Workshops :	crafts involving large scale machinery/ equipment	8.4
	crafts requiring work benches and smaller scale machinery/equipment	5.6
Craft rooms:		5.6

19. In the case of non-specialised accommodation, the areas calculated include space for the teacher and demonstration facilities. It is expected that variations will occur according to circumstance and course in the specialised and workshop categories, especially where accommodation is shared between departments, where multiple use accommodation is provided, and where space utilization is fully implemented.

20. Storage space and rooms, and preparation and service room areas are calculated roughly as a percentage addition to the teaching room area. These rough additions are:

Geography rooms; language laboratory; boardwork room; work study:	10%
Non-advanced science; radio and TV service laboratories; machine workshops; typewriting and accounts rooms:	15%
Craft room and electrical workshops:	20%
Advanced science and engineering; motor vehicle; brickwork and plumbing workshops:	25%
Carpentry and joinery workshops:	30%
Hairdressing salon; laundry and reception areas	40%

21. *Non-teaching areas: further education other than polytechnics*

Area allowances are made according to the number of full-time equivalent students for whom the accommodation is intended. Evening students are discounted from this calculation because the DES bases its utilization calculations on day time college use. FTEs are here calculated as: one each for full-time and sandwich students; two ninths for part-time day students; one third for block release students. The usable areas according to type of accommodation then are as follows.

22. Libraries in colleges with at least 30% advanced work: 390m^2 for the first

500 FTE students, and $0.44m^2$ for each additional FTE student. Libraries in colleges with less than 30% advanced work: $300m^2$ for the first 500 FTE students, and $0.38m^2$ for each additional FTE student. These allowances are intended to allow full library services and one reader's seat to every eight FTE students. It might be noted that these are high standards. Colleges may find that their libraries are able reasonably to function with less floorspace, albeit short of the ideal.

23. Administrative accommodation is calculated (including storage space, for which up to 15% should be given within the allowance) on a graduated scale:

FTEs	*Usable Area in m^2*
500 or fewer	255
1,000	330
1,500	395
2,000	450
2,500	495
3,000	530
3,500	560
4,000	585
above 4,000	For every 500 FTEs add $25m^2$

24. Academic staff workroom provision attracts a separate allowance of $0.36m^2$/FTE student. This allowance does not extend to heads of department as their offices are categorised as administrative accommodation. It is insufficient to allow each staff member her or his own room but, by room sharing in some cases, individual accommodation will be made available for others.

25. Non-academic staff attached to departments have a workroom recommended allowance equivalent to $0.2m^2$/FTE student.

26. Communal accommodation[5] allowance may be supplemented by $0.5m^2$ allowance for each full-time and sandwich student. The basic allowances are:

FTEs	*Usable area in m^2*
500 or fewer	590
1000	840
1500	1020
2000	1140
2500	1250
3000	1350
3500	1430
4000	1500
above 4000	For every 500 FTEs add $25m^2$

---

5 Communal accommodation has a wide definition, and includes: physical recreation spaces, with changing rooms (which in a school would be accounted as teaching area); staff and student common rooms; committee rooms; rooms used for recreation; and storage for any of these rooms.

27. Catering accommodation is subject to great variability in that size depends on demand, the presence of alternative facilities and the type of service offered. The graduated DES scale below therefore is no more than a basic guide.

FTEs taking meals	*Usable area in* m^2
500 or fewer	310
1000	555
1500	785
2000	1000
above 2000	For every 500 FTEs add 210m^2

28. The usable area – the sum of the types of accommodation instanced above – is then increased by what is known as the balance area. The balance area includes: corridors, stairs, entrance foyer, and access to the main offices' inquiry counter; cloakrooms, locker space and lavatories; cleaners' and gardener's stores; maintenance workshops; boiler house; plant room and service ducts; electricity sub-station and meter room; general delivery bay; and porters' rooms where these are not part of the administrative accommodation allowance. It will be seen therefore that even by using costing guidance, it is not possible to arrive at precise information on serious matters such as the provision of lavatories and washing facilities in areas of a college where the Factories Act and Offices, Shops and Railway Premises Act do not apply. Presumably, no college's provision would be such as to lead to action by a public health inspector but in older buildings especially – and where buildings are extended – it will be a matter for the authority, college administrators and safety representatives seriously to bear in mind. The balance area allowances are:

Type of accommodation	*Balance as % of usable area*
Teaching other than workshops	40
Workshops	25
Library	25
Administrative accommodation	50
Academic staff workroom	50
Non-academic staff workroom	40
Communal	30
Catering	25

29. The DES recommends that car parking facilities should be provided only outside the building and on the surface of the site at a scale of one car space per ten FTE students. There are cost limitations to this provision. Where circumstances are such that a car park has to be provided under or within the building, the recommended scale including spaces provided on the site surface is not to exceed one car space per 300 FTE students. Five motor cycles are to occupy one car space, and do not attract extra allowances. No allowance is made in the DES formula for deliveries or bicycle storage.

30. *Teaching and non-teaching areas: polytechnics*
Area allocations are the same as for further education, except where instanced below:

31. In specialised accommodation, greater allowances may be made in subject areas not treated separately under the further education recommendations. For example, mathematics is allotted $5.3m^2$ in usable area, and a management suite $5.1m^2$.

32. According to circumstances, library provision may be up to an area of $1.29m^2$ per FTE student.

33. Administrative accommodation is allotted at $0.44m^2$ per FTE student for the first 3000, and thereafter at the rate of $0.36m^2$ per FTE student.

34. Academic staff workrooms allowance is determined at the rate of $0.69m^2$ per FTE student. Usable area for communal accommodation is calculated at $1.65m^2$ per FTE student. Non-academic staff workroom allowances are determined at two rates: $0.5m^2$ per FTE student for technicians, clerical and administrative staff in science and technology departments, and $0.3m^2$ per FTE student for staff in other departments.

35. Allowances for research space are made for polytechnics on the presumption that provision will be made for 50% of the staff. Humanities academic staff are allotted $0.29m^2$ per FTE student; and science, technology and art and design staff $0.58m^2$ per FTE student.

36. **DES design advice**
The DES acknowledges that while its procedural *Notes* determine prescribed cost limits, the area encompassed by the whole college (within those cost limits) represents the total provision for the time spent in a college by staff and students. The Department recognises that how this provision is best divided cannot be subject to particular rules as the determination will depend on the circumstances of the college. There is therefore great flexibility within the cost breakdown. The purpose of the Design Notes 8 and 9 is to put forward some general conclusions and questions of design for further education and polytechnics. Very few prescriptions are made. A summary of significant matters is provided below.

37. *Further Education*
In making design provision and use projection the DES accepts that colleges are subject to an inevitable and often unpredictable pattern of growth and change. This can be mitigated by planning which takes account of local circumstance – for example, potential industrial growth or decline. There should be the greatest possible intensity of use, and provision which in both costing and use allows the maximum possible overlap, interchange and virement between different categories of accommodation. Not only may student numbers change, but the types of course which are likely to grow and be developed must be considered.

38. In attaining the economical use of a site, where there is a design choice, the Department recommends in an urban area a ratio of floor area to site area "of, say, 1:1 and 1.5:1", subject to town planning considerations. Compact layout is recommended as it allows easy communication, the development of possibilities of accommodation interchange, and promotes homogeneity in the student body. Consideration is advised in the siting of workshops: single storey construction does not make economical use of the site: the floor loading problems associated with multi-storey sites are only avoided where workshops are on the ground floor. Good landscaping gives a high amenity value in proportion to its cost. The DES recommends that car parking space should be adequate to meet the needs of essential users, but that it should also be considered as part of the total parking and traffic problem of its locality: colleges and authorities may, for example, jointly operate some separate fee paying facility.

39. The DES recommends that accommodation should be looked at as a whole: little, if any, general teaching space need have departmental allocation. Communal accommodation should be easily accessible. There should be the maximum sharing of facilities. Flexibility should be such as to allow maximum future alteration at minimum cost. Distinct provision in teaching accommodation has to be provided for: art and design, business and administration, chemistry and biology, physics and mathematics, construction, electrical engineering, and mechanical, civil and production engineering. Design Note 9 here makes few recommendations but contains observations on several issues.

40. In its recommendations for administrative accommodation the Department advises that: the college layout should be displayed at the main entrance, and clear and consistent signposting provided; the offices of the principal, principal's secretary and registrar, and a committee room should be readily accessible to visitors; the main office should occupy a central position; and that except where secretarial services are shared, departmental offices should be closely associated with their departments. Staff workrooms should contain desks, paper storage and filing facilities. There should be "some provision" of first aid and rest room facilities. The library should be accessible and, where it is to be used by the public, easily accessible from outside. Full consideration needs to be given to the consequences of the library's nature and potential types of use.

41. The DES recommends that a college's social aims should be determined before any assessment of its communal accommodation needs. Central provision will generally be appropriate in colleges with up to 3000 FTEs, although this will have to be balanced against educational needs where teaching is to take place in less formal settings. Any central provision is to be readily accessible from all parts of the college. Although both staff and students will probably require some exclusively reserved space, the DES states that it "would be unreasonable for it to cover the whole range of provision." Clear social focal points are useful – for example, for notice display – and there should be a quiet area. The DES considers that there is evidence sufficient to show that maintenance and cleaning staff require their

own rest rooms, and that such accommodation should be near to their place of work and allow them to have refreshments. It is important to remember that maintenance staff can here include persons not employed at the college, such as local authority direct labour employees, and staff employed by contractors.

42. In determining catering accommodation, demand has to be estimated. This estimate has to recognise the total number likely to use the facilities, and the kind of facilities they are likely to require. There is evidence to show that many students prefer a cooked snack to a full lunch, and that many require even less substantial comestibles. The DES considers that the arguments against staggered lunch breaks have to be particularly strong to justify the large extra accommodation cost. Catering and communal accommodation may overlap. The remainder of the DES catering advice deals only with generalities, a circumstance entirely understandable given that it is primarily for design purposes and pre-dates the Health and Safety at Work etc. Act. Reference on particular health and safety matters will have to be made to the Food Hygiene Regulations (see Section **5.5.** 4-10) but the DES general advice where it touches upon this context is worth noting:

(i) there must be adequate access to the catering facilities for staff, customers, incoming goods and waste disposal;
(ii) food storage and preparation techniques should be suitable for the number and types of meals to be provided; and
(iii) catering staff should have good working conditions, including adequate cloakroom and office facilities.

43. Matters of building design recommended by the DES relevant to health and safety matters not dealt with elsewhere in this sub-section are:-

(i) a room height of about three metres is adequate for most activities (art and design may need up to five metres);
(ii) rooms which are more than six metres deep from an external wall require permanent supplementary artificial lighting, and may require supplementary mechanical ventilation;
(iii) vibration problems caused by machinery can be reduced by damping, using suitable mountings;
(iv) suitable grades of PVC or linoleum with continuous surfaces which reduce water penetration, and are not subject to high polishing or cleaning which creates slipperiness, are considered normally acceptable as floor coverings;
(v) building users should be supplied with specific maintenance guidance (appropriate to their college function);
(vi) rubbish chute locations should be checked with the fire officer, screened areas provided where rubbish awaits disposal, and the relevant statutes observed when dealing with waste disposal;
(vii) fume cupboard extraction should be regarded in design as part of the ventilation system,[6] and "it should be axiomatic" for an extract fan to be positioned near to its discharge vent;

6 This somewhat loose advice does *not* mean that fume cupboard extraction should be linked directly to the general college ventilation system.

(viii) the electricity distribution system should be easily adaptable, have full maintenance instructions, have special screening cages where appropriate in certain radio and electronics laboratories, and there must be care taken in the ventilation, storage, acid use, overnight charging and transporting where portable battery supplies are used;

(ix) there should be careful definition of any environmental control which may be necessary for certain equipment and experiments;

(x) storage facilities offering "some degree of security" (such as lockers and lockable clothing racks) should be available for students and of sufficient size to store clothing briefcases and crash helmets (see also Section **5.7.**11-13 and **5.5.**15);

(xi) laboratory worktop heights of about 850mm are suitable, as are surfaces of about 700mm for written work, and;

(xii) laboratory storage should be arranged in its own part of the laboratory space.

44. Further reference to DES safety advice which may be relevant under the Health and Safety at Work etc. Act is obtainable from the DES Safety Series, Nos. 2-5. These documents are not summarised here. One purpose of the foregoing investigation was to bring to attention certain advice which may be determined by the courts as constituting "standards" or "codes" relevant under the Act and which may be seen especially in the context of welfare, for which a general duty is imposed on every employer, as the only available DES source of reference. Details concerning the provision in design made for students will be relevant to the student's employer where he or she is required to ensure for block release students that adequate arrangements under the Act have been made.

45. *Polytechnics*

DES advice in Design Note 8 follows the broad theme of its further education advice. There are few exact recommendations and therefore for the purposes of this publication there is little need to provide any summary. It will be useful however to note gross area recommendations, and the Department's recommendation headings for the drawing up of a development plan.

46. For the purposes of site planning only, the DES recommends the following approximate gross areas per FTE student, including balance area additions:

Subject	*Teaching area (m^2)*	*Non-teaching area (m^2)*
Arts and social sciences	6	7
Science and technology	9	7
Art and design below Dip AD	11	7
Art and design, Dip AD	18	7

47. In drawing up a development plan, the DES recommends procedure under the following heads: a forecast of the framework of academic development; the calculation of the total gross floor areas for teaching and non-teaching

activities likely in successive years; an assessment of current available gross area, including buildings under construction and those with a limited life; a determination of whether additional sites are needed, including car parking and residence, community and environmental criteria; the possible adjustment necessary to the academic development plan caused by difficulties in site acquisition; the planning of new buildings in a rational framework, including an assessment of FTE capacity; the co-ordination of finance, site acquisition and places in the building programme; and a plan review procedure which will allow adaptation where circumstances change.

48. Provision for the handicapped has not been mentioned in this sub-section but is dealt with under Section **12.11** below.Reference should also be made to: Selwyn Goldsmith, *Designing for the Disabled,* RIBA.

REFERENCE

The Building Regulations 1976, Statutory Instruments 1976 No. 1676, HMSO.

The Building (First Amendment) Regulations, Statutory Instruments 1978, No. 723, HMSO.

The Further Education Regulations 1975, Statutory Instruments 1975, No. 1054, HMSO.

The Health and Safety at Work etc. Act 1974, DES Circular 11/74, 6 November 1974.

Acoustics in Educational Buildings, DES Building Bulletin 51, 1975, HMSO.

Code For Interior Lighting Design, Illuminating Engineering Society, 1977.

Constructional Standards For Maintained and Direct Grant Educational Building in England, DES Administrative Memorandum 2/79, 9 February 1979.

Designing For Further Education, DES Architects and Building Branch Design Note 9, DES, 1972.

Guidelines For Environmental Design And Fuel Conservation in Educational Building, DES Architects and Building Branch Design Note 17, DES, 1979.

Notes On Procedure For The Approval Of Further Education Projects (Other Than Polytechnics), DES/Welsh Office, 1972.

Notes On Procedure For The Approval of Polytechnics Projects, DES.

Polytechnics: Planning For Development, DES Architects and Building Branch Design Note 8, DES, 1972.

Design Notes are available free of charge from:

Publications Despatch Centre, DES, Honeypot Lane, Canons Park, Stanmore, Middlesex.

4 ENERGY CONSERVATION

1. It is no exaggeration to state that energy conservation represents one of the most critical problems currently facing the country. As well as the wide issue of the nation's energy needs and consumption, the education service has also to face the simple practical issue that as the costs of energy rise, so budgetary considerations in an institution may result in there being less resources available for direct educational provision. Conservation measures in an institution may result in the present balances being maintained; but there may be circumstances whereby energy saving could release monies for other educational uses. It may also be the case that an LEA might wish to use such "saved" money for purposes other than education.

2. Resources have been allocated by the Department of Energy to local authorities for energy conservation measures in educational and other non-domestic buildings. These allocations, in later years, will, it is estimated, be recovered from the savings made; or else set against the amounts available for school building and FE minor works. However, the allocations also include some deductions from previously planned expenditure by way of enforced savings. The details will be settled within the context of the annual rate support grant negotiations and in actual capital allocations. Although it remains open to authorities to use their allocations (including additional provision for the employment and training of staff in energy matters) as they see fit, Government advice suggested that priority be given to heating control installation, insulation, and the better management of buildings.[1] It was expected that part of an authority's energy manager's job would be to advise principals on building management. Government estimates on energy saving suggested that improved management can result in an up to 20% saving, and heating controls result in a further saving of up to 15%.

3. It is important to realise when considering the real cost of a building that over a life span of, for example, 40 years, the total costs are approximately 20% to design and furnish and 80% to operate. Thus, despite the concentration in building programme decisions on the initial capital cost, it is appropriate to consider in the design of any new building or the adaptation of existing premises how the total operating cost can be reduced, even though that may entail incurring extra costs at the design and construction stages.

4. In a pilot monitoring scheme in a district of one authority, it was discovered that buildings ranged from 50% below target fuel consumption to over 900% above.[2] The over-consumption was not caused by mismanagement alone:

---

1 *Energy Conservation Measures,* Department of the Environment Circular 56/78; DES Circular 10/78; Welsh Office Circular 100/78, 24 August 1978.

2 Geoffrey Hamlyn, "Prospects for Change," *County Councils Gazette,* December 1978, pp.284-286.

much could be attributed to plant malfunction and faulty building design. When a good housekeeping campaign was implemented, fuel consumption dropped by 19.6% (£41,500). It is estimated that substantial improvement can be attained, and that at a conservative estimate at least 20% of the authority's fuel bill could be saved – representing over £600,000 at current prices. The authority exceptionally for a two year period decided to return the net savings from the fuel monitoring scheme to the relevant committees in order to assist their budgeting problems in a period of severe restraint. The lessons and potential opportunities for colleges are very plain. Few LEAs would wish to resist a practical offer from a college to save energy and to involve the students in the exercise. A campaign mounted without consulting the LEA, however, is less likely to result in the college receiving full benefit.

5. Fuel monitoring is required of authorities in any case in return for their resource allocation. It may well be that individual institutions will be required to furnish the authority with detailed fuel use information. Whether or not this is the case, it will be sensible for any institution in monitoring its fuel consumption to include information on the use of its buildings. This will include the total number of hours and days when the institution is open for normal use as well as special uses, including evening, social, weekend and vacation use. Full monitoring requires professional expertise and will usually be the responsibility of an LEA. Required data will include full details of construction, design and engineering; weather information; and fuel consumption as well as user information.

6. The legal position regarding buildings has been referred to above under Sections **1.3** and **5.3.** It will be remembered however that the advice of the DES as contained in its administrative memoranda, building bulletins and design notes is intended to obtain compliance with the Building Regulations. In the matter of fuel conservation, the relevant DES publications are: *Guidelines For Environmental Design And Fuel Conservation In Educational Buildings,* Design Note 17; and *Energy Conservation in Educational Buildings,* Building Bulletin 55. The purpose of the remainder of this sub-section is to provide a digest of the matters discussed. Much of the information contained in these DES publications is of a technical nature, and some of it will not be readily understood by laymen. Specific reference ought to be made to these publications, however. The items discussed below are intended to provide an introduction to the topic. It is appropriate to note in passing that the DES welcomes further comment, suggestions and information on successful methods of energy conservation.

7. The obvious aim is to save energy but this must be done in ways which are cost effective. Cost effectiveness is generally determined in the DES publications as being the ways by which any capital outlay is recouped within a short period. The riders must be added therefore that total cost provisions should be considered, and that cost effectiveness is subject to rapid change: fuel price increases will render further savings measures appropriate which previously were too expensive. Any conservation policy will also need to have regard to the purpose of the buildings: varied patterns of use and intermittent occupancy require consideration, and so do educational needs.

The object is to secure the lowest possible running costs compatible with the human and educational requirements.

8. **Good management**

It has been demonstrated above that good housekeeping can achieve dramatic savings. It also provides a quick return for little expenditure. Many authorities have issued advice regarding fuel saving by good management. Any advice will recognise that the nature of the building will largely dictate many conservation practices. The DES offers the following general advice:

9. *Teaching staff and students*

(i) As supplementary heaters, such as electric fires, are costly to run, they should be used only in exceptional circumstances, for example, during cold spells outside the normal heating season when the main heating system is not in use, or when a room is occupied after the main heating period.

(ii) Lights and electrical appliances should be switched off when no longer needed, and nor should lights be used in rooms with blinds or curtains after the need for such facilities has passed. The minimum necessary number of lights and appliances should be used when people are working late.

(iii) Heating systems should be adjusted when rooms become overheated during the heating season. Ventilation should be used only in exceptional circumstances and then at minimal levels. Excess ventilation will usually activate thermostats so that more heat is supplied.

(iv) Subject to the needs for hygiene and cleanliness, hot water should be used economically.

(v) Heat can be conserved overnight by up to 20% by preventing loss through windows if blinds and curtains are closed at dusk (or when it is clear that artificial lighting will be required for the rest of the working day). Maximum use should be made of daylight, for both lighting and heating purposes, by fully drawing back blinds and curtains during the day.

(vi) Clothing appropriate to the temperatures at which the institution is necessarily maintained ought to be worn.

(vii) Rooms should be allocated in such a way, where separate areas of a building can be heated independently, to allow economical use whereby heat and light are not supplied to unused areas.

(viii) Windows should be closed overnight, and external doors kept closed as much as possible during cold periods.

(ix) High power consumption equipment ought not to be used during the winter months in circumstances whereby the accumulation of other electrical demands will lead to loads in excess of the Maximum Demand Tariff (see paragraphs 11-12 below).

10. *Maintenance and caretaking staff*

(i) Thermostats should be set to provide the appropriate heat for the various uses of the premises.

(ii) Hot water thermostats should be set to the lowest acceptable temperature, not exceeding 40°C, and where warmer water is required, consideration should be given to the provision of "topping up" or a separate supply.

(iii) There should be immediate replacement of faulty washers, especially in hot taps.

(iv) Windows should be closed at night, and external doors kept shut as much as possible.

(v) Cleaners should be instructed to use lights sparingly, and to extinguish them when no longer required.

(vi) To avoid heating the whole building, rooms used for evening, weekend or vacation use should wherever possible be those which can be heated independently.

(vii) Although heating can usually be turned off before people have vacated a building, where automatic controls are not available to guard against weather damage, a temperature of about 5°C or 6°C (or higher if there is a serious condensation problem) will be necessary to afford protection against frost.

(viii) The times at which heating comes into operation will need to be varied: it should be started no earlier than is necessary to achieve normal working temperatures and consequently later during mild weather.

(ix) Plant maintenance is essential: boilers should be maintained in good working order and operated at their designed temperature; thermal insulation should be regularly checked; the heating load should be supplied by the minimum number of boilers; and boilers not in operation, where practicable, isolated from the heating system.

11. Electricity tariffs are a complex topic, but some brief explanation will be useful. There are twelve Electricity Boards serving different areas of the country. Each board operates its own practices and tariffs. Thus, although these are broadly similar, it will be necessary for a college itself to ascertain its particular position. Maximum Demand Tariffs are only a part of a range of tariffs. In general, the Maximum Demand Tariff will be the highest demand recorded in the premises in a month or a year, according to the particular rate at which an establishment is charged, and this will determine a part of the charge for the electricity used. The amount may be significant. To give examples, there is a rate charged by the London Electricity Board which comprises a demand charge and a unit charge: the demand charge consists of the maximum demand which has occurred over a twelve month period; and the unit charge consists of the price of the number of kilowatt hours used over monthly periods. At another rate, the demand charge comprises the maximum demand incurred during the month. Consumers of electricity can, within reason, choose the rates at which they are charged. Each rate has its specific rules, and some tariffs are available only from particular electricity boards.

12. It will be appreciated that consequences for colleges can be considerable. It will be necessary for the college and LEA to review existing electricity

consumption, and to discuss with the relevant electricity boards other rates of charge which might be applied. It is imperative that staff and students are informed of the consequences of any proposed changes in the nature of electricity supply, and that the ways in which electricity might be saved are fully discussed. To provide a final illustration, a Maximum Demand operated by the London Electricity Board demonstrates the need for good housekeeping, at least: "The maximum demand in kilowatts at any point of supply in any month shall be deemed to be twice the largest number of units supplied in any half hour in that month. Where the supply to the premises is metered at more than one point the maximum demand in any month shall be deemed to be the arithmetical sum of the maximum demands at any of those points in that month."

13. It is important that users of colleges are made fully aware of conservation advice. There will be a need for the clear definition of responsibilities. It is also important, and relevant to the general duties imposed by the Health and Safety at Work etc. Act, that there is no unauthorised alteration of a college heating or any other power supply system.

14. **Energy conservation and the design of buildings**

Items discussed here are relevant to new buildings and to the adaptation of existing premises. Although the main elements of the conservation of energy – ventilation, lighting, insulation, and heating – will be discussed separately, overall conservation clearly depends on the interaction of those elements.

15. *Ventilation*

Where a building is well insulated, over half of the total heat loss is due to ventilation. Control of ventilation is therefore important. In either the design of new buildings or in improvements to existing buildings it will be appropriate to consider the following, subject to cost effectiveness limitations:

(i) Draught stripping can be fitted to ill-fitting external doors and windows. Either, or both, door closers and draught lobbies can be installed where external doors are used frequently. Joints between, for example, walls and window frames or in panelling, may result in heat loss and the problem therefore remedied by the use of draught exclusion materials.

(ii) Where buildings are exposed to a prevailing wind, it may be appropriate to provide screening by tree or hedge planting, or even the construction of walls or earth barriers.

(iii) In older buildings, although many window frames may be suitable for the use of draught stripping, others may require replacements. This may not be cost effective. Double glazing for energy conservation purposes alone is not at present considered cost effective.

(iv) The use of mechanical ventilation by such means as air extractors will be necessary in certain parts of a college. Use of a warning device or time switch may be appropriate however in ensuring that an extractor is not left to operate unnecessarily.

(v) If costs continue to rise, it will be necessary to consider the benefits of heat recovery whereby ducted air systems are adapted to transfer heat from extracted air to incoming fresh air.

16. *Lighting*

Although colleges constructed during the past three decades have generally made full use of daylight, consideration of the following may be appropriate:

(i) Economic use of electric lighting can be assisted if lights in a room can be operated independently: thus, lights furthest from a source of daylight can be switched on independently.

(ii) Research is currently proceeding on the automatic controlling of lighting which will eliminate abrupt and annoying changes of level. This control of lighting would be achieved by a photoelectric process whereby an on/off switch or dimming device was activated, causing the lights to come on or be raised or lowered in accordance with given illumination requirements and the incidence of daylight.

(iii) Ease of maintenance of any lighting system is relevant, as is the choice of the most efficient sources and lighting fittings.

(iv) In new buildings factors to be taken into account include the advantage of a southerly orientation, the full exploitation of daylight and the cost effectiveness against fuel consumption of more glazed areas, including side windows and roof lights.

(v) In older colleges built with very large windows which cause large winter heat loss and summer overheating the situation could be remedied by: reduction of loss by means of refitting or reglazing using opaque material; use of blinds and curtains; and the sealing of some windows where the original provision of opening windows was excessive.

17. *Insulation*

Although the effectiveness of thermal insulation depends on where it is placed, its cost effectiveness has increased dramatically as fuel prices have risen. In general, the most effective measures are roof or ceiling insulation, according to conditions. Wall insulation has also become important. Double glazing, however, becomes economic only where a high cost fuel such as electricity is used. The purpose of thermal insulation is to retain as much heat, from whatever source, as is possible. Insulation can also reduce condensation and in this respect the following points should be considered:

(i) The insulation should not be by-passed by cold air entering a cavity behind it, nor allowed to become wet.

(ii) It is cheapest and easiest to insulate pitched roofs or roofs with large, accessible voids. Problems arise with flat roofs, however, and the high humidity conditions prevailing in kitchens and swimming baths demand a careful consideration of any insulation decision. In some circumstances it may be appropriate to cover or add to an existing roof an additional insulation, such as expanded plastic board; or to add a suspended ceiling under a flat roof. At present, however, these methods are not considered to be cost effective.

18. *Heating*
Opportunities occur naturally to change the type of fuel used, since the efficient life of a heating system is of about 20 years' duration. Where old or inefficient systems are reaching the end of their period of useful existence, they should be replaced. In this instance, planned maintenance programmes are often available. Changing of a fuel system at any time is appropriate if sufficient cost effectiveness can be achieved. At present, coal is the cheapest fuel, closely followed by gas. Oil is the next cheapest fuel, and electricity decidely expensive. It is predicted, however, that market forces will operate to narrow the gap between oil and solid fuel prices, whereas the electricity price differential is likely to continue. In selecting a heating system it may be worthwhile to consider: the advantages of a warm air system, particularly in lightly constructed buildings, as it provides a short heat-up period; the recovery of heat from exhaust air; and the benefits of utilizing solar radiation where appropriate.

19. Installation of further heating control systems now repays the investment. To keep temperature fluctuations to a minimum is the main requirement for a control system: a rise in room temperature of 1°C can mean an increase of fuel consumption of 10%. It is important that space heating controls should be reliable, fully automatic, accessible only to responsible personnel and be proof against unauthorised interference. Overall control alone has been found to be economic only in small premises, and controls which respond to localised heat changes are recommended instead. For example, local controls would respond to sudden temperatures rises caused by sunshine and obviate the need for ventilation which would entail heat loss. Control devices known as optimum programmers or optimum start controllers give frost protection and also allow for the most efficient pre-occupation heating of a building. Any controls used must be properly maintained and regularly checked to ensure the most efficient operation. User manuals should be available, and LEAs and their colleges should ensure that all appropriate staff are fully conversant with the operation and controls of all heating and ventilation plant.

20. **General improvements and modifications**
Avenues for improvement will have become apparent from the preceding paragraphs. However, consideration of the following will also be worthwhile:

(i) Where a choice of heating system exists, an option should be kept open to allow change from one type of fuel to another in accordance with price developments. Systems whereby heat is conveyed by warm air or hot water could be converted to coal, gas, oil or electricity. The DES states that of the alternative energy sources currently available, and then only after further research, only heat pumps are likely to prove cost effective.

(ii) Temporary buildings, such as concrete framed huts, timber huts and "portakabins" have high running costs. The DES advises their removal or replacement with a permanent building as soon as possible. Where this not possible, efforts should be made to save energy by cost effective means.

(iii) Water consumption can be reduced and energy saved by up to 50% by the use of spray taps in wash basins. Modifications to the plumbing system can also reduce water consumption. Spray nozzles in showers are much more economical than roses.

(iv) Advice is not yet available on energy savings which can be made in kitchens. While awaiting the advice, however, it will be worthwhile considering what measures may be appropriate.

REFERENCE

Energy Conservation, Department of Energy Circular 1/75, HMSO.
Energy Conservation Measures, Department of the Environment Circular 56/78; DES Circular 10/78, Welsh Office Circular 100/78.
Energy Conservation in Educational Buildings, DES Building Bulletin 55, HMSO, 1977.
Energy Conservation, Current Paper 56/75, Building Research Establishing Working Party Report, BRE, 1975.
Energy Consumption and Conservation in Buildings, Building Research Establishment Digest 181, HMSO, 1976.
Guidelines for Environmental Design and Fuel Conservation in Educational Buildings, DES Architects and Buildings Branch Design Note 17, DES, 1979.
Design Notes are available free of charge from:
Publications Despatch Centre, DES, Honeypot Lane, Canons Park, Stanmore, Middx.

5 LAW CONCERNING FACTORIES, OFFICES AND CATERING AS IT AFFECTS COLLEGES

(NB: This sub-section must be read in conjunction with Section **11.10**)

1. Where activities carried on in a college are such that they are relevant to the provisions of statute governing such practices, then their environmental and welfare standards must be observed. Thus, kitchens are subject to the Food Hygiene Regulations, and administrative areas to the Offices, Shops and Railway Premises Act. Workshops are directly subject to the Factories Act only if in them articles are made or adapted for sale in the course of employment. However, under the Health and Safety at Work etc. Act, the standards set in the Factories Act apply to those college activities and workplaces which are construed as carrying out factory activities. The same conditions apply concerning the Offices, Shops and Railway Premises Act. This will remain the case until regulations specific to education are made under the Health and Safety at Work etc. Act. There are no indications that this will occur soon. In practical terms, the situation can be summed up as meaning that the welfare provisions of the Factories Act and Offices, Shops and Railway Premises Act apply directly where relevant, and otherwise through the Health and Safety at Work etc. Act. Thus colleges possess a statutory welfare standard base, albeit one which is qualified. However, if standards are not adequate, and the statute under which that is determined is the Health and Safety at Work etc. Act, the matter can be determined only by the courts and under the powers of the Health and Safety Executive (HSE) and its inspectorate. Only the HSE can institute criminal proceedings. Subject to regulations which might be made under the Health and Safety at Work etc. Act, breach of that Act cannot result in a civil action. Therefore, although standards required by the Act can be enforced, personal redress for injury or loss resulting from inadequate provision can be obtained only at civil law, such as under the Occupier's Liability Act (see Section **5.7**). Rather than deal separately with factory and offices legislation, it will be convenient in this sub-section to investigate in turn the various areas of welfare provision.

2. **Cleanliness**
The Factories Act requires that places of work are kept clean and free from smells. Rubbish and dirt must be removed daily; floors cleaned weekly; inside walls and ceilings be washed every 14 months, and white or colour washed every 14 months or else painted every seven years. It is worth observing here that severe problems have been experienced in some colleges regarding air extraction, especially with regard to fumes, dust and where woodworking is being carried out. Common examples are: the explosion risk arising from wood dust, and the dangers from toxic fumes used in glass fibre moulding (used, for instance, in the repair of canoes). There is a need in many cases for a thorough review of air extraction provision. As the brushing of dust and waste can create considerable air pollution, it is preferable that such cleaning be undertaken outside working hours.

3. Under the Offices, Shops and Railway Premises Act there are only general requirements concerning cleanliness. The premises, equipment and fittings have to be kept clean; there should be no accumulation of rubbish or dirt, and steps and floors have to be cleaned weekly.

4. **Cooking and eating areas**
Kitchens are subject to the Food Hygiene Regulations. There are cases in which the Public Health Act itself may be relevant, as well as statute relating to the supply of energy. Where food is stored, prepared or handled, then there has to be compliance with the standards laid down in the Food Hygiene Regulations, and the areas in which food is kept or prepared are subject to the inspection of the public health inspectors. The main provision of the Food Hygiene (General) Regulations, is that no food business (ie, preparation, storing and handling) is to be conducted at insanitary places, or where the condition, situation or construction of premises are such as to expose food to the risk of contamination. Food must be hygienically handled, and contamination avoided. Persons engaged in food handling are required to maintain a standard of cleanliness. There must be provision of a constant water supply and washing facilities. Arrangements for the proper disposal of waste materials must be made. Certain foods are to be kept at specified temperatures.

5. Those engaged in food business are required as far as reasonably practicable to keep clean all parts of their persons and clothing likely to come into contact with food; to cover cuts and abrasions with suitable waterproof dressings; and to refrain from smoking and spitting. There are special regulations which apply to persons suffering from certain infections.

6. Sanitary conveniences must be suitably sited, not communicate directly with any room where open food is handled, and be equipped with hand washing notices. Washing facilities must be suitable, efficient; and equipped with a constant hot and cold water supply, wash basins, soap, nail brushes, towels or other drying facilities.

7. First aid materials must be available. There must be accommodation for clothing. Food and equipment washing facilities must be suitable and adequate. Food rooms must be suitably and sufficiently lit, ventilated, kept in good order, and be of a repair and condition such as to allow effective cleaning and prevent – as far as reasonably practicable – infestation by rats, mice or insects. Waste storage and disposal facilities must be adequate, and no refuse is to be deposited or allowed to accumulate except where unavoidable. As well as persons working with food, those with management responsibilities for the activity can be guilty of an offence if all reasonable steps have not been taken to prevent contravention of the food hygiene regulations.

8. It has been found on occasion that college kitchens have been sub-standard. In some cases the wrong sorts of fabric have been used in construction: porous walls and ceiling fabrics have allowed germ retention to occur. Laminated work surfaces have been found to be unhygienic: when the

laminate has worn, it too has allowed germ rentention. The remedy is to ensure that stainless steel is used on all food preparation surfaces, and similarly on all serving or counter surfaces. Floors have been found to be both dangerous and unhygienic. The regulations require that catering premises are cleaned frequently and regularly; floor surfaces should be non-slip.

9. There have been cases where kitchens have been closed because ventilation was inadequate or insufficient. This circumstance can arise when staff interfere with the ventilation provided. It is important for staff to be made aware, therefore, of both the need for ventilation and the possible penalties which an institution can suffer where this is tampered with. That consideration will be appreciated to be applicable in other catering circumstances. By way of example, reference may be made to the provisions of the Gas Act. The Gas Corporation is empowered to cease to supply gas where there is improper use by a consumer, or interference with the supply. Should an unauthorised alteration be made to the supply, pipes, meter or fittings then the person wilfully, fraudulently or by culpable negligence perpetrating the action will be guilty of an offence and may be fined.

10. While it is presumed that the environmental conditions concerning heating, lighting, ventilation and noise level will prevail as satisfactorily in an eating area as elsewhere in a college, it may be useful to consider spatial requirements. Suggestions for provision are made by the Department of Employment:[1]

Dining room areas (including space between tables and aisles).	*Sq. ft per person*
To seat at tables for 4	12 (1.12m^2)
To seat at tables for 6	10 (0.93m^2)
To seat at tables for 8	8 (0.74m^2)
Seating as in a coffee bar	4-6 (0.37 - 0.56m^2)
Tea making areas (where no seating is provided)	
Up to 25 teas served at one time	2 (0.19m^2)
25-30 teas served at one time	1¾ (0.16m^2)
50-100 teas served at one time	1½ (0.12m^2)

11. **Thermal environment**

The general requirement of the Factories Act that there be a "reasonable" temperature (subject to certain specific stated levels in special

1 *Canteens, Messrooms and Refreshment Services,* Department of Employment Health and Safety at Work booklet series No 2, HMSO. Measurements are given in square feet. Metric equivalents are given in brackets therefore in the table above.

circumstances) and the similar requirement of the Offices, Shops and Railway Premises Act (except that here there should be a minimum temperature of 16°C after one hour's work, and a thermometer be available to check this) means that in practice reference should be made to the DES standards referred to under Section **5.3.**11 above. Similar recourse may be taken in the matter of ventilation. However, it should be noted that the Factories Act requires not only adequate ventilation but that all practicable measures should be taken to give protection against fumes and dust; and that ventilation implies the supply of fresh air.

12. **Working space provisions and facilities**
The Factories Act requires that there should be 400 cubic ft. ($11.32m^3$) of space allocated for each worker, and that there should not be overcrowding which will cause risk of injury or to health. The Act requires the posting of a notice specifying the number of people who may be employed in the workroom. Students and staff, where their activities are construed as being the same as would obtain in a factory, are subject to this requirement.

13. In calculating spatial requirements under the Offices, Shops and Railway Premises Act, account has to be taken of both the number of persons working in a room but also the space occupied by all furniture, equipment and fittings. This Act stipulates 400 cubic feet ($11.32m^3$) per person (but also refers in some cases to 40 square feet ($3.7m^2$) per person).

14. Both the Factories Act and Offices, Shops and Railway Premises Act require seating facilities to be provided wherever work can be satisfactorily undertaken when seated. Where a large portion of work may be so undertaken, seating must be of a design, size and construction suitable for both the work and the person; and where necessary for comfort, a footrest has to be provided.

15. **Cloakrooms, lavatories and washrooms**
Under the Factories Act and the Offices, Shops and Railway Premises Act there is an obligation to provide suitable and adequate cloakroom space for clothing not worn during working hours, and arrangements for drying wet clothes. While it is not easy to define "suitable" or "adequate", such provision should include space for changing of clothing and footwear, adequate lighting and ventilation, separate pegs or lockers, and a high standard of cleanliness. Although it is not clear how far the provider of the accommodation is required to guard against theft, the case of McCarthy v Daily Mirror Newspapers Ltd, Court of Appeal 1949, has made it clear that some action is an element to be considered when determining if accommodation is adequate (see Section **5.7.**13). There may be grounds for action if provision is inadequate under the Occupier's Liability Act (see Section **5.7**) or other law.

16. Requirements concerning lavatories made by the Factories Act and Offices, Shops and Railway Premises Act and regulations made under them are similar, with the exception that the latter Act requires that a suitable and effective means of disposal of sanitary towels be provided where the total

number of women exceeds ten. Incinerators must be constantly maintained, and the contents of bins suitably and regularly disposed of. There is no such provision in the Factories Act. Main statutory provisions common to both Acts may be summarised thus:

(i) If conveniences for men and women adjoin, the approaches must be clearly indicated and separate. Lavatories for each sex must be so screened or placed in other that, although the door may be open, the interior is not visible where persons of the other sex have either to pass or work.

(ii) There must be at least one suitable convenience for every 25 employees of each sex. In the case of men, this suitability does not include urinals. Where college activities under the Health and Safety at Work etc. Act would be subject to Factories Act provisions, then where there are over 100 male persons so engaged in such activities and sufficient urinal accommodation is provided, one seated convenience may be supplied for every 25 men up to the first 100, and thereafter one for every extra 40.

(iii) There must be sufficient ventilation and, except through the open air or an intervening ventilated space, a lavatory must not communicate directly with any workroom.

(iv) Except for urinals, every lavatory must be covered and partitioned to allow privacy and have an adequate, locking door. Urinals must be so screened and sited for them not to be visible from elsewhere in the workplace. Lavatories must be easily accessible.

17. There must be a supply of clean, running, hot and cold water. Means of cleaning and drying must be supplied, a provision which includes soap and clean towels. One wash basin for every 20 employees is recommended by the HSE inspectorate.

18. **Medical rooms and first aid**

As regulations made under the Factories Act require that medical rooms have to be provided in certain industries where the numbers employed in most circumstances are 500 or more,[2] larger colleges undertaking activities which include building, metalwork, woodworking and work with chemicals appropriate to regulations will probably on aggregation of numbers be required to comply with these provisions. Similarly, when a college is engaged in these activities, a responsible person must be readily available during working hours to call an ambulance or other means of transport.

19. The Factories Act requires that an accessible first aid box or cupboard must be provided and maintained by a responsible person. Where more than 150 people are employed (including in the case of colleges any persons engaged in activities subject to the Act), an additional box must be provided for

2 This fluctuates in building and shipbuilding, the figures being determined within the 500 ceiling according to the site capacity and distance from a hospital. The figures are 250 where 500 have or may be employed in building, and 100 in both where the distance from a hospital is 10 miles or over.

every additional 150. Where there are more than 50 employees or persons in colleges protected by the Act, there must be a person in charge of first aid who is trained in the subject. Notices must be provided in each work area giving the person's name, and that person must be readily available during working hours. He or she must undergo further training or a refresher course every three years and have her or his certificate renewed. While that person is undergoing further training, the post must be filled by a suitably trained replacement.

REFERENCE

Factories Act 1961, Chapter 34, HMSO.
Food and Drugs Act 1955, Chapter 16, HMSO.
Gas Act 1972, Chapter 60, HMSO.
Offices, Shops and Railway Premises Act 1963, Chapter 41, HMSO.
Public Health Act 1936, Chapter 49, HMSO.
Public Health Act 1961, Chapter 64, HMSO.
Food Hygiene (General) Regulations, Statutory Instruments 1970 No. 1172, HMSO,
*The Materials and Articles in Contact with Food Regulations,*Statutory Instruments 1978, No.1927, HMSO.

NB: There are many food and hygiene regulations. The first quoted will be the most usual to which reference should be made. The second may be relevant where a domestic science department manufactures food articles for sale.

Department of Employment Health and Safety at Work Booklets series:-
No. 2 *Canteens, Messrooms and Refreshment Services,* HMSO.
No. 5 *Cloakroom Accommodation and Washing Facilities,* HMSO.
No. 36 *First Aid in Factories,* HMSO.
No. 48 *First Aid in Offices, Shops and Railway Premises,* HMSO.

6 FIRE PRECAUTIONS

1. Building regulations and other buildings provisions have been referred to above. Advice from the DES, and also local fire officers, concerning fire precautions centres exclusively on the personal safety of users and occupants. Parts of colleges – those previously subject to the Offices, Shops and Railway Premises Act – are subject in the case of the means of escape to the Fire Precautions Act 1971. Safety provision under the Health and Safety at Work etc. Act is also relevant. Otherwise, maintained colleges are exempt from local bye-laws but subject to certain arrangements made under DES administrative memoranda and to parts of the DES Building Bulletin 7, *Fire and the Design of Schools* as well as other DES safety advice. The Building Bulletin is designed in places to achieve uniformity with the Building Regulations. In the matter of structural fire precautions, the provisions contained in the Building Bulletin apply with statutory force. A further consideration applies in that insurance companies are now becoming increasingly interested in the resistance of buildings' fabric to fire. The companies' reasons for this are purely financial, but there are clear implications for colleges and LEAs.

2. It is the purpose of this sub-section to provide a summary of DES recommendations and to discuss fire precautions issues. DES recommendations do not apply to residential accommodation. This is considered by the Department on an individual basis. As design responsibilities rest with an authority rather than its colleges, and are an adjunct to a college building programme rather than its purpose, emphasis is placed here mainly on the precautions for occupants.

3. In considering means of escape, precautions have to be taken against smoke and fumes as well as flame and heat. The DES recommends therefore that there should be no "dead end" corridors – escape should be possible in both directions. Corridors should be constructed with fire-resistant materials. Stairs should be virtually incombustible and surrounded by fire-resistant walls or partitions. The DES recommends the use of self-closing fire doors. However, it has been argued that such doors present greater risk of crushed and bruised limbs than the remoter possibility of saving life. To restrict the danger of panic, large rooms should have more than one exit. The number of room exits should relate to the size, occupancy and purpose of the room. Where halls are licensed for public assembly, it will be necessary for the approval of the local licensing authority to be sought regarding fire precaution arrangements. Where ground floor windows do not allow a means of escape, consideration should be given to the provision of further safeguards. It may be necessary to install emergency lighting. Extra stairways in buildings over two storeys are preferable to external fire escapes. Escape distances and door opening widths are subject to standard recommendations. No alterations without professional advice should be made to any structure which may afford a means of escape. It is inadvisable to seek the advice of a fire officer without LEA officers being present at the meeting.

4. It is impossible to give even general advice on matters such as room planning for, while they may follow DES schools recommendations, much will depend on the nature and purpose of the college. There is, however, a method of numbers calculation used to determine the maximum number of students using a stairway. These figures are used in the planning of minimum stairway widths according to the height of a building in storeys. The number of students may be taken as 80% of the maximum full-time equivalent student capacity of the accommodation on the upper floors.

5. In the case of structural fire precautions, colleges are subject to Schedule 1 of the Building Regulations as interpreted in Appendix 2 of Building Bulletin 7 and pp. 25-27 of that Bulletin, and as modified by the appendix to Administrative Memorandum 2/79. Compliance with the standards is essential to life, but also limits damage to property. In general, the necessary precautions deal with limiting spread of fire from building to building, the restriction of spread of smoke and flame, the use of fire resistant construction, and limiting the use of combustible materials. Recommendations here do apply to residential accommodation.

6. Fire warning systems should preferably be such that, once activated, they continue to sound an alarm. They should be tested weekly, the results recorded, and any fault immediately rectified. The DES considers it preferable for such installations to be uniform throughout an institution, and if possible, throughout a local authority's area. The alarm sound should be distinctive to avoid confusion with any other sound devices, and operating power should be from an independent source. Call-points are recommended to be in prominent positions; within 30m walking distance on every floor; of the "break-glass release" type; and provided in or near every kitchen, laboratory, workshop, housecraft and craft room, and assembly hall. Indicator boards which show the points from which warning has been given may be necessary in some colleges. There should be an extinguisher adjacent to every call-point.

7. Water supply and ready means of access to the building for the fire brigade will be necessary. Dry risers or internal hydrants may be necessary in special circumstances and where the building is of over four storeys. Consultations between the chief fire officer and the authority and college will be required at the planning stage.

8. All the Department's recommendations in Building Bulletin 7 concerning fire fighting and fire prevention by a building's occupants are relevant to colleges. The usual types of fire fighting equipment are hosereels, portable fire extinguishers, buckets of water, buckets of sand, and blankets. Consultation with the chief fire officer regarding the types of equipment suitable in each circumstance will be necessary but it must also be borne in mind that equipment should generally be such as to allow effective use with little training.Extinguishers expelling water or soda-acid are suitable for fires involving ordinary combustible materials. Foam, carbon dioxide or dry powder extinguishers are suitable for fires which involve flammable liquids such as cooking fats, oils and solvents. Extinguisher provision should be of

the type suitable to the circumstances, and instruction given to ensure the use of the appropriate means of effective extinguish. Almost all laboratory fires can be dealt with by the use of either or both of extinguishers or sand. Buckets of water are the cheapest and least effective of fire fighting devices. Blankets of either asbestos or glass fibre can be used to smother small fires which involve flammable liquids, and are recommended in dealing with persons whose clothing is alight (they should be wrapped and rolled in the blanket). If the presence of live electricity is thought or known, fire fighting equipment must not be used. It is recommended that the equipment should be standardised throughout an institution in accordance with the relevant British Standard, be maintained and recharged according to manufacturers' instructions, and positioned well away from heat sources.

9. The DES recommends that in the following high risk areas there should be:

   (i) a water or soda-acid extinguisher in every craft room, workshop and assembly hall stage;
   (ii) a foam, carbon dioxide or dry powder extinguisher in every laboratory, housecraft room and kitchen, except that dry powder or carbon dioxide may be preferable in laboratories where there are voltatile liquids or fragile equipment, and that those extinguishers may similarly be preferable where cooking takes place and there is no fixed frying equipment; and
   (iii) a foam extinguisher in every boiler room where oil fuel is used.

10. In the event of fire the DES recommends that safety of occupants takes precedence over fire fighting, and that: however small the fire, the fire brigade should immediately be called; and although small fires may be fought by occupants, evacuation procedures agreed with the chief fire officer should be carried out.

11. A variety of everyday precautions are recommended by the Department. These are:-

   (i) Locking doors across escape routes must be unlocked while the building is occupied. Exit doors should not be obstructed and be capable of being opened during occupation of the building from within. It should be explained that the purpose of fire doors is to prevent escape routes being blocked by gas or fumes.
   (ii) Stairways should be kept clear, in good repair, and not to have accumulated in their enclosures any combustible material. Storage cupboards, for example, should not be set up in stair-wells or on landings.
   (iii) Materials, furniture and fixed equipment should not be allowed to block escape routes, especially in open areas.
   (iv) Combustible rubbish and waste material should not be allowed to accumulate. All flammable materials should be stored carefully. Intending arsonists ought not be aided by the accessible storage of combustible material outside the building.
   (v) Heating appliances should be protected against misuse. Open fires

should have the relevant British Standard specified guard. The Department strongly recommends regular maintenance.

(vi) Only the correct fuse wire should be used to repair blown fuses. Wiring work should be undertaken only by a competent electrician. There should be regular inspections of flexible cable to electric fittings. The cable should be as short as possible and replaced if worn immediately.

(vii) In laboratories, it is recommended that dangerous experiments do not take place near doors. Further reference is recommended to DES Safety Series 2, *Safety in Science Laboratories* (see also Section **11.10**, Appendix 1).

(viii) Petrol storage on the premises should be limited. Not more than 14 litres may be stored, and then in separate half litre containers. This is a statutory provision (see Section **11.10**, Appendix 1) unless a local authority has granted a licence.

(ix) Where irons are used, the Department recommends that guidance is given on their nature and use: they should have pilot lights, efficient stands, and be put away only when cool and without damage to the cable by winding it around the appliance while hot.

(x) Furnishings and equipment should be fire retardant where possible. Materials should be selected for their fire resistance, and advice sought where appropriate.

(xi) Where smoking occurs, there should be a sufficient supply of adequate ashtrays.

(xii) Where premises are used by the public, information should be supplied concerning fire escape routes and procedures. Before a building is locked for the night the premises should be thoroughly checked.

12. It is worth noting in addition that fire and safety precautions are sometimes held to be an obstacle in making provision for the handicapped. Resolution of the problem may not be too difficult: escape routes should be clearly marked and have been made known. In the event of fire where a handicapped person requires assistance, the DES suggests[1] that there be a person willing to be responsible for such help, for example, in assisting their movement down stairs. Undoubtedly there may be extreme circumstances where this would be difficult, but fire precautions should not be used simply as a pretext for inaction where a handicapped student is being considered for admission. Clear procedures regarding assistance for a handicapped person in the event of fire are necessary.

13. Among the periodic actions recommended by the Department are the regular inspection of the premises and fire drills. Inspections may be made by fire brigade officers or other competent persons. Safety representatives, who may in any case wish to operate their own procedures, must be informed if an inspection is to be made. Recommendations for fire drills procedure may be obtained from a chief fire officer.

---

1 This information was given orally to the author.

REFERENCE

Fire Precautions Act 1971, Chapter 40, HMSO.
The Fire Precautions Act 1971 (Modifications) Regulations 1976. Statutory Instruments 1976 No. 2007, HMSO.
The Building Regulations 1976, Statutory Instruments 1976 No. 1676, HMSO.
The Building (First Amendment) Regulations, Statutory Instruments 1978, No 723, HMSO.

Constructional Standards For Maintained And Direct Grant Educational Building In England, DES Administrative Memorandum 2/79; Welsh Office Administrative Memorandum 3/79, 9 February, 1979.
Fire and the Design of Schools, DES Building Bulletin 7, 5th Edition, 1975, HMSO.
Safety in Science Laboratories, DES Safety Series No.2, HMSO,
Safety in Practical Departments, DES Safety Series No.3, HMSO.

A.J. Elder, *Guide to The Building Regulations 1976,* The Architectural Press, 1977.

7 OCCUPIER'S LIABILITY

1. Every occupier of premises owes a duty to have reasonable care for the safety of lawful visitors on those premises. The rules of common law in this sphere were complicated, but the matter is now governed by the Occupier's Liability Act 1957.

2. The occupier of premises is the person (natural or legal) who is in actual occupation or possession of them for the time being, whether he or she is the owner of them or not. Doubtless in the case of colleges of further and higher education that occupier is the local education authority. It has, however, been held by the courts that there may be cases where there may be two or more occupiers of premises at the same time. Exclusive possession is not required; the test is whether a person has some degree of control arising from his or her presence, or use, or activity in the premises. This might arise where a part of college premises is handed over to contractors carrying out work there, or where rooms are hired out for occasional use by another body.

3. Lawful visitors are any persons who enter the premises other than as trespassers; hence in colleges the term lawful visitors will include staff, students and all other persons who may have lawful occasion to enter. The term "premises" is defined in the Act as not only premises which would have been regarded as such at common law, but also any fixed or movable structure, including any vessel, vehicle or aircraft. Premises consist of everything within their confined boundary, thus including grounds. Fixed structures would certainly include not only buildings but garden sheds and even swings; and, in one case, the premises involved were a tunnel in the ground.

4. The nature of the duty owed by the occupier is set out in the Act as a common duty of care: "The common duty of care is a duty to take such care as in all the circumstances of the case is reasonable to see that the visitor will be reasonably safe in using the premises for the purposes for which he is invited or permitted by the occupier to be there". Whether the standard of care required is attained will be a question of fact to be determined by the court, but the Act provides that the circumstances relevant include the degree of care, and of want of care, which would ordinarily be looked for in such a visitor, so that, for example, in proper cases:
   (i) an occupier must be prepared for children to be less careful than adults; and
   (ii) an occupier may expect that a person, in the exercise of his calling, will appreciate and guard against any special risks ordinarily incident to it, so far as the occupier leaves him free to do so.

   Thus, in one case, specialists called in to seal leaks in a boiler flue were warned not to remain in the sweep-hole unless the fire was out. They ignored the warning and were asphyxiated by carbon monoxide fumes. As specialists they should have appreciated the dangers, so the occupier was not liable.

5. The common duty of care does not impose upon the occupier any obligation to a visitor in respect of risks willingly accepted as his or hers by the visitor, The question of whether a risk is so accepted is to be decided on the same principles as in other cases in which one person owes a duty of care towards another. It should be noted that the common duty of care is owed only to visitors who are "using the premises for the purposes for which they are invited or permitted to be there". If a visitor exceeds the area of permission or invitation, he or she may become a trespasser. As Lord Justice Scrutton put it, in a case at common law before the enactment of the Occupier's Liability Act: "When you invite a person into your house, you do not invite him to slide down the banisters".

6. In determining whether an occupier of premises has discharged the common duty of care to a visitor, regard is to be had to all the circumstances, so that, for example:
   (i) where damage is caused to a visitor by a danger of which he had been warned by the occupier, that the warning is not to be treated "without more", as absolving the occupier from liability unless in all the circumstances it was enough to enable the visitor to be reasonably safe; and,
   (ii) where damage is caused to a visitor by a danger due to a faulty execution of any work of construction, maintenance or repair by an independent contractor employed by the occupier, the occupier is not to be treated "without more" as answerable for the danger if in all the circumstances he had acted reasonably in entrusting the work to an independent contractor and had taken such steps (if any) as he reasonably ought in order to satisfy himself that the work had been properly done.

7. The effect of these provisions is that the mere exhibiting of a notice will not be enough to avoid liability unless reasonable steps are taken to bring the effect of the notice to the attention of the visitor; but where danger arises because of faulty work done by a contractor, the occupier will not be answerable unless he or she has personally been negligent. Thus, in O'Connor v Swan & Edgar Ltd and Carmichael (Contractors) Ltd (1963), a woman was injured in a West End store when part of the ceiling fell on her. She sued the owners of the store, who brought in the contractors who had installed the ceiling. Since the ceiling would not have fallen if it had been properly put up, the contractors were held liable. So also in Cook v Broderip and Ford (1968); a cleaner was hurt when she received an electric shock from a fire which was not switched on. She sued the owner of the flat, by whom she was employed. He had engaged an apparently competent contractor to install a new switch-fuse, and it appeared that the switch had been wrongly connected and that the contractor had failed to test it for "reversed polarity". Hence the contractor not the owner of the flat was liable for the injury to the cleaner.

8. However, the occupier will not be able to avoid liability where he or she entrusts the work done to unqualified persons, or where the occupier can readily satisfy him or herself that the work has been properly done. Here the

common law remains unaltered, and is illustrated in Woodward v Mayor of Hastings (1945). A pupil had been injured on any icy step at a school. The step had been negligently left in a dangerous condition by a cleaner. Even assuming that the cleaner was an independent contractor, no technical knowledge was required to ascertain the state of the step. Accordingly, the occupiers of the school were liable.

9. Persons who enter premises for any purpose in the exercise of a right conferred by law are to be treated as entering by permission of the occupier, whether they have that permission or not. The occupier will also owe the common duty of care to all persons who enter or use or bring goods to the premises in consequence of a contract between the occupier and themselves; and the duty will also be owed to persons whom the occupier is obliged to allow to enter under a contract to which those persons are not themselves parties, for example, the workmen of a contractor. In the latter case, the Act does not allow the occupier to limit by means of that contract liability towards those who are not party to the contract; but, generally speaking, the Act permits an occupier to extend, restrict, or exclude his or her duty to any visitor by agreement or otherwise.

10. This freedom is, however, now limited by the Unfair Contract Terms Act 1977, which provides that a person cannot by contract limit his or her liability for causing by negligence death or personal injury to another; nor exclude liability for any other form of damage from negligence, unless, the exclusion clause is *reasonable* in all the circumstances of the case. This is a question of construction, to be determined by the court.

11. In the matter of students' possessions, it is held by some legal authorities that the common duty of care placed upon every occupier by the Occupier's Liability Act extends to the personal belongings of lawful visitors. However, the occupier is free to extend, modify or restrict the extent of the duty to persons who enter the premises in virtue of a contract with the occupier. Although the Unfair Contract Terms Act forbids any contract which relieves the occupier from the results of negligence resulting in a visitor's death or personal injury, such a contract would be valid in respect of damage to goods or chattels (unless the contract is unreasonable, which would be a matter of fact for a court to determine).

12. Most, if not all, students enter a college in virtue of a contract. Most, if not all, LEAs make it clear, in their conditions of acceptance of students to their courses, that the authority will not be liable for any loss or injury to students' personal belongings. Acceptance of that condition by students makes them, in the eye of the law, willing parties to the arrangement – even though they have no alternative but to accept.

13. The same principle applies to the personal belongings of members of staff. At common law, an employer has no duty of care for the personal belongings of employees (Edwards v South Herts Hospital Committee (1957)). Liability can, however, arise under the provisions of the Factories Act 1961 where, and only where, that Act applies (see McCarthy v Daily Mirror Newspapers Limited 1949, Court of Appeal).

14. The Occupier's Liability Act 1957 affords no rights to trespassers, and, at common law an occupier of premises owes no duty of care to trespassers. They must take the premises as they find them, though it is not permissible to deliberately inflict injury upon them – save in justifiable self-defence. Reasonable force may be employed to eject trespassers if they do not remove themselves when requested to do so.

15. However, the severity of the common law towards trespassers has, in recent times, been modified by the courts in respect of child trespassers. Here courts have decided that there is a duty to take such steps as common sense and common humanity would dictate, having regard to the occupier's economic resources and knowledge of the probability that trespassers will come on to the premises. In Pannett v McGuiness & Co (1972) contractors' men on a demolition site lit bonfires in order to get rid of rubbish. They warned trespassing children and chased them away. But the men left the fires burning when they left work, and in their absence the children again entered the site and one of them fell into the fire and was burned. The contractors were held liable.

16. If an occupier habitually acquiesces in the trespassing of children on to his premises, those children will be deemed to become "licensees", that is, lawful visitors. Hence, in Cooke v Midland G.M. Railway of Ireland (1909); the defendants kept an unlocked turntable on their land. Their employees knew that children habitually trespassed and played on the turntable. One of the children was injured by the turntable. The defendants were held liable for that child's injuries.

17. So too, if any occupier permits children to play on his premises, he may become liable in respect of any injury that those children cause to other people. In Hilder v Associated Portland Cement Co (1961), an occupier of land adjoining the highway permitted children to play there. From time to time those children kicked a ball into the road. On one occasion the ball caused a passing motor-cyclist to have an accident which killed him. The occupiers were held liable in negligence, for the risk was a reasonably foreseeable one and should have been guarded against.

18. These examples may be relevant in the cases of colleges which have car parks or other areas within their precincts where, owing to lack of supervision, children are accustomed to trespass in order to play or ride cycles; and the occupiers of such colleges should be alert to ensure that liability of this kind does not arise, for it may have expensive consequences. The precautions to be taken are obvious.

REFERENCE

Occupier's Liability Act, 1957, Chapter 31, HMSO.
Unfair Contract Terms Act, 1977, Chapter 50, HMSO.

8 ACCOMMODATION USE AND ALLOCATION

1. The use and allocation of accommodation in colleges has been the matter of some debate. Surveys have shown that the level of utilization may often be lower than is necessary. If higher utilization levels can be attained, provided that this does not entail disadvantages in other respects, then the resulting gain in efficiency will only be of benefit. It will be appreciated that the matter is complex. Educational and human needs must not be ignored in any reallocation of accommodation. More effective use of college space cannot be approached in a simplistic manner. For example, energy might appear to be conserved by a room allocation system which provided for more teaching to occur in less space. However, whether a room left unused for part of a week represents an energy saving depends upon the nature of the college heating supply.

2. There has been a considerable growth in the study of space utilization. For the purposes of colleges, there are two basic ways of determining accommodation usage. One is termed "space budgeting" and involves the theoretical simplicity of the available space being costed at its market rent value: teaching departments then negotiate for the use of space within their total budgets. The other involves formulae using the frequency and type of room occupancy, the hours available, the numbers of students and the available space. This approach is illustrated in some detail in the DES/UGC publication, *Space Utilization In Universities and Polytechnics,* Design Note 12, and it is this document which will be discussed below.

3. The principles outlined in the Design Note are obviously relevant to universities and polytechnics, but the DES also offers them for consideration to all further education institutions. It may be felt that further education has to be too flexible to adopt any particular processes for room allocation, and also that such processes will be inappropriate because much further education accommodation has been obtained by the adaptation of other buildings. This ought not be the case, for use of a suitable computer programme in timetabling (see paragraphs 12-13, below) should resolve such difficulties.

4. In order to obtain a quantitative analysis of accommodation use, the DES Design Note adopts the formulae of Utilization Factors, Room Frequency Factors and Seat Occupancy Factors. The factors are expressed thus: [1]

$$\text{Utilization Factor} = \frac{\text{seat-hours used}}{\text{seat-hours available}}$$

$$\text{Room Frequency Factor} = \frac{\text{room-hours used}}{\text{room-hours available}}$$

$$\text{Seat Occupancy Factor} = \frac{\text{Utilization Factor}}{\text{Room Frequency Factor}}$$

---

1 *Space Utilization in Universities and Polytechnics,* UGC/DES Architects and Building Branch, University Building Note/Design Note 12, p.1.

5. The purpose of the Utilization Factor is to compare "activity" with space "capability". The other factors break this down into proportions: the time that rooms are in use and the places then occupied. Therefore, the Utilization Factor can also be expressed thus: Utilization Factor = Room Frequency Factor x Seat Occupancy Factor. Utilization Factors are always less than 1. They are usually expressed as percentages. Surveys have shown that in educational buildings the optimum utilization factors will be of the order of 0.7 - 0.8 (70% – 80%) according to activity.

6. Various empirical studies in higher education have demonstrated that: average room sizes are two or three times greater than average class sizes; at least one third of rooms in many institutions are unused at peak teaching times; there are frequently twice as many classes per hour in the morning as in the afternoon; the larger the institution, the fewer hours per week the room is used; and the larger lecture theatres are the least used rooms. Even where overall utilization was low, overcrowding could still be a problem at certain times. Although the studies suggest that Utilization Factors of 20% - 25% are common, it appears that the users of accommodation in the institution studied considered that they were overcrowded. The problem, therefore, is less that of the overall utilization of a building, but the activities within its various areas. The Design Note makes several observations and suggestions.

7. Library use is uneven. Monitoring of such use might demonstrate the need for the temporary adaptation or use of other nearby accommodation at peak periods, such as the approach of examinations. Monitoring of canteen use could show the arrival pattern, the speed at which the food providing service is required to operate if queues are not to form, and the maximum number of seats which are likely to be occupied. Study of timetabled space (ie, teaching rooms) in higher education showed that approximately one fifth of the available seat hours and half the available room hours were used, and that the rooms were only one third full. The figures would probably be higher in non-advanced further education, for although the percentage of timetabled space is higher there are greater attendance requirements.

8. The Design Note survey established that there is a cumulative loss of utilization as the number of separate room types and departments increase. It can be argued that there will be a loss of utilization because space should not be designed or adapted so rigidly as to prevent freedom for alternative use. However, the survey found institutions where overcrowding seemed to be a problem although they possessed in the levels at which they were operating a complete freedom to alter accommodation use. Five limitations concerning utilization levels were found: many institutions possess accommodation with too many large rooms which are difficult to subdivide; highly specialised rooms can be unsuited to any but their particular design use (although current DES recommended laboratory design does allow a wider use); utilization will be low where teaching space is not shared between departments; people appear to perceive space as being more crowded than it actually is; and most important in the opinion of the Design Note, is excessive loyalty to traditional teaching times and arrangements:

"while there may be no apparent reason for a particular lecture to change from one year to the next, the aggregation of many fixed events leads to excessive space requirements at certain times (and may also restrict students from taking certain combinations of courses and inhibits course development)".[2]

9. Since under-utilization of accommodation represents a loss of educational provision, it is necessary to determine how accommodation use can be improved. In design matters, this may be summarised as: development of buildings to allow easy working links between different departments; to surround departments requiring a core of accommodation which is exclusively their own with rooms which can be shared with others; to design rooms which, including their furniture, can be quickly and easily adapted to a variety of uses; and to ensure that buildings contain a variety of room sizes suitable for multiple use, enabling course and teaching method changes to be accomplished mainly by timetabling alteration. Most of these recommendations will not be easy to accomplish without cost in existing buildings, but where possible should be considered. All are clearly highly relevant in new buildings. In all existing buildings, however, consideration should be given to utilization issues when furnishings and equipment are renewed.

10. The Design Note recommends improvements in management in order to improve accommodation utilization. These are: to pool for the shared use of all college departments, or among groups of departments, as much accommodation for teaching purposes as possible; to classify rooms by their facilities, shape and size in order to ascertain all potential users; to re-examine traditional timetabling methods and criteria; and to spread scheduled activities as widely as possible in order to avoid unnecessary crowding peaks (bearing in mind the effects this could have on non-teaching activities, such as catering).

11. In effecting such management improvements, there will be a need for a full management information system, and for timetabling to occur on a college basis. The Design Note suggests that two essential steps towards better utilization are room type reduction and a better match between activities and space. The Note emphasises that as course structures evolve and become more complex, ways of utilization improvement must allow for personal preference and student choice. To this must be added staff involvement in timetabling design, and the effects upon the college of the use of its premises by the community (see Section **5.10.**). Although timetabling matters are discussed under Section **2.2.**46 above, it is necessary here also to consider the topic.

12. Effective accommodation use clearly requires college, or department/faculty group timetabling. This, in turn, requires sophisticated timetable design techniques which will probably necessitate the service of a computer

---

2 *Ibid*, p.9.

programme. A particular programme is advocated in the Design Note,[3] but colleges ought to consult with their LEAs concerning choice, nature and operation of a programme, especially since the LEA will probably possess the computing facilities which a college may lack. If necessary, advice and facilities will also be available from commercial enterprises and computer time and service sharing bureaux. To provide the information necessary for any computed timetabling system, teaching staff will need to provide course details and personal and educational requirements; due regard to conditions of service agreements will have to be paid; meals and refreshment breaks times will have to be determined; staff-student groups and room availability be determined; and activities detailed, meeting lengths specified, and spatial requirements also specified. With this information it will be possible for a computer matching process to begin. Full information, and full involvement of all concerned will be necessary if an acceptable timetable is to be devised. In such a timetabling process, those needs and activities most difficult to fit represent the information required first by the computer programmer. Thus special requirements, such as leaving one staff day free, or ensuring that consecutive days or times are available for certain activities, have to be investigated and stated fully. It must also be appreciated that this is a complex and time-consuming exercise, probably inappropriate for a small institution, and one which will require final, manual, adjustments.

13. The most obvious constraint on any further education institution in timetabling design aimed at acceptable space utilization is the amount of flexibility required to provide optional courses. *Ad hoc* courses for the unemployed, "walk-in" literacy courses, and special provision for disadvantaged groups all require flexibility. A computer programme will have to recognise this, and also allow for certain courses failing to operate because of poor recruitment or cuts in expenditure. Hence, there needs to be a further planned element of utilization loss.

14. The Unit for Architectural Studies of University College London, which prepared the Design Note, carried out pilot studies using computer timetabling techniques in an existing institution, and in the planning of a new institution. In both cases, the results were encouraging. In the existing institution, space savings could be made and a satisfactory timetable produced. In the new institution, use of the techniques resulted in a reduction of the gross building area which in turn allowed expenditure to attain higher environmental services. A study[4] inspired by the Design Note has also demonstrated that savings can be made, but the emphasis it places on changing certain existing practices demonstrates the need for caution. As the Design Note implies, traditional practices operated for no reason other than inertia clearly require removal. But any space utilization programme must be the servant and not the determinant of educational provision. Its aim

---

3 The Dynamic Space Allocation Model. Information concerning the use of this programme is available from The Unit for Architectural Studies, University College London, Gower Street, London WC1E 6BT.

4 Ken Ridings, "A Detailed Investigation Into the Utilization of Accommodation At Stockport College of Technology," *Use of Resources in College Management,* Coombe Lodge Reports Vol. 11, No, 11, 1978, pp 420-432.

will be the creation of better educational provision by the more economical use of accommodation resources. The educational constraints on the exercise must first be established, as with the computer programme, and those may or may not represent the 20%-30% recognised inevitable loss of the total space available for use.

REFERENCE

Assessment of Curricular Activity and Utilization of Staff Resources in Polytechnics and FE Colleges, Councils and Education Press, 1972.

Grace Kenny, *Polytechnics: The Shared Use of Space and Facilities,* DES Architects and Building Branch, 1977.

Notes on Procedure For The Approval of Further Education Projects (Other Than Polytechnics), DES/Welsh Office, 1972.

Notes On Procedure For The Approval of Polytechnic Projects, DES.

Ken Ridings, "A Detailed Investigation Into the Utilization Of Accommodation At Stockport College of Technology," *Use of Resources In College Management,* Coombe Lodge Reports, Vol.11, No.11, 1978, pp. 420-432.

Space Utilization In Universities and Polytechnics, University Grants Committee/Department of Education and Science Architects and Building Branch, University Building Note/Design Note 12, DES, 1974.

9 SECURITY OF PREMISES

1. It is not the purpose of this sub-section to give detailed advice on security. Apart from such advice probably being counter productive, the circumstances of colleges vary widely and provisions in each establishment will be according to needs. Moreover, any action will depend upon the relationship between the college and the local education authority. Except where the college has the right to commit large expenditure, it would be extremely unwise for it to become involved in detailed discussions with, for example, a crime prevention officer without having first alerted the LEA. LEA, and fire officer, advice will be essential, for security considerations may conflict with necessary fire precautions.

2. Security problems can be categorised under five headings: break-ins; theft; intruders; threats to staff holding or carrying cash; and student and others' vandalism. Responsibility for security is not clear. The principal has a responsibility both to the employer under the terms of the contract of employment and under the Health and Safety at Work etc. Act. The LEA and college governing body have a responsibility for security. Some security responsibility will form a part of the employees' duty under their contracts and under the Act.

3. Colleges and their staffs increasingly possess valuable equipment. The personal effects of students in residence can also include items of value. Break-ins inspired by these factors certainly occur although the spoils are generally not large enough to attract skilled professional criminals. Break-ins occur usually at night or during vacations. The obvious preventive step is the installation of burglar alarm systems. Cost here is a determining factor. Such systems are expensive and protection of an entire campus in this way may not be financially possible. Selection of premises and areas within them, therefore, will probably be usual. Such selection, as well as the selection of the most suitable alarm system, is probably best carried out with the advice of the police crime prevention officer or accredited security experts. LEAs may have other priorities for expenditure: a principal would be well advised to inform the authority that the crime prevention officer was being consulted, and to discuss the advice received with the authority as soon as possible. The presence of alarms presumes that there is someone to take action when they are activated. Therefore, they ought to be connected to a police station or caretaker's residence or similar source where immediate action can be taken. Alarms should also be regularly checked and serviced; apart from causing severe annoyance to those dwelling in the vicinity, defective alarms left to ring unanswered will be ignored also when they are announcing that an unauthorised entry has occurred. It is generally the case that the mere presence of an alarm system acts as a deterrent and outbalances the consideration that it is an advertisement that a building contains items of value. Some colleges employ security firms to patrol buildings at night and during vacations. It is the policy of other colleges and authorities, however, that security firms should be employed only where access to premises has been made easier by circumstances such as building operations.

4. While an obvious consequence of a break-in is burglary, thefts can also occur while the college is open. Although this problem is closely linked to that of intruders, dishonest behaviour remains a part of the human condition. Colleges, therefore, need not only to make staff and students well aware of the necessity to safeguard their own and college property, but also to give advice on insurance. Staff and students should be clearly advised of the general insurance cover provided by the college's own policies as well as being strongly encouraged to ensure that their own insurance policies fully cover their property (see Section **12.6.**19).

5. Losses from burglaries and theft can be minimised if a number of precautions are taken. Portable equipment should not be left unattended and should be safely locked away when not in use. Equipment should be taken off the premises only with written or clear permission. Sums of money should not be left lying around. Keys should always be kept in a safe place, and the number issued restricted to the minimum necessary. Equipment should be marked with the name of the college or authority, preferably with an engraving tool or a soldering iron. Such a practice makes the equipment less attractive to thieves and easily identifiable if subsequently recovered. In the event of a loss, it is important to know what has been stolen, and stock records should be kept up to date and a complete stock check carried out at least once a year.

6. The greatest problem encountered by most colleges is that of intruders during the time of normal college operation. This problem can be especially acute in urban areas of high youth unemployment, and at its worst during bad weather. The problem moreover is complicated by considerations beyond those of security. It can be maintained that colleges are community institutions and that, therefore, the community ought to be able to use the premises; ex-students ought not to be debarred from using their former place of education and that to allow free access to the college is to encourage recruitment to courses. Where the instrument and articles of government permit, and in the case of student bars and clubs where licensing and membership regulations permit, it is entirely possible for student unions to open their facilities to whom they wish. Similarly, many colleges open their libraries to the public (an arrangement which allows similar purchasing arrangements to those enjoyed by public libraries) and it is usually necessary in such cases to operate a more sophisticated security system. It can be difficult, therefore, to separate these social and security issues. The only general advice which can be offered is that there should be full consultation, and that any action should depend upon the size of the intrusion problem. For any security system to be at all effective it has to operate with consent, and preferably with the active assistance of all college members.

7. In any event, an agreed college policy is essential. Where there is confusion – for example, where an intruder may be supported by some college members and be subject to the wish of other members for removal – then trouble will almost certainly follow. It is generally accepted that few intruders wish to cause trouble: most are attracted by student facilities, society, the refectory, and heat, light and warmth. Even when intentions are

peaceable, however, trouble can occur. While violent incidents are rare, they nonetheless represent the greatest danger of all: people may suffer considerable injury. This risk must clearly be recognised as a most important factor in determining any college policy.

8. It is the usual practice of authorities to take action only where a problem has arisen. Courses of action are determined by two issues. The first is that of recognition: in an institution of any size, it can be established clearly if a person is an intruder only if there is an identification and checking system. Secondly, apart from statute such as the Occupier's Liability Act (see under Section **5.7**), colleges will also be subject to local legal requirements. Bye-laws on matters such as disorderly behaviour on educational premises will indicate penalties and forms of action.

9. Essential to any recognition process is the carrying of an identity card. It is not unusual for access to be obtained to large student unions, libraries, and other educational institutions where security is important, by means of an identity card with a photograph of the bearer affixed. A registration slip may be all that a college will require. In any event, the consent of staff and students to such a system is essential.

10. Recognition systems will be greatly aided if entrance to the institution or building is limited. Preferably there should be one entrance only, with reception facilities which will allow anyone who enters the building who is not recognised to be stopped. Where the problem is acute, barriers or turnstiles could be installed. Compliance with safety regulations can be secured by ensuring that while there is only one way of entering the building, there are more exits. Such exits could be on the usual fire exit door systems; easy to open from the inside, but not from outside. Again, such provision requires the consent of the college members and their active assistance: if exit doors are left open, the whole purpose of the exercise is wasted.

11. Halls of residence do not usually present such a problem as the main college premises. Given their nature, the recognition of intruders does not create difficulty. Nonetheless, agreed procedures need to be established and similarly liaison with the police so that assistance where required can be readily available. This latter precept applies also to student bars.

12. The employment of full-time security staff is not a usual authority policy unless difficulties are exceptionally acute. Since the practice has been established in some areas, however, it may become more widespread. Where such staff have been employed, colleges have reported that the number of thefts has declined and the intrusion problem has been virtually eliminated. The type of security staff employed varies. In some cases specialist firms have been used; in some cases additional porters or stewards were recruited. It must be stressed that where specialist security staff are employed, the carrying by staff and students of identity cards is essential, especially when the system is first put into operation.

13. Security staff ought not to be employed without there having been

consultation with the college members: it is easy to imagine circumstances in which unpleasant incidents could occur if there was considerable objection to the security personnel. There will also be a tendency for staff and students to forget their own responsibilities and leave security entirely to the security staff. Where that occurs, much of the value of the specialist staff will have been lost: a security system can operate only with the co-operation of all involved. Once security staff have been employed, albeit as a temporary measure, it can be difficult to manage without them: behaviour and management patterns will have been established. Such staff will be most effective when they have been employed for some time and consequently know the college procedures and its occupants.

14. The most serious issues in the employment of security specialists are those of contract and liability. The procedures which the security staff are to operate must be very clearly specified; and the consequences of any excess of duty especially emphasised. Procedures for staff and students ought to make clear their application to security arrangements, and the security staff must be in no doubt as to their authority, and to their own functions and procedures, in all instances. Liabilities will depend upon both the law and the nature of the contract as well as whether the security staff are employed directly or supplied by a contractor. In the latter case the provisions of the Health and Safety at Work etc. Act relating to sub-contractors ought also to be remembered (see Section **11.10.**8).

15. The fact that many colleges may on occasions have significant amounts of cash to store, distribute or transport creates a particular security risk, and staff may reasonably object to undertaking the responsibility of transporting cash to or from banks (except, of course, where this security function has been included in their contracts of employment). An elimination of a part of the problem is the encouragement of those workers who have the right to be paid in cash to be paid by cheque. It is obviously sensible practice not to keep large amounts of cash on the premises overnight, and when this does occur for there to be safes of sufficient size and reliability to house it.

16. At enrolment time there can be a significant amount of cash on college premises. Potential dangers can be reduced by encouraging the payment of fees by cheque and by ensuring that cash is not collected centrally but at different points in the college. Again, where justified by the circumstances, it is possible to use a security firm to collect and transport cash to a bank.

17. Student vandalism is not necessarily restricted to colleges in localities where vandalism is common. Whatever the original causes of this behaviour, vandalism begets vandalism. It is important that damage is repaired as quickly as possible. A college suffering from vandalism can expect the problem to worsen unless it takes action. It has been reported by colleges who have employed recognisable security staff, generally uniformed, to patrol the premises that the problem quickly disappears.

18. Regard should be paid to the college's external protection. Most colleges can be easily seen from a roadway. It will be readily apparent if work has

ceased.Entrance to the college grounds can be very easy. In most instances there will not be a great need to protect the college further than in the usual ways. Where further protection is necessary the most effective means have been found to be, in descending order: the employment of security firms; building walls and improving external lighting; and the raising of the heights of existing walls by the use of weld mesh fencing. The fencing can be highly effective but it is unsightly and may well not receive planning permission. The unsightliness of a wall depends upon its siting and character; undeniably a sense of claustrophobia can be engendered in those who work within it and younger students may associate such provision with school. While both these exercises are expensive, given the continuing cost, they are not as expensive as security firms.

19. It remains undeniable that many colleges see their role as community institutions which perform many social functions. Restricted entry would be a barrier to the practice of some colleges to provide open access to literacy and numeracy workshops for non-enrolled students, especially those who are unemployed with nowhere to go and nothing to do. It has been argued that the presence of security staff in a college should also be accompanied by the appointment of youth workers to serve both in the college and the community; and that the money spent could be better devoted to education. It is the continuing problem of a liberal society to determine how to defend its liberal values. Such social and ethical considerations apart, however, where security problems are encountered cost will be a determining factor. Perhaps the best test to apply is that established in the operation of the Factories Act and applied to the Health and Safety at Work etc. Act: where possibility of injury is such that action is necessary, that action should be all that is reasonably practicable; and that reasonable practicality should be determined by the cost of the preventive action necessary balanced against the risk of injury.

20. It is useful to recall that the principle of crime prevention is deterrence. No security system can ever be total: the determined burglar will be able to enter almost any building. A college's procedures ought to provide deterrents sufficient for acts of unauthorised entry not to be worthwhile.

10 USE OF PREMISES

1. This sub-section must be considered together with Section **5.4-7**, and Section **12.6**. Its purpose is largely to deal with particular circumstances which may arise, the most common of which is lettings (see paragraphs 5-7). Advice concerning racialist activities is contained in Sections **2.2**, Appendix 4 and **11.6**.3.

2. Colleges may be used for the purposes of the Representation of the People Act 1949, under s82(3) of that Act which refers to "meeting rooms situated in the constituency the expense of maintaining which is payable wholly or mainly out of public funds or out of any rate or by a body whose expenses are so payable." If in complying with its duties under the Act, the authority has prepared its area lists of meeting rooms which candidates in any constitutency are entitled to use and the list includes rooms in a college, then that college may be so used. This provision relates to parliamentary elections. In the case of local government elections, colleges will be affected only where they use the rooms of county or voluntary schools; in local government elections use is not made of actual college premises.

3. The entitlement for candidates to use premises in pursuit of their candidature is restricted in the case of parliamentary elections to the times between the receipt of the writ and the date of the poll. The right of use of premises by the candidates does not apply outside the times specified. Moreover, the right to use can only be exercised where reasonable notice is given and subject to the provision that "this section shall not authorise any interference with the hours during which a room in the school premises is used for educational purposes or any interference with the use of a meeting room either for the purpose of the person maintaining it or under a prior agreement for its letting for any purpose."

4. S.5 of the Public Order Act 1936 makes it an offence for any person in a public place or at a public meeting to use threatening, abusive or insulting words or behaviour or distribute or display any writing, sign or visible representation which is threatening, abusive or insulting with intent to provoke a breach of the peace or whereby a breach of the peace is likely to be occasioned. The public place is defined as including any "highway or any other premises or place to what at the material time the public have or are permitted to have access." If a principal or member of the college staff feels that persons gathering outside the college premises are likely to cause a breach of the peace, the police should be contacted immediately.

5. Practices vary in dealing with lettings. In many instances authorities and/or governors issue guidance and instructions: in other cases decisions rest with the principal. It has been advocated that in making a decision a simple test can be taken: to allow the letting, the organization seeking accommodation should be seen to have objectives which match those of the college. However, some local education authorities regard the allowing of the use of their colleges by outside bodies as part of their community function; and

some principals actively welcome and encourage such bodies and meetings, even though the college as an academic institution has no direct role to play. Where lettings are made, it will be necessary for the college to specify clearly to the lessee the safeguards which the LEA or it requires, and the duties regarding the use of the premises which must be fulfilled.

6. The extent to which an institution's facilities are used by the community will depend not only on LEA and college policy but also the amount of space available (see Section **5.8**) and the availability to the community of other sources of supply. There may be few or many large halls in an area, for example. There are certainly differences which obtain in charging arrangements. Some institutions make either no or low hiring charges where activities are of an educational or cultural nature (although there are generally specific charges made if extra caretaking staff are required). In polytechnics, research has demonstrated that determination of charges and the designation of activities varies according to institution.[1] Most polytechnics make charges based on the user's status, but do not take into account the real cost of providing accommodation. It is usual in polytechnics for students from other institutions, schoolchildren, industrial and commercial users, and the general public to have some access to the library.[2] The Council of Polytechnic Librarians (COPOL) issues a vacation reading card which allows students to use polytechnic or university libraries during a vacation. This facility allows library use without a student having to make an individual application supported by a recommendation. A similar process is operated by the Standing Conference of University and National Libraries (SCONUL).

7. Wherever the public is admitted to college premises, it is necessary to ensure compliance with legal and other requirements. These requirements are not just those of fire precautions and occupier's liability but also include the arranging of appropriate insurance cover, and the acquiring of licences for the sale of alcohol and for public performances. Licensing requirements may entail restricting numbers or making improvements to the premises. A licence for public performance is necessary if entry fees are to be charged (unless, for example, a charge is made for a programme but not for the performance of which it supplies details). There are usually bye-laws which relate to letting of educational premises. These may be complex. For example, they may require that only "seemly" events occur, and are conducted by persons of "right standing". There are often bye-law prohibitions concerning Sunday lettings.

8. S.8 of the Misuse of Drugs Act, 1971, makes it an offence for an "occupier" or person "concerned in the management of premises" knowingly to "permit or suffer" the production or supply of *any* controlled drug on the premises or the smoking of opium or cannabis. It is not an offence to allow people to use other drugs on the premises. The word "occupier" includes a student living in a college hostel or hall of residence.

---

1 Grace Kenny, *Polytechnics: The Shared Use of Space and Facilities*, DES Architects and Building Branch, 1977, pp 4, 17.
2 *Ibid*, p.7.

9. The police may legally search college premises only where they possess a warrant issued by a magistrate or where the person responsible for the premises allows access. A warrant is valid for one month. Except where the police enter the premises specifically to arrest someone, all other searches are unlawful. However, the courts do allow illegally obtained evidence to be used against defendants. It is a defence where the police have been obstructed in pursuit of their enquiries by a person responsible for the premises if the police either did not possess a warrant, or if the warrant were to be defective or invalid. The police are entitled to take away anything they think can be used as material evidence to show that a crime has been committed. The police will issue a formal receipt for the property removed in due course, but if a receipt is required at once, it will usually be given informally. The police are entitled to retain the property for a reasonable period to decide whether it will be used as evidence; a magistrate may order the return of the property if such action is in the interests of justice; and there are circumstances in which a court may order the confiscation of property.

REFERENCE

Misuse of Drugs Act 1971, Chapter 38, HMSO.
Public Order Act 1936, Chapter 6, HMSO.
Representation of the People Act 1949, Chapter 68, HMSO.

Grace Kenny, *Polytechnics: The Shared Use of Space and Facilities,* DES Architects and Building Branch, 1977.

11 DAY NURSERY PROVISION

1. It should not be necessary to rehearse the arguments for day nursery provision. In this time of expenditure restraint, however, a summary may be appropriate: such provision is an essential social and educational good in itself; it creates opportunity for intending or enrolled students who would otherwise be unable to pursue their studies because of family commitments; it allows staff applications and appointments which for the same reasons might otherwise not occur; and, developed in a community sense, can represent a significant contribution by the college to its neighbourhood. Nursery provision should occupy a high priority in any college development plan, especially where the college already operates courses in nursery education and nursery nursing, and also must accord with LEA policy. A significant number of colleges, especially those concentrating on advanced further education, have already established child care facilities. Demands for such facilities can be expected to increase. Given the different recruitment patterns in further education of men and women staff and students, administrators may feel that the provision of child care facilities requires more attention as a means of improving the recruitment of women to further education. Nurseries may well be operated in conjunction with the student union, or with community groups.

2. It will be essential to establish current and projected nursery needs. As a preliminary, it is important to estimate the numbers and ages of children, the times during which provision will be required, and whether, intially or as a continuing policy, the nursery is to be for the children of all, or only some of the college users; or the whole community. Potential students for certain courses, such as YOP and TOPS courses, or access courses for women such as "NOW" (New Opportunities for Women) and "WOW" (Wider Opportunities for Women), may particularly benefit from nursery provision. In establishing estimates of potential demand, it will be useful to consider that where college nurseries have been provided, actual demand has almost always been greater than the envisaged potential. Any demand survey will need to take account of estimates provided by the college student welfare division, the student union, teaching departments and, if appropriate, the social services departments of the locality.

3. Types of facilities provided will vary according to circumstances, but availability time will have to be such as at least to cover college hours and the working weeks of staff and students. The greatest shortage of day care facilities is for the 0-3 age groups. Minimum standards for provision are established by law but there may be additional local legal variations.

4. The Nurseries and Child Minders Regulations Act 1948, as amended by the Health Services and Public Health Act 1968, requires health authorities to maintain registers of premises in their area, other than premises wholly or mainly used as private dwellings, where children are received to be looked after for the day, or a period of two hours or longer, or for any longer period not exceeding six days. Persons intending to receive children must apply for

registration. Registration is to be refused if the persons or premises are unfit. The health authority is empowered to make an order concerning the number of children who can be accommodated. The premises are to be safe and adequately staffed, equipped and maintained. A suitable diet has to be provided, and there must be provision for access to medical supervision. The premises are open to inspection by the health authority. In making nursery provision, therefore, it will be necessary for the college and LEA to determine with the health authority the standards of staffing and accommodation.

5. The crucial issue in nursery provision is that of cost. As running costs tend to be high, it is not generally possible to recover costs from student fees or charges on staff. Given many of the cost constraints under which local authorities now have to operate it may well be that they will prefer to discuss college nursery provision in the context of provision for the community rather than individual college needs. There are, however, a variey of finance routes which are worth exploration.

6. There are authorities which have provided a subsidy specifically for college nursery provision. In some cases this has been a direct annual subsidy, in others capital costs have been covered by an LEA loan. There has been joint provision made between a voluntary college and a local authority, provision made by a voluntary college, and in another case a local authority has made provision with a priorities stipulation concerning use: students, then teachers, then non-teaching staff. In other cases where no direct authority provision has been made, college accommodation has been provided free of charge.

7. There are other sources of finance. Loans have been extended and funds allocated by colleges themselves; allocations have been made from funds established for use in inner city areas; student unions have made contributions to nursery costs; and pilot schemes exist for provision for the children of students financed partially by the EEC Social Fund and Home Office funding.

8. A board of management will be required to oversee any nursery provision. The constitution of the board will need to recognise all the groups involved in the provision. Representation will need to include the college, its staff, students and governing body; the LEA; trade unions and professional associations; parental groups, and representatives of any external funding agencies.

9. The Education (No.2) Bill of 1979 contains (Clause 26) authorisation whereby nursery school teachers may provide educational services in day nurseries. However, the definition of "day" is such as normally to exclude a college crèche; the powers appear to be intended to allow an LEA to deploy its nursery teachers in social services' day nurseries.

REFERENCE

The Health Service and Public Health Act 1968, Chapter 46, HMSO.
The Nurseries and Child Minders Regulations Act 1948, Chapter 53, HMSO.
Nurseries and Playgroups: A Plan for Action, NATFHE.
The Under Fives: Report of a TUC Working Party, TUC.

Section 6

THE EUROPEAN ECONOMIC COMMUNITY

1 THE EEC: STRUCTURE AND LEGAL PROCESSES

1. Belgium, France, Holland, Italy, Luxembourg and West Germany were the signatories to the Treaty for the Establishment of the European Economic Community ("Treaty of Rome") on 25 March 1957. The Community was enlarged under the Treaty of Accession: Denmark, Eire, and the United Kingdom joined on 1 January 1973. The member states of the community are bound by the terms of the Treaty of Rome. The aspirations of the Community are contained in Article 117 of the Treaty: the states agree to promote better living and working conditions, allowing them "to be equalised as they improve." Such a development is to follow from the operation of the common market, for its operation is held to favour the harmonisation of social systems, and also from the Treaty provisions "and from the approximation of provisions, imposed by law, regulations and administrative action."

2. The Commission of the European Communities has the tasks of drawing up legislation proposals, and the monitoring of the proper implementation of the Treaty's provisions. It is subdivided into various departments, known as Directorates-General (DGs). Legislation is drafted by the DGs, and then sent to the Commissioners for approval. If approved, the draft is forwarded to the Council of Ministers.

3. The Council of Ministers comprises representatives of the governments of member states. The nature of the representation depends upon the business under discussion. Once the Council has approved a measure, that item has reached the final stage of the EEC process. Thereafter, the member states have to ensure that they have legislation which conforms to the EEC requirement. There are generally time limits – usually of two years – by which this has to be achieved.

4. The European Parliament is a consultative body only. Its consent to legislation is not required. However, especially through its committee structure, it has considerable influence, for it engages in consultation with the Commission concerning draft legislation. The Council of Ministers will normally consult Parliament before making its final decision on a proposal of the Commission.

5. The Economic and Social Committee has the appearance of importance in that it is the sole EEC body concerned with legislation upon which workers and employers have to be consulted and have direct representation. The Economic and Social Committee has to be consulted on many topics before a Council decision can be taken, and it can also submit opinions on its own initiative. In practice the Committee's influence is small. This is partially because of the agenda presented for its discussions, and because there is no wish at present from workers or employers for the Committee to have a decision-making or negotiating function. The potential of the Committee is clearly not being fully realised. The trade unions acknowledge that they

have failed to achieve the degree of consultation for which they had hoped. This is seen to result from conflicting employer interests, which cause issues to be watered down to a low but acceptable level.

6. Employers and unions can represent their own views by presenting their cases to their national governments but also through their membership of European associations. For example, the TUC is affiliated to the European Trade Union Confederation (ETUC). Neither the employers' nor unions' associations are EEC institutions. They are concerned also with matters other than the Community. However, the associations seek to influence policy where appropriate.

7. The European Communities Act 1972 brought UK obligations under the Treaty into national law. All rights, powers, liabilities, obligations and restrictions arising under the Treaty, without further enactment, were "to be given legal effect and used in the United Kingdom, [and to] be recognised and available in law, and be enforced, allowed and followed accordingly." Existing and future legislation is to take effect and be construed accordingly. Therefore, provisions which are directly applicable under EEC law apply to the UK regardless of any inconsistent national legislation, as long as that legislation preceded the 1972 Act. EEC law does not prevail over inconsistent national legislation passed after the 1972 Act, although it is to be construed in the light of it. The European Communities Act allows the making of subordinate statute to render specific, or to enlarge upon, directly applicable obligations and rights. This provision is in accord with the decision of the Court of Justice (see paragraphs 14-19) that if an EEC enactment is directly applicable, it is for national authorities to decide how it is to be given effect. However, national legislation cannot modify EEC law and only the Court of Justice can give a binding interpretation.

8. EEC provisions which apply directly to the UK are: parts of the Treaty itself, regulations, and, according to circumstance, certain provisions of Community decisions and directives. For a term of the Treaty to apply directly it has to have a wider application than between relations of member states, must be precise, clear and not require further EEC implementation, and leave little discretion to either the Commission or national governments. The Treaty empowers the Commission and the Council to "make regulations, issue directives, take decisions, make recommendations or deliver opinions" (Article 189). The choice of instrument depends on particular provisions of the Treaty.

9. Regulations are binding throughout the Community, just as is national legislation within a state. Most regulations are issued by the Commission. Regulations are enforceable in national courts without the need for national legislation.

10. Directives are binding (as to the result to be achieved) upon each member state to which they are addressed. However the Treaty stipulates that national governments have the choice as to the form and methods of implementation. Directives require governments to implement policies within a certain time

period (generally, two years). Usually, directives are binding upon governments only. A decision of the Court of Justice against a government department allowed the direct enforcing of a directive by an individual.[1] Thus, where a directive's provisions are similar to those contained in the Treaty, and where the narrow defining of a directive's application to governments only would limit the usefulness of the directive, it may be that – in these very restrictive circumstances – it might be directly enforceable by an individual. National legislation is required, however, before directives can be enforceable in national courts. Labour law directives set only minimum standards, upon which governments and employers are encouraged to improve.

11. Decisions can be issued by either the Commission or the Council. They can be addressed to individuals (who may be natural or legal, and therefore decisions can go to a particular party or parties) or to one or more member states. They admit no discretion in the way in which they are to be implemented, being binding in their entirety. Authorities so designated under national law are empowered by Article 192 of the Treaty to pay such money for persons as may be required under a decision. The authorities must be made known to the Commission and Court of Justice. It is this Article which allows the disposal of EEC monies by, for example, the MSC (see Section **6.3**.4 below). National legislation is required before decisions can be enforceable in national courts. The direct applicability of decisions is the same as that for directions described above.

12. Recommendations and opinions can be issued by both the Council and the Commission. They are not binding. Recommendations are intended to promote action; opinions express no more than a point of view. Thus, in 1975 the Council of Social Ministers recommended that by 1978 the working week should not exceed 40 hours, and that there should be a minimum of four weeks' paid annual leave. There has been little progress on this recommendation (the UK complies with the first recommendation in many areas of employment, but less than half of UK manual workers have achieved the holiday recommendation).

13. Conventions may be concluded on specified subjects between member states. States which joined the EEC under the Treaty of Accession are bound by the conventions signed by the original EEC members.

14. The Court of Justice has jurisdiction over the application and interpretation of the laws of the EEC. It is not able to interpret or rule on the validity of national law. There is no system of precedent: it is possible for the Court in different cases to provide contradictory interpretations of EEC law. Thus far, the judgments of the Court have been followed. The Court itself does not have the physical means with which to enforce judgment. A failure to

1 Van Duyn v Home Office (1974) ECR 1337. Ms Van Duyn was refused entry to Britain as a matter of "public policy" because she intended to work for the Church of Scientology (although that religion was not an illegal organization). In finding for the Home Office, the Court also held that directive 64/221, which deals with freedom of movement exceptions, was directly applicable thus, in this instance, allowing Ms Van Duyn's case to be heard).

follow a judgment may represent a breach of obligations under the Treaties. In this case, the Treaty of Rome requires that where the Court of Justice finds that a member state has failed to fulfil a Treaty obligation, "the State shall be required to take the necessary measures to comply with the judgements of the Court of Justice" (Article 171). There is no appeal from the judgements of the Court.

15. The Court decides disputes in two areas: between member states and the authorities of the EEC; and between individuals and the EEC. When requested by a national court, the Court of Justice is enabled to give a binding interpretation of provisions of EEC law. This power is intended to aid uniform interpretation throughout the EEC, for as courts in member states are required to apply those Community provisions which have become directly part of their national law, so they are bound by Court interpretations. The Court consists of nine judges. It is assisted by four Advocates-General. An Advocate-General suggests a legal solution on an issue before the Court. The Court is assisted in making judgements by an Advocate-General but does not have to accept the offered advice.

16. In practice, it appears that the Court hears two types of case. These are *preliminary rulings* and *direct actions.* Preliminary rulings are allowed under Article 177 of the Treaty in three areas: Treaty interpretation; the validity and interpretation of acts of the institutions of the Community; and the interpretation of the statutes of bodies established by the Council where the statutes so provide. If a question under any of these headings is raised in a court of a member state, that court may request a Court of Justice ruling if it considers that necessary in enabling it to give a judgement. Where a court is such that there is no right of appeal under national law, a request for a Court of Justice ruling must be made where any of the areas instanced above are in question. Case law at the Court of Justice has established the types of questions which can be asked. The Court *cannot* rule on the application of the Treaty to specific cases; interpret national legislation; consider why a national court made a request, or whether the request should have been made under national law; make factual investigations; or decide the compatibility of national and EEC law. The Court has ruled on these types of question: the scope and meaning of Treaty provisions and EEC law; the applicability of an EEC legal provision; which legal provisions are governed by EEC or national law; whether clarification under national law or EEC law may or must occur; and the effects of a Community rule regarding time. As case law develops, so the area of possible jurisdiction may be widened.

17. Despite a construction which might be put on Article 177 of the Treaty of Rome, UK law currently holds that actions on EEC law may be taken only in the courts, and not in industrial tribunals.[2] This has considerable

---

2 Amies v ILEA (EAT 334/76); Snoxell v Vauxhall (EAT 504/76). The rule established was that as "creatures of Statute", tribunals could deal only with the matters for which they have specific powers. Since the National Insurance tribunal has considered cases involving EEC provisions, and the National Insurance Commissioners have referred questions to the Court of Justice, this view appears to be arguable where national law has been amended by EEC law.

consequences, for there are instances where EEC law is more beneficial to employees than national law. Examples are the EEC's less restrictive time limits, and legislation concerning equal pay (see paragraphs 21-25). However, it may be open to those contemplating legal actions in Britain under a particular Treaty provision (for example, Article 119 concerning equal pay) to bring the case not in a tribunal, but in an action directly in the relevant court. Except where an appeal to the Court of Justice is required by the nature of the court, the court in which proceedings are brought is the one which decides whether or not to make a reference to the Court of Justice. Under UK law, the wishes of the parties concerned are to be taken into account in making a decision to refer. There have been few UK references to the Court of Justice. There is legal argument concerning whether an action may be brought under EEC law when alternative legislation is available under national law. That argument can only be resolved by case law. It must be remembered here, however, that Court of Justice interpretations of EEC law in references from other courts are binding throughout the Community. Thus an interpretation of a reference from, for example, an Italian court, is binding upon UK courts.

18. The Court of Justice is also concerned with direct actions against member states, or EEC institutions, for failure to fulfil an obligation under the Treaty. Direct actions can be brought only by the Commission, the Council, or a member state, and not by individuals.[3] Direct action can be taken by the Court against EEC institutions for failure to act, or in the annulment of measures taken.

19. Member states have the right to represent their views before the Court. This has resulted in the Court appearing on occasion to make somewhat pragmatic decisions. For example, the British government has argued on more than one occasion in equal pay cases for judgments which would deny benefits since their possible effect could have had severe financial consequences in Britain. The arguments were successful in that the Court judgments were limited.

20. It now remains to indicate how and where EEC provision affects, or may affect, UK law. It will often be possible to identify only areas where problems may arise, for interpretation through case law is necessary before it is possible to be positive. In many instances, commentary is necessarily restricted to matters of small detail since much of Britain's social and employment legislation of last decade is in harmony with EEC law. This is scarcely surprising since it was the presence of the EEC law which required the making of the UK statute in many instances. It is also this presence which, while it allows our Government to modify certain provisions of employment law which are more generous than EEC provision, does not allow its reduction below EEC requirements. Current UK employment law is

---

3 There is, however, the somewhat tortuous possibility of an individual in a national court alleging Treaty breach and by that means indirectly causing action to be taken.

investigated in Section **11**. Issues which affect that provision are discussed below.

21. **Equality of treatment in employment**

EEC law concerning equality is made by a Council directive and Treaty Article 119. This Article provides "that men and women should receive equal pay for equal work ... [and] ... 'pay' means the ordinary basic or minimum wage or salary and any other consideration, whether in cash or kind, which the worker receives, directly or indirectly, in respect of his employment from his employer." Further, equal pay without sex discrimination is defined as the calculation of pay at the same rates in piece work on the basis of the same unit of measurement; and that "pay for work at time rates shall be the same for the same job." The Court of Justice has held that this part of the Treaty is directly applicable. Therefore, it can be enforced by individuals before their national courts.

22. In most cases, the Equal Pay Act 1970 appears to comply with the EEC directive, although where it does not, the matter does not appear to be directly applicable and therefore is not enforceable by individuals. However, there are issues arising under the EEC directive concerning equivalent work. In April 1979 the EEC Commission began infringement proceedings against the UK in order to make it comply with EEC provision. The Commission believes that the "equal value" of work stipulation in the Equal Pay Act (Section **11.6.**15) is restrictive for where job evaluation studies have not been carried out, female employees in the UK cannot claim equality under the "work rated as equivalent" heading. If Britain is forced to comply with the Commission's requirements, this may have consequences in the employment of college non-teaching staff.

23. The Defrenne[4] case concerning equal treatment was the one in which Article 119 was found to be directly applicable, and thus allows cases under that Article to be heard in UK courts. Therefore, since Article 119 is binding, the Equal Pay Act must be construed according to it. Principles established in the Defrenne case are therefore highly relevant in considering the application of that Act. The Article is concerned with employment where men and women do *equal work* (not *like work*, as under the Equal Pay Act, which is therefore restrictive – until the proceedings for infringement against the UK are concluded and the anomaly removed). The Defrenne case has also showed that it is currently legal for the UK government not to equalise retirement ages in state pension schemes[5] (although there should in principle be equality in private schemes), and, importantly, that Article 119 does not apply to discrimination in the terms of employment other than in

---

4 Defrenne v Sabena (ECJ(1976) ICR 547); Defrenne v Belgium (EJC(1974) CMLR 494).
5 *IDS International Report*, July 1978, 76.5

pay (even though such discrimination can have financial consequences).[6] References to UK courts under Article 119, therefore may usually refer to cases concerning equal work.

24. The equal treatment for married women directive of February 1976 corresponds broadly with the UK Sex Discrimination Act. However, there are two important possible exceptions: it may be that the indirect discrimination clauses of the Sex Discrimination Act are inadequate; and that the UK government may not adequately be publicising the terms of its anti-discriminatory provision. However, actions cannot be brought under the directive by individuals. Again, an EEC judgement that the UK is not complying may result in changes being caused in its employment law.

25. The EEC directive on group dismissals is, again, largely satisfied by UK law. There are, however, areas of possible conflict. In the management of redundancies, it appears that UK law stresses compensation rather than the punishment of the employer for failing to implement procedures (especially to consult). It appears that the UK is paying much less heed to the requirement to consult over group dismissals than elsewhere in the EEC. The directive requires consultations with workers' representatives; in the UK, EAT decisions have demonstrated a limitation in that representatives (ie unions) must have a relationship with the employer in order to be consulted: this means that the union must have a continuing relationship with the employer which goes further than occasional participation in dismissal matters, or negotiations with employers' associations at national level. There is no EEC directive at present concerning individual or unfair dismissal, except by inference to discrimination legislation.

26. Article 48 of the Treaty requires the free movement of workers within the EEC. This Article may be used by individuals before national courts. Articles 49-51, and regulations made under them and Article 48, supplement the provisions. EEC workers[7] (this vague term is employed here since it is used in Article 48) are entitled freely to enter and stay in EEC countries for employment purposes. The workers have to be nationals of an EEC country. The freedom of entry and residence is further defined under regulations and directives. The worker may: enter a member state without formality, accompanied by spouse and children (aged under 21 or dependant), with a

---

6 *Ibid,* April 1978, 70.5.The UK government argued for this result. It is important to remember here that precedent is not binding on the Court of Justice. Thus, in October 1979 in referring a case of two Lloyds Bank employees who claimed that the company's scheme discriminated against them to the Court of Justice, Lord Denning observed that the employees had a "fair chance" of success. The point of the original judgment in the Defrenne case was that Mlle Defrenne won the case for private equal pension rights in principle, but the Court declared also that there could be no retrospective claims from any persons whose cases had not already gone before the Court. In the matter of private equal pension rights therefore, it appears that – if Denning is correct – each individual case has to be taken on its merits through the national system and thence to the Court of Justice. The result, while the Court's rulings preserve fine distinctions, is, in pensions equality, one of possible contradiction. It is a nice point, for example, to distinguish pension as meaning pay.

7 This may be construed as meaning those who would normally be employed under a contract of employment.

view to obtaining employment[8]; enter, together with family, even if not a national of an EEC country in order to take up an employment offer which has actually been made[9]; settle with family once employment has been obtained[10]; remain in the host country for a year at least in the case of incapacity or temporary involuntary unemployment[11]; and acquire rights of permanent residence in the host country, subject to certain requirements, upon permanent incapacity, or on taking up employment in another member state, or after attainment of normal retiring age (permanent residence may, subject to certain conditions, be acquired by the worker's family after his or her death).[12]

27. Although there are exemptions from Article 48 on grounds of public policy, security or health, EEC states' discretion is limited.[13] In one case, the Court of Justice stated that entry restrictions on public policy grounds could only be implemented where there was a genuine and sufficiently serious threat. Failure to complete entry formalities does not justify deportation. Regulation 1612/68 supplements the Article on race discrimination. Taken with Article 48, the regulation offers generally the same rights in the UK as the Race Relations Act. However, since actions can be brought in UK courts under Article 48 and regulation 1612/68, provided that they are not barred because other legal recourse is available under national statute, there may be instances where litigation under the Article is preferable (if for no other reason than because time limits are longer).

28. Article 48 provides for an exemption from the freedom of movement laws in "employment in the public service." The exact meaning of this phrase has yet to be tested. It was intended to exclude only civil servants, but it may be argued that it is sufficiently wide and vague possibly to refer to teachers (and also health workers). If teachers are excluded by the definition, a further anomaly arises, for many teachers in Europe are employed by religious bodies: for example, there could be the case that a Belgian teacher in a Catholic institution could have the protection of the freedom of movement laws in moving throughout the EEC to similar institutions, but a Belgian teacher working in a state establishment could not. (80% of Belgian education occurs in denominational institutions, and only 20% in state institutions; and in this latter case the teacher is employed directly by the state). In other words, there may be an anomaly whereby denominational teachers have freedom of movement protection, but "public service" teachers do not. Protection against discrimination in employment, therefore, rests only on the national laws of the EEC states. It must be stressed that this "public service" issue is unclear, and requires definition.

---

8 Council Regulation 1612/68, 15 October 1968; Council Directive 68/360, 15 October 1968. Work permits and visas are not required except where members of workers' families are not nationals of an EEC country.

9 Council Regulation 1612/68.

10 A residence permit is necessary for longer stays, (in Britain six months or more, except in the case of Eire nationals) and is valid for five years, renewable automatically. Employment can begin before residence formalities are complete.

11 Council Directive 68/360.

12 Commission Regulation 70/326, 29 June 1970.

13 Council Directive 64/221, 25 February 1964.

The EEC Commission has assured the author that in principle the public service exclusion does not apply to teachers and health workers, but admits that there is a potential problem. In practice at present the issue scarcely arises since there is currently very little movement of teachers through the EEC. The Education Committee, however, is proceeding on the basis that teacher mobility will occur. In *Towards A European Education Policy,* Bulletin of the European Communities 1/77, teacher mobility in nursery, primary and secondary education is accepted; and the document gives evidence that student and teacher mobility in further and higher education is being studied. The practical difficulty at present relates to the transferability of qualifications. The processes in the EEC concerning academic recognition are continuing, albeit slowly (cf Section **6.2.**5). Progress is hampered by the difficulty presented by language, and by the growing practical problem of teacher unemployment.

29. It remains briefly to consider the types of legislation which can be expected to affect the UK. A directive of 1977[14] will result in a small amendment to the Health and Safety at Work etc. Act: where employers have safety signs at workplaces, they are to be required to use the standard EEC signs. There are exemptions to this requirement, but education is not included among them.

30. By a study of directives currently in draft, areas of UK law change can be predicted. These may be itemised as: in employment merger and tranfer, the automatic transfer of the contractual relationship, information and negotiation rights, union representation safeguarding, and safeguarding against dismissal arising solely from the merger; changes in company law; and the eradication of "conflict of law" in employment relationships.[15] The latter item is intended to provide equality in contract law across the EEC. This provision will be important in the UK for contract law currently presents formidable conflict. Contract law in its "conflict" rules differs generally from liability law regarding accidents at work, and both in turn differ from public law in relation to employment contracts. Substantial reform can be expected.

31, A draft directive concerning illegal work was adopted in October 1978 by the European Parliament. There are four constitutional stages to complete before a decision by the Council of Social Ministers renders it a legal document. Changes may, of course, occur during this process. The draft directive appears to require member states to have legislation penalising employers who employ illegal migrants. The definition of illegal migrants is wider than that currently operated in the UK. It includes not only illegal entrants but also those legal entrants whose permission to stay has expired. The draft directive requires employers to check on their employees' credentials (instead of just by immigration officers at points of entry),

14 To comply with the rough two year rule, the UK should have made legislation in 1979 (to take effect in 1981). At the time of writing this had not been done.

15 "Conflict" is the circumstance which arises when some aspects of the contract appear to be in accordance with the law of one state and other aspects of the transaction appear to fall under the differing law of another state. English law applies complex rules for the resolution of such conflicts.

includes the possible sanction of imprisonment, and stipulates that employers should bear repatriation costs. UK representatives at the European Parliament strenuously opposed the adoption of this draft directive.

32. There is sound evidence[16] to suggest that directives can be anticipated concerning individual dismissals, the raising of social security benefits[17] and special employment rules for young workers. There are more possible proposals than these; only those most likely directly to affect education have been selected.

33. This sub-section has dealt with the Community structure and law at some length. This has been necessary in order that the status of the law quoted in the following sub-sections can be appreciated, to indicate changes which can be expected to occur in the law summarised in Sections **11.6**, Appendix 7 and **12.10**, and to demonstrate the possible alternatives to legal action under current UK employment law.

REFERENCE

Schedule of Community Acts Concerning Right of Establishment and Freedom to Provide Services, Commission of the European Communities, Doc. 111/1418 77-EN (and addenda).
Treaties Establishing The European Communities, Office for Official Publications of the European Communities, Luxembourg, 1978. (This publication is available from HMSO. An abridged version was published in 1979).
On Freedom Of Movement For Workers, Council Regulation 1612/68.
On the Right of Workers to Remain in the Territory of a Member State after having been Employed in that State, Commission Regulation 70/326.
On the Abolition of Restriction on Movement and Residence within the Community for Workers of Member States and their Families, Council Directive 68/360.
Proposal for Council Directive concerning the approximation of the member states in order to combat illegal migration and illegal employment. Official Journal of the European Communities, C 97, Vol 21.
Towards a European Education Policy, Bulletin of the European Communities, 1/77.

European Communities Act 1972, Chapter 68, HMSO.

IDS International Reports, Incomes Data Services (especially nos. 76 and 103 (indices), and 70.5, 76.5, 84.3 and 95.2).
The EEC and the UK Employer, IDS Handbook series no 7, 1977.

16 cf *The EEC and the UK Employer,* IDS Handbook series No 7, October 1977. pp 87-95.
17 This may be a contentious issue. For example, if the UK were to follow the Belgian pattern, an unemployed qualified teacher would receive an unemployment benefit, according to qualification level, which may be up to 50% of the regular salary were the teacher to be employed.

2 EDUCATIONAL AND TRAINING POLICIES IN THE EEC

1. Education is not mentioned at all directly in the Treaty of Rome. However, Article 57 makes some provision concerning the mutual recognition of diplomas, and Articles 118 and 128 make specific reference to vocational training. The latter Article makes provision for a common vocational training policy. In the last decade the Community has begun to develop educational policies, albeit haltingly and to a very limited extent. These are considered below. Vocational training is clearly of significance to the Community's economic policies. Hence as early as 1963 the Council established a number of binding principles for a common policy on vocational education, including rather anodyne references to the needs for retraining, "éducation permanente", manpower planning, research, dissemination of education, exchanges and study visits, improved instructor training and the harmonisation of qualifications. More significantly, the Council Decision stressed that vocational training was inseparable from a liberal education. The vocational training policies of the Community are funded by the European Social Fund, and are the concern of Directorate-General 5 (Social Affairs). They are discussed below in paragraphs 16-22.

2. The Education Ministers of the EEC did not meet together until 1971. Although annual meetings were planned, they have been cancelled frequently by one or other of the member states. Only four subsequent meetings have taken place. At the 1971 meeting the Ministers recognised a need for co-operation in education, and established initiatives from which stem current EEC education policies. A working party was set up whose report (The Janne Report) argued for Community harmonisation in three areas: 16-19 education, educational technologies and "éducation permanente" (or, continuing education). The report was too visionary for the Commission, which reduced it to the more limited and less costly objectives of the equivalence of qualifications, the mobility of teachers and administrators, the development of foreign language teaching, and the education of the children of migrant workers.[1]

3. An administrative structure for implementing Community education policies was sought, and a Directorate-General for Research, Science and Education (DG 12) was established in 1973. A forum for meetings of Education Ministers was formalised but, in response to opposition from some member states to Community involvement in education, this was implemented by a formula – the Council of Ministers and Education Ministers Meeting in Council – which precluded the broader legislative role held by other meetings of ministers, such as Agricultural Ministers. An Education Committee, comprising officials of each of the member states and of the

---

1 *For a Community Policy on Education,* Commission of the European Communities, 1973.

Commission, was set up with the tasks of preparing for meetings of ministers and of producing a Community action programme for education.[2] In 1976 a programme of educational co-operation was agreed (Council Decision of 9 February 1976), with the broad aims of promoting European unity and greater equality of opportunity throughout the community. More specifically, an action programme was adopted (Council Decision of 13 December 1976) which recognises the strategic importance of education within the EEC and its inseparability from employment and vocational training policies. This integrated policy for education and training clearly has far reaching consequences.

4. The action programme covers 6 major areas. The first is the education of migrant workers and their children. Under a 1977 directive, member states were required to provide reception classes for teaching the host country's language, tuition in language and culture of the country of origin, and specialised training for the teachers of migrants' children. A number of pilot programmes have been established in support of the directive, and are considered in paragraphs 10-14 below. The second area is that of transition from school to work. Priority has been given to the promotion of information exchanges, studies of common problems, the educational and training needs of school leavers, ways of stimulating higher participation levels by young people in school and work, the development of educational and vocational counselling, and the training of appropriate teacher groups. Special attention is given to migrants, to young girls (reflecting the Treaty of Rome's advocacy of equal treatment for men and women), and handicapped young persons. The other four action programme areas are foreign language teaching, student and teacher mobility, the study of European problems in their geographical, historical and political aspects, and the extension of international information networks and cooperation between education systems. These have a number of implications for teacher training which are discussed below. The action programme with its pilot projects has been approved for four years, until the end of 1980, but is expected to be extended for another year.

5. **Teacher training and retraining**

Because the primary concern of the creators of Europe has been with economic integration, the founding treaties ECSC[3], EEC[4], and EAEC[5] reveal little interest in educational matters. As an example, Article 57 of the EEC treaty, although bearing on the mutual recognition of diplomas, does not implement schemes to cope with the actual integration problems resulting from the language and cultural differences between the member states. Ways had to be devised to align the different educational systems in order to lead to a greater teacher and student mobility. However, it was not until 1974 that the EEC Ministers of Education agreed upon the institution of an Education Committee. As stated above, the Committee's task was to

---

2 Resolution of the Council and of the Ministers of Education Meeting within the Council, OJ C 38/1 of 19/2/1976.
3 European Coal and Steel Community (1951).
4 European Economic Community (1957).
5 European Atomic Energy Community (1957).

set up an action programme for the harmonisation of education in the Community.

6. The committee may claim some results, as will be demonstrated below, but progress has been particularly slow in teacher mobility. This is due. at least partially, to the great diversity of qualifications, duration and type of teacher training in the various countries. Table 1 demonstrates that studies appear to range from: a two-year training at a non-academic institution (Belgium, France, Luxembourg); a fully graduate three-year course (Germany, Ireland, United Kingdom from 1980) for nursery and primary school trainees; and from four to six years of academic training for secondary school candidate teachers. In Belgium, Denmark and Germany, teacher training for junior secondary schools is part of level 1[6]. In the other countries, training for secondary education constitutes a discrete (and often indivisible) programme. It is in the field of teacher training itself, however, that differences are most marked. Level 1 training, as a rule, is integrated within the curriculum of teacher training colleges; at level 2 it may be part of the formal training at the university (Belgium, Netherlands, France), or be a post graduate course as in Italy and Luxembourg. In Germany, teacher training is a supervised, paid, probationary period of teaching experience leading to the final state examination.

7. Not all countries give similar consideration to the retraining needs of their teachers. In some of the Community states, teachers can attend only short term refresher courses varying in length from one day to a series of afternoon lectures. In Italy regional "Teachers' Centres" have been set up: all teachers can exchange experience and undertake research according to their individual training needs. Denmark and the UK may grant their teachers study leaves which allow longer periods of absence from the regular job in order to update initial training and assimilate new methods and techniques. The Education Committee believes that if "external mobility", or the facility of one teacher to take up a post in another Community country, is to succeed, teacher training will have first to allow an internal mobility. This would necessitate adapting the curriculum to the assessed realistic needs of society and the stimulation of interaction with other professions. France has taken a step in this direction by providing for adult education: teachers are given a one-year specialised training course to prepare them for on-the-job training of adults. After two years, they can resume their former duties, having acquired considerable experience in a training rather than a directly educational area. Further, in a number of countries "credit hours" can be used by the employed to attend language courses; this occurs in Belgium, for example.

8. This overview clearly demonstrates the scale of difficulties to be overcome before the integration of all teacher training in the EEC. Not only will the nature of training have to be reconsidered – for example, in its substance and duration – but those responsible for education policy making will be increasingly confronted with the problem of permanent retraining (the claim

---

6 for explanation see legend under table 1.

Table 1

EEC Teacher Training

Country	*Duration* (years) Level 1	Level 2A	Level 2B	*Type of Training* Level 1	Level 2A	Level 2B	*Teacher Practice at Level 2B*
BELGIUM	2	*Ibid*	4	Ed. Col	Ed. Col	Uni	theory and teaching practice as part of "Aggregaat" (4th year/Uni)
DENMARK	$3\frac{1}{2}$	4	6	Ed. Col	Ed. Col	Uni	"Pedagogicum" written exam on history of education teaching method after 4/5 months' preparation
FRANCE	2	1+2 (PEGC) 3+1 (CAPES)		Ed. Col	Uni (1)+ Reg. Uni (3)+ Reg.	Centres (2) Centred (1)	at Regional Centres at Regional Centres
GERMANY	3	*ibid*	4	Uni status	Uni status	Uni	theory integrated in Uni curriculum practice in probationary period of 18 months in schools.
IRELAND	3	3+1	3+1	Ed. Col/Uni	Uni	Uni	post graduate training for the Higher Diploma in Education.
ITALY	3/4	4	4	Ed. Col	Uni	Uni	a six months' post graduate course
LUXEMBOURG	2	4	4	Ed. Col	Uni (Abroad)	Uni (abroad)	three years' probationary experience in schools
NETHERLANDS	4 (2nd/3rd grade)	*ibid*	6 (1st grade)	Ed.Col/Uni	Ed. Col/Uni	Uni	theory and practice integrated in initial training
UK	3 3+1	3 3+1	3 3+1	degree c. (After 1980)	degree c. (after 1980)	degree c.	– integrated in BEd – BA+1 (Post Graduate Certificate of Education)

For United Kingdom and the Netherlands, apparent over-simplification of a complex educational teacher training network results from ommission of current systems that are in the process of being phased out. Illustration is made complex since systems as well as qualifications differ.

Legend Level 1 = nursery and primary school
Level 2 = secondary school: A junior
B senior
ibid: where the training for junior secondary schools is part of level 1 training.

for continuing education in all professions). The Association for the Training of Teachers in Europe (founded in Liége in 1976) may assist by its promotion of the sharing of experience between institutions of different nationalities.

9. **Professional mobility**

Presumably at least partially because of doubts concerning teachers' eligibility under the freedom of movement laws (see Section **6.1.**28), progress towards teacher mobility has been slow. Co-operation has been more successful concerning the other professions. This is especially the case between the institutions of higher education concerned with nuclear sciences, data processing, the environment and medical and energy research. Dating from the foundation in 1976 of the Advisory Committee on Medical Training, regular reports have been issued on comparable basic and clinical training standards for doctors. Similar initiatives were taken in 1978 for veterinary surgeons and dentists to guarantee transferability of qualifications. It is now a legal right for nationals qualified in one of the professions (other than lawyers) to establish a practice in another EEC state.[7] These developments are a consequence of Council Resolution 6/6/74 on the mutual recognition of diplomas, certificates and other evidence of formal qualifications. Agreement concerning transferability has been based largely on norms of professional skill, however defined: quantitative criteria have been found to be inappropriate.

10. **A Common Education Policy?**

The vision of the Janne Report has little place in present Community educational policies. The budget devoted to education is minute by Community standards – in 1978 only £3.5m, or a mere 0.0004% of the total Community budget. The areas of current action reflect the short-term needs of member states, in spheres where national interests are least likely to be challenged. Fundamental disagreements between member states about the rights of the EEC to consider education at all persist, and have led to the cancellation of the last two scheduled meetings of Education Ministers. Attempts to overcome problems have focused upon Treaty Article 235, which empowers the Commission to take action in areas other than those specified and therefore could provide the means for a major Community educational programme. But there are few signs at present of the political will within the Community necessary for such a programme, and the aspirations catalogued below are as yet unfulfilled throughout the Community.

11. The harmonisation of teacher training is only a part of the overall problem of initiating a truly European education policy. For this reason Council Decision 9/2/1976 recommended measures to be taken by all member states to increase integration efforts. The most urgent resolutions and strategies were brought to the attention of the national education representatives by the European Commission.[8] The Education Committee frequently finds that

7 Council Decisions 24/8/1978 (dentists) and 23/12/1978 (veterinary surgeons); *Twelfth General Report on the Activities of the European Communities 1978*, Brussels, 1979.
8. *Towards a European Education Policy*, Commission of the European Communities, European documentation, 1977/2.

lack of command of languages proves to be the main handicap to professional mobility, or even cultural exchange. Pending a solution to the problem of whether one or more foreign languages should be introduced at the primary school level, the Education Ministers urged their governments to improve language teaching in general, to organize training periods for language teachers, and to encourage exchanges for students and pupils. Inter-Community state exchanges for education administrators and educational staff to observe and discuss language teaching techniques are also considered necessary. The status of language teaching is said to require alteration: the successful example of the educational institutions for the children of EEC officials demonstrates that a foreign language can be used effectively for the teaching of other subjects. Bi-lingual education of this nature is stated to be an excellent expedient in the acquisition of a thorough grounding in languages. Moreover, freedom of movement of labour is considered utopian unless language programmes are set up for the in-service training of adults.

12. When the Education Ministers launched their action programme in 1975, they fully realised that all integration efforts would fail if the EEC peoples did not acquire a better understanding of European problems and developments. Documentation is now available from the Commission. It is claimed that effective insight is being delayed as long as European Studies are not introduced as a compulsory subject to all primary and secondary schools curricula. Some universities have a European documentation centre; some may also provide courses in European Affairs. A positive and hopeful achievement is the founding in 1972 of the European Institute in Florence. Since it was officially opened in 1976, it has functioned as an intellectual depository for post graduate work on European history and civilization, economics, law and political and social sciences.

13. The most noteworthy example of where the European idea has been given a concrete shape is in the education of migrant workers' children. The problems facing these children are manifold: apart from the language barrier there is the psychological shock to children confronted with an alien and sometimes hostile environment. The older immigrant children are the more likely to experience frustration and integration difficulties. Articles 7 and 12 of EEC Regulation 1612/68 (October 1967) therefore stipulate that all national governments should increase their efforts to break down language and cultural barriers for the children of resident immigrants, and to ensure their access to the normal educational facilities under the same conditions as nationals[9]. For children aged under five who interact with children of their age in the host country, and who receive pre-school education, integration into the new environment is a quick and natural process with few adaptation problems. After these formative years, immigrant children receive special language tuition in the form of crash courses where specialised teachers train small classes using intensive language acquisition methods. If the "foreign" population does not exceed 20% of the native

9 see *Education of Migrant Workers' Children in the European Community*, European Documentation, 1975/1.

children, cultural and social integration may be achieved in one or two years, after which the children can attend normal classes. These "reception classes" have been organized successfully in some of the member states: Denmark, Germany, France, Luxembourg and Belgium. In a number of cases special tuition is extended even after transfer to the regular classes in special remedial classes.

14. However important adaptation to the new environment may be, reintegration means that the cultural and social system of the home country must be stimulated, not only to permit the return of children to schools, but also to facilitate the access of adolescents to employment in their own country. This is why the study of the native language and cultural background is considered essential in the education of migrant workers' children. In Germany these studies are part of the normal school curriculum at both the primary and secondary level. To cope with these special needs language teachers, in particular those intending to take reception classes, should be familiarised with the cultural and religious background of the children, and trained in the use of intensive methods. In Germany, which sets an example in a number of integration measures, foreign teachers are recruited to supplement native staff.

15. Other significant developments include the establishment of an information centres network to serve policy makers, exchange information and support the priority areas of the current education action programme. A descriptive handbook of member states' education systems is also planned. However, the major part of the small education budget is expended on a programme of 28 pilot projects, evaluation studies, study visits and workshops on the transition from school to work, reflecting the common concern throughout the Community for youth employment. These focus upon the educational and training needs of young people who experience difficulty in finding and retaining work, who are poorly motivated, or who belong to certain disadvantaged categories – girls, migrants and handicapped young people. Altogether they absorb over 70% of the EEC education budget, which may well reflect the overlapping concerns of two Directorate-Generals here: for Social Affairs; and for Research, Science and Education. The former is responsible for the administration of the EEC Social Fund, which has supported vocational training and retraining on a scale totally different from the meagre investment in education, disbursing over £350m in 1978 – a hundred times as much as the education budget. The deployment of the Social Fund budget is considered below.

16. **Adult vocational training and further education**

The 1963 Council decision establishing ten general principles for the implementation of a common EEC policy on vocational training has been referred to in paragraph 1, above. These principles have not been carried into effect, a result of their idealism and subsequent practical difficulties. However, the guidance which they established remains and certain positive results have occurred. The European Centre for the Development of Vocational Training (CEDEFOP) was set up in Berlin in 1975. Its tasks are to promote and develop vocational training and in-service training for adults at Community level; and to investigate the relationship between school systems and vocational training schemes, paying special attention to language training for adults (in order to facilitate the free movement of labour).[10] The Commission is sponsoring research to analyse the assistance provided by the broadcasting media in the teaching of languages to adults. Action is to be taken to improve access to language courses, especially because migrant workers do not have ready access to vocational training institutions in the host country. It is an EEC intention to make vocational training an integral part of general civic and cultural training. The hope is expressed that unions, professional associations, industry, and governments will consult together to determine the education structures necessary to meet the individual's working, cultural, civic and family needs. To assist this process, the European Parliament has requested the Commission to provide information concerning EEC adult education, and opportunities for action by the Community.

17. **The European Social Fund**

The European Social Fund (ESF), in compliance with a decision by the Social Affairs Ministers in June 1974, is in a position to meet half the bill for the organization of special courses for migrant children and for training schemes for social workers and teachers. When the European Social Fund was set up in 1958 "to improve employment opportunities for workers in the common market"[11] the full scope of its future activities was not foreseeable in the social and economic context of the time. Fundamental reforms in 1971 greatly extended the activities of the ESF. One of the first initiatives taken in 1972 was the financial aid for reconversion programmes for people wanting to leave agriculture and seek employment in non-agricultural areas.[12] Similar measures affecting an entire economic sector were taken in 1976 to protect the textile and clothing industries, in the main by assisting member states in their retraining programmes. These programmes were submitted by national,public and private training authorities[13] . But it was not until 1975,

10 In 1978 the Centre gave priority to work concerning how vocational training can improve the employment prospects of young people (specifically during the transition from school to work) and to the collection and dissemination of information to achieve a better understanding of the national vocational training systems and their financing. The Centre follows EEC policies in devoting attention to young people, women and migrant workers. It also deals with the issue of continuing vocational training, and the effect of the development of qualifications on vocational training. The Centre carries out its work by means of studies, surveys, conferences and seminars. It has an initiative and experimental role. For example, it developed an action programme concerning equal opportunities and vocational training for 1978-79, is carrying out work on the effects of technological development for vocational training, and has undertaken comparative studies on national vocational training systems. The Centre publishes *The Vocational Training Bulletin*, responsibility for which it took over from the Directorate-General, Employment and Social Affairs in 1977. The *Bulletin* is aimed at a general educational readership, and seeks to provide authoritative information concerning training in the EEC. The Centre has participated in its work with bodies such as the ETUC, OECD, UNESCO, and other organizations.

11 Article 123 of the Treaty for the Establishment of the European Economic Community (i.e. The Treaty of Rome).

12 Council Decision 72/428 of 19/12/1972, amended by CD 77/802.

13 Council Decision 76/206 of 9/2/1976 amended by CD 77/802.

when the full impact of the economic recession became clear, that most of the interventions of the European Social Fund were geared to coping with youth unemployment. Youth unemployment is perceived by the Commission as the most serious manifestation of the economic crisis.[14] The total figure for unemployment throughout the Commmnity in 1978 was 5,969,000, 38% of which (2,200,000) represented young people under 25.[15] In the light of this alarming situation, and also because of the great number of job vacancies registered with the national public employment services [16], vocational training programmes were set up together with effective placement services to facilitate geographical mobility in the Community. It is these undertakings which give the European Social Fund an important role in further education.

18. The other fields of intervention of the European Social Fund are: migrant workers and women (grouped under Article 4), and "regions", groups of firms and the handicapped (Article 5). This categorisation is meant to distinguish the fields of permanent intervention (Article 5) from those eligible for temporary aid (Article 4). It is worth mentioning that the European Social Fund is not a public service in the English sense of the word, but rather an Employment Training Fund intended to lead to new, stable employment. Individuals cannot apply for aid (see Section **6.3.**12). In the following breakdown by field of intervention, emphasis is laid on existing vocational training programmes or on current EEC measures affecting further education.[17]

19. **Article 4: Temporary Aid**

Five categories of person benefit under this article of the Social Fund. They are:

(i) *Persons leaving agriculture*

Approximately 8,000 persons benefited in 1978 from programmes that provided training for people who were seeking a different kind of job (building, metallurgy, electronics, electrical, services, processing and agricultural products), and for those who wanted to supplement their agricultural occupation with a different activity (tourism, craft industries, management of skiing and camping).

(ii) *Workers in the textile and clothing industries*

Community finance was spent in areas of high unemployment where public training authorities provided in-firm training in centres linked with a number of firms (13,500 recipients).

(iii) *Young people*

Assistance given under this heading was of the following type:

(a) vocational preparation for school leavers;

---

14 Council Decision 75/459 amended by CD 77/802 and 78/1036.

15 See *Seventh Report on the Activities of the European Social Fund. Financial year 1978*, p.4.

16 A total number of 685,000 by June 1978 in seven of the member states.

17 Full statistical and numerical information may be found in the *Seventh Report on the Activities of the European Social Fund. Financial Year 1978*, Brussels, 1979.

(b) supplementing inadequate initial training with vocational training;
(c) professional training in para-medical occupations; and
(d) vocational preparation for semi-skilled jobs.

Moreover the Council has ruled[18] that assistance shall be granted for the creation of additional jobs with a vocational content, making it easier for young people under 25 to find a stable job. This regulation became effective as of 1 January 1979. The recent widening of the scope of aid granted to the young unemployed benefited about 300,000 persons under 25; expenditure amounted to 388m EUA[19].

(iv) *Women*

1978 was the first year of applications in a new field opened up by Council Decision 77/804. This aimed at providing women aged 25 and over – both the recently unemployed and those wanting to resume work after a period of absence – with training leading to employment. Three of these programmes had been financed as pilot projects in an attempt to devise means to prepare women for jobs from which they had been thus far excluded. Pursuant to Article 4 of Council Decision 71/66, the cost for the training and preparing of instructors was included in the expenditure for the training programmes.

(v) *Migrant workers*

Although free movement of labour has been one of the major objectives since the foundation of the EEC, the global percentage of Community workers finding employment in another country is only 1.6% of the domestic working population.[20] In order to promote geographical and occupational mobility, an earlier Council Decision of 1971 was amended by CD 77/803 which extended assistance to all integrated programmes and integration measures to facilitate adaptation of the adult migrant workers to the working and social life of the host country. In 1978, such programmes included in-company language courses and basic and advanced training of social workers. Integrated programmes were submitted by almost all member states and provided for:
(a) the schooling of 100,000 children of migrant workers;[21]
(b) language and training courses of about 130,000 adult migrants; and
(c) the training of about 4,000 teachers and social workers.

---

18 Council Decision 78/1036.
19 million European Units of Account; 1 EUA = Dkr 7.01; DM 2.59; Bfr 40.19; FF 5.82; £0.629; Lir 1,064; Fl 2.77.
20 Horst Reichenbach, *The Impact of European Integration on its Members – a Political and Economic Overview*, forthcoming. The figure excludes workers who commute to work across national frontiers.
21 No provision is made for the normal education covered by the national public services.

20. **Article 5 : Permanent Intervention**

(i) *Regions*

The Social Fund was also established to raise the standard of living of all Community members, especially in the less developed regions.[22] This is why 37.6% of the Fund's total resources are committed to the five absolute priority regions: those which, besides structural deficiencies, face the most serious employment problems. The priority regions are: Greenland, the French Overseas Departments,[23] Ireland, Mezzogiorno and Northern Ireland. For the same reason, and pursuant to paragraph 9 (2) of the same Council Decision, 50% of the actions making provisions for persons (Article 4) are to be carried out in the ERDF regions.[24] The Commission under this heading promoted national training programmes to maintain people in employment in their own regions; and to prepare management staff or to supply necessary training in case of industrial reconversion. Under this provision the regional authorities of Rhône-Alpes and the University of Lyon were granted aid to employ 5,000 people on a three-year developmental programme of the Ardèche. Likewise, the Scottish Development Agency could train small craft firms in rural zones with Fund assistance.

(ii) *Groups of firms and occupational areas*

Very often regional assistance is connected with groups of firms which apply for the training of management staff and personnel for innovative technology in the chemical, metal or publishing industries. The aggregate amount in 1978 for Regions and Technical Progress was 281m EUA, affecting 385,000 people.

(iii) *Handicapped workers*

By Council Regulation 2893/77 measures were also taken for the reintegration into working life of the handicapped after functional rehabilitation, vocational adaptation and re-adaptation. Finance was extended to the training and advanced training of personnel.

21. Applications for ESF finance in all fields of intervention should be addressed to the national employment authorities of the member state. These authorities alone can submit applications to the Commission. In its decisions concerning programme eligibility, the Commission is advised by the Social Fund Committee. This comprises representatives of governments, and employers' and workers' organizations.[25] The kind of aid granted by the ESF normally covers:

(i) expenditure incurred by the preparation and management of training courses, including the training of instructors;

---

22 Article 5 of Council Decision 71/66, sub-paragraph 1(a).

23 Guadaloupe, Martinique, Réunion, St Pierre, Miguelon, French Guiana.

24 European Regional Development Fund. These regions are the regional development areas as determined by the member states.

25 cf Section **6.1.**5-6.

(ii) tuition fees and the payment of trainees' salaries while attending courses; and

(iii) the cost of transfer of the trainee and family, and their integration in the social and working environment. Appendix 1 demonstrates the total figure of recipients per country and per field of intervention through 1978 and parts of 1979.

22. Although the amount of EEC educational action may appear small, it must be appreciated that there is considerable co-operation between DG5 and DG12 on educational issues. Many surveys have been undertaken, there has been a large amount of discussion, and educational policy is subject to considerable thought within the EEC.

APPENDIX 1

SOCIAL FUND RECIPIENTS 1978/79

Countries	Field of intervention	Number of recipients
Belgium	Migrant workers	166
	Young people	4800
	Women	30
	Regions	6600
	Groups of firms	375
	Handicapped	220
	Total	12191
Denmark	Migrant workers	8042
	Young people	17352
	Women	1500
	Regions	11083
	Groups of firms	450
	Handicapped	1600
	Total	40027
France	Agriculture	9182
	Textile	871
	Migrant workers	15301
	Young people	139089
	Women	11203
	Regions	34912
	Groups of firms	834
	Handicapped	5012
	Total	216404
Germany	Agriculture	1080
	Textile	2665
	Migrant workers	1023105
	Young people	8809
	Women	60
	Regions	26497
	Handicapped	2433
	Total	1064649
Ireland	Agriculture	1365
	Textile	160
	Migrant workers	400
	Young people	22888
	Women	12
	Regions	38833
	Handicapped	12410
	Total	76068

6.2

Countries (cont)	Field of intervention (Cont)	Number of recipients (Cont)
Italy	Agriculture	450
	Textile	3543
	Migrant workers	118494
	Young people	117202
	Women	930
	Regions	213109
	Groups of firms	7076
	Handicapped	7328
	Total	468132
Luxembourg	Young people	630
	Handicapped	217
	Total	847
Netherlands	Agriculture	350
	Textile	2000
	Migrant workers	80400
	Young people	6000
	Women	2000
	Regions	1800
	Groups of firms	1000
	Handicapped	1890
	Total	95440
United Kingdom	Textile	4213
	Migrant workers	16450
	Young people	72726
	Regions	81156
	Handicapped	41890
	Total	216435

REFERENCE

Council of Europe, *Eudised R & D Bulletin,* Documentation Centre for Europe, Strasbourg, 1978.

European Centre for the Development of Vocational Training, *Annual Report 1978,* Office for Official Publications of The European Communities, Luxembourg, 1979.

European Social Fund-Official Texts, Commission of the European Communities, Brussels, 1979.

Education of Migrant Workers' Children in the European Community, Commission of the European Communities, European Documentation, 1975/1.

Grants and Loans from the European Community, Commission of the European Communities, Division 1X D11, 1978.

Le développement européen de l'éducation permanente, Commission of the European Communities, Collection Études, Brussels, 1976.

Practical Guide on the Submission and Consideration of Applications for Aid from the European Social Fund, Directorate General for Research and Documentation of the European Parliament, 1978.

Seventh Report on the Activities of the European Social Fund-Financial Year 1978, Commission of the European Communities, Brussels, 1979.

Teacher Training in the European Community, Commission of the European Communities, European Documentation, 1976/2.

The European Community and Education, European file, E 18/79.

Towards a European Education Policy, Commission of the European Communities, European Documentation, 1977/2.

Twelfth General Report on the Activities of the European Communities, Commission of the European Communities, Brussels, 1979.

Horst Reichenbach, *The Impact of European Integration on its Members-A Political and Economic Overview,* forthcoming.

3 THE EEC: EDUCATION AND TRAINING IN ENGLAND AND WALES

1. As the previous sub-section has explained, the direct impact of the EEC upon education and training in the member states is still relatively slight, but is growing rapidly. This sub-section outlines some of the ways in which the activities of the European Community are affecting education and training in England and Wales, and suggests some likely developments.

2. **The European Social Fund**
The major current influence of the EEC upon education and training in the Community is through the operations of the European Social Fund. The Fund's objectives are described above in Section **6.2.**17, where it is pointed out that the Fund is mis-named, as it is used exclusively for the encouragement of employment and associated training activities in the member states. The United Kingdom, like the other member states, benefits from five types of Social Fund aid. These are: aid to facilitate training including both the operating expenses of training courses and grants to participants; aid to ease the movement of workers and their families forced to change their place of residence; aid which facilitates integration into new social and working environments; aid which eases access to available employment for handicapped persons and workers over 50 years of age; and aid which promotes better conditions of employment in less-developed and declining regions of the Community. In no circumstances is aid available for social security and other medical benefits, for capital expenditure, or for the normal education of children of migrant workers.

3. Social Fund aid is limited to 50% of the total national public expenditure eligible for aid, or, if the scheme is undertaken by a private organization, an amount equal to the contribution of the public authorities. Public authorities must also be able to guarantee the scheme's completion (although they need not be the authorities providing financial support), and aid cannot be extended over more than three years. In Britain, public authorities comprise government departments and agencies, including the MSC, local authorities, nationalised industries and Industrial Training Boards. In general terms training programmes must be aimed at providing new stable employment for their participants within a defined area, industry, company or category of persons. They should normally last for at least 100 hours, and offer reasonable expectations of improved status or salaries, and normally should be large enough to have some impact upon problems of unemployment.

4. Social Fund aid is provided under three budget headings, under Articles 4 and 5 of the reformed Fund and Article 7 of the regulations administering the Fund.[1] These are described in detail in the previous sub-section. Five areas have so far been identified by the Council as eligible for assistance

---

1 Articles of the Council Decision 71/66/EEC of 1/2/1971, as amended by Council Decision 77/801/EEC of 20/12/1977; Regulations governing the administration of the Fund, Regulation EEC 2398/71 as amended by EEC 2893/77.

under Article 4 in order to improve the balance between manpower supply and demand, or to compensate for Community policies which affect employment prospects. Of these, one – the assistance of former agricultural workers seeking non-agricultural occupations – has so far been of little significance in the United Kingdom. In 1979 the Commission has established top priority for programmes promoting the transition to tourist and craft activities, and for mountain and hill farming and other low-income areas.

5. Persons employed in the United Kingdom's textile and clothing industries may benefit from programmes which facilitate occupational or geographic mobility, with top priority currently given to workers having to leave those industries in areas of high unemployment, and to programmes for workers remaining in the industries where structural changes might enable the industry to become viable competitively. In 1978, programmes under the auspices of the Manpower Services Commission affected nearly 3,000 workers with grants from the Social Fund of over 5 million EUAs[2] (i.e. about £3.2m). Individual textile and clothing companies received aid of nearly £0.5m (matched by equivalent aid from public authorities).

6. Migrant workers may benefit from Social Fund aid for integrated programmes which facilitate mobility between member states, the reception and integration into a new social and working environment of such workers and their families, and the development of basic and advanced training programmes for social workers and teachers. Currently such programmes are given top priority, as are language tuition programmes for young people who have left school, and activities which demonstrate improvements in the adaptation of teaching methods for the children of migrant workers. However, migrants entering an EEC country from a non-EEC country (ie most migrants to Britain) qualify only for limited aid which can facilitate integration – language training, but not vocational training. In the United Kingdom the Home Office, in association with local authorities and the Department of the Environment, was the major recipient of such aid in 1978, obtaining nearly £0.5m for over 5,000 beneficiaries. The other organizations funded under this heading were the Manpower Services Commission and the London Council of Social Service.

7. Women over the age of 25 may benefit from aid to programmes designed to help them gain employment, a first professional qualification, or improved qualifications. The Commission has also stressed the importance of equal treatment of men and women at work, and of accompanying measures such as information concerning available jobs. In 1980-82 top priority is given to programmes preparing women for jobs in which they are under-represented and in new occupations. As yet requests for aid under this heading have not come up to available designated aid, and the United Kingdom made no eligible claims in 1978, partly because aid is restricted to programmes preceded by pre-vocational training, and followed by assistance in finding an appropriate job.

---

2 European Units of Account. These are currently equivalent to £0.629. Throughout the rest of this sub-section EUAs have been converted to £ sterling at this rate.

8. Young people under the age of 25 may benefit when unemployed or seeking employment. Although priority is given to assisting young people seeking their first jobs, the Fund cannot support the initial training of young people immediately after the end of their compulsory schooling. For 1980-82 the Commission has established specific and complex priorities to aid training programmes and to promote employment.[3] First priority is given to vocational preparation measures for young people under 20 years of age with no other opportunity to receive vocational training, which incorporate modern and appropriate teaching methods, vocational guidance and practical work experience, and active and regular liaison with employment services and potential employers. Skill training should carry the assurance of a subsequent job. Top priority is also given to basic training in certain occupations, to the retraining of those young people unemployed for at least six months and excluding university graduates whose basic training is not in demand, and to skill training for young women which seeks a balance between men and women and which encourages the access of women to occupational areas where they have been under-represented. With the exception of this last category, such aid is available only in the Community's five "absolute priority regions";[4] and to regions with youth employment levels above the national average or the community average as specified by the Commission.[5] Lower priority has been given to applications, also from these regions, for vocational training programmes which follow from the vocational preparation measures referred to above, and to training provided under employment-training contracts or traineeships in firms. Programmes promoting recruitment in the absolute priority regions are given top priority in the aid to employment category; lower priority is given to similar programmes in the other specified regions, and to large urban areas with high youth unemployment rates. As applications for aid under this heading far exceed available funds, the chances of successful application for second priority operations are relatively slight. In 1978 operations in the United Kingdom funded by the Manpower Services Commission received nearly £23m in Social Fund aid, for 71,000 young people. Other recipients were some Industrial Training Boards and some youth associations.

9. Article 5 permits Social Fund interventions where they alleviate long-term structural unemployment and train a highly skilled labour force in certain specified regions, occupational areas, groups of undertakings or involving handicapped persons capable of vocational rehabilitation. Regional aid, designed to help solve problems where under-development or economic decline is responsible for serious and prolonged economic difficulties, is available for regions specified in member states' internal regional aid systems. Five levels of priority have been established by the Commission for 1980-82 as applications in this largest of Social Fund categories are far in

---

3 OJ C 159, of 26/6/1979.

4 Greenland, the French Overseas Departments, Ireland, Northern Ireland and the Italian Mezzogiorno.

5 In 1978 the Community average was 12.4%: the United Kingdom average was 13.1%. Similar priorities have been established in the UK specified regions. Priority regions specified in the UK are in the North and North West of England, Scotland and Northern Ireland. OJ C 159 of 26/6/79.

excess of available funds. First priority is given to programmes of vocational training for unemployed workers and workers needing new qualifications in the five absolute priority regions (see footnote 4) and for basic courses of vocational training where employment prospects exist.[6] Second priority is given to operations in certain regions eligible for aid from the European Regional Development Fund. These currently include, in England & Wales, the "assisted areas" as identified by the Department of Employment. At third level are operations in other regions eligible for European Development Fund aid – including the remaining "non-assisted areas" in England and Wales. Second and third level programmes must contain the assurance of a job at the end of them. Fourth level priority is given to programmes in the areas specified at second and third levels for unemployed people with insufficient skills to benefit from vocational training, and at fifth level of priority are other programmes of training for the unemployed in those regions. In 1978, nearly 80,000 people in the United Kingdom benefitted from Social Fund regional aid amounting to nearly £28m, over £25m of which went to the Manpower Services Commission. Other recipients of such aid included the Departments of Health & Social Security, Agriculture and the Environment, various Industrial Training Boards, one of the major brewers (Whitbread & Co) and Durham University, which received about £7,000 for the development of entrepreneurial in-company training programmes at its Small Business Centre.

10. Although Social Fund aid is available for specified economic sectors with problems of adaptation to the requirements of technical progress, and to groups of undertakings forced to adjust to changed production and marketing circumstances, in 1978 the United Kingdom received no aid in either category. However, substantial aid was received in the fourth area of assistance, for handicapped persons capable of undertaking employment. For 1979 top priority was given to operations facilitating the placement of such persons in open employment, including agriculture, where such programmes employ adequate teaching methods and means of social and occupational integration. New demonstration activities designed to improve methods of rehabilitating and placing handicapped people in employment were also given top priority. For 1980-82, top priority is given to schemes for the handicapped in the priority regions identified above, and for innovatory and experimental operations. In 1978 the major recipients of the £6.7m of Social Fund aid in the United Kingdom were the Manpower Services Commission (about £6m) and the Department of Health and Social Security, benefiting about 40,000 handicapped persons.

11. **Pilot schemes and preparatory studies**

The third and smallest budget heading of the Social Fund is that, under Article 7, financing pilot schemes and preparatory studies where they might guide the Commission either in its choice of future areas of intervention or in the more efficient use of existing funds. Pilot schemes, which have priority over preparatory studies, may receive grant-aid at 50%, and must involve

---

6 OJ C 159 of 26/6/1979.

fewer than 30 people. They should be innovatory, designed to facilitate improved or additional employment, and to raise training standards, in ways potentially applicable throughout the Community, and concerned with youth unemployment, setting up small craft industries, creating new jobs for women, training for new skills arising from technological change, or training instructors. British pilot schemes in 1978 included an Engineering Industrial Training Board scheme which examined the possibilities of training women as technicians in the engineering industry, schemes for the handicapped by the Spastics Society and Alcoholics Recovery Project, and for the training of textile workers. Other schemes have assisted the establishment of experimental day-care centres to look after the children of student-mothers, under the action-research programmes to combat poverty.[7] Preparatory studies, which are smaller and more theoretical than pilot studies, may be financed completely by the Fund. The Commission selects bodies or institutions to undertake pilot and preparatory studies after needs have been identified.

12. **Applying for Social Fund aid**

The machinery whereby assistance is obtained from the Social Fund is complex but need not be lengthy. Individuals do not have the right to claim assistance from the Fund. Instead the Fund aids "operations", paying grants to the responsible public or private body. There are at least 9 types of application form, according to the type of aid being requested (the five headings under Article 4, and the four under Article 5). Applications must be forwarded by the member state to the Commission, necessitated by the requirement that Social Fund aid must be matched by public authorities in the member state.[8] Although the European Parliament has recommended that direct intervention by the Social Fund should on occasions be possible, this has not yet been acted on by the Council.

13. In the United Kingdom, the Department of Employment is the public authority in contact with the Social Fund, through which applications must be submitted. The Department will advise and help at every stage of application including, where necessary, the quest for public authority support. The relevant address is included at the end of this sub-section. Although the Commission required in 1972 that each member state inform the Commission of the procedure it has laid down for submission of applications for assistance, so that the information might then be published in the Official Journal of the European Communities,[9] such information has not yet been published.

14. The member states must submit their applications in groups to the Commission, either before 21 October for operations due to commence in the first half of the following year, or by 1 April for those due to commence in the second half of the year, provided that the nature and size of the

---

7 One such scheme is based at Hackney College, acting as an "area resource centre".
8 Except in the five "absolute priority regions" where a 10% higher rate of intervention automatically applies.
9 Council Regulation 858/72 of 24/4/1972.

operation had been notified before the previous 21 October. Single applications can be submitted only in response to unforeseen developments or in place of grouped applications. The Social Fund Advisory Committee receives the applications from the Commission and considers them for approval. The Committee, set up under Article 124 of the Treaty of Rome, is chaired by a Commissioner, and comprises 54 members, 18 each from the governments, the trade unions and the employers. The Committee uses a complex system of weightings and priorities when considering applications, as the volume of applications amounts to nearly double the size of the Fund. The major current priorities set by the Commission have been indicated above. The weighted reduction system applies in those categories where eligible applications exceed available funds, and is based upon each member state's national unemployment rate and gross national product in comparison with the Community average.

15. The Committee's decisions are considered and normally confirmed by the Commission in the following December and June respectively. Should the Commission disagree with the Committee's advice it must give its reasons within six weeks. The Commission may request further information from the member state, and should this not be forthcoming within the specified time limit, the application is then deemed to have lapsed. Once approval has been granted, assistance is paid to the responsible body, normally in three instalments, 30% in advance as soon as the member state notifies the Commission that the operation has commenced, 30% upon notification that half the operation is complete, and the remainder on receipt of a report on the scheme's completion, and after inspection by a Commission inspector.

16. In 1978 United Kingdom requests amounted to nearly one quarter of all requests, but well over half of these were rejected. Altogether, over £70m were allocated to UK operations.[10] It is not possible from the published figures to distinguish the proportion of these in England and Wales. Northern Ireland's status as one of the absolute priority regions ensured that a substantial proportion of available resources was deployed there.

Table 1

Social Fund applications and grants. 1978.[11] **(£ millions).**

	Amounts requested (£m)	*Amount Agreed*	*Not Eligible*	*Non Priority*	*Linear Reduction*	*Total Refused*
UK	165.7	70.3	0.2	60.0	35.2	95.4
EEC Total	688.0	357.3	2.3	199.2	130.2	331.7

17. It is not possible to identify Social Fund aid which has entered the further education system of England and Wales. It seems probable that most of such

10 *Seventh Report on the Activities of the European Social Fund – Financial Year 1978.*
11 *Ibid.*

aid has come through Manpower Services Commission sponsored schemes, as the MSC received a major part of Social Fund assistance in 1978, amounting to well over £50m. No identifiable educational organization (except Durham University) received aid directly from the Social Fund. This is a pattern of distribution very different from that pertaining in other member states. Thus in Ireland, the major recipient of aid in 1978 was the Industrial Training Authority, which might be compared to the MSC, but over 10% went to the Irish Department of Education. In Luxembourg the bulk of the (very limited) aid went to the Education Ministry, and in Italy the "scuola edile" – local authority funded vocational training centres – were major recipients of aid.

18. **The European Investment Bank**

Social Fund aid cannot be used for capital projects. However, the European Investment Bank may grant long-term loans to finance investment designed to solve regional problems. Vocational training centres are among the projects that the Investment Bank has funded. But although the United Kingdom was the largest single recipient of Bank loans in 1977, no support has been given to education or training developments other than those associated with specific industries. The Bank draws a clear distinction between activities which generate wealth, eligible for support, and other ineligible activities, in which latter category it includes national and local authority education and training programmes.

19. **Demonstration projects for energy saving** (cf Section **5.4.**2)

The Community grants financial support for projects designed to demonstrate a significant improvement in the efficiency with which energy is used. Financial aid can be between 25% and 49% of total costs, for schemes which have been preceded by a feasibility study, are capable of more general adoption in the Community, or involve risks or large investments so that other sources of finance are not readily available.

20. **Community education policies**

The activities of the Community's Education Committee and its Directorate-General for Research, Science and Education have been described in sub-Section **6.2**, above. The Community's Education action programme has not had a dramatic influence upon the education system in England and Wales. Experimental programmes for the children of migrant workers, and for language tuition outside the traditional school system have been encouraged. European Studies teaching has been promoted in schools and colleges (although, of course, European Studies were undertaken in some parts of England and Wales before accession to the EEC). Some students and teachers have benefited from the European schools established for the children of EEC officials,[12] from the European University Institute, and from moves to facilitate student mobility. A number of higher education institutions have received grants to foster courses where students spend part of the course in a foreign institution. English academics and civil servants

---

12 The first such school in Britain has recently been established at Culham in Oxfordshire.

have attended a wide variety of conferences and study groups examining aspects of education in the Community, including teacher-training, vocational training, and scientific and technical co-operation.[13] The total EEC education budget in 1978 was only £3.5m, of which the UK received only £0.5m

21. However, the Community is committed to education as a strategic part of its social and economic development, and EEC research has suggested that education is a powerful determinant of national industrial practices and organization. EEC perspectives see education as inseparable from employment and training policies, and recent evidence of significantly lower levels of *per capita* expenditure in the United Kingdom than in most of its EEC partners [14] may well have implications for the further education service. The EEC Education Ministers' current four-year action programme gives priority to action projects to facilitate the transition from school to work, to coordinate the activities of educational guidance, training and employment agencies, to improve job motivation, to encourage greater cooperation between schools and employers, to improve the in-service and initial training of teachers of those in transition from school to work, and to help specific groups – young girls, young migrants and the young handicapped. Already a major curriculum development project has been initiated under the auspices of the DES,[15] and experimental schemes for young school leavers, involving further education colleges, have been established in London, Bradford and Sheffield. Other schemes, to improve foreign language teaching and promote greater educational mobility for those under 18 years old, are benefiting increasing numbers of students, although the total sums available remain small. The community's initiatives in establishing a European educational information network are also of increasing significance.[16]

22. In a period when national and local government funds for education are being cut back, and when Britain's contribution to EEC funds exceeds receipts by £1,000 millions, it could well be an auspicious time for the further education sector to look more closely than hitherto at the Community's policies and activities. Support might well be found in Europe for developments and initiatives which domestic provision is currently unable or unwilling to sustain.

---

13 The Central Bureau for Educational Visits and Exchanges (See Section **2.6.**2) administers a programme of one week study visits for administrators and advisers, and inspectors with responsibility for educational institutions providing for the 11-19 age range. Other study visit grants are available to specialists in vocational education and guidance, and to teachers, administrators and researchers in higher education institutions. A limited number of bursaries is available each year for LEA advisers and inspectors.

14 *Per capita* expenditure on education in 1975 was Denmark £277, Netherlands £239, Belgium £209, Germany £197, France £166, Luxembourg £165, United Kingdom £144, Ireland £89, Italy £82; *Euroforum*, 12/79.

15 The Careers Guidance Integration Project organized by the National Institute for Careers Education & Counselling.

16 These include the EURONET computer-based information retrieval system, and the experimental Education Policy Information Centre based in the UK at the National Foundation for Education Research, to investigate how UK policy-makers might use an international information exchange service.

23. Other European educational organizations

Brief reference should be made to the educational influence of two other international organizations, the Organisation for Economic Co-operation and Development (OECD) and the Council of Europe. The OECD's Education Committee has been established since 1970 and is concerned largely with comparison and analyses of policies influencing economic and employment issues. Its small budget (£0.6m in 1978) supports a number of study groups including those examining policies affecting young people and work, policies for post-compulsory education, and educational building. Thirteen UK polytechnics and universities are involved in OECD's research and training programmes into institutional management in higher education. OECD's Centre for Educational Research and Innovation is funded separately (about £1.1m in 1978) and promotes research and development activities including surveys of innovations in higher education, studies of recurrent education and positive discrimination policies, and a project involving nine UK centres of further provision for the handicapped adolescent. The Council of Europe finances the Council for Cultural Co-operation, whose budget of £0.8m in 1978 was used to support a "preparation for life" study for 14-19 year olds, adult education projects, a bursary scheme (although only one of the 200 places on national short courses abroad available through the DES was taken up in 1978), and the European Document and Information System for Education which is designed to facilitate the exchange of education and research information.

REFERENCE

Grants and Loans from the European Community, Commission of the European Communities, 1979.

Guidelines for the management of the European Social Fund during 1980-82, Official Journal of the European Communities, OJC 159, 26/6/1979.

Practical Guide on the submission and consideration of applications for aid from The European Social Fund, Directorate-General for Research and Documentation of the European Parliament, 1978.

Seventh Report on the Activities of the European Social Fund – Financial Year 1978, Commission of the European Communities, Brussels, 1979.

The European Community and Education, European File 18/79, Commission of the European Communities Directorate-General for Information, 1979.

Towards A European Education Policy, Bulletin of the European Communities, European Documentation 1/1977.

European Education Co-operation and the UK, Department of Education and Science, 1979.

Fred Jarvis, *The Educational Implications of Membership of the EEC,* National Union of Teachers, 1972.

16-20: Current Developments in Europe, Coombe Lodge Report Vol 8, No 15, 1976.

The European Social Fund; a guide for possible applicants, Department of Employment, 1979.

Applications for and enquiries concerning Social Fund aid should be made to: Department of Employment, Caxton House, Tothill Street, London SW1H 9NA. 01-213 4305.

Information and EEC publications are available from the European Communities Information Office, 20 Kensington Palace Gardens, London W8 4QQ. 01-727 8090.

Section 7

THE DEPARTMENT
OF
EDUCATION AND SCIENCE
AND
THE WELSH OFFICE
EDUCATION DEPARTMENT

1. This sub-section will deal largely with the Department's policy and broad administrative functions. It should be read in conjunction with Section **1**, above.

2. The Education Act, 1944 provided for the replacement of the Board of Education by a Ministry of Education. The function of the Minister of Education under the Act was to "promote the education of the people of England and Wales and the progressive development of institutions devoted to that purpose." The Minister's duty was further "to secure the effective execution by local authorities under his control and direction, of the national policy for providing a varied and comprehensive educational service in every area." Thus, the Minister had a responsibility for maintaining minimum educational standards although, as will have been seen from Section **1**, the education service was to be operated as a partnership between local and central government.

3. In 1964 the Ministry of Education and Office of the Minister of Science were amalgamated to form the Department of Education and Science. The post of Minister then became that of Secretary of State. The DES also acquired further functions in that it took over from the Treasury responsibilities for liaison with the University Grants Committee; and the post of minister with special responsibility for arts was created. This office, which in 1979 was passed to the Chancellor of the Duchy of Lancaster, will not form any significant part of the discussion below. It may be that the office will return to the DES in the future.[1]

4. The Secretary of State for Education and Science is a member of the government of the day, has a place in the cabinet, and is presently assisted by a Minister of State and by two Parliamentary Under Secretaries of State. Ministerial responsibility is currently distributed as follows:
   (i) Secretary of State: formulation of general policy; questions involving senior Ministers in other departments and the Lord President and Chief Whip; public expenditure; major pay issues; major appointments.
   (ii) Minister of State: all matters relating to schools including special schools and nursery education; the curriculum and examination system: Schools Council matters; school meals and milk: urban programme; educational problems of ethnic minorities; sex discrimination; educational technology; local government finance and related matters; devolution; teacher employment, recruitment, qualifications, pay and superannuation.

---

1 Administrative irregularity resulting from political and personal ministerial considerations is an occasional feature of British government. For example, Gladstone held the offices of First Lord of the Treasury (Prime Minister) and Chancellor of the Exchequer between 1880 and 1882. Salisbury was Prime Minister and Foreign Secretary from 1895 to 1900, as was Ramsay MacDonald in 1924. Combination of offices is usually the result of necessity or personal preference. In the case of the Ministry of the Arts, there can be little good reason for its retention by the Chancellery of the Duchy of Lancaster after the cessation of office of the present incumbent.

(iii) Parliamentary Under Secretary of State (1): universities (including the Open University) and academic salaries; polytechnics; adult and further education; training of teachers; students' awards and student affairs; educational broadcasting. This Under Secretary of State is currently also responsible for answering in the House of Commons on matters relating to schools, including legislation.

(iv) Parliamentary Under Secretary of State (2): science, including the research councils, international matters; education and vocational preparation of 16-19 year olds; training for science and engineering; industrial training; youth and community service, National Youth Service Forum.

5. In April 1978 responsibility in Wales for all non-university institutions of higher and further education, the youth and community services and adult education was transferred to the Secretary of State for Wales. The Secretary of State for Education and Science continues to exercise responsibility in Wales, as in England, for the universities, the Research Councils, mandatory and post-graduate awards to students, and the pay, superannuation, qualifications, probation and medical fitness of teachers and cases of teachers' misconduct. The Secretary of State also exercises responsibility for government support for civil science, and is responsible for the Science Museum and the Victoria and Albert Museum.

6. The Department of Education and Science is staffed by civil servants, whose appointments are not dependent upon political decisions or considerations. The Department is under the general direction of a Permanent Secretary who is assisted by four Deputy Secretaries. The Deputy Secretaries deal respectively with schools, higher and further education, planning, and science and international relations. The Permanent Secretary is also assisted by the Department's Legal Adviser and Senior Chief Inspector, both of whom have Deputy Secretary rank.

7. The DES has as its main tasks the following:

(i) the broad allocation of resources for education;

(ii) the control of the rate, nature and distribution of educational building;

(iii) the agreement with local authority associations on the forecast level of local authority expenditure on education in relation to the central decisions on the rate support grant for local government spending; and

(iv) the training, supply and superannuation of teachers.

These duties represent important powers, and they give to the DES a crucial control over education. (Although the Education (No.2) Bill 1979 allows local authorities more power in some areas, such as the closure or significant enlargement of schools, in the exercise of its cost limit powers and influence over building design, the Department retains important controls over LEA activities).

8. The Department is responsible for the recognition of teachers as qualified practitioners, for administering the Teachers' Superannuation Scheme, and

for supporting financially by direct grant a number of educational institutions of a special kind. Those institutions providing teacher education and training – colleges, university departments of education and departments of education in polytechnics – are therefore directly affected by the decisions made by the DES on the recruitment of intending teachers, their courses of training, their qualifications and "recognition", and particular superannuation arrangements.

9. While the extension of the size and scope of the education service, the continuing increase in public and political interest in education, and the general growth of government involvement in the ordering of national life have resulted in more open debate and the obscuring of certain former administrative divisions, it remains the local authorities who possess theoretical control over and routine administration of most of education, and the DES which is largely occupied with policy. Since it is occupied with the formulation of national educational policies and has only narrow executive functions (for example, teachers' pensions), in comparison to other departments of state the DES is relatively small. In effect, the education service is decentralised for administrative purposes. However, by reason of its actual statutory powers the Department has a theoretical control; but it is through its function concerning the broad allocation of resources and its influence that it seeks to implement policy. It is this which has provoked the view in some local authorities that the DES ought be to more firm, the accusation being that powers which could be exercised are not. However, the fairness of such a view depends upon the circumstances from which it emanates: local authorities vary in their commitment to certain educational matters.

10. Although having a concern for educational standards and working with the assistance of HM Inspectorate, the DES has no direct control over teaching methods or education content. However, indirect control is considerable. Like all departments of state, the DES in administering resources works within estimates which have been approved by Parliament, and may deploy its own funds appropriately.

11. Since it is a department of state, the DES exercises a function in the formation of government policies in the areas for which it is responsible. Governmental annual reviews are made for public expenditure, and the DES has only the share of financial resources allotted to it as a result of estimates which are based on expenditure reviews. Therefore, the Secretary of State contributes to discussions concerning allocation and must work within the final estimates. The DES is associated with the Treasury in its planning, as are all departments of state. However, there is increasingly close co-operation not only with central departments of government such as the Treasury and Cabinet Office, but with others such as the Departments of Health and Social Security, the Environment, Employment, Industry, and the Scottish and Welsh Offices. The DES therefore has to estimate the resources needed to implement the policies which have been decided upon, and to represent those needs within the framework of national economic planning. Examples of specific collaboration with other departments are: with DHSS

on welfare benefits; DoE on energy conservation; DE on careers, training and the MSC; and Industry on the training of engineers.

12. In 1978/79 the educational services for which the DES has a policy responsibility were estimated to involve public expenditure of over £6,500m and to involve the employment of over one million people. However, the monies which the Department directly disburses amount to less than 15% of public expenditure on education, the residue of expenditure being made by the local authorities. The Department makes a block financial allocation to the University Grants Committee and also gives grants to certain colleges, schools, and educational bodies. The DES commissions research,[2] and is responsible for the support of government for civil science. Policy responsibility for museums, libraries and the arts has been transferred to the Duchy of Lancaster, although the Office of Arts and Libraries is still based at Elizabeth House.

13. Since the DES operates less by the direct use of its legal and financial powers and more by influence, guidance, persuasion and the promotion of ideas, the processes of educational policy often involve extensive discussions with other authorities operating the education service. In some cases the DES has established standing advisory machinery for this purpose. Two examples, which illustrate differing advisory functions, are the Advisory Committee on the Supply and Education of Teachers (ACSET), and the Expenditure Steering Group for Education (ESGE). ESGE has a greater status than ACSET. The latter is an advisory body with a fairly wide representation, but ESGE is an official consultative group primarily, but not exclusively, concerned with assessing the implications of policy and finance within the context of the rate support grant, and represents a channel of communication between central and local government. ESGE has been said to have resulted in a greatly improved flow of information between local authorities and the Department, and to have improved working relationships. Advisory committee advice may be published, and may or may not be accepted and implemented. The DES also establishes or sponsors organizations which are necessary to fulfil national needs but are outside the competence of individual institutions or local authorities. Recent examples are the Council for Educational Technology, (CET) and the Further Education Curriculum Research and Development Unit (FEU). Certain voluntary bodies with an important national function may receive grants from the DES, for example, The National Bureau for Handicapped Students. In arts and civil science, policy is generally implemented by independent bodies, although as principal paymaster the DES has a general policy responsibility. These bodies, such as the various research councils, consist of members wholly or mainly appointed by Ministers, and are financed mainly by the DES. The Office of Arts and Libraries, presently part of the Duchy of Lancaster, has responsibility, *inter alia,* for grants to the Arts Council.

14. The Department has to maintain the capacity to evolve, not only to match

---

2 A list of research projects supported by the DES is published annually and available free from the Planning Unit, DES, Elizabeth House, York Road, London SE1 7PH.

the changes which occur in the bodies with which it deals (for example, the firmer exercising of central power in certain areas and increased local autonomy in others) but also adequately to perform its most important roles. Those roles may be summarised as the maintenance of minimum educational standards; the securing of a sufficient financial allocation and its equitable distribution; and ensuring that the supply, training and superannuation of teachers are properly arranged.

15. Until 1976 the style of the DES was said to reflect the nature of the former authoritarian world for which it had responsibility. Ironically, it took some years before the movement towards greater participatory democracy in education formalised by Circular 7/70 was reflected by changed attitudes in the Department. The DES is not a department of state in which secrets of great national importance are kept, although premature disclosure of delicate issues still under consideration may be held in some quarters not to be desirable, and it was not until concessions to the principles of open government were made that the public debate of issues was seen by the Department other than in terms of unhelpful premature speculation. Similarly, the Department did not display an enthusiasm towards advisory committees or consultative bodies which might have contributed to policy formulation. The current way in which the Department operates is indeed more open, but the degree of approval it might receive is rather dependent upon the circumstances and point of view of the observer. A machinery possessing such power but operating in an indirect fashion is not one about which objective judgements can readily be made. Where the Department clearly operates on an executive basis, there is evidence to show in an instance concerning administration and justice, that decisions at law have not always upheld DES judgement (cf Section **11.5**, appendices 1 and 2).

16. **The structure and work of the Department**

The Permanent Secretary delegates the work of the Department. Except for finance and establishment, which are delegated to officials of under secretary rank but who report directly to the Permanent Secretary, the work of the Department is delegated to the four deputy secretaries. These secretaries delegate further to under secretaries who have charge of branches. The Legal Adviser has deputy secretary rank and reports directly to the Permanent Secretary. Each of the four deputy secretaries has an area of responsibility. These are:

(i) Schools education (Schools Branches I, II and III) and educational building (Architects and Building Branch).

(ii) Higher and further education (Higher and Further Education Branches 1, 2, and 3).

(iii) Teachers matters (Teachers Branch), statistics (Statistics Branch), planning (Departmental Planning Unit), educational research policy and the utilization of the contribution of HM Inspectorate to educational planning.

(iv) Civil science matters and international relations (Science and International Relations Branch). Arts and libraries matters, until 1979 grouped under this heading, and the function of Arts and Libraries Branch, are currently transferred to the Duchy of Lancaster.

17. The DES branches can be said to be of two types: those which are concerned with the work of the whole Department, and those which deal with specific areas of policy. The Departmental Planning Unit is responsible for the promotion of the Department's planning work.

18. **The schools branches**
The schools branches deal with the entire range of schools provision. Schools I is concerned with the general organization and supply of schools, dealing with provision, organization, management and attendance. Regular contact is maintained with local education authorities by means of staff teams organized on a territorial basis. Among the work of territorial teams is schools provision, which will include opening, closure, enlargement or character change, and the handling of matters concerning individual pupils which have been referred to the Secretary of State by parents. Because of their liaison with LEAs and the Inspectorate, the territorial teams should have a comprehensive view of local practices, variations and provisions. Much of the work of the territorial teams refers to schools buildings provision and responsibility for ensuring that statutory requirements are observed. Schools I also has teams which are concerned with voluntary and direct grant schools, and with nursery schools. The branch advises on questions relating to the acquisition of land for educational purposes, and on matters involving school pupils (such as the education of children of British subjects living abroad).

19. Schools II has three divisions. One division has responsibility for educational disadvantage, the education of immigrants, the education welfare service, and matters relating to truancy and indiscipline. Another division is concerned with school meals and milk, education maintenance allowances and clothing, and school transport. The third division deals with the special education of handicapped pupils, liaison with the Department of Health and Social Security on matters relating to school health, and liaison with the Employment Medical Advisory Service. The special education for which this third division has responsibility can be that in special schools or classes or in specialised institutions for further education provided by the LEAs, voluntary bodies, or in other ways. Although the Medical Adviser and the professional medical staff are employed by the DHSS, they advise the DES – particularly Schools II and III branches – on general questions of health concerning handicapped pupils and teacher employment.

20. Schools III is divided in two. One division is concerned with the school curriculum, careers guidance and education, work experience and liaison between schools and industry. The other division is concerned with school examinations, the Assessment of Performance Unit (APU), liaison with the Schools Council, and DES policy relating to educational technology.

21. **Higher and further education branches**
There are three branches with responsibility for policy in post-school education.

22. Higher and Further Education 1 is responsible for public sector higher

education development planning, management and control. This includes course approval, the Dip HE and liaison with the CNAA. The branch is responsible for policy concerning overseas student admissions, fees, pooling and recoupment, direct grants, catering and residence charges; and the administration, government and finance of voluntary colleges. It is also concerned with all public sector further and higher education building programmes. The branch is responsible for the organization of further education, including course approval and college government matters, and for the development of polytechnics.

23. A division of HFE 1 has a particular responsibility for art, design, music and other vocational subjects, for further education for agriculture; and for all aspects of adult education, however it is actually provided. Another division is concerned with further education provision for handicapped students, equal opportunities, certain other matters affecting further education students, and the operation of the Further Education Information Service (see Section **12.1.**8).

24. Higher and Further Education 2 branch is divided into three. One division is concerned with special measures for the young unemployed, general education and industry matters, manpower planning as it affects further education, education for engineering and associated industries, the Youth Service (including grants to the national voluntary youth organizations), the training of full-time youth and community workers, and the financing of certain youth work and youth and community projects.

25. Another division is concerned with young persons' vocational preparation (including the Unified Vocational Preparation programme and day release), education for industry, and liaises with the Manpower Services Commission and Industrial Training Boards on such matters as industrial training policy and the Training Opportunities Scheme. In conjunction with MSC the division provides a Secretariat for the Training and Further Education Consultative Group. This body provides a liaison link between the DES and MSC. The DES provides the chairman. The group also contains local education authority representatives. The Group's function is to resolve training and further education conflicts, for example, problems concerning the location of Skillcentres: see Section **4.**6. The division has also a concern with the vocational education activities of international organizations, the EEC and OECD among them.

26. A third division deals with TEC, BEC, CGLI, and the FEU, with educational provision for the 16-19 age group in further education (including both full-time education and vocation preparation release) and the relation with the provision made in schools, and careers guidance and counselling in further education. This division also deals with curricular matters, management and business studies, and trade union education.

27. Higher and Further Education 3 branch has four divisions. It is largely responsible for university matters. Two divisions are concerned respectively with: university government, educational and institutional research,

university students' health and welfare, and international affairs; and universities' resources and running costs, and the development of the university system to fulfil national requirements. Both divisions liaise closely with the University Grants Committee.

28. A third division is responsible for financial support policy for higher education students in England and Wales, advising on the application of grants regulations, administering postgraduate studentships and bursaries for which the Department is responsible, and co-ordinating with the various research councils postgraduate research policy.

29. The fourth division provides the secretariat for the Computer Board for Universities and the research councils. HFE 3 also authorises grants for the Open University, the British Academy, the Royal College of Art, and the Cranfield Institute of Technology.

30. Teachers Branch has six divisions. It deals with employment matters affecting teachers and has policy responsibility for teacher supply and demand, and the equitable distribution of teacher resources. Within this responsibility are the national planning of initial teacher training, numbers control and the balance of training, further education teacher training, in-service training, and teachers' training research. The branch is responsible for the supervision and approval of the government of teacher training institutions. It also issues advice concerning teachers' salaries. The main responsibilities of the divisions of the Teachers Branch are:

31. Division A : teacher demand and supply;
Division B : DES representation on the Burnham Committees, and the pay of university academic staff;
Division C : the administration of regulations concerning teachers' and prospective teachers' misconduct;
Division D : the preparation of Burnham salaries documents;
Division E : qualified teacher status, probation and the medical fitness of teachers; and
Division F : the national planning of teacher training, including college intakes.

32. The Science and International Relations Branch is concerned with DES responsibility for civil science, and because international relations are an important aspect of the civil scientific work, the branch has responsibility for that and all other DES international work. Because the DES finances civil science research but has no managerial responsibility since that is mainly exercised by the universities and research councils, the branch is largely concerned with supporting the Advisory Board for the Research Councils (ABRC). This body advises the Secretary of State on matters such as the allocation of funds to the research councils, and certain scientific questions affecting the councils, universities and government. The branch also deals with scientific issues, generally concerning fundamental research which, for reasons such as their involvement in relations between other countries or their implications for public expenditure, cannot be delegated to an individual research council.

33. The Architects and Building Branch has a responsibility for the handling of all building projects in England and Wales sponsored by the Teachers, and Higher and Further Education Branches, and Schools Branches in England. It is responsible for the scrutiny and approval of educational building projects, checking that statutory requirements are met and that costs incurred are not excessive. It supervises the co-ordination of building programmes and the progress of work. The branch has a Chief Architect and a large staff. It works closely with members of HM Inspectorate. For schools matters, one staff inspector has an assignment which loosely attaches her or him to the branch; for further education, a staff inspector and an HMI are linked with the branch for part of their work in connection with various aspects of building and equipment. The branch maintains statistics concerning educational building, undertakes in conjunction with other branches, LEAs and the Inspectorate, consideration of the technical and architectural implications of educational developments. The branch also issues guidance and information concerning design matters, the content of which varies in legal status (see Section **1.3.**5, and Section **5.3.**1).

34. The Statistics Branch has three divisions. These deal respectively with: statistics for adult, further and higher education, manpower and science; statistics for school and pre-school education, school leavers, teachers, and libraries and arts; data processing services, educational finance statistics, international and United Kingdom statistics, and branch administration. The Statistics Branch works closely with the Finance Branch. It produces the annual six volume *Statistics of Education*, and also the annual single volume *Education Statistics for the United Kingdom.*

35. Of the DES service branches, Establishments and Organisation, and Legal, are not discussed here since their functions are obvious. The Finance Branch is responsible for consultations with the Treasury and the Department of the Environment. It plays the major role in the forecasting of relevant rate support grant expenditure for education; provides the educational information for public expenditure white papers; and includes the Financial Services Division which, *inter alia*, services the Pooling Committee, and carries out annual student/staff ratio surveys. The Financial Services Division is currently investigating ratios for non-teaching staff in polytechnics and major establishments.

36. Although not a branch in name, the Planning Unit has that status in that it is headed by an under secretary. The Unit staff co-ordinate and service the work of the Department's standing policy groups. There are three such groups: Policy Group A, which is concerned with higher and further education policy, Policy Group B, which deals with schools; and the Policy Steering Group. The Planning Unit also has administrative responsibility for the DES programme of educational research, responsibility for the Department's interest in matters such as devolution and local government issues; and includes economics staff and a Financial Modelling Team which serve both the Unit and the needs of others of the Departments' branches.

37. DES planning occurs on a collective basis, and is carried out through a

flexible committee network. Planning involves the relevant operational branches, the analytical and advisory services and the Planning Unit. Together these bodies form the Departmental Planning Organisation. A deputy secretary has overseeing responsibility for the planning services. The link between the DES planning processes and its involvement in educational research is provided by a chief inspector. However, main planning responsibilities remain with individual policy branches although they are assisted by the Statistics Branch and the Planning Unit.

38. It will have been seen that the Department operates through policy branches and service branches. However, although several of the Departments' policy branches are organized on a territorial basis, there is no regional organization. Only the Pensions Branch at Mowden Hall, Darlington, which deals with superannuation (and also compensation for relevant staff under The Colleges of Education (Compensation Regulations) employs significant numbers of staff outside London. This branch was located at Darlington as part of the policy to make government employment available outside London. The DES is at considerable pains to avoid its outpost staff becoming too isolated.

39. The Department and the Welsh Office implement their concern with educational standards in various ways. These include close co-operation with the Inspectorate, the setting up of official committees of inquiry into various educational issues (the recommendations of which may or may not be accepted), the funding of research projects, and through the establishment of certain units.

40. In August 1974 there were established within the Department the Educational Disadvantage Unit (EDU), and the Assessment of Performance Unit (APU). These units have relatively small staffs of their own but also draw on the services of DES officials from the various branches. The EDU functions as the DES forum for the consideration of educational disadvantage, multi-cultural education, and truancy and behaviour problems in schools. The EDU seeks to influence resource allocation in the interests of the educationally disadvantaged. The APU exists to promote the development and use of better forms of assessment of school pupils' achievement. Because of the considerable involvement of the Inspectorate and its location at the DES, the APU is seen by many as a considerable force. It has attracted critics and supporters. The supporters claim that the APU functions mainly as a measuring instrument; the critics see it as eventually being more influential than the Schools Council, and a possible instrument to enforce not only a core curriculum but also to influence personal and social development.

41. The structure of the Department reflects the nature of its work, but the machinery is such that there is always a need for evolution, flexibility, and for the central organization to keep itself informed of local developments. Thus, policy branches have to make effective use of the information reposing in the territorial teams, and with the Inspectorate. As with any bureaucratic organization, failures in communication occur. As the heads of branches,

under secretaries have considerable freedom in the management of their work but in any decision or policy making, the official's limit of discretion varies: there is often a clear need to consult within the Department; the implications of a decision may be sufficiently wide for it to be referred to the departmental planning machinery, and from thence to higher levels. Thus, critics of the DES complain of the length of time required for decisions to be made. The reasons for delay can be the wholly valid – the need for consultation and further referral, or the pressure of work within the Department – but there are those who would maintain that such is not always the case. The Department is acknowledged usually to consult interested bodies, such as the teachers' associations, when it is considering policy and practice changes, but there are complaints that it allows too little time for this process.

42. **HM Inspectorate**

HM Inspectorate was established in 1839. Its function, to inspect and report, has now changed. Under s.77 of the Education Act, 1944, the Secretary of State is required to cause inspections to be made. The Act does not define the purpose or the nature of such inspections, but they are clearly designed to assist the Secretary of State in the performance of her or his functions. Thus, the primary responsibility of the Inspectorate is to Ministers and the Department.

43. The Inspectorate has three functions. Its main function is to assess standards and trends throughout the educational system, to report to the Permanent Secretary and to the Secretary of State and to advise on the state of the system nationally. In performing this function, the basis is inspection, but the form of that inspection varies. Inspection can take the form of visits to institutions, but such a visit may be brief, informal and by one individual; or it may be visits by teams of inspectors to various establishments in pursuit of a particular investigation. It is from the knowledge acquired from visits that the Inspectorate is able to contribute to the formation of government educational policy. Inspection is of necessity exercised selectively. The greatest proportion of the Inspectorate's time, nearly 45%, is spent in visting educational establishments.

44. The Inspectorate has an advisory, central and regulatory function. HMI are available when necessary to explain the implications of current policy to local authorities and educational institutions. The Inspectorate may act on behalf of the Secretary of State on, for example, the approval of advanced courses of further education. It plays a role in the consultative process, both in the dissemination and collation of information, by which the DES formulates policy.

45. A further function of HMI is the concern to improve the work which they are called upon to inspect. This may be represented as a partial fulfilling of the Secretary of State's duty to ensure the maintenance of standards, and will vary in nature from the provision of national short courses for teachers, to giving individual advice, to the publication of information, discussion documents, and advisory materials. The Inspectorate co-operates with other

departments of government in the inspection of educational estalishments for which those departments are responsible and also inspects independent educational establishments. (All schools of whatever kind, public or private are open to inspection, as are colleges maintained from public funds or, in the case of the independent colleges, those which have been recognised as efficient). In practice, the Inspectorate is sensitive to the delicacies of relationships with other governmental bodies. Thus it has not inspected MSC courses in colleges except with MSC approval.

46. The Inspectorate can be seen to exist in parallel with the Department's branches. The Permanent Secretary is accountable to Parliament for the expenditure incurred by the Inspectorate. However, the Inspectorate maintains a degree of professional independence: thus, HMI have substantial freedom to develop and manage both their professional response to the needs of government and also the services offered to LEAs, institutions and individuals.

47. The Inspectorate is headed by the Senior Chief Inspector who has the right of direct access to the Secretary of State, and has deputy secretary rank. There are five chief inspectors, each of whom has a responsibility for a broad area of education. The chief inspectors' areas are divided thus: primary education, middle schools, publications, programming of HMI activities; initial and in-service training of teachers, teacher probation, educational technology; secondary education, independent schools, European schools, careers education and counselling; further and higher education (excluding teacher training), safety and safety education in schools and colleges, Inspectorate representation on all outside bodies and committees other than the Schools Council, Services education, international relations; and educational disadvantage, special education, multi-racial education, religious and moral education, health education.

48. In order to provide for awareness of national patterns, the Inspectorate is organized territorially. Within the territorial designations, organization is further qualified according to subject(s), and the type of education provided. Territorially, the Inspectorate is divided into seven divisions, each of which is headed by a divisional inspector. There are 59 staff inspectors who are responsible for individual subjects, "phases" (the type of education, for example: primary, secondary) and aspects of education. Certain HMI based in a division may be placed on "first call centre". This system is operated by way of Elizabeth House and may result in a selected HMI being placed anywhere in the country and given particular assignments (for example, participation in the secondary school survey).

49. Roughly three quarters of the Inspectorate deal mainly with school education, and roughly a quarter with higher and further education. However, HMI who report on teacher training, 16-19 education, education research, educational technology, and those engaged in monitoring expenditure are drawn from both groups. Each group is comprised of inspectors who combine their general duties with a particular specialism.

50. Except for the Senior Chief Inspector, chief inspectors and staff inspectors,

all HMI are assigned to one of the seven divisions. Each division is headed by a divisional inspector who is responsible for the routine management of territorial work. Two HMI, one for schools and one for post-school education, are nominated as district inspectors to each local education authority. Educational institutions are obviously well advised to foster their contacts with the district inspectors and, through them, the divisional inspector. However, an inspector's work is not confined to an assigned division; a district inspector will not spend the majority of her or his time with the assigned LEA. There is a strong HMI presence at the DES in London, because of the need for regular consultation, but that consultation is not exclusive. Regional staff inspectors have specific functions in respect of the approval of advanced courses and also have certain territorial functions. Under FECL 1/80, RSIs have been asked in their course assessments to take into account expenditure restraint: course proposals will have to show unmet student demand, and existing courses be provided from existing resources (unless there is an expressed vocational need and specific employment opportunities for students). FECL 1/80 appears to emphasize the powers of RSIs.

51. An inspection programme will have both formal and informal outcomes. The formal will include the making of reports on specific institutions, issues or aspects of education; the preparation of publications and papers which may be either confidential or for public knowledge; and the provision of short courses. Where a formal report on an institution is made, it is made to the Secretary of State but it will also be received by the responsible authority. The informal, or less formal, will include: discussions with practising teachers and teachers' associations; the giving of advice within the DES and to LEAs; responsibilities concerning initial and in-service teacher training; action as assessors or observers of many educational bodies; relations with other departments of government; and the undertaking of international projects and study visits, and addressing conferences.

52. The establishment strength of the Inspectorate of 430 is not usually attained, recruiting difficulties being the reason offered by the DES. A criticism sometimes made of the operation of the Inspectorate is that its varied responsibilities occupy disproportionate amounts of time, resulting in classroom contract with teachers and regular local authority contact being too restricted. The increased co-operation between HMI and local authority advisers and inspectors has been largely welcomed. Given the importance of HMI advice concerning, for example, buildings and AFE course approval, colleges are well advised to maintain strong links with their HMI, and Regional Staff Inspector.

53. The Inspectorate in Wales is "on loan" from HM Inspectorate. The Welsh Inspectorate is headed by a chief inspector who is assisted by eight staff inspectors. The total strength of the Welsh Inspectorate is about fifty. The organization and practices of the Welsh Inspectorate are similar to those obtaining for England.

54. **The Welsh Office Education Department**
The Secretary of State for Wales has been responsible since 1970 for primary and secondary education in Wales, and since April 1978 for higher and further education, with the exceptions stated in paragraph 5, above. The Transfer of Functions (Wales) (No.2) Order provided that, apart from the exceptions, the Minister's functions as laid down in the Education Acts should lie with the Secretary of State for Wales. In order to assist the Secretary of State to discharge these new duties, a new Education Department was established within the Welsh Office. This Department superseded the Welsh Education Office which had functioned as a joint Welsh Office/DES unit.

55. The transference of function in theory allows the Secretary of State for Wales complete independence of the DES in the exercising of the designated duties and responsibilities for education. In practice, there is close consultation between the DES and Welsh Office, and a general uniformity of policy. There is close liaison between the two Departments on matters with general policy implications. Departmental papers are commonly exchanged and officials attend meeting whenever necessary. The DES and Welsh Office act jointly where issues refer to education in both England and Wales. Thus, circulars, guidance, and discussion papers are frequently issued jointly, and committees of inquiry may be jointly established. For example, the Committee of Enquiry into the Teaching of Mathematics in Primary Schools in England and Wales (among the terms of reference of which were to have regard to the mathematics required in further and higher education) was established jointly.

56. As might be expected, it is in areas of particular interest to Wales that the Education Department acts with independence. For example, the Education Department has issued a series of publications designed to stimulate discussion of current educational issues in Wales; the Department's research programme includes projects designed to lead to the preparation of Welsh language teaching materials; and, like the DES, the Education Department makes grants for particular purposes: during 1978/79, the Schools Broadcasting Council for Wales was given a grant to help meet the cost of Welsh language publications produced in support of schools broadcasting whose viability was threatened.

57. As in the exercise of its functions, so in its organization does the Educational Department mirror the DES. The Department is headed by an under secretary. The under secretary is responsible to a deputy secretary who has responsibility for education, health and social work, local government, and housing. The Education Department therefore can be compared to a DES branch.

58. The Education Department is comprised of four divisions, each of which is headed by an assistant secretary. The Schools Division administers Government policy concerning all matters relating to maintained, and voluntary independent schools in Wales with the exception of building programmes. It also deals with matters relating to the curriculum and examinations.

59. Further Education Division 1 is responsible for higher education, the supply and training of teachers, and liaison with the University of Wales, UGC and CNAA. It is also concerned with tuition fees and other student matters.

60. Further Education Division 2 is concerned with non-advanced further education, 16-19 provision, student grants, liaison with the Manpower Services Commission, adult education (including State Bursaries), the youth service, and grants for village halls and community centres.

61. The Education Services Division is responsible for educational building, school meals, milk, transport and other services, publications, statistics and research.

62. **Possible DES changes**

At the time of writing, press reports [3] indicated that as a consequence of public expenditure restraint, there would be changes in the organization of the DES. The proposed cut in manpower would result in: a reduction of the advisory services to local authorities concerning building, health, safety and catering, and a reduction in DES services to overseas services; the removal of equipment controls for further education; a reduction in commissioned research work; and less involvement generally by the Department in further education. Staffing level reduction may also entail cuts in the statistical and pensions advisory services. If all the proposed cuts are implemented, the Department will be reduced to the staffing levels of the Ministry of Education in 1964. There are also various bodies supported by the DES whose future at the time of writing appeared uncertain.[4]

63. In recent years, criticisms of the DES have been made by the OECD, the House of Commons Expenditure Committee, and a former Minister.[5] The substance of the criticisms – although not all were expressed by the same source – may be summarised thus:

(i) too much DES planning takes place in secret;
(ii) the Department tends to react to events rather than anticipating or acting as an initiator;
(iii) planning does not sufficiently take account of the needs of society, or the changes which occur in its nature, and does not sufficiently involve outside interest groups; and
(iv) broad educational objectives should be given more prominence than the DES allows in its concentration on the allocation of resources.

There is certainly a degree of agreement[6] that the DES does not have a clear policy for further education (possibly because of inadequacy in its own resources). The complaint of lack of leadership is double edged for there are many who would oppose the presumably ensuing firmer central control.

3 *Daily Telegraph*, 18 September, 1979.
4 It has been announced that one of these, the Centre for Information on Educational Disadvantage, is no longer to be supported by the DES, presumably resulting in its closure.
5 cf *THES*, 9 May 1975; *Policy Making in the DES*, 10th Report from the Expenditure Committee, HMSO 1976; *THES*, 7 May 1976.
6 cf L.M. Cantor and I.F. Roberts *Further Education Today A Critical review*, Routledge and Kegan Paul, 1979, p13.

7

The organisation of the DES: January 1980

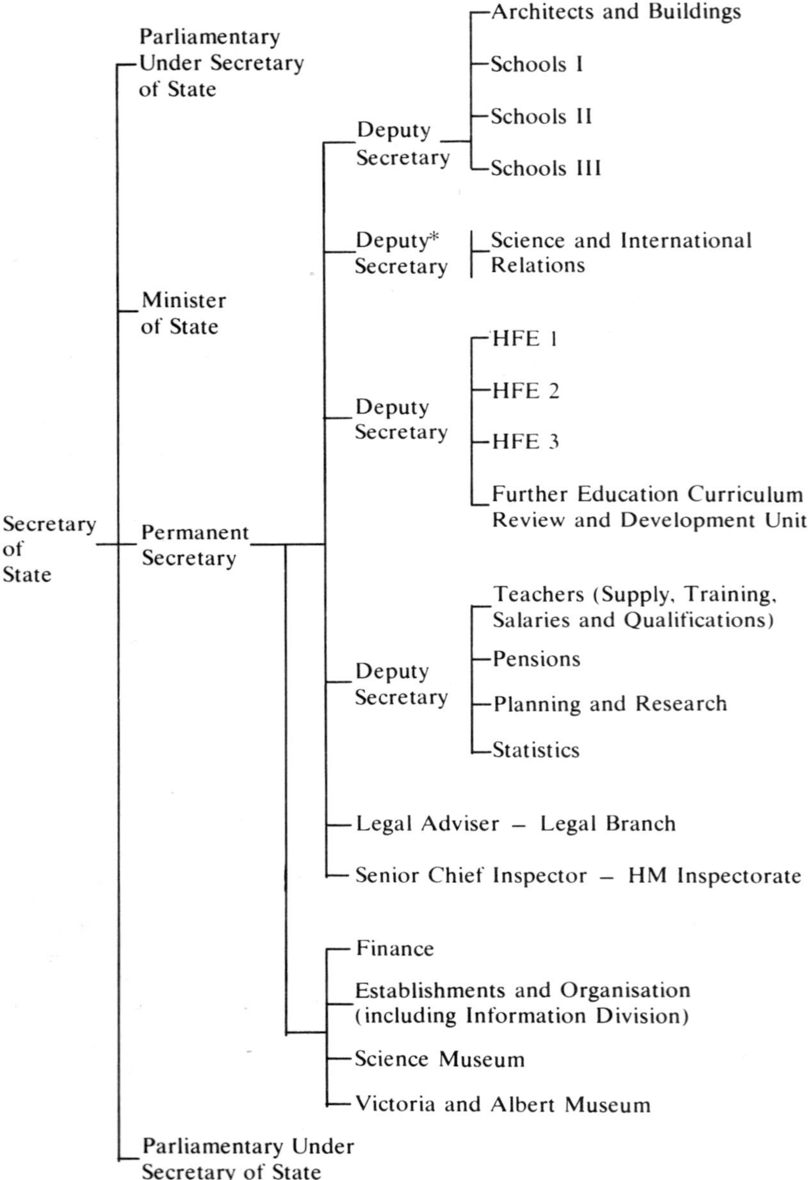

*This Deputy Secretary formerly also had responsibility for Arts and Libraries.

64. In response to the criticisms expressed by the OECD and in Parliament, the DES undertook a management review.[7] The review concentrates on the Department's organization and procedures. The various initiatives which have been taken, such as by way of the FEU, may be taken to be an answer to criticism. In so far as conclusions are apparent from the review, it would appear that the evolutionary process is preferred (thus rendering initiative somewhat difficult) and that the Department considers that no basic change is required because, although the DES is more open than when the criticisms were made, the present structure is considered adequate to meet needs. In January 1980, a House of Commons committee began another investigation into the way the DES has discharged its responsibilities.

65. **Note to appendices**

The appendices below refer to administrative memoranda, circulars, and college letters by which the DES (and Welsh Office) issue formal communications. Discussion of the status of these documents is contained in section **1.3.**5 above. The DES publishes past circulars and administrative memoranda annually in book form. We are grateful for DES and HMSO permission to quote from this material. The present Government is committed to the issuing of fewer circulars. (see Section **1.3.**46).

REFERENCE

Government Publications, Sectional List No.2, Department of Education and Science, HMSO, 1978.
How the DES is Organised, DES, 1976.
The Department of Education and Science – a brief guide, DES, 1978.
The education system of England and Wales, DES, 1978.
Education in Wales 1978, A report to Parliament by the Secretary of State for Wales.
Management Review 1977-78, Report of the Steering Committee, DES.
Sir William Pile, *The Department of Education and Science*, George Allen and Unwin, 1979.
As will be appreciated from the appendices to this section, and other DES material quoted elsewhere in this book, the Department issues a considerable volume of publications. If the publication is priced, it is sold through HMSO. If the publication is free, it is available from the Department of Education and Science, Elizabeth House, York Road, London SE1 7PH. 01-928 9222. On occasions, publications (such as Design Notes) are available from the Publications Despatch Centre, Department of Education and Science, Honeypot Lane, Canons Park, Stanmore, Middlesex. However, where particular reference has not been given, it is advisable first to write to the Information Division at Elizabeth House. Enquiries concerning Wales should be addressed to: Welsh Office Education Department, Government Buildings, Ty Glas, Llanishen, Cardiff CF4 5PF. 0222 753271.

---

7 *Management Review 1977-78*, Report of the Steering Committee, DES (unpublished, but available on application to the Department).

7

APPENDIX I

LIST OF DES/WELSH EDUCATION OFFICE/WELSH OFFICE ADMINISTRATIVE MEMORANDA CURRENT AT 1 JANUARY 1980

No. of AM	*Date of Issue*	*Subject*
25	26.1.45	Instruments, articles of government and rules of management (including schedule showing model instrument and articles of government for a county secondary school).
35	7.3.45	Boarding accommodation in connection with voluntary secondary schools.
134	12.3.46	Release of teachers to industry and commerce.
137	29.3.46	Married women teachers.
156	27.5.46	Power to ensure cleanliness: administration of Section 54 of the Education Act 1944.
295	31.8.48	Members of HM Forces : facilities for further education.
359	18.4.50	Civil Defence Act, 1949 Regulations relating to the evacuation of the civil population (S.I. 1949, No. 2147) (including Memo. F.V.I. and Ministry of Health Circular 37/50).
377	5.1.51	School records (including memorandum of guidance issued by the British Records Association).
437	17.12.52	Training arrangements: Air Training Corps (superseding AM No. 241).
440	26.2.53	Education in prisons and Borstal institutions.
440 (Addendum No.1)	10.4.56	Education in prisons, Borstal institutions and Detention centres.
440 (Addendum No. 2)	24.6.63	Education in prisons, Bostal institutions and Detention Centres.
455	8.9.53	Section 12 of the Education (Miscellaneous Provisions) Act, 1953, (including Appendix).
491	16.2.55	Houses for teachers.
517	9.11.55	Restrictions on the use of certain types of glazes in the teaching of pottery.

No of AM	*Date of Issue*	*Subject*
526	16.3.56	Local education authorities and responsible bodies for adult education.
531	10.5.56	School registers and records (superseding AM No. 301).
533	18.6.56	War office warning to children.
542	21.11.56	Verification of qualifications, service, etc., of teachers from overseas (superseding AM No. 352).
557	15.7.57	Introduction of Part III of the Education Act, 1944.
	3.10.58	Training and testing of child cyclists.
3/59	28.4.59	Approval of courses in establishments of further education.
11/59	13.8.59	Arrangements for pooling educational expenditure.
4/60	18.2.60	General Certificate of Education.
9/60	18.10.60	Handicapped children of service parents.
12/60	16.11.60	Examinations for the qualification offered by the Institutional Management Association (superseding AM No 152)
8/61	10.4.61	Training and testing of child cyclists.
10/61	21.4.61	General Engineering courses.
13/61	25.7.61	Approval by the Ministry of Education of Courses leading to the Diploma in Art and Design.
14/61	27.7.61	Teachers' qualifications: teachers of music.
15/61	10.7.61	Welfare foods for school children (superseding AM No. 483 and addenda).
15/61 (Addendum No. 1)	1.1.62	Welfare foods for school children under five.
18/61	29.9.61	Measures to encourage the recruitment of teachers for service in the Commonwealth and other countries overseas.
20/61	11.9.61	Industrial safety and the education service (superseding AM No 534).

No. of A.M.	Date of Issue	Subject
5/62	4.5.62	Fees in establishments of further education.
6/63	2.8.63	Adult education (accommodation and staffing).
9/63	9.10.63	Training and testing of child cyclists.
1/64	3.3.64	Records of teachers.
2/64	23.3.64	Children and Young Persons Act, 1963.
9/64	22.9.64	Council for National Academic Awards.
13/64	16.12.64	Building work for aided and special agreements schools.
2/65	1.2.65	Poisonous substances in pencils and other allied materials used in schools.
2/65 (Amendment)	14.10.68	Poisonous substances in pencils and other allied materials used in schools.
6/65	11.8.65	Education for the nursing services: pre-nursing courses in secondary schools and establishments of further education.
2/66	26.1.66	Revised agreement between The City and Guilds of London Institute and the Regional Examining Boards.
2/66 (Addendum No.1)	10.8.66	Revised agreement between The City and Guilds of London Institute and the Regional Examining Bodies.
6/66	28.4.66	Visits by parents to handicapped children boarded away from home.
8/66	6.6.66	Information for applicants for full-time advanced courses in further education.
16/66	24.11.66	Approval of courses in establishments of further education.
16/66 (Addendum No.1)	29.3.67	Approval of courses in establishments of further education.
16/66 (Addendum No.2)	12.7.67	Approval of courses in establishments of further education.
1/67	5.1.67	Overseas students – admission arrangements.
3/67	1.2.67	Computer education.

No. of A.M.	Date of Issue	Subject
8/67	5.4.67	Polytechnics.
10/67	11.4.67	Teachers' Superannuation Regulations.
11/67	12.4.67	Development of post-diploma studies in art and design.
14/67	20.4.67	Fees for students from outside the United Kingdom attending full-time and sandwich courses in establishments of further education.
16/67	24.5.67	Development of courses leading to the Diploma in Art and Design.
17/67	9.6.67	National Water Safety Campaign.
22/67		Liability for pupils and students visiting industry.
23/67	1.9.67	Procedure for introducing superannuation arrangements for part-time teachers in primary and secondary schools.
23/67 (Addendum No.1)	28.12.67	Procedure for introducing superannuation arrangements for part-time teachers in primary and secondary schools.
25/67	25.10.67	Joint planning of industrial training and associated further education.
2/68	30.1.68	Physical education apparatus in schools and colleges.
8/68	11.6.68	Technical college resources – the use of buildings and equipment.
10/68	20.8.68	Probation of qualified teachers (replaces AM No. 4/59).
11/68	17.9.68	Teachers' Superannuation (Amending) Regulations, 1968.
14/68	2.12.68	Metrication in the construction industry.
14/68 (Addendum No. 1)	18.7.69	Metrication in the construction industry.
2/69	20.1.69	Joint planning of industrial training and further education-craft studies courses in engineering.
8/69	2.6.69	Fees for quantity surveyors.

No. of AM	Date of Issue	Subject
8/69 (Addendum No.1)	1.9.70	Fees for quantity surveyors.
9/69	15.7.69	Arts facilities in educational and other establishments.
17/69	12.12.69	Writers in schools.
21/69	16.12.69	Technician courses and examinations.
23/69	8.12.69	Requests by school pupils for information from public and other bodies.
23/69 (Addendum)	28.1.70	Requests by school pupils for information from public and other bodies.
3/70	23.1.70	Avoidance of carcinogenic aromatic amines in schools and other educational establishments.
4/70	9.1.70	The Teachers' Superannuation (Amendment) Regulations, 1970.
5/70	21.1.70	Licensing of closed circuit educational television systems.
7/70	20.2.70	Use of lasers in schools and other education establishments.
12/70	17.4.70	Joint planning of industrial training and further education.
22/70	25.6.70	Teachers' records.
25/70	10.9.70	Report of the Joint Committee of the NACAE and the NCDAD on the structure of art and design education in the further education sector.
26/70	11.9.70	In-service courses for teachers: financial and administrative arrangements.
26/70 (Addendum No.1)	23.3.71	In-service courses for teachers: financial and administrative arrangements.
26/70 (Addendum No.2)	20.12.71	In-service courses for teachers: financial and administrative arrangements.
26/70 (Addendum No.3)	7.11.72	In-service courses for teachers: financial and administrative arrangements. Open University courses.

No. of A.M.	Date of Issue	Subject
5/71 (Welsh Education Office AM 2/71)	14.4.71	Removal of temporary defence works.
6/71 (Welsh Education Office AM 3/71) (Welsh Education Office AM 5/71)	29.4.71	Acquisition of land – new arrangements for loans.
1/72	7.1.72	Transfer to colleges of education of full financial responsibility for field studies, modern language courses and exchanges and teaching practice by students.
4/72	25.1.72	Reports of the Committee of Enquiry into Teacher Education and Training.
6/72	1.2.72	Training for the Future. A Plan for Discussion.
8/72 (Welsh Education Office 2/72)	11.2.72	Educational Visits to ancient monuments and historic buildings in the care of the Secretaries of State for the Environment, for Scotland and for Wales.
12/72	15.3.72	Approval of courses leading to the Diploma in Art and Design.
12/72 (Addendum No.1)	27.9.73	Approval of courses leading to the Diploma in Art and Design.
11/72 (Welsh Education Office 4/72)	27.4.72	Section 115 – Education Act 1944.
18/72 (Welsh Education Office 5/72)	13.6.72	Licences for television broadcasts receiving sets in schools and other education institutions.
22/72	24.8.72	Review of Teachers' Superannuation Scheme.
1/73 (Welsh Education Office 1/73)	10.1.73	The Standards for School Premises Regulations, 1972.
2/73 (Welsh Education Office 2/73)	19.1.73	Reorganisation of local government: allocation of new reference numbers to local education authorities and establishments.
2/73 (Addendum No.1) (Welsh Education Office 2/72)	2.5.73	Reorganisation of local government: allocation of new reference numbers to local education authorities and establishments.

No. of AM	Date of Issue	Subject
2/73 (Addendum No.1)	9.5.73	Reorganisation of local government: allocation of new reference numbers to local education authorities and establishments.
Amendment (Welsh Education Office 2/73)		
3/73 (Welsh Education Office 3/73)	28.2.73	Arrangements for distribution of HM. Inspectors' Reports.
4/73 (Welsh Education Office 5/73)	6.3.73	Immigration Act, 1971.
5/73 (Welsh Education Office 5/73)	27.3.73	Town and Country Planning Act, 1968 – Structure Plans.
6/73 (Joint AM with Welsh Education Office)	22.3.73	Report of the Committee of Inquiry into Adult Education in England and Wales.
7/73		Establishment of the Technician Education Council.
8/73	3.4.73	Organisation of the Department.
10/73 (Welsh Education Office 6/73)	22.5.73	Cost limits for educational building in England and Wales.
11/73 (Welsh Education Office 7/73)	24.5.73	Constructional standards for maintained and direct grant educational building in England and Wales.
14/73	22.6.73	Teachers' Superannuation Scheme – Actuarial Valuation 1966/71.
15/73 (Welsh Education Office 8/73)	27.6.73	Royal Ballet School and Yehudi Menuhin School.
21/73	10.12.73	The staffing of nursery schools and classes.
22/73	19.12.73	Report of the Working Party on School Transport.
1/74	11.374	Teachers' Superanuation Scheme – new rates of contribution.

No. of AM	*Date of Issue*	*Subject*
2/74	26.3.74	Future arrangements for the handling of School Health Service Records and Statistical Returns.
3/74	29.3.74	The Teachers' Superannuation (Added Years and Interchange) Regulations, 1974.
4/74 (Welsh Office 1/74)	10.4.74	Constructional standards for maintained and direct grant educational building in England and Wales (Amendment).
5/74	26.4.74	Report of the Working Group on Vocational Courses in the Design Technician Area.
9/74 (Welsh Office 4/74)	11.6.74	Metrication.
12/74	1.7.74	Report of the Joint Advisory Committee on Agricultural Education.
13/74	28.6.74	Exchange and interchange of teachers and assistants with overseas countries, 1975-76.
13/74 (Amendment)	10.7.75	Exchange and interchange of teachers and assistants with overseas countries, 1975-76.
13/74 (Amendment)	4.12.75	Exchange and interchange of teachers and assistants with overseas countries, 1975-76.
14/74	27.6.74	Amalgamation of the Council for National Academic Awards and the National Council for Diplomas in Art and Design.
17/74 (Welsh Office 5/74)	22.8.74	Rent Act 1974: The Protected Tenancies (Exceptions) Regulations, 1974.
5/75 (Welsh Education Office 1/75)	2.5.75	The General Certificate of Education Ordinary Level Examination: grading of results
6/75	10.7.75	Exchange and interchange of teachers and assistants with Overseas countries, 1976-77.
6/75 (Amendment)	4.12.75	Exchange and interchange of teachers and assistants with overseas countries 1976-77.
9/75	20.8.75	In-service courses for teachers: financial and administrative arrangements.
12/75	19.9.75	Grants to postgraduate students.

No. of AM	Date of Issue	Subject
12/75 (Welsh Office 2/75)	25.11.75	Reports of the Committee on catering arrangements in schools and of the working party on nutritional aspects of school meals.
1/76	16.2.76	Silver Jubilee 1977.
2/76	17.3.76	The use of Ionising Radiations in Education Establishments.
3/76	29.4.76	Salary scales for teachers in primary and secondary schools.
4/76	26.5.76	Salary scales for teachers in establishments of further education (including Colleges of Education) and Farm Institutes and for teachers of agricultural (including horticultural) subjects.
5/76	2.6.76	Salary scales for teachers in primary and secondary schools.
6/76 (Welsh Office 4/76)	25.6.76	The laboratory use of Dangerous Pathogens.
7/76 (Welsh Office 5/76)	2.7.76	The use of Asbestos in Educational Establishments.
8/76	19.7.76	Exchange and Interchange of Teachers and Assistants with Overseas Countries.
9/76 (Succeeding AM 14/75)	20.10.76	Programme of Long Courses for qualified teachers.
10/76	29.10.76	Professions Supplementary to Medicine: Use of Further Education facilities.
11/76 (Welsh Office 6/76)	31.12.76	Implementation of the Report of the Joint Planning Group on the links between the Training Services Agency and the Education Service.
12/76	31.12.76	Salary Scales for Teachers in Primary and Secondary Schools.
1/77	12.1.77	The Teachers' Superannuation Regulations 1970.
2/77	14.1.77	Salary scales for teachers in establishments for further education.
3/77 (Welsh Office 1/77)	31.1.77	Constructional standards for maintained and direct grant educational building in England and Wales (Revision).

No. of AM	*Date of Issue*	*Subject*
4/77 (Welsh Office 2/77)	10.2.77	Further education for unemployed young people.
5/77 (Welsh Office 3/77)	18.2.77	Commonwealth Day.
6/77 (Welsh Office 4/77)	3.3.77	Approval of fees at non-maintained special schools and establishments for the further education and training of disabled persons.
7/77	4.3.77	Salary scales for teachers in primary and secondary schools.
8/77 (Welsh Office 5/77)	18.3.77	Educational Building – minor works.
9/77	26.5.77	Training and retraining of teachers in Mathematics, Physical Sciences and Craft, Design and Technology.
10/77	30.5.77	Salary scales for teachers in primary and secondary schools.
11/77	18.7.77	Exchange and interchange of teachers and assistants with overseas countries 1978-79.
12/77 (Welsh Office 6/77)	1.8.77	Links between the training and further education services.
13/77	8.9.77	Salary scales for teachers in establishments of further education.
14/77 (Welsh Office 7/77)	11.11.77	Threatened industrial action in the fire services.
15/77 (Welsh Office 8/77)	7.12.77	Health education in schools.
1/78	4.1.78	Guide to Making Induction Work.
2/78 (Succeeding AM 9/78)	15.3.78	Programme of Long Courses for qualified teachers 1978/79.
3/78	20.3.78	Report of the Working Group on Management of higher education in the maintained sector.

No. of AM	Date of Issue	Subject
4/78 (Welsh Office 2/78)	18.4.78	Training and retraining of teachers in mathematics, physical science and craft design and technology.
5/78	24.5.78	Teachers' Superannuation: Social Security Pensions Act 1975.
6/78 (Welsh Office 3/78)	17.7.78	Exchange and Interchange of teachers and assistants with overseas countries 1979/80.
7/78	31.7.78	Salary scales for teachers in primary and secondary schools.
8/78	1.8.78	Salary scales for teachers in primary and secondary schools.
9/78 (Replacing AM 10/78) (Welsh Office 5/78)	24.8.78	Probation of qualified teachers.
10/78	29.8.78	Salary scales for teachers in further education.
11/78	27.9.78	Salary scales for teachers in further education.
12/78 (Welsh Office 6/78)	20.11.78	Making Inset Work.
13/78	22.11.78	Programme of Long Courses for qualified teachers 1979/80.
14/78 (Welsh Office 4/78)	12.12.78	Research and experiment on volunteers in nonmedical institutions.
15/78	4.12.78	Salary Scales for teachers in further education.
26/78 (Addendum No. 4)	19.12.78	In-service courses for teachers: financial and administrative arrangements.
4/77 (Amendment No.1)	10.2.78	Further Education of unemployed young people.
1/79	16.1.79	Teachers' Superannuation Scheme Actuarial Valuation 1971/1976.
2/79	9.2.79	Constructional Standards for Maintained and Direct Grant Educational Establishments in England.

No. of AM	*Date of Issue*	*Subject*
3/79	26.2.79	Experiments in Genetic Manipulation.
4/79	10.4.79	Training and retraining to teach mathematics, and physical sciences, business studies and craft, design and technology. Further training for teachers, in mathematics and the physical sciences.
5/79	9.4.79	Salary Scales for Teachers in Primary and Secondary Schools.
6/79	24.9.79	Salary Scales for Teachers in Primary and Secondary Schools.
4/77 (Amendment No.2) (Welsh Office 2/77) (Amendment No.2)	31.12.79	Further Education for Unemployed Young People.

APPENDIX 2 –

CIRCULARS CURRENT AT 1 JANUARY 1980

No of Circular	*Date of Issue*	*Subject*
87	20.2.46	Regional organisation of further education (including Appendices A and B).
94	8.4.46	Research in technical colleges
133	19.3.47	Schemes of further education and plans for county colleges (including addendum and pamphlet No.8).
133 (Addendum No.1)	30.5.47	Schemes of further education and plans for county colleges.
133 (Addendum No.2)	16.7.47	Schemes of further education and plans for county colleges.
139	25.4.47	Plans for county colleges.
151	18.7.47	School records of individual development.
172	30.4.48	Teachers (Superannuation) Acts, 1918-1946; National Insurance (Modification of Teachers Pensions) Regulations, 1948 (including Appendix and correction).
179	4.8.48	The school health service and handicapped pupils: effect of the establishment of the national health service.
183	8.10.48	Provision of Clothing Regulations (including the Regulations – S.I. 1948, No.2222).
232 (Home Office 31/1951)	31.3.51	Childrens Act 1948: allocation of functions as between local authority and local education authority (including S.I. 1951, No. 472).
268	17.8.53	Education (Miscellaneous Provisions) Act, 1953.
270	27.8.53	Advanced short courses for scientists and technologists engaged in industry.
270 (Amendment No.1)	20.3.57	Advanced short courses for scientists and technologists engaged in industry.

Where a circular has been issued jointly with another government department both departmental references are given in the first column.

No. of Circular	Date of Issue	Subject
272	15.1.54	Prevention of food poisoning in school canteens.
275 (Min of Agric. & Fisheries 5)	7.5.54	Working Party on Agricultural Education: joint circular from the Ministry of Agriculture and Fisheries and the Ministry of Education (including Carrington Report).
275 (Addendum No.1)	26.4.61	Local education authorities and the National Agricultural Advisory Service.
275 (Addendum No.2)	18.2.64	Local education authorities and the National Agricultural Advisory Service.
295	8.11.55	Education grants for service children.
295 (Amendment No.17)	19.9.75	Education grants for service children.
299	29.2.56	Technical education (including White Paper on development of technical education).
302	3.5.56	Milk in schools scheme (superseding Circulars 278 and 296 and A M Nos 238, 469, 481 and 492).
302 (corrigendum)	9.5.56	Milk in schools scheme.
302 (Addendum No.1)	29.3.65	Milk in schools scheme.
305	21.6.56	Organisation of technical colleges (out of print).
320	1.3.57	Hostels at technical colleges.
322	12.4.57	Libraries in technical colleges.
322 (Amendment No.1)	18.6.57	Libraries in technical colleges.
323	13.5.57	Liberal education in technical colleges.
336	12.2.58	Recruitment of teachers for technical colleges.
348	10.3.59	Special educational treatment for maladjusted children.

No of Circular	Date of Issue	Subject
350	24.3.59	Local Government Act, 158: changes in administrative procedure (cancelling Circulars 89, 100, 106, 112, 129, 156, 208, 230, 237, 252, 255, 285, 297, 304, 237, 333 and 334 and A.M. Nos. 255, 277, 291, 436, 442, 444, 470, 474, 475, 478, 490, 499, 502, 507 and 549).
1/59	13.4.59	Technical education – the next step.
5/59	11.6.59	Further education in commerce.
7/59	10.8.59	Governing bodies for major establishments of further education.
7/59 (Addendum No.1)	7.9.61	Governing bodies of major establishments of further education: farm institutes.
9/59	21.8.59	Education Act, 1959.
10/59	3.9.59	The remodelling of old schools.
12/59 (Min of Health 26/59)	9.10.59	Health visiting service.
2/60	1.3.60	Land questions.
4/60	17.3.60	"Your Future in Industry".
10/60	12.9.60	Teaching Service in the Commonwealth and other countries overseas.
10/60 (Addendum No.1)	28.1.64	Teaching Service in the Commonwealth and other countries overseas.
10/60 (Addendum No.2)	21.7.65	The National Council for the Supply of Teachers Overseas.
14/60	27.9.60	Report of Working Party on assistance with cost of boarding education (superseding A.M. No. 225)
1/61	5.1.61	"Better opportunities in technical education".
3/61	13.3.61	Regional colleges.
11/61	3.7.61	Special educational treatment for educationally sub-normal pupils (superseding Circular 79).

No. of Circular	Date of Issue	Subject
15/61	24.8.61	Organisation of business studies in colleges of further education.
4/62	18.4.62	The Education Act, 1962.
4/62 (Addendum) (Revised Appendix No.1)	10.10.69	School leaving dates. The Family Law Reform Act, 1969.
3/63	18.1.63	Organisation of further education courses.
4/63	26.3.63	The Certificate in Office Studies – Rules 128.
4/63 (Addendum)	11.2.64	The Certificate in Office Studies.
6/63	28.4.63	Sandwich courses – National Advisory Council on Education for Industy and Commerce. Report of Advisory Sub-Committee.
9/63	23.5.63	The Certificate of Secondary Education.
10/63	4.7.63	Training of part-time youth leaders and assistants. Conference on training the trainers.
1/64	28.2.64	Industrialised building and educational building consortia.
2/64	2.3.64	Provision of language and export courses for business firms.
2/64 (Amended Appendices A and C)	14.3.66	Provision of language and export courses for business firms.
2/64 (Amended Appendix A)	21.2.68	Provision of language and export courses for business firms.
3/64	20.3.64	The education service and nuclear attack.
4/64	18.3.64	A higher award in business studies.
10/64	16.7.64	Council for National Academic Awards.
11/64	27.8.64	Provision of facilities for sports.

No. of Circular	*Date of Issue*	*Subject*
Ministry of Housing and Local Government 49/64)		
12/64	27.8.64	Education Act, 1964.
13/64	29.9.64	The Schools Council for the Curriculum and Examinations, Secondary School examinations.
14/64	6.10.64	The Henniker-Heaton Report on day release.
17/64	16.12.64	The public relations of further education.
4/65	9.3.65	Public Libraries and Museum Act, 1964.
6/65	18.5.65	Part-time teaching in the schools.
7/65 (Min. of Housing and Local Government 53/65)	14.6.65	The education of immigrants.
9/65	8.7.65	Refresher and supplementary courses for nursery and allied staff.
(Home office 143/65: Ministry of Health 13/65)		
11/65	19.8.65	Post diploma studies in art and design.
2/66	10.1.66	Management studies in technical colleges.
3/66	26.1.66	The nutritional standard of school dinners.
7/66	3.3.66	Courses of further training for teachers in further education.
8/66	24.5.66	A plan for polytechnics and other colleges.
11/66	12.4.66	Technical colleges resources: size of classes and approval of further education courses.
12/66	20.4.66	Pre-diploma studies in art and design.
19/66 (Ministry of Land & National Resources 3/66)	12.9.66	Use of reservoirs and gathering grounds for recreation.

No. of Circular	Date of Issue	Subject
20/66	5.9.66	School meals service – technical advice and inspection.
21/66	13.9.66	Training of teachers for further education and schools: teaching practice.
22/66	18.9.66	Agricultural education
24/66	12.12.66	Relations between colleges of education and schools; teaching practice.
25/66	15.12.66	Local Government Act, 1966 – School Meals and Milk.
27/66	21.12.66	Fees for students from outside the United Kingdom attending full-time and sandwich courses in establishments of further education.
2/67	7.2.67	The government of colleges of education.
3/67	22.367	Education Act, 1967.
8/67	21.7.67	Immigrants and the Youth Service.
11/67	24.8.67	School building programme – school building in Educational Priority Areas.
3/68	10.1.68	Co-operation between libraries.
4/68	17.1.68	Teachers' misconduct – Revision of Statutory Instruments.
9/68 (Ministry of Health 6/68)	4.6.68	Head-worn hearing aids for children.
12/68	30.4.68	The Education Act, 1968.
16/68	15.8.68	The teachers and the school meals service.
22/68	9.10.68	The Education (No. 2) Act, 1968.
6/69	11.4.69	The future supply and training of librarians.
7/69	2.4.69	Provision of milk, meals and other refreshments.
8/69	10.4.69	The Education (No. 2) Act, 1968: Colleges of Education.
11/69	28.5.69	Special education for children handicapped by spina bifida.

No. of Circular	*Date of Issue*	*Subject*
16/69	19.8.69	The staffing of the schools.
19/69	16.12.69	Bachelor of Education degree: arrangements for serving teachers.
3/70	4.3.70	Basic training of youth workers and community centre wardens.
7/70	4.3.70	Government and conduct of establishments of further education.
11/70	30.7.70	Awards for postgraduate study (superseding Circular 14/66) given by the research councils, government departments and local education authorities.
12/70	30.7.70	The education of young children with defects of both sight and hearing.
13/70 (Dept. of Health and Social Security Circ. 12/70 Min of H, L.G. Circular ROADS No. 20/70 (Min. of Transport)	17.8.70	The Chronically Sick and Disabled Persons Act, 1970.
14/70	27.8.70	In-service courses for teachers: financial and administrative arrangements.
15/70	22.9.70	The Education (Handicapped Children) Act, 1970.
18/70 (Welsh Office Circ. 108/70)	3.11.70	Primary and secondary education in Wales.
19/70	26.10.70	The Children and Young Persons Act, 1969, and the enforcement of school attendance.
3/71	9.2.71	Revised arrangements for school meals.
6/71 (Welsh Office Circ. 91/71)	17.6.71	Education of autistic children.
7/71	12.7.71	The structure of art and design education in the further education sector: Report of the Joint Committee of the NACAE and NCDAD.

No. of Circular	Date of Issue	Subject
8/71 (Welsh Office Circ. 139/71)	24.8.71	Raising the School Leaving Age to 16.
9/71 (Home Office Circ. 147/1971)	24.8.71	Tidal flooding in Greater London.
12/71 (Welsh Office Circ. 147/71)	26.8.71	Provision of Milk and Meals (Amendment No. 2) Regulations, 1971.
13/71	15.11.71	Capital grants to voluntary youth service village hall and community centre projects: new arrangements.
2/72 (Welsh Office Circ. 151/72)	31.7.72	Financial Arrangements for social work training (Joint Circular with the Department of Health Social Security and the Home Office).
3/72 (Welsh Education Office 162/72)	1.8.72	Provision of Milk and Meals (Amendment) Regulations, 1972.
(Welsh Office Circ. 22/73)	16.1.73	Local Government Act, 1972. Reorganisation of local government: the education function.
2/73 (Welsh Office Circ. 39/73)	31.1.73	Nursery Education.
3/73 (Welsh Office Circ. 51/73)	2.3.73	Provision of Milk and Meals (Amendment Regulations, 1973) School Meals: remission of Charges.
4/73 (Welsh Office Circ. 47/73)	6.3.73	Staffing of special schools and classes.
5/73	29.3.73	Local government reorganisation and the public library service.
6/73	29.3.73	Constitution of district councils in Wales as public library authorities.
7/73	29.3.73	Development of higher education in the non-university sector.
8/73 (Welsh Office Circular 86/73)	29.3.73	Local government reorganisation. Arrangements for the establishment of Education Committees.

No. of Circular	Date of Issue	Subject
9/73	13.6.73	Local Government Act 1972. Reorganisation of local government: museums and galleries and the arts.
10/73 (Welsh Office Circ. 169/73)	3.8.73	The Provision of Milk and Meals (Amendment No. 2) Regulations, 1973. School meals.
11/73	31.12.73	The qualification of teachers.
13/73 (Welsh Education Office Circ. 289/73)	14.11.73	Action to conserve energy supplies.
14/73 (Welsh Office Circ. 289/73)	12.12.73	Local Government Act 1972 – Local Government (Voluntary Schools and Education Charities) Order, 1973.
1/74	4.1.74	The NHS Reorganisation Act 1973. Future arrangements for the provision of school health services and of health advice and services to local education authorities.
(Dept. of Environment 19/74) (Home Office 16/74) (Dept. of Health and Social Security Local Authority Circ. 11/74) (Welsh Office 35/74)		
3/74 (Dept. of Health and Social Security HSC (IS) 9) (Welsh Office WHS (IS) 5)	14.3.74	Child guidance.
4/74 (Welsh Office 112/74)	16.4.74	The organisation of secondary education.
5/74 (Dept. of Health and Social Security HSC (IS) 37)	21.5.74	The education of mentally handicapped children and young people in hospital.

No. of Circular	*Date of Issue*	*Subject*
6/74	17.6.74	Development of higher education in the non-university sector: Interim arrangements for the control of advanced courses.
7/74 (Welsh Office 135/74)	14.6.74	Work experience.
8/74 (Welsh Office 154/74)	12.6.74	Education building 1974-75.
9/74 (Welsh Office 153/74)	9.7.74	The Provision of Milk and Meals (Amendment) Regulations, 1974.
10/74 (Welsh Office 181/74)	19.7.74	School building 1974-75.
11/74 (Welsh Office 226/74) (Dept. of the Environment 171/73) (Home Office 233/74) (Dept. of Employment 1/74) (Dept. of Prices and Consumer Protection 1/74) (Dept. of Health and Social Security Local Authority Circ. (74) (36)) (Welsh Office 282/74)	6.11.74	Health and Safety at Work etc Act, 1974.
13/74 (Welsh Office 281/74)	31.12.74	Educational building after 1974-75.
1/75 (Welsh Office 49/75)	12.3.75	Revised arrangements for school meals.

No. of Circular	*Date of Issue*	*Subject*
2/75 (Welsh Office 21/75)	17.3.75	The discovery of children requiring special education and the assessment of their needs.
5/75	18.7.75	The reorganisation of higher education in the non-university sector: The Further Education Regulations 1975.
6/75	25.7.75	The Colleges of Education (compensation) Regulations 1975.
7/75 (Welsh Office 126/75)	30.7.75	Phasing out of direct grants to grammar schools.
8/75 (Welsh Office 137/75)	6.8.75	School Building 1976-77.
9/75 (Dept. of the Environment 79/75) (Dept. of Employment 1/75) (Dept. of Prices and Consumer Protection 6/75) (Welsh Office 140/75)	21.8.75	The attack on inflation – remuneration charges and grants. Implications for local authorities.
10/75 (Dept. of the Environment 88/75) (Home Office 149/75) (Dept. of Health and Social Security Local Authority Circular (75) (10)) (Welsh Office 142/75)	3.9.75	Local authority expenditure in 1976/77; forward planning.
11/75	10.10.75	Awards to Students.

No. of Circular	*Date of Issue*	*Subject*
12/75 (Welsh Office 167/75)	15.10.75	Provision of Milk and Meals (Amendment No. 2) Regulations 1975.
13/75	2.12.75	Revised Conditions of the Recognition as efficient of independent establishments of further education.
1/76 (Welsh Office 18/76)	15.1.76	Determination of Hardship: treatment of mobility allowances.
2/76 (Welsh Office 20/76)	20.1.76	Sex Discrimination Act 1975.
6/76	21.7.76	Government Statement on unified vocational preparation.
11/76	25.11.76	Education Act 1976.
13/76 (Welsh Office 160/76)	25.11.76	Provision of Milk and Meals (Amendment No. 2) Regulations 1976.
1/77	14.1.77	Tuition Fees in Further Education 1977-78
2/77	15.3.77	Provision of Milk and Meals (Amendments) Regulations 1977.
4/77 (Dept. of the Environment 54/77) (Home Office 87/77) (Dept. of Health and Social Security 11/77)	10.6.77	Race Relations Act 1976.
7/77 (Welsh Office 119/77)	26.7.77	Provision of Milk and Meals (Amendment No. 2) Regulations 1977.
3/77	14.11.77	Tuition Fees in Further Education (Overseas Students).
10/77	30.9.77	Unemployed young people.
11/77	17.11.77	The training of teachers for further education.

No. of Circular	*Date of Issue*	*Subject*
12/77 (Welsh Office 128/77)	18.11.77	Provision of Milk and Meals (Amendment No. 3) Regulations 1977.
13/77	17.11.77	Approval of equipment purchases at establishments of further education.
14/77 (Welsh Office 185/77)	29.11.77	Local Education Authority arrangements for the school curriculum.
2/78	11.1.78	Tuition Fees in Further Education.
3/78 (Welsh Office 186/77)	20.1.78	The School Meals Service.
8/78	20.6.78	Tuition Fees in F.E. (Overseas Students).
9/78	2.8.78	Entry to initial teacher training courses in England and Wales.
11/78 (Replacing Circ. 4/75) (Welsh Office 111/78)	18.8.78	Medical fitness of teachers and of entrants to training.
12/78 (Replacing Circ. 3/69) (Welsh Office 112/78)	18.8.78	Control of tuberculosis; protection of children at school against the risk of infection by non-teaching staff.
14/78	11.10.78	Admission arrangements.
17/78	6.12.78	Boarding charges: Race Relations Act 1976.
1/79 (Dept.of Environment 6/79) (Local Authority Circular (79) 2 (DHSS)) (Home Office 6/79) (Dept.of Transport 6/79) (Dept.of Employment 1/79)	24.1.79	Rate Support Grant Settlement 1979-80.

No. of Circular	Date of Issue	Subject
(Dept. of Prices and Consumer Protection 1/79) (Welsh Office 7/79)		
2/79 (Dept. of the Environment 15/79) (Local Authority Circular (76) 6 DHSS) (Home Office 52/79) (Dept. of Transport 7/79) (Dept. of Employment 2/79) (Dept. of Prices and Consumer Protection 3/79) (Welsh Office 28/79)	29.3.79	The Government's Expenditure Plans (Cmnd. 7439): Implications for Local Authority Expenditure 1979-83.
3/79	27.3.79	Tuition Fees in Further Education 1979-80.
4/79 (Dept. of the Environment 21/79) (Local Authority Circular (79) 9 DHSS) (Home Office 111/79) (Dept. of Transport 7/79) (Dept. of Employment 3/79) (Dept. of Trade 1/79) (Welsh Office 51/79)	9.7.79	Local Authority Expenditure in 1979-80.
5/79	12.7.79	Tuition fees and admissions to further education establishments and awards 1979-80; Race Relations Act 1976.

APPENDIX 3

COLLEGE LETTERS CURRENT AT 1 JANUARY 1980

Number	*Date of Issue*	*Title*
CL 7/67	21/3/1967	Colleges of Education: Model Scheme of Government.
CL 14/68	29/8/1968	Records of Trainee Teachers, including Notes of Guidance for Colleges of Education.
CL 20/68	20/12/1968	Amendment No. 1 to CL 18/68.
CL 1/69	24/1/1969	Revised Notes on the Procedures for the Approval of College of Education Building Projects (Red Booklet).
CL 4/69	12/2/1969	The Design of Libraries in Colleges of Education (Detailed guidance on provision required in new College Libraries).
CL 18/69	25/9/1969	Instrument and Articles of Government for Voluntary Colleges of Education (Student membership of governing bodies: student membership of Academic Board: Committees of the body and Academic Board; representation of students: disciplinary procedures).
CL 16/69	30/9/1969	Staff-Student Ratios in Colleges of Education. (Enclosing Memorandum from Pooling Committee on unit costs and staff-student ratios in colleges of education).
CL 21/69	21/11/1969	Records of Trainee Teachers, Trainee Teacher Record Card. (including Notes of Guidance).
CL 3/70 VCL 3/70	19/2/1970	The Balance of Training.
CL 8/70 VCL 13/70	17/4/1970	Expenditure by Specialist Students on Books, Equipment, Clothing and Materials.
CL 9/70 VCL 14/70	5/5/1970	B.Ed Candidates: Selection for Fourth Year (See also CL 15/71).
CL 10/70 VCL 15/70	12/5/1970	B.Ed Degree: Terms on which studies for the B.Ed degree may be interrupted
CL 13/70 VCL 17/70	28/5/1970	Some aspects of the Education of Immigrants.

(CL – College Letter: VCL – Voluntary College Letter: TTCL – Teacher Training College Letter)

Number	Date of Issue	Title
CL 15/70 VCL 19/70	8/6/1970	Referred stuents (Students referred for further study or teaching practice through failure in part of their Certificate examination).
CL 18/70 VCL 25/70	10/8/1970	Payment of Fees in 1970-71 for Students and Teachers undertaking Preparatory and Substantive B.Ed. degree courses.
CL 3/71 VCL 4/71	2/4/1971	Cash Grants for Students in Colleges of Education. (Pilot Scheme in eight colleges 1971-72).
CL 7/71 VCL 8/71	1/6/1971	Half Term Breaks in Colleges of Education.
CL 8/71 VCL 9/71	18/5/1971	Financial Responsibility for Field Studies, Vacation Course, and similar activities of College of Education Students.
CL 10/71 VCL 12/71	9/7/1971	Film Library for Teacher Training.
CL 12/71 VCL 14/71	6/8/1971	Admission of Students to Intial Teaching Training Courses (See also Circular 11/71).
CL 13/71 VCL 15/71	6/9/1971	Determination of Boarding Fees in Teacher Training Establishments.
CL 14/71 VCL 16/71	31/8/1971	Report of the Working Party on Emoluments for Colleges of Education Staff.
CL 15/71 VCL 17/71	8/9/1971	B.Ed Candidates: Selection for the Fourth Year. (See also CL 9/70).
CL 16/71 VCL 18/71	6/9/1971	Expenditure by Specialist Students on Books, Equipment, Materials, and Clothing.
CL 19/71 VCL 21/71	8/10/1971	Capital Investment Programme – Minor Works. Revision of normal limits and tolerance as from 1st April 1972 (See also Administrative Memorandum 15/71).
CL 21/71 VCL 23/71	6/12/1971	Catering and Residential Costs in Colleges of Education.
CL 1/72 VCL 1/72	7/1/1972	Pilot Scheme for Cash Grants for Resident Students in Colleges of Education (First Interim Report).
CL 3/72 VCL 3/72	28/1/1972	Referred Students: Tutition Fees and Examination Fees.

Number	Date of Issue	Title
CL 6/72 VCL 8/72	23/3/1972	Governors' responsibility for drawing up rules of disciplinary procedure.
CL 8/72	14/4/1972	Arrangements for Field Studies and Vacation Courses, Modern Language Courses and Exchanges, and Teaching Practice.
CL 13/72 VCL 14/72	22/6/1972	Colleges of Education as Residential Communities. (Questionnaire on residential places for students, residential accommodation for staff, and residential emoluments and charges).
VCL 15/72	27/6/1972	The Superannuation Act 1972. (Superannuation for non-teaching staff under a new local government superannuation scheme).
CL 15/72 VCL 16/72	11/9/1972	Returns of Student Numbers at the beginning of the Academic Year: Forms 6TT (1972) and 7TT (1972).
CL 17/72 VCL 18/72	7/8/1972	Pilot Scheme for Cash Grants for Resident Students in Colleges of Education.
CL 3/73 VCL 6/73	30/3/1973	Field Studies, Vacation Study and Courses, Teaching Practice.
CL 8/73 VCL 11/73	21/6/1973	Pilot Scheme for Cash Grants for Resident Students in Colleges of Education (enclosing copy of Working Group's Full Year Report for 1971-72).
CL 8/73 VCL 11/73	21/6/1973	Pilot Schemes For Cash Grants for Resident Students in Colleges of Education.
CL 9/73 VCL 12/73	3/9/1973	Safety in Outdoor Pursuits.
CL 10/73 VCL 13/73	11/9/1973	Forms 6TT and 7TT.
VCL 14/73	12/9/1973	Voluntary College Estimates 1973/74.
VCL 15/73	19/9/1973	Annual Statement of Accounts Form 23TT.
VCL 16/73	20/9/1973	Student/Staff Ratios in Colleges of Education.
CL 11/73 VCL 17/73	25/9/1973	Colleges of Education Cost Tables.
VCL 18/73	25/10/1973	Expected Claims for Grant Up to March 1974.

Number	*Date of Issue*	*Title*
CL 13/73 VCL 19/73	17/12/1973	Admission of Students from outside England and Wales to Initial Teacher Training Courses.
CL 12/73	28/9/1973	Cost bands in LEA Colleges of Education 1972-73.
CL 1/74 VCL 1/74	1/2/1974	Courses in France for Students taking French as a main subject.
CL 2/74 VCL 2/74	5/2/1974	Return of Student and Teaching Staff Nos. Form 19TT.
VCL 3/74	12/2/1974	Voluntary Colleges Cost Tables 1972-1973.
VCL 4/74	18/2/1974	Voluntary Colleges: Current Expenditure 1973-4 and 1974-5.
VCL 5/74	20/3/1974	Cost bands in Voluntary Colleges of Education 1972-3.
CL 4/74 VCL 6/74	22/4/1974	College of Education Libraries.
CL 6/74 VCL 7/74	10/5/1974	Safety in Outdoor Pursuits.
CL 7/74 VCL 8/74	7/6/1974	List of Authorities with Vacancies for Teachers 1974 (+ Appendix).
VCL 9/74	24/7/1974	Voluntary Colleges of Education Annual Statement of Accounts, Form 23TT.
CL 8/74 VCL 10/74	11/9/1974	Forms 6TT and 7TT.
CL 9/74 VCL 11/74	24/10/1974	Financial Arrangements for B.Ed. Courses University Fees.
VCL 12/74	24/10/1074	Voluntary Colleges of Education Current Expenditure 1974/75.
VCL 13/74	30/10/1974	Expected Claims for Grant up to March 1975.
CL 10/74 VCL 14/74	13/11/1974	In-Service Education and Training for Teachers in Schools.
CL 3/74	14/2/1974	Colleges of Education – Cost Table 1972-3.
CL 5/74	26/4/1974	Colleges of Education maintained by LEAs. Annual Statement of Accounts (Form 22TT) 1973-74.

Number	Date of Issue	Title
VCL 1/75	8/1/1975	Educational Building After 1974-5.
CL 1/75 VCL 2/75	19/2/1975	Return of Student Teaching Staff Nos. Form 19TT.
VCL 3/75	27/2/1975	Voluntary Colleges' Current Expenditure 1974-75 and 1975-76.
CL 2/75 VCL 4/75	4/3/1975	Course in France for Students taking French as a main subject 1975-76.
VCL 5/75	25/3/1975	Central Register and Clearing House.
CL 3/75	15/4/1975	Maintained Colleges – Cost Tables 1973/74.
CL 4/75	15/4/1975	Colleges of Education maintained by LEAs Annual Statement of Accounts 1974/75 Form 22TT.
VCL 6/75	15/4/1975	Cost Tables 1973/74 Voluntary Colleges of Education.
CL 5/75 VCL 7/75	15/4/1975	Financial Arrangements for University Validation of College Education Courses.
CL 6/75 VCL 8/75	9/6/1975	List of Authorities with Vacancies for Teachers 1975 and Revised appendix.
VCL 9/75	9/7/1975	Payment of Maintenance Grant to Voluntary Colleges and Form 67TT.
CL 7/75	21/7/1975	Colleges of Education Libraries.
VCL 10/75	21/7/1975	College of Education Libraries.
CL 8/75 VCL 11/75	15/8/1975	Fees for Courses of Teacher Training.
VCL 12/75	29/8/1975	Further Education Major Building Programme 1976-77.
CL 9/75 VCL 13/75	8/9/1975	Forms 6TT and 7TT.
VCL 14/75	15/9/1975	Voluntary College of Education Annual Statement of Accounts Form 23TT 1974/75.
VCL 15/75	17/11/1975	Provisional Allocation of Total Teacher Training Places in 1981.

Number	*Date of Issue*	*Title*
VCL 16/75	19/11/1975	Approval of Estimates and Current Expenditure 1975/76.
VCL 17/75	Nov. 1975	Pay of Non-Teaching Staff in Voluntary Colleges of Education – Incomes Policy.
CL 10/75	17/11/1975	Provisional Allocation of Total Teacher Training Places in 1981.
CL 11/75	Dec. 1975	Colleges of Education Maintained by LEAs Cost Tables 1974/75.
CL 1/76 VCL 1/76	23/1/1976	Rationalisation of Initial Teacher Training Provision.
CL 2/76 VCL 2/76	23/2/1976	Return of students and teaching staff Nos. Form 19TT.
VCL 3/76	4/4/1976	Voluntary Colleges' Current Expenditure 1975/76.
CL 3/76 VCL 4/76	23/4/76	Catering and Residence for students.
VCL 5/76	28/4/1976	Cost Tables.
CL 4/76 VCL 6/76	May 1976	Courses in France for students taking French as a main subject 1976/77.
CL 5/76	18/6/1976	Colleges of Education maintained by Local Education authorities Annual Statement of Accounts (Form 23TT) 1975/76.
VCL 7/76	June 1976	Tuition Fees for teacher training courses.
VCL 8/76	3/9/1976	Tuition Fees for teacher training courses.
CL 6/76 VCL 9/76	6/9/1976	Forms 6TT C1976 and 7TT (1976).
VCL 10/76	17/9/1976	Current Expenditure – cash limits
VCL 11/76	23/9/1976	Annual Statement of Accounts 1975/76 (Form 23TT).
VCL 12/76	19/10/1976	Central Register and Clearing House.
CL 7/76 VCL 13/76	29/10/1976	Financial Arrangements for University Validation of College Courses.
CL 8/76 VCL 14/76	10/12/1976	Courses in France for students taking French as a main subject.

Number	Date of Issue	Title
CL 1/77 VCL 1/77	7/1/1977	Circular Letters on Teacher Training Matters.

(This was the last college circular letter. After this the DES issued Teacher Training Circulars. These are listed at the end of each year).

Number	Date of Issue	Title
VCL 2/77	30/3/1977	Return of teaching staff and student numbers. Form 19TT.
VCL 3/77	25/4/1977	Voluntary College Current Expenditure 1976/77 and estimates. Form 20TT.
VCL 4/77	May 1977	EEC Education Programme and Covering Letter.
VCL 5/77	30/8/1977	Central Register and Clearing House.
VCL 6/77	9/9/1977	Voluntary Colleges of Education Statement of. Accounts 1976/77. Form 23TT.
VCL 7/77	Sept. 1977	Cost Tables 1975/76.
TTCL 1/77	7/2/1977	Admissions to Intitial Teacher Training.
TTCL 2/77	June 1977	Cost Tables 1975/76 Maintained Colleges of Education.
TTCL 3/77	26/8/1977	Training and re-training of teachers of Maths, Physical Sciences and Crafts Design and Technology.
TTCL 4/77	Nov. 1977	Programme of short courses for teachers.
TTCL 5/77	21/11/1977	Financial Arrangement for University Validation of College Courses.
VCL 1/78	Jan. 1978	Return of student and teaching staff numbers. Form 19TT.
VCL 2/78	March 1978	Voluntary Colleges of Education Preparation of Estimates 1978/79.
VCL 3/78	April 1978	Tuition Fees 1978/79.
VCL 4/78	27/5/1978	EEC Private Mini-buses on international journeys.
VCL 5/78	July 1978	Tutition Fees, Admission to Further Education Establishments, Awards, Race Relations Act 1976.

Number	Date of Issue	Title
*VCL 6/78	30/11/1978	Cost Tables 1976/77.
VCL 7/78	6/9/1978	Annual Statement of Accounts 1977/78 (Form 23TT).
VCL 8/78	25/8/1978	Central Register and Clearing House.
VCL 9/78	27/10/1978	Financial Arrangements for University Validation of College Courses.
*Also issued as FECL 6/78		
TTCL 1/78	10/1/1978	Training and re-training of teachers of mathematics, physical sciences and craft design and technology.
TTCL 2/78	10/1/1978	Intensive Courses for teachers of French 1978.
TTCL 3/78	10/1/1978	Courses for students taking French as a main subject.
TTCL 4/78	Oct. 1978	Arrangements for medical examinations and entrance to initial teacher training.
TTCL 5/78	20/11/1978	Despatch of Form 13TT [for above].
VCL 1/79	Jan. 1979	Return of teaching staff and student numbers. Form 19TT.
VCL 2/79	10/4/1979	Tuition fees 1979/80.
VCL 3/79	11/4/1979	Preparation of estimates 1979/80.
VCL 4/79	28/6/1979	Voluntary College of Education Cost Tables 1977/78.
VCL 5/79	30/7/1979	Financial Arrangements for University Validation of College Courses.
VCL 6/79	10/8/1979	Annual Statement of Accounts 1979-80.
VCL 7/79	20/8/1979	Central Register and Clearing House.
VCL 8/79	5/10/1979	Return of Students and Teaching Staff Numbers. Form 19TT.

There have been no 1979 TTCLs.

APPENDIX 4

FURTHER EDUCATION CIRCULAR LETTERS (FECL)
current at 8 February 1980

Presentation differs here from the previous appendices: the style adopted follows that of the DES in its listing of FECLs.

1954

1/54. Ministry's Art Examinations (1954).
2/54. Further Education Building Programme for 1955-56.
3/54. Ministry's Art Examinations – move to new Premises.
4/54. Release of Teachers to Industry and Commerce.
5/54. New courses in Establishments for Further Education.
6/54. Further Education Statistical Returns 1953-54.
8/54. Two year Retail Trades Junior Certificate Course.
9/54. Approval of Courses leading to the Ministry's Art Examinations and Eligibility of Candidates for the Examinations.
10/54. Research Associations.
11/54. Return of Enrolments 1954-55.
12/54. Confidential. Scholarships in Work study.
13/54. Further Education Building Programme for 1955-56.
14/54. Building Craft Classes – Distribution of Pamphlet.
15/54. Records of Careers of Students Successful in the Examinations for the National Diploma in Design.

1955

1/55. Technical College Equipment.
2/55. Evening Use of New Schools.
3/55. Scholarships in Work Study.
4/55. Employment of Trained Technical Teachers.
5/55. Visits of Art Students to Art Galleries.
6/55. Further Educational Statistical Returns 1954-55.
7/55. Approval Withdrawn from Certain Courses.
8/55. Scholarships in World Study.
9/55. Shortage of Suitably Qualified Officers available for the Nautical Teaching Profession.
10/55. Whitworth Foundations Awards 1956.
11/55. Courses Requiring Approval by outside Bodies.
12/55. Physical Training and Recreation Act 1937.

1956

1/56. Further Education Building Programme for 1957/58.
2/56. Further Education Building Programme for 1958/59.
3/56. 1955-56 and 1956-57 Building Programmes for Further Education.
4/56. Further Education Statistical returns 1955-56.
5/56. Research Associations.
6/56. European Productivity Agency. Training in the United States of European Teachers in Business Administration.
7/56. Amendments to Rules 110, Governing the Ministry's Art Examinations 1957.
8/56. Gauge Testing Scheme.
9/56. Further Education Building Programme for 1959/60.
10/56. Whitworth Foundation Awards 1957.
11/56. Preliminary Nursing and Pre-nursing.

1957

1/57. Regional co-ordination and Inter-authority payments agreement.
2/57. Building Craft Classes-Distribution of Pamphlet.
3/57. Approval of New Courses in Establishments for Further Education Session 1957-58.
4/57. Physical Training and Recreation Act; Social and Physical Training Grant Regulations.
5/57. European Productivity Agency Training in the United States of European Teachers in Business Administration E.P.A Project No. 329/5.
6/57. European Productivity Agency Summer Seminar for Management Teachers E.P.A. Project No. 404.
7/57. 1. National Coal Board Scholarships, 1958.
2. British Coking Industry Association Scholarships, 1958.
8/57. Further Education Statistical Returns 1956-57.
9/57. Approval of New Courses in Establishments for Further Education Session 1958-59.
11/57. Overseas Students in Establishments of Further Education.
12/57. Whitworth Foundation Awards, 1958.

1958

1/58. Further Education Building Programme for 1960-61.
2/58. Recruitment of Former Members of the Armed Services to Teaching Posts in Establishments of Further Education.
3/58. The National Institute of Houseworkers Limited.
4/58. 1. National Coal Board Scholarships, 1959.
2. British Coking Industry Association Scholarships, 1959.
5/58. Overseas Students in Establishments of Further Education.
6/58. Amendment to Rules 110 Governing the Ministry's Art Examination.
7/58. Whitworth Foundation Awards, 1959.
8/58. 1. Ministry of Labour and National Service.
2. The Professional and Executive Register.
9/58. Short Courses of Professional Training for Teachers in Establishments for Further Education.
10/58. Approval of Courses in Further Education.

1959

1/59. Whitworth Foundation Awards, 1960.
2/59. Deferment of National Service Admission of Students to one-year Farm Institute courses.
3/59. National Retail Distribution Certificates and Certificates in Retail Management Principles.
4/59. Further Education Statistics.
5/59. Academic Qualifications of Full-time Teachers in Major Establishments of Further Education.
6/59. 1. National Certificates and Diplomas.
2. Revision of Scale of Fees.
7/59. National Diploma in Hotel Keeping and Catering.
8/59. 1. National Coal Board Scholarships, 1960.
2. British Coking Industry Association Scholarships, 1960.
9/59. Agricultural Education Farms Maintained for Educational Purposes.
11/59. Governing Bodies of Farm Institutes.
12/59. One-Term Courses of Professional Training for Serving Teachers in Establishments of Further Education.

1960

1/60. Ministry's Art Examinations.

3/60. Whitworth Foundation Awards, 1961.
4/60. Further Education Major Building Programme.
5/60. Endorsed Higher Certificates in Applied Biology.
6/60. Meeting of Heads of Departments of Chemistry.
8/60. The National Institute of Houseworkers Limited.
9/60. Academic Qualifications of Full-time teachers in Major Establishments of Further Education.
10/60. National Certificates and Diplomas in Metallurgy.
11/60. 1. Ministry of Labour and National Service.
2. The Professional and Executive Register.
12/60. National Certificates and Diplomas in Electrical Engineering.
13/60. 1. National Coal Board Scholarships, 1961.
2. British Coking Industry Association scholarships, 1961.
14/60. Higher National Certificates in Civil Engineering.
15/60. Agricultural Education Major Building Programme 1961-62.
16/60. Programmes of Work in Major Establishments for Further Education including Farm Institutes.
17/70. Surplus Equipment hitherto sold to Educational Authorities at concessional prices.
18/60. National Certificates and Diplomas in Metallurgy.
19/60. Further Educational Statistics.
20/60. Practical Training for College-based Sandwich Course Students.
21/60. Diploma in Management Studies Approval of Courses.
22/60. Integrated Courses of Education and Initial Apprenticeship Training.
23/60. The National Joint Apprenticeship Board of the Building Industry.

1961

1/61. National Craftsman's Certificate for a Motor Vehicle Service Mechanic.
2/61. National Certificate and Diplomas in Building.
3/61. Further Education Major Building Programme.
5/61. Meeting of Heads of Department of Chemistry.
6/61. Agricultural Education – Major Building Programme 1962/63.
7/61. Academic Qualifications of Full-time Teachers in Major Establishments of Further Education.
8/61. Diploma in Management Studies rules and notes for guidance.
10/61. Use of "V" bricks in Building Courses.
11/61. The National Institute of Houseworkers Ltd.
12/61. English for Foreigners.
13/61. Advisory and instructional films for use on courses of Further Education in Agriculture and Horticulture.
14/61. 1. National Coal Board Scholarships, 1962.
2. British Coking Industry Association Scholarships, 1962.
15/61. Registers for Major Establishments of Further Education, Colleges of Art and Evening Institutes.
16/61. National Certificates and Diplomas in Applied Physics.

1962

1/62. Local Authorities Committee on Inter-Authority Payments under Section 7 of the Education (Miscellaneous Provisions) Act, 1953.
2/62. "Accidents; how they happen and how to prevent them" (The Ministry of Labour quarterly magazine dated January 1962).
3/62. Academic Qualifications of Full-Time Teachers in Major Establishments of Further Education.
4/62. Outline Schemes of Development for Further Education for Agriculture.
5/62. National Institute of Houseworkers Limited.
6/62. ONC in Engineering.

7/62. Agricultural Industry.
8/62. Agricultural Education – Major Building Programme 1963/64.
9/62. Rule 122. Higher National Certificates in Chemical Engineering.
10/62. Whitworth Foundation Awards, 1963.
11/62. Local Authorities Committee on Inter Authority Payments under Section 7 of the Education (Miscellaneous Provisions) Act 1953.
12/62. FE Major Building Programmes.
13/62. Ordinary National Diplomas in Engineering.
14/62. Forestry Education.
15/62. Survey of Accommodation in Technical Colleges and Colleges of Commerce.
16/62. General Studies in Technical Colleges.
17/62. Teachers of the History of Art.
18/62. Ordinary National Certificates in Engineering.
20/62. Training of Laboratory Technicians.
21/62. Candidates for courses Leading to the Diploma in Art and Design.
22/62. 1. Ministry of Labour.
2. The Professional and Executive Register.
23/62. Survey of Accommodation in Technical Colleges and Colleges of Commerce.
24/62. Report of the Committee on the Selection and Training of Supervisors.
25/62. Integrated Courses of Education and Initial Apprenticeship Training.
26/62. Amendment to Rule 110 Governing the Ministry Art Examinations.
27/62. Higher National Certificate in Foundry Technology.
28/62. Agricultural Education – Major Building Programme 1964/65.
29/62. Commonwealth Immigrants Act, 1962 – arrangements for Students.
30/62. Local Education Authority Advisory Committee on Inter-Authority Payments for Further Education under Section 7 of the Education (Miscellaneous Provisions) Act, 1953.

1963

1/63. Intermediate Certificate in Art and Crafts National Diploma in Design.
2/63. Higher National Certificate in Applied Biology.
3/63. Endorsed Certificates and Diplomas in Printing.
4/63. Teaching in Technical Colleges.
5/63. Admission of students to courses leading to the Diploma in Art and Design.
6/63. Training of Dispensing Assistants.
7/63. Approval of Courses leading to Diploma in Technology.
8/63. Nursing Cadet schemes.
9/63. Intermediate Certificate in Art and Crafts, 1964.
10/63. Ordinary National Certificates in Engineerings.
11/63. Ordinary National Certificate in Naval Architecture.
12/63. "Further Education for School Leavers".
13/63. General Course in Construction.
14/63. General Course in Mining.
15/63. General Course in Science.
16/63. General Course in Shipbuilding.
17/63. Termination of B.I.M. Examinations
18/63. National Certificates and Diplomas in Mining.
19/63. Problems arising in Connection with the Introduction of the Diploma in Art and Design.
20/63. LEA Advisory Committee on Inter-Authority Payments for Further Education under Section 7 of the Education (Miscellaneous Provisions) Act 1953.
21/63. Approval of Courses leading to Diploma in Technology.
22/63. 1. National Coal Board Scholarships, 1964.
2. British Coking Industry Association Scholarships, 1964.

1964

1/64. Alternative Entry Scheme for Marine Engineers.
2/64. Advice for Students in Overseas Countries on Professional and Technician Qualifications in Engineering and Building.
3/64. Admission to Art Training Centres – Defective Colour Vision in Students.
4/64. Alternative Entry Scheme for Marine Engineers.
5/64. Return of Full-time and Sandwich Advanced Places.
6/64. Diploma in Management Studies: New Examination arrangements.
7/64. Ordinary National Certificates in Engineering.
8/64. National Certificates and Diplomas in Textiles.
9/64. Agricultural Education.
10/64. National Awards in Business Studies Oral Language Examinations.
11/64. Forestry Education.
12/64. Management Studies – Teacher Development Courses.
13/64. New Two-year Ordinary Certificate Courses in Construction.
14/64. The Industrial Training Act, 1964, The Training of Training Officers and Craft Instructors.
15/64. Diplomas in Art and Design: Future Admission to pre-diploma courses.
16/64. Transfer from the Ordinary National Certificate in Business Studies to the Certificate in Office Studies.
17/64. New arrangements for Foremanship Examinations.
18/64. Ordinary National Certificate and Diplomas in Sciences.
19/64. 1. National Coal Board Scholarships, 1965.
2. British Coking Industry Association Scholarships, 1965.
20/64. Organochlorine Pesticides.
21/64. National Certificates and Diplomas in Mining.
22/64. The Industrial Training Act, 1964: Membership of the Central Training Council Industrial Training Boards.
25/64. The Art Examinations of the Department of Education and Science,1964/1965.
26/64. Higher National Certificates and Diplomas in Electrical and Electronic Engineering.
27/64. National Diplomas in Baking.
28/64. Ionising Radiations.
29/64. Education and Training of Supervisors.
30/64. The Education of Computer Personnel.
31/64. Candidates for Courses leading to the Diploma in Art and Design.
32/64. Capital Investment – Further Education Programme 1966/67.
33/64. Research Associations.
35/64. New two-year Ordinary National Certificate Courses in Construction.

1965

1/65. The Industrial Training Act, 1964. Full-time integrated courses of further education and industrial training in technical colleges.
2/65. The Certificate in Office Studies.
3/65. Ordinary National Diplomas in Engineering.
4/65. Higher National Certificates and Diplomas in Electrical and Electronic Engineering.
5/65. National Certificate and other courses, and the Certificate of Secondary Education.
6/65. Fees and National Certificate and Diplomas Examinations.
7/65 Short full-time courses for training officers. Grants for students.
8/65. Ordinary National Certificate and Diplomas in Business studies.
9/65. Ordinary National Diploma in Nautical Science.
10/65. Higher National Certificates and Diplomas in Mechanical, Production and Aeronautical Engineering.
11/65. Higher National Diploma in Applied Biology.

12/65. The Education and Training of Supervisors.
13/65. Approval of courses leading to Awards by the Council for National Academic Awards.
14/64. Industrial Training Act, 1964. Information on the work of the Industrial Training Boards.
15/65. Advertising and Marketing.
16/65. Ordinary National Certificates and Diplomas in Sciences.
17/65. National Diplomas in Hotel Keeping and Catering.
18/65. Ordinary National Certificates and Diplomas in Engineering.
19/65. Ordinary National Diploma in Nautical Science.
20/65. Industrial Training Act, 1964. Levy/Grant Proposals of the Iron and Steel Industry Training Board for 1965/66.
21/65. Industrial Training Act, 1964, Levy/Grant Proposals of the Construction Industry Training Board for 1965-66.
22/65. Refresher and supplementary courses for Nursery and allied staff.
23/65. The Clothing Institute Examinations.
24/65. Agricultural Education Courses and examinations in animal husbandry, minor operations on animals.
25/65. Industrial Training Act, 1964. Levy/grant arrangements of the Wool Industry Training Board for 1965/66.
26/65. National Craftsman's Certificate for a Motor Vehicle Service Mechanic.
27/65. Approval of Advanced Courses.
28/65. 1. National Coal Board Scholarships, 1966.
2. British Coking Industry Association Scholarships.
29/65. Public Relations of Further Education.
30/65. Training in Safety.
31/65. Industrial Training Act, 1964. Levy/Grant Proposals of the Shipbuilding Industry Training Board for 1965/66.
32/65. Candidates for courses leading to the Diploma in Art and Design.
33/65. Industrial Training Act, 1964, Levy/Grant Proposals of the Engineering Industry Training Board for 1965/66.
34/65. Higher National Certificates and Diplomas in Chemistry and Applied Chemistry.
35/65. Industrial Training Act, 1964.
1. Certification by Colleges of Further Education of attendance by a student at a course of associated Further Education.
2. Ministry of Labour grants for sandwich courses.
36/65. Whitworth Foundation Awards 1966.
37/65. Industrial Training Act, 1964. Central Training Council: Report to the Minister.
38/65. National Nursery Examination Board – Revised Regulations.
39/65. Training for teachers of the mentally handicapped.
40/65. Post-Registration courses for State Registered Nurses.

1966

1/66. Quality and Reliability Year.
2/66. Capital investment – Further Education building programme 1967/68.
3/66. Industrial training in Technical Colleges: Fees for Integrated Courses.
4/66 Programmed Instruction.
5/66 Higher National Certificate and Diplomas in Electrical and Electronic Engineering.
6/66 Higher National Certificates and Diplomas in Mathematics, Statistics and Computing.
7/66. National Certificates and Diplomas in Mining and Mining Surveying.
8/66. Higher National Certificates and Diplomas in Applied Physics.

9/66. "Industrial training and Further Education" – Central Training Council Memorandum No.4.
2. "An approach to Industrial Training" – Central Training Council Memorandum No. 5.
10/66. National Certificates and Diplomas in Business Studies: Fees for Oral Language Examinations.
11/66. 1. Agricultural Education.
2. The Safe Use of Agricultural Chemicals for Crop Protection.
12/66. The Industrial Training Act, 1964. Demand for Places in Further Education courses in the 1966/67 session.
13/66. Agricultural Education: minor operations on animals.
14/66. The Council of Engineering Institutions.
15/66. National Certificates and Diplomas in Printing.
16/66. Higher National Certificate in Engineering.
17/66. Courses for the training of Training Officers.
18/66. Agricultural Education.
19/66. Industrial Training Act, 1964. Engineering Industry Training Board: First Year training for Craftsmen and Technicians.
20/66. National Diplomas in Baking.
21/66. Ordinary National Certificates and Diplomas in Sciences. Arrangements for Medical Laboratory Technicians.
22/66. Approval of Advanced Courses in Art and Design.
23/66. The Certificate in Office Practice.
24/66. National retail distribution Certificates and Certificates in retail management principles.
25/66. National Coal Board scholarships, 1967.
26/66. Courses of training for Instructors.
27/66. Industrial Training Act, 1964. Training grant scheme of the Furniture and Timber Industry Training Board for 1966/67.
28/66 Report of the Commercial and Clerical Training Committee of the Central Training Council.
29/66. Industrial Training Act 1964. Engineering Industry Training Board Supplementary grant for extra first-year Training Places.
30/66. Students Union Subscriptions.
31/66. Vacancies in Advanced Courses approved to start in 1966/67.
32/66. Approval of Courses leading to awards of the Council for National Academic Awards.
33/66. Industrial Training Act, 1964. AM 9/66: Charges for Industrial Training provided by Colleges of Further Education. Application of the Prices and Incomes Standstill.
34/66. Capital Investment – Further Education Building Programme 1968/69.
35/66. Whitworth Foundation Awards 1967.
36/66. Joint Committee for the National Certificates and Diplomas in Metallurgy.
37/66. Sandwich Courses for the Diploma in Art and Design.
38/66. Industrial Training Act 1964 AM 9/66 – Application to 48 week integrated courses.

1967

1/67. The Certificate of Office Studies.
2/67. Higher National Certificates and Diplomas in Applied Physics.
3/67. Further Education Information Service, 1967.
4/67. Joint Committee for National Awards in Building.
5/67. National Certificates and Diplomas in Business Studies.
6/67. Ministry of Labour Grants for Sandwich Courses.
7/67. Agricultural Education: Approval of full-time and sandwich courses.
8/67. Higher National Certificate in Engineering.

9/67. Report of the Committee on the problem of noise.
10/67. Higher National Certificates in Medical Laboratory Subjects.
11/67. Pilot courses in functional aspects of management.
12/67. Preliminary Nursing Courses – Discontinuation of the Preliminary State Examination for Student Nurses.
13/67. Placing Overseas Nationals in Industrial Training in Britain.
14/67. Ordinary National Certificates and Diplomas in Sciences.
15/67. Ordinary National Certificates and Diplomas in Engineering.
16/67. National Craftsman's Certificate for a Motor Vehicle Service Mechanic.
17/67. Transitional Arrangements for the HNC in Building.
18/67. 1. Agricultural Education
2. Stockmanship.
19/67. Higher National Certificates and Diplomas in Medical Laboratory Subjects.
20/67. Industrial Training Act 1964: First year Off-the-job Training; disposal of surplus machine tools by the Ministry of Labour.
21/67. "The Further Education of the General Student".
22/67. The Council of Engineering Institutions: exemptions from their examinations – Higher National Certificate or Diploma.
23/67. Higher National Certificates in Applied Biology.
24/67. National Awards in Agriculture.
25/67. The Management Training and Development Committee of the Central Training Council.
26/67. Whitworth Foundation Awards 1968.
27/67. Central Training Council Committee on the Training of Training Officers.

1968

1/68. Higher National Diplomas in Civil Engineering.
2/68. Nigerian Students affected by Civil War in their Country.
3/68. Proposals for CNAA Courses.
4/68. Change-over to the Metric system – FE Syllabuses and Examinations.
5/68. Further Education Information Services, 1968.
6/68. The Second Report of the Commercial and Clerical Training Committee of the Central Training Council – "Training for Office Supervision."
7/68. Decimal Currency.
8/68. Ordinary National Certificate in Public Administration
9/68. Higher National Diplomas in Food Technology.
10/68. Higher National Certificates and Diplomas in Foundry Technology.
11/68. Industrial Training Act 1964: Joint Planning of Industrial Training and Associated Further Education. Training for Engineering Craftsmen.
12/68. "Training Standards for Occupations Common to a Number of Industries."
13/68. Safety in the use of Woodworking Machines City and Guilds of London Institute Carpentry and Joinery Courses.
14/68. Advisory and instructional films for use on courses of Further Education in agriculture and horticulture.
15/68. National Awards in Agricultural Subjects: Ordinary and Higher National Diplomas.
16/68. Ordinary National Diplomas in Hotel and Catering Operations.
17/68. Higher National Certificates and Diplomas in Medical Laboratory Subjects.
18/68. Ordinary National Diplomas in Food Technology.
19/68. "Training for Skill".
20/68. Ordinary National Diplomas in Institutional Housekeeping and Catering and Higher National Diplomas in Institutional Management.
21/68. Higher National Certificate in Building Subjects of Supplementary Study.
22/68. National Certificate and Diploma Examinations – Students' Records.

1969

1/69. Whitworth Foundation Awards 1960.
2/69. Recruitment and Training of Medical Secretaries and Receptionists for Consultants and General Practitioners.
3/69. "Training of Export Staff". A Report by the Commercial and Clerical Training Committee of the Central Council.
4/69. Award of National Retail Distribution Certificates and Certificates in Retail Management Principles embodied in Rule 121.
5/69. Second Report of the Management Training and Development Committee of the Central Training Council.
6/69. Higher National Diplomas in Computer Sciences.
7/69. Higher National Certificates and Diplomas in Electrical and Electronic Engineering.
8/69. 1. Ordinary National Diploma in Institutional Housekeeping and Catering.
2. Ordinary National Diploma in Hotel and Catering Operations.
9/69. Further Education Information Service 1969.
10/69. Ordinary National Diplomas in Food Technology.
11/69. Agriculture (Tractor Cabs) Regulations 1967.
12/69. Day and Block Release – Action by Industrial Training Boards.
13/69. Industrial Training Act 1964. Demand for places on courses of Further Education.
14/69. Higher National Certificates in Engineering and Higher National Diplomas in Mechanical, in Production and Aeronautical Engineering.
15/69. Further Education Major Building Programme.
16/69. Higher National Certificates and Diplomas in Civil Engineering – Rule 107.
17/69. Drama Courses in Colleges of Further Education.
18/69. Higher Certificate in Office Studies.
19/69. Higher National Certificates Diplomas Computer Studies.
20/69. National Awards in agricultural subjects, National Stockman's Certificate in Poultry Practice.
21/69. Construction Industry Training Board – Plan of Training for operative skills.
22/69. Occupational Guidance units.
23/69. Engineering Industry Training Board – Recommendations for the training of technician engineers.
24/69. Ordinary National Certificates and Diplomas in Sciences.
25/69. Whitworth Foundation Awards 1970.

1970

1/70. Safety Training in colleges of Further Education.
2/70. Higher National Certificates and Diplomas in Applied Physics.
3/70. Report of the Commercial and Clerical Training Committee of the Central Training Council "The training of women returning to the office after a break, and adults entering this field of work for the first time."
4/70. National Certificates and Diplomas in Textiles.
7/70. National Certificates and Diplomas in Naval Architecture and Shipbuilding.
6/70. Ordinary and Higher National Certificates in Surveying, Cartography and Planning.
7/70. Further Education Information Service 1970.
8/70. Joint Committee for Ordinary National Certificates and Diplomas in Engineering.
9/70. Safety in Colleges of Further Education: Colour coding of Flexible Cords.
10/70. Further Education Major Building Programme.
11/70. Engineer Cadet Training Scheme of Merchant Navy Training Board.
12/70. Higher Certificate after Ordinary National Certificate in Public Administration,
14/70. Basic Certificate in Computer Programming.

15/70. National awards in Agricultural subjects: Ordinary and Higher National Diplomas and the National Stockman's Certificate in Poultry Practice.
16/70. Revised structure of Courses in Distribution.
17/70. Proposed courses leading to Ordinary National Certificate in Nautical Science.
19/70. External degrees of the University of London.
20/70. Circular 7/70: Submission of Draft Articles of Government.
21/70. Part-time Courses leading to award of the Certificate in residential care of young people and children.
22/70. Fees for National Certificates and Diploma Examination.
23/70. Student Union Facilities and Finance.
24/70. Higher National Certificates in Diplomas in Electrical and Electronic Engineering.
25/70. a. Higher National Diploma in measurement and control.
b. The option of a common first year for Higher National Diploma in Mechanical Production, Aeronautical and Electrical Engineering and in measurement and control.
26/70. Proposals for CNAA Diploma Courses.

1971

1/71. Polytechnic Development Plans (P).
2/71. 1. Agricultural Education
2. Short Courses for Teachers in the safe use of chemicals in agriculture.
3/71. Exemptions grants from the Department of Trade and Industry examinations for certificates of competency to students who have completed the engineer cadet training of the Merchant Navy Training Board.
4/71. National Distribution Certificates and Certificates in distributive management Principles.
5/71. National Certificates and Diplomas in Building (Welsh copies only).
6/71. Further Education Information Service 1971.
7/71. National Awards in Business Studies and Public Administration.
8/71. Joint Advisory Committee on Agricultural Education.
9/71. University Administration and National Certificate and Diploma Examinations.
9/71. University Administration and National Certificate and Diploma Examinations (Welsh).
10/71. Higher National Certificate and Diplomas in Chemical Engineering.
11/71. Higher National Certificate in Engineering and Higher National Diploma in Production and in Aeronautical Engineering.
12/71. Further Education Major Building Programmes.
13/71. Higher National Certificate and Diplomas in Medical Laboratory Subjects.
14/71. Engineering Industry Training Board: Training awards scheme for first year integrated courses in Engineering in 1971/72.
15/71. Training Courses provided in Colleges of Further Education under the Government Vocational Training scheme.
16/71. Regional Centres of Management Education.
17/71. 1. Joint Committee for National Diplomas in Hotel and Catering administration.
2. Joint Committee for National Diploma in Institutional Housekeeping and Catering and Institutional Management.
18/71. Joint Committee for National awards in Business Studies and Public Administration Higher National Certificates in Business Studies.

1972

1/72. Joint Committee for Ordinary National Certificates and Diplomas in Engineering Ordinary Diploma in Technology (Engineering).

2/72. Higher National Diploma courses in Printing.
3/72. Arrangements and Conditions for the awards of National Certificates and Diplomas in Nautical Science.
4/72. London External Degree arrangements.
5/72. Council for National Academic Awards course proposals.
6/72. Ordinary and Higher National Certificates in Estate Management and Valuation
7/72. Further Education Information Service.
8/72. Machine Tools.
9/72. Report of a Working Party on Shop Steward Education and Training.
10/72. The United Kingdom Machine Tool Industry.
11/72. Survey of Accommodation in Establishments of Further Education.
12/72. Engineering Industry Training Board: Training Awards scheme for first year integrated courses in Engineering in 1972/73.
13/72. Higher National Diploma courses in Medical Laboratory Subjects.
14/72. The employment of Art College Leavers.
15/72. The training opportunities scheme arrangements for 1972/73.
16/72. Machine tools – the placing of orders.
17/72. Education and Training in work study.
18/72. Higher National Certificates and Diplomas in Chemistry and in Applied Chemistry.
19/72. Ordinary National Diplomas in Hotel and Catering Operations/Institutional Housekeeping and Catering. Higher National Diplomas in Hotel and Catering Administration/Institutional Management.
20/72. New craft courses in construction.
21/72. Joint committee for National Certificates in Distribution. Rule 121 Revised January 1971 – Amendment to paragraph 15.c.

1973

1/73. Fees for students attending sandwich courses leading to first degree and designated comparable courses.
2/73. Further Education Information Service 1973.
3/73. Certificates and Higher Certificates in Office Studies.
4/73. Higher National Certificate in Estate Management and Valuation. Higher National Certificate in Estate Management and Valuation (Welsh).
5/73. Fees for National Certificate and Diploma Exchange. Charges for Industrial Training.
6/73. Pilot Scheme of "Directed Private Study" courses in Distributive Subjects.
7/73. National Certificates and Diplomas in Textiles.
8/73. Report of the Commission on Industrial Relations on Industrial Relations Training.
9/73. Courses leading to an Ordinary National Certificate or Ordinary National Diploma in Nautical Science.
10/73. Joint Committee for Ordinary National Certificates and Diplomas in Engineering, Ordinary National Diploma in Technology (Engineering).
11/73. Technician Education Council. Joint Committee for National Certificates and Diplomas.
12/73. Fees for National Certificate and Diploma Examinations.
13/73. The Training Opportunities Scheme arrangements for 1973/74.
14/73. Education and Training for offshore oil and gas development.
15/73. Ordinary National Certificate in Nautical Science (fishing).

1974.

1/74. Further Education Information Service 1974.
2/74. Joint Committee for National Certificates and Diplomas in Building Higher National Certificate in Building.

3/74. Certificate in Distributive Management Principles.
4/74. Joint Committee for National Diplomas in Hotel, Catering and Institutional Management.
5/74. National Distribution Certificate.
6/74. Fees for National Certificate and Diploma Examinations.
7/74. Training Opportunities Scheme. Arrangements for 1974/75.
8/74. Joint Committees for National Certificates and Diplomas.
9/74. Joint Committee for Food Technology.
10/74. Nautical science.
11/74. National Certificates and Diplomas in Applied Biology.
12/74. Agriculture.
13/74. Adult Illiteracy, Establishment of a Resources Agency.

1975

1/75. FE Major Building Programme.
2/75. FE Information Service.
3/75. Advanced Courses: Failure to start because of low enrolments.
4/75. National Diplomas in Baking.
5/75. National Certificate and Diplomas Examination: Entry Requirements.
6/75. Joint Committee for HNC & D in Civil Engineering.
7/75. Engineering craft courses.
8/75. Joint Committee for HNC & D in Applied Physics.
9/75. ONC/OND in Sciences and Notes for Guidance to Elective Medical Physics and Physiological Measurement
10/75. HNC & D in Electrical and Electronic Engineering.
11/75. Joint Committee for National Awards in Business Studies and Public Administration.
Joint Committee for National Certificate in Distribution.
National Committee for Certificate in Office Studies.
12/75. Fees for National Certificate and Diploma Examinations.
13/75. FE Major Building Programme 1976/77.
14/75. Engineering Cadet Training Scheme of the Merchant Navy Training Board (Corrigendum to FECL 6/75).
15/75. The Manpower Services Commission Job Creation Programme.
16/75. Joint Committee for NC and D in Building HNC in Building, New Courses for Building Services Technicians.

1976

1/76. Further Education Information Service 1976.
2/76. (P) UGC Working Party Report on Building Services Engineering
3/76. Fees for NC & D Examinations.
4/76. O & HNC In Estate Management and Valuation.
5/76. Health Services on F/T and Sandwich Courses.Health Services for Students.
6/76. Approval of Courses leading to the Higher Awards of the TEC and the BEC.

1977

1/77. Further Education Programmes 1976/77 and 1977/78.
2/77. National Certificate and Diplomas in Building.
3/77. Further Education Information Service 1977.
4/77. Computer Purchases for Establishments of FE.
5/77. National Certificates and Diplomas in Printing.
6/77. HNC and D in Chemistry and Applied Chemistry.
7/77. Tops Revised Arrangements for Charging.
8/77. Fees for National Certificate Examinations 1977/78.
9/77. National Craft Certificate for Motor Vehicle Service Mechanics.
10/77. Approval of Courses leading to the Higher Awards of the BEC.

11/77. Tests of Professional Competence for operators or their transport managers in the road haulage and road passenger transport industries.
12/77. The Effect of Employment Legislation on Sandwich Course Students.

1978

1/78. ONC/D in Engineering.
2/78. Adult Literacy.
3/78. Further Education Information Service.
4/78. Examinations.
5/78. (1) Reorganisation of the Manpower Services Commission.
(2) Liaison between the MSC and DES.
6/78. ((VCL) 9/78) Financial Arrangements for University and Validation of College Courses.
7/78. Accommodation and Boarding Charges for Students coming from outside England and Wales.

1979

1/79. Further Education Information Service 1979.
2/79. Agricultural Education.
3/79. Student Exchange Schemes.
4/79. Rhodesian African Training Programme (and note)
5/79. Training Courses in Computer Programming and Systems Analysis.
6/79. The Management of Simians (and note) – (Being held).
7/79. Fees for National Certificate and Diploma Examinations.

1980

1/80. Regulation 8 of The Further Education Regulations 1975.

Section 8

LOCAL AUTHORITIES

1. This Section examines some aspects of the local government service which influence the administration of further and higher education. The focus is, largely, upon the work of the local education authority, but the development of more complex and more integrated structures of local administration in the last decade require that some consideration be given to the broader aspects of local government.

2. The present structure of local government in England and Wales is shaped by the Local Government Act 1972, which abolished all local authorities except for those in the Greater London area, which had been re-structured in 1965. In their place, from 1 April 1974, 53 counties were established, 47 of them "non-metropolitan counties". The remaining 6 were designated metropolitan counties, for the major conurbations of Greater Manchester, West Yorkshire, South Yorkshire, Merseyside, West Midlands and Tyne and Wear. All counties were sub-divided into a number of districts, and 333 district councils were established. A third tier of parish councils was maintained in non-metropolitan counties, and in some metropolitan counties, with mainly advisory responsibilities. The division of responsibilities between county and district councils differs in metropolitan and non-metropolitan (or "shire") counties. Education, libraries, personal social services and youth employment services are the responsibility of non-metropolitan county councils and of metropolitan district councils. Fire and police services, and responsibilities for consumer protection, refuse disposal and the broader aspects of planning and transport are the concerns of the county councils. District councils are responsible for housing, refuse collection, and more detailed aspects of planning, transport and highways. Environmental health is a district responsibility, but the major health and medical concerns of the National Health Service were separated from the local government system and under the National Health Service Reorganisation Act 1973 are administered by Area Health Authorities. The division of responsibilities between county and district councils is without any obvious rationale, and is subject to change. Thus counties seem likely to lose most of their planning powers in the near future.[1]

3. The London Government Act 1963 established the Greater London Council, with powers similar to those of metropolitan county councils, and 32 London boroughs. The 20 Outer London borough councils have powers which resemble those of the metropolitan district councils, but the education services for the 12 Inner London boroughs are undertaken by the Inner London Education Authority, a special and separately elected committee of the Greater London Council with extensive delegated powers. The singular position of the Inner London Education Authority (ILEA) has led to a number of current proposals for its amendment or abolition. The Isles of Scilly also have special local government arrangements, with a council which undertakes both county and district functions.

1 The Rt. Hon. Tom King MP, Minister of State for Local Government, stated the Government's intention of transferring these powers to district councils, (House of Commons, 18 July 1979). It has been argued that a rationale – of strategic county powers and local district functions – does exist, but has not worked well.

4. Thus responsibilities for the education service are discharged by, in total, some 105 local education authorities, comprising 47 counties, 36 metropolitan districts, 20 Outer London boroughs, ILEA and the Isles of Scilly. Technically the full councils are, under the Education Act, 1944 (s.6)[2], the local education authorities, comprising all the elected council members. However, the Education Act, 1944 required such councils to appoint education committees, whose composition had to be approved by the Secretary of State[3] and had to "include persons of experience in education and persons acquainted with the educational conditions prevailing in the area for which the committee acts".[4] Although this does not specifically demand co-option of members to the education committee, DES Circular 8/73 made it clear that the Secretary of State would only approve the composition of committees which included at least two-thirds elected members but between one quarter and one third co-opted members. In practice only one authority, whose committee structure was established before 1973, has no co-opted members.[5]

5. The Local Government Act 1972 confirmed the special status of education committees endowed by the 1944 Act, which laid down that councils had to consider reports from their education committee before exercising their education powers.[6] Only the police and social services similarly have to be governed by specified committees. DES Circular 8/73 went further and pointed out that, under the Local Government Act, a council could "not arrange for the discharge of any of its functions in respect to education by any committee or sub-committee other than its education committee or a sub-committee of its education committee"[7]. Hence considerable disquiet has been expressed when some authorities have, on occasions, permitted committees other than their education committee to undertake certain educational responsibilities. These have occurred most commonly when corporate planning structures have been adopted. These are described in paragraphs 9 to 11, below.

6. Most authorities delegate some of their educational powers and duties to their education committee, as they were encouraged to do by the DES,[8] thus further increasing the significance of what is normally the largest council committee. However, a minority of education committees have no delegated powers, and some others have very few such powers. The education committee chairman is usually a senior member of the ruling political group, and must be an elected member of the council.[9]

7. A distinctive feature of education committees is that most contain co-opted employees of the council in the form of teacher representatives. The Local

---

2 Confirmed in s192 of the Local Government Act 1972.
3 Education Act, 1944. First Schedule, Part II.
4 *Ibid*, Paragraph 5.
5 The London Borough of Croydon.
6 Education Act, 1944. 1st Schedule, Part II, Para 7.
7 DES Circular 8/73, Paragraph 9. The statutory basis for this is s101 (9) and (10) of the Local Government Act 1972.
8 *Ibid*, Paragraph 8.
9 *Ibid*, Paragraph 11.

Government Act 1972 permitted teachers and others employed in an authority's schools, colleges and higher educational institutions to be appointed – though not elected – members of education committees.[10] DES Circular 8/73 encouraged the co-option of teachers from primary, secondary and further education, and recommended the co-option of teachers in colleges of education.[11] Representatives of industry, commerce, religious denominations and even parents are also co-opted by the elected members of the education committee, who must comprise at least two-thirds of the committee.

8. The tasks of the education committee are in turn deputed to a number of sub-committees. There is no central control over the number, type or composition of the sub-committees that an education committee may establish. A common pattern is for some sub-committees to undertake sectoral responsibilities, including schools, further education and the youth service, while other sub-committees discharge resource responsibilities for buildings, finance, etc. Sub-committees tend to be the arenas for the detailed discussion of policies and problems, whose resolution at sub-committee level tends then to go to the full education committee for formal ratification. In turn, education committee decisions go to the full council which, acting in its capacity as local education authority, ratifies the education committee's decisions. Clearly the extent to which such ratification is a mere formality depends largely upon the extent of powers delegated to the education committee. In the shire counties fairly extensive delegated powers often mean that full council meetings are quite infrequent, in some cases not more than quarterly. In the urban authorities, delegation tends to be less extensive, with the consequent need for more frequent council meetings. One result of this can be a heavy programme of sub-committees, education committee and council meetings for many councillors. These commitments can be compounded by service as school and college governors, working party membership, and, increasingly in recent years as local government has become politicised on national party political lines, attendance at party meetings.[12] Indeed, a major part of some education authorities' decision-making tends to take place in private meetings of the ruling political party group rather than in formal committee or council meetings, as is the case in other authorities. This trend has probably increased since the Public Bodies (Admission to Meetings) Act 1960 compelled authorities to open council and education committee meetings to the public, except where this would be prejudicial to the public interest. In recognition of the demands made upon elected councillors, ss173 to 178 of the Local Government Act 1972 established the entitlement of councillors (except parish councillors) to attendance allowances (currently £13.28 per day) in respect of any loss of earnings, and travelling and subsistence allowances. Such allowances are available for attendance not only at council, committee and sub-committee meetings, but at all other relevant meetings and conferences, including those

10 Local Government Act 1972, ss81 and 104. In practice non-teaching staff do not seem as yet to have benefited from this.

11 DES Circular 8/73, Paragraph 13. Circulars are not usually mandatory, but their advice is not lightly ignored by local authorities.

12 Only three local authorities with educational responsibilities – Cornwall, Gwynnedd and Powys – are not organized along party political lines.

of governing bodies and their various committees, except meetings which are convened by "a body the objects of which are wholly or partly political".[13] The Local Government, Planning and Land Bill of 1979 proposed that some councillors with special responsibilities (such as an Education Committee chairman) should receive appropriate allowances, in addition to those described above.

9. **Corporate management**

In the last decade a large number of local authorities have developed systems of management rather different from the traditional pattern of separate committees dealing with the major areas of local administrative responsibility. These have become known as "corporate planning" or "corporate management". Although it had evolved in some authorities before local government reorganization in 1974, its adoption was hastened by the resultant changes, and particularly by its advocacy in the 1972 Bains Report,[14] the recommendations of a study group set up to examine appropriate management structures for the new local authorities. The traditional committee system had been extensively criticised for its inefficiency, with poorly co-ordinated services, wasted resources – financial, human and material – and its ineffective and even unlawful personnel management procedures, with no consideration of relative priorities. Bains recommended that authorities should establish a Policy and Resources Committee which would function as a management board consisting of senior elected members, including the major committee chairman. The committee's task would be to establish priorities, to set objectives for the authority, co-ordinate policies, manage the authority's resources and review its performance. In such a system, the service committees, including the Education Committee, are required to serve the objectives fixed by the Policy and Resources Committee. Such objectives would take account of concerns broader than just the needs of the education service, or any other sectoral interest. Similarly, the resources available to the service committees, including education, would be determined by the priorities set by the Policy and Resources Committee, and not just the perceived needs of the education service.

10. The integration of services and other activities has been taken further by some authorities with the adoption of complex organizational or financial management planning systems. These include Management by Objectives (MbO) and Planning Programming Budgeting Systems (PPBS – also known as Output Budgeting or Programme Budgeting). The distinctions between these are technical and there are many forms of each.[15] They share in common the definition of specified objectives and their refinement into sub-

---

13 S.175, Local Government Act 1972.

14 *The New Local Authorities: Management and Structure.* HMSO, 1972.

15 For a fuller discussion of their features, differences and applicability to local authorities see J.L. Davies, "A Discussion of the Use of PPBS and MBO in Educational Planning and Administration," in ed. L. Dobson, *Management in Education: Some Techniques and Systems.* Ward Lock Educational, 1975.

objectives, which in turn are related to specified activities. The evaluation of the extent to which objectives have been achieved leads to their reconsideration and to the examination of possible alternative strategies. The thorough implementation of such systems could well result in the establishment of sub-objectives for individual components of the local authority, including its colleges, and in the subsequent assessment of the extent to which they had been achieved.

11. Most local authorities have probably adopted some features of corporate management, commonly in co-existence with the traditional committee structure. A few have rejected the innovations, and returned to the traditional pattern, after a change in political control. The extent to which corporative management impinges – if at all – upon the authority of the Education Committee varies from authority to authority, but Winter[16] found substantial concern amongst Chief Education Officers that the effectiveness of the Committee's work had been reduced by some forms of corporate planning. Significant areas of decision-making which rest with the Policy and Resources Committee might include the establishment of new policy, the priority to be given to the development of educational services, financial control over capital programmes and the appointment of the Chief Education Officer (CEO). Furthermore, in some authorities Personnel Committees, or Manpower Sub-Committees of the Policy and Resources Committee, undertake some staffing functions traditionally undertaken by the Education Committee, including the appointment of non-teaching staff and, in a few authorities, consideration of the appointment and conditions of service of teachers and lecturers. In other authorities Leisure and Recreation Committees have acquired responsibilities more usually those of the Education Committee, most contentiously in the case of community education and the youth services. In these respects a number of authorities would seem to be acting in breach of the Education Act, 1944[17], by exercising educational duties and powers without first considering a report from the Education Committee. In some cases this has been pointed out by the DES. Paragraphs 28 to 34 explore some of the implications of corporate management structures for local authority departments, and paragraphs 58 and 59 examine some implications for establishments of further and higher education.

12. In spite of some criticism of corporate management, it seems likely that forms of it will increasingly characterise local government in England and Wales, particularly in large authorities, and it is desired by many elected members. As authorities find it more difficult to obtain desired resources, and as pressures increase for the more integrated use of local authority services and facilities, there are heightened demands for management systems which emphasise the implications for all local authority departments of decisions made in any one sector. Similarly, approaches are sought which improve communication and understanding between local authority

---

16 G. Winter, *The Position of the Education Service following Local Government Reorganisation*, Society of Education Officers, 1977.
17 Education Act, 1944; First Schedule, Part II; Para. 7.

departments. However, as the education service is by far the largest consumer of local authority resources, such approaches are likely to seek means for controlling and examining the effective deployment of those resources – and this seems likely to reduce the autonomy of the Education Committee. Furthermore, corporate management approaches are attractive for political reasons to some councillors, especially where the "cabinet" of the ruling political party can form itself into the Policy and Resources Committee.

13. **Local authorities' educational responsibilities**

Whatever the system of management, local authorities are required by statute to undertake a number of specified duties, and have the discretion to discharge a further large number of powers, as specified by Parliament. Should any local authority attempt to undertake any activity or responsibility not so specified by legislation, it would be acting *ultra vires* (beyond its powers) and may be restrained by the courts. An authority's educational responsibilities arise from the Education Act, 1944 and its subsequent amendments and additions. Apart from the duty to establish an education committee, authorities are required to appoint a suitable person to be Chief Education Officer – one of only three such specified appointments.[18]

14. Most of the educational duties demanded of a local authority refer to the provision and maintenance of schools. Ss 41 and 42 of the Education Act, 1944 required merely that "it shall be the duty of every local education authority to secure the provision for their area of adequate facilities for further education", and that authorities should prepare schemes of further education and present them for the approval of the Minister of Education. In practice such schemes were not updated, and have not been required since (except when the London Government Act 1963 required their re-statement by the newly established London boroughs and ILEA), although this does not mean that a Secretary of State who so chooses might not again require their presentation. Nor has any definition of just what would be considered to be "adequate facilities" been anywhere defined. Indeed further education itself was defined only in the most general terms as full-time and part-time education for persons over compulsory school age; and leisure-time occupation, in organized cultural training and recreational activities for persons over compulsory school age.[19] The 1944 Act specified in far more detail the bases of a system of "county colleges" for persons over compulsory school age, but these clauses were never implemented, and were overtaken by the development of the further education system in subsequent years.

15. The 1944 Act imposed very few other duties upon local authorities with respect to further education. S.43 required every authority to provide adequate facilities for recreation and social and physical training, as part of primary, secondary and further education provision. S.48 obliged authorities to encourage and assist pupils to take advantage of any medical provision,

---

18 The other two are Finance Officer and Director of Social Services: (ss 112 & 151, Local Government Act 1972).
19 Education Act, 1944, s 41.

and to provide facilities for the medical and dental inspection of students by what is now the Department of Health and Social Security.[20] S.55 made it the duty of every authority to provide either free transport where it considers it necessary (or as the Secretary of State might direct), or reasonable travelling expenses of students attending establishments of further education as well as schools. The Education (No.2) Bill of 1979 proposed the repeal of s55, and to allow authorities to make whatever transport arrangements they consider appropriate, including the imposition of charges and the payment, in whole or in part, of reasonable travelling expenses.

16. Legislation following the 1944 Act imposed further obligations on authorities. The Education Act 1962 required them to make awards to students accepted for certain courses of higher education who have the requisite educational qualifications.[21] Although initially this applied almost entirely to the university sector, the subsequent development of higher education in the maintained sector has greatly extended its applicability. Furthermore, the courses for which grants are mandatory were extended by the Education Act 1975 to include courses leading to the Diploma in Higher Education, the Higher National Diploma and courses of initial teacher training.

17. The Education (No.2) Act 1968 is the only major legislation of considerable and specific relevance to further education. It established the present system of college government, requiring authorities to prepare instruments of government for each college, constituting the institution's governing body (see Section **2.1**). Articles of government which determined the functions of LEA, governing body, principal and academic board (if any: see Section **2.1.**15) were to be prepared and presented for the Secretary of State's approval. Such approval was also required for the instruments of government of colleges of education. Apart from the above, other significant duties demanded of local authorities by the law include those of the Health and Safety At Work etc. Act, 1974, and the other extensive labour legislation of the last decade. They are discussed in detail in Sections **5.3**, **5.5**, **11.6** and **11.10**.

18. Beyond this unco-ordinated and gradually acquired portfolio of duties, the local authorities are expected to develop and maintain their further education service with a considerable degree of discretion. Under the 1944 Act the Secretary of State can intervene in the prescribed circumstances, should the local authority, or college governors, exercise its powers "unreasonably" (s68), as determined by the Secretary of State or through the Courts. S.99 allows the Secretary of State to intervene when an authority has failed to discharge a duty. The procedure then is for the Secretary of State to declare the authority in default, as the sole judge of what constitutes a justifiable intervention, and to give directions for the enforcement of the duty. In practice these powers have been very rarely used since 1944, and on the

---

20 DES Circular 1/74 explained the new relationship between LEAs and Area Health Authorities arising out of the National Health Service Reorganisation Act 1973.

21 Currently, under The Further Education Regulations 1975, two passes at GCE Advanced level.

occasions they have been called upon have involved schools rather than further education establishments.

19. Reference should be made to the requirements of the Town and Country Planning Act 1971. County councils were required to produce a structure plan, outlining the social and economic development planned for the area. Such plans naturally incorporated suggested educational developments, including proposals for further education. Draft plans were to be made available to the public, and were expected to stimulate a participatory planning debate before finalisation. Economic difficulties have since hindered their implementation, while the regional economic planning network which had been expected to co-ordinate neighbouring counties' proposals is now in the process of being dismantled, and many of the requirements on local authorities are about to be withdrawn. [22]

20. In contrast to the rather limited range of duties demanded of local authorities, they have considerable discretionary powers in further education. The differential exercise of these powers by authorities since 1944 has resulted in the remarkable diversity of provision from authority to authority, in scale of provision, type of establishments and range of available courses therein. Without any specified levels of acceptable provision, authorities have interpreted their duties under s41 of the 1944 Act very differently. Some have built upon substantial pre-1944 provision to provide a wide range of institutions of further, higher and adult education which serve not just the authority's own population, but a regional or even national demand. Other authorities seem to have made only the most minimal provision, or to have depended upon facilities provided either by local voluntary establishments or neighbouring authorities. As just one example of the diversity immediately before local government reorganization. Blackpool provided only one college of further education while Bolton, with an almost identical population, provided a college of education and no less than six FE colleges.

21. Other powers especially relevant to further education which have been, and are still very differently exercised between authorities are those obtained through the Education Act 1962, allowing authorities to bestow discretionary awards on persons over compulsory school age attending full- or part-time courses of further education. The enormous diversity both in the range and type of courses qualifying for such awards, and in the levels of financial support provided by different authorities, has often been commented upon critically (see below, para. 53).

22. Local authorities also have powers to inspect any educational establishment maintained by them,[23] to accept gifts for educational purposes,[24] to purchase land compulsorily where required for educational purposes,[25] and to make provision for educational research and conferences where they might lead to

22 cf *Central Government Controls over Local Authorities*. Cmnd. 7634, HMSO, 1979.
23 Education Act, 1944, s.77.
24 *Ibid*, s.85.
25 *Ibid*, s.90.

the improvement of the area's educational facilities.[26] Authorities also might make grants to universities for the purpose of improving facilities for further education in their area.[27]

23. Although district and metropolitan county councils have no educational responsibilities they are empowered by s137 of the Local Government Act 1972, to spend up to the product of a 2p rate on "expenditure which in their opinion is in the interests of their area or any part of it or all or some of the inhabitants". This can include contributions to the funds of any non-profit-making public body. A recent Appeal Court judgment[28] has confirmed that this can include educational expenditure, even where this might be counter to the policies of the local education authority. It seems possible, therefore, that further education establishments might be influenced by the educational policies of local authorities other than LEAs, who already have some influence through joint provision and dual-use schemes. These have been encouraged in recent years, to maximise utilization of facilities and provide as wide a community service as possible.[29]

24. **The Chief Education Officer**

In order that the local authority might exercise its statutory powers and duties, it is authorised to "appoint such officers as they think necessary for the proper discharge by the authority of such of their or another authority's functions as fall to be discharged by them".[30] it has already been noted that one such officer which every local education authority must appoint is the Chief Education Officer (CEO), sometimes entitled (although less frequently than previously) the Director of Education. The requirement of the Education Act, 1944 that the Secretary of State examine an authority's short-list when appointing a CEO and eliminate any applicants considered not fit persons to be the chief education officer has been repealed.[31] Hence authorities can now appoint whomsoever they choose as CEO. However, when in 1978 one authority advertised the post in such a way as to suggest that it might select someone without the usual background in teaching and educational administration, protests by the Society of Education Officers and others led to assurances that such an appointment was not intended. Thus, although no formal professional training or qualifications are required, virtually all CEOs have similar backgrounds, with an honours degree from a British university, a period of teaching experience, followed by experience in educational administration, usually in a local authority's education department, although a few have come straight from senior posts in educational institutions, such as principal of a college of further education.

---

26 *Ibid*, ss. 82 & 83.
27 *Ibid*, s.84.
28 Manchester City Council v the Greater Manchester Council, 1979. The latter was given permission to maintain a trust fund to send pupils to independent schools, although the former was given leave to appeal to the House of Lords, and, at the time of writing the issue is *sub judice*. *Guardian*, 7 July 1979.
29 DES Circular 2/70, and *Towards a Wider Use*, report of an inter-local authority association working party, 1976. Statutory powers for such projects obtain from the Local Government Acts of 1972 (ss101, 103 and 145) and 1976 (s19).
30 Local Government Act 1972, s112.
31 Local Government Act 1972, s272.

25. In spite of the requirement that a local authority appoint a CEO, there are no regulations or guidelines as to what he (or she)[32] should do once appointed. In consequence the role differs from authority to authority. In part this depends upon the relationship between the CEO and the Education Committee, and in particular with its chairman. This relationship is complicated still further where authorities have employed systems of corporate management – and in at least two cases the resultant tensions have led to the resignation of the CEO. The traditional distinction between elected members as policy-makers and officials as executives of that policy certainly does not hold today in many authorities. Distinctions between policy formulation and implementation are blurred, and most CEOs – as research in the last decade has amply demonstrated[33] – take an active part in the determination of the authority's educational policies. However, the CEOs are not the administrators and providers of professional services in quite the same ways that the chief officials of the other local authority departments operate, as responsibilities for educational institutions are diffused through governing and managing bodies. Their control of institutions of further and higher education is more indirect since the changes instituted by the Education (No.2) Act 1968, if no less real. On the other hand legislation such as the Health and Safety at Work etc. Act 1974 and the Employment Protection Acts have laid considerable duties upon the employer, and, where this is specified as the CEO, have emphasised his controlling role (cf Section **11.10.**33). The result is a complex and dynamic system of local authority management which differs in every authority, and within authorities over time, which owes a great deal to the personality, the vision and the interpersonal and political skills of the CEO and the other chief officers, as well as to the party political structure and the attitudes and priorities of the leading elected members.

26. **The Education Department**

The one management role clearly specified for the CEO is that of managing the Education Department. In common with the other local government departments, this has grown substantially in recent years. However, it differs from the other departments in that most of its professional administrators tend to specialise only in educational work, and move between the education departments of different authorities, rather than between education and other local government departments. The administrative structure varies from authority to authority, but normally comprises a Deputy Chief Education Officer, with below him Senior Assistant Education Officers, one of whom is commonly responsible for FE, then Assistant Education Officers, with Professional Assistants at the junior professional level. Normally – and this is a further area of difference between education and other departments – some teaching experience is a necessary pre-requisite for appointment, and officers are usually graduates of British universities. Nowadays the department is augmented by professional administrators without previous

---

32 Only two of the 104 CEOs in June 1979 were female.

33 See, for example Maurice Kogan & William van der Eycken's conversations with three CEOs in *County Hall*, Penguin, 1973. Also the work of R. Saran, *Policy Making in Secondary Education*, 1974 and M. David, *Reform, Reaction and Resources*, 1977.

teaching experience, and by specialist officers with professional qualifications such as accountants, statisticians and architects. Furthermore, as part of the rationalization of local government services following reorganization, the education department increasingly is likely to make use of the services of other specialist local government departments. In the larger authorities an area administrative structure has been established, for education and other local government services. Each area has its separate administrative department, headed by an Area Education Officer, but the autonomy of such areas is normally considerably less than that of the Divisional Executive and Excepted Districts which were abolished in 1974, because of a statutory bar against divisional committees holding executive powers [34]

27. In addition to the administrative officials of the Education Department, local education authorities also employ a number of Advisers, Inspectors, or Organizers. Their tasks are to give advice to both schools and administrators, to inspect schools and colleges, to monitor standards, to advise upon appointments and to stimulate and review innovations. There are very considerable differences between the sizes and composition of advisory teams between authorities. It is probable that few authorities meet the recommendations of the Taylor Report [35] that they should appoint one adviser for every 20,000 people in the authority. Inspectors and Advisers are, like most administrators, drawn from the teaching profession, although the point of transfer is usually somewhat later in their career. Unlike administrators, whose salaries like those of other local government officers are related to size of authority, the salary scale for advisers and inspectors, the Soulbury Scale, is linked to the Burnham Committee Scale for Head Teachers. Advisory Services, except in the smallest authorities, are organized under a Chief or Principal Adviser. Senior Advisers can hold sectoral responsibilities, including further and/or community education, area responsibilities, where the authority is organized in areas, or subject responsibilities. Advisers normally are concerned either with a sector or a curricular area. Bolam *et al.*[36] found that only 5% of their sample of advisers held responsibilities for further and adult education, but the sphere of responsibility of many, if not most of the curriculum subject area advisers (70% of Bolam's sample), and of the advisers with district responsibilities would include further – and possibly also adult and community – education.[37] Bolam also found that about a quarter of the sample had previous teaching experience in colleges of education, and half had previous experience in colleges of further education. In 1979 only about 20 LEAs seem to have appointed advisers with specified responsibilities for further education.

28. **The other local authority departments**

It has already been noted that the local education service increasingly utilizes

---

34 Local Government Act 1972, s192 (2).

35 *A New Partnership for our Schools*, Para 6.42, HMSO, 1977.

36 R. Bolam, G. Smith and H. Canter, *Local Education Authority Advisers and Educational Innovation*, University of Bristol, 1976.

37 See para. 55, below.

the services of other local government departments. The integration of educational and other services is normally greatest where a system of corporate management is employed. The corporate structure described above in paragraphs 9 to 11 is served by a team of chief officers acting as a Management Team in accordance with the recommendations of the Mallaby[38] and Maud Management[39] Reports. The Team, headed by the Chief Executive, is expected to ensure the integrated pursuit of the authority's objectives by each of its departments, whose chief officers should operate as a unified group of managers. The relative importance of the Education Department in both financial and employment terms argues for the inclusion of the Chief Education Officer in the Management Team, as is usually the case. In a few authorities, however, an "inner cabinet" of some chief officers has excluded the CEO, and has led to some conflict between educational and other local authority objectives. Winter[40] found substantial criticism that the existence of a Management Team had inhibited the effective development of the education service. Particular criticisms were that Education Committee agenda had been manipulated, that the Management Team had prevented some Education Committee reports reaching the key Policy and Resources Committee, and that a great deal of time was wasted in Team meetings. However, in other cases the Management Team and Education Department's closer liaison were thought to have contributed to the greater effectiveness of local authority services.

29. One effect of the adoption of corporate planning systems by local authorities has been that tasks traditionally undertaken by the Education Department are now undertaken by or in consultation with other departments. Certain broadly educational responsibilities are thus partly or wholly under the control of committees other than the Education Committee, and undertaken by officials other than the CEO and his staff. The key commitee in a corporate management system is the Policy and Resources Committee (or its equivalent). Commonly it has not only taken over the traditional tasks of the Finance Committee, but has impinged on areas previously those of the Education Committee by exercising control over education's capital programmes, including the acquisition of sites, by deciding the scale, priority and nature of educational building programmes, by fixing fees and charges, and by negotiating with employees' associations and unions over conditions of service, as well as influencing or controlling the appointment of the Chief Education Officer. In consequence, tasks formerly undertaken by the Education Department have fallen to the Treasurer's (or Finance) Department, or to the Legal and Administrative Department, including the clerking of Education Committee and sub-committee meetings, the production of reports and the preparation of budgets. This has led to criticism of the resultant duplication of effort, lack of expertise, and consequent time-wasting.

---

38 *Report of the Committee on the Staffing of Local Government*, Ministry of Housing and Local Government, HMSO, 1967.

39 *Report of the Committee on the Management of Local Government*, Ministry of Housing and Local Government, HMSO, 1967.

40 *The Position of the Education Service following Local Government Reorganisation*, Society of Education Officers, 1977.

30. The Establishment Committee and its Personnel Department have also taken over a number of activities and responsibilities from the Education Committee/Department in some authorities. These include the consideration of institutional establishments, the monitoring of all appointments, the review of non-teaching staff establishments, the administrative work involved in staff appointments, and the appointment, secondment and approval for conference attendance of Education Department staff. While in almost all authorities, attempts to transfer the responsibility for the appointment of teaching staff from the Education to the Personnel Department have been strenuously resisted so that the Education Committee retains responsibility for appointing teaching staff, the Personnel Department has been criticised for delays in decisions concerning the appointment of temporary staff, the approval of secondments and leave of absence and the payment of expenses to teaching and other staff. Delays are compounded in some authorities where appointments have to be approved not only by Education and Establishment Committees but also by the Management Team. It seems possible that recent financial restrictions are leading to an increase in the development of such complex controls on staffing procedures with consequential delays in appointments procedures. Against that, many local education authorities have benefited from Personnel Department expertise in the sphere of labour relations.

31. In many authorities the development of Recreation and Leisure (or Amenities) Departments has led to encroachments upon Education Department territories. This has led to the rationalization of recreational facilities in educational and other establishments, and to standardised maintenance procedures for playing fields and other open spaces. Problems have arisen where the Recreation Committee has taken on responsibility for the community uses of educational premises, for the provision and administration of community centres, and the allocation of grants to village halls and other centres providing adult education. However, the Recreation Department is probably better placed than the Education Department to negotiate with district councils over joint use projects, in that the Education Department otherwise has no district council responsibilities.

32. A number of committees and departments liaise with the Education Department in the spheres of land and buildings. In some authorities the Land and Buildings Committee undertakes the sale and acquisition of sites, the rental of premises, including school houses, and the control of non-operational property. The Surveyor's/Engineer's/Buildings/Architect's Department might control the maintenance of playing fields and buildings, the acquisition of sites, the submission of planning applications, the application for and consideration of tenders, and the supply and maintenance of educational transport. While this has made possible the integration of acquisition and maintenance policies for educational with other local government services, it has led to complaints about delays and lack of consultation concerning educational needs and priorities.

33. The establishment of a local authority Purchasing Department usually has implications for education. In some authorities this department has

organized a central purchasing system, and has placed contracts for supplies, including those for schools and colleges. Some implications of this are considered in paragraph 50. Other responsibilities might include the purchasing, storage and disposal of equipment, goods and vehicles.

34. Other committees and departments which in some authorities undertake responsibilities exercised in other authorities by the Education Committee and Department include the Road Safety Committee, the Library Committee, and the General Purposes Committee (which in some authorities elects members to governing bodies of schools and colleges and to other educational bodies). The Social Services Department might undertake responsibilities for educational welfare officers and for some aspects of the Educational Psychology service.[41] An authority's Central Research Unit might produce formulae for staffing levels in and for the allocation of resources to educational establishments. The Computer Unit in some authorities handles salaries and the processing of invoices to and from schools and colleges.

35. **Local government staff: numbers, training and organization**
The local government service employs about 2 million workers (full-time and full-time equivalent). The education service accounts for nearly half of this total, and for over half of the total local government salary bill, as the educational labour force includes a higher proportion of professional employees than the other major departments. Appendix 1 indicates some features of the local government and LEA employment structure.

36. The training of some groups of employees, including teachers, educational psychologists, police and firemen, is organized nationally, with arrangements for pooling the costs of such training. Most other local government employees, including Education Department officials, have since 1967 come under the auspices of the Local Government Training Board for their training needs. The Board is financed by deductions from the needs element of the rate support grant, and it aims to increase local government efficiency by providing appropriate in-service training to all levels of staff. Thus, in recognising the particular needs of education officers, the Board has published detailed recommendations for a suitable four-stage training programme.[42] The Board, however, stresses that the prime responsibility for training its employees rests with the local authority, and some authorities have established comprehensive internal training programmes for both officers and manual workers. Colleges of further education and polytechnics are substantial providers of training programmes at all levels, including ONC and HNC courses in public administration, Certificate in Municipal Administration programmes, and courses leading to the Diploma in Management Studies, as well as those for over a hundred different professional examinations. Non-teaching staff in schools and colleges are

---

41 Only three authorities (Cheshire, Coventry and Somerset) have transferred educational welfare offices to the Social Services Department.

42 *Management Development in Education Departments,* Supplement to Training Recommendation 7, Local Government Training Board, 1977.

eligible as local government employees for appropriate training programmes. The Further Education Staff College, the Institute of Local Government Studies, some regional management centres and NALGO are amongst the providers of such programmes and courses (see Section **2.2.**54).

37. The staff associations of local government employees have been prominent in the organization of training programmes for their members. Education officers are represented by the Society of Education Officers, founded in 1970. It has over 1100 members, drawn from all local authorities, and has an active regional structure. It maintains a small salaried secretariat, and has become increasingly active in promoting the interests of its members and the local education service, by seeking representation on outside bodies, promoting research and publications, meeting regularly with appropriate civil servants and politicians and with other groups with related concerns, drawn from local authorities and national bodies. Regional branches have considered the Local Government Training Board proposals for training education officers, and other training possibilities. The Society has also intervened when local authority policies have appeared to threaten its members' interests, by investigating problems and, on occasions, warning members not to apply for specified posts. Advisers, inspectors and organizers have their own association, the National Association for Inspectors and Educational Advisers, with about 1300 members and concerns similar to those of the Society of Education Officers. It publishes a journal and undertakes a variety of training and other developmental activities.

38. Local government employees are represented by a large number of other professional and staff associations, indicative of the fact that over 500 different occupations are found in local government. Professional groups tend to be represented by specialist organizations such as the Association of Educational Psychologists and the Institute of Careers Officers. A recent development has been the establishment of "white-collar" trade union organizations which have grown out of and are related to some of these professional associations. Thus chief executives are represented professionally by the Society of Local Authority Chief Executives (with appropriate acronym) and in conditions of service negotiations by the twin Association of Local Authority Chief Executives. More recently the Association of Education Officers (AEO) has grown from the Society of Education Officers as a trade union with membership restricted to SEO members, and is represented on the negotiating body for chief officers' conditions of service.

39. In contrast to these diverse and frequently highly specialist staff and professional associations, local government is unusual in that the great majority of employees are represented by one major trade union, whose membership extends broadly across occupational and hierarchical categories of employment. The union is NALGO, the National and Local Government Officers Association. It represents administrative, professional, technical and clerical staff in all sections of local government, including Education Departments and schools and colleges. Its membership is now over 700,000,

the fourth largest trade union in Britain. NALGO's major activity remains the consideration and negotiation of its members' salaries and conditions of service. It is the major union represented on the National Joint Council for Administrative, Professional, Technical and Clerical Services, and its Provincial Councils (on which each local authority is represented), whereby local government salaries and conditions of service (the "Purple Book") are negotiated. NALGO has a substantial national secretariat, employing over 300, a district structure allied to the 13 APT & C Provincial Council Areas, and a branch organization based on individual local authorities. It maintains an active educational and training programme, including correspondence courses and residential courses. Other significant activities include the provision of legal services, insurance and holiday facilities, and welfare services including convalescent homes for its members. A number of other trade unions operate within local government. Many local government workers are represented by their craft unions. Manual workers tend to be members of the National Union of Public Employees, the Transport and General Workers Union and the General and Municipal Workers' Union. Establishments of further and higher education could well, therefore, include amongst their staff, members of a score or more different associations and unions. Their activities are discussed in detail in Section **9.**

40. **The college and the local authority**

It will be appreciated from the previous paragraphs that the considerable diversity of the local government system means that relationships between establishments of further and higher education and their local authority are both complex and vary greatly between – and even within – authorities. In general terms the LEA is responsible for the general educational character of the college and for its place in the local education system. The authority is legally responsible both as LEA and as employer, and cannot (nor would it normally wish to) delegate these responsibilities to the establishment's governing body. The major variations in both formal and actual structures of control and communication preclude any confident generalizations about resultant relationships. In consequence, all that can be offered here is an outline of the most usual manifestations of local authority control, and of the most common points of contact between college and authority. A major proviso is that these will vary according to an indeterminate number of variables, including the nature of the authority's political structure, its management system, and the proportion of advanced work in the college. However, consideration of some significant differences of practice is intended to illustrate the extent of local authority discretion.

41. Local authority control has become more indirect, if in some cases no less effective, as a result of the changes in college government instituted by the Education (No.2) Act 1968, with the delegation of powers to governing bodies, to principals and directors, and to the college academic board. The Department of Education and Science's insistence that its model articles of government be adopted by polytechnics, colleges of education and the major institutions of further education has resulted in substantial autonomy in some areas for these institutions. Smaller establishments, undertaking a lower proportion of advanced work, were given less freedom by many

authorities – a cause of considerable complaint within those colleges. Indeed, these complaints are echoed in some major establishments, where the actual degree of local authority control is stated to be considerably greater than is laid down formally, and than had been intended in the model articles of government.

42. Conversely, complaints are heard from local authorities that, helped by the pooling of all expenditure on advanced work, the major establishments are no longer effectively under local authority control at all. Such concern contributed to the establishment of the Oakes Committee, but its Report[43] has not as yet led to any changes in the existing system. However, the articles of government, specifying the powers, duties and modes of conduct within a college, cannot be altered without the permission of the Secretary of State. It would seem that very powerful arguments for change would have to be presented before such approval might be obtained, and it would seem that, when granting any such approval, the DES commonly insists on a reduction of LEA powers.

43. The major direct influence of the local authority upon any of its colleges is financial. The articles of government normally specify that a college's financial estimates should be submitted by the governing body to the Education Committee which not only either approves or amends those estimates, but also authorises any capital expenditure. Capital programmes have significant long-term revenue consequences not only for loan charges and repayments, but also for staffing and other expenses arising from the new development. Central governmental constraints upon capital expenditure are described in Section **3**.9-17. It is the local authority's decision whether to apply to the DES for the inclusion of a further education capital project in the latter's further education standing building programme. It is further an authority decision whether or to what extent the DES allocation for minor works should be taken up, and how far, if at all, further education capital developments should be financed out of the "locally determined" sector of approved loan sanctions, where such developments are in competition with the schemes of other local authority departments. Authorities decide whether or not minor capital works should be financed out of revenue, or from the sale of capital assets. They are also expected to liaise with neighbouring authorities when planning capital expenditure on the provision of further education. In making any of these decisions the authority can influence fundamentally the size and nature of its further education establishments.

44. Local authority control of revenue expenditure varies considerably between institutions. To some degree such variations arise from differences in virement practices,[44] for the greater the permitted virement, the greater the institution's financial autonomy. Major differences also arise from local authority practices and policies with regard to staffing establishments for

---

43 *Report of the Working Group on the Management of Higher Education in the Maintained Sector*, Cmnd. 7130, HMSO, 1978 (see Sections **1.2.**18 and **2.1.**44, *passim)*.
44 Virement is explained in Section **3** (note 49 and Appendix 2).

both teaching and non-teaching staff,[45] purchasing and supplies, and the extent to which institutions might retain income from student fees, letting and other college services, including catering, and grants.

45. Staffing costs amount to over two-thirds of total expenditure on further education, as the table below indicates. Institutional expenditure is considered in detail in Section **3.**62 *et seq.*

Table 1

Estimated expenditure, polytechnics and other establishments of further and higher education, 1979-80[46]

(Adult education centres exluded: staff categories explained in note to table 3, para. 48 below).

	%
Teaching staff	49
Educational support staff	7
Premises related staff	4
Administrative & clerical staff	5
Total employees	65
Premises	7
Supplies & services	8
Other expenditure	20
Total expenditure (excluding Boarding & catering)	100%

Course developments requiring the acquisition of new staff involve the local authority in substantial long-term financial commitments. In consequence, although technically the appointment of staff other that the principal, vice-principal and chief administrative officer of a college is commonly the decision of the principal or the governing body, in practice staffing establishments are normally carefully vetted by the local authority, whose formal control lies in the annual estimate for teaching and non-teaching staffing establishments. Institutions are in many authorities required to conform with authority-wide appointment procedures, which may well involve not only the Education Department, but also the Personnel Department and possibly the Establishment or Policy and Resources Committees, with reference to the Management Team. Thus the initial request for new staff by a college might well have to proceed through an elaborate process of examination and discussion in departments and committees before permission is received to advertise the post. The advertisement procedures might then be the responsibility of a local authority department (not necessarily the Education Department) rather

45 See Section **11.2**.
46 *Education Statistics 1979-80 Estimates*, CIPFA, 1979.

than of the college. Selection procedures thereafter might well be subject to local authority influences, through the presence of an Adviser or Education Officer, or through the presence of councillors as members of the governing body's (or principal's) Selection Committee.

46. As is discussed in Sections **11.1** and **11.2**, the Burnham FE Committee's annual salary agreements permit quite substantial areas of discretion for local authorities in fixing the proportions of staff and the various salary grades. Inevitably, some authorities implement the agreement more generously than others, in permitting appointments at the more senior grades. For example, the proportions of senior lecturer posts created in respect of non-advanced work can vary between 0% and 5%. Some LEAs (e.g. Cleveland) have adopted the minimum, others (e.g. Cheshire) have adopted the mid-point, while a few (e.g. Barking) permit the maximum. Another area of discretion is the amount of enhancement to be given under the premature retirement scheme (see Section **11.4**). Again, while local authorities are no longer free to establish the rates paid to part-time teachers previous discretion has led to considerable variations between the regional rates set by the Burnham salaries document (Appendix IV). For example the rate for Category I work in Oxfordshire is currently £7.27, while in Liverpool it is £6.19 per hour (plus January 1980 increase). Similarly the variations in locally negotiated conditions of service agreements for teaching staff, which supplement the model agreement between CLEA and the recognised unions,[47] result in variations between establishments' student:staff ratios, etc., which are not accounted for only by differences in levels and types of work.

47. Many differences occur between authority policies with regard to permitted levels of secondment and study leave. It is very largely the authority's decision as to what priority should be given to full-time one-year secondment, in relation both to other forms of in-service activities and other educational expenditure. Estimated secondments for further education lecturers (one year full-time) for 1979-80 range from none at all in 22 LEAs to 215 in one (ILEA – and not including secondments from the authority's five polytechnics).[48] Table 2 illustrates the very different policies of two of the largest authorities, with similar numbers of teaching staff. Other, if less striking variations occur in the estimated secondments for less than one year. With a few exceptions the authorities which are not seconding staff for one year are also not seconding staff for shorter periods: in all, 18 authorities plan no secondments for further education staff in 1979-80, and no staff will be seconded from ten of the polytechnics in England and Wales.[49]

---

47 See Section **11.7**.
48 CIPFA. *op.cit.*
49 *Ibid.* These figures may well have been revised downwards as part of the economic measures following the June 1979 budget.

Table 2

Numbers of secondments and support staff planned for 1979-80 Hants. and Lancs.[50]

	No. of instns	*Total nos. of students*	*Total nos. of lecturers (FTE)*	*Nos. of lecturers seconded (1 year or more)*	*Total no. of support staff*
Hants.	15	57,926	2,925	3	1,272
Lancs.	21	61,232	2,825	26	829

48. The table illustrates also the major variations in staffing levels for non-teaching staff established in different authorities (see Section **11.2**). The constraints on staffing levels arising out of the model conditions of service agreements for teaching staff have as yet no equivalent for non-teaching staff.[51] In consequence authorities have allowed colleges to establish very different patterns and proportions of non-teaching staff, which are by no means wholly explained by differences in types of courses and levels of work between colleges. As a result, whereas the ratio of non-teaching to teaching staff in Hampshire is 1:2.3, in Lancashire it is only 1:3.4. Furthermore, the control and deployment of non-teaching staff varies considerably between colleges and authorities. In some authorities, whereas teaching staff are the responsibility of the Education Department, non-teaching staff come under the Personnel Department, which may well seek to establish and maintain staffing establishments applicable throughout the authority's services. Table 3 illustrates how four smaller authorities apportion their non-teaching staff expenditure differently, in spite of similar overall employment figures.[52] Similar variations have been noted between individual polytechnics.[53]

---

50 *Ibid.*

51 The Pooling Committee is currently examining the possibility of recommending "norms" for non-teaching staff involved in advanced level work. Current agreements between CLEA and LACSAB and the unions do not specify an "establishment" for any institution.

52 To some degree the variations might be explained by the different forms of allocation to expenditure headings, in the absence of any standardised form for presenting such information.

53 Polytechnic Finance Officers Group, *Annual Report*, 1978-79.

Table 3

Nos. and expenditure on non-teaching staff: four local authorities [54]

Expenditure on non-teaching staff (£000s)

	No. of instns.	*No. of lecturers (FTE)*	*Educ. support staff* i.	*Premises related staff* ii.	*Admin & clerical staff* iii.	*Total no. of non-teaching staff* iv.
Calderdale	1	160	77	85	108	34
Hillingdon	1	153	5	43	170	39
Isle of Wight	1	135	127	49	77	45
Rochdale	3	193	92	76	46	43

i. inc. laboratory and workshop technicians, librarians, storekeepers and models.
ii. inc. caretakers, cleaner, stokers, porters, etc. employed under NJC for Local Authorities' Services (manual workers).
iii. inc. all direct administrative and clerical staff.
iv. inc. clerical and general assistants, laboratory and workshop technicians, librarians, storekeepers, models, secretaries and administrative staff, but excluding manual workers & domestic staff.

49. The extent to which colleges are required to make use of specified local authority services varies considerably between authorities. Some establishments are required to employ the authority's direct labour system for all or a specified part of its repairs and maintenance programme. Others, within the overall budget heading approval, can seek tenders for such work within only the constraints of s135 of the Local Government Act 1972, which governs contracts for the supply of goods and materials and the execution of work for local authorities.

50. Similar variations occur with respect to a college's supplies and purchasing system. A number of authorities operate centralised purchasing schemes, organized through a Supplies or Purchasing Department. Colleges, like other educational establishments, can then be required to purchase all, or a specified proportion of certain items of expenditure through that department, thereby benefiting from the discount arrangements negotiated by the authority which can involve very substantial savings. In 1979-80 at least seven local authorities operate schemes of this nature which are so extensive that they extend to the purchase of books.[55] Centralised

---

54 CIPFA, *op.cit.*
55 Manchester, Kent, Leicester, ILEA, Bromley, Newcastle upon Tyne, Warwickshire.

purchasing arrangements have been criticised not only for the limited choices available, but also for long delays in the supply of items from the Supplies Department. More commonly, most authorities arrange contracts with some suppliers for certain items of educational equipment and materials, including books. Colleges then must order those materials from the specified suppliers, in some cases being restricted to a limited range of possible choices. Again this has been the subject of some criticism from colleges.

51. Perhaps a more serious cause of concern in many colleges is the considerable diversity of budgetary provision for supplies, including books, equipment, stationery and other educational materials. Single items of equipment which cost more than £10,000 have needed to obtain the approval of the Secretary of State,[56] but otherwise local authorities can decide themselves what levels of expenditure within these headings are permissible, with the proviso only that the articles of government permit widely different degrees of virement between budget headings for different colleges. Table 4 illustrates the resultant differences between four medium-sized authorities, with very similar levels of expenditure on staff salaries.

Table 4

Estimated expenditure on supplies and services: four medium-sized authorities, 1979-80

Total expenditure (£000s)

	No. of instns.	*No. of lecturers*	*Salaries & wages*	*Books & equipment* i	*Other supplies & services* ii
Brent	2	592	5,024	280	87
Lincs.	9	618	5,235	466	102
Sheffield	6	716	5,452	538	53
West Sussex	5	626	5,415	598	241

i. Text-books and library books (inc. public library service charge) educational and physical education equipment; educational stationery and materials. Inc. any education museum service apportionment.
ii. Inc. wages of laundry workers.

56 The Government has announced its intention of removing this requirement, *Central Government Controls over Local Authorities*, Cmnd. 7634, HMSO, 1979; see Section **1.3.**44.
57 CIPFA. *op.cit.*

It must be emphasised that such figures are merely illustrative of variations between different institutions with different needs, at one point in time, without reference to previous or planned future levels of expenditure. They do illustrate, however, that different authorities seem to employ very different criteria when deciding upon appropriate levels of expenditure in this sphere of further education.

52. Similarly, the priority given to this area of expenditure in relation to the other sectors of education varies very considerably between authorities Comparisons of unit costs are particularly difficult in further education because of the problems of defining full-time equivalent students, a problem compounded by the inability of authorities to agree as yet upon a standardised method of calculation. There is no nationally agreed definition of a full-time equivalent (FTE) student. The Pooling Committee has recommended a formula for advanced further education, whereby the total number of class-contact hours of students per course or department in the spring term is divided by the number of class contact hours that a typical full-time student on a normal equivalent full-time course would undertake during that term, to obtain the number of full-time equivalent students. However, some authorities use a weighting system which takes account of type and level of course as well as mode of attendance. For non-advanced further education, a method has been devised by education officers of the Outer London boroughs which weights students according to mode of attendance, with part-time day students amounting to 0.25 FTE, part-time day and evening students 0.33, and evening students 0.08. A different set of weighting factors is used by the DES when calculating FTE students for building purposes. However, it would seem that in 1977-8 the *per capita* expenditure on books, educational equipment and other materials and equipment for schools and colleges varied substantially between primary, secondary and further education sectors, as is shown in Table 5.

Table 5

Per capita expenditure on capitation allowances, England & Wales 1977-8 (all enrolled students)

		£ s	
	Primary	*Secondary*	*Further education*
Books	3.69	6.20	3.79
Educational Equipment	7.48	14.20	12.63
Other equipment	0.71	0.97	1.32
Total	11.88	20.37	17.74

The variations indicated here hide much wider variations of sectoral provision in individual authorities. Although the further education figures are notionally supplemented by elements within student awards, in practice these are small and benefit only a minority of students attending non-advanced further education.

53. One further sphere of financial decision-making by the local authority which has considerable import for its further education colleges concerns discretionary student grants. This is discussed in detail in Section **12.5**. Once again minor differences in local authority practices occur. Ss1(4) and 2 of the Education Act 1962 empower local authorities to make awards for both "designated" courses[58] to students not eligible for mandatory awards, and non-designated courses. The latter include most courses below first degree or HND levels (except DipHE), a variety of vocational postgraduate courses, courses of professional training for youth leaders, social workers and other groups, and courses undertaken outside the UK and in private institutions. They also include part-time degree courses such as those of the Open University, and those leading to external degrees of London University. Although the Secretary of State has drawn local authorities' attention to the undesirability of wide variations of practice both in policy in making discretionary awards and in the rates and conditions applicable to them,[59] wide variations between authorities' policies and rates of grant do occur. Concern has been expressed that, in a period when demand for such awards is increasing, many local authorities have reduced both the numbers and the size of their discretionary grants.[60] The local authority associations have advised their members that rates and conditions for grants for students over 19 should not differ from those currently applicable to mandatory awards, and that students under 19 should receive assistance equivalent to that available had they stayed at school (ie, free tuition, books and equipment allowance, subsidised meals, and where appropriate travel and hardship maintenance allowances).[61] In spite of this, differences between local authority practices would seem to be increasing, while financial difficulties are causing more and more authorities to cut back on the levels and availability of their discretionary grants, with at least two authorities (Cheshire and Oxfordshire) about to discontinue virtually all such awards.

54. **Secondary and further education**

Other major areas of local authority decision-making which profoundly affect the nature of its further education service are those involving

---

58 "Designated" courses are those so defined in Regulation 6 of the Local Education Authorities Awards Regulations, 1975. See Section **12.5**.3.

59 *Awards to Students,* DES Circular 11/75, 1975.

60 *Discretionary Awards 1975/76 to 1977/78.* Report of a DES survey, DES, 1978; *Grants Handbook and Survey of LEA Awards,* National Union of Students, 1978. An example of the variations of practice revealed there is that students over the age of 19 attending non-advanced full-time courses received grants of £601-£700 if resident in the London borough of Barking; of £401-£500 if in Ealing; and nothing at all if in Bromley or a number of other London boroughs.

61 Advice given before 1974 by the then local authority associations, re-affirmed by CLEA at its fourth meeting, 31/10/1974, minute 17. The advice is cited in DES *Discretionary Awards, op.cit,* para 31. A recent CLEA Working Party Report *Student Awards* (CLEA, 1979) has expressed concern at the existing anomalies and has recommended some fundamental changes, including the payment of mandatory awards for courses leading to basic professional qualifications and for part-time degree courses.

educational provision for 16-19 year old students, and for community and adult education. The development of "O" and "A" level courses in many colleges of further education has brought them into direct competition for students with the secondary schools, at a time when the establishment of 11-18 and 13-18 comprehensive schools has commonly had the effect of encouraging a larger proportion of the 16-18 age group to remain at school. Resultant problems are now being intensified by falling secondary school rolls, and the stabilization of the proportion staying on at 16.[62] Where 11-16 comprehensive schools have been established, the choice is often clearer for 16 year olds between sixth-form colleges and colleges of further education, but the sixth form colleges are particularly vulnerable as school populations contract, and class sizes dwindle. Some authorities are attempting to rationalize 16-19 education, by restricting competitive course developments in further education colleges, or by encouraging co-operation between further education colleges, and schools and sixth-form colleges, in order to minimise uneconomically small classes. In so doing the authority, stressing its right to control the college's general educational character and its place in the local education system, can come into conflict with the college's principal and governing body. Arguably the absence as yet of any policy for 16-19 year olds from central government has not helped, although the recent publication of two consultative papers jointly by the Departments of Employment and Education and Science, and the establishment of the Macfarlane committee (see Section **10.2.**72), might indicate forthcoming changes here (see Section **1.2.**41 and Section **4**). Some authorities have attempted to rationalize further, by establishing tertiary colleges, incorporating the functions of both sixth-form and further education colleges. To date, however, only eight authorities in England and Wales have adopted this solution. One stumbling block is the conflict of interests between those wishing such institutions to come under The Further Education Regulations, and those who see advantages in their coming under regulations for schools, as do sixth-form colleges (see also Section **5.1.**5).

55. **Adult and community education**

Local authority policies with regard to community and adult education can similarly have a major influence upon the shape and nature of further education. Further education colleges are normally the major providers of adult education, but it is the authority's decision whether such provision should be made within secondary schools, further education colleges, or in separate centres for adult and community education. Some authorities have clearly defined policies maintained by a distinctive community and adult education service, including relevant advisers and administrators. Problems have occurred where the service has been made the responsibility of a department and committee other than the Education Department/Committee (usually the Recreation and Leisure Department).

---

62 The proportion of the 16-18 age group remaining at school increased by nearly one-third between 1966-7 and 1972-3. However, since 1973-4 the proportion of students over the minimum school leaving age has remained steady (at about 17% of the total age group), while the proportion in full-time further education has increased from 7% to 10% of the total age group. *16-18: Education and Training for 16-18 year olds,* DES, 1979.

56. In a number of authorities developments have occurred piecemeal with little or no authority co-ordination. Colleges which have thus developed a substantial commitment to community education can now find themselves affected adversely both by recent and current cutbacks in financial provision for a sector of the education service which usually is first to suffer from any economic stringency, and by the authority's attempts belatedly to rationalize such provision. In a period of declining secondary school rolls, the pressure to utilize spare school capacity for such activities can be considerable. DES forecasts of student numbers in the 1980s[63] indicate, however, that further education is likely to face similar problems of contraction, and many establishments are likely to depend increasingly upon the provision of community education services. Although local authorities are obliged under the Education Act, 1944 to ensure the provision of adequate facilities for adult education as a part of further education, the nature of that provision is at the discretion of each authority. Some depend heavily upon provision by voluntary bodies and the Workers' Educational Associations. Others have drastically cut their provision, or even suspended it completely, even though by so doing they would seem to be in breach of the 1944 Act. Fees for courses are fixed by local authorities and vary considerably between authorities, or between regions (see also Section **1.3.**22). Thus many authorities have attempted to make adult education classes more self-financing, by drastically increasing fees and by increasing the minimum viable class size. The consequences have commonly been still further reductions in provision of adult and community education.

57. **Contact and communication between college and local authority**

While always numerous, these again differ between authorities. The following paragraphs are no more than a check-list of common contacts. The Education Department personnel most likely to come into direct contact with the college are the Senior Education Officer and/or Assistant Education Officer for further, adult and community education, and the Adviser (or Inspector) for further and/or adult and community education. To some extent their roles are likely to overlap, where the latter exists, although, as explained earlier, some authorities have established structures without specialist advisory responsibilities for further education. Education Officers with resource responsibilities are likely to influence strongly local authority decisions concerning college developments which demand extra resources, such as building programmes. In many authorities the advisory service also holds resources which are released to stimulate desired curricular developments and to stem glaring deficiencies. These extra resources, over and above the college's capitation allowances, can sometimes make significant differences in specific departments and curricular fields.

58. Contacts with departments other than the Education Department vary according to the authority's management system. Winter[64] found that, in

---

63 *Higher Education into the 1990s,* DES discussion document, DES, 1978. See Section **1.2.**37.
64 Society of Education Officers. *op.cit.*

about three-fifths of the authorities in his sample, chief officers other than the CEO communicated directly with colleges and schools without reference to the CEO. The main contacts are with the Treasurer's Department, concerning salaries and wages, invoicing and the collection of money, accounting and auditing arrangements, and enquiries about superannuation. The role of the auditor is discussed in more detail in Section **3.**76 *et seq.*, where the distinction between the district and internal auditor's functions is discussed. In general terms the district auditor is likely to examine the extent to which local authority policies with financial implications are being pursued, and district auditors are becoming increasingly interested in the substantial differences of student: staff ratios between establishments. Whereas the district auditor is a civil servant, employed to examine all aspects of local government finance, the internal auditor is the agent of the local authority, responsible to the authority's Treasurer or Finance Officer. His task is to examine the details of the college accounts, and he usually pays particular attention to the petty cash and the catering budget.

59. Where centralised supply schemes operate, contacts between the college and the Purchasing Officer and his or her staff are inevitably frequent. Similarly repair and maintenance queries are dealt with in some departments by a separate department. Problems can occur for colleges where a Recreation and Leisure (or Amenities) Department has been established with areas of interest which overlap with those of the Education Department. Activities within further and adult education can become matters of conflict between the two departments or, at the very least, responsibilities and lines of communication can become blurred, particularly in areas involving the community use of college premises, community activities and youth services.

60. Officials of the Personnel Department are likely to come into contact with colleges where systems of corporate management are employed which delegate substantial staffing responsibilities to that department. In some authorities it is the Personnel Department which handles negotiations concerning conditions of service for both teaching and non-teaching staff, and union negotiators have found some advantage in dealing with employers' representatives with substantial experience of such negotiations in varied occupational spheres. In spite of the nominal responsibility of the governing body for the employment and deployment of non-teaching staff, the Personnel Department is likely to be interested in staffing levels, particularly if attempting to implement a common staffing policy throughout the authority. It is thus possible that it might attempt to influence the procedure for selecting, deploying and training all local authority staff, including those in colleges. The Department may well thus seek to influence, if not control, policies for the secondment and staff development of teaching and non-teaching staff. It is here that problems can arise, where such policies might come into conflict with the policies of the institution and the Education Committee.

61. **The elected members**

The most likely contact between a college and local authority councillors is with those appointed as members of the institution's governing body. As establishments of further and higher education are often the largest establishments controlled by the authority, their governors usually include senior councillors from the ruling political party, including commonly the Chairman of the Education Committee. The involvement of such members can extend far beyond attendance at quarterly governors' meetings and meetings of the governing body's various committees and sub-committees. It has been shown to extend to the acceptance of individual students by institutions, and the nature and existence of courses and departments.[65] In consequence the distinction between politicians and officials has sometimes become blurred, a matter of some concern to at least one CEO who has warned that "politicians will take care to tell the truth and nothing but the truth. It may sometimes fall to officers to see that the whole truth is also told." [66]

62. **The local Ombudsman**

While the above paragraphs indicate that a substantial area of further educational administration is controlled externally to the college, there is now at least a means of possible redress where this is considered to have led to injustice or maladministration. The Local Government Act 1974 established Commissions for Local Administration for England and for Wales, which comprise Local Commissioners (along with the Parliamentary Commissioner). Their tasks are to investigate complaints of "injustice in consequence of maladministration in connection with action taken by or on behalf of an authority."[67] Complaints can be made by an individual or a body of persons, but not by an institution such as a college. They must concern an individual member of the public, but the Ombudsman cannot investigate matters affecting all or most of the authority's inhabitants. Nor can he or she investigate matters where alternative remedies, such as legal action, appeal to a tribunal or to the Secretary of State (as under ss68 and 99 of the Education Act, 1944)[68] are possible. Furthermore, Schedule 5 of the Act precludes investigation of secular and religious instruction, or the conduct, curriculum, internal organization, management or discipline in colleges of education and further education. The Commissioner's reports are made public, and he or she must be told by the authority the action it proposes to take, or has taken, in response to the report. If not satisfied the Commssioner can then issue a second report, but has no powers to enforce the implementation of any recommendations. Between 1976 and 1979 only seven complaints concerning further and higher education were investigated, all but one concerning student grants.

63. **Local authority associations**

Local authorities are represented nationally in consultation and negotiation with central government and with other national organizations by a number

65 A recent high court case, Central Council for Education and Training in Social Work *et al.* v North East London Polytechnic *et al.*,1978 revealed a remarkable degree of political intervention in these areas within an institution with, formally, more autonomy than many colleges, governed as it is by a Joint Education Committee from three LEAs. *New Statesmen,* 21 April 1978, pp 521-3.

66 Dudley Fiske, Presidential address to Society of Education Officers, *Education* 21/1/78.

67 Local Government Act, 1974; s26(1).

68 See para. 18, above.

of powerful associations, two of which represent those authorities with educational responsibilities. These are the Association of County Councils (ACC), representing the non-metropolitan counties, and the Association of Metropolitan Authorities (AMA), representing the metropolitan districts and counties, the Greater London Council and the London Boroughs. They exist to safeguard their members' interests, to provide a forum for discussion of matters of common concern to their members and others, and to provide appropriate central services. The latter includes a secretariat for each association, each run by an education officer, answerable to the association's Education Committee. Their Education Committees are increasingly active, and their officers send out circulars to constituent members as well as advising individual authorities. Furthermore, the committees are represented on a wide variety of national and international bodies, including the Expenditure Steering Group for Education (see Section **7.**13) which forecasts educational expenditure for the Consultative Council on Local Government Finance, in the annual rate support grant negotiations.

64. Although the interests of AMA and ACC commonly differ, they have established a joint body for education, the Council of Local Education Authorities (CLEA). This comprises 12 AMA and 12 ACC members, and has a small secretariat. CLEA undertakes a wide variety of negotiating tasks on behalf of all local authorities. Thus it has established in negotiation with NATFHE and the other recognised unions model conditions of service for lecturers in further and higher education (see Section **11.7**), has advised on the clearing house for teacher training applicants, issued circulars on pooling arrangements and awards, and it has been active in its advocacy of a re-constructed system of regional machinery for English further education (see below). CLEA's Further Education Advisory Team – comprising an education officer and a finance officer – has been established to investigate the uses of resources in advanced further education. It has examined, first in polytechnics, then in other establishments providing advanced further education, unit cost variations and problems arising from the open-ended nature of the pooling system. It has sought standardised means of measuring unit costs, and has looked at the information needs of any organization which might be established to ensure the equitable distribution of pooled resources. CLEA's size and range of activities is restricted, partly by the limitations of being able to operate only in those areas where AMA and ACC interests and policies coincide, but largely because of both Associations' distrust of any powerful organization which might represent local education authorities nationally, and thus perpetuate the education service's distinctiveness from the rest of local government. One illustration of this has been CLEA's inability to maintain levels of grant support for the six bodies recommended under s 2 (7) of the Local Government Act 1974 by the local authority associations for funding by the Secretary of State for the Environment.[69] One of CLEA's major functions,

69 The six bodies are the Schools Council, the National Foundation for Educational Research, the National Committee for Audio-Visual Aids in Education, the Field Studies Council, the Further Education Staff College and the National Institute for Adult Education. Their recommended grants were reduced in 1978 by the Policy Committees of AMA and ACC, in spite of CLEA's recommendations otherwise. The Associations argue that this type of funding reduces local authority discretion.

that of negotiating conditions of service for teachers in further and higher education has been transferred to a new National Joint Council for Further Education Teachers in England and Wales under an independent chairman, wherein LACSAB (see below, paragraph 69) and the Education Officers of ACC and AMA form the secretariat for the employers' side. CLEA has recently agreed to form a joint working party with the DES (the Macfarlane Committee), to investigate local authority provision for 16-19 year olds. This is referred to in more detail in Section **10.2.**72.

65. **The Regional Advisory Councils**
One of CLEA's first initiatives was to propose a structure of regional bodies which would consider, promote, monitor, and advise on the planning, co-ordination and development of all forms of further education in the public education system. This was but one of a number of proposals for replacing the existing unsatisfactory system of Regional Advisory Councils (RACs). This system, established in 1946,[70] comprises nine such Councils for England. It was intended to co-ordinate the provision of further education within regions and thus between LEAs, and to ensure that further education responded to the needs of industry. The nine English regions are territorially anomalous, neither coinciding with the boundaries of existing LEAs and other regional planning structures, nor indeed, in some cases even having clearly defined boundaries at all. Furthermore, the Councils differ in the extent to which they concern themselves with non-advanced further education, as they have been allowed to develop separately in response to local circumstances. The full Councils are large, with up to 100 members, but meet infrequently. They are financed by constitutent local authorities and include representatives of the LEAs – both elected members and officials – principals and teachers from further education and, anomalously, university representation, for while the latter might comment upon the provision of education in the maintained sector, the RACs do not effectively influence university provision. Most Council activities are delegated to their Standing Committees and Regional Academic Boards, which, along with associated sub-committees, are serviced by small secretariats.

66. The RACs' major function is the scrutiny of proposals for advanced courses of further education, before their submission to the Secretary of State for approval as required by The Further Education Regulations 1975. Recently the RACs have been required to approve proposals for Diploma in Higher Education and initial teacher training courses, part-time non-degree courses and courses leading to a post-graduate award without further reference to the Secretary of State.[71] For other courses the RACs (or rather their executive standing committees) forward recommendations to a committee of the Inspectorate, after discussion with the Regional Staff Inspector. The committee's decisions are then normally endorsed by the Secretary of State. RACs are expected to bear in mind the new criteria by which RSIs are to assess advanced course proposals (established by FECL 1/80 under

70 DES Circular 87 (HMSO, 1946) in response to the Percy Report, *Higher Technological Education.*
71 DES Circular 10/76.
72 The Further Education Regulations 1975; regulation 7.

regulation 8 of The Further Education Regulations: see Section **7.**50). RACs are further required[72] to ensure that not only are courses not duplicated unnecessarily in neighbouring authorities, but that fees charged do not vary substantially between authorities. Thus the RACs have attempted to cope with the rapid expansion of advanced further education provision in the last decade, and to rationalize it, against pressures from local authorities and colleges for course approval. The result has been some rather unsavoury horse-trading, which has intensified pressures for the replacement or abolition of the RACs – whose reputations further suffered when the DES failed to consult them concerning either the location of the new polytechnics or the closure or merger of colleges of education, even though they have provided an administrative structure for teacher education since the abolition of the university-based Area Training Organizations. The Oakes Committee[73] recommended that the RACs be replaced by nine new Advisory Councils with functions including non-advanced further education, with rationalized boundaries, funded by the constitutent local authorities. Their tasks would be to "consider, promote, monitor and advise on the planning, co-ordination and development in the regions of higher education outside the universities, including the initial, induction and in-service training of teachers".[74] As yet these proposals have not been implemented, although the previous government's abortive Education Bill (1978) attempted to establish new Advanced Further Education Councils. Reform or abolition of the regional machinery for further education in England seems likely in the near future.

67. **Joint education committees**

The RACs' functions in Wales are undertaken by the Welsh Joint Education Committee (WJEC). Unlike the RACs this is a statutory body under Part II of Schedule 1, Education Act, 1944, which permitted joint committees of local education authorities with executive responsibilities. The WJEC comprises representatives of all eight Welsh LEAs, and co-opted members representing other interests, including teachers, industry and the University of Wales. It undertakes a heterogeneous collection of functions, as well as those of an RAC. It co-ordinates activities in special education and in-service education. It acts as the only examining body with responsibilities for CSE and GCE examinations, and is responsible for technical examinations. More generally, it facilitates the regulation of Welsh LEAs' interests, and acts to express Welsh educational concerns, including the promotion of Welsh langage teaching, and the administration of the Welsh National Youth Orchestra.[75]

68. Other joint education committees have been established with more specific tasks. Thus several polytechnics are responsible to a joint education committee of two or more local authorities. Less formal organizations of

73 *Report of the Working Group on the Management of Higher Education in the Maintained Sector*, Cmnd. 7130, HMSO, 1978.

74 *Ibid*, s 9 (13).

75 *Annual Report 1977-8*, Welsh Joint Education Committee, 1978. The political and administrative activities of WJEC are discussed in detail in L.M. Cantor and I.F. Roberts, *Further Education Today: A Critical Review*, 1979.

local education authorities occur in several parts of England, including the London boroughs and Yorkshire and Humberside. They serve to make recommendations on a host of administrative matters, to reconcile differences and to act, when necessary, as a regional pressure group. In some areas an RAC sub-committee provides a structure for discussion and co-ordinated action by CEOs.

69. A host of other local authority organizations undertake activities with educational implications. Some, such as the Local Government Training Board (paragraph 36, above) have already been mentioned. Reference to just a few of the others is possible here. The Local Authorities' Conditions of Service Advisory Board (LACSAB) is of major and increasing significance in further education. Established in 1948, it exists to co-ordinate the activities of local authorities as employers, in their negotiations on wages, salaries and conditions of service. As such it provides the employers' secretariat for most of the national negotiating organizations such as the Joint National Council and the Burnham Committees, it collects and disseminates information, and advises individual authorities on their roles as employers, and represents local government in discussions with central government concerning employment and manpower. The Board comprises 19 members, appointed by the local authority associations, the Greater London Council, and the employers' side of the major national negotiating bodies, including the Burnham Committees. A secretariat of about 70 has grown rapidly in recent years, in response to the massive labour legislative activity of the last decade. It is financed by the local authorities,[76] and the provincial councils which deal with local authorities' collective bargaining on pay and conditions of service. It is important to stress that LACSAB is an advisory body, and its advice is not always taken. Advice is in the form of commentaries and interpretations in individual cases, and through handbooks such as the *LACSAB Employee Relations Handbook.* LACSAB's involvement in further and higher education is extensive, providing the secretariat not only for the employers' side of the Burnham Further Education Committee, but also for the negotiating bodies dealing with wages and conditions of service for non-teaching staff. Furthermore, it will now become the focal point of the management secretariat in the reorganized negotiating machinery for conditions of service of teachers in further education, thus aligning salary and conditions of service negotiations more closely together.

70. The Local Authorities' Management Services and Computer Committee (LAMSAC) was established in 1969 to assist local authorities with the introduction and use of computers and management sciences in local government. It is funded principally through s2 (7) of the Local Government Act 1974. It comprises four advisory panels for Computers, Organizations & Methods and Productivity, General Management, and Purchasing. LAMSAC collects and disseminates information, offers advice and proposes guidelines, and operates a more detailed consultancy service. It also provides training in management techniques, and undertakes research into new systems of computing, and management. It has undertaken comparative studies of non-

---

76 Under s2 (7) of the Local Government Act, 1974.

teaching aspects of the education service with planning and the social services. A more specialist service is provided by the Local Government Operational Research Unit of the Royal Institute of Public Administration, which seeks rational, systematic approaches to decision-making which can be expressed and evaluated quantitatively. Its studies have included school transport, and the development of more effective decision-making approaches to educational administration. Reference also should be made to a number of local authority consortia. Six building consortia were established between 1957 and 1966 to apply industrialised building methods and standardised designs to school buildings, initially, but the expertise thus acquired has since been applied to college building. Consortia have also been formed to plan and advise upon the design and purchase of furniture, science equipment and kitchens.

71. **Conclusion**

The establishment and development of the local authority associations and organizations described above are indicative both of the changing needs of local authorities and the increasing pressures upon them. Authorities face an unprecedented series of complex problems, many of which they are no longer capable of dealing with individually. Many powers have, therefore, already been delegated to powerful local authority associations. Central government seeks to occupy other areas traditionally held by local government, and particularly in its demands for sharp reductions in spending levels, not only challenges the autonomy of local authorities, but even makes it difficult for some authorities to carry out their statutory responsibilities. The education service, as the major consumer of local authority resources, is under particular pressure, and the long-held concept of a national service locally administered is in danger of collapse. Demands for more effective management systems have disturbed traditional patterns of authority. Claims for greater institutional autonomy on the one hand, and for the national, or at least regional application of employment and operating conditions on the other threaten the powers of the local education authority. At the same time, the statutory education service is shrinking as numbers of pupils fall sharply, while high levels of youth unemployment have led to the development of a major education and training service outside the local authority sphere of influence. The absence of national educational objectives, and the subordination of local educational needs to the broader priorities of a corporately managed local authority inhibit the development of any effective planning or accepted sense of direction in the local education service. The resultant confusion is perhaps most marked in the fields of public sector further, higher and community education, where the diffusion of policy making between (and within) institutions, local authorities, local authority organizations and central government agencies makes for both unwieldy and perplexed bureaucracies. It is not surprising that demands for rationalization, whether through national bodies or through directly elected *ad hoc* education authorities persist.

APPENDIX 1

LOCAL GOVERNMENT EMPLOYMENT

Table 1

Numbers employed in local government, England & Wales, June 1979 (thousands)

	Full-time	*Part-time*	*Full-time Equivalent*
Lecturers and teachers	543	150	573
Other education	213	504	430
Construction	135	1	135
Social Services	137	166	207
Transport	22	0	22
Libraries & museums	25	16	33
Recreation, parks & baths	73	21	81
Environmental health	22	2	23
Refuse collection	50	0	50
Housing	44	12	50
Town & Country Planning	22	1	23
Fire Service	40	2	41
Police service	150	8	154
Probation, Magistrates' Courts and agency staff	16	4	18
Other services	248	49	269
Total	1,740	936	2,109

Source: *Department of Employment Gazette*, Nov, 1979. Part-time includes employees normally working for not more than 30 hours per week. Full-time equivalents calculated by factors derived from a 1974 analysis of hours worked by local authority employees, to convert part-time employees to approximate full-time equivalent: i.e., teachers and lecturers in further education 0.11; teachers in primary and secondary education, and all other non-manual employees 0.53; manual employees 0,41.

Table 2

Teaching, administrative and related staff employed by local education authorities, estimated 1979-80

	Full-time equivalent (thousands)
Teachers (qualified: schools)	484
Teachers (other: schools)	5
Nursery assistants	9
FE teaching staff (polytechnics)	31
FE teaching staff (other FE establishments)	92
Other FE teaching staff (inc. adult education)	10
Advisers, inspectors & organizers	3
Education welfare officers	3
Administrative and support staff	21
Educational psychologists	1
Youth service wardens and leaders	5
Careers service staff	6
Total	670

Source: CIPFA, *Education Statistics 1979-80 Estimates.*

APPENDIX 2:

LOCAL AUTHORITY RETURNS

The following information is required of local authorities and voluntary colleges by central government departments, concerning further and higher education.

Form	*(1979) When required*	*By whom*	*Subject*
CO1	1 Aug.	DoE	Local authority transaction on capital account (including FE).
RO1	1 Aug.	DoE	Local education authority revenue & expenditure and income, divided between polytechnics, agricultural colleges, other major establishments of further education, evening institutes, other further education, teacher training.
510F (Pools)	31 Oct.	DES	Provisional actual (for current year) estimated (for next year) and forecast (for following year) revenue expenditure on teacher training, advanced further education and "no area" pupils.
512F	no specific date	DES	Audited revenue expenditure to be pooled, via District Auditor.
UG1	30 Sept.	DES	Estimated expenditure on mandatory awards to students.
UG8	no specific date	DES	Certified actual expenditure on mandatory awards, via District Auditor.
503G	15 Dec.	DES	Full-value awards to students.
ST2 (LIB)	July	DES	Library provision in major FE establishments, including expenditure on employees, books, periodicals, etc.
FESR (Further Education Statistical Record)		DES	Computerised information including details of students' age, sex and type of course, and of course enrolments.
618G	Oct.	DES	Details of all teachers employed on a specified day.
19TT (3195)	31 Oct.	DES	Numbers of students and teachers in establishments on 31 Jan in teacher training establishments.
7TT	7 Dec.	DES	Student numbers at beginning of academic year in teacher training (technical) establishments.
20/23TT	Nov.	DES	Statistical accounting summary including student numbers, tuition costs, and catering and residential cost.

REFERENCE

Education Act, 1944, Chapter 31, HMSO.
Education Act 1962, Chapter 12, HMSO.
Education (No.2) Act 1968, Chapter 16, HMSO.
Education Act 1975, Chapter 2, HMSO.
London Government Act 1963, Chapter 33, HMSO.
Local Government Act 1972, Chapter 70, HMSO.
Local Government Act 1974, Chapter 7, HMSO.
National Health Service Reorganisation Act 1973, Chapter 32, HMSO.
Public Bodies (Admission to Meetings) Act 1960, Chapter 67, HMSO.
Town and Country Planning Act 1971, Chapter 78, HMSO.
The Further Education Regulations 1975, Statutory Instruments 1975, No. 1054, HMSO.

Regional Organisation of Further Education, DES Circular 87, 1946.
The Chance to Share, DES Circular 2/70, 1970.
The National Health Service Reorganisation Act 1973, DES Circular 1/74, 1974.
Approval of Advanced Further Education Courses: Modified Arrangements, DES Circular 10/76, 1976.
Central Government Controls over Local Authorities, Cmnd 7634, HMSO, 1979.
Regulation 8 of The Further Education Regulations 1975, DES FECL 1/80, 1980.

Towards a Wider Use, Report of an Inter Local Authority Association working party, 1976.
Student Awards, Report of a CLEA Working Party, 1979.
Discretionary Awards 1975/76 to 1977/78, Report of a DES survey, 1978.
Higher Education into the 1990s, DES Discussion Document, 1978.
16-18: Education and training for 16-18 year olds. A consultative paper, DES and DoE, 1979.
Providing educational opportunities for 16-18 year olds. A consultative paper, DES, 1979.
A Better Start in Working Life, A consultative paper, DES/DE, 1979.
Management Development in Education Departments, Supplement to Training Recommendation 7, Local Government Training Board, 1977.
Government of the Colleges of Education, Report of the Study Group under the Chairmanship of T.R. Weaver, HMSO, 1966.
A New Partnership for our Schools (Taylor Report), HMSO, 1977.
Report of the Working Group on the Management of Higher Education in the Maintained Sector, (Oakes Report), HMSO, 1978.
Report of the Committee on the Staffing of Local Government (Mallaby Report), Ministry of Housing & Local Government, 1967.
Report of the Committee on the Management of Local Government (Maud Management Report), Ministry of Housing and Local Government, 1967.
The New Local Authorities: Management & Structure (Bains Report), HMSO, 1972.

D. Birley, *The Education Officer and His World,* Routledge & Kegan Paul, 1970.
R. Bolam, G Smith and H. Cantor, *Local Education Authority Advisers and Educational Innovation,* University of Bristol, 1976.
J. Bourn, *Management in Central and Local Government,* Pitman, 1979.
L.M. Cantor and I.F. Roberts, *Further Education Today A Critical Review,* Routledge & Kegan Paul, 1979.
Chartered Institute of Public Finance and Accountancy, *Educational Statistics 1979/80 Estimates,* CIPFA, 1979.
M. David, *Reform, Reaction and Resources,* NFER Publishing Company, 1977.
L. Dobson, T. Gear, and A Westoby (Eds), *Management in Education: Some Techniques and Systems,* Ward Lock Educational, 1975.
R.E. Jennings, *Education and Politics: Policy Making in LEAS,* Batsford, 1977.

M. Kogan and W Van der Eyken, *County Hall: the role of the Chief Education Officer,* Penguin, 1973.
Local Government Training Board, *Management Development in Education Departments,* LGTB, 1977.
J. Mann, *Education,* Pitman, 1979.
National Union of Students, *Grants Handbook and Survey of LEA Awards,* NUS, 1978.
Polytechnic Finance Officers Group, *Annual Report 1978-79,* Sheffield City Polytechnic, 1979.
K. Poole, *The Local Government Services,* George Allen and Unwin, 1978.
D.E. Regan, *Local Government and Education,* George Allen and Unwin, 1977.
R. Saran, *Policy Making in Secondary Education,* Oxford University Press, 1973.
Society of Education Officers, *Management in the Education Service: Challenge & Response,* Routledge & Kegan Paul, 1975.
Society of Education Officers, *The Position of the Education Service Following Local Government Reorganization,* SEO, 1977.
Welsh Joint Education Committee, *Annual Report 1977-78,* WJEC, 1978.

Section 9

THE UNIONS

1. This Section provides brief details of the major unions representing teaching and non-teaching staff in public sector further and higher education which have full recognition for the purposes of salaries and conditions of service negotiations. LACSAB's advice to local authorities on the question of recognition is that they "should not recognise for collective bargaining purposes at local level unions which are not represented on provincial or national negotiating bodies,"[1] All the organizations covered are certified as independent trade unions under the certification procedures described in Section **11.6**, Appendix 1. Reference is made in Section **8.**37 to professional associations with members employed in local authorities.

2. The Section concerns itself primary with the structural organization of the unions, concentrating particularly on their form of organization at local level. Further information on relations with the unions, and salaries and conditions negotiations is given in Sections **2.4**, **11.7** and **11.8**. There are of course many professional organizations and other specialist groupings to which education staff belong. Some of these are referred to elsewhere in this book and most are listed in Section **1.4**.

3. **Teaching staff**
The further education teacher unions nationally recognised in England and Wales for the purpose of salary and conditions of service negotiations are: the Association of Agricultural Education Staffs, the Association of Principals of Colleges; the National Association of Teachers in Further and Higher Education and the National Society for Art Education. These are the organizations which constitute the Teachers' Panel of the Burnham Further Education Committee and form the Teachers' Side of the new National Joint Council for Teachers in Further Education in England and Wales in which conditions of service are negotiated (see Sections **11.1.** and **11.7**). Seats on the Burnham FE Committee Teachers' Panel and the Teachers' Side of the NJC are distributed as follows:

Association of Agricultural Education Staffs	1
Association of Principals of Colleges	2
National Association of Teachers in Further and Higher Education	12
National Society for Art Education	1

4. Salary scales for agricultural education staff are negotiated through the Agricultural Education Sub-committee of the Burnham FE Committee which replaced the former Burnham Farm Institutes Committee in 1976 (see Section **11.15**). The Association of Agricultural Education Staffs holds six of the eight seats on the Teachers' Panel of the Sub-Committee, the other two being held by NATFHE. Conditions of service for agricultural education staff are governed by a Code of Good Practice agreed between the AAES and Association of County Councils.

---

1 *The LACSAB Employee Relations Handbook*, 1977, p.45.

5. Salary scales and conditions of service for penal education staff are negotiated through the Joint National Council for Further Education Teachers Assigned to Prison Department Establishments (see Section **11.14**). Seats on the Teachers' side of the JNC are distributed as follows:

Association of Principals of Colleges	1
Association of Teachers in Penal Establishments	2
National Association of Teachers in Further and Higher Education	4

6. **National Association of Teachers in Further and Higher Education (NATFHE) – 73,000 members**
The National Association of Teachers in Further and Higher Education is the largest organization representing lecturers in all sectors of further education. NATFHE members work in colleges of further education, colleges of technology, polytechnics, institutes of higher education, colleges of education, adult, agricultural, art and penal education. Approximately 85% of full-time lecturers covered by The Further Education Regulations 1975 are members of NATFHE.

7. NATFHE is both a trade union and professional association and the scope of its activity is, therefore, very broad indeed. It is the major trade union representing post-school, public sector lecturers in all negotiations on salaries, pensions and conditions of service at both national and local levels. NATFHE members work in all areas of the post-school public sector of education and the Association's involvement in educational policy-making and the promotion of public sector further and higher education reflects the wide interests and expertise of its membership. The Association has access to the Secretary of State for Education and Science, is regularly consulted by the DES on major policy matters and invited to participate in policy-making initiatives. It is also a significant influence in the international educational field (see Appendix 3 for details of international teachers' organizations).

8. The Association is represented on many official educational bodies, including the Further Education Curriculum Review and Development Unit, the National Consultative Group on links between the Training Services Division and the education service, and the Advisory Committee on the Supply and Education of Teachers. NATFHE members sit on examining and validating bodies such as the Council for National Academic Awards, the City and Guilds of London Institute, the Business Education Council, the Technician Education Council and some GCE Boards, as well as a wide range of professional and advisory institutions. Many hundreds of members represent the Association on committees within the sub-structures of these bodies and on numerous other educational bodies.

9. NATFHE publishes a variety of explanatory and policy material on trade union and educational matters, a list of which is appended (Appendix 1).

10. **Membership**
Membership is open to all lecturers in public sector post-school education

whether working full-time or part-time. Students in full-time training for teaching service in further education are also eligible for membership. There is a category of membership for the unemployed which includes student members and unemployed members seeking posts in further education.

11. The Association has a number of joint membership arrangements with other trade unions and professional organizations in post-school public sector education designed to minimise the conflicts which can arise from competitive recruitment and maximise the services available to members.

12. A joint partnership scheme with the National Union of Teachers eliminates competitive recruitment through its provision for joint membership and also provides for cross representation on Executive and other national committees of the two organizations and for NUT representation on NATFHE's National Council.

13. Under a joint membership and partnership scheme with the Association for Adult and Continuing Education (see Appendix 2) competitive recruitment is restricted through NATFHE being responsible for recruiting adult education teachers in further education colleges and the AACE for recruiting adult education teachers elsewhere, and the benefits of each organization being available to members of the other in accordance with the scheme. NATFHE members whose duties are wholly or substantially in adult education and AACE members are entitled to Joint Ordinary or Associate membership of both organizations. Teachers in colleges whose duties incorporate a minority concern with adult education are entitled to Joint Associate membership of AACE. Teachers in further education colleges who have an interest in adult education by virtue of an additional part-time contract are not eligible for joint membership but may become affiliate members of AACE on payment of an additional subscription.

14. Under a joint membership scheme with the Association of Agricultural Education Staffs, new teachers in agricultural further education establishments are entitled to receive full joint membership rights of the two organizations and enter the scheme via the AAES; new teachers of agriculture in other FE establishments are entitled to full joint membership rights, also via NATFHE.

15. Under a joint membership scheme with the Association of Teachers in Penal Establishments, teachers in penal education automatically qualify for full rights and membership of both Associations. Teachers in the field of penal education pay their subscription to the ATPE.

16. A joint membership scheme with the Association of Teachers of Domestic Science provides that members of the ATDS who move into further education may retain their ATDS membership and have joint membership of both Associations.

17. A joint membership scheme with the Further Education Lecturers' National Section of the Educational Institute of Scotland provides for close co-

operation between the two organizations and cross representation at Executive Committee and Annual Conference levels. The EIS is considered the appropriate national organization for further education lecturers in Scotland and NATFHE for further education lecturers in England, Wales and Northern Ireland.

18. **Structure**

The basic organizational unit of NATFHE is the Branch. NATFHE's Branch structure is workplace-based and there is a NATFHE Branch in each college. In the larger institutions which operate on several sites (the majority of polytechnics, for example) there may be several Branches. Where there is more than one Branch in an institution, a Co-ordinating Committee is established.

19. The NATFHE Branch is responsible for representing the interests of members through negotiation with the principal or director and governing body of the institution where there is only one NATFHE Branch in that institution. A committee and officers conduct the daily work of the Branch, each Branch having a chairman, secretary and treasurer. Most Branches have a membership secretary too and many have other officers also, such as an assistant secretary, a publicity officer, etc. NATFHE encourages Branches to operate systems of departmental representation and departmental representatives will normally be included on the Branch Committee.

20. Co-ordinating Committees, as their name implies, co-ordinate the activities of the Branches in an institution and make representations to the principal or director and governing body on behalf of constituent Branches on matters concerning the institution. Model rules for Branches and Co-ordinating Committees are incorporated in NATFHE's *Constitution and Rules.* The rules under which Branches and Co-ordinating Committees operate are subject to approval by the appropriate Region of NATFHE.

21. NATFHE Liaison Committees cover all Branches in each local authority area. These are established by the Regional Councils of the Association and have in membership representatives of all Branches in the area and of appropriate organizations with which NATFHE has joint membership schemes (AACE and AAES). A Liaison Committee makes representations on behalf of constituent Branches to the authority and conducts negotiations with the authority on conditions of service, trade union facilities and other matters.

22. NATFHE Branches are grouped into 14 Regions covering England, Northern Ireland and Wales. Each Region has a Regional Council on which all Branches are represented. Each Region is required to establish such Regional Standing Committees as it considers necessary having regard to the pattern of committees at national level. The Association's Inner London Region is effectively both Region and Liaison Committee in that it covers the London boroughs in the scope of the Inner London Education Authority and conducts negotiations with the ILEA. Regional Rules are incorporated in NATFHE's *Constitution and Rules* and changes are subject to approval by the Association's National Council.

23. The supreme policy-making body of the Association is its Annual Conference. Between Annual Conferences policy is decided by the National Council, a body comprising the national officers, General Secretary, 100 regional representatives, representatives of organizations with whom NATFHE has joint membership arrangements and representatives of certain specialist educational areas. The National Executive Committee of NATFHE is elected by and from the National Council. The NEC (which normally meets monthly) conducts the business of the Association between meetings of the National Council.

24. **Policy-making in NATFHE**

As has already been mentioned the Association's Annual Conference consisting of the NEC, National Council and Regional representatives is the supreme policy-making body of the Association. Annual Conference policy is contained in resolutions approved by the Conference which have been debated in conjunction with a report of work carried out in the preceding year presented to Conference by the NEC.

25. The Association has a democratic structure involving its basic organizational units together with specialist committees at regional and national level for the formulation of, for example, specific policy and responses to new developments and Government initiatives.

26. **Committee structure**

The National Executive Committee conducts much of its business through three sub-committees, one of which is specifically concerned with educational policy. There are five national Standing Committees covering different areas of education – higher education, further education, teacher education, art education and adult education. Every Region has one member on each of these committees. The Standing Committees make recommendations to the National Executive Committee on new policy, and have delegated powers to act on matters within their spheres of activity and in furtherance of established Association policy. In addition to these, there are four Standing Panels covering women's rights, research staff, international relations and polytechnics. As mentioned in paragraph 22, Regions too are expected to set up appropriate machinery having regard to the pattern of national Standing Committees. Thus there is an effective structure for channelling the views of the membership through to national level.

27. **Policy statements**

Draft policy statements on major areas of the Association's educational interests are drawn up within the committee structure. Comments from Branches and Regions are sought before a policy statement is discussed by the Association's National Council. The Association regularly responds to educational initiatives by the Government or other bodies and is frequently asked to submit evidence to the House of Commons Expenditure Committee.

28. NATFHE employs a team of officials at national and regional level to advise and assist members with professional or trade union problems, to represent

members (where necessary), to negotiate, to develop trade union training programmes and to promote the work of the Association.

29. NATFHE is affiliated to a number of organizations including the Trades Union Congress, Irish Congress of Trade Unions, Wales TUC, National Federation of Professional Workers and World Confederation of Organizations of the Teaching Profession.

30. **Association of Agricultural Education Staffs (AAES) – 1,000 members**

The Association of Agricultural Education Staffs is both a trade union and professional association. AAES members work in county agricultural colleges and centres of agricultural education. (Details of the organization of agricultural education and terms and conditions covering teaching staff therein can be found in Section **11.15**). The AAES takes into membership all grades of agricultural education lecturer including principals. Details of the joint membership and partnership scheme between the AAES and NATFHE are given in paragraph 14.

31. AAES members are organized in college-based Branches which are usually county-based too, there being no agricultural colleges in metropolitan authorities. Joint members of AAES and NATFHE who enter the joint scheme via NATFHE because they teach in further education establishments other than agricultural colleges, have the right to participate in the appropriate AAES Branch.

32. AAES Branches are entitled to representation on the NATFHE Liaison Committee (the body which negotiates with the local authority: see paragraph 21). The degree to which AAES Branches operate through the Liaison Committee will vary from area to area. Because of the specialised nature of their membership and the institutions in which agricultural education is provided, it is common for AAES Branches to make representations to and negotiate directly with their county authorities.

33. AAES Branches are grouped into nine Regions. Each Region has a member on the national Executive Committee which also includes representatives from certain specialist areas, for example, agricultural engineering, which may not be represented through the Regions. The Executive Committee conducts the business of the Association through three main committees, including an education and a salaries committee. Members of the AAES salaries committee form the teachers' side of the Agricultural Education Sub-committee of the Burnham FE Committee. Overall Association policy is formed by the AAES Annual Conference which is open to all members.

34. **Association of Principals of Colleges (APC) – 500 members**

The Association of Principals of Colleges (originally the Association of Principals of Technical Institutions) is both a trade union and professional association and has in membership principals of all types of college in public sector further and higher education. The majority of APC members are also members of NATFHE.

35. The objectives of the Association include: the discussion of all matters relating to the work now conducted, or which may be conducted, in colleges, and relevant action; representation on educational, professional and other appropriate bodies; co-operation with other educational, industrial, commercial, professional and other bodies; advice to members upon appropriate standards of professional behaviour; and the issue of publications dealing with the work, interests or functions of the Association. The Association is represented on the Teachers' Panel of the Burnham FE Committee. It publishes reports and memoranda on topics of current concern in further and higher education and comments on proposals emanating from the DES, other government departments and professional, examining or other bodies which may affect colleges.

36. APC members belong to regional Branches, each of which usually meets once a term. Branches elect members to the Association's Council which meets regularly throughout the year and, subject to the overriding control of the twice-yearly general meetings, is the main policy-making body. General meetings are open to all APC members. The APC has a panel of Liaison Officers consisting of recently retired principals available to advise members in difficulties.

37. **Association of Teachers in Penal Establishments (ATPE) – 265 members**

The Association of Teachers in Penal Establishments is both a trade union and professional association. Teachers in penal establishments are employed by local education authorities within an education service administered nationally by the Home Office. (The structure of penal education and terms and conditions covering those employed therein are dealt with in detail in Section **11.15**). ATPE members work in prisons, borstals, detention centres (junior and senior), remand centres and women's penal establishments. The ATPE also has members who work at Broadmoor (which is classified as a hospital, falling within the purview of the Department of Health and Social Security). Brief details of the joint membership scheme between the ATPE and NATFHE are given in paragraph 15.

38. ATPE members are organized in Branches based on the four Home Office Regions covering the North, Midlands, South East and South West (England and Wales). Joint members of the ATPE and NATFHE are entitled to participate in the appropriate NATFHE Branch and Region.

39. The ATPE does not have any formal organizational structure at workplace level. Each Branch communicates with all its members, a course made feasible by the fairly small numbers involved. At establishment level, penal education staff are responsible to the governor for day-to-day matters and ultimately to the chief education officer. Penal education officers would expect to have direct access to the governor of their institutions. Where problems arise of concern to penal education staff as ATPE members it is customary for an Association Executive member and, if necessary, a NATFHE representative to be called in to assist.

40. The supreme policy-making body of the ATPE is its annual General Meeting to which all members are invited. In between these meetings a national Executive Committee consisting of three officers, two elected members, two co-opted members and representatives of appropriate affiliated organizations, such as NATFHE, conducts the business of the Association. Individual Executive Committee members take on responsibility for particular aspects of ATPE work. There is also a consultative committee, consisting of Home Office and ATPE representatives presided over by a Prison Department official with senior education officers of the prison service, which discusses general educational matters such as education finance, teaching equipment and conferences.

41. **National Society for Art Education**

The National Society for Art Education is both a trade union and professional association with members in primary and secondary education, post-school public sector education and the universities. At institution level the Association operates a system of college representatives. Members are organized into 16 Departments, each run by a District Committee. The Districts elect members to the NSAE Council which in turn elects an Executive. The supreme policy-making body of the NSAE is its Annual General Meeting. The Executive is responsible for implementing policy and acting on the decisions made by the Council.

42. The NSAE's main interest lies in subject development. It is nationally recognised as one of the professional bodies for art and design teachers, has representation on a wide range of bodies, including the Association of Art Institutions, and direct access to the Secretary of State on matters of policy-making in art and design. The NSAE's AGM is primarily concerned with national topics related to subject development; it organizes a variety of lectures and conferences on matters of current concern in art and design and issues publications, a list of which may be found in the Association's journal. The Association employs a team of experts at its head office specialising in particular subjects – for example, fine arts, craft subjects, training of designers – and dealing with salaries and conditions of service. Members of the NSAE in post-school public sector education, many of whom are members of NATFHE, are covered by the salaries determined by the Burnham Further Education Committee on the Teachers' Panel of which the NSAE is represented, and by conditions henceforth determined by the new NJC.

43. **Non-teaching staff**

The trade unions nationally recognised for the purpose of salaries and conditions of service negotiations for non-teaching staff manual workers are the General and Municipal Workers' Union, the National Union of Public Employees and the Transport and General Workers' Union. These are the unions which constitute the trade union side of the National Joint Council for Local Authorities Services – Manual Workers.

44. Seats on the NJC for Local Authorities Services – Manual Workers are distributed as follows:

General and Municipal Workers' Union	12
National Union of Public Employees	9
Transport and General Workers' Union	9

The Provincial Councils are similarly constituted to the National Joint Council.

45. The unions so recognised in respect of white-collar non-teaching staff are the National and Local Government Officers' Association, the white collar sections of the General and Municipal Workers' Union and the Transport and General Workers' Union, and the National Union of Public Employees. These unions, together with the Confederation of Health Service Employees and direct representation from the Provincial Councils, form the staff side of the National Joint Council for Local Authorities' Administrative, Professional, Technical and Clerical Services.

46. Seats on the NJC for Local Authorities' APT & C services are distributed as follows:

National and Local Government Officers' Association	8
General and Municipal Workers' Union (Managerial, Administrative, Technical and Supervisory Association)	3
National Union of Public Employees	2
Transport and General Workers' Union (Association of Clerical, Technical and Supervisory Staff)	1
Confederation of Health Service Employees	1
12 Provincial Councils	12
Greater London District Whitley Council	4
Scottish Council	4

47. The Provincial Councils are similarly constituted to the National Joint Council. The Greater London Whitley Council for Administrative, Professional, Technical, Executive and Clerical Grades, involves also the Greater London Council Staff Association, a TUC affiliated trade union covering the same type of membership as NALGO.

48. **General and Municipal Workers' Union (GMWU) – 970,000 members**

College non-teaching staff belonging to the General and Municipal Workers' Union are organized at local authority level in Branches which may cover all an authority's GMWU members or may be more specialised, having an education staff Branch, for example. The pattern of Branch organization is not uniform and manual and white-collar staff may be in the same Branch in one Authority and in different Branches in another. The white-collar section of the union is known as MATSA, the Managerial, Administrative and Technical Staff Association. The union operates a shop stewards system at workplace level. In large workplaces there may be a convenor steward. Branch members elect a Branch Committee to co-ordinate activity. Branch members elect representatives to the union's Regional Councils and Committees. There are ten Regional Councils covering England, Northern Ireland, Scotland and Wales. The Regional Committees are responsible for ensuring the effective organization of Branches, the development of union officers, supervising Branch finance, administering strike benefit and other matters. The supreme policy-making body of the GMWU is its annual Congress. Between Congresses the Executive Council, which is representative of all ten Regions on an elective basis, is the main decision-making body.

49. The GMWU employs a team of full-time officials at national, regional and local level. In 1974 a scheme of District Officers was introduced. The District Officer comes under the authority of the Regional Secretary and is now taking the place of many of the former full-time Branch Secretaries and administrative officers. MATSA has its own officials. The union is affiliated to the TUC, Irish Congress of Trade Unions, Scottish TUC, Wales TUC and Labour Party.

50. **National Union of Public Employees (NUPE) – 710,000 members**

College non-teaching staff members of the National Union of Public Employees are organized locally into Branches based on local authorities. Non-teaching staff will therefore be in Branches alongside other local government workers. At college level a system of shop stewards operates, the number and election of whom is determined by the staff themselves. In a large institution there will probably be stewards for individual groups of workers, for example, refectory staff, caretakers or groundsmen. The election of each steward is reported to the local Branch for ratification and the issue of credentials, and notification is given to the college authorities. Convenor stewards may be appointed to represent a group of stewards, for instance, all the education stewards in an authority. All stewards and Branch Officers in a particular local authority form the Branch District Committee which co-ordinates local negotiations conducted by stewards, assists where necessary and negotiates with the local authority.

51. Branch District Committees elect representatives to Area Committees which are service-based. Non-teaching staff come under the auspices of NUPE local government Area Committees. Areas are grouped into 11 Divisions covering England, Northern Ireland, Scotland and Wales. Delegates from Area Committees plus two women elected by Divisional Conference form Divisional Councils. These apply and develop overall union policy within the Division, and are responsible for administration, ballot arrangements, union affiliation arrangements and liaison with regional organizations of the TUC and Labour Party. A national local government committee covers the service interests of non-teaching staff. The union also has a number of National Advisory Committees which cover the special occupational interests of members within or across a service, for example, nursery nurses. The overall general management of the union is the responsibility of the Executive Council. The supreme policy-making body of the union is its National Conference which meets annually. NUPE employs a team of full-timhe officials who operate at area, divisional and national levels of the union. The union's affiliations include those to the TUC and the Irish Congress of Trade Unions, the Scottish TUC, the Welsh TUC and the Labour Party.

52. **Transport and General Workers' Union (TGWU) – 2,091,489 members**

The Transport and General Workers' Union is a multi-industrial union with members in a large number of trade groups. Non-teaching staff in colleges fall within the Administrative, Clerical, Technical and Supervisory group or the Public Services group. The constitution of the union is dual in character, the decision-making bodies being elected partly on a geographical basis and partly on an industrial or trade group basis.

53. College non-teaching staff belonging to the TGWU are organized locally into Branches which are generally local authority-based. Manual and white-collar workers (who belong to ACTS, the Administrative, Clerical, Technical and Supervisory section) are normally, though not invariably, in separate Branches. Workplace representatives or shop stewards are elected to represent the members on matters affecting their employment. District officers of the union are required to notify the employer concerned of the names of elected representatives. Branch members elect a Branch Committee to conduct the business of the Branch.

54. The trade group business of the union is conducted by Regional Trade Group Committees or District Committees. Where the trade group structure operates, non-teaching staff manual workers would come under the auspices of the Public Services Committee. Regional Committees are the principal committees of the TGWU Regions, of which there are 11 covering England, Ireland, Scotland and Wales. These are composed of representatives of each of the Regional Trade Group or District Committees. The Regional Committees constitute the first administrative co-ordinating link in the structure. The Trade Group or District Committees deal with matters specific to the type of employment they cover.

55. National Trade Groups or Section Committees are the principal trade bodies of the union. They are composed of members from the Regional Trade Group. These committees deal with the industrial interests of the group membership, formulate wages and conditions policies and develop organization.

56. The Biennial Delegate Conference is the supreme policy-making body within the union. The General Executive Council governs the union in between Conferences. The TGWU employs a team of full-time officials and staff at Head Office, Trade Group and Regional levels. The TGWU's affiliations include those to the TUC, the Irish Congress of Trade Unions, the Scottish TUC, the Wales TUC and the Labour Party.

57. **National and Local Government Officers' Association (NALGO) – 745,000 members**

The National and Local Government Officers' Association is the major union for white-collar non-teaching staff in further education. NALGO is the fourth largest trade union in Britain and claims to be the largest white-collar union in the world.

58. The basic unit of NALGO organization is the Branch, which is normally made up of members working in the same service in the same area. Some polytechnics, particularly those administered by more than one authority, may have their own Branch. In some institutions there are sub-branches, the powers of which are determined by the main Branches. The 1977 NALGO conference approved a report recommending the development of a steward system to facilitate better member representation at workplace level to increase the involvement of members and improve communications between members and the union. Many Branches operate a shop steward or workplace representative system but the pattern and level of development varies from Branch to Branch. Branch members elect officers and executive committees to run the Branch.

59. Each Branch sends representatives to a District Council. NALGO has 12 Districts covering England, Scotland and Wales. The Districts provide the main link between neighbouring Branches and the National Executive Committee. Each District Council has a local government committee which nominates NALGO members for the staff side of the Provincial Council (see paragraph 47) and other negotiating bodies, appoints or elects a member to the National Local Government Committee, discusses issues affecting other local government members within the District and policy relative to national agreements, co-ordinates Branch activity and formulates District policy.

60. At national level, NALGO's policy in respect of the salaries and conditions of service of members employed in local government is the responsibility of the National Local Government Committee. The main functions of this committee are: to nominate NALGO's representatives to the staff side of the NJC for APT & C staff (see paragraph 46) and other national bodies, such as the Local Government Training Board; to discuss national principles governing the conditions of service of local government staff and decide overall policy, to formulate claims for presentation to the employers, and to consider references from District Local Government Committees. The national committee has a number of sub-committees and is empowered to establish working groups to consider matters of importance to particular groups of staff.

61. There is also a National Joint Consultative Committee (local government) whose object is to secure co-operation between professional and sectional organizations in local government and NALGO, in all matters relating to conditions of service and other matters in which there is a common interest.

62. General policies of the union are decided by its Annual Conference. The Local Government Group meets on the first day of each Annual Conference to decide policy matters particular to local government. In between Conferences the National Executive Council conducts the work of the union.

63. NALGO employs a large number of full-time officers at national and district level. The senior professional officer covering college non-teaching staffs is the Local Government Service Conditions Officer. Full-time officers cover

each NALGO Branch. Some Branches have their own full-time administrators. NALGO is affiliated to the TUC, the Scottish TUC and Wales TUC. NALGO is also discussed in Section **8.**39, above.

64. **Union rules and membership**

Under s5 of the Trade Union and Labour Relations Act 1974 every worker has the right not to be excluded or expelled from membership of a trade union or branch or section of a trade union by way of arbitrary or unreasonable discrimination.[2] Exclusion or expulsion would not be deemed to be arbitrary or unreasonable if the worker is of a description different from that or those of the majority of the members of that union, branch or section, or does not possess the appropriate qualifications for membership. Any worker aggrieved by exclusion or expulsion can apply to an industrial tribunal for a declaration that he or she is entitled to be a member, and if the union branch or section does not implement such a declaration within a specified period or, if no period is specified, within a reasonable period, the worker has the right to apply to the High Court for an injunction, interdict or other relief (including compensation) which the Court may prescribe. The rights of employees not to have any action taken against them individually by an employer because of their membership of or participation in an independent trade union and their rights to time off for trade union duties and activities are dealt with in Section **11.6.**27 and 66.

65. On joining a union a member usually receives a copy of, or will certainly have access to, the union's rules. The rules of every trade union must contain provisions in respect of certain matters specified in s6 of the Trade Union and Labour Relations Act 1974. These include: the name of the union and address of its principal office; the objects for which the union was established; the purpose and manner in which its funds or property can be used or invested; the amount of any financial benefits available to members from union funds and the circumstances in which they are available; the manner in which the rules can be changed or revoked; arrangements for the election of the governing body, officers and officials, and for their removal from office; election and ballot arrangements; conditions of membership and application procedures; disciplinary procedures and penalties for offences; and the procedure for settling disputes between a member and the union or officer of the union. The Employment Bill published in December 1979 proposes that unions should carry out ballots, to be secret so far as is reasonably practicable, in certain circumstances including elections to full-time trade union officer posts, to the executive or other governing body and in relation to the amendment of union rules (see Section **11.6**, Appendix 7).

66. Most union rule books lay down the basis of organizational structure. The benefits and services for which members are eligible and the arrangements and procedures under which such benefits are made available are sometimes specified in rule books and usually also publicised through pamphlets, notes of guidance, training courses and the like. Unions normally have procedures,

2 cf also Section **12.6.** 39 n5.

for example, for determining when individual cases will be taken up which take into account the particular circumstances, the attitude of the Branch, and other matters; for handling problems when one member or group of members is in dispute with another member or group; and for making available legal assistance.

67. Every trade union has to keep proper accounts and is required to submit an annual return to the Certification Officer (see Section **11.6**, Appendix 1) who has to keep this available for public inspection. Every trade union is obliged at the request of any person to supply him or her with a copy of its rules and most recent annual return, either free of charge or on payment of a reasonable charge.

APPENDIX 1

NATFHE PUBLICATIONS[1]

Policy Statements

The Young Unemployed, 1977.
The Education, Training and Employment of the 16-19 Age Group, 1977.
Art and Design Education, 1978.
Teacher Education, 1978.
Higher Education, 1978.
The Education and Training of Teachers for Further and Higher Education, 1978.
Further and Teacher Education in a Multi-cultural Society, 1979.
Special Educational Needs. A response to the Report of the Committee of Inquiry into the Education of Handicapped Children and Young People, (Warnock Report), 1979.
Student Counselling, 1979.
Education for Adults, 1979.
The Future Development of College Government, !979.
The Education, Training and Employment of Women and Girls, 1980.
General Studies, 1980.
Submission to the Standing Commission on Pay Comparability, the Teachers' Panel of the Burnham Further Education Committee, 1979.

Discussion Papers
Assessment, 1977.
Education and Training for the 16-19s, 1979.

Journals
NATFHE Journal (monthly during term time).
Journal of Further and Higher Education (three issues a year).

Miscellaneous
Annual Reports.
Conference Resolutions.
Press and Public Relations Guide, 1977.
NATFHE Constitution and Rules.
Nurseries Photographic Exhibition.

A variety of recruitment, information, organization and campaigning material.

---

1 Details of the prices of these publications and order forms may be obtained from the Publications Officer, NATFHE, Hamilton House, Mabledon Place, London WC1H 9BH.

APPENDIX 2

ASSOCIATION FOR ADULT AND CONTINUING EDUCATION (AACE) – 2,600 MEMBERS

1. The Association for Adult and Continuing Education does not have direct representation on the Burnham Committee (though its General Secretary, who sits on the NATFHE Executive, is a member via NATFHE) but the organization does have an important union role and it seems appropriate, therefore, to include details of the structure of AACE as an appendix.

2. AACE is both a trade union and professional association. Details of the joint membership and partnership scheme between AACE and NATFHE are given in paragraph 13. AACE members are organized in Branches which are usually based on local authorities. (In Inner London there are a number of Branches in the scope of the ILEA). At adult education centre and institute level the Association is developing a representatives' system primarily for the purpose of building membership. Negotiations with centre or institute management are the responsibility of the Branch. NATFHE members engaged in adult education may become members of their local AACE Branch if they wish.

3. AACE negotiates at local authority level through the NATFHE Liaison Committee (see paragraph 21) on which it is entitled to one representative under the joint membership agreement. Branches are grouped into 13 Regions covering England and Wales. A National Executive Committee conducts the overall business of the Association.

4. National negiotiations on salaries, superannuation and conditions of service for adult education staff are conducted through NATFHE. A joint AACE/NATFHE committee draws up policy in these areas. AACE has an education policy and strategy committee which considers educational matters, draws up policy statements and responds to initiatives and developments in adult education. The Association is also represented on various education and salaries committees of NATFHE and on its National Council.

APPENDIX 3

INTERNATIONAL TEACHERS' ORGANIZATIONS

1. *World Confederation of Organizations of the Teaching Profession (WCOTP).* NATFHE is amongst the 120 or so national teachers' organizations from 80 countries which belong to the World Confederation of Organizations of the Teaching Profession. Founded in 1952 through a merger of three major international federations of teachers, WCOTP exerts independent political influence to promote equality of opportunity through education and quality in education, to defend the interests of teachers, to give expression to their views on educational and professional issues and to secure the advancement of their status. WCOTP seeks to encourage co-operation between the four international teachers' organizations. It is financed by its affiliates.

2. WCOTP co-operates with the United Nations and its specialised agencies, in particular, UNESCO and the International Labour Office, and maintains contacts with regional inter-governmental organizations such as the Commission of the European Communities, the Council of Europe and the Organization for Economic Co-operation and Development.

3. There are three other international federations of teachers. FISE (Fēdēration International Syndicat de l'Enseignment), IFFTU (International Federation of Free Teachers' Unions) and WCT (World Confederation of Teachers). FISE is numerically the largest organization with a membership based on the communist countries and with affiliates also from Asia, Africa and South and Central America. FISE and IFFTU are effectively the trade secretariats of the World Federation of Trade Unions and the International Confederation of Free Trade Unions. WCT is predominantly a body based on trade unions with close religious links, having membership only where trade unions are split by religion as well as politics.

APPENDIX 4

TEACHING AND NON-TEACHING STAFF UNION ADDRESSES

Association for Adult and Continuing Education
Honorary General Secretary: Mr S. Macdonald,
"Crossways",
Breachwood Green,
Hitchin,
Herts SG4 8PL

Association of Agricultural Education Staffs
General Secretary: Mr E.W. Yates,
43 St John's Road,
Mogerhanger,
Bedford MK44 3RJ

Association of Principals of Colleges
Honorary Secretary: Mr L.K. Street,
Principal's Office,
East Herts College,
Turnford,
Broxbourne,
Herts EN10 6AF

Association of Teachers in Penal Establishments
Joint Secretaries: Mr G. Todd,
1 Waltham Road,
Ravenshead,
Nottingham NG15 9FP
and
Mr J.D. Jones,
Tregastel,
Mile Street,
Usk, Gwent.

General and Municipal Workers' Union
National Officer, Local Government: Mr C. Donnet
Thorne House,
Ruxley Ridge,
Claygate,
Esher,
Surrey KT10 0TL

National Association of Teachers in Further and Higher Education
General Secretary: Mr P. Dawson,
Hamilton House,
Mabledon Place,
London WC1H 9BH

National and Local Government Officers' Association
Local Government Service/Conditions Officer: Mr. A. Jinkinson
NALGO House,
1 Mabledon Place,
London WC1H 9AJ

National Society for Art Education
General Secretary: Mr. D. Gleason
Champness Hall,
Drake Street,
Rochdale,
Lancs. OL16 1PB

National Union of Public Employees
National Officer, Local Government: Mr R. Bickerstaffe.
Civic House,
8 Aberdeen Terrace,
London SE3 0QY

Transport and General Workers' Union
National Secretary, Public Services: Mr M. Martin,
Transport House,
Smith Square,
London SW1P 3JB

World Confederation of Organizations of the Teaching Profession (WCOTP)
Secretary General: Mr J.M. Thompson,
3 Avenue du Moulin,
1110 Morges,
Switzerland

REFERENCE

Employment Protection (Consolidation) Act 1978, Chapter 44, HMSO.
Trade Union and Labour Relations Act, 1974, Chapter 52, HMSO.

Disputes Principles and Procedures, TUC, 1980 (a revised code on inter-union disputes).
Employee Relations: Reference Guide for Chief Officers and Managers in Local Authorities, Local Authorities Conditions of Service Advisory Board and Local Government Training Board, 1978.
The LACSAB Employee Relations Handbook, Local Authorities Conditions of Service Advisory Board, 1977.

Trade Union rule books have to be made available free or for a reasonable charge to any person on request. A list of union addresses is contained in Appendix 4.

Section 10

CURRICULUM IN FURTHER AND HIGHER EDUCATION

1 INTRODUCTORY NOTE

1. This Section is intended primarily to be descriptive. Its essential aim is to provide information concerning curriculum in further and higher education. The historical foundation of further education courses is response to a perceived need; curricula study as a whole has never yet been taken forward, and even the Further Education Curriculum Review and Development Unit has preferred to investigate areas where needs require fulfilling. For that reason, and because of both the constraints of space and the overall purpose of this book there is no significant discussion of curriculum philosophy. The extent to which our curriculum philosophy entails the provision of an education largely supportive of the state, whether it is dominated by the needs of industry, or how much of it represents a combination of the needs of society, vocational education and a skill-orientated tradition dating back to nineteenth century technical and elementary education as opposed to the "generalist" traditions of the grammar schools and universities, represent indeed serious and vital propositions in any consideration of the whole curriculum. To leave aside the full philosophical debate may seem a significant omission but it must also be appreciated that the fragmented and often *ad hoc* approaches to curriculum design made necessary by the very nature of further education makes difficult the consideration of any all embracing philosophy, if indeed one exists.

2. There are philosophies which will be apparent, however, from the following text. Similarly, while the prime descriptive aim remains, it is necessary to provide comment on current urgent issues. Consideration of 16-19 education, for example, since it is still developmental, must include some comment. However, comment is restricted mainly to the more readily encompassable issues: full debate, for example, of by whom courses should be run – colleges, local authorities, the DES, employers, the MSC – is one beyond the scope of this book. However, many of the constraints, sources and impetuses acting upon the curriculum will be apparent from other Sections. An indication of the development of further education can be gained from Sections **1.2** and **1.5**.

3. The extent to which curriculum design is a political, educational, social – or combined – process is one for the reader to determine. Certainly, until fairly recently, curriculum design may be described as having been largely intuitive and content based. While colleges have and continue to respond to needs, few – in specifically further education at least – have a specialist curriculum design support team. Pressures resulting on staff lead in turn, as well as to staff development, to pressures on LEAs and validating bodies. The Council for National Academic Awards (CNAA) and more especially the Technician Education Council (TEC) and the Business Education Council (BEC) as recently created validating bodies in higher and further education, represent major curriculum initiatives in the post school sector. Each of these bodies has issued guidelines on aspects of curriculum development. Each has been concerned to establish comparability with some existing component of the education and training system, yet each has been

concerned to establish a distinctive approach to curriculum design. Thus the CNAA sought to establish parity with university degree awards but at the same time was keen to see the establishment of innovatory part-time and sandwich degree courses. TEC and BEC are concerned to establish parity with existing technical and commercial sub-degree awards but each has postulated a distinctive (albeit different) approach to curriculum design. TEC has adopted a module (unit) structure based largely on well defined pre-requisites, behavioural objectives and analytical assessment plans. BEC has adopted a more integrated approach with compulsory inter-disciplinary studies and assessment. Within most FE colleges, at least two of these validating bodies have to be dealt with and most LEAs will come into contact with all three. Whilst all three bodies would deny that they are over-prescriptive in defining their own particular curriculum model, there is no lack of evidence to indicate that some teachers find them restrictive, confusing and demanding. These issues are therefore discussed below. One crucial issue which emerges is that of staff development. The array of courses, constant course development, and staff participation demonstrates that the need for planned, effective and coherent staff development is vital. A survey of practice and theory of staff development is contained in Section **11.11**.

4. The following sub-section has been edited from the contributions of three authors. Paul Bennett has written on the CNAA and Jean Bocock on higher education. Jack Mansell's work, however, represents by far the greatest contribution.

2 CURRICULUM IN FURTHER AND HIGHER EDUCATION

1. The range of curriculum in further education is immense. It stretches from an overlap with schools, to "vocational education" from operative through craft technician to graduate and professional qualifications, and postgraduate work. There are many agencies which impact on the curriculum at varying levels; there is no single mode of approach to the design of the whole of curriculum in further education; sources of curricula may be local, regional or national. The system includes work at all levels in the humanities and the sciences, and a vast range of activities for adults.

FURTHER EDUCATION AND THE SCHOOLS

2. **Linked courses**
Linked courses (links between schools and colleges) have been developed since 1969. Their number has grown to c.140,000 students, although that number is fairly stable. The courses enable school pupils to attend a college for one or one and a half days per week. Most courses are pre-vocational, and since they provide insights into occupational areas are sometimes referred to as "sampling" or "taster" courses. Some courses lead to a qualification, such as under the Mode III of the Certificate of Secondary Education (CSE) which may be used, for example, as a route into a City and Guilds of London Institute (CGLI) Craft course.[1] Linked courses facilitate effective co-operation and liaison between schools and colleges, and can also assist in the transition between school and work.

3. **CGLI Foundation Courses**
The CGLI sponsors one year full-time Foundation Courses. These are broad-based with a vocational content, and are designed for those of average ability who enter further education in preference to staying on at school. However, Foundation Courses can be provided by schools and colleges, both of which are free to design their own courses subject to CGLI approval. The vocational content of the courses is intended to give a basis for further vocational study. They are often provided on a linked basis, and have the advantages of being able to be adapted to local industrial and occupational needs and available for the use of the young unemployed.

4. **The Schools Council**
The Schools Council (for Curriculum and Examinations) is an independent body, established in 1964 to promote education by research and by reviewing curricula, methods and examinations in schools. Its structure was radically altered in 1978; this had the effect of reducing the teacher-majority in some sections of its committee structure. By definition the Council is concerned with the curriculum in *schools* but this embraces the 16-18 year age groups and as many further education colleges anyway offer schools-based examinations, a significant overlap exists between the interests of the Council and FE. Under the 1978 structure, a Higher and Further Education

---

1 CSE and CGLI are discussed in paragraphs 10 and 18, below.

Liaison Group was set up as an attempt to overcome the criticism that further education is inadequately represented on the Council, but on the other Council committees the further and higher education representation remains, perhaps unavoidably, minimal. Curriculum development is carried out by the Council. It is related to the schools examination system and to the promotion of other curriculum discussions, research and innovation. Much of this work appears sometimes to be undervalued. The Council's *Index* of research and development projects describes a formidable list of work ranging from pre-school to 18+ activities, covering subject areas such as English, Welsh, Humanities, Languages, Creative Studies, Mathematics and Science. The single-subject examination orientation of many of these projects cannot be denied. Although a number have their origin in CSE Mode III development, many other projects exist, including significant sections of work on inter-related studies and special education. At the 16-18+ area of overlap, in addition to the conventional school subjects, work of interest to many in further education exists in projects on General Studies, The Environment, Political Education, Engineering Science, Mass Media, Industry and Computers. The general awareness of further education teachers of the Council's curriculum development however, may not be high. There are good reasons for this: much of the material requires some translation into FE vernacular to be effective and this is not the responsibility of the Schools Council, which would undoubtedly maintain that it has yet to solve its own problems of effective dissemination and implementation of curricula ideas in the schools sector.

5. At the time of writing, the Council is developing its strategy for work in 1980-83. This will come under five broad headings:[2]
   (i) purpose and planning in schools;
   (ii) helping individual teachers to become more effective;
   (iii) developing the curriculum for a changing world;
   (iv) individual pupils; and
   (v) improving the examination system.

   Planning groups have been set up to produce programmes of work under these headings. It is interesting to note that in the guidelines for these groups an emphasis is apparent on links with the outside world, more effective dissemination and low-cost budgets. There is also a major shift from centrally conrolled to regionally and locally based schemes and diffusion centres.

6. **GCE "O" and "A" levels**

   Although General Certificate of Education (GCE) courses occupy only 16% of further education work, more than a quarter of all GCE students are in further education establishments. There are significant differences between colleges and schools in the organization and provision of GCE courses: college students have greater opportunity – because of greater college resources – to study subjects such as sociology, economics, and certain science subjects; sometimes college GCE courses differ because LEAs do

2 A more detailed description of the activities to be carried out under these headings will be found in the Schools Council's *Principles and Programmes* report, published in July 1979.

not allow duplication with school work; and since colleges cater for the whole community, its demands are reflected in course availability. The more adult atmosphere of a college, as well as its "second chance" provision, can be attractive to students of school leaving age.

7. There has been debate concerning proposals to replace the present GCE "A" level examinations by "N" (Normal) and "F" (Further) levels. These are single-subject, consecutive one year courses, involving the study of five subjects at two levels. Colleges have been included in the case studies used in the construction and testing of the proposed scheme.[3] The Secretary of State in June 1979 stated that "N" and "F" levels were not at present to be implemented: GCE "A" levels would remain.

8. At the time of writing, major proposals for a radical restructuring of the GCE and CSE examinations and their replacement by a common examination system were under consideration by the DES. The Secretary of State announced in February 1980 that the examination boards were to be merged and invited to devise national criteria to cover both the new 16+ syllabus and assessment. The new system, which is not expected to operate until 1986, will preserve "O" levels: the GCE boards will determine the top three grades. The present boards are to be reduced to five for GCE and five for CSE, the boards to arrange their own merging and regrouping. The present GCE boards consist of:
Oxford and Cambridge boards;
Welsh Joint Education Committee;
University of London;
Northern Universities' Joint Matriculation Board;
Associated Examining Board (AEB);
Southern Universities Joint Board; and
Northern Ireland Board.
Regional preferences are exercised in the choice of board examinations but in further education these are not so distinct as obtains for schools where local authority restrictions are often in force. Many colleges will deal with more than one board. However, the AEB is a board of great significance in further education. It was set up in 1953, and had its origins in the CGLI. Its creation was based on a desire to provide an examining body not coupled directly with a university, and the result has been a close association with further education.[4] Approximately 20% of GCE examining now takes place by way of the AEB. The structures and operation of the GCE boards are generally similar. Each has a general policy-making board supported by a sub-committee structure which deals with executive and educational matters. Each subject area has associated with it a subject panel serviced by a full-time administrator, and has the services of teachers and other educationalists who advise the board, the chief examiner and his or her assistant examiners as appropriate. There is an involvement of further education in GCE

---

3 cf "Examinations at 18+: The N and F studies", *Schools Council Working Paper* 60, Evans/Methuen Educational, 1978; *Examinations at 18+*, Schools Council Examinations Bulletin, 38, Evans/Methuen Educational, 1978.

4 see H.G. Earnshaw, *The Associated Examining Board – Origin and History*, AEB, 1974.

examining board subject committees and examining boards – particularly with the AEB. The growth of college GCE work may be attributed to the attractions of the teaching and other facilities, and also to the particular growth in the numbers of adults taking GCE examinations.

9. An alternative to GCE "A" levels is provided by the International Baccalaureate Diploma (IB). The IB differs from GCE "A" levels, for candidates are required to follow a grouped curriculum which consists of a broad range of subjects. An obstacle to the IB's growth has been the difficulty caused to some students by its mathematics requirements. An alternative mathematics course is now being devised. The IB is currently offered by several colleges. Since it has an appeal to overseas students and may well fulfil the needs of the proposed "N" and "F" levels since they are not be introduced, it may be that more institutions will make IB provision. However, the broad nature of the IB, as with "N" and "F" levels, may make it unattractive to evening and part-time students.

10. **CSE courses**

The 13 CSE boards serve sharply defined regional areas. The boards' constitution is specified by the Schools Council. CSE courses offered by further education colleges are on a scale much smaller than GCE provisions, and where colleges are associated with CSE examinations they act invariably through a local school. Whilst both the GCE and CSE boards offer syllabuses based on externally examined (Modes I/II) or internally set and examined and externally moderated (Mode III) examinations, the CSE boards encourage local curriculum development and internal examining to a greater degree than the GCE boards. Hence colleges involved in CSE courses of a linked nature are involved in such curriculum development.

11. **Certificate of Extended Education courses**

The CEE is available to both schools and colleges, and while analogous to the CSE is suited to older students. The basic concept of the CEE is a single subject examination, taken after a one year course of study, designed for students over 16 years of age who had gained broadly grades of 2 to 4 in CSE. A number of CEE pilot schemes have been introduced but the Secretary of State limited further development in 1976. However, in December 1979 the Keohane Committee[5] recommended that the CEE should be introduced nationally. The Report (*Proposals for a Certificate of Extended Education*, Cmnd. 7755, HMSO, 1979) states that all certificates should be introduced nationally (a proposal surprisingly rejected by the AMA in February 1980). The Report states that all certificates should include the

---

5 The Keohane Committee was set up in 1978 under the chairmanship of Professor K.W. Keohane, CBE, Rector of the Roehampton Institute of Higher Education, with the following terms of reference:
"To consider the Schools Council's proposals for a Certificate of Extended Education (CEE) in relation to other courses and examinations for those for whom the CEE is intended; to study and advise upon the pilot CEE schemes, to consider possible developments in the provision of relevant courses and examinations in schools and further education, and report to the Secretary of State."

results of obligatory proficiency tests in English and mathematics. The committee estimates that by 1991, the number of potential candidates for the CEE would be between 52,000 and 60,000. The committee intends the examination to cater for those whose examination achievements at 16 plus were in the range covered by CSE grades 2-4 who have no clear career intentions, wish to continue their education for a further year, and do not aspire to "A" levels. In stressing that it considers the preparation of young people for employment crucial, the committee observes that the taking or re-taking of "O" levels or CSEs is generally inappropriate (for such courses may, for example, have the disadvantages of representing the repetition of study or of being designed primarily for younger pupils). The Report stresses that if the one year course is to satisfy the needs of those about to start work, it must ensure basic communication and numerical skills, provide some element of vocational preparation, assist in the development of personal and social skills relevant to work and offer certification which will give such assurance to employers. The Keohane Report observes that the Schools Council's 1976 proposals do not satisfy adequately these requirements. It is recommended that the tests should be set by the examining boards and marked by schools and colleges. Marking is recommended to occur on two or three fixed dates, one of which would be at or near the beginning of the academic year. The Report states that CEE results should not be linked with "O" level or CSE grades; CEE certificates should list subjects which the candidates had "passed" or "passed with merit".

12. **Common examinations proposals: problems and comment**

Although the Secretary of State has stated that "N" and "F" levels will not be implemented, it is still appropriate to consider grounds on which they were criticised. Because "N" and "F" level courses are broadly based, they have an attraction to further education since they appear to be less dominated by the requirements of the universities. However, the former proposals of the Schools Council would be unsuitable to many further education students. If higher education institutions demanded two "Fs" and "Ns" as effective entrance requirements, this would impose too great a workload on part-time and particularly evening students in further education. Also, since many further education students undertake GCE or similar courses with very precise objectives – such as achieving the required entry qualifications to another course, the nature of the proposed examinations would for them be less satisfactory than the existing "A" level courses. The five subject basis of the proposed system would also cause difficulty for students who at present take one-year full-time "A" level courses at further education colleges. As well as these problems for part-time and adult students, the proposed system has also been criticised for making the present complex system still more complicated because of its implications for existing equivalences between general and vocational qualifications and entrance requirements to other courses. The question of equivalences raises that of grading. A Schools Council Report *(Standards in public examinations: problems and possibilities)* published in December 1979 states that any meaningful comparison of the results obtained by pupils in public examinations is impossible under the present grading system: employers, parents and other users of examination results are said to be confused by what public examinations meant, often attributing far too precise a degree of equivalence to examination results. In recommending the development of a new system under which grades awarded in GCE and CSE examinations would be based on a common set of nationally agreed criteria related to specific levels of attainment and mastery of skills, the report calls for a reduction and rationalization of the diversity of syllabuses and examinations, and the creation of nationally agreed grade definitions. There has, of course, been debate on this matter for some time. The Secretary of State's proposals (see paragraph 8) seem broadly to meet the Council's recommendations, but it appears at present that the Schools Council will not be significantly involved in establishing the new 16+ GCE and CSE examinations.

13. The discussion of the relationship of general and vocational education in the education of adolescents, which is certain to be sharpened as a result of the Keohane Report and the "O" level/CSE merger, should not obscure the debate concerning the need for a common system of examining at the age of 16 plus. The balance to be achieved is a system appropriate to the needs of two groups: school fifth year and above pupils; and also the considerable proportion of further education students, aged 16-18, adult, full-time and part-time who currently undertake at college the types of course provided by and under examining bodies for both schools and colleges.

VOCATIONAL EDUCATION: HIGHER EDUCATION

14. Colleges can be distinguished from schools in their provision for the 16 plus age group by the vocational courses which they operate. Non-advanced vocational courses, for example at operative and craft levels, can be either ends in themselves leading to or the development of skilled employment, or else to advanced courses in the same or another institution. Opportunities are considerable, and the curricula wide and varied.

15. **The Further Education Curriculum Review and Development Unit**

The Unit, generally known as the Further Education Unit (FEU) was established in 1977 as a long overdue response to the pressure of various bodies (including the APC and NATFHE) for a further education analogue to the Schools Council. The aim of the FEU is to contribute to the general development of further education curricula by:

(i) reviewing the range of existing curricula and identifying overlap, duplication and deficiencies;
(ii) determining priorities for action to improve the total provision and suggesting ways in which improvement can be effected;
(iii) carrying out specific duties, helping with curricular experiments, and contributing to the evaluation of objectives; and
(iv) disseminating information about the process of curriculum development in FE.

The FEU was initially set up by the DES (see Section **7.**16) in association with the 1976 policy on Unified Vocational Preparation (UVP) (see paragraph 73, below) and whilst the FEU has developed guidelines for UVP, its policy and action so far has ranged over a wider spectrum. It is independent of, but financed via the DES. Its basic reason for existence is to promote the rationalization of FE courses, to investigate inadequacies in provision and to suggest action for improvements. The FEU is tiny compared to the Schools Council, despite its function being similar. However, although the FEU is small and under resourced, it has produced work of value (for example, *A Basis for Choice*) and has demonstrated its ability to act effectively. It has a Board of Management of 12 members representing the local authorities, the TUC, industry and training services, teachers in further and higher education (NATFHE is represented), the educational departments of England, Wales and Northern Ireland, and it has an observer from the Schools Council. The Unit has a full-time Director, backed by a full-time staff of twelve including five development officers on secondment from the FE/training field. As such its full-time staff is less than one-tenth of the Schools Council. As a matter of priority the Board chose to concentrate on areas of non-advanced further education (NAFE) and initially much of its attention has been concerned with vocational preparation. Consequently its major publications have related to the Youth Opportunities Programme (YOP) (see Section **4.**12, and paragraph 84, below), UVP and one-year full-time pre-employment courses.[6] Mention is made in paragraphs 73 and 87 of the work done on social and life skills by the Unit. A full-time development officer is engaged on evaluating some aspects of the Technician Education Council (TEC), and a similar evaluation of the work of the Business Education Council work is planned. In addition to these projects, the Unit has also commissioned other studies, mainly though not entirely, related to the 16-19 age group: low level courses in ILEA[7], day-release, styles of curriculum development and the learning strategies of young people are projects in hand. Many of these studies are near completion and future plans include more work on the curriculum opportunities for women and girls, staff development, industrial tutors and caring courses.

16. With an annual budget of the order of £¼m, there is a limit to the output of the Unit. There is also, perhaps inevitably, a problem with respect to dissemination and awareness of the Unit's activities, but an experimental link

---

6 *A Basis for Choice*, FEU, 1979, describes a curriculum structure for 16+ school-leavers who are as yet uncommitted to a particular vocation. By specifying a common core of learning and a standardised profile method of describing achievement, the report claims that some form of national validation is possible, thus reducing the confusion and disparity that now exists in this area of pre-employment courses. [This report, the Mansell Report, is a significant document, for it identifies a possible core curriculum for all young people and takes into account the demands of adult and working life. Ed. See Section **1.5** and cf Bob Doe, "Mansell may be the core that Whitehall wants". *TES*, 23/11/1979].

7 ILEA's Curriculum Development Project in Communication Skills has aroused considerable interest and stimulated some lower-level course development in further education. A number of college based workshops have been set up to develop teaching materials. Garnett College's Research and Development Unit comes under the aegis of the ILEA.

with the West Midlands Advisory Council through a Regional Curriculum Unit may, if extended, help this problem. In the meantime, its output over two years is at least respectable, and is increasing. The Unit was threatened with closure in 1979 as part of public expenditure restraint, but at March 1980 it appeared to have survived.

17. It is now appropriate to begin consideration of the examining and validating bodies in further education. These will be discussed within the pattern of the major further education examining and validating bodies at present. It should be noted however that this approach is adopted for reasons of clarity, and not with the implication that all curricula is based upon sources determined by authority. Much of a college's curriculum development is home grown to meet the needs of individuals or target groups as identified by local employers, local community groups, or the college. In many cases a need is identified, and a matching course found.

18. **The City and Guilds of London Institute**
The CGLI was founded in 1878[8]. It is an independent body occupying a dominant position in technical examining, particularly at craft level. It deals with approximately half a million candidates yearly through about 850 different examinations in over 200 different subject areas. Established by the Livery Companies "to provide and encourage education adapted to the requirements of all classes of persons engaged, or prepared to engage, in the manufacturing or other industries", it is today predominantly an examining rather than a providing body. It still has links with Imperial College London and with the Livery Companies but over 90% of its income is now derived from examining and testing fees. It examines through over 1000 educational and training institutions in the UK and overseas. Like other examining bodies it operates via a structure of senior committees and subject area committees, with panels of lay members responsible for examining and moderating; in all of these industrial representation is significant.

19. Over the last decade the Institute has developed a comprehensive and increasingly sophisticated system of objective testing. In 1968, largely as a result of the Industrial Training Act 1964, the CGLI set up a Skills Testing Service through which it provides mainly practical tests for training and other interests outside the conventional FE system. Since 1973 it has progressively taken over the function of administering the Joint Committee National Certificate and Diploma schemes (see paragraph 25) and the administering responsibility for TEC and BEC. Although retaining a predominant position in craft education, the Institute is progressively phasing out many of its technician-level schemes in favour of the Technician Education Council. On the other hand it is developing an increasing role in the area of 14-18 pre-employment and training schemes. Its Foundation Course, available for use at the school-college interface, is a major example of this type of activity. In 1978 the Institute modified its structure of awards and now offers a senior Licentiateship award which reflects the significant

---

8 To celebrate its centenary, the CGLI published in 1978 a special *Broadsheet* describing its development over the last hundred years.

number of schemes at advanced level offered by the Institute, such as in supervisory and instructional skills. Although the content of some of its schemes involves an element of in-course assessment (and often this has to be devised by the college) other schemes allow local curriculum options to be generated by colleges in response to the needs of local industry and, should a need be large and consistent enough to justify the generation of a separate local scheme, colleges can apply for a special CGLI certificate. These can produce within colleges a considerable amount of curriculum activity. In general the production of vocational schemes by the CGLI is acknowledged to be a major factor in determining technical skill levels in most of our conventional trades.

20. **The Royal Society of Arts**

The RSA was established in 1734; it has examined since 1854. It is concerned mainly with commercial education and skill at "craft" level but like the CGLI it examines over a wide range of subjects at all levels including computer studies, languages, English as a foreign language (EFL) and teacher training. It provides for over 500,000 subject entries each year, tending to concentrate on single-subject examinations rather than a more prolonged and integrated course structure. Its committee structure comprises a Council, an Examining Board and subject-area Advisory Committees. It examines within and without the FE system and is involved overseas. Like the CGLI it is concerned with vocational preparation at school and college level: it has worked in conjunction with the CGLI and Schools Council on the Foundation Course and CEE. Unlike the CGLI, the RSA has been involved in examining at National Certificate level but much of its "technician" level work is likely to pass over to BEC. Indeed, the RSA suffered a political set-back when the Haslegrave Report[9] recommended that the CGLI undertake the administration of both TEC and BEC. The RSA is involved in Mode II and Mode III examining in schools and colleges: it validates experimental schemes in conjunction with local authorities and colleges. The RSA is thus a major provider of curricula and is undoubtedly the predominant certifying body in clerical and secretarial skills.

21. **The Regional Examining Bodies**

These comprise six examining boards which, with the exception of the Welsh Joint Education Committee (WJEC), generally restrict their examining and curricula activities to the post-school sector. They are:
East Midland Educational Union (EMEU);
Northern Counties Technical Examinations Council (NCTEC);
Union of Educational Institutions (UEI);
Union of Lancashire and Cheshire Institutes (ULCI);
Welsh Joint Education Committee (WJEC);
Yorkshire and Humberside Council for Further Education (YHCFE).

9 *Report of the Committee on Technician Courses and Examinations*, HMSO, 1969. Chaired by Dr H.K. Haslegrave (former Vice-Chancellor of Loughborough University of Technology), its main recommendations were to set up a Technician and a Business Education Council, to be administered by the CGLI. A note of dissent by Mr W.F. Crick in the Report objected to the CGLI administering BEC, but in the eventual implementation of this report in 1973, the majority recommendation prevailed.

These boards, by definition, are much more locally based than are the nationally based bodies. Their membership reflects this and they have strong links with local colleges, industry and commerce. The REBs examine in a variety of subjects, both technical and commercial. As such they overlap and sometimes complete with bodies like the CGLI and RSA. Much of the competition with the CGLI has, over the years, been restricted by a concordat agreement, which has been revised from time to time, but significant overlap remains.

22. The Haslegrave Report recommended that the CGLI and Regional Examining Bodies should consider "...drawing closer together to form a unified administrative organisation for the examination, testing and general assessment of performance." This pressure to rationalize their activities has increased with the setting up of TEC and BEC, under which the REBs have no specific examining or validating role in technician education. Consequently, almost without exception, the REBs have since 1974 re-structured themselves and on occasion merged with Regional Advisory Councils for Further Education (see paragraph 23). With the CGLI, the REBs set up a Council of Technical Examining Bodies (CTEB) in 1955, which over the period 1968-73, under the DES Administrative Memorandum 25/67,[10] played an important role in preparing new and revised schemes to fit the training recommendations being issued by the Industrial Training Boards. Of recent years, however, the CTEB has been virtually moribund but at the time of writing it appears likely that in 1980 a new CTEB agreement will exist, establishing a framework for a national examination system sponsored by the CGLI and the REBs. Such a system will cover England and Wales and will have the primary tasks of identifying education and training needs, the development of appropriate syllabuses, and their examination and certification. Cross representation between the CGLI and REBs will increase. A uniform fee structure and method of certification will be worked towards. REBs will still examine on a regional basis but it is generally anticipated that overlap and competition with the CGLI will be eliminated eventually, and that the curriculum development role of the regional bodies will expand. The position of the REBs vis-a-vis the RSA, which is not a member of CTEB, will presumably remain unchanged.

23. **The Regional Advisory Councils**

The RACs are associated with the following regions:-

London and Home Counties;	East Anglian;
Southern Counties;	*Yorkshire and Humberside;
South West;	*North West;
*West Midlands;	Northern Counties;
East Midlands;	*Wales.

(*These RACs have a definite organizational relationship with a Regional Examining Board).

The functions of the RACs are numerous but in the main they are concerned with providing a forum between further and higher education, industry and

10 *Joint Planning of Industrial Training and Associated Further Education*, DES Administrative Memorandum 25/67, 25 October 1967.

commerce, and with advising on the provision of further education. They make recommendations with respect to the location of advanced courses (invariably with DES support via a regional staff inspector) and some RACs have a machinery concerned with the location of non-advanced courses. Their role in teacher training may become more significant since the issue of Circular 11/77, concerning further education teather training (see Section **11.12**); a further explanation of their role and the debate concerning their future is contained in Section **8.**65.

24. On curriculum, the RACs are required to publish reports and memoranda, to stimulate research and to arrange conferences. Some RACs do generate curriculum activity. RACs have set up workshops on new techniques required, such as the writing of objectives; they sponsor working groups of FE teachers concerned with various aspects of curriculum implementation such as laboratory work in a given area; some, through an associated REB, support new examination concepts such as the Certificate of Further Education (CFE).[11] The Yorkshire and Humberside Council for FE has developed a special course for industrial operatives (TRADEC)[12] and the West Midlands Advisory Council has set up in conjunction with the Further Education Unit a Regional Curriculum Unit, whose activities are co-ordinated by a full-time development officer. RACs therefore can be concerned with curriculum development; but this type of involvement is generally *ad hoc* and varies considerably from region to region. Their relationship with the national examining and validating bodies is tenuous: some are represented on various committees of these bodies but their influence on curriculum at this level is indeterminate.

25. **The Joint Committee for National Certificates and Diplomas**

The Haslegrave Report considered that the pattern of technician courses was unsatisfactory, providing as it did for considerable overlap in technician courses arising from CGLI and Joint Committee courses, and recommended new national administrative and co-ordinating machinery. This led to the creation of the Technician Education Council (TEC) and the Business Education Council (BEC). It involved the phasing out of Joint Committee courses as well as those of the CGLI already referred to. Especially in the case of the National Certificates, this has caused some controversy. The National Certificate Scheme was set up in 1921 with, what was then, Board of Education sponsorship. It had three basic aims, which summarised are:

(i) to provide a qualification of national standing;

(ii) to provide a high degree of teacher participation; and

(iii) to provide well qualified personnel for industry.

---

11 The CFE is a one year full-time vocational course devised by the REBs. It is broad-based; open to students of average ability; and aims to enhance a student's employment prospects, allowing the student to make an informed career choice and, where possible, to have a transferability value into other FE courses. The CFE is more structured than the CEE, and it can provide a more direct route to other vocational courses. There are two specific CFE schemes (in engineering/construction and pre-nursing) but its future remains uncertain. It will be affected by the outcome of the debate referred to in paragraph 12, above.

12 TRADEC (Trade - Education) is a course structure, covering Mechanical Trades Principles, details of which are published by the Yorkshire and Humberside Council for Further Education.

26. Each course structure is administered by a Joint Committee comprising representatives of industry, commerce, professional institutions, teachers and other educationalists, with DES representatives (invariably HMI). In some cases the DES provided the secretariat: in others, appropriate professional institutions provided this service. It is possible under this system for colleges to prepare their own syllabuses and examination schemes to meet local needs. Such curricula, provided they were compatible with published guidelines, were approved by the appropriate Joint Committee. Course work and final examinations were college set and externally moderated by an "assessor" appointed by the Joint Committee. In many respects this system, providing as it did for local college curriculum development and a high degree of internal control, was remarkably progressive. Some would maintain that over the years the system did not always manage to keep pace with the growing complexity of curriculum change: standards of moderation within and between Joint Committees were claimed to be too variable. The changes in structure brought about by the 1961 White Paper, *Better Opportunities in Technical Education,* (see Section **1.5**), the growth in CGLI technician courses, the effective demoting of many Higher National Certificates by the professional institutions and greater opportunities available via CNAA courses, were some of the other factors which, during the late 1960s, tended to reduce the popularity of sections of the Joint Committee system. There is little doubt that the Joint Committee system represented a significant stage in curriculum development in further and higher education. The Certificates at Ordinary and Higher Level were based on part-time day release and so complemented a growing industrial experience on the job. This part-time route did and does produce in good quality students a blend of technical and operational knowledge that made a valuable contribution to productive manpower in the UK. In 1971 the Ordinary National Diploma in Technology (Engineering) represented a brave attempt to bring at least part of the Joint Committee system more into line with the demands of modern curriculum design: meant as a technological alternative to university entrance via "A" levels it has proved to be a demanding course. Although not entirely successful in numerical terms, it nevertheless provided in the colleges an example of a progressive curriculum development in which staff could participate.

27. **The Technician Education Council**

TEC was set up in 1973 as a registered limited company, DES funded, but with the aim of ultimate self sufficiency secured by fee payments. TEC arose from the main recommendations of the Haslegrave Report. Its terms of reference are largely concerned with the development of policies in technical education: to plan, administer and keep under review the development of a unified national system of technician courses; to devise or approve suitable courses, establish and assess standards of performance and to award certificates and diplomas as appropriate. It has a committee structure responsible to its Council, comprising representatives of industry, the local authorities and teachers. Its curriculum policy is now guided by an Education Committee and its implementation is via a series of sector and programme committees. TEC published its major policy statement in 1974 and its courses are being progressively introduced into colleges, replacing the CGLI and Joint Committee courses described above.

28. From the outset TEC has concentrated on its role as a validating rather than as an examining body. TEC considers its function to be (thus saving resources), to review and innovate, and to endorse initiatives from colleges and other bodies. It has adopted a curriculum design model based largely on a behaviourist approach, requiring syllabuses to be defined in terms of aims and objectives and accompanied by a systematic plan of assessment based on an analysis of those objectives. Its preferred curriculum structure is modular, based on *Units* of study at various levels, each unit subject to the design and assessment explained above. An approved combination of units, validated by an appropriate TEC committee, makes up a programme which, on satisfactory completion by the student gains him or her an award. TEC has adopted four basic awards: Certificate; Higher Certificates; Diploma and Higher Diploma, having a range of entry qualifications starting at CSE grade 3. There are two types of TEC course approach: the Standard Units prepared by TEC, and the TEC validated Units which are designed in colleges. Notwithstanding the issue of numerous Guidelines, Circulars and Standard Units, the amount of curriculum development required by the colleges has been considerable. The consequential burden of the validation of individual college programmes by TEC has also proved to be formidable. The adoption of this particular curriculum model has proved to be a particularly demanding task for the colleges, especially for those with little or no experience of design and assessment. The task of maintaining standards represents to TEC a complex moderating function, and in much of its work effective moderating is essential.

29. Most students on TEC courses follow Certificate courses, the minimum entry to which is completion of a five year secondary school course and the attainment of a standard recommended by the appropriate programme committee. This standard is roughly comparable to that of the ONC, and falls between that of Parts I and II of CGLI Technicians' Certificate. TEC Diploma entry requirements are similar, although the Diploma consists of a broader range of studies. A successful Certificate student can add the necessary units, or else qualify in additional endorsement procedures, to obtain a Diploma. Higher Certificate and Higher Diploma entry is based on either TEC certificates and diplomas or else GCE "O" and "A" levels. Higher Certificate may be taken by a two year day-release course, and the Higher Diploma by a two-year full-time or sandwich course.

30. College TEC programmes have to contain a significant (15%) element of general and communication studies; all TEC programmes have to contain health and safety material to complement the training which employers are obliged to provide (see Section **11.10**). By means of a system of "levels", entry qualifications to subsequent stages of a TEC programme can be attained: a level is ascribed to a particular unit so that a means of comparison

with other units is available. TEC awards, therefore, are intended to allow both vocational and academic progress, with standards safeguarded, and to allow a progression which can reach from the minimum entry level to a higher award (and, for example, if the Finniston Report is implemented (see Section **1.5**) a progression to high professional qualification).

31. **Review of TEC progress**

TEC's tasks have not been easy. Its progress is reviewed here since, as a new major force, some discussion is essential. This discussion should not be taken to imply that the previous, and other continuing course systems are above reproach: certain CGLI courses, for example, have aroused considerable controversy. In a short time TEC has validated a wide range of courses. The necessary speed of action has brought with it certain problems for colleges. These may be summarised as:

(i) *Resources*

Since TEC allows colleges considerable discretion in the composition of curricula, assessment practices of necessity vary (and have been criticised in some instances) but more important, perhaps, is that because of its own lack of resources TEC cannot always offer an external examination to the colleges which want one. As TEC has to be satisfied that colleges and staff can provide the resources for a programme, it has had to attempt to control colleges' own assessement procedures. This has put considerable pressure upon college staff. College submissions to TEC involve invariably a considerable amount of paper-work. This burden has involved great difficulties for teaching and administrative staff at a time when financial restraints do not allow the resources and facilities for the tasks effectively to be carried out. There has also been criticism of TEC for both the expense of its own structure, and the resources wasted by duplication of functions.

(ii) *Course provision*

Although an intention of TEC was to replace CGLI and National Certificate and Diploma courses, in the case of the latter concerns have been expressed. One criticism is that TEC's minimal entry requirement, while generous, in certain circumstances might disbar a student from course entry whereas previously a course would have been available. It seems that it will be some time before TEC courses replace the OND and HND. Some colleges have argued that whereas TEC courses provide routes to higher education, their design in certain subjects does not, as obtains in the OND Technology (Engineering) course for example, allow transference to higher education. It can generally be said that arrangements for the replacement of the HNC and HND, both concerning their nature and speed, are current causes of concern.

(iii) *Representation*

TEC has been criticised for the under-representation of the education service in its structures. However, at the curriculum level (for example in syllabus design) there is considerable teacher involvement, as can be seen from the TEC *Directory*, and further involvement is clearly possible.

(iv) *Curriculum*

TEC has been criticised for giving the impression in its procedural conduct that structure is more important than the curriculum. This may or may not be fair, but without doubt TEC has a commitment to curriculum design based on behavioural objectives. This may be both educationally desirable and an invaluable aid to assessment, but critics have maintained that procedural precision must not be assumed to be a substitute for good teaching. Whether the criticism is valid or not, the relative novelty of the behavioural objectives approach indicates a need for appropriate staff development. The concern which has been expressed about overall standards is also one which clearly demands attention.

32. TEC's progress has nonetheless been impressive, and its tasks enormous. It affords great opportunities, and has stimulated curriculum development. The brief review above is intended to be constructive. Many interests have to be brought together; none would dispute the aim of promoting better education.[13]

33 The Business Education Council

BEC was set up in 1974, arising out of the main recommendations of the Haslegrave Report. Its terms of reference are similar, but not identical, to those of TEC: they require the planning, administration and review of a unified system of non-degree courses; to devise or approve suitable courses, establish and assess standards of performance and to award certificates and diplomas as appropriate. As such, BEC is able to cover both "craft" and "technician" levels of education in so far as these terms are applicable to business education, and to interpret "business" as including education, other than the technical and scientific, for work in industry, commerce, and local and central government. Its committee structure, responsible to Council,

---

13 Review of TEC's progress can be found in Patricia Santinelli, "Two part revolution of 1960s comes to fruition," *THES*, 27/1/1978; J. Mansell, "TEC: NATFHE Opinion", *NATFHE Journal*, October 1976, pp 8-9; J. MacRory *et al*, "Backwards from TEC", *Journal of Further and Higher Education*, Vol.1, No.1, Spring 1977, p.3; Keith Ebbutt, "What is to be done about TEC", *NATFHE Journal*, March 1977, p.14; J.R. Rudling, "Should anything be done about TEC?", *NATFHE Journal*, October 1977; and L.M. Cantor and I.F. Roberts, *Further Education Today A Critical Review*, Routledge and Kegan Paul, 1979, pp 57-70. Cantor and Roberts provide a well researched and considered appraisal of TEC. Although supportive of TEC, NATFHE is concerned about its nature and progress. An indication of this can be found in the number of resolutions appearing at NATFHE conferences:
In 1977 a resolution was carried indicating that Conference was disturbed at the introduction of these new course structures without adequate consultation and remission. The resolution instructed the National Executive to negotiate for extra staff and facilities, adequate representation on TEC/BEC committees and a variety of safeguards concerning the students.
In 1978 three resolutions devoted to TEC/BEC were given a high priority. These were concerned again with resources, remission standards and "the undue haste" with which these courses were being introduced. A delay of implementation of these courses was supported, should extra resources not be made available. In 1979 two resolutions were passed, again expressing concern at the lack of resources, opportunities, representation, standards and the burden of assessment. NATFHE is not the only source of discontent: in October 1979 the East Midlands RAC sent to TEC a catalogue of complaints on TEC validation procedures.

comprises the usual senior committees responsible for Finance, Educational Policy, Planning, *et cetera,* (although the structure is based upon the named committees) together with a number of Boards responsible for the development and implementation of curriculum in various sectors of the business world.

34. BEC published its first policy statement in 1976 and its major *Initial Guidelines* statement in 1977. As such its courses are being introduced into colleges some two years later than those of TEC. It has adopted three basic levels of awards: General, National and Higher National, having entry requirements ranging from none to "O" and "A" levels respectively. For each level of award there is a Certificate or Diploma. Like TEC the differences between Certificates and Diplomas are claimed to be based on breadth rather than on depth of study. BEC General Certificate and Diploma courses are largely designed to provide "second chance" opportunities (hence there are no formal entry requirements), and are aimed at providing a broad educational foundation stressing literacy and numeracy.

35. The curriculum model adopted by BEC appears more pragmatic that the strict analytical approach of TEC. It uses a course structure comprising core and optional modules. The core modules are compulsory study-areas concerned with Money, People, Communication and Problem Solving. The assessment system is part external and part internal, the latter including in some cases requirements from BEC to set up cross-modular assignments and oral tests. Again, as for TEC, internal assessments will be externally moderated.

36. BEC National Certificate and Diploma courses take students to present ONC and OND Business Studies level. The former BEC course takes two years part-time. These courses recruit at credit level from the General courses, or the equivalent of at least four "O" levels. National level qualifications, or a combination of GCE "O" and "A" levels, lead to the Higher National courses. Study time for Higher National courses is the same as for national courses, and minimum entry requirements for both may be waived according to circumstance. BEC awards are recognised for entry to DipHE and degree courses (and also as carrying exemptions from both degree courses and the examinations of professional and qualifying bodies). BEC awards may be gained by way of a variety of study patterns.

37. **Review of BEC progress**

This review is undertaken, as in the case of TEC, because of the novelty, scope and impact of BEC. Again, previous and continuing course systems, concerning the RSA, for example, have aroused controversy. While much of BEC's approach differs from that of TEC, many of the criticisms have a similar base:

(i) *Resources*

BEC's progress is not as advanced as that of TEC (one reason being that there was less foundation on which to build) but it is clear that its courses entail and will enable substantial organizational change. This in turn, requires resource support – for example, in staff development and teaching materials.[14]

(ii) *Representation*

Although BEC has consulted colleges, and undertaken substantial consultation generally, there has been criticism that it has not involved sufficiently those who will be teaching its courses.

(iii) *Curriculum*

While many will support BEC's view that a broad rather than subject base is necessary, one consequence is the need for staff to be prepared to undertake such teaching. Whereas TEC has included an assessed element (of at least 15%) of general studies in its Certificate and Diploma courses, BEC's attitude is that general studies need not be imposed, and are at the college's discretion. Together with the development (in both TEC and BEC schemes) of more easily assessed communications skills courses, there is a concern that – while the acquisition of communications skills is necessary and important – it should not be at the expense of general studies courses which aim at the personal development of the individual and his or her increased understanding of society. As with TEC, there is a concern that the curriculum should not be so constrained as not to allow some freedom in the development of learning processes. Since BEC aims to fulfil employer needs, identification of those needs is clearly important. The curriculum development task falling on the colleges has proved to be a complex and demanding one, bringing in its wake a similar articulation of stress to that described above in connection with TEC.

38. It is important also to remember that the Haslegrave Report, which gave rise to both TEC and BEC, did point out that while a single body might not be acceptable to all concerned, it admitted equally that such an arrangement might be appropriate, and accordingly framed its recommendations so that such an event would not be more difficult to achieve.[15] Differences between the Councils have already created problems in joint TEC/BEC schemes where issues concerning entry levels, college participation and grades of pass have proved difficult to resolve. Although BEC has perhaps the major promotional task, (business education has never had, for example, the tradition of day-release that existed in technical education) both Councils are investigating innovatory study methods and both are to some extent committed to distance-learning techniques (see Appendix 1).

---

14 As a reflection of its concern that curriculum innovation should be adequately resourced, a 1979 NATFHE resolution was "not to implement BEC Higher or National Schemes until the following additional resources are provided..."

15 Review of BEC's progress can be found in: Santinelli, *op.cit;* G. Mace, "BEC – Which Way Now?", *NATFHE Journal*, August/September 1977, p.7; D. Brace, "General Studies versus Communication" *Liberal Education*, No.35, 1978, pp 18-22; P. Morris, "The Proposals of the Business Education Council: A Critical Appraisal of BEC as an Exercise in Curriculum Development, *Journal of Further and Higher Education*, Vol.1, No.3, Winter 1977, p.6, and Cantor and Roberts, *op.cit.* As in its attitude to TEC, NATFHE is generally supportive but has concerns about representation, resources and support. The differences between TEC and BEC in terms of awards and grades of certification do not in the Association's opinion contribute to the hope that the two Councils might eventually merge.

39. **Professional bodies**

Professional bodies cover many fields from learned professions such as law, and through a variety of trades. The major associations exercise control over the particular profession with which they are concerned and qualify individuals to act in a professional capacity. Professional bodies therefore have a strong influence on the content of many courses and many colleges and polytechnics offer courses leading to professional qualifications. Often these examinations are set by the professional body itself. The range is extremely wide: from social work qualifications to those in engineering or accountancy. Many professional institutions accept recognised qualifications as partial or complete exemption from their own examinations (as do elements of the armed services) and most publish a list of degrees or qualifications which they accept. [16]

40. Many professional and sub-professional institutions hold examinations concerned with membership; the Civil Service holds examinations for entry into the service; certain areas of industry, such as mining and sea-going, use examinations as a statutory safeguard of either safety and/or essential competence. The Board of Trade is concerned with the issue of mariners' qualifications and there are many other occupations, apart from those obviously in the field of medicine which require either statutory or quasi statutory certificates prior to practice. The standard school or college-based examinations tend in these cases only partially to contribute towards these qualifications and further study and/or accredited experience is required.

41. Among the best known professional bodies are the Institute of Chartered Accountants, the Hotel, Catering and Institutional Management Association, the Royal Institute of Chemistry, the Institute of Bankers, the Institute of Marketing, and the Council of Engineering Institutions. A considerable amount of college work is concerned with professional bodies' courses. Indeed, in some polytechnics, such work can form a considerable proportion of the institutions' work.

42. **The Council for National Academic Awards**

The CNAA was established by Charter in 1964, following a recommendation in the Robbins Report on Higher Education. The principal purpose of the CNAA is to validate higher education courses and award degrees and diplomas to students in maintained institutions outside the university sector. The Council also awards degrees based on research. It took over the role of the National Council for Technological Awards, and had from the outset a much wider scope than its predecessor. The scope of the CNAA has continued to expand in recent years with, for example, its expansion into teacher education and, following its amalgmation in 1974 with the National Council for Diplomas in Art and Design, its responsibility for the award of

---

16 Lists and reviews of the main professional bodies and the courses which they operate may be found in ed. Barbara Priestley, *British Qualifications*, Kogan Page, 1977; the *Careers Encyclopedia*, Cassell; and *The CRAC Job Book*, Hobsons Press. A critical survey is contained in W. Bonney Rust and H.F.P. Harris, *Examinations: Pass or Failure*, Pitman, 1967.

degrees in art and design. The CNAA is also responsible for Diploma in Management Studies courses.

43. The CNAA operates to a considerable extent through its subject boards and panels, which include teachers from both the public sector of higher education and the universities. Nominations are invited from university departments, from further education institutions with degree courses in the subject area, and, for teacher education degree courses, the relevant teachers' associations. The Council requests nominations and then selects from the nominations received, attempting to ensure not only coverage of all aspects of the subject area, but also a geographical spread of representatives. The boards consider degree course submissions put to them by institutions. These submissions are generally subjected to a process of rigorous scrutiny including visits to the institutions concerned (see paragraph 46 below). However, the system does allow individual institutions, and faculties or schools and departments within them, considerable scope in the planning of courses and, once the CNAA is satisfied with the standard of the course and the staffing resources of the institution, in the operation of the courses. Examination papers are marked within institutions and submitted to external examiners, with the CNAA monitoring results to check on standards.

44. The CNAA system has achieved a considerable degree of flexibility and variety in course patterns and modes of study (including part-time and modular) in entrance requirements and assessment techniques. It has assisted institutions in obtaining additional resources, and has also promoted a much greater amount of planning, including in many instances greater participation by teachers than existed hitherto. In the introduction to its *Principles and Regulations* the Council states that "while the Council remains sensitive to the differing traditions of undergraduate study out of which its work has developed, it is also sensitive to the evolution of course design and it welcomes a considerable diversity of course patterns depending on the aims and objectives of the courses concerned."[17]

45. In preparing CNAA submissions, institutions will need to consider a number of factors:
   (i) objectives of the course in academic and, where appropriate, in vocational or professional terms, and in the context of the overall regional or national demand for courses of that type;
   (ii) the level and integration of the components and the years of the course, and progression within the course;
   (iii) the resources (including staff) required both within the teaching departments or other units concerned, and in the institution as a whole (for example, whether the number of relevant books is held in the library, or the necessary quality and quantity of laboratory accommodation is available);
   (iv) methods of assessment, in their relationship to the objectives of the

---

17 Introduction to *Principles and Regulations for the award of the Council's First Degree and Diploma in Higher Education*, CNAA 1979.

course and the balance between examinations, project work and course work;

(v) relations with other courses within and outside the institution concerned, in particular with linked DipHE and degree courses, and modular and combined studies schemes; and

(vi) in the organization of multi-disciplinary courses in the increasing number of degree course submissions in which the study of two or more subjects is involved, the Boards concerned are likely to look for evidence of a well thought out course clearly based on either an integrated inter-disciplinary approach or a multi-disciplinary approach in which the subjects are studied quite separately. Adequate provision for meetings of teaching teams will also be needed where these are based in more than one school or faculty.

46. The CNAA boards or panels and secretariat have generally been willing to offer more or less formal advice to institutions prior to the finalising of a written submission. The CNAA may respond to the submission with a written response, followed by a relatively informal meeting between a small delegation from the institution and a few representatives of the validating board or panel. Alternatively, the course team may wish to respond in writing to criticism of the submission made by the CNAA. Following these stages, the CNAA will send a visiting party to the relevant board or boards who are likely to ask searching questions about the aspects of new courses outlined in paragraph 45. The visit is clearly more productive if the course team has given thought to the provision of background information to be used in explaining why particular proposals have been made. In the case of a submission linking two or more degrees or a degree linked with a DipHE, a Working Party comprising representation from relevant boards and/or panels may be formed to deal with validation of the linked submission. If a Board rejects a submission at any stage, it will normally give its reasons and advice, which may provide the opportunity for a successful resubmission. The resubmission must then clearly indicate in what respects it differs from the original and satisfies the criticisms previously made.

47. In addition to visits in connection with particular courses, the CNAA carries out full visitations of institutions when they first seek to operate a CNAA validated course and at periodic intervals (hitherto normally quinquennial) thereafter. These will look at the whole institution as an academic community, its government and management structures, its general planning and organization, its level and standards of resources and staffing, student services and other factors. Members of visiting parties will assess an institution's performance not only by formal discussions with senior staff, but by meeting staff and students at all levels. While these visitations have been seen as useful both in the immediate relationship between the CNAA and the institution, they have also been criticised on a number of counts. Charges levelled at this process include the superficiality of some aspects of visits, and a lack of appreciation of the difficulties under which institutions often operate, or of the consequences of adverse criticisms (sometimes of individual teachers or members of the management team). Concern has also been expressed at the comments made on areas outside the direct concern of

the CNAA, such as the structures of governing bodies and academic boards. Opinions are divided on the usefulness and desirability of the involvement of the CNAA in issues of finance and resources which relate to the courses it validates. Concern is sometimes expressed by institutions or LEAs at the highly specific requirements sometimes made by the CNAA with regard to resources or staffing. However, there is general agreement that the insistence by the CNAA on certain levels of resources has assisted many institutions in obtaining needed resources.

48. In the field of higher degrees, the CNAA has encouraged some institutions to set up Research Degrees Committees, which have streamlined the process of registration and the CNAA has allowed the institutions a measure of greater individual responsibility. The CNAA has made a number of proposals for allowing institutions greater independence in validation.

49. Institutions with a satisfactory record have been given approval for modifications to established courses more or less automatically, rather than being required to go through a lengthy process of resubmission. The CNAA's major initiative to pass a more general responsibility for some stages of validation back to the individual institutions, in its discussion document, *Partnership in Validation,* published in 1975, met with a mixed but generally unenthusiastic response from the institutions themselves. However, the CNAA has in 1979 published a new document, *Developments in Partnership in Validation,* which, although adopting a more evolutionary approach than the earlier document, does seek to give more freedom and responsibility to individual institutions. The new document includes provision for appropriate courses to be given indefinite periods of CNAA approval, subject to regular progress reviews. (Also, it is intended to replace the periodic renewal of course approval procedures by more flexible progress reviews, and to extend the limits within which institutions can change approved courses). Institutions will also have the opportunity to propose variations from the normal validation methods. At the time of writing, these new proposals have been adopted but still have to be put into practice. Institutions will wish to examine carefully the advantages of these new procedures.

50. A new key body of the CNAA, the Committee of Institutions, will have oversight of the new procedures from the academic year 1979-80. It will also act as a final body of appeal for institutions which believe that the CNAA should place greater reliance on its internal institutional procedures, and to examine other issues raised by CNAA institutional visits. The full responsibilities of this committee are set out in an appendix to the CNAA's *Developments in Partnership in Validation.*

51. Current developments in CNAA policy would appear to indicate that, while some aspects of the operation of the CNAA continue to give cause for concern, institutions generally find the relative objectivity, the protection of academic standards, and the support for more resources afforded by the CNAA to be of considerable value. It remains to be seen how far the CNAA's approach to validation will influence curriculum development

throughout the further education system. Without doubt the CNAA has an influence upon staff development: by its scrutiny of course objectives, content, and staff capabilities, it forces teachers to consider the rationale of what they teach.

52. **Degree and degree equivalent courses**
There is no sharp divide between further and higher education in the public sector. Nonetheless, higher education is often regarded as synonymous with degree or degree equivalent courses and these do form the greater part of higher education provision in this country. There are over 100 colleges in Great Britain offering one or more degree courses, although the major providers are the polytechnics and the colleges and institutes of higher education (see Section **1.2.**16-17).

53. There are now a wide variety of courses leading to the award of a degree: Bachelor of Arts (BA) and Bachelor of Science (BSc) are still the most common awards but they have now been augmented by BHum (Humanitites), BEd (Education), BSocSci (Social Sciences) and many other nomenclatures (cf the Finniston Report, Section **1.5**). Institutions in the public sector do not award their own degrees. Prior to the establishment of the CNAA, colleges awarded the degrees of a university. In particular, London University external degrees were offered by a number of institutions although this practice is now being phased out and the university will no longer register or examine full-time students from public sector colleges. The only university-validated degrees now tend to be offered by former colleges of education whose BEd (and previously Certificate of Education) courses were validated by a local university and who have to continue this practice. In a few cases these universities have also agreed to validate other degree courses as the colleges diversified their programmes.

54. The scope and pattern of CNAA degree courses has undergone considerable change. The CNAA has promoted greater variety of course patterns and modes of study and made entry requirements more flexible. There are now almost 1,000 CNAA degree courses available in colleges and polytechnics, including some in subject areas not covered by the universities. The main areas excluded from the public sector colleges are medicine and related disciplines such as veterinary science which are to be found in the university sector. The awards of the CNAA are now fully established as being comparable in standard with those granted by universities.

55. Entry to CNAA degree courses is normally by two or more "A" levels or Ordinary National Certificate or Diploma but there is a special provision for mature students, (25 and over) with appropriate experience and motivation to enter without either qualification. The CNAA will also accept TEC and BEC awards of an appropriate standard. Students on full-time degree courses normally spend three years studying while part-time courses often take up to five years. About 10% of CNAA students are studying on part-time degree courses, while approximately one third are taking sandwich courses. The latter alternate periods of academic study with related

industrial or commercial or other appropriate experience. The non-academic experience is either all concentrated into a single year, a "thick" sandwich, or alternates at six monthly intervals to provide a "thin" sandwich. In either case the period of study is four years with the student being paid by the relevant employer for the period of study away from the college.

56. Many colleges also make a special feature of their modular course patterns with students being offered a great variety of units or modules to build up a coherent course or programme more tailored to their individual wishes. Such a course structure can also offer a certain flexibility in qualifications, particularly if the first two years are built around a Diploma in Higher Education (DipHE).

57. **The Diploma in Higher Education**
DipHE is a qualification which derives from a recommendation of the James Committee on Teacher Education for a two year course of general higher education. As it eventually materialised (via the 1972 White Paper *Education: A Framework for Expansion*) it was with a wider remit designed to serve a number of purposes. Courses must be equivalent in standard to the first two years of a degree course and entry qualifications are equivalent to those of degree courses. The award is made both by CNAA and the universities although the CNAA validates the overwhelming proportion.

58. The DipHE is designed to serve a number of purposes. It can be a terminal qualification in its own right and used as a qualification for entry to appropriate jobs. It can also be "topped up" by a further one or two year course to give a degree or an appropriate professional qualification. This can be in the same institution or by transfer elsewhere – to another college, polytechnic or university. It has particularly been used by the former colleges of education both as a basis for their BEd degrees and for their programmes of diversification.

59. The first DipHE courses were run in 1974-75. There are now some 45 courses, almost all of them full-time, and most linked to a number of other degree qualification via further periods of study. It is, as yet, unclear whether over the next few years more students will use the DipHE as a terminal qualification, but there are considerable pressures which militate against this, including its acceptability by employers as an advanced qualification. Nonetheless the DipHE has proved, in a relatively short time, a valuable mode of entry to higher education, particularly for mature students.

60. **Teacher education**
In 1977[18] the Secretary of State announced the phasing out of the Certificate of Education courses. The last entry is in 1979/80 although one year courses for specialist qualifications in craft, design and technology, music and

---

18 *Entry to Initial Teacher Training Courses in England and Wales,* DES Circular 9/78; Welsh Office Circular 99/78.

business studies will continue until 1983/84. This decision means that teaching will be an all graduate profession with only two routes to qualified teacher status. Students can either take a BEd degree – three years for an ordinary BEd, four years for honours – or a Postgraduate Certificate of Education (PGCE) which is a one year course taken by students who are already graduates in a given discipline or area. The former course combines a study of one or more disciplines together with education and required periods of teaching practice. Entry is by normal matriculation requirements but from 1983 intending students will also have to satisfy requirements in English Language and Mathematics[19] which will normally mean a pass at Grade C or above in these subjects at GCE "O" level or Grade 1 in CSE. Special provision is also made, once again, for mature candidates. PGCE students will also have to satisfy the mathematics and English requirement, but their course will concentrate on education and teaching practice.

61. Course patterns vary from one institution to the next. A very few run four year courses only. Many run the first two years as a DipHE programme with students then completing a BEd or BA or other degrees depending on their interests. Many colleges and polytechnics also provide in-service BEd courses for serving teachers who have a Certificate of Education and want to upgrade their qualifications. In-service MEd courses, full-and part-time, are available in some colleges. Most also provide a wide range of in-service specialist courses for teachers either on a full-time or part-time basis. There has been a considerable growth of in-service teacher education, instanced for example, in the development of Diploma in Professional Studies in Education courses. In addition, there are many short, non-award bearing courses.

62. **Special courses in preparation for entry to higher education**

In 1978, in the light of the general move towards an increase in the level of qualifications required for entry to professional training courses, and courses of teacher education in particular, the DES wrote to seven local authorities [20] asking them to consider mounting special preparatory courses for entry to higher education. These courses are designed to meet the needs of those who have left school without acquiring the necessary qualifications to enter higher education. The DES would like particularly to attract applicants from ethnic minority groups who may have arrived in this country at an age which made it difficult to take advantage of the full range of educational opportunities, or who have experienced difficulties in doing so for cultural or linguistic reasons. The DES identified the need for such courses primarily in relation to initial teacher training but stressed that it

19 *Ibid.* A recent report, *Swings for the schools,* Policy Studies Institute Report No. 584, suggests that there should be greater flexibility in the use of schools and that teachers should be able to undertake either primary or secondary work. This, says the report, means that there should be a shift from reliance on full four year courses of teacher training to the use of non-education graduates who had taken a one year postgraduate diploma in education (with a consequent restructuring of the PGCE).

20 The seven authorities were: Avon, Bedfordshire, Birmingham, Haringey, ILEA, Leicestershire and Manchester.

would also welcome courses to prepare students for entry to other professional training courses such as social work or for entry to other higher education courses. Unfortunately, owing to the current economic climate, only four local authorities seem likely to mount such courses in 1980/81.

63. **College diplomas**

Many colleges and polytechnics offer their own awards either to meet particular, often local, demands or to meet demands in new fields where there are no established or recognised qualifications. The level of such qualifications can vary considerably but they are often linked with other recognised awards, for example: professional examinations or CNAA degrees.

64. **Postgraduate and post-experience courses**

All polytechnics and many colleges offer postgraduate qualifications though not necessarily in all fields of study which they offer at undergraduate level. Many offer one year taught masters' programmes in fields of special expertise or masters' and/or doctoral qualifications for students undertaking research programmes. These will usually be validated by the CNAA and can be undertaken on a full- or part-time basis.

65. Many colleges also offer a range of short courses, lasting from one day to several months, for practitioners in a given field who want to update their knowledge or learn of new techniques or developments. Entry to such courses is not necessarily restricted to graduates. There are also some courses for students with a degree or equivalent qualification (HND or HNC) who have also had a period of employment. The Diploma in Management Studies (DMS) is perhaps the best known and this validation now comes under the auspices of the CNAA.[21] The course varies from six months full-time to three years part-time. There are, once again, opportunities for mature students, without qualifications, but with substantial experience, to gain entry to DMS courses. Such courses are usually offered by one of the regional management centres throughout the country.

66. **Credit transfer in higher education**

On the whole the system of higher education in this country has not encouraged mobility between institutions. Courses, while of equivalent standards, tend to be particular to a given institution, and students generally expect to remain in the same institution reading for the same degree for which they enrolled. There have been two major influences in recent years which have opened up the possibility of student mobility. The first was the establishment of the Open University[22] and its adoption of a "credit" system leading to its awards. This meant many students could gain exemption from part of its programmes by virtue of holding existing qualifications – such as the exemptions from professional examinations referred to above. This led,

21 Management education is discussed in Section **2.2.**52-57.

22 See Appendix 1.

in turn, to several direct links between the Open University and other institutions, both other universities as well as colleges and polytechnics, with appropriate credit transfer arrangements.

67. The second influence was the establishment of the DipHE[23] in 1974, and the requirement not only that this should be regarded as equivalent to the first two years of a degree programme but also that institutions offering the course must show that there is provision for students to get a degree without loss of time. This raised the problem of the credit transferability of the DipHE. In 1977 a major step forward was taken when a joint credit transfer scheme was officially agreed between the Open University and the CNAA[24]. This enables students who have gained a number of credits towards an Open University degree to be admitted to the later stages of a CNAA DipHE or degree course, and alternatively allows students who wish to complete their degree course by correspondence to transfer from a full- or part-time course in a college to the Open University.

68. In response to growing pressures about credit transfers, the DES in 1978 funded the Educational Credit Transfer Feasibility Study under the direction of Peter Toyne at the University of Exeter. The report of this project is to be circulated in Spring 1980 and comments invited from interested parties, but it has yet to be established whether its proposals to set up a credit transfer information service will be accepted.[25]

69. **Credit transfer within the EEC**

An "action programme in the field of education" was published by the Resolution of the Council and of the Ministers of Education meeting within the Council of February 1976. One important aspect of the action programme has been the provision of grants for the development of joint programmes of study between institutions of higher education in member states of the European Community.[26] This tended to encourage mobility of students between two or more institutions for the purpose of studying a jointly developed course. The more recent consultative document, *Admissions to Institutions of Higher Education of Students from other Member States* (Brussels, February 1978)[27] has also opened up the possibility of a wider circulation of students within the context of negotiated institutional arrangements – much as is beginning to happen in Britain. It must however

---

23 See also Section **1.2.**15.

24 Further information is available from either the CNAA or the Open University.

25 NATFHE has strongly supported a continuance of the project, and the funding of an initial pilot project for a two year period, while acknowledging that many of the detailed proposals will need further careful consideration.

26 Resolution of the Council and of the Ministers of Education meeting with the Council, 9th February 1976, *Action Programme in the Field of Education,* OJC 38/1. cf. Sections **6.2** and **6.3**, above.

27 Not formally published but copies are available in limited quantity from either the Department of Education and Science or the Information Office, Commission of the European Communities, 20 Kensington Palace Gardens, London W.8.

be stressed that the EEC developments are so far very tentative and have had little impact on curriculum development, particularly in institutions of higher education in the public sector. Nonetheless it may well become a more important area of development in the future.

70. **Art and design**

As far as distinctions can be made, art education can be described as referring to fine art (such as painting and sculpture) and design is concerned more with the needs of commerce, involving graphics, textiles and other materials. Courses are available at all levels throughout the further education system, extending from recreational courses to those leading to a degree and postgraduate qualification. A variety of foundation courses exist, usually one-year full-time. Some colleges offer longer foundation courses, and also pre-foundation courses. Despite pressure from interested parties there is not yet a national validating body for foundation courses. Non-advanced courses may lead to CGLI or regionally validated examinations. Art and design vocational courses tend often to be mainly full-time. TEC has the responsibility for non-advanced vocational art and design courses (despite opposition, and against the recommendations of the Gann Report of 1974 which recommended an autonomous validating body for art and design). TEC's committee for art and design, DATEC, will be running courses on TEC lines from 1980. Art and design has long had a tradition of curriculum development. It is anticipated that DATEC may increase regional participation in course design. The former Diploma in Art and Design (DipAD) and Higher Diploma awards have been subsumed into CNAA BA and MA awards. There has been an increase in CNAA sandwich courses. Art and design are increasingly components of BEd and DipHE courses. Art teacher education qualifications can be gained by this route, and by way of the one year full-time postgraduate course leading to the award of a diploma or certificate.

71. **Agricultural education**

Reference is made to specialist institutes in Section **11.15**. However, a considerable amount of agricultural education occurs in colleges. There are OND, general three year sandwich, a one year National Certificate, BEC Diploma, and various college awarded courses at the non-advanced level (full-time). However, most college-based agricultural education is part-time, leading at both craft and technician levels to CGLI or REB awards. HND courses are offered by some colleges of agriculture. There has been a long standing debate on the nature of the national body to be responsible for this field of education. In 1974 the Hudson Report recommended an independent national validating and examining body to be administered by the CGLI. So far no decision has been arrived at on this recommendation. Because of its nature, agriculture does not fit easily, if at all, into any strict division between levels. In its recent report, *The Years Ahead,* the Agricultural Training Board outlines a programme calling for more training provision by colleges, the agricultural industry, and the training agencies. Perhaps more than any other area, agriculture is illustrative of crucial debates in further education: the issues of education and training, and the relationship between craft and technician levels.

EDUCATION AND TRAINING

72. Recent developments in further education

Various initiatives, most notably by way of the Manpower Services Commission, have in recent years entailed considerable development in the further education system. The current consultative documents, *16-18,* and *A Better Start in Working Life* are referred to in Section **1.2.**41, above. The DES 1979 consultative paper, *Providing educational opportunities for 16-18 year olds,* also contributes to the debate. Late in 1979, CLEA and the DES set up a joint working party, the Macfarlane Committee, to review local authority educational provision for the 16-19 age group in England and Wales. Within the Committee's general remit to take due regard of factors affecting demand and related types of provision are the following further remits:

(i) to take account of the effect on the demand for various types of education of:
  - (a) the expectations of young people and their families;
  - (b) the perceived requirements of employers and industrial training boards;
  - (c) expected technological change and levels of economic activity;
  - (d) co-existent training and apprenticeship provision;
  - (e) known demographic trends to the mid 1990s;
  - (f) geographically and socially disparate rates of participation in 16-plus education;
  - (g) the financial policies of central and local government;

(ii) to consider, from the point of view of the providers of education, the relationship between education and training agencies.

(iii) to examine the relationship between schools and further education, and in this connection:
  - (a) the compatibility of the legislative framework associated with the sectoral divisions in education; college and school structures, articles of government;
  - (b) manpower;
  - (c) LEAs' allocation of resources to secondary and further education;
  - (d) provision of systematic vocational guidance, careers education and information; and

(iv) to survey work already done by LEAs and groups of LEAs in rationalizing 16 to 19 education, and to assess the evidence of cost-effectiveness of existing provision.

73. Unified Vocational Preparation (UVP)

The role of the DES is generally described in Sections **1.3.** and **7**. It will be seen that although the DES has no direct control over the curriculum, its indirect control is considerable. It relies largely on influence, guidance, persuasion and the promotion of ideas, often by its assessors appointed to the many influential committees that exist. The DES does nevertheless take curriculum initiatives where it feels this to be necessary: acting as the secretariat to some of the joint committees of the National Certificate system, sponsoring the Certificate of Office Studies, and funding educational research are three typical examples. In July 1976 the UVP[28] programme was launched for an initial period of three years in response to concern about the inadequate provision for those school-leavers who go into jobs where they receive no further education and little or no systematic training. Some 24 schemes were due to be started in FE colleges in 1976 but only 11 actually commenced. The main reason for this slow start was the reluctance of employers to release young people to participate: not a surprising attitude when it is considered that the grant available to employers was £4 per day of release. More resources were made available; two field organizers were appointed; at the request of the DES, the CGLI provided a national curriculum framework for colleges which wished to use it, comprising three sections: Induction, Skill and Knowledge, and Communication and Social Skills. The FEU produced suggestions regarding the design and implementation of such schemes and the NFER was commissioned to evaluate the scheme.[29] An extension of the pilot programme until 1981 was approved and at the time of writing, some 80 schemes are claimed to exist, covering about 1000 young people. There has been recent adverse DES comment concerning UVP, but a UVP Field Officer has demonstrated that the pilot project is fulfilling a real need (for example, in providing a consolidating expansion from YOP courses), that demand is increasing, and that expansion is worthwhile.[30]

74. Considering the Industrial Training Boards' pre-occupation with skilled man-power and the MSC's pre-occupation with the unemployed, the UVP scheme aimed as it was at those young workers in "dead-end" jobs, was generally welcomed by most educational bodies. Possible limits to its success could have been predicted on the basis of past neglect, but its survival has enabled colleges to gain experience in operating curricula aimed at vocational preparation. In April 1979, the then Government, in acknowledging the valuable practical experience with the pilot schemes of unified vocational preparation and with certain elements of the Youth Opportunities Programme, published *A Better Start in Working Life,*

---

28 Unified Vocational Preparation was launched by the Labour Government as a joint venture between the MSC, the Department of Education and Science and the Welsh and Scottish Offices. Aimed at the 300,000 school-leavers who enter employment and receive no further education and little or no systematic training, the aims of UVP were to assist young people:

(i) to assess their potential and think realistically about jobs and careers;
(ii) to develop the basic skills which will be needed in adult life generally;
(iii) to understand society and how it works; and
(iv) to strengthen the foundation of skill and knowledge on which further education and education can be built.

The same document also announced the setting up of the Further Education Curriculum Review and Development Unit.

29 *General Employment Award Pilot Scheme,* CGLI No 362; *Experience, Reflection (and) Learning,* FEU, May 1978. Aimed at college staff involved or about to be involved in UVP schemes, it provides an explanation of the UVP philosophy, makes suggestions on designing programmes and offers a learning model based on "experiential learning".

30 Albert Weedall, "UVP Towards 1981", *NATFHE Journal,* Vol.4, No.8 November 1979, pp 10-13. Weedall states, "It is certain ... that a valuable experiment in the on-going education and training of the young worker has been carried out."

suggesting a comprehensive scheme of vocational preparation for employed young people in Great Britain. Although the 1979 general election interrupted the essential national debate on this proposal, which many saw as a last attempt to find a voluntary solution to this problem,[31] at the time of writing consultations were still continuing.

75. **The Industrial Training Boards**
ITBs and their relationship with the MSC are discussed in Section **4**. The ITBs were set up under the Industrial Training Act 1964 which came from a growing realisation that we were not producing the skilled work force required by a competitive industrial nation. 29 (now 24) Industrial Training Boards were set up covering approximately 60% of the nation's working population. Each ITB consists of persons appointed by the Secretary of State for Employment, nominated by employers, trade unions and, to a lesser extent, by the educational sector. Their collective function is to ensure that their industries are provided with sufficient skilled manpower. Before 1974, the way in which the levy grant system (see Section **4**.9) was applied by the ITBs varied considerably. The Engineering Industry Training Board imposed a levy of 2.5% of each firm's total wage bill which netted many hundreds of millions of pounds; whereas the Electricity Supply ITB had a levy only of the order of 0.2%. The EITB and similar Boards thus paid out relatively large grants for approved training whereas the Electricity Supply ITB had no grant system but relied on an agreement with its industry to provide training as recommended. The operation of ITB policy was heavily monitored by the Department of Employment; levy-grant, training recommendations and statistical returns were all subjects to the scrutiny of the DE.

76. Over the eight years following the setting up of the ITBs a considerable amount of training activity was generated by the Boards and in many industries training was upgraded and improved. However, the Industrial Training Act 1964 with its ITBs and Central Training Council did not prove to be the piece of social engineering that many in education hoped for. It had been seen by many as the mechanism by which day-release could be introduced for all young workers and initially there were Ministerial statements implying that further education should be an essential part of the training for all young trainees. In fact, in spite of brave attempts by a few ITBs, further education tended to be associated only with training programmes of a duration of one year or more. This meant that only those young people designated as trainees in craft and technician type programmes received further education. The net effect was that young workers in designated training received as a result of the 1964 Act, a better training and education than before, but those not so designated received no further education and no real increase in day-release occurred; indeed it declined. By 1972 as a result of a Department of Employment review of the Industrial Training Act, most ITBs no longer accepted that they might be the agents for

31 The consultative document illustrates not only a typical DES curriculum initiative but also a growing recognition that the 16-19 problem requires a comprehensive solution which can only be brought about by an inter-departmental approach. NATFHE has long subscribed to this view, and also maintains that any voluntary system is doomed to fail: some form of legislation is considered necessary.

bringing about universal day-release and came to regard it as a matter of government policy rather than the responsibility of ITBs.[32] Notwithstanding this, there is no doubt that in many sectors of industry and commerce such as printing, furniture, catering, distribution and the hotel industry, new areas of training and FE were developed and over the period 1965-1972 a greater awareness of industrial training was generally developed. Whether this increased awareness resulted in the permanent shift in attitude in British industry with respect to training, claimed by the Department of Employment in its 1972 *Training for the Future* discussion document, remains a matter of some debate. Similarly, any permanent improvement in manpower planning, particularly at local level, is difficult to discern.

77. The Employment and Training Act 1973 set up the MSC, abolished the Central Training Council and significantly reduced the autonomy of the ITBs. Those ITBs associated with the public utilities of gas, water and electricity ceased to exist as such. The remaining ITBs come under the control of the MSC, from whom they get the bulk of their monies. The role of the ITBs has, perhaps inevitably, shifted from the directive to the advisory. The major thrust of the curriculum design has perhaps abated and with it many of the points of conflict that arose between the ITBs and the further education system on curriculum matters. In many respects the activities of the MSC have tended to overshadow the work of the ITBs, although some ITBs are far from quiescent in curriculum matters. In 1977 the EITB published a major research report which examined the relevance of school experience to later performance in industry, the Rubber and Plastics ITB has since 1975 published three reports on the Education and Training of Young People, and in 1979 the Man-Made Fibres Producing ITB published a consultative document suggesting changes in its craft and technician training which, if implemented, would undoubtedly have an impact on school and further education curricula. Even so, at the time of writing many people now associate training initiatives and curriculum change more with the centralised agencies than with the ITBs, especially where these initiatives are directed towards those young people with whom the ITBs have little contact.

78. In July 1979, the MSC set up a body[33] to review the Employment and Training Act 1973. It is likely that a fundamental appraisal of the role of the

32 In February 1972 the Department of Employment published a discussion document, *Training for the Future*, in which it asked for comments on possible radical changes to the Industrial Training Act. It was in the responses to this document that many ITBs were forced to state their attitude on day-release. The EITB statement in its *Information Paper* No.31 is a typical example.

33 The Review Body is chaired by Richard O'Brien, MSC Chairman, and comprises 14 invited members who appear in the main to represent employers, unions and ITBs. Two members are associated with the education service. The review is inviting evidence under such main headings as:

(i) the aims of a national training system;
(ii) formulation of national training objectives;
(iii) strengths and weaknesses of the present system;
(iv) relations between education and training services; and
(v) regional and local training needs.

In its request for evidence the Review Body was at some pains to indicate that "...no alternatives to the present system can be excluded from consideration". NATFHE believes that any revised system should include a more equal and representative educational view than now exists.

ITBs will be a major part of this review. The result of this review however is not to appear until mid 1980. It is argued by many that the ITB system, greatly weakened by the 1973 Act, should be either extended so that it covers the whole of the workforce or that it should be replaced by a more comprehensive and co-ordinated system of education and training.

79. **The Manpower Services Commission**
The Commission is considered in Section **4**, above. The purpose here is to deal only with curricular aspects of its work. The Commission has ten members, one of whom[34] is intended to relate to professional education interests. Those divisions of the MSC which relate to further and higher education are the Training Services and Special Programmes Divisions. The Training Services Division (TSD) has responsibilities for the Industrial Training Boards and the Skillcentres, with their annexes. Many of these Skillcentres were, before 1973, Government Training Centres. They tend to concentrate on engineering, construction and automotive trades. In some of them, trainees are prepared for CGLI/TEC examinations. As this can be seen as a competitive threat to colleges, especially if a local college has spare capacity on similar courses, from time to time activity and expansion in this sector of MSC activity is criticised.[35]

80. The Training Opportunities Scheme (TOPS) is primarily aimed at retraining unemployed adults via full-time courses of usually up to one year in length. The level of these courses ranges from basic clerical skills to the post graduate. The great majority of TOPS courses however are run in either Skillcentres or in colleges of further education. The colleges tend to provide clerical, commercial and higher level courses. An interesting development has taken place in some colleges whereby, to assist those with minimal qualifications, "pre-TOPS" courses have been introduced. In 1978/79 the further education system provided for half of the 70,000 TOPS completions, of which almost 25,000 were in clerical and commercial subjects. Within the TOPS time constraint of one year, many conventional FE courses can be offered, although they have to be approved by the TSD. Many other courses however are of a much shorter duration and these are designed exclusively for TOPS, hopefully as a co-operative venture between the college, LEA or sometimes RAC and TSD Regional Training Advisers. Inevitably, all the conflicts and constraints involved in curriculum development apply in the development of joint TOPS curricula. The concept of FE and MSC joint curriculum exercises, provided there is adequate consultation and support, is generally acceptable. Colleges and their LEAs however remain nervous of mounting courses which require a heavy

34 At the time of writing this was Roy Helmore, Principal of the Cambridge College of Arts and Technology. He attempts to carry out this difficult task by chairing an informal Educational Consulative Group comprising representatives of the AUT, APC and NATFHE. NATFHE acts as the secretariat to the group.

35 The Training and Further Education Consultative Group, set up in 1976, often acts as a forum for discussions on topics such as demarcation. Its *Bulletin* No. 3 records a discussion on CGLI entrants in which fuller use of the machinery recommended in the DES Administrative Memorandum 12/77 was urged. Its *Bulletin* No.5 records a discussion on the setting up of a Skillcentre at Ashford, apparently in competition with the local FE college. A new Skillcentre is currently being built at Accrington at a time when the local further education college has had a number of MSC courses withdrawn.

investment of capital and/or staff since MSC courses may be withdrawn with little notice (cf Section **4.**18).

81. A comprehensive review of TOPS was carried out by the TSD in 1978 and this is commented on in the 1978/79 *Annual Report* of the MSC. One theme of the review report was that "...TOPS management should have much closer contact in future with the further education sector and with Industrial Training Boards to enable TOPS to develop as an independent but complementary part of the national system."

82. Because of the administrative and financial system and the level of resources the MSC has at its command, it is able through the TSD rapidly to generate curriculum activity in response to identified needs. This it does, often at a pace beyond that of the education service. The result of this, some would maintain, is a reduction in the innovative role of further education in technical training, especially in the fast moving technologies. Thus in computer subjects, off-shore oil related industries, industrial languages, and micro-electronics the TSD has been able to finance and generate curriculum development far more quickly than the FE sector.

83. The Special Programmes Division of the MSC has its origin in a growing awareness during the mid-1970s of the increasing number of young unemployed people. From 1975 the MSC took a series of initiatives to minimise this situation: the Job Creation Programme (JCP) and Work Experience Programme (WEP) were major examples. In 1978, resulting from the proposals of the Holland Report,[36] JCP and WEP were replaced by a wider, more coherent range of schemes intended to meet the needs of the young and long-term unemployed. These schemes come under the general headings of the Youth Opportunities Programme (YOP) and the Special Temporary Employment Programme (STEP). YOP is concerned with unemployed 16-18 year olds; STEP is concerned with the over 18s, especially the long term unemployed and in its first year of operation in 1978/79 about half of the STEP entrants were over 25 years of age.

84. It is however the YOP schemes that have had a significant impact on the further education system. Local authorities acting as sponsors have provided, via the colleges, many YOP schemes. Indeed it remains the opinion of many that the objectives and age group of YOP make it as much an educational as a training process. The pressure of the problem and the rapidity with which resources could be obtained by the MSC were, however, generally acknowledged as inevitably producing a training rather than an educational solution.[37] In the first year of YOP operation in 1978/79 over 162,000 young people entered YOP schemes; of these 90% were between the

---

36 The Holland Report: *Young People and Work* was the result of a Working Party chaired by Geoffrey Holland of the MSC. Published in May 1977, the report concluded that the levels of unemployment among school leavers were unlikely to decrease for some years and so recommended a coherent programme of action designed to offer "each young person an effective bridge to permanent employment...".

37 NATFHE is generally supportive of YOP, but insists that the further education system should be a fully participative partner to ensure wherever possible "a fully integrated element of further education" as proposed in the Holland Report.

age of 16 and 17 years. Half of that first year total had no educational qualifications. The range of YOP schemes comprises:

(i) Work Preparation Courses – ranging from two-week assessment and induction courses, 13 week courses, leading to operative or semi-skilled competency – to longer, basic remedial courses.

(ii) Work Experience – comprising Work Experience on Employers' Premises; Project Based Work Experience Training Workshops.

85. Not surprisingly, Work Experience on Employers' Premises (WEEP) attracted the most work experience entrants in the first year of operation, mainly because of the employers' familiarity with the concept under the previous work experience schemes and the low capital investment required. Training workshops, on the other hand, requiring considerable investment and curriculum development are slower to develop. Even so, in 1978/79 over 100 such workshops were approved for MSC funding and 90 became operational.

86. With the general exception of WEEP, the FE system is largely involved in all aspects of the YOP programme and in many cases it represents the major provider. Some local authorities, such as Coventry, seek to provide a co-ordinated programme of training and work experience under YOP, using not only conventional further education premises but also utilizing other premises for training workshops, where goods are produced for sale to the local authority and other public bodies. At the other end of the scale some colleges provide an FE element in a Work Experience Programme. It follows from the above that curriculum development for the many aspects of YOP has represented a considerable load on the further education service. Many see it as a worthwhile investment, contributing towards an eventual policy of some form of day-release for all school-leavers. All this activity has already given rise to a general discussion on the nature of the provision and educational environment best suited to the YOP entrant. With more operational experience many of the issues posed will probably be solved but, for the next few years, many problems remain. Many YOP courses are short (although some can last for a year), none lead to recognised qualifications, and a considerable overlap exists with some FE courses, in content and ability range. There is a wish [38] for feasibility studies to be mounted to explore the possibility of some form of facilitation and accreditation of YOP with respect to FE courses.

87. As an aid to curriculum development for YOP schemes, the FEU (see paragraph 15, above) set up a priority project in 1977 to survey the types of courses already being offered in further education for the young unemployed. The resultant 1978 report [39] provided many colleges with a

38 By NATFHE, the NUS and other bodies. The MSC is at present opposed to accreditation.

39 *Postal Survey of FE Provision for the Young Unemployed, 1977,* FEU, June 1978. It comprises an analysis of over 150 college replies to a questionnaire on course design, curriculum content and teaching approaches in this area of work. This analysis is accompanied by a description of provision in five colleges and by a further analysis of the further education component of Work Experience Schemes. It was followed in July 1979 by a further publication, *Supporting YOP.*

timely aid for much of their own curriculum design for YOP schemes. The Further Education Unit has also sponsored work on Social and Life Skills which is a curriculum element associated not only with YOP but with many other schemes of education and training for the 16-19 age group. Many young people find it difficult to make the transition from school to work and to cope with the every day requirements of life as a young adult in a community. Being unemployed makes this transition more difficult and the teaching of social and life skills is claimed by many to ease this problem. There is however much confusion with respect to the nature of these skills, and generally there exists a lack of experience as to how and where they are best learned. YOP schemes therefore, like any other curricula innovations, create teacher training needs. This not only applies to further education teachers but to all those engaged in this type of work. One of the Holland proposals was to use a large number of unemployed craftsmen and other skilled workers to act as tutor-supervisors for YOP entrants. This too created a staff training problem and among the various solutions adopted perhaps the most significant is the development of a joint CGLI/MSC course leading to a recognised Instructor/Supervisor Award. Apart from this, the TSD trained in the first year of YOP, some 600 staff. (The training occurred largely in MSC instructor colleges, rather than in further education institutions).

88. Although not strictly a part of YOP, the Community Industry Scheme, sponsored by the National Association of Youth Clubs, is also overseen by the Special Programmes Division. In this scheme young people are employed by the NAYC and are paid a wage rather than the standard YOP allowance. The schemes gives special emphasis to the needs of young people who are personally and socially disadvantaged. The young people work in teams, under an adult supervisor, on tasks which benefit the community. It is within this environment that the teaching of social and life skills and basic literacy takes place. Some 6000 young people go through CI each year. Murray[40] has produced an evaluatory study of the scheme. Research into generic skills has been undertaken by the MSC and ILEA.

89. The Special Programmes Division of the MSC has generated in the post-school sector a considerable amount of curriculum development. In its wake are not only significant staff training problems and new areas of curriculum activity, but also a growing awareness that a significant amount of "education" is taking place outside the formal further education college and training system. Indeed, organizations like Youthaid are highly critical of the formal education system in its help to young people, maintaining that concern about jobs and the economy is obscuring the failings of the education system. Whether or not such criticisms are justified, there is little doubt that under the MSC much of this work is being done by people who do not claim to be professional teachers or instructors. Only time will tell whether a permanent change is taking place in the way we design learning situations for young people, in the way we prepare young people for adult society, and in the way we structure our post-school curriculum provision.

---

40 Christopher Murray, *Youth Unemployment: A socio-psychological study of disadvantaged 16-19 year olds*, NFER, 1978.

The lack of effective co-ordination between the education and training systems is leading to a pattern of provision more reliant on *ad hoc* finance than on long term planning, leading inevitably to the accusation that the provision is cosmetic rather than based on a genuine appraisal of young people's educational needs. This in turn raises the question as to what are these needs if unemployment is to become a permanent element of adult life. For this question adequately to be answered we require a better assessment of possible future employment prospects. Not surprisingly, such an assessment is not forthcoming and our education system remains committed to the inculcation of the work-ethic. With this potential dilemma in mind the FEU commissioned Youthaid to study FE curriculum alternatives in areas of high and prolonged unemployment but, at the time of writing, this study is proving somewhat inconclusive.

90. In organizational and administrative terms, there exist rigid divisions between education and training. From Ministerial level downwards schisms appear between the education and training functions, and at college level these appear often in the form of differential fee and grant structures, in curriculum organization and in the methods of monitoring and certification. There are differences between the further education system and training institutions concerning *inter alia,* salaries, working conditions, types of staff, types of teaching, professional bases, and resources. The reasons for this are historical; there is an unresolved debate in the UK as to where and how training should occur; economic arguments and conflict in policy have perpetuated the division. It is instructive to note that the EEC, which tends to consider education in the context of manpower and its preparation (see Sections **6.2** and **6.3**) sees education and training as a single entity. However, to give a specific example, the disadvantage which the DES suffers in relation to the MSC is that whereas the MSC can fund directly, and thus act as an initiator and innovator, there is currently no guarantee that DES initiative (since its direct funding opportunities are restricted) can actually be implemented.

91. Both education and training draw upon teaching methods and learning strategies which have common philosophical bases. However, Skillcentre training tends not to provide a general education, thus leaving the student him or herself to acquire personal and educational development. The curriculum development instigated by BEC, for example, is an indication of the substantial opposition to this view. In particular educational or training schemes, emphases may vary and objectives may differ but there is little discernible difference between the actual activities. While it may indeed be true to say that the further education system may be more concerned with productivity and job-specific skills, overlap remains considerable and the problems of curriculum design in essence similar. For example, under the TEC curriculum model it is possible to have an award comprising both "education" and "training" units, and for many years "integrated" training and education courses have been a feature in off-the-job craft and technician training. The education and training issue is discussed also in Section **4**, above. Not all training, of course, occurs in Skillcentres.

ADULT EDUCATION

92. Reference has been made to adult education in Section **1.2**. It will be appreciated that although adult education is an integral part of the further education system, its scope is immense, the activity takes place in a variety of institutions and manners, and the courses available encompass the whole of the post-school curriculum. Discussion of adult education here will be limited to the forms of provision not so far discussed in this sub-section.

93. Adult education centres provide through LEAs and alongside the Responsible Bodies a wide range of educational and recreational activities. While a part of the role of adult education will emerge from the paragraphs below which discuss disadvantage, it will be appreciated that the role of the teacher is particularly demanding: counselling skills, a breadth of knowledge, and particular abilities are required. The resource availability to promote and consolidate such skills, as with much else in adult education, is often lacking. As important elements of adult education result from the identification of a need, the teacher has a particularly vital role in the development of schemes of work.[41]

94. The Russell Report's recommendations (see Section **1.5** and **1.2.**20) have been only partially implemented. However, the broad interpretation of adult education as "continuing education" contained in the report and its acknowledgement of the needs of disadvantaged groups may have been influential in at least facilitating some later developments.[42] In order to provide continuing education – which is seen as being necessary not only in personal terms, but also to allow for facilitating career change, providing "second chance" education, equality of opportunity, retraining to cope with technological change, and what may be described as life skills,[43] development is clearly necessary. Colleges are already providing this type of education, and on an increasing scale. Continuing education (recurrent education or éducation permanente) may be described in summary as the principle that people throughout their lives should be able to return to education, alternating or accompanying periods of organized education with work, or other activities. The further education system with its huge range of academic, vocational and recreational courses is already the main provider

---

41 Through its journal, *Adult Education,* the National Institute of Adult Education describes the range of curricula tackled by this sector of the education system and much of its curriculum expertise can apply directly, and profitably, to the more conventional colleges. Its range of interests is considerable, dealing as it does with programmes associated with the running of pre-school playgroups, conventional examinations, YOP, TOPS, adult basic education and retirement. *Adult Education* is published by the NIAE each month for six months each year. The NFER is currently engaged in a project investigating the needs of adults in an inner city area and the extent to which those needs are met.

42 Chaired by Sir Lionel Russell (best known in further education perhaps for the 1966 Russell Report on further education teacher training), the committee was appointed by the DES "To assess the need for and to review the provision of non-vocational adult education in England and Wales...". It would be the opinion of many that in effectively ignoring the concept of education permanente (cf Section **6.2**) "...a long term concept and we do not have time to wait for it," the status of the report as a major educational document was diminished.

of such education: the most significant amount of current continuing education at present takes the form of part-time day release. It will have been noted already that numbers here are small (see also Section **1.2**) and are restricted to the 16-21 age group. The highly important issue of part-time day release can, however, be linked to the more general issue of Paid Educational Leave (PEL). This term represents leave of absence from employment for educational purposes without loss of income. Paid educational leave may be defined as leave within normal working hours (excluding arrangements for the granting of leave on condition that employees attend for a proportion of their own time), at no cost (in wages, pensions rights or other benefits) to those taking leave, and with the right to return to the workplace. It may be that such leave would be for a specified period for educational purposes, granted under statutory provisions or collective agreements, and not dependent on the education being job related. Paid education leave could be granted for leisure and recreational pursuits. The UK has signed the International Labour Office convention concerning PEL, endorsing its commitment in a White Paper (Cmnd. 6236). The DES and MSC have funded a current research project concerning PEL. As well as the general issues of PEL and continuing education, it must also be noted that current activity in the further education system demonstrates that there are growing numbers of part-time advanced and degree courses available. Although resource difficulties may make progress towards continuing education slow, it is clear that some development is likely to occur. Already there has been a significant growth in trade union education. Colleges provide both facilities and courses. The greatest growth has been in courses concerned with health and safety.

SPECIAL AREAS OF NEED

95. This subject should not be thought of as being restricted. Perhaps the best context in which to approach it is that of the Warnock Report. The

---

43 For example, education for newly elected representatives; marriage; and retirement. In its 1979 policy statement, *Education for Adults,* in identifying needs for development NATFHE stresses the urgency of increasing provision and opportunities for the disadvantaged (specifically: women and girls with a view to expanding opportunities in work areas not traditionally associated with female employment such as technical, supervisory, and managerial posts where numbers are declining; ethnic minorities; the handicapped; and mature students lacking formal qualifications). The document stresses the needs of the elderly (including the need for courses allowing preparation for retirement), education for trade union members, and education to assist in adjustment to changes in life-style (for example, parenthood, and changes in the nature of employment such as work sharing or reduced working weeks). In stressing its belief that adult education must become an integral part of the education system, the policy document observes that it is estimated that only 5% of those in need of help have availed themselves of current adult literacy provision. As the lack of resources has led to the use of volunteer tutors in adult education (especially, for example, in the adult literacy campaign) NATFHE states that:

(i) Volunteer tutors should be used only after full consultation and agreement, only for recognized schemes (such as adult literacy, adult numeracy and Parosi); and only in one-to-one teaching (or if in group teaching, under the supervision of a teacher remunerated under the provisions of the Burnham Further Education salaries documents – and the group taught not to exceed ten); and

(ii) appropriate training schemes for volunteer tutors should be supervised and validated by teachers as defined in (i), above, who would also provide continuing support and supervision.

Secretary of State announced in March 1980 that the Warnock Report was to be implemented; a Bill to establish the legal framework was to be prepared. Warnock recommended that planning should be based on the assumption that about one in six children at any time will require some form of special educational provision.

96. **Adult literacy and numeracy**

Whatever the roots of the problems of illiteracy or innumeracy, in many cases the solution is made more difficult because of the atrophy of a neglected skill and the stigma associated with adult illiteracy. Since the early 1970s however, the climate has changed and the problem is now more openly discussed. This in part at least was due to the campaign waged by the British Association of Settlements (BAS) which estimated in 1973 that over two million adults in England and Wales were unable to read as well as the average nine-year old. With extra support from the BBC, the Government in 1975 allocated £1 million to LEAs and voluntary organizations via a new Adult Literacy Resource Agency (ALRA) for a programme of schemes for one year. This has been extended to 1980, albeit on a different funding basis since 1978, with the LEAs gradually taking over a greater share of the funding. In December 1979 the Secretary of State announced that Government support for adult literacy was to be continued for at least a further three years, and that a grant of £½ million was to be made available in 1980-81 for the development of an adult literacy and basic skills unit. In 1977 the Secretary of State for Education set up the Advisory Council for Adult and Continuing Education (ACACE), to advise on a "coherent strategy for basic education provision" for adult literacy. ACACE in 1979 published a report[44] which if anything describes a problem larger than that originally identified by BAS.

97. In curriculum terms, one major problem of adult basic education is the initial point of contact. The formal enquiry and enrolment procedures of FE colleges and adult education centres have obviously not proved successful in this respect and more popular and anonymous modes of contact were necessary. BBC, and later ITV, programmes coupled with a confidential telephone referral network have proved to be an effective combination whereby adults in need lose their sense of isolation and can obtain sympathetic advice. The referral service[45] has recruited both students and volunteer tutors and there is no doubt that tens of thousands of adults have at least been brought into touch once more with some form of educational process. Once the contact has been made however, motivation has to be sustained through the inevitable plateaux of learning that occur. Also

---

44 *A Strategy for the Basic Education of Adults*, ACACE, 1979. In this report the Council estimates that at least three million adults are in need of basic education. It goes on to propose that the various agencies in the field of adult basic education should be co-ordinated by a Development Board working via the Regional Councils.

45 The Adult Literacy Support Services Fund (ALSSF) provides a national telephone referral service for those seeking help and information on adult basic education: England 01-992 5522; Scotland 041 332 4028; Wales 0222 869444; Northern Ireland 0232 22488.

because the lack of literacy is often accompanied by a lack of numeracy and of other skills, there has to be made for many adults a satisfactory transition to basic education if their disadvantage is to be minimised. Thus the adult literacy campaign has generated new materials, methods and curricula not confined to literacy.[46] It has also brought forth, at last, some fundamental research sponsored by the DES.[47] The curriculum development in this area is undoubtedly radical and exciting; it has to be. But it is inevitably expensive; many would claim that as yet only the surface of the problem has been scratched and the dominant constraint is not a lack of curriculum ideas but an uncertainty of funding.

98. **Prison education**

One area of adult basic education very much at the mercy of inadequate resources is that associated with prisoners and offenders. The constraints obtaining on the curriculum are described in Section **11.14**. The need for better provision if anything is greater, the curriculum problems are immense and, in spite of good co-operation between the Prison Education Service, the Probation Service, LEAs, colleges and the adult education system, there is almost by definition a need for some unification in this field, backed up again by better conditions in many prisons.[48] In the meantime there are a few progressive educational experiments in Manchester, Swindon, Reading and elsewhere, showing that with local authority support, FE colleges can make a contribution to the rehabilitation and resettlement of offenders and ex-prisoners.[49]

99. **The handicapped**

Provision for the handicapped is discussed in detail in Section **12.11**. Discussion here will be restricted therefore to certain curriculum implications. Few existing colleges have really adequate facilities for the handicapped, few have trained staff with special responsibilities for providing for special educational needs and few offer a range of curricula wide and stable enough to satisfy the needs of all the disadvantaged. The Warnock Committee, in line with its thinking that education is the right of

---

46 David Stringer's study of IBA's *Make it Count,* a learning package comprising 13 television progammes, supporting material, workbook and tutor's manual, describes the need in this area and illustrates some of the curriculum development that is taking place in adult basic education. *Make it Count,* National Extension College, 1979.

47 The NFER in 1979 is due to complete a two-year research project surveying attainment and progress in adult literacy programmes. To date very little research has been carried out in this area and there is an almost complete lack of diagnostic instruments and criteria against which these tests (and courses) can be validated.

48 The May Report was published in late 1979 and has drawn attention to the problem of accommodation in our prisons.

49 The National Association for the Care and Resettlement of Offenders (NACRO) is the principal voluntary organization in the penal field concerned with rehabilitation and resettlement of offenders, alternatives to prison, and the prevention of crime. Most of its income derives from Government sources, it works closely with the Probation and After-Care Service and its major areas of concern have been promoting the provision of accommodation and employment opportunities for offenders, establishing the use of volunteers and contributing to the development of community alternatives for juvenile offenders. Education is increasingly being seen as one of the main factors in the resettlement process. NACRO has committed some of its resources to various educational experiments; it has recently established an Education Advisory Committee.

all, defines the problem (para 3.19) as:

(i) the provision of special means of access to the curriculum through special equipment, facilities or resources, modification of the physical environment or specialist teaching techniques;

(ii) the provision of a special or modified curriculum; and

(iii) particular attention to the social structure and emotional climate in which education takes place.

100. Adequately resourced, the Warnock Report's philosophy of integration would undoubtedly ease the problem for many handicapped people who wish to enter further education; an increasing number of colleges are improving their facilities and means of access. Few institutions however are at present adequately equipped to cope with the needs of those with severe physical handicaps. Inevitably, the Warnock Committee had to suggest here some concentration of resources. (NATFHE responded by suggesting that a small number of colleges, polytechnics and universities should be especially designated and funded to provide a suitable level of provision).

101. Handicapped students may have sensory and manipulative disabilities which have to be catered for. In vocational education especially, the use of equipment, and methods of assessment, present problems over and above those usually associated with information processing. The NFER, in addition to researching into the education of handicapped children in ordinary schools,[50] is also involved in three further education projects. One of these is in association with Hereward College of Further Education (Coventry), which was established in 1971 to fill a gap in national provision for relatively severely physically handicapped students who cannot be provided for in ordinary colleges. Another project is concerned specifically with blind and visually handicapped students at the Queen Alexandra College, Birmingham and at the Hethersett Centre for Blind Adolescents in Reigate. Both of these FE projects are concerned with monitoring, testing and other assessment procedures, and both are also concerned to determine how much of this expertise can be made more generally available. The Hereward project is broader in scope and in its later phase; over twenty other further education establishments doing innovative work with the handicapped are being surveyed. It is hoped that this report in particular will produce for local authorities an evaluative record of a wide variety of practices and policies. The third project is seeking to follow up disabled college leavers to discover what their employment prospects have been.

102. The Employment Service Division (ESD) of the MSC has a special staff of Disablement Resettlement Officers who seek to secure more and better employment for disabled people (see also Section **11.6.**57). In 1979 the MSC began a major promotional campaign to persuade employers to adopt positive policies towards the employment of disabled people (of whom about 200,000 are registered as unemployed). The MSC has set up several special

---

50 Following a report in 1977, the NFER is now engaged in a three-year project, sponsored by the DES, seeking to identify the factors that make for the successful integration of handicapped children (physical, sensory and intellectual retardation, but excluding maladjustment) into ordinary schools. A report is due in late 1980.

grant schemes to improve the employment of disabled people of which the "Fares to Work" scheme appears successful. In its 1978/79 *Annual Report* however, the MSC was forced to comment that "...the number of employers taking advantage of the grants to adapt premises and equipment in order to employ severely disabled people, ... remained disappointing". It appears therefore that there is a need for a stronger link to exist between the FE and manpower services to aid the investigation of any special curriculum needs necessary to improve the employment prospects of handicapped people. However, the MSC has been less than helpful in supporting educational courses for the handicapped in colleges because of an arbitrary and long standing distinction between "educational" and "training" programmes.

103. The National Bureau for Handicapped Students in its 1977 policy statement suggests that "As increasing numbers of handicapped students are accepted for courses in post-school education, institutions should examine how far existing courses meet the demands of these students".[51] While distance learning techniques will obviously extend educational opportunities for many disabled students, there is a need for course evaluation. This, and the increased integration of handicapped students, will create a need for staff development. Garnett College, a college of education (technical) has a special unit responsible for development courses for teachers of disadvantaged students. The CGLI has designed an in-service course for the Teaching of the Handicapped in Further Education.[52] The Warnock Report's priorities include provision for young people over 16 with special needs and an urgent need for development in teacher education, and education and training.[53]

104. **Women and girls**

The Sex Discrimination Act 1975 makes sex discrimination in employment, training and education, unlawful. Legislation alone will not of course eliminate a pattern of disadvantage that has been with us for generations and whilst education can perhaps play a significant role in eliminating this, it will require a major shift of attitude from all sections of

---

51 *An Educational Policy for Handicapped People,* November 1977.

52 CGLI Course No 731. This is a course aimed at FE teachers in contact with handicapped students in colleges. It deals with subject areas such as provision for the handicapped, reports and legislation, types of handicap, agencies and support services, teaching method and curriculum development. The DES Report on Education, Number 69 (1971), *The Last to Come In,* is appositely titled in this respect: it makes a significant contribution to the destruction of the concept of the "ineducable" and in its way helped progress towards the Warnock Report.

53 The Report had been with the Secretary of State for two years before the proposals outlined in paragraph 95 were announced. The question of the allocation of resources to give the proposed Education Bill any real meaning remains unanswered. NATFHE (1979) has published a response to Warnock, generally welcoming the report, although voicing a reservation that unless the concept of integrating the handicapped into the normal educational environment is sufficiently resourced, it could degenerate into a policy of "no action". Certainly the Warnock Report draws attention to the neglect of post-school needs and provision. Warnock tends to distinguish between *disability* as a medical term, *disadvantage* as a social phenomen and *handicap* as educational in nature. This distinction may be helpful to those outside education, but to those in education it is less helpful, particularly to the classroom teacher, who would tend to see any of these categories under the generalised heading of those with "special educational needs".

society for a total solution. Weiner[54] has analysed how far current educational practices support undesirable sex-stereotyping and concludes that although the Act is an important piece of legislation, educators cannot assume that discrimination will soon disappear from schools and colleges. There is also no lack of evidence that many women and girls are disadvantaged as a result of entrenched attitudes. This shows in post-school education where fewer women than men get day-release, where girl apprentices are rare, where medical schools appear to favour men, and where the proportion of women employed (especially in higher education) is small (cf Section **11.11.**9). In the Open University too, women students are in the minority. The situation may have been improving slowly but higher unemployment levels and recent government policy have, *inter alia,* exerted disproportionate pressures on women and girls. The Equal Opportunities Commission has pressurised LEAs to make more fair their selection procedures for school employment and the EITB has set up with the help of EEC funds a special scholarship scheme encouraging the training of women technicians.

105. In post-school curriculum, the FEU has made a start. In its proposed curriculum for pre-employment courses it indicates that some positive discrimination may be necessary for girls. The Mansell Report, *A Basis for Choice,* in suggesting a diagnosis of individual student needs, states: "Such diagnosis may also reveal some systematic differences between groups of students: for instance, girls' mathematical and technical skills, because at school their opportunities or attainment in these areas may have been such as to unduly restrict their vocational options." Elsewhere in the report, when describing that part of a common-core related to making a realistic decision about their future, a specific warning is given about sex-stereotyping. The FEU has also sponsored an NFER study of Bridging Courses for women; the interim report indicates that specific guidance may be forthcoming on curricula and teaching strategies.[55] The Unit has also sponsored a further research project investigating in particular the availability and suitability of science and technology courses in further education colleges and polytechnics.

106. The Equal Opportunities Commission and SSRC in 1979 launched a three year £¼ million research programme, comprising 13 projects, investigating the general theme of "Women and Underachievement". Most of the projects are concerned with achievement in employment but at least two are concerned with curricula: one on the Science Achievement of Schoolgirls, the other on the Effects of Company Training on Women's Employment Opportunities.

107. The European Economic Community has always been generally supportive of the promotion of equality of opportunity for girls and boys. The Standing

54 Gaby Weiner, "Education and the Sex Discrimination Act", *Education Research,* NFER, June 1978.

55 A study of Bridging Courses For Women is a one-year project due to be published in 1980. "Bridging courses" are defined for the study as any educational opportunity which helps a mature person to take the *first* step towards either further or higher education.

Conference of European Ministers of Education at the Hague in September 1979 had as its main theme equality for girls and women, and a major resolution was adopted by the Council of European Communities in late 1979.

108. Generally however, many would maintain that the major obstacle to sex equality is not so much curriculum design and implementation, but *accessibility,* and to overcome this a significant support framework in the form of crèche and nursery provision is required if women and girls are to be able to sustain the regular attendance so necessary for equality in education, training and employment. A NATFHE policy document elaborates many of these arguments.[56]

109. **Those for whom traditional courses are not satisfactory**
Those who are unable to gain educational opportunities at 16-19 may never find their way back into the educational system in later life. The growing awareness of this problem can be instanced in the activities of TRADEC (see paragraph 24, below). We are all different in our basic abilities, motivation and personalities. A teacher's primary task is to optimise the pupils' learning. Each individual should be given the opportunity to match learning ability in the best possible way to the educational task before him or her. The perceptive teacher will identify the strengths and weaknesses of a pupil's capacity to learn, seek to provide a supportive educational environment and will choose or facilitate the choice of the teaching methods and pace to match best these strengths and weaknesses. However, as well as the identification of needs being potentially problematic, so is what is taught.

---

56 *The Education, Training and Employment of Women and Girls,* NATFHE, 1980. calls for, *inter alia:* substantial expansion of appropriately staffed pre-school education; the elimination of discriminatory practices and attitudes in primary and secondary schools, and the development of positive policies; examination of the formal and hidden curriculum; the positive encouragment of girls to consider choices traditionally regarded as male prerogatives; the review of entry requirements and greater grant provision to enable more girls to continue in full-time education; a review of LEA, college, and employment practices; particular attention, for example, by way of special college courses, bridging courses, and promotional material, to encourage the participation in education of women in minority ethnic groups; new study routes, including part-time provision, to enable study to continue from one level to another, and easier access for women to return to study after a break; eradication of constraints on academic, vocational and professional study and career choice; new student places to be created to compensate for the rundown of teacher education and the development of new college courses to provide equivalent education and career opportunities for women to compensate for those lost with the reduction of entry to the teaching profession; the protection and development of opportunities for part-time study at advanced levels; the development of recurrent education to meet specific needs, such as the recreational, self-developmental and compensatory, as well as providing a means of enabling women to re-enter employment after a break; the recognition of the curricular, teacher training and resources implications of the development of college courses meeting the educational and vocational needs of different groups of women; the development of educational opportunities for adults in the workplace through community organizations and within the trade union movement; promotion of research into the education, training and employment prospects faced by women and girls and increased action and participation by the trade unions. NATFHE is committed to pursue policies which will both open access for women and girls to further and higher education, and extend opportunities, facilities and conditions for women teachers and students in the system.

110. The factors impeding solutions are formidable and not entirely unknown. For the teacher correctly to identify students' individual educational needs and to provide optimal teaching strategies for each, requires a student:staff ratio and a level of support quite beyond that which is conceivable in conventional educational policy formulation. Added to this, the choice of curriculum by the teacher or student cannot be assumed always to be the best. The teacher, individually or corporately, has obviously a limited number of educational programmes on offer. The ideal solution described above assumes a curriculum structure able to be well matched to the particular needs of any individual. In those areas where the constraints of national, examined standards are not applicable, the range of programmes on offer can be wide and varied, and there is no doubt that many schools and colleges are able in this way to contribute towards the essential development of disadvantaged pupils and students. The adult literacy campaign is a good example of this. Where recognised skills and competence levels are sought however, usually via examinations of some kind, the programmes on offer are inevitably restricted and invariably constrained by time. A mismatch between an individual's needs and the available curriculum is thus more likely. This is particularly so in vocational education, where viable numbers, well specified skills and uncompromising assessments are normally essential.

111. The choice of curriculum by the student is another possible source of mismatch. In intellectual terms, experienced teachers may be able to judge how well suited students are to cope with the choices they make, and few teachers would deny the motivation that usually accompanies an active choice. If there is only marginal doubt as to intellectual ability, most teachers will give the benefit of that doubt to the student. However, teachers' judgements on pupil choice are of necessity limited. Very often the choice made is not well matched, due perhaps to inadequate and unrealistic advice or counselling, to gross under or over self-estimation or to stereotyping. On the other hand there is the view that the curriculum must not be taken as "given", whereby pupil needs are moulded to fit what is available. The problem may be seen essentially as moulding the curriculum to meet student needs. (Hence, for example, there is a need for curriculum development for those who require little technical training).

112. Perhaps the most difficult aspect of choice however, is where the school-leaver has become so allergic to education that he or she opts out of any further formal education and thus makes no curriculum choice. For obvious reasons, there is not a lot known about the 16+ school leaver who opts out of any further education (although the education service may well ponder upon what makes it unattractive in these circumstances). Longitudinal studies tend to stop at 16+, coinciding with a discontinuity in record-keeping. The National Children's Bureau is attempting a fourth follow-up in its longitudinal study of a sample born in 1958. There is a desperate need to evaluate the data already available at 16+ as to why young people opt out of education and training. Ironically, the current period of high unemployment of young people is providing an opportunity to study some aspects of this group of the disadvantaged. The Northern Ireland

YOUTHWAYS[57] project is typical. An impetus, of course, comes from the Holland Report, and from the teachers' associations.[58]

113. People have different rates of learning. The label of "slow-learner" is one originating in the school system, and may not have the same relevance in further education. Damage is caused when arbitrary thresholds of achievement are imposed on those with low or variable rates of learning. Such people can attain respectable levels of conventional achievement, given the opportunity.[59] Under the present school examination system at 16+, the "slow-learner", likely to fall within the bottom 40% of (conventional) ability of this age group, is unlikely to have any conventional examination success on leaving secondary school. Both the Schools Council and the NFER are investigating ways in which the slow learner can be better dealt with in secondary schools;[60] so far there is evidence that in curriculum terms at this level there is room for improvement. In further education, in spite of an open-entry to many of its courses, the evidence so far available from the secondary sector could also form some useful guidelines for improvement.

114. The use of objectives defining as far as possible the skills to be achieved by all students, is now a familiar concept in further education. What is needed perhaps is a radical approach to the amount of time to be allowed for the attainment of these objectives. Similarly, a difficulty encountered in schools is the way in which a pupil's performance and experiences are evaluated and recorded. By describing well defined objectives and experiences to be fulfilled, and by developing a non-competitive profile method of recording achievement, there is scope for improving these defects where they exist in further education. Indeed, the FEU proposed curriculum for the uncommitted school leaver does include these features. Where more work needs to be done is in the analysis of each individual's needs so that a realistic range of objectives and experiences can be worked for by the student and somehow the resultant level of achievement be fully accredited.

115. **Ethnic groups**
The problems of disadvantage in this area are concentrated by factors such

---

57 YOUTHWAYS is a course programme established by the Department of Education in Northern Ireland, with the primary aim of meeting the needs of unemployed young people who are unqualified, untrained and unmotivated. Experience has confirmed that these young people are more at ease in small units separate from formal educational buildings "...it has been difficult to persuade some young people to attend the local FE college or training centre for sampling and development work, even in jobs they were interested in."

58 NATFHE has recorded its belief that the urgent need to develop an overall strategy to meet the needs of the 16-19 age group cannot be overstressed. Hence, while welcome, the Holland Report's proposals are not seen by the Association as going far enough towards an overall strategy of NATFHE's statements, *The Young Unemployed* and, *The Education Training and Employment of The 16-19 Age Group.*

59 cf. ed. J. Block, *Mastery Learning, Theory and Practice,* Holt, Rinehart and Winston, 1971.

60 (i) Schools Council Working Paper 63 (1979): W.K. Brennan, *Curricular Needs of Slow Learners,* is a survey of over 500 primary, secondary and special schools.

(ii) The NFER project: Provision for Slow Learners in the Secondary School, is a three-year review of policy and organization with respect to slow learners in ordinary schools. The completion date is scheduled for December 1981.

as ignorance, political and personal sensitivity, prejudice, the incompatibility of education and racist views, and culturally biased educational and assessment materials. Some published views have aroused particularly strong feelings[61]; it was not until 1979 that a committee[62] was set up to enquire into the education of children from ethnic minority groups.

116. There is now a growing amount of literature on the subject of multi-ethnic education[63]. NATFHE has published a major document on this issue[64]. The Community Relations Commission published in 1976 *A Second Chance*, which was concerned particularly with further education in multi-racial areas. It analysed the use made of the further education system by ethnic minorities. The lack of national data was acknowledged and much of its detailed information is based on local studies. The publication made several recommendations concerned with curriculum matters: all colleges should appoint a full-time member of staff with special responsibility for the education of ethnic minority students; an adequate counselling and diagnostic service should be available and staff development for those engaged in the teaching of different ethnic groups. It is less specific on curriculum, recognising the many specialisms that exist in FE: in acknowledging that in some inner-city colleges, certain courses such as pre-nursing and radio/TV servicing "have become almost entirely the preserve of black students", it suggests that colleges may like to consider providing specialised courses in race relations or ethnic studies, and it describes an outline Mode III "O" level course on the black and white role in the economic and social development of the UK and the Caribbean.

117. A later study by Guildford Educational Services[65] attempts to define specific problems of West Indians, Pakistanis and Sikhs. Although primarily

---

61 Jencks's study on inequality; Jensen's and to a lesser extent Eysenck's work on intelligence, tended to produce between them evidence, based on American experience, questioning the effectiveness of compensatory education. Their combined arguments, crudely summarised, indicated that the inequalities associated with disadvantaged groups such as ethnic minorities were so fundamental that there was little that the school system could do to improve the situation. This (not unfamiliar) "nature v nurture" argument became polarised to an extent that an objective analysis of the factors of inequality and their possible minimisation at the classroom level, was never really translated into terms which teachers could understand and discuss.

62 In March 1979, Rt. Hon. Mrs Shirley Williams, the then Secretary of State for Education and Science, announced that Mr Anthony Rampton had accepted her invitation to lead an independent enquiry, arising from the 1978 White Paper, *The West Indian Community* (Cmnd. 7186), into the education, attainment and needs of children from all ethnic minority groups. Early attention would be given to pupils of West Indian origin. The terms of reference were announced by the Rt. Hon. Mark Carlisle, MP, the new Secretary of State. They include not only a review in relation to schools but also factors outside the formal education system "...including influence in early childhood and prospects for school leavers".

63 Perhaps the most useful short publication is *Multi-Ethnic Education*, a newsheet giving details of recent literature, research and news. It is published at present by The Centre for Information and Advice on Educational Disadvantage. See also Section **12.10**, appendices 2 and 3.

64 *Further and Teacher Education in a Multi-Cultural Society*, NATFHE, 1979.

65 *Educational and Community Provision for the Unemployed School Leaver*, Guildford Educational Services Limited, 1979. This was a report commissioned by CET in order to inform itself about the possible contribution which educational technology might make to the provision being made for unemployed school leavers.

concerned with unemployment, it comments on the possible unsuitability of some learning materials (eg. for non-conformist Rastafarians); the possible need for effective diagnostic instruments, for remedial languages classes and for the need to build on the successful experiences of teaching staff, rather than measures introduced "from outside".

118. The problem confronting further education with respect to the vocational education of ethnic minorities is complex because if these students are to succeed in this field they must eventually obtain the qualifications offered by the educational system. The temptation to produce special curricula in vocational education is thus generally rejected on the grounds that in terms of vocational competence such students could be regarded as sub-standard. Consequently, recognising that many of them are already disadvantaged at the point of entry to a college, the curricula problems centre around:
(i) adequate and realistic counselling, and the guiding of students into courses matched to their abilities and to their employment prospects;
(ii) the diagnosis of specific learning difficulties and the organization of learning situations to meet these difficulties; and
(iii) the design of special *preparatory* curricula to facilitate entrance to the more conventional vocational courses.
It must be noted, however, that the needs of immigrant students and those of students from ethnic minority groups are not synonymous. Colleges make provision according to needs. For example, a number of colleges have provided programmes for newly arrived immigrants.

119. There are risks associated with the implementation of item (iii), above. There could be a degeneration into stereotyping convenient to the system, or a segregation resulting in separate classes for minority ethnic groups and whites. Although unlikely if the further education service provides the needed training and education, there is a possibility that students might stay too long in the educational system and thus become unable effectively to compete for employment because of their age. Given rising costs and public expenditure restraint, the pressure on further education and on the MSC to provide an education and/or training solution to the problem of disadvantaged ethnic minorities could well represent a major issue facing colleges over the next decade: certainly, there is a need for funding. Administrative difficulty, such as in the obtaining of EEC monies for migrant students (see Section **6.3**), does not help.

TOWARDS AN OVERVIEW

120. Post-school curriculum research and evaluation

Vernon-Ward[66] estimated that only 0.13% of the total educational expenditure in the UK went on educational research. At that time the further and higher education share anyway was low and there is no doubt that the amount of research on the post-school curriculum was negligible. In 1968, supported by an initial grant from the DES, the Brunel Further Education Group was set up at Brunel University under the direction of Professor

66 A. Vernon-Ward, *Resources for Education Research and Development*, NFER, 1973.

Furneaux. However, the DES funding was temporary and the Group has all but disappeared. It did in 1971 publish a survey of research in further education[67] in which it noted that the current spending by the DES on research in this sector was of the order of £26,000 ! More recently, however, the DES and others such as the NFER have paid increasing attention to educational research in the post-school sector. Many of the above paragraphs have described relevant projects. Some polytechnics publish educational research bulletins from time to time[68] but these tend to be occasional, not to say ephemeral, publications. The Scottish Council for Research in Education (SCRE) has occasionally sponsored and published research data relevant to further education[69] but not all of this is easily transferable to England, Wales and Northern Ireland. Mention has also been made in preceding paragraphs that some of the work done by the Schools Council is relevant to further education, as is some of the work done by the ITBs and TSD.

121. The Further Education Research Association (FERA) has made a brave effort to raise the level of awareness of the further and higher education system with respect to educational research. It offers a platform to relevant researchers through its conferences and bulletin.[70] Generally, however, the level of educational research in further education remains low. This is perhaps an inevitable consequence of designating a sector almost entirely in terms of *teaching* institutions. In curriculum research the activity has been even less and there is little doubt that our knowledge-base in many areas of curriculum is weak. There is an uncertainty as to the amount of school-based research that can be transferred to further education. This is due not only to a lack of knowledge about the extent to which such factors as intelligence, parental attitudes and teacher-expectations relate, if at all, to further education, but it is also due to the many varied curricula groupings of small size that are found in nearly all colleges.

122. The lack of a cohesive body of research into day-release is, against this background, understandable. For many years much of the work in this area rested on researchers such as Venables[71] and the Brunel Further Education Group described above. More recently, the FEU has commissioned surveys of research into this area[72] and whilst these have identified many small-scale

67 Hilda Cole and Willam van der Eyken, *Survey of Current Research in Further Education,* Monograph 1, Brunel Further Education Group, 1971.

68 A typical example is the *Bulletin of Educational Research,* Newcastle Polytechnic.

69 An example of this is *A Day Off Work* by A.D. Weir (1971) which looked at motivation in FE Craft Courses. The study was restricted, to four colleges in Central Scotland.

70 Details of FERA and its Bulletin can be obtained from its Secretary: Ann Robinson, Southgate Technical College, London N14 6BS.

71 The publications most associated with this aspect of Ethel Venables's work are:
(i) *Leaving School and Starting Work,* Pergamon Press, 1968
(ii) *Intelligence and motivation among day-release students,* NFER, 1974. Both of these publications are largely based on work done in the 1960s. Thus, whilst they provide much needed insights into the technical college system of that time, many would now maintain that because full-time further and higher education has creamed off many able students, the value of these studies is diminishing.

72 Marjorie Holt, *Review of Research into Aspects of the Education and Training of Young Part-time Students,* 1977 (unpublished, but available from the FEU).

projects, they have also confirmed that severe constraints and deficiencies exist. Constraints such as teacher training and curriculum support have been described earlier. Deficiencies too have been mentioned: the disadvantaged, the training-education interface and the contribution of the day-release FE curriculum to the personal development of the less able, are three such examples of where more curriculum expertise is required.

123. The amount of formal curriculum evaluation, until recently, has also been at a low level. For many years, the effectiveness of the further education system has been described in terms of its level of acceptability to industry and commerce and of its examination success rates. As the major examining bodies have always had on their committees a healthy sprinkling of interested and articulate employers, these two factors have been normally complementary. The Industrial Training Act 1964 and the creation of the ITBs, with their more structured training recommendations, sharpened to some extent the appraisal of further education curricula and one or two examples of curriculum evaluation began to appear.[73] These, however, were still related to examination success and the technical education of skilled workers. At about the same time a growing awareness of the general need for curriculum evaluation appeared and the Schools Council began to include in its curriculum budgets an evaluatory element. A framework for curriculum evaluation theory also began to appear in educational literature and whilst there is no unique theory, the growing experience of evaluators has resulted in some agreement on the aims and techniques of curriculum evaluation.

124. The creation of UVP schemes by the DES with their emphasis on non-skilled workers, vocational preparation and no formal examinations, obviously demand evaluation techniques related to factors other than examination successes and technical skills. With this in mind the FEU was set up, although since then the NFER has undertaken the evaluation of the UVP schemes. However, the FEU, although not evaluating UVP, has set up evaluatory studies in other FE curriculum areas. It has an interest in TEC and BEC evaluation, but in addition to this it has, relevant to its remit, sponsored other curriculum studies.[74]

125. As explained in Section **10.1**, this is not the publication in which to

---

73 Two interesting examples are:
(i) B.M. Moore, *Block or Day Release*, NFER, 1968. This was a DES sponsored comparative study of engineering apprentices attending FE colleges on two different modes of attendance. The project was largely inconclusive, because the ability levels of those apprentices on block and day-release differed significantly.
(ii) S.M. Kannett Barry, *Engineering Craft Studies*, NFER, 1974. This was a CGLI sponsored study of the effectiveness of the FE system in implementing a new curriculum. The result was far from complimentary to FE management and it identified a lack of uniformity between the various examining boards and a deficiency in the dissemination of curriculum change in the colleges.

74 (i) *Dissemination of Curriculum Information in Further Education*, Blackpool College of Technology and Art, FEU, 1979.
(ii) *Review of the Major Styles of Curriculum Design in Further Education*, Coombe Lodge, FEU, 1980.
(iii) *FE Curriculum Analysis Project*, University of Keele/FEU, 1980.

undertake a discussion of the relative merits of, say, illuminative versus analytical curriculum evaluation. Many would maintain that any evaluation is better than none because it more often than not identifies deficiencies of support and/or resources. Certainly the work in this area so far sponsored by the FEU has indicated that further education curriculum dissemination is poor; that the central curriculum bodies tend to over-estimate the ability of colleges to respond to curriculum change; and that our knowledge of the curriculum process is primitive. Each of these is enough to justify a significant increase of resources. On the other hand, some would maintain that curriculum evaluation is uncomfortably too near the concept of *accountability*. Becher and Maclure[75], in suggesting CNAA type visitations to schools as a pattern of accountability, have implied that the curriculum is an integral part of accountability. Few would deny this, but if this sub-section has achieved one of its aims, fewer may now accept that the post-school curriculum or indeed any other curriculum, can be encapsulated, analysed and evaluated as if it were a simple, static and apolitical process.

---

75 Tony Becher and Stuart Maclure, *Accountability in Education*, NFER, 1979.

10.2

APPENDIX 1

THE OPEN UNIVERSITY: A MODEL FOR DISTANCE LEARNING IN FURTHER EDUCATION?

1. The OU is by definition a radical departure from conventional curriculum development and implementation. Set up in 1969, it is predominantly associated with higher education although in recent years it has been developing courses at sub-degree level. It employs distance learning techniques and strategies: radio, television, correspondence texts, self-assessment tests, computer marked assignments (objective testing) and tutor-marked assignments. These are backed up by a nation-wide system of tutorials held usually in the evening in schools, colleges and polytechnics; together with a series of (compulsory) summer schools (of a duration of one week or more) basic to some courses. An integral support system, in the form of its own Institute of Educational Technology, is an essential feature of its curriculum design and evaluation. The OU degree courses comprise a modular system of credits and half-credits: an ordinary degree is the aggregate of six credits, an honours degree eight credits. Exemptions related to previous qualifications are possible and the effectiveness of the OU exemption system has undoubtedly given support to a more universal system of accreditation. The University is largely intended for adults. DES limits applv to the OU student body. Teachers are the largest occupational group in the OU, some of whom go on to study for a higher degree (not necessarily within the Open University). An experiment was set up in 1974-75 whereby a restricted number of young people under the age of 21 were allowed to enrol on OU courses. This was a government idea; it was not a great success, and had a high wastage rate.

2 The original financial thinking was that the OU would operate at something like one-third of the cost of conventional higher education institutions but it has never been possible to make a firm analytical comparison. An estimated unit productivity is that one academic, backed by an appropriate support team, is able to produce in a year one to three units of a 32-34 full credit course. A credit is estimated to involve some 400 hours work (excluding summer school) from students. Translating this into further education sub-degree terms obviously raises major resource questions and what evidence has emerged from the various projects in this sector, makes difficult to assess the overall costs of distance learning. With a success rate of about 70% for each year of study however, the OU has undoubtedly proved that for its type of students, this curriculum model does work. Moreover, the OU has undertaken significant involvement in continuing and pre-vocational education.

3. As an innovation in the process of curriculum development, the OU is widely acclaimed and its systematic approach to course design is regarded as an example of good educational technology in action. Its material is used by many outside the OU system and its publishing activity is a successful enterprise. All this success has prompted a growing interest in the concept of an OU analogue in the form of an"Open College" (cf Section **12.1.**5) for sub-degree work. Although curriculum methods might not differ significantly from those already existing in the OU, many in further and higher education, would now give no more than a cautious welcome to such a concept on the grounds that its application to a heterogeneous sub-degree ability range is as yet unproven, and that it would also involve a considerable resource commitment of a nature not yet fully investigated. The comparative data possible to adduce from the OU provides an essential base from which this system of curriculum development and provision could be appraised.

4. However, the preparation of material is crucial in any distance learning programme. Techniques and materials should also be transferable for use within colleges (either as course material, or as part of educational technology provision). Preparation of such materials should clearly be undertaken by teachers experienced in the course needs of the users. If there is to be an extension of techniques pioneered by the Open University, direct transference of course material cannot be wholly suitable. Rather, the material, instead of being an extension of OU methods, will require to be designed specifically by and for those with extensive further education experience. The observation can also be made that no firm conclusion concerning a wide application to further education of distance learning methods can be reached until there have been sufficient effective and monitored pilot programmes.

APPENDIX 2

SOME ORGANIZATIONS RELEVANT TO THE STUDY OF EDUCATIONAL DISADVANTAGE[1]

(Further lists, specific to their subjects, are contained in appendices to Sections **12.10** and **12.11**).

Advisory Centre for Education,
18 Victoria Park Square,
Bethnal Green,
London E2 9PB
01-980 4596

Advisory Committee for the Education of
Romany and Other Travellers,
Mary Ward Centre,
9 Tavistock Place,
London WC1H 95P
01-387 1918

Adult Learning Trust,
10 Barley Mow Passage,
Chiswick,
London W4 4PH
01-994 6477

Adult Literacy Unit,
52-54 High Holborn,
London WC1V 6RL
01-405 4017

Aslib Social Welfare Group,
c/o 5 Tavistock Place,
London WC1H 9SS

Association of Dramatherapy,
136 Oxford Street,
Rugby,
Warwickshire
0788-73856

Association for Recurrent Education,
c/o School of Education,
The University,
Nottingham NG7 2RD
0602-56101

Association of Teachers of Ethnic Minorities,
c/o 8 Coles Close,
Rushey Mead,
Leicester.

British and Foreign School Society,
The Richard Mayo Hall,
Eden Street,
Kingston-upon-Thames,
Surrey
01-546 2379

1. List supplied by the Centre for Information and Advice on Educational Disadvantage.

British Association of Early Childhood Education,
Montgomery Hall,
Kennington Oval,
London SE11 5SW
01-582 8744

British Association for the Retarded,
17 Pembridge Square,
London W2 4EP
01-229 1855

British Association of Social Workers,
16 Kent Street,
Birmingham B5 6RD

British Library Social Welfare Information
Resources Project.
c/o National Institute of Social Work,
5 Tavistock Place,
London WC1
01-387 9681

British Psychological Society,
48 Princess Road East,
Leicester LE1 7DR
0533-549568

British Sociological Association,
BSA Office,
13 Endsleigh Street,
London WC1 0DS.
01-387 3627

Cambridge House Literacy Scheme,
131 Camberwell Road,
London SE5 0HF
01-701 4221

Cambridge Specific Learning Disabilities Group,
Lucy Cavendish College,
Cambridge CB3 0BU.
0223-63409

Catholic Education Council,
41 Cromwell Road,
London SW7 2DS
01-584 7471

Centre for Information on Language
Teaching and Research,
20 Carlton House Terrace,
London SW1
01-839 2626

Child Poverty Action Group,
1 Macklin Street,
London WC2 5NH
01-242 3225

Community Service Volunteers,
237 Pentonville Road,
London N1 9NJ
01-278 6601

Community and Youth Service Association,
82 Great Bridgewater Street,
Manchester M15 5JY
061-236 6623

Confederation for the Advancement of State Education,
4 Stafford Street,
Helensburgh,
Dumbartonshire G84 9JT

Co-ordinating Committee for Mother Tongue Teaching,
c/o 62 Chandos Place,
London WC2

Council for Educational Advance,
c/o Hamilton House,
Mabledon Place,
London WC1H 9BD
01-387 2442

Council for Education in World Citizenship
43 Russell Square,
London WC1B 5DA
01-637 8321

Educational Development Association,
The Castle,
Museum Square,
Wisbech,
Cambridgeshire

Educational Publishers Council,
19 Bedford Square,
London WC1B 3HJ
01-580 6321

Educational Resources Information Centre,
Box 40,
Institute for Urban and Minority Education,
Teachers College,
Columbia University,
New York NY 10027

English Teaching Information Centre,
British Council,
10 Spring Gardens,
London SW1A 2BN

European Bureau of Adult Education,
Nieuwveg 4,
PO Box 367,
Amersfoort,
Netherlands

Family Service Unit,
207 Marylebone Road,
London NW1 5PQ
01-402 5175/6

Friends' Community Relations Committee,
Friends' House,
Euston Road,
London NW1 2BJ
01-387 3601

General Synod Board of Education,
Church House,
Dean's Yard,
Westminster,
London SW1P 3N2
01-222 9011

Harmony,
64 Ashbourne Road,
Mitcham,
Surrey CR4 2BA

Health Education Council,
78 New Oxford Street,
London WC1A 1AH
01-637 1881

Home and School Council,
81 Rustlings Street,
Sheffield S11 7AB

Independent Assessment and Research Centre,
53 Marylebone High Street,
London W1M 3AE
01-486 6106

Institute for Research into Mental and Multiple Handicap,
16 Fitzroy Square,
London W1P 5HQ
01-387 6066

Inter-Action,
I.A. Advisory Service Limited,
15 Wilkin Street,
London NW5 3N6
01-485 0881

International Bureau of Education,
Palais Wilson,
1211 Geneva 14,
Switzerland

Institute for Family and Environmental Studies,
7a Kidderpore Avenue,
London NW3 7SX
01-435 5919

International Round Table for the Advancement of Counselling
Livingstone House,
Livingstone Road,
London E15 2LL
01-534 0085/534 7845

Links Association,
Old Lamb House,
7 Strad,
Rhondda,
Mid-Glamorgan
044-372 2380

MIND
22 Harley Street,
London W1N 2ED
01-637 0741

Minority Rights Group,
36 Craven Street,
London WC2
01-930 6659

National Association for the Care and Rehabilitation of Offenders,
169 Clapham Road,
London SW9
01-735 1151

National Association for Gifted Children,
1 South Audley Street,
London W1Y 5DQ
01-499 1188

National Association of Governors and Managers,
40 Garth Drive,
Liverpool L18 6HW
051-724 3273

National Association of Asian Youth,
46 High Street,
Southall,
Middlesex
01-574 1325

National Association for Multi-Racial Education,
The Northbrook Centre,
Penn Road,
Slough, Berks SL2 2IP
0753-23416

National Association for Remedial Education,
77 Chignal Road,
Chemsford,
Essex

National Association of Social Workers in Education,
8 Ryeleaze
Potterne,
Devizes,
Wiltshire

National Association for the Teaching of English,
Fernleigh,
106 Thornhill Road,
Edgerton,
Huddersfield HD5 5AU
0484-20728

National Association of Tutors in Education and Health,
14 Gair Park Hill,
Newport,
Gwent NPT 3NQ

National Committee for Adult Literacy,
2 Rutland Avenue,
Liverpool 17

National Confederation of Parent Teacher Associations,
1 White Avenue,
Northfleet,
Gravesend,
Kent DA11 7JB
0474-60618

National Conference of Teacher's Centre Leaders,
c/o Enfield Teachers Centre,
Craddock Road,
Enfield EN1 3ST
01-363 4148

National Council for Special Education,
1 Wood Street,
Stratford-upon-Avon,
Warwickshire CU37 6JE
Day-time 021-744 9162
Evening 0789-5332

National Council for Social Service,
26 Bedford Square,
London WC1B 3HU
01-636 4066

National Educational Research and Development Trust,
32 Trumpington Street,
Cambridge
0223-59126

National Elfrida Rathbone Society,
11a Whitworth Street,
Manchester
061-236 5358/9

National Foundation for Educational Research,
The Mere,
Upton Park,
Slough,
Berks SL1 2DQ
0753-28161

National Federation of Community Associations,
26 Bedford Square,
London WC1B 3HU
01-636 4066

National Gypsy Education Council,
82 Eversham Road,
London E15 4AJ
01-555 3648

National Institute of Adult Education,
35 Queen Anne Street,
London W1M 0BL.
01 637 4241

National Youth Bureau,
17-23 Albion Street,
Leicester LE1 6GD
0533-554775

Parents' National Educational Union,
Murray House,
3 Vandon Street,
London SW1H 0AJ
01-222 7181

Personal Social Services Council,
Brook House,
2-16 Torrington Place,
London WC1E 7HN
01-323 4757

Pre-school Playgroups Association,
Alford House,
Aveline Street,
London SE11
01-582 8871

Project Fullemploy Trust,
Project Fullemploy,
Token House,
14-18 Copthall Avenue,
London EC2

Rowntree Memorial Trust,
Beverley House,
Shipton Road,
York
0904-29241

Social Research Co-ordinating Unit,
SRCo Unit,
Cabinet Office,
Queen Anne Chambers,
Tothill Street,
London

Teachers' Advisory Council on Alcohol and Drug Education,
2 Mount Street,
Manchester M2 5NG
061-834 7210

United Kingdom Reading Association
General Secretary,
63 Laurel Grove,
Sunderland,
Co Durham SR2 9EE

Volunteer Centre,
29 Lower Kings' Road,
Berkhamsted,
Herts HP4 2AB

Workers' Education Association,
Temple House,
9 Upper Berkeley Street,
London W1H 8BY
061-402 5601

World Council of Churches,
Secretary for Migration,
Programme Unit on Justice and Service,
150 Route de Ferney,
PO Box No. 66,
1211 Geneva 20.

Young Volunteer Force Federation,
c/o Community Service Volunteers,
237 Pentonville Road,
London N1
01 278 6601

Youth Aid,
Tress House,
3 Stamford Street,
London SE1 9NT
01-928 6424/5

REFERENCE

Tony Becher and Stuart Maclure, *Accountability in Education*, NFER, 1979.

Tony Becher and Stuart Maclure, *The Politics of Curriculum Change*, Hutchinson, 1978.

ed. J. Block, *Mastery Learning, Theory and Practice*, Holt, Rinehart and Winston, 1971.

Adrian Bristow, *Inside the Colleges of Further Education*, HMSO, 1976.

Tyrell Burgess, *Education After School*, Penguin, 1977.

Eileen M. Bryne, *Planning and Education Inequality*, NFER, 1974.

L.M. Cantor and I.F. Roberts, *Further Education Today A Critical Review*, Routledge and Kegan Paul, 1979.

L.B. Curzon, *Teaching in Further Education*, Cassell, 1976.

Developments in Partnership in Validation, CNAA, 1979.

H.G. Earnshaw, *The Associated Examining Board – Origin and History*, AEB, 1974.

ed. Ron Glatter, *Control of the Curriculum: Issues and trends in Britain and Europe*, University of London/NFER, 1977.

ed. Richard Hooper, *The Curriculum: Context, Design and Development*, Oliver and Boyd/Open University Press, 1971.

A.V. Kelly, *The Curriculum, Theory and Practice*, Harper and Row, 1977.

E.G. King *et al.*, *Post Compulsory Education: The Way Ahead*, Sage Publications, 1975.

Ronald King, *Schools and Colleges*, Routledge and Kegan Paul, 1976.

Denis Lawton *et al.*, *Theory and Practice of Curriculum Studies*, Routledge and Kegan Paul, 1978.

Michael Locke and Jane Howells, *Britain and the EEC: Admission to Higher Education in the United Kingdom:* papers presented for a conference organized by North East London Polytechnic.

Michael Locke and John Pratt, *A Guide to Learning After School*, Pelican, 1979.

Patricia Macmillan and Len Powell, *An Induction Course for Teaching in Further Education and Industry*, Pitman, 1973.

David Matthews, *The Relevance of School Learning Experience to Peformance in Industry*, EITB, 1979.

Christopher Murray, *Youth Unemployment: A socio-psychological study of disadvantaged 16-19 year olds*, NFER, 1978.

ed. Guy Neave, *Research Perspectives on the Transition from School to Work*, Swetz and Zeitlinger, Amsterdam, 1978.

Audrey and Howard Nicholls, *Developing a Curriculum: A Practical Guide for Teachers at Primary, Secondary and Tertiary Levels*, George Allen and Unwin, 1978.

John Pratt *et al.*, *Costs and Control in Further Education*, NFER, 1978.

ed. Barbara Priestley, *British Qualifications*, Kegan Paul, 1977.

Review of Craft Apprenticeship in Engineering, Information Paper 49, EITB, 1978.

G.J. Russell, *Teaching in Further Education*, Pitman, 1972.

ed. J. Russell and J. Latcham, *Curriculum Development in Further Education*, Coombe Lodge, 1973.

W. Bonney Rust and H.F.P. Harris, *Examinations: Pass or Failure?*, Pitman, 1967.

J. Springett, *Further Education Outside the Polytechnics*, ACFHE, 1975.

P.H. Taylor and M. Johnson, *Curriculum Development – A Comparative Study*, NFER, 1974.

A Vernon-Ward, *Resources for Educational Research and Development*, NFER, 1973.

Gaby Weiner, "Education and the Sex-Discrimination Act", *Education Research*, NFER, June 1978.

Section 11

STAFF

1 SALARIES: TEACHING STAFF

1. **The Burnham Further Education Committee**
Among the provisions of the Education Act, 1944 is the requirement for the payment to teachers in England and Wales of a standard scale of salaries. The Remuneration of Teachers Act 1965 gave statutory authority to the schools and furthur education negotiating committees responsible for determining teachers' pay. In fact, until recently, there were four negotiating committees: the Burnham (Primary and Secondary) Schools Committee, the Burnham Further Education Committee, the Burnham Farm Institutes Committee and the Pelham Committee. The Houghton Report recommended a unified further and higher education salaries system, proposing identical scales in the establishments previously covered by the separate Burnham Further Education Committee and the Pelham Committee (which covered colleges of education). When, in 1975, teacher education and further education were brought under a common set of regulations, The Further Education Regulations 1975, it seemed appropriate to the Secretary of State to merge the Burnham FE Committee and the Pelham Committee. This was done by a determination made by the Secretary of State in 1976. The opportunity was also taken to absorb the Burnham Farm Institutes Committee into the reformed Burnham FE Committee. Hence, there are currently two statutory committees which deal with the salaries of teachers: the Burnham (Primary and Secondary) Schools Committee and the Burnham Further Education Committee.[1] The Burnham Further Education Committee determines the remuneration of teachers in all maintained establishments of further and higher education (within the meaning of The Further Education Regulations 1975) including teachers in adult education establishments. It covers full-time and part-time teachers. Teachers seconded to non-maintained bodies which reimburse the employing LEAs the amount of their salaries, and teachers paid "Burnham equivalent" salaries in, for example, outdoor centres, are not subject to the jurisdiction of the committee.

2. The committee consists of two panels, one of which represents the teachers and the other the LEAs and the DES. The committee chairman is independent and is appointed by the Secretary of State for Education and Science. Membership of the Burnham FE Committee is:
Management Panel
Association of County Councils (8)
Association of Metropolitan Authorities (6)
Welsh Joint Education Committee (1)
Department of Education and Science (2)
(Observers from certain Church Boards[2] may attend)

---

1 Agricultural establishments and penal establishments are discussed in Sections **11.14** and **11.15**, below. Adult education is referred to under paragraphs 40-43 below.
2 The denominations represent actual employers in voluntary colleges. However, there is no denominational representation, even with observer status, on the Burnham Primary and Secondary Committee, because, although the governors of aided *schools* are employers, the LEAs are the paymasters, and Burnham is concerned wholly with pay.

Teachers' Panel
National Association of Teachers in Further and Higher Education (12)
Association of Principals of Colleges (2)
National Society for Art Education (1)
Association of Agricultural Education Staffs (1)
The Joint Secretaries to the Committee are the Secretary, Local Authorities Conditions of Service Advisory Board (LACSAB), and the General Secretary, National Association of Teachers in Further and Higher Education (NATFHE).

3. When the Committee has agreed new salary scales and other provisions, subject to the approval of the Secretary of State, statutory instruments are made. These give statutory authority to the reports of the Committee (the salaries documents) which are normally issued by the DES each year. When a report is not issued, an amendment order may be made to amend the previous report. There are two circumstances which can lead to arbitration in the event of a failure of the Committee to reach agreement. Firstly, if the Management and Teachers' Panels resolve that breakdown has occurred, the issues are referred to arbitration. Secondly, if the chairman believes together with one of the panels that no further progress can be made on any issue, he or she can decide that arbitration should take place. The arbitral body is established by the Secretary of State and is provided with a chairman by the Arbitration, Conciliation and Advisory Service (ACAS). The Burnham FE Committee has rarely resorted to arbitration: since the Committee was reformed in 1976 it has not been used at all. The Secretary of State can "veto" the findings of the arbitrators, by securing in the national financial interest a majority vote in both Houses of Parliament against the recommendations. There is a sub-committee of the Burnham FE Committee which deals with grading of courses (see Section **11.2.**6 *et seq.*, below); there is also a Joint Committee of Reference which may meet to settle questions relating to the provisions of the report. Another committee, the Further Education Joint Working Party, deals with matters referred to it by the Burnham FE Committee for detailed consideration. This body also received references from the Council of Local Education Authorities/Further Education teachers' negotiating group which dealt with conditions of service: this function is now undertaken by the National Joint Council for Further Education Teachers in England and Wales. A Commentary on the Burnham FE Report is published by the Joint Secretaries. In some circumstances, the Joint Secretaries issue an agreed circular which outlines the understandings reached in the Committee (see also note to Reference list).

4. Those to whom the Committee Report applies

(i) *Full-time teachers*
There is a distinction in the rates and methods of calculation of pay between full-time and part-time teachers. Mainly administrative positions inside

teaching, such as head of department and principal, are treated as being teaching posts. Where posts involve divided service, a circumstance where, for example, a teacher is employed in two discrete areas of education, then the issue of differing salary rates is resolved thus: the teacher is paid on the salary scale appropriate to the post in which the majority of time is spent: where the time is split equally, the teacher is paid at the higher of the two rates. The lower rate of salary applies where this is not the case. For the full-time teacher to receive by law the Burnham FE Committee rates of pay, the teacher must work in an institution which can be categorised as a further education establishment for the purposes of the Committee Report.

(ii) *Part-time teachers*
The Burnham FE Committee has agreed that part-time hourly rates of pay should be based on full-time salaries and that one set of national part-time hourly rates will be introduced on a phased basis in the future. In the meantime, Appendix IV of the Burnham salaries document contains the mandatory determined rates for part-time teachers. These rates are determined by the Committee on a regional basis. Generally, the rates in a region are fixed by reference to the categories of work. However, in some regions a further, lower rate has been authorised for certain non-advanced further education courses. These remain in existence, for the time being, where, prior to the determination by the Committee of part-time rates, the local authorities in the regions concerned had adopted such a rate (see paragraph 6 (iv) below).

(iii) A different system of remuneration applies to teachers employed in part-time service in colleges and departments of education. Included also in this category are "such other part-time teachers as may, at the discretion of the authority be determined". These teachers are paid a proportion of the annual salary that would be appropriate if they were paid as full-time teachers. A parallel provision was made by the CLEA/FE teachers negotiating group. This provides for the creation of Associate Lecturer posts (see Section **11.7.**11).

5. **Salary scales**
There are nine salary scales: Lecturer Grade I, Lecturer Grade II, Senior Lecturer, Principal Lecturer, Reader, Academic Post above Reader, Head of Department, Vice-Principal, Principal. There are six grades of department, each with an appropriate salary scale upon which their heads are paid; there are twelve groups of colleges. The salaries of vice-principals and principals are on fixed points determined by their employers from the ranges of salaries for each group. Where there are exceptional circumstances in the cases of principals, vice-principals and heads of department grade VI which justify a salary higher than that permissible within the appropriate salary range or scale, then application may be made to the Secretary of State for approval of payment of the higher salary.

6. Salary scales and points ranges: 1 April 1979

(see note to Reference list)

An interim salary award made in January 1980, and effective from 1 January 1980, gave an increase of 7½% on the scale points printed below, or £288 *per annum,* whichever is the greater.

i) *Further Education*

Scale/Incremental Point	
Lecturer I	£
0	3480
1	3630
2	3780
3	3930
4	4083
5	4245
6	4401
7	4581
8	4761
9	4944
10	5124
11	5298
12	5472
13	5643
14	5814
15	*5988
Lecturer II	£
0	4470
1	4746
2	5019
3	5289
4	5550
5	5811
6	6072
7	6333
8	6597
9	6873
10	7149
Senior Lecturer	
0	6597
1	6873
2	7149
3	7422
4	7701
5	7977
6	8253
Principal Lecturer/Reader	
0	7680
1	7962
2	8241
3	8523
4	8799
5	9081
6	9360
7	9639
Heads of Department	
Grade I	
0	6435
1	6660
2	6888
3	7113
4	7338
Grade II	
0	7338
1	7572
2	7812
3	8046
4	8283
Grade III	
0	8031
1	8268
2	8502
3	8742
4	8976

**With effect from 1 September 1979*

Grade IV		
0		8655
1		8916
2		9180
3		9441
4		9702
Grade V		
0		9420
1		9681
2		9945
3		10206
4		10467
Grade VI		
0		10185
1		10449
2		10710
3		10971
4		11232
Vice-Principal	(Min)	(Max)
1	7155	7737
2	7845	8424
3	8589	9168
4	9342	9921
5	10071	10653
6	10734	11316
7	11340	11916
8	11967	12477
9	12489	12999
10	13008	13518
11	13530	14040
12	14052	14562
Principal	(Min)	(Max)
1	8400	9093
2	9222	9915
3	10110	10815
4	11022	11715
5	11886	12495
6	12585	13194
7	13218	13827
8	13890	14499
9	14511	15123
10	15138	15744
11	15762	16371
12	16383	16995

Lecturer IA Agriculture	
0	3480
1	3630
2	3780
3	3960
4	4083
5	4245
6	4401
7	4581
8	4751
9	4944
10	5124
11	5298
12	5472
13	5643
14	5814
15	*5988
Lecturer IB Agriculture	
0	3921
1	4071
2	4221
3	4371
4	4527
5	4686
6	4842
7	5022
8	5202
9	5385
10	5565
11	5739
12	5913
13	6084
14	6255
Lecturer II Agriculture	
0	6066
1	6273
2	6474
3	6678
4	6882
5	7086
6	7293
7	7494

**With effect from 1 September 1979*

Lecturer II Agriculture (Cont.)		12	9177
8	7701	13	9414
9	7905	*Principal Agriculture*	
10	8109	0	8109
11	8316	1	8316
12	8526	2	8526
Vice-Principal Agriculture		3	8730
0	6678	4	8940
1	6882	5	9177
2	7086	6	9414
3	7293	7	9651
4	7494	8	9885
5	7701	9	10125
6	7905	10	10359
7	8190	11	10596
8	8316	12	10833
9	8526	13	11070
10	8730	14	11304
11	8940	15	11544

(ii) The 1979 salaries settlement included a reference to The Standing Commission on Pay Comparability (Chairman, Professor Clegg). From 1 April 1979 an addition of £6 per month has been paid to every teacher on account of the expected award. Following the interim award of January 1980, arrangements have been made for recouping the £6 payment made on account. The payments made will be recouped over the period 1 January 1980-30 April 1980. The interim award is a separate settlement, and will not affect negotiations arising from the Clegg Report. However, the interim award will be subsumed in the Clegg settlement. It was agreed that 50% of the settlement arising from the Clegg Commission's report would be paid on 1 January 1980, and 50% on 1 September 1980.

(iii) *Part-time hourly rates*
The part-time hourly rates by regions of the country and categories of work, effective from 1 April 1979 (and in the case of category II/III work, from 1 September 1979) are as follows (but see also sub-paragraph (iv), below):

1. In the Counties of Buckinghamshire, East Sussex, Essex, Hertfordshire, Kent, Surrey, the Greater London Council area, and the area of Berkshire within the former county of Buckinghamshire:

Category I	£7.21 per hour
Category II (II/III)	£7.21
Category III*	£7.21
Category IV	£6.00
Category VA	£5.03
Category VB	£4.47

2. In the Counties of Berkshire, excluding the area within the former County of Buckinghamshire, Hampshire, Isle of Wight, Oxfordshire and West Sussex:
(NB: The category V rates in this region are separated into two rates, VA and VB from 1 April 1979).

Category I	£7.27 per hour
Category II (II/III)	£6,91
Category III*	£6.69
Category IV	£5.56
Category VA	£4.96
Category VB	£4.78

3. In the Counties of Avon, Cornwall, Devon, Dorset, Gloucestershire, Isles of Scilly, Somerset and Wiltshire:

Category I	£6.97 per hour
Category II (II/III)	£6.97
Category III*	£6.97
Category IV	£5.74
Category VA	£4.70
Category VB	£4.01

4. In the Counties of Hereford and Worcester, Salop, Staffordshire and Warwickshire and the Metropolitan Districts of Birmingham, Coventry, Dudley, Sandwell, Solihull, Walsall and Wolverhampton:

Category I	£7.21 per hour
Category II (II/III)	£6.75
Category III*	£6.19
Category IV	£5.58
Category V	£4.47

5 In the Counties of Derbyshire, Leicestershire, Lincolnshire, Northamptonshire and Nottinghamshire:

Category I	£6.89 per hour
Category II (II/III)	£6.89
Category III*	£6.47
Category IV	£5.60
Category VA	£4.60
Category VB	£4.01

6. In the Counties of Bedfordshire, Cambridgeshire, Norfolk and Sussex:

Category I	£7.09 per hour
Category II (II/III)	£6.44
Category III*	6.27
Category IV	£5.27
Category VA	£4.47
Category VB	£4.01

7. In the Counties of Humberside and North Yorkshire and the Metropolitan Districts of Barnsley, Bradford, Calderdale, Doncaster, Kirklees, Leeds, Rotherham, Sheffield and Wakefield:

Category I	£7.29 per hour
Category II (II/III)	£7.29
Category III*	£7.29
Category IV	£6.05
Category VA	£5.00
Category VB	£4.01

8. In the Counties of Cheshire and Lancashire, and the Metropolitan Districts of Bolton, Bury, Manchester, Oldham, Rochester, Salford, Stockport, Tameside, Trafford, Wigan, Knowsley, Liverpool, St Helens, Sefton, and Wirral:

Category I	£12.38 per two hour session
Category II (II/III)	£12.38
Category III*	£12.38
Category IV	£10.12
Category V	£ 8.28

9. In the Counties of Cleveland, Cumbria, Durham and Northumberland and the Metropolitan Districts of Gateshead, Newcastle upon Tyne, North Tyneside, South Tyneside and Sunderland:

Category I	£7.12 per hour
Category II (II/III)	£7.12
Category III*	£6.91
Category IV	£5.41
Category VA	£4.93
Category VB	£4.23

10. In the Counties of Clwyd, Dyfed, Gwent, Gwynedd, Mid Glamorgan, Powys, South Glamorgan and West Glamorgan:

Category I	£7.07 per hour
Category II (II/III)	£7.07
Category III*	£6.97
Category IV	£6.02
Category VA	£4.71
Category VB	£4.01

**NB. These rates were to be used from 1 April to 31 August 1979 only. From 1 September 1979 the category II/III rate applied.*

(iv) The 1979 agreement on part-time hourly rates incorporated the equivalent of the "£6 per month on account" referred to in sub-paragraph (ii) above. The rates from 1 January 1980 will incorporate similarly the recoupment. A formula has been agreed by the Burnham FE Committee which ensures that the basic rates have been increased by 7½% and the minimum increase will be 6p per hour.

(v) The Burnham Further Education Committee is committed to introducing nationally uniform hourly rates, according to the category of work done, for part-time teachers. However, there is no indication at this stage when such rates will be introduced and, of course, recent settlements on part-time rates, restricted as they have been by incomes policies, have not made major moves in this direction. The Burnham FE Committee has approved a formula which seeks to relate together the median salaries from the relevant full-time salary scales, the proportions of full-time posts, and the category of work in order to produce an appropriate part-time rate for each category of work. The Committee could not agree on an appropriate hourly divisor to be used in this formula, but the figure of 972 has been used for illustrative purposes in recent negotiations.

7. **Transfers and bars** [3]

There are circumstances in which Lecturers Grade II can transfer to the Senior Lecturer scale. The final three points of the Lecturer Grade II scale are the same as the first three points of the Senior Lecturer scale. If an individual, whilst on point 8 of the Lecturer Grade II scales is responsible for a significant amount of work in categories I and/or II/III (formerly categories I and/or II and/or III) and satisfies the efficiency requirements, then he or she is entitled to transfer to the Senior Lecturer scale when next due to receive an increment. Instead of progressing to point 9 on the Lecturer Grade II scale, the teacher will move to point 1 on the Senior Lecturer scale. These points carry the same monetary value. The individual will then proceed up the Senior Lecturer scale as if appointed to that scale. If the work and efficiency requirements are not satisfied at the earliest point of eligibility, there is an opportunity at the subsequent later points on the scale to transfer when these conditions are satisfied: transfer will then take place at points 9 or 10 of the Lecturer II scale.

8. The requirements for the transfer from Lecturer Grade II to Senior Lecturer need further explanation. It has been agreed that it is inappropriate and probably impossible to lay down criteria for the definition of "efficiency". Local authorities have been advised that the case of a person who becomes eligible for transfer should be reviewed in good time by the principal of the college. Such advice and information should be laid before the principal and the governors as is necessary to enable a decision to be made. The principal ought then to submit the name of the teacher concerned to the governors, or to the authority, as appropriate and to specify in each case whether the individual has satisfied the requirements. The teacher should be told of the

3 College administrators should note the need to maintain records of an individual teacher's incremental point in order to determine when the question of going through bars will arise; and to ensure that unwarranted changes of timetable either in favour or against advanced work do not take place at such times. There is also a need to maintain records of decisions regarding the efficiency requirement for the benefit of any appeal machinery.

decision as soon as possible. If the decision is against transfer, then the teacher should be advised of the right to appeal. Where a decision to appeal is taken, the principal ought to prepare a report on the matter and to issue copies of that report and such documents as are relevant to the appellant. The appeal should be heard within the processes of the agreed grievance procedure (see Section **11.7**.9 and Sections **2.4;** and **11.9**).

9. In an assessment of a "a significant amount of work", in relation to the transfer of a lecturer Grade II to the Senior Lecturer scale and passage through the bar on the Senior and Principal Lecturer scales, cognizance should be taken of the following interpretations of the phrase. The Further Education Reports define this amount as at least 50% of work time.
Work time can be defined in two ways:
(i) the workload in the year immediately preceding consideration of transfer or passage through the bar;
(ii) the average workload in the three previous years.
Whichever is the more favourable of these alternatives is to be applied. Further, the phrase "a significant amount of work" refers to more than class contact time. It has been agreed that time spent in the administering of work of others can be taken into account. Where a teacher has class contact remission, these hours should be considered according to whether or not they relate to advanced level work courses. Hence, if a teacher had an allocation of 18 contact hours, three of which were remitted, then unless those hours were legitimately spent on advanced level work, at least 9 hours of advanced teaching would be required in order to qualify for bar transfer.

10. As has been seen, salary bars apply to the Senior Lecturer and Principal Lecturer scales, although it is important to note in these instances that there is no efficiency requirement. In the past, the provisions concerning passing the bar on the Principal Lecturer and Senior Lecturer salary scales were very complicated. For example, a Principal Lecturer could only pass the bar on the basis of work in categories I and II. This applied also to Senior Lecturers but for them there were, in addition, no less than four other routes. For example, a Senior Lecturer (in post on 1 March 1975) could pass the bar when it was reached if the individual had a significant amount of work in categories I, II or III in a Grade IV, V or VI department. The merger of work categories II and III has simplified the arrangements for passing the bar on the Principal Lecturer and Senior Lecturer salary scales. From 1 September 1979, any Senior Lecturer or Principal Lecturer who is at the bar and who in the year spent on the bar is responsible for a significant amount of his or her time for advanced level work (old categories I, II and III; new categories I and II/III) is entitled to pass the bar. Hence, in relation to Lecturers Grade II, Senior Lecturers and Principal Lecturers, the Burnham Report now defines advanced level work in a uniform way.

11. Since once teachers are transferred to the Senior Lecturer scale or pass through the bar, they will continue to progress up their scales, the Joint Secretaries advise that the balance of their timetables between advanced and non-advanced work in future years ought to be broadly maintained unless there are compelling educational reasons to the contrary. Similarly, there

ought not to be a sudden change in advanced work without good reason during the year immediately before passage through the bar.

12. The Burnham FE Report states that an authority is not to be prevented from promoting a Lecturer Grade II to a post of Senior Lecturer before eligibility to transfer by the operation of the transfer critieria.

13. **Allowances**

NB. All the amounts of allowances quoted in this sub-section are subject to review and alteration. Figures given were correct at the time of writing.

The Burnham FE salaries document contains a number of provisions for additional payments and allowances. Teachers serving in the London area receive payments according to the area in which they serve:
Inner Area: £609 per annum
Outer Area: £408 per annum
Fringe Area: £177 per annum
These allowances are revised from time to time. The rates above were agreed in January 1980, and are effective from 1 April 1979. In the case of teachers who before 1 October 1974 were employed in a maintained further education establishment outside Greater London but within the Metropolitan Police District, then for as long as they remain in service in that area they receive a safeguarded allowance of £267 per annum. Where a teacher works in a split site institution which has premises in more than one designated area, an allowance appropriate to the location at which more than half of the time is spent will be received. Teachers serving in the London area, but temporarily employed elsewhere, continue to receive their London allowance. London area payments are the subject of negotiations in the Burnham and Primary Secondary Committee; any increases agreed within that committee are normally automatically applied to those to whom the provisions of the Burnham FE Committee apply. The London areas are defined thus:
Inner Area: the ILEA area and the boroughs of Barking, Brent, Ealing, Haringey, Merton and Newham;
Outer Area: Greater London, excluding the Inner Area;
Fringe Area: Surrey, and certain districts in Berkshire, Buckinghamshire, Essex, Hertfordshire, Kent and West Sussex.

14. A teacher who takes charge of a department or undertakes the duties of a vice-principal or principal in the absence of those appointed to such posts, or pending their appointment, may be eligible to receive an acting allowance. The payment of such an allowance and its amount is at the discretion of the employing authority. The amount of the allowance must not cause the total remuneration received to exceed that which would be payable if the recipient were to be appointed to the post in question.

15. At the discretion of the authority, a temporary allowance can be paid to a teacher who returns from a period of seconded overseas service. While payment is discretionary, the amount of the allowance is mandatory. The allowance cannot be paid for more than two years. It consists of an amount

which brings the teacher's remuneration to the level of the salary earned in the post held immediately before the secondment. The allowable circumstances for the payment of the temporary allowance are that the secondment was under arrangements approved by the Ministry of Overseas Development; to Ministry of Defence schools which provided for the education of the children of members of HM Forces; or any such other service approved by the Burnham Committee for this purpose.

16. It is no longer possible to appoint a Lecturer Grade I with a special responsibility allowance. Such persons appointed before this change was made (1 March 1975) continue to receive that allowance. The allowance is now £282 per annum (plus 7½% from 1 January 1980), is adjusted from time to time, and will continue for as long as the teacher remains in post and continues to carry the responsibilities which had justified such payments.

17. It is mandatory to establish a full-time vice-principal post in establishments of Group 4 or above, except where a head of department was appointed before 25 February 1972 to undertake the duties of vice-principal in addition to head of department duties, and continues to be so employed. Most colleges, even those below Group 4 where it is not mandatory, have established Vice-Principal posts. However, where this has not occurred in establishments below Group 4, a head of department often has been appointed to undertake, in addition, tne duties and responsibilities of a vice principal. Where this is so, it is mandatory to pay an allowance to the head of department in question. Further, it has not always been mandatory to create Vice-Principal posts in colleges above Group 4. Hence, in a few cases, heads of department are still holding "Vice-Principal" allowances to which they became entitled several years ago in establishments above Group 4. The allowances applying to both groups of staff are as follows. The normal *maximum* allowance for a head of department appointed to undertake, in addition, the duties of vice-principal in establishments below Group 4 is £783 (plus 7½% from 1 January 1980). The allowance for a head of department (appointed before 25 February 1972 to undertake, in addition, the duties of vice-principal) in an establishment of Group 4 or higher, is between £783 and £1194 (both figures increased by 7½% from 1 January 1980); the actual amount between these limits is at the local authority's discretion.

18. Where departments in a Group 5 or higher establishment are grouped into faculties and a head of department exercises co-ordinating responsibilities within the faculty, the authority may pay an allowance not exceeding £696. An allowance not exceeding £549 will be paid to a head of department exercising faculty duties in an establishment below Group 5 where he or she received an allowance under the corresponding provisions of the 1974 Further Education salaries document. Both allowance figures were increased by 7½% from 1 January 1980.

19. The adoption of scales and regulations common between the former colleges of education and other further education establishments resulted in the removal of many special allowances. However, where a Principal Lecturer in

a college of education was in receipt of a special allowance and has not had the post converted to that of head of department, there is a continuing entitlement to the payment of that allowance, which is adjusted from time to time, provided that the recipient continues to discharge the duties for which the allowance was paid.

20. **Safeguarding**

The Burnham Further Education and Primary and Secondary documents make provision for the safeguarding of a person's salary in certain circumstances where his or her post formerly held is lost. When that individual receives the safeguarding entitlement, he or she continues to be paid on the salary scale applying to the lost post for as long as this is beneficial. For safeguarding to apply, *mandatorily,* the individual has to have lost the post in one of the following circumstances:

(i) the loss had occurred because of the closure or reorganization of an educational establishment and the teacher continues as a full-time teacher in the employment of the same authority in a school or college; or

(ii) the loss had occurred in a teacher education establishment and was due to reorganization, closure, or a direction of the Secretary of State concerning initial teacher training, and the teacher continues in full-time employment in any educational establishment which is covered by either the Further Education or Primary and Secondary Burnham Reports.

It can be seen from these conditions that a teacher who loses a post in a teacher education establishment due to a direction of the Secretary of State (of closure or reorganization) is entitled to receive a safeguarded salary if he or she moves to a new teaching post in England and Wales, provided that the post falls within the scope of the Burnham Reports. However, where a teacher loses a post because of the closure or reorganization of an institution which is not one of teacher training, there is only a safeguarding entitlement if he or she moves to a new teaching job with the same local education authority. In both cases, the teacher must remain in continuous service: there must not be a gap between the date of termination of the lost employment and the commencement of the new employment.

21. Certain conditions apply to the receipt and continued receipt of a safeguarded salary. These may be summarised thus:

(i) the teacher must not unreasonably refuse to accept an alternative post with the employer;

(ii) the employer must approve any subsequent move to other employment (however the employer must not unreasonably withhold such approval); and

(iii) a teacher holding a post which is a fixed term appointment and, at the time of closure, reorganization or direction, has held that post for less than two years, will not be entitled to safeguarding.

It is important to note that the safeguarding arrangement does not apply to non-teaching staff, or to teaching staff who move to jobs which do not fall within the scope of the Burnham Reports.

22. Following an identical clause introduced in 1979 by the Burnham Primary and Secondary Committee, the Burnham FE Committee has agreed that a new form of safeguarding should be introduced from 1 April 1979. This provides that, *at the discretion of the employing authority*, a person who would suffer a financial disadvantage for any reason and continues in employment can be safeguarded. In the schools context this provision was introduced to facilitate staff transfers in response to falling school rolls. However, as can be seen, the wording is very wide and the circumstances of suffering a financial disadvantage are not confined to any particular cause. Whilst this provision is discretionary on local authorities, it might be felt that it changes radically the traditional safeguarding clauses described above. These clauses are mandatory upon LEAs but apply *only* to staff who lose their posts, or whose salaries would otherwise be diminished, for specific reasons – such as college or departmental reorganization or, in the case of teacher education establishments, a direction of the Secretary of State.

23. Again, following agreement reached in the Burnham Primary and Secondary Committee, the Burnham Further Education Committee agreed in the 1979 negotiations that staff who lose their posts in teachers' centres, and also peripatetic and home visiting teachers who lose their posts, and who immediately following this loss enter a further education establishment in the same authority, shall be entitled to safeguarding.

24. Some questions of interpretation of the safeguarding arrangements have been dealt with by the Joint Secretaries or have been the subject of comment in LACSAB publications.[4] The most important of these items are as follows:

   (i) The right to safeguarding should be beyond doubt if the teacher receives notice that the post will be lost, and that the loss is due to a direction, or to the closure or reorganization of the college. However, where a college has been directed to cease teacher training and, as a consequence of that direction, the college will cease to function on a particular date, then all the teaching staff may be held to have been affected, irrespective of whether or not notices have been issued. In these circumstances a teacher may leave in advance of a personal redundancy notice and, nonetheless, claim safeguarding, providing that the college agrees to the teacher leaving at that time.

   (ii) The Further Education Joint Working Party has discussed the doubt which exists as to whether the safeguarding provisions apply to a teacher who, having lost employment, moves to a post with a lower maximum, but who is entitled to an *immediate* increase on transfer to the new scale. The Working Party's recommendations was that such a teacher should remain on the previous scale: the teacher should receive neither an immediate increase nor a long term decrease. The 1979 salaries documents have made this point clear: a teacher who moves to a scale with a lower maximum shall be entitled to safeguarding providing, of course, that the other requirements are met. The Joint Secretaries have agreed that any revisions in teachers' salaries arising from this interpretation shall take effect from 1 April 1979.

---

4 *Redundancies of Teaching and Non-Teaching Staff*, Local Authorities Conditions of Service Advisory Board, revised edition 1978, para 4, pp. 47-49.

25. Agreement of interpretation has been reached on the position of teachers qualifying for safeguarding who would have passed through their salary bars but have lost their posts before doing so. A former Senior or Principal Lecturer in receipt of a safeguarded salary should be allowed to pass through the salary point and to the end of the scale if during the last academic year before the date of the loss of post, the provisions of the salaries document regarding responsibility for advanced work were satisfied. As from 1 September 1978 the period of three years preceding the date of loss may be used for the assessment of advanced level work if this method is more favourable.

26. The above criteria apply also to a Lecturer Grade II transferring to the Senior Lecturer scale and to that person's progress through that scale. In this instance, the efficiency criterion is also considered. In order to avoid future doubt about the eligibility of a safeguarded teacher to make a scale transfer or passage through the bar, the college from which the individual loses his or her post ought to issue in writing to the individual concerned a statement concerning his or her eligibility for progression or transfer under the safeguarding arrangements.

27. **Categories of work and staffing establishments**

Although it is necessary to understand work categories before the unit totals referred to in paragraphs 28-33 below can be fully comprehended, consideration of this topic, and staffing establishments, properly belongs to the vital subject, which determines so much of the character of our further education system, discussed in Section **2.2**. Reference here should be made to that sub-section therefore, and particularly to paragraph 11.

28. **Unit total**

The unit total of a college or department is the device whereby departments are graded and the group of the college is calculated. The latter provision determines the salaries of vice-principals and principals. Unit totals are calculated retrospectively. The unit total for a particular academic year is based on the student hours for the immediate past academic year. To find the unit total, the authority calculates student hours and applies divisors thus:

Divisors

Category of Work	
I	for each 100 student hours count..1 unit
II/III	for each 300 student hours count..1 unit
IV and V	for each 600 student hours count..1 unit

29. **Student hours**

Student hours are calculated by four methods;

(i) The actual registered hours spent in the college by part-time and block release students are counted. An exception is to be found where students attend courses of less than one term's duration. In this case the actual registered hours are increased by 10%.

(ii) Where full-time students are following courses of a duration of more than one term but less than one year, then the number of enrolled students on the various courses is counted and credit given for 95% of the student hours for the particular course as determined under sub-paragraph (v), below. Where the course is not in excess of a term's duration, credit is given for 110% of the actual full-time student hours.

(iii) In respect of other full-time students, the number is counted of those enrolled on 1 November according to the year of the course being undertaken. Credit is then given for 95% of the student hours for the year, as determined under sub-paragraph (v), below.

(iv) For each sandwich course, credit is given for 100% of the student hours spent in the college or department during the year, as determined under sub-paragraph (v) below, for each sandwich course, together with an addition determined by the authority according to the duties and responsibilities of the college staff for students during the period (if any) of the year spent in industry. The Burnham Committee recommends that this addition be of 10% of the student hours for the year of the course.

(v) The student hours of a particular course is the time spent in the college or department as determined by the authority in consultation with the principal of the college. The Burnham Committee expects the maximum time spent in the college or department during normal hours, whether in normal lectures, practical work, tutorials or individual work (for example in the library) to be taken into account.

30. **Grading of departments**

When the unit total for a department has been calculated, its grade is determined thus:

Unit Total	*Grade*
76-140	I
141-250	II
251-400	III
401-600	IV
601-900	V
over 900	VI

In the grading of a department, the following further provisions apply:

(i) If the staffing of a department includes the post of Senior Lecturer, its grade shall not be less than II; if the staffing includes a Principal Lecturer or Reader, the grade shall not be less than III. If the principal lecturer is entitled to pass the bar in a department graded lower than IV, the authority is empowered, at its discretion, to upgrade the department to IV.

(ii) Where a department of Grade III or higher normally undertakes work of category I or II/III standard and the authority considers its grading to be inadequate, then the authority may place the department into such higher grade as it considers appropriate. The authority's decision should have regard to the volume and standard of research or educational development work undertaken.

(iii) Pending the reorganization of a department, the authority can establish a temporary grade for the department, or make other arrangements for the direction of the work without establishing a departmental post. Such an arrangement should not obtain for more than two years. The restriction that, apart from satisfying the unit totals, for a department to be above IV at least 250 units of the work had to derive from work in categories I and/or II and/or III, ceased to apply with effect from 1 April 1979.

31. As the grading of a department and the grouping of a college (see paragraph 32) depends on student hours, it is possible for them to decline with a fall in student numbers. This clearly affects the salaries of principals, vice-principals and heads of department. In this instance the grade of a department or group of a college is reckoned to be one above that calculated on the basis of the actual figures: the *status quo* obtains where the grade or group falls by one. Where, however, the fall is by greater than one, the salary is determined within the grade or group which is one above that which obtains after the decline. In such circumstances, however, a personal allowance would be paid to the member of staff concerned. The allowance would be the amount necessary to bring the salary to the level which was being received, within the grade or department or group of the college, immediately before the decline. The allowance, however, is subject to reduction: as the new salary scale moves upwards, the amount of the allowance declines.

32. **The grouping of a college**

When the unit total for the college has been calculated, its group is determined thus:

Unit Total	*Group*
Up to 250	1
251-500	2
501-1000	3
1001-1750	4
1751-2750	5
2751-3750	6
3751-5000	7
5001-6500	8
6501-8500	9
8501-11000	10
11001-13500	11
Over 13500	12

33. The authority can determine the group of the college on the basis of an estimate of its work for the third complete academic year after its opening or reorganization. This condition is similar to that obtaining for departments which are newly opened or reorganized.

34. **Individual salaries: salary on first appointment**

On first appointment to the education service as a Lecturer Grade I, salary is the total of:

(i) the minimum of the scale;

(ii) three increments if the teacher possesses a degree or a qualification approved as a degree equivalent;
(iii) one additional increment where the qualification in (ii) is a first or second class honours degree, or a higher degree, or a qualification equivalent to such degrees;
(iv) one increment if certain teacher education qualifications such as the standard certificate or the certificate in education (technical) are held;
(v) one increment for each year of full-time study, training or research in excess of three after the age of 18 (normally up to a maximum of three);
(vi) increments for previous educational, industrial or professional experience after the age of 18 which, in the authority's opinion, is *relevant* to service as a Lecturer Grade I.

Where, after appointment, a Lecturer Grade I fulfils for the first time the requirements of (ii) – (iv) above, he or she will receive such incremental credit provided that the maximum of the scale is not exceeded. An additional, 15th, increment was added to the Lecturer Grade I scale with effect from 1 September 1979. Those currently in service, new entrants, and re-entrants on 1 September 1979 are eligible for placement on the 15th incremental point with effect from that date, provided that the normal criteria for incremental award on the Lecturer I scale are satisfied.

35. Salary scales from Lecturer Grade II upwards are treated in a different way. The scales are consolidated and have no allowances for qualifications. A new appointee receives:
(i) the minimum of the scale;
(ii) increments for previous educational, industrial or professional experience which, in the opinion of the authority, is *equivalent* to service as a lecturer at the appropriate level.

It is important to notice the differences between the words "relevant" (34 (vi)) and "equivalent" (35 (ii)). What is relevant is generally more easy to determine; most experience is relevant to teaching in further education. Equivalent means generally that the experience was in a post which commanded the same or a higher salary than that which the teacher would have received if he or she had been a Lecturer Grade II or higher at the time. The authority may determine a higher salary on the scale if it considers the award of extra increments appropriate. Reference is made usually to the salary of the individual before appointment. Increments awarded in respect of pre-1971 experience are lower and have in the past been somewhat complex to implement. The process has now been simplified and is operative from 1 September 1978. Another recent development is that an entrant, or re-entrant to the Lecturer Grade II scale, is entitled to a salary which is in no circumstances less than the salary to which the individual would be entitled as a Lecturer Grade I.

36. **Salary on promotion**

The provisions of this paragraph apply also to the appointment of a former school teacher to a further education establishment. The Burnham salaries document awards "whichever is the highest" of two methods of calculating salaries. The first method is that outlined in paragraphs 34-35 above; this calculation usually produces a lower figure than the second method. The basic provision of the second method is to take the previous salary and add to it one and one half increments on the higher scale. Such a calculation often produces a figure between two incremental points. Where this occurs, the salary is rounded up. In some cases the addition of one and one half increments does not bring the total to the minimum of the new scale. Where this is so, the teacher enters the new scale at point 0. On the 1 September following promotion the teacher will receive a full increment on the new scale. There is an important extra provision whereby an authority is entitled to place a teacher promoted from Lecturer Grade I to Lecturer Grade II on any point up to and including the sixth point of the higher scale.

37. **Increments**

As changes take place at each salary negotiation, an individual's salary position is not always easily reckonable by making the simple equation between years of service and incremental points. The standard incremental date of 1 September does simplify matters however. All teaching staff have been paid since 1 September 1975 on whole incremental points; on each successive 1 September a new or re-entrant teacher who has served for at least six months in the previous year receives a complete increment.

38. **Non-teaching staff paid on Burnham rates**

The Joint Secretaries have advised that research staff, librarians and other staff who are paid on Burnham scales "as a matter of convenience" should be paid the appropriate increases which accrue to teachers under the statutory provision of the Burnham documents. The Burnham FE Committee has agreed that the Further Education Joint Working Party should examine the remuneration and grading of research staff, which varies considerably between local authorities, to determine whether a measure of uniformity can be introduced.

39. **Credit given for unremunerated activity in determining salary**

It has been claimed in the Teachers' Panel that a teacher's experience in bringing up a family could be relevant to teaching employment. In response to this, the Committee has noted that authorities already have discretion to take into account such periods when assessing the salary of a Lecturer Grade I. The 1979 Burnham salaries document was drafted to allow unpaid maternity leave to be reckoned for the purposes of incremental credit.

40. **Adult education**

As was stated in paragraph 1, teachers in adult education establishments are included in the provisions of the Burnham reports. A teacher of adult education is defined as one employed as a teacher of adult education for 50% or more of the working time, except that in the case of a principal or vice-principal, as one whose responsibilities are concerned directly with adult teaching for 50% or more of the working time. An adult education establishment is that part of the adult education service of an LEA recognised by the authority as a separate unit, irrespective of the number of centres it comprises.

41. Staff in adult education establishments were brought within the scope of the Burnham Further Education salaries document in recent years. Such staff who were formerly paid on Burnham Primary and Secondary School scales are to be transferred to further education scales when the local authority so decides. However, if such a transfer leads to a lower salary, the member of staff shall be protected on his or her former salary. All other adult education staff (except those in colleges of further education) who are in charge of adult education establishments have their salaries determined as set out below.

42. The group of the establishment is determined from 1 April 1978 (to 31 August 1979), and thereafter in the normal way, on the basis of the establishment's unit total. Where the unit total is 160 or more the provisions set out in paragraph 32 above, apply. That is to say, the teacher in charge is paid from the appropriate principal ranges of salary points. Where the unit total is 80-159, the Head of Department Grade II scale, the upper limit of which can be extended, should be used. Where the unit total is less than 80, the top six points of the Lecturer II scale are used. However, from 1 April 1979, local authorites have discretion to extend this scale upwards. Further, in respect of appointments on these ranges and scales, upward adjustments, if the student hours do not reflect the responsibilities involved, or downward adjustments, if the post does not call for the exercise of the full range of responsibilities normal to a further education principal, may be made.

43. The appointment of a vice-principal is mandatory where the unit total exceeds 1000. Otherwise, it is at the discretion of the local authority. Where a vice-principal is appointed in an establishment with a unit total of 160 or more, the appropriate Vice-Principal salary range is used. In other cases, the salary scale is between 80% and 85% of that used to remunerate the principal.

44. The principles outlined in paragraphs 30 (iii), 31 and 33 above also apply to the grading of principal and vice-principals posts in adult education.

APPENDIX 1

SALARY SCALES: DIAGRAMMATIC REPRESENTATION

The diagram below is intended as both a means of representing salary scales, and to allow updating. In the diagram, ranges for principals and vice-principals are represented by broken lines, scales for heads of departments by rope ladders, and the remaining scales by ladders.

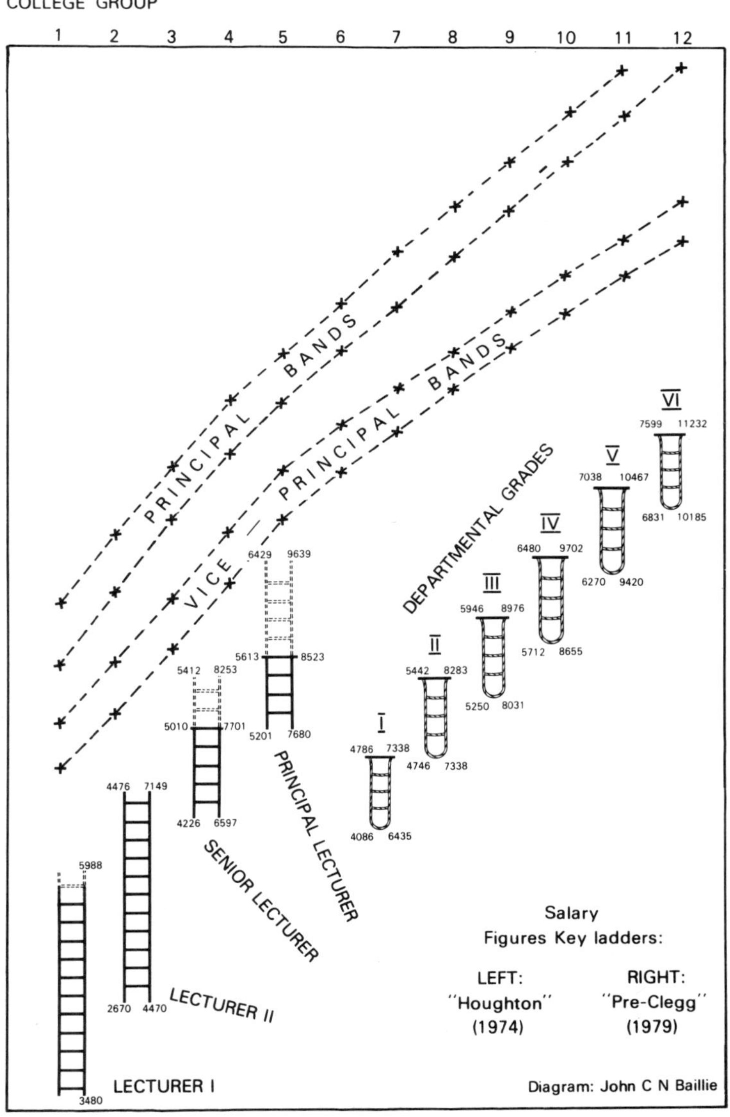

REFERENCE

Remuneration of Teachers Act 1965, Chapter 3, HMSO.
Department of Education and Science, *Scales of Salaries for Teachers in Establishments for Further Education, England and Wales 1978*, HMSO.
Department of Education and Science, *Scales of Salaries for Teachers in Establishments for Further Education, England and Wales 1979*, HMSO.

Joint Secretaries of the Burnham Further Education Committee, *Commentary on the Further Education Salaries Documents 1974 and 1975*.
Joint Secretaries of the Burnham Further Education Committee, *Commentary on the Further Education Salaries Documents, 1976*.
Joint Secretaries of the Burnham Further Education Committee, *1978 Salary Circular*, BAC/84.

Redundancies of Teaching and Non-Teaching Staff, Local Authorities Conditions of Service Advisory Board, Part 4 Salary Safeguarding, revised edition, 1978.
Salaries, NATFHE Information Series No. 2, revised June 1977.

NB. The salary scales printed in paragraph 6 above, will be revised in any further editions of this book. However, it may be noted that the *NATFHE Pocket Book and Diary* publishes the annually reviewed salary scales as well as the amounts of certain allowances; and that in the time between the making of new scales and the publication of the Burnham Report, the latest agreed scales are published by the Joint Secretaries in circulars obtainable from LACSAB. The Joint Secretaries publish commentaries and give advice in respect of specific queries which may be raised by LEAs, by governors of voluntary colleges, or by teachers through the recognised teacher unions. Further, the Joint Secretaries consider which qualifications shall entitle a holder to be treated as a graduate or good honours graduate for salary purposes, or be entitled to receive the merit addition in respect of teacher training. The addresses of the Joint Secretaries are:

Teachers' Panel:
The General Secretary,
NATFHE
Hamilton House,
Mabledon Place,
London WC1H 9BH
Tel: 01-387 6806
01-388 2745

Management Panel:
The Secretary,
LACSAB
41 Belgrave Square,
London SW1X 8NZ
Tel: 01-235 9801

2 STAFFING ESTABLISHMENTS AND THE GRADING OF COURSES

1. **Introduction**

This sub-section reviews the methods used to determine the numbers and gradings of teaching and non-teaching posts in colleges. These matters are of crucial importance to those engaged in college administration and to staff, generally, in further and higher education. Clearly, the total number of teaching and non-teaching staff to which a college or polytechnic is entitled considerably influences the efficiency of the institution and its management. It affects staff relations and represents a highly important element in an institution's budget. Naturally, in times of expenditure restraint the number of staff in a college's establishment will be carefully monitored and controlled by the local education authority. An under supply of staff affects staff relations in that it imposes strains on teaching and non-teaching staff and may raise conditions of service problems. However, the phrase "staffing establishments" does not just refer to the number of staff which a college can employ. It refers also to the grading of the posts which they occupy. The grading of posts directly determines the type of management structure possible in the college and its departments. From the staff point of view, the grading of posts determines directly promotion opportunities and career development. The wrong balance in this is a major factor in staff turnover and the relative contentment of staff with college life. A staff which feels that despite its efforts to develop college work there is no promotion available, is unlikely to have the same identity with the aims of the college as a staff which can see promotion opportunities open to it (cf Section **11.11.**9).

2. In this context, the methods used to determine the number of staff and the grading of their posts can have a major influence on the educational character of the institution. A system which offers rewards in respect of certain types of work, as against other types, encourages the development of one type of work against another. For example, a grading system which offers more rewards in respect of advanced further education, as against non-advanced work, tends to encourage the development of advanced courses.

3. Paragraphs 36 to 40 of this sub-section deal with the staffing establishment of teaching staff; paragraphs 41 to 44 deal with non-teaching staff. In order to understand teaching staff establishment it is necessary to understand the complex matter of the grading of further education courses. The grading attached to courses offered in colleges determines, amongst other things, the grading of teaching posts and, often, the number of such posts.

4. **The Grading of Courses**

The grading of courses system has attracted, in recent years, a good deal of criticism from a number of quarters[1]. Its ways may seem mysterious. To many, it is a puzzling reflection that the system was introduced in an attempt to provide an objective method of relating the salary teachers earned and their promotion opportunities to the perceived nature of the work which they did. It was believed that teachers and their employing local education authorities should be able to determine jointly the categories of the large variety of courses, and years of courses, taught and administered by staff paid under the Burnham Further Education salaries document. Indeed, when the scheme was first introduced it led to a large number of promotions and established a national procedure for determining the proportion of staff in different grades in colleges. In doing this it moved away from a system whereby the employer alone determined promotion possibilities for teachers as well as the grading of Principal, Vice-Principal and Head of Department posts. However that may be, the present system has attracted two types of critical comment. Firstly, there are those who complain that the basis of the system is elitist and out-moded in educational terms, for its use favours advanced or academic work against non-advanced and vocational work. Secondly, there are those who, whilst not opposing the basis of the system, complain about the grading actually awarded to particular courses. In order to assess these opinions, the technical details of the system and its origin must be examined.

5. The national grading of courses system was introduced in 1967. At that time a fourfold classification of courses was developed by the Burnham Further Education Committee. This was as follows:

"A.1. Study above Advanced level of the General Certificate of Education, Ordinary National Certificate or equivalent standard leading directly to a university degree or an examination which satisfies the academic criteria accepted for graduate status for salary purposes.

A.2. Study of equivalent standard to that in category A.1. but not necessarily leading to the qualifications mentioned in that category.

B. Study or courses above the Ordinary level of the General Certificate of Education or comparable level leading directly to Advanced level of the General Certificate of Education or the Ordinary National Certificate or courses or parts of courses of a comparable standard.

C. Study or courses or parts of courses which do not satisfy the above criteria."

---

1 For example, in May 1978 NATFHE's Annual Conference adopted the following resolution: "Conference deplores the use of categories of work as a basis for salaries negotiations and instructs the National Executive Committee to devise an alternative scheme." However, in reporting to its National Council, in July 1979, the NATFHE National Executive Committee proposed that no alternative schemes were any more desirable than the grading of courses, and many were less desirable: a proposition which the National Council endorsed. (See Appendix to *Minutes of Council Meeting 7th July 1979*, Appendix J.6(7a), NATFHE). See also, Donald Gold, "Time to burn 'em?" *Education and Training*, October 1979, p.288.

6. A Committee known as the Grading of Courses Committee was established (which in turn later established a Working Group) to carry out the monumental task of placing courses in the categories outlined above. The Committee and Working Group consisted of representatives of the local education authorities and the recognised further education teachers' associations. The Secretariat work was undertaken by the DES and the Department also provided specialist advisers, in the form of HMI, to assist the Committee and Working Group. In 1968, the Committee was in a position to publish the first graded course list,[2] a document some 76 pages long, and attached to it a statement setting out the considerations of which it had taken regard in reaching its conclusions.

7. These considerations have shaped the work of the Grading of Courses Committee from that time on and, whilst variations have occurred, it is worth dwelling on them at some length in order to explain the original methodology of the grading of courses exercise. The 1968 statement referred to the following principles:
   - (i) It was necessary to break up courses so that, in many cases, parts of them fell into different categories.
   - (ii) Account was taken of more than purely academic factors. Examples of other factors quoted are the age of the students and the need to recruit specialist and experienced staff.[3]
   - (iii) It was not felt generally practicable for the Committee to grade college courses. In the main, only courses leading to external examinations and recognised qualifications would be classified. It was believed that local education authorities could grade individual college courses, following the principles laid down by the Committee.
   - (iv) Normally, it was not practicable to grade non-vocational courses. However, the Committee felt it important that such courses should be graded (presumably by local education authorities) according to the principles adopted for vocational courses, for example, to grade a course in parts where it involved progression by parts; to have regard to the character and standard of the course and the calibre and expertise of the teacher required.
   - (v) It was felt right to classify the final examinations of professional bodies (eg, Associateships and Licentiateships) as A2 where such studies were beyond the OND/ONC or GCE "A" level standard. However, the earlier years of these courses, which were not clearly of an advanced nature, were to be graded below this level.
   - (vi) Courses accepted as poolable under the Rate Support Grant (Pooling Arrangements) Regulations, 1967, were classified as A2 or, where they led to a qualification entitling a lecturer holding such a qualification to receive a graduate equivalent incremental allowance, as A1.

---

2 Grading of Courses Sub-Committee, *List of Courses Graded by the Sub-Committee*, 1968, Burnham Further Education Committee.

3 For example, in relation to Mine Deputies' courses the Committee has this to say: "In grading this course account was taken not only of the academic content of the course but also that this was preparing persons of mature age for posts of considerable responsibility. It was felt that such work could only be undertaken by teachers with appropriate industrial experience and this warranted a B grading for the course." *Ibid*, p.1, para 5.

(vii) Postgraduate courses in the same field or technology as first degree courses should be graded A1. However, where this was not so the particular course should be considered from the point of view of its content and the previous education of the students taking it.

(viii) The main purpose of the grading exercise was to ensure that an adequate level of staffing was provided at further education colleges.

8. To reach the numbers of decisions set out in their first list, the Committee must have done a great deal of work in 1967 and 1968. In the later sixties and early seventies the Committee and Working Group continued to meet, publishing from time to time amendment sheets to the original list.[4] The development of new courses, curricular changes affecting old ones and requests for guidance from local authorities, teachers and administrators, meant that the work of the Committee and the Working Group assumed a continuing character. In 1975, the Committee was reconstituted following changes in the composition of the Management and Teachers' Panel of the Burnham Further Education Committee, and the secretariat work passed from the DES to LACSAB.

9. A much more fundamental change occurred in 1975, following the recommendations of the Houghton Committee. This Committee recommended that a new fivefold classification of courses should be used.[5] This classification, as adopted by the Burnham Further Education Committee, was as follows:

"I (i) Taught courses or research programmes, or combinations of the two, leading to a higher degree.

(ii) Courses leading to qualifications agreed to be of post-graduate standard, where a first degree or equivalent qualification in an appropriate discipline would normally be a pre-requisite for a student taking the course. (Where an extra period of time is required to bring a student up to the entry requirements of a post-graduate course, such a "bridging course" will normally be graded Category II).

II Courses above Ordinary National Certificate standard and leading directly to degrees of Universities of the United Kingdom or degrees of the Council for National Academic Awards; and courses with entry standards equivalent to one or two "A" levels and which lead directly to qualifications which satisfy the academic criteria accepted for graduate status for salary purposes.

III Study of equivalent standard to that in Category II but not necessarily leading to the qualifications mentioned in that Category.

IV Study or courses above the Ordinary Level of the General Certificate of Education or comparable level leading directly to the Ordinary National Certificate, or courses or parts of courses of a comparable standard.

V Courses other than those described above".

---

4 In fact, in 1972 a revised edition of the list was published. Department of Education and Science, *Burnham Further Education Committee Grading of Courses*, 1972, HMSO.
5 *Report of the Committee of Inquiry into the Pay of Non-University Teachers*, 1974, p.44, para 170, HMSO.

10. Later in 1975, a further revised edition of the Grading of Courses List was published.[6] This replaced categories A1, A2, B and C with categories I, II, III, IV and V and dealt with many new courses. Discontinued courses were deleted. The recommendations of the Houghton Committee also meant that teacher education courses (see paragraph 28 below) had to be graded for the first time and the decisions of the Grading of Courses Committee on this area of work were set out in the new list. Following previous practice, purely individual college courses were not graded and, in fact, those that had been included, for guidance, in previous editions, were deleted.

11. The final major change which has occurred in the grading system came in 1979 when the Burnham Further Education Committee agreed to merge work categories II and III. The new fourfold classification is now defined as follows.

"I (i) Taught courses or research programmes, or combinations of the two, leading to a higher degree.

(ii) Courses leading to qualifications agreed to be of post-graduate standard, where a first degree or equivalent qualification in an appropriate discipline would normally be a pre-requisite for a student taking the course. (Where an extra period of time is required to bring a student up to the entry requirements of a post-graduate course, such a "bridging course" will normally be graded Category II).

II/III Courses above Ordinary National Certificate standard and leading directly to degrees of Universities of the United Kingdom or degrees of the Council for National Academic Awards; and courses with entry standards equivalent to one or two "A" levels and which lead directly to qualifications which satisfy the academic criteria accepted for graduate status for salary purposes or study of an equivalent standard but not necessarily leading to the qualifications mentioned.

IV Study or courses above the Ordinary Level of the General Certificate of Education or comparable level leading directly to the Ordinary National Certificate or courses or parts of courses of a comparable standard.

V Courses other than those described above."

12. Clearly, this change has a major impact on the work of the Grading of Courses Committee. It simplifies the grading of advanced level work by dispensing with the distinction between degree courses and courses giving graduate status, on the one hand, and courses of the same academic standard, but not leading to such qualifications, on the other. It is expected that, following the revision of gradings caused by this change, a new edition of the Gradings of Courses List will be published in 1980.

---

6 Burnham Further Education Committee, *Grading of Courses, List of Courses 1975*, LACSAB, 1975.

13. **The present Committee and reference to it**

The composition of the present Committee is as follows:

Management Side		*Teachers' Side*	
Association of County Councils	2	APC	1
Association of Metropolitan Authorities	2	NATFHE	4
Welsh Joint Education Committee	1	NSAE	1

In addition, an assessor from the DES also attends meetings of the Committee. There are two joint Chairmen of the Committee, one from the Management and one from the Teachers' Side. By custom and practice one of the AMA representatives is a member of Her Majesty's Inspectorate.

14. References to the Committee can be made only by local education authorities, via the Management Panel, and by teachers, via the Teachers' Panel. Correspondence should be addressed, as appropriate, to the Secretary of the Management or Teacher' Panel (see Section **11.1**, Reference). There is one exception to this requirement. The Committee's work obviously depends on the receipt of up-to-date information concerning examination regulations and curriculum changes from the examination bodies and the professional institutes. Hence, where a course has already been graded, the Committee does consider references from these bodies about relevant changes.

15. Whilst the Committee does not publish decisions about individual college courses, it does give advice to local authorities (or teachers) about their grading. Local authorities in grading college courses, or in grading other courses not so far graded by the Committee, are under a statutory obligation to grade courses "in accordance with the ... criteria" for the classification of courses [7] Obviously, a teacher who feels that a particular course has been wrongly graded by the local education authority, can refer this matter for determination by the Grading of Courses Committee via the Teachers' Panel (assuming it supports the case). Once a course has been considered by the Committee, the local authority is obliged to grade it in the way advised by the Committee.

16. Recently, the Committee has developed a proforma to assist in the recording of details about courses to be graded. A copy of this proforma is set out in Appendix 1.

17. The Committee meets roughly twice every academic term, and sometimes more frequently than this. As in the past, it continues to receive advice from HMI and publishes, periodically, amendment sheets to the Graded Courses List.

---

7 Department of Education and Science, *Scales of Salaries for Teachers in Establishments for Further Education, England and Wales 1978*, HMSO, Appendix IIA, p.16, para 2.

18. **Using the Graded Courses List**
Since 1968 the Graded Courses List has been arranged in two parts. Part I deals with General Courses, such as the General Certificate of Education and National Certificate and Diploma Courses. It also deals with the industrial parts of integrated training courses. Part II is split into two schedules. Schedule A deals with City and Guilds Courses: Schedule B with Professional and Vocational Subjects. City and Guilds courses are listed under their DES and City and Guilds numbers and are arranged under subject area. The courses in Schedule B are listed under their DES number where they have one, and again, are arranged according to subject, or, under the Council, Union of Institutes or Committee offering the examination. The course as a whole is classified under its category or, where it has been considered in parts, the various parts are listed under the appropriate categories. On occasion, a particular year of a course (e.g. the final year) will be listed under the appropriate category and the remainder of the course listed under a lower category.

19. In using the Graded Courses List to determine the grade of a course or part of a course, it is necessary always to check the amendment sheets published subsequent to the 1975 edition of the List.

20. **The decisions made by the Committee**
The general methodology adopted by the Committee, as established in 1967-1968, is described in paragraph 7, above. It can be seen from that methodology that three considerations have determined the grading of courses. Firstly, the academic standard of the course has, in the vast majority of cases, determined its grading. Secondly, consideration has been given to the age of the students taking the course. Where the students are mature this may lead to a higher grading. Thirdly, the need to recruit specialist staff, or staff in short supply, has had an influence on the grading of courses.

21. The Committee has taken the view that the academic standard of a course is dictated primarily by the entry requirements laid down for intending students. This means that the fact that all the students on a particular course have certain high level qualifications is, of itself, irrelevant unless those qualifications were required for entry. Further, the fact that a course may be mounted with the intention that it should recruit students of a particular calibre, is also irrelevant, unless the course regulations require the inclusion only of students possessing such qualifications. Again, it is not sufficient for grading purposes if colleges are only *advised* to accept students with certain qualifications, if the advice can be disregarded. Often, courses will "lay down" certain intended entry qualifications but allow students not possessing these qualifications to enter the course at the discretion of the principal or the college. Such an arrangement may incline the Committee to give less weight to the envisaged entry requirements attached to the course.[8]

---

8 It is perhaps understandable that advocates of open access to certain courses do not always find decisions of the Grading of Courses Committee particularly palatable (cf Section **12.1.**18).

22. This is not to say that the Committee does not consider curriculum matters in deciding the academic nature of a course. Indeed it considers not just the academic complexity of the syllabus but also features such as the numbers of hours of teaching laid down in the course details and, on occasion, examination papers. However, the Committee does expect that there will be a general correlation between these features and entry requirements.

23. The "specialist staff" criterion has had some interesting consequences. One suspects that it was a criterion more readily relied upon in the past when there was a chronic difficulty in recruiting staff from certain backgrounds, for example, accountants. The maturity of students criterion is also interesting. The Committee will not be impressed by the fact that all the students following a particular course are over a certain age. The maturity of student criterion is relevant only where the course *requires* the recruitment of older people. Clearly, the operation of these two "minor" criteria can lead to anomalies if courses are compared purely at the academic level. However, it should be noted that the Committee said in its 1968 statement that the point of the grading exercise was to ensure an adequate level of college staffing.

24. It is not possible to provide a complete summary of the decisions reached on the generality of courses in further education. However, the following comments may assist in an understanding of the pattern of decisions made.

25. *National Certificate courses.* The GCE "O" level and the ONC/OND are the foundations of the system. Courses at "O" level and below are graded in Category V. Courses at ONC/OND level are graded in Category IV. Hence, a day release ONC course is graded the same as a full-time OND course, even though the latter has required many more hours of teaching. GCE "A" level courses are graded in Category IV.

26. *Craft and technician courses.* Generally, years 1 and 2 of craft courses are graded in Category V, years 3 and 4 in Category IV and the remaining years in the new Category II/III (formerly in Category III). Again, in a very general way, year 1 of a technicians' course is graded in Category V, years 2 and 3 in Category IV and the remaining years in Category II/III. In grading the ultimate stages of certain craft courses as Category II/III, the Committee has been anxious to ensure that this category is awarded only where there is an extension to the depth of work. Part 2 subjects studied subsequent to the Part 2 stage should not, for example, be graded in Category II/III. Where the Part 3 stage of a craft studies course involves specialised craft subjects, the study of which is based upon the knowledge gained in earlier stages of the course, or, where the Part 3 stage involves the treatment in greater depth of a subject studied at an earlier stage, the grading should be Category II/III providing there is an extension of work undertaken at Part 2 or there is a basis in Part 2 studies as a prerequisite. However, where the Part 3 stage involves only a sideways step, such as an appreciation study of another craft, or an optional study from an earlier stage of the same course, but not previously taken up by the student, the grading will normally be at Category IV.

27. *TEC and BEC courses.* The Committee has devised a generic grading for TEC courses and intends to devise a generic grading for BEC courses. TEC courses leading to ordinary certificates and diplomas are graded Category IV. Those leading to higher certificates and diplomas are graded II/III. Supplementary studies to ordinary level courses are graded II/III provided that there is an extension in the depth of work. It is expected that the grading of BEC courses will be published early in 1980.

28. *Teacher education courses.* When, under the fivefold classification system, the Committee had to classify teacher education courses, it made some very interesting decisions – decisions which subsequently had a considerable influence on the agreement to merge Categories II and III. A course with an "O" level entry requirement, such as the three year certificate of education, would normally have its first year, at least, graded in Category IV. Yet the Committee graded the whole of the certificate in Category III. Similarly, the Post Graduate Certificate of Education was graded in Category II even though it evidently was not a degree course, nor a course giving graduate status for salary purposes. Other teacher education "post experience" courses were also graded in Category II and the Committee made a general decision that post experience courses were not to be graded less than Category III. Decisions of this sort made the distinction between courses in Category II and III less and less reliable.

29. *CNAA Diploma courses.* The introduction of Category I has caused the Committee to look in some depth at CNAA and other diploma courses which are aimed at postgraduate students. It was decided that CNAA post-graduate diploma courses which form an integral part of a Master's taught degree course should be graded Category I. So should other CNAA diploma courses for which the normal entry requirement is a first degree, or its equivalent in a subject of direct relevance to the subject matter of the diploma and in which the content was such as to involve study *beyond the level associated with a first degree.* Where this is not so, for example, where the course involves a broadening, rather than a deepening, of knowledge required at the first degree level, the diploma is graded as Category II/III.

30. **The purposes of grading courses**

It is indicated in paragraphs 7(viii) and 23, above, that the Committee sees that the main purpose of the grading of courses exercise is to ensure an adequate level of staffing exists in further education instititions. That is to say that when applied in conjunction with the proportion of posts ranges laid down by the Burnham Further Education Committee in Appendix IIA of the salaries document, the grading of courses determines the grading of posts at the Lecturer I, Lecturer II, Senior Lecturer and Principal Lecturer level. In many cases, a college's size of establishment, as well as its proportions of these grades of post, is determined by the grading of courses offered by the college. Hence, the grading of courses has a direct bearing on promotion opportunities and the staffing structure of colleges. This is discussed in detail in paragraphs 36 to 40, below.

31. However, there are a number of other purposes to which grading of courses decisions are put, either by intention of the Burnham Further Education Committee or by other bodies. In Section **11.1.**27-33, an explanation is given of the unit total system, and its relationship to the grading of departments and the grouping of colleges. Clearly, the grades of courses offered in colleges directly detemines the college's and its departments' unit totals and hence, the salary of the principal, vice principal and heads of department.

32. Another major purpose of grading courses is outlined in Section **11.1.**7-12, which deals with the arrangements for transfer from the Lecturer II to the Senior Lecturer scale and with passage through the bars on the Senior and Principal Lecturer scales. Here, again, the grades of courses taught by staff directly determine whether or not they will proceed past certain points on their salary scales.

33. The grade of a course also determines the hourly rate paid to part-time staff teaching on it (see Section **11.1.**6). However, in some regions a rate below that applicable to Category V work is still used for some non-vocational studies (see Section **11.1.**6 (iii)).

34. Finally, the grading of courses has been used to determine the student fee structure for courses, inter authority payments for courses, and, has relevance to whether or not expenditure for a course is poolable.

35. Given the ramifications of decisions reached in the grading of courses committee, the work of the committee is clearly crucial to the further education salaries system. The following paragraphs deal with the relation of the grading of courses to academic staffing establishments.

36. **Academic staffing establishments**

The Burnham salaries document lays down a scheme for determining the proportion of Lecturer Grade I, Lecturer Grade II, Senior Lecturer and Principal Lecturer posts in a college. This scheme does not necessarily determine the total number of posts though in one method of its application, in fact the most popular one, it can be used to determine the size as well as the structure of the academic staff establishment.

37. There are three basic methods, not necessarily mutually exclusive, for determining the size of the establishment of a college. Firstly, as indicated above, the Burnham proportions of posts can be applied to the volume of work in the college, measured in staff or student hours, so as to produce an overall figure for the number as well as the grades of staff. Secondly, a student: staff ratio can be used to determine the number of staff required. Thirdly, the number of posts can be determined by a political decision of the LEA based on budgetary considerations. There has, of course, been a good deal of argument about the use of student:staff ratios, especially in respect of advanced further education work.[9] Some have argued that such ratios

---

9 cf Pooling Committee, *Assessment of Curriculum Acitivity and Utilization of Staff Resources in Polytechnics and FE Colleges*, Councils and Education Press, 1972; and Sections **3.**51, and **8.**46, above.

provide a valuable tool for analysing and monitoring educational developments. Others have sought to use student:staff ratios as a means of economic control on the development of education and the viability of certain courses. The ratio applied can be crude, for example where an overall ratio of full-time equivalent student hours to staff is applied to the volume of work in a college or, more sophisticated, for example, where the ratio is weighted to take account of the level of work, the type of work, whether or not the students are full or part-time and the length of the courses. In recent years another ratio, the class size ratio, has been developed as a further analytical tool. An examination of this and other developments in the use of ratios can be found in Norma Whittaker's paper on the allocation of resources in further education and the monitoring of their use.[10] We are not concerned here with an analysis of the large variety of student:staff ratio calculations as such. For the purposes of this sub-section it is important only to note that with varying degrees of sophistication the student:staff ratio can be used to determine the size of the academic staff establishment before any consideration is given to the proportion (or numbers) in which that establishment is allocated between the various lecturer grades.

38. The Burnham salaries document does not lay down *a* method for determining the size of the establishment or its structure. Rather, it lays down certain parameters within which the size of the establishment *may* be calculated and within which the structure of the establishment *must* be determined. It is this latter consideration, the proportion of posts at the various levels, which in fact concerns the Burnham Further Education Committee. The Committee negotiates a range of proportions of posts by category of work from which LEAs have to adopt particular proportions for determining the balance between the grades. LEAs can be "generous" in this matter, by adopting the maximum proportion of senior posts for each category of work, or "ungenerous", by choosing the minimum proportion. Most LEAs choose the mid point of the range of proportions laid down in the salaries document. The current range of proportions in respect of each category of work is as follows:

Category of Work	Grade	Proportion of Posts: Estabs of FE	Proportion of Posts: Coll. of Educ. (Technical)
I	Principal Lecturer	20-30%	35%-40%
	Senior Lecturer and Lecturer Grade II	70%-80%	60%-65%
II/III	Principal Lecturer	10%-25%	25%-35%
	Senior Lecturer and Lecturer Grade II	75%-90%	65%-75%

10 Norma Whittaker, "The Allocation of Resources and the Monitoring of their Use", *Use of Resources in College Management,* Coombe Lodge Report, Vol.II, No.11, 1978.

Category of Work	Grade	Proportion of Posts Estabs of FE / Coll. of Educ. (Technical)
IV	Senior Lecturer	0-5%
	Lecturer Grade II	40%-65%
	Lecturer Grade I	30%-60%
V	Senior Lecturer	0-5%
	Lecturer Grade II	15%-25%
	Lecturer Grade I	70%-85%

39. A popular method of using these proportions in fact gives rise not just to the particular ratio of posts in any college but also to the overall number of posts. This method can be illustrated by the following formula which is based on the mid points within the range of proportions set out in paragraph 38.

Number of Lecturer Grade I Posts:

$$\left(77.5\% \times \frac{D}{LI}\right) + \left(45\% \times \frac{C}{LI}\right)$$

Number of Lecturer Grade II Posts:

$$\left(20\% \times \frac{D}{LII}\right) + \left(52.5\% \times \frac{C}{LII}\right)$$

Number of Senior Lecturer Posts

$$\left(2.5\% \times \frac{D}{S}\right) + \left(2.5\% \times \frac{C}{S}\right)$$

Number of Principal Lecturer Posts

$$\left(17.5\% \times \frac{B}{P}\right) + \left(25\% \times \frac{A}{P}\right)$$

Number of Lecturer II and Senior Lecturer Posts:

$$\left(82.5\% \times \frac{B}{S}\right) + \left(75\% \times \frac{A}{S}\right)^{*}$$

Where,

A = Volume of category I work	P	=	Class contact level for Principal Lecturers
B = Volume of category II/III work	S	=	Class contact level for Senior Lecturers
C = Volume of category IV work	LII	=	Class contact level for Lecturers Grade II
D = Volume of category V work	LI	=	Class contact level for Lecturers Grade I

*As is indicated in paragraph 40 (vi), below, the actual number of Lecturer Grade II posts derived from this part of the formula must not exceed 50% of the total. In this example the Senior Lecturer class contact level is used as the denominator. In some cases an average of the Lecturer Grade II and Senior Lecturer levels is used.

40. There are certain features of the application of the range of proportions of posts which should be noted.

(i) The establishment of a college is college based. This apparent truism is important – the Burnham Committee does not lay down the internal departmental allocation of the establishment. At its most basic, the provisions of the salaries document are satisfied if the minimum points in the range of proportions of posts exist in a college. To take an extreme example: all the senior posts could be allocated to one department, and all the junior posts to the other departments, irrespective of the balance of advanced and non-advanced work between departments. In fact, of course, most colleges work on a principle of equity in distributing the posts in the establishment but that this is not always automatically the case is evidenced by the heat generated in most head of department meetings about the departmental share out of the college's establishment.

(ii) The fact that work in categories I and II/III generates only posts at Lecturer Grade II and above, does not mean that lecturers Grade I (if they exist in the college) cannot be called upon to teach work in these categories. Further, there is no compulsion on LEAs or college administrators to promote staff teaching advanced work to the senior posts which this work generates. Again, in equity, many colleges do have regard to the level of work attached to a post in deciding its grading or regrading but, again, there is no automatic connection between these two considerations.

(iii) The general principle that college establishments are college based admits of some exceptions. The Burnham salaries document lays down that in respect of departments in Grade III or above there must be a minimum number of Senior Lecturer posts. These minima are as follows:

Grade III Department	1 Senior Lecturer
Grade IV Department	2 Senior Lecturers
Grade V Department	2 Senior Lecturers
Grade VI Department	3 Senior Lecturers

(iv) The salaries document does not put any limit, apparently, on the number of Head of Department or Vice-Principal posts in a college. Again, it does not lay down a basis for determining the number or proportion of Reader posts or Academic Posts above Reader. However, it does express certain conditions under which Reader and Academic Posts above Reader can be established.[11] Clearly, these posts are intended for use in colleges with a major commitment to advanced work. It is nevertheless worth commenting that few institutions have developed these posts, which represents a

11 See Department of Education and Science, *Scales of Salaries for Teachers in Establishments for Further Education, England and Wales 1978*, Appendix IIA, Part II, p.17-18, HMSO.

significant difference between such institutions and the universities. Presumably, this is due to the financial restraints imposed by LEAs.

(v) It is worth noting that it is not possible to create, on a mandatory basis, Principal Lecturer posts in respect of work in categories IV and V. This can cause administrative difficulties in colleges of further education solely committed to this type of work. It means, for example, that apart from the Principal Lecturer posts protected from previous years in which it was possible to create such posts in respect of non-advanced work, there is no mandatory creation of Principal Lecturer posts for the administration of often large departments. Those engaged in college administration in institutions which do a mixture of category V, IV and II/III work with a majority of work at the lower level, may find other establishment problems facing them. For example, the senior lecturers regarded as the deputy heads of department may not have sufficient category II/III work to enable them to pass the bar on their salary scales whereas those whose work they apparently administer may have sufficient work at this level to pass the bar. The Burnham proportions of posts table and the provisions regarding scale transfer and bar passage have been amended in piecemeal ways in recent years: this has resulted in some anomalies both within and between institutions.

(vi) It will be noticed that in respect of work in categories I and II/III, there is no separate range of proportions for Senior Lecturer and Lecturer Grade II posts. This is necessary because of the transfer arrangement between the Lecturer Grade II and Senior Lecturer grades in respect of work in these categories (see Section **11.1.**7). This arrangement makes it very difficult to distinguish these posts for establishment purposes. In the extreme case, a college doing only work in these categories which experienced no mobility of staff out of the institution, would have eventually all lecturers at the Senior and Principal Lecturer level. The Burnham Committee has made provision to avoid the reverse situation of all posts being graded at the Lecturer Grade II and Principal Lecturer levels. It has been agreed that, at any point in time, no more than 50% of the posts created in the Senior Lecturer and Lecturer Grade II grades in respect of advanced work, should be at the Lecturer Grade II level.[12]

41. **Non-academic staffing establishments**

It should be apparent from the above review of academic staffing establishments, that the Burnham Committee lays down only parameters at national level within which LEAs and colleges have some flexibility in determining the number and grades of posts in the academic establishment. There are not even these general national parameters for determining the number and grading of non-academic staff posts. This contrasts with the situation in the universities where, as Fielden and Lockwood[13] show, a

---

12 See Joint Secretaries of the Burnham Further Education Committee, *Commentary on the Further Education Salaries Documents 1974 and 1975*, pp.6-7, para 17, LACSAB.
13 J. Fielden and G. Lockwood, *Planning and Management in Universities*, Chatto and Windus, 1973.

more precise approach to the determination and allocation of technical and secretarial staff is common (for example, by way of the use of ratios between staff in these categories and academic staff).

42. Local authorities vary greatly both as to whether or not they use a formula for determining the number of non-academic staff and, where one is used, the type of formula adopted. In fact where formulae are used there seem to be as many formulae as there are LEAs. Some formulae, but by no means all, relate the number of staff, but rarely their grading, to student hours. The most common method of determining grading relates grades to the type of college or its size. These general factors seem to differentiate academic and non-academic establishment calculations. In the latter, organization and method studies have a bearing on the calculation in many colleges and the decision on staffing will more often than not be taken outside of the Education Committee, and certainly outside of the college. In this context the positions of administrative, technical and manual staff are reviewed, briefly, in turn below.

43. There are no national prescriptions of the scales to be applied to administrative posts and NALGO, the relevant union, does not have a policy for the negotiation of such arrangements nationally. However, the Association of College Registrars and Administrators has proposed a grading scheme for registrars based on the unit total of the college.

44. Laboratory and workshop technicians are covered by the "Purple Book" (paragraph 28(14)) which sets out nationally prescribed scales.[14] The agreement makes a distinction between degree and non-degree level work. However, NALGO's policy specifically excludes the negotiation of a national formula for the gradings and numbers of technicians employed, in favour of local negotiations on these issues.

45. The establishment of manual workers in a college is, again, dependent on local conditions and the policy of the LEA. NUPE generally presses, at local level, for a staffing structure in colleges which reflects the different catering arrangements as between schools and colleges. Similarly, whilst there is no specific regulation governing the establishment of caretaking and cleaning staff in colleges, NUPE believes that arrangements in colleges should be at least as good as those provided in the national agreement covering schools.

---

14 See Section **9.**43 and **11.8**.

APPENDIX 1

BURNHAM GRADING OF COURSES SUB-COMMITTEE:

Pro-forma for consideration of a course to be graded.

1. Title of Course ....

2. *Duration of Course ....

....

....

....

3. Mode of Study ....
   (full-time, part-time, sandwich, block etc).

4. Total Number of Hours of Study Required ....

5. Entry Qualifications or Requirements

....

....

....

6. Final Qualification(s) Obtained

....

....

....

....

7. Is the Final Qualification a qualification satisfying the Burnham "Degree Equivalent"?

YES/NO

Details of the course subjects, syllabuses and examination requirements and/or assessments should be attached to this form.

*Note: Please indicate the number of years and weeks per year. In the case of courses divided into sections state name of each section i.e. Part 1, Part 2, Stage 1, Stage 2, Inter, Final, etc, and give duration of or hours of study required for each stage.

REFERENCE

Burnham Further Education Committee, *Grading of Courses List of Courses 1975*, LACSAB, 1975. (See also, *Amendment Sheet No.1*, February 1976, *Amendment Sheet No.2*, March 1977, *Amendment Sheet No. 3*, November 1978, and *Amendment Sheet No.4*, August 1978, LACSAB).

Department of Education and Science, *Burnham Further Education Committee Grading of Courses*, 1972, HMSO.

Department of Education and Science, *Scales of Salaries for Teachers in Establishments for Further Education, England and Wales 1978*, HMSO.

Department of Education and Science, *Scales of Salaries for Teachers in Establishments for Further Education, England and Wales 1979*, HMSO.

J. Fielden and G. Lockwood, *Planning and Management in Universities*, Chatto and Windus, 1973.

D. Gold, "Time to burn 'em?", *Education and Training*, October 1979.

Grading of Courses Sub-Committee, *List of Courses graded by the Sub-Committee*, 1968, Burnham Further Education Committee.

Joint Secretaries of the Burnham Further Education Committee, *Commentary on the Further Education Salaries Documents 1974 and 1975*, LACSAB.

Pooling Committee, *Assessment of Curricular Activity and Utilisation of Staff Resources in Polytechnics and FE Colleges*, Councils and Education Press, 1972.

Report of the Committee of Inquiry into the Pay of Non-University Teachers, HMSO, 1974.

N. Whittaker, "The Allocation of Resources and the Monitoring of their Use", *Use of Resources in College Management*, Coombe Lodge Report, Vol.11, No.11, 1978.

3 SUPERANNUATION

1. The regulations for the administering of the Teachers' Superannuation Scheme are made by the Secretary of State under s9 of the Superannuation Act 1972. These regulations, The Teachers' Superannuation Regulations 1976, Statutory Instruments 1976 No. 1987, therefore have the force of statute. Comment on the regulations is available in leaflet form in some detail from the DES Pensions Branch, the address of which is given in the Reference list, below. Any comment on the regulations, however, cannot override statutory provisions. A guide to the regulations is published by NATFHE (*Teachers' Pensions,* Information Series No.4).

2. **Eligibility**
The scheme is compulsory for those employed full-time in schools, colleges and other educational establishments maintained by local authorities or, in some cases, in receipt of government grants. Voluntary colleges within the purview of The Further Education Regulations 1975 participate in the scheme. Youth leaders, youth employment officers and educational organizers are among those in educational employment who can participate in the scheme. Many independent schools participate; they are given the status of "accepted" schools, provided that the terms of their employment so allow.

3. Not all educational service qualifies for benefit under the scheme:
   (i) A modified version of the scheme was operated in some independent schools until 30 April 1975. Service in such an "admitted" school affects pension. Details of the effect are available in the DES leaflet, 430 Pen.
   (ii) Part-time teachers who receive a proportional Burnham salary and who work regularly for a regular proportion of the week may choose whether or not to participate in the scheme. Part-time teachers paid on hourly rates are *not* eligible for participation.
   (iii) Teachers who enter the service after the age of 55 may choose to participate if they wish.
   (iv) Contributions to the scheme cease when a teacher has completed 45 years of service; a serving teacher over 70 pays no contributions. Any service after such times does not count for pension purposes.

4. **Contributions**
Employment pensionable under the teachers' scheme is called reckonable service. "Reckonable service" is defined in a number of ways in the regulations. It includes full-time employment as a teacher, certain kinds of part-time employment as a teacher, war service, in certain cases, and purchased added years. It also includes leave on full pay. Sick leave is included unless either the teacher has been continuously absent for more than 12 months (18 months in the case of pulmonary tuberculosis) or, he or she is not entitled to at least half pay, disregarding any reduction or refund provided for by the terms of his or her employment. Teachers in reckonable service pay contributions of 6% of their salary. Salary is the amount

appropriate under the Burnham salaries document and includes London and other relevant allowances. The larger part of the cost of the scheme is financed[1] by contributions made by employers. Contributions to the new state pension scheme have been lowered by the Secretary of State's decision to "opt-out" of that arrangement. Pensioned teachers will still receive the basic pension benefit but the bulk of their income after retirement will come from the teachers' scheme. Contributions to the teachers' scheme are allowed as a deduction from income in the assessment of income tax liability. This is normally done by the employer.

5. **Repayment of contributions**

Except as indicated below, there is no automatic right to repayment. Although a teacher may leave reckonable service the entitlement to pension remains; hence, should the teacher re-enter reckonable service, pension is based on the whole period of participation in the scheme. Service does not have to be continuous. Once contributions are repaid, the service is no longer reckonable. Repayment is made when a teacher reaches the age of 70 without having qualified for benefits; and to a teacher who has been out of reckonable service for three months unless:

(i) since 31 March 1972 the teacher has completed five years' reckonable service;

(ii) is entitled to retirement benefits immediately on leaving reckonable service;

(iii) has at any time during reckonable service received a salary of £5,000 a year or more. (Under regulations in draft form at the time this book went to print, this restriction was due to be removed for staff leaving service after 6 April 1980).

6. Repayment includes compound interest of 3% per year on the teachers' contributions, reduced by half of any payment in lieu of graduated national insurance contributions which the DES has had to make to secure for the teacher a national insurance pension as if all graduated contributions at the full rate had been paid during the relevant service period. A standard tax charge of 10% is then made.

7. Contributions are also repaid on the death in service of a teacher to her or his estate where the benefits paid to her or him were less than accumulated contributions and interest.

8. **Return of contributions previously repaid**

Eligibility for this provision is limited to teachers who:

(i) withdrew their contributions before 1 June 1973, and

(ii) have returned to reckonable service or external service (external service is that under relevant schemes in Scotland, Northern Ireland, Guernsey, Jersey and the Isle of Man), and

(iii) the amount required to reinstate the previous service is normally not less than £200.

---

1 The scheme operates on the basis of a notional fund and money, as such, is not collected into a real fund. There is a good deal of controversy about the funding of the scheme: see, for example, Peter Knight, "Pay Now – Live Later", *The Technical Journal,* December 1975, pp. 6-7.

Tax relief on repayment applies only where repayment is made by regular and equal instalments. Further details can be found in DES Leaflet 240 Pen.

9. **Benefits: eligibility and amounts**
Application for benefit is made to the Department on Form 14 Pen; part of this form has to be completed by the employer. In order to receive benefits promptly, application should be made at least four months before they become due. Benefits consist of an annual allowance (pension) and an additional allowance (lump sum) and are paid to:
(i) a teacher aged 60 or over who has retired;
(ii) a teacher aged under 60 who, because of infirmity, has become permanently incapable of serving efficiently;
(iii) a teacher who is entitled to claim superannuation benefit under a scheme of premature retirement (see Section **11.4**, below). These conditions are subject to a minimum service provision: the teacher must have rendered at least five years' service. The only exception is a teacher who has rendered service before and after 1 April 1972 or 6 April 1975 but was not actually in service on that date: such an individual must serve either five years from 1 April 1972 onwards, or a total of ten years.

10. Where a person possessing at least five years of reckonable service leaves the teaching service before benefits are due to be paid, the right to a pension based on the length of actual teaching service has nonetheless been established. Pension benefits will be received, on application, from the age of 60; the size of the pension will have increased under the terms of the Pensions (Increase) Act during the period between leaving service and the receipt of the pension. All periods of service are aggregated: a gap in service has no significance apart from the reduction in the length of possible reckonable service. The Pensions (Increase) Act allows for pension increases according to inflation rates, and is applicable from the age of 55.

11. Both pension and lump sum are based on the "average salary". The average salary is the highest for the best consecutive 365 day period of salary in the last 1095 days of reckonable service. In most cases this will mean the last year of service. Pension is calculated as $\frac{1}{80}$ of the average salary for each year of service. A teacher with 30 years of reckonable service would receive a pension of $\frac{30}{80}$ of the average salary. This pension is subject to income tax, and may be reduced on account of national insurance.

12. The lump sum is calculated at two rates. For each year of reckonable service from 1 October 1956, the rate is $\frac{3}{80}$ of the average salary; the rate for each year or reckonable service before 1 October 1956 is $\frac{1}{30}$ of the average salary. Odd days count at 1/365 of the appropriate rate for a year.

13. It is important to remember that the average salary is calculated exactly. The calculation therefore will be the sum of the periods 1 September – 31 March (including the September increment) and 1 April - 31 August (including any salary supplement or increase) averaged over the whole year.

Example:

A teacher with 30 years of reckonable service and an average salary of £8,664 retires in 1979.

£8,664 x 30 x $\frac{1}{80}$ = £3,249

Lump sum will be:

(i) On service before 1 October 1956

£8,664 x 7 x $\frac{1}{30}$ = £2,021.60

(ii) On service from 1 October 1956

£8,664 x 23 x $\frac{3}{80}$ = £7,472.70

£9,494.30

The lump sum has not been subject to taxation. The provisions of the Finance Act 1978 may affect the tax liability of staff who receive in the same tax year a variety of lump sum payments connected with redundancy which amount in total to more than £10,000. At the time of writing the precise effect is not clear and, in particular, the tax liability of those who receive a lump sum under their pension scheme, or extra lump sum by way of compensation for loss of office and a redundancy payment, needs to be the subject of further scrutiny and legal test.

14. Where a teacher had an increment withheld as a result of incomes policy (but not an anticipated increase in a salary scale) such increments are included in the average salary. As cited in paragraph 10 above, pension is increased annually under the provisions of the Pensions (Increase) Act. The maximum amount of reckonable service which can count for lump sum is 45 years but, if total service is in excess of this amount, deduction is made from the beginning of the service so that as much of the lump sum calculation can be made at the rate of 3/80 as possible.

15. **Infirmity benefits**

A teacher aged under 60 who has become permanently incapable of fulfilling duties while in reckonable service, or in circumstances which are directly linked to ill-health which began during reckonable service, becomes eligible to pension and lump sum as calculated above. Such calculations are subject to the following forms of enhancement:

(i) service of the last five years, but less than ten years counts as double subject to what could have been completed by age 65;

(ii) ten to 13½ years reckonable service counts as 20 years, subject to what could have been completed by age 65;

(iii) more than 13½ years' reckonable service qualifies for an addition of six and two thirds years subject to what could have been completed by age 60, or, if more favourable, counts as 20 years limited by what could have been completed by the age of 65.

16. Where teachers have served for at least one year and suffered a breakdown in health but who have not served the five year qualifying period, there is an entitlement to a short service gratuity. This gratuity, which is a single

payment, is calculated as $\frac{1}{12}$ of the average salary for each year of reckonable service. As for a normal pension, days of service are included in the calculation.

17. **Death gratuities**

Without being subject to the five year qualifying period, where a teacher dies in reckonable service, or within 12 months of leaving reckonable service because of ill-health but without having received an ill-health retirement pension, a death gratuity is paid to the teacher's estate. The gratuity is whichever is the greatest of:

(i) the salary in the best 365 day period in the final 1095 days of reckonable service;

(ii) the lump sum which would have been paid if the teacher had retired because of ill-health, including the enhancement provisions;

(iii) repayment of the teacher's accumulated contributions with compound interest at 3% per annum.

The gratuity payment will be reduced by the sum of any benefits previously paid.

18. Where a teacher aged under 60 dies after having left reckonable service at some previous date, the estate receives whichever is the greater of:

(i) a lump sum without enhancement calculated by the normal method on the amount of actual service completed or

(ii) repayment of contributions with compound interest at 3% per annum less any benefits previously paid and less half of any payment-in-lieu of graduated national insurance contributions. This form of benefit is subject to the five year qualifying period.

19 **Dependants' benefits**

Benefits are paid to persons dependent on a teacher. The main beneficiaries are the widows and children of male teachers, but a female teacher or an unmarried male teacher may make application to the DES to nominate a financially dependent close relative to receive benefits. The conditions for nomination are:

(i) that the Department is notified of nominations while the teacher is in reckonable service;

(ii) the nominee is wholly or partly dependent on the nominator and is:

  (a) the teacher's parent; or

  (b) an unmarried dependant of either of the teacher's parents; or

  (c) the teacher's widowed stepmother or stepfather; or

  (d) any unmarried descendant of the deceased wife of a man teacher; or

  (e) the husband of a woman teacher.

Nomination becomes void when the Department receives written notice of revocation; when the nominee dies or marries; when the nominee is a child and becomes of age; and where the teacher is a man, on his marriage.

20. Automatic provision for dependants' benefits was made only on 1 April 1972. Before this date there was a voluntary scheme and, both when that scheme and the 1972 improvements were instituted, it was possible for a

teacher to supplement an earlier superannuation record by undertaking to pay additional contributions for dependants' benefit purposes. The main provision of the dependants' benefit scheme may be summarised as follows for someone who has all years of reckonable service covered for dependants' benefit purposes:

(i) where a male teacher dies after retirement, the widow is entitled to one half of his pension;

(ii) where a male teacher dies in service, the widow is entitled to one half of the ill-health retirement pension he would have received had his health broken down (enhancement therefore is included);

(iii) where there is one dependent child, the fractions referred to above become three quarters; the whole pension is awarded where there are two or more dependent children;

(iv) where there is no widow, the pension for one child is one third and the pension for two or more children is two thirds of the husband's pension.

A child is defined as: a child of the teacher, legitimate or illegitimate, an adopted or accepted member of the family, wholly or mainly dependent, either under 17 or if over receiving full-time education or a specified two year training course, and who is not married or receiving a disqualifying income.

21. Where a part of the teacher's reckonable service is not applicable for dependants' purposes. the benefits under (i), (ii) and (iii) above are calculated according to the proportion of service which has been covered for these purposes. Calculation of reckonable service depends for this purpose upon whether voluntary contributions were made to the widows and orphans scheme before April 1972 and/or the number of years bought into that scheme.

22. **Short-term pensions**

Where a male teacher who has qualified for the above benefit dies, the widow will receive, for the first three months after his death, the salary or pension he was receiving rather than the lower pension which she will ultimately receive.

23. If there is no entitlement to dependants' benefits, the period over which the salary is paid to the widow is increased to four and one half months if there is one dependent child, and to six months if there are two or more dependent children. If there is no widow, the period is two months for one dependent child and four months for two or more dependent children. No subsequent benefits are payable in these cases. Similar payments are made in respect of dependants nominated under paragraph 19 above, where the teacher dies without sufficient qualifying service for a dependant's pension.

24. **Modification**

Teachers who entered service from 1 July 1948 onwards, together with those in service on that date who opted accordingly, pay contributions very slightly less than 6% and consequently have their pension reduced. The reduction is never greater than £67.75 per year. The technicality, known as "modification", derives from previous national insurance arrangements.

25. **Absence from service**
A teacher who leaves reckonable service for a period may be allowed to continue to pay employer's and employee's contributions for up to three years, and up to six years in respect of certain educational employment outside the United Kingdom. Application must be made within three months of leaving service, or six months in the case of employment outside the UK.

26. **Pensioners returning to service**
If a retired teacher in receipt of a pension decides to return to full-time reckonable service, the pension will be either reduced or suspended according to the amount of the new salary received. A comparison is made of the earnings from the re-employment with the salary of reference. [2] If the new earnings exceed the salary of reference, the pension is suspended. If this is not so, the pension is abated so that it does not exceed the difference between the salary of reference and the new earnings. If the new earnings and the pension are together less than the salary of reference, payment of the pension is not affected.

27. If the re-employment is as a part-time teacher (i.e. an engagement to teach regularly for part only of each day or week or as a relief teacher) the pension may be affected if the new earnings are paid out of public funds. If, in any pension quarter, the earnings are less than the difference between one quarter of the teachers annual pension (as increased by the Pensions (Increase) Act) and one quarter of the salary of reference (similarly increased) the payment of his or her pension will be unaffected. However, if in any pension quarter, the earnings are more than the difference between one quarter of the annual pension and one quarter of the salary of reference, the quarter's pension is reduced by the amount of the excess. Where one quarter of the teacher's annual pension (as increased by the Pensions the pension is suspended. The phrase "pension quarter" means either each quarter commencing from the teacher's birthday or the conventional quarter the first day of which starts on 1 January of any year.

28. The arrangements described in paragraph 27, above, apply also to other types of re-employment, the earnings from which are paid out of public funds, *if the employment could be pensionable (if it were full-time) under the teachers' superannuation scheme.* The italicised words are important. They mean that most non-teaching re-employment does not affect the payment of pension. Also, some types of teaching are exempted, for, example: part-time teaching in an independent school (since, even though such teaching if done full-time could be reckonable, the earnings do not come from public funds).

29. Paragraphs 26-28, above, deal with the abatement of pension when a teacher takes up re-employment after he or she has commenced the receipt of a pension. We now turn to look at a different pension effect of re-employment: the further pension benefit which might be obtained from that employment.

---

2 The basic salary of reference is the highest annual rate of salary received during the last three years of pensionable service prior to retirement. In most cases it will be the rate in payment at retirement (cf DES Leaflet 192 Pen).

30. Re-employment in teaching is pensionable and involves the deduction of contributions in most cases. The exceptions are:
    (i) where the teacher is over 70 or reaches this age during the re-employment, in which case the time spent over 70 is not pensionable;
    (ii) where the teacher has 45 years' reckonable service or achieves this during the re-employment, in which case the time in excess of 45 years' total service is not pensionable.

    In other cases, the pension position of someone ceasing re-employment is as follows. If the average salary is equal to or higher than that on which the benefits were originally calculated, pension and lump sum will be calculated on the new total of service. If the new average salary is less than that on which the original benefits were calculated, the original pension is resumed and a separate pension and lump sum is awarded in respect of the re-employment. Both these provisions relate to re-employment of 365 days or more. Teachers re-employed for less than this can withdraw any contributions paid during the re-employment. None of the provisions described in this paragraph apply to re-employment in part-time teaching, except in the case where re-employment is of an individual who is in receipt of an infirmity pension.

31. **War service**

    The war service of those who served in the Armed Forces of the Crown may be reckonable for pension purposes under certain conditions. Briefly, these are as follows:
    (i) the teacher must have been engaged in contributory teaching service which he or she left to join the Forces; or
    (ii) the teacher must have completed a teacher training college course (but not taken up his or her first teaching post) prior to joining the Forces; or
    (iii) the teacher must have left such a course to join the Forces; or
    (iv) the teacher must have been registered for such a course but could not take up his or her place due to joining the Forces.
    (v) Unless the teacher earned more by way of Forces pay than he or she would have done as a teacher, the service is counted free.
    (vi) The period eligible for consideration as "war service" is that between September 1939 and the end of March 1949. There is another scheme for the *part coverage* of war service which provides for those who after war service entered reckonable service for the first time before July 1950. This scheme also applies to those entering reckonable service later than this on completion of an emergency training course, a course in respect of which grants were paid to him or her under the Ministry of Education (Further Education and Training) Grant Regulations 1946 (or the equivalent Scottish Scheme), or any other course of training providing it was begun before July 1950. Those who began the final year of a four year combined degree/teacher training course before November 1950 are also covered. Male teachers who satisfy these qualifications and who served in the Armed Forces, the Merchant Navy or the Mercantile Marine at any time during the Second World War (3rd September 1939 - 1st April 1949), are able to reckon one half of their service for pension purposes. Similarly, women who satisfy the

qualifications and who served at any time in the same period in one of a large variety of women's services (e.g., the Queen Alexandra's Royal Naval Nursing Service), are also able to reckon one half of the service for pension purposes.

32. **Added years**

The purchase of added years ("buying in") is the arrangement by which a teacher may fill a gap in a superannuation record by purchasing the required number of years' service at full cost. The main restrictions on the scheme are that the period in question must be when the teacher was over the age of 20; that it was not superannuable in any other scheme and that the teacher made the election to purchase before the age of 55. Employers make no contributions to the purchase of added years; the intent of the buying-in tables is that they should provide "value for money". However, as the "value for money" consideration does not take into account the operation of the Pensions (Increase) Act, election to purchase added years may be found by some generally to be beneficial.

The three methods of buying-in are:

(i) The payment of between 1% and 9% of salary until the amount of money due has been paid. These periodic payments will attract tax relief.

(ii) The payment of a lump sum, but this payment does not attract tax relief.

(iii) The payment of fixed instalments over a period between five and ten years. This method avoids the linking of payments to a progressively higher salary as in the first method; and the whole of the payments attract tax relief.

Contributions for all superannuation purposes, including the purchase of added years, must be kept within the Inland Revenue limits concerning levels of pension contributions. This limits pension contributions to 15% of salary.

33. **Allocation of pensions**

Allocation of pension may be made only by a retiring teacher, or a teacher over the age of 60 whose length of service qualifies for retirement benefits but who does not wish to retire immediately. Allocation may be made in addition to the normal family benefit provision. Before any allocation is allowed, the applicant must satisfy the Department's conditions regarding good health. There are two forms of allocation:

(i) An allocation which would ensure to the beneficiary a pension payable from the date of death of the allocator.

(ii) An allocation made in favour of the spouse only which provides:

  (a) an annuity payable from the date of commencement of the pension (this annuity is payable only during the lifetime of the beneficiary and ceases on his or her death);

  (b) a pension of double the amount of this annuity, payable to the beneficiary after the death of the allocator.

Allocation in favour of a spouse may be made under either option, but provision for another person may only be made under the first option. In making any decision to allocate, it is highly important to note that under either option, if the beneficiary dies first, the pension of the allocator will continue to be reduced by the amount allocated (or will be reduced by the amount allocated when the pension is eventually put into payment).

34. It is not possible to allocate more than one third of the gross pension or make an allocation of a size which would exceed the balance of the beneficiary's pension against that of the allocator. Both the pensions of allocator and beneficiary remain subject to income tax, but only to such proportions as they receive. The Pensions (Increase) Act applies similarly here. As this is a somewhat complex matter, a person considering the allocation of pension should consult DES advisory leaflet 207 Pen.

35. **Transferability**

Provision for transferability should, in time, reduce substantially the need for purchase of added years. Where a person enters teaching service from another superannuation scheme, the teachers' scheme is prepared to accept from the administrators of that scheme a transfer value; similarly, the teachers' scheme is prepared to offer reciprocal arrangements. It must not be assumed that such a transfer will be on a year for year basis, since the transfer will be governed by the benefits and rules of the respective schemes. However, transfers between public sector schemes will normally be on a broadly comparable basis. For example, the teachers' scheme accepts the transferability of the university teachers' scheme at a value of 90%.

REFERENCE

Pensions (Increase) Act 1974, Chapter 9, HMSO.

Teachers Superannuation (War Service) Act, 1939, Chapter 95, HMSO.

The Teachers' Superannuation Regulations 1976, Statutory Instruments 1976 No. 1987, HMSO.

The Pensions Increase (Teachers) Regulations 1974, Statutory Instruments 1974, No.831, HMSO.

TheTeachers' Superannuation (Amendment) Regulations 1978, Statutory Instruments 1978 No. 422, HMSO.

Re-employment of Retired Teachers – Effect on Age Pensions, DES Leaflet 192 Pen.

Information for Teachers applying for Retirement Benefits on the grounds of age, DES Leaflet 193 Pen.

General Information for Teachers about Retirement Benefits on the grounds of age, DES Leaflet 194 Pen.

General Information for Teachers about Infirmity Benefits, DES Leaflet 198 Pen.

A Guide to Teachers' Superannuation, DES Leaflet 199 Pen.

Allocation of Pension, DES Leaflet 207 Pen.

Teachers' Superannuation: Return of contributions previously repaid, DES Leaflet 240 Pen.

The Teachers' Superannuation Scheme – Past Added Years, DES Leaflet 374 Pen.

Teachers' Superannuation Regulations: Repayment of Contributions, DES Leaflet 381 Pen.

Teachers' Superannuation Regulations: Teachers from Overseas, DES Leaflet 425 Pen.

Service in Independent Schools Admitted to the Special Superannuation Arrangements of the Teachers' Superannuation Regulations, DES Leaflet 430 Pen.

Teachers' Superannuation Regulations [Death: General Information], DES Leaflet 450 A Pen.

Teachers' Superannation Regulations: General Information about benefits payable in respect of teachers who die after leaving pensionable teaching service, DES Leaflet 450B Pen.
Superannuation Arrangements for part-time teachers in primary and secondary schools and establishments of further education, DES Leaflet 476 Pen.
Teachers' Superannuation Regulations: payment of combined contributions during absence from reckonable service, DES Leaflet 721 Pen.
Teachers' Superannuation – A guide to preservation and transfer, DES Leaflet 735 Pen.
Teachers' Superannuation – A guide to widows', children's and adult dependants' benefits, DES Leaflet 861 Pen.
Teachers' Pensions, NATFHE Information Series No 4, 1977.

Enquiries about income tax in relation to superannuation should be sent to:
Office of HM Inspector of Taxes, PD3, Ty Glas Road, Cardiff CF4 5X3.
Pension payment is operated by the Paymaster General. Questions about payment or, for example, the effect on pension of fluctuating earnings in re-employment, should be addressed to:
The Paymaster General (T/P),
Russell Way,
Crawley, Sussex.
Enquiries about national insurance can be addressed to the local Social Security Office or to:
The Department of Health & Social Security,
Benton Park Road,
Newcastle upon Tyne NE98 1YX.
An immediate source of advice upon superannuation is:
The Department of Education & Science (Pensions Branch),
Mowden Hall,
Staindrop Road,
Darlington, Co Durham,
DL3 9DG (0325 60155).

4 PREMATURE RETIREMENT COMPENSATION

1. The reasons advanced for the introduction of the premature retirement scheme are that: it is an extension of schemes applying to local government and the civil service; falling rolls require staff reorganization; and promotion blockages can be removed with consequent benefits to morale. The enabling regulations, The Teachers' Superannuation (Amendment) Regulations 1978, Statutory Instruments 1978 No.422, came into effect on 17 April 1978 and have retrospective effect from 1 April 1976. The regulations which deal specifically with enhancement and other provisions are expected to come into operation in the future and to have a similar retrospective effect. At the time of writing, these regulations are in the form of a first draft only. Therefore, comment upon these provisionally entitled Teachers' (Compensation for Premature Retirement) Regulations can be general and anticipatory only.

2. **The Amendment: main provisions**

The Teachers' Superannuation (Amendment) Regulations contain two main provisions; the other provisions set out consequential changes in the principal regulations so as to extend the existing position relating to purchase of added years, allocation of pension, and payment of family benefits to those who retire prematurely. The principal changes are:

(i) Where a teacher ceases to be employed in reckonable service having attained the age of 50 but not having attained the age of 60, provided that the service was not terminated by incapacity, then that individual is eligible to receive the normal superannuation allowances if the employer gives written notice to the Secretary of State that the employment was terminated by:
   (a) the reason of redundancy, or
   (b) in the interests of the efficient discharge of the employer's functions.

(ii) A teacher whose service was terminated under the above conditions after 31 March 1976 but before 1 January 1977 (the date from which the amendments have effect) may elect to be dealt with under the Amendment as if it had effect on the date of the termination of employment.

3. The ages mentioned in the Amendment are specific. A person at the time of redundancy aged under 50 does not qualify for the scheme, even if on attaining the age of 50 that person has not been employed since their loss of employment. A teacher aged, for example, 49 at the time of her or his loss of employment would not qualify for the payment of superannuation allowances until the minimum retirement age of 60. If benefits are not claimed by an eligible individual, then other forms of public pension compensation received (for example, under the Colleges of Education (Compensation) Regulations) could be reduced by the sums to which the individual is eligible, whether they have been claimed or not.

4. Application for superannuation allowances is made in the usual way on Form 14 Pen at least four months before the allowances are due to be paid. In this instance, however, the employer must certify on the form that the reason for the termination of reckonable service was either because of redundancy or in the efficient exercise of the employer's functions.

5. The way in which premature retirement legislation should be operated has been the subject of an agreement between the teachers' unions represented on the Burnham Committee and CLEA, acting on behalf of the Association of County Councils and the Association of Metropolitan Authorities. The agreement indicates that it does not prejudice the teachers' organizations' general policy of opposition to redundancy, or any existing provisions of statute or collective agreements. The agreement may be summarised thus:
   (i) As the Employment Protection Acts require consultations about redundancy, the joint consultations between employers and teachers' organizations must begin at the earliest opportunity, and should comprise a thorough examination of all courses of action. For example, the need for redundancies may be obviated by redeployment and retraining.
   (ii) The authority will disclose in writing to teachers' associations' representatives:
      (a) the reason for its proposals;
      (b) the number and descriptions of teachers whom it is proposed to dismiss as redundant;
      (c) the total numbers of teachers of these descriptions employed at the institutions concerned;
      (d) the proposed method of selection for redundancy; and
      (e) the proposed method of effecting such redundancies including the period over which they are to take effect.

   During the course of the consultations, the authority must consider and reply to any representations made by the teachers' representatives, including proposals for courses of action to avoid redundancies. Reasons for rejection, if applicable, must be made in writing by the authority.
   (iii) Where redundancies are contemplated, the authority will seek volunteers for premature retirement. In determing the enhancement to be given (see under paragraph 10, below) there should not be discrimination between teachers in similar professional circumstances. For example, it would be wrong to discriminate between staff of equal length of reckonable service.
   (iv) Application of the premature retirement regulations in respect of the efficient exercise of the employer's functions should not be dissimilar to that applied to redundancies. However, the application of the agreed arrangements in individual cases of premature retirement in the interests of the efficiency of the service will be a matter between the authority and the individual teacher. The authority ought nonetheless to advise the teacher to consult the relevant professional association.
   (v) Problems of interpretation of the agreement may be referred for joint consideration to the secretaries of the appropriate authorities' or

teachers' organizations. Particular grievances ought to be referred to the appropriate agreed grievance procedures.

6. Within an agreement on redundancies between CLEA and the further education teachers' organizations, there are further provisions relevant here (the agreement is summarised in Section **11.7.**10).

7. **The Teachers' (Compensation for Premature Retirement) Regulations**

It must be stated again that these regulations were in preliminary draft form only when this book was written. It is not expected, however, that the main details of the enhancement scheme will differ significantly from those set out by the Department of the Environment for local government officers.

8. **Eligibility**

The regulations will apply to full-time teachers of at least five years' reckonable service, subject to the conditions set out below. Part-time teachers will qualify only if their posts are superannuable under the Teachers' Superannuation Scheme and they have elected that they be so. Teaching posts are specified as:

(i) in a school; or
(ii) a maintained or voluntary establishment of further education; or
(iii) a polytechnic wholly assisted by a local education authority; or
(iv) an opting direct grant school.

Employment by a local education authority, or by a local authority otherwise than in one of the above capacities will also be eligible but the person must nonetheless be subject to the Teachers' Superannuation Regulations. Further conditions currently proposed are:

(v) that on or after 1 April 1976 the individual suffered a loss of employment certified to the Secretary of State by the employer to be due to redundancy or the efficient discharge of the employer's functions;
(vi) at the date of the termination of employment, the age of 50 but not the age of 65 had been attained; and
(vii) the teacher is not eligible for compensation under local government schemes or schemes made under s1 or s24 of the Superannuation Act 1972.

9. Condition (vi) means that whereas the Teachers' Superannuation (Amendment) Regulations lower the age at which retirement is possible to between 50 and 60, the compensation regulations allow for the consideration for compensation of a teacher aged in excess of the normal minimum retiring age. Thus a teacher aged, for example, 63 could qualify for a compensation payment. Condition (vii) refers to regulations such as the Colleges of Education (Compensation) Regulations which are made under section 24 of the Superannuation Act; a teacher eligible to be considered for such compensation is likely to be disqualified from *compensation* under the premature retirement scheme.

10. **Enhancement**
The compensating authority has the discretionary power to credit the eligible teacher with an additional period of service. The amount of such service awarded is again discretionary, subject to a maximum limit. The limit of such service will be the shortest of:
(i) a period of ten years;
(ii) a period equivalent to the teachers' reckonable service;
(iii) a period which, when added to reckonable service, does not in aggregate exceed 40 years;
(iv) a period equal to the time between ceasing to hold the terminal employment and reaching the age of 65.
Enhancement will not apply where the teacher has already been credited with an equal or greater period of enhancement in a previous post (for example, long term compensation under the Colleges of Education (Compensation) Regulations). Where the period of enhancement in such an instance is less than the shortest period itemised in (i-iv) above, the authority will obtain the maximum figure for its discretionary award by subtracting the previous award from that shortest period. Payments generated by enhancement, including increases in those payments under the Pensions (Increase) Act, will be borne directly by the compensating authority (see paragraph 19) and not the superannuation fund.

11. **Annual allowance and lump sum: compensation**
While the lump sum and pension received are enhanced forms of the benefits usual under the teachers' scheme, because of the years of service which an authority can add they are described as compensation. Annual compensation is calculated in the same way as annual allowance (pension) except that reckonable service has been extended by the discretionary award. The annual compensation (pension) will be $\frac{1}{80}$ of the average salary multiplied by the number of years of reckonable service, including the discretionary award. As usual, this sum is subject to taxation.

12. Lump sum compensation (additional allowance) will be $\frac{3}{80}$ of the salary of reference multiplied by the number of years of reckonable service, including the discretionary award. The taxation position regarding this sum is referred to in Section **11.3.**13.

13. Compensation will not be payable if the sum of the annual compensation and the annual amount of any occupational pension resultant from an employment prior to that in which the redundancy or discharge occurred is equal to, or exceeds, one half of the average salary. Where a teacher possesses the sort of pension referred to above and it is less than one half of the average salary, annual compensation will be reduced to an amount which allows the maximum pension/compensation permissible.

14. **Short term compensation**
Where a teacher's widow or widower is entitled to a short term pension under the Teachers' Superannuation Regulations, then under the Teachers' (Compensation for Premature Retirement) Regulations that person will receive, for three months following the day of the death of the

teacher, a short term compensation payment. This payment will be at an annual rate equal to the annual compensation payable to the teacher before his death.

15. **Dependant's benefits**
Where a teacher dies leaving a widow or widower entitled to a pension under the Superannuation Regulations, then that beneficiary will be entitled to receive long term compensation [1] of one half of the annual compensation paid to the teacher before death. No account is taken here of any reduction in, or suspension of compensation which may have occurred. If, prior to death, the teacher had been re-employed then the payment to the widow will be without compensation enhancement: the pension received will be calculated solely in accordance with the Superannuation Regulations. The beneficiary is entitled to one-half of the ill-health retirement pension the teacher would have received had a breakdown in health been suffered (including therefore the enhancement benefit of the ill-health scheme).

16. Where there is one dependent child, three quarters of the annual compensation of the deceased is awarded. The whole of the annual compensation is awarded where there are two or more dependent children. Where there is no surviving widow or widower, the benefits are: one third of the annual compensation for one child and two thirds for two or more children. Where the deceased teacher had been re-employed, these benefits are calculated on the basis of compensation received during re-employment.

17. These benefits are payable until the death of the beneficiary or, in the case of a child, on ceasing to be a child within the meaning of the Superannuation Regulations. Eligibility for payment commences at the time of the cessation of short term compensation, if applicable, or on the day after the date of death. Where the widow or widower remarries then unless the Secretary of State directs otherwise, the whole compensation shall cease to be payable, except that: if the remarried widow has reached pensionable age, her annual compensation will be restored but reduced where, when added to the pension payable under the Superannuation Regulations, it exceeds her guaranteed minimum pension. These conditions relating to remarriage apply similarly to cohabitation. If cohabitation ceases or the remarriage is terminated, compensation becomes payable again should the Secretary of State so direct.

18. **Adjustment and reduction of compensation**
(NB: these draft abatement provisions represent the least clear or firm part of the proposed regulations). Amounts payable under the Redundancy Payments Act will be reduced (or extinguished) by the payment of lump sum compensation. In the case of the Colleges of Education (Compensation) Regulations, resettlement compensation is subject to such reduction and this form of compensation (an enhanced redundancy payment) is paralleled in the draft Teachers' (Compensation for Premature Retirement) Regulations. Should authorities award compensation payments outside the scope of the

---

1 This compensation must not be confused with the long term compensation payable under the Colleges of Education (Compensation) Regulations.

Premature Retirement Regulations, it is certainly the intention of the draft regulations that lump sum compensation should be reduced by the amounts of any such "termination payment" which an authority may award. However, in this instance, short or long term payments to beneficiaries would not be affected.

19. A teacher to whom the regulations apply is required to give notice to the compensating authority not later than 28 days after either entering or ceasing re-employment. The compensating authorities will normally be either the DES or the local authority but in special circumstances these bodies may act jointly.

20. **Allocation**
Allocation may still be carried out within the terms of the Superannuation Regulations (and subject to the provisions discussed under Section **11.2.**33, above). If allocation has not been made, notice of intent must be given not later than two months after receipt of the written notification of the entitlement to annual compensation.

21. By analogy with the relationship between Colleges of Education (Compensation) Regulations and the Superannuation Regulations, it is fair to state that in re-employment or any circumstance which would entail eligibility for reduction of compensation, allocation is not a route by which to increase benefits. Under the Colleges of Education (Compensation) Regulations it is stipulated that any portion of a pension allocated, and therefore that amount by which the pension is reduced, shall be regarded as having been received in full for the purposes of compensation. Thus, even though one third of the pension may be allocated, it is the whole pension which is used to determine any reductions in compensation.

REFERENCE

The Teachers' Superannuation (Amendment) Regulations 1978, Statutory Instruments 1978 No. 422, HMSO.
The Teachers' (Compensation for Premature Retirement) Regulations (Draft).

5 THE COLLEGES OF EDUCATION (COMPENSATION) REGULATIONS

1. **The Crombie context: an introductory note**
Of all the regulations with which those involved in college administration have to deal, the Colleges of Education (Compensation) Regulations are probably the most complex and unclear. Made in 1975, and coming from a stable of similar regulations known collectively as the Crombie Code, these regulations have suffered from a combination of bad drafting and an attempt to stretch regulations, designed for use in the civil service and local government, to cover the teaching service. The meaning of some parts of the Crombie Code is so unclear that in a leading case brought under the local government version of the Code, a High Court Judge indicated that it was clear to him that the two Counsel before him failed to understand the regulations: a fact he did not find surprising since he failed to understand them himself! Because of the complexity of the regulations this sub-section is, inevitably, long. It seeks to provide not only a guide to the regulations but also a summary of their latest judicial interpretation. It is hoped that this will prove useful not just to those involved in the administration of teacher education, but to those working elsewhere in further and higher education. One of the purposes here is to provide an historical account of the regulations and their interpretation so that readers will be aware of their virtues and vices and thereby more able to assess suggestions that the Crombie Code should be extended to other fields of education.

2. Law which is obscure invites litigation and the Crombie Code has stimulated a large number of references to industrial tribunals and the higher courts. Many believe that these cases have been unnecessary and, certainly, a clearer code and a greater mutual understanding between the DES, local authorities and the teachers' associations would have avoided them. It is a sad commentary on the regulations that, to date, over 100 references have been made to tribunals. Unfortunately, college administrators cannot ignore the results of these cases since they provide a scheme of interpretation of the regulations which does not always accord with the intentions of those in the Government, the local authorities and the teachers' associations who "negotiated" the regulations in the early 1970s.

3. What did those negotiators think they were about and why did the Government feel it was necessary to apply the Crombie Code to teacher education? The early seventies were exciting years for those concerned with the organization of higher education. They were years of heated debate about the role of teacher education in our higher education system. Most contributors to the debate felt a change was needed: a change which would involve the reorganization of teacher education to remove it from its monotechnic basis; and inevitably such changes would lead to the displacement of certain staff. It was expected that this would be a relatively small number, and just as such displacements in the context of civil service

and local government reorganization had been facilitated by the Crombie Code, so too, the argument ran, should teacher education reorganization. It might, at the time, have seemed curious that such a large hammer was being applied to crack such a small nut. After all, the then apparent scale of the envisaged teacher education reorganization was hardly as great as the earlier reorganization of local government. That, it seems, was not the point. The point of similarity in the different exercises was that they both involved a change in government policy and the displacement of staff. The cause and effect thus envisaged was the statutory origin for the special compensation provisions which the Crombie Code enshrines.

4. Of course, history didn't work out as the different parties in the early seventies had expected and, indeed, there must be considerable doubt that the parties had the same view of the future anyway.[1] In fact, by the time the Colleges of Education (Compensation) Regulations appeared in 1975 a parallel set of regulations, the Further Education Regulations, had also been made.[2] These latter regulations gave the lie to all versions of reorganization which suggested that the process would be exclusively one of merger between institutions. In fact, they gave the Secretary of State one power, though a draconian one, and that was to reduce by way of directions to colleges and LEAs, the number of students following teacher education courses. Whatever people believed was going on in the early seventies, by the middle of the decade the Secretary of State was armed with an axe sufficiently sharp as to close colleges of education at a stroke, by reducing their intakes of students to nil. The exciting context of the reorganization and reformation of teacher and higher education which existed in the early seventies, had become, by the late seventies, one in which the closure of over 30 colleges of education had been planned. It is hardly surprising that a version of the Crombie Code negotiated in the earlier period has provided an inferior tool for dealing with problems of the later one.

---

1 David Hencke, *Colleges in Crisis*, Penguin, 1978, started a debate taken up by Hugh Harding *(Education*, 29 December 1978, Volume 152, Number 26, pp.631-633 and 5 January 1979, Volume 153, Number 1, pp.11-12) about the differences between apparent collaborators in the process of college reorganization.

2 Regulation 3(2) of The Further Education Regulations 1975 (SI 1054) states:

"An authority or (in the case of a voluntary establishment) the governing body shall comply with any direction by the Secretary of State given after consultation with them and expressed to be given for the purpose of facilitating the reorganisation referred to in paragraph (1) above –

(a) as to the discontinuance of any course or courses for the training of teachers; or

(b) as to the numbers and categories of students to be admitted for the purpose of attending such courses at:-

(i) any institution provided by them which immediately before 1st August 1975 was conducted as a training establishment within the meaning of the Training of Teachers Regulations 1967 as amended; or

(ii) any other institution provided by them which includes a department which immediately before 1st August 1975 was conducted as is described in sub-paragraph (i)"

5. **The main provisions of the regulations**
For many staff the attempt to gain Crombie compensation must seem like entering on an assault course with hurdles which get progressively bigger as the course goes on. The first hurdle is that of basic qualification – to whom do the regulations apply? There are two basic regulations to be satisfied here. Firstly, the member of staff must have been employed in a training establishment immediately before a "material date" (regulation 3(a)). Secondly, the loss of employment or diminution in emoluments which stimulates the claim must be attributable to a direction (under The Further Education Regulations, 1975) of the Secretary of State (regulation 4). In this context, though not in others, "material date" means the date on which the direction was given. What constitutes a direction is hardly clear, especially since the DES has sent a number of letters to colleges about reorganization and reductions since 1975. In fact, a letter of direction is one which is signed by an authorised agent and quotes the Secretary of State's powers under The Further Education Regulations 1975, as the basis of the letter. "Training establishment" is defined in the compensation regulations as an institution which immediately before 1 August 1975 was conducted as a training establishment within the meaning of the Training of Teachers Regulations 1967, or an establishment of further education (within the meaning of The Further Education Regulations 1975) which includes a department which, immediately before 1 August 1975, was conducted as such a training establishment. Hence, the typical college of education and a teacher education department in a polytechnic are both included.

6. It is important to note that the loss of employment must be attributable to a direction and not due to some other cause, for example, a failure to recruit students. As we shall see, both these innocent looking phrases "loss of employment" and "attributable to a direction" have led to industrial tribunal and high court cases. (See paragraphs 24 to 33 below).

7. Having passed that hurdle all the claimant has acquired is the right to have his or her case considered under the regulations. There is then the question as to which, if any, of three types of compensation: resettlement, long term and retirement, is the claimant entitled. There is a good deal of confusion – understandably given the terms used – about the meaning of "resettlement", "long term" and "retirement" as types of compensation. In essence, resettlement compensation is an enhanced redundancy lump sum payment. It has very little to do with resettlement in the geographical sense and is not paid simply because someone losing a job in a college has to move his or her home in order to acquire another job. Long term compensation is a periodic payment and has been thought by some to be an early retirement benefit. It is not. In essence, long term compensation is a protection against loss of income. It is not really expected to be a long term payment since someone who is in receipt of this type of compensation is, as we shall see, expected to seek other employment to mitigate his or her loss. Finally, retirement compensation seeks to compensate an individual for reduction in pension benefit as a result of his or her loss of employment or diminution in emoluments.

8. An individual whose case falls to be considered under the regulations will become entitled to compensation if he or she satisfies the following provisions.
   (i) He or she has suffered loss of employment (in the case of all three types of compensation) or emoluments (in the case of long term and retirement compensation) attributable to a direction within ten years of a material date and has made a claim (within 13 weeks of the date of loss for resettlement, and within two years for long term and retirement compensation) to his or her compensating authority.
   (ii) He or she has been employed continuously for two years (for resettlement compensation) and five years (for long term and retirement compensation) in relevant employment, either full-time or part-time immediately prior to a material date.
   (iii) He or she has not reached normal retirement age at the date of loss.
   (iv) His or her loss has not been because of misconduct or incapacity to perform his or her duties.
   (v) After notice of termination or intention of termination of employment has been given in writing, he or she has not been offered, in writing, any relevant employment which is reasonably comparable or, in the case of resettlement compensation only, any employment which is suitable for him or her and in which he or she performs substantially the same duties, at the same place or in the same locality.

9. Some of the terms used above require explanation. The term "material date" in this context is defined differently from that outlined in paragraph 5. Here it means the date of loss or the date on which the direction comes into effect, whichever is the earlier. "Relevant employment" is defined in a number of ways on page 7 of the regulations. For most staff the employment defined as "by any person, authority or body, for the purposes of a training establishment" will be their relevant employment. But the term also covers school teaching, university teaching, local government and civil service employment and service not covered in the definition but which, in the opinion of the Secretary of State, should be regarded as relevant employment. As we shall see this last definition of relevant employment (giving powers to the Secretary of State to count any employment as relevant) is not all it may seem. The "compensating authority" is the LEA in the case of maintained colleges and the DES in every other case. The continuous employment for two or five years referred to in paragraph 8(ii), admits of breaks of six months and 12 months respectively. "Normal retirement age" means 65, in the case of teachers, and 60 for women and 65 for men, for other employees in colleges.

10. It will be noticed that two crucial phrases used in paragraph 8(v) above, are not defined in the regulations. These are "reasonably comparable relevant employment" and employment which is "suitable for a member of staff in which he or she performs substantially the same duties at the same place or in the same locality." Offers of these two types of employment, by the same or a different employer, remove the member of staff from eligibility to compensation as is indicated in paragraph 8(v). The offer, which must be made in writing, can come as a result of the individual's search for

employment or, unsolicited, from the employer. A restrictive interpretation of these terms could hence rule most people out of benefit. A lot, therefore, lies in the hands of the compensating authority. It is understandable, perhaps, that given this feature of the regulations, the bulk of references to tribunals and the courts in matters of dispute between claimants and their compensating authorities, have arisen in the context of this particular regulation.

11. If the claimant manages to mount these hurdles, he or she has established an entitlement to compensation. Those who are just seeking resettlement compensation have now reached their goal and will be paid out. For those seeking long term and retirement compensation there are more hurdles to overcome. The regulations lay down how the actual amount of resettlement compensation is to be calculated for the individual. They lay down only how the *maximum* amount of long term compensation is to be calculated. (See paragraph 15 (ii) below for the methods of calculation). The actual amount of long term compensation paid, up to the maximum, and also whether or not it should be paid at all, is a decision made by the compensating authority in the light of the following factors:
(i) the conditions attached to the lost employment, especially its security of tenure;
(ii) the emoluments and other conditions attached to any new employment undertaken as a result of the loss;
(iii) the extent to which the claimant has sought suitable employment and the emoluments which he or she might have acquired by accepting other suitable employment offered to him or her in writing, following written notice of termination or likely termination of his or her employment.

12. It is unlikely that a compensating authority will pay much, or any, long term compensation to someone who loses employment by way of the demise of a temporary contract. The compensating authority is likely to argue, on the basis of 11(i) above, that the security of tenure was slight. (There has already been a tribunal decision on this point and others concerning temporary staff: see paragraph 40 below). Of more importance is the rather sweeping provision set out in paragraph 11(iii). What constitutes "seeking suitable employment"? The term "suitable" is not defined in the regulations – nor has it yet been the subject of judicial interpretation in the courts under the regulations. However, it has been widely used and interpreted in other employment law statutes. It might be held that it does not mean the same as in paragraph 8(v) above where offers of suitable employment also have to be in the same place or locality and in performance of the same duties. Nor need this suitable employment be relevant employment as described in paragraph 9. As we shall see, some commentators have sought to infer, from cases arising under different regulations, the precise meaning of this clause. For the moment the following point needs to be noted. Staff notified of their loss, or likely loss, of employment must make a search for suitable employment. This requirement continues also for as long as they are in receipt of long term compensation. If they do not make such a search they could lose some, or all, of their long term compensation. Further, if the

search results in an offer of reasonably comparable relevant employment, they lose entitlement to long term compensation anway. It is this emphasis, perhaps even a "Catch 22" emphasis, on the requirement to mitigate the loss that makes it clear that whatever else long term compensation might be, it is not a premature retirement payment.

13. The final hurdle facing staff once they have acquired long term compensation and retirement compensation, comes with the obligation on the compensating authority to review periodically the awards made. Review in the first two years must be at least at six monthly intervals. Given pressure of work and economies in staffing it is unlikely that compensating authorities will, in fact, meet this timetable. Further, a review can be stimulated by any material change in circumstances and, to parallel this, a claimant is required to inform the compensating authority of any such changes. Compensating authorities must have regard to the following in making reviews:
    (i) the factors set out in sub-paragraphs 11(i) – 11(iii) above;
    (ii) whether there has been a change in circumstances; and
    (iii) whether or not to increase, reduce or discontinue compensation, or otherwise change the original decision, and whether or not to reduce the compensation on account of any other emoluments received.

14. Other important aspects of the review process are as follows:
    (i) The compensating authority must give fourteen days notice of the intention to make a review, unless the review is carried out at the request of the claimant.
    (ii) The claimant can require a review to be carried out within the first two years.
    (iii) After the two years have expired, the compensating authority must make a review, if requested to do so, if it took into account new emoluments in the original award and there has been a loss or reduction in these not due to misconduct or incapacity, and the compensating authority is satisfied that the loss or reduction is causing hardship.
    (iv) Reviews are automatically made during or after the two year period if the claimant takes up employment in which the emoluments come from public funds and the aggregate of the current emoluments, superannuation benefits and the long term compensation exceeds the emoluments lost or diminished due to a direction.
    (v) In making reviews, increases in new emoluments due to cost of living changes, have to be disregarded. The DES takes the view that this means that annual salary increases below the level of changes in the Retail Price Index will be disregarded; increments and promotion increases will not.

15. The amount of resettlement and retirement compensation is fixed by formulae set out in the regulations. The maximum amount of long term compensation is also laid down. These formulae are as follows.
    (i) *Resettlement compensation*
    The greater of
    (a) an amount equal to 13 weeks' emoluments plus, in the case of a

claimant who has attained the age of 45, one additional week's emoluments for each year of age after 45 and before loss of employment, up to a maximum of 13 additional weeks; or

(b) an amount equal to

(i) one and one half weeks' emoluments for each year of service in which the claimant was not below the age of 41;
(ii) one week's emoluments for each year of service (other than in paragraph (b) (i) above) in which the claimant was not below the age of 22, and;
(iii) one half of one week's emoluments for each year of service not included in (b) (i) and (b) (ii) above; providing that where a claimant has completed more than 20 years' service, only the 20 years immediately prior to the loss of employment shall count.

(ii) *Long term compensation*
The maximum rate, in any individual case, will be the lesser of
(a) an amount made up of one sixtieth of the emoluments lost in respect of each year of reckonable service, plus, for teachers aged 40 or over at the date of loss, extra sixtieths as follows:

Age	**Years of Service**	**Extra Sixtieths**
40 – 49	less than 10	one for each year over 40
40 – 49	10 to 14	one for each year over 40 plus one (maximum 10)
40 – 49	15 to 19	one for each year over 40 plus two (maximum 10)
40 – 49	20+	one for each year over 40 plus three (maximum 10)
50 – 59		one for each year over 40 (maximum 15)
60+		one for each year over 45;

or,
(b) two thirds of the emoluments lost.

(iii) *Retirement compensation*
The amount of retirement compensation is
(a) the claimant's accrued pension benefit, plus

(b) if the claimant has reached the age of 40 at the date of loss, additional years as follows:

age 40 .... 2 years
age 41 .... 4 years
age 42 .... 6 years
age 43 .... 8 years
age 44 .... 10 years

and for each subsequent year up to the date of loss, one additional year providing the additional years so credited do not exceed, either:

(i) the number of years which, when added to his or her actual reckonable service, could have been served by the time the claimant reached normal retiring age; or

(ii) the period of his or her reckonable service; or

(iii) 15 years;
whichever is the least.

16. Long term compensation is usually paid in monthly instalments and retirement compensation at the same intervals as the claimant's pension, unless otherwise agreed. Reckonable service is defined more generously than in most pension schemes. All relevant employment is reckonable. So is war or National Service, undertaken by an individual on his or her ceasing to hold relevant employment. However, it does not include service reckonable under any pension scheme other than the last scheme of which the individual was a member and for which he or she has become entitled to receive a pension. A person who has, say, a substantial record in a pension scheme for which a benefit is due (such as the Local Government Scheme) and subsequent service in the Teachers' Superannuation Scheme as his or her last pension scheme, will find that service in the other scheme is not reckonable for determining the amount of compensation. Also, where loss of employment occurs within three years of normal retirement age, for the purpose of paragraph 15(i)(a) above, and within one year, for the purpose of paragraph 15(i)(b), the compensation will be proportionately reduced.

17. There are a number of circumstances which can lead to reduction or increase in compensation in certain cases. Some of these may be summarised as follows:

(i) Resettlement compensation is reduced by the amount of redundancy payment receivable under the Redundancy Payments Act.

(ii) Long term compensation can be reduced, as indicated in paragraphs 13 and 14, by the amount by which the emoluments in a new post plus compensation exceed the emoluments at the time of loss of employment or diminution in emoluments. Should the emoluments in the new post (ignoring cost of living changes) exceed the emoluments at the time of redundancy, then, long term compensation will be discontinued.

(iii) Long term compensation is reduced by a sum, equal to the amount by which the aggregate of a single person's National Insurance benefit or retirement pension and the long term compensation that would otherwise be paid, exceeds two thirds of the emoluments lost. It follows from this, and is also important in the matter of seeking suitable employment, that a claimant should register as unemployed and claim any due benefit, including state retirement pension at 60 in the case of a woman. The compensating authority will make a reduction irrespective of whether or not the benefits have been claimed.

(iv) Long term compensation will be reduced by the amount of any pension benefit to which a claimant is entitled under his or her last relevant pension scheme.

(v) For those below the age of 55, there is no inflation proofing, but when a claimant reaches 55 or is 55 or over at the time of the award, long term compensation is subject to inflation proofing under the Pensions (Increase) Act. This provides for increases in benefits based on the increase in the Retail Price Index. A person in receipt of long term compensation will have his or her benefit adjusted at age 55 to reflect increases awarded under the Pensions (Increase) Act from the date of his or her award to the age of 55.

18. The connections between long term compensation, retirement compensation and benefits under the claimant's standard superannuation scheme, are important. Long term compensation continues to be paid, in the case of a teacher, to 65. At that point, it ceases, and any entitlement to retirement compensation is received. In view of the fact that long term compensation is reduced by any entitlement to benefit under the pension scheme, from age 60, long term compensation will be reduced. It is even likely that with the introduction of premature retirement compensation (see Section **11.4**) under the Teachers' Superannuation Scheme, a teacher who is aged between 50 and 60, and is made redundant, will find his or her long term compensation reduced by the amount of his or her entitlement to premature retirement benefit (i.e. the benefit due to an individual under his or her superannuation scheme where that individual is made redundant, or dismissed in the interests of efficiency of the service, between the ages of 50 and 60). For reasons which are not very clear the DES draws a distinction between age retirement benefit at 60 (which it says will be deducted from long term compensation), and premature retirement benefit available between 50 and 60, which it says will be deducted only if it is claimed. NATFHE has advised its members to claim all their pension benefits (including premature retirement pension) as early as they can, if they are redundant due to a direction. This protects them against the possibility of deduction of any entitlement to premature retirement benefit, which they have not claimed, being made from their long term compensation. There is a further advantage in claiming premature retirement benefit. This is, that in many cases the premature pension payment will represent a substantial part of their long term compensation figure. Yet it, as opposed to long term compensation, cannot be reduced as long term compensation can, for example, on account of a failure to seek suitable employment. When a teacher claims premature retirement benefit and Crombie compensation, then, assuming he or she satisfies the qualifying regulations, he or she will receive:

(a) resettlement compensation;
(b) the lump sum from the Teachers' Superannuation Scheme;
(c) the premature retirement pension;
(d) long term compensation (reduced by c).
At 55, (c) and (d) will attract inflation proofing. At 65, (d) will cease but the claimant will receive:
(e) retirement compensation composed of an additional lump sum and a further pension payment.

The additional lump sum will represent the difference between (b) and the lump sum he or she would have received at age 65. In both cases, of course, the limits placed on the calculation of retirement compensation, as set out in paragraph 15, apply.

19. Finally, in this review of Crombie's main provisions, we have to look at the most obscure part of the regulations. Part V, which deals, *inter alia*, with payments on death, retirement compensation and compounding of awards. The following comments may be helpful.[3]

(i) It is generally believed that the amount of retirement compensation a person receives is fixed as set out in paragraph 15(iii) above. However, regulation 17 (5) provides that if the last relevant pension scheme has a provision allowing discretionary enhancement of the pension in certain circumstances, the retirement compensation may also be enhanced. It seems that the Teachers' Superannuation Scheme and the Local Government Scheme have assumed this character with the introduction of premature retirement compensation, and it may be worth those claiming retirement compensation, but not achieving the maximum, to seek an increase under regulation 17(5).

(ii) The Teachers' Superannuation Scheme and the Local Government Pension Scheme make provision for an infirmity pension. A claimant who becomes incapacitated after losing his or her post and before reaching 60, is entitled to receive, under the regulations, the infirmity pension he or she would have received under the Teachers' Superannuation Scheme.

(iii) Retirement compensation is paid in respect of diminished emoluments as if this event were a loss of employment. In the case of loss of emoluments the compensation will be:

$$C1 = \frac{C2\,(X - Y)}{X}$$

Where C1 is the compensation for diminution of emoluments;

C2 is the compensation for loss of employment;

X is the total amount of the emoluments before their reduction; and

Y is the emoluments after their reduction.

3 I am indebted to W.L. Browne, Director of the Colleges of Education Redeployment Bureau, for his permission to base the whole of this paragraph on a paper he and I produced in 1977, *Compensation and Superannuation*.

However, if a person pays superannuation contributions as if there had been no reduction in emoluments (as he or she may be entitled so to do under his or her pension scheme) no compensation will be payable.

(iv) If someone who is entitled to retirement compensation enters employment which is pensionable, the entitlement to retirement compensation may end in respect of the period covered by the new employment. If the new employment gives a salary, on entry, in excess of the emoluments of the lost employment, no retirement compensation is payable. However, if the new salary is lower than the one lost, some entitlement will remain which will be calculated by reference to the difference between the two salaries.

(v) The Teachers' Superannuation Scheme and the Local Government Scheme make provision for dependant's benefit and this is reflected in the regulations governing retirement compensation. The regulations are, however, obscure on this point. Under regulation 23(2)(b), the dependant seems to become entitled to compensation, where death occurs before 65, calculated by reference to the retirement compensation which would have been payable if incapacity or age retirement rather than death had occurred. Presumably, this means that the dependant receives up to one half of the incapacity retirement compensation (if the death occurs before age 60) just as, under the pension scheme, the dependant receives up to one half of the infirmity pension, or, up to one half of the age retirement pension if death occurs between 60 and 65. If death occurs after 65 it seems that, just as reference under the pension scheme is made to pension for determining dependant's pension (the surviving benefits being usually up to one half), in the case of dependant's retirement compensation, reference is made to the amount of the retirement compensation. In each case child dependants' benefits are dealt with in the same way.

(vi) The Teachers' Superannuation Scheme and Local Government Pension Schemes provide for a death grant where death in service occurs. The grant equals the lump sum that would have been paid if the individual had become infirm rather than died. Under the Crombie Code this is preserved. The sum payable is ascertained in accordance with the pension scheme's provisions as if the person had died when he or she had lost employment. Additional service is added, subject to the individual's maximum entitlement to retirement compensation, to his or her service record at the date of loss, to the extent of the period between the date of loss and the date of death.

(vii) All these benefits are reduced by the amount of any corresponding benefits under the last relevant pension scheme.

There is a complex provision, with relevant tables, which allows the compounding of awards. This enables certain claimants to receive in a lump sum a portion of their entitlement to periodic payments under the regulations. Where a person has been awarded long term or retirement compensation, the compensating authority may, on a request from the individual compound up to one quarter of its liability to make periodic payments to the individual, by the payment of an equivalent amount as a lump sum. In deciding on such requests, compensating authorities must have regard to the state of health of the claimant and the other circumstances of the case.

20. **The pooling of compensation payments**

LACSAB's advice to authorities on the poolability of compensation payments is as follows[4].

"3.72 Crombie compensation payments are only poolable when made 'to persons who, in consequence of a direction given by the Secretary of State under Regulation 3(2) of the Further Education Regulations 1975, have ceased to be employed as teachers in colleges for the training of teachers and become employed either by a local authority in a different capacity or as teachers in voluntary schools'. (See the Rate Support Grants (Adjustment of Needs Element) (Amendment No.2) Regulations, 1977).

"3.73 It follows that payments to teachers in other circumstances, and all payments to non-teaching staff, are excluded from the pool. Payments made only to teachers displaced from colleges of education are poolable, but not payments made to teachers displaced from departments of education.

"3.74 The use of the term 'local authority' in the regulations quoted in paragraph 3.72 above is not to be read as being confined to 'local education authorities.' For example, compensation paid to a redundant lecturer who becomes an officer in a housing department, or a parish clerk, is poolable, even though the new occupation has no obvious connection with the education service.

"3.75 The anomalies which the provisions described in the foregoing three paragraphs represent can only be resolved by an amendment to the Local Government Act 1974. Whilst there is general agreement that compensation for the other categories of teachers (notably those in departments of education), and non-teaching staff, should be admitted to the pool, at the time of issuing this document (June 1978) it was not possible to say when a Bill to make the necessary amendment would be included in the Parliamentary timetable."

21. At the time of writing the Government had produced proposals, in the Education (No. 2) Bill (1979), to rectify these anomalies.

22. **Interpreting the Crombie code**

The remaining paragraphs of this sub-section seek to interpret the complex regulations made in 1975 under the Colleges of Education (Compensation) Regulations by referring to some commentaries on the regulations, but more commonly by reference to the industrial tribunal and high court decisions on disputes between claimants and compensating authorities. Decisions reached in the courts do, of course, set legal precedents for interpreting the Code. This is not so with tribunal decisions. Whilst tribunals are bound by decisions in the courts the reverse is not true. Also, tribunal decisions do not bind other tribunals. However, tribunal decisions are important as "persuasive" on other tribunals. The regulations provide that within thirteen

4 See *Redundancies of Teaching and Non-Teaching Staff in Colleges and Departments of Education*, A LACSAB Information Booklet, revised edition 1978, pp. 45-46.

weeks of a decision by a compensating authority, an aggrieved claimant can petition an industrial tribunal to seek redress. Similarly, an application can be made within thirteen weeks of the expiry of the prescribed time if the compensating authority fails to make a decision within the prescribed time. The prescribed time is one month after the receipt of the claim. Appeals against decisions of tribunals, which have to be made within 42 days of the date of promulgation of the decision, are made to the Queen's Bench Division of the High Court and not, as is common in other cases, to the Employment Appeal Tribunal. The way industrial tribunals interpret the time limits can vary. In the case of Hart v ILEA[5] the tribunal found that the application to the tribunal was made within time even though it had been made several months after the *first* decision of the compensating authority on the claim. The reason for this was that the ILEA had shown, by indicating a willingness to review their decision and by referring to a final decision in later correspondence, that they had not in the first instance made a decision at all. Mr Philips, in Philips v The Secretary of State for Education and Science[6], did not fare so well. It was found that he applied to the tribunal more than two years out of time and whilst the DES was criticised for not notifying the applicant of the address of the Secretary of Industrial Tribunals, as they are obliged to do by regulation 34(5)(c), the tribunal did not feel that this failure justified the hearing of such a late application. Clearly, those involved in the administration of the Crombie code need to take great care over time limits and the advice they give about them.

23. Relevant employment

The concept of "relevant employment" is important in relation to a number of qualifying and other regulations. For example, one of the qualifying conditions for all three types of compensation is that an individual has been engaged in relevant employment on a full-time or part-time basis. Again, any offer of relevant employment which is reasonably comparable with the lost employment will remove an individual's right to compensation. Finally, the length of a person's relevant employment determines the amount of compensation he or she receives or can receive. A clause in the definition of relevant employment (p.7, clause (h)) allows service to be counted as relevant employment at the discretion of the Secretary of State. It seems that the DES, on behalf of the Secretary of State, adopts the view that any service which could have been covered by the Teachers' Superannuation Scheme or any other pension scheme, but which for some reason was not covered (for example, by reason of the claimant's choice not to cover it at the time), will not be allowed by the Secretary of State as relevant employment. This has created particular difficulties in relation to overseas service. In some cases this will be relevant employment under clause (a) – " employment under the Crown or by any person, authority or body for the purposes of the Crown". However, in other cases, teachers have worked abroad for a foreign government often on a basis arranged by the British Government. This does not count as relevant employment unless the teacher took steps at the time, to secure that the employment was reckonable for the purposes of his or her

5 Hart v ILEA, 1978, London C/10361/78/LS.
6 Philips v the Secretary of State for Education and Science. 1979. Gloucester. C11697/79.

last relevant pension scheme. In the case of Burnett v DES[7] the tribunal found that the Secretary of State's decision not to count his overseas employment as relevant could not even be challenged in the tribunal, and that it was not service under the Crown. The tribunal held that the DES, in deciding for the Secretary of State whether or not some employment was relevant employment, was not acting in its capacity as a compensating authority. Hence, the tribunal could not intervene on this point. When the DES said, in its capacity as the compensating authority, that the employment was not service under the Crown, this was a question which the industrial tribunal could determine, and it did so in favour of the DES. Since the Burnett case the DES has developed a new criterion, for determining the relevance of overseas service, which relates to whether or not the service was done in a country which by its constitution was or was not independent of Britain.

24. **Loss of employment**

An early qualifying condition for consideration of one's case under Crombie is that there has been a loss of employment (or, in some cases, a diminution in emoluments). One would have thought it straightforward that if a person received a redundancy notice, was dismissed from his or her college and had taken up new employment in a school, he or she had lost his or her employment and gained new employment. This view has not been adopted by all LEAs. Following advice from LACSAB, some LEAs took the view that where an individual was offered new employment, by the same employer, there had been no loss of employment. To take an extreme example: a college principal could be displaced from his or her job and acquire, with the same employer, a job as a Scale I teacher in a school and be held not to be entitled to have his or her case considered under the regulations since, given continuous employment with the same employer, there had been no loss of employment. This view was based on the findings in a case heard under the Redundancy Payments Act. In the case in question, Woods v York City Council,[8] concerning a local government employee, it had been held that continuity of employment had been established by the serial issue of contracts to Mr Wood. This was a point in Mr Wood's favour since by taking all the contracts together he qualified for redundancy payment. York City Council had sought to show that each yearly contract was a separate employment and in none of these separate employments had Mr Wood served for two years and, hence, had no right to redundancy pay. Some LEAs sought to apply the apparent corollary of this to Crombie. If serial contracts gave continuity of employment there could be no loss of employment. There have been two cases heard on this point. In the first, Heywood v Doncaster Metropolitan Borough Council,[9] the authority argued that, whilst Mr Heywood had lost his post as a Senior Lecturer, his continued employment as a Scale I teacher with the authority meant that he had not lost his employment. In the second case, Murray v Durham County Council[10], Durham argued that no loss of employment had occurred when Mr Murray's

---

7 Burnett v DES, 1977, Middlesbrough.
8 Wood v York City Council (1978) IRLR. 228.
9 Heywood v Doncaster Metropolitan Borough Council. 1978. Sheffield 31690/78.
10 Murray v Durham County Council, 1979, Newcastle upon Tyne. C34222/78.

job at Middleton St George College had come to an end, on the grounds that he had acquired a new job at a local comprehensive school in County Durham. In both cases, the tribunals rejected the LEAs' arguments, finding the Wood v York City Council case had no corollary for Crombie compensation. The term "loss of employment" is to have its commonsense meaning. If a person is made redundant where one contract is terminated, although it may be replaced by another, there has been a loss of employment. Wood v York City Council was not about loss of employment but about continuity of employment. The fact that an individual may or may not be removed from entitlement to redundancy *pay*, by virtue of the fact that he or she has been offered suitable alternative employment, does not detract from the fact that that person has suffered a loss of employment. The decisions in the Heywood v Doncaster Metropolitan Borough Council and Murray v Durham County Council cases may be felt to be at variance with the decision in one of the few cases involving non teaching staff, that of Butler and Others v Coventry City Council.[11] The applicants were employed at the Coventry College of Education which merged with the University of Warwick. Upon the merger the applicants accepted work with the University on terms which indicated distinctly that continuous service would continue to be calculated from the date when they took up their appointments with the Coventry Corporation. The tribunal held that there was no loss of employment at the time of the merger. The applicants became redundant from the university service roughly six months after the merger. Clearly here was a loss of employment: but was it attributable to a direction? The tribunal decided that it was not so in these cases. This raises the difficult question of the meaning of "attributable".

25. **Attributable to a direction**

The uncertainty compensating authorities have felt in interpreting the term "loss of employment" has paled into insignificance when compared to the uncertainty about the meaning to be given to the requirement that the loss has to be attributable to a direction of the Secretary of State. "Attributable" is not a commonly used word in statute. It clearly has something to do with cause and effect. The direction must cause the loss of employment. But how directly must the Secretary of State's direction be responsible for the loss, for the loss to be attributable to it? Must the direction be the sole cause or must it simply be the case that there was a reasonable probability that the loss would not have occurred if the direction had not been given? These philosophical questions have also teased the minds of tribunals.

26. The first context in which this question has occurred has been in the cases of full-time and part-time staff on fixed term contracts, who have suffered loss of employment by virtue of the fact that the contracts have not been renewed. In cases where the Secretary of State has directed the cessation of teacher training in their establishments, is it fair to conclude that the non-renewal of the contracts would not have occurred but for the direction, or, alternatively, might one say that the loss would or may have happened anyway by the effluxion of time?

11 Butler and Others v Coventry City Council. 1979. Birmingham. 35976/78 - 35827/79.

27. LACSAB's advice to LEAs on this matter[12] relies on cases heard outside the Colleges of Education (Compensation) Regulations. These are the Court of Appeal decisions in Tuck, Moody and Wray v National Freight Corporation[13] and Mallet v Restormel Borough Council.[14] In the first case, Lord Denning said "in every case the question is whether the 'worsening of [the man's] position' is 'properly attributable' to the relevant event". He observed "if the new company, soon after the transfer, decides to effect economies or eliminate over-manning, which the old company would not have done, the worsening might well be said to be properly attributable to a transfer. But if some years pass and there is a depression in business which forces the new company to economise, the worsening will not be due to transfer but the supervening depression in business." Lord Justice Jeffrey Lane concluded that " 'attributable to' is a wider expression than 'caused by'. It embraces a number of possible causes." Similarly, Lord Justice Eveleigh was of the view that the words "properly attributable to" are wider than the words "caused by". In Mallet's case the Court of Appeal held that Crombie Compensation was payable only if a cause like a direction "contributed to the existence of the situation which resulted in his loss of employment, as where an employee of an old authority was not offered employment by the new authority." The Tuck and Others v National Freight Corporation[15] case ended up in the House of Lords. In judgment, Lord Wilberforce had this to say: "There remains the question of proper attributability which, as in all questions relating to causation and similar concepts, is one of considerable difficulty. I think that two things can be said. First, the expression is not identical with 'caused by'. Secondly, it not identical with having [the relevant event as] a *sine qua non.* There must be a nexus or linkage less exclusive than the one but stronger than the other. If there is no causal link whatever between the event and the worsening, if the latter is caused exclusively by something else, the claimant does not succeed."

28. In this context there have been six cases heard by industrial tribunals on the Colleges of Education (Compensation) Regulations, all of which involve the question as to whether or not a person whose employment ends due to the expiry of his or her fixed term contract has lost employment in a way attributable to a direction. Appendix 1 summarises the decisions reached in these cases. As can be seen in this Appendix the findings have varied. In all these cases, the compensating authority has argued that the employment has been lost due to the expiry of a fixed term contract and that the contract was made fixed term as a result of, or in anticipation of, the receipt of a direction to cease teacher training. In the cases of Wood v DES[16] and Beaumont v DES.[17] evidence was brought to show that the true reason for the temporary nature of the contract was that these teachers were replacing staff on secondment and that this employment was continued even when the

---

12 See LACSAB, *op.cit.,* pp 5-9.

13 Tuck,Moody and Wray v National Freight Corporation, Court of Appeal, 6th December 1977.

14 Mallet v Restormel Borough Council, Court of Appeal, 28th February 1978.

15 Tuck, Moody and Wray v National Freight Corporation, House of Lords, 23rd November 1978, ICR (1979) 123-14.

16 Wood v DES, 1977. London C/6218/77/B.

17 Beaumont v DES. 1978. Newcastle upon Tyne, C/40673/77.

secondments came to an end. Further, it was shown that the contracts were first entered into prior to the direction being given and were renewed because in both cases the seconded staff did not return to employment, and hence there was a permanent vacancy. The tribunals accepted here that there had been a loss of employment due to a direction. The fact that the contract had been issued before a direction to cease training was given (even though it was known that such a direction was due) seems to have been an important point in interpreting the word "attributable" in these cases. However, it is not a litmus test. In the case of Jones v City of Bradford Metropolitan Council[18] the applicant held a contract under which he had waived rights to unfair dismissal appeal and redundancy pay, and the contract specified that it was temporary due to the reorganization of teacher training. Nevertheless, the tribunal found that the loss of employment was attributable to a direction. It also found that no reduction should be made in resettlement compensation by way of redundancy pay since Mr Jones's inability to claim redundancy pay, caused by his waiving his right to claim it, meant that there was no redundancy payment to take into account.

29. The tribunal hearing the Pearson v Kent County Council[19] case took an altogether different view of the word "attributable". Mrs Pearson had been employed prior to the receipt of the direction to cease training, had replaced someone on secondment and on his resignation at the end of the secondment had gone on to fill the vacancy so created. Referring to the Wood v DES case, the tribunal said "with the greatest respect to the argument propounded before us that our London colleagues applied a principle that temporary employment should generally be protected as offering a hope or expectation of future engagement of an indefinite duration and whilst the premature determination by a direction of temporary employment secured contractually or otherwise by law or practice may be available for consideration in appropriate circumstances, we could not recognise that temporary employment of itself conferred a right to protection or gave security of tenure after the expiry of a term fixed by contract ... contractually no loss occurred ... We have therefore come to the conclusion that Mrs Pearson did not lose anything she had by way of employment or earnings, though she may have felt a hope that she herself might have her contract renewed. She had everything she was entitled to and lost nothing which she had". That decision was appealed, successfully, in the High Court and represents the only case under the Colleges of Education (Compensation) Regulations which has been heard on appeal, though, at the time of writing, other appeal cases are pending. The High Court[20] took a less restricted view of the meaning of "attributable", finding that the tribunal had misdirected itself. On the meaning of "attributable", Mr Justice Forbes said "it must be a cause; there must, in other words, be no break in the chain of causation. It need not be the proximate cause or the only cause. As long as it can be said to be one of the causes, then whatever follows can be said to be 'attributable'." The appeal by Mrs Pearson was allowed.

18 Jones v City of Bradford Metropolitan Council. 1978. Leeds C32074/78.
19 Pearson v Kent County Council. 1977. Ashford. 28080/77.
20 Pearson v Kent County Council, QBD, 12th February 1979.

30. Another interesting case involving the meaning of "attributable" is the case of Talbot v Mayor, Alderman and Burgesses of the London Borough of Bromley.[21] Mr Talbot became Director of the Bromley Institute of Higher Education on 1st January 1977, a month or so before the Secretary of State indicated her intention to close the Stockwell College of Education, one of the constituent colleges of the new institute. Mr Talbot was declared redundant but was refused compensation on two grounds, one of which was that it was the LEA decision not to go ahead with the "proposed" merger to form the Bromley Institute which led to the redundancy. The redundancy was not attributable to the direction. The tribunal found that the loss was attributable to the direction and not merely to a decision of the Borough not to proceed with the merger. This is significant, since had the LEA won, it would, presumably, have been open to any LEA to argue that its decision to make someone redundant, and not the direction, was the cause of that person's loss of employment even though the direction may have led to its decision. Again, a narrow, hair splitting definition of "attributable" had been rejected. The second reason for refusing compensation was that the Bromley Institute, since it had never been properly formed – its instrument and articles of government has never been approved by the Secretary of State – was not a training establishment. As we have seen, the regulations apply only to those employed in training establishments. The tribunal rejected this view, finding that Mr Talbot had been appointed and acted as Director of a merged college which contained a training establishment (the Stockwell College) and hence, was itself a training establishment.

31. These cases on the meaning of "attributable" have a significance far outstretching the circumstances of staff on fixed term contracts or, like Mr Talbot, appointed to institutions which are new and not traditional training establishments. The significance for college administrators is clear. The letters which often they will be responsible for sending to staff, concerning their loss or change of employment, and the records about the implementation of directions and the consequences on staffing, can all be called into question in tribunal cases. The need for accurately worded letters and properly kept records should be evident.

32. There is a deeper significance which is likely to have further implications for college administrators and their staff. The loss of employment which entitles staff to Crombie Compensation, not only has to be attributable to a direction of the Secretary of State, but has to occur within ten years of a material date. Why has this ten year clause been introduced when the redundancies in question take place within one or two years, at the latest, of the date on which the directions to cease training come into effect? This has raised the further question: are subsequent redundancies covered by Crombie? Could it be that someone who loses employment due to a direction and takes another post which also terminates in redundancy can claim compensation at that stage providing the subsequent loss is within ten years of a material date? If this interpretation is possible it makes the causal relationship between a direction and loss of employment, embraced by the word

21 Talbot v Mayor, Alderman and Burgesses of the London Borough of Bromley. 1978. London C/3693/78/LS.

"attributable", very loose indeed. LACSAB's Information Booklet, *Redundancies of Teaching and Non-Teaching Staff in Colleges and Departments of Education* comments on this point in some detail: "It can be concluded that a claimant who seeks to discharge the burden on him to show that his loss of employment, or diminution of emoluments, occurring sometime after the material date ... was attributable ... to the original direction of the Secretary of State can be required to produce evidence to prove that the direction 'contributed to the existence of the situation which resulted in his loss of employment'. In effect, the claimant would have to establish that, for example, in the case of a member of staff redeployed from teacher training to another department of a polytechnic, a reduction in student numbers which later brought about his redundancy in his new department would not have occurred but for the direction ... As the years pass, any chances of such a member of staff successfully establishing that his dismissal on grounds of redundancy from the post in which he was redeployed was attributable to the original direction of the Secretary of State becomes even more remote."[22] In general, that would seem to be fair comment in that it admits of the possibility of compensation, in the event of a subsequent redundancy. However, it does not get to grips with the meaning of the ten year clause.

33. The ten year period dates from a material date and in this connection the "material date" means "the date specified in the direction as the date on which it is to take effect, or the date on which the loss or diminution occurred, whichever is the earlier" (regulations 7(1)(a) and 11(1)(a)) When the latter definition is substituted, the regulation reads "he has suffered loss of employment attributable to a direction not later than ten years after that date on which the loss or diminution occurred." This is, apparently, meaningless. It has been said by one Counsel, in a tribunal hearing, to be impossible of construction. Is this yet more bad drafting? I think not, since if a precise date, say 31st August 1977, is substituted for "the date on which the loss or diminution occurred", the regulation now reads "he has suffered loss of employment attributable to a direction not later than ten years after 31st August 1977." If this construction is put on the regulation its meaning becomes clearer and the obscure ten year clause and, perhaps, the intended wide meaning of "attributable" becomes significant. This is speculation and has not yet been tested in tribunals or the courts. College administrators may feel, however, that this argument at least provides a further reason for the accurate keeping of records about the effects of directions on their colleges or departments, and for keeping in close touch with the compensating authority about them.

34. **Reasonably comparable employment**

The majority of tribunal references made, so far, have been made by claimants who, having been made redundant and acquired another job, have been refused compensation on the grounds that the offer they have received is reasonably comparable relevant employment (see paragraph 10 above). The regulations do not define the meaning of the phrase "reasonably

22 LACSAB, *op.cit,* para 1.7, p.8.

comparable relevant employment" but they do specify that "in ascertaining for the purposes of this regulation whether a person has been offered [employment which]... is reasonably comparable with the employment which he has lost, no account shall be taken of the fact that the duties of the employment offered are in relation to a different service from that in connection with which his employment was held or are duties which involve a transfer of his employment from one place to another within England and Wales" (regulation 7(2)). This means that a claimant who moved from Plymouth to Newcastle could not acquire resettlement compensation solely on the grounds that his or her new job was not comparable because it was in a different place. Similarly, the same claimant who took up a new job in Plymouth would not be debarred from resettlement compensation just because the two jobs were in the same place.[23] The meaning of reasonable comparability has been determined by tribunals in the context of claims for resettlement compensation, though the criteria adopted could be applied in claims for long term and retirement compensation to which the same regulation applies. All the cases have had a common theme. A member of staff has lost employment, the loss being due to a direction, and has taken up employment with the same or a new employer in a school or a college, without loss of salary. All, therefore, that has been at issue has been whether or not resettlement compensation is due. That question, in turn, has rested on whether or not the lost and new posts are reasonably comparable. Appendix 2 shows the findings in all the cases, to date, which have come before tribunals. None has yet been to the High Court.

35. The reason that, in all these cases, there has been no loss of salary is the existence of the salary safeguarding provisions of the Burnham Reports (see Section **11.1.**20). If the salary safeguarding arrangements had not existed the pattern of cases and decisions would have been very different. Some staff would have experienced several thousand pounds drop in salary and that would have established the lack of comparability immediately. It must be acknowledged that the existence of safeguarding has stimulated appeals to tribunals since it has led compensating authorities to take a very particular view of claims made to them. Initially, the DES, the main compensating authority, took the view that any job which carried a safeguarded salary constituted the offer of a reasonably comparable job. In extreme cases this would have led to the DES refusing compensation to a head of a college department, or, presumably, even the principal, who had acquired a safeguarded scale 1 teaching post in a school. By contrast, NATFHE adopted

23 This may seem to make the use of the term "resettlement" peculiar. However, it has been suggested that the term applies to resettling in a professional sense into a new job. "The place of new employment, of course, cannot be taken into account, but it may be worthwhile for tribunals to ask themselves the basic question – would the reasonable man settle without difficulty into this new post offered, or will it involve a material change in approach, methods of work, prospects and status? Will the employee have to make a substantial adjustment in his or her working life. From this basic principle, the various criteria already adopted by industrial tribunals will flow." (See Keith Scribbins, Graham Clayton, Joan Gordon, "Where Crombie Went Wrong", *Education*, 4 May, 1979). This view seems to accord with the view of at least one tribunal chairman. In Cope v DES, Mr B.H. Cato declared "it would appear that the nature of compensation is a solatium for the 'dislocation' in the sense of an individual having to engage in not reasonably comparable employment."

the view that whilst salary could not be the only factor, a job which carried the payment of a safeguarded salary was not comparable with the post lost. Those two positions provided a recipe for conflict which has led to so many tribunal references. We shall see that tribunals have arbitrated in this matter in a very painstaking way.

36. Tribunals have rejected the DES view that safeguarding entails comparability. In this they have relied on the decision of the High Court in a case brought under the Local Government Crombie Code. In the case of Tolley and Craske v Hereford and Worcester County Council,[24] Mr Justice Phillips stated that "salary is not irrelevant to comparability; but, if the employments were not otherwise at all comparable, the fact that Mr Tolley was being paid more cannot make them so. Speaking generally, salary, it seems to me, can only be important in a marginal case of comparability where it may tip the balance one way or the other." In following this approach, tribunals have rejected any simplistic formula for determining comparability. They have favoured, instead, making a commonsense decision based on weighing together factors of difference and similarity between posts. In doing so they have evolved a number of criteria or headings under which they have assessed the evidence put before them. Obviously, as time has gone on the number of headings has increased and tribunal decisions have become more elaborate. In the early cases taken in 1976 and 1977 (e.g., Harvey v DES,[25] Bull v DES[26]) the tribunals considered four or five headings.[27] Two years later a dozen or more headings were being used. In many cases no single heading or criterion has won or lost the claimant's case. The approach has been to take them all together. This approach was first laid down in the case of Fletcher v DES,[28] in which the Chairman, Mr R.B. Lauriston, remarked "it is instructive in this case to look at a number of .... marginal matters ... some of these matters ... may sound trivial but again when added up all are in favour of Mrs Fletcher."

37. The headings or criteria which have been used by tribunals can be summarised as follows.

(i) *Salary.* Tribunals have rejected the view that the mere fact that a new job carries the same salary by way of safeguarding makes it comparable. They have, by contrast, in some cases, accepted the view that since salary scales are determined nationally by the profession, the employer and the government, differences in the salary grading applied to jobs signify a real difference, in professional terms, in the jobs themselves. In Siviour v DES[29] the tribunal found that "the

24 Tolley and Craske v Hereford and Worcester County Council, QBD, 17th February 1976.
25 Harvey v Secretary of State for Education and Science. 1977. London C/38105/76/D.
26 Bull v Secretary of State for Education and Science. 1977. London 40680/76.
27 In his article, "Redeploying College Lecturers in the Classroom," *Education*, 5 August 1977, Leonard Sheen analysed the cases of Harvey v DES, Bull v DES, Loose v Northumberland County Council and Oliver v DES. He showed that five criteria had been used in these cases.
28 Fletcher v DES, 1978. Middlesbrough C/30982/7.
29 Siviour v Secretary of State for Education and Science, 1978, London 10017/78/B.

difference in the salary scales seems to indicate that well qualified persons in the educational field do not rate the two jobs reasonably comparable." However, this test has not been universally approved by tribunals. Remarking on salary scale differences in the case of Cope v DES,[30] the chairman said, "it may well be that this is due to historical reasons. We would prefer to look at other factors to see whether there is a difference in the responsibility of the post."

(ii) *Conditions of service.* Whilst not a major factor, some tribunals have taken note of the differences between class contact hours and holiday periods, especially in cases involving a move from a college to a school. Conditions are likely to be taken into account in certain circumstances. In Fletcher v DES the tribunal had this to say: "...the question of holidays has been brought up and Mrs Fletcher in her present job gets something like 3 weeks holiday less than in her previous job. It is true and we accept, that in the teaching profession it is necessary to do certain work during the holidays but in Mrs Fletcher's case this marginal matter of holidays is of some importance because it prevents her from now completing a summer term's lectures at the Open University." By contrast, in Heaton v DES,[31] whilst finding in favour of the applicant, the tribunal wished to lay down a general principle about conditions of service as follows: "we do not think that changed conditions of work in themselves can be decisive. Lecturing in a College of Education, from its nature, is most likely to involve some personal facilities, such as the provision of a study, and shorter teaching hours and longer holidays which are not to be found other than in other Colleges of Education, Polytechnics or Universities. To make such conditions decisive would ... restrict 'reasonably comparable' and limit it to employment in those establishments."

(iii) *Working facilities.* In spite of the reference made above in Heaton v DES, differences in features like office accommodation, library facilities, etc. have played an important part in some cases. In Howarth v DES[32] the tribunal remarked that "the actual places of work were not only less congenial but less well equipped."

(iv) *Age of students.* In most cases this has been seen as a significant difference, especially where the applicants have been able to show that they have been involved in in-service work. For example, in Harvey v DES the tribunal was aware that in his new school teaching job "the biggest age band is a good deal less in years."

(v) *Academic level.* Tribunals have generally rejected the view taken in the case of Loose v Northumberland County Council,[33] that there is not much to choose between sixth form and college level work. Most applicants have been able to show an involvement in degree level work and that its loss, in many cases, can be regarded as a loss of a career in higher education. In one case, Brown v DES,[34] great store was put on the Burnham categories of work and the changes in work category

30 Cope v DES. 1978. Newcastle upon Tyne C41447/77.
31 Heaton v DES. 1978. Newcastle upon Tyne C10529/78.
32 Howarth v DES. 1978. London C13869/78/E.
33 Loose v Northumberland County Council. 1976. Newcastle upon Tyne C/22534/76.
34 Brown v DES. 1978. London C/41738/77/LS.

which Mr Brown had to make in moving from his Lecturer Grade II job at a College of Education to his Lecturer Grade I job at Bury Metropolitan College of Further Education. In Taylor v DES[35] this was a decisive factor: "from the evidence given before us the employment at St Mary's was far more akin to that of a lectureship at a University than that of a school master. The applicant was rather expected to engage himself in research at St Mary's but is probably not expected to do at Ashlyns [school]. The atmosphere is probably far different. Nearly all of those at St Mary's were probably people who wanted to learn whereas at Ashlyns there may be many that do and quite a few that don't."

(vi) *Research opportunities.* Tribunals have been impressed by applicants who have been able to demonstrate that they have done research in their college jobs and in their new jobs have lost this opportunity. However, this is not likely to be a decisive factor in itself.

(vii) *Responsibility.* Most tribunals have been reluctant to accept the view that, in its very nature, training teachers imposes greater responsibilities than other forms of teaching. However, when it can be demonstrated that either the former or the new post involves responsibility for administering the work of others, responsibility has proved to be a key factor. This was so in Allford v ILEA[36] where, as a head of department. Mr Allford had greater managerial responsibilities in relation to other staff than he came to have as vice-principal of an adult education centre. In Fletcher v DES the tribunal found, unequivocally, that "...in her present job Mrs Fletcher now has nothing like the responsibility or flexibility that she enjoyed in her previous job." In Heaton v DES the tribunal was as direct. "It is true that the applicant" (in his new job) "has 3 subordinates but this only represents a small amount of man management ... it is very difficult to put the element of responsibility into words ... perhaps the only way of doing so is to use the rather simple formula. 'Is the applicant such an important man in the educational process?' Our impression is that the applicant's position as a scale 3 teacher is not as important ... as that ... in his former employment as a Senior Lecturer." The same Chairman concluded in the Cope v DES case that ... "we place our major emphasis upon [responsibility]. As we have indicated, the responsibility at the college was a horizontal responsibility based upon a particular course. The present responsibility is a vertical responsibility with considerable responsibility in man management."

(viii) *Career implications.* This has been regarded in several important ways. Firstly, tribunals have looked at the relative career prospects in the two jobs. Inevitably this has involved a degree of speculation, but where it has been possible to show that in the new job expectations are reduced, this has sometimes been a telling factor. In the decision in Cope v DES, this appears: "we regard the present position of the applicant as one which will give him substantial experience in a position of responsibility ... and which will positively assist him in the future." In Siviour v DES the tribunal found a great deal in the

---

35 Taylor v DES, 1977 and 1978, London C31795/77/C.
36 Allford v ILEA. 1979. London C/33526/78/D.

following argument advanced by Dr Siviour. "Dr Siviour asked us to look at the picture in terms of his career prospects outside the two colleges ... Had he stayed where he was, his experience in terms of administration, command and responsibility generally would have deepened and broadened and thus put him in line for higher things, whereas his reversion to a less responsible post means that the longer he stays in it the less relevant will his previous experience become. At the present moment, no doubt, and perhaps in a year or two, he would be able to point to both jobs as useful experience but in practical terms his career prospects over the years have worsened." Secondly, tribunals have looked at what might be called "career congruity". In some cases, applicants were moving to the same type of job that they held several years before entering teacher training. In such cases it has been held that they have taken a step backwards. For example, in Mr Heaton's case, he had been employed as a scale 3 teacher prior to entering teacher training. At his redundancy he acquired another scale 3 job and the tribunal found that he "has now had to revert to what is virtually the same position." In Oliver v DES [37] it was said that "Dr Oliver had a right to consider that the effort involved in taking the PhD course would entitle him to take a step upward in the teaching profession, and make him more able to take on a job which his additional skills would enable him to perform." By contrast, where particularly young lecturers have moved to school jobs several grades above those they have previously held in schools, the tribunals have found against them. This was so in the Loose and Cope cases.

(ix) *Status.* This was dismissed in one early case (Loose v DES) as a "slippery concept." Later decisions have defined differences between "social" and "professional" status and whilst concluding marginal differences in the latter, no tribunal has been prepared to admit of differences in the former. In Siviour v DES, the tribunal declared "we do not see how it can be argued that there is no difference in status between a senior lecturer and a lecturer. The difference may not amount to much to an outsider but we are satisfied that within the profession a drop from senior lecturer to lecturer amounts to a drop in status." In Fletcher v DES, the tribunal was "unanimous" in its view that "there has been a loss of professional status."

(x) *Job satisfaction.* Again, this is a rather nebulous concept. Some tribunals have been disinclined to take account of it at all (see, for example, Taylor v DES); others have regarded it as a marginal factor (see, for example, Fletcher v DES).

(xi) *Training teachers.* In all cases applicants have argued that they made a positive career decision to enter teacher training and that their new jobs removed this feature of their work. Whilst this factor has influenced some tribunals, it has never been regarded as decisive. After all, if it were, no jobs outside teacher training would be "reasonably comparable" and the regulations state that any other forms of relevant employment may or may not be regarded as comparable. In Harvey v DES we find some emphasis on teacher training. "At Sarum St Michael ... he was teaching prospective teachers

37 Oliver v DES. 1977. Birmingham. 7823/77.

how to teach music. Now he is solely concerned with teaching an instrument to young school children in a class." But, more commonly, the view of Mr Cato, in Cope v DES, has prevailed. He said "...we would deem it inappropriate for an individual to base a claim solely on the proposition: 'formerly I taught the teachers, now I teach those who are learning the subject', i.e. that the very change in the nature of the work entitled the person to compensation. To accept this principle would mean that no employment could be regarded as reasonably comparable unless it contained this element of 'teaching teachers' and the scope of reasonably comparable would be restricted to employment in training establishments which, in our view, is not the intention of the enactment."

38. As can be seen from Appendix 2, certain patterns have emerged from the careful sifting of evidence, made by tribunals, under the headings set out in paragraph 37. Firstly, most applicants have won their cases. Secondly, with the exception of the Bull v DES case, college teachers who have moved to scale 1, 2 or 3 jobs in schools have won resettlement compensation. It is understood that, except in exceptional circumstances, the DES will now pay compensation in such cases and LACSAB has advised LEAs to make payment in cases involving a move to scale 1 or 2 posts. In fact, most LEAs follow the DES line. Thirdly, with the exception of the Siviour v DES case, tribunals seem disinclined to look sympathetically on applicants (as in the Gray v DES [38] and Pick v DES [39] cases) who move from a Senior Lecturer to a Lecturer Grade II post. In these cases, the fact that Lecturers Grade II in higher education transfer to the Senior Lecturer scale and that there has been no change in the academic level of the work involved in the two posts, has had a bearing on the decisions. Finally, in cases of movement from Senior Lecturer or Lecturer Grade II posts in colleges of education to Lecturer Grade I posts in colleges of further education, the changes in grading and in the nature of the establishments has secured successful decisions for the applicants.

39. **Suitable employment in the same place with the same duties**
In paragraph 8(v) it is made clear that another bar to the achievement of resettlement (but not long term or retirement) compensation is that the claimant has received an offer of employment which is suitable, is in the same place or locality and involves the performance of substantially the same duties as those undertaken in the lost employment. There have been no industrial tribunal decisions involving teaching staff in which only the meaning of these words has been at issue, though, in the Heywood v Doncaster case the compensating authority argued, not just that there had not been a loss of employment, but also that the scale I post offered to Mr Heywood was an offer of suitable employment in the same locality and in which he performed substantially the same duties. This argument fell on the third leg of the test, the tribunal finding that the new job, as a scale I teacher, did not involve work requiring substantially the same duties as in his previous senior lecturer post. It is important to note certain features of this regulation.

---

38 Gray v DES. 1979. Middlesbrough C21672/78.
39 Pick v DES. 1979. London C/369093/78/F.

(i) All the tests, that the job is suitable, is in the same place or locality and involves performance of substantially the same duties, have to apply together. A job offer which is suitable but not involving substantially the same duties would not debar the claimant from compensation.

(ii) The suitability of a post is likely to be established by the claimant's acceptance of it.

(iii) There is no definition of place or locality in the regulations. LACSAB gives the following advice on this matter. "Until definitive guidelines are established, it would be reasonable to regard [locality] as meaning the area close to the place where the person was employed. This may be an unsatisfactory definition, but any particular interpretation of it may depend on the type of area in which his place of work was located; *locality* could mean the area of a small town, a limited area of a large city, or a more extensive part of a rural area, but it may be unsafe to regard it as such, as in the Concise Oxford Dictionary it is defined as 'things, position, place where it is; site or scene of something.' "[40]

(iv) The offer does not have to be of relevant employment – any kind of job offer can count. Clearly, something wider is intended than in the case of reasonably comparable offers which have to be of relevant employment to debar the claimant. There has been an industrial tribunal case involving a non-teaching member of staff in which attention was given to regulation 7 1(f)(ii). In that case, Brown v Coventry City Council,[41] the tribunal drew an interesting distinction between "reasonably comparable" employment and "suitable" employment. It held that in the latter, purely personal considerations could be taken into account, but not so in the former. It was found that the employment offered was not suitable to *her* since, taking into account the pattern of her husband's working week, acceptance of the new employment would lead to a disruption of their domestic circumstances and result in their seeing each other much less.

(v) Whilst, as is made clear above, the only case of a teacher decided by a tribunal on this issue is that of Heywood v Doncaster, it may be useful for college administrators, and others, to know the outcome of a case which was registered for tribunal hearing on this point but which was conceded by the DES prior to the hearing. This case involved a teacher who had been a principal lecturer and who had, on his redundancy, become a senior lecturer in a college of education in the same city. In preparing its submission to the tribunal, the DES found that the teacher's responsibilities as a principal lecturer, which involved the supervision of teaching practice, did not, after all, involve substantially the same duties as he acquired as a senior lecturer, a post in which he had no supervisory duties. It cannot be assumed, of course, that the DES or other compensating authorities will make the same decision in other cases of movement from principal lecturer to senior lecturer.

(vi) It is understood that the DES will not regard most jobs in schools as involving substantially the same duties as most jobs in colleges.

---

40 *Op. cit.*, para 1. 24, p.10.
41 Brown v Coventry City Council. 1978. Birmingham. 16649/78.

40. **Regulation 12 : the payment of long term compensation**
We know next to nothing about how regulation 12 should be interpreted. This regulation lists the factors to be taken into account in determining whether or not to pay long term compensation and, if so, its amount (see paragraph 11). In only one case, that of Beaumont v DES, has this regulation been brought into question. Mr Beaumont won his claim for resettlement compensation in that the tribunal held that, in spite of the fact that he had been employed on a fixed term contract, he had, nevertheless, lost his employment and this loss was due to a direction. For the same reason he was entitled to long term compensation, but the tribunal went on to determine that the amount of long term compensation should be nil because he had no security of tenure in his employment, and one of the factors listed in regulation 12 to be taken into account, is the conditions attached to the lost employment, including its security of tenure.

41. Of greater significance is regulation 12(iii) which allows a reduction in long term compensation according to the extent to which a claimant has sought suitable employment (see paragraph 12). There has been no tribunal case under the Colleges of Education (Compensation) Regulations in which a claimant has sought redress against a compensating authority which has used this regulation to pay less than the maximum long term compensation. However, LACSAB has given advice to LEAs on the policy they might adopt in relation to this requirement. LACSAB quotes one compensating authority as accepting evidence of applications for three posts as acceptable for the purposes of review. This, LACSAB states, "is not unreasonable, bearing in mind the state of the labour market and that reviews occur every six months in the first two years, but it cannot be recommended as a policy to be adopted generally by compensating authorities."[42] LACSAB suggests that the following factors are also relevant:
(i) the age of claimant (those below 50 are expected to make strenuous efforts to obtain suitable employment, and it is acknowledged that for those over 60 the chances of such efforts being successful are remote);
(ii) the health of the individual; and,
(iii) the evidence provided by the claimant of effort to find suitable employment.

42. NATFHE advises all long term compensation claimants to register as unemployed, register with the Colleges of Education Redeployment Bureau (see Section **11.7.**15) and to keep copies of applications made.

43. LACSAB's advice ignores people between 50 and 60 when this is, in fact, the most difficult age group with which to deal. It is possible that a tribunal would hold that a claimant over 60 has, if he or she is a teacher, retired, and cannot be expected to seek other employment. In spite of the fact that someone over 50 may have claimed his or her premature retirement pension from the TSS (see paragraph 18) it is not likely that a tribunal would see that person as retired. (However, that person would have protected some of his or her compensation from reduction; see paragraph 18). Nevertheless, this

42 *op.cit.* paras 3.44 - 3.45, pp 39-40.

prematurely retired status may have some bearing in the minds of tribunals on regulation 12(iii).

44. The DES has issued no guidance as to how it, as a compensating authority, interprets regulation 12 (iii), though LACSAB states that, broadly speaking, the Department would expect the considerations set out in paragraph 41 above to be taken into account. In the absence of any more precise guidance from the DES, we are left wondering whether or not there is any geographical limit to the search for suitable employment or a limit in terms of the numbers or types of applications which have to be made.

45. LACSAB puts some store by an industrial tribunal decision on the Local Government Compensation Regulations, in which there is a similar power vested in compensating authorities to reduce long term compensation on account of the failure of the claimant to seek suitable employment. In this case, Maude v East Devon County Council,[43] Mr Maude, a 49 year old claimant, was appealing against a decision to reduce long term compensation from £1355 to £678 per annum on account of the fact that he had applied for only seven posts between 1974 and 1976. There was a ten month period during this time when no applications had been made. However, Mr Maude had been ill from April until November 1974 and he also showed that he would be penalised if he sold his house to facilitate a move since he had undertaken not to sell it for five years as part of a discount purchase arrangement he had made in 1973. The tribunal reached a compromise decision, reducing the long term compensation to £1221 and not to the £678 the Council had intended. It is hard to say, as LACSAB recognises, what inferences can be drawn from this case in respect of college staff. It is likely to have greater relevance for non-teaching staff, given the differences in the job market for them and teaching staff. If tribunals accept that "suitable" for a college lecturer means jobs in other colleges, polytechnics and universities in his or her subject specialism, then seven applications might be sufficient to satisfy the regulations, as it was not in the Maude case. However, if any teaching job, anywhere in the country, is taken as suitable, teaching staff will be likely to find themselves penalised if their job applications do not reflect this. At the moment, we can only guess at the policies the DES and other compensating authorities might adopt and, more importantly, how tribunals will interpret this obligation on claimants to mitigate their loss.

46. **The meaning of "emoluments"**

The amount of a claimant's compensation is determined in part, by the emoluments which have been lost or diminished. Regulation 38(i) defines emoluments as "all salary, wages, fees and other payments paid to or made to an officer as such for his own use, and also the money value of any accommodation or other allowances in kind appertaining to his employment, but does not include payments for overtime which are not a usual incident of his employment, or any allowances payable to him to cover the cost of

43 Maude v East Devon County Council. 1976. Exeter 24223/76.

providing office accommodation or clerical or other assistance, or any travelling or subsistence allowance or other monies to be spent, or to cover expenses incurred, by him for the purposes of his employment." An obvious query which has been stimulated by this definition is how are residential emoluments to be evaluated? LACSAB advises that in any case where the monetary value of accommodation cannot be agreed, the services of the local authority's valuation officer should be sought. It also suggests that "it may be considered reasonable to regard essential occupiers of provided accommodation, and those who, whilst not necessarily essential occupiers, are from time to time *contractually required* to perform certain residential duties ... as being eligible for compensation if they lose their accommodation for a reason attributable to a direction."[44] NATFHE agrees with the idea of arbitration by an auditor but does not share the view that only essential users, or those contractually required to be in residence, are entitled to compensation in the event of loss of a residential emolument. Clearly, this difference of opinion is likely to form the basis of a future tribunal case.

47. NATFHE has suggested that the following formula can be used to define emoluments:

Emoluments = (S+ MR + K + A) - (R)
where S = salary including fees;
MR = market rent of provided property;
K = allowances in kind;
A = monetary allowances, and;
R = rent actually paid.

The DES and LACSAB seem to agree with this definition.

48. The one case which has been heard by a tribunal on the meaning of emoluments, Minton and Kewley v Barnsley Borough Council[45] resulted in a rather puzzling decision which is now being appealed in the High Court. Dr Minton and Dr Kewley were, respectively, Principal and Vice-Principal of the Wentworth Castle College of Education – two residential posts in which they enjoyed free furnished accommodation, free heating and lighting, free food, free laundry and free domestic service. The claimants contended that the money value of these emoluments was their reasonable cost of replacement in the open market. The compensating authority contended that the proper criterion for valuation was the actual cost to the local authority of supplying these facilities. The tribunal supported neither view. It sided with the claimants in deciding that " 'money value' must apply to a person entitled to compensation and not a person who is liable to pay compensation." However, the claimants "received some benefits which they might not have thought fit to buy and enjoy if they have lived extra murally." The tribunal found that the assessment should include a reasonable rent, rates and the cost of food and other services which the applicants would have had to pay to the provider if they had not been provided free. It went on to say that

44 *Op.cit.* paras 3.3 - 3.6, pp 27-28.

45 Minton. and Kewley v Barnsley Metropolitan Borough Council. Sheffield. 6744/79 and 6745/79.

since the local authority is not a profit making concern, the cost can only be calculated with reference to the full cost to the authority of providing these benefits without consideration of any hidden or artificial subsidy. Hence, the full cost of preparing meals, providing domestic services, laundry etc. should be taken into account. As has been said this decision is the subject of appeal. However, if it is sustained, or in any case followed by compensating authorities, the burden they and the administrators of their colleges will be under, to quantify the actual cost of providing benefits, will be considerable. There are two further cases, to which it is worth referring, concerning how the regulations dealing with the diminution in emoluments, and how those dealing with the acquisition of new emoluments, should be construed.

(i) In the case of a non-teaching member of staff, Elve v Coventry City Council,[46] the tribunal held that when the University of Warwick offered Mrs Elve a job for 35 hours per week in place of the one held with the respondent for 37½ hours per week, the respondent was obliged to pay long term compensation amounting to the difference in wages involved in the two employments.

(ii) The case of Roots v Lincolnshire County Council[47] raises a different point. Mr Roots had been awarded long term compensation and, subsequently, took on a supply teaching job for 38 days. The compensating authority reduced his compensation to nil, for these days, by construing the annual rate of his new emoluments to be 5/7 x 365 x his daily rate of pay. The tribunal found this to be wrong. It held the annual rate to be the rate he could have earned by working for 200 days (the length of his school teaching year) at his daily rate.

49. **Crombie and college administrators**

Finally, it may be useful to summarise some of the major lessons for college administrators which emerge from this review of the Colleges of Education (Compensation) Regulations and the industrial tribunal cases which have so far arisen from them.

(i) Senior college staff will often be called upon to give advice to teaching and non-teaching staff about their probable entitlements. It is hoped that this chapter will enable college administrators to do this, subject to the general proviso that only the compensating authority can make a decision on a claim. The regulations, and the case law based on them, are so complex that administrators may feel that they can give only the most general kind of advice and should refer would-be claimants to other agencies.

(ii) In this sub-section it has become clear that a great deal depends upon the dates of letters sent to the college or authority from the DES, and the date and type of letter sent to staff about their loss of employment. Care should be taken to ensure that these are accurate and unambiguous. In the case of maintained colleges, the LEA should be closely consulted about the wording of such letters.

(iii) A lot hinges, too, on the type of work done by staff, and evidence about this may have to be produced long after the member of staff has lost his or her employment. The need for accurate records should be

46 Elve v Coventry City Council. 1978. Birmingham 3114/78.

47 Roots v Lincolnshire County Council. 1979. Nottingham. C/14480/79.

clear. Some colleges have achieved this by sending to staff on their redundancy, a complete and objective account of their work profile in the college and the reasons for their loss of employment.

(iv) Many college administrators have been, and will be, called upon to act as witnesses in industrial tribunal cases, both for compensating authorities and claimants. Whilst tribunals are intended to be informal "courts", they are regulated, nevertheless, by procedure and in most cases respondents and applicants are represented by specialists, often lawyers. Evidence is elicited by means of examination and cross examination, and is given on oath. This procedure can often make witnesses, including college administrators, uncomfortable. Senior staff who have no experience of such procedures and who may be called upon to act as witnesses may find it useful to attend a tribunal, in advance, to get the feel of the thing. It is hoped, but by no means with certainty, that the number of tribunal cases will reduce in the future and that compensating authorities, claimants and their representatives will be able to agree, without reference to tribunals, the meaning of this complex and badly drafted Crombie code.

APPENDIX 1

The following table analyses the cases brought under the Colleges of Education (Compensation) Regulations in which industrial tribunals or the High Court havehad to decide whether or not a claimant whose temporary contract to work in a college of education has come to end is entitled to receive compensation. The question before industrial tribunals in these cases has been "Has the claimant lost employment and, if so, is the loss attributable to a direction?"

CASE	CIRCUMSTANCES	DECISION
Almond v Leicestershire	Appointed before direction to do research on contract for a limited period.	Compensation not payable.
Beaumont v DES	Appointed before direction to replace seconded member of staff; contract renewed during course of employment.	Compensation payable
Griffin v DES	Appointed before direction; contract renewed during course of employment. Had acquired another temporary job and tribunal found this to be reasonable comparable.	Compensation not payable
Jones v Bradford	Appointed after direction on contract indicating that temporariness of employment due to reorganization of teacher education.	Compensation payable
Nouri v DES	Appointed before direction as a French Assistant.	Compensation not payable
Pearson v Kent	Appointed part-time before direction; temporary contract renewed on a full-time basis during couse of employment	Tribunal found compensation not payable; High Court reversed this decision
Wood v DES	Appointed part-time before direction; contract renewed during course of employment.	Compensation payable

The case references for four of the cases listed above appear in the appropriate footnote to the text. The case references in the three remaining cases are: Almond v Leicestershire County Council, 1979. Leicester C33527/78; Griffin v DES 1978. Middlesbrough C6267/78; and Nouri v DES 1978. Nottingham C10190/78.

APPENDIX 2

The following table analyses the cases brought under the Colleges of Education (Compensation) Regulations in which industrial tribunals have had to decide whether or not the claimant has been offered relevant employment which is reasonably comparable with the employment which he or she has lost, (Regulation 7(1)(f)(i)).

CASE	EMPLOYMENT LOST	EMPLOYMENT OFFERED	DECISION
Allford v ILEA	Head of Department Grade V	Deputy Principal Adult Education Centre	Not reasonably comparable
Brown v DES	Lecturer II	Lecturer I in College of Further Education	Not reasonably comparable
Bull v DES	Senior Lecturer	Scale III Teacher	Reasonably comparable
Cope v DES	Senior Lecturer	Scale IV Teacher	Reasonably comparable
Fletcher v DES	Senior Lecturer	Scale II Teacher	Not reasonably comparable
Gray v DES	Senior Lecturer	Lecturer II	Reasonably comparable
Harvey v DES	Senior Lecturer	Scale II Teacher	Not reasonably comparable
Heaton v DES	Senior Lecturer	Scale III Teacher	Not reasonably comparable
Howarth v DES	Senior Lecturer	Scale III Teacher	Not reasonably comparable
Jones v Barnsley	Head of Department Grade IV	Senior Teacher at Educational Development Centre	Not reasonably comparable
Loose v Northumberland	Senior Lecturer	Scale IV Teacher	Reasonably comparable
Pick v DES	Senior Lecturer	Lecturer II	Reasonably comparable
Oliver v DES	Lecturer II	Scale I Teacher	Not reasonably comparable
Siviour v DES	Senior Lecturer	Lecturer II	Not reasonably comparable

11.5

CASE	EMPLOYMENT LOST	EMPLOYMENT OFFERED	DECISION
Smith v DES	Senior Lecturer	Lecturer I in College of Further Education	Not reasonably comparable
Taylor v DES	Senior Lecturer	Scale III Teacher	Not reasonably comparable

Unless otherwise stated the Senior Lecturer and Lecturer II posts referred to in the table are posts in colleges of education. The case references for most of the cases appear in the appropriate footnote to the text. The case references to the two cases, listed above, to which no reference is made in the text are: Jones v Barnsley Metropolitan Borough Council, 1979. Sheffield 11901/79 and Smith v DES 1977. London 28497/77/A.

REFERENCE

The Colleges of Education (Compensation) Regulations, 1975, Statutory Instrument 1092 HMSO.
The Further Education Regulations, 1975, Statutory Instruments 1054, HMSO.
The Teachers' Superannuation Regulations, 1976, Statutory Instruments 1978, HMSO.
Public Service Pensions Guide to Annual Review Provisions Pensions (Increase) Act 1971, HMSO.

Redundancies of Teaching and Non-Teaching Staff in Colleges and Departments of Education, A LACSAB Information Booklet, 1978.
The Colleges of Education (Compensation) Regulations 1975 An Explanatory Guide for Claimants in Voluntary Colleges, Leaflet 3000 Pen C, Department of Education and Science, 1975.
Teacher education – Safeguarding and Compensation, National Association of Teachers in Further and Higher Education Information Series No 3, 1976.

W. Browne and K. Scribbins, unpublished paper, *Compensation and Superannuation,* 1977.
L. Sheen, "Redeploying College Lecturers in the Classroom", *Education,* 5th August 1977.
K. Scribbins. "The Compensation Regulations," *NATFHE Journal,* October 1977.
K. Scribbins and J. Gordon. "Crombie Four Years On ... Making the Promises Stick," *NATFHE Journal,* March 1979.
K. Scribbins, G. Clayton and J. Gordon, "Where Crombie Went Wrong", *Education,* 4th May 1979.
I. Waitt, *Low v The Department of Education and Science: An Exercise in the Simulation of an Appeal to an Industrial Tribunal,* NATFHE, 1979.

6 EMPLOYMENT LAW

1. It is not the purpose of this sub-section to provide an exhaustive guide to employment law. Detailed comment on and reference to the law may be obtained from *The LACSAB Employee Relations Handbook* and the guides published by the Department of Employment, Equal Opportunities Commission and the Commission for Racial Equality. This sub-section is intended to itemise in outline the provisions of the laws of which administrators in colleges ought to be aware. In any particular instance, administrators ought to consult also the guides referred to above and the statutes themselves. There are important restrictions and qualifications concerning UK law which arise as a consequence of EEC membership: this sub-section should be read in conjunction with Section **6.1**, above. Proposed changes in current employment law are discussed in Appendix 7, below; items in the text which may be affected by such changes are marked by an asterisk*. Some comment on the law is given in Section **11.9**.

2. **Advertisement of posts**[1]

The advertisement, including the further details, will usually include a detailed job description and the salary range. The salary offered, as well as the salary subsequently paid, must have regard to the Equal Pay Act 1970. The purpose of this Act is to eliminate discrimination between men and women in regard to pay and other terms of their contracts of employment. For the purposes of colleges, the Act will probably be mainly relevant to non-teaching staff. Under the Sex Discrimination Act 1975 and the Race Relations Act 1976 it is unlawful to publish or cause to be published an advertisement which indicates an intention to discriminate on grounds of sex or race, except where there is a *genuine occupational qualification* of sex or race for the post in question. Examples of this genuine occupational qualification would be:

(i) where a person of a particular sex should hold the post because of considerations of decency or privacy; and

(ii) where education or a similar service could best be provided by a person of a particular racial group.

Employers have a duty to ensure that advertisements and job descriptions do not contain racial or sexual connotations: where there is doubt, a specific statement that there is no intention to discriminate ought to be included in the advertisement.

3. **Selection for employment: discrimination**

In the selection of persons for employment there must again be regard to legislation relating to discrimination. The Rehabilitation of Offenders Act is referred to under paragraphs 53-54 below. Discrimination on the grounds of sex and race is unlawful. This paragraph refers, therefore, not only to selection for interview and employment but also to selection for promotion, transfer and training; and to opportunities for benefits such as services or facilities. Both the Sex Discrimination Act and the Race Relations Act

---

1 NATFHE policy concerning appointments is reproduced as Appendix 1 to Section **11.9**.

envisage two types of discrimination: direct and indirect. Under the Sex Discrimination Act, direct discrimination involves treating a woman less favourably than a man because she is a woman. Indirect discrimination means that conditions are applied which favour one sex more than the other but which cannot be justified. These provisions apply equally to men and women unless the discrimination is equally applied against single persons or, in respect of a woman, to maternity provisions. Married persons are discriminated against if they are treated less favourably than single persons. A further discrimination occurs if a person is victimised as a result of proceedings taken, or information given, under either the Sex Discrimination or Race Relations Act.

4. A person seeking to complain of discrimination may question the person whose conduct is the subject of grievance. The questions and answers are admissible in evidence. Cases of discrimination in employment are first subject to the jurisdiction of an industrial tribunal. The burden of proof is on the employee.

5. **Contracts of employment**

The provisions of the Contracts of Employment Act 1972 as amended by several subsequent Acts are now included in the Employment Protection (Consolidation) Act 1978.

6. A contract of employment, unless it is a contract of apprenticeship, does not have to be written. A contract of employment exists as soon as the employee proves acceptance of the employer's terms and conditions of employment by starting work. Whatever form the contract takes, the law demands that the employer should provide the employee with a written statement of the main terms and conditions of employment within 13 weeks of the commencement of the contract., The written statement must contain an additional note concerning disciplinary procedures.

7. These requirements may be summarised thus:

Written statement

This must contain:

(i) the names of employer and employee, the date of commencement of employment and whether any employment with a previous employer counts as continuous service (including, if so, the date of that commencement) and at a date not more than seven days before the issue of the statement;

(ii) the scale or rate of remuneration, or the method of its calculation;

(iii) the intervals at which remuneration is paid;

(iv) terms and conditions relating to: hours of work; entitlement to holidays, including public holidays and holiday pay (the information to be sufficient to allow precise calculation on termination of employment of the employee's entitlement); incapacity for work due to sickness or injury, including sick pay provisions; pensions and pension schemes (except where employees are covered by statutory schemes and whose employers are already obliged by law to provide information).

(v) the entitlement to notice of termination of both employer and employee, including the date of the expiry of the contract if it is for a fixed term; and
(vi) the employee's job title.

Additional note
The note refers to matters of discipline and grievance procedure. The note must:
(i) specify any disciplinary rules (other than those relating to health and safety as that matter is the subject of other legislation) relevant to the employee, or else refer to a document reasonably accessible to the employee which specifies the rules;
(ii) specify the person, and the manner of application, to whom the employee can apply if the employee is dissatisfied with any disciplinary decision, or for the purpose of seeking redress of any grievance relating to employment; and
(iii) explain any further steps which follow an application or refer to a reasonably accessible document containing such information.

8. The written statement does not itself have to provide all the required information. Reference may be made by the statement to other reasonably accessible documents. For example, an employer may refer an employee to a collective agreement if all or any of the terms of employment are contained therein. Where there is a change in the terms of employment, the employer must amend the statement and/or other relevant documents within one month of that change.

9. Provided that the employee has a copy, or access to a copy, of a written contract which contains all the details required for the written statements, then the employer need not issue a written statement. The additional note must still be issued where there is such a written statement, or else access to it ensured. There is no requirement for an employee to sign a written statement. Where employees are asked to sign for a written statement, agreement to sign should only be on the basis of receipt of the statement. Disputes concerning written statements may be referred to an industrial tribunal; disputes concerning failure to observe the terms of a contract of employment are not within the jurisdiction of tribunals (except in certain instances of unfair dismissal).

10. **Rights to notice**
Rights to notice of termination of employment under the Employment Protection (Consolidation) Act for the purposes of colleges will refer in effect mainly to non-teaching staff, part-time employees and temporary staff appointed on fixed term contracts.

11. The employer is required by the Act to give an employee notice of:
(i) at least one week if there has been continuous employment for four of more weeks;
(ii) at least two weeks if there has been continuous employment for two or more years; and

(iii) one additional week's notice for each further complete year of continuous employment up to 12 weeks' notice if the employee has been employed continuously for 12 or more years.

An employee after four or more weeks of continuous employment is required to give the employer notice of at least one week. This period is not subject to increase with longer service. The Act lays down minimum provisions only: it does not alter the provisions in a contract of employment for longer periods of notice.

12. The Act applies to part-time employees if they work, or are normally expected to work, 16 hours a week or more; and also to employees continuously employed for more than eight but less than 16 hours a week after a period of five years. Again, individual contracts of employment may well allow a period of notice longer than provided for by the Act, or where there is no entitlement to notice under the Act. Employees whose periods of employment are not expected to last for more than 12 weeks and who are not employed for longer than this period have no right under the Act to minimum notice.

13. In the case of temporary employees, if it is agreed at the commencement of the contract that the contract is to last for a fixed period, then the rights to notice will not generally apply. Notice will, in fact, have been given at the start of the contract. However, where an employee is working under a contract which is for a fixed term of four weeks or less, but the contract has been renewed so that the employee has remained in employment for 12 weeks or more, the contract will have effect as if it were for an indefinite period, and thus have applied to it the minimum notice rights. In addition, an employee who has a fixed term contract may, if that contract refers to the conditions of service of permanent full-time teachers, have an implied right to notice.

14. An employee may accept payments in lieu of notice; employer and employee alike may waive their rights to notice.

EMPLOYMENT

15. **Equal treatment**

Legislation regarding discrimination already referred to in paragraphs 2-3 continues to apply in employment. It remains necessary, however, to refer to the rights established by the Equal Pay Act. This Act applies both to men and women. It establishes the right of an individual to equal treatment in respect of the terms of the contract of employment when that employment is:

(i) on work of the same or a broadly similar nature to that of a person of the opposite sex; and

(ii) in a job which, though different from that of a person of the opposite sex, has been given an equal value to that person's job under job evaluation.[2]

---

2 cf Section **6.1.**21-24; UK law concerning equality does not at present conform to EEC requirements.

16. The Central Arbitration Committee is empowered to remove discrimination in matters affecting employment. A person suffering from discrimination may make application to an industrial tribunal. "Equal treatment" means that each term in a contract must not be less favourable than the corresponding term in the contract of the person of the opposite sex (apart from maternity provision). Comparisons for the purposes of establishing equal treatment may be drawn with establishments other than the place of work if the terms and conditions of employment are common between them. Where it is sought to make a comparison of "like work", the two jobs considered will not be like work if the differences between them are "of practical importance in relation to terms and conditions of employment" "Job evaluation" is defined as being a study undertaken with a view to evaluating (in terms of work demands such as effort, skill and decision) the jobs to be done by any or all of the employees in an establishment or establishments. Where job evaluation has shown that equal treatment is being denied, then that entitlement can only be disallowed where the employer can show that the variation between the two contracts is "genuinely due to a material difference (other than the difference of sex)".

17. **Terms and conditions of employment** *

Schedule 11 of the Employment Protection Act 1975 makes provision for the reporting to ACAS, which may refer the matter to the Central Arbitration Committee (CAC), of claims that an employer is not observing the relevant recognised terms and conditions of employment (or, if such recognised terms do not exist, the relevant general level of terms and conditions). The "recognised terms and conditions" are those settled nationally and locally by agreement between employers' associations and independent trade unions, or by arbitration. Where the relevant agreement or award establishes minimum terms and conditions, these constitute the recognised terms and conditions. The "general level of terms and conditions" is that general level observed for comparable employees by other employers engaged in the same undertakings, in the same district, and in similar circumstances.

18. The schedule disallows the reporting of claims where "workers whose remuneration or terms and conditions ... is or are fixed .. in pursuance of any enactment," Because teachers are paid under statutory provisions, the reporting of salary claims under the schedule is therefore not allowed. It had been thought that the expression "remuneration or terms" was conjunctive: that is, because teachers' salaries were excluded so were their terms and conditions of employment. The balance of legal opinion is now that the expression is disjunctive: it is possible to report a claim relating to terms and conditions but not relating to salaries. Claims can be reported only by an employers' association or an independent trade union (see paragraph 28 below) which is a party to the agreement or award which constitutes the recognised terms and conditions. If the matter cannot be settled by ACAS, it is referred to the CAC. A CAC award becomes an implied term of contract of employment for employees of the description identified in the award.

19. **Guarantee payments***

The Act provides that when an employee is not provided with work which under contract would normally be required to be done because of either a reduction in the employer's requirements, or any other occurrence affecting the natural workings of the undertaking, then the employee is entitled to a guarantee payment. Such payments can only be made in respect of complete working days lost. For the purposes of colleges it can be said that guarantee payments will *not* be made where:

(i) the employee is a part-time employee who fails to satisfy the conditions set out in paragraph 12 above;

(ii) the employee has no normal working hours prescribed by his or her contract of employment;

(iii) the employee has unreasonably refused an offer from the employer of suitable alternative work; and

(iv) the lay off or short time results from a trade dispute involving any employee of the employer (or of an associated employer).

20. The amount of a guarantee payment is calculated by the multiplication of the number of normal working hours for the day in question by the guaranteed hourly rate, subject to an upper limit (currently £6.60 per day). Payments are further limited to no more than five days per quarter. Payments made by the employer under a contract of employment are offset against the employer's liability under the Act, and *vice versa.* An employee who does not receive a guarantee payment but considers that there is an entitlement can complain to an industrial tribunal.

21. The appropriate Minister under certain conditions may grant an exemption from the Act where employers and employees have their own collective agreement concerning guarantee pay. Unemployment benefits cannot be paid for a day in respect of which any guarantee payment is payable.

22. **Itemised pay statement**

The provisions of the Act concerning pay statements will apply to all college staff other than those part-time staff specified in paragraph 12 above.

The pay statement must specify:

(i) the gross amount of the wages or salary;

(ii) the amounts of any fixed deductions such as trade union subscriptions and the purposes for which they are made (unless a written standing statement of fixed deductions is issued);

(iii) the amounts of any variable deductions and the purposes for which they are made;

(iv) the net amount of wages or salary payable; and

(v) where different amounts of the net amount are paid in different ways, the amount and method of payment for each part-payment.

23. An employer may issue either a pay statement which specifies the amounts and purposes of every fixed deduction separately, or a pay statement specifying only the aggregate amount of all fixed deductions. In the latter case, the employee must be provided with a standing statement of fixed deductions at or before the time that latter form of pay advice was adopted. The employer is required to notify the employee in writing of any change in the amount, purpose or number of fixed deductions. The standing statement

of fixed deductions must be reissued within 12 months beginning with the date on which the last statement was issued. Apart from questions concerning the accuracy of an amount, disputes concerning pay statements may be referred to an industrial tribunal.

24. **Time off for public duties**

Employers are required under s29 of the Employment Protection (Consolidation) Act to permit employees holding public positions time off in which to perform their public duties. For the purpose of college staff, the persons not eligible to time off are part-time employees failing to satisfy the conditions set out in paragraph 12 above. The relevant public positions may be broadly defined as:

(i) Justices of the Peace;
(ii) members of a local authority;
(iii) members of any statutory tribunal; and
(iv) in England and Wales, members of a regional or area health authority, a water authority, the managing or governing body of a maintained educational establishment.

25. The duties of the employee for which an employer is required to permit time off are those which arise from the office or membership held, and are defined as: attendance at meetings of the body or any of its committees or sub-committees; and the performance of duties approved by the body concerned which are required to fulfil its functions. The amount of time off permissible under the Act is that which is "reasonable in all the circumstances", having regard to:

(i) the amount of time off required in general to perform the particular public duty, and the amount required on the particular occasion in question;
(ii) the amount of time off the employee has had already for this purpose as well as time off for trade union duties, if any; and
(iii) the circumstances of the employer's undertaking and the effect thereon of the employee's absence.

26. An employer is not obliged to pay an employee for time taken for public duties, but may do so at his or her discretion, or as a result of an individual or collective agreement. An aggrieved employee has the right to complain to an industrial tribunal where the employer has refused to allow time off.

27. **Trade union membership and activities***

Employees employed under a contract of employment have the right not to have any action taken against them individually by the employer in any of the following:

(i) prevention or deterrence from joining or belonging to an independent trade union, or to be penalised for doing so;
(ii) prevention or deterrence from participation in independent trade union activities at any appropriate time, or to be penalised for doing so;
(iii) compulsion to join or belong to a union which is not independent, or to any union if the employee has genuine religious objections.

Infringement of these rights does not necessarily have to be caused by the employer; where others are acting on the behalf of the employer infringement can occur, and the employer is answerable for such actions. An employee dismissed because of trade union membership or activities or because of refusal to join a *non-independent union,* will have suffered unfair dismissal. This is a provision of the Trade Union and Labour Relations Act 1974. The Employment Protection Acts deal with actions short of dismissal. Under those Acts, infringements of employee's rights would include matters such as: unjustified refusal of promotion, training or job transfer; threats of dismissal or redundancy; the docking of pay or benefits; and disciplinary measures. In order to prove that employee rights have been infringed, it is necessary to show that the employer's actions were intended to have the effect of putting pressure on employees in respect of their union membership or activities. Nonetheless, at an industrial tribunal, the onus of proof is on the employer to show that the employee's rights have not been infringed: once the employee has proved that an action pressurising him or her was taken, the employer must satisfy the tribunal that the action was not intended to infringe the employee's rights.

28. Under the Trade Union and Labour Relations Act 1974, amended by the Employment Protection Act 1975, "independent trade union" means a union which:
    (i) is not under the domination or control of an employer or group of employers or of one or more employer's associations; and
    (ii) is not liable to interference by an employer or any such group or association tending towards such control.

    The employee does not have to prove that the union to which he or she belongs, or wishes to join, is independent before seeking a remedy for infringement of rights. Proof of a union's independence is the holding of a certificate of independence issued by the Certification Officer. Action by an employer under a closed shop arrangement to ensure that an employee joins a particular union is not an infringement of rights, but where with the consent of the unions concerned an employee seeks to take out dual membership of independent unions, any employer action to prevent such membership will be an infringement of rights.

29. The kind of trade union activity in which an employee is entitled to take part is not defined. The Act establishes rights to time off for members of unions to participate in the affairs of the union, and to representatives of the union (for example, shop stewards, branch officers and persons otherwise acting on behalf of the union) to execute the duties of their office. Protection would also be afforded for activities connected with the election and appointment of union officials. The activities however must occur at an "appropriate time". The right to time off to participate in activities is a right to time off without pay (although it may be considered good practice if pay were given). The right to time off to perform union office is a right to time off with pay. Employers are required to permit reasonable time off for participation in union affairs during working hours (not necessarily with pay). There is no definition of what is reasonable time off but the ACAS Code of Practice states that the amounts "are those that are reasonable in all the

circumstances, having regard to any relevant provision of this Code of Practice".[3] Although written in a very general sense, the Code of Practice will be of use in cases of doubt or dispute.

30. **Maternity***

The Employment Protection (Consolidation) Act makes three important provisions concerning maternity: the right not to be dismissed (pregnancy is not a valid reason for dismissal); the right to return to work after the birth of the child; and the right to maternity pay. These rights apply to all women, married or unmarried, provided that:

(i) in the case of employment for more than eight but less than 16 hours a week they have been employed continuously for five years or more; and

(ii) in the case of employment of 16 hours or more they have been continuously employed for 26 weeks (to acquire the right not to be dismissed because of pregnancy), or two years (to acquire the rights to return to work and maternity pay). The Act does not affect the right to better conditions extended under a contract of employment.

31. Dismissal of a pregnant employee for the reason of her condition alone is possible only if her pregnancy makes it impossible for her adequately to do her job, or where it would be unlawful for her to work while pregnant. In these circumstances, an employer must offer suitable alternative employment if it is available. If an offer of such employment is refused then the employee will be considered to have resigned, and to have lost her rights. Disputes can be referred to an industrial tribunal. The onus of proof is on the employer.

32. A woman is entitled to return to her employment at any time up to 29 weeks after the commencement of confinement. Rates of pay, holidays and other conditions of service are continued as if she had not stopped work. Rights concerning seniority and pensions, however, are subject to a restriction: absence because of maternity does not break continuity of service, but it does not count towards it. The following conditions apply to the right to return to work:

---

3 ACAS, *Time off for Trade Union Duties & Activities*, Code of Practice 3, HMSO. In finding for the applicant in the case of Ratcliffe v Dorset County Council, the tribunal stated that in terms of the law it could not make a direction as to what time should be allowed off for public duties. However, in organizing the applicant's timetable to free him of teaching duties in order to allow him to attend the meetings of the Bournemouth Borough Council, but in still requiring him to perform his full functions – which meant that he had to do work at home and at weekends – the respondents were found by the tribunal to have "contravened the applicant's right under s.59 of the Employment Protection Act to time off during his working hours to perform public duties ... Since the applicant still had to do the work at some other time, his work load was not diminished .... Swapping time around is not giving time off." *Industrial Relations Law Reports*, Vol. 7, No. 5, May 1978, 191. EAT decisions have shown that union officials' duties ranking for paid time off must not be narrowly construed; that employers restrictively rely too much on the ACAS code; that union officials are entitled to paid time off for matters other than meetings with management; that duties are not confined to the existing industrial relations structure; and that a test is whether the time off is required to enable the official to carry out his or her duties in connection with a matter arising in relations between employer(s) and employees. cf Incomes Data Services, *Brief 166*, October 1979, pp. 4-6.

(i) The employee must have continued her employment with her employer up to the 11th week before the birth is due (as certified in a Certificate of Expected Confinement by a midwife or doctor). At her own discretion the employee may continue to work after the 11th week, and even until confinement (but see paragraph 31 above).

(ii) At the time of the 11th week of pregnancy, the woman must have been employed by her employer for at least two years.

(iii) At least 21 days before stopping work, the woman must inform her employer that she intends to stop work because of her condition and also state that she intends to return to work after the birth. The employer is entitled to require such notice in writing, and to see the Certificate of Expected Confinement.

(iv) If it is not reasonably practicable to give the notice required in (iii), such notice must be given as soon as is reasonably practicable.

33. The employee must notify the employer at least seven days before the date of her intended return. That date is at the discretion of the employee, provided that it is at any time before the end of the period of 29 weeks beginning with the week in which the date of confinement falls. The employer may delay the employee's return to work for up to four weeks from the notified date, provided that reasons are given and she is told when she may resume work. The employee may similarly delay her return for up to four weeks from either the notified date or at the end of the 29 weeks if she is ill and produces a medical certificate; but she can only do this once. If the return to work is prevented by an interruption of work, such as an industrial dispute, the employee should return as soon as practicable, but not later than 14 days, after the end of the interruption. Where an employer does not allow the employee to return to work, the employee may complain to an industrial tribunal. According to the circumstances, if the application is successful, the tribunal may order reinstatement, an entitlement to redundancy payment or a cash award in compensation.

34. Where an employer appoints a temporary replacement for an employee who has stopped work in order to have a baby, that person should be advised in writing at the time of the engagement that the employment will be terminated on the return of the absent employee; and for the reason of the absence of the permanent employee. If the replacement is dismissed in order to allow the return to work of the person to whom the maternity provisions apply, that dismissal will not normally be unfair.

35. A woman who ceases to work in order to have a baby is entitled to claim maternity pay from her employer. This entitlement is subject to the same conditions as those required for the right to return to work (except that the provisions concerning notice to return do not apply here; the employee is entitled to maternity pay whether or not she intends to return to work).

36. Employers are required to pay maternity pay for the first six weeks of the employee's absence, starting on or after the 11th week before the expected week of confinement. The payment due for each week is nine-tenths of a week's pay, less the amount of the flat-rate national insurance maternity

allowance (whether or not this is due to the employee). No account should be taken of any earnings related supplement. Maternity pay is taxable. The employer should deduct tax under normal PAYE arrangements where a contract of employment is in existence at the date of payment of the maternity pay. Where the contract was terminated before the date of payment, no tax should be deducted by the employer; but the employee should show the payment as untaxed income in her return to the Inland Revenue. Tax liability will be taken into account by the Inland Revenue in dealing with any repayment claim. If they have an authority from the employee, employers may deduct other amounts from maternity pay, such as pension contributions. Employers must also calculate and pay over their share of national insurance contributions on the gross amount of maternity pay.

37. The Act does not state the method of payment of maternity pay. Therefore, it could be paid in weekly or monthly instalments, or as a lump sum. However, since the intention of maternity pay is to maintain earnings during the weeks of absence, payment of a lump sum at the end of six weeks would be contrary to this intention. Employers can claim back maternity payments from the Maternity Pay Fund. However, this rebate is limited to the statutory amount of maternity pay calculable according to the employee's contract; if an employer has paid more than the statutory obligation, that excess portion is not recoverable from the fund.

38. Where an employer has not made a maternity payment and the employee has exhausted all methods of obtaining that payment, she may apply to the Department of Employment for a direct payment. An employer who has unreasonably refused to make payments may be charged for those payments by the Department and also lose the right to a refund. Guidance on maternity benefits under the national insurance scheme is to be found in leaflet N1 17A, *National Insurance Maternity Benefits,* published by the Department of Health and Social Security and available from any of its offices.

39. **Continuous employment**

In order to qualify for most of the employee rights under the Employment Protection Acts, the individual must have been continuously employed for the period stipulated for the right. Where there is a dispute as to whether service is continuous, the employee's service is presumed to have been continuous unless the employer proves otherwise.

40. Service is worked out in weeks, the week ending with a Saturday. In all cases where the employee is under contract for the necessary number of hours a week, whenever service is terminated other than on a Saturday it is treated as though it had terminated on the next following Saturday.

41. An employee may be able to establish that a week should count either on the basis of the hours worked in that week (irrespective of the terms of the contract); or on the basis of contractual hours irrespective of the actual hours worked. Any week counts in which an employee is employed by the employer for 16 hours or more (but see also paragraphs 12 and 42). This

applies if the employee actually works those hours, even if the maximum hours normally worked, or which could be required to be worked, are less than 16. Any week also counts if in any part of it an employee is covered by a contract with the employer which normally involves employment for 16 hours or more weekly. In effect, this means that so long as the contract continues, a week will count even if the employee does not actually work as much as 16 hours in it. Therefore, absences through sickness, pregnancy, temporary lay-offs and holidays automatically count as part of the period of continuous employment *provided that the contract still continues.*

42. If a contract which normally involves employment for 16 hours or more weekly is temporarily varied to provide for less than 16 hours but not less than eight each week, then up to 26 weeks involving such reduced contractual hours will not break the continuity: they will count towards the period of continuous employment, provided that the employee then reverts to a contract providing for not less than 16 hours. These 26 weeks are in addition to any weeks which would count by means of another provision: the principle is more understandable, perhaps, if expressed as there being a pool of 26 weeks or reduced contractual hours available to be counted (and not necessarily consecutively) in addition to any weeks which can be brought within one of the other provisions. Continuity is not, therefore, automatically broken by a period of more than 26 weeks between two contracts. It must be noted, however, that if the contracted working hours are not restored to 16 or more before the 26 weeks plus any intervening countable weeks have elapsed, then the period of continuous employment will be regarded as having terminated in the last week covered by the original contract.

43. If an employee is employed under a contract which normally involves employment for eight hours or more per week, but less than 16, and has been so employed for five years, then the whole of that period and subsequent employment on these terms will count. Even if some weeks during the five year period would count in any event, the position is the same.

44. There are also circumstances in which a week may count even if the contract has ended and the employee has not been employed as much as 16 hours. This applies if the employee is away for all or part of the week because of:
(i) sickness or injury, so long as the absence does not exceed 26 weeks; or
(ii) a temporary cessation of work, but not if the employee is on strike; or
(iii) circumstances relating to a particular employment where, by custom or arrangement, the employment is regarded as continuing; or
(iv) pregnancy or maternity, so long as the absence does not exceed 26 weeks.

45. When an employee has qualified for rights by the completion of the necessary period of continuous employment, these rights are retained until such time as the contract is varied to provide for less than eight hours a week. Rights may still be retained even with such a variation if the employee actually works 16 or more hours a week despite the varied terms of the contract.

46. When an employee has qualified for an individual right which increases with further service (the rights to notice, redundancy payment or the basic award of unfair dismissal compensation), he or she will be allowed to build up entitlements to further service under a contract, providing that the contracted weekly hours are not less than eight.

47. If a complaint of unfair dismissal is upheld and the employee is reinstated or re-engaged (or engaged by a successive or associated employer), all the weeks falling between the date when the dismissal took effect and that of the resumption (or commencement) of work count towards the employee's period of continuous employment as though the dismissal had never occurred.

48. In the case of reinstatement or re-engagement following leave for pregnancy or maternity, all the weeks which fall between the date of the woman's first absence from work (wholly or partly because of her pregnancy or maternity) and the date of return to work count towards her period of continuous employment as though she had been working for her employer for that time and had never been absent.

49. No week beginning on or after 6 July 1964 in any part of which the employee is on strike is to count. Weeks in which strikes have taken place before 6 July 1964 are all to count. Weeks in which lock-outs have occurred all count. Weeks in any part of which the employee was on strike do not break the period of continuous employment.

50. If an employee is absent on service with the armed forces with reinstatement rights under the National Service Act 1948 or related legislation and afterwards resumes work with the former employer within six months of the end of the service, the two periods of employment are linked and counted as one. The intervening period of service does not count.

51. **Calculation of a week's pay**

Once continuity of service for the relevant rights is established, in many instances payments arising from those rights are calculated on the basis of a week's pay. The calculation of a week's pay is dependent upon whether the employee's pay in normal working hours is subject to variation. For the purposes of colleges, the categories of employee whose calculation of a week's pay may be subject to difficulty are hourly paid employees and employees whose pay varies with the amount of work done. For cases other than these, or where difficulty arises, reference should be made either to the Department of Employment booklet, *Continuous Employment and a Week's Pay,* or to the nearest office of the Department.

52. Where employees are paid entirely by an hourly time rate or by a fixed wage or salary and the pay for work done in normal working hours does not vary, then a week's pay is the pay obtaining for normal weekly hours as at the date of termination of employment. All non-variable bonuses and allowances (except expenses allowances) are included. Where the employee's pay varies with the amount of work done, a week's pay means pay for the normal weekly hours worked. This is calculated over a 12 week period. The hours to

be taken into account are only those, including overtime hours, when the employee was working. Any week in which the employee did not work should be replaced by the last previous week in which work was done. This process is continued until the 12 week period is established. The pay to be taken into account is the pay for all the hours when the employee was working (including overtime but subject to the adjustment of overtime pay), but excluding any pay for hours not worked. The hourly rate is obtained by dividing the pay to be taken into account by the hours to be taken into account. Apart from special cases such as output bonuses, it is generally the case that where pay for overtime is greater than the pay for the same work at the normal rate, the reckonable amount will be the lower sum which would have been payable had the work been done in normal working hours.

53. **Rehabilitation of offenders**

Under the Rehabilitation of Offenders Act 1974, persons convicted of offences for which sentences, suspended or otherwise, of up to two and a half years were imposed, after completing the prescribed rehabilitation period have the right to have the conviction regarded as "spent". In many instances this means that the offence is treated as if it had never occurred: a spent conviction may not be used as "a proper ground for dismissing or excluding a person from any office, profession, occupation or employment, or for prejudicing him in any way in any occupation or employment". However, by virtue of an Exemptions Order made under the Act there are certain types of employment to which the Act does not apply. For colleges' purposes, the relevant types of exempted employment are:

(i) Employment which is normally carried out within the precincts of a prison, remand centre, detention centre, borstal institution or young offenders' institution.

(ii) Teachers in schools or establishments for further education, and any other employment which is carried out wholly or partly within the precincts of a school or further education establishment which involves access to persons under the age of 18 as part of the employee's normal duties. The definition of a "teacher" includes youth workers, wardens of community centres and leaders of youth clubs and similar institutions.

(iii) Employment connected with the provision of social services which involves access to persons under the age of 18 or over 65; the mentally or physically handicapped; drug addicts; the blind, deaf or dumb, or the chronically sick or disabled.

(iv) Employment concerned with the provision of health services which involves access to patients.

(v) Persons employed for the purposes of, or to assist the constables of, a police force established under any enactment.

54. Applicants for such posts are not protected by the Act if they fail to disclose the existence of a spent conviction, provided that they are told that in completing the application forms, or at interviews, that spent convictions must be disclosed because of the effects of the Exemption Order. There is not normally a legal penalty for failure to disclose spent convictions but the application can be rejected, or the person subsequently dismissed, if the employer learns of a spent conviction of the individual concerned.

55. **Suspension on medical grounds**
An employee suspended on medical grounds under any of the regulations listed below should receive from the employer a normal week's pay for every week suspended up to a maximum of 26 weeks. An employee with a right to pay under a contract of employment while suspended should continue to receive that pay. The employer will not have to pay suspension pay in addition but, if the actual pay is less than a normal week's pay, the employer must make up the difference. Provisions relating to the suspension of teachers on medical grounds are contained in Appendix 4. The regulations are:

(i)	The Paints and Colour Manufacture Regulations 1907	S.R. & O. No 1907 17 Reg 5
(ii)	The Yarn (Dyed by Lead Compounds) Heading Regulations 1907	S.R. & O. 1907 No. 616 Reg 4
(iii)	The Vitreous Enamelling Regulations 1908	S.R. & O 1908 No. 1258 Reg 10
(iv)	The Tinning of Metal Hollow-ware from Drums and Harness Furniture Regulations 1909	S.R. & O. 1909 No 720 Reg 6
(v)	The Lead Smelting and Manufacture Regulations 1911	S.R. & O. 1911 No. 752 Reg 13
(vi)	The Lead Compounds Manufacture Regulations 1921	S.R. & 0. 1921 No 1443 Reg 11
(vii)	The India Rubber Regulations 1922	S.R. & O. 1922 No 329 Reg 12
(viii)	The Chemical Works Regulations 1922	S.R. & O. 1922 No. 731 Reg 30
(ix)	The Electric Accumulator Regulations 1925	S.R. & O. 1925 No. 28 Reg 13
(x)	The Lead Paint Regulations 1927	S.R. & O. 1927 No. 847 Reg 6
(xi)	The Pottery (Health & Welfare) Special Regulations 1950	S.I. 1950 No. 65 Reg 7
(xii)	The Factories Act 1961	1961 c. 34 Sections 75 (2) including as extended by Section 128
(xiii)	The Ionising Radiations (Unsealed Radioactive Substances) Regulations 1968	S.I. 1968 No 780 Regs 12 and 33
(xiv)	The Ionising Radiations (Sealed Sources) Regulations 1969	S.I. 1969 No. 808 Regs 11 and 30
(xv)	The Radioactive Substances (Road Transport Workers) (Great Britain) Regulations 1970	S.I. 1975 No. 1522 Reg 3 of the Employment Protection (Medical Suspension) Order 1976

56. Employees are not entitled to medical suspension pay:
(i) if they have not been in continuous employment with the employer for four weeks before suspension begins; or
(ii) if they work less than 16 hours a week or eight hours after five years' continuous service; or

(iii) for any time when unable to work because of illness or physical or mental disability; or
(iv) so long as suitable alternative work offered by the employer is unreasonably refused; or
(v) if any reasonable requirements imposed by the employer to ensure availability for work when necessary are refused.

An employer engaging a temporary replacement for a suspended employee should inform that person in writing at the time of the appointment that employment will only be until the suspended employee returns. If the replacement is then dismissed to allow the suspended employee to return, this will not normally be unfair dismissal. An employee who considers that suspension pay is not being paid in full may complain to a tribunal. Complaints of unfair dismissal can also be entered if an employee is dismissed where he or she would otherwise have been suspended for medical reasons. In this case, the length of continuous employment necessary to establish the right is four weeks.

57. **Disabled persons: the quota scheme**
The Disabled Persons (Employment) Act 1944 and its subordinate legislation imposes a duty on every employer of not less than 20 employees to give employment to a quota of registered disabled people. A percentage of such an employer's total staff must consist of registered disabled people. Failure to employ the quota does not of itself constitute an offence, but it remains the duty of employers to allocate to registered disabled people vacancies as they occur on the staff until the quota is reached. The employer is subject to two restrictions:
(i) In all engagements of staff (except where statutory reinstatement rights apply) the employer must not engage a person who is not a registered disabled person if the employer is below quota, unless a permit is obtained to allow such action.
(ii) An employer must not discharge a registered disabled person without "reasonable cause" if he or she is below quota, or if the discharge would result in the quota being breached. The 1944 Act does not provide a remedy where the registered disabled person is dismissed without reasonable cause. In that event, the person would have redress under the Employment Protection Acts. Every employer (under the Act the employer may be an individual or body corporate) has a duty to ensure that the quota obligations are being fulfilled and that offences are not being committed in respect of the engagement or discharge of employees. The disablement resettlement officers of the Department of Employment will assist any employer below quota who is seeking registered disabled persons to fill current vacancies.

58. An employer's quota is determined by applying the appropriate percentage to the numbers of employees employed for more than ten hours a week. A person normally employed from ten to 30 hours a week is counted as a half unit, a person normally employed more than 30 hours a week is counted as a full unit. There are two kinds of percentage: standard and special. Where no special percentage is fixed, the standard percentage will apply. A special

percentage is fixed after consultation between associations of employers and employees according to the nature of the employment(s) in a particular concern. As the quota is determined by percentage, it varies with changes in the employer's total staff; where a change in staff could result in an offence being committed, the employer must obtain a permit to justify his action. The standard percentage is three per cent (although at the time of writing the Government was considering lowering the percentage). An employer may apply for a reduction in quota, but cause for the reduction has to be shown.

59. An employer below quota must not engage a person who is not registered as disabled, either for full-time, casual or part-time work without having obtained in advance a permit to do so; nor may such a person be engaged without a permit if as a result the employer would then be below quota. Permits are granted subject to conditions, and may relate to one or more persons specified, or to a specified number of people. A permit will not be granted if a suitable registered disabled person is available for the job. Where an employer objects to the refusal of a permit or to the imposition of conditions under the Act, application may be made to a district advisory committee and thence to the Secretary of State, with whom the final decision rests.

60. Every employer subject to quota obligation is required to record information necessary to demonstrate compliance with the law, and to produce those records for inspection. The records should show the total number and names of all employees as well as the dates of engagement or termination of employment. The record must also give such information as is necessary to identify the following individual employees:
    (i) a registered disabled person, including a person whose registration has lapsed during employment with the employer;
    (ii) a person in an employment to which a special percentage applies and the figure of that percentage;
    (iii) a person who has been engaged by virtue of reinstatement rights;
    (iv) a person employed under a permit;
    (v) a person whose employment ordinarily involves less than ten hours work per week; and
    (vi) a person whose employment ordinarily involves not less than ten but not more than 30 hours work per week.

61. Although the purpose of this sub-section is to provide guidance rather than comment on employment law, some attention has to be drawn to the implementation of the Disabled Persons (Employment) Act. The Act was designed originally with a consideration towards persons disabled in warfare. The register of disabled persons now contains fewer numbers of that category; some of those registered persons being less easy to place than war victims. It is considered by the Department of Employment that only about half of the disabled persons in employment are registered; and about three quarters of those disabled persons who are unemployed. Only registered disabled persons count towards the quota. The number of registered disabled persons fell from 906,008 in 1951 to 610,107 in 1972. It is, therefore, not the policy of the Department of Employment rigorously to

enforce the law, although it still wishes to emphasise to employers their statutory obligations. Moreover, recalcitrant employers can still have action taken against them under the Act. If an employer dismissed a registered disabled person without reasonable cause, of if a dismissal caused the employer to fall below quota, then an offence has been committed. The penalties for such an offence are a fine or imprisonment or both.

LOSS OF EMPLOYMENT

62. **Dismissal**

Legal provisions concerning dismissal are contained in the Employment Protection (Consolidation) Act 1978. The right to receive a written statement of reasons for dismissal is provided for by this Act.

63. Dismissal is defined as the termination of employment by:
   (i) the employer, with or without notice;
   (ii) the employee's resignation, with or without notice (where the employer's conduct is such that it demonstrates an intention not to be bound by the contract of employment – i.e. "constructive dismissal" – cf Section **11.9.**21);
   (iii) the expiry of a fixed term contract without its renewal; and
   (iv) the refusal of an employer to allow an employee to return to work after the birth of her child.

Where an employee gives notice to terminate a contract of employment after dismissal by the employer at an earlier date than that required by the employer, the employee will still be regarded as dismissed by the employer. In this case, the effective date of termination of employment will be the date that the employee's notice takes effect.

64. The effective date of termination of employment is:
   (i) the date on which the notice expires, where the employee worked through the notice period given by either party (except where the employer gave shorter notice than required by law: the effective date here is that of when the longer notice would have expired); or
   (ii) the last day on which the employee worked for the employer (except as in (i) above) where the contract was terminated without notice by the employer, or where the employee has received a payment in lieu of working part or all of the notice period; or
   (iii) the last day on which the employee worked for the employer where the contract was terminated without notice by the employee; and
   (iv) the date of the expiry of a fixed term contract.

65. Employees whose employment is terminated with or without notice, or whose fixed term contracts expire without being renewed, have the right to receive from their employers a written statement of the reasons for their dismissal. The employee must ask for such a statement, however. The written statement may be used in evidence in any subsequent proceedings. The employee may complain to an industrial tribunal if the employer unreasonably fails to provide a statement, and also if he or she considers that the statement is inadequate or untrue.

66. **Unfair dismissal***

An employee who works under, or worked under a contract of employment, has the right to complain to a tribunal of unfair dismissal. For college purposes, those who cannot complain of unfair dismissal are:

(i) those who are not employees (for example, free-lance agents);

(ii) employees who have not completed 52 weeks'[4] continuous employment with the employer at the effective date of termination. (This qualification is reduced to four weeks for certain dismissals following periods of statutory medical suspension. Employees dismissed for union membership or activities do not have to serve a qualifying period);

(iii) except in the case of dismissal for union membership or activities, part-time employees who normally work less than 16 hours a week, unless they have been employed by the same employer for eight or more hours a week for 5 years;

(iv) except in the case of dismissal for union membership or activities, employees who before their effective date of termination had reached the normal retiring age for their employment, or where there is no normal retiring age, had reached the age of 60 for women or 65 for men (but cf Section **11.9**.29, below);

(v) employees with fixed term contracts for two years or more where the dismissal consists only of the expiry of the contract without renewal, and the employee had previously agreed in writing to forego the right of complaint in such circumstances; and

(vi) employees with fixed term contracts for two years or more where the dismissal consists only of the expiry of the contract without renewal and that contract was entered into before 28 February 1972 or, in the case of dismissal on grounds of pregnancy, 1 June 1976.

67. Unfair dismissals for reasons of trade union membership or activities and maternity leave have been referred to under paragraphs 27-38 above. Dismissals for reasons of sex or race are also unfair. If, at the date of dismissal, there is an industrial dispute, a tribunal will not determine the fairness of the dismissal unless it is shown that not all the relevant employees have been treated equally (in respect of either dismissal or re-engagement).

68. Where complaints of unfair dismissal to an industrial tribunal are successful, the law provides for three remedies: reinstatement, re-engagement and compensation. Where the employee is reinstated he or she is to be treated in all respects as though the dismissal had not occurred. If the employee is re-employed, the re-employment may not necessarily be in the same job or on the same terms and conditions of employment. In deciding whether to make an order for reinstatement or re-engagement, the tribunal will consider the employee's wishes, the practicability of his or her returning to work for the employer, and if it would be just to make such an order where the employee was partly to blame for the dismissal. Awards of compensation are made in

---

4 The substitution of a 52 week qualifying period instead of the previous 26 week period is operative from 1 October 1979 and results from the provisions of The Unfair Dismissal (Variation of Qualifying Period) Order 1979, S.I. 1979 No. 959. The Order applies where the effective date of termination falls on or after 1 October 1979.

two forms: the basic award and the compensatory award. The basic award is calculated according to service and subject to a current maximum of £3000 which can be reduced where the employee was 59 (female), 64 (male), or partially contributed to the dismissal, or received a redundancy payment or payments under the Sex Discrimination Act or Race Relations Act. The compensatory award is subject to a current maximum of £5,200 and may be reduced where the employee was partly to blame for the dismissal or, failed to mitigate the loss by making efforts to obtain another job; and by the amount of earnings in subsequent employment between the dismissal and the hearing, and by payments made *ex gratia* by the employer or in lieu of notice. Complaints of unfair dismissal should be presented to an industrial tribunal within three months of the effective date of termination.

69. **Fair dismissal**

The reasons which would justify dismissal are:

(i) a reason related to the employee's capability or qualifications for the job; or

(ii) a reason related to the employee's conduct; or

(iii) redundancy; or

(iv) a legal duty or restriction on either the employer or employee which prevents the continuance of the employment; or

(v) some other substantial reason which could justify the dismissal.

The dismissal can only be fair if the employer can show that its reason was one of the criteria listed above. Moreover, the employer has to show that he or she acted reasonably in the circumstances in treating that reason as sufficient to justify the dismissal. Unfair selection for redundancy is investigated below under paragraph 78.

70. **Redundancy**

The law concerning redundancy is contained in the Employment Protection (Consolidation) Act 1978. Redundancy is defined as:

(i) where the employer has ceased, or intends to cease, to carry on the business giving rise to the employment, or to carry on the business in the place at which employees were contracted to work; or

(ii) the requirements of the business for employees to carry out work of a particular kind have ceased or diminished, or are expected to cease or diminish, or that such diminution applies or will apply in the place at which the employees were contracted to work.

71. Where a redundancy occurs, the employee is entitled to a redundancy payment. Redundancies can be suffered by persons whose employment is subject to substantial change, and by employees who are laid off or kept on short time. For college purposes, persons not eligible to a redundancy payment are:

(i) an employee who has not had at least two years' continuous employment (at 16 hours a week or more, or five years' continuous employment for between eight and 16 hours a week) with the employer;

(ii) an employee whose reckonable service ends on or after the age of 60 (female) or 65 (male) (but see Section **11.9.**29);

(iii) a person performing services under a contract of service as distinct from a contract of employment;

(iv) an employee engaged on a fixed term contract of two years or more if the contract was entered into before 6 December 1965;

(v) an employee engaged on a fixed term contract of two years or more entered into on or after 6 December 1965 if he or she has made a written agreement with the employer to forgo any right to a redundancy payment in the event of there being no re-engagement when the term of the contract expires.

If the case of (v), if the person becomes redundant before the expiry of the contract then, the written agreement notwithstanding, provided the two year qualifying period of continuous employment has been served, full entitlement to a redundancy payment is retained. Any agreement to forgo a redundancy payment must relate only to a particular contract; where a contract is renewed for a further term, the parties will need to make a fresh arrangement, if required, to forgo rights to a redundancy payment. There are also circumstances in which an apprentice may be eligible for a redundancy payment.

72. Losses of employment here suffered (see paragraphs 62-65 above) may be defined as dismissal by reason of redundancy. Such dismissals carry the right to a redundancy payment. Where an employer asks for volunteers for redundancy, the volunteer does not lose entitlements provided the employer terminates the contract. Whether an undertaking is to continue or not, where an employer requires fewer employees, their dismissals will be because of redundancy. An employee is taken to be dismissed if he or she leaves employment with or without notice where the employer's conduct justifies such action; entitlement to a redundancy payment will depend on the circumstances of the case. There is no dismissal, and consequently no right to redundancy payment, where an employee accepts an offer of alternative employment with the employer (or an associated or successive employer) and continues in the new employment beyond the end of the trial period (see under paragraph 76 below).

73. Where an employee is under notice of redundancy but wishes to leave before the expiry of the employer's notice, provided that the employer does not object to his or her leaving, entitlement to a redundancy payment is not affected (except that the date of the employee's notice becomes the dismissal date for the purposes of reckoning service). If the employer objects to the employee leaving prematurely, the employer is entitled to serve a written notice on the employee requesting the withdrawal of the employee's notice and warning that, unless this is done, the employer will contest liability to make a redundancy payment. If the employee proceeds with the premature departure, he or she may apply to an industrial tribunal for consideration of the case.

74. If a dismissal was wholly or mainly due to some cause other than redundancy, there is no entitlement to a payment. Any dispute concerning the cause of dismissal will have to be settled by a tribunal; the onus of proof is on the employer to establish that the employee was not redundant.

75. **Redundancy entitlements where offers of further employment are made**

An employee is not entitled to a redundancy payment if, when under notice of redundancy but before its expiry, he or she accepts the employer's offer of further employment on the same terms starting not later than four weeks after the end of the current contract. If an employee refuses such an offer there is no entitlement to a payment, unless there were reasonable grounds for such a refusal.

76. The provisions of the above paragraph apply where an employee is offered work by the same, associated or successive employer on different terms or in a different place except that the employee is allowed a trial period to determine whether or not the new post is suitable. The trial period is of four weeks' duration but it may be extended where retraining is required (and subject to a specified agreement). During the trial period, the employee may terminate or give notice of termination of the new contract, and be treated as though he or she had been dismissed on the day the old job ended. There will be an entitlement to a redundancy payment if the usual conditions are satisfied. The employer, after consulting the Department of Employment, would have to consider whether or not to make a redundancy payment. In any industrial tribunal proceedings, it would be for the employer to prove that the alternative employment was suitable and that it was terminated unreasonably by the employee. There is no entitlement to a redundancy payment where an employee unreasonably refuses an offer of continued employment in suitable alternative work.

77. It is important to remember, in the context of college reorganization and possible contraction in the education service, that in law it is a post, not its occupant, which becomes redundant. Thus, a person dismissed or under notice of dismissal is not redundant if he or she is replaced by another person appointed full-time to exercise the same duties and not previously an employee. Further, it is possible that technical redundancies can occur where the nature of a post is changed by a change in the employer's activities. In this instance it is the advice of ACAS that if the nature of work done in the post changes by 50% or more, then a redundancy has occurred. Entitlements to redundancy payments and the operation of the trial period therefore are relevant here and subject to the conditions outlined above.

78. **Unfair selection for redundancy**

Dismissal on grounds of redundancy will be unfair if:

(i) the employee was selected for dismissal because of trade union membership or activities; or

(ii) the employer unreasonably disregarded the customary arrangements or agreed procedure relating to selection of employees for redundancy; or

(iii) the selection was unfair for some other reason (such as a failure to consider alternative employment for the employee).

79. **Time off for job finding or the arranging of training**

An employee under notice of dismissal because of redundancy who has worked for the employer continuously for two years or more is entitled to reasonable time off with pay in working hours in order to look for another job or make arrangements for training for future employment. Employees who work, or are normally expected to work, less than 16 hours a week are excluded from this provision.

80. The employer should allow the employee reasonable time off. The employee should be paid the appropriate hourly rate for the period of absence from work. An employer does not have to pay more than once for the same period; any payments made will be offset against either the provisions of the contract of employment or the Employment Protection Acts.

81. **Procedure for handling redundancies**[5]
Part IV of the Employment Protection Act 1975 requires employers to consult appropriate recognised trade unions whenever a redundancy is proposed, and to notify the Secretary of State if it is planned to make ten or more employees redundant at one establishment within a specified period.

82. For the purposes of colleges there are only three categories of person excluded from these provisions: anyone who is not an employee; those employed for a fixed term of 12 weeks or less; and employees covered by collective agreements on redundancies who have been excluded from the provisions by an Order made by the Secretary of State for Employment. The provisions apply regardless of how long an employee has worked for the employer, or for how many hours per week he or she is employed.

83. Employers are required to consult appropriate trade unions[6] about proposed redundancies so that, before individual redundancies are announced, the unions can discuss the plans to see if the effects of the redundancy can be mitigated or numbers reduced. An employer who proposes to dismiss as redundant any employee, and who recognises an independent trade union for the group or category of employees to which the redundant employee belongs, must consult a representative of that union about the dismissal before it occurs. The employer must consult the recognised trade union whether or not the employee is a member. The person consulted should be a union representative authorised by the union to carry on collective bargaining.

84. Where an employee is to be made redundant, the employer should begin consultation with the union concerned at the earliest opportunity. If it is proposed to make ten or more employees redundant within a short period, the employer must begin consultation not later than the specified minimum time before the first dismissal takes effect.[7] The minimum time is:

---

5 cf Section **6.1.**25.
6 EAT decisions have required that for consultation to occur, the union must have a continuing relationship with the employer: see Section **6.1.**25.
7 The original time specifications of the Employment Protection Act 1975 have been amended with effect from 1 October 1979 by The Employment Protection (Handling of Redundancies), Variation Order 1979. S.I. 1979 No. 958, resulting in the consultation time in para 84 (i), above being reduced from 60 to 30 days.

(i) if ten to 99 employees may be dismissed as redundant at one establishment over a period of 30 days or less, at least 30 days; or

(ii) if 100 or more employees may be dismissed as redundant at one establishment over a period of 90 days or less, at least 90 days.

Nonetheless, wherever practicable, consultation should begin as soon as the possibility of redundancy arises. An employer who has already begun consultations on proposed redundancies and later finds it necessary to make more employees redundant does not have to add both groups together to calculate the appropriate period for consultation. The minimum times for consultation with the unions may run concurrently with the individual periods of notice of the employees concerned.

85. In order that consultation should be effective, employers must disclose information to the union(s) in writing. The information to be disclosed is:

(i) the reason for the proposals;

(ii) the numbers and descriptions of employees proposed for redundancy;

(iii) the total number of employees of such description employed at the establishment in question by the employer;

(iv) the proposed method of selection of employees who may be dismissed as redundant; and

(v) the proposed method of carrying out the dismissals, taking account of any agreed procedure, including the period over which the dismissals are to take effect.

The employer must consider the comments, if any, of the union(s), and reply to them, giving reasons if any of them are rejected.

86. Where a union complains that an employer has not fulfilled the consultative obligations, the employer must show that the requirements were fully complied with, or that there were special circumstances which prevented full compliance, and that all possible action which was reasonably practicable was taken to secure compliance.

87. In cases of complaint of an employer's failure to consult, and if no conciliation has been possible, a tribunal will make a declaration if it considers the complaint justified. If the complaint was about failure to consult in time, the declaration will be an indication to the employer to postpone dismissal notices to enable consultation to occur. In appropriate cases, whether or not employees are still employed, the tribunal may safeguard the employee's remuneration by making a protective award. This award requires the employer to pay the employees covered by the award their normal week's pay for a specified period: the protected period. Where offers of new or renewed employment or a trial period for a different type of job are received, but are refused or rejected without good reason (or in the trial period where the employee is fairly dismissed), the right to payment during the protected period is lost.

88. If an employer is proposing to make ten or more employees redundant at one establishment within a relatively short period, then the Secretary of State for Employment must be notified. This provision exists so that the manpower services can take any necessary measures for redeployment or retraining, and

to consider further steps necessary to avoid or minimise the redundancies. The Special Temporary Employment Programme, for example, may be of assistance (see Section **4.**14). The minimum times for notification are the same as for consultation with unions, but there is no obligation to notify the Secretary of State of redundancies of fewer than ten employees (although in borderline cases and where numbers are uncertain, it is advisable to give notification). Notification forms are obtainable from any office of the Department of Employment or the Employment Service Division. The employer must do all that is reasonably practicable to meet fully the requirements for minimum notification periods, and the requirement to disclose in writing to the Department of Employment the proposals for the carrying out of the employer's functions. Non-compliance could result in a fine, or the reduction by up to one-tenth of the amount of any redundancy payment rebate.

89. **Redundancy payments**

There is no need for an employee to submit a formal claim if the employer accepts liability for a redundancy payment and makes a satisfactory payment at or soon after the date of dismissal. If the payment is not satisfactory, or not made, the employee should take up the matter with the employer (where appropriate, through the union representative) and then make a written claim. If neither a written claim to the employer nor a reference to a tribunal is made within six months of the effective date of termination, then the employee is "time-barred" and the employer no longer has a statutory obligation to make payment.

90. The amount of a redundancy payment depends on how long the employee has been continuously employed with the dismissing employer, no matter whether in different jobs. The number of complete years of continuous employment is reckoned backwards from the date of expiry of the statutory notice. Completed years of service up to a maximum of 20 are counted for the making of redundancy payments. The scale of payments is:

(i) for each year of employment at age 41 or over but under 65 (60 for women), one and one half weeks' pay;

(ii) for each year of employment at age 22 or over but under 41, one week's pay;

(iii) for each year of employment at age 18 and over but under 22, half a week's pay.

Reckonable employment, excluding weeks which do not count but which do not break continuity, must be aggregated to make complete years. No payment is due for a fraction of a year. Excess reckonable employment in a higher age bracket will count towards employment in the bracket immediately below. There are circumstances where service can be added to make a complete year. In such an event Service Calendar RPL4 (obtainable from a redundancy payments office of the Department of Employment) should be used to assist calculation. In general, the ready reckoner in Appendix B of the Department's *Redundancy Payments Scheme* booklet will be adequate in the making of calculations. In all cases there is an upper limit (currently £120) on the calculation of a week's pay.

91. Employees aged 60 (female) or 65 (male) at the date of termination of employment are not entitled to redundancy payments. Employees aged over 59 (female) or 64 (male) at the date of termination of employment receive reduced payments: payment is reduced by one-twelfth for each complete month over the relevant ages.

92. An employer can offset pension and lump sum payments made under occupational schemes against redundancy payments, but other payments by the employer (such as payment in lieu of notice) do not affect the amount of redundancy payments due. Employers who operate a more advantageous voluntary redundancy or severance pay scheme are advised to make clear in the scheme's provisions that obligations under the Act will be met and then supplemented to the extent specified in the voluntary scheme. The Secretary of State for Employment has power to make exemption orders whereby employees who are covered by the provision of a scheme agreed with the trade union concerned for payments on termination of employment have no entitlements to payments under the Act.

93. Redundancy payments do not affect entitlement to unemployment benefit. Employees receiving a redundancy payment will not be subjected to taxation on that account alone but where the aggregate of superannuation lump sum, redundancy payment and any other severance pay exceeds £10,000 there may be taxation of a proportion of the sum in excess of that figure (cf Section **11.3.**13).

94. At the time at which a redundancy payment is made, or earlier, an employer is required to give the employee a written statement indicating how the amount of the payment has been calculated. An employer who makes a redundancy payment as required by the Act may claim a rebate from the Redundancy Fund of 41% of the cost. An employer who, although not liable under the Act to make a redundancy payment, contributes to the Redundancy Fund in respect of the employees concerned may claim a payment equivalent to rebate if a payment equivalent to a redundancy payment is made under that employer's own arrangements.

95. **Codes of practice**
The legal status of codes of practice is referred to under Section **11.10.**7. A failure to observe a provision of a code of practice does not of itself render an individual liable to any proceedings, but the code is admissible in evidence and breaches of it will be taken into account. Of the three current ACAS codes dealing with employment, that concerning time off for trade union activities has been referred to already under paragraph 29, above.

96. *Code of Practice 2* refers to information which employers may have a duty to disclose which would be in accordance with good industrial relations practice to disclose.[8] Broadly, the information to be disclosed is that without which a trade union representative would be impeded to a material extent in bargaining. Examples of such information would be: job evaluation systems

8 ACAS, *Disclosure of information to trade unions for collective bargaining purposes,* Code of Practice 2, HMSO.

and grading criteria; total pay bill; details of non-wage labour costs; policies on recruitment; redeployment, redundancy, training, equal opportunity and promotion; appraisal systems; manning standards, planned changes in work methods, materials, equipment or organization; cost structures; and details of financial assistance. It is advised that employers and authorised trade union representatives should agree the means and procedures by which information is to be disclosed. For fuller details it is necessary to refer to the Code.

97. *Code of Practice 1* gives guidance on how to draw up and implement disciplinary roles and procedures.[9] Management, whose responsibility such procedures are, is advised fully to consult the employees in drawing up rules and procedures. Rules should be readily understandable and accessible. Employees should be made aware of the rules, the likely consequences of their breach and also be given a clear indication of the type of conduct which may warrant summary dismissal. Disciplinary procedures ought not to be seen as methods of imposing sanctions, but rather be designed to emphasise and encourage improvements in individual conduct. The code states that disciplinary procedures should:

(i) be in writing and specify to whom they apply;
(ii) provide for matters to be dealt with quickly;
(iii) indicate the disciplinary actions which may be taken;
(iv) specify the various forms of management which have the authority to take the various forms of disciplinary action;
(v) provide for individuals to be informed of the complaints against them and to be given an opportunity to state their case before decisions are reached;
(vi) give individuals the right to be accompanied by a trade union representative or by a fellow employee of their choice;
(vii) ensure that, except for gross misconduct, no employees are dismissed for a first breach of discipline;
(viii) ensure that disciplinary action is not taken until the case has been carefully investigated;
(ix) ensure that individuals are given an explanation for any penalty imposed; and
(x) provide a right of appeal and specify the procedure to be followed.

98. Where the facts of a case appear to call for disciplinary action, other than summary dismissal, the following procedure should be observed:

(i) according to the severity of the offence, oral or written warnings should be given, together with the likely consequences of further offences and advice that such a warning constitutes the first formal stage of the procedure;
(ii) further misconduct might warrant a final written warning which should contain a statement that recurrence would lead to penalisation; and
(iii) if allowed for expressly or by implication in the contract of employment, the final step could be transfer, suspension without pay

---

9 ACAS, *Disciplinary practice and procedures in employment,* Code of Practice 1, HMSO; cf Section **11.9.**34.

or dismissal. Suspension without pay should not normally be for a prolonged period.

99. The employer will need to satisfy the test of reasonableness in all circumstances and, as far as possible, should take into account the employee's record and any other relevant factors. In the case of trade union officials, the code recommends that while they should have normal disciplinary standards applied to them, no disciplinary action beyond an oral warning should be taken until the case has been discussed with a senior union representative or a full-time official. The code recommends that criminal offences outside employment should not be treated as automatic reasons for dismissal, regardless of whether the offence has any relevance to the duties of the individual as an employee. It is advised that the main consideration should be whether the offence is one that makes an individual unsuitable for his or her type of work, or unacceptable to other employees. It is recommended that employees should not be dismissed solely because a charge against them is pending or because they are absent through having been remanded in custody.

100. ACAS observes that grievance procedures are sometimes used for disciplinary appeals but states that it is normally more appropriate to keep the two kinds of procedure separate, since it considers that such issues are generally better resolved within the organization. However, the code advises that the external stages of a grievance procedure may be the machinery appropriate for dealing with appeals against disciplinary action where a final decision within the organization is contested or where it becomes a collective issue between unions and employers.

APPENDIX 1

INDEPENDENT UNIONS: THE CERTIFICATION OFFICER

1. The Certification Officer is responsible under the Employment Protection Act and the Trade Union and Labour Relations Act for:
   (i) maintaining lists of trade unions and employers' associations;
   (ii) determining the independence of trade unions;
   (iii) seeing that trade unions and employers' associations keep accounting records, have their accounts properly audited and submit annual returns;
   (iv) ensuring the periodical examination of members' superannuation schemes;
   (v) securing observance of the statutory procedures for transfers of engagements, amalgamations and changes of name; and
   (vi) supervising the statutory requirements as to the setting up and operation of political funds and dealing with complaints by members about breaches of political fund rules.

2. For trade unions, entry in the lists is an essential preliminary to applying for a certification of independence under the Acts. Listing also entitles unions to tax relief for expenditure on provident benefits. Employers' associations do not have corresponding advantages.

3. The Certification Officer is required to keep a public record of all applications for certificates of independence, and of all decisions reached. In making a decision, the Officer must take into account any relevant information submitted by third parties. Reasons for refusal must be given; the union concerned has the right of appeal to the EAT. A certificate may be withdrawn if the officer is of the opinion that the union in question is no longer independent. Where a question concerning the independence of a particular union arises in proceedings before ACAS, or certain other bodies, statute enables the question to be referred to the Officer for a decision.

4. *The Annual Report of the Certification Officer* gives a full account of the Officer's activities. The address of the Certification Office is: Vincent House Annexe, Hide Place, London SW1P 4NG 01-921 6144.

APPENDIX 2

THE ADVISORY, CONCILIATION AND ARBITRATION SERVICE

ACAS is set up on a statutory basis. It offers industrial relations advice, provides a conciliation service and may arrange for arbitration. It can conduct enquiries into industrial matters and publish its findings. ACAS also publishes codes of practice on industrial relations. If the parties concerned agree, ACAS may refer disputes to the Central Arbitration Committee. ACAS officers receive copies of applications to industrial tribunals. The conciliation officer will try to promote a settlement, if asked to do so by the employee and employer concerned or their representatives, or on his or her own initiative if it is considered that such action has a reasonable prospect of success. Where the parties concerned desire conciliation they should not wait to be contacted by the conciliation officer but themselves contact their regional ACAS office. ACAS regional addresses are:

Northern Region	Westgate House, Westgate Road, Newcastle upon Tyne NE1 1TH 0632-612191
Yorkshire & Humberside Region:	City House, Leeds LS1 4JH 0532-38232
South East Region:	Clifton House, 83 Euston Road, London NW1 2RB 01-388 5100
South West Region:	16 Park Place, Clifton, Bristol BS8 1JP 0272-291071
Midlands Region:	Alpha Tower, Suffolk Street, Queensway, Birmingham B1 1TZ 021-643 9911
North West Region:	Boulton House, Chorlton Street, Manchester M1 3HY 061-228 3222
Wales:	Phase 1, Ty Glas Road, Llanishen, Cardiff CF4 5PH 0222-762636

APPENDIX 3

INDUSTRIAL TRIBUNALS[1]

Industrial Tribunals may consider questions relating to the following major statutes, plus a number of others not referred to below.

Trade Union and Labour Relations Act 1974: Employment Protection (Consolidation) Act 1978.

Right not to be unfairly dismissed (see also *Employment Protection Act 1975).*

Time off with pay for safety representatives (operative from 1 October 1978).

Redundancy Payments Act 1965: Consolidated into the *Employment Protection (Consolidation) Act 1978.*

Right to receive redundancy payment or rebate and questions relating to the amount of such payments.

Equal Pay Act 1970.

Right to receive the same pay or other terms of contract of employment as an employee of the opposite sex working for the same or an associated employer if engaged on like work or work rated as equivalent under job evaluation.

Contracts of Employment Act 1972: Consolidated into the *Employment Protection (Consolidation) Act 1978.*

Right to receive a written statement of terms of employment or any alteration to them with sufficient details to meet the requirements of the Act.

Sex Discrimination Act 1975

Right not to be discriminated against in employment, training and related fields on the grounds of sex or marriage, or victimized for pursuing rights under this Act or the Equal Pay Act 1970.

Employment Protection Act 1975; Employment Protection (Consolidation) Act 1978.

Right to be paid by the Secretary of State certain debts owed by an insolvent employer.

Right to be paid by the Secretary of State occupational pension scheme contributions owing on behalf of employees of insolvent employers.

Right of a recognised independent trade union to be consulted by the employer about proposed redundancies.

Right to receive payment under a protective award made by an industrial tribunal.

Right of an employer to appeal against reduction of redundancy payment rebate for failure to notify proposed redundancies.

Right not to be unfairly dismissed for reasons connected with pregnancy and the right to return to work following absence because of maternity. Right to reeive maternity pay.

Right to receive reasonable time off in the event of redundancy to look for work or make arrangements for training or to receive payment for such time off.

Right to receive guarantee pay from employer during lay-offs.

Right not to be unfairly dismissed on medical grounds relating to health and safety regulations. Right to receive pay on suspension on medical grounds.

Right not to have action other than dismissal taken either because of an employee's trade union membership or activities or because of a refusal to join a trade union on religious grounds.

Right to receive an itemised pay statement.

Right to receive a written statement of reasons for dismissal.

Right not to be unfairly dismissed.

Time off for public duties.

Time off for trade union duties and activities.

Race Relations Act 1976

Right not to be discriminated against in the employment, training and related fields on grounds of colour, race, nationality or ethnic or national origin, or victimized for

1 There is a restriction concerning industrial tribunals and EEC law: see Section **6.1.**17.

pursuing rights under the Act.
Superannuation Act 1972
For example, the Colleges of Education (Compensation) Regulations 1975 give a right to apply to a tribunal if dissatisfied with a decision of a compensating authority.

2. Forms for the making of an application to a tribunal are available from any local employment office, Jobcentre or unemployment benefit office. Advice about tribunals is given in the Department of Employment booklet ITLI, *Industrial Tribunals Procedure.* Communications about proceedings before a tribunal in England and Wales should be made to the Secretary of the Central Office of the Industrial Tribunals: 93 Ebury Bridge Road, London SW1W 8RE 01-730 9161.

3. Appeals against tribunal decisions are allowed normally only on points of law. It is advisable but not obligatory to have the services of a professional representative when applying to a tribunal.

APPENDIX 4

MEDICAL FITNESS OF TEACHERS IN FURTHER EDUCATION[1]

1. There is no requirement in regulations for persons appointed to teaching posts in establishments of further education to satisfy the Secretary of State of their medical fitness for teaching. However, the Secretary of State expects employers to make arrangements for checking the medical fitness of all teachers appointed to teach young persons in further education; and states that it is for employing authorities to satisfy themselves of the medical fitness of such persons before offering them employment. Such an examination should include a chest X-ray, unless there is evidence of a satisfactory X-ray carried out within the preceding 12 months.

2. There is a provision in regulations under which the Secretary of State for Education and Science or the Secretary of State for Wales may require that on medical grounds a teacher shall not be employed in a maintained or grant aided establishment of further education, or that the employment shall be restricted. These are reserve powers, however, and are not intended to remove from the employing authorities the responsibility for taking under their own procedures whatever action may be necessary when teachers become medically unfit. Particularly where there may be risk to students, employing authorities are advised to ensure that a teacher does not continue to perform teaching duties.

3. Where a teacher is either unable to continue duties or has no intention of resuming them until declared fit to do so, suspension will amount to no more than a formality; but in a few cases it may be needed in order to ensure that the teacher does not stay at work or resume duties when his or her presence entails a risk to students or other staff members, or the teacher concerned is unable to give efficient service. Authorities are requested to inform the DES or Welsh Office Education Department whenever suspension or prolonged absence occurs. While it is the responsibility of the employing authority to decide whether a teacher is fit, the DES advises that greater consistency in dealing with cases will be achieved if the Department's Medical Adviser is consulted whenever there is doubt in the matter. The Medical Adviser will also offer advice on the action to be taken in the case of any disorders other than those instanced below.

4. While the medical conditions which may lead to the suspension of a teacher from duty are wide ranging, the most frequently encountered are: pulmonary tuberculosis (including tuberculous pleural effluxion), psychiatric disorder and epilepsy.
   (i) *Pulmonary tuberculosis.* A teacher found to be suffering from active pulmonary tuberculosis should be suspended immediately and not permitted to return until a report from his or her consultant physician indicates that the teacher is fit to resume duties and free from the risk of conveying infection. Continued teaching should be made conditional upon the receipt by the authority of satisfactory medical certificates at six monthly intervals for as long as the teacher's physician considers necessary.
   (ii) *Psychiatric disorder.* Ignoring short breaks, a teacher absent from duty for more than three months because of psychiatric disorder (a term which includes conditions described as nervous illness and depression) should be advised that when he or she feels fit to resume duties that it should be arranged for a consultant psychiatrist, preferably one familiar with the case, or else the family doctor where referral to a psychiatrist has not been considered necessary, to submit a report to the authority indicating whether the teacher is sufficiently fit and recovered to teach young people and be a member of the college community. The teacher should not be permitted to return unless satisfactory evidence of fitness has been provided.

---

1 cf Section **11.7.**7 and **12.4.**4.

(iii) *Epilepsy.* It is usual for there now to be available complete, or almost complete, control of this ailment. However, should a teacher suffer severe or recurrent attacks, the Specialist in Community Medicine (Child Health) should be informed and his or her advice sought on the need for temporary suspension while investigations occur and treatment is established. Where a teacher suffers occasional attacks and his or her condition was known at the time of appointment, suspension should not be necessary. Seizures occurring in a teacher not previously known to be subject to them should be fully investigated. Physical education teachers suffering epileptic attacks however should always be suspended from specialist duties pending further investigation. Before allowing any suspended teacher to return to service, the authority should normally require a report detailing the circumstances of the case, including treatment and prognosis. It will also be necessary to consider the age ranges of the students in the teacher's charge and the circumstances of his or her employment; whether, for example, the teacher is engaged in work involving particular physical risks in instances such as physical education, home economics, laboratory and craft work. When seeking the advice of the DES Medical Officers it will be helpful if the fullest information is made available about the nature, frequency, location and duration of the attacks.

5. A decision to terminate a teacher's employment on medical grounds is one for the employing authority to take unless the Secretary of State has prohibited the teacher's continued employment. It will be sensible to seek the advice of the DES Medical Officers. It would also be advisable to contact the DES to enquire as to its view if the teacher were to apply for an infirmity pension. Teachers whose employment may be terminated on medical grounds should seek also the advice of their relevant professional association.

APPENDIX 5

TEACHERS FROM OVERSEAS

Teachers from overseas, other than those who are EEC nationals, who wish to work in the United Kingdom, need to hold a work permit issued by the Department of Employment, in respect of a specific post with a specific employer, before they can enter the country. Qualified teachers from the Commonwealth are no longer admitted for a limited period in order to seek employment. However, certain persons may be admitted for employment without work permits, provided that they hold a current entry clearance or other satisfactory documentary evidence. Among these categories are: ministers of religion and members of religious orders; Commonwealth citizens seeking teaching posts which are incidental to a holiday in this country, and who do not intend to remain here indefinitely; and teachers and language assistants under exchange schemes approved by the Education Departments or administered by the Central Bureau for Educational Visits and Exchanges or the League for the Exchange of Commonwealth Teachers. (see Section **2.6.**2-10).

APPENDIX 6

RESTRICTION ON EMPLOYMENT OF TEACHERS ON GROUNDS OF MISCONDUCT

Regulation 14 of The Further Education Regulations 1975, Statutory Instruments 1975 No. 1054, provides that:

"A person who is on grounds of misconduct or conviction of a criminal offence determined by the Secretary of State to be unsuitable for employment as a teacher or suitable for employment as such only to a limited extent, shall not be employed as a teacher or, as the case may be, shall be employed as such only to the extent determined by the Secretary of State".

If a teacher is convicted of a criminal offence, the DES may refuse to allow her or him to continue in teaching employment. In making its decision, the Department may require medical reports. The teacher has a right to receive a written statement detailing the reasons for the Department's action. If the teacher is not satisfied with these reasons, there exists a right of appeal. The appeal is before a senior official of the Department and the appellant has the right to be accompanied and represented by a friend.

APPENDIX 7

POSSIBLE CHANGES IN EMPLOYMENT LAW

1. Changes in UK law which are predictable consequences of proposed EEC legislation are indicated in Section **6.1.**29-32. In the autumn of 1979, the Government outlined proposals for the amendment of employment protection legislation. In December 1979 the Government introduced an Employment Bill (intended to become the Employment Act 1980). There are differences between the autumn proposals and the contents of the Bill. This causes two problems. Firstly, although certain proposals are not included in the Bill, because they refer to legislation which can be effected by statutory instruments, they may nevertheless be implemented in some form. Secondly, because a proposal does not appear in the Bill it may still subsequently be included in the passage through Parliament of the Bill in the form of amendments. Of course, amendments to the Bill may also take the form of deletion. Should the proposed or other changes be carried into effect, readers of this book should refer to the new statute, to interpretation of it by the courts, and to comment made in relevant publications.

2. It is made clear below if a proposal does not appear in the Bill, but may be effected by statutory instrument. The proposals contained in the working papers of autumn 1979 gave indications of where codes of practice might be made. The Employment Bill contains a clause allowing the Secretary of State to make codes. Therefore, the text below indicates those areas of the law for which the Secretary of State may make codes, since specific intentions in this respect were contained in the working papers.

3. *Unfair Dismissal*
   Four major changes have been proposed by the Government, three of which appear in the Employment Bill of 1979:
   (i) the onus of proof to be neutral as between employers and employees (contained in working papers only; may be effected by statutory instruments);
   (ii) the period of a fixed term contract in which it is permissible to waive unfair dismissal rights to be reduced from two years to one;
   (iii) tribunals to have the power to reduce (perhaps to nil) the minimum award available in a successful unfair dismissal action (the current minimum is two weeks' pay) if an employee has failed to mitigate his or her loss or if misconduct has come to light beteeen the date of the dismissal and the date of the hearing; and
   (iv) new firms with less than 20 employees will be exempted from unfair dismissal provisions for the first two years of trading (and the tribunal specifically to be required to take into account the circumstances, such as the size and resources of the undertaking, in determining whether an employer has carried out a dismissal reasonably).

4. Comment here, as throughout this Appendix, will be restricted to possible effects on colleges.[1] At present the burden of proof that dismissal was fair rests with the employer who must show that reasonable action was taken in making the dismissal. A neutral burden of proof will place a considerable onus on a tribunal for neither applicant nor respondent presumably will have to demonstrate the absence or presence of fairness. To create precedent binding upon tribunals, there will have to be several cases (and an appeal to a higher court) before this issue is clarified. It must be noted

1 Comment on the proposals as they affect employment legislation overall can be found in Roy Lewis *et al., Industrial Relations Law and the Conservative Government,* Fabian Trade Union Special, NCLC, 1979; LACSAB *Advisory Bulletins;* Incomes Data Services *Brief 166,* October 1979; *Employment Digest* No 56, 9 October 1979; and Keith Scribbins and Ian Waitt, "Changes in Employment Law" *NATFHE Journal,* Vol 4. No.9, 1979 and Vol.5 No. 1, 1980.

that this provision is not in the Bill, but may be effected by statutory instrument. The increase already made in 1979 in the qualifying period to 52 weeks is likely to have a serious effect on the previous ability of some part-time staff, and other staff on fixed term contracts, to appeal against unfair dismissal. Further, the reduction proposed by the Employment Bill of the period from two years to one in respect of a fixed term contract in which it is permissible to waive dismissal rights has to be considered with the now operative amendment to the law which has increased the qualifying period for an unfair dismissal complaint to one year. Staff engaged on one-year temporary contracts will find that they have no protection against unfair dismissal (even if the initial contract is renewed for a further year) should they have waived their rights at the time in relation to these contracts. The Bill's proposal concerning the reduction of the minimum award for unfair dismissal in certain circumstances raises a startling proposition: failure subsequently to mitigate loss or the revelation of previously unknown misconduct implies that dismissals might be made yet subsequently be justified by knowledge which was not available at the time of dismissal. A curious route to dismissal is here being offered to employers; it can only be said that it should be approached with extreme caution – if at all – for legal processes stemming from its implementation may well be both lengthy and expensive.

5. *Industrial tribunal procedure*
Three changes are proposed, but they do *not* appear in the Employment Bill of 1979. However, they may be effected by statutory instruments (and in March 1980 the Government indicated that the changes were to be effected by statutory instruments). The working paper proposals are:
(i) tribunals to be allowed to conduct proceedings in whatever manner they consider most suitable;
(ii) tribunals to be able to advise either party that the case is weak, and that costs may accordingly be awarded against them; and
(iii) that costs may be awarded against a party who brings or conducts a case unreasonably.
At present costs in tribunal hearings are awarded only if either party acts in a frivolous or vexatious way. The proposals would seem to have the object of reducing tribunal applications. As will be appreciated, recourse to law is only advisable where all other approaches have failed; in this instance, more legal activity can be anticipated if the proposals become regulations – if only in order to determine what "unreasonably" means.

6. *Maternity*
Some of the proposals in working papers are known to have been abandoned. One proposal not contained in the Bill in an obvious sense related to the Government's wish to simplify the maternity pay system. The items outlined below, however, are all contained in the Employment Bill.

7. The Bill proposes changes in the reinstatement provisions, and a greater flexibility allowed to the employer concerning the post which can be offered to the woman on her return to work. On reinstatement, the proposal is to increase the period of seven days' notice of the intention to return to work, to 21 days. After 49 days after the expected week of confinement, or the date of confinement, where the employer requests *in writing* that *written* confirmation should be given to him that she still intends to return, she must reply within 14 days or, if not reasonably practicable, as soon as is reasonably practicable. If she does not do this, she loses the right to return. For the right to maternity pay, notice must be given in writing *only* if the employer wishes; for the right to return, written notice is obligatory.

8. Proposals concerning the greater flexibility which can be exercised by the employer concerning the woman's resumption of her employment as set forward in the Employment Bill may be summarised thus: they allow employers to be able to offer a

suitable and appropriate alternative post, on terms and conditions not substantially less favourable, even if there is no question of redundancy, if it is not "reasonably practicable" to offer the post occupied before maternity. An appeal to a tribunal will be available in the case of a dispute. Current law provides for reinstatement in the original post, and the offer of suitable alternative and appropriate employment only in the case of redundancy. The term "reasonably practicable" is not defined in the proposals but its interpretation could well be one involving a balance of cost, such as arises elsewhere in law (cf Section **11.10.**13).

9. *Gurantee pay*
The Bill proposes to reduce the guarantee pay rights by providing that no more than five days' guarantee pay will be payable by an employer over any period of three consecutive months.

10. *Picketing*
The law currently allows persons in contemplation or furtherance of a trade dispute to attend at or near a place where another person works or carries on business, or any other place where another person happens to be (except the place of residence), for the purpose only of peacefully obtaining or communicating information, or peacefully persuading any person to work or abstain from working. The Government proposes in the Employment Bill to restrict this provision. Pickets are to be those who are party only to the trade dispute which occasions the picketing, and to the picketing which they carry out at their own place of work. It is further proposed that where the new provisions are contravened, it will be possible for an employer to take legal action if it was considered that his or her enterprise was being damaged; and that the employer would have legal recourse for actions involving breaches of contract (other than contracts of employment). A code of practice concerning picketing was proposed in the working papers.

11. These proposals return to the legal concept of "in restraint of trade" which can be followed from the medievals guilds to the Taff Vale case of 1906 and beyond. What is of immediate importance for education is how, if the proposals become law, the employer's business and breach of contract are defined. If the limitation of contract protection is strictly to the contract of employment, it may be possible for pickets to be proceeded against, for example, for preventing the operations of a particular college.

12. *Closed shop and dismissals*
The law currently provides that the dismissal of an employee for not being a member of a union, in compliance with a union membership agreement, is fair unless the employee genuinely objects on grounds of religious belief to being a member of any union. Union members may be expelled from their unions only in accordance with the union's rules and under the principles of natural justice (see Section **12.6.**25).

13. The Employment Bill proposes to extend the protection against dismissal for non-membership of a union in a closed shop to the following categories of employee: those in the employment of the employer before the closed shop agreement was made (provided they have not subsequently joined the union) and those who object to membership of the union on the grounds of religion, conscience, or other deeply held personal convictions. Where a closed shop agreement is irregular, or, where regular and the employee had not joined the union after the agreement, the Bill proposes that it shall be unfair to dismiss the employee in either of those circumstances for failure to join the union. Closed shop agreements are proposed only to be approved (i.e. regular) where an overwhelming majority (80%) of the employees involved vote in favour by ballot which, so far as is reasonably practicable, is secret. The Bill proposes legal recourse (including an award of compensation against the union) for an employee arbitrarily excluded or expelled from a union where a closed shop agreement is in

operation (cf Section **12.6.**25). In addition, if in response to an unfair dismissal claim the employer claims that he or she was induced to dismiss the employee by pressure which a trade union or other person exercised on him by calling, organizing, procuring, or financing a strike or other industrial action, or by threatening to do so, and that this pressure was exercised because the employee was not a member of any trade union, or the particular trade union, the employer may require the person[2] involved to be joined as a party to the proceedings. Where this occurs and the tribunal finds the claim of the employer to be well founded, it may order the person concerned to pay a contribution to the employer in respect of any compensation awarded to the dismissed employee. The working papers proposed a code of practice concerning picketing.

14. *Union ballots*
It is proposed in the Bill that unions should carry out ballots, to be secret so far as is reasonably practicable, in: elections to full-time trade union officer posts and to the executive or other governing body of an independent trade union; and the calling or ending of strikes. The Bill refers to a scheme to be operated by the Certification Officer (see Appendix 1, above) for some reimbursement of expenditure incurred. The autumn 1979 working papers referred to expenditure as being reasonable postal costs and, possibly, certain administrative costs.

15. *Schedule 11 of the Employment Protection Act 1975*
This provision, for the purposes here of education, currently allows remedy where an employer is not observing the relevant general level of recognised terms and conditions of employment. The Employment Bill proposes the repeal of the schedule. The consequencies of such an event are possibly far reaching. It may be that opposition to this measure is such that an amendment is made on the basis of the working paper proposals. These proposals offered the choices of: repeal; the repeal of the "general level" provision; and amendment to allow, *inter alia*, the CAC to take into account the effect of awards on employers' pay structures. It must be said, however, that at the time of writing repeal appeared the most likely course.

16. *Trade union recognition*
The Employment Bill proposes the repeal of the statutory procedures regarding trade union recognition. The Bill does not state how recognition issues are to be settled but the autumn 1979 working papers suggested that this be done in a voluntary manner (with the assistance of ACAS presumably being available). Recognition here means the recognition of a union by an employer, or associated employers, for the purpose of collective bargaining.

17. *Union recruitment*
The Bill proposes to afford statutory protection against coercive union recruitment activities.

Appendix 7

Reference

Because this appendix is of necessity of a speculative nature, a reference list for its particular purpose is given below. The reference list for the sub-section follows separately.

Employment Bill, HMSO, December 1979.

Working Papers on Proposed Amendment to the Employment Protection Legislation, Department of Employment, September 1979.

Working Paper for Consultations on Proposed Industrial Relations Legislation, Department of Employment, October 1979.

---

2 Persons in law may be natural or legal (i.e. corporate bodies).

11.6

Chris Curson, "Changes ahead in the employment laws", *Education*, 16 November 1979.

Employment Digest, Nos 55 and 56, 25 September/9 October 1979.

Alun Gronow, "How LEAs should deal with the coming militancy", *Education*, 28 September 1979.

Incomes Data Services, *Brief 166*, October 1979.

Roy Lewis *et al.*, *Industrial Relations Law and the Conservative Government*, Fabian Trade Union Special, NCLC, 1979.

Keith Scribbins and Ian Waitt, "Changes in Employment Law", *NATFHE Journal*, Vol. 4. No.9, 1979 and Vol.5. No.1, 1980.

REFERENCE

Disabled Persons (Employment) Act, 1944, Chapter 10, HMSO.
Equal Pay Act 1970, Chapter 41, HMSO.
Employment Protection Act 1975, Chapter 71, HMSO.
Employment Protection (Consolidation) Act 1978, Chapter 44, HMSO.
Race Relations Act 1976, Chapter 74, HMSO.
Redundancy Payments Act 1965, Chapter 62, HMSO.
Rehabilitation of Offenders Act 1974, Chapter 53, HMSO.
Sex Discrimination Act 1975, Chapter 65, HMSO.
Trade Union and Labour Relations Act 1974, Chapter 52, HMSO.
The Employment Protection (Handling of Redundancies) Variation Order 1979, Statutory Instruments, 1979, No. 958, HMSO.
The Unfair Dismissal (Variation of Qualifying Period) Order 1979, Statutory Instruments 1979, No. 959, HMSO.

ACAS, *Disciplinary Practice and Procedures in Employment*, Code of Practice 1, HMSO.
ACAS, *Disclosure of Information to Trade Unions for Collective Bargaining Purposes*, Code of Practice 2, HMSO.
ACAS, *Time Off for Trade Union Duties and Activities*, Code of Practice 3, HMSO.
Immigration Act 1971, DES Administrative Memorandum 4/73; Welsh Office Administrative Memorandum 4/73, 6 March 1973.
Medical Fitness of Teachers and of Entrants to Teacher Training, DES Circular 11/78; Welsh Office Circular 111/78, 18 August 1978.

A comprehensive range of leaflets and booklets on employment law is published by the Department of Employment and available from any of its offices. The most useful of these are guides to: *Contracts of Employment Act 1972; Dismissal – Employees' Rights; The Redundancy Payments Scheme.*
Guides to legislation on discrimination on the grounds of sex or race are available from Citizens Advice Bureaux and from the relevant commission:

Equal Opportunities Commission
Overseas House,
Quay Street,
Manchester M3 3HN
061-833 9244

Commission for Racial Equality
Elliot House,
10-12 Allington Street,
London SW1E 5EH.
01-828 7022

7 CONDITIONS OF SERVICE: AGREEMENTS AFFECTING TEACHING STAFF

1. It is one of the remarkable features of education that teachers' pay and other conditions of service are determined separately. As explained above, salaries are established under statute. Conditions of service are determined by negotiation and have no statutory basis, except for the possibility of their enforcement under Schedule 11 of the Employment Protection Act. This provides that a report may be made to the Advisory Conciliation and Arbitration Service and in turn to the Central Arbitration Committee of claims that the employer is not observing the relevant recognised terms and conditions of employment. (See Section **11.6.**17 and Appendix 7).

2. Until 1974 representatives of local authorities' and teachers' organizations drew up model recommendations for the consideration of individual authorities. There is no regional machinery for the joint enforcement of the terms of any of the documents embodying these recommendations or of documents agreed subsequently. Following the reorganization of local government in 1974, the Council of Local Education Authorities (CLEA) was formed by the Association of County Councils and the Association of Metropolitan Authorities as a convenient forum between the two Associations to deal with educational matters of common interest. Both Associations have their own education committees which deal with a considerable range of business; there are often differences of emphasis between the two Associations. CLEA has negotiated matters affecting conditions of service with the representatives of teacher organizations represented on the Burnham FE Committee. Where the title of an agreement is headed, for example, "recommendations", this should not be taken to mean that it can be lightly disregarded. The recommendations amount to a national collective agreement and can be enforced as indicated in paragraph 1, above. The arrangements for negotiating teachers' conditions of service have been formalised by the formation of a joint negotiating body between the local authority associations and the recognised further education teachers' unions: the National Joint Council for Further Education Teachers in England and Wales.

3. The law relating to conditions of service has been referred to in Section **11.6.**17 above. However, neither of the parties responsible for the framing of national conditions of service agreements think it desirable for such agreements to be statutory, or for there to be a position created which necessitates frequent recourse to legal action, or one which creates the need to draft provisions in a legalistic sense. The negotiators believe that readily understood collective agreements are the most effective and acceptable way of establishing national conditions of service. Recourse to law remains possible, subject to legal advice, where agreements are being disregarded without good reason. Proposals concerning the establishment of an efficient machinery for the settling of local disputes have been made. These should be seen in the context of the wish of both the local authority associations and the teachers' unions to secure the repeal of the Remuneration of Teachers

Act and establish a more convenient means of collective bargaining. This would allow salaries, staffing establishment, gradings and conditions of service for both full- and part-time teachers to be negotiated together and incorporated within one document. Until such a time, however, the present system obtains. The agreements referred to below all have the force of national collective agreements, having been made by the local authorities' organizations and the teachers' organizations. They refer to colleges of further and higher education within the meaning of s.41 of the Education Act, 1944, and The Further Education Regulations 1975. The agreements summarised below are agreements for teaching staff. These agreements have been made over a long period of time, many of them dating back to before the formation of CLEA. Some of them, for example, the sick pay arrangements, apply to schools as well as colleges and polytechnics; others, for example, the 1975 conditions of service agreement, apply only to colleges and polytechnics. Whilst one or two of the agreements have been revised recently, such as the redundancy procedure agreement, most of them remain in their original form. This means that a number of the agreements are in need of revision to take into account changes in employment law which have occurred since their promulgation. Also, changes in the organization of further and higher education have necessitated further revision. For these reasons, and also to facilitate ease of reference, the local authority associations and the recognised further education teachers' unions have agreed to codify the various agreements and to bring them together in one document. The codified conditions of service agreements relating to further education teachers should be published in 1980 and will provide, for the first time, a comprehensive statement of the relevant conditions. Those responsible for college administration will no doubt find it necessary to refer regularly to the codified document. The details of agreements summarised below are not intended as a substitute for reference to the agreements either in their present form or in the forthcoming codified version. The agreements summarised below are not dealt with chronologically. Those agreements dealing with the rights and conditions of individuals are dealt with first: the agreements dealing with collective rights follow.

4. In 1973 an agreement was made covering what might best be called conditions of tenure, since its major part sets out the rights of a teacher under contract and a teacher's rights in the event of dismissal. However this agreement deals with a number of other items as well, including topics like insurance against loss or damage to personal property. The main features of the agreement are as follows:
   (i) The teacher's conditions of tenure should indicate that the employment is subject to the provisions of: the Burnham FE Report, the Teachers' Superannuation Scheme, the general regulations of the LEA and the instrument and articles of government of the college.
   (ii) The year should be regarded as comprising three terms: the spring term (1 January to 30 April), the summer term (1 May to 31 August) and the Autumn term (1 September to 31 December). Salary, payable monthly, should be paid from the originating dates of terms as set out above or from the actual date of the start of term, if this is earlier, unless the teacher starts working during term time in which case the

salary should originate from the first day of work. When an appointment is coming to an end, salary should be paid up to the last day of the notional terms set out above or where a teacher is taking up a new appointment in an establishment in another authority and the summer or autumn terms start earlier than 30 April or 1 September, respectively, the final salary from the old authority should date to the day preceding the date of commencement of work with the new authority. The same arrangement applies if the teacher is leaving teaching. His or her salary should be paid up to 30 April, 31 August or 31 December, as appropriate, or to the day preceding the date of commencement of the new appointment, whichever is the earlier.

(iii) The agreement also defines a week for the computation of sessions as running from Monday to Friday and as being composed of morning, afternoon and evening sessions. A teacher should not be required to undertake more than 10 sessions (of which not more than two should be evening sessions) in any week.

(iv) The agreement makes provision for notice of termination of the employment. Where the LEA is giving notice, written reasons must be supplied. The period of notice applicable to either side is two months in the spring and autumn terms and three months in the summer terms, except in the case of principals, vice-principals and heads of department for and by whom the notice is three months in the autumn and spring, and four months in the summer terms. In all cases the terminal date must be the end of term dates as defined in sub-paragraph (ii) above.

(v) The main part of the agreement is the provision made concerning appeal by a teacher against termination of her or his employment by the LEA. The teacher has the right to appear, assisted by a friend, before the appropriate committee of the LEA or governing body if he or she feels dismissal is unreasonable or unjustified. It is also provided that in circumstances where consideration is being given to dismissing the teacher for misconduct or any other urgent cause, the matter should be referred to the appropriate body not less than ten days after the teacher has been notified of the fact that dismissal is being considered, and of the charge, complaint or adverse report against him or her. Again, he or she has the right to appear before the appropriate body with a friend. Where the appropriate body recommends dismissal to the LEA, there shall be a further right of hearing to appeal against the recommendation. Alongside these provisions the governing body, CEO and sometimes the principal, have powers to suspend the teacher from office (with pay unless the LEA expressly decides there is a compelling reason to the contrary).

5. The 1973 agreement has some minor but significant *ad hoc* features as well. Some of these are set out below.

(i) The teacher cannot be required to perform duties except those connected with the work of the establishment, or to abstain from any occupation unless the governing body decides it would interfere with his or her teaching duties.

(ii) The principal should be supplied with a copy of representations made to the LEA by the teacher concerning her or his employment.

(iii) The agreement envisages that a teacher will retire at the end of the term in which she or he reaches 65. However the teacher and the LEA can mutually agree to extend the retirement date. This is, of course, without prejudice to a teacher's right to leave teaching on pension before 65 under the various provisions of the teachers' superannuation scheme on this matter (See Sections **11.3.**15 and **11.4**).

(iv) Where the teacher is taking up a first appointment, the first year can be regarded as probationary. However, the dismissal procedure set out above (paragraph 4(v)) should apply if the LEA terminates the appointment at the end of the probationary year.

(v) Finally, the agreement proposes that LEAs should make provision for indemnification against risk of assault (on the same basis as recommended by the NJC for Local Authorities Administrative Staff) and against loss of, or damage to, personal property.

6. The most far reaching agreement made for teachers in further and higher education was the one made in 1975 concerning their day-to-day *conditions of service*. This agreement does not seek to indicate, as has often been wrongly assumed, what constitutes the maximum professional workload for a teacher, or less still what a teacher must do. The agreement lays down what can be reasonably required of the teacher. The agreement is unique in education and has been the subject of a good deal of misinterpretation both by those who would disparage it (it was called a "Skiver's charter" in the *Daily Mail*) and by those who would wish to see it as a straight jacket on the working arrangements of college staff. In fact, the corner stone of the agreement is intended to be reasonableness and flexibility. Given the multi-sessional and extended year character of further education, the agreement seeks to ensure that further education teachers should have reasonably comparable conditions to those applying to teachers in other parts of the education service where these features do not exist. The main provisions of the agreement are as follows:

(i) The agreement sets out the length and distribution of the teacher's year as being, at maximum, 38 weeks of which not more than 36 shall be teaching weeks. There should be no continuous period exceeding 14 weeks for which the teacher is required to teach, and between the beginning of June and the end of September arrangements should be made for at least six, and preferably seven weeks' continuous holiday for the teacher. Holiday schedules should be made available by the end of October at the latest. It will be noticed that these provisions relate to individual teachers and not to the college year. Subject to the closure of all classes for at least seven consecutive days at Christmas and Easter, the college, if appropriately staffed, could operate throughout the year. Union representatives are entitled to have access to detailed information about timetables to enable them to check that the provisions of the agreement are being observed.

(ii) The next section of the agreement deals with teaching load. This is limited in two ways. Firstly, no teacher can be required to attend for more than ten sessions in a week (see paragraph 4 (iii) above); a session should not normally exceed three hours, and never exceed four hours. Hence a teacher's duty period is 10 x 3 hours, giving 30 hours per week. No evening session should last more than three hours for a teacher; and an evening session is defined as one lasting at least half an hour after 5.30pm. Secondly, the maximum class contact hours to be taught by teachers is laid down according to the grade of lectureship held. The national agreement indicates bands for these maxima and local authorities and local negotiating committees of the recognised teacher unions are expected, and (in nearly all cases) have negotiated the maxima to apply in their area. The national bands are

Lecturer I	20-22 hours
Lecturer II	17-20 hours
Senior Lecturer	15-18 hours
Principal Lecturer	13-16 hours

(iii) The agreement defines class contact hours as time spent in actual teaching, invigilating and supervising examinations and tests, and tutorial and supervision work with individual students or groups. Clearly the work of a teacher encompasses a great deal more than this class contact time and hence the agreement conceives that certain duties should attract class contact remission to assist the teacher and the college. The agreement gives examples of these duties ranging from approved research projects to liaison with students' unions. But these are only examples. The agreement envisages that, again, local negotiations will determine an appropriate scheme of remission related to the duties relevant in the case of particular institutions. Most LEAs have met this provision by agreeing a percentage of the college's class contact total hours as hours available for remission. The actual decisions as to which teachers get remission has then to be made in the colleges following consultation with the recognised further education teachers' unions. In a time of restricted expenditure LEAs have not been free to award large percentages for remission hours. Nevertheless the amount and distribution of remission hours is a matter which is very important for those involved in the administration of colleges.

(iv) The agreement goes on to deal with those circumstances in which a teacher may be entitled to receive extra payment. As is well known, extra payments in further education are governed by the hourly rates of pay negotiated for part-time teaching staff. The agreement makes it quite clear that systematic additional teaching duties should not exist. Clearly college administrations should seek to avoid a situation in which full-time teachers regularly do "overtime" hours. However, the agreement envisages that in circumstances like a late decision to mount a course or the temporary shortage of staff, it may be necessary for a full-time member of staff to fill the breach and teach hours outside of the normal working arrangements for full-time staff. Where this occurs a separate contract should be issued as would be issued to a part-time member of staff. Greater difficulty comes where short term situations (such as those caused by the absence of a member of staff) occur. Generally, where the additional teaching is in an evening session, or outside the teacher's ten sessions, or inside the ten sessions, but above his or her class contact maximum, extra payment should be made at the appropriate part-time hourly rate. However, there are certain exceptions to this general provision. Firstly, no entitlement to additional pay exists where the teacher substitutes for a member of staff who is absent for three consecutive working days or less or in the event of a sudden and/or short term emergency. However, where the absence stretches past three working days, payment should be made for the whole of the period in question. Secondly, it is possible for the teacher to agree to receive paid leave of absence instead of additional payments for periods of additional teaching duties.

(v) When the agreement was made it was known that working arrangements varied even between colleges in the same LEA. Hence a safeguarding clause was agreed. This takes two forms. Firstly, where existing conditions are better than those laid down in the agreement, or local versions of it, the better conditions should apply to serving teachers in their existing posts. Secondly, only in respect of contact hours and the teacher's year provisions, where the agreement would worsen the arrangements in a college, the existing arrangements in the college should be retained. An example may make this clear. If a college had a 35 week teaching year, then that teaching year should be retained for existing and new staff. Where a college had an arrangement to pay all staff who substituted for absent teachers immediately (without the three day "waiting" period referred to in paragraph 6(iv) above), then those staff in post in that college at the time of making the new agreement should be protected on the better existing arrangement for as long as they hold their posts.

7. The Teachers' Sick Pay Regulations,[1] common to schools and colleges, are of an earlier vintage than the conditions of tenure and Conditions of Service Agreement. The provisions are complex and will, hopefully, be simplified in the codification exercise. However, the main provisions can be summarised as follows.

(i) The amount of sick leave entitlement depends on length of service. During the first year of service the entitlement is full pay for 25 working days and (after four months' service) half pay for 50 working days. In the second and third years, the entitlements are full pay for 50 and 75 working days respectively plus half pay for the same respective periods. In the fourth and successive years, full pay lasts for 100 days and half pay for a further hundred. However, if the sick leave results from an accident occurring in the course of performing college duties, the teacher is entitled to six months' full pay and, at the discretion of the LEA, six months' half pay. In addition there are variations in these periods where absence arises from pulmonary tuberculosis or where absence occurs because the teacher resides in a house in which some other person is suffering from an infectious disease.

(ii) The sick leave year runs from 1 April to 31 March. A teacher on sick leave on 31 March is not entitled to a fresh allowance until she or he has resumed teaching duty.

---

1 cf Section **11.6**, Appendix 4.

(iii) There is a general principle that no one should benefit from sick leave to an extent greater than the benefit of full salary. Hence sickness benefit receivable under the National Insurance Acts is deductible during the period of full sick pay. The precise meaning of "receivable" in this connection is not clear and it is hoped that the codification exercise will result in greater clarity. However, it is clearly intended that where a teacher fails to claim national insurance benefit there shall nevertheless be a deduction made from the sick leave pay.

(iv) A married woman teacher who pays the reduced national insurance contribution will nevertheless find the deductions made from full pay to correspond to the sickness benefit she would have received had she paid the full national insurance contribution.

(v) A teacher who is absent for more than three college days owing to illness is required to submit a medical certificate to the LEA and can be required to submit certificates at the end of each month of duty and on return to duty. If entry to hospital is necessary, medical certificates submitted on entry and discharge stand as substitutes for periodic certificates.

(vi) In circumstances in which damages are recoverable from a third party in respect of an injury occasioning sick leave, the LEA can claim back some of the allowances paid. Also, allowances are not paid, unless the LEA resolves otherwise, where the accident occurs due to active participation in sport as a profession.

8. The Maternity Leave Scheme for women teachers has recently been revised to take account of the maternity provisions of the Employment Protection (Consolidation) Act 1978 (see Sections **11.6.**30 and **11.9.**22). The new scheme provides the following main arrangements.

(i) The basic provisions apply to women teachers who have one year's full-time service with one or more LEAs, or equivalent part-time service. In addition, teachers with two years' or more continuous service have additional rights as set out in paragraph (viii) below.

(ii) The teacher must notify the LEA of her intention to take leave as soon as practicable and, unless she can show good cause, not less than 14 weeks before the expected confinement date. If she wishes to return to work in the job in which she is employed she should, at the same time, so inform the employer.

(iii) The teacher may absent herself from work at the beginning of the 11th week before expected confinement, or at a later date unless certified unfit to work.

(iv) She may remain absent for 18 weeks from the commencement of the leave. (In the case of still birth this period is limited to up to six weeks after the week of confinement).

(v) She is entitled to maternity pay as follows:

(a) 100% pay for the first four weeks;

(b) 90% pay for the next two weeks;

(c) 50% pay for the remainder of the 18 weeks.

In (a) and (b) maternity allowance, at the full national insurance rate, is deducted in all cases; and in (a), earnings related and dependants' additions to the allowance are deductible, except to the extent that the net payment would be less than that payable in (b). In (c) it is not deducted unless, when added to the half pay, the sum exceeds full pay, in which case the excess is deducted.

(vi) These payments are made on the condition that the teacher returns to work for at least 13 weeks full-time (or the equivalent, if agreed with the LEA, part-time). If this condition is not met, the LEA may reclaim the payment made, except that in the case of teachers with two years' continuous service the first six weeks' pay may not be reclaimed. This 13 week period runs from the date on which the teacher returns to duty, or the date during any college holiday on which she is deemed available for duty.

(vii) Absence due to illness attributable to the pregnancy occurring outside the period of leave is treated as ordinary absence on sick leave, provided it is covered by a doctor's statement.

(viii) The ways in which these provisions are varied for a teacher with two years' continuous employment with one or more LEA by the eleventh week before expected confinement, are as follows:

- (a) she may remain absent for up to 29 weeks beginning with the week of confinement;
- (b) the employer may postpone the date of return by up to four weeks after her notified date of return provided written notice giving reasons for the postponement is given to the teacher.

(ix) The employer may at discretion extend to adoptive parents the relevant post natal sections of the maternity leave provisions.

9. Following the requirements of the law, the LEAs and recognised further education teachers' unions drew up, in 1973, model procedures relating to individual grievances and disputes. As will be seen the procedure needs modifying slightly to apply to heads of department, vice-principals and principals. However it will not be uncommon for staff in these positions to find themselves nominated as the aggrieving party in particular cases. The procedure has informal and formal stages and the main provisions of the agreement are as follows.

(i) The informal procedure is intended to solve the problem and in it the teacher is encouraged to approach the other member of staff involved and, if the matter remains unresolved, his or her head of department. At this stage she or he can be accompanied by a friend, and similarly at all other subsequent stages, and the interview with the head of department should take place within five working days of the request for it. Finally, in the informal procedure, an interview can be held with the principal and this should be arranged within ten working days of its request.

(ii) The formal procedure has two stages. Firstly, the aggrieved party should submit a written notice of the grievance to the chairman of the governing body. The aggrieving party and the principal should receive a copy of that notice. Unless the principal is the aggrieving party, he should report to the governors in writing. Within five and ten working days of the submission of this report a hearing should be held to which both parties should be invited. Secondly, there should be a right of appeal against the findings of the body hearing the grievance for either of the parties involved. The constitution of the appeal committee should be agreed between the LEA and the recognised further education teachers' unions. Documents should be submitted within ten working days of the notice of appeal and the appeal heard not more than twenty-one working days after receipt of the notice.

10. In 1975 a revised redundancy procedure agreement was made. This is an agreement unique to further and higher education and governs the procedures to be adopted in an instance of expected redundancy. The point of the agreement is to seek to avoid redundancy. This agreement should be read alongside certain other provisions. Firstly, there is a more recent "statement of intent" concerning redundancies in teacher education establishments. Secondly, there is an agreed procedure concerning the use of the premature retirement compensation arrangements of the teachers' superannuation scheme (see Section **11.4**). Thirdly, the redundancy procedures agreement must be studied alongside the procedures laid down in the Employment Protection (Consolidation) Act 1978 for handling redundancies. The main provisions made in the agreement are summarised below.
   (i) The scope of the procedure is limited. It is intended to cover redundancies which arise in further education due to year by year contraction and changes in work patterns. It is not intended to cover the large scale redundancies caused in recent years by the reorganization of teacher education, though many LEAs and colleges have found it valuable to apply the procedure to such redundancies. In essence such redundancies should be the subject of separate local agreements.
   (ii) The procedure envisages the earliest possible discussion with the recognised further education teachers' unions where redundancies are thought likely to arise. Every effort should be made to find alternative employment and this should include consultation with neighbouring authorities.
   (iii) Notice of at least one year should be given to the teacher(s) concerned and a right of hearing against the redundancy should be afforded to the individual(s).
   (iv) Secondment to facilitate retraining should be given to the redundant teacher(s). This period may overlap or run consecutively with the notice period.

11. The agreements reviewed so far deal with the individual rights of full-time teachers in respect of tenure, conditions of service, sick leave and pay, maternity leave and pay, grievances and redundancy. For a very important group of further education staff – those paid on part-time hourly rates – no such agreements exist. However there is an agreed arrangement, known as the Associate Lecturer agreement, which governs the circumstances in which part-time staff can be treated in similar ways to full-time staff in the areas so far reviewed. It may be the case that claims currently being made by the recognised further education unions will lead to agreement about the terms of employment of hourly paid staff but at the moment only the following, Associate Lecturer provisions, apply where relevant to some part-time staff.

(i) The Associate Lecturer agreement is one which enables LEAs to employ part-time staff, as it should choose, on terms which are proportional to those applying to full-time staff. These appointments count against the full-time establishment of the college.

(ii) The appointments entail that the staff concerned should play a full part in college life. Hence, the appointments should be expressed as a proportion of 30 hours and the pay and other entitlements should be calculated on this basis. For example, a half-time Associate Lecturer I contract would involve college attendance for 15 hours over five sessions and a class contact commitment of half that applicable to a full-time Lecturer Grade I.

(iii) The contract should state the salary and class contact time and indicate that proportional benefits to sick pay, superannuation and other conditions of service for full-time staff exist.

12. We now turn to look at the two further education teachers' agreements which are more collective in character. These are the *Arrangements for Consultation and Negotiation: The Collective Disputes Procedure* and the *Agreement on Facilities for Representatives of the Recognised Teachers' Organisations.*

13. The Arrangements for Consultation and Negotiation document begins with a recital of the purposes of the agreement and points LEAs and local negotiating committees of the recognised further education teachers' unions in the following direction. Existing arrangements where they are satisfactory should not be disturbed, and where it is customary for matters raised first to be examined by LEA Officers, this practice should continue. The procedure should allow negotiations to occur by way of meetings arranged within agreed time limits when either party considers it necessary. The procedure should define as far as possible the scope of items appropriate for negotiation. The agreement goes on to deal with collective disputes and the recommended procedure for resolving them. The following form the main parts of this procedure.

(i) Disputes at establishment level should be resolved if possible by discussion between the principal and union representative and, if necessary, by discussion with representatives of the governing body. If delays occur, exacerbating the problem, that matter can be raised by either side with the LEA.

(ii) Where a dispute involves more than one establishment, recourse should be made to discussion between the recognised further education teachers' unions and the CEO or his or her nominee. There should be an agreed time period for these discussions followed by an opportunity for the matter to be discussed between union representatives and the LEA. There should also be a limit on the period allowed to elapse between the termination of discussions at officer level and their commencement at LEA level.

(iii) There are two stages for conciliation if the problem is not resolved at LEA level. Firstly, if both sides agree, reference can be made to the national representatives of the LEA and the recognised further education teachers' unions. Secondly, if this fails, each side locally should consider reference to ACAS.

(iv) A clause exists allowing agreed variation in the procedure in a particular case and it is indicated that where a dispute arises out of an attempt to change existing circumstances, the *status quo* should prevail until procedures have been exhausted.

14. The agreement on facilities for union representatives is more elaborate. Representatives are categorised as national, regional, local authority and college representatives; and it is recognised that the limits of appropriate leave and/or remission from college duties will need to be negotiated locally for each category of representative, and be related to the numbers of members employed in the LEA's area and serviced by the representatives. The level of the actual demand on the representative should be that upon which leave and/or remission is granted. Authorities are also encouraged to give support to representatives wishing to attend trade union education courses. The main articles of the agreement are as follows:

(i) The unions have responsibility for notifying the LEA of the names of their accredited representatives at the different levels.

(ii) The primary functions of representatives are dealing with matters of grievance and dispute, executing responsibilities to their unions, executing responsibilities in connection with the interests of their members in colleges, and, attending courses.

(iii) Reference is made to the need for representatives to attend meetings and to convene meetings of newly appointed teachers.

(iv) The LEA should provide lists of newly appointed teachers and annually a list of all teachers employed. Arrangements should also be made for accommodation for meetings, use of the LEA distribution system and for the deduction of union subscriptions from salary.

(v) Also, the following amenities should be offered to college representatives. There should be a free noticeboard, charged use of telephone, typing and duplicating services and provision or access to a small room for use as an office and for private consultations.

(vi) Finally, the representatives at local authority level should be provided with copies of documents produced by the LEA which are relevant to pay, conditions and LEA regulations. College representatives should also receive these documents plus information on the staffing of their college and a copy of the instrument and articles of government of the college.

15. *Redeployment: The Colleges of Education Staff Redeployment Bureau.* It is appropriate to deal here with this bureau since it has an important bearing on the conditions of staff employed in teacher education. The Bureau was formed in 1974, under a Management Committee consisting of representatives of ATCDE and the DES, as a direct consequence of the decision to reorganize the colleges of education. This reorganization involved the closure of many colleges, substantial reductions in student numbers in most others, and the creation of several merged and diversified establishments. In January 1976, NATFHE took over the ATCDE responsibility for the Bureau and provided office accommodation. The main

function of the Bureau is to assist academic staff faced with redundancy to find other suitable employment and to advise on problems inevitably associated with redeployment. The services of the Bureau are available, free of charge, to all members of the teaching staff of colleges of education, colleges of higher education (including those staff in diversified institutions no longer responsible for teacher education) and polytechnic departments of education. At present (March 1980) there are over 900 persons registered with the Bureau but it is estimated that by the early 1980s nearly 3,000 staff will have been made redundant, many of whom will not have secured redeployment within their institutions or authorities and consequently will need to seek alternative employment elsewhere. Those eligible to register are advised to do so (and as registration is considered as one method of partially fulfilling the requirements of the Colleges of Education (Compensation) Regulations to seek suitable alternative employment, this is a recommended course). Such persons should write to the Director of the Bureau at the address given below, asking for registration forms. These forms are dealt with in the strictest confidence.

W.L. Browne MA
Director, The Colleges of Education Staff Redeployment Bureau, Hamilton House, Mabledon Place, London WC1H 9BH 01-388 0659.

REFERENCE

The following agreements, which may be obtained from NATFHE or CLEA, have been used in writing this sub-section. They are listed in order of their treatment in the sub-section.

Conditions of Service of Teachers in Establishments for Further Education: Recommendations of Joint Conference of the Association of Education Committees, Association of Municipal Corporations, County Councils Associations, Welsh Joint Education Committee, Association of Principals of Technical Institutions, Association of Teachers in Technical Institutions, National Federation of Continuative Teachers' Associations, National Society for Art Education. Issued 1973, replacing those issued in 1959.

Recommendations for Local Conditions of Service for Further Education Teachers: CLEA and FE Teachers' Organisations. Issued 1975.

Teachers' Sick Pay: Model Scheme recommended by a Joint Conference of representatives of the Association of Education Committees, County Councils Association, Association of Municipal Corporations, Welsh Joint Education Committee, National Union of Teachers, Joint Committee of the Four Secondary Associations, National Association of Head Teachers, National Association of School Masters, to govern the payment of allowances to teachers during absence from duty owing to illness, injury or other disability. Reprinted with amendments, 1973, to take the place of the Model Scheme issued in 1946 and revised in 1949, 1958, 1960, 1968 and 1972.

CLEA/School Teachers Maternity Agreement: Adopted by CLEA and the FE Teachers' Organizations in 1979.

Teachers' Conditions of Service (Further Education) A Model Grievance Procedure for Teachers in Further Education to meet the requirements of the Contracts of Employment Act 1972: Association of Education Committees, Association of Municipal Corporations, County Councils Association, Welsh Joint Education Committee, Association of Principals of Technical Institutions, Association of Teachers in Technical Institutions, National Federation of Continuative Teachers' Associations, National Society for Art Education, Association of Teachers in Colleges and Departments of Education.

The Recognised Further Education Teachers' Organisations and the Council of Local Education Authorities Further Education Redundancy Procedures. Issued in 1975, revising recommendations made in 1973.
Contractual Agreements for Associate Lecturers in Further Education: The Council of Local Education Authorities and the Further Education Teachers' Organisations. Issued in 1977.
Further Education Consultation and Negotiation Arrangements Procedure for Collective Disputes: The Council of Local Education Authorities and the Further Education Teachers' Organisations. Issued in 1977.
Agreement on facilities for Representatives of Recognised Teachers' Organisations (Further Education): The Council of Local Education Authorities and the Recognised Further Education Teachers' Organisations. Issued in 1976.

It is indicated in paragraph 3 that at the time of writing (March 1980) the recognised further education teachers' organizations and the Council of Local Education Authorities are engaged in an exercise of codifying the agreements referred to above. The codified set of agreements is likely to be published by the Council in 1980 under the title *Conditions of Service for Further Education Teachers in England and Wales.*

8 SALARIES AND CONDITIONS OF SERVICE: NON-TEACHING STAFF

1. Non-teaching staff generally are subject to pay and conditions of service schemes negotiated by the National Joint Council for Local Authorities Services (Manual Workers) and the National Joint Council for Local Authorities' Administrative, Professional, Technical and Clerical Services.[1] The National Joint Councils are bodies comprised of representatives of employers and employees. A majority of each side of an NJC is required before an agreement can be reached.

2. There are 28 Provincial Councils (14 for manual and 14 for white-collar workers) whose principal functions include: the implementation, interpretation and augmenting of national agreements, the provision of conciliation and arbitration and the control of entry into and training for local authorities' services. Terms and conditions covering certain groups of workers are primarily determined at this level: for example, college caretakers and inner London polytechnic white-collar workers. White-collar staff dissatisfied with their grading can appeal to the appropriate Provincial Council if the matter cannot be resolved at local authority level.

3. Negotiation also takes place at local authority level, normally through a local joint committee. Authorities have a wide range of discretion in the application of national terms and conditions (though they set a base which is binding on authorities) and it is common for local improvements to be negotiated.

4. Details of the nationally negotiated terms and conditions are contained in the handbooks of the National Joint Council for Local Authorities Services (Manual Workers) and the National Joint Council for Local Authorities' APT & C Services (often known as the "Purple Book"). Local authority colleges will be able to acquire copies of these handbooks from their authorities; voluntary colleges can obtain copies from LACSAB. In addition to the national handbooks are provincial handbooks detailing constitutions, wage rates, occupational classifications, conditions of service, NJC decisions, ratings, interpretations and amendments. Thus for many provisions provincially and nationally negotiated affecting employees, reference should be made to Provincial Council handbooks obtainable from local authorities or, in the case of voluntary colleges, from the relevant provincial employers' secretariat. Addresses of these secretariats are included as an appendix to this sub-section. In addition to this information will of course be that on agreements negotiated at local authority level.

5. Some local authorities have codified the various agreements and recourse

---

1 It should be noted however that there are separate national bodies for craftsmen:
JNC for Local Authorities' Services (Building and Civil Engineering);
JNC for Local Authorities' Services (Engineering Craftsmen);
Standing Conference for Electricians; and
Standing Conference for Heating, Ventilating and Domestic Engineers.

therefore ought to be taken to such documents. As agreements continue to be made and modified, it is essential to have access to the up-dating services. The volume of information, however, is detailed and formidable and for this reason precise details of current provisions are not given here. It would be a considerable task for college administrators to become entirely familiar and expert in all areas affecting non-teaching staff. There should, therefore, be close liaison with the local authority education and personnel departments and such other channels of reliable advice. Colleges must adopt any local agreements reached by the authority with the unions and it would be wise for voluntary colleges to adopt such agreements where circumstances are similar. Such action in the latter case also obviates the need for a separate agreement and forestalls difficulties between the college and the unions. Nonetheless, college administrators will need to become familiar with the general pattern of agreements, and also to impress upon their local education authorities that they ought to be consulted when changes in conditions for non-teaching staff are proposed. Most authorities will offer consultation.

6. There are two issues to which it is necessary to draw attention: the interpretation of agreements, and procedures. Regional differences in the interpretation of agreements, particularly for manual workers, have caused difficulties in colleges. Reference therefore should be made to the authority (or, where appropriate, the provincial employers' secretariat). While the point may seem elementary, the largest difficulty in colleges has been caused by procedures: the role and powers of the governing body under the instrument and articles of government notwithstanding, it remains essential to keep procedures, as far as possible, in line with those of the authority when dealing with unions or individuals. Voluntary colleges would be well advised to follow the procedures of the authority in which they are situated. It is essential for the provisions of the articles of government concerning where powers and responsibilities lie in dealing with non-teaching staff to be understood, and thereafter for the agreed procedures to be followed. Procedures must clearly be observed but ought not, unless warranted by the occasion, to become too formal. This appeal for commonsense has to be seen within the context of change in further education: revisions of articles of government, because of the policy of the DES, generally give more authority to governing bodies. However, employer liability remains with the local authority, unless the college is the employer (which will rarely be the case), and the college must ensure that the LEA's conditions and procedures are followed exactly: this is obligatory, not a matter of recommendation.

7. Negotiations for all staff are becoming more complex, and as agreements for non-teaching staff have a wider employment application than those for teaching staff, difficulties can be compounded. An obvious example is the hours of employment: irregular college hours may involve the variation of national and regional agreements for non-teaching staff.

APPENDIX 1

PROVINCIAL EMPLOYERS' SECRETARIATS

Eastern, Essex and Hertfordshire Provincial Councils
St Edmunds House, Lower Baxter Street,
Bury St Edmunds
Suffolk IP33 1ET
Tel: 0284 63681

East Midlands Provincial Council
County Hall, Leicester Road,
Glenfield, Leicester LE3 8RN
Tel: 0533 871313

Greater London Joint Council
Alembic House, 93 Albert Embankment,
London SE1 7TQ
Tel: 01-735 7554

Mid-Southern Provincial Council
10 City Road,
Winchester SO23 8SD
Tel: 0962 69587

Northern Provincial Council
7th Floor, Northern Rock House,
Regent Farm Road, Gosforth,
Newcastle upon Tyne NE3 4PF.
Tel: 0632 850431/2

North Wales Provincial Council
Station Road,
Ruthin, Denbighshire LL15 1BP
Tel: 082 2773

North Western Provincial Council
Washington House,
The Capital Centre,
Manchester M3 5ER
Tel: 061 834 9362

South Eastern Provincial Council
33 Queensway,
Crawley, Sussex
Tel: 0293 34066/7

South Wales Provincial Council
41 Eastgate,
Cowbridge, Glamorgan
Tel: 044 63 2432

South Western Provincial Council
Post House, Church Square,
Taunton, Somerset,
Tel: 0823 86391

11.8

West Midlands Provincial Council
Rutland House,
148 Edmund Street,
Birmingham B3 2JS
Tel: 021 236 6943

Yorkshire & Humberside Provincial Council
5th Floor, Arndale House, Arndale
Centre, Headingley, Leeds LS6 2UU.
Tel: 0532 787471

REFERENCE

Reference may be made to the following handbooks (available from LEAs or LACSAB).

National Joint Council for Local Authorities' Administrative, Professional, Technical and Clerical Services (the "Purple Book").

Auxiliary Workers in Local Authority Employment, England and Wales, Rates of Wages and Conditions of Service.

Available from LEAs or provincial employers' secretariat:

Provincial Council for Local Authorities' Services (Manual Workers) Handbook.

9 COMMENTARY ON THE LAW AND CONDITIONS OF SERVICE AGREEMENTS

1. The purpose of this sub-section is to provide some comment on the conjunction of the law and conditions of service agreements, identifying areas where problems may be encountered. Attention will not be drawn to differences readily apparent from a reading of sub-sections **6-8** above. Numbers in brackets after sub-headings below refer to the sub-section paragraphs to which cross reference might be made. In each case, only the paragraph introductory to the topic is cited. Reference should also be made to Section **11.6**, Appendix 7 where the possible effects of proposed changes in the law are discussed.

2. **Fixed term contracts**[1] (**6.**5; 39; 63; **7.**4)
Under employment law and interpretations of it provided by the courts, an individual holding a fixed term contract will be held as having been dismissed at the expiry of the contract. Provided that the service qualifications are satisfied, then the individual has the right to petition an industrial tribunal that the dismissal was unfair. This right has been established at law and has consequences for the education service where such contracts have become common. The exception is where a person appointed to a fixed term contract of two years or more has waived the right to complain of unfair dismissal.

3. Changes in employment law in 1979 have serious consequences for temporary staff. Until that year, a person employed continuously for 26 weeks at a rate of 16 or more hours a week, or continuously for five years at a rate between eight and 16 hours per week qualified for the right to petition against unfair dismissal. The Variation Order operative from 1 October 1979 extended the 26 week qualifying period to 52 weeks. (NB: the other rights which the 26 week/16+ hours a week period conferred, such as redundancy provisions and maternity leave and pay have not been affected). This 52 week provision means that certain employees have now lost, or may have seriously qualified, their former statutory rights concerning unfair dismissal (see also para. 5 below). It will be possible, for example, for an employer to construct contracts of employment for temporary staff which last for, say, one day less than a year.

4. The more drastic effect of the Variation Order concerns part-employees.

---

1 NATFHE accepts that there are occasions when it is necessary to employ a member of staff on a temporary basis, but it believes that such contracts should be used only in these cases: to allow the replacement of a seconded staff member; for a period of up to a year to replace a woman teacher while she is on maternity leave; to allow the appointment of a member of staff who cannot satisfy the medical requirements for permanent employment; and to facilitate the employment of a member of the research staff who is to be employed on a personal research programme leading to a higher degree (but such a contract should not be used in other types of research staff employment). NATFHE further advises its members not to waive rights concerning the complaint of unfair dismissal either at the time of the making of the contract or during its course.

The former requirement of 26 weeks' continuous employment gave rise to difficulty, for the word "continuous" is not easily reconcilable with the nature of many part-time contracts. In some cases it might be held that vacation periods broke the continuity of employment; in other cases that might not be so: resolution of the question largely depends on the wording of the contract. If continuity is broken, then the rights do not apply; where the contract or circumstances of employment are held to be continuous throughout vacations, then the rights do apply. However, the introduction of a one-year qualifying period seems virtually to have removed statutory protection from part-time employees against unfair dismissal: the qualifying period now includes the long summer vacation which usually falls outside the period of employment for which part-time staff are contracted. There is less difficulty over what actually constitutes a dismissal. The demise of a contract by the effluxion of time where it is a limited or fixed term contract should be regarded as a dismissal in the case of part-time staff just as it is in the case of full-time temporary staff (and, of course, it may not be an unfair dismissal).

5. **Continuous employment** (**6.**39; 5)
It is always for the employer to show in any disputed case that employment has not been continuous. The application of the provisions of the Employment Protection Acts concerning continuous employment to colleges is no easy matter, especially in respect of part-time staff. The main rights under the EPAs which are affected by continuous employment are:
(i) a statement of employment particulars;
(ii) a minimum period of notice;
(iii) a written statement for reasons of dismissal on request;
(iv) not to be unfairly dismissed (but NB para 3, above);
(v) statutory maternity leave and maternity pay; and
(vi) redundancy pay.

6. The central issue is that of the contract of employment. (However, it is important to remember the circumstances in which a week can still count even though the contract no longer exists). Where a contract states or implies, or has been supplemented by conditions of service agreements, or modified by custom and practice, so that employment is continuous, then breaks such as vacations will not interrupt continuous service. For example, a cleaner or member of the kitchen staff in a college qualifying for rights because of the hours normally worked (16 hours a week or eight hours or over for five years), would have vacation periods counted as continuous employment if he or she was normally expected to recommence work as soon as the college began its new term and this was recognised by the payment of a retainer. Where an individual experiences periods which are not paid, greater difficulties arise. For example, there has been a question in the past as to whether a part-time hourly paid teacher who has worked in the autumn and spring terms has achieved 26 weeks' continuous employment. The doubt arises in such a case because of the unpaid period of the Christmas vacation. Whether or not such a person has continuous employment will be determined by the contract. Where two separate contracts covering the autumn and spring terms have been issued, it is unlikely that such a person will be able to demonstrate continuous employment over the two terms.

However, where the contract first issued implied employment in both terms (for example, where it employed the teacher to teach a particular class which it was known was going to run over the two terms in question) then, that person might be able to demonstrate continuous employment. In the case of any part-time staff where there is no reasonable or normal expectation of a recommencement of employment after a vacation (and obviously where excluded by the contract or its modifications), that vacation period will not count as continuous employment, service will have been broken and rights consequently lost. Difficulties occur here usually in the case of hourly paid employees.

7. The position of hourly paid part-time employees is one which can create further difficulty, especially where variations of hours below the fixed minima occur. If these variations continue for more than the pool of 26 weeks (plus additions occurring because of other provisions), then continuity is broken. This raises again the question of vacations, and will be compounded by the particular provisions of the individual's contract. All that can be given by way of advice in these circumstances is that while compliance with statute is the minimum requirement, subject to any conditions of service agreement, part-time hourly paid staff ought to have the difficulties of their positions recognised by colleges and not be subjected to unfair treatment.

8. In the interpretation of what constitutes hours of work for a part-time teacher, it had been held that a teacher marginally below the relevant hours threshold (16 hours a week or eight hours after five years) in contact time did qualify for a reference to a tribunal if employment was terminated, since there was more actual work involved in the contract, such as preparation and marking, than just the class contact. However, in the leading case in this matter, Essex County Council v Lake[2], the decision of the EAT that the hours of employment were greater than the hours Mrs Lake was contracted to teach, was overturned on appeal. It was decided that the difference of two hours between the qualifying threshold and the actual contact time was a disqualification. This decision that it is not competent for tribunals to take into account hours of work not governed by the contract means that little, if any, discretion exists in making an allowance for marking and preparation time.

9. **Research staff**

There are no national conditions of service for research staff, and nor are there national pay agreements. Such staff have generally been paid on scales adapted from the Burnham Further Education Reports; their conditions of

---

2 Lord Denning stated that difficulties would be posed if it was said that Mrs Lake was required to work outside the hours stipulated in her contract: "She might be expected to do so and would normally have to do so by way of preparation. But it would depend very much on the nature of the subject, the qualities of the teacher, or the amount of knowledge she had. I cannot find any suggestion that she was required to do this extra work. It was unpaid work by way of expectation". Lord Justice Lawton said that it would be impossible for a local education authority to supervise or measure the work required for the preparation of lessons. Mrs Lake had said that she used to spend up to one and a half hours each evening in preparation and marking. (*Industrial Relations Law Reports,* Vol.8, No.6, June 1979, 241).

service vary from NJC to teaching terms of employment. NATFHE has sought to have pay for research staff included in the Burnham FE proceedings and while this has not been agreed, the Joint Secretaries and LACSAB have agreed that where they are paid on Burnham salaries, they should receive any increases awarded in the FE Committee.

10. In one part of the country there are consultations concerning research staff which occur on a relatively formal basis. While the issue awaits formal resolution, it may be helpful to colleges to consider the following propositions which are included here for discussion purposes only.[3]
   (i) Research staff could be categorised below the level of research fellow thus:
      (a) staff primarily employed on personal research programmes leading to a higher degree;
      (b) staff primarily employed on the development of the institution's research programme;
      (c) staff providing leadership in the development of the institution's research programme, including the supervision of staff in advanced work.
   (ii) Research staff roles could be clearly defined within the development of their institution's research programme and have applied to them:
      (a) an appropriate Burnham FE teaching scale according to the level of their work and responsibilities;
      (b) an appropriate career structure/clearly defined staff development opportunities; and
      (c) further education teachers' conditions of service, modified and amended where appropriate to their particular research function.

11. **Academic and non-academic appointments**
A problem has arisen concerning the position of staff who are not readily classified as either academic or non-academic. An example of such staff is librarians. It is fairly common for librarians to receive Burnham salaries and teachers' conditions, but some receive NJC salaries and conditions, and others a Burnham salary but NJC conditions. While it would be convenient if such a situation did not obtain, the area of "hybrid appointments" is such that it is difficult to offer advice. The problem is subject to negotiation, and is the cause of concern to several unions and associations, since a variety of practices obtain.[4]

12. **Rehabilitation of offenders** (**6.**53)
For the purposes of colleges, an offender whose conviction is spent is not

3 NATFHE is producing a policy statement which will deal with the development of research in further education institutions and the terms and conditions of employment of the staff who undertake the research.

4 NATFHE believes that tutor-librarians (that is, librarians who also have a clearly designated teaching function and who are usually responsible for managing a college library) should be paid on a Burnham head of department scale. However, it is not easy to determine whether or not a particular librarian is a teacher in the formal sense. Hence, there are likely to be disagreements between, for example, NATFHE and NALGO concerning whether or not particular posts in college libraries should be paid according to Burnham scales. College administrators will need to tread cautiously in this area.

required to divulge the conviction unless asked. If an undisclosed offence subsquently comes to light, then the employer appears to have the right of dismissal on grounds of deception. However, legal opinion is that such a dismissal would probably be unfair, unless the circumstances of the offence were such as to justify dismissal (i.e. that the circumstances were such as to affect the employer's business adversely).

13. In a specific reference to education, the Exemptions Order under the Act states that where employment is carried out wholly or partly within the precincts of a school or further education establishment involving "access to persons under the age of 18 as part of the employee's normal duties", then the offender must divulge the conviction if asked, and may be liable otherwise to dismissal. This raises two problems: the case of an individual applying for a post to teach students aged 18 or over in an establishment which provides teaching for students from the age of 16; and where an individual guilty of an offence is redeployed, transferred or otherwise moved as a consequence of reorganization from an institution catering for 18 year olds and over only, to one catering for those aged from 16. In both cases the job specification is important. "Access to persons" is defined as meaning those who are taught by the individual, or those for whom the individual has responsibility. Therefore, an offender need not disclose a conviction where his or her duties will be in relation to 18 year olds and over, even though persons under that age may be being taught in the same institution. Further, if a "spent" offence came to light, the employer would have to disregard it; it could not be used as a reason for refusal to employ an applicant for a job, or to dismiss an employee, or to withhold a promotion for which an employee would otherwise be eligible. However, where as a result of redeployment or reorganization an individual with a spent conviction was to teach students below the age of 18, then the Exemption Order would apply: if asked, the conviction would have to be disclosed and if not disclosed the dismissal liability would remain. It may still be, however, that such an individual would lose benefits under employment law (and also, for example, National Insurance unemployment benefit regulations) if he or she were to refuse such an offer of re-employment or redeployment as being unsuitable. The individual would probably be wrong to reject the offered employment: he or she would probably be expected by a tribunal to have gone through the procedures, disclosing information if asked. If the offered post were then withdrawn, if all other relevant provisions were satisfied, the individual would qualify for a redundancy payment.

14. Particular provisions relevant to individual cases would probably be contained in a college's instruments and articles of government, and have relevance to criminal offences generally (see paragraph 32 below).

15. **Contracts** (**6.**5;**7.**4)

Many of the common issues at employment law revolve around the question of the contract. A contract of employment exists from the time that a definite offer of employment is unconditionally accepted. Unless both parties agree, statements made after the contract are excluded. Unless the employee agrees to a change in the contractual agreement, or the contract gave the employer power to vary its terms, it is a breach of contract for an employer to require an employee to perform duties other than those for which he or she was originally appointed. However, agreements arrived at through collective bargaining machinery become implied terms in individual contracts of employment.

16. Many articles of government refer to collective agreements, such as conditions of service, as being part of the contract of employment. Such agreements can form part of a contract; it is generally advisable for the letter of appointment to make clear whether the employee is covered by any collective agreements in existence or which may be negotiated, and whether or not they are part of the contract. Subject to Schedule 11 of the Employment Protection Act (claims that an employer is not observing the relevant general level of terms and conditions of employment), collective agreements themselves between employers and unions are not normally contracts in law and therefore are legally unenforceable by the parties to them, though – as mentioned above – they may introduce binding terms into the contracts of individuals affected.

17. Rules of employment form, or can form, part of a contract. Dismissal for the breach of rules, provided that the employee has been made aware of the rules, can therefore be justified. However, in such a case where the employee can demonstrate that such contravention of the rules was common and that a custom had been established, a tribunal may consider that the rules had been amended by custom and thus consider the dismissal to have been unfair.

18. A contract does not exist alone; it also carries implied duties. An employee must be willing to work within the scope of the contract but where work is not provided, or work of a different nature offered, there may be legal redress. The Employment Appeal Tribunal found it "a startling proposition" that all teachers could be asked to teach any subject at any time. Further, the tribunal found that "no doubt there is a need for flexibility and for teachers normally engaged in one type of teaching at a particular level to be ready to undertake teaching at different levels ... provided that the request is reasonable ... [which] ... will depend on circumstances ... and it would be relevant to take into account the custom and practice of the Profession".[5] In this case, a teacher who had refused to teach a timetable because the post to which she had been appointed had been "eroded to the point of destruction", was found to have been unfairly dismissed. Thus although the employee has the implied duty to work within the scope of the contract and

---

5 London Borough of Redbridge v Fishman, *Industrial Relations Law Reports*, Vol 7. No. 2, Feb 1978, 69.
cf Darnton v Essex County Council (Chancery Division 4 December 78; *Daily Telegraph* 5 December 1978). Mr Darnton was a school teacher appointed to teach mathematics, economics and sociology. Instead, he was required to teach humanities (including history and geography) and physical education. This he did without complaint during his probationary year. Thereafter he complained that his original terms of employment were not being observed. The judgment was that he had adopted a much too legalistic approach, that his teaching requirements were within his capabilities, and that he was being too pernickety: a declaration that he was being improperly required to teach beyond his contract was refused.

cannot refuse to comply with an order within that scope, unless it is illegal or involves unreasonable danger, the employer does not have the right to make unrestricted demands on the employee.

19. Employees have an implied duty to take care of the employer's property, and may be disciplined or have to make financial reparation where property is damaged either deliberately or by negligence. This duty extends to confidential information. Although there is no legal precedent, it has been maintained that the misuse by a lecturer of confidential information (relating, for example, to students) would mean a breach of contract.

20. An employee is in breach of contract under the common law if he or she acts dishonestly against the employer. Such an offence would also carry criminal implications. However, such dishonesty does not automatically justify dismissal: it is regarded in the same way as any other kind of misconduct under employment law and must be dealt with accordingly. In consideration of dishonesty, it is relevant to refer to acting in good faith and employees being prohibited from competing with their employer. For example, it would be an abuse of position for a lecturer to accept bribes from students, and for a lecturer to advise students not to enrol at college but instead attend his or her private tuition classes. To use college materials for private enterprise and gain could be a breach of contract (as well as the crime of theft, or the civil wrong of conversion). The issue will normally be determined according to the terms of the particular contract, unless the case has been proven in the criminal courts. While the law is reluctant to restrain spare time activities unless they are in competition with the employer, there are circumstances where if those activities are so substantial, a breach of contract may be held to have occurred.

21. There are differences of opinion over whether an employer has fulfilled contractual obligations by providing salary, or whether work must also be provided. This can be an issue where an employee is suspended on full pay or where, for example as an interim but unspecified consequence of college reorganization, there is no work for the employee to do. It is possible under such circumstances that the employer may be constructively dismissing the employee. (Constructive dismissal may be defined as where an employee resigns from employment in circumstances in which the employer has acted so unreasonably that such behaviour is held to be tantamount to repudiating a contract, and that dispute over the issue will be resolved in accordance with the law of contract).

22. **Maternity leave** (**6.**30; **7.**8)

The terms of the teachers' national conditions of service maternity agreement differ from those of the Employment Protection (Consolidation) Act. These differences, which generally although not wholly favour the teachers' scheme, are investigated below. The question has been raised as to whether a person has to choose between the two "schemes", and the teachers' scheme has recently been amended in an attempt to integrate the differing provisions.[6] This is a highly complex area. Table 1, and the following paragraphs illustrate points of comparison which may in any case be useful in considering the situation of non-teaching staff.

23. In considering EP(C) A and maternity conditions of service agreements, it is also necessary to have regard to local agreements. Points of difference between the EP(C)A and the national agreement will be apparent from Table 1. The main items concern: qualification; notice of absence and the date of absence; maternity pay; and the use of "capacity" in the teachers' scheme definition of "job" in the right to return to work. In general, the teachers' scheme represents superior conditions – for example, a greater amount of maternity pay; and although the EP(C)A offers longer maternity leave in certain circumstances, the sick leave entitlements of the conditions agreement (since they cater for health difficulties which may arise after pregnancy) will usually offer superior benefit. Again, in the case of a teacher of two or more years' service, under the conditions of service scheme any period of absence outside the 18 week period not covered by a medical certificate would be leave without pay; but under the EP(C)A provisions, all leave after six weeks is leave without pay. Changes proposed in the Employment Bill of 1979, if enacted, make the teachers' scheme even more attractive in many instances than the EP(C) A.

24. Item 6 in Table 1 concerns the post to which a woman may return. The conditions of service agreement seems here to be more restrictive than the EP(C)A. The Act provides for the return to the former job; the maternity conditions of service agreement definition of job (which is not defined in the Act) introduces the phrase "the same capacity". Job and capacity may not be held to be synonymous. The Act also provides, in the case of the former post not being available by reason of redundancy, that a new contract of employment must be offered in which "the work to be done ... is of a kind which is both suitable in relation to the employee and appropriate for her to do in the circumstances." Appropriate is the key word: the sort of employment available under the maternity conditions of service scheme (or even by way of other conditions of service agreements) may not be

---

6 Both the teachers' associations and the LEAs have acted in the belief that there was no requirement on a teacher to choose between the previous provisions of the maternity conditions of service scheme and those of the EP(C)A. This view seems to have been adopted in spite of the case of ILEA v Nash (*IRLR*, Vol.8, No.1, Jan 1979, 29). Mrs Nash's conditions of service were established under the ILEA staff code, not the national agreement, although that circumstance does not qualify what follows. In giving judgement, the EAT stated that: "A contract of employment can certainly substitute conditions which are superior to the rights conferred under statute but it cannot detract from them ... [the respondent] cannot, of course, have both; she cannot opt in and out, choosing what she likes from the Staff Code and rejecting others ... The two sets of conditions are, in effect, optional packages and the employee must choose one or the other". However, since these observations were not concerned with the actual point of the case and the judgment given, they represent *obiter dicta. Obiter dicta* represent a judicial expression of opinion uttered in arguing a point or in giving judgments but not essential to the decision – and therefore do not have binding legal authority. However, *obiter dicta* can be significant in guiding decisions in other courts, and are not lightly disregarded. The local authority associations and teachers' associations have always considered that there is generally a right to combine the provisions of the conditions of service and EP(C)A schemes.

Table 1

	National conditions of service maternity agreement	Employment Protection (Consolidation) Act
1.	Applies to all full- and part-time teachers with at least one year's full-time, or equivalent part-time service, whether with one or more LEAs. Additional rights and conditions for women teachers with at least 2 years' continuous service.	Applies to all female employees, full- or part-time, provided they work for the employer at least 16 hours a week or 8 hours if they have so worked for more than 5 years. Service requirement: continuously employed by the same (or successor or associated employer) for at least 2 years (and for the right not to be dismissed for the reason of pregnancy, 6 months).
2.	Must notify LEA of intent to take leave as soon as practicable, unless good cause is shown, not less than 14 weeks before expected confinement date, and at the same time inform LEA of wish to return to work. Must notify LEA at least 21 days before absence begins; notify return to work (for right to return) at same time.	Shall notify employer at least 21 days before absence begins that she will be absent due to pregnancy, and (for the right to return) notify intention to return at the same time. (Employment Bill 1979 proposes written notice obligatory for right to return: written notice for maternity pay only if employer requires).
3.	May remain absent for 18 weeks from commencement of leave (up to 6 weeks after confinement if still birth occurs). May absent herself from work at beginning of 11th week before expected confinement, or later, (unless certified unfit to work). Women with 2 years' continuous employment may remain absent for up to 29 weeks beginning with week of confinement; additional 4 week discretionary period (employer); (and employee	May work until confinement, if fit; may return at any time before end of 29 weeks period beginning with the week of confinement; 7 days' notice of return; additional 4 week discretionary period (employer); (and employee if certified incapable); interruption of work (e.g. industrial dispute) provisions. (Employment Bill 1979 proposes 21 days' notice of return).

National conditions of service maternity agreement	Employment Protection (Consolidation) Act
only if ill because of pregnancy – absence as in sick leave scheme); 7 days notice of return; no interruption of work provisions	
4. On condition that teacher returns to work for at least 13 weeks (or agreed part-time equivalent), 100% maternity pay for the first four, 90% for the next two, 50% for the remainder of the 18 weeks. A woman with at least two years' service is allowed to retain the first six weeks' pay whether or not she returns to work. Absence due to illness because of pregnancy outside the leave period treated as sick leave. Full pay if need for absence because of risk of rubella, provided she does not refuse unreasonably to serve in another institution where there is no risk.	9/10 of a week's pay for the first 6 weeks whether returns to work or not.
5. Employer may extend at discretion post-natal provision to adoptive parents.	Does not apply to adoptive parents.
6. Right to return to former job, defined as "the nature of the work which she is employed to do in accordance with her contract, *in the same capacity** in which, and in the same place where, she is so employed". (By reference to other conditions agreements, certain redundancy entitlements; no "appropriate" alternative post, however).	Right to keep the job, or in the case of redundancy a suitable and appropriate alternative; protection against unfair dismissal except where condition makes employment illegal or impossible. (Employment Bill 1979 proposes that employers can offer a suitable and appropriate alternative post, on not substantially less favourable terms, even if no question of redundancy, if not reasonably practicable to offer old job back).

*editor's italics

appropriate. It must be remembered that this EP(C)A provision refers only to redundancy.[7] However, the amendments proposed by the 1979 Employment Bill allow the offering of another job, if it is not reasonably practicable for the former post to be offered, on terms and conditions *not substantially less favourable.* If enacted, this amendment – especially since its provisions apply even where there is no redundancy – has significant implications.

25. Part-time employees who do not qualify for the maternity conditions of service scheme, or have not had discretion operated on their behalf, also do not qualify for the EP(C)A provisions if they do not meet the hours and continuous employment requirement. In this case they will receive only the National Insurance maternity grant and maternity allowance, and on its cessation supplementary benefit may be justified by the circumstances (and sickness benefit similarly if appropriate).

26. If an Associate Lecturer is eligible for maternity benefits, she will receive the benefits of the conditions of service scheme on a proportional basis; rights under the EP(C)A are the same as for full-time staff provided that the hours and service requirements are fulfilled. Any teacher not eligible under the conditions of service scheme may benefit from the scheme solely at the discretion of the employing authority.

27. In maternity leave cases, where the period of leave ends during a vacation and the teacher is fit to return to service, the authority should be advised, and since the teacher is available for duty, salary will be resumed (where the employer's discretion to defer the return to work is not exercised).

28. A question may arise concerning superannuation. The DES has promised the local authority associations that it is to amend the superannuation regulations, and they have therefore advised LEAs, that if they treat maternity leave as if it were sick leave, superannuability will follow here the sick leave arrangements (See Section **11.3.**4).

29. **Dimissal (6.**62; **7.**4)

The disqualification of age in petitioning for unfair dismissal has now been qualified by a judgment of the House of Lords.[8] Formerly, an employee aged over 65 (male) or 60 (female), or over the normal retirement age for the particular type of employment had no protection against unfair dismissal if either condition were not satisfied. The Lords' decision means that the position is reversed: protection exists if either condition is satisfied. Thus a woman teacher aged, for example, 61 now has right to petition in respect of unfair dismissal.

---

7 Because the maternity agreement gives a right to be absent rather than a right to return, the contract of employment must subsist throughout the whole of the period of absence, and if redundancy arises during or at the end of the period of absence, then protection against redundancy as implied by statute in the contract of employment continues to subsist. The EP(C)A makes specific provision for this possibility because the rights created by the EP(C)A may exist independently of the contract of employment.

8 London Borough of Barnet v Nothman, *IRLR,* Vol.8, No.1, Jan 1979, 35. Chapter 16 of the *LACSAB Employee Relations Handbook,* para 17.5(v) must now be read in the light of this decision: the phrase "whichever is the earlier" no longer applies.

30. The statement which the employee is entitled to request giving the reasons for dismissal has to be adequate. One word reasons are not enough; a brief description of the circumstances leading to the dismissal is required. College administrators should note that procedural matters are important: petitions in respect of unfair dismissal have been successful where employers or their agents have not followed procedures.

31. While it is obviously necessary to make a distinction between gross misconduct and general misconduct, a comprehensive definition is difficult to supply. Gross misconduct may be said to be conduct which makes it intolerable for the employer to continue the employment of the offender. However, gross misconduct in one type of employment may not be so in another. Tribunals have held that dismissal for gross misconduct in the education service has been justified in the cases of a failure over a considerable period of time of a teacher to teach allocated classes, in various instances of sexual relationships with pupils, and the persistent failure of a head teacher to carry out the authority's curriculum policy. The nature and number of warnings concerning misconduct ought to be within procedures outlined in Sections **11.6**.96-100 and **11.7**.4 above. It has been suggested that two or three written warnings may be appropriate in cases of relatively minor offences such as persistently bad time-keeping.

32. The question of criminal offences has been raised in relation to contract (paragraph 14). It is necessary here to distinguish between offences committed at work and those committed outside employment which may have an effect on an employee's suitability for a job. There is no automatic right for an employer to suspend on full pay or dismiss an employee accused of a criminal offence, or to dismiss that employee if he or she is found guilty.[9] Where the alleged offence occurs during employment, the employer has a duty to investigate the circumstances as far as possible, and to act reasonably. In order to justify action, the employer does not require proof but must have reasonable grounds for supposing that an offence justifying disciplinary action has occurred.

33. Offences committed outside employment cannot be investigated by the employer. It is generally the case that such offences are not grounds for dismissal. However, education is subject to the requirement that there must be public confidence in the employees' ability fully to carry out their duties. Where public confidence in an individual guilty of a criminal offence outside employment can be established to be lacking, a tribunal would probably

---

9 cf Norfolk County Council v Bernard (*IRLR*, Vol.8, No.6, June 1979, 220) Despite the DES having told Mr Bernard that his conviction for the possession and cultivation of cannabis, while warranting a severe warning, would not result in action being taking concerning his suitability as a teacher, the disciplinary sub-committee of his LEA dismissed him because of the offence. The dismissal was found to be unfair by a tribunal, and by the EAT. For conviction of an offence outside employment to constitute reason for dismissal depends upon the circumstances; it is by no means automatic justification. For example, the tribunal in the Bernard case found that: "no reasonable person or committee properly directing themselves and weighing fairly and honestly the evidence which we know was put before them could arrive at the decision to dismiss."

conclude that dismissal is justified. Between the preferring of charges and the outcome of the trial, suspension on full pay in such circumstances is usually the employer's only recourse.

34. Dismissal on grounds of incapacity (see Section **11.6**, Appendix 4) are again better divided under two headings. Where incapacity and incapability arise for reasons other than health, procedures should follow those outlined in Sections **11.6.**97-100 and **11.7.**4. It has been said, however, that tribunals may attach less importance to procedural steps than in misconduct cases. Warnings should be related to a reasonable assessment of the employee's incapability, whether it is of such a nature as to warrant dismissal and to what degree the employee would be able to improve performance after receipt of a warning. This is not to say that statutory, code of practice and conditions of service provisions should be disregarded. Obviously, they must be followed: the point here is that cases must be treated on their merits and be subject to reasonable flexibility. However, where principals are acting as agents of the LEA, they are advised to be especially scrupulous in procedural matters (cf paragraph 30, above).

35. Where an employee absent for a prolonged period because of sickness is dismissed, the usual reason would be his or her lack of physical capability to carry out the employment. (Discharge in the interests of the efficiency of the employer's business is one of the means to premature retirement). Teachers' conditions of service carry an entitlement not to be dismissed until the exhaustion of the sick leave period. However, notice of dismissal can be given before the end of that period although it might be felt that such action would be unsympathetic.

36. Employers are entitled to request medical information concerning the employee's condition and this may contain an assessment of the time required before work could be resumed. Unless the circumstances are exceptional, employees must be given an opportunity to express their opinion on their health and fitness. Where appropriate, suitable alternative employment should be offered. One test of the fairness of a dismissal on the grounds of ill health is how long an employer can be expected to wait before taking action.

37. In the case of mental illness, the essential test on the resumption of work is fitness to carry out employment. The Secretary of State may rule upon the question in certain cases. There is no obligation to disclose a mental illness before taking employment. Where such an illness is subsequently discovered and be of a nature to justify concern, again application may be made to the Secretary of State. Nonetheless, in most cases a dismissal would be unfair if the employee was able to carry out his or her contractual duties.

38. **Redundancy** (**6.**70; **7.**10)
Selection for redundancy has to be fair. Dismissal on the grounds of redundancy may be unfair where the selection procedure was unfairly applied, or where the procedure was arbitrary, or where an agreed procedure has been disregarded. Any dismissal for redundancy is

automatically unfair if warning has not been given or is inadequate; and similarly with regard to consultation with the employee's representatives. Unless there are good reasons, favourable treatment cannot be extended to one person at the expense of another. It is unfair to select higher grade staff for redundancy in order to reduce costs; and to dismiss lower graded staff in order to retain their seniors. Selection on the basis of sex, race and marital status is also unfair. Arbitrary percentage cuts are not allowed. A balance is essential, and is evidence of reasonable behaviour. Whereas a selection which disregards long and satisfactory service is likely to be unfair, the "last in, first out" basis of selection is too crude to have general application to education. Selection must depend on the circumstances creating the redundancies. For example, if a failure to recruit caused redundancies in a college, it would be unfair to select for redundancy the most junior member of a department on the grounds of service alone: it would be necessary to establish how recruitment failure affected the courses taught by all members of that department (and also the courses upon which they were appointed to teach).

39. As any selection contravening procedures agreed with the unions concerned is unfair dismissal, the first obvious step is to consult with those bodies. A selection procedure can be established, presumably within existing agreements. Where redundancies cannot be prevented, volunteers should be sought. Any volunteer should have all issues which refer to the redundancy, procedures and compensation fully and carefully explained. In practical terms, the compensation arrangements for staff in teacher education and the premature retirement provisions[10] offer some appeal to persons aged 50 and over. While age might therefore be a criterion assisting the drawing up of any selection procedures, it cannot be a general determining factor. There is also an obvious constraint in accepting volunteers for redundancy where a college or department could suffer severely from an exodus of staff in any particular area.

40. **"In loco parentis" (12.6)**

Teachers act *in loco parentis* (in the place or position of a parent) where students are under the age of majority. The law requires a teacher to take such care of those pupils as would a careful parent.[11] This provision is relevant to colleges where students are aged between 16 and 18. However, the extent of teachers' responsibilities is limited by the consideration that a minor aged 16 and over is expected to a very large extent to look after her or himself. Care should be taken where students aged under 16 attend, or are transported[12] to, a college for the purposes of link courses or other activities. However, general advice to college administrators is that they

---

10 See Sections **11.5** and **11.4**

11 Shepherd v Essex County Council (1913) 29 TLR 303. True parental authority prevails, however, (Price v Wilkins (1888) 58 LT) and the authority of the teacher is to be exercised reasonably (Fitzgerald v Northcote (1865) 4 F & F 656.

12 Where students are carried in a teacher's car, it is the duty of the teacher to ensure that his or her vehicle is insured for the purpose for which it is being used. In the event of an accident, liability can arise only if it is shown that injury has been suffered as the result of some negligent act or omission to act on the part of the teacher (and each case must be considered on its merits).

should act reasonably. It would be unreasonable, for example, for a principal to insist that teaching staff of a college should supervise students who are minors in getting onto and off buses (since parents would not normally exercise such supervision). Little more need be said on this issue as there have not been as yet any cases concerning *in loco parentis* and colleges.

APPENDIX 1

NATFHE APPOINTMENTS POLICY

There is not at present an agreement between the employers' associations and NATFHE concerning appointments and interview procedure. In order to demonstrate the principles NATFHE wishes to have adopted, its policy statement is reproduced below:

Introduction

1. In 1966 the Association of Teachers in Technical Institutions published a policy statement which offered advice to employers and employees on the procedure to be adopted in appointing to posts and the conducting of interviews. This advice was intended to ensure that in this difficult area problems were minimised and selection was made, and seen to be made, fairly.

2. Since 1966, with the growth in further and higher education, the Association has become aware of the growing intensity of problems connected with appointments. Many of these problems have been the subject of complaints made by Association members and, consequently, a growing volume of casework. In addition, many worrying reports have been received about discrimination in appointments and interviewing against women. It is for these reasons that the Association has decided to review and amend its policy, where necessary, to cater for problems which have been reported. It is hoped these new guidelines will be adopted by local authorities, governing bodies and the profession as contributing to greater fairness in the selection of teachers for the posts for which they apply.

The Details of the Post

3. Information about the college and the particular vacancy shall be sent to prospective candidates with the application form or the details of how the application should be made. This initial information shall include a brief description of the work of the college and the physical, social and industrial environment of its locality. The structure of the college and its departments shall be described and related to any special area the successful candidate will be expected to develop. A specification of the duties, both teaching and administrative if applicable, and the nature of the courses involved shall be included amongst the details provided about the post.

4. The initial details shall contain also a full description of the conditions of employment and service attaching to the post.

5. The initial details of appointment shall state whether or not the satisfactory completion of a medical examination is a pre-condition of appointment. (If this is so only the candidate eventually offered the post shall be required to undergo a medical examination. This shall take place as soon as possible after the offer of the post is made).

6. It is essential that the post shall be advertised at a specific salary or grade which shall not be varied subsequently in the appointment process. The Association is concerned about the practice adopted by some local authorities whereby a post is advertised at one grade and offered at a lower one. In general this should not occur. However, where an internal candidate is selected to fill a Lecturer Grade II post and a Grade I post is thereby created, it is reasonable for this post to be offered to one of the candidates who unsuccessfully applied, and was interviewed for, the Lecturer Grade II post.

7. Where several posts in one field are advertised together at different grades, the candidate is advised to indicate whether or not he or she is only interested in the post or posts advertised at the higher grade(s).

Application forms and references

8. Candidates shall not be required to submit more than one copy of the application form and supporting documents.

9. Candidates shall not be required to indicate their marital status on the application form.

10. The benefit of testimonials is dubious and in the Association's view a prospective employer should not request they they be provided. The candidate shall not be required to submit the names of more than three referees.

11. NATFHE advises candidates who are teachers at the time of making their application to request that reference be made to their Principal or Head of Department. Principals and Heads of Department should be prepared to show the reference to the applicant and should, in any case, indicate any adverse comments which they may have made in the reference.

12. The candidate's present employer shall not be contacted without the explicit permission of the candidate.

13. References shall be made in writing and not given by telephone.

Shortlisting

14. Shortlisted candidates shall receive as much notice as possible of the date set for their interview and not less than seven days notice. In addition, the expected dates on which the interview might take place shall be included in the details of the post.

15. Candidates selected for interview should receive, where practicable, a copy of the college prospectus with the letter which details interview arrangements. Where this is not possible a copy of the prospectus shall be made available to candidates on the day of the interview.

16. Shortlisted candidates shall be invited to visit the college in advance of the interview in order to meet members of the teaching staff of the relevant department and form an impression of the college. This will benefit both the prospective employer and employee since it is important that the person offered the post shall have sufficient information upon which to base a decision to accept or reject any offer which is made. In some cases it will be possible to arrange the visit to take place on the same day as the interview.

17. Candidates who apply for posts in their own college and are not shortlisted shall be informed of this prior to interviews taking place. Such a candidate shall be entitled to seek an explanatory interview with his or her Principal or the Principal's nominee.

Interviewing

18. Over the years many different methods of interviewing have developed. All of them have advantages and disadvantages and the Association does not wish to advocate one method in preference to the others. The Association's prime concern is that whatever method is chosen it is applied fairly between the candidates. In some cases, candidates have claimed that their interviews were biased and included questioning on matters which, in fairness, ought not to have concerned the interviewing panel. (This matter is dealt with below where the general theme of discrimination in appointments is considered).

19. Concern has been expressed about the role of lay members serving on interviewing panels. The Association recognises that this is a delicate area since lay members cannot

be expected to be versed in interviewing techniques or always distinguish thoroughly the appropriate from the inappropriate question. It may help to avoid these problems if the interviewing panel decides in advance the nature of the questions which are to be put to the candidates.

20. The Association believes that it is important to keep the size of the interviewing panel to a reasonable size. The size of the panel should allow for the proper representation of interested parties but overlarge panels should be avoided.

21. Prior to the start of the interview, the candidate shall be informed whether or not the interviewing committee has the power to appoint or only to recommend appointment. When a teacher accepts an appointment by a committee which has the power to appoint, he or she should not subsequently withdraw from an acceptance of the appointment. However, where a local authority has to confirm the offer of appointment, it is unreasonable to expect candidates to give a committed acceptance until the offer has been confirmed. Wherever possible, the interviewing committee should allow the candidate offered the post a period of time to consider whether or not he or she wishes to accept it.

22. It is very desirable that interviewed candidates should be provided with a provisional assessment of the salary they would receive if appointed. This assessment shall be as accurate as possible in order to avoid the difficulties which have sometimes arisen in cases where the provisional salary quoted is much higher than that to which the candidate is shown eventually to be entitled. It is recognised that a salary assessment can be only as accurate as the information on which it is based. Accordingly, candidates are advised to provide details of their existing salary (excluding any earnings received for work outside their full-time employment, e.g., extra hourly part-time payments) experience and qualifications. Exact dates shall be specified as part of these details.

23. "Double interview" procedure is acceptable provided that no candidate is required to attend for more than two consecutive days.

Administration following interview

24. Normally all candidates who attend for interview should be reimbursed for the travel and subsistence expenses they sustain. Payment shall be made immediately or as soon as possible after the interview.

25. The Association is concerned about the practice adopted by some Authorities which do not reimburse candidates who are selected for appointment but who decline the offer. It is necessary to distinguish between cases in which such a candidate was aware of the grounds for rejecting the offer prior to his or her visit to the college and the interview, and cases in which a candidate makes a decision to decline the offer due to information gained only during his or her visit or interview. In the former case the Association believes it is reasonable to withhold reimbursement; in the latter case reimbursement shall be made.

26. Every applicant shall be advised that the post has been filled when an appointment has been made.

27. The precise salary payable to the appointed candidate shall be stated in the formal letter of appointment which shall be sent to the teacher as soon as possible and well in advance of the start of his or her duties.

Unfair discrimination

28. The Association is concerned by reports of unfair discrimination in interviews and during the appointment process. Grounds of alleged discrimination are membership of a

teachers' union, political views, religious conviction and the race or sex of the applicant. The Association cannot countenance such discrimination on any grounds and will seek to eliminate it in those cases where it is thought to exist by appropriate negotiations. The Association is sufficiently concerned about unfair discrimination as to have agreed the following resolution at its first Conference in 1976. "Conference calls upon the National Executive Committee to enter into negotiations with the Secretary of State for Education and Science for a revision of Circular 7/70 to embody ... the setting up of appointments procedures and Committees to ensure elected staff representation on panels for internal and external appointments, this procedure to ensure that no discrimination takes place on the grounds of sex, sexuality, age, family status, race, nationality, creed, political belief or record."

29. The Association is concerned about reports it has received of alleged discrimination against women applicants. There is a marked imbalance betweeen the proportion of men and women members of the profession. There are clearly a number of reasons for this trend in general and for the failure of further education to recruit women into senior posts in particular. The Association is determined that discrimination in appointments should be eliminated from amongst these factors.

30. Some women members have reported that they have been asked detailed questions about their plans for a family. In some cases, this has extended to questioning about the method of contraception they use. Similarly, it has been suggested to women candidates that they would find difficulty in coping with family and teaching responsibilities and concern has been expressed that a woman's continuing employment will depend on the location of her husband's job. In addition, women members have gained the impression that interviewing committees have often defined jobs as being exclusively "male" or "female" ones.

31. The Association regards this sort of questioning as totally unnecessary and offensive. There seems no good reason to put to women candidates any questions which are not equally appropriate to male applicants. Whilst this guideline will not solve all the problems which cause the failure to recruit more women into further education, it will at least create a fairer approach to interviewing and the making of appointments.

32. The Association is aware of the recent developments of legislation which deal with discrimination, particularly racial and sex discrimination. It trusts that this policy statement will be seen in the light of this legislation and the Association intends to issue detailed guidance, at a later date, on the implications of this legislation for interviews and appointments procedure and its implications for other areas which concern those involved in further and higher education.

Reference

Sex Discrimination Act 1975, Circular 2/76 (DES); Circular 20/76 (Welsh Office), 20 January 1976.

G.R. Barrell, *Teachers and the Law*, Methuen, 1978.
Christopher Curson, *Education Guide to Industrial Relations*, Swift Publications, 1977
Employment Law and College Management, Coombe Lodge Report, Vol.11, No.7, 1978.
Handbook on the Trade Union and Labour Relations Act 1974, Local Authorities Conditions of Service Advisory Board, 1974.
John Harris, *Employment Protection*, Oyez, 1975.
Joan Henderson, *A Guide to the Employment Protection Act 1975*, The Industrial Society, 1975.
ed. B.A. Hepple and Paul O'Higgins, *Encyclopaedia of Labour Relations Law*, Sweet and Maxwell, 1972.
ed B.A. Hepple, *et al.*, *Labour Relations Statutes and Materials*, Sweet and Maxwell, 1979.
J. McMullen, *Rights at Work*, Pluto Press, 1978.
ed E.B. Pollard, *Croner's Reference Book for Employers*, Croner Publications, 1977.
Sex discrimination and equal pay: How to prepare your own case for an Industrial Tribunal, Equal Opportunities Commission, 1979.
Norman Singleton, *Industrial Relations Procedures*, Department of Employment Manpower Paper No.14, HMSO, 1975.
G. Taylor and J.B. Saunders, *The Law of Education*, Eighth Edition, 1976.
The LACSAB Employee Relations Handbook, Local Authorities Conditions of Service Advisory Board, Revised edition 1977.
Unfair Dismissal, Incomes Data Services Handbook Series, No.1, 1976.
ed P. Wallington, *Butterworth's Employment Law Handbook*, Butterworths, 1979.

10 HEALTH & SAFETY AT WORK

1. **The Robens Report**
In May 1970 a committee of enquiry, chaired by Lord Robens, was established to enquire into the then current health and safety legislation, the nature and extent of voluntary action concerned with those subjects, and to consider whether more needed to be done to safeguard the public from hazards arising from industrial and commercial activities. The committee had the power to make recommendations; its final report was published in July 1972. This report criticized severely the existing system of legislation and recommended that a radical revision was necessary.

2. Robens stated that "perhaps [the] most fundamental defect of the statutory system is simply that there is too much law". The plethora of statute and statutory instrument had resulted in a "sheer mass of this law ... [which] ... may well have become counterproductive". Not only was the legislation vast, detailed and confusing to those to whom it purported to afford protection, but it had been largely instrumental in creating apathy: there was little realisation of the fundamental issues. Every year, approximately 1,000 people were killed at work, half a million injuries occurred and 23 million working days were lost annually because of industrial injury and disease; the annual economic cost amounted to approximately £200 million. Robens concluded that: "The primary responsibility for doing something about the present levels of occupational accidents and disease lies with those who create the risks and those who work with them ... Our present system encourages rather too much reliance on state regulation, and rather too little on personal responsibility and voluntary, self-generating effort. This imbalance must be redressed." [1]

3. The committee found that the bulk of the existing provisions dealt with physical circumstances (for example, the safeguarding of machinery) "to the neglect of equally important human and organizational factors, such as the roles of training and joint consultation, the arrangements for monitoring safety performance and the influence of work systems and organisation upon attitudes and behaviour." [2] Reform of the system of jurisdictions, protection of those employed at premises not then subject to statutory provision; rationalization of the various inspectorates and the need for national policy making and law making bodies were further recommended by the committee. In stating its future objectives, the committee emphasised that:

4. "The most fundamental conclusion to which our investigations have led us is this. There are severe practical limits on the extent to which progressively better standards of safety and health at work can be brought about through negative regulation by external agencies. We need a more effectively self-regulating system. This calls for the acceptance and exercise of appropriate responsibilities at all levels within industry and commerce. It calls for better systems of safety organisation, for more management initiatives, and for

---

1 *Safety and Health at Work, Report of the Committee, 1970-72,* Cmnd. 5034, para.28.
2 *Ibid,* para 31.

more involvement of work people themselves. The objectives of future policy must therefore include not only increasing the effectiveness of the state's contributions to safety and health at work, but also, and more importantly, creating the conditions for more effective self-regulation."[3] This widely quoted statement is often utilized to explain the philosophy of the Health and Safety at Work etc. Act 1974.

5. Robens's recommendations achieved wide acceptance. The Health and Safety at Work etc. Act became law under a government different from that which had set up the Safety and Health at Work Committee, an indication of the support for Robens's proposals. Not all of the Act's provisions were implemented until 1978 and, while it is clear that the Act was based largely upon Robens's report, it is necessary to observe that Robens's vision of a single enabling Act to be supported by new regulations and codes of practice has not, as yet, been achieved; and that the time necessary to attain such a position may be long. Many complex existing statutes remain in force; the educational service is subject to the Act but it is not always easily apparent to the college administrator to which legislation an institution is subject. (Guidance is given on this issue under paragraphs 9-15, below). Robens's recommendations quoted above, however, will give an indication of the spirit in which all ought to view their responsibilities under the Act.

6. **The Health and Safety at Work etc. Act 1974 amended by the Employment Protection Act, 1975: summary of the Act**

The principles of the Act, all derived from the Robens Report, can be summarized under five headings:

(i) *Action rather than reaction.* Employers and managements should plan safety policies and anticipate incidents, rather than follow events.

(ii) *Co-operation.* In their safety planning, employers should attempt to gain the co-operation of their employees through trade union representatives. These representatives should have the rights of consultation and inspection.

(iii) *Clarity.* Safety law should be easily understandable and capable of quick modification as and when the need arises.

(iv) *Incentive enforcement.* Enforcement procedures should be flexible, but also carry penalties sufficient to be an incentive to observation of the law. Hence use is to be made of criminal law.

(v) *Unrestricted protection.* Employers should protect not only their employees from danger, but also all members of the public who are affected by their undertakings.

7. The Act is an enabling device. It establishes principles and general duties but, unlike the Factories Act, 1961 or the Offices, Shops and Railway Premises Act, 1963, only to parts of which the education service was previously subject, it contains no detailed provisions on the standards to maintain in the consideration of specific risks. Detailed safety measures required of employers will be made under the Act by regulations and codes of practice. At present, the only regulations and code made directly under

3 *Ibid*, para 41.

the Act which have an immediate application to education are those concerned with safety representatives and safety committees.[4] Regulations, being statutory instruments, have the force of the law. A code of practice can be said to stand in the same relation to the Act as does the Highway Code to the road traffic laws: contravention of the code is not necessarily an offence given all the circumstances of the event, but the code is admissible in evidence and the onus of proof will rest on the contravenor of the code to prove that actions were justifiable. Notes of guidance on the regulations and codes are written in that type of easily understood language which can be exploited at law: they have no legal stature, are intended to provide guidance on compliance with the Act and not as authoritative statements of the law, but could be used to assist the establishment by counsel of an argument to be presented at law. To disregard any such guidance, however, would be to court danger.

8. The Health and Safety at Work etc. Act contains 85 sections and 10 schedules. Ss1-9 will be summarised individually, the other sections referred to only for the immediate purposes of this book.

S.1 lays down the purposes of the first part of the Act: the maintenance and improvement of health, safety and welfare standards of people at work; the protection of others against risk arising from work activities; the control of the use and storage of dangerous substances; and the control of the emissions into the atmosphere from certain premises.

S.2 imposes a general duty on employers to ensure the health, safety and welfare of their employees. The employer is required to consult the employees on matters concerning joint action on health and safety affairs. At the request of trade union representatives, the employer is required to establish safety committees. A written statement of safety policy and arrangements is required of the employer, as is its publication. (Discussion of the term "employer" will be found under paragraphs 32-33 below).

S.3 requires of employers and the self employed a general duty to ensure that the prosecution of their business does not endanger employees or the public and, where applicable, to provide information to the public about any potential dangers which their activities involve.

S.4 requires those responsible for places and premises of work to ascertain that those places, as well as their contents, do not endanger the people using them. Reference is made under subsection (3) to "risks to health arising from plant or substances in any such premises". "Plant" has a wide legal definition: it is a term which includes any machinery, equipment or appliance. An unsafe chair, for example, would come under this heading.

S.5 refers to the general duty of persons in control of certain premises in relation to harmful emissions into the atmosphere: the best practicable means have to be applied to render harmless and inoffensive such noxious substances as may be emitted.

---

4 *Health and Safety. The Safety Representatives and Safety Committees Regulations 1977*, Statutory Instruments 1977 No. 500. These regulations and also the code of practice are reproduced in *The LACSAB Employee Relations Handbook*, revised edition 1977.

S.6 requires that anyone who designs, manufactures or supplies an article or substance for use at work should ensure, so far as is reasonably practicable, that such items are safe when used according to that person's instructions. Necessary testing, research and inspection must be carried out, and necessary information supplied. Installers of plant are required to ensure that it is safely installed.

S.7 states that all employees while at work have a duty to take reasonable care to ensure that they neither endanger themselves nor others by their work activities. The employee must co-operate with the employer so far as is necessary for the employer to fulfil statutory duties.

S.8 forbids the misuse of, or interference with, anything provided for health and safety purposes under a statutory requirement.

S.9 prevents employers from charging employees for any equipment provided for health and safety purposes or for anything done in compliance with statute.

Ss10-12 relate to the establishment, functions and powers of the Health and Safety Commission and the Health and Safety Executive.

Ss 15-17 refer to regulations and codes of practice.

Ss 18-26 refer to enforcement, powers of inspectors and notices of improvement and prohibition.

Ss 27-28 refer to the obtaining and disclosure of information. Health and Safety Executive inspectors are required to supply certain information to employers or their safety representatives. However, s.28 provides for a restriction of the information which an employer is required to supply.

Ss 29-32 apply to agriculture;

Ss 33-42 refer to offences; and

S 43 is concerned with financial provisions.

Ss 44-54 are concerned with miscellaneous and supplementary provisions.

S.47 refers to civil liability. It is intended that proceedings in respect of any infringement of the Act may be brought only by the Inspectorate, except by permission of the Director of Public Prosecutions. Similarly, it is intended that civil actions are not to be based on alleged breaches of the Act. Whether these intentions are carried out depends upon the interpretation of the Act in the courts: a right of action to civil proceedings may arise under regulations made under the Act, provided that such regulations do not bar such actions. However, the common law route remains open to employees seeking redress to injuries caused whilst pursuing their employment.

Ss 55-60 refer to the Employment Medical Advisory Service.

Ss 61-76 refer to building regulations.

Ss 77-85 are miscellaneous and general provisions.

Schedule 1 lists existing enactments which are statutory provisions relevant to the Act.

9. **Further and higher education and the Act**
The education service is one to which the term "new entrant" to health and safety legislation applies. The term is used to identify those sectors of the economy which were not covered, or covered only incidentally, by former statutory provision. All those employed in education now come within the jurisdiction of the Act. Students are not directly covered, but they are afforded protection under s.3: as members of the public they have protection against the acts or omissions of all those who are responsible for, or work in, the institutions which they attend. Student protection is further investigated under paragraphs 72-74, below.

10. The Health and Safety at Work etc. Act, however, is not, as has been explained, a detailed codification of health and safety law. Establishing to which statute various educational activities are subject is not an easy process. The legislation which directly applies is:
(i) The Health and Safety at Work etc. Act 1974: general duties only.
(ii) Offices, Shops and Railway Premises Act, 1963: statutory requirements for the provision of a safe and healthy working environment for those employed in offices, including lighting and ventilation, sanitary accommodation, space and guarding of machinery.
(iii) The Petroleum (Regulations) Act 1963: requirement concerned with the storage of defined petroleum spirits.
Contrary perhaps to expectation, The Standards for School Premises Regulations, 1972, do *not* apply directly to further and higher education, although it would be unwise to ignore such relevant guidance as they supply.

11. As the making of regulations and codes of practice under the Act will take a great deal of time, most of the current statutes governing occupational safety are to continue in existence. The difficulty is that many of such statutes are relevant to the activities of further and higher education but do not have a direct legal bearing thereon. It is necessary, therefore, to attempt to interpret requirements and obligations in the light of existing established legal precedent. It must be noted, however, that the arguments set out in paras 12-15 below will not be confirmed until established by sufficient legal precedent.

12. The Factories Act, 1961, has an application wider than its title. Whilst the definition of a factory under s.175 of that legislation refers to "premises in which ... the work is carried out by way of trade or for the purposes of gain", s.175 (9) states that "any premises occupied by the Crown or by any

municipal or other public authority ... shall not be excluded ... by reason only that the work carried on is not carried on by way of trade or by purposes of gain." Therefore, subject to decisions at law, it will be generally the case that this Act will apply directly to local authority colleges where people are employed in any of the activities specified in the Act. A storekeeper, for example, would have the same protection under the Factories Act while working in an authority college as he would have had if his employment had been in a factory. Further implications for colleges of the Factories Act are discussed in paragraph 13.

13. The key duty conferred on the employer in the Health and Safety at Work etc. Act is the requirement to do all that is "reasonably practicable" for the purposes of safeguarding health, safety and welfare. The Act does not indicate what is and what is not reasonably practicable, although in using such a phrase it relies upon a well tried expression taken from the common law. It has been suggested by several writers on the law that one of the tests for reasonable practicability should be that of the standards set out in factory and other occupational legislation. Thus, while such statute would not have a *direct* application, it sets out the standards which ought to apply and the contravention or observance of which moreover could be taken to be a key test as to whether there is a case to answer under the Health and Safety at Work etc. Act. Support for such a view comes from the case of Butt vs ILEA. (*Times Law Reports*, 6 March 1968; *Local Government Reports* 66 LGR 379; *Knights Industrial Reports*, IV 2 p.iii) In this case it was held that, even though the student who was injured at a machine in a technical college was neither employed nor subject to the Factories Act, the standard of safety which should apply in such a college when operating such machinery should be that of the Factories Act and its associated legislation. It can be said, therefore, that it would be an unwise college which contravened statutory occupational legislation where that legislation was relevant to any college activity or undertaking.

14. The Health and Safety Executive (HSE) has issued a list of statutory instruments which provide guidance in complying with the Health and Safety at Work etc. Act. This list is reproduced as Appendix 1. The list can be said to apply to the argument outlined in paragraph 13, above.

15. The Health and Safety Executive has also issued a list of its advisory publications, together with that of the DES, which apply to colleges. This list forms Appendix 2 of this sub-section of the handbook. However, these advisory publications fall short of being codes of practice under the Act. They are best understood as fulfilling the same function as HSE notes of guidance. They are not legal documents and have no legal status. If they were to be referred to in legal proceedings, observance thereof may be held to have illustrated an attempt to take all reasonably practicable steps to have avoided hazard, but that would not necessarily be the case. Again, it would be an unwise institution which disregarded such advisory publications, but mere adherence to them could well be insufficient to satisy the requirements of the Act. The only certain way of complying with the Act is to take all possible measures to ensure health, safety and welfare. Advisory

publications are an assistance, ought not be ignored lightly, but in themselves are no real protection against prosecution.

16. **The Health and Safety Commission (HSC)**
The Commission came into being on 1 October 1974. Its membership consists of not fewer than six members and not more than nine, including the chairman. Three members are appointed by consultation with employers, three by consultation with the trade unions, and the others after consultation with the local authorities and any other bodies deemed appropriate by the Secretary of State. The functions of the HSC are:
(i) to take action which will further the purposes of the Act;
(ii) to promote research and training;
(iii) to furnish advice and information (for example, by way of the Employment Medical Advisory Service);
(iv) to carry out enquiries and investigations (usually via the HSE);
(v) to establish advisory committees;
(vi) to establish an Executive which will enforce the law and provide advice on how best to comply with it.
Thus far 7 advisory committees have been set up under the HSC:
(i) Advisory Committee on Major Hazards;
(ii) Advisory Committee on Asbestos;
(iii) Medical Advisory Committee;
(iv) Advisory Committee on Dangerous Substances;
(v) Advisory Committee on Toxic Substances;
(vi) Agriculture Industry Advisory Committee;
(vii) HSE/Local Authority Enforcement Liaison Committee.
With the exception of the Agriculture Advisory Committee, there is local authority representation on all these committees.

17. The HSC has identified three areas as central to its strategy of anticipating rather than following events: the review of existing legislation; the encouragement of positive attitudes to safety, health and welfare; and the better provision of information.

18. **The Health and Safety Executive**
The HSE was created on 1 January 1975. It has a director and two deputy directors. Its staff consists mainly of the previous occupational health and safety inspectorates. With the exception of the Railway Inspectorate, all previous inspectorates are now under the aegis of the HSE. The Executive has further defined its functions under eight headings:
(i) providing the HSC with the information and advice necessary for it to carry out its functions;
(ii) the securing of the observance of the Act and other relevant legislation by all to whom they apply;
(iii) the maintenance and improvement of all the services to industry and commerce in existence before the 1974 Act;
(iv) the development of services to the new entrants;
(v) the development of the capacity to protect the general public against risks arising from work activities;

(vi) the provision of advice and information to departments of government and other relevant bodies;

(vii) the representation of the government on relevant matters at the EEC and other international organizations;

(viii) the maintenance and extension of research work.

19. The Executive has reformed the location of inspectorate organization. Over 100 district offices of the former Factory Inspectorate have been closed down; the organization is now concentrated upon a limited number of local offices and 21 area offices. This concentration has been the subject of some criticism. The locations of these area offices are reproduced as Appendix 3, below. Each area office will have an inspector or group of inspectors who specialise in a particular sector of employment.

20. The Commission, by way of the HSE and its inspectorate, has the power of enforcement, but it is a power shared in certain circumstances by the local authorities. However, local authorities do not have any enforcement or inspection powers in the new entrant areas. Education, therefore, remains within the purview of the HSE, although this may be subject to future alteration. "Self-inspection" by local authorities is not allowed; nor can one local authority inspect the premises of another. As far as colleges are concerned, therefore, the position is likely to remain unchanged, except for that of voluntary institutions. (See also Appendix 5).

21. **Regulations and codes of practice**

Regulations and codes of practice have already been referred to above, but it remains necessary to refer to their origin. Regulations must be made by the Secretary of State, but they will normally follow from proposals by the HSC and consultation with relevant bodies. The delay of some 18 months in the implementation of the regulations relating to safety representatives and committees was caused by local authorities' concern over cost.

22. Non-statutory or quasi-statutory approved codes of practice relating to health and safety represent a concept relatively new to this country. The Act (s.16) gives the codes the status of practical guidelines relating to the requirements of the general duties under the Act. Codes may be issued by the HSE, or approved by the HSE after their issue by some other body. This retrospective approval is presumed to be intended to refer to standard specifications issued by the British Standards Institute and to codes issued by authorised professional bodies.

23. This reliance upon outside bodies can be easily explained. Many statutory provisions dealing with health and safety are out of date; not only are the required standards inadequate, but the terminology used has become obsolete. For example, the 1941 Lighting Regulations have been repealed: metrication of lighting standards was required and the standards of the 1941 regulations were anyway inadequate. Moreover, the standards of lighting provided for by the Offices, Shops and Railway Premises Act 1963 are also

out of date. Therefore, the lighting standards currently used are those of the Illuminating Engineering Society (IES).[5]

24. Codes of practice cannot be approved by the HSC without the consent of the Secretary of State and are subject also to the same processes of consultation as are regulations. The status of codes in law has been referred to already. There is no certainty as to how codes will be used. They could be used mainly in support of regulations or, as Robens intended, have a widespread use as an alternative to regulations. It seems most likely that the use of codes will be dependent upon the weight given to them in legal proceedings; it will be necessary for colleges to keep themselves informed of the status accorded to codes in law.

25. **Notices of improvement and prohibition**

When an investigator or inspector discovers what he or she considers to be a breach of statute, or that a breach has occurred in circumstances which make it likely that such a breach will continue, then he or she is empowered to serve a notice on the person or organization concerned. This notice will state the alleged breach of statute, the reasons why it is considered that an offence has been committed and may go on to require that the breach is remedied in a specified period of not less than 21 days from the date of the notice. This notice is an improvement notice.

26. Improvement notices refer only to a breach of statute. There is no power to issue such a notice where a code of practice has been contravened. Improvement notices will usually contain advice on remedies; they may be withdrawn by the inspector before expiry but presumably only after the defect has been remedied and checked. The recipient of an improvement notice may appeal to an industrial tribunal if he or she considers the notice unjustified. The tribunal may cancel, affirm or modify the notice; the notice is suspended until the tribunal hearing is concluded. Unless an appeal is pending or has been upheld, once the time limit of the notice has expired without improvement taking place, then an offence has been committed. Prosecution will almost certainly follow.

27. When an inspector believes that work activities are causing a risk of serious personal injury, he or she may serve a prohibition notice. A prohibition notice must state the inspector's opinion of which statute may be being breached and the circumstances creating the risk. The inspector in this instance does not have to allege a breach of statute. The prohibition can become operative at once. If a time limit is stipulated, the notice is termed usually a "deferred prohibition notice". Appeal machinery is similar to that against improvement notices, except that the prohibition will not be suspended during the appeal unless the employer is successful in making a *separate* application to continue the practice subject to the prohibition.

28. It is not the policy of the HSE to issue notices whenever contravention of

---

5 Lighting, and other matters relevant to "welfare" under the Act are discussed in Section **5.3**, above.

statute is discovered. The usual procedure is for the inspector to allow the employer opportunity to remedy matters (unless the risks are grave, or the employer is a persistent offender). However, colleges are subject to many restrictions, especially when expenditure is necessary. Thus, in order to ensure that any requirement of an inspector is implemented, colleges will require swift communication with those persons and bodies authorised to allow expenditure. (Normally the college will need to be in contact with the appropriate LEA officer). Speed of action is of importance when an improvement notice is under consideration, essential when the issue is one of prohibition. It is worth observing that notices are not issued lightly. In 1976 the HSE issued 6100 notices. Of the 40 appeals against notice, only three achieved modification; no notices were cancelled. Already there have been cases in schools and colleges where conditions were such that it was necessary to issue notices of improvement and prohibition.

29. Although the rights and duties of employers are investigated below under paragraphs 31-36 it is apposite here to draw attention to two further matters concerning notices. While notices relate to contravention of legislation and require improvements to be made within specified periods, and as such are not particularly appropriate for individuals, there is nonetheless no legal reason why they should not be served on employees. If a notice were to be served on an employee, he or she would have to comply with the conditions set out above or else face the legal penalties. The employee is involved in notices in a second way. One of the functions of a safety representative is to represent members in consultations at the place of work with the HSE inspector; in the event of an inspector issuing a notice under the Act, the inspector would also have a duty to issue a copy of the notice to a safety representative (or else arrange for its publication at the work place).

30. **Employment Medical Advisory Service (EMAS)**

The EMAS consists of a medical staff of some 100 and is in the employment of the HSC. The tasks of the service are the identification of health hazards; to function as a central information bank; to advise on environmental control necessary as a result of work activities and monitor such action as is taken; to advise employers and employees of any risks to health to which they may be exposed; to advise on the medical aspects of any employment problems, particularly the employment of the handicapped and rehabilitation for employment; and to attempt to act as a focus for the development of occupational medicine in Britain. The service will advise on the effects of a particular job on health, undertake medical examinations and study the medical requirements for varieties of work, taking special cognizance of the handicapped. It is recommended that, wherever problems arise relating to occupational health, early recourse by employers or safety representatives should be taken to the local EMAS area office. Appendix 4 provides a list of EMAS locations.

31. **Duties under the Health and Safety at Work etc. Act**

Employers

Before investigating this topic, it is necessary to define for the purposes of this sub-section, who in the education service is an employer, and also those upon whom certain of the employer's responsibilities and liabilities devolve.

32. Where colleges are maintained by a local authority, then invariably the local authority will be the employer. In the case of a voluntary institution, the employer is the governing body. In both cases the employer is a corporate body.

33. S.37 (1) of the Act states that "where an offence ... committed by a body corporate is proved to have been committed with the consent or connivance of, or to have been attributable to any neglect on the part of, any director, manager, secretary or other similar officer of the body corporate or a person who was purporting to act in any such capacity, he as well as the body corporate shall be guilty of that offence and shall be liable to be proceeded against accordingly". Therefore, an individual can be prosecuted as well as the corporate body of which he or she is an employee. It would be possible to construe principals, vice-principals, senior administrative officers and senior staff generally as fulfilling the functions of managers on their employer's behalf. Such a construction must be qualified, however. It is the advice of the HSE that for senior college staff to have a criminal liability under the Act, one or all of the following conditions would need to be satisfied.

(i) that the senior college staff would have to have fulfilled a policy making role within the body corporate (i.e. to have had a position of consultation within the LEA [or in a voluntary college, the governing body] analogous to that of a member of the board of directors of a company); or

(ii) that the senior staff had a responsibility for the implementation of a safety policy; or

(iii) that the senior staff have been given designated safety responsibilities by the employer.

34. Whilst this advice offers some clarification, further qualifications are necessary. If the contract of employment or the instrument and articles of government lay such responsibilities as enumerated above upon a senior staff member, then a liability is incurred. It is the general view of the HSE that most principals of colleges are "too far down the chain of responsibility" to incur liability under s.37(1) but it is admitted that the courts alone can decide the ultimate interpretation. It can be stated with confidence, however, that where a senior staff member failed in designated duties, or to implement designated duties under a safety policy, then that individual could be liable to criminal prosecution. (NB: the matter of the imposition of duties on teachers is discussed in paragraph 39, below). Senior staff, the principal particularly, have a general duty under s.4(2) of the Act to ensure that the premises of the college are safe and without risks to health. Derelictions of this duty notwithstanding, the conditions for criminal liability are those itemised above (although in any instance of dereliction of duty it would clearly be difficult to separate the issues). Until legal precedent has been established the advice to be offered to senior staff is:

(i) while in general liability to criminal prosecution may be unlikely, any issue would be decided on the whole circumstances of the case; and

(ii) where duties have been clearly designated, there is the possibility of liability.

It must be stressed, however, that the HSE states that its general policy is to place responsibility on employers and that employees should not be required to undertake duties, responsibilities and liabilities which were not intended under the Act to apply to them. An instance of employee liability under s.37(1) is discussed in paragraph 43, below. This instance refers to neglect. The "consent or connivance" referred to in s.37(1) can be defined thus: "consent" means conscious acquiescence; "connivance" means active participation (in bringing about the contravention of the Act). Therefore, as well as having their individual duties as employees under the Act, the managerial staff of colleges have clear duties while acting as their employer's agents and also one liable to penalties under the Act if they fail properly to discharge their health and safety functions on their employer's behalf. An example of such circumstance could be found in a failure to fulfil duties under an employer's agreed safety policy.

35. The majority of duties imposed by the Act fall upon employers. These general duties have been represented as being so broad that they differ little from obligations under the existing common law. The difference is that, whereas the common law provided – and provides – for civil liability and civil damages, the Act imposes the sanction of criminal offence for disregard of statutory duties. Under s.2 of the Act the employer's duties are:

(i) to provide and maintain safe plant and systems of work;

(ii) to ensure the safe using, handling, storing and transporting of articles and substances;

(iii) to provide instruction, information, training and supervision;

(iv) to provide a working environment which is safe and without risk to health;

(v) to provide adequate welfare facilities;

(vi) to ensure that the employer's activities do not expose the public to risk;

(vii) to make no charge for any equipment or materials (such as goggles), which are required by statute for the safety of the employee;

(viii) to provide a safety policy and to ensure that the policy is brought to the notice of employees;

(ix) to consult safety representatives and, when requested, to establish safety committees;

(x) to prevent offensive or noxious fumes from entering the atmosphere;

(xi) to give information concerning health, safety and welfare in the shareholders' reports.

36. These duties are all qualified by the phrase "so far as is reasonably practicable". This terminology has a considerable history of interpretation resulting from its use in the Factories Act. It is safe, therefore, to assume that such interpretation will be applied here. In order to consider whether any action was "reasonably practicable" it has been established that the test is that of the cost of the preventive or remedial action concerned balanced against the possibility or likelihood of any injuries resulting from the action not being taken. The term "reasonably practicable" should be contrasted with the term "practicable". "Practicable" is taken to mean whatever is

possible, given the current state of knowledge on the subject without taking cognizance of the cost involved. S.40 of the Act, however, indicates that the burden of proof lies with the accused: it is for the accused to show that a safety precaution which could have ameliorated, mitigated or prevented an event was not reasonably practicable, or practicable, as the case may be. To emphasize the point: it is for the accused to prove that in any circumstance he or she did all that was reasonably practicable.

37. As the functions and work systems of colleges vary so considerably, it would be both tedious and futile to attempt to provide a detailed commentary on each of the employers' duties and upon each remedial step to be taken. Two observations, however, can be made. A local authority was successfully prosecuted following an accident at an outdoor pursuits centre: fumes emitted from a boiler resulted in a fatal accident involving the gassing of four girls. It is the clear duty of the employer and his managers under the Act, and for the purposes of this book the local authority or governing body and their senior staff in their colleges, to ensure that the working environment for which they are responsible is, as far as is reasonably practicable, safe, healthy and without risk to all who work therein or are within its premises or environs. This duty extends to the adequate provision of facilities and arrangements for welfare at work. Guidance for such duties can be found under the publications and information cited in the bibliography and appendices of this sub-section.

38. *Employees*

The general duties imposed on employees are less specific than those laid upon the employers, but have a scope which has been the cause of considerable concern amongst teachers. The duties are:

(i) to take reasonable care for themselves and for others who may be affected by their acts or omissions;

(ii) to co-operate with the employer so far as is necessary for the execution of the employer's duties; and

(iii) to refrain from recklessly or intentionally interfering with anything provided in the interests of their health, safety and welfare.

The third duty, abstinence from reckless behaviour, ought not to create difficulty. The other duties have been the cause of debate and concern. The HSE has commented wryly that the main concern in education seemed to be that of the teachers for their responsibilities to their pupils, whereas the real cause for worry was the inadequate health and safety systems in certain areas of education.[6]

39. It was thought that employees in colleges would have little difficulty in complying with the provision to co-operate with the employer. However, the HSE has found this not to be the case and has pronounced trenchantly upon the subject: "There has been considerable misunderstanding about the extent of the teacher's duty under Section 7(a) and there has been a tendency to assign to teachers duties which they do not have. The argument has been that the HSW Act requires local education authorities to provide safe

---

6 *Pilot Study, Health and Safety in Schools and Further Education Establishments,* Health and Safety Executive, paras.132, 145, *passim.*

conditions, including safe apparatus, fittings and laboratory space etc. This having been done, the teacher, it is said, is responsible if unsafe procedures or inadequate apparatus are used.

"This widely held view is misleading in two respects. First because it lays upon teachers duties far beyond those set out in the Act, and second because it changes the thrust of the Act and directs it towards the protection of students and pupils, whereas it is, in fact, the teacher as an employee who is equally entitled to this protection. Only by due process of delegation could an LEA shift the substantial part of its responsibility to teachers. Delegation is an individual overt act, precisely defined in the authorities.

"A teacher is paid to exercise control, but the principal responsibility for carrying out the provisions of the HSW Act lies with LEAs because they are the employers. Their main duty is towards their employees, the teachers, lecturers, technicians and multifarious non-teaching staff. These duties extend beyond the provision of safe conditions (apparatus, premises), to include safe systems of work and the maintenance of such systems and such apparatus and premises, and the like. The teacher is often the instrument whereby these duties are carried out, but does not himself thereby necessarily assume the LEA's responsibility." [7]

40. The requirement on the employee to take reasonable care is not one upon which it is easy to be specific. Blatant failure to observe this regulation could result in prosecution, even if the culpable individual had suffered personal injury as a result of his or her behaviour and could moreover offer evidence sufficient of misconduct to justify dismissal. Many college activities are hazardous, although these hazards are reduced by the processes entailed being largely occasional – or, at least, below the frequency of occurrence in similar circumstances on a factory production line. It has been shown that the more frequent process and the more experienced operator combine to increase the risk of accident. However, presuming that the teacher is implementing the relevant published guidelines on safety and health, and exercising "reasonable care", then the obligations may be fulfilled. It will only be when the courts have decided on the interpretation of "reasonable care" that firmer advice can be offered. It can be argued that the emphasis which the courts will lay will be upon commonsense rather than particular safety expertise. Until a definitive judgement occurs, employees ought all at least to observe guidelines, attempt to fulfil their statutory duties, report to their safety representative and college authorities (and, in the case of senior staff, to their employers and governing bodies) any hazards of which they are aware. Students should receive information on hazards and should not be left unsupervised without the employer's consent in potentially dangerous situations. Where a college safety committee has devised a code of practice, it should be observed.

41. *Others*

S.6 of the Act (suppliers of goods and materials to colleges) has been referred to under paragraph 8 above, as has s.3 which places duties on the self-employed (relevant to colleges where contractors and sub-contractors

---

7 *Ibid*, paras 185-187.

are employed on any activity[8]). It would be wise nonetheless for colleges to check deliveries and activities wherever possible. Students, other occupants of colleges who are not employees, and indeed all members of the public have a duty under the Act. S.8 provides for prohibition of the misuse of materials relevant for health and safety; everyone is subject to the offences provision of s.33 (for example, the obstruction of an inspector in the exercise or performance of his or her powers of duties), and s.36 is relevant where an offence is due to the act or default of some other person (in which case that other person shall be guilty of the offence).

42. **Prosecution**

It is for the enforcing authority – in the case of colleges the HSE – to decide whether to institute proceedings and, where there is a choice, if they are to occur in a crown court or a court of summary jurisdiction (magistrates' court). Penalties vary according to venue. The maximum penalty at a magistrates' court is £1000. If the HSE elects for indictment in the crown court, fines are without limit and an offender is liable for up to two years' imprisonment. A continuing fine of £50 per day is incurred for non-compliance with notices of improvement or prohibition.

43. It is HSE policy in most cases to prosecute only where the law is being deliberately and persistently flouted. However, it is worth recalling that if a manager of a corporate body is found to be responsible for a statutory offence committed with his or her consent or connivance, or for the offence to have been attributable to his or her neglect, then he or she is liable to prosecution. The director of roads for Strathclyde Regional Council was found guilty of five charges concerning the accidental death of a council employee. The charges related to neglect. In the appeal judgment it was stated that s.37(1) of the Act referred "to any neglect, which means neglect in duty, however constituted." The judgment continued: "the Council's statement of Safety Policy, ... imposed on the appellant the duty to prepare ... a written general safety policy in relation to the work of his department. His failure to do so thus constituted neglect." The director was fined. (*Industrial Relations Law Reports,* Vol.6, No.8, August 1977, 310). Fines of up to £6,000 have thus far been incurred under the Act.

44. On conviction, a court may issue an order which will compel specified remedial action within a given time. Orders may also be issued for purposes such as the destruction or removal of dangerous substances.

45. **Safety representatives**

On 1 October 1978 the Safety Representatives and Safety Committee Regulations made under s.2(4) of the Act came into operation. These regulations provide for a wide trade union function in the implementation of the Act. It is important to realise the spirit which guides the regulations: this is an attempt to attain Robens's ideal of a safety consciousness throughout all working activities by closely involving the representatives of the work force in the provision of safe and healthy conditions. Such a

8 This provision extends also to lecturers who design or make machinery for use in college, even if the exercise is not carried out for gain.

concept has been praised as furthering industrial democracy and attacked as removing responsibility from management; the potential costs involved have given rise to protest. Whatever the causes for praise and complaint, the regulations are now in force and if the Act is to be successful in its intentions must be implemented fully.

46. Only recognised trade unions are allowed to appoint safety representatives. The definition of recognised trade unions is derived from the Trade Union and Labour Relations Act 1974 and the Employment Protection Act 1975 and means an independent trade union recognised by the employer for the purposes of collective bargaining. As far as college and polytechnic teaching staff are concerned, this means effectively that unions represented on the Burnham Further Education Committee may appoint safety representatives. While authorities may make local agreements with unions not represented on Burnham, CLEA has advised local education authorities to recognise only the Burnham unions. Other recognised unions who have members working in colleges among the non-teaching staff are also entitled to appoint safety representatives.

47. Selection of safety representatives should occur via the procedures issued by the unions involved, and once they have been appointed the employer should be notified in writing. The employer is the local education authority (except in certain polytechnics and in voluntary establishments), and safety representatives make their representations to the authority and not to principals and senior academic staff unless those persons have been so designated by the authority. The representatives must be employed in the workplace where they are to carry out their functions (except in the cases of members of Actors' Equity or the Musicians' Union) and, where reasonably practicable, should have had at least two years' employment with their present employer or two years' experience in similar employment. Where, as in colleges, there are situations in which several unions have representation, the HSC has advised that a safety representative can represent more than one group of workers where there is "mutual agreement between the appropriate unions". In this eventuality, the TUC recommends that the most appropriate way of securing nominations is by way of local existing or *ad hoc* bodies representing all union members.

48. The numbers of safety representatives to be appointed are not specified: such a decision rests clearly on circumstance. Some colleges will have diverse functions resembling those of industry, some will have several sites and some will be relatively easily inspected monotechnic institutions. Any decision on the numbers and location of representatives rests with the relevant unions, but it may be helpful to identify issues worthy of their consideration. Some regard will need to be paid to cost: not only the costs involved in training and time off, but also the personal costs resultant from conscientious self education. The HSE *Pilot Study* on education in the North West has demonstrated that the more advanced the work, the older the students and the greater the complexity of curriculum, then the greater is the danger and eventuality of risk. Such circumstances call clearly for several representatives, and moreover persons who can share experience of

different complexities of process. In the simplest terms of human nature, an isolated safety representative is less likely to function efficiently than one who has a colleague readily available with whom to discuss functions and the problems encountered. It has been suggested that small establishments should be grouped with others and served by one representative; the TUC suggests that in large colleges there should be separate representation for teaching and non-teaching staff.[9] For the purposes of colleges "small establishments" should be taken to mean only small annexes. All colleges should have their own safety representatives.

49. An employee ceases to be a safety representative when the union which appointed him or her has notified the employer in writing that the appointment has been terminated. The appointment would also be terminated by the resignation of the representative or where the employer dismissed, or transferred him or her from the place or places of work represented.

50. The functions of the safety representative are set out in the regulations and are therefore statutory. They may be summarised as:

(i) to investigate hazards, dangerous occurrences, the causes of accidents and complaints by employees;

(ii) to make representations to the employer arising from the investigations made on general matters affecting health, safety or welfare;

(iii) to consult with inspectors and receive information from them;

(iv) to attend meetings of safety committees in connection with his or her functions;

(v) to make formal inspections at three monthly intervals or where there has been a substantial change in the conditions of work and to make formal inspections following notifiable accidents, occurrences and diseases; and

(vi) to inspect and take copies of any relevant information which the employer is required to keep by virtue of statute.

51. The regulations, 4(1), go on to state that "but without prejudice to Sections 7 and 8 of the 1974 Act, no function given to a safety representative by this paragraph shall be construed as imposing any duty on him." The HSE is instructed not to prosecute a safety representative. Thus the risk of criminal liability is removed from the representative's functions: immediate responsibility in that capacity is to those who choose him or her. However, representatives retain liabilities under the Act which appertain to them as employees. A pessimistic view is taken by some legal authorities regarding the degree of protection against criminal liability arising from the function of safety representatives but any such legal action is perhaps unlikely. There is, however, no protection afforded to a representative against civil liability.

52. The emphasis on the representative's functions is that of prevention. Rather than react to events, the representative is expected to perform his or her

9 The HSE *Pilot Study, op cit.*, para. 212, showed that the incidence of accident in education establishments was far greater among non-teaching staff: "Ancillary workers suffer over 80% of known accidents and yet they do not appear to receive adequate attention so far as safety organisation, safety rules and advisory literature is concerned."

functions on a day to day basis, attempting to prevent accidents before they can occur – an expectation which will require ease of access by the representative to the employer and senior college staff, as well as the need to keep proper records and to liaise with inspectors.

53. Inspection is clearly a vital part of a representative's duty, the pursuance of which may be the cause of dissension in colleges. It is highly important, therefore, to indicate precisely the scope of a representative's powers and to state that the Act makes no distinction between public and private undertakings: college managements can expect a rigorous inspection to take place and they are required to place no unnecessary barriers in the way of such inspection.

54. The forms of inspection which are directly permissible under the regulations are:
    (i) regular inspections of the place of work, these to be carried out at least once a quarter;
    (ii) inspections following a notifiable accident, a dangerous occurrence or the identification of a notifiable disease within the place of work;
    (iii) inspections where there has been a substantial change in the conditions of work (for example, the introduction of new machinery);
    (iv) inspections resultant from the publication by the HSC and HSE of information relevant to the hazards of the place of work;
    (v) the investigation of complaints by employees relating to their health, safety or welfare at work;
    (vi) the inspection and the taking of copies of any document relevant to the workplace or the employees which the employer is required to keep by virtue of any relevant statutory provision (excluding health records on an identifiable individual).

The latter point is one worthy of expansion. While the regulations do not so indicate directly, the code shows clearly that employers ought not to assume that disclosure is limited to minor areas: the code allows for information about "the plans and performances of their undertaking and any changes proposed insofar as they affect the health and safety at work of their employees". Such provision includes also technical information relating to work processes.

55. Where inspections follow notifiable accidents or dangerous occurrences, there is no requirement that the employer is present when the representative consults with his or her constituents. Whilst formal inspections are no substitute for regular informal monitoring, they do provide opportunities for full examination of the work premises, consultations between representatives and discussion with employers and their managers concerning remedial action. It will be necessary for the arrangements for formal inspections to be agreed with employers (and in multi union concerns for all the relevant unions to be consulted). During joint inspections, representatives are allowed private discussions with their members but have no right to exclude employers or their managers during inspections. Listed below are a series of categories useful to adopt in the making of formal inspection criteria:

(i) the number of representatives taking part in an inspection;
(ii) the kinds of inspection to be carried out;
(iii) the precise notice of timing to be agreed for inspection; arrangements for more frequent inspections of high risk or changing areas of work;
(iv) the sub-division of the premises into areas more manageable for inspection;
(v) the different parts of the place of work to be inspected by different groups of representatives; and
(vi) the provisions for consulting with and calling in independent and accredited advisers.

It should be noted that safety representatives have the right immediately to investigate dangerous occurrences, potential hazards, the causes of accidents and complaints from their members without waiting for the occasions of formal joint inspections. The HSC envisages joint formal inspections between employers (managers) and safety representatives.

56. Representatives should complete a report form after an inspection has been carried out. This form records the date, time and details of an inspection: one completed copy should be sent to the employer and the other retained by the representative. Where inspection has been the result of a serious occurrence, the representative should complete the hazard report form, copies of which are distributed as above. Once the employer has completed the "remedial action or explanation" part of the form, it should be returned by him to the representative.[10]

57. HSE inspectors (and, where appropriate, local authority inspectors) have a duty to disclose to representatives certain kinds of information following a visit to college premises. The information includes the result of monitoring or sampling, testing, measurements and any action which the inspector proposes to take. A representative ought to be informed by the employer when an inspector is on the premises and the time of any intended visit; the representative ought also, where necessary, to have the opportunity of private consultation with the inspector and be permitted to accompany the inspection.

58. Employers are required to furnish such "facilities and assistance" to representatives as they may reasonably require to assist them in their inspectoral duties. Representatives are allowed to take samples of any substance used at work for the purposes of analysis. There is no definition of the term "facilities" but it may be useful to refer to the facilities recommended by the TUC:
(i) a room and a desk;
(ii) facilities for storing correspondence, papers and inspection reports;
(iii) access to telephones;
(iv) access to typing and duplicating facilities;
(v) provision of notice board;
(vi) use of internal mailing system;
(vii) noise meters, dust level samplers, detector tubes; and

10 Books of forms of inspection and report are available from HMSO.

(viii) copies of all relevant statutes, regulations, codes, guidance notes and all legal and international standards relevant to the work place.

Where employers refuse to make arrangements, or provide facilities which are inadequate, resort may be made to an industrial tribunal (a provision which extends to time off for training and other areas of employer duty). This is clearly a resort to be avoided by means of consultative arrangements. Cost, however, will clearly be a factor. Large colleges which possess already facilities for trade union activities ought to encounter few problems, but the issues may be more acute in smaller institutions. The employer's duty to provide facilities, therefore, needs to be well indicated. Reference may be made to an industrial tribunal if the facilities are considered to be inadequate.

59. **Time off and training**

Under the Safety Representatives and Safety Committee Regulations, safety representatives have the rights to take time off work in order to carry out their safety functions and to be paid for time taken off work in order to undergo union training courses for safety representatives in accordance with the HSC Code of Practice on Time Off. There is no right given to a representative to demand time off with pay; such a circumstance must be negotiated and agreed with the employer. Under the Act, employers have a duty to train all employees in basic job safety. The initial training of safety representatives is generally a matter for unions alone.

60. As soon as possible after appointment, a safety representative should be allowed paid time off to attend a course of basic training approved by the TUC or by the independent union or unions responsible for the appointment. Further time off for training should be allowed as and when needs arise. When a trade union wishes its safety representatives to receive training, the employer ought to receive details of the particular approved course, a copy of the syllabus and contents (if required) and a satisfactory notice of absence from work. Clearly the numbers of representatives attending a course at any one time ought to be reasonable and not disrupt the operation of the college. Consultation will be both advisable and necessary.

61. **Safety committees**

There are few statutory requirements which relate to safety committees. The regulations require the employer to establish a safety committee where at least two safety representatives have requested it in writing. Such establishment must follow consultation with representatives of the recognised trade unions. A notice stating the composition of the committee must be posted and the committee established within three months of the receipt of the written request. Safety committees which were in existence in colleges before the Act ought either to be dissolved and replaced by new bodies or reconstituted as recommended by the HSE.

62. Advice is given in some detail in the HSC Notes of Guidance, but there is no code of practice covering safety committees. The notes emphasise that arrangements for committees should result from negotiations between employers and safety representatives and that the areas of reference should

include health and welfare as well as safety. Functions of the committees are specified thus:

(i) to study trends and statistics concerning accidents and notifiable diseases and make recommendations for corrective action;
(ii) to examine safety audit reports; to consider reports and information provided by the inspectorate and safety representatives;
(iii) to assist in the development of safety rules and safe systems of work;
(iv) to maintain a watch on the effectiveness of the safety content of employee training;
(v) to monitor the adequacy of safety and health communications and publicity in the place of work;
(vi) to provide a link with the appropriate inspectorates of the enforcing authority; and
(vii) possibly to carry out inspections as an addition to those done by management and safety representatives.

63. The HSC emphasises that the number of management representatives should not exceed the number of employee representatives, and that management representatives should possess knowledge, expertise and "adequate authority". Safety representatives are not responsible to the committee, nor are they its agents, and nor are they bound by its findings. It is clear that representatives of employees other than safety representatives should have seats on the committee. The guidance notes stress the need for regular meetings and quick decisions by managements on recommendations of the committees. Also recommended is the presence of *ex officio* members, such as doctors or professional workers in the field of health and safety, and the stricture that the committee ought not to be unwieldy in size.

64. There is a variety of opinion on the role and structure of safety committees, but for the purposes of colleges it is possible to make observations which ought to have value. The regulations do not remove health and safety from the arena of collective bargaining between employer and employees' recognised representatives. Therefore, any safety committee decision may be subject to renegotiation. The effectiveness of any committee depends upon the dedication, expertise and energies of its members: an obvious danger for colleges to avoid is that a sudden rush of improving zeal is allowed to dissipate into apathy once immediate problems have been solved. Such is the variety of college work, even within one local authority, that it is likely that each college will require its own safety committee and, in some cases, that there will be a need for one committee per site. In these instances it may be difficult to arrange for the inclusion on each committee of a representative of each relevant recognised union. The situation may be ameliorated by the establishment of local authority joint safety committees. This is the case in Devon. A simple example is illustrated below:

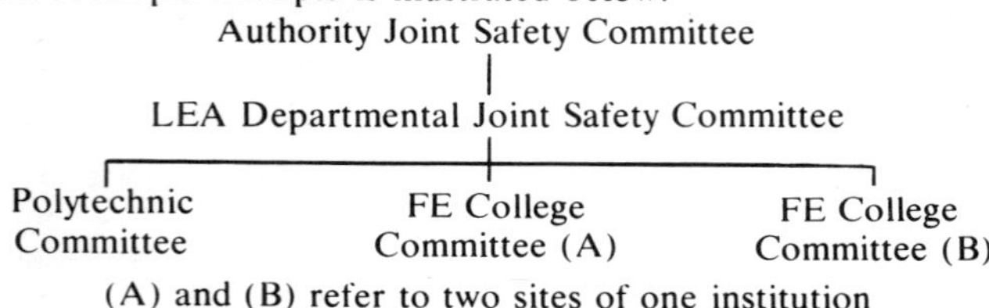

(A) and (B) refer to two sites of one institution

65. Ultimately the matter here is one for negotiation. Committees may cover education as a whole or separate arrangements may be made for colleges and schools. Whichever the case, colleges will require an effective system of safety and joint safety committees. Difficulties in the resolution of such procedures ought to be resolved under the agreed appropriate disputes procedure before reference is made to outside agencies such as ACAS or the HSE.

66. **Safety officers**

Safety officers are regarded at law as the representatives of the employer on health and safety. They fall into the managerial category and have no protection against criminal liability should they clearly fail in their duties. Colleges, therefore, are advised not to follow a practice common before 1978 of appointing teaching (or ancillary) staff as safety officers. Such staff have their general duties under the Act as explained previously, but an additional appointment as a safety officer would be to impose obligations which are not those of the ordinary employee but which are, once entered into, inescapable.

67. Given the obligations on the employer under the Act, it would be surprising if professional safety officers were not appointed.[11] Where a college has a full-time safety officer, or where an authority safety officer has specific duties regarding a college, employees have a statutory duty not to obstruct him or her, and to co-operate with the officer in the pursuit of the employer's safety provisions.

68. **Safety policies**

Under the Act, all employers have a duty to draw up and bring to the attention of their employees a written statement of their safety policy. This statement must be revised whenever necessary. It has been suggested that the posting on a notice board of a safety policy may be inadequate: the employees' attention needs to be directed positively to the policy. Colleges should consider issuing policies to each employee. The term "safety policy" is one capable of wide definition, and the means of notification of the policy can be varied. The whole policy, if it included items such as codes of practice, could become a document so bulky that it could defeat its purpose and be subject to the kinds of criticism Robens directed at previous health and safety legislation. There could be occasions, therefore, when safety policies ought to be designed to meet particular needs: each employee could be issued with a précis of the policy which would be accompanied by such further information relevant to that employee; and supplemented by an advisory statement specifying the details and locations of other documents, as well as that of the whole policy.

69. The HSE advises that the safety policy should be in three parts: a general statement, the organization for implementation and the arrangements for

11 Given the possibility of criminal liability, it is highly important that the safety officer has a clear, defined responsibility. *Safety in Colleges: The Legal Requirements,* Coombe Lodge Report, Information Special, Vol.11, No.8 pp.304-5 reproduces a job description for a full-time safety officer.

ensuring health and safety. The general declaration should indicate the intention to provide a healthy and safe working environment. LACSAB suggests this formula: "The Authority recognises and accepts its responsibility as an employer for providing a safe and healthy workplace and working environment for all of its employees." The organization for the implementation of the policy should detail the allocation of responsibility within the institution. Therefore, individuals exercising responsible functions should be named, the structure of the joint consultative machinery explained and the means stated by which resources will be allocated to cope with health and safety matters. The third part of the policy should cover the full extent of the employer's enterprise and itemise detailed safety procedures or else, where appropriate, refer to other printed information on safety available to the employees.

70. Unless the safety policy contains analyses of precautions, possible hazards and relevant legal standards, it is unlikely to have great value, and may constitute a failing under the duties imposed by the Act. Policies can be supplemented by the inclusion of HSE material: the HSE has deliberately released copyright to allow for such eventualities.

71. As the employer has a duty to inform employees of his or her safety policies, he or she may wish to supplement written statements by the provision of specialist library facilities. Moreover, any training programme for its employees and users which a college might introduce, while it could not replace the right of safety representatives to attend approved training courses, would not only be a contribution to the purposes for which the Act was designed, but also the fulfilling of one of the employer's obligations.

72. **Students**

The general protection under the Act of students has been referred to under paragraph 9, above. While civil proceedings cannot themselves arise from s3(1) of the Act, the civil liability of the college is not removed by the Act. Should the relevant regulations be made under s15 of the Act, however, then they could give rise to both civil and criminal liabilities. Ss3 and 4 of the Act cover all students attending a college (i.e. the right, as far as is reasonably practicable, not to be exposed to risks to their health and safety). General protection of students, and of all other lawful visitors, is given by the Occupier's Liability Act 1957. Breach of this Act gives rise to civil actions for compensation (see Section **5.7**).

73. Further protection is afforded to day-release, sandwich and other part-time students. These students have the benefit of the protection of s2: *their employer* must continue to fulfil his or her duties. The HSE advises that the student's employer to fulfil his obligations must:

"(i) before sending his apprentices to the college, he should ask for and receive an assurance from the college that it is complying with the known safety standards in respect of machinery etc.,

"(ii) issuing to the apprentice whatever protective clothing and equipment (overalls, goggles etc) the apprentice will need during his attendance at the college.

(iii) telling the apprentice, preferably in writing, that if any of the protective clothing or equipment is lost or damaged, he should report such loss or damage to his employer."

74. The term "apprentice" can be applied to any person undergoing training or instruction at any type of training establishment. Should the student suffer an accident at college not attributable to any failing in his employer's duties, then his employer is absolved of responsibility. Responsibility for the accident, were this any other than the student's own responsibility, would rest with the college, subject to the circumstances of the case.

75. **Notification of accidents and dangerous occurrences**

There is not at present any requirement for the "new entrants" under the Act to notify accidents and dangerous occurrences. The notification of accidents generally within education is haphazard, unsystematic and subject to local variation. The HSE *Pilot Study* complains of the inadequate provision of accident notification and statistical record in education.[12] To remedy this and other similar situations, the HSC has circulated proposals for new regulations concerning notification to be made under the Act. It must be stressed that these are proposals only, but until such time as they or their equivalent become statutory, colleges may wish to base their notification systems upon them. In the reduction of accident levels and the improvement of safety performance, accident notification records play an important part in giving guidance as to necessary remedies and improvements.

76. The HSC has proposed that serious accidents and dangerous occurrences should be reported immediately and confirmed in writing within three days. Notification for college purposes should include all who have a function within the premises. Serious bodily injury would be defined as:

(i) fracture of skull, spine, pelvis, arm or leg;
(ii) amputation of hand or foot or a substantial portion thereof;
(iii) loss of sight of an eye;
(iv) dislocation of major joint or spine; and
(v) other injury which, at the time of the accident, appeared likely to endanger life, cause prolonged or permanent incapacity for work, or substantially impair the physical condition.

77. **Welfare**

The employer has a duty under s2(2) (e) of the Act to provide a working environment which is "so far as reasonably practicable ... adequate as regards facilities and arrangements for their welfare at work". It is not entirely clear as to what precisely welfare means other than in the most general interpretation of the whole working environment. Matters such as washing facilities, drinking water supply, cloakrooms, first aid and sitting facilities are referred to as welfare provisions under Part III of the Factories Act. Reference to such topics has been made in Sections **1.3**, **5.3**, and **5.5**, above.

---

12 HSE, *Pilot Study, op.cit.*, paras. 133, 145, *passim.*

78. **Health and Safety and the Common Law** [13]

An employer has duties placed upon him or her by the common law. These common law duties are all embracing. It is necessary to refer to cases in some detail to explain them (Tennyson called the common law "that wilderness of single instances, that maze of precedent").

79. **Duties at Common Law**

Every employer has a duty of care for the safety of those employed by him or her. This duty is personal to the employer, and though he or she may delegate the performance of the duty, he or she cannot delegate the responsibility for ensuring it is done. At common law the duty is that of taking *reasonable* care, i.e. that degree of care which a reasonable man would take in all the circumstances of the case. In Wilson's and Clyde Coal Company v English (1937), the House of Lords stated that the duty of care is three-fold: the provision of safe plant and machinery, the provision of a competent staff, and the maintenance of a safe system of work. In Paris v Stepney Borough Council (1951), it was pointed out that there are not three separate duties, but that these are merely aspects of one comprehensive duty.

80. Breach of a duty of care, if damage results, constitutes the tort of *negligence*. Negligence, in the sense here used, means something more than mere carelessness or inadvertence. Negligence, as a legal wrong, was defined by Lord Wright in the following terms: "In strict legal analysis, negligence means more than heedless or careless conduct – whether in omission or commission – it properly connotes the complex concept of duty, breach and damage thereby suffered by the person to whom the duty was owing" (Lochgelly v M'Mullen (1934). This complex concept cannot adequately be analysed or illustrated briefly, but one can perhaps attempt to give a sketch of the way it has been interpreted in a variety of concrete instances.

81. *The extent of the duty.* In the leading case of Donoghue v Stevenson (1932), Lord Atkin laid the foundation for the modern view as to the general extent of the duty: "You must take reasonable care to avoid acts or omissions which you reasonably foresee would be likely to injure your neighbour. Who, then, in law, is my neighbour? The answer seems to be persons who are so closely and directly affected by my act that I ought reasonably to have them in contemplation, when I am directing my mind to the acts or omissions which are called in question". Translated into the sphere of employment, this doctrine means, not that the employer must eliminate every possible danger, but that he must take such precautions as experience has shown to be necessary.

82. In considering such precautions, it is often said that the extent of the duty of care is the product of three variables:

(i) the likelihood of the occurrence of the harm;
(ii) the magnitude of the harm if it should occur; and
(iii) the burden of taking precautions sufficient to prevent its occurrence: (Morris v West Hartlepool Navigation (1956)).

---

13 Paras 79-89 have been written by Jack Hendy, Paras. 90-91 rely heavily on his unpublished paper, *The Duty of Care: Employer's Liability,* NATFHE document 0633-79.

83. This rule may be illustrated by the following cases:-
In Tremain v Pike (1969) the plaintiff, a herdsman, had contracted a very rare disease – known as Weil's disease (or leptospirosis) – which is caused by contact with the urine of rats. He brought evidence that the rat population on the farm where he worked was increasing. The court held that though a reasonably prudent farmer would wage war on rats to protect his milk supplies and animal feed, such a farmer would have no valid reason to anticipate the possibility that his staff would contract such a rare disease as leptospirosis. Hence the farmer was not liable for not taking precautions against it. As Viscount Dunedin put it, in Fardon v Harcourt-Rivington (1932): "people must guard against reasonable probabilities; they are not bound to guard against fantastic possibilities".

84. On the other hand, if the possible damage is large, then even a small risk of its happening must be guarded against. In Paris v Stepney Borough Council a one-eyed workman was given the job of removing some rusty bolts under a vehicle. He was not provided with goggles. A sliver of metal entered his good eye and rendered him totally blind. His employers were held liable for not having taken adequate precautions. The loss of only one eye is a serious inconvenience, but the loss of the other is disastrous.

85. However, an employer is not bound to guard at any cost against all possibilities. In Latimer v AEC (1953) a violent rainstorm flooded a factory. When the waters subsided they left an oily film on the floors. The management caused sand and sawdust to be spread everywhere, but despite this a workman carrying a heavy barrel trod on an oily patch, fell, and was injured. It was held that the employers had not been guilty of negligence. They had done what was reasonable in the circumstances. There were not bound to shut down the works until the floors has been washed down thoroughly, nor to send everyone home till this had been done.

86. An employer will not be liable in negligence except where the damage is the reasonably foreseeable consequence of his or her act or omission. There is no liability without fault, and even then only for the foreseeable result of the fault. This general principle was established with finality in the Wagon Mound case (1961) by the Judicial Committee of the Privy Council. It was applied to employer's liability in Doughty v Turner Manufacturing Co (1964). Here a factory heat treatment room contained cauldrons of hot metal, one of which held molten sodium cyanide at 800° centigrade. The cauldron was fitted with a cement-asbestos lid. The lid slipped into the metal, causing a splash, but injuring no-one. A few minutes later there was an eruption of molten liquid which struck and severely burned a workman nearby. The cause of the eruption was a reaction between the metal and the cement-asbestos. Such a reaction was hitherto unknown and unsuspected. Hence the firm was held not liable to the workman. It was not bound to foresee the unforeseeable.

87. Many commentators have suggested that though the concept of no liability without fault is eminently just, it places the work people at risk from the dangers of innovation; and innovation is essential to go-ahead concerns.

However, if the *kind* of harm can be foreseen, the fact that its *extent* is not foreseen will not excuse common law liability: Smith v Leech Brain and Company (1962). Here a workman was, through inadequate protection, struck on the mouth by molten metal. The burn promoted cancer of the face, from which three years later the man died. It was held that the fact that the man had a pre-disposition to cancer was irrelevant; the employers were liable not merely for the burn, but for the death which was its result.

88. Needless to say, workmen also are under a duty to take reasonable care for their own safety and the safety of others. They must use the skill and care which the work demands, and, as was said in one case, "use that degree of care which an ordinary, prudent crane driver would have used": Staveley Iron Company v Jones (1956). If the workman's negligence contributes to the damage sustained, then the employer's liability will be diminished in proportion to the degree of fault, but here the court will "give due regard to the actual conditions under which men work in a factory or mine, to the long hours and the fatigue, to the slackening of attention which naturally comes from constant repetition of the same operation, to the noise and confusion in which a man works, to his pre-occupation with what he is doing at the cost perhaps of inattention to his own safety" – *per* Lord Wright in Caswell v Powell Duffryn (1940).

89. If the workman's negligence is the *sole* cause of the harm, then the employer will not be liable at all. So it was in O'Reilly v National Rail Appliances (1966), where two men working in a scrapyard found what appeared to be a live shell. They tested it by striking it with a 14lb hammer. The result was not the fault of the employer, for the men had voluntarily accepted the risk.

90. **Statutory duties**

In addition to the common law duties outlined briefly above, certain legislation, such as the Factories Act or Building Regulations, impose a code of statutory duties. Some of these duties have been referred to above and under Sections **5.3** and **5.5**. It will be remembered that the Factories Act applies directly to colleges only in certain circumstances. It is beyond the scope of this book, therefore, to investigate case law which has arisen under that Act. However, it may be useful to outline general principles concerning the duties imposed by statute.

91. The general rule of English law is that if a statute provides that breach of its provisions is punishable by the inflicting of a fine or other criminal punishment, then a person injured by such breach has no right to sue for damages. However, the courts have held that where a statute is passed for the protection of a class of persons, then a member of that class may sue – whether or not the breach also incurs a penal sanction. A claim in negligence, and a claim for breach of statute must be separately pleaded. If one claim fails, then it is not permissible to fall back on the other, unless both were pleaded together or in the alternative. The standard of duty in negligence is that of reasonable care: in breach of statutory duty, the standard is strictly fixed by the actual words of the statute itself. Further, in negligence the resulting harm must be foreseeable; in breach of statutory

duty it need not. It must be shown that the breach was a cause of the damage, but where harm occurs which the statute was intended to prevent, and it is shown that there was a breach of the statute, then the court will need little persuasion to find that the breach was in fact the cause. As in common law negligence, contributory negligence on the part of the person harmed will reduce the liability for the breach of statute, and the damages will be diminished proportionately. If the statutory duty breached is one imposed upon the employer – or upon both employer and employee – the defence that the risk was voluntarily undertaken will not be accepted. There are, of course, other questions of "*volenti*" (i.e. questions relating to the voluntary running of risks) but their discussion is beyond the scope of this publication.

APPENDIX 1

STATUTORY INSTRUMENTS WHICH PROVIDE GUIDANCE IN COMPLYING WITH THE HSW ACT

Title	*Activity or situation*	*Scope of the guidance offered*
Abrasive Wheels Regulations 1970	Teaching and maintenance workshops in schools and colleges.	Detailed requirements for the use of abrasive wheels.
Asbestos Regulations 1969	Maintenance by staff and visiting contractors.	Detailed requirements for the handling and disposal during the course of construction and demolition and the maintenance of buildings and plant.
Casting (Castings and other Articles) Regulations 1949.	Engineering laboratories of some polytechnics.	Detailed requirements for the cleaning of metal castings.
Construction (General Provisions) Regulations 1961.	Construction, demolition and maintenance work in all buildings used in education. Craft and certificate courses in colleges of building and other further education establishments.	Detailed requirements for excavations, dangerous atmospheres, use of vehicles, demolition work, safeguarding of machinery and temporary structures.
Construction (Lifting Operations) Regulations 1961.		Safeguards in connection with, and the examination of, lifting appliances, chains, ropes and lifting gear and hoists. The carriage of persons on hoists. Safety at working places on and above the ground. Access and egress.
Construction (Working Places) Regulations 1966.		
Chromium Plating Regulations 1931.	Limited number of specialist circumstances in higher education.	Specific requirements for the health of persons employed at chromium plating baths.
Electricity Regulations 1908.	Installation and use of electrical systems and apparatus in buildings and on teaching courses in schools and colleges.	General requirement for the safe use of low and high voltage electricity.
Factories Act 1961.	All aspects of education.	General and detailed standards for safeguarding the environment in teaching establishments.

Title	*Activity or Situation*	*Scope of the guidance offered*
Highly Flammable Liquids and Liquefied Petroleum Gases Regulations 1972.	Technical college workshops and chemical labs, and particular apparatus in other college courses.	Detailed requirements for the safe storage and manipulation of flammable liquids.
Horizontal Milling Machine Regulations 1972.	Teaching and maintenance workshops in secondary schools and colleges.	Detailed requirements for the safeguarding of horizontal milling machines.
Non-Ferrous Metals (Milling and Founding) 1962.	Craft courses in schools, sculpturel fine arts departments in art colleges and polytechnics.	Detailed requirements for the protection of persons against burns and fumes.
Ionising Radiations (Sealed Sources) Regulations 1969.	Schools and college teaching and research laboratories.	Keeping of records, basic principles of inspection, radiological supervision, organization of work, monitoring, radiography and x-ray crystallography and spectrometry measuring and detecting devices, maximum permissible doses, in connection with sealed and unsealed sources of ionising radiations.
Pottery (Health and Welfare) Regulations 1950.	Craft courses in schools, in further education colleges, including art colleges and polytechnics.	Detailed requirements for the minimising of lead and silica risks in all processes in the manufacture of potteries. Welfare provision, including ventilation, storage and consumption of food and drink, temperature and cleanliness.
Power Press Regulations 1965.	Engineering workshops in schools and further education colleges.	The examination and testing of safety devices on power presses and press brakes.
Protection of Eyes Regulations 1974.	Chemical laboratories, metal working shops, maintenance shops and other workshops in schools and colleges including on-site maintenance work.	Standards for and use of approved eye protection in specified processes.

Title	*Activity or Situation*	*Scope of the Guidance offered*
Woodworking Machinery Regulations 1974.	Teaching and maintenance workshops using woodworking machinery in schools and colleges.	Detailed requirements for the safeguarding of all woodworking machines including circular saws, narrow band sawing machines, planing machines, vertical spindle moulding machines. Standards for ventilation, lighting and noise levels where such machines are worked.
School Premises Regulations.	Buildings constructed for use as schools.	Standards for heating, lighting, ventilation space, in new schools.

APPENDIX 2

HSE AND DES ADVISORY PUBLICATIONS WHICH MAY PROVIDE GUIDANCE IN HEALTH AND SAFETY FOR EDUCATION AUTHORITIES, TEACHERS AND STUDENTS.

Title	*Activity or situation*	*Scope of the guidance offered*
HSE		
Abrasive Wheels Training Leaflets 1 and 2 and Explanatory leaflet.	Maintenance and teaching workshops.	Precautions in training in the working and installation of abrasive wheels.
Dermatitis: Effects on Skin of Mineral Oil.	Maintenance and teaching workshops. Art colleges.	Precautions against dermatitis from certain substances.
Dermatitis from Synthetic Resins.		
Fire Alarms, Fire Drills, Fire Prevention.	All buildings.	Advice on fire precautions to appointed security, fire and safety officers.
First Aid – Advice on First Aid Treatment.	All employees and students.	Advice on first aid to all employees and senior students and, in particular, those with a first aid responsibility.
Foundries (Protective Footwear & Gaiters) Regulations 1971: An Introduction.	Metal work teaching workshops.	Metal work teachers.
Highly Flammable Liquids & Liquefied Petroleum Gases Regulations 1972: An Introduction.	Maintenance workshops, chemical and physics laboratories, art colleges and courses.	Maintenance managers, teachers in chemistry and physics and certain art courses.
Lead Poisoning; Cause & Prevention leaflet for workers. Code of Practice for Health Precautions.	Painters shops and courses. Pottery shops.	Maintenance workers and metal work and pottery teachers and lab technicians.

Title	*Activity or situation*	*Scope of the guidance offered*
Mercurial Poisoning Preventative Measures in Handling Liquid Mercury & Removal of Contamination.	Chemistry lab.	Teachers of chemistry and lab assistants.
Milling Machines – Safe Operation of, Guide for Instructors.	Maintenance shops, metal working workshops.	Maintenance workers, metal work teachers.
Power Presses Fencing & Other Safety Precautions for – leaflet.	Metal workshops.	Metal work teachers.
Protection of Eyes	Maintenance workshops, teaching workshops and laboratories.	Employees, teachers, students and pupils.
Safe Use of Ladders	All buildings.	Maintenance workers, teachers and students on building courses.
Woodworking Machinery Safety Hints.	Joiners shops, woodworking classrooms.	Joiners, woodworking teachers and pupils.
Precautions needed on Dangerous Machines Advisory Booklet.	Offices.	Office managers and staff.
Food Slicing Machines – Safety in the use of.	Canteens and kitchens.	Canteen managers and staff.
DES (see also appendices to Section **7**).		
Administrative Memorandum 5/64 – Offices Shops & Railway Premises Act 1963.	Offices and shops in local education authorities, colleges and schools.	LEA administrative offices and office staff in colleges and schools.

Title	*Activity or situation*	*Scope of the guidance offered*
Administrative Memorandum 1/65 – The Use of Ionising Radiations in Schools, and Establishments of Further Education and Teacher Training Colleges.	Secondary schools, FE, teacher training college demonstration and practical work with radioactive substances and x-rays.	Administrative teachers and technicians.
Administrative Memorandum 1/65 Addendum No. 1.		
2/65 Poisonous Substances in Pencils & other allied materials used in schools.	Pencils & a variety of illustrative materials used in schools.	Persons responsible for the purchase of school materials.
20/67 Inhalation of Asbestos Dust.	Laboratories and the maintenance of buildings.	Teachers, technicians and lab assistants in laboratories, maintenance staff and persons responsible for purchasing.
2/68 Education Apparatus in Schools and Colleges.	Gymnasia.	PE staff.
12/69 Work Experience.	Work by school pupils in industrial and other undertakings.	Local education authorities and principals of major establishments and school principals.

Title	Activity or situation	Scope of the guidance offered
3/70 Avoidance of Carcinogenic and Aromatic Amines in Schools & other Educational Establishments.	School and college laboratories.	Science teachers, lab. technicians.
7/70 Use of lasers in schools and other educational establishments.	CW lasers in physics and optical laboratories.	Physics teachers and laboratory technicians and assistants.
*Safety in Outdoor Pursuits. DES Safety Series No. 1.	*as indicated by the title. Stresses the need for training, experience and skill, including planning and leadership. References are given to outside sources of expertise and advice.	
*Safety in Science Labs DES Safety Series No. 2 (Revised 1976).	*as indicated by the title. Covers a wide range of potential hazards in laboratories and is of particular use to non-scientific personnel. It is broad rather than particular in its approach. The purposes of, and duties under, the Health & Safety at Work etc. Act are covered.	
*Safety in Practical Departments 1973. DES Safety Series No. 3.	*as indicated by the title. Deals with workshops, arts departments and home economics. It recommends seeking HM Inspectors of Factories advice, though it recognises that the Factories Acts do not apply directly. It is broad in its approach, but mentions goggles, respirators and protective clothing. General information on toxic hazards; woodworking machinery, other machinery, pottery, asbestos and fire precautions are included.	
*Safety in Physical Education. DES Safety Series No.4.	*as indicated by the title. Covers the safety of pupils and bystanders. Covers ordinary school activities, plus wrestling, judo, aikido and karate.	
*Safety in Further Education. DES Safety Series No.5.	*as indicated by the title. Suggests procedures by which colleges and other further education establishments might promote safe working. Identifies hazards and recommends authorities. Covers the provision and operation of safety organizations. Mentions hazards to pupils and staff and provides a starting point for reference to particular aspects and subjects.	

APPENDIX 3

HSE AREA OFFICES

Area	*Address and Telephone No.*
South West	Inter-City House, Mitchell Lane, Victoria Street, Bristol BS1 6AN. 0272-290681.
South	Priestly House, Priestly Road, Basingstoke RG24 9NW. 0256-3181.
South East	Paymaster General's Building, Russell Way, Crawley, West Sussex RH10 1UH. 0293-511671.
London NW	Chancel House, Neasden Lane, London NW10 2UD. 01-459 8844.
London NE	Maritime House, 1 Linton Road, Barking, Essex. 01-594 5522.
London S	1 Long Lane, London SE1 4P9. 01-407 8911.
East Anglia	39 Baddow Road, Chelmsford CM2 0HL. 0245-84661.
Northern Home Counties	6th Floor, King House, George Street West, Luton LU1 2DD. 0582 34121
East Midlands	5th Floor, Belgrave House, 1 Greyfriars, Northampton NN1 2LQ. 0604-21233.
West Midlands	McLaren Buildings, 2 Masshouse Circus, Queensway, Birmingham B4 7NP. 021-236 5080.
Wales	Brunel House, 2 Fitzalan Road, Cardiff CF2 1SH. 0222-497777.
Marches	2 Hassell Street, Newcastle-under-Lyne, Staffordshire ST5 1DT. 0978-262 5324.
North Midlands	Birbeck House, Trinity Square, Nottingham NG1 4AU. 0602-40712.
South Yorkshire & Humberside	Sovereign House, 40 Silver Street, Sheffield S1 2ES. 0742-739081.
West & North Yorkshire	8 St Paul's Street, Leeds LS1 2LE. 0532-446191.
Greater Manchester	Quay House, Quay Street, Manchester M3 3JB. 061-831 7111.
Merseyside	The Triad, Stanley Road, Bootle, Merseyside L20 3PG. 051-822 7211.
North West	Victoria House, Ormskirk Road, Preston, PR1 1HH. 0772-59321.
North East	Government Buildings, Kenton Bar, Newcastle-upon-Tyne, NE1 2YX. 0632-869811.

APPENDIX 4

EMAS: LOCATION OF REGIONAL OFFICES

Region	*Areas covered*	*Addresses & telephone nos. of Senior Employment Medical Advisers*
North Eastern	Metropolitan County of Tyne & Wear, Counties of Cleveland, Durham, Northumberland.	Government Buildings, Kenton Bar, Newcastle upon Tyne, NE1 2YX. 0632-863411.
Northern	Metropolitan Counties of South Yorkshire, West Yorkshire, Counties of Derbyshire, Humberside, Lincolnshire, North Yorkshire, Nottinghamshire.	8 St Paul's Street, Leeds LS1 2LE. 0532-446191.
Eastern and SE Midlands	Bedfordshire, Buckinghamshire, Cambridgeshire, Essex, Hertfordshire, Leicestershire, Norfolk, Northamptonshire, Oxfordshire, Suffolk, Wawickshire.	4 Dunstable Road, Luton LU1 1DX. 0582-415722.
London and S Eastern	Greater London, Kent, Surrey, East Sussex, West Sussex.	Atlantic House, Farringdon Street, London EC4A 4BA 01-583 5020 (Ext 303).
S Western	Avon, Berkshire, Cornwall, Devon, Dorset, Gloucestershire, Hampshire, Isle of Wight, Somerset, Wiltshire.	Beacon Tower, Fishponds Road, Fishponds, Bristol BS16 3HA. 0272-659573.
Wales	Wales	St David's House, Wood Street, Cardiff CF1 1PB. 0222-43984.
W Midlands	Metropolitan County of West Midlands, Counties of Hereford & Worcester, Salop, Staffordshire.	Auchinleck House (5th Floor), Broad Street, Birmingham B15 1DL. 021-643 8441/4.
N Western	Metropolitan counties of Greater Manchester, Merseyside, Counties of Cheshire, Cumbria, Lancashire.	Quay House, Quay Street, Manchester M3 3JE. 061-831 7111.

APPENDIX 5

THE INSPECTION OF EDUCATIONAL ESTABLISHMENTS

The following guidelines have been issued by the HSE concerning its approach to the inspection of educational establishments:

"1. Inspection of large and complex establishments such as universities and the larger colleges of higher education will require initial visits by appointment to meet senior officials of the university or college and explain the purpose and arrangements for inspection and to determine the management structure and organisation of the establishment. The safety policy and the delegation of duties under the policy will be discussed at this stage. Before visiting establishments under the control of Local Education Authorities, inspectors will normally seek an appointment with the director of the department to determine the safety organisation of the department and the most efficient method of liaison concerning the programme of inspection.

"2. The initial discussion will seek to determine the areas to be visited and identify the responsible persons to be contacted. Details of the trade union and staff association consultative arrangements and of safety representatives and committees will also be requested.

"3. The first objective of inspection will be to ensure that each employing body has an adequate safety policy and has set up the necessary organisation for health and safety within its management structure. This will include a definition of the various levels of responsibility at which the duties described in the policy are to be carried out. The approach will be similar to that followed in other areas of employment but inspectors will seek to ensure that the arrangements for implementing the policy also cover the safety and health of non-employed persons, particularly students and pupils.

"4. The safety policy statement should cover matters such as plant, machinery and electrical equipment. In addition, it should cover dangers arising from the activities carried on both inside the premises, e.g. engineering workshops, research laboratories and the use of ionising radiations, and outside the premises where field work is undertaken. It should set out the arrangements which have been made for occupational health and the procedure for identifying, recording, investigating and monitoring accidents, dangerous occurrences and cases of occupational disease. It should refer to the methods of control of dangerous or toxic materials and substances used in laboratories and the storage and use of flammable and explosive liquids and gases. Where appropriate the precautions should be set out in further detail in departmental safety policies and arrangements or rules or codes or practice. It is important that a senior member in the organisation should be appointed to co-ordinate the implementation of the policy and monitor its effectiveness.

"5. In addition to being employees, a number of employed persons will, as in other spheres of activity, exercise managerial functions in varying degrees, or in the case of academic staff within departments or promoted teachers within schools exercise quasi managerial control and authority over other staff, students or pupils. It is accepted that in practical terms the employer who cannot be omni-present will need to delegate the performance of some of his function to others in respect of day to day matters. At the same time, it must be pointed out that it is not possible for him to delegate his overall responsibility. Where duties concerning health and safety are delegated within institutions or authorities, it should be made clear in any departmental or subsidiary safety policies to what extent duties have been further delegated and where these lie. Inspectors will pay particular attention to the way in which duties have been assigned to ensure compliance with the employer's overall responsibilities.

"6. Because students and pupils greatly exceed the number of employees in educational establishments, inspectors will give particular attention to examining the measures taken to comply with the employer's responsibilities under Sections 3 and 4 of the Health and Safety at Work Act. They will, of course, bear in mind that the duty of care is not a concept new to educational establishments and is indeed implicit in the whole educational process. They will, however, wish to satisfy themselves for example that employers in education establishments have taken appropriate measures to ensure that any machinery or plant used by students or pupils is safe and that where necessary protective equipment, such as eye protection or respirators, is supplied and used.

"7. Inspectors will also be concerned to examine the measures taken to protect teachers and other employees from the hazards which could arise from the activities of students and pupils. They will, therefore, wish to establish that effective arrangements have been made for the health and safety of students and pupils and for their instruction, training and supervision in these matters and still expect to see a reference to these matters in the written safety policy.

"8. A satisfactory level of health and safety training in educational establishments is considered to be of fundamental importance if everyone is to be made aware of the risks involved in his place of work and the precautions to be observed. There are four main areas of training; on the academic side the training of teachers in their duties to other employees as well as to students and pupils and the training of students and pupils themselves; and on the non-academic side the training of managers and supervisors of maintenance and other service departments and the training of service or supporting staff. Inspectors will seek to ensure that the standard of training in all these areas is of an acceptable level. The work of laboratory technicians, cleaners and security officers, particularly in research laboratories in universities and other further education establishments, may expose them to special dangers. It is important that the arrangements for health and safety in such establishments should cover the special training needs of these workers.

"9. In deciding whether to inspect with or without having given prior notice to the management, the Inspector will take account not only of the needs of effective inspection in the particular circumstances of the case, but also the need not to cause disruption which may adversely affect the teaching process. He will, as in the case of other premises, be guided by considerations such as the purpose of his visit, the part of the premises to be inspected, the need to see one or more particular people in order to make the visit fully effective as well as his previous dealings with the establishment in question.

"10. It is the intention of the HSE that employees in education establishments shall receive no less degree of protection against risk or injury or danger to health than persons in other areas of employment. The Inspectorate recognise, however, that financial and staff resources will not always be available to remedy immediately all the matters identified by the Inspector as requiring attention. As in the case of other employers, Inspectors will be prepared to discuss priorities with management with a view to phasing less urgent matters and will endeavour where possible to agree any programme with management. They will also discuss the matter with the trade union and staff associations. All matters of significance and any agreed programme of implementation will be confirmed in writing to both the management and employees' representatives.

"11. Inspectors will establish contact with safety representatives when appointed and in the interim with shop stewards and other staff association representatives. However, in view of the complexity of the staff organisation in some establishments, Inspectors will seek to establish central points of contact for the disclosure of information in accordance with their duties under Section 28(8) of the HSW Act.

"12. Inspectors will be familiar with many of the processes, hazards, plant and equipment found in education establishments and where appropriate will apply them to similar standards as in other premises. Certain guidance on health and safety precautions in the form of booklets, pamphlets, notes, rules or codes of practice already exists in universities, colleges of further education and schools. Where the DES, SED, Universities, Local Authorities or Professional Associations have issued technical guidance, this will not be queried at Area level. If Inspectors consider that this guidance is unsatisfactory either generally or in particular circumstances, they will refer the matter to the National Industry Group which will if necessary take it up centrally with the appropriate body. The aim will be to ensure that consistent standards of precautions and safety performance are achieved in all establishments. Where remedial measures are not covered by any national standard, it will be for the management to decide whether the implications of the problem are sufficiently important to merit the matter being referred through the normal channels to the Authority, Committee or appropriate Department of State concerned for discussion with the National Industry Group. It is intended that all standards of technical guidance affecting the health, safety and welfare of persons employed in education establishments will eventually be reviewed by the Health and Safety Executive and discussed with the issuing body so that the standards can be agreed and recognised.

"13. Some departments of universities and further education establishments are subject to inspection by HM Nuclear Installations Inspectorate. Factory Inspectors are aware of these designated premises and will work in close liaison with the Nuclear Installations Inspectors, so that duplication of inspection is avoided. The majority of premises where ionising radiations are used will be inspected by the Factory Inspectorate. Factory Inspectors may use the services of the National Radiological Protection Board for inspections in these premises on an agency basis as they do in factories.

"14. Parts of educational establishments subject to the Factories Act or ORSP Act are designated under the Fire Precautions Act 1971 and fire certification and requirements for fire precautions are the responsibilities of the Fire Authority, with the exception of Crown educational establishments which are the responsibility of HM Inspectors of Fire Services of the Home Office and the Scottish Home and Health Department. In other parts which have not as yet been designated under the Fire Precautions Act, the Fire Authorities have traditionally advised on a goodwill basis and are also empowered under Section 10 of the Fire Precautions Act to apply to the courts for orders in cases of serious risk. Factory Inspectors will not examine the fire precautions nor will they inspect the structure of fittings of buildings other than the extent to which these may affect the process fire risk. If, however, matters of serious fire risk come to their attention, they will be brought to the notice of the management, the Fire Authority or the Inspector of Fire Services and employees' representatives as a matter of urgency.

"15. Except for those with Crown status, education establishments will be subject to normal enforcement procedures provided for the HSW Act. The small number of Crown employers are being told separately of the special procedures that will apply to them. Inspectors will prefer to achieve health and safety standards by advice and recommendation but as in other areas of work activity will take enforcement action when the situation demands it.

"16. The information available to date from the two pilot studies and from the feedback of information from the inspection programme already underway in HSE Areas suggest that there are many problems to be overcome. Measures to control health and safety in many educational establishments are in certain respects below those in industry. The occurrence of accidents, however, appears to be less than in industry from the accident information available and this seems to indicate that maintenance staff, technicians and ancillary workers such as cleaners, groundsmen and catering staff are more at risk than teaching staff or pupils. There is considerable variation in standards within establishments depending largely on the initiative of the head of department and between one similar establishment and another. From the examples of high standards found, it would seem that there is the know-how to achieve conditions which are safe and without risks to health inside all educational establishments providing performance can be equalised. The question of resources is raised repeatedly, but could be less significant than the correct deployment of existing resources.

"17. Universities, colleges of further and higher education and local education authorities have in many cases taken the initiative to produce safety policies and a safety organisation before the HSE inspection programme began. The professional associations and trade unions representing teaching and non-teaching employees are being noticeably active in appointing safety representatives and in providing training for them to meet the Safety Representatives and Safety Committee Regulations. In response to this a number of employing bodies have organised management training courses and are discussing proposals for safety committees with the unions concerned. This interest and response is encouraging. A prime objective of the HSE will be the establishment of an effective organisation for health and safety covering each establishment. Inspection of individual establishments will measure the performance and effectiveness of that organisation. The HSE will take a part in the formulation of national standards for health and safety but in the main these standards can best be set by the many existing organisations in the educational field."

REFERENCE

Health and Safety at Work etc. Act 1974, Chapter 37, HMSO.
The Safety Representatives and Safety Committees Regulations 1977 S.I. 1977, No 500, HMSO.
Safety and Health at Work, Report of the Committee, 19070-72, Cmnd. 5034, 1972, HMSO.
Health and Safety Commission, *Safety Representatives and Safety Committees,* the Regulations, Code of Practice and Guidance Notes to the Regulations, 1978, HMSO.
Health and Safety Commission, *Advisory Leaflets,* HMSO:
HCSI *Health and Safety at Work etc. Act 1974: some legal aspects and how they will affect you.*
HSC2 *The Act outlined.*
HSC3 *Advice to employers.*
HSC4 *Advice to the self-employed.*
HSC5 *Advice to employees.*
HSC6 *Guidance notes on employers' policy statements for health and safety at work.*
HSC7 *Regulations, Approved Codes of Practice and guidance literature.*
HSC8 *Safety committees: guidance to employers whose employees are not members of recognised independent trade unions.*
Health and Safety Executive, *Pilot Study, Health and Safety in Schools and Further Education Establishments,* HMSO/HSE, 1978.
Health and Safety Executive, *Sectional List 18,* Revised 1977, HMSO [lists all statutory instruments, advisory publications and the titles of the *Health and Safety at Work* series of leaflets].
The Code of Safety Practice for Engineering Training Centres, Booklet 18, Engineering Industry Training Board, Watford.
Recommendations for Health and Safety in Workshops of Schools and Colleges, British Standards Institution, BS4163, 1975.
Code of Practice, *Safeguarding of Machinery,* British Standards Institution, BS5304, 1975.
Health and Safety at Work etc. Act 1974, DES Circular 11/74; Welsh Office Circular 226/74, 6 November 1974.

Alison Broadhurst, *The Health and Safety at Work Act in Practice,* Heyden, 1978.
H. Cavanagh, *The Health and Safety at Work Act and its Application to Educational Establishments,* Association of Colleges for Further and Higher Educaton, 1978.
Christopher Curson, *Health and Safety at work in the public services,* Councils and Education Press (Longmans), 1978.
J. Hendy and K. Scribbins, "The Health and Safety at Work Act," *NATFHE Journal,* Vol. 3, Nos. 7-9, October-December 1978.
LACSAB, *Handbook on the Health and Safety at Work Act 1974,* 1975.
Safety in Colleges: The Legal Requirements, Coombe Lodge Report, Information special, Vol.11, No.8.
The LACSAB Employee Relations Handbook, Revised Edition 1977, pp87-94.
TUC Handbook on Safety and Health at Work, Second Edition 1978.

Bibliographical Note
There is a considerable canon of writing on the Act. The list quoted above represents only a selection of further reading. Fuller bibliographies will be found in the *TUC Handbook,* and in the works of Broadhurst and Curson.

Broadhurst's book gives an indication of the scope of the Act and its place in occupational legislation. Curson does not deal with education in any detail, but discusses the Act within the broad context of the public services. The *LACSAB*

Handbook on the Act has been somewhat overtaken by events; the *LACSAB Employee Relations Handbook* provides brief comment only on the Act and reprints verbatim the Regulations, Code of Practice and Guidance Notes on safety representatives and committees. The *TUC Handbook* provides an easily comprehensible survey of the Act and detailed comment on the prevention of hazard; its bibliography is worthy of attention. The articles of Hendy and Scribbins give both comment and information, and provide a sound starting point for a study of the legislation. The Coombe Lodge Report contains examples of a safety checklist, hazard notification form and a safety officer job specification, and some discussion of the Act.

Cavanagh's pamphlet contains a short summary but is devoted mainly to the reproduction of the HSC guidelines on inspection detailed in Appendix 5, above.

Essential reading is to be found in the HSE *Pilot Study:* more than any other publication, this report demonstrates the need for the education service seriously to consider its obligations under the Act.

A comprehensive bibliography is contained in the NATFHE statement: *Safety in Colleges.*

11 STAFF DEVELOPMENT

1. Staff development is an important issue. However, although it has gained an increasing importance in Britain in the last decade, there remain many doubts concerning philosophy and methods of implementation. This sub-section, therefore, in contrast to most of the rest of this book, is presented as a discussion essay. It is not intended to be prescriptive. This is not to obscure the need for review and some resolution of the issues of staff development. In simple terms, the nature of the teaching profession and, indeed, the education service in the next decade may depend upon it. This sub-section should be read in conjunction with Sections **2.2**; **11.12**; and **11.13**.

2. Essentially, staff development is concerned with the professional in conjunction with the personal development of staff, whether academic or non-academic. Many colleges and LEAs have appreciated the importance of the topic, and indeed may have pursued staff development policies. Unfortunately, to inject an element of flippancy rare in this book, the object of the pursuit may be likened to the Holy Grail: it represents indeed a consummation devoutly to be wished; most are in favour of it without knowing very much about it; it is elusive and not readily quantifiable; it is ardently pursued by a few; it means different things to different people; and those who claim to have found it do not always find an audience wholly receptive to their explanations. Researchers in the field have elicited comment such as: "staff development is looking at the job advertisements each week"; and "my headmaster is a self-made man who worships his creator and rules his school with a whim of iron". Published guidance does exist. As the Reference list shows, it is necessary also to consider works prepared for the use of schools and universities as well as further education. Staff development suffers from another difficulty in that it requires resource provision. Yet, without it, especially in a time when the education service is likely to become increasingly static, it is no exaggeration to state that the education service will become increasingly impoverished.

3. **Current general practices**

The Haycocks Reports have given great impetus to staff development.[1] The DES has provided a number of significant courses. Various education management institutions have developed the theme. There has been a general increase in emphasis on further education teacher training[2] and in the place of staff development in its curricula. A staff development communications network is based on Bolton College of Education (Technical), Ealing College of Higher Education, and Wolverhampton Polytechnic Faculty of Education. Various bodies exist to promote staff development.[3] The Further Education Staff College has provided various models.[4] The kinds of course provision (and as such only one mode of staff

---

1 see Sections **1.5**; **2.2**.54-59; **11.12**. In the consultative document, *A Better Start in Working Life*, 1979. Annex D, the Secretaries of State for Employment, Education and Science, Industry, Scotland and Wales advocated a staff development programme in order to implement improved vocational preparation for employed young people.

2 see Section **11.12**.

3 see Reference list.

4 cf. *College Management Readings and Cases*, Vol.3.

development) currently made for staff may be roughly categorised in four areas: professional teacher training (often for teachers of non-advanced courses); further academic qualification by examination or research (often for teachers of advanced courses); management education; and the wide variety of courses available for the various needs of non-teaching staff. It is fair to observe that as the further education curriculum changes, so staff development is required – as the pressures created by the introduction of DipHE, TEC and BEC courses and the various MSC programmes have demonstrated (see Section **10.2**). Staff development, of course, does not necessarily mean course attendance.

4. At institutional level, many colleges have adopted staff development policies. These may or may not include provision for non-teaching staff. A staff development unit may be established with a support services department. Organizational responsibility can be an academic board committee function. Staff development officers have been appointed at some colleges. These officers are often principal or senior lecturers. Vice-principals on occasion undertake staff development roles; the function may be undertaken by education departments. Professional tutors have been appointed at some colleges. Such tutors are generally responsible for staff induction programmes, counselling, the co-ordination of internal and external teaching programmes, and for the advising of all staff on matters such as retraining and further professional training.

5. CNAA's expectation that staff are provided with research, consultancy and staff development opportunities has acted as an impetus in higher education. Most polytechnics provide an induction course for new members of staff. These courses are designed to make staff aware of the philosophy, organizational structure and facilities of the institution. A number of large institutions provide teaching method courses, often of an initial short block followed by regular contact; such courses generally attempt to relate content to the students' practical experience. In some polytechnics such courses are designed to allow the teaching methods course to lead into a further course, leading in turn to a teaching qualification. Seminars, workshops and short courses are also often offered to polytechnic staff; most polytechnics appear to offer staff undertaking development programmes opportunity for self-evaluation[5]; and, in the case of administrative staff, while much of their training takes place in the normal course of employment, national collaboration in considering development has begun at specialist level by way of bodies such as COPS (Conference of Polytechnic Secretaries), PARG (Polytechnic Academic Registrars Group) and PFOG (Polytechnic Finance Officers Group). These "functional groups" are normally recognised by the Committee of Directors of Polytechnics (although the CDP has not nationally considered administrative staff development).

6. To discuss regional or national structures within which staff development might occur before considering how it might take place may seem like acceptance of an assumption that teachers are unable to identify their own

5 Harriet Greenaway and Derek Mortimer, "Britain (polytechnics) – a case of rapidly evolving institutions" in ed. David C.B. Teather, *Staff Development in Higher Education, An International Review and Bibliography*, Kogan Page/Nichols 1979, p.69.

needs.[6] This assumption is not accepted. Rather, current proposed structures stem from the Russell[7] and Haycocks Reports, which argue strongly for the training of further education staff, and from the belief of the teachers' associations that a pattern of education and training to graduate equivalent for all lecturers is necessary to meet the needs of both those in service and new entrants.[8] For example, NATFHE believes that there should be continuing professional education, that there should be trained professional tutors in all colleges to provide limited professional training for all further education teachers; and that – in agreement with Haycocks – there should be a rationalized pattern of institutions or centres offering courses for teachers within each Regional Advisory Council area (adding that provision for all teachers at all levels within further and higher education should be made). Thus, while a national framework has not yet been fully established, there is clearly agreement on the basic form which it might take. Such a structure, however putative, demands consideration of individual institutional structures. It is here, therefore, that the debate on staff development must be considered.

7. The essence of the staff development debate can be expressed thus:
   (i) The form which it is to take: by secondment, study or sabbatical leave, in-service training, research, in-post training, job interchange, consultancy; by a combination of several of these provisions; and whether direct or indirect or both.
   (ii) Should the development be primarily for the good of the teacher, or for the institution; or should it attempt to combine the requirements of both?
   (iii) Responsibility for development policy: by way of the "top down route" where decisions on selections and methods are made by the principal, acting either alone or through a senior committee; through an agreed college policy which recognises the needs of both individuals and the institution but operates within its own terms of reference; via a participative process involving all college staff members; or the leaving of the greater responsibility for development mainly to the individual?
   (iv) As development tends to presume assessment, the question is how and by whom appraisal and assessment of staff performance is to be carried out.
   (v) The issue of whether staff development policies are to be exclusive to academic staff; or whether non-academic staff will have equal, less, or no provision.
   (vi) How will the cost be borne?

8. These are the main areas of contention. Of themselves, they demonstrate little more than that staff development is a topic for which it is easier to

---

6. cf. David S. Ireland, "Changing Teachers: The Top Down Way", *Journal of Further and Higher Education*, Vol.2, No.2, Summer 1978, p.83.
7 *The Supply and Training of Teachers for Further Education*, Report of the Standing Sub-Committee on Teachers of the National Advisory Council on the Training and Supply of Teachers, 1966, HMSO.
8 cf. *The Education and Training of Teachers for Further and Higher Education*, NATFHE, 1978.

provide questions than answers. To proceed in some measure towards resolution, the issues of promotion, and the current nature and response to staff development, will now be examined (since the pressures which these issues exert may determine part of policy), then the various philosophies discussed, and finally practical models put forward for discussion.

9. Promotion

Research was recently carried out at the NFER into further education teaching as a career. A summary of the findings concerning promotion is given below. [9]

(i) Staff promotion prospects have been substantially reduced by cuts and reorganization. Decreased establishments, and the high proportion of senior posts occupied by persons likely to continue in tenure for a considerable time has created an "apparently intractable promotion blockage". The Burnham grading of posts and courses has caused dissent and disagreement, the prime examples of which are cited as referring to individuals unable to progress beyond the ceiling of their scale and those engaged in non-advanced work. The authors note the "widespread dissatisfaction within the profession that the opportunity to assign senior posts to staff with major responsibility for non-advanced work is severely limited." [10]

(ii) Concern was expressed that promotion almost always involved less teaching and more administration. Some of those interviewed put forward promotion schemes based on dual routes: teaching ability and administrative ability. Very few teachers understood the reasons for promotion. One head of department had advised a recruit: "Promotion, and future prospects, courses and level of work cannot be guaranteed and may appear to be based on no rational grounds." The survey showed, however, that promotion prospects were greatly enhanced by possession of academic qualifications, particularly doctorates. Professional teaching qualifications had virtually no effect. (The authors note, however, that NATFHE's policy stressing the need for professional training to cater for 16-19 provision [as well as the Government's intention to expand non-advanced further education] is expected to have an effect, and that such training will become increasingly important).

(iii) Geographical mobility clearly assisted career advance. Although women could reasonably expect promotion to a Lecturer Grade II post, their chances of becoming principal lecturers were less than half of those of men; women principals and vice-principals are rare." [11] This imbalance was attributed to women being less geographically mobile, tending to have lower academic qualifications, being unable to teach courses associated with trades and professions from which they were traditionally discouraged from entering, and the grading of

---

9 Judy Bradley and Jane Silverleaf, *Making the Grade*, *NFER*, 1979, pp.58-99; cf Bradley and Silverleaf, "Promotion in F.E. Teaching", *NATFHE Journal*, Vol.4, No.1, February 1979, pp. 8-9.

10 cf Section **11.2**. It can also be argued that the presumptions of Burnham appear to relate gradings and seniority to the volume of advanced work, but that there remain areas of discretion which may or may not be exercised: ILEA, for example, is an authority which does operate this discretion.

courses procedure which has entailed an absence of senior posts in departments where women staff are most numerous.

(iv) It was clear from the survey that there was a discrepancy in the views of senior staff as to the current criteria for promotion. However, there was greater consensus in identifying ideal criteria. Teaching ability was given the highest priority, but there was no agreement as to how this was to be assessed. Student assessment and student examination performance were among the suggested methods.

10. The survey demonstrated that teachers would clearly welcome a statement from senior staff outlining their own views on promotion – "teachers on the whole held very pessimistic views regarding their prospects for the future" – and that, whilst it would be impossible for any career structure ever to satisfy all staff, nonetheless, the current promotion procedures could be criticised "on a wider basis". Although the survey is valuable, one result is that further questions are raised: Burnham grading is subject to national negotiations (see Sections **11.1** and **11.2**); for some time at least, promotion issues will continue partially to be subject to provisions made outside the colleges. As to the provisions which a college or LEA might make, Bradley and Silverleaf discovered that a marginal majority of teachers favoured in-service training, but very few teachers regarded induction courses as particularly valuable; under a fifth of those surveyed had been offered an induction course. In-service courses, or some instruction in college administration and in specialist method were favoured by all staff. Teachers appear to regard the opportunity to design new courses as the major factor influencing promotion prospects. It was agreed that secondment, in-service, and retraining opportunities were not readily available, and that opportunities for secondment to industry or commerce were rare (many teachers in these areas were concerned that their knowledge was becoming out of date). The survey confirmed that staff development practices at institutional level vary widely: it was here suggested that "a crucial initial step must be the clear identification both of institutional objectives and of their relation to the needs of individual teachers." Bradley and Silverleaf

---

11 In "Women in Education: Some Points for Discussion", *Journal of Further and Higher Education*, Vol.1, No.3, Winter 1977, pp17-39, Keith Scribbins identifies the covert and overt practices which, by way of sexual disadvantage, and inequality of opportunity, amount to a pattern of discrimination against women. His findings were: the distribution of women workers in education is inversely proportional to the academic status and resources given to its different sectors; distribution of women staff shows a marked decrease as rise occurs in the hierarchy of posts and salary scales; that male teachers in further education outnumber women by 5:1; three quarters of women FE teachers occupy low paid posts; and that teacher education, an area which did offer women significant career prospects, because of contraction and reorganization, no longer affords such wide opportunities. Whether the roots of this disadvantage are social, or partially a result of women's self perception, Scribbins identifies various factors which contribute: the grading of courses/categories of work system (which places many courses taught by and studied by women in low categories); discrimination in entry to trades and professions;negative discrimination against women in selection for first jobs, and subsequently promotion; the awkward pattern of the working week for women with children, and inadequacies in maternity and paternity leave, crèche and nursery facilities. Scribbins also observes that "there is a clear pattern of sex difference in recruitment of students by area of study and course choice and a clear pattern of sex difference in the recruitment of staffing for these courses." (*Ibid*, p.35).

state that "perhaps the most important role of staff development should be seen as seeking to produce better practising teachers and administrators with increased job satisfaction at all grades and in all subjects." [12]

11. **Philosophies of staff development**

The debate has occurred throughout education, and has been partially obscured by presumptions of the various sectors concerning the aims of staff development. Attainment of the aim of "better teaching" has been advocated in two distinct ways: formal systems using evaluation techniques referring to student attainment and the acquisition of further staff qualifications may be defined as seeking the improvement of the institution; greater imponderables such as an increase in teacher confidence and the ability to select from a greater variety of teaching techniques, may be referred to as routes to individual expansion. Neither of these considerations are necessarily mutually exclusive, but weight given to either, or their synthesis, will be a determinant in the choice of structures outlined below. These structures have been identified as "management", "shop floor", and "partnership" models. [13]

12. **The management model**

This model, which enjoys a certain popularity in the United States of America, presumes that the needs of the institution are the foremost consideration. [14] The teachers' functions are examined, present and future roles considered and a training programme formulated. Staff appraisal is carried out, and management intervention occurs where it is believed that the teachers' performance is inadequate. Responses from student questionnaires are collected with reports written by staff detailing their past activities and future aspirations. This latter activity – where an individual discusses with senior staff his or her current progress and hopes for the future – is currently practised in some British institutions.

13. The most frequently criticised facet of the management model is the lack of provision for individuals to contribute to their own professional development. Modifications of the model to attempt to accommodate the individual have been attempted but may be said to be prone in practical terms to create confusion (since the specific aim has been changed). The ACFHE/APTI paper follows the management model but added a provision for "the enhancement of job satisfaction".[15] The practice at one college of technology is for the head of staff development and education section to utilize both his particular expertise and personal knowledge of, and his relationships with, his colleagues "to look at each teacher's function in college, to assess the levels at which he performed, to endeavour to supply his weaknesses and to fit him for future advancement."[16] Such practices

12 *op.cit* p.150.

13 Mantz Yorke, "Staff development in further and higher education: a review," *British Journal of Teacher Education,* Vol.3, No.2, May 1977, p.162.

14 cf. J. Latcham, "An American System of Staff Appraisal", in ed. D.L. Parkes, *College Management Readings and Cases,* Coombe Lodge, 1974.

15 *Staff Development in Further Education,* Report of the Joint ACFHE/APTI working party, ACFHE/APTI, 1973.

16 Frank Bacon, The Practicalities of Staff Development, *Journal of Further and Higher Education,* Vol.1, No.3, Winter 1977, p.57.

have been criticised on the grounds of inconsistency: the staff development officer has to act as an internal inspector, and as such has an inquisitorial function, as well as being the fount of professional support, which involves issues of confidence. At the very least, therefore, the post of staff development officer (or professional tutor) calls for a trained person of considerable tact, judgement and knowledge, and for great confidence in his or her probity by the other members of staff. While this scheme as an example of the modified management model clearly suits that institution, it is not necessarily to be given a blanket recommendation.

14. **The shop floor model**

This model was developed to allow greater individual freedom, and to avoid rigid institutional programmes, as the educational climate was expected to demand flexibility. Any member of staff who identifies a personal need may instigate procedures which may involve support from staff development resources. The process could be instigated by groups of staff. The essential principle is the emphasis on staff needs; managerial functions only operate within their limits. This raises vital considerations however: to place the onus for their development completely upon staff demands that they find time to become acquainted fully with avenues potentially open to them; to remove staff development from managerial involvement entails its practical removal from easy access to crucial funding decisions. While small internal groups, such as within the Department of Applied Community Studies in Manchester Polytechnic, have implemented this model, as Yorke remarks, a "massive act of faith is required on the part of management to finance this approach."[17]

15. **The partnership model**

This model obviously involves a synthesis of the two preceding, and requires both management and staff to surrender some functions. As Yorke states, "Management withdraws from direct intervention while supplying funds to enable initiatives to be taken by staff development personnel operating autonomously and, where necessary, on a confidential basis. The staff in turn accept that, in addition to responding to their own perceptions of needs, staff development may initiate activities which offer some promise of benefit to the institution ... The precise balance would be for each institution to decide in full and open debate: anything less would establish a fertile breeding ground for uncertainty and suspicion which could wreck the partnership on the rocks of either side's mistrust."[18] Such a solution must clearly be reached with very close consultation with the unions and professional associations involved. It has all the disadvantages of imprecision and compromise, but that is a circumstance indivisible from the English educational system. One of the provisions of the Belgian system, for example, is that a teacher takes several years to reach a "stage" and may subsequently be nominated to a particular post. The teacher may never actually occupy that post and may indeed, either by negotiation and appointment or individual initiative, broaden his or her experience by teaching or working elsewhere for prolonged periods; the post remains to be claimed on demand. This system is difficult to operate in practice, mainly for

17 Yorke, *op.cit.*, p.166.
18 *Ibid*, p.167.

administrative and political reasons. The point in considering staff development in our country is that it is a part of a whole system, and one which demands compromise. Neither of the pure models will easily suit our institutions; despite its conflict potential, it is likely that only a partnership scheme will be suitable; and indeed essential in view of the current educational system.

16. Models and procedures have to be considered. The items below refer in part to those implemented in an existing college[19] and rely heavily on considerations put forward by Geoffrey Lyons.[20] They ought not to be taken as either exclusive or exhaustive: final resolution rests with the circumstances of particular institutions.

17. **Discussion model for a staff development programme**

(i) *General aims*

The programme could have the following general aims:

to improve the effectiveness of individual teachers:
to improve the communications, organization and function of the college;
to improve individual career prospects; and
to enhance job satisfaction.

(ii) *Particular aims*

(a) For individuals:

to assist academic staff to do their jobs as effectively as possible;
to enable them to keep up to date;
to encourage positive responses to change;
to broaden experience;
to increase job satisfaction;
to prepare for different and/or increased responsibilities; and
to identify and prepare those ready for advancement (in either the particular or other institutions).

(b) For institutions:

to increase the institution's capacity to predict, cope with, and fully respond to changing circumstance in terms of pedagogic, organizational and subject development; and to facilitate the planning of effective management succession.

18. **Guidance criteria in the drawing up of a programme**

The programme will need to recognise:

(i) the need for partnership and full consultation;
(ii) that staff training and development is a continuous process, relevant to each stage of a teacher's career;

---

19 ed. Royston McHugh and Edward Miller, *Staff Development: The Individual and the Organisation,* in Open University Educational studies: A Third Level Course, E321, Management in Education, *Broadcast Notes,* Open University Press, 1978, pp.36-39, cf also, D.E. Billing, "The nature and scope of staff development in institutions of higher education", in ed. L. Elton and K. Simmonds, *Staff Development in Higher Education,* SRHE, Guildford, 1977.

20 Geoffrey Lyons, *Head's Tasks, a handbook of secondary school administration,* NFER 1976, pp.133-177. Lyons' work is especially deserving of full consideration, cf also, *College Management Readings and Cases, op.cit.,* Vol.3.

(iii) policy must be sufficiently wide and flexible to meet the needs of all staff;
(iv) individual consultation should be the basis for all proposals made for or by any staff member;
(v) that as job satisfaction comes from doing any job well, it is not to be associated only with those offered hopes of advancement;
(vi) that wherever appropriate and possible the institution will use its own resources to further development; and
(vii) that whilst the college declares its intent to provide opportunities for the development of individual abilities, not every teacher will be able to claim a particular development at a particular time.

19. **Guidance criteria in determining the overall needs of the institution**

Whilst it is assumed that the interests of any college may largely coincide with those of its inhabitants, it may nonetheless be helpful to indicate that the development programme will benefit from such identifications as:
(i) the aims of the college in terms of its entire function;
(ii) the ways in which the college fulfils, or proposes to fulfil these aims;
(iii) the planned college development programme for the next five years, alternative options, and the timing of developments; and
(iv) consideration of the consequences for staff of these developments, implications to be expressed as fully as possible.

20. Staff development, therefore, will not necessarily be self-generated or occurring in a vacuum; there will be instances where college and individual needs will exactly coincide. To expand further: retraining in order to continue in employment in a particular college will be the more effective if the potential and actual recipients have time to prepare; and the college's needs will be better met by knowing how its structure and personnel will change.

21. **Limitations requiring early attention**

Before any practical machinery can be set up – whether a staff development unit, or a further duty for the principal – it will be necessary for any programme to recognise actual and potential limitations and, where possible, to mitigate or overcome them. These limitations may be summarised under the following headings: career planning; appraisal; counselling; training and opportunity; programme responsibilities; identified common errors; secondment; and research. Each will be discussed in turn.

22. *Career planning*

The dissatisfaction at promotion procedures has been indicated under paragraphs 9-10 above. This may be attributed partially to individuals not having equipped themselves at a sufficient early stage, if at all, with a career map. This view does not presume a linear development, but rather considers that an awareness of career geography and the concomitant career possibilities is essential to the achievement of advance. If it is correct, the implications are uncomfortable, especially for those who discover that they have identified too late in their lives the route which might have carried them further. Other considerations, such as the wish of some not to have a planned existence and the cynicism that the favoured will rise to the level immediately above their actual competence, may also enter the debate but any staff development programme will have to recognise both career planning and the needs of individuals unlikely to rise above their current posts. In particular, attention will need to be paid to:

(i) general career planning;

(ii) the advice to be offered (preferably at interview or an early stage in employment) to a late entrant to the profession;

(iii) the consequences for individuals who have reached the end point of their career within teaching; and

(iv) the consequences for the college of a static (and therefore aging) staff, especially in a time of contraction in education.

23. *Appraisal*

This emotive team is used deliberately. Any staff development programme requires information. That information will include the needs and performance of a teacher, and a review of development both inside the college and as a result of external courses undertaken. It has been suggested that it would be better to use the word "review" but this is to dodge the issue: the element of threat will be found in the minds of some, and not necessarily without justification. Any appraisal system must recognise this, and procedures must be seen to be totally scrupulous and related to the needs of staff development rather than as a preliminary to disciplinary action. This raises the issue of confidentiality: it will need to be clearly established where the boundaries of further disclosure are, and is one of the most potent arguments against the principal being the sole recipient of all information. Counselling is essential to staff development, but will be negated if the professional tutor's or counsellor's role does not have a considerable area of designated discretion.

24. Closely linked to any appraisal system is the need for staff references to be as exact as possible. It is usual for principals to rely on the advice and information received from senior staff as well as their own perceptions when compiling a reference. Like all practical, if occasionally subjective and haphazard, systems this has its undeniable virtues and it is not the purpose here to suggest its replacement by some rigid bureaucratic process. However, appraisal and reference systems must be considered together: where the one exists, the other inevitably does. To state that an appraisal system must result from full staff consultation is not to attempt to avoid a difficult issue. To put forward an actual model, however, could be unnecessarily prescriptive. The guidelines below therefore are taken from other works,[21] are included without comment, and expected only to provide a basis for debate:

25. *Performance appraisal*

(i) each teacher to give a written description of his or her present post, using a standard format which gives direction towards objectives;

---

21 J.L. Davies and I. Newton, *Staff and Organization Development of Management Departments*, Discussion paper for East Anglian Regional Advisory Council Conference, 1973; Markwell and Roberts, *Management Career Planning:* both quoted in Lyons, *op.cit*, p.146; cf also Section **11.9**. Appendix 1, above.

(ii) the teacher to agree the job description with the relevant superior;
(iii) the teacher to agree performance standards and specific short term targets for achievement within the department's overall plans;
(iv) these standards and targets regularly to be reviewed;
(v) the needs for training will be identified via (iii) and (iv) and then appropriate action can be agreed and begun. These needs will vary but will probably be a mixture of the individual and the job-related.

26. *Potential appraisal*
It is argued that the purpose of potential appraisal is to assist each teacher to realise fully his or her potential as an education practitioner independently of institutional allegiance. Markwell and Roberts suggest this strategy: Each teacher draws a career line on a graph. One axis represents time. The other represents career level or particular function. The line is recommended to be historical to date, and to be projected into the future. Where teachers have been previously employed in industry, it is suggested that the career level can be determined according to salary on the termination of (each) employment. The career line then forms the basis for guidance discussion. Those who offer guidance will need knowledge of the field and level to which the individual aspires.

27. These systems can be contrasted with the techniques practised at one college where, as part of the staff development programme, the principal carries out an annual interview with each teacher.[22] These interviews are "not meant to be an assessment or evaluation session, but a chance for the individual to discuss his professional development with the chief executive of the organisation." The interviews can be extended but they "are not always easy and not necessarily successful." Their value is seen to be an improvement on casual corridor conversations and, while acknowledging that the teacher may for personal or professional reasons not wish to speak to the principal, as an important part of the communications system.

28. While both the management sciences approach and that quoted from one college are intended to further staff development, their differences demonstrate the choices which have to be made: a useful programme can certainly be mounted without the deployment of the full range of the management battery, but the ultimate results may be less rewarding.

29. The role of the professional tutor has been referred to in paragraph 4, above. Without a tutor/counsellor or a counselling service, any staff development programme will have little value. The teacher's career needs will usually be drawn from the combination of the motives which caused entry into the profession, career goals, the areas of work which give satisfaction, and external pressures. To advise on how to meet those needs or, sadly, to indicate avenues of adjustment where they cannot be met, require skilled counselling. Principals may fill this role without difficulty[23] but apart from this being a further requirement to their acting as super being and the issue

---

22 ed McHugh and Millar, *op.cit*, p.37.
23 A digest which might provide assistance is given by Colin M. Turner, *Inter-Personal Skills in Further Education*, Coombe Lodge, 1978.

of confidentiality already raised, a full staff development programme clearly demands the presence of a person, persons, committee or unit with a designated and specified counselling function. Such a function must also have access to the means of action and information: it would be pointless to have established that a teacher's needs would best be fulfilled by redevelopment within the college if such redevelopment could not take place.

30. *Training and opportunities*

The training an individual will require depends upon needs, but the opportunities for such training will vary according to the structure of the institution, its staff development programme, and funding policies. Close liaison between the college, the governors and the local authority will be necessary in several instances, especially in the provision of in-service training. However, it will be useful to itemise possible training areas:

(i) In-service training. Such training can include induction and opportunities to experience other areas of college work. Usually however it occurs elsewhere, which raises the question of how the skills newly acquired are to be fully transferred to the context of the current employment. Among suggested programmes are: specialist short courses; regular staff training sessions and lectures at the place of work; a regular quota of teachers seconded each term of the year for teacher or other training courses, some of whom will undertake long advanced courses.

(ii) Secondment. Although the field remains largely unexplored, there is evidence of colleges seconding staff to other institutions. While this has been in a directly educational context (ie. to work upon a specific educational project) it need not be so. Experience, or further experience, in industry will assist those responsible for giving careers advice. More ambitious schemes are known, [24] but while this wide use of secondment remains rare it is worthy of serious consideration. Its advocates stress the breadth of experience which can be acquired, and as a consequence improved awareness; there is also benefit to an institution of regular and fresh contact with employment outside education.

(iii) Consultancy. While this has generally developed as the preserve of higher education and of the professional consultants – inspectors, advisers, teacher trainers, and education management teachers – it has been argued that serving teachers have a greater role to play than in giving the occasional visiting or in-service course lecture.

(iv) Establishment interchange. This idea is relatively new to the educational world. Its implementation requires the approval, participation and encouragment of the local authority. While administrative considerations cannot be ignored, it is a cheap and flexible method whereby teachers can directly acquire wider experience. Such a method can be supplemented by visits to other colleges.

(v) Job rotation. The object is to avoid staleness and for rotation to be a part of an institution's development programme. The method clearly

24 For example, one college seconds teachers to local broadcastings stations.

involves practical difficulties and may be unsuitable in many instances: experiment and evaluation would be useful.

(vi) Expansion of current opportunities. It has been advocated that current development methods such as research, project participation and working party membership should be part of a coherently planned programme.

31. The discussion above has referred largely to direct factors in staff development. Staff development may also occur indirectly, and independently of a structured programme. For example, in the course of their employment staff may be elected to various college committees and working parties, or serve as examiners or on course committees outside the college. This indirect development may be consolidated by instruction and guidance. The administrative areas in which staff are most likely to become involved are: organization; finance; and communications, records and office procedure. Experience, at college or departmental levels (and perhaps on a rotation basis) may be provided thus:

(i) organization: responsibilities in timetabling; student selection procedures; enrolment arrangements; examination arrangements and timetables; short course organization and publicity; educational technology arrangements.

(ii) finance: sub-estimate production; purchasing and order book procedures; financial and stock records; and stock check procedures.

(iii) communications, records and office procedure: establishing an information storage/retrieval system; routine documentation; preparation of reports and minutes; drafting of memoranda and instructions.

32. The development issues discussed above are as relevant to non-teaching as to teaching staff. Specifically, a development programme for non-teaching staff may be easier to arrange in that significant development will occur during the course of employment, and may be consolidated by attendance at relevant courses operated by the college. Responsibility for development here may be part of the college's overall developmental structure, or perhaps be part of a CAO's duties in acting as training officer for non-teaching staff. Course attendance may be by day-release, or other arrangement. Heads of department may have a responsibility for the development of in-post training scheduled for their ancillary staff. It is the practice in some institutions that support for non-teaching staff development by way of fees payment, library access, and release is conditional upon the courses being undertaken within the college. While the policy of providing opportunity for personal as well as vocational development may obtain as it does for teaching staff, non-teaching staff development policies may lay a stress on institutional needs. For example, the training of technicians may be required to cover all laboratories or workshops within a department; individual staff are often appointed to specific laboratories, but some institutions "pair" technician staff, encourage opportunities for working together, and anticipate that job interchange may on occasion result. (This practice demonstrates the care necessary in developmental policies: against it, if abused or unwanted, have to be set the protections given by employment law and conditions of service agreements).

33. In summary, whichever means are adopted it is axiomatic to development that the end should be constructive. Such a teleological view will require full consultation, and the consent of all participants. There will always be cases to which ready answers are not easily available, such as the best path of development for a principal, or a person who has become an inveterate time-server, but recognition of the problem at least could begin in advance. It may also be the case that a number of staff may find full satisfaction in the current post, have no wish for promotion, have finance sufficient to needs, and not wish to have any involvement in staff development.

34. The common means of identifying training needs is by a questionnaire. This, too, will require full consideration of the ends to be attained. The details required will usually include: personal details; education; courses attended; application of skills; self-evaluation of courses; specialist professional work; managerial work; and immediate and long term aspirations.

35. *Promotion*

General findings concerning promotion have been referred to under paragraph 9. It is presumed that a staff development programme will assist towards the achievement of promotion in another institution (one college as a part of its programme provides coaching in interview techniques). In view of the concern expressed about internal promotion criteria it may be necessary for colleges to ensure that the criteria are well known and well understood. Information will therefore need to be supplied concerning the college establishment, and the actual promotion possibilities which may or do exist. Further, how teachers' selection and eligibility for promotion are determined is likely to cause concern. A commonly advocated method of selection is that of "peer rating". It is argued that this method is both the most effective and the least disruptive. If it is to be successful however, it must be clearly established: procedures should be known to all and to have been formulated by consultation. This may involve the staff collectively or through elected committees responsible to the whole staff.

36. If peer rating is adopted, the kinds of criteria – within the establishment structure and operation of market forces – will probably include: academic, administrative and pastoral responsibility; distinction in service; general service to the college; and other activities which demonstrate dedication, ability and service. By giving agreed weighting to each element, it would be possible to arrive at statistical totals.

37. The Engineering Industry Training Board recommends the use of a matrix system in which an individual's eligibility for promotion is determined as immediate, within two-three years, or unlikely according to the following factors:[25] age, length of service, time in present job; education and qualifications; performance in present job (outstanding, above average, below average, poor).

38. Whatever system is adopted it is clear that it must be seen by all to be fair,

25 *Training Managers on First Appointment*, Booklet 19, Engineering Industry Training Board, 1973.

and not to rest upon unchallengeable autocratic decision, however wise and beneficent the autocrat. Staff will need to accept the system on their own terms, unions and associations will need to be full consulted, and it will have to be appreciated that development of the system will not only of necessity be slow, but that it will have to operate within the confines of the college establishment and statutory provisions.

39. *Responsibility for the programme*

It may well be felt that responsibility should be open and shared; decisions may rest with the staff of the college: it is their programme, after all; but on the other hand, institutional needs and managerial objectives have also to be reconciled. A structure which demonstrates full consensus is more likely to win the approval of most, but it will need to recognise factors which can be either limitations or the means of advance. These will include:

(i) The executive unit. This could be a sub-committee of the academic board; a college department (such as one entitled Central Educational Services which has responsibility for audio-visual aids systems, guidance and counselling, in-service training and staff development); the principal/staff development officer; or a standing committee consisting of heads of department, principal, vice-principal and CAO.

(ii) Liaison. The amount of formal involvement of LEA officers and advisers, inspectors, representatives of relevant training institutions and employers, and professional associations will require attention. The attitude of the local authority to secondments and job interchange will be crucial.

(iii) Counselling. If a professional tutor, staff welfare or development officer exists in the college, roles and responsibilities will require definition. Where existing posts or responsibilities are enlarged, cognizance will have to be taken of the roles performed by the principal and local authority advisers.

(iv) Cost. Any new scheme will require careful budgetary provision.

40. *Wider considerations*

While participative management may be said to be common in many areas of employment, the structure of our education service does not always encourage it. "Top-down" routes of staff development are hardly surprising when so much of funding has a central source and salary structures are nationally determined (not that this circumstance is unique to education). As the need for regional development has been voiced for some time, it may be that staff development programmes will not be satisfactorily constructed until such time as there is adequate national and regional machinery. It can be argued that while this is being too conservative, real viability will only occur when schemes are constructed which are common to a local authority. In making its decision however, every college ought to consider its particular needs. The discussion model above is no more than that: prescription is not intended. [26]

26 Alternative models are to be found *inter alia* in *College Management Readings and Cases, op.cit,* Vol.3.

41. It may be useful in conclusion, however, to itemise common errors in staff development programmes:[27]

(i) Timing. Development staff ought not to be designated or appointed until decisions concerning the basic nature of the programme have been established; consensus of all aims and objectives is necessary before a programme is begun; resources and methods must be established before programme commencement.

(ii) Parochialism, over-administration and other constraints on colleges' autonomy. Parochialism is used as a term to describe the appointment to a job according to other than the job specification's criteria; and over-administration to describe over-standardised selection, structure and promotion criteria.

(iii) Lack of capacity at top management level. Overloaded or inadequate top management tends to produce a vicious circle of under briefed and inadequately supported middle management. Staff development, among other matters, invariably suffers.

(iv) Errors in structure and objectives (compounded where the development programme allows no feedback of comment and information) produce a wrongly briefed and trained staff.

(v) Incomplete analysis and communication.

(vi) While this is often beyond colleges' control in that reorganization is invariably imposed upon them, for any development programme to proceed satisfactorily, rates of change should be organized and phased over long periods.

(vii) Lack of experience, and difficulties in obtaining consensus. It is cited as a crucial difficulty that a lack of skill, confidence and willingness to begin the kinds of counselling work necessary can afflict staff with executive functions.

42. *Research*

Research, for itself, a higher degree, or to lead to publication is the most common form of current staff development. It is of obviously high value to the individual, the institution, and the education service. NATFHE states that it should be a basic right of all members of any academic community to have the necessary time and facilities to undertake research. The CNAA has stated that: "the leaders of each branch of study should ... have relevant teaching experience together with research or industrial experience. The Council will expect some members of the staff to be undertaking research."[28] Any development of research will require resource provision if staff are to have a realistic opportunity of engaging in research. Such provision will include: accommodation, library and laboratory facilities, consideration of staffing ratios, and remission of class contact hours. NATFHE believes that there should be no arbitrary terminal point for the availability of research opportunities, whether in institutional terms or according to level of work; and that opportunities should not be restricted according to the type of institution: it argues that wherever staff with

27 These are drawn from P.C. Webb "Staff Development in Large Secondary Schools", *Educational Administration Bulletin*, Vol.2, No.1, 1973, quoted in Lyons, *op.cit.* pp.160-161.

28 *Memorandum on courses leading to the Council's first degrees*, CNAA statement No.3, CNAA, November 1965.

particular expertise or contacts with industry and commerce exist, they ought not to be denied access to the sources of research finance. Despite the severe restrictions imposed on polytechnics by resource controls, it is clear that much research takes place in those institutions, even though while there is usually a senior committee concerned with research, the activity is seldom directly related to staff development.[29]

43. Teachers in further and higher education have long claimed an entitlement to a sabbatical (study) leave. The colleges of education have a provision in some cases for one term in seven years to be available for refreshment; there has been some extension of sabbatical provisions in universities. The arguments have become rather confused, for sabbatical provision does not presume approval for a particular course of study but rather for the individual to pursue means to personal and intellectual refreshment, and the term has been used loosely to embrace both this concept and that of the commoner study leave/secondment which does require course or activity approval.[30] Whether such distinctions are preserved in any negotiated resolution remains imponderable but at present they ought to be appreciated. Study leave provision varies (in polytechnics, in percentage terms from almost nil to about 3% of the full-time teaching staff per year). The main use of study leave remains the acquisition of a further qualification in the teacher's own discipline but increasingly staff are seeking leave to gain qualifications in other areas. Criteria for the award of study leave, as well as length of tenure, may include further professional and industrial experience, academic research, and the development of learning resources.

44. **Coda**

The survey contained in this sub-section is limited. It is confined, for reasons of clarity and space, to an encompassable consideration of the subject. It could be argued that awareness of the law is a part of staff development, and that EEC educational developments should be considered. Information on those topics is provided elsewhere in this book, and perhaps the book itself may be regarded as a staff development manual. Ultimately however, whatever the pressures exerted on the nature and scope of staff development in further and higher education, as a commentator remarked to the author, "staff development lacks a point of view". Perhaps it is time for one to be formed.

REFERENCE

A Better Start in Working Life, DES, 1979.

The Supply and Training of Teachers for Further Education, Report of the Standing Sub-Committee on Teachers for Further Education of the National Advisory Council on the Training and Supply of Teachers, HMSO, 1966.

---

29 cf Teather, *op.cit*, p.68.

30 cf. Jeff Brass, "Sabbatical Leave", *NATFHE Journal*, Vol.4, No.1, February 1979, pp.7,9. Brass makes few distinctions but offers wide ranging arguments. The issue is more fully discussed in Catherine Goyder, *Sabbaticals for All*, NCLC, 1977, and by H. Greenaway and A.G. Harding, *The Growth of Policies for Staff Development*, Monograph 34, SRHE, Guildford, 1978.

The Training of Teachers for Further Education: a report by the Sub-Committee on the Training of Teachers for Further Education relating to the training of full-time teachers in Further Education, ACSTT, June 1975 (DES 1977).
The Training of Adult Education and Part-Time Further Education Teachers: a report by the Sub-Committee on the Supply and Training of Teachers, ACSTT.
Training Teachers for Education Management in Further and Adult Education: a report by the Sub-Committee on the Supply and Training of Teachers, ACSTT, August 1979.

Annual Conference Report, BEAS, Vol.1, No.1.
Frank Bacon, "The Practicalities of Staff Development", *Journal of Further and Higher Education,* Vol.1, No.3, Winter 1977, pp.56-63.
Judy Bradley and Jane Silverleaf, *Making the Grade,* NFER, 1979.
Judy Bradley and Jane Silverleaf, "Promotion in F.E. Teaching", *NATFHE Journal,* Vol. 4, No.1. February 1979, pp.8-9.
J. Brass, "Sabbatical Leave", *NATFHE Journal,* Vol. 4, No.1 February 1979, pp.7-9.
L.M. Cantor and I.F. Roberts, *Further Education Today: A Critical Review,* Routledge and Kegan Paul, 1979.
College Personnel Management, Coombe Lodge Report, Vol.3, No.3, 1970.
ed. L. Elton and K. Simmonds, *Staff Development in Higher Education,* SRHE, Guildford, 1977.
Catherine Goyder, *Sabbaticals for All,* NCLC Publishing Society, 1977.
H. Greenaway and A.G. Harding, *The Growth of Policies for Staff Development,* SRHE Monograph 34, SRHE, Guildford, 1978.
I.W. Hannaford, *Staff Development Practice,* Coombe Lodge Reports, Vol.7, No.5, 1974, pp.299-306.
A.G. Harding, *Training of Polytechnic Teachers,* Society for Research in Higher Education, 1974.
R.G. Havelock, "The Utilization of Educational Research and Development," *British Journal of Educational Technology,* Vol.2, No.2, pp.84-98.
S. Hilsum and B. Start, *Promotion and Careers in Teaching,* NFER, 1974.
David S. Ireland, "Changing Teachers: The Top-Down Way", *Journal of Further and Higher Education,* Vol.2, No.2, Summer 1978, pp.76-84.
Issues in Staff Development, Staff Development in Universities Programme/University Teaching Methods Unit, 1975.
Geoffrey Lyons, *Head's Tasks, a handbook of Secondary School Administration,* NFER, 1976.
Management Information Systems, Coombe Lodge Reports, Vol.6, No.3, 1973.
ed. Royston McHugh and Edward Milner, *Staff Development: The Individual and the Organisation,* pp.33-47 of *Broadcast Notes,* Open University Third Level Course Management in Education, E.321 BN, 1978.
D. Warren Piper and R. Glatter, *Changing University,* NFER, 1979.
Register of Educational Development Services in Polytechnics, SCEDSIP, (available from PETRAS, Newcastle upon Tyne Polytechnic).
Research in Further Education, Coombe Lodge Reports, Vol.6, No.14, 1973.
Report of the working party on resources for research in polytechnics and other colleges, CNAA, 1974.
T.J. Russell, *The Training of Teachers for Further Education Establishments,* Coombe Lodge Reports, Vol.6, No.5, 1973 pp.224-30.
S. Sayer and A.G. Harding, "Causes for Concern in Training Lecturers", *Times Higher Education Supplement,* No.258, 1 October 1976, p.10.
Keith Scribbins, "Women in Education: Some Points for Discussion", *Journal of Further and Higher Education,* Vol.1, No.3, Winter 1977, pp.17-39.
ed. Donald D. Simmons and D.L. Parkes, *College Management, Readings and Cases; A Staff Development Handbook,* Vols 1-5, Coombe Lodge, 1971-76.
Staff Development in Further Education, Report of the joint working party, ACFHE/APTI, 1973.

Staffing, Coombe Lodge Reports, Vol.5, No.4, 1972.
Staffing, Coombe Lodge Reports, Vol.9, No.3, 1976.
Staffing and Staff Development, Coombe Lodge Reports, Vol.6, No.1, 1973.
ed. D.C.B. Teather, *Staff Development in Higher Education, An International Review and Bibliography,* Kogan Page, 1979.
The Education and Training of Teachers for Further and Higher Education, NATFHE, 1978.
G. Tolley, "Problems of Staff Development in Polytechnics", in Coombe Lodge Reports, Vol.6, No.15, 1974, pp.708-713.
Training Managers on First Appointment, EITB, 1973.
Colin M. Turner, *Inter-Personal Skills in Further Education,* Coombe Lodge, 1978.
Mantz Yorke, "Staff development in further and higher education: a review", *British Journal of Teacher Education,* Vol.3, No.2, 1977.

Bodies Concerned with Staff Development

SCEDSIP is concerned with educational development, including staff development. It produces bulletins and publications, arranges meetings and conferences, and liaises with various bodies (such as the CDP); Secretary, Dr P. Griffin, Learning Systems Group, Middlesex Polytechnic, Bounds Green Road, London N11 2NG. The Society for Research into Higher Education (SRHE) is located at the University of Surrey, Guildford, Surrey GU2 5XH. The National Association for Staff Development produces an occasional *Journal.* The Institute of Professional Tutors produces a newsletter (issued from South Downs College of Further Education, Havant).

12 FURTHER EDUCATION TEACHER TRAINING

1. The overlap between staff development and initial (teacher) training is particularly marked in further education, largely because most initial training is done on an in-service basis. This is completely different from the situation in schools where now the normal requirement is that all teachers must have undertaken a pre-service training course (usually BEd, PGCE or Cert. Ed with the final entry to the latter courses in 1979) leading to qualified teacher status. While some new entrants to further education will have attended a pre-service training course, usually at one of the four specialist training centres for further education teachers,[1] many will enter without professional teacher training. There is therefore a backlog of training needs amongst serving teachers in further and higher education, and staff development, for many of these, takes the form of release to undertake initial training, often on a day or block release basis.

2. **The present structure**

The present system of training for teachers in further and higher education is very diffuse. A number of different courses and patterns of courses are available in a wide variety of institutions, but the overall ouput is small and the system lacks coherence. Only now are attempts being made to develop a greater unity of provision and a national pattern of training (see below).

3. At present the main providers of full-time and sandwich training are the four specialist colleges of education. These institutions have concentrated on courses of initial training leading to a certificate of education. A number of course patterns have been developed to help to meet the needs of differing groups, including full-time pre-service courses and sandwich and day release courses for serving teachers. The pre-service courses are for students who wish to be trained as teachers before seeking appointments. They last for one academic year and entrants must have a qualification in the subjects they intend to teach, for example: a university degree or diploma, Higher National Certificate or Diploma, Full Technological Certificate of the CGLI or Advanced RSA Certificate in shorthand and typewriting. Usually there is one course for non-graduates with relevant qualifications and appropriate industrial or commercial experience who are over 24 years of age, and a further course for students with graduate or graduate equivalent qualifications who can be admitted at a younger age. Similar courses but on a sandwich or block release basis are run for serving teachers wishing to gain professional teaching qualifications where the entry qualifications are comparable.

4. In addition to the courses offered by these four colleges of education, several institutions such as Bristol, Middlesex, Oxford and Portsmouth polytechnics now provide, or are hoping to provide shortly, courses for unqualified teachers in further education. Similar full-time (pre-service and sandwich

---

1 Bolton College of Education, Huddersfield Polytechnic, Garnett College, London and The Polytechnic, Wolverhampton, Faculty of Education.

courses) are provided in Wales jointly by University College Cardiff, the University of Wales Institute of Science and Technology and the North East Wales Institute of Higher Education. A number of universities, such as Brunel, Bath and London University Institute of Education, now have some further education option within their PGCE.

5. The number of students on full-time and sandwich courses has remained fairly stable in recent years (by 1974 there were 1,288 full-time; 383 sandwich[2]). There has, however, been a rapid growth in the number of serving teachers taking part-time courses at local centres linked to one of the main institutions where student numbers have grown from 78 in 1968 to 765 in 1974. Over 30 extra mural centres now exist to cater for this demand. These centres are being rationalized and strengthened in the regional plans in response to Circular 11/77 (see paragraph 8 below). Their role seems likely to expand, therefore, in the foreseeable future.

6. Thus the main routes developed by the specialist institutions are full-time, sandwich or part-time courses of initial training leading to certification roughly analogous to the PGCE pattern for school teachers. These courses, together with certain others, are recognised for incremental purposes for certain grades of staff in further education.[3] The main types of course which have developed outside this pattern are the CGLI 730 course for serving teachers and the RSA courses with substantial numbers of teachers studying Office Studies and English as a Foreign Language. These are available almost exclusively via part-time day and/or evening routes in many colleges and represent the major route by which existing teachers in further education receive a basis of professional training. Other City and Guilds courses, including specialisms such as Administration, Educational Technology and Achievement Testing are available in a number of colleges for serving teachers. The College of Preceptors also offers teacher training courses for teachers in further education.

7. Some universities, such as Newcastle, Manchester and Bristol, also offer post initial courses for further education. Some curriculum courses, such as the one at Sussex University, are predominantly oriented towards further education.

8. **Recent developments: The Haycocks Report and Circular 11/77**

The report was approved by ACSTT[4] in June 1975 and published by the DES, together with the DES response (Circular 11/77) in November 1977. (The main recommendations and a summary of Circular 11/77 form appendices 1 and 2 below). The Secretary of State supported the proposals in principle and called for an early start on implementing them "so far as this is possible within existing resources".

2 Advisory Committee on the Supply and Training of Teachers report on *The Training of Teachers for Further Education* June 1975. cf Annex A.

3 *Scales of Salaries for Teachers in Establishments of Further Education, England and Wales 1978*, Annex B, Appendix III.

4 Advisory Committee on the Supply and Training of Teachers sub-committee report on *The Training of Teachers for Further Education.*

9. Since then all Regional Advisory Councils have submitted proposals, some of an interim nature, in response to Circular 11/77. It is clear from these that there is considerable regional disparity in existing provision and patterns of provision. There is now a real danger that the impetus to establish a national pattern of training and provision will be lost. No commitment, for example, has yet been forthcoming to make induction training compulsory by 1981, and it is unlikely that this target date will now be met. No national forum has been established for consultation between validating bodies. Perhaps the most important regional variation is in those currently proceeding, or envisaged as likely to proceed in the future, to full certification even under the new proposals. NATFHE was critical of the Haycocks assumption that only a proportion of lecturers, which the report envisaged as about one third, should proceed to full certification. Unless existing resources are increased this variation seems likely to continue to the detriment of the profession.

10. Since the first Haycocks report there have been two further reports[5] published, although they have not yet been endorsed by ACSET which, although reconstituted, has met only once since the final meeting of its predecessor, ACSTT, in March 1978. While their formal status is currently that of reports sent out to interested bodies for comment, a number of RACs have already begun to incorporate proposals for adult education and part-time further education teachers within their overall regional plan in response to Circular 11/77.

---

5 *The Training of Adult Education and Part-time Further Education Teachers; Training Teachers for Education Management in Further and Adult Education.*

APPENDIX 1

MAIN RECOMMENDATIONS OF THE HAYCOCKS REPORT

Advisory Committee on the Supply and Training of Teachers Sub-Committee. Report on the Training of Teachers for Further Education.

Training Requirement

1. Not later than 1981 there should be a training requirement for all new entrants to full-time teaching in further education, who have less than three years full-time equivalent teaching experience. This requirement will be met by those who have satisfactorily completed a course of pre-service training for teachers in further education or who possess some other recognised teacher training qualification. All other entrants must take a systematic induction/training course, normally during their first year of service. This requirement should if possible be introduced before 1981.

Pre-Service Training

2. Planning should be for a modest growth, to some 1,700 places by 1981.

3. At present there should be no increase in the number of centres providing one year full-time pre-service courses. Should further provision be called for in the future the criteria set out in the Report should be useful.

4. Consideration should be given to the possibility of further education teachers, and indeed some prospective school teachers, undertaking teaching practice in both schools and further education during their training.

College Introduction Arrangements

5. All new staff joining further education colleges should have an introduction to their role in their new institution. These arrangements should be separate from and additional to the arrangements from the induction to teaching of new entrants.

Induction Arrangements for Trained New Entrants

6. Although our intention is that there should be a full year's programme of induction for new entrants who have completed a one year full-time pre-service course of training when resources permit, we accept that in the first instance their induction training should be restricted to release for the equivalent of one day a week for one term.

7. Release should normally be during the first term of service.

8. Part of the release period should be spent with other new teachers appointed to schools or further education colleges as appropriate and this will often mean spending it outside the college at which the teacher is employed.

Induction/Training Arrangements for Untrained New Entrants

9. All new entrants to full-time teaching in further education who have less than three years full-time equivalent teaching experience, and who do not already meet the training requirements set out in the report should:
   (i) undertake not more than three quarters of a full-time teacher's normal contract hours (and preferably less) during their first year.
   (ii) be released for professional training for at least the equivalent of one day a week throughout one academic year together with a period of block release equivalent to not less than four weeks; and
   (iii) receive support within their institution during this time.

In very exceptional circumstances, it may be necessary to defer these arrangements until the second year of service, but every endeavour should be made to avoid this. At the earliest possible date, and in any case not later than 1981, these induction arrangements should be made a requirement for the teachers concerned (see also recommendation 1).

10. The full-time block release referred to in recommendation 9 need not necessarily be taken as a single block.

11. The content and structure of the proposed first year courses should be such that modules of study in them find a natural place in Certificate of Education courses.

12. The emphasis of the first year should be related to practice and to those aspects of theory directly related to the needs of the teacher in his first year.

13. It would not be appropriate to make a final overall assessment in the limited time available during the first year course, but a future validating body and the teacher himself may wish to have some form of assessment.

14. Opportunities should be available for a significant proportion (perhaps a third or so) of the new entrants referred to in recommendation 9 to go on to a further year's study on a similar basis, either immediately thereafter or after further (but normally not more than four years) teaching experience. In the event of more than a third of these new entrants wishing to undertake a further year's study, further consideration should be given to the resources available.

Validation

15. We would expect the further year's study referred to in recommendation 14 to lead to a certificate awarded by a university or the CNAA, which would enable its holder to be considered where appropriate for qualified teacher status on the same terms as those which apply to teachers who have satisfactorily completed a pre-service course of training for further education teachers.

16. A national forum should be established for consultation between those concerned with validation. It is hoped that the present number of validating bodies will not be greatly increased.

17. There should be an appropriate body in each region (either an institution or, more probably, an inter-institutional committee), to secure the co-ordination of arrangements so that they may be acceptable for validation, and to ensure that where devolution occurs it does not lead to differing standards, fragmentation and lack of continuity in the studies undertaken.

18. The first year induction course should contribute some credit towards the certificate. The extent of the credit will be a matter for the validating bodies who will therefore need to be associated with both years of the courses.

19. Possible credit for qualifications awarded by other bodies should be a matter for the validating bodies. A common view on such credit would be important.

Further In-service Training

20. Opportunities for in-service training should be more generous for teachers in further education than for teachers in schools, and in any event they should be at least on the same scale. Release for in-service training should be increased to five per cent of the further education teaching force at any one time as soon as resources permit.

21. Teachers' Centres could well be used more generally by further education teachers.

Organisation of In-Service Courses

22. Regional bodies should be asked by the Department to draw up and submit plans for their areas, on the basis of the guidance offered in this report, in the light of the needs of their areas for initial and further in-service training.

Professional Tutors

23. There should be at least one professional tutor in every further education college, on either a full- time or part-time basis, who would normally be a member of the full-time staff of the college.

24. Professional tutors should be trained.

25. All colleges of education (technical) in consultation with local authorities and institutions of further and higher education in their regions, should develop pilot schemes to examine further the roles of professional tutors in further education, taking into account developments in the schools sector, in order to establish appropriate training objectives, taking into account the existing arrangements.

Timing

26. The aims should be to reach the target for each element in the programme of expansion for teachers in further education by 1981.

APPENDIX 2

DES RESPONSE TO THE HAYCOCKS REPORT

1. In Circular 11/77, the DES reproduced the main Haycocks recommendation (the training of new entrants without pre-service training) and the two complementary recommendations concerning induction, and summarised the recommendation concerning increased provision of in-service training.

2. The Secretary of State's response was to support the proposals in principle, and to wish that an early start be made on their implementation "so far as this is possible within the limit of existing resources." While recognising that the Sub-Committee took account in its proposals of probable constraints on finance, the then Secretary of State nonetheless recorded her belief that "more effective use could be made of the considerable resources already devoted to teacher training in this field" by way of the colleges of education (technical), extra mural and other part-time provision, "if their deployment could be better organised in accordance with the report's recommendations."

3. Although the White Paper, *The Government's Expenditure Plans*, Cmnd. 6721, indicated that no increase would occur in the number of staff employed in further education, the DES believed it possible "to introduce over a period the report's recommendations for induction training" whilst also making "some progress towards a target of 3% for in-service training." However, even if the recommendation concerning the release for in-service training being increased to 5% were to be left aside, the Government doubted whether the report could be fully implemented by 1981. It was the governmental view that priority should be given to the recommendation concerning "the institution of systematic induction arrangements" for teachers without previous experience or training.

4. The Government proposed that, pending the outcome of the Working Group on the Management of Higher Education, in connection with recommendation 22, LEAs should request RACs to draw up and submit plans for their areas in consonance with the report's guidance, and that priority be given to the induction training recommendations. It was stated that all regions would wish with reference to paragraphs 40-47 of the report to make the best possible use of existing resources, and that some may wish to prepare plans on a sub-regional basis. In itemising the available resources, the circular drew attention to the colleges of education (technical), extra mural centres, and the resources released by the cuts in initial teacher training. The Secretary of State agreed with the report that a further pre-service training centre was unlikely to be justified.

5. Further consideration would be given to the recommendation concerning the making of induction training compulsory by 1981 after RACs had submitted progress reports (by September 1978 in the first instance) and there had been an examination of other priorities and resources in the education service.

REFERENCE

The Training of Teachers for Further Education: a report by the Sub-Committee on the Training of Teachers for Further Education relating to the training of full-time teachers in Further Education, ACSTT, June 1975 (DES November 1977).

Scales of Salaries for Teachers in Establishments of Further Education, England and Wales 1978, HMSO.

The Training of Adult Education and Part-time Education Teachers: a report by the Sub-Committee on the Training of Teachers for Further Education, ACSTT.

Training Teachers for Education Management in Further and Adult Education: a report by the Sub-Committee on the Training of Teachers for Further Education, ACSTT, August 1978.

The Training of Teachers for Further Education: DES Circular 11/77, 17 November 1977.

With the exception of the Burnham Further Education report, all these publications are available upon request from the Department of Education and Science, Elizabeth House, York Road, London SE1 7PH.

13 COOMBE LODGE, THE FURTHER EDUCATION STAFF COLLEGE

1. Coombe Lodge, the Further Education Staff College located near Bristol, resulted from a recommendation in the 1957 Willis Jackson Report[1] that a residential staff college be established to provide management training for senior college lecturers and administrators.[2]

2. The college was founded in 1960. Its establishment was assisted by a £100,000 grant from industry. Operation of courses began in 1963. Since that time its short courses have been attended by more than 18,000 members of the further education service and industry. There are few college or polytechnic principals and vice-principals who have not received formal management training at Coombe Lodge.

3. The staff college runs an extended series of conferences on the management of colleges for principals and vice-principals as well as a developmental series of conferences and workshops for heads of departments and their deputies. Courses on the management of college departments are run in a series of four weeks which cover the following area:
   Phase I Improving the Efficiency of Departments
   Phase II The Skills of Department Management
   Phase III The Use of Resources
   Phase IV Change and Development

4. In addition to the management courses which form the basis of much of the work of the staff college, Coombe Lodge also plays an important innovative role in the FE service. It has been instrumental in bringing together college staff working on TEC and BEC courses. Its workshops have played a vital role in helping staff find their way through the intricacies of the new councils. Coombe Lodge has also done valuable work in bringing together college staff and officers of the Manpower Services Commission.

5. The college also runs courses on more specialised areas of interest. Its current programme includes, for example, a seminar on the study of dispersed institutions of higher education.

6. The aim of the college is to provide a place where members can learn and think effectively. That effectiveness comes from the total of activity – meeting together, listening to lectures, studying papers, considering cases, confronting experts, questioning witnesses, working in groups of various sizes or making visits. Part of the work of the conference is done in plenary sessions with visiting speakers. Members then usually break up into syndicate groups where they are often asked to complete various projects and exercises.

---

1 *The Supply and Training of Teachers for Technical Colleges,* Report of a Special Committee appointed by the Minister of Education in September 1956, Ministry of Education, 1957.
2 cf Section **2.2.** 54-59 and **2.2**, Appendix 1.

7. The Coombe Lodge full-time academic staff of 11 is supplemented by visiting tutors and outside experts and witnesses.

8. The fee for the conference does not cover the whole cost. The balance is met by grants from local education authorities in England, Wales and Scotland and from the Department of Education, Northern Ireland.

9. The staff college's unique information service is available to anyone in further education. The Coombe Lodge Information Bank has more than 3,000 papers, case studies and reports on virtually every aspect of further education. Most of these papers were originally written for use in conferences. Copies are available from the Coombe Lodge library for a small charge. The college also publishes regular reports on subjects of general interest to the FE service. Most reports are the result of Coombe Lodge conferences, but some cover subjects which cannot be fitted into the conference programme. Most college libraries subscribe to the Coombe Lodge report service; individual copies are available by post. A list of current publications is given in paragraph 14.

10. The staff college provides an advisory service to colleges and to individuals in FE. Its aim is to make the knowledge and expertise of the staff college readily available to all those who think they might benefit from it. The precise nature of assistance given will be in keeping with the requirements and wishes of the authority or college seeking help.

11. Coombe Lodge is prepared to help with any problems within its competence. It has established a mode of operation which consists, in the main, of meeting individuals and/or groups concerned, talking problems through, and making relevant written materials available for further examination. The Coombe Lodge contribution may be limited to one such meeting or it may continue over a period of months or years with a number of meetings involving different individuals and groups of college staff. The degree of formality of these exchanges is largely in the client's hands, and rarely are formal written reports presented.

12. Some clients find it more convenient to visit Coombe Lodge for consultation and this is particularly appropriate where it is likely that they have a number of related problems on which they are seeking information or guidance. The college will respond readily to requests for information by letter or telephone.

13. These are some examples of the help given in the past two years: a review of a number of major issues of college policy; the structure of the academic board and its committees; the management of new learning methods; improvement of personal relationships among the college management team; rationalization of "A" level provision; staff development schemes; methods of staff selection; student selection; improvements in the college management information system; organizational difficulties stemming from growth, help with curricular innovation – notably in relation to TEC and BEC; and help with research projects into aspects of the administration of FE.

14. Coombe Lodge has recently established a research programme and is currently engaged in a project commissioned by the Further Education Curriculum Review and Development Unit (FEU) to review the major styles of curriculum design in FE. It is also conducting a survey of colleges of FE currently operating open learning systems for the Council for Education Technology (CET).

15. The college is an independent charitable trust of which the chairman and governors are appointed by the Secretary of State for Education and Science. The governors are drawn from local authority associations of England and Wales, the staffs of colleges, polytechnics, universities, industry and the professions, the TUC, and the staff of the college itself. One governor is appointed by the Secretary of State for Scotland. An assessor to the governing body is appointed by the DES. Committees of the governors include co-opted members from CBI, TSD and the City and Guilds of London Institute, as well as former governors.

Current Coombe Lodge Publications:

(i) *Reports*

Volume Ten

No.1. Art and Design Education
No.2. Management & Organization of Sociology Studies in FE.
No.3. Management & Organization of English Studies in FE.
No.4. Women in Further Education.
No.5. The Employment of Staff in FE.
No.6. Overseas Students in Further & Higher Education.
No.7. Phoenix from the Ashes? Prospects for Teacher Education.
No.8. The Vocational Preparation of Young People.
No.9. Industry, the Training Services Agency and Further Education.
No.10. College Management.
No.12. Cost & Educational Effectiveness in FE.
No.13. Post Compulsory Education in Western Europe.
No.14. The Organization of Legal Education and Training.
No.15. The Training Services Agency: Clerical, Secretarial and Office Studies.

Volume Eleven

No.1. Mathematics in TEC and BEC.
No.2. Language Studies in Further and Higher Education.
No.3. The Management of 'O' and 'A' Level Courses.
No.4. Manpower Services Commission: Securing a Future for Young People.
No.5. NEBSS: Report of a Conference/Workshop of the National Examinations Board for Supervisory Studies.
No.6. Establishing International Understanding through Further Education.
No.7. Employment Law and College Management.
No.8. Safety in Colleges: The Legal Requirements.
No.9. College Libraries and FE Development.
No.10. A Handbook for College Governors.
No.11. Use of Resources in College Management.
No.12. Current Developments in Further Education.
No.13. The Impact of MSC/TSD on 16-19 FE.
No.14. College Administration.

Volume Twelve

No.1. Education for the Young Unemployed.
No.2. BEC Assignments.
No.3. Craft Education and Training.
No.4. Education Priorities in FE/HE for the 1980s.
No.5. FE in Inner City and Urban Colleges.
No.6. Evaluating TEC Programmes.
No.7. Developing Youth Programmes.
No.8. Resources in FE: The Role of Management Information.
No.9. Art & Design DATEC Developments.

(ii) *Comparative Papers in Further Education*

No.1. The Netherlands: 16-19 Education.
No.2. An Anglo-German Report.
No.3. The FE System of England and Wales.
No.4. The German Vocational Education System.
No.5. Craft Apprenticeship in Europe.

(iii) *Curriculum Development in Further Education*

Revised Edition. A series of papers published in response to the greater demand for curriculum development made on colleges by TEC, BEC, CNAA, C&GLI and MSC. Price includes the rights to reproduce for internal staff development purposes.

(iv) *College Management: UK and European Case Studies*

Case studies and material based on researched situations in UK and European further education. The British section consists of material on organization and policy developments of current interests in FE. The European material includes profiles of Italian vocational and technical education and training of educational managers in Norway.

(v) *Inter-Personal Skills in Further Education: A Collection of Papers for In-Service Development*

A book written for staff in colleges and other educational institutions who are not highly trained in the skills of inter-personal relationships but who are involved in work with or management of other people. It is an introduction to inter-personal skills and forms a basis for further study or training.
Further details are available from Coombe Lodge, Blagdon, Bristol BS18 6RG.

14 PENAL ESTABLISHMENTS

1. **Introduction: the administration and character of education in penal establishments**
In order to understand the regulations, conditions of service arrangements and salary provisions affecting teaching staff in penal establishments, it is necessary to know something of the character and administration of the prison education service. This service is based on a tripartite contribution made by the Home Office, local education authorities and teachers employed by local education authorities to work in the prisons in their areas. In theory these are equal partners: in fact whilst local authorities employ the teachers, the important partners in the process are the teachers and the Home Office with the local authorities sometimes having only a peripheral interest in the education provided. All expenditure on the service is met by the Home Office: the main regulations, guidance and policy statements emanate from the Home Office (often following extensive consultation with the teachers); and, the further education provided in prisons cannot easily be integrated with the wider provision made by the local authority. Much of this is inevitable, given the context of penal education. Further, there is an extensive system of instruction and training which is carried out in prisons, not by teachers, but by prison officers and instructors who are employed by the Home Office on the relevant prison and civil service pay and conditions. The distinction between education and training, discussed elsewhere in this book (cf Sections 4 and **10.2.**72) in relation to the general social provision of further education is, in fact, an institutionalised distinction in the prison service.

2. The prison education service is administered, nationally, by the Home Office's Chief Education Officer and his staff. They work closely with a team of regional officers who provide guidance to particular establishments in their region. In most establishments there is a full-time education officer who is responsible for devising the education programme in the prison, administering it on a day to day basis, liaising with the prison governor, assistant governors, prison officers and specialists such as the medical officer, and liaising with the local education authority and the college to which he or she may be attached. A further, major, task facing the prison education officer and his or her staff is the difficult process of advising inmates on appropriate classes and allocating them accordingly. This is not, as it is in a college, a process which occurs primarily during certain weeks of the year. A penal establishment's population is constantly changing and, particularly in institutions which receive a large number of prisoners awaiting allocation to other institutions, the administration of class assignment and registration is a permanent and time consuming task. In short, the prison education officer has to act as a college principal, registrar and head of department in what is a microcosm of a college within a system of external contraints. Part of this work also involves the supervision of the work of other teaching staff. Most prisons have at least one full-time teacher – some have many more – and scores of part-time teachers. The education officer may not be able to use, easily, the clerical support which exists in a

prison, given competing demands for its use. Consequently, a reliance is often built up on inmate assistance for the performance of certain clerical and administrative duties. This brings its own problems, especially in short stay institutions.

3. The range and intensity of a prison's education programme vary considerably between institutions. In a young offenders' establishment certain mandatory provision has to be made. For inmates under school leaving age at least ten sessions of full-time education must be provided. In addition, for those between 16 and 21 in Borstals, it is mandatory to provide six hours per week as evening classes for each inmate. In adult offenders' establishments there is no particular mandatory provision.[1] However, Home Office policy entails certain types of provision. For example, any offender with a reading age below nine should have the opportunity to receive ten hours per week remedial education during working hours. Again, a prisoner or young offender who prior to entry to the institution was following a particular examination course should have the opportunity to "maintain" that education in the prison. These policies have major consequences for the administration of prison education. The system has to accommodate all ranges of ability from remedial and basic skills education to Open University and degree standard education. In any one institution there will be a range of vocational and non-vocational classes and the education officer and his or her staff have to administer the examination systems relating to these classes, including the General Certificate of Education and the City and Guilds examinations. It is important to emphasise that there is a great variation in the work of education officers and teachers, according to the type of institutions in which they work. Clearly, the pattern of education, and the problems posed in administering it, is not the same in young offenders' establishments such as a Borstal or junior detention centre as it is in, say, a remand centre. The pattern will differ again in an adult institution which may have, primarily, long stay offenders. In all institutions, but particularly in young offenders' establishments, attention has to be given to the social education of the prisoners. The education officer has to integrate social education with the formal education curriculum. Social education finds expression in such things as personal relationship courses, social skills classes, careers advice and counselling, money management and pre-release courses. The arrangement of cultural activities (for example, in the prison at Portsmouth there is a very successful drama group), leisure activities and "hobby" based classes, is an important part of the education officer's role. Again, the education officer has overall responsibility for the institution's library which, given the penal environment, is itself a major undertaking.

4. The prison environment influences considerably the character of the education provision. Prisons vary from high security closed institutions to

---

1 However, education is a feature of all penal establishments, its existence being specifically required in the statutory rules for these establishments. The providing body is the local education authority, acting under Section II(I) Schedule 1, of the Education (Miscellaneous Provisions) Act, 1948. The circular instructions issued by the Home Office, setting out the major policy decisions, are logged by the prison administration officer.

open institutions. They vary, too, in the types of offenders they deal with and the length of the sentences they have to serve. The strict registration of prisoners in classes, the escorting of prisoners to and from classrooms and workshops, the checking of tools and equipment, and the general observance of security rules all impose strictures on the prison education system which are absent, or less marked, in colleges. Further, prisoners have certain rights – such as a right of interview on application within 24 hours with the education officer – which also influence the work of that officer and his or her staff. Finally, the general culture of a prison, involving as it does the overall supervision by the prison governor, the attitudes concerning education adopted by prison officers and the attitudes of the prisoners themselves, exerts a considerable influence on the work of education officers and teachers.

5. The prison education service does not operate on a 38 week teaching year. It is not restricted, either, in the balance of day time and evening work on the normal college pattern. It is not unusual for the services of the education officer and teachers to be required every morning, afternoon and evening of every week of the year. This being so, particular arrangements have been made to deal with the conditions and remuneration of these staff. It also means that in most institutions one of the teachers will act as the deputy for the education officer. As we shall see, it is certainly open to question whether or not the conditions and grading arrangements for teachers in prisons is, at present, sufficiently sophisticated to deal with these features of the prison education service.

6. **Negotiating arrangements for teachers in penal establishments.**

Until recently the arrangements for determining the salaries and conditions of employment for teachers (including education officers) in penal establishments, were relatively informal. A tradition had developed whereby education officers and teachers in prisons were paid on scales derived from the Burnham Further Education Report, though their conditions of service varied greatly from prison to prison and did not always reflect the conditions applied to further education teachers in the relevant local authority. In the late 1960s attempts were made to systematise the salary arrangements and the contractual position of such staff. This was done through agreements reached by the Prison Department, the DES, local authorities, and the further education teachers' associations represented on the Burnham FE Committee, at the time, plus the Association of Teachers in Penal Establishments. These agreements, published in the form of circulars by the Home Office, covered all full-time teaching staff in penal establishments except those in junior detention centres who were (and are) paid on scales from the Burnham Primary and Secondary salaries document.

7. In the 1970s, the further education teachers' associations sought to make more formal collective bargaining arrangements for teachers in penal establishments by introducing claims on their behalf in the Burnham Further Education Committee. However, the determinations made by the Secretary of State for Education and Science in 1976 under the Remuneration of

Teachers Act 1965, concerning the scope of that Committee, excluded from its scope teachers in penal establishments. As a consequence, the local authorities, the further education teachers' associations plus the ATPE (with the support of the prison department of the Home Office), agreed to establish a joint negotiating committee to deal with the salaries and conditions of employment of prison teachers.

8. The JNC so established, in 1977, is called the Joint Negotiating Committee for Further Education Teachers Assigned to Prison Department Establishments. It is an interesting body, since it represents the only JNC for further education teachers which allows the determination, in one forum, of salaries and other conditions of service. Also, it is not established by statute and is free of influence from the Department of Education and Science. In December 1979, its constitution was amended to include staff in Junior Detention Centres but, at the time of writing, no negotiations have yet taken place on their behalf.

9. The constitution of the JNC provides, amongst other things, the following arrangements.
   (i) The Committee considers the remuneration and conditions of service of teachers employed by local authorities in England and Wales to work in Prison Department establishments, having regard to the Burnham Further Education salaries document and the agreements reached between CLEA and the further education teachers' associations.

   (ii) The representation is:

Management Side	*Teachers' Side*
Association of County Councils......2 members	NATFHE......4 members
Association of Metropolitan Authorities......2 members	APC......1 member
Welsh Joint Education Committee......1 member	ATPE......2 members

   Additionally, a non-voting representative of the Secretary of State for Home Affairs may attend on the Management Side.

   (iii) The Committee can form sub-committees and ask advisers to attend.
   (iv) The Committee appoints a Chairman and Vice-Chairman. In the first year the Management Side nominates the Chairman and the Teachers' Side the Vice-Chairman. Thereafter the positions are reversed annually.
   (v) Resolutions of the Committee are formed by there being a majority on *both* sides.
   (vi) Either side may refer matters on which it is not possible to reach agreement in the Committee to ACAS for either conciliation or submission to any appropriate form of arbitration.

10. It will be noted from the title of the JNC that staff who work as teachers and education officers in prisons are, in fact, employed by local education authorities but assigned to work in particular penal establishments. This has important implications for the contractual position of these staff.

11. **Contracts and conditions of service**
In 1969 the outcome of the consultations, referred to in paragraph 6 above, between the relevant teachers' associations, the Prison Department of the Home Office, the DES and the local authorities, was the issue of Home Office Circular 65/1969, *Full-Time Tutor Organisers and Full-Time Teachers, Salaries and Conditions of Service.* This circular set out the salary and contractual arrangements for the staff and these remained the basis for their employment until the establishment of the JNC in 1977. As is described below, the JNC amended the salary arrangements and supplemented the contractual arrangements by introducing the conditions of service agreement.

12. The main contractual provisions made in Circular 65/1969 are as follows:
(i) Full-time staff should be employed by the education authority and assigned, where possible, to specific further education colleges in order to have available to them the advice and support of college principals and the resources of the college.
(ii) There should be no time limits on the appointment to work in a prison, as there had been in the past.[2]
(iii) The first year of the appointment should be probationary.
(iv) In the event of serious disciplinary problems, the governor is expected, except in emergencies, to consult with the member of staff concerned and the local education authority. However, where the difficulty cannot be resolved, the local authority is expected to withdraw, forthwith, the member of staff concerned from the establishment. In this event the teacher or education officer should be able to state his or her case before representatives of the Prison Department, the governor and the local authority, prior to a final decision in the matter. If, following this, the Prison Department feels that the member of staff should not return to that institution, the local education authority should seek to provide the individual with alternative and comparable employment. If they are unable to do so, or if such an offer is refused, the local education authority should dismiss the teacher under its procedures, giving the appropriate rights of appeal, relating to the dismissal of teachers. At such appeal hearings the Home Office Prison Department should be represented.
(v) In general, local education authorities should provide parallel conditions of service to those enjoyed by further education teachers in their areas. This should include a ten session week.

13. The clause set out in sub paragraph 12(v) above refers to the general

---

2 Prior to the issue of Circular 65/1969 there were time limits on the period of the contract to work in a prison and appropriate fixed term contracts were issued. It is interesting to note that there are, currently, some suggestions to reintroduce such time limits. These developments are discussed, briefly, in paragraph 18 and in footnote 5.

conditions of service of further education teachers (existing in 1969) which are described in Section **11.7**. Hence, the general provisions concerning items like sick leave and pay entitlement and maternity provisions, applying to further education teachers, are also applied to teachers assigned to prison department establishments. The degree to which arrangements made for further education teachers since 1969 apply to prison education staff is not clear. The JNC intends to carry out a codification exercise (of the sort described in relation to further education staff in Section **11.7.**3) and this should clarify the full conditions of service of prison education staff.

14. The JNC has, already, reached agreement on the application of the 1975 further education teachers' conditions of service agreement to prison education staff. (For details of the 1975 further education teachers' conditions of service agreement, see Section **11.7.**6). The agreement in the JNC provides that the general provisions of the 1975 agreement should be applied to prison education staff in the following way:

(i) The teaching year shall be the *equivalent* of not more than 36 weeks, the working year not more than 38 weeks. This is to allow for the fact that administration in prison departments takes place throughout the year rather than in one identifiable two week period.

(ii) Class contact hours shall be in accordance with local conditions of service agreements for further education teachers. Education officers should undertake class contact work in line with local practice (applying to heads of departments) in the colleges. Deputy education officers should undertake class contact work in line with the provisions of the 1975 conditions of service agreement.

(iii) Teachers shall have not less than seven consecutive days' leave at Christmas and Easter.

(iv) Teachers are entitled to take a period of not less than six weeks' continuous weeks' leave between 1 June and 30 September.

(v) Because the JNC is still discussing the number of evening sessions that a teacher could expect to work, the *status quo* in each local authority should prevail for the time being.[3]

15. **Salaries**

It is indicated in paragraph 6 above, that customary salary scales for prison education staff (except those in junior detention centres) are adopted from the Burnham Further Education salaries document. Circular 65/1969 recognised this, indicating that, in 1969, education officers were being paid as Lecturers Grade I, with a special responsibility allowance, and teachers as Lecturers Grade I without an allowance. The circular suggested that in a limited number of cases a higher salary scale for the education officer was desirable. Subsequently, an arrangement was introduced for relating the grading of the education officer posts to unit total ranges (slightly amended) and four of the head of department salary scales set out in the Burnham

3 The letter to local education authorities under reference BAC/109 and titled *JNC for Teachers assigned to Prison Department Establishments: Gradings of Posts and Conditions of Service,* which sets out the agreement of the JNC on conditions of service, is dated 27 April 1979. At the time of writing the *status quo* provision referred to in sub-paragraph 14(v) above, still holds good since there is still no conclusion to the JNC discussions on evening sessions.

Further Education salaries document (see Section **11.1.**6). By 1977, as a result of these developments, 46 education officers were paid on the minimum agreed scale of Lecturer Grade II, 22 on Head of Department Grade I, 38 on Head of Department Grade II, four on Head of Department Grade III and one on Head of Department Grade IV.

16. The JNC further developed this system in 1978 and the following provisions, for the grading of education officers' and teachers' posts, now apply:

(i) *Grading of education officers' posts*

(a) The following table sets out the unit total range and the relevant grading to be applied to the education officer's post.

Unit Total [4]	*Grade of Post*
51-100	Head of Department Grade I
101-210	Head of Department Grade II
211-350	Head of Department Grade III
Over 350	Head of Department Grade IV

(b) As in colleges, the unit total is to be calculated in accordance with the provisions of the Burnham Further Education salaries document (see Section **11.1.**28). Hence the unit total is derived from work undertaken in the academic year ending on 31 August immediately before the year in which the grading of the post comes into effect. There is one variation from the "Burnham" system. The education officer is awarded 30 units for each civilian instructor employed within the establishment in respect of vocational training.

(c) Where the unit total is below 51, the education officer is graded as Lecturer Grade II.

(ii) *Grading of deputy education officers' posts*

(a) In cases where the education officer is graded as a Head of Department Grade III or IV, the appointment of a deputy education officer is mandatory.

(b) These can be graded as Lecturer Grade II or Senior Lecturer. However, they are always likely to be graded as Senior Lecturer in Grade III and IV departments since, as is the case in colleges, it is mandatory in Grade III departments to have at least one, and in Grade IV departments at least two, Senior Lecturer appointments. The deputies graded as Senior Lecturer are not additional to these mandatory posts. However, they do not count against the national pool of promotions posts described below.

(iii) *Grading of other posts*

(a) The JNC has devised an intriguing system for determining the grade of teaching posts other than the post of education officer and that of his or her deputy. This is based on a global approach

4 It will be noticed that the unit total ranges used are considerably more favourable than those applied in colleges to determine the grades of a department. These more favourable ranges have been agreed in recognition of the different educational environment in a prison and the problems it poses.

in which all the work done in prison departments is accumulated and used for determining a staffing establishment as if all the work were done in one college. The posts so created are then distributed between establishments to provide promotion opportunities for teachers. As will be seen, there is an opportunity for the recognised teachers' associations to make representations on the distribution of the posts so created.

(b) The number of promotion posts (i.e. Lecturer Grade II posts) is 20% of the global pool of otherwise Lecturer Grade I posts, calculated on the proportions for Category V work (see Sections **11.1**.30 and **11.2**).

(c) The machinery for the distribution of promotion posts is, essentially, a management prerogative. However, the following consultative procedures are adopted. The recognised teachers' associations, locally, are given warning of the proposed distribution so that they can make representations. In addition to local representatives, representations can be made at national level via the Joint Secretaries to the JNC. The teachers' side of the JNC is, in any case, given access to the proposed promotions list.

17. **Future developments**

The JNC for Further Education Teachers Assigned to Prison Department Establishments is a relatively new JNC but has managed to deal successfully with conditions and salary negotiations in a collective, non-statutory forum. It is regarded by some as a possible precursor of such arrangements in further education generally. It is hoped that this review of its work and of the salary and conditions of service arrangements affecting teachers in prisons will be of use to education officers, their staff, local authorities and college administrators to whose colleges the staff are attached.

18. At the time of writing, there are some signs, judging by items currently under discussion in the JNC, that the link between college administrators and education officers, and their staffs, will become closer in the future[5]. Indeed, the relationship between local authorities and prison education departments is currently under review, and, whilst not all participants in that review would share the same educational views about the relationship between prison and general further education, most parties would accept that a closer and more supportive relationship between the two is a desirable future development.

REFERENCE

Education (Miscellaneous Provisions) Act 1948, Chapter 40, HMSO.

Department of Education and Science, *Scales of Salaries for Teachers in Establishments for Further Education, England and Wales 1978,* HMSO.

---

5 One scheme, under discussion in the JNC, is that proposed in the Cheshire authority. This seeks an integration of prison education work between the three penal establishments in the county and with a local college. The scheme is controversial since it envisages a limited term appointment for education officers and "mixed" appointments involving work in the college and the prison(s) for the teachers.

Prison Department, *Full-Time Tutor Organisers and Full-Time Teachers' Salaries and Conditions of Service*, Circular Instruction 65/1969, Home Office.

Joint Secretaries of the Joint Negotiating Committee for Further Education Teachers Assigned to Prison Department Establishments, *JNC for Teachers Assigned to Prison Department Establishments: Grading of Posts and Conditions of Service*, 27 April, 1979, BAC/109, LACSAB.

Joint Secretaries of the Joint Negotiating Committee for Further Education Teachers Assigned to Prison Department Establishments, *JNC for Teachers Assigned to Prison Department Establishments: 1979 Burnham Salary Award*, 26 September, 1979, BAC/127, LACSAB.

A number of circular instructions, which have important effects on the administration of prison education, have been issued by the Prison Department of the Home Office in recent years. Unfortunately, the Home Office was not prepared for security reasons to allow the author to include a list of recent circulars.

15 AGRICULTURAL EDUCATION

1. The function of county agricultural colleges is the provision of a sound technical education for workers at all levels in the agricultural industry. Not only do these often small specialist colleges cover courses at all levels below degree level, but in their scope they accommodate the full range of activities currently present in this highly technical and rapidly developing industry. The ranges of courses are:-

   (i) Part-time studies courses at craft, operative, supervisory and management levels extending to 5 year schemes.

   (ii) Full-time courses

National Certificate	– 1 year residential
Advanced National Certificate	– 1 year residential
Ordinary National Diploma	– 2 year residential – 1 year supervised industrial sandwich
Higher National Diploma	– 2 year residential – 1 year supervised industrial sandwich

2. The county college is the centre for the agricultural education service for the county as a whole. In many cases, the principal of the college is designated County Agricultural Education Officer responsible for the provision of all aspects of agricultural and horticultural education throughout the county. He or she is often responsible for the staffing of day release courses accommodated at local colleges of further education, and in many instances controls the provision of vocational and non-vocational evening courses in agriculture and horticulture offered by adult centres.

3. The college may often be the base for the county advisory services for such subjects as beekeeping, rural studies, home economics and horticulture.

4. Another function is the service the college offers to the rest of the county education service, particularly through the schools, as a centre for rural education and environmental studies. Many counties have large urban populations and the college plays an important and developing role in bridging the gap between town and country life. Thousands of children and their teachers visit county agricultural colleges annually for a variety of educational activities from one day visits to residential courses.

5. A most important role as far as the agricultural industry is concerned is as a focal point for adult education and training and careers advice. Considerable time and effort are expended upon the provision of advice for those seeking a career in agriculture. The initial point of contact includes visits to schools, careers talks and panels, and the mounting of two to three week residential "taster" courses to provide an insight into agricultural work in the real commercial world of work. In the past, much of the formal training and re-training available to the industry has been through the colleges and this has been recognised recently with the courses now being approved by the

Training Boards. Staff of colleges frequently provide the secretarial and organizational skills needed for the operation of the National Practical Proficiency Testing Service on which the industry relies and whose qualifications it recognises in its pay structure. Educational courses from operative to management level are provided to meet a clear demand from the industry. Most colleges are used for meetings of farmers' groups and technical conferences, and staff are closely associated with the organization and running of such groups. Assistance is given to County Federations of Young Farmers' Clubs and other rural organizations.

6. The college farms and horticultural holdings, in addition to their normal educational function, provide physical and financial data as a basis for management education courses and for discussion of farming topics. They demonstrate modern techniques and are in consequence a first hand source of technical information for all branches of the industry.

7. The county colleges as centres for technical education of young agriculturalists, have a number of differences from other establishments of further education. One of these is that, through their farms and commercial operations, the colleges are part of the industry itself, and this is intended to bring a commercial reality to the education offered at all levels to the benefit of both students and teachers.

8. The second difference is that these colleges have residential accommodation and are able to provide for those employed in the industry the experience of residential college life. This is particularly important for those young people who, by virtue of their rural background, may have had a reduced opportunity for social contact.

9. The greatest proportion of full-time and part-time students coming under the agricultural education service comprises agriculturalists in the purest sense. For example, in October 1978, of the students enrolling for the part-time agriculture and horticulture courses, 58.7% were employed in agriculture, 30% in commercial and amenity horticulture and 11.3% in agricultural mechanics.

10. Other students are employed in the service industries, a major sector being farm machinery servicing, although there are courses available for those wishing to take up employment in farm secretarial work, veterinary nursing, agricultural merchanting and food technology. Some colleges are national centres in subjects such as forestry, arboriculture, fish farming and horse management. These have established and maintained a national standard in these disciplines.

11. The salary arrangements for agricultural education reflect the special needs of the service and the foundations were laid down by the former Burnham Farm Institutes Committee. This became part of the enlarged Burnham Further Education Committee in 1976 but the new body has established a Sub-Committee to deal with this area of work.

12. The basic scale is known as Lecturer Grade 1A. It is identical in every respect to the Lecturer Grade I scale for further education: for example, the figures, the arrangements for graduate allowances, incremental placement, etc. The next scale is known as Lecturer IB. In September 1979 this scale was £441 higher than the Lecturer Grade 1A scale at all points except that there is no equivalent of the maximum point 15; it is one increment shorter. The arrangements for allowances and incremental placement are as on the Lecturer Grade I and IA scales.

13. Where a teacher is promoted from Lecturer Grade 1A to 1B, he or she "moves across", at the same incremental point and is not subject to the usual "one and a half increments" procedure. Lecturer IB is considered to be the grade normally appropriate for a teacher who, as an integral part of his or her duties, has responsibilities of an administrative or practical nature, such as:
    (i) responsibility for a part of the activities arising from the practical education in the establishment;
    (ii) responsibility for the organization, care and maintenance of equipment or stores or demonstration facilities required for educational purposes;
    (iii) responsibility for the organization and operation of the establishment library where no librarian is employed;
    (iv) responsibility for the organization of part-time and short full-time courses.[1]

    The Lecturer Grade II scale is completely different from the scale of the same name in further education and covers a salary range of thirteen points from near the top of the FE Lecturer Grade II scale to a position close to the bar on the Principal Lecturer scale. The local authority selects a scale of five points from the range according to the responsibility carried by the individual teacher.

14. The Burnham Further Education Committee gives advice in the Burnham Report on the criteria to be used in selecting points. This is as follows. "The Burnham Further Education Committee expect the lower part of the appropriate salary range set out in Appendix 1B to be used where the Lecturer II is in charge of a small department or has responsibility for advanced work or for activities arising from the practical education in the establishment."[2]

15. The Vice Principal and Principal's scales are also constructed on a similar basis. The Vice-Principal's range has 14 points and the Principal's scale 16. The local authority selects a scale of five points from these. The Burnham FE Report specifies the following criteria for determining the relationship between the salary of a vice-principal and that of the principal. "The normal percentage relationship between the maximum of the Vice-Principal's scale and the maximum of the Principal's scale shall be 80% within a range of 75% at minimum and 85% at maximum. Examples of factors which might

---

1 *Scales of Salaries for Teachers in Establishments for Further Education, England and Wales 1979,* Appendix IIB.
2 *Ibid.*

appropriately be taken into account in determining whether it would be appropriate to appoint a Vice-Principal to a scale with a maximum excess of 80% of the maximum of the Principal's scale are:
(i) responsibility as an agricultural or horticultural adviser for the county;
(ii) responsibility for farm or horticultural management;
(iii) responsibility for an extra-mural centre."[3]

16. It will be seen that the salary system is a flexible one giving considerable discretion to the local authority. It is noteworthy that there is no specific grade of Head of Department. The title is often used as one of convenience and the holder will be a Lecturer Grade II paid on an appropriate scale selected from the range.

17. The criteria for selecting scales from the ranges also demonstrates the wide range of responsibility carried by some staff. The existence of commercial units and the responsibility for managing the college farm are major examples of the way in which this area differs from education as a whole. The responsibility for residential facilities is also different for most of its students will be under 18 years of age and the concept of "*in loco parentis*"[4] plays a larger role than in other colleges with residential facilities.

18. The conditions of service of teachers in agricultural colleges are governed by recommendations in a "code of good practice" negotiated between the Association of County Councils on the one hand and the Association of Agricultural Education Staffs on the other.

19. The Agricultural Code of Practice recommends that no member of staff is required to undertake college duties for more than 42 weeks in a year. A period of teaching longer than fourteen weeks must be followed by at least one week of leave. A teacher is entitled to at least one week's holiday at both Christmas and Easter at least four weeks' continuous holiday between the beginning of June and the end of September.

20. A teacher should not normally be required to attend for more than ten sessions per week; a session normally not exceeding three hours and in no circumstances exceeding four hours. There should normally be a break of one hour between sessions and no teacher should be required to teach for more than three hours after 5.30pm with a normal maximum of two evening teaching sessions per week.

21. Normally a teacher shall not be required to undertake more than 20-22 hours of class contact in any week and never more than 24 except in circumstances in which additional payment is made.

REFERENCE

Scales of Salaries for Teachers in Establishments for Further Education, HMSO, 1979.
Code of Good Practice (Incorporating Conditions of Service and Terms) For staff in Colleges of Agriculture (ie, paid under the Burnham Farm Institutes Report) (ACC document 1737/75), Association of County Councils, 1975.

---

3 *Ibid.*
4 In the place or position of a parent. See Section **11.9.**40.

Section 12

STUDENTS

1 ADMISSIONS

1. The diversity of courses and institutions makes presentation of admissions information somewhat untidy. Admissions to teacher education, and the procedures of the Central Register and Clearing House are investigated under Section **12.2** and **12.3**, and provision for overseas students forms Section **12.10**.

2. Applications for courses in further education are usually made directly to the institution, except where clearing house arrangements apply. In the case of art colleges, for foundation and vocational courses, applications are made by the individual directly to the institution, and for degree courses by way of the Art and Design Admissions Registry. The clearing houses are:

   Art and Design Admissions Registry
   Imperial Chambers
   24, Widemarsh Street
   Hereford HR4 9EP.

   Central Council for Education and Training in Social Work
   Derbyshire House
   St. Chad's Street
   London WC1H 8AD.

   Central Register and Clearing House Limited
   3, Crawford Street
   London W1H 2BN.

   Chartered Society of Physiotherapy
   14, Bedford Row
   London WC1R 4ED.

   Occupational Therapy Training Clearing House
   British Association of Occupational Therapists
   20, Rede Place
   London W2 4TU.

3. There are two clearing houses which deal with admissions to employment in surveying and accountancy. These are:

   Chartered Accountants Students Introduction Service
   38, Finsbury Square
   London EC2A 1PX.

   Royal Institute of Chartered Surveyors
   29, Lincoln's Inn Fields
   London WC2A 3DG.

4. General course information is contained in a variety of directories. These directories are usually published annually. They are:

Directory of Further Education, CRAC/Hobsons Press.
Directory of First Degree Courses, CNAA, (344-54 Gray's Inn Road London WC1X 8BP)
Compendium of Advanced Courses in Colleges of Further and Higher Education, Regional Advisory Councils For Further Education.
Graduate Studies, CRAC.
The Handbook of Degree and Advanced Courses in Institutes/Colleges of Higher Education, Colleges of Education, Polytechnics, University Departments of Education, NATFHE/Lund Humphries.
Each RAC produces a directory for its area. The Central Council for Education and Training in Social Work (CCETSW; address in paragraph 2, above) operates an information service which provides advice on careers, education and training in social work. The DES publishes the *Choose Your Course* Series. These publications are revised annually and distributed to careers teachers, careers officers and colleges. Further copies are available from the DES, Room 2/11, Elizabeth House, York Road, London SE1 7PH.

5. The Open College is a federation of institutions in the north west of England. Its courses can provide entry to Lancaster University, Preston Polytechnic and certain colleges of higher education. These courses require no formal qualifications and are especially suited to mature students and persons who left school early. Prospective applicants should contact the Information Officer, University of Lancaster, University House, Bailrigg, Lancaster.

6. There are four colleges of education (technical) which train teachers for further education: Bolton College of Education (Technical), Garnett College, Huddersfield Polytechnic and Wolverhampton Polytechnic. Applications should be made directly to the institution. Further education teacher training is discussed in Section **11.12**.

7. **Training opportunities scheme**

Entrance to further education may be gained by way of TOPS. This scheme may assist students who do not possess qualifications. Although the scheme is investigated under Section **4.**7 and also has recently been restricted by cuts in public expenditure, it is appropriate here to outline the general provisions. TOPS courses are available to all who are at least 19 years old, have been out of full-time education for a total period of more than three years, and who intend to take up employment using the skill for which training is given. The conditions may be more generous in the case of a handicapped person. TOPS courses are also available to unemployed people and to persons willing to give up their present job to take a full-time training course, provided that they have not taken a government training course in the past five years (except that for advanced courses there are variations to this rule). A weekly allowance is paid to the student by the Training Services Division of the Manpower Services Commission for the duration of the course. There are two types of TOPS course: exclusive courses, run only for TOPS students; and "infill" courses, which are courses that are already running, and on which TOPS students are placed. TOPS runs courses at all levels in a wide range of subjects. Details for applicants are available from local employment offices, job centres or the Training Services Division (TOPS), 180, High Holborn, London WC2V 7AT.

8. **Further Education Information Service**

This service is operated by the DES. The primary function of the FEIS local advisory officers is to inform intending students about courses available within the further education system, particularly those with an entry requirement of one "A" level or above, and how to apply for a place on one of those courses. As the service operates in August and September when schools are closed, education authorities are asked to supply the names and addresses of the local advisory officers to all secondary schools as soon as possible in order that publicity can be given and young people informed of how the service operates before they leave school. Each local advisory officer can provide the names and addresses of other officers so that intending students temporarily resident outside their local education authority area may continue to have access to advice. Colleges should inform themselves of the names and addresses of local advisory officers.

9. The service advises on courses available which are full-time and sandwich courses leading to degrees. DipHE or HND. Colleges may include those Higher Diploma courses leading to awards of TEC or BEC and for which the entry requirement is normally at least one "A" level or the equivalent. By arrangement with the Central Register and Clearing House, the service will also include courses leading to the degree of BEd.

10. The service is available for all establishments of further and higher education which offer the courses specified above. The DES provides local advisory officers with regular vacancy lists of courses in establishments which participate in the FEIS scheme. Local education authorities will usually draw the FEIS to the attention of colleges. Colleges are asked to submit vacancy returns at regular specified intervals.

11. As it is important for each local advisory officer to have particulars of all available relevant courses, the DES requests the establishments concerned to arrange for the necessary college prospectuses or extracts to be sent to all local advisory officers. The DES issues a complete set of address labels to colleges for this purpose.

12. The Department arranges publicity in schools and issues regional press notices. Currently the Department sponsors local radio publicity and also issues a television public service announcement. The Department is grateful for assistance in publicity, and colleges may be asked, or wish, unasked, to provide local publicity material.

13. **Admissions procedures**

Admissions procedure and policy will greatly affect colleges' academic organization and planning. It will involve central and departmental administrative procedures, publicity, and record keeping.

14. A college needs to supply clear information on its courses and procedures. It is necessary to distinguish between the college prospectus and particular course leaflets. The prospectus should supply all the basic information which an applicant will require, and course leaflets the particular requirements and procedures for a course. Applicants have also to be informed of the data they are required to supply, the entry qualifications which are necessary, the closing dates which have to be met, and of the ways in which applications are processed. It will be necessary to specify how further course information can be obtained, whether applicants will be called for interview, and when and how payment of fees is required. Information concerning grants (or at least advice as to where it might be discovered), entry exemptions which might apply, and also any particular requirements which a college might have should also be provided.

15. Successful applicants should receive clear guidance concerning enrolment procedures. Where appropriate, this should include more detailed course information and information concerning the relevant college facilities. Unsuccessful applicants should be notified as soon as possible. In this case it will be helpful to supply appropriate information concerning other relevant college courses, and also courses operated in other institutions. Administrative work here can be reduced by devising standard letters and forms.

16. Admissions policies and procedures will be monitored by the academic board. They will require adaptation according to changes in the college's clientele. For courses which have local recruitment this will usually involve liaison with the LEA, schools, youth and careers workers, and local employers. The process will also involve course validating and providing bodies. For nationally recruited courses, the college will need to publicise itself, and liaise with the relevant bodies and institutions. Liaison with the Regional Advisory Council concerning recruitment and admission will be necessary. It is essential that a college should be able to supply, at the appropriate time and in the formats required, all the information required by the various national clearing houses and directories.

17. It is necessary to establish the duties of academic admissions tutors and admissions administrative staff. A college may have a specifically appointed admissions officer, and there may be academic departmental admissions staff. In any event, policies should be clear and functions well designated. Admissions practices, as far as possible, should be uniform and equitable. The senior member of staff responsible for admissions will usually need to call meetings at appropriate stages in the college year, and to issue written admissions procedures guidelines. Care should be taken here, for disgruntled students may resort to litigation (see Section **12.6.**14-16). It will be necessary to establish special measures of support, both in welfare, counselling and careers advice, and by way of information concerning discretionary grants. Such measures will require the active support of the local education authority.

18. Colleges are continuing to develop progressive admissions policies which

endeavour to afford greater opportunities to disadvantaged groups. However, in many areas of study, national validating bodies as well as the grading of courses procedures impose constraints on more open admissions policies. Therefore, in considering the needs of the communities which they serve, colleges will need to liaise where appropriate, and to identify the ways in which admissions requirements can become more flexible without diminishing course standards.

19. **Enrolments**

The successful conduct of the enrolment process is highly important. The enrolment period brings the college and its clients together. It is an important public relations exercise. Its publicity and progress must be well and carefully planned. Not only is enrolment a major activity for a college, but for many of those registering for courses it represents a considerable decision, and one which will have an effect upon their lives. It is essential therefore that the college is able to be sympathetic, and in devising its procedures allow for the means to reassure the nervous.

20. In planning enrolment, it is essential that all publicity material gives some guidance. While this will appear in the college prospectus, there are many intending students who arrive at enrolment without having first informed themselves fully of what they might study. Therefore provision has to be made for opportunity for personal interviews, for course guidance, and for procedures for changing courses to be made clear. It will be necessary for help to be available in filling in enrolment forms. Intending students may first be directed to a department for course advice before undertaking any of the form filling procedures. It is important to remember that once a student has been enrolled, a contract has been formed (see Section **12.6.**14).

21. The logistics of the enrolment period represent a major activity. Large numbers of people are involved, and the resultant problems of crowd handling can be severe. Direction notices should be prominent and clear. It may be necessary to inform the police where large numbers are expected. The issue of security at enrolment is referred to under Section **5.9.**16. Refreshments should be made available, lavatory provision adequate, attention paid to occupiers' liability (see Section **5.7**) and care exercised concerning the demands which are made upon staff. An information desk, staffed by experienced personnel, can be beneficial to intending students.

2 THE CENTRAL REGISTER AND CLEARING HOUSE

1. The Central Register and Clearing House was established as a co-ordinating body in order to meet the needs of colleges of education in dealing with applications for admission to courses. To facilitate the selection of entrants it has operated a scheme for the central registration of these applications. College reorganization has increased the types of institution which make use of the Clearing House. It is now used by colleges of education, colleges of higher education and polytechnic departments of education. Application through the Clearing House to these institutions is no longer restricted to teacher training: application may be made for whichever advanced courses are being offered. The Clearing House assists candidates by the supply of detailed course information and by ensuring consideration by a number of institutions through the submission of one application; it assists institutions by its centralised procedures which avoid duplication of applications.

2. The Graduate Teacher Training Registry is housed in the same premises as the Clearing House and works with it closely. Its purpose is to assist graduates, and undergraduates in the final year of a degree course, to secure admission to a course of professional teacher training leading to the award of a Postgraduate Certificate of Education and recognition as a qualified teacher.

3. The Clearing House has been established for over 40 years. The present organization was formed in 1962 as a non-profit making limited company (Central Register and Clearing House Ltd.), registered as a charity. The majority of shares are held by nominees of NATFHE but shareholders also include representatives from other educational associations. The Company's work is directed by a council of management consisting of members representing the institutions concerned, schools, and observers from local education authorities and the DES.

4. All further education institutions in England and Wales providing courses for initial teacher training other than the four colleges of further education (technical) recruit students via the Clearing House. Many also recruit for DipHE and degree courses not leading to, or necessarily leading to a teaching qualification in this way. All university departments of education recruit students for the postgraduate certificate course via the GTTR, as do the colleges and polytechnics providing such courses. Applications through the Clearing House for 1978 entry numbered 19,222 (15,891 for teacher education courses and 3,331 for other courses in higher education). There were 15,061 applications through the Graduate Registry.

5. **Procedures**

Both offices issues preliminary literature to enquirers, check requests for application forms, issue forms and explanatory literature and subsequently file master registration/receipt cards and master forms ("2" forms). If "3" forms (the Clearing House and GTTR application forms) are returned by the colleges or departments, they are linked with their corresponding "2" forms for further action. This action can be despatch for consideration elsewhere, or for enquiry letters to be sent where candidates had originally stated that they did not wish to be considered elsewhere or had sought to withdraw completely after having started their applications. The registries also select institutions to which to send the forms of candidates willing to be considered elsewhere. Forms are passed on to institutions for consideration each week, accompanied by check lists. Candidates are advised at the same time of the despatch of their forms. To prevent candidates selecting institutions which are full, vacancy information is included with application forms.

6. The registries also answer many enquiries both from prospective candidates and registered institutions. Telephone enquiries from schools, careers advisers and colleges are welcomed but neither registry accepts telephone enquiries from candidates and the registry numbers are not listed in telephone directories. The collection of statistical information is a very important feature of the work of both registries. Senior staff members give talks at careers meetings, to groups of teachers and careers advisers and act as consultants at careers conventions. The Company issues an Annual Report every March.

7. The Clearing House organizes the publication of an annual handbook published by NATFHE. There is also an information updating service which is supplied to candidates with their application forms. The 1980 Handbook is *The Handbook of degree and advanced courses in Institutes/Colleges of Higher Education, Colleges of Education, Polytechnics, University Departments of Education* and was published in July 1979. The registries issue the documents *Clearing House Procedures (CRCH)* and *Notes on Administration (GTTR)*. The procedures document deals with procedures for application to institutions other than universities, and the administration notes refer to institutions providing postgraduate courses. Both documents are indexed.

8. All organizations concerned with recruitment to higher education courses are represented on the Clearing House Committee. This body meets twice a year to consider procedures for candidates applying through the CRCH and reports to the Colleges Committee of NATFHE. Matters concerning admission to postgraduate courses and GTTR procedures are considered at meetings of the NATFHE Colleges Committee, and at meetings of Standing Committee B of the Universities Council for the Education of Teachers.

9. **CRCH: difficulties experienced in operation**

The registrar, Miss E.B. Sowerbutts, has identified areas which can cause difficulty. These are:

(i) Application and registration returns. If college administration departments delay in returning information to the Clearing House, two difficulties can be caused:

(a) where the college selectors have returned the "3" forms to the

Clearing House for onward transmission but the administration department has not returned the "2" forms, then delays occur in the candidates' applications being forwarded; and

(b) since the Clearing House quotes national application figures as early as possible in November, where colleges with a large number of first choice applications have delayed in sending forms to the Clearing House, the total figure for applications can be distorted.

Therefore, the Clearing House requests that where delays unavoidably arise, that it is informed, and that if there is insufficient time for the banking of fees then arrangements can be made for the forms to be sent in advance of the fee slips.

(ii) The Clearing House will provide colleges with extra copies of its *Clearing House Procedures* notes, *Notes on Administration (GTTR)* and *Notes for Interviewers.* It asks colleges to pay special regard in the interview and selection process to: delays in making a final decision for a candidate's chances elsewhere may be damaged; the recording of interview comments; and the preservation of confidentiality of the reports of referees and the comments of interviewers.

(iii) As both registers issue vacancy information and Further Information sheets daily, or weekly, as necessary, it is requested that institutions notify any changes immediately by telephone or first class post.

(iv) When institutions are asked for returns, the object is to provide statistical information for committees, or for inclusion in the Annual Survey. Notification is requested where institutions experience any difficulties with a questionnaire or in observing the due date for its submission.

(v) Many institutions continue their selection of entrants into the spring and summer terms. While it is an understandable saving of time to interview sizeable groups of candidates at intervals, some institutions may take a term or longer to interview and notify candidates of the results. Thus, when forms are returned the vacancies remaining elsewhere are limited. The registries state that forms should not be held for longer than a month, particularly where candidates have applied late in the year.

(vi) The Clearing House suggests that college careers officers avail themselves for careers convention purposes of its bibliographical service. A source list of literature on teaching as a career is given in the *Clearing House Procedures* document.

10. The registries came into existence because of the need of educational institutions for some centralised procedures. These procedures cannot be operated efficiently without the continued co-operation of colleges and their staffs. The registries are very conscious that admissions procedures represent only a small portion of college administration. If problems arise,

the registrar requests that she or the deputy or assistant registrar be contacted. The registries welcome visitors from colleges and departments but request prior notification where possible.

REFERENCE

The Handbook of degree and advanced courses in Institutes/Colleges of Higher Education, Colleges of Education, Polytechnics, University Departments of Education, NATFHE, 1979 (published annually each July).

Annual Report of the Central Register and Clearing House and Graduate Teacher Training Registry, Central Register and Clearing House Ltd.

Clearing House Procedures, Central Register and Clearing House Ltd.

Notes for Interviewers, Central Register and Clearing Houe Ltd.

Notes on Administration, Graduate Teacher Training registry.

Admissions procedures have not been summarised in this text as they are stated in the registries' publications which colleges receive. Extra copies of these publications are available from the Clearing House on request. Enquiries concerning the registries should be addressed to:

Miss E. Beryl Sowerbutts
Registrar/Secretary
Central Register and Clearing House Ltd.
3 Crawford Place
London W1H 2BH.

3 ADMISSION TO INITIAL TEACHER TRAINING COURSES

1. The last general entry to non-graduate Certificate in Education courses was in the academic year 1979/80. All who expect successfully to complete a course of initial training leading to qualified teacher status, whether at undergraduate or postgraduate level, at the end of the academic year 1983/84 will, on entry to the course, be expected to provide evidence of a level of competence in the understanding and use of the English language, and in mathematics. In order to safeguard the supply of teachers in certain shortage subjects, the final entry to one year non-graduate certificate courses for holders of specialist qualifications in business studies, music, craft and design and technology (handicraft) will be deferred until the academic year 1983/84. Special dispensation should not be sought from the entry qualifications for the BEd degree other than those available for entry to other degree courses. Where there are mature students entering training with qualifications between a degree and GCE "A" level, it will remain permissible at present for such students to be accepted on an individual basis for suitably shortened BEd courses as with other degrees.

2. Passes at Grade C or above in the GCE "O" level examination, or a Grade I in the CSE examination in both mathematics and English language (or English where the course has contained a significant amount of language work) are recommended as broadly appropriate. However, it is open to intending entrants otherwise to satisfy the institution and validating body concerned of their competence in the subjects. The alternative arrangements to admit suitable candidates without formal English and mathematics qualifications are restricted to: candidates mostly aged 25 or over; applicants for the one year non-graduate certificate courses; or those who wish to seek recognition as qualified teachers under the arrangements for holders of qualifications designed for the training of teachers of further education.

3. The provision of certificate courses designed for the training of teachers for further education is not affected by the above arrangements. However, the provision whereby local authorities may apply for the holder of such a certificate to be accepted as a qualified teacher for the purpose of teaching in schools is affected in the instance of non-graduates only: the arrangement will not apply to non-graduate holders of certificates gained on successful completion of a course begun in or after the academic year 1980/81; unless they have been offered a post teaching craft, design and technology, business studies or music, so long as they obtained the certificate on successful completion of a course begun in the academic year 1983/84 or earlier.

4. With the integration of courses leading to a teaching qualification with other advanced further education courses, and the development of unit-based courses which enable students to defer commitment to teaching as a career and permit those who may ultimately obtain a BEd, BA, or DipHE to study alongside one another, The Further Education Regulations 1975 include no

statutory requirement for a medical examination on entry to teacher training such as was contained in the former Training of Teachers Regulations. However, the Secretaries of State for Education and Science and Wales consider it important that institutions continue to ensure that persons unsuitable for health reasons are not admitted to courses which include practical experience in schools. Because of the medical requirements necessary in entering school teaching (see Section **12.4.**4) it is in the interests of students before admission to an initial teacher training course first to be medically examined.

5. In deciding a teacher's fitness in the matter of health and physical capacity for employment, the matter is determined by the local authority if it has not been considered by the Secretary of State. The initial onus of considering the fitness of a person for teaching falls on the college or department of education when deciding whether or not to accept that person for training. The Secretary of State does not have to be satisfied as to medical fitness at that stage but is concerned with the health and physical capacity of those completing their training and wishing to take up teaching employment. It is advisable for medical officers to consult the DES before arriving at a decision in any instance of uncertainty about an applicant's fitness either for training or ultimately for teaching employment. Early consultation is especially advised where applicants have a history of epilepsy, psychiatric disorder, or have particular physical, visual or aural disabilities which could affect their efficiency as teachers. A full medical report, including a specialist's report where relevant, should be sent under confidential cover addressed to the Medical Adviser to the Department. Where a special report is considered necessary by the examining medical officer or by a candidate appealing against a decision of the training authorities, one should be obtained from a specialist selected by the candidate (usually on the advice of his or her family doctor) and approved by the examining medical officer.

6. It will be helpful to both the student and the institution if the medical examination occurs in good time to avoid any delay in admission to the course (or the component of a course directly involved with teaching). An examination is not considered necessary before a student undertakes periods of observation in school as part of a course not generally involving close contact with school pupils and not leading directly to a teaching qualification. A chest X-ray is not required as part of the examination except at the discretion of the examining medical officer. Medical reports on candidates for admission should be made on Forms 13TT (held by training institutions) and on Forms 14TT (Med) (held by Area Health Authorities). Form 13TT is issued by the college or department to each candidate offered a provisional place. Form 14TT (Med) is completed by the medical officer after the examination and must not be seen by the candidate. After the examination the two forms are sent to the college medical officer who should immediately advise the college of the candidate's suitability or otherwise on medical grounds for acceptance for training.

7. The forms are retained by the college medical officer where the candidate is acceptable on medical grounds, and is offered and confirms acceptance of the training place. If the candidate is judged unfit and the college does not

offer a place, the reports should be returned to the Specialist in Community Medicine (Child Health) in the candidate's home area. However, where the college medical officer considers that the candidate possesses a defect rendering her or him unsuitable for a place at that particular college but which may not disbar acceptance elsewhere, then, with the candidate's permission, the medical reports may be sent in confidence to the Central Register and Clearing House (see under Section **12.2.**5; 9). Medical reports may also, with the candidate's consent, be sent to the registries if the college's rejection is for other than medical reasons. If the candidate does not agree to the forms being sent to the registries, or where a student applies to transfer from a course of advanced further education at one institution to a course of initial training at another (and hence does not use the central registries) and the medical officer considers that the candidate possesses some defect rendering him or her unsuitable for such a place, then the forms should be returned to the Specialist in Community Medicine (Child Health) of the candidate's home area.

8. Medical examination of candidates is made by the school medical officer under arrangements between the local education authority and the Area Health Authority. Examination and reports are free of charge except in the case of students from Scotland seeking admission to initial training courses in England and Wales, where the fees charged will be the responsibility of candidates. The cost of specialist examination of candidates for admission to training is met by the National Health Service where the candidate is still at school: in all other cases candidates for admission and entrants to the teaching profession are responsible for the expenses incurred unless the LEA concerned is prepared to arrange with the Area Health Authority for the cost to be met or the person involved has made arrangements with her or his doctor under the National Health Service. X-ray examinations are free of charge.

9. The Secretary of State's jurisdiction over the misconduct of teachers (see Section **11**, Appendix 6) extends to persons proposing to become teachers. If applicants for training have behaved in ways which would render them liable to exclusion from the teaching profession if they were serving in schools, they should not be admitted to training. Where the matter is in doubt, colleges should discuss the case confidentially with the DES, initially with the appropriate territorial officer. It is important to ensure that previous academic and employment records and references are checked before candidates are accepted for training.

REFERENCE

Admission of Students to Initial Teacher Training Courses, DES College Letter 12/71; Voluntary College Letter 14/71, 6 August 1971.

Entry to Initial Teacher Training Courses in England and Wales, DES Circular 9/78; Welsh Office Circular 99/78, 2 August 1978.

Medical Fitness of Teachers and of Entrants to Teacher Training, DES Circular 11/78; Welsh Office Circular 111/78, 18 August 1978.

4 FIRST SCHOOL TEACHING APPOINTMENTS

1. There is an interviewing arrangement for first appointments.[1] Because of the current over supply of qualified teachers, this agreement has rather less relevance than formerly. It relates only to local authority block interviews: students may respond to press advertisements for individual posts in the usual way and at any time. The agreement is circulated by CLEA after consultation with NATFHE, the Universities' Council for the Education of Teachers, and the Joint Council of Heads. The purpose of the agreement is to regulate and synchronise appointments mechanisms, and to avoid undue competition between authorities. The agreement is reviewed annually and applies to all general appointments to the school teaching service of a local education authority.

2. Under the agreement dates are fixed between February and April of each year for:
   (i) the first date on which colleges may supply reports on applicants;
   (ii) the first date for the interviewing of applicants; and
   (iii) the first date for the offering of appointments.

3. It is important that college reports are submitted as early as possible. The late receipt of reports creates administrative difficulties for local education authorities and lessens their ability to comply with the terms of the agreement. Students are disadvantaged if college reports are not submitted in time to be considered prior to interviews, a disadvantage increased by the current pressure on teacher employment.The agreement recognises college difficulties however: it is accepted that some students may make significant progress in their final year, and that the compression of the one year Post-graduate Certificate in Education can render early meaningful assessment difficult.

4. **Medical requirements for school teaching employment**
All teachers taking up their first appointment in a maintained primary or secondary school, special school, or direct grant school are required to satisfy the Secretary of State of their health and physical capacity for teaching; with the exception that untrained qualified teachers and qualified teachers trained outside the United Kingdom will have to satisfy their employing authority of their fitness. Training institutions therefore should arrange for the medical examination (conducted by the college medical officer or an officer made available by the Area Health Authority) to take place before the end of their course in sufficient time to forward the result to the DES by 30 June. Where the Secretary of State can make a favourable decision, subject to conditions such as a satisfactory chest X-ray, the local authority first employing the teacher will be informed and asked to obtain

---

1 *Agreement on the Interviewing of Students applying for their first teaching appointment,* CLEA Circular 79/3.

any further evidence and to clear the matter on the Secretary of State's behalf. Medical examination of newly qualified entrants to the teaching profession is provided free of charge (see also Section **12.3**.8).

5. In the case of postgraduate and other one-year students, a general medical examination is not required if the college medical officer is able to make a satisfactory report based on information already available. Medical reports are not required for students who taught before training and can produce evidence of having already satisfied fitness requirements unless the college medical officer has sufficient reason to deem otherwise. An applicant placed in medical category A may be accepted as being medically fit. An applicant placed in category B may be accepted unless for any reason it is decided that his or her health requires further investigation. An applicant placed in category C should be rejected as unfit.

6. The college is responsible for making arrangements via the Area Health Officer of the Area Health Authority for the arrangement of the compulsory chest X-ray for all teachers on first entry to the profession.

7. If a specialist's report is considered necessary by the Secretary of State, LEA, or the intending entrant appealing against an examining medical officer's recommendation, any such consultation must be with a specialist selected by the entrant. This selection will usually be on the advice of his or her family doctor and approved by the DES or LEA.

8. The Department sends annually the forms used in connection with the medical examination to the Area Health Authority and to the LEA or other body responsible for the college, together with guidance on their completion. All medical reports should be sent in confidence. Colleges are asked not to send reports, or copies of them, to employing local education authorities; any requests for reports, or copies, from an employing local education authority must be referred to:

   Teacher's Salaries and Qualifications Division
   DES
   Mowden Hall
   Staindrop Road
   Darlington DL3 9BG

9. **Probation of qualified teachers in schools**
   The initial service of a qualified teacher is probationary. The probation normally lasts one year if the teacher has satisfactorily completed an approved teacher training course in the UK. Any other teacher will usually have to serve a probationary period of two years. A qualified teacher who has gained recognition because of a combination of training and experience serves a one year probation. Special arrangements are made where initial service is part-time; and in certain circumstances, the Secretary of State may waive or extend the probation requirement.

10. Probation is a statutory requirement for initial employment in maintained nursery, primary and secondary schools; in direct grant schools other than direct grant grammar schools; and in maintained and non-maintained special

schools. There is no statutory probation requirement for service in further education establishments (although LEAs may operate probation), independent schools or direct grant grammar schools; and consequently persons who began their teaching employment in such institutions must serve their probationary period if they subsequently gain employment at an institution for which probation is a requirement.

11. Employing authorities are responsible for all decisions concerning teachers having completed satisfactorily their periods of probation after demonstrating their practical classroom proficiency. The granting of an extension of probation, and the taking of decisions that teachers are unsuitable for such further employment remains that of the DES (in which case it is advised by HM Inspectorate). Authorities inform the DES and Inspectorate where it is considered that an extension of probation is required, or where a teacher is held not to have demonstrated sufficient capability during the probationary period to be acceptable. Teachers may make representations concerning the latter event before a decision is taken. Authorities inform the Inspectorate where probation has been satisfactorily completed.

12. There is no specified period during which teachers are required to serve their probation. Probation is held in abeyance until such time as a teacher gains the relevant employment. Teachers who leave their posts before their probation period is complete may, if they have served the larger part of the period, have their probation regarded as completed. In this case, authorities make a recommendation to the DES, which the Department may or may not accept. The teacher will be notified if the recommendation is successful.

13. Following the induction recommendations of the James Report,[2] the introduction of pilot schemes in certain authorities, and government support generally to encourage LEAs to develop more extensive and systematic induction arrangements, central government has expressed the wish that authorities put such schemes quickly into effect, or at least ensure that guidance is available to supplement the help of head teacher and staff, and that probationers be informed of to whom to turn for advice.

14. The DES recommends probationers are given help and advice, and should be employed in conditions which allow reasonable opportunity to demonstrate practical proficiency. The DES advises authorities and head teachers that part-time employment for probationers is less satisfactory than full-time employment, and that employment on peripatetic duties or supply work is particularly undesirable. The Department recommends that where a probationer is not making expected progress, he or she should be transferred and given a trial period in another school.

REFERENCE

Agreement on the Interviewing of Students applying for their first teaching appointment, CLEA Circular 79/3.

---

2 *Teacher Education and Training*, HMSO, 1972.

12.4

Medical Fitness of Teachers and of Entrants to Teacher Training, DES Circular 11/78 ; Welsh Office 111/78, 18 August 1978.

Probation of Qualified Teachers, DES Administrative Memorandum 9/78; Welsh Office Administrative Memorandum 5/78, 24 August 1978

The Qualification of Teachers, DES Circular 11/73.

5 GRANTS

1. Local authorities have a legal obligation under the Education Acts of 1962 and 1975 to make an award (i.e., grant) to every student resident in their area who attends a course which is "designated", is not disqualified in any way and who satisfies the conditions of the regulations. Regulations made under the Acts deal with the implementation of this legal obligation and themselves have the force of law The amounts of awards are subject to annual review, and payment must be made at the prescribed rate. The DES issues circulars which comment upon the regulations but while these represent advice on what constitutes a reasonable interpretation and method of application of the regulations, and if followed do allow consistency, actual application of the regulations remains a matter for the individual authority. The regulations concerning grants are complex and as they are implemented by authorities rather than colleges are dealt with here only in outline. However, as it may be necessary for colleges to advise students of their grant entitlements, reference should be made to the sources cited at the end of this sub-section.

2. **Mandatory awards**
Authorities are required to make grants to students resident in England or Wales who are accepted on designated courses. Such courses are full-time or sandwich, and for college purposes are ones which lead to: a university or CNAA first degree; the DipHE, the HND and the higher diplomas of TEC and BEC; initial teacher training qualification, including the PGCE or Art Teachers' Certificate or Diploma; and other qualifications specifically prescribed as being comparable to first degree courses (see also Section **1.3**, Appendix 1). Updated lists of these latter and certain part-time courses are available from the DES and local education authorities. If a student not in receipt of an award is following such a course when it becomes designated, he or she will qualify, if other conditions are satisfied, for a mandatory award. The mandatory award includes the payment of tuition and student union fees. Certain part-time initial teacher training courses are designated for grant purposes.

3. A student admitted to a designated course must satisfy certain eligibility conditions. These are:-
   (i) to have been resident in the UK for the three years immediately preceding the academic year in which the course begins (or would have been so if the student, spouse or either parent had not been temporarily employed abroad; except that special provisions apply to the children of EEC nationals who are working or have worked in the UK);
   (ii) except for intending PGCE and Art Teachers' Certificate or Diploma students, not to have previously attended any one of certain courses of further education (up to one term's attendance on one such course is disregarded);
   (iii) to have ensured that written application for an award was made to the providing authority (i.e. the one in whose area the student was normally resident on 30 June preceding the start of the course, or 31 October or

28/29 February for courses beginning in the spring or summer) before the end of the first term of the course;

(iv) to have given the providing LEA a written undertaking to repay any sum paid in excess of grant entitlement;

(v) in the opinion of the providing LEA not to have demonstrated by his or her conduct unfitness for the receipt of an award; and

(vi) in the case of awards for courses prescribed as comparable to degree courses, to have obtained certain prescribed qualifications (not necessarily those prescribed for course entry).

Grants may still be awarded where not all the eligibility conditions are fulfilled, but such action is at the discretion of the authority.

4. Payment of grant is usually made termly through the college office. The basic maintenance grant covers term-time attendance and vacations other than the summer vacation. Calculation of the amount of grant due to a student is made by assessing her or his maintenance requirements. These are the basic maintenance grant plus any additional grant appropriate to the student's circumstances. The student's resources in personal income and parental or spouse's contribution are deducted from the maintenance requirements and the balance represents the net grant due. Where the net grant is below a certain figure, a minimum payment is made (except in certain prescribed instances, such as college of education resident students and assisted students). The minimum payment is also usually made if the student or his or her parents or spouse prefer not to declare their income.

5. The standard rates for the basic maintenance grant are determined each April and are payable from September. There are differential rates according to circumstance. These are, in descending order of the size of sum paid : students living in hall/lodgings attending London area establishments; students living in hall/lodgings attending establishments outside London; students living in the parental home; students on teacher training courses provided with full board and lodging. The providing LEA may apply the parental home rate instead of a higher rate if it considers that the student could conveniently attend the course from the parental home, except where the student is married or has satisfied an independent status condition. Special arrangements apply to students provided by their college with free board and lodging. In these cases where the students' resources exceed their maintenance requirements the excess has to be paid towards the board and lodging cost, subject to a specified maximum payment to ensure that the student receives benefit in kind equivalent to the basic maintenance grant minimum sum.

6. The determination of the student's resources represents a means test for the calculation of grant. A student in receipt of a private income or earnings (except vacation earnings) during the course will have its residual value, after income tax and national insurance contributions, deducted from the grant. In determining the residual value of income, the student is allowed to retain an initial amount, and certain other sources of income are disregarded. These sources are: scholarship and sponsorship sums up to a

maximum figure; disability pensions not subject to taxation; forces bounties; family allowances; DHSS benefits; vacation earnings; tax and national insurance contributions; and earnings by sandwich course students resulting from periods of industrial or other experience.

7. The grant is reduced by an amount calculated on parental income. There is no obligation on parents to make their contributions although if they neglect to do so the student's resources will be less than her or his assessed needs. Contributions are not expected from the parents of a student who has: attained the age of 25 before the academic year for which the grant is being assessed; or been self-supporting from earnings for any three years before the first year of the course; or held an award under previous regulations or grant arrangements to which a parental contribution was not applicable. The student will then be judged to be of independent status. Contributions are not expected from parents who cannot be traced. Only actual or legally adoptive parents are subject to a means test. Step parents are not subject to such a test. The three year self support period may include periods during which the student was in receipt of sickness benefit, invalidity pension, maternity allowance, and the first six months of registered unemployment. Periods spent at home caring for children by married students will also be included.

8. To calculate parental contribution, deductions are made from the gross income in the financial year preceding the academic year for which the grant is being assessed. Allowable deductions to determine this residual income are: sums for dependent adults and other dependent children; interest payment for which income tax relief is given or option mortgage interest; contribution to a dependant's income tax relieved pension scheme; the amount up to 15% of gross income of any other contribution to a pension or superannuation scheme if those schemes attract tax relief, and any life assurance premium allowed for tax relief; in some circumstances, and up to a prescribed maximum, the wage cost of domestic assistance; a discretionary extra allowance where the parents live outside the UK; and an allowance against gross income which may be made for parents who are themselves in receipt of a grant. Once the parental residual income has been established, parental contribution is calculated on a sliding scale. Special arrangements apply: where two or more children in the family are eligible for awards; to sandwich course students (because no maintenance grant is paid for any year in which there are no periods of full-time study); to students on part-time initial teacher training courses; to "assisted" students (for example, students given paid leave from employment to attend a course); to students married before the course but whose marriage has terminated; and to members of religious orders.

9. When a married student does not satisfy one of the independent status criteria, his or her grant is assessed with reference to the parental income. The spouse's contribution is only made where the parental contribution is not applicable. The calculation of the spouse's contribution is again based on residual income and determined according to a different sliding scale.

10. Where appropriate, students are entitled to an additional maintenance grant. These additional allowances are added to the student's maintenance requirements. The additional allowances are for: permissible travelling expenses over a certain amount; special equipment expenditure; required course attendance in excess of 39 weeks and three days of the academic year; vacation hardship; disabled students; the maintenance of two homes; mature students previously employed during at least three of the previous six years and aged over 26; and dependants' allowances. Some of these allowances are made at the LEA's discretion, although most are obligatory. Students ineligible for dependants' allowances payments may qualify under separate regulations administered by the Students' Unit of the Department of Health and Social Security at Blackpool, for which application forms are available from LEAs. Additional grants in certain cases are also available for any expenditure resulting from study away from the college during term time, up to a prescribed maximum (normally by application to the college); for vacation study, payable by the LEA only in colleges not wholly maintained out of public funds and otherwise by the institution; for students required to study abroad (see Section **2.6.**8), including the cost of medical insurance, and determined according to whether or not the country is classified as one of high cost; and for students whose marriage has terminated.

11. **Discretionary awards**

If a student does not qualify for a mandatory award then, other than grants made by the Manpower Services Commission (see Section **4.**7, 12) the most immediate recourse is application to a local education authority for a discretionary award. An authority may decide on the value of the award and the conditions under which it will pay it. Often an authority will have a policy as to the courses for which it is prepared to make a grant. Previous examination results may be taken into account as discretionary grants are usually competitive. A person may be required to study locally if a relevant course is available. It is always advisable to apply early for a grant, especially so where the award is discretionary. It may be possible to appeal against a decision. Discretionary awards are available to students on non-designated courses, and to students on designated courses who for one reason or another are not eligible for a mandatory award. These are normally students who have become ineligible by receiving an earlier award.

12. Where a student leaves school at 16 in order to undertake a further education course, provided that study is undertaken locally, there is no requirement for her or him to pay tuition fees, other than for evening courses, until the age of 18. Although many colleges waive tuition fees for certain courses up to the age of 19, there are some which make fee charges. Small special grants may be made by authorities to assist towards the maintenance costs of students aged 16 and over undertaking a course of further education.

13. Response to a DES survey of discretionary awards[1] made between 1975 and

---

1 *Discretionary Awards 1975/76 to 1977/78*, A report of a DES survey, DES, 1978. The survey revealed what the LEAs already knew: that severe expenditure restraint meant a restriction in discretionary provisions. CLEA undertook, with the support of the DES, a fundamental review of discretionary awards policy. The result of the review was the report referred to in paragraph 13.

1977 indicated that authorities were making fewer awards, that demand was increasing by 10%; that there was a decline in comparability with mandatory award amounts; that a 12% increase in expenditure would have been necessary to maintain the 1975-76 position; and that with regard to students on non-advanced courses: 45% of authorities make grants to the under-19s which are more restricted than those recommended by the local authority associations; and 80% make grants to the over-19s which are less generous than those recommended. Figures quoted represent the national average. There are substantial differences between the practices of individual authorities and also in the demand for awards and the availability of courses. By reason of their discretionary status, discretionary awards felt the impact of expenditure restraint imposed on LEAs in 1976. As this kind of pressure, or an even greater, has been and is likely to continue to be put on LEAs by the present Government, it is possible that awards will be further restricted. CLEA produced in 1979 a report arguing for wider coverage of courses by mandatory awards, but since the effect would be to increase public expenditure, significant change in the present system may not be likely.

14. **Private students**

Students ineligible for mandatory awards and discretionary awards are responsible for their own fees and maintenance (should they not be in receipt of sponsorship). The DES has advised however that where a student's circumstances change during the course and result in extreme hardship being suffered, then a college should consider the mitigation of fees and hostel charges. Particular cases should be reviewed carefully, however, for colleges would scarcely wish themselves to create unintentionally a further system of discretionary awards. Private students living in rented accommodation may be able to claim rent allowances from the State.

15. Students in receipt of sponsorship, even where they receive reimbursement of travelling and subsistence allowances, should consult their tax inspector to determine whether any further necessary expenditure incurred as a result of study may be offset against tax liability.

16. **Other financial assistance**

Many industrial organizations and some government departments have schemes whereby subsidies are afforded to promising students. Details of these schemes are to be found in *Sponsorship and Supplementary Awards*, published by the Careers and Occupational Information Centre. There are various educational charities which offer supplementary grants, usually small. Details may be found in *Educational Charities*, published by the National Union of Students.

17. Students are eligible to claim supplementary benefit, and there are also circumstances in which they may be eligible for unemployment benefit. A college may find it appropriate to provide students with literature concerning state social security provision, as well as guidance concerning the circumstances in which it is advisable to continue the payment of national insurance contributions. Most students are debarred from claiming

supplementary benefit during term time because of the condition of availability for work. The exception is that of part-time further education students, unemployed and continuing to register as unemployed and available for work, who are undertaking a genuinely "fill-in" course until such time as they gain employment. The advice given by the DES[2] is that unemployed young people may attend further education courses for up to three days a week, or the equivalent in half days, without losing their entitlement to supplementary benefit, so long as they remain available for work. Long term unemployed people aged 21 or over benefit similarly. Claimant and college principal must accept that study can be terminated where employment is available; the student must register at a careers or unemployment benefit office, and seek, and take up work as soon as it is available; and the claimant must not give up a full-time course to undertake a part-time course. Students in receipt of an award (mandatory or discretionary) will have the vacation element for the two short vacations deducted from any payment. Students in receipt of grants will be eligible to make claims, provided other relevant conditions are fulfilled, for the summer vacation. Students on advanced courses with no grant, subject to the usual means test, will be eligible for benefit for all vacations. As postgraduate awards are normally made for a whole year, persons in receipt of such awards are not usually eligible for benefit.

18. Students following full-time non-advanced courses are usually debarred from supplementary benefit during vacations as the Supplementary Benefit Act excludes persons "receiving full-time instruction of a kind given in schools". This instruction has been interpreted to mean not just "O" and "A" level courses but also vocational courses in subjects such as photography, hairdressing and radio technology. Exceptions regarding students on non-advanced courses in eligibility to supplementary benefit are: heads of households; disabled students unlikely ever to be able to work to support themselves; those irrevocably estranged from their parents; and where they have attained the age of 19 by the end of the summer term of the course or will reach that age before the beginning of the next academic year.

19. On other matters concerned with social security and national insurance, students should be referred to the local DHSS office and the publications of the NUS. An aggrieved individual has the right to appeal to an independent appeal tribunal in the case of the refusal of supplementary benefit or unfair treatment. Appeals should be made in writing within 21 days of a decision being given.

20. **Department of Health and Social Security awards**

The DHSS makes awards for certain courses which are similar to awards made by LEAs under the Local Education Authorities Awards Regulations. The awards are discretionary. Courses for which awards are made are those for: dental auxiliaries, dental hygienists, occupational therapists, orthoptists,

---

2. *Further Education for Unemployed Young People*, DES Administrative Memorandum 4/77; Welsh Education Office 2/77, 10 February 1977, and *Amendment No. 1*, 10. February 1978; *Amendment No. 2*, 31 December 1979.

physiotherapists, radiographers, remedial gymnasts, and the postgraduate Certificate of Qualification in Social Work (CQSW). Information on these courses and awards is available from the Department of Health and Social Security, Branch P2D2, Room 344, Friar House, 157-168 Blackfriars Road, London SE1 8EU.

21. **Postgraduate Awards**

Apart from private sponsorship, (and those courses in education such as MA, M.Phil and doctorates undertaken by research which, because they do not fall into the designated courses under The Postgraduate, etc. Courses (Exclusion from Discretionary Awards) Regulations 1973, attract for that reason only discretionary grants);[3] there are two systems of awards for postgraduate courses. A bursaries scheme is administered by the DES for students taking certain vocational full-time postgraduate courses in the humanities. State bursaries are offered to educational institutions on a quota basis. They are not tenable for part-time study. Candidates should normally be under 27 (but if older they may be eligible for TOPS sponsorship); have been ordinarily resident in the UK for a period of at least three years, discounting any periods spent in further and higher education; hold a degree or its equivalent; not be in receipt of other equivalent sponsorship; and not normally to have undertaken previous postgraduate study, be a qualified teacher or be in possession of two first degrees. A bursary includes maintenance grant, fees, travel expenses and may include dependants' grants and other additional grants. Parental contributions are assessed and applied only in respect of students under the age of 25. Student contributions are made only where a maximum earning ceiling is exceeded. Applications are made via the college. Students are advised to consult the college authorities as soon as possible. Colleges must normally forward their nominations by mid-July at the latest, and by the end of that month, bursaries not allocated are liable to be pooled, and re-allocated to other institutions. Students should not apply direct to the DES. Successful candidates are notified by the DES as soon as possible, but candidates placed on the reserve list will be notified only if their application is successful. As reserve lists relate to individual institutions, students are advised to maintain contact with their college concerning the progress of their application.

22. The DES also administers the State Studentship Scheme. Ordinary state studentships may not be held for more than one year but major state studentships may be held for up to three years. Awards for postgraduate study in the social and natural sciences are the responsibility of the research councils. These councils are: Science Research Council, State House, High Holborn, London WC1R 4TA; the Social Science Research Council, 27-33 Charing Cross Road, London WC2H 0AX; and the Medical Research Council, 20, Park Crescent, London W1. All these studentships are competitive. Eligibility conditions are normally the possession of a British degree (in practice, of first or upper second class); the satisfaction of the UK residence qualification; and being aged under 27. Special arrangements exist for candidates aged 27 and over but under 35 who obtained their first degree

3 Apart from the PGCE, all postgraduate awards are discretionary.

not earlier than 1975. Other candidates over 27 and all over 35 have their cases considered on their special merits.

23. The awards made include fees, certain travel and other expenses, and maintenance grant. Additional grants may be made for dependants, disabled students, further travel and special expenses. A student's income from other sources may reduce the grant, and student income is assessed in addition to the income of a spouse. Applications for DES awards are made via the college, which will supply the application forms. Candidates may apply either through their own institution, or the one at which they are intending to undertake the postgraduate study. Candidates should not apply direct to the DES. Candidates are advised to consult the college authorities and to apply for an award as early as possible. Colleges must normally forward their nominations by the end of April at the latest. An independent selection committee advises the Secretary of State as to selection for state studentships. Criteria for selection include academic attainments, and aptitude and ability for postgraduate study. Successful candidates are notified during the summer but, particularly for candidates placed on the reserve list, it may be late September before notification is received. Double applications for state studentships and major state studentships are encouraged. Such application will not prejudice opportunities for a major award. In the case of research council awards, application is again made through the institution, but where subjects to be studied fall on the borderline between the DES and research councils' responsibilities, a candidate should submit her or his application to the most appropriate body without delay. Early application (by the end of March) is vital to ensure that, if redirection of a borderline case occurs, deadlines are met. A student can apply to only one source of public grant for a particular course. It appears that, in general, the research councils have a greater fund availability than the DES for the making of awards. However, postgraduate awards have never been easy to obtain, and their availability has recently been further decreased as a result of cuts in public expenditure.

24. **Adult education**

State bursaries for adult education are available from the DES for students attending one year or two year full-time courses of liberal adult education at certain long-term residential colleges. These bursaries are not available where students are eligible for LEA discretionary awards. The eligibility requirements are: to be over 20 at the start of the course; to have been offered a place and recommended for a bursary by the college; and to have satisfied the UK residence requirements. Application is made to the college on form SBAE1, and the form is forwarded by the college to the DES. The grant is payable at the same rate as for students taking first degree or comparable courses and includes tuition fees. Additional grants may be made for married students; widows, widowers, divorced and separated students; vacations; and travelling expenses. No parental contribution is expected from students aged 24 or who have supported themselves by the beginning of the course for at least three years (including up to six months of registered unemployment). A student's and spouse's income may result in the value of the bursary being reduced.

REFERENCE

Education Act 1962, Chapter 12, HMSO.
Education Act 1975, Chapter 2, HMSO.
Education Act 1976, Chapter 81, HMSO.
Local Government Act 1974, Chapter 7, HMSO.

The Local Education Authorities Awards Regulations 1975, Statutory Instruments 1975 No. 1207, HMSO.
The Local Education Authorities Awards (Amendment) Regulations 1975 Statutory Instruments 1975 No. 1697, HMSO.
The Local Education Authority Awards Regulations 1978, Statutory Instruments 1978 No. 1087, HMSO.
The Postgraduate, etc. Courses (Exclusion from Discretionary Awards) Regulations 1973, Statutory Instruments 1973 No. 1232, HMSO.
The Students' Dependants Allowances Regulations 1978, Statutory Instruments 1978 No. 1098, HMSO.

Awards to Students, DES Circular 11/75, 10 October 1975.
Further Education for Unemployed Young People, DES Administrative Memorandum 4/77, Welsh Education Office 2/77, 10 February, 1977; *Amendment No 1,* 10 February 1978.
Further Education for Unemployed Young People, DES Administrative Memorandum 4/77, Welsh Office 2/79, *Amendment No.2,* 31 December 1979.

Finance and Awards 1976, DES Statistics of Education Vol. 5, HMSO, 1978.
A Guide to State Bursaries for Adult Education, DES. Designated Courses Discretionary Awards 1975/76 to 1977/79, A report of a DES survey, DES, 1978.
Getting a Grant, Choose your course series, DES, 1979.
Grants to Students: A Brief Guide 1979, DES
Guide to Postgraduate Awards 1, State Bursaries for Postgraduate Study in the Humanities, DES, 1979.
Guide to Postgraduate Awards 2, For Postgraduate Study in the Humanities, State Studentships and Major State Studentships, DES, 1979.
Teacher Training, part-time courses designated for grants purposes. Education Information series, DES, 1975.
Undergraduate Income and Spending, Summary report of a survey, DES 1976.

Most of these publications are free and obtainable from Room 1/27, Department of Education and Science, Elizabeth House, York Road, London SE1 7PH. Enquiries regarding postgraduate awards should be sent to the DES (HFE IV), Honeypot Lane, Stanmore, Middlesex, HA7 1AZ. Enquiries concerning first degree courses and equivalents should be sent to the DES, Elizabeth House, York Road, London SE1 7PH.

Directory of Grant Making Trusts, Charities Aid Fund of the National Council of Social Service (48 Pembury Road, Tonbridge, Kent).
Educational Charities, National Union of Students.
Grants Survey – A reference work for advisers, National Union of Students.
Grants for higher education, Advisory Centre for Education/Barrie and Jenkins, available from WBR Distributors, Book Centre Limited, PO Box 30, North Circular Road, London NW10 (currently out of print).
Sponsorship and Supplementary awards, Careers and Occupational Information Centre, Pennine Centre, 20-22 Holly Street, Sheffield S1 3GA.
Student Welfare Manual, NUS, The relevant leaflets available singly or as part of the manual are:
Your Grant; Vacation Grants; Grants for Mature Students; Dependants' Allowances; Supplementary Benefit; Benefits for F.E. Students; Students and Income Tax; and *Students and Social Security (National Insurance).*
The Grants Register, Macmillan.

6 STUDENTS: LEGAL RIGHTS AND LIABILITIES

1. Legal protection afforded under the provisions of the Health and Safety at Work etc. Act and by the Occupier's Liability Act are referred to under Section **5.7**, and Section **11.10.**72. General provisions regarding sexual and racial discrimination are referred to in Section **11.6.**3. The matters requiring explanations here are:

2. **Sexual and racial discrimination in education**

Discrimination here means direct and indirect discrimination, and victimisation. In maintained educational establishments and certain other establishments providing full- or part-time education which are designated by an order of the Secretary of State it is unlawful to discriminate:

(i) as regards terms of admission to the establishment;

(ii) by refusing or deliberately omitting to accept an application for admission;

(iii) in the way it affords a student whom it has admitted to the establishment access to any benefits, facilities or services, or by refusing or deliberately omitting to afford such access; or

(iv) by excluding such a student from the establishment or treating him or her unfavourably in any other way.

NB: An establishment providing education or training which does not fall into the categories mentioned above may still be within the provisions of the Acts relating to employment and the provision to the public of goods, facilities and services.

3. **Other discrimination by local education authorities**

It is unlawful for an authority to discriminate in the performance of its functions under the Education Acts. Examples of such functions are the award of discretionary grants, access to equal opportunities in the curriculum, and the provision of facilities for social and physical recreation. Authorities are also required not to discriminate in the performance of their function under Section 8 of the Employment and Training Act 1973.

4. **General duty**

A general duty is imposed on responsible bodies for educational establishments in the public sector to ensure that educational facilities, and any ancillary benefits provided, are provided without discrimination. This duty is enforceable by the Secretary of State.

5. **Exceptions**

Exceptions are made in the case of sexual discrimination only. These are:

(i) single sex establishments;

(ii) admissions to communal accommodation (provided that the accommodation is managed for men and women as fairly and equitably as circumstances permit);

(iii) educational charities; and

(iv) further education courses in physical training and courses for teachers of physical training.

6. **Complaints**
Complaints of discrimination in education must first be notified to the appropriate Education Minister, by way of:

The Permanent Secretary
Department of Education and Science
Elizabeth House
York Road
London SE1 7PH.

The Secretary for Welsh Education
Welsh Office Education Department
Government Buildings
Ty Glas
Llanishen
Cardiff CF4 5PL

A complaint in respect of a body subject to the Education Ministers' powers can be brought before the courts in the normal way two months after the complaint has been notified by the complainant to the appropriate Education Minister, or before the end of the two months if the complainant is informed that further time is not required to consider it.

7. **Discrimination in the provision of goods, facilities and services and premises**
This provision of both Acts is also referred to in Section **11.6.** While it applies to persons who are concerned with the provision of goods, facilities and services to the public or a section of the public, its relevance to students ought not to be ignored.

8. **Exceptions**
Exceptions are made regarding charities and sport. Certain exceptions are made with regard to sex discrimination in the provision of communal accommodation. There is a general exception for acts of both racial and sexual discrimination which are necessary in order to comply with the requirements of other statutes, instruments or Orders in Council. Also excepted from the Race Relations Act is discrimination on the basis of nationality, place of ordinary residence or length of residence in or outside the United Kingdom or in an area within the United Kingdom, where the discrimination is in pursuance of arrangements made by, or with the approval of, a Minister of the Crown, or to comply with a condition imposed by a Minister.

9. The Race Relations Act also contains a general exception for acts done to enable the special needs of particular racial groups to be met as regards education, training or welfare or ancillary benefit. It permits access to facilities, services or benefits to be restricted, or to be allocated first, to members of the particular racial group in question, provided it can be shown

that members of that racial group have a special need in regard to their education, training, welfare or ancillary benefits, which is met by such a restriction or preferential allocation.

10. A general exception for racial discrimination applies in the affording of access to facilities for education or training or ancillary benefits where the discrimination is for the benefit of a person who is not normally resident in Great Britain and where it appears to the provider that the person in question does not intend to remain in Great Britain after his or her period of education or training here. Further, discriminatory acts are allowed if they are done to further any arrangements made by, or with the approval of, or for the time being approved by, a Minister of the Crown.

11. **Positive action**

Neither the Sex Discrimination nor the Race Relations Act permits "reverse discrimination". Both Acts however permit certain forms of positive action which are relevant to the education service. Where it appears to a relevant training body[1] that at any time within the previous 12months there were no, or comparatively few, members of a particular racial group or of one sex engaged in particular work in an area of Great Britain, although not for Great Britain as a whole, the training body may lawfully discriminate in relation to affording such members of the minority sex or racial group who appear likely to take up that work in that area access to facilities for relevant training, or encouraging persons of that sex or racial group to take advantage of opportunities in the area for doing that work. There is nothing in the Sex Discrimination Act which makes unlawful any discriminatory act done by one of the eligible training bodies, in, or in connection with, affording access to training to people who, in the view of the training body, are in special need of it because of periods for which they have been discharging domestic or family responsibilities to the exclusion of regular full-time employment. The most obvious example is that of married women who have given up work to bring up a family and now wish to be able to return. While employers may similarly discriminate positively in providing facilities for training, it is not lawful for an employer to select for such opportunities in order to achieve a sexual or racial balance in his or her concern. The body providing the training course would be able to discriminate positively in facilitating access to that course, however.

12. **Liability of employers and "principals"**

A person (a "principal") is vicariously liable for any discriminatory act done with his or her authority (whether express or implied, and whether given before or after the act) by his or her agent; and an employer is vicariously

---

1 These bodies are: the Manpower Services Commission (including the Training Services Division and the Employment Service Division) and industrial training boards. Other bodies may take advantage of the provisions but only if they have been specifically designated for the purpose by an order made by or on behalf of the Secretary of State. Training bodies which must be specifically designated in order to be eligible to claim the positive action exceptions in the case of sex discrimination may be designated in respect of "minority sex" training only, or in respect of training of people returning to work only, or both.

liable for any act done, with or without his or her knowledge or approval, by an employee in the course of employment. Thus, the "principal" and the agent, and the employer and the employee are vicariously liable for the unlawful act, and if convicted of an offence would be liable to incur a fine. The Acts provide a defence to an employer or "principal" otherwise liable for an unlawful act by an agent or employee if it can be proved that he or she took such steps as were reasonably practicable to prevent that person from committing the unlawful act(s).

13. **Local authorities' statutory requirement (Race Relations Act)**
The Race Relations Act applies to the acts of local authorities in the same way as it applies to the acts of private persons. In addition, it imposes a duty on all local authorities to make appropriate arrangements with a view to securing that their various functions are carried out with due regard to the needs to eliminate unlawful racial discrimination; and to promote equality of opportunity and good relations between persons of different racial groups.

14. **Contract**
Once a student has enrolled, a legally binding relationship known as a contract is created. Contracts are enforceable at law. Should either party – student or college – be in breach of any of the terms of the contract, there may be a claim to damages and/or specific performance of the contract. It is not straightfoward to determine what constitutes a contractual term. However, statements made in college prospectuses, course advertisements, course handbooks and literature, correspondence, and interviews may (usually) amount to contractual terms. Almost certainly, the college rules and regulations will have the status of contractual terms. In addition, terms will be deemed by the courts on the basis of custom and convention to be implied.

15. A student may have a right to sue for damages if the college is in breach of contract. Such a breach could be where the contract has not been observed at all, where only part of it has been performed, or where it has been performed fully but inadequately. The withdrawal of a course by a college when students have already undertaken a part of it could be the subject of an action for breach of contract, as could an attempt to levy an extra fee half way through the course. Colleges ought to be able to guard against breaches of the whole or part of the contract, but the issue of inadequate performance is inevitably more difficult since it would probably involve allegations of professional incompetence by teaching staff. Where inadequate performance is considered over a failure to teach an entire syllabus, it ought to be borne in mind that whereas teachers have a professional responsibility to cover the majority of a syllabus, it appears that the responsibility for the coverage of the whole syllabus is the students'.

16. Although it is possible in legal terms for colleges to include disclaimer clauses whereby an attempt is made, for example, to exempt liability for the withdrawal of a course, or part of a course, in any issue at law the courts may be subject to the Unfair Contract Terms Act 1977. Under this Act the courts are bound to declare that such a disclaimer clause will have effect

only if it is reasonable in all the circumstances of the case. The courts are also directed, *inter alia,* to consider the bargaining power of the parties: a college would be well advised to bear this in mind when attempting to exclude any contractual liability. Disclaimer clauses regarding fees and alterations to courses are found in the literature of some institutions, and such clauses may often be wide. The nature of certain courses may imply some contractual variation. The contractual relationship is less clear when applied to the student's employer (for example, the employer of a day release student): the contract is between college and student, and any dissatisfaction an employer might feel would depend for legal redress on the circumstances of the case, but such redress would probably be difficult to obtain. The law may be complex here, for such a problem may entail several different contracts.

17. Halls of residence contracts are often unclear and consequently may lead to legal difficulties. Colleges should be aware of the need, in this and other matters, for clear regulations and disciplinary procedures (see paragraphs 25-42).

18. **Negligence**

Actions for negligence may be taken by a student if reasonable care has not been taken by the college for his or her physical safety and the safety of property. Injuries occurring because of the condition of the premises and the arrangements within laboratories and workshops may, depending upon the circumstances, enable a student to sue the college. Unless the college has specified its disclaimed responsibility in such a manner as to bring it clearly to attention, losses of personal property from cloakrooms may allow a student to sue for negligence. This topic is complex, and reference must be made to the operation of occupier's liability law (see Section **5.7**). Unless security was inadequate, it would probably be viewed as unreasonable for a college to be held to be responsible for all the property of students – for example, property housed in a room of a hall of residence.

19. Insurance of property is the student's responsibility, although the college might consider warning students that their insurance should be sufficient to cover the relevant property, and that they should indeed possess insurance. This observation is pertinent especially where residential students keep valuable items in their rooms. It would be prudent for a college regularly to review its insurance cover: that cover should be such as to meet claims for injuries and other eventualities. Student property is sometimes insured by way of policies effected by their parents ("all-in" policies) but these are sometimes invalidated where the student lives away from home. Equipment used by the disabled is sometimes on permanent loan, and insurance against damage or loss provided by the owners. It could be, however, that the owners will expect the student to insure such equipment. College authorities should ascertain responsiblity here.

20. Negligence in the giving of advice is a matter to which attention should be paid. It is open for a student to sue where following advice given by a staff member (especially, perhaps, in a guidance capacity) has demonstrably led to

hardship or loss. In this case the local authority (or governing body in a voluntary college) would be sued as it retained the final responsibility as the staff member's employer. It would then be open to the authority to sue the individual staff member.

21. A college and its authority would be liable to a negligence action where it arose from an event or incident occurring at a student union function only if the constitution of that union, or its status established under the instrument and articles, did not give it autonomy. Thus, for example, an injury because of over-crowding at a student union dance (subject to occupier's liability law, and the responsibility for providing stewards) where the union was autonomous, would be the responsibility of the union. If the injury however occurred not because of over-crowding but because of the state of the premises which the college had allowed the union to use, responsibility for negligence would largely rest with the college. The college and student union might also be jointly responsible for negligence, according to circumstances. Even where a student union is autonomous, that does not necessarily mean that there will not be college liability.

22. **Trespass: student illegal occupations**

Students may be sued for trespass to land where they have participated in demonstrations or illegal occupations of premises. It has been the practice in some institutions to obtain injunctions where demonstrations and sit-ins have occurred; and there may be further legal redress where premises and property are damaged. Trespass is investigated further under Section **5.7.**14. It should be noted, however, that trespass is a tort which is actionable *per se:* there is no need to prove damage. Any damage done will rank for compensation, which otherwise in the absence of damage will be only nominal in amount. The issue of occupations is concerned more with the obtaining of possession, and the legal routes most commonly adopted here are applications for possession orders or injunctions. Actions for criminal trespass might arise, for example, in the threatening of forcible entry (whereby staff might be intimidated), and where trespass is effected with offensive weapons.

23. **The law of associations**

This law relates to "persons". Persons in its operation may be either human, or legal entities – that is, corporate bodies. Where representative bodies are not corporate, the law operates in a somewhat complex way. Student unions and student clubs which are unincorporated cannot be sued as bodies for the price of goods or services supplied to them: a person or persons must be sued, and therefore the persons liable are usually the officers or trustees of the union or club (or, exceptionally, a member or members, of the club). Legal procedures and enforcement can here be complex, and to an extent might be overcome by incorporation. Incorporation would replace the necessity for trustees where the union acquires or wishes to acquire property. There are severe disadvantages to incorporation, however, and consequences of registration at Companies House and the need to present annual accounts may involve more complex administration than is worthwhile. The topic of student unions' finance is discussed further under Section **12.7.**24.

24. **Criminal law**

An offence can be "compounded" where a person discovers that another has committed an offence and does not report it. However, where, for example, a permanent official of a student union discovered that an elected representative had taken union funds and reported the matter, not to the police, but to the executive committee, then the official would not be guilty of compounding the offence since the responsibility was now the committee's.

25. **Constitutional law**

College regulations form part of the contract between college and student. Such regulations are those made by, in, under and including the instrument and articles of government. Decisions made by college officers, authorities, boards and committees so empowered by the college constitution are binding – provided they are made known – on both sides in the contractual sense. This domestic law, provided that it is not *ultra vires* (beyond its powers) generally takes precedence over general law: courts will only turn to general law where a college's domestic law contains no provisions for a particular matter, or where it is determined that it is in the general interest to do so. This circumstance raises important issues:

(i) Delegation: Under common law, powers of academic and personal discipline cannot be delegated, unless particularly allowed under the instrument and articles of government. Thus a college's domestic law must usually be implemented solely by those persons entitled to do so. For example, a student dismissed from an institution by a faculty would have to be reinstated where the right to take such action did not properly belong to the faculty but to a superior body of the institution.

(ii) In most cases a student will have an ultimate course of appeal against any official action taken against him or her by the college. Thus, in an expulsion case, a student would have no redress at all if he or she had not followed the full domestic appeals procedure. Where a student is following a course validated by a university, the ultimate appeal may be to the university visitor.

(iii) For the very reason of its supremacy, it is clear that makers and executors of college domestic law have a heavy responsibility. Procedures should be clear, efficient, and designed to cover most eventualities. Vague phrases such as "bringing the college into disrepute" should be avoided. It will also be necessary to distinguish clearly between procedures for academic matters and regulations concerning discipline. The principles of natural justice should be observed. In disciplinary cases this may be taken to mean that at least: the student is informed of the precise nature of the complaint; the disciplinary tribunal should act in good faith, fairly, without bias, give each party the opportunity of adequately stating its case, and not hear the cases of both sides separately; the student should have the right to representation by a friend; and there should be full opportunity for the student's case to be presented to a tribunal which does not include the other party to the dispute. These matters are discussed more fully in paragraphs 26-40 below. It will be necessary to consider special appeals procedures for students aged 16-18.

26. **Disciplinary and appeals procedures**
Although there exists a series of pieces of advice from the DES to voluntary colleges of education which are still current,[2] it is more appropriate here to refer to the DES Circular 7/70.[3] The model articles and notes contained in the annex to the circular recommended in the case of matters of student discipline, where the student body is largely composed of full-time students aged over 18, that the governors establish a disciplinary committee including representatives in equal numbers of staff or students, provided that if governors are appointed (other than staff or student governors) their numbers do not exceed one third of the total. Rules governing student discipline are to be made by the governors after consultation with student representatives and the academic board; and these rules should provide amongst other matters:
(i) for the principal to have power to suspend a student for good cause, pending consideration of the case by the disciplinary committee within a stated period, and for such action to be promptly reported to the chairman of governors;
(ii) for decisions concerning suspension, other than in (i) above, or expulsion to be taken by the disciplinary committee, and for the student concerned to have the right of appeal to the governors or a relevant governors' committee (and for any governor involved in the earlier proceedings not to participate at the appeal stage);
(iii) for the student to have the right to appear and be heard (accompanied by a friend if so desired) at any disciplinary or appeal hearing.

27. In the matter of the exclusion of a student from the college because of an unsatisfactory standard of work, it is further recommended that this be carried out by the governors in most circumstances on the recommendation of the academic board, subject to the student's having a right of hearing (accompanied by a friend where desired) before the governors or relevant governors' committee. Circular 7/70 is here referring to academic appeals.

28. The DES recommended minima concerning appeals must be considered in the light of the legal status of college domestic law and the need for a college to safeguard both itself and its students.[4] Set out below therefore are discussion principles for the devising of disciplinary and academic appeals procedures:

29. **Academic appeals**
By way of preamble it must be stated that appeals made in consideration of nationally awarded qualifications, such as GCE "O" and "A" levels, cannot be based on internal college procedures, and similarly where a student is following a course in college which is validated by a university and the

---

2 College Letter 7/67 (DES reference R436(3)/42); College Letter 18/69 (reference R 26/23/01); Voluntary College Letter 10/70 (reference R26/23/01).

3 *Government and Conduct of Establishments of Further Education*, DES Circular 7/70. See also Sections **2.1**; **2.3** and **1.3.**17

4 Students have been able, with legal assistance, successfully to challenge a disciplinary ruling on procedural grounds.

appeal is against the university decision; but that it is important to consider areas of overlap. However, the CNAA recommends that all colleges which run CNAA validated courses should establish appeal procedures.

30. The manner of assessment does not materially affect an appeals procedure: the considerations will apply equally to continuous assessment and to assessment by examination, but it may be appropriate to draw up different appeals rules. Offences relating, for example, to cheating in examinations are regarded as disciplinary rather than academic offences,[5] and should be subject to other procedures. As with any recourse to law or quasi legal procedures, there should be strenuous effort made to avoid activating the full machinery unnecessarily: it may remove the necessity for an appeal if a procedure allows a student to be warned that failure is imminent, and is allowed to argue the case on academic grounds before any further formal steps are taken.

31. General principles for consideration are:
   (i) That there should be an appeals procedure must be considered axiomatic. If one does not exist, either a student is left without method of appeal or else a procedure will need to be devised when the need arises.
   (ii) Procedures should be formulated and where necessary revised[6] in consultation and agreement with the student union or, where a student union does not exist, representatives of the student body.
   (iii) Except in the case of some courses assessed on a national basis, one set of academic procedures should cover an entire institution. If there are several different procedures (often resulting from negotiations at different faculty boards) it is likely that confusion will be created.
   (iv) All students should be given a copy of the procedure on enrolment, and all documents either re-issued or prominently displayed when assessment results are given, both during and at the end of the course. This advice is given so that time limits may be fully known and observed, and to prevent a student prejudicing his or her case by appealing in the wrong way.
   (v) It is presumed that the committee hearing the appeal will have a constitution which allows for student representation. The selection of such representation will normally be the business of the student union. The union should be informed officially before the committee is allowed to sit.
   (vi) Except where the appeal committee is a full academic board, the staff involved in the original assessment should not normally sit on the appeal committee, although they would clearly need both to address it

5 Once a student has demonstrated academic capability by being accepted for a course, the only academic reason for the early termination of that course can be failure to fulfil academic requirements. This therefore means failure to achieve a required standard in a prescribed examination or other method of assessment, rather than being the means by which attempts were made to gain that standard.

6 The types and natures of student change in accordance with changing educational provision. It is important therefore that procedures are revised to accommodate new types of student.

and provide it with full information.

(vii) The student should be sent in writing a full explanation of the reasons for the academic failure.

(viii) The student should be invited to attend the hearing with a friend, and access to the information required to assist the conduct of the appeal should be furnished.

(ix) In appeals meetings the student representatives should be present throughout. For example, if the appeals committee is the full academic board, no part of the discussion bearing upon the case should be a reserved area of business.

(x) The student may appeal further to the governing body or academic board, where appropriate, against the decision of the appeals committee on the grounds that the appeal procedure was not correctly adhered to.

(xi) The ultimate recourse of appeal should be specified, and the procedural route made clear.

(xii) All appeals procedures should be clearly timetabled: whenever possible all appeals should be decided before the commencement of the next session.

(xiii) It will probably be necessary to classify appeals, and to draft rules for the different categories, for example:

(a) appeals against dismissal for academic failure not involving examinations;

(b) appeals against dismissal for academic failure which involves solely internal examinations; and

(c) appeals against dismissal for academic failure involving examinations subject either to external control or influence.

32. A student wishing to appeal against failure in an examination set and marked externally is at something of a disadvantage. The City and Guilds of London Institute and the GCE examining boards, among others, do not accept appeals from individuals. However, if a college principal writes to the board explaining that the examination result is out of character with the student's previous course performance, the board may agree to a re-assessment. It is in the students' interest if such possible recourse is drawn to their attention.

33. **Non-academic offences and appeals**

It is most important to ensure that disciplinary and academic offences are subject to separate procedures. Once again, however, it is vital that the procedures are clearly laid down, known to all, and to have been drawn up in consultation and with the agreement of the student representatives. It will probably be useful in devising procedures if there are distinctions made between minor and major offences. Each will be considered in turn, although it is appreciated that there may be borderline cases in practice which might require the establishment of a preliminary machinery which will determine into which category the offence falls. It is impossible here to give examples, for the gravity of an offence depends upon circumstances. The breaking of a window may normally be a minor offence; but if done deliberately in a room in which the college governors were meeting may well be considered a major offence.

34. *Minor offences*
Such offences can be dealt with in the first instance by a disciplinary committee containing equal staff/student representation. The staff or student member concerned with the offence would furnish information in the usual manner but, if a disciplinary committee member, would not be party to the decision. The student should be allowed the assistance of a friend, if desired, and the rules of natural justice (see paragraph 25 (iii) above) should be observed. The penalties which a minor offences disciplinary committee may impose could include: oral reprimand, with or without a written apology; written reprimand; temporary suspension of certain college rights; the requirement to make good in whole or in part any damage caused; a small fine; and a written warning concerning the consequences of future or persistent offences. Appeal could be made to higher college disciplinary bodies, including the governors. Again, it is important for the full procedures to be clear and known.

35. *Major offences*
Basic procedures should not be markedly different from those outlined above in considering academic appeals. However, the significant areas of difference concern the initiation of proceedings and the period between the complaint and its resolution. With regard to the provisions of Circular 7/70 and by analogy with criminal and employment law (see Section **11.9.**32) it is possible to consider the following as a basis for discussion.

36. Where the principal or chief administrative officer decides that a *prima facie* case exists, the student concerned is sent a written statement of the charge, and notification of the time, date, and place of the hearing before the relevant disciplinary committee or tribunal. The student should also receive in good time before the hearing copies of any statements and relevant documents. It may be necessary for some time to be allowed in order for the student to prepare his or her case.

37. The student should be allowed the assistance of a friend or representative, have the right to call witnesses, and produce statements and documents. The student should be able to admit the charge prior to the hearing, and to request mitigation of the penalty; to object before the hearing, in writing and in good time, concerning the composition of the disciplinary committee; and to have the usual right of the presumption of innocence until guilt is proved.

38. The consequences for a student suspended from college can be considerable, not the least of which is the reduction of grant. It is appropriate therefore to consider that in criminal cases, bail is not refused unless an accused is likely to influence witnesses or to leave the country: in cases involving employees, the employers' powers of suspension are usually limited to persons committing offences during the course of their employment. Therefore, unless the student's continued presence in the college could be construed not to be in the public interest or to represent a danger to him or herself or the college community, there is a strong case, Circular 7/70 notwithstanding, for the student not to be placed under suspension pending the hearing.

39. The hearing should follow the example of legal processes: for example, the student be able to submit that the offence does not breach a college regulation; the case against the student be presented first; and for the charge not to be proved against the student unless it has been established beyond reasonable doubt.[7] Consideration should also be given to the danger of over-administration. The operation of natural justice ought not to be such that a student is subjected unreasonably to the intimidation of too formal legal processes. Rather than submit to such an ordeal a student may well decide that it is a price too high to pay for continued membership of the college. The necessity for consultation with student union representatives in drawing up procedures can be seen here. In any event, however, the right of appeal should be allowed.

40. Although disciplinary and appeals procedures are almost inevitably cumbersome, and may often end in a result which would have been obtained more speedily by the principal acting on behalf of the governors, it is worth considering that justice ought to be seen to be done. The very fact of the importance of college domestic law made under the instrument and articles of government demands a full consideration for all those subject to its jurisdiction.

41. **Student complaints against staff**

The issue of student complaints against members of staff is one fraught with difficulties. It will be necessary for a principal to investigate fully the allegations made, and for such investigation to be carried out tactfully. Where a complaint is substantiated and of a major nature, the college can institute its own disciplinary proceedings against the staff member (see Sections **11.6.**97 and **11.9.**30) and a student, if necessary, can have the relevant legal recourse. Where the complaint is of a minor nature, there is a need once more for clear procedures. It may be appropriate, for example, to arrange for the double marking of a student's work both as a response to a student's complaint, and to safeguard the position of the teacher where professional probity has been questioned. Whatever procedures are adopted they will need to guard against frivolous complaints and, as well as protecting the member of staff against widespread publicity of ill founded allegations, also afford the student the opportunity to express a genuine complaint. It is, after all, more usual for a student to nurse a grievance than to institute proceedings, for reasons of feared victimisation if no other.

---

7 It might have been thought that since breaches of rules in educational bodies are civil matters, the proof required would be on the civil test of "the balance of probabilities." This is not the case. The courts have held that "punitive" rules in such cases must be construed strictly. Thus where a breach of rules may result in a penalty – for example, exclusion or expulsion – such matters must involve a burden of proof similar to that used in criminal cases. Therefore, the burden of proof for college purposes here must rest upon the party bringing the complaint, with the prosecutor having to prove the case "beyond reasonable doubt". Any doubts (including, for example, whether the rules allegedly breached were punitive) must be resolved in favour of the person complained against. (Kelly v NATSOPA (1915) TLR 632; Blackall v National Union of Foundry Workers (1923) 39 TLR; Lee v Showmen's Guild (1952) 2 GV 239, Court of Appeal). All these cases involved the disciplining of members in consequence of alleged breach by them of the rules of the organization of which they were members. The courts held that such rules must be strictly construed – and, further, that any arrangements to exclude the jurisdiction of the courts of law will be void.

42. In order to establish the seriousness of a complaint, and indeed during the process of the complaint, strict confidentiality should be maintained. A principal may wish to consult those of her or his staff who also teach the student who is making the complaint in order to determine its motivation. However, a student of unfortunate reputation may still have a genuine grievance. The accused teacher may have a right of action against the student for defamation if the complaint is unsuccessful – and possibly, even if it is successful. However, such a course of action in law may be subject to the defence of privilege. Generally, statements in judicial proceedings are absolutely privileged, and no redress can be obtained, however outrageous or damaging the statement might be. However, in college disciplinary proceedings, qualified rather than absolute privilege may obtain (since it will depend on whether the proceedings are seen as judicial or quasi-judicial). In determining an issue, the courts may well attempt to find some level of privilege; but the defence of privilege is not likely to obtain where the complaint was frivolous.

REFERENCE

Race Relations Act 1976, Chapter 74, HMSO.
Sex Discrimination Act 1975, Chapter 65, HMSO.
Unfair Contract Terms Act 1977, Chapter 50, HMSO.

Government and Conduct of Establishment of Further Education, DES Circular 7/70.
Sex Discrimination Act, 1975, DES Circular 2/76; Welsh Office Circular 20/76.

R.H. Jones, *Constitutional and Administrative Law*, Macdonald and Evans, 1968.
David Foulkes, *Law for Managers*, 2nd Edition, Butterworths, 1971.
The legal department of the National Union of Students has considerable expertise in the matter of students' legal rights and obligations but colleges should appreciate that the prime responsibility of the NUS is to advise student unions and individual students.

7. RELATIONS WITH STUDENT UNIONS

1. The annex to Circular 7/70, paragraph 7a, provides the model article that: "The Governors shall make arrangements for the Students' Union or other body representing the students to conduct and manage its own affairs and funds in accordance with a constitution approved by the Governors." The notes to the annex observe that such provision will be suitable for any college with a substantial proportion of (full-time equivalent) adult students but that modifications may be considered necessary in the case of other colleges. Where, for example, no students' union exists, it is recommended that the articles of government "should at least require arrangements to be made whereby representations on matters of proper concern to the students may be made by their representatives" to the relevant college authorities. Provision could be made for a Joint Consultative Committee which might include equal representatives of the governors, teaching staff, and students (and, the notes suggest, such provision could also be appropriate where a students' union is in existence).

2. The nature of student representation in higher education may be reasonably well known. The issue of such representation in colleges offering mainly non-advanced courses, and in small colleges generally, does require comment however. The National Union of Students is currently conducting a union development campaign, part of which is its wish to have adopted its charter for small colleges, and as part of that campaign is advising the lobbying of trade union members and approaches to college administrators, it is necessary to consider here both the operation of student unions and to provide discussion of the NUS aims.

3. As a preamble to the discussion, even though in many colleges student unions have long been accepted as an integral part of both education and college life, it is proper to review the reasons for their existence. The natural rights of representation, the necessity for consultation fora, and the value of associations which can provide social, recreational and welfare facilities for their members are reasons well sufficient for allowing the formation and support of student unions. To those reasons must be added the immense educational value to young persons of being able to develop their capacities of responsibility, participation and self-government. It may be necessary however for the college to provide guidance to its student union, especially in a small non-advanced institution: items of guidance are discussed below.

4. Crucial to any student union is the matter of union fees. Payment of union fees in higher education does not usually create a problem, for where the student's providing local education authority pays the mandatory grant, a part of that grant consists of the union fee agreed between the college and the particular student union (but see para. 7, below). The fee is sent to the college and automatically transferred to the union. The amount of fee, however, is settled by negotiation. How the student union draws up its budget and conducts its negotiations is its own business (in which it may turn to the NUS for advice, as well as to the college).

5. Where colleges provide non-advanced courses, most of the students are drawn from the immediate locality, and the local authority provides maintenance grants, tuition and union fees only at its discretion. Thus the level of union fees agreed between the union and the college is not automatically agreed to and paid by the LEA. The authority has the right to veto this agreement, and to pay minimal union fees for students or none at all. Therefore, while it remains the business of the student union to conduct its own campaign for an increase in fees, or their establishment, the college can expect not only to be involved but will require to establish its own policy of whether and how to support, and to what extent. Liaison with the LEA will be vital. The students will require details from the college. The minimum of these will be: the date by which college estimates need to be drawn up; the dates of forthcoming governors' meetings; and advice of at which governors' meeting the estimates will be approved. Staff, governors, local authority officials and elected representatives may well be lobbied by the student union. As the estimates have ultimately to be considered by the local authority, the union may well request both support from the college and information as to the persons to approach at this final stage of its submission. Where the matter of the union submission is subject to college disagreement, it will be necessary for college administrators not only to fulfil their duties under the provisions of college government and to their students and employers, but also to be seen to be acting fairly. This observation may be extended from the topic of fees to all matters involving student union submissions to governing bodies and local authorities.

6. There are at present a variety of union fees and methods of payment:

   (i) Registration fee. This is a common source of income for many student unions in non-advanced further education. When the college collects individual student registration fees, some or all of such monies may be passed to the student union. In some colleges, the fees are passed to a student welfare fund. The unions often have no control over the money, and the college is under no obligation to give income details to the union. In many cases, where money is given to the union, the college reserves supervisory rights.

   (ii) Block grant. In this case a fixed sum is given by the college or the maintaining college authority to the union. The problems associated with this method of funding are that the sum does not always increase with a growth in student numbers, and that unions may well resist the college designating the ways in which the money is spent.

   (iii) *Per capita* union fee. The students' grant awarding bodies, or they themselves, pay a fee which has been negotiated between the union and the college authorities. The fee is collected by the college acting as the union's agent. This is the type of fee usual in universities, polytechnics and colleges of higher education.

   (iv) *Per capita* block grant. The fee is paid by the local education authority maintaining the college and represents an agreed fixed amount for every student in the college. As the majority of students undertaking non-advanced courses do not receive discretionary awards, this system ensures the viability of the student unions: the same level of union fee is paid for each student. There is, however, a constitutional disadvantage in that the maintaining LEA has to support students from other authorities as well as its own, unless some reciprocal agreement is made with the other authorities involved.

7. In February 1980 the Secretary of State proposed that from 1981-82 the system under which local authorities have to pay – through mandatory student grants – whatever fee the college fixes would be replaced by college provision of the money out of its normal funds. The amount of money available for each union would be a matter for settlement at institutional and, where appropriate, local authority level. In the case of voluntary institutions, the new system would leave the negotiation of union funds entirely with the institutions concerned; in public sector colleges, the LEA would be involved. Since a student union would thus become just one of the facilities to be paid for out of an institution's funds, the Government proposes to abolish *per capita* fees. At the time of going to press, the proposals were the subject of considerable debate.

8. Levels of union fee vary considerably. The lowest polytechnic union fee is currently £20 per student, college of higher education fee £10 per student; and whilst some larger technical colleges have union fees of £10 per student, the highest recommended (by ILEA) further education college fees are just over this amount (and subject to college negotiation up to that maximum figure). In May 1978 the DES issued a discussion paper on the financing of student unions, the main suggestion of which was that an upper limit (possibly £15 to £20) should be set on the amount which could be paid through the Awards machinery in respect of student union subscriptions, be reviewed periodically, and that this could be supplemented from an institution's own resources, following local negotiations. The paper also suggested a minimum level of subscription, possibly £1.25 for full time students (and by using the full-time equivalence system of 4 or 5 part-time students being the equivalent of one full-time student, a minimum part-time student subscription of 25p) would be recommended in guidance to local authorities for payment. It was proposed that these suggestions should be implemented in 1979-80 or 1980-81.

9. In its union development campaign, the National Union of Students is seeking to have accepted the following claims: automatic union membership for all students; guaranteed union fees paid by the LEA; student representation on college committees; time off for union meetings during the day; union affairs free from staff control; a permanent, properly equipped union office; access to college rooms for meetings; sabbatical leave for the president; funds for a part-time secretary; and a students' permanent common room. As these claims merit consideration of themselves and also provide a useful framework within which to discuss relations with student unions, apart from the fees issue discussed above, each will be investigated in turn. As a preface to the discussion it will be noted that several of the claims have a clear relationship with the provisions of employment law: and it can be argued that student rights morally should be analogous in a college to those provided by statute for the employees of a college. The counter argument is that a student union is not a trade union, and ought not to be treated as if it were. The issue is complicated by reason of many students being aged under 18, for although they may be eligible to enter employment,

it can be held that as they are not adult they require guidance and protection as well as being given opportunity to learn and mature. Students who are minors may attend governing body meetings, but they are not allowed to vote on matters concerning the allocation of public funds.

10. Automatic membership of the union for full-time students has been considered a right for some time. Voluntary membership can result in the services and facilities afforded by the union being disrupted by membership fluctuation, as well as allowing a union to be taken over by a minority and the possible imposition of members only rules which can have a disruptive effect on a college's life. Membership for all part-time students is complicated by the nature of those students: it can be administratively difficult for a college to ensure that this occurs, however desirable it is for part-time students to be involved in the life of the college, and in such cases it will be appropriate to seek the assistance of the union in bringing part-time students into membership. Where a student (or in the case of a part-time student, perhaps her or his employer) objects to compulsory membership, the issue may be determined in several ways. The college instrument and articles of government may provide the answer, and if not, the rules and regulations operated by the LEA. In extremity, a principal may use the powers of suspension. It will be preferable if the matter is settled by conciliation, using the good offices of the student union.

11. The matter of student representation in college and academic affairs is not a topic upon which it is easy to give guidance. Paragraph 4 ix of Circular 7/70 advises that in the case of colleges with a substantial proportion of advanced work, or a substantial proportion of adult students (whether or not they are following advanced courses) that in the establishment of membership of governing bodies "consideration should be given to the inclusion of students appointed through the students' union". The circular states that authorities may also wish to consider the representation of students in other cases, and indicates that where specific provision is not made that the general power of co-option can be used. However, the circular advises authorities when determining the articles of government of a college to have regard in matters of representation to the age composition of the student body; and the proportions of full-time, sandwich, and part-time day or evening students. The statement that governors "shall also make arrangements whereby representation on matters of proper concern to the students may be made by their representatives to the Governors, the Academic Board or the Principal as may be appropriate" was intended to apply to full-time students.

12. In the case of a student body largely comprised of full-time adult students it can be held that, since the Department advises consultation generally, and especially in disciplinary matters, it should certainly occur. Student representatives should be selected by the union, not by the college. In determining representation matters the issues are: the numbers of students involved and their voting rights; where and at which levels representation occurs, and what policies are implemented concerning reserved business. Representation should mean that there are at least two student representatives upon any body upon which they serve, and that they ought to

have voting rights: other students designated by the union may attend as observers (and in the case of the business of some committees it may be appropriate for representation to consist of observers only). Representation on bodies dealing with the business of the college, such as the academic board and its committees, is not the whole issue however.

13. As students are the consumers of education, and may also be able to make contributions to its progress, the argument exists that their representatives' involvement should extend beyond business, disciplinary, and social and welfare matters to academic representation: that is, to be involved in the designing, preparation and review of courses. Such representation ought to be given careful consideration. While it may be most appropriate in a large college where the union enjoys the services of an academic affairs office, the benefits to students and colleges of academic representation (the nature of which will depend on the courses and their levels) should not be underestimated or rejected without the most careful thought. It may be necessary for there to be reserved business in certain college committees. However, this business ought to be as limited as possible, refer only to matters of absolute confidentiality and not be a device to limit student participation. The designation of agenda into parts A and B, for example, where part B requires student withdrawal, can allow items to be discussed under the cloak of confidentiality which properly belong to an open agenda.

14. In considering any system of student representation, whatever the nature of the college, it ought obviously to fit the needs of the students and to allow a form of representation for all students. For example, in the case of students on sandwich courses, machinery ought to exist for their representation during the times at which they are absent from college; and in the case of part-time students where their direct participation is impractical, maximum efforts made to represent their views. Structures in such cases may be difficult to devise, especially in the case of evening students, but in all events, no matter the ages of the students, representation ought to exist and be as full as possible. Such representation should extend to sub-committees of the academic board and governing body. It will be necessary for there to be careful examination of the means by which students aged under 18 are represented.

15. The wish for time off for daytime union meetings may become acute where class attendance is a condition of the course. As the effectiveness of any student union depends on its officers having time to perform their functions as well as the members being able to attend meetings, it will be necessary for colleges and unions to reach an agreement as to how time can be allowed without major disruption of classes. Where unions are required to hold evening meetings, attendance is usually poor. It ought not to be too difficult to arrange for the extension of a lunch time meeting into class hours where this is necessary. The amounts of time off allowed to a student officer will be subject to negotiation. It may be considered that the following suggestions are appropriate: students are allowed the minimum of one hour release from class hours to attend general meetings, of which there are not more than two per term; union officers are granted minimum release of one hour per week;

there be further time off allowed for union officers or representatives to attend college committee meetings, and to carry out agreed designated union functions; and that a union president who does not have sabbatical leave should be allowed a further hour per week allowance. However, while many would view sabbatical leave (see paragraph 19) as essential, it can also be argued that trade unions and student unions are not analogous. Hence, whereas an employee absent on union business will either be covered by a colleague or else have her or his work delayed or adjusted, a student absent from class will be missing something of value which cannot be wholly replaced.

16. Students certainly, and rightly, will resist staff control of their union. There will always be a need for good and close liaison, especially where the use of the college premises is involved (see Sections **5.7** and **5.10**). The balance between liaison and interference can be a fine one. It is the practice in some colleges to designate staff advisers whose role is to assist the union. In many cases such advisers have been able to give well appreciated assistance, Problems arise, however, where their role is not clearly defined, where the wrong kind of help is extended at an inappropriate time; and where the advisers are inexperienced. It is recommended therefore that the college and the union negotiate an agreement which will allow staff assistance and prevents unreasonable interference. Probable issues for negotiation will include legal and financial liabilities (see Section **12.6.**23); the autonomy of the union; and the role of staff advisers. Union nomination of the staff adviser, subject to college approval, will be advisable, as will a role definition which includes technical advice and assistance but does not include involvement in the formulation of union policy.

17. It may be appropriate for staff advisers to have negotiated roles which include: assisting in the conduct of union elections; advising on technical matters associated with the union's responsibilities, including financial obligations; and advising where required at meetings. The staff adviser may have a responsibility for ensuring the union receives adequate information, and also adequate access to college facilities. If the staff adviser is a co-signatory to cheques drawn on the union account, it is important that she or he should not be held accountable for any payment made which has been agreed by the union in accordance with its constitution. Even where the staff adviser considers that a union's failure to follow advice is sufficiently grave to require further action, it will still be preferable for informal action to precede any formal procedures.

18. While most unions possess an office, desks, typewriter, telephone, filing cabinet and at least access to reprographic facilities, the National Union of Students stresses that many unions' effectiveness is limited by their having an office which is too small or else situated too far away from the main activities of its members.

19. In most colleges the student union will not possess a separate building. Access to college rooms for meetings and social events is obviously necessary to the union. It will be prudent therefore if the student union is consulted at

the time of termly or annual room timetabling. A period of advance notice necessary for the booking of the college hall will need to be agreed. Supervision of events such as dances will require careful negotiation. The union will need to be fully informed of its legal obligations and security provisions will have to be agreed. Where staff have warden duties they too will need to be consulted. While student volunteers may replace ancillary staff in some instances (subject to their and their unions' agreement) on social occasions, responsibility for college security cannot rest with the student union. Agreement on procedures in this instance is highly important. Where porters or security staff have to be employed late at night, as they have a responsibility for college rather than student union security, it would be reasonable if any necessary overtime payments were made by the college. However, if the late work was necessary because of the union being open, it would be reasonable for the cost, or part of it, to be charged to union funds.

20. Although common in higher education, the sabbatical student union president remains a rarity in other areas of further education. The obvious reason for this is cost. It is argued by the NUS that without a sabbatical officer it is impossible for a student union to provide an effective service to its members. This view was shared by the ATCDE, one of the predecessors of NATFHE: "The contribution which a good student union president can make to the relationship between the college authorities and the student union is inestimable ... we feel that colleges and student unions should seek to provide the optimum conditions for this difficult and demanding job."[1] College authorities were here advised to avoid laying down formal academic commitments as a precondition for granting sabbatical leave to student officers. Financial support, to the equivalent of a full student grant plus reasonable expenses, was to be met from union funds (because the options of a full LEA grant or college subsidy had been found not to be viable).

21. Only the larger unions are able to employ secretarial, administrative or book-keeping assistants. Such assistance is obviously a great help to the union and especially where there are no full-time union officers, may be seen as an important way in which to ensure the efficiency of the union. Where a union cannot afford to employ a secretary and an authority or college is unable or unwilling to provide such a service, the union should at least have a definite access to the secretarial and accountancy resources of the college. Some of the larger unions have appointed permanent secretaries or research officers. It is important for the status of such persons in the college management structure to be established.

22. Almost all unions have common rooms for their use. In some instances in small colleges however these facilities have been reported to be inadequate. Complaints vary from restrictions on opening times, to the room(s) being used for teaching, to the facilities consisting of ill-equipped, uncomfortable, rudimentarily converted classrooms. As students are entitled to be able to

---

1 *Sabbatical Leave for Union Officers in Colleges of Education*, a statement by the ATCDE and NUS, 1973.

relax and enjoy one another's company, at the very least they ought to have common room facilities sufficiently comfortable and attractive to ensure that they are looked after, and to have space sufficient to allow a lounge area, recreational activities, and the sale of tea, coffee or fruit juice. More generous provision will entail items such as a stage, store room, an uncarpeted area suitable for dancing, screen and projector facilities, and facilities necessary for a permanent or temporary bar.

23. Student union bars on occasion present problems for colleges, especially the smaller colleges. It is advisable that the bar is part of a registered club. In this case the licensee is the club rather than an individual. It is essential that the club has a constitution which makes provision for rules and officers. Full consultation in the drawing up of the constitution of the club is essential. Where the club is on college premises, however autonomous the union, there will be a need for the college to be represented on the management committee. Some principals have advocated that after consultations have been held and general agreement reached, the constitution should then be drawn up by a solicitor. The solicitor, or some other competent person, then makes the application for a licence to the clerk to the magistrates. The application will then be considered by the bench; the fire officer will inspect the premises; and it is advisable that the police are informed once a licence has been granted. Officers of the club retain certain legal liabilities in respect of the club's activities, the most obvious of which is the observance of licensing hours. It is not possible to advise on the day to day running of the club: some colleges have found that the bar is best managed by the students themselves; others have found management best left to professional stewards. [2] Opportunities for dishonesty and incompetence clearly exist. Where student clubs are on college premises, they are required to act within the rules of the college, and fall under the general jurisdiction of the governors and the authority. How the club is operated – whether, for example, the college porter or security staff are responsible for ensuring that the premises are vacated, and whether the club employs its own cleaner – will depend upon the circumstances of the college. In any operation upon college premises of a student bar however, it is essential that good relationships exist between the college authorities and the students, and the rules and procedures are agreed, well known and understood.

24. There is a real need for student unions to be strictly accountable concerning the manner in which funds are expended. This accountability should be seen as not merely to the governing body of the college, but also to the student membership itself. As such a statement may appear to breach the principle of student union autonomy, it is important to consider the context in which that word is used. Colleges, and therefore student unions, are in receipt of public funds. Even the "autonomous" universities are required to account for expenditure and public sector institutions are subject to stringent financial controls. Where defalcations occur in student union finances, this represents both a loss of public money and a diminution of resources available to the

---

2. The NUS recommends the employment of stewards (who work under the direction of a management committee).

general body of students, many of whom may be unaware of how their finances are being used. Although mention has been made of students' legal liabilities (see Section **12.6.**23), it is obviously preferable to prevent defalcation rather than subsequently obtain redress. Some authorities insist on making student union funds available in two separate block grants, the second of which is not made available until the first has been fully audited. Some governing bodies monitor the observance of the student union constitution. Whatever practice is adopted, accounting should be rigorous. The greatest argument for student unions is the facility they allow for the appreciation and participation in democratic procedures. The continuity of democratic organization can well depend upon financial accountability. The NUS Finance Pack, which is recommended by the DES and CLEA, provides models for a student union financial control system.

25. A well administered student union can only be of great benefit to the college and its students. It is proper for that union to have the greatest possible autonomy within the constraints demanded by finance, and the college's responsibility for security, legal liabilities, and safety. Inefficiency in student unions can generally be attributed to a lack of resources, both financial and in the time constraints imposed upon officers. The movement towards greater student representation in the past decade aroused many fears but has proved to be a very valuable exercise. The rather loose expression "good relationships" can only be given meaning where college authorities are fully sensible to the rights, opinions and aspirations of their students, however difficult such a response occasionally may be; and where student unions too are sensible of the needs of the college.

26. There is a NATFHE/NUS/NUT joint committee which meets to consider issues of interest to the parties concerned. Discussions may result in joint action or the publication of joint advice after agreement has been reached between the associations involved. The NUS also liaises in this manner with other unions. Discussions are currently well advanced on the conduct of teaching practice. NATFHE and NUS are preparing a joint protocol concerning the role and conduct of academic staff in relation to student union affairs. The protocol seeks to protect the autonomy of the student union whilst also providing for advice and technical assistance by academic staff to the union. Reference should be made to this protocol when it is ratified and made available. The NUS has agreements with several unions such as NALGO and NUPE which relate to areas of common concern, for example, procedures concerning campus disputes.

REFERENCE

Government and Conduct of Establishments of Further Education, DES Circular 7/70.
A Guide to Academic Representation, National Union of Students.
Digby Jacks, "The Students' Union," *Student Life in Further Education,* Coombe Lodge Reports, Vol 6, No 11, pp 531-533.
NUS Finance Pack, National Union of Students.
Sabbatical Leave for Union Officers in Colleges of Education, ATCDE/NUS, 1973.
Union Development Campaign Pack, National Union of Students.

8 STUDENT WELFARE

1. Welfare provision varies enormously, and not only according to the type of institution. In larger colleges there may be a well staffed student services division which offers full welfare provision; in some small colleges provision may be minimal. The essential questions regarding student welfare are those of width and liaison: whether provision is adequate depends not just on the current use of services, but also in the ways in which the services can be developed; and while the welfare role of the student union, or that of outside agencies, ought not to be duplicated, it is necessary for liaison to be thorough and for the various bodies involved to be fully aware of the others' functions and services. The age of majority being 18 ought not to be taken as an excuse for inaction. Certainly, many students may exercise their rights as adults to take a responsibility for their existence; but nonetheless advisory and practical services ought to exist to be used as required. In discussion of student welfare provision, it will be convenient to identify areas thus: accommodation; health; finance; advisory and counselling services; religion and college life.

2. **Accommodation**
Advice and action concerning accommodation will usually consist of: dealing with allocations for hall and hostel places; the finding of lodgings and flats; liaison with landladies and landlords; assistance in the resolution of tenancy problems; the maintenance of contact with the local education and housing departments, and local housing associations; and the advising on questions of eligibility for rent and rate rebates, and rent allowances. Advice ought always to be available to students undertaking a tenancy, and where difficulties arise over rent, notice to quit, deposits and repairs. A college accommodation officer may be required to approve lodgings, especially for students aged under 18.

3. Even in higher education there are few instances of a college providing residence for all its students. Apart from the perennial reason of cost, this has also occurred because for at least part of their time at college, significant numbers of students have chosen to live outside the academic community. This choice is the result of both financial and social considerations. Where students have exercised this right to opt out of college residence, it is a harsh interpretation of their action which presumes that the college has therefore no further duty towards them. Advice to such students, as well as to the many for whom anyway there are no residential places available, in coping with the jungle of private and public tenancies, will be essential in many cases.

4. While liaison with landlords and landladies is an essential task, it must be remembered that a very large proportion of further education students live at home. This ought not to mean that it is merely presumed that the college has no responsibility. Consideration ought to be paid to the personal position of such students, especially since their lives might be further complicated by their receiving no or little income. The difficulties which can occur within family relationships as a result of a member undertaking a college course,

while they more properly belong to the topic of counselling, might nevertheless be seen as partially an accommodation problem.

5. **Health**

The minimum provision for a college to afford consists of: attempting to ensure that each new student registers with a doctor and makes arrangements for dental and ophthalmic care; that literature describing the National Health Service is available (a provision especially relevant to overseas students); and to remind sandwich course students to change their doctor when they move to another area for their industrial experience if they move for more than three months. A list of all dentists, ophthalmic medical practitioners and opticians who may provide NHS general dental and ophthalmic services might be obtained from the Family Practitioner Committee and be made available to students by the college authorities. A sick bay, and a matron or day/night nurse, full- or part-time according to numbers, are essential in a residential college. Where a college does not have the services of a nurse, it will be necessary for there to be designated staff members within the college to deal with minor injuries and accidents, maintain an accident record book, and to accompany injured students to hospital. It may be appropriate for certain members of staff to possess a First Aid certificate. Where a college is residential, or is some distance from a doctor's surgery, it is advisable for there to be a doctor either in attendance, or available for attendance, for some hours each week. It is not usual for there to be a college doctor on site, but it is a sensible practice for there to be a college doctor available to the institution. The Area Health Authority decides on the supply of clinically trained staff to public sector institutions. This authority has the power to refuse to allow a college to employ such staff. Students have the right to refuse to register with a college doctor.

6. Where an employer or local authority requires a student to undergo a medical examination, for example before sandwich course employment, the student is required to pay for the examination unless the requirer of the examination agrees to meet the cost. Teacher education students do not have to pay for medical examinations for teaching posts. Colleges ought to keep application forms for free examinations, and for chest X-rays, or else they might arrange for students to attend the nearest X-ray unit.

7. As part of its medical services, it is advisable for a college to have available information concerning such matters as family planning, and health education generally, as well as maintaining a list of addresses to which to apply for further information. Health education might well be part of the college curriculum.

8. **Finance**

It is important that there be ready advice available to students on matters such as grants, allowances, sources of finance, social security and legal problems – or at least advice as to where the matters might be better pursued. Colleges may also wish to consider the formal or informal provision of some sort of hardship fund. Even if such a discretionary system is not operated, a college ought certainly to be able to supply advice in the first instance; and the students should be fully aware that such advice is available. Although grants to students are discussed under Section **12.5** it is appropriate to mention here that local charities might well assist students experiencing financial difficulties.

9. **Advisory and counselling services**
Counselling services can never be successful unless they are integral to the total activity of the college. It can be argued further that whatever the formal provision of welfare services, those too will not operate effectively without full staff awareness and involvement. Whilst a counselling service may operate alongside advisory welfare services or those concerning careers advice, or be part of a staff development division, and indeed ought to have strong liaison links with such bodies, it remains important that its function is the receipt of information and that its non-directive relationship with its clients is fully known and understood. The differences between guidance and counselling are becoming increasingly well known but the essential point is still worth making: guidance is concerned with the identification and satisfaction of needs, and invariably entails the giving of advice; counselling is a method whereby the individual becomes involved in a process of self-awareness and self-discovery.

10. It is important that counselling appropriate to the needs of all students is available throughout the further and higher education service. Whilst by reason of their contact with their students, teaching staff are often able to identify persons in need of counselling, both the demands on their time and the possible need for professional services require the availability of full-time trained counselling staff. The appointment of counsellors in universities and polytechnics has been usual for some time but it is clear that there is an equal if not greater need in non-advanced further education. As colleges respond to educational developments involving the disadvantaged, so student counselling services are increasingly required, as are fully trained counsellors. Both teaching and other professionally trained staff will be involved. In the larger institutions, the necessary arrangements may well occur in student services divisions which embrace all aspects of student welfare – a sensible development which allows easy and close liaison but which to be fully effective ought not to be isolated from teaching departments. In the smaller institutions, responsibility may well devolve upon an individual who works in conjunction with a team of tutors whose main work is academic.

11. The nature and operation of the counselling service ought to be fully known to the staff and students alike. Where a college appoints residential wardens, it will be necessary for them to receive training in counselling, and also for them to consider, because of the range of their responsibilities, a difference from the usual counselling role. It is usually considered that a disciplinary function is incompatible with counselling. Course tutors and personal tutors necessarily retain a certain counselling role (for which both professional training and contact time remission is necessary). However, a problem may occur where such staff see their function as being primarily academic and disciplinary: they may not wish to assume such a role, may not be competent

without training to undertake it, and it would be unsuitable for such a role to be thrust upon them. It is wrong to expect staff to undertake a counselling role which they do not feel competent to fulfil. It should be considered that since the role of personal tutor may be primarily concerned with counselling, staff might volunteer for the responsibility, rather than be selected for it. It must also be remembered that students require assistance at various levels: their problems may be academic, personal, or social; and while a counselling service has to attempt to fulfil each of these needs, the personal tutor's main responsibility will be academic. Personal tutors should be required to act only in a tutorial role, and not have a disciplinary function within that capacity. Should they so desire, students ought to be able to change their personal tutor.

12. The professional student counsellor should wherever possible be appointed on a college basis. While needs and practices will vary, it has been suggested that the appropriate minimum staffing level ratio is that of 1 student counsellor to 700 full-time equivalent students. This ratio is not adequate to make suitable provision for the 16-19 age groups, however. Counselling is most effective on an individual basis; group counselling can be undertaken effectively only by appropriately trained staff.

13. In the attainment of the necessary full integration of the counselling service it will be appropriate if the counsellor is involved in planning at appropriate college levels, and, while additional to the teaching establishment, should be considered to be a full member of the academic staff. Such recognition is important also in the development of the counsellor's role: while many counsellors like to retain a teaching connection, others equally consider that in order to function effectively they must be seen by the students to be removed from formal teaching and disciplinary tasks. Resolution of this matter ought not to be too difficult: it can generally be said that it is desirable for the counsellors to continue to have a teaching role, but that such a role ought not to be one which involves him or her in taking disciplinary action. It is important that the counsellor's integrity is respected. Unless the student client expressly permits the divulgence of information, the matter must remain confidential; and such confidentiality will be required to be respected by all college administrators and staff. The right to professional discretion must also be extended to the counsellor by both staff and students: the counsellor will need to refer some clients to legal, medical or psychiatric services. It is also necessary for counsellors to be accorded the status necessary in the college for the performance of their duties. For example, the counsellor may have become aware that particular institutional practices are harmful to the students and will therefore require both status and access to the relevant authorities to begin the discussion of methods of reform.

14. **Religion**

It is appropriate for colleges not only to advise their students of chaplaincy arrangements and the local whereabouts of clergy of all relevant denominations, but also to afford facilities for religious worship and observance. This latter provision can be of especial value to overseas students. Only a few colleges now have resident chaplains; in some instances, chaplains may be appointed to the student union rather than the college. Advice can be obtained from the National Ecumenical Agency for Further Education, a body to which the DES gives support. Colleges will generally liaise with the local clergy, however, as part of their involvement in the life of the community.

15. **College life**
More particularly in non-advanced further education institutions perhaps, there is a proportion of students which rejects much of college life. Whatever the public relations benefits to the adult and outside world, functions such as open days have not enjoyed universal student popularity for some time. While college clubs, student union activities, drama, joint staff-student activities and particularly sport have both considerable appeal and use, it has been argued that such activity does not of itself provide the whole stuff of college life. Further, it is argued in some quarters that such activities and their special provisions are élitist and, intentionally or unwittingly, are designed to isolate college and students from the community which subsidises them and which they ought to serve. That there is a movement to fuller involvement between colleges and the community is inescapable, and it is proper to consider some of the implications.

16. Public educational institutions usually make a contribution to their local communities. Such practices must now be considered in the light of predictable educational events. Despite public expenditure restraint, there is a response to adult education provision; responses to unemployment can be seen both in youth opportunities programmes and retraining schemes; there is increasing provision for the handicapped; and there has been a growth in continuing and remedial education. Social amenities outside the homes of young people, particularly those living in large conurbations, are often poor. It has been argued that students and parents ought to be helped in dealing with their home relationships. There have been for some time many advocates of community schools and colleges, and it has been argued that colleges should provide amenities and accommodation for the whole community, especially as exemplified by those groups for whom recent educational provision has been made. Hence, a college's social and recreational facilities might be shared with the community. If colleges are to consider providing social centres for young people, then that provision will necessarily require to be continued at weekends and during vacations. Administrative difficulties may well be daunting, but the task of the administrator is not the arrangement of circumstances to suit her or himself, but to enable whenever possible a desired policy to be implemented. However, in designing such policy, it will be necessary to liaise closely with the LEA.

17. There is an assumption, inherited perhaps from the *mores* and myths of public schools, that all students ought to find complete fulfilment within the college. It is often presumed that a student should integrate totally into the institutional existence. In pursuit of this goal, attempts have been made to integrate part-time students into college life. as well as worthily striving to

make college life as full as possible for all. No solution to the problem has been propounded. One reason, perhaps, is that part-time students have a life outside the college which is time consuming – and may be preferable. There have always been students who have rejected the sometimes artificial, narcissistic, hot-house environment of college. To turn the argument of the preceding paragraph around, therefore, there are those who would wish, instead of bringing the community into the college, to take the college into the community. The resolution of the arguments is the same: in the provision of social, recreational and educational functions, colleges will need to consider how and to what extent they involve themselves in the community. This process will require consultation with the LEA (see also Section **5.10**).

REFERENCE

Health Services for Students on Full-time and Sandwich Courses, DES Further Education College Letter, 5/76.

Counselling and Guidance, Coombe Lodge Reports Vol. 1, No.4.
Schools and Colleges: Personal Counselling and Careers Guidance, Coombe Lodge Reports, Vol. 4, No.11.
Student Counselling, NATFHE, 1979.
Student Life in Further Education, Coombe Lodge Report, Vol. 6, No.11.
Student Welfare Manual, National Union of Students, 1978.

Association for Student Counselling, Harrow College of Technology and Art, Northwick Park, Harrow, Middlesex, HA1 3PT. 01-864 4411.

9 CAREERS ADVICE

1. **Statutory provision**

The Employment and Training Act 1973 requires local education authorities to provide certain careers services. Authorities are required to make arrangements:

(i) to assist persons attending, either full-time or part-time, educational institutions other than universities to determine what forms of employment will be suitable for them and available to them (having regard to their capabilities) when they leave the institutions, and what training will then be required and available to fit them for such employment;

(ii) to assist such persons to obtain relevant employment and training;

(iii) to make such arrangements available to persons who seek to make use of them; and

(iv) for officers of the authority to be appointed to administer the arrangements.

2. The authority may also extend these arrangements in order to assist other persons not specified in the main provision who are seeking employment or a change of employment, and/or training. Authorities may consult with one another and make joint arrangements. An authority may arrange for the Manpower Services Commission to carry out its functions as specified in (i) above.

3. The authority must keep records of advice given on its behalf. Where a person who had received such advice attends an institution in another authority area then, on request, the first authority must furnish the other with records of vocational advice given.

4. In carrying out its statutory duties, the local education authority must act in accord with guidance of a general character issued by the Secretary of State, and to provide that person with such information as may be required. Currently, this general guidance is given by the Department of Employment in *The Careers Service*, a publication shortly to be revised. Among its other suggestions, the *Government Statement on Unified Vocational Preparation*, encouraged further education establishments as well as other institutions to provide vocational preparation for young people making the tıansition from work to school.[1] The unified vocational preparation scheme is experimental, and may be described as being still at the pilot stage (see Section **10.2.**73).

5. The careers service is linked with the other statutory employment service, the Employment Service Division of the Manpower Services Commission, in that it is under the direction of the Secretary of State for Employment and has to undertake a large amount of statistical work. This latter function is an

---

1 *Government Statement on Unified Vocational Preparation*, Circular 6/76 (DES) and 104/76 (Welsh Office); cf *A Better Start in Working Life*, DE/DES, 1979 (See also Section **1.2.**45).

essential part of national manpower recording, and is highly relevant to planning.

6. **Procedures and methods**
How an authority might carry out its statutory duties and colleges might best arrange their careers services are questions to which there are at present no definite answers. The purpose here therefore will be to draw attention to existing practices and to demonstrate possible procedures. Careers advice in any institution will necessarily overlap with general guidance and counselling services (see Section **12.8.9**) and may well form an integral part of a student welfare system. The remainder of this sub-section is to be seen as a discussion mainly relating to further education.

7. It is the practice in some authorities to operate the careers service in colleges in a similar fashion to that obtaining in many schools: an authority careers officer visits the establishment, for example, one day a week; and the college may have a liaison system concerning its internal arrangements and the officer's function. The strength of such a system is dependent on the nature and efficiency of the liaison as well as the full development of the service and facilities. In other authorities, the view is taken that a careers service should always be fully available and be an integral part of the college's function. To this end, therefore, the practice exists of a full-time local authority careers officer being present in every large and medium sized college, and smaller colleges having the service of such a person for one half or three quarters of the time. There is also the belief that such local authority careers officers should be fully involved in college life: their presence should be recognised on the academic board, in the planning and operation of courses, and in admissions procedures. The responsibility of such officers remains to the local authority rather than to the college: responsibility to the college is only in the meeting of its requirements as agreed with the authority. The argument advanced in favour of this approach is that a careers service should be permanently available. Such availability allows the pattern of college life not to be disrupted by students having to miss classes to attend careers interviews; the students may seek advice formally and whenever necessary; better relationships can be formed and hence guidance will be more fruitful; and the student's potential career development will become part of his or her college life.

8. It is the practice in some colleges for a careers education system to be implemented. Such a system provides careers and further course information, individual guidance as well as indications of general "career geography" (that is, the demonstration of career routes and development), and arranges work experience. Some colleges possess a careers teacher as part of the staff establishment; such appointments may prove to be part of a developing trend. Where such appointments exist, the role of the local authority careers officers becomes of a more general advisory nature whereby contributions are made to the careers education programme where their experience is relevant and in the implementation of courses such as interview techniques, and methods of obtaining employment. Although there is overlap, it appears to be usual that where colleges have careers teachers

who are engaged in careers education and also have the services of a careers officer, they tend to allocate individual guidance to the careers officer. Whatever system is adopted it is important to avoid professional tensions between careers officers and teachers; specific functions should be designated, and full collaboration encouraged.

9. Some authorities have requested colleges to consider incorporating within their prospectuses a statement detailing careers policy, guidance and implementation. The benefits of such a statement are obvious, but colleges will need to be aware that such a statement involves making a contractual obligation (see Section **12.6.**14).

10. However a careers service is operated, it will require certain facilities. Basic physical necessities include: a room equipped with telephone, filing cabinet and bookshelves; full use of the college reprographic facilities; space for display materials; and an information point which contains all essential literature. Some colleges issue careers news-sheets and bulletins. How job vacancies are displayed is a subject of debate. It is argued that to provide a student with the best service is to allow maximum convenience by displaying all information in the college, rather than requiring the individual to leave the college premises to consult vacancy lists in a job centre or local authority careers office. If this practice is adopted, the college will need to decide whether "job sifting" on behalf of individuals should occur.

11. Whether the service is college or authority based, it is obvious that there will be staff able to contribute to it. Such persons, apart from their contact with the students whom they regularly teach, will be able to contribute to careers tutorial groups; to employ their personal knowledge or general interest in the field; and to extend the benefits of their experience where they have recently been working outside the education system. There is a clear link here with staff development policies (see Section **11.11.**17). A warning must be sounded however: the careers service of one authority at least has complained of college staff giving careers advice which was out of date; there must be provision for the continuing training of careers lecturers and teachers. In achieving the desired close collaboration between careers officers and teachers, there will probably be a need both for a careful demarcation of function, and for there to be a continuing emphasis on training.

12. Apart from the statutory requirements to keep records of advice given to students, it is generally felt that such records ought to be used as a basis for improving the service. The records obviously provide statistical information useful in advising future students, and can be linked to selected studies of employment in a particular field. Such follow-up of students leaving college can provide valuable information for both staff and students. It is useful if student comments on both the service and how they found employment are also collected. The keeping of records is normally the function of the local authority careers officers but, as part of the general need for close co-operation between careers teachers and officers, careers teachers or staff will also benefit from its provision. It is necessary to add that to safeguard both the

individual adviser and the institution, it is imperative that records of advice given are kept: students' legal rights and their remedies for discrimination and negligence must be remembered and observed (see Section **12.6.**20).

13. Although the practice is in decline, it continues to be a remarkable feature of existence that persons are selected for employment and other functions on the basis of an interview lasting half an hour. The careers interview of a set, short time has come under similar attack. The suggested alternative is that there should always be opportunities for follow up and further and continuing interview, as well as the student having ready access to the careers adviser. This practice clearly argues for a careers presence continually in the college.

14. The earlier careers advice is available, the better the service to the student. The student will also require early advice of how to contact careers personnel, and the procedures which have been adopted. In some colleges, careers staff are involved in the admissions and selection process, and similarly in induction. In many cases they are consulted as part of the referral process where a student has been rejected for a particular course but where it may be possible to advise of existing vacancies elsewhere; where a potential student clearly lacks motivation; and where a student requires advice on which course might be undertaken since at the time of application he or she has no clear idea of which career might be pursued.

15. It is important when undertaking a course that the student is made aware of the opportunities afforded. Careers officers have discovered that a student is often unaware that the course being followed is not one which will usually lead to employment, but rather a course enabling the student to undertake further study which does offer more reasonable employment propsects. Such an observation extends to work experience: in making the arrangements, colleges may need to consult with careers specialists concerning the needs and career prospects of the individual student. The preceding sentences tend to presume a student following a low level course. Careers officers have observed that much of their work is often with the less able but stress that advice should be given to all students, and that information provided by the service ought to be used by colleges, rather than be allowed to exist as a token fulfilment of an obligation.

16. Careers conventions in colleges have an important function. It is argued that a full involvement of employers both here and as a normal part of careers education is of great value, especially where employers and staff have full opportunity to meet and discuss their aims and needs. Platitudinous this may sound, but the wider such contact, the better the education service.

17. **The role of LEA careers officers in colleges of further education : discussion model**

Where careers officers currently function for most of their time in a college, their roles may be summarised thus:

(i) to provide information about careers, industries, occupations, employment, and further training and educational opportunities;

(ii) to establish and maintain a well publicised career information library which is readily available to students and staff;

(iii) to provide individual careers guidance based on a development process whereby such guidance is available to students throughout their course; and also to students who change their course, fail, or leave college prematurely;

(iv) to provide job vacancy information and introduce students to employers, to inform employers about colleges as sources of recruitment, and to keep students and staff informed of labour market trends and developments;

(v) to liaise with senior LEA careers officers, the Employment Service Division, Training Services Division, Professional and Executive Recruitment (an ESD service), and other local, regional and national agencies so that the college is linked into the main stream of careers, training and vacancy information;

(vi) to contribute to the careers education and vocational preparation of all courses at the planning, execution and evaluation stages, and to contribute to such college working parties and committees which have a bearing upon students' careers and employment;

(vii) to follow up students who have completed courses, where possible, in order to offer further help if required, and to obtain and maintain statistics relevant for the use of staff and students; and

(viii) to liaise closely with college careers teachers whose major responsibility is with careers education in its widest interpretation.

18. Careers advice provision: discussion check list questions

(i) If a college has a declared careers policy, where and how is it documented and to whom is it publicised?

(ii) In the staffing of careers education and guidance, where does the ultimate responsibility lie, and what are the time allowances and training and support allotted to all careers staff?

(iii) Where careers staff contribute to course planning, are they also involved in student selection, the provision of work opportunities, and in the vocational elements of the course?

(iv) Resource availability. The careers service will require finance, space, furnishing, reprographic facilities and clerical support.

(v) Information provision, housing, and access. What provision is made for the updating and expansion of information?

(vi) The careers provision content of each course will require investigation: what materials and methods are used; and is it to be voluntary, timetabled, or integrated?

(vii) In providing individual guidance and assessment, how are individual consultations organized, how are records kept and used, is there provision for psychological testing, and are parents involved?

(viii) Facilities for students to learn about job vacancies. In determining the effectiveness of the college in helping students to gain employment, it will be necessary to ask: if employment agencies are used, if the college arranges job interviews with employers; and if employers are encouraged to visit the college, provide work experience, and job vacancy lists?

(ix) Where provision is made for follow-up, how is the information collected and used, and with what success?

(x) In liaison with the community guidance services what is the involvement of the local careers service, the MSC, and the Further Education Information Service? (FEIS is discussed under Section **12.1.**8).

(xi) Course records. Where these are kept, are there recorded: the number of information queries, interviews, and specific careers education sessions; and placement activities?

19. **Careers advice in polytechnics**

It is usual for polytechnic careers services to be operated in a manner similar to that of university appointments boards. The careers service here tends to be institution based: staff in most instances are the employees of the institution itself rather than of the local careers service. While use of the polytechnic careers service is often by way of student self-referral, it has been found in some establishments that where well publicised group and tutorial careers sessions have been operated that student attendance and participation has demonstrated the merits of the exercise.

20. The employment market is well organized and clearly defined by way of the Association of Graduate Careers Advisory Services (AGCAS); the Standing Conference of Employers of Graduates (SCOEG); and the Central Services Unit (CSU) which is the national agency for the collection and dissemination of vacancies to universities and polytechnics.

21. The annual event occurring between January and March, popularly known as "the milk round", at which employers interview students is generally administered in accordance with a code of practice agreed by AGCAS, SCOEG and the NUS. The annual "job shop summer fairs" held in July in various regions are intended to fill new and still outstanding job vacancies. Other means of job finding, apart from via the press, include: direct introduction of students by careers staff to employer contacts; the CSU *Current* and *Forward Vacancy Lists* which are available to all final year and past students; the annual job vacancy directories; the AGCAS *Register of Graduate Employment and Training* (generally available to students for reference at Careers Centres); polytechnic sector vacancy lists; and the placing agencies of the various professional, private and national bodies.

REFERENCE

Employment and Training Act, 1948 Chapter 46, HMSO.
Employment and Training Act 1973, Chapter 50, HMSO.

The Careers Service, Dept. of Employment, 1975.
Government Statement on Unified Vocational Preparation, Circular 6/76 (DES) and 104/76 (Welsh Office).

Catherine Avent, *Practical Approaches to Careers Education,* Hobsons Press for CRAC, Bateman Street, Cambridge.
Exercises in Careers Education and *Further Exercises in Careers Education,* Careers Consultants, 12-14 Hill Rise, Richmond Hill, Richmond, Surrey TW10 6UA.
Michael Kirton, *Career Information : A Job Knowledge Index,* Heinemann, 1979.
Lesley Perrins, *Handbook,* Careers and Occupational Information Centre, Pennine Centre, 20-22 Holly Street, Sheffield S1 3GA.

10 OVERSEAS STUDENTS

1. Britain's law of nationality is confused by its relationship with immigration law. Successive Immigration Acts, EEC membership (see Section **6.1**) and responses to colonial responsibilities have rendered the law complex – illegal in international law according to some authorities – anomalous in places, and also subject to the wide discretionary powers of the Home Office. Governmental use of these powers varies. It is impossible therefore to give clear legal guidance as to what might be overseas students' rights in all cases (for example, under international law).[1] In order to provide an outline of the situation as it applies to colleges, the regulations in operation, and the advice of the Department of Education and Science are summarised below. These policies are those which obtain in practice at present. The subject of overseas students, therefore, will be considered in an overall sense.[2]

2. Rules made under the Immigration Act 1971 control the entry into and stay in the United Kingdom of persons who are not "patrial". Such persons are subject to immigration control. The Rules include provision for the admission of people ("passengers") coming for employment, or as students, visitors, or dependants.[3] They allow for the temporary admission of "passengers" seeking entry as students. A passenger will be admitted as a student if evidence satisfying each of the following conditions is produced:
   (i) that the person has been accepted for a course of study at a university, college of education or further education (maintained and non-maintained) or an independent or direct grant school; and
   (ii) that the course will occupy the whole or a substantial part of the person's time; and

---

1 A summary of these complex issues is contained in Ann Dummett, *Citizenship and Nationality*, Runnymede Trust (62, Chandos Place, London WC2). A shortened version is contained in *Further and Teacher Education in a Multi-Cultural Society*, NATFHE, 1979, pp.74-90.

2 It is possible to categorise overseas students in several ways. For example, divisions could be made thus: those who join existing courses; those for whom special courses are provided; those undertaking study on inter governmental agreements negotiated by the British Council; and refugee students. Operation of any such categories, however, is determined by the arrangements set out in this sub-section. Further, as the sub-section shows, there is the anomaly that some overseas students may be reckoned not as overseas students for fees purposes but still have to be classified as overseas students for awards purposes. (The Government is to categorize all EEC students as home students for fees purposes).

3 Copies of the Rules and their amendments can be obtained from HMSO. They are: *Statement of Immigration Rules for Control on Entry: Commonwealth citizens:* HC79; *Statement of Immigration Rules for Control after Entry; Commonwealth Citizens:* HC80; *Statement of Immigration Rules for Control on Entry: EEC and other non-Commonwealth nationals:* HC81; *Statement of Immigration Rules for Control after Entry: EEC and other non-Commonwealth nationals:* HC82. A person must be accepted for a full-time or sandwich course in order to be treated under the Immigration Rules. A full-time course is one which generally entails not less than 15 hours a week in organized day time study. A person wishing to visit this country for 6 months or less and attend a course of study which can be completed in that period may be treated as a visitor: studies here therefore will not be relevant to entry.

(iii) that the person has the means of meeting the cost of the course, and her or his own maintenance and that of any dependants during the course, and that he or she will leave when the course is completed.

An offer of a place at a maintained school does not entitle a passenger who does not otherwise qualify for admission to enter the United Kingdom as a student. The Government is proposing to make changes in the Immigration Rules. These proposals are summarised in Appendix 4, below. Paragraphs 2-13 and 29-31 should be read in conjunction with Appendix 4.

3. **The Race Relations Act and overseas students**

A discriminatory act is lawful if it is done to further any arrangements made by or with the approval of, or for the time being approved by, a Minister of the Crown. Thus, the decision by the Secretary of State, in the interests of containing public expenditure and working within limited educational resources, to offer guidance on the restriction of the numbers of overseas students admitted to the United Kingdom was not a contravention of the Race Relations Act 1976. Similarly, this exemption from the Act allows discriminatory arrangements in differential fees, hostel charges, admissions and discretionary awards.

4. **Admission to educational establishments**

The right of appeal against refusal of entry to the United Kingdom exists for all persons seeking admission as students. It is possible therefore that immigration officials, witnesses and students will wish to contact colleges in cases of doubt. Colleges may also be consulted by the immigration service over other cases of difficulty arising at the ports, and may be invited to provide or nominate a qualified person to assess the academic suitability of an intending student. The DES observes therefore that it would be helpful if academic staff with knowledge of overseas students were available at colleges during the summer vacation.

5. Generally, the immigration service will regard a firm letter of acceptance from a college as *prima facie* evidence of the holder's ability to follow the course, and thus be eligible for entrance. The decision as to whether a student complies with the institution's academic entrance standards remains with the institution. Where a college is unable initially to make a firm offer to a student (because of doubts concerning her or his financial resources, for example) it is appropriate to issue a letter of conditional acceptance which states the points requiring further verification. Advice on educational qualifications can usually be obtained via the British Council. The firm acceptance letter should be sent as soon as the verification matters have been resolved. Where in cases of serious doubt immigration officials call for an independent academic assessment, this is usually carried out by the college concerned but occasionally it may be necessary to arrange in consultation with the college for local academic assessors to be involved. Final decisions on academic suitability, however, are always taken by the college. As immigration officers are required by law to satisfy themselves that a candidate is willing and able to follow a course of study, it is advisable for students to establish their *bona fides*. They can do this by providing

suitable documentation before leaving their home countries. This will usually entail completing the entry clearance procedures operated by the United Kingdom high commissions and embassies.

6. Except where students come from countries for which the UK has visa requirements[4] (which entail students being required to hold a visa on every occasion on which they enter the country), an entry clearance is optional. However, colleges may wish to advise students that use of the clearance system can help to avoid difficulty at the port of arrival since it is only on exceptional grounds (medical, for example) that possessors of entry clearance are refused admission; and to equip themselves with a certificate of medical examination and vaccination from their homeland in order to satisfy the requirements of the port of arrival medical inspection. In order that clearances and certificates can be obtained in time, colleges should send their letters of final acceptance as soon as possible

7. Most overseas students on whose behalf the British Council (see Section **2.6.**11) makes application are sponsored by a government department, such as the Ministry of Overseas Development, or by international or other official scholarship agencies. Correspondence here should be with the British Council and not the student unless prior agreement with the Council has been made. Colleges may also wish to contact the Council to check the equivalence or otherwise of British and overseas qualifications. As colleges should ensure that sponsorship carries full financial support, first correspondence should always be to the relevant embassy, consulate, or high commission where application has originated from such a source, as it is to be assumed that such bodies are applying on behalf of government sponsored nationals. Where applicants approach colleges individually claiming sponsorship, colleges are advised to refer to the appropriate body for verification.

8. Very few students are sponsored. The DES advises certain procedures for private overseas students. The entry clearance system by means of entry certificates is known and used in Commonwealth countries. If colleges advise students of the system, they are asked to send a copy of the letter to the appropriate British Mission. Students using this system have to provide the entry certificate officer (ECO) with documentary evidence of educational qualifications. Colleges should identify precisely the written qualifications required. The ECO will have regard to the applicant's financial standing, and may refer the matter to the Home Office which may in turn contact the college. The college will be notified by the ECO of the decision. The college remains the assessor of educational standards.

---

4 Countries for which the UK has visa requirements are:- Afghanistan, Albania, Angola, Benin (formerly Dahomey), Bhutan, Bulgaria, Burma, Burundi, Cambodia (now Kampuchea), Cameroon, Comoros, Cape Verde, Central African Republic, Chad, China, Congo, Cuba, Czechoslovakia, Egypt, Gabon, German Democratic Republic, Guinea, Equatorial Guinea, Guinea Bissau, Hungary, Indonesia, Iraq, Jordan, Korea (North), Laos, Lebanon, Liberia, Libya, Madagascar, Mali, Mauritania, Mongolia, Mozambique (Maputo), Nepal, Oman, Philippines, Poland, Romania, Rwanda, Sao Tome e Principe, Saudi Arabia, Senegal, Somali Democratic Republic, Soviet Union, Sudan, Syria, Thailand, Togo, Upper Volta, Vietnam, Yemen (North), Yemen (South), Zaire.

9. In the case of students coming from countries for which the UK requires a visa, British representatives in those countries can advise about visas but are not usually in a position to verify *bona fides*. Where advice on visa procedures is required, colleges should contact the Visa Section, Migration and Visa Department, Foreign and Commonwealth Office, 4th Floor, Clive House, Petty France, London SW1H 9HD. Foreign nationals who do not require a visa may apply to a British embassy or consulate to ascertain in advance if they are eligible for admission.

10. Where a student applies through his or her own country's authorities, receives their support and has their placing services made available, it must be remembered that such sponsorship does not necessarily guarantee academic suitability. Therefore, Commonwealth citizens should still apply for entry clearance. Even in sponsorship cases the Visa Officer or ECO will still need to assess suitability by checking qualifications documentation.

11. The DES advises that except where an applicant's fees will be met out of public funds, in all cases students – indigenous and from overseas – be required to pay a substantial fee deposit before acceptance is made. However, the Department concedes that deposit procedures should not be too rigid, in order to cater for students from countries with stringent exchange control legislation. Deposits should be returned if a student does not take up an allotted place. It is important, especially for the purposes of the immigration officer, that students' deposit receipts and letters of acceptance should be such as to demonstrate their authenticity beyond doubt.

12. As there are restrictions on overseas visitors taking employment in Britain (see also Appendix 4) colleges should warn applicants that their finances should be such as to maintain themselves unaided throughout their stay. Overseas students may obtain vacation employment only with the consent of the Department of Employment, the conditions in each case of employment being: confirmation of the applicant's student status; that the terms of employment offered are similar to those prevailing in a similar area for similar work; and that no suitable local labour is available. Employers must apply to the Employment Service Division of the Manpower Services Commission for consent. Students refused permission on entry to Britain to take employment may apply to the Home Office (Immigration and Nationality Department, Lunar House, Wellesley Road, Croydon CR9 2BY) for a variation of the entry conditions. In the case of students following sandwich courses, application by the student or the college giving full details (full name, date of birth, address in the UK, passport number and issuing country, course and duration of study) to the Department of Employment, Overseas Labour Section, (Training Unit), Ebury Bridge House, Ebury Bridge Road, London SW1W 8PY will normally result in a letter of approval being given, on the condition that the employment is certified by the college to be an integral part of the course. Subsequent employment resulting from and as part of the course will not require further ratification.

13. Since applicants for an extension of their residence period have no right of

appeal if they apply after the expiry of their stay and are refused, it is important for application to be made before the relevant date. Overseas students are admitted for a limited period, generally a year, but leave to remain will usually be given provided certain conditions are observed and the course continued. Colleges here may be asked to confirm that the student is continuing the course. It can be permissible for visitors to have their stay extended if the purpose of their visit has changed (for example, to undertake a course of study). In accepting a student for a course under such circumstances, colleges should indicate in their letters of acceptance that admission is subject to a Home Office decision to extend the stay.

14. Regardless of their purpose, EEC nationals are normally admitted for six months but if they wish to stay longer they should apply for a residence permit, sending evidence to the Home Office of course enrolment and their means of support. Commonwealth students do not have to register with the police but all foreign students, including EEC nationals staying for more than six months, are required to register and pay the registration fee.

15. The DES uses the term "specified student" to describe students not resident in the UK, nor ordinarily resident in the UK, Channel Islands or Isle of Man, for a period of three years prior to the beginning of a course of study. The period is one year where a student had previously attended a full-time or sandwich course of advanced further education in the UK. Specified students are liable to the operation of the quota restricting the numbers of overseas students in further and higher education and also to the payment of larger fees. Fees for ordinary students are at present less by approximately one quarter than those for which specified overseas students are liable under the Department's annual recommendations. The restrictions imposed by the creation of the specified student category have meant that young persons joining their families in this country have become liable to the larger fees and quotas, as have persons who formerly qualified for more generous treatment by having been over 21 and being with one parent ordinarily resident here for one year, or being married for at least a year to someone ordinarily resident in the UK. However the specified category was devised as a result of the Race Relations Act which distinguished between ordinary residence and residence: because the Act refers only to discrimination in respect of a person's ordinary residence or residence but not that of his or her parents or spouse, the Secretary of State has not found it possible to approve arrangements in favour of those categories of student previously subject to more generous treatment. Specified students are also liable for the payment of further fees charged by external examining and validating bodies and by student unions. There are two exceptions to fees liability:-

(i) a person who does not attain the age of 19 before the end of the academic year in question is not to be charged a tutition fee above the standard fee for the course in that year; and

(ii) fee arrangements are to be without prejudice to fee remission in the case of particular students or classes of students where such action is appropriate and does not involve discrimination against other students. This provision is made to prevent unlawful discrimination under the Race Relations Act.

16. It was announced in July 1979 (and confirmed in the White Paper, Cmnd. 7746, of November 1979) that from September 1980 the Government intended that new students from overseas should be charged the "full cost" of their tuition fees.[5] At current prices and fee levels, this would raise the annual fee cost for a degree course by over 150%. (Fees are also discussed in Section **1.3.** 33). It is essential that individual students should be advised of exactly what "full cost" is. At present the charging of "economic costs" appears to be somewhat muddled, for in the case of accommodation and boarding charges (see paragraph 21) it appears that some local authorities have indirectly provided subsidies.

17. Since the large increases of fees for overseas students during the last decade, while recruitment of such students has also risen, there has been a decline in numbers of those coming from the poorer countries. Half of the overseas students currently in Britain come from the Commonwealth. Certain grants are provided for Commonwealth students (see Section **3.**13), and this practice is to continue. In November 1976 there were 27,260 Commonwealth students undertaking public sector courses in England and Wales, and 20,386 foreign students. Of those numbers, the Commonwealth students were evenly split between advanced and non-advanced courses; whereas two thirds of the foreign students were pursuing non-advanced courses.[6] The United Kingdom Council for Overseas Student Affairs (UKCOSA) considers that the charging of full cost fees will cause many overseas students to go elsewhere.

18. The Department has advised in Circular 8/77 that the numbers of specified students should be restricted. The restriction is to be to the numbers of such students, irrespective of when they began their course, who were studying in the relevant institution during the academic year 1975/76. Thus the "quota" of overseas students for admission in any year is to be that which will maintain "as nearly as may be" the same level of overseas student presence in a college as obtained in 1975/76. However, this quota has the appearance, if not the reality of being discretionary. The Department's advice exempts colleges from the provisions of the Race Relations Act, and may be seen as returning to authorities the discretion removed from them by the Act. Where colleges recruit significantly more students than would maintain the 1975/76 level, they are no longer covered by the exemption obtained for them by the Secretary of State. The DES has no direct power to influence college policy

---

5 The DES has stated that the subsidy for overseas students amounted annually to £100m but, using the same official figures, the London Conference on Overseas Students and UKCOSA have calculated that an annual profit of £50m is made from overseas students. The difference in approach is: the DES takes the average cost of a student, multiplies by the number of overseas students, and deducts fees paid; and the other method is to assume that our education system exists primarily for home students, to calculate the extra costs incurred in providing for overseas students, and to estimate the financial benefits from overseas students' imports of foreign exchange, research input, and from overseas trade spin-off.

6 *Further Education,* DES Statistics of Education 1976 Vol. 2, England and Wales, HMSO, 1979, table 14, pp.22-3. The largest numbers of Commonwealth students were from Malaysia (6,859) Nigeria (4,243), Hong Kong (2,804), Sri Lanka (2,219), Kenya (1,171) and Cyprus (1,127); and the largest numbers of foreign students were from Iran (7,105), Greece (1,500), Jordan (806), Pakistan (762), USA (673) and Venezuela (647).

here. Colleges taking unilateral action however have two main factors to consider. Firstly, if they act outside the Department's advice they are fully liable under the Race Relations Act: there must be no discrimination. In practical terms, one obvious danger is where colleges attempt to pick and choose on grounds other than the strictly academic in their recruitment of students. Such action would be unlawful. Secondly, there are budgetary considerations. If recruitment results in the 1975/76 levels of overseas students in a college being significantly exceeded, then the college will need to have the extra budgetary considerations approved by its maintaining authority. If the authority approves the increase, and provided that the provisions of the Race Relations Act are observed, then a college may recruit as it wishes. It will be appreciated, however, that, to put it mildly, these conditions may not be easy to obtain in all circumstances (see also Section **1.3.**7).

19. Authorities may refuse to make awards to overseas students not qualifying as home students, but awards may be made where this appears appropriate to the authority and does not involve discrimination against other students which is unlawful under the Race Relations Act. The DES has asked authorities "to consider sympathetically exceptional cases of hardship" for fee exemption. There remains another route to obtain an overseas student quota at variance with 1975/76 levels. It is possible to apply to the Department for the Secretary of State to make a further exemption under the Race Relations Act, or to include such special provisions under the exemption already made. Thus an authority may have special arrangements made on its particular behalf. This is the case in respect of the Inner London Education Authority.

20. Although the quota of specified students may have been admitted, further specified students may be admitted where there are exceptional circumstances which justify such action in each particular case. Where an institution has expanded as the result of a merger since 1 September 1975 and consequently has more facilities available, its specified student quota is nonetheless determined in accordance with the 1975/76 figures for the single institution then in existence: it is not possible to combine figures where a new institution is composed of others which have now ceased to exist. A college should inform and seek advice from the DES where it has difficulty in making arrangements for its overseas student quota because, for example, abnormally small numbers of such students were admitted in the year beginning 1 September 1975.

21. **Accommodation and boarding charges**

The Secretaries of State for Education and Science and Wales have approved arrangements which provide for economic costs to be charged to specified students for the provision of residential accommodation with or without board. Such arrangements do not apply to a person admitted, or seeking admission, to a course for whom the sections of the Race Relations Act apply concerning the special needs of racial groups in regard to education or the provision of education for persons not ordinarily resident in Great Britain (see under Sections **11.6.**3 and **12.6.**2-13). Hence, except where authorities have decided to treat overseas students as home students, the DES considers that the full economic cost of board and accommodation should be met by specified students or their sponsors; and that such cost includes:

(i) loan charges, rent or other capital expenditure on hostel buildings and on their equipping and initial furnishing;

(ii) the cost of maintaining the fabric of the buildings;

(iii) rates, taxes and insurance premiums payable in respect of the buildings; and

(iv) any allowances or salary paid to any warden residing in the buildings.

22. The Secretaries of State have approved arrangements whereby students ordinarily resident in Scotland, Northern Ireland, the Channel Islands or the Isle of Man are to be charged full economic costs. This is because, although not overseas students, such persons do not belong to England or Wales. However, it should be noted that in the case of students from Scotland and Northern Ireland supported by the Northern Ireland or Scottish Education Departments that those departments have made arrangements for the direct payment of the difference between the standard subsidised cost and the full cost. Colleges and authorities should send claims to the relevant Departments and not to individual students.

23. So that students or their sponsors may know in advance the amount of fee to be paid, it will be advisable to make early estimates. It is important also to consider the law of contract (see Section **12.6.**14): students are entitled to know the fees for which they are liable, and that the amounts of such fees are subject to annual review.

24. The Department states that no residual costs in respect of accommodation for students from other than England or Wales should fall on the pooling system.

25. **Welfare** (see also Section **12.8**)
The Department has issued a circular containing recommendations for the welfare of overseas students in further education. These are summarised below together with other issues which are relevant.

26. It is important for the student to be made aware of the full costs entailed in undertaking a course. Students should be advised to arrive in the UK equipped with sufficient initial currency, and on a weekday in working hours so that the college might assist in any difficulties arising at the port of arrival. Colleges are recommended to request the submission of a medical report prior to acceptance even though it may be difficult for the college to check its validity.

27. Consideration could be given by colleges to devising an information pack for both tutors and staff covering all arrival and welfare procedures. This is especially important in that overseas students generally attach great significance to their relationships with tutors. Staff therefore will probably find themselves expected to undertake a wide role and will need to possess

knowledge of the students and available welfare services. As in other welfare areas, the questions of staff contact time remission may be appropriate as well as a full integration of college welfare operations, which should include: personal tutorial facilities, regular welfare interviews, student union involvement; and advisory and counselling services equipped to deal with the problems of anxiety, loneliness, overwork, and the strain of having to communicate in a foreign language, to all of which overseas students are particularly prone.

28. It is important, especially where families are involved, that overseas students obtain suitable living accommodation. They are likely to experience more difficulties in the search for suitable accommodation than those encountered by indigenous students. Colleges should not only make such difficulties clear but inform the students of the degree to which they can assist, encourage students to travel ahead of their families in order to search for accommodation, or make its securing easier. A college approved lodging system has been found to be most appropriate in many cases. It may be appropriate to send intending students lists of local guest houses to conduct their search. Information concerning overseas student hostels is available from the British Council.

29. Accommodation officers will require full knowledge of the problems which overseas students are likely to face. Whilst college accommodation provides one answer, students ought to be fully informed of its cost and also of its catering facilities. This latter observation extends to general catering arrangements: the form of diet provided by our educational institutions may not be entirely suitable to overseas students, whatever accolades it achieves from British citizens accustomed to its particular virtues.

30. In giving financial advice, it will already have been noted that it is advisable to inform students of their full liabilities, which will include annual fee revisions and vacation employment. It will also be appropriate, however unwelcome, to inform students of the rates of inflation to which Britain is subject. Guidance on educational charity provision might be considered, and colleges may wish in advance to consider arrangements which may be made when political events in a student's home country separate him or her, temporarily or permanently, from the means of financial support (and similarly where the student's sponsor does not make grant payments promptly). UKCOSA can assist those in financial difficulties by representing cases of hardship to appropriate charities.

31. The Department recommends that students new to Britain should have introductory talks and courses which might include the following:-
   (i) life in lodgings and college;
   (ii) information about the National Health Service and the necessity of registering with a doctor;
   (iii) social conventions, local services and facilities;
   (iv) methods of study;
   (v) immigration requirements and employment restriction, including police registration, renewal of permission to stay before expiry, re-entry procedures; and

(vi) availability of English language teaching and tuition facilities, and peculiarities of colloquial and local expressions.

To this list might be added items such as transport, including student rail travel arrangements, banking facilities, vehicle licensing laws and insurance regulations. The Department advises consultation of the biannual British Council publication: *How to live in Britain.* The advice of the British Council, NUS, and UKCOSA should also be sought. The DES also advises colleges to be prepared to give help in English reading and linguistic skills. English testing services are available through the overseas and regional offices of the British Council. Introduction to the local community is both necessary and advisable: religious, voluntary, cultural, social, sporting, and political bodies should be involved.

32. Regional organizations for overseas student welfare exist in some areas. Information concerning them is available from the British Council or UKCOSA. The DES advises that staff with responsibilities for the welfare of overseas students should be able regularly to attend training courses and conferences wherever possible. UKCOSA, among other organizations, operates such courses. Other bodies have argued that as welfare problems associated with overseas students should not be treated lightly, nor easily be delegated to teaching staff, that the DES should positively encourage local authorities to appoint properly trained welfare officers who would deal with all college welfare issues. It is certainly important that there should be a designated staff member with responsibility for overseas students.

33. NATFHE has campaigned vigorously on the issue of provision for overseas students. Its policy is set out in its publication, *Further and Teacher Education in a Multi-Cultural Society.* Reference might be made especially to pp 90-2.

APPENDIX 1

ADDRESSES OF BRITISH MISSIONS OVERSEAS

ANTIGUA*	Labour Commissioner, Labour Department, St. John's.
AUSTRALIA	British Passport Office, British High Commission, Commonwealth Avenue, (P.O. Box 15) Canberra.
	British Consulate-General, 8th Floor, 70 Pirie Street, Adelaide.
	British Consulate-General, BP House, 193 Northquay, Brisbane.
	British Consulate-General, CML Building, 330, Collins Street, Melbourne.
	British Consulate-General, Prudential Building, 95, St. George's Terrace, Perth, Western Australia.
	British High Commission, Gold Fields House, 1, Alfred Street, Sydney Cove, Sydney, 2,000, New South Wales.
BAHAMAS	British High Commission, Bitco Building, (3rd Floor), East Street, P.O. Box N7516, Nassau.
BANGLADESH	British High Commission, 75, Indira Road, Tejgaon, (P.O. Box 90), Dacca.
BARBADOS	United Kingdom Entry Certificate Office, c/o British High Commission, Barclays Bank Buildings, 147/9 Roebuck Street, Bridgetown.
BELIZE	Officer-in-Charge of Immigration, Immigration Department, Queen Street, Belize.
BERMUDA	Chief Immigration Officer, Allenhurst Building, Hamilton.
BOTSWANA	British High Commission, (Private Bag No. 23), Queen's Road, Gaborone.
BRITISH VIRGIN* ISLANDS	The Administrator's Office, Tortola, British Virgin Islands.
BRUNEI	British High Commission, Jalan Residency, Bander Seri Begawan.
CANADA	British High Commission, 80 Elgin Street, Ottawa, 4, Ontario.
	British Consulate, Centennial Building, 10th Floor, 1645 Granville Street, Halifax, Nova Scotia.
	British Consulate, 500 Grand-Allee Est, Suite 707, Quebec, P.Q.
	British Consulate-General, 635 Dorchester Boulevard West, Montreal, 2, PQ.
	British Consulate-General, 8th Floor, 200 University Avenue, Toronto, Ontario.

	British Consulate-General, Suite 1404, Three McCauley Plaza, 10025, Jasper Avenue, Edmonton, Alberta.
	British Consulate-General, 4th Floor, Bank of Nova Scotia Building, 602 West Hastings Street, Vancouver, 2, British Columbia.
CAYMAN ISLANDS	Chief Immigration Officer, Department of Immigration, Cayman Islands, BW1.
CYPRUS	British High Commission, Alexander Pallis Street, (P.O. Box 1978), Nicosia.
DOMINICA*	The Labour Commissioner, Department of Labour, Roseau.
FALKLAND ISLANDS	The Chief Secretary, Port Stanley.
FIJI	British High Commission, Civic Centre, Stinson Parade, P.O. Box 1355, Suva, Fiji.
GAMBIA (THE)	British High Commission, 78B Wellington Street, (P.O. Box 507), Banjul.
GHANA	Consular Section, British High Commission, Ring Road East, P.O. Box 296, Accra.
GIBRALTAR	United Kingdom Entry Certificate Office, Colonial Secretariat.
GILBERT ISLANDS	Principal Immigration Officer, Bairiki, Tarawa.
GRENADA*	Labour Commissioner, St. Georges.
GUYANA	Passport Office, British High Commission, (P.O. Box 625), 44 Main Street, Georgetown, Guyana.
HONG KONG	Director of Immigration, The Immigration Department, International Building, 141 Des Voex Road Central.
INDIA	British High Commission, Chanakyapuri, New Delhi, 21, 1100-21.
	British Deputy High Commission, Mercantile Bank Building, Mahatma Gandhi Road, Bombay, 1.
	British Deputy High Commission, 1 Ho Chi Minh Sarani, Calcutta, 16.
	British Deputy High Commission in South India 150A Anna Salai, (P.O. Box 3710) Madras, 2.
JAMAICA	British High Commission, P.O. Box 575, Trafalgar Road, Kingston 10.
KENYA	British High Commission, Bruce House, Standard Street, P.O. Box 30465, Nairobi.
LESOTHO	British High Commission, (P.O. Box 521), Maseru.
MALAWI	British High Commission, Victoria Avenue, P.O. Box 479, Blantyre.

MALAYSIA	British High Commission, (P.O. Box 1030), Wisma Damansara Jalan Semantan, Kuala Lumpur.
MALTA	British High Commission, 7, St. Anne Street, Floriana, Malta GC.
MAURITIUS	British High Commission, P.O. Box 586, Cerne House, Chaussee, Port Louis.
MONTSERRAT*	The Labour Commissioner, Labour Department Plymouth, Monserrat.
NEW HEBRIDES	Acting Commandant of Police, British Residency, Vila.
NEW ZEALAND	The British High Commission, Reserve Bank of New Zealand Building, 9th Floor, 2 The Terrace, (P.O. Box 1812), Wellington, C1.
	British Consulate-General, 9th Floor, Norwich Union Building, Queen Street, Auckland, 1.
NIGERIA	British High Commission, Eleke Crescent, Victoria Island (Private Mail Bag 12136), Lagos.
	British Deputy High Commission, Finance Corporation Building, (Private Mail Bag 5010), Lebanon Street, Ibadan.
	British Deputy High Commission, United Bank for Africa Building, (Private Mail Bag 2096), Hospital Road, Kaduna.
PAKISTAN	British Embassy, Diplomatic Enclave, Ramna 5 P.O. Box 1122, Islamabad.
	British Consulate-General, York Place, Runnymede Lane, Port Trust Estate, Clifton, Karachi.
PAPUA NEW GUINEA	British High Commission, United Church Building, (3rd Floor), Douglas Street, Port Moresby.
ST. CHRISTOPHER* (ST KITTS)	The Labour Commissioner, Labour Department, Basseterre.
ST HELENA	Superintendent of Police and Immigration Officer, Police Headquarters, Jamestown.
ST LUCIA*	The Labour Commissioner, Labour Department, Manoel Street, Castries.
ST VINCENT*	The Labour Commissioner, Labour Department, Kingstown.
SEYCHELLES	British High Commission, P.O. Box 161, Victoria.
SIERRA LEONE	British High Commission, Standard Bank, Sierra Leone Building, Wallace Johnson Street, Freetown.
SINGAPORE	British High Commission, Taglin Circus, Tanglin Road, Singapore 10.
SRI LANKA	British High Commission, Galle Road, Kollupitiya (P.O. Box 1433), Colombo 3.

SWAZILAND	British High Commission, Allister Miller Street, Mbabane.
TANZANIA	British High Commission, Permanent House, Independence Avenue, (P.O. Box 9200) Dar es Salaam.
TONGA	British High Commission, P.O. Box 56, Nuku'alofa.
TRINIDAD AND TOBAGO	British High Commission, P.O. Box 778, 4th Floor Furness House, 90 Independence Square, Port of Spain.
TUVALU	Chief of Police, Funafuti, Tuvalu (Ellice Islands) via Fini.
ZAMBIA	British High Commission, Independence Avenue, (P.O. Box RW50) Lusaka.

*All entry certificate applications made to offices in Antigua, British Virgin Islands, Dominica, Montserrat, St. Christopher, St. Lucia and St. Vincent are dealt with by the entry certificate officer in Barbados.

No correspondence should be sent to these territories or to Anguilla. All applications to the Grenada Office are dealt with by the ECO at Port of Spain, Trinidad: no correspondence should be sent to Grenada.

APPENDIX 2

FURTHER SOURCES OF ADVICE

The following bodies are among those which will be able to advise on matters affecting overseas students:-

British Council,
Overseas Students Services Department,
11, Portland Place,
London W1N 4EJ.

Central Bureau for Educational Visits and Exchanges,
43, Dorset Street,
London W1H 3FN.

Commission for Racial Equality,
Elliot House,
10/12 Allington Street,
London SW1E 5EH.

CRE Regional Offices:
Daimler House,
33, Paradise Circus,
Queensway,
Birmingham B1 2BS.

Third Floor,
Scottish Life House
Bridge Street,
Manchester M3 3BG.

Birbeck House,
Trinity Square,
Nottingham NG1 4AX.

133, The Headrow,
Leeds LS1 5QX.
(A list of Community Relations Offices, which are situated throughout the country, can be obtained from the CRE).

Commonwealth Institute,
Library and Resource Centre,
Kensington High Street,
London W8 6NG.

Commonwealth Students' Children's Society,
4, Cambridge Road,
London NW1.

Community and Race Relations Units (CRRU),
British Council of Churches,
10, Eaton Gate,
London SW1W 9BT.

Centre for Information and Advice on Educational Disadvantage,[1]
11, Anson Road,
Manchester M14 5BY.

Educational Grants Advisory Service,
26, Bedford Square,
London WC1.

Institute of Race Relations (IRR),
247 Pentonville Road,
London N1 9NG.

International Students' House,
229, Great Portland Street,
London W1.

Joint Council for the Welfare of Immigrants,
44, Theobalds Road,
London WC1.

National Union of Students,
International Department,
3, Endsleigh Street,
London WC1H 0DU.

The Runnymede Trust,
62, Chandos Place,
London WC2 4HG.

United Kingdom Council for Overseas Student Affairs (UKCOSA),
60, Westbourne Grove,
London W2 5FG.

Voluntary Committee on Overseas Aid and Development (VOCAD),
Parnell House,
25, Wilton Road,
London SW1V 1JS.

World University Service,
20 Compton Terrace,
London N1.

---

1 In November 1979 the Government announced its intention to withdraw financial support from this body, thus presumably forcing it to close.

APPENDIX 3

ETHNIC ORGANIZATIONS AND CENTRES

Africa Centre,
38, King Street,
London WC2.

Afro-Caribbean Education Resource Project,
275, Kennington Lane,
London SE11.

Black Peoples Information Centre,
301, Portobello Road,
London W.10.

Hindu Centre,
7, Cedars Road,
London E15.

or:-

39, Grafton Terrace,
London NW5.

Islamic Cultural Centre,
Regents Lodge,
146, Park Road,
London NW8.

India Centre
83, Plumstead Common Road,
London SE18.

Pakistan Society,
37, Sloane Street,
London SW1.

West Indian – African Community Association,
206, Evelyn Street,
Deptford,
London SE8.

West Indian Students Centre,
1, Collingham Gardens,
London SW5.

APPENDIX 4

PROPOSALS FOR REVISION OF THE IMMIGRATION RULES

1. The White Paper[1] published in November 1979 indicated the Government's intention shortly to lay before Parliament a statement of comprehensive new Immigration Rules. The proposals have been subject to considerable criticism. It is impossible at the time of writing exactly to predict which changes will be carried into effect. However, the proposals affecting education itemised below are likely to be implemented. Interestingly, the proposals were issued at the same time as the Commission for Racial Equality began proceedings against the Home Office concerning its refusal to allow the Commission to carry out a formal investigation into its immigration procedures.

2. It is proposed to consolidate all the provisions affecting Commonwealth and foreign citizens into one Immigration Rules document.

3. Passengers seeking entry as visitors for the purpose of study are to be required to satisfy the entry clearance officer that they can meet maintenance, accommodation, (including that of any dependants) and course costs without having to work, or have recourse to public funds. Entry may be granted for a period appropriate to the length of the course and the student's means, with a strict condition restricting freedom to take employment: refusal would be the normal course if foreign students applied to be allowed to take work after their entry. Entry may be allowed for a short period where the conditions are not satisfied, but the passenger can satisfy the Immigration officer that study intentions are genuine and realistic. Otherwise, a passenger arriving without an entry clearance seeking entry as a student is to be refused admission. It is proposed that dependants of students would be prohibited from taking employment.

4. In addition to the present requirements regarding the duration of a student's stay, it is proposed that unless attendance on the course is and was regular, and that the student is able to maintain and accommodate him or herself without working or have recourse to public funds, an extension of stay is to be refused. Extension is proposed also to be refused if there is reason to believe that the student does not intend to leave at the end of his or her studies. It is further proposed that extensions of stay should not be granted to students who appear to be moving from one course to another without any intention of bringing their studies to a close: extension is proposed to be refused if it would lead to more than four years being spent on short courses (a short course is defined as being one of less than two years, but includes a longer course where this is broken off before completion). Overseas students financed by the UK Government, an international scholarship agency, or by their home government, are proposed to have their stay limited to the duration of their award, and not thereafter normally to be eligible to remain for further studies. Visitors and students currently may be granted extensions to stay as trainees if the Department of Employment considers the offer of training to be satisfactory; but it is proposed that the qualification be added that the intention to leave the UK on completion of training be not in doubt.

5. One significant overall effect of the proposals is that persons admitted for temporary purposes such as visits or studies would not be eligible to remain for another temporary purpose if this carried with it the prospect of eventual settlement.

---

1 *Proposals for revision of the Immigration Rules*, Cmnd. 7750, HMSO, 1979.

REFERENCE

Commonwealth Immigration Act 1968, Chapter 9, HMSO.
Immigration Act, 1971, Chapter 77, HMSO.
Immigration Act 1971; A General Guide for Commonwealth Citizens, HMSO.
Immigration Act 1971; A General Guide for E.E.C. and other Non-Commonwealth Nationals, HMSO.
Proposals for revision of the Immigration Rules, Cmnd. 7750, HMSO, 1979.
Race Relations Act 1976, Chapter 74, HMSO.

Fees for Students from Outside the United Kingdom Attending Full-Time and Sandwich Courses in Establishments of Further Education, DES Administrative Memorandum 14/67, 20 April 1967.
Immigration Act, 1971, DES Administrative Memorandum, 4/73; Welsh Education Office 4/73, 6 March 1973.
Health Services for Students on Full-time and Sandwich Courses, DES Further Education College Letter, 5/76, 30 September 1976.
Tuition Fees in Further Education 1977-78, DES Circular 1/77, 14 January 1977.
Tuition Fees and Admissions to Further Education Establishments and Awards: Race Relations Act 1976, DES Circular 8/77, 18 August 1977.
Tuition Fees and Admission to Further Education Establishments and Awards: Race Relations Act 1976, DES Circular 8/78; Welsh Office Circular 80/78, 20 June 1978.
Tuition Fees and Admission to Further Education Establishments and Awards: Race Relations Act 1976, DES Voluntary College Letter 5/78.
Admission of Overseas Students to Courses of Further Education, DES Circular 14/78; Home Office Circular 160/78; Welsh Office Circular 131/78, 11 October 1978.
Welfare of Overseas Students in Establishments of Further Education, DES Circular 15/78; Welsh Office Circular 110/78, 11 October 1978.
Accommodation and Boarding Charges for Students Coming from Outside England and Wales, DES Further Education College Letter, 7/78, 5 December 1978.
Race Relations Act 1976: Accommodation and Boarding Charges, DES Circular 17/78; Welsh Office Circular 161/78, 6 December 1978.
Tuition Fees and Admissions to Further Education Establishments and Awards 1979-80 Race Relations Act 1976, DES Circular 5/79, 12 July 1979.

Ann Dummett, *Citizenship and Nationality,* Runnymede Trust.
Education Charities, NUS.
Freedom to Study, a report by the Grubb Institute, Overseas Students Trust, 1979.
Further and Teacher Education in a Multi-Cultural Society, NATFHE, 1979.
How to live in Britain, British Council.
Higher Education in the United Kingdom: a handbook for overseas students and their advisers, British Council and the Association of Commonwealth Universities.
NUS Student Welfare Manual, NUS. (The leaflets, *Overseas Students – Immigration Regulations* and *Tuition Fees for Home and Overseas Students* are particularly relevant. The leaflets are available separately or as part of the set comprising the *Manual.*
Overseas Students in Britain: a handbook for all who are interested in their well-being, British Council.
Overseas Students in Further and Higher Education, Coombe Lodge Report, Vol. 10 No.6, 1977
Scholarships Guide for CWPG Students, Association of Commonwealth Universities.
Statistics of Overseas Students in Britain, British Council.
Study Abroad, UNESCO.
The Grants Register, Macmillan.
The Loss of the Right of Appeal, Joint Council for the Welfare of Immigrants.
UKCOSA News: Journal of the U.K. Council for Overseas Student Affairs.
UKCOSA Guidance Leaflets: a source of reference for those working with overseas students.
Young Visitors to Britain, Central Bureau for Educational Visits and Exchanges.

11 PROVISION FOR THE HANDICAPPED

1. Legal provision for the handicapped is made by the Chronically Sick and Disabled Persons Act, 1970, Amended 1976. The Act may be summarised for the purposes of colleges thus:

   (i) All local authorities have a duty to inform themselves of the number of persons within their area to whom the Act applies, to publish general information on the services for them provided by the authority, and to ensure that persons availing themselves of those services shall be informed of other services relevant to their needs.

   (ii) Where satisfied that the case applies, the authority must provide for chronically sick and disabled persons where they have need: lecturers, games, outings or other recreational activities outside the home, or assistance to allow access to available educational facilities.

   (iii) Where satisfied that the case applies, the authority must provide facilities for, or assistance in, travelling to and from home for the purpose of participating in any relevant services provided.

   (iv) As far as is practicable and reasonable, access to and within buildings, and in parking facilities and sanitary conveniences, must make provision for the needs of the disabled. In a planning application for a building, whether by new construction or adaptation of existing premises, approval will be subject to the condition that, as far as is practicable and reasonable, provision is made for the disabled. Such provision is to be in accordance with the recommendations of the British Standards Institution Code of Practice CP96 Part 1 (*General Recommendations*), or such subsequent code of practice as the Secretary of State may direct.

   (v) Where public sanitary conveniences are provided, so far as is both practicable and reasonable, the authority must make provision for the needs of disabled persons. Whereabouts of such conveniences must be indicated.

   (vi) A building intended for the purposes of education must, as far as is both practicable and reasonable, in the means of access both to and within the building, and in parking and sanitary facilities, make provision for the needs of disabled persons using the building.

   (vii) Every local education authority must, when required, provide the Secretary of State with information on its provision of special educational facilities for children suffering the dual handicap of blindness and deafness, or acute dyslexia, autism or other forms of early childhood psychosis. So far as is practicable, such provision shall be in any school maintained or assisted by the authority.

2. A Private Members' Bill to amend the Act, giving a person legal redress by personal application to a county court where an authority had not made statutory arrangements within a reasonable time, was about to proceed to the committee stage when it was lost because of the dissolution of Parliament in April 1979. Such a Bill was thought necessary because the present duties are not backed by penalties. However, there are no special resources available to pay for the building work; and it has been said that

provision for the handicapped can be costly to an authority where it provides special facilities in a college for a certain type of handicap which may not be used again until another person with a similar handicap is enrolled. In this latter case, a co-ordination of resources and provision within (and across) authorities is clearly necessary.

3. **The Warnock Report**

This report contains recommendations which have wide implications for colleges. Fundamental to Warnock's thinking is the belief that education is the right of all, and that even where a person suffers severe handicap then, for many reasons, and ultimately for no other reason than humanity, that person ought to be entitled to educational provision. The principle of integration of the handicapped in education also underlies the report. While this is not the place to summarise the Warnock Report, it will be helpful to itemise some of its recommendations relevant to further and higher education:

(i) The "designated person". Every institution of further education should designate a member of staff as responsible for the welfare of students with special needs in the college and for briefing other members of staff. Warnock advocates a "named person" to whom an individual might turn to for help and advice, the concept applying from birth and through education. In post-school education, this person for Warnock's purposes is the careers officer.

(ii) The report recommends the necessity of skilled careers advice, particularly for those who are handicapped, and the need for early assessment. Effective counselling is also advocated.

(iii) Every institution of further and higher education should formulate and publicise a policy on the admission of and provision for handicapped students.

(iv) A range of link and other courses which colleges might offer is recommended. Similarly, emphasis is placed on the links between education and training for handicapped people and their employment prospects.

(v) It is emphasised that progress will occur by the devoted attention of teaching staff in developing or adapting appropriate courses. Further ancillary staff are recommended to assist this process.

(vi) There should be a number of additional facilities such as accommodation and the provision of special units.

(vii) All initial teacher training should include a special educational element, and there should be extensive provision of in-service training. The report also sets out ways in which people with disabilities can take advantage of increased opportunities to become teachers.

(viii) The report emphasises the need for research to be undertaken.

(ix) Warnock stated that post-sixteen education and training, and the development of teacher education and training, were areas which should receive high priority for action.

---

1 *Special Educational Needs: Report of the Committee of Enquiry into the Education of Handicapped Children and Young People*, Cmnd. 7212, HMSO, 1978. See also Section **10.2.**95; 99-103.

4. It has been established that provision for handicapped students is subject to considerable variation,[2] and that a low percentage of those considered likely to benefit from further education actually receive it.[3] There are few readily accessible collations of information on provision for the handicapped. However, the East Midlands RAC has issued a guide to provision within its area,[4] which demonstrates the need for such information. The work and function of the National Bureau for Handicapped Students is referred to under paragraph 22 below.

5. It is not known how many handicapped students there are in Britain. A survey[5] has shown that handicapped university students often tried to conceal their disability in applying to an institution on the assumption that it might jeopardise chances of admission; that handicapped students were highly motivated; that once an institution had accepted a handicapped student it was found that anxieties about catering for others lessened; and much can be done without large scale and expensive renovation of buildings. Some universities, and also colleges,[6] remain firm in their refusal of entry to the handicapped. Many public sector institutions have now made statements of intent concerning the handicapped (for example, "It then follows that once an individual student has been accepted as a *bona fide* student, the Polytechnic accepts the obligation to ensure by all means available that the student can further his/her education within the Polytechnic to a level commensurate with his/her ability": North East London Polytechnic, 1971). Many institutions also issue handbooks or specific information (for example, Bradford College, and Huddersfield Technical College). However, in order to provide a form of guidance on how provision for the handicapped might be made, the model below is offered for discussion:

6. **Discussion model provisions for the handicapped**

These model provisions are drawn from policies operated by some institutions. Wherever possible provisions are given in summary form.

(i) *Statement of Intent*

Such a statement concerning the admission of handicapped applicants to be inserted in the prospectus and handbook, and a shortened version to appear in all course literature.

(ii) *Admissions*

(a) Although buildings may not be fully suited to persons with

---

2 Paul Bennett. "Patchy Provision for Handicapped Students", *NATFHE Journal*, Vol.3, No.7, October 1978, p.4. See also Appendix 1, below.

3 G.D.C. Tudor, "Further Education for the Handicapped School Leaver", *Educare*, Vol.1, No.4, pp.9-10.

4 *Further Education for Handicapped People 1978-9*, Regional Advisory Council for the Organisation of Further Education in the East Midlands. Copies are available from the Secretary, East Midlands RAC, Robins Wood House, Robins Wood Road, Apsley, Nottingham, NG8 3NH.

5 Alex Gunn, *Physically Handicapped Students in Universities*, Upjohn Travelling Fellowship Report to the Royal College of General Practitioners, 1975.

6 See Appendix 1.

particular handicaps, no such person will be rejected without being given an opportunity to discuss with the relevant authorities how difficulties may be overcome.

(b) Applicants stating their disability in their initial enquiry or application shall receive from the admissions officer an individual letter of acknowledgement stressing that college staff will assist in every way possible. Applicants to be informed that they will have to visit the college for an interview. Where a written enquiry has been made, the admissions officer is to send copies of the letter and reply to the co-ordinator for handicapped students, where such exists (see sub-paragraph iv, below), and the appropriate admissions tutor.

(c) When an application is made, the admissions officer shall send a copy together with appropriate information to the co-ordinator for handicapped students.

(d) On the day of the academic interview, arrangements will be made for the applicant to tour the site and to discuss environmental, medical and social difficulties which may have to be resolved. The applicant will also meet the co-ordinator, the student adviser and, if justified by the level or nature of the handicap, other members of staff responsible for student services.

(e) If the applicant is to live away from home, arrangements must be made with the accommodation officer to ensure that suitable accommodation can be made available.

(f) The decision to accept a handicapped applicant remains with the appropriate department, as far as academic criteria are concerned, but all members of staff who have seen the applicant should meet and discuss the case before a final offer of a place is made. In the event of a disagreement, the case should be referred to the principal, vice-principal or other person with designated responsibility, for further discussion with the interested parties, including the applicant.

(iii) *Premises*

(see also Sections **5** and **11.10**)

Evaluation of access and internal movement for the handicapped should be carried out. Major improvements will require budgetary provision over several years. Lifts will be a major item of expenditure. Paternoster lifts are not regarded as suitable for use by handicapped people. Regard will have to be paid to both fire regulations and safety provisions where premises are to be adapted. There are no grants available for modifications to buildings to make them accessible to students. Funds must be obtained from the normal source, although finance for modifications has been raised by voluntary committees, and obtained in some cases from trusts. Grants have been provided by local authorities, especially for adaptations and the installation of lifts. The following initial improvements will not require great expenditure:

(a) construction of ramps;

(b) provision of handrails where necessary for safety;

(c) adaptation of a number of lavatories to allow access by wheel chairs and provision of other necessary facilities;

(d) provision of suitable emergency call systems in lavatories or where there are particularly difficult access points;
(e) alteration of lift buttons to allow lifts to be operated from wheel chairs;
(f) provision of clearly marked car parking spaces for use by handicapped persons only; and
(g) issuing to all handicapped students, and those staff with responsibility for them, special emergency instructions.

(iv) *Student Services*
(see also Section **12.8-10**)

(a) A member of staff to be designated or appointed as co-ordinator for handicapped students. Such an appointment should carry remission time, or be a specific appointment stating the proportion of time to be allotted to co-ordination, according to the size of the institution. Responsibilities of the co-ordinator to be:

maintenance of personal contact with all handicapped students in the institution, and to monitor their progress;

to advise on preliminary enquiries made to the institution by handicapped people and liaise with all persons concerned in the admission of students;

to liaise with academic staff, particularly admission tutors, course leaders and placement staff, concerning special equipment which might be required by handicapped students in their academic studies together with other matters, such as examination arrangements, which may require variations in the students' academic courses;

to liaise with relevant staff concerning other appropriate arrangements which might assist handicapped students, including planning;

to have responsibility for publications dealing with the handicapped; and

to liaise with local authority departments, public bodies such as the DHSS, and voluntary organizations.

In brief, the co-ordinator would be fulfilling the role of the "designated person" advocated by Warnock. It would be necessary to specify the roles of the co-ordinator and, where there is provision, the student adviser or counsellor.

(b) Medical services. Although there may be student reluctance in some cases, it remains advisable that handicapped students should have contact with the student medical officer or health centre.

(c) Careers advice services should take early recognition of handicapped students. Their need for careers advice will often be greater, and career preparation should be undertaken early. In some cases it will be necessary to prepare handicapped students for unemployment. Similarly, early contact where courses involve placements with employers is necessary.

(d) Accommodation services will require early advice of the needs of handicapped students;

(e) It will be necessary to arrange special facilities for physical education and recreation; and

(f) In matters concerning grants and fees, the relevant administrative officers will need to be able to extend specialist advice to the handicapped.

(g) Detailed information on all the college's support services should be readily available to handicapped students, and to all academic and non-academic staff who may have a role in advising and helping them during their courses.

(v) *Academic Arrangements*

(a) to deal successfully with examination and assessment problems of handicapped students it will be essential for staff to identify the likely difficulties well in advance; and any special provision (such as the use of amanuenses, separate rooms, examination in the home or specialist centre, use of special equipment, extra time, briefing or invigilators, consultation with examining boards) should be similarly subject to early arrangements;

(b) to allow them to be of effective assistance, personal tutors should receive advance information of any handicaps which their students may have;

(c) it will be necessary to maintain a list of equipment for use by handicapped students, and to budget for the provision of special learning aids;

(d) it is vital that good study facilities be provided, especially in the library, be subject to regular review; and

(e) it will be necessary for staff to examine the ways in which courses are presented in order to determine whether changes could improve conditions for handicapped students without harming the requirements of other students.

7. This model scheme has been drawn from the provisions made by or recommended in two institutions. Obviously, any course adopted will depend on the size and purpose of the college in question. As well as having regard to Warnock, however, colleges ought to consider the statement of a Minister for the Disabled that there should be in educational planning and provision a measure of positive discrimination in favour of handicapped students.

8. **Libraries**

It will be essential to ensure that the library and its access is adapted. Guides on the designing of premises for wheelchairs are issued by the Centre on Environment for the Handicapped and the Royal Association for Disability and Rehabilitation, among others. College libraries will also need to give attention to the following:

(i) A clear uncluttered layout of items such as shelves, tables, carrels and study facilities will be of great assistance to the visually handicapped.

(ii) Regulations which bar dogs from a library should be formally relaxed in respect of guide dogs, and it be recognised that blind or partially sighted students will need fullest access to all parts of the library and its services.

(iii) It will be necessary to provide sound-proof carrels with power points, tapes, playback and recording equipment, typing facilities, reading aloud services for books and journals, and large print material. Provision of talking calculators and other study aids should be considered. Persons confined to a wheelchair will require assistance to obtain books from high shelves, or else the use of a clench. Those with residual sight will benefit from systems which greatly enlarge print or transfer it to a screen.

(iv) Access and facilities notices for handicapped students should be displayed prominently inside the library, in common rooms and at other focal points in the institution. Guiding on shelves should be adequate and legible. Because of their handicaps, it is possible that some students may have little experience of libraries; full instructions on the library and its methods will, therefore, be necessary.

(v) Borrowing arrangements will need to be reviewed, especially in the cases of the visually handicapped (where, for example, a reader will require time to transfer the material to tape) and for those for whom it is difficult frequently to visit the library. Such concessions could also be accompanied by provision of free or reduced cost photocopying.

9. **The visually handicapped**

The Royal National Institute for the Blind will give guidance to any college which has not previously considered an application from a visually handicapped student. As well as noting the advice given above, colleges may wish to give attention to the following further information:

10. Where accommodation is provided, a visually handicapped person using braille will require strong shelving, spaced at least 1'6" (0.46m) apart, since braille volumes are large and heavy. Working space large enough to accommodate a Perkins Brailler, typewriter, tape recorder and Talking Book machine will be necessary, as will a number of power points.

11. Tactile maps of the college site can be made on request to the RNIB. It will be helpful to a visually handicapped student if he or she is allowed to spend some time at the college before the start of the first term in order to acquire familiarity with the premises. As most students will have been educated as visually handicapped, they will have become accustomed to negotiating even old and awkward buildings. Once familiar with basic location of amenities and their routes, they are likely with the aid of a cane, dog or human escort to be able to travel freely. It will be helpful if unexpected obstacles are not left in corridors, or doors half open.

12. While there are many academic texts available in braille and on tape, as they represent only a small proportion of such texts, the RNIB libraries request that students should be able to give sufficient advance notification of required books. As soon as a student is offered a place, the RNIB libraries should be sent a list of recommended books with essential texts marked accordingly. (It can take up to three months to tape a book, and longer to braille). As it is unlikely that the RNIB libraries will be able to supply all a student's needs, there will be recourse to reading assistance, either in the

form of readers, or tape recordings. Fellow students may volunteer to read, and a rota system can minimize the time commitment of individuals. College reader services can be supplemented by arrangements made with local authorities and community groups. The RNIB initial grant is intended to meet the cost of equipment and services.

13. It will assist visually handicapped students if they are allowed by lecturers to make notes on a small braille machine or use a cassette tape recorder. Lecturers should give verbal descriptions of visual material, and distribute printed lecture notes and handouts in advance so that they can be transcribed into braille or large print. Visual diagrams can be rendered into tactile diagrams by use of three methods: Melinex paper sleeves, drawing with a ball point pen on aluminium sleeves and the use of a multi-headed embossing tool.[7] The first method is probably the simplest.

14. The printed question papers for public examinations can be transcribed by the RNIB Students' Library. The normal procedure is for the college or department concerned to inform the examining body that the candidate is blind and wishes the question papers to be in braille. It is then essential that the examining body sends the question papers as soon as possible to the RNIB. The majority of students type internal examinations, but for external examinations many students prefer to dictate to an amanuensis (because of concern over the speed and accuracy of the typing). It is necessary for the student to take the examination in a separate room and, where not dictating to an amanuensis, it helps if an invigilator is immediately available to read back what has been typed and, if required, to check or read the printed examination papers. There are precedents for granting additional time allowances to visually handicapped students. An allowance of either an additional half hour, or a quarter of an hour per hour on a three hour paper, is usually considered adequate for a straightforward arts paper. Up to half an hour per hour has been allowed where translation or textual criticism of a prose passage has been involved. For mathematics, science, geography and music, additions of up to 50% can also be justified because of the special communications problems. Where such time allowances are granted, the paper may last up to four and a half hours. It is usual here for a student to be given a supervised break of a quarter or half hour.

15. **The deaf and hearing impaired**

A list of examination arrangements made by various examining bodies for the pre-lingually hearing impaired has been compiled by the National Study Group on Further and Higher Education for the Hearing Impaired, and also a paper, *The Language of Examinations*, which contains suggestions for the modification of the language of examination papers to be taken by hearing impaired candidates. The Group has compiled a directory of courses followed by the hearing impaired. Information on special provision and courses for the deaf offered by colleges of further education is contained in *Educare*. Vol.1, No.3, April 1977, pp 9-13.

---

7 All these items are available from the RNIB Sales Department.

16. Cassette tape recorders and radio microphone hearing aids can be important aids for the hearing impaired. Particular provision will depend upon the student and the severity of the handicap.

17. **The physically handicapped**
Again, provision will be dependent on the nature and severity of the handicap. Tape recorders and typewriters can be essential aids. Special arrangements for matters such as examinations and library use will need to be made in accordance with the recommendations made above. Where students suffer from severe handicaps, it is important to consider provision of "bridging" facilities. The Warnock Committee commented on the high proportion of physically handicapped students from the specialist Hereward College who were able to progress to further and higher education, and while such bridging may occur in specialist regional units, colleges and authorities ought to consider the contributions which they can make.

18. **The mentally handicapped**
The majority of school children ascertained as handicapped are those described as educationally sub-normal (ESN), maladjusted, or "delicate". These conditions can often involve mental as well as physical difficulties. Statutory special school provision is made for the ESN, but after the age of 16 a variety of practices apply. Between 50% and 60% of mentally handicapped adults (both in the community and in hospital) are not receiving education, training or occupational therapy.[8] A certain provision is made for the mentally handicapped in adult training centres and in hospitals. Some further education institutions have links with these establishments, but it is worth quoting Warnock's recommendation "that there should be a specifically educational element in every adult training centre and day centre and that the education service should be responsible for its provision."[9] It is NATFHE's belief that in many areas clients at adult training and day centres should be able to use further education facilities. Some colleges have experience in making provision for the mentally handicapped.

19. In its response to the Warnock Report,[10] NATFHE stated its belief that there was a need to develop courses in further education (ie, separate from the adult training centres and within the education system) which would parallel, but not be identical to, the secondary phase of school education. Already this occurs for those whose handicap is mild (ESN(M)), and it is NATFHE's belief that similar success could be attained with those whose handicap is severe (ESN(S)), the courses extending for students from the age of 16 until the early twenties. At that age, the student could then enter an adult training centre to receive adult education to meet individual needs. Such a provision would increase the possibility of the severely handicapped reaching their full potential.

---

8 Eileen Baranyay, *A Lifetime of Learning*, National Society for Mentally Handicapped Children, 1976, p.13.

9 *Special Educational Needs*, *op.cit*, para. 10.53.

10 *Special Educational Needs*, NATFHE, 1979, para. 3.17 *et seq*.

20. It has been established that although there is a tendency to dispense with categorisation of mental handicaps into ESN (M) and ESN (S) wherever practicable, it appears that actual provision of further education and leisure activities are less extensive within the community than within hospitals and privately operated enterprises.[11] Warnock recommended that LEAs accept the responsibility for providing continuing education for those who require hospital care. The further education service in this event has a contribution to make in distance learning; and where students, more commonly, are required (often because of physical handicap) only to spend short-term periods in hospital then, as occurs in some instances at present, colleges have to arrange both visits and close liaison with the hospital.

21. Where students suffer handicaps so severe that their education has to occur in hospitals and/or special units, it is important that courses are appropriate, and that the intellectually more able receive education suited to their needs. This observation applies wherever the severely handicapped are taught: special needs must be met, and *ad hoc* courses will only be satisfactory if colleges can supply adequate care and access. In making any provision for those suffering mental handicap, it is essential to appreciate that objectives should be "drawn from the real needs of the mentally handicapped and not from erroneous views of them as overgrown children."[12]

22. **The National Bureau for Handicapped Students**

Students and colleges will find the services of this bureau invaluable. It acts as an information centre, co-ordinates where necessary the work of organizations and institutions, offers or arranges specialist advice, promotes the extension of careers guidance and placement, and initiates study and research in education and employment. One of its prime functions is to inform handicapped school leavers of opportunities offered by colleges. The NBHS provides a variety of services, including information, advice, publications, and consultation with Government and other departments, institutions and organizations. These services are available to teaching and other professional staff and employers as well as to handicapped students. There are three kinds of NBHS membership: institutional, individual and student. The Bureau publishes a newsletter, *Educare.*

23. **Financial assistance for disabled students**

A special allowance may be claimed by disabled students in receipt of a mandatory award, in addition to their normal grant. This allowance may be claimed where additional expenditure is incurred as a result of the student's presence on the course. It is the decision of the local authority as to whether the particular expenditure is necessarily incurred. Authorities have reimbursed expenditure incurred in the provision of such items as typewriters, physical aids, and assistance with readers and other paid helpers. These allowances may also be applied for by students in receipt of discretionary awards: the authority, however, is not obliged to make any payment in this circumstance.

---

11 Baranyay, *op.cit,* pp.68-69.

12 Statement at the 1973 Conference "Education for Mentally Handicapped Adults", Newton Le Willows, quoted *ibid,* p.67.

24. Although the operation of the Manpower Services Commission is investigated under Section **4**, it will be useful here to indicate arrangements of special relevance to disabled persons. Eligibility conditions for courses operated by the Training Services Division may be relaxed for handicapped people. For example, a disabled person can be accepted for training even though under 19 years of age (but 16 or over), and may be given a second course in less than five years. A disabled person may be accepted for part-time training or for training by means of a correspondence course in schemes operated under TOPS and its allied arrangements. Such courses may involve training of longer than a year. The Professional Training Scheme provides financial assistance, subject to an income test, for disabled people who wish to train for a professional career but who are unable to obtain a normal educational grant. Graduates may be eligible for postgraduate courses but in most instances must be over 27. All courses taken under TOPS are free, and trainees receive a weekly tax free allowance. This allowance may include an earnings related supplement and benefits such as travelling expenses, lunch, free credit of National Insurance contributions and an accommodation allowance for those who have to stay away from home. Further information on the operation of TOPS for disabled people may be found in the leaflets, *Training opportunities for disabled people*. TSA L15 and *Training opportunities for young disabled people*, TSA L84. Details of financial assistance are contained in leaflet TSA L65. These leaflets are available from local employment offices. Full details of TOPS for handicapped people may be obtained from Disablement Resettlement Officers who can be contacted through any Job Centre, Employment Office, or TSD District Office.

25. Details of benefits and allowances provided by the Department of Health and Social Security are to be found in the leaflet *Help for Handicapped People*, HB1. Supplementary benefits legislation is more generous in its treatment of disabled students than of others undertaking educational courses. These benefits are summarised below:

26. *Students on advanced courses*
Students who are severely handicapped or registered as disabled, and whose prospects of employment are such that they would be unlikely to obtain a job if they were not in further education, could claim supplementary benefit during term time if they have been refused a grant from their local authority. Disabled students applying for supplementary benefit during term time will probably be required at regular intervals to produce medical certificates.

27. Disabled students in receipt of grants which are means tested and whose parents are either unwilling or unable to meet the parental contributions in full can claim the difference between supplementary benefit level plus (£2) per week and the amount of grant actually received each week.

28. The rates of supplementary benefit are regularly revised. Disabled students may be entitled to "exceptional circumstance additions" for items such as extra heating costs, special diets and high laundry bills. There are higher weekly scale rates for blind persons.

29. *Students on non-advanced courses*
Although students following educational courses of a kind given in schools are normally excluded from claiming supplementary benefit, exceptions are made in the cases of students who are so severely disabled as to be unlikely to be able to work to support themselves. These students can claim supplementary benefit from their 16th birthday.

30. Unemployed young persons may claim benefit under certain circumstances if they are undertaking part-time further education (see Section **12.5.**17). Such students are subject to certain requirements, but it is likely that disabled students would be treated more sympathetically.

31. *Vacations*
Students are not normally allowed to claim supplementary benefit during the Christmas and Easter vacations, even if their parents are not paying the assessed parental contribution in full. Where disabled students are by reason of a disability, in comparison to other students, unlikely to obtain employment within a reasonable time, this condition does not apply. Such students therefore, ought to receive benefit which ignores the vacation element of the mandatory grant, all or any additional grant from the local authority to cover extra expenses because of a disability; and makes good any shortfall in the full grant because the student's parents do not pay their assessed contribution in full.

32. *Attendance allowance*
Physically handicapped persons who need considerable care or frequent attention for at least six months are entitled to a tax free allowance. If this care and assistance is provided by the college, and the student is in receipt of the allowance, the college may claim it from the student to defray expenses. The student may use the allowance to pay for such services or private attendance which may be required. There are two rates of allowance; the higher is for day and night attention, and the lower for day or night attention. Fuller details are available in Leaflet N1 205.

33. *Mobility allowance*
Where a person is unable, or virtually unable, to walk because of a disability which is likely to last longer than a year, application may be made for the mobility allowance. This flat rate benefit is taxable. Further details are available in leaflet N1 211.

34. *Invalid care allowance*
This allowance is payable to a man or single woman who gives up work in order to care for a severely disabled person. The test of qualification is that the disabled person is in receipt of the attendance allowance. The claimants must fulfil certain conditions. Further details are available in leaflet N2 212.

35. *Non-contributory invalidity pension*
This is mainly applicable to only the more severely disabled student apparently medically unfit for any but academic work. It is primarily for people of working age who have not been able to work for some time and

who do not qualify for sickness or invalidity benefit because they do not have sufficient national insurance contributions. If the recipient is in full time education, he or she must be at least 19. The pension is tax free and is not subject to a means test. Details are available from leaflet N1 210.

36. *Voluntary organizations*

The Royal National Institute for the Blind makes a grant of up to £250 for the whole course available for students entering full-time further education or studying for Open University degrees. The grant is given for expenditure related to study, such as the purchase of equipment or payment of readers. In certain circumstances the grant may be extended. Further details are available from the RNIB.

37. Some national voluntary organizations may be able to offer assistance in special cases of hardship. The directory *Educational Charities*, published by the NUS, gives information on trust funds which makes grants and loans to students. Local authorities have information concerning local trusts; colleges and student unions themselves may make grants.

APPENDIX 1

EXISTING COLLEGE PROVISION FOR THE HANDICAPPED

1. An unpublished survey[1] reveals that of the 182 institutions supplying information: 54% made special provision for handicapped students; another 11% make provision on an individual basis; and a further 9% admit students able to cope with existing facilities. 9% demonstrated that the nature of their courses made admissions impracticable. 21% stated that the handicapped were not admitted because there were no facilities for them.

2. Of the colleges which do make provision, most provide ramps, many provide lifts and suitable lavatories, and a few provide handrails. Only a very small number of colleges provide special academic facilities, and only a few make full physical provision. Many institutions at the time of the survey, however, were planning on undertaking conversion, although funding remained a difficulty.

3. Where special courses for the handicapped are provided, they tend to be: handicraft-based, guidance, or designed to help fit the student into society. Other colleges accepting the handicapped tend not to operate special courses but to integrate the students into normal classes.

4. It appears that handicapped persons applying for admission generally receive guidance and practical advice, but thereafter advice seems to be given individually when needed. In many cases, the final decision concerning the suitability of facilities is left to the student.

5. Transport is usually provided by the DHSS and LEA, supplemented sometimes by the college and by voluntary organizations. Some colleges offer no help at all, expecting students to make their own arrangements. (This practice should not be seen as being necessarily harsh: it can be argued in some cases that for the student to develop and fit into society, it is necessary to encourage independence of action where possible).[2]

6. A few colleges appear to operate a quota system whereby only a certain percentage of handicapped students are admitted.

---

1 *Provision for Handicapped Students in Colleges.* Analysis of positive responses to a survey of NATFHE branches, March-May 1978, document nos, 1685-78/1686-78.
2 cf Julia Carter, "Taking the next step", *Guardian*, 11 September 1979.

APPENDIX 2

SOURCES OF FURTHER INFORMATION AND ASSISTANCE

Association of Blind and Partially Sighted Teachers and Students, Secretary; Mr T. Moody, Dept. of Political Economy, University of Glasgow, Glasgow G12 8RT.

Association of Disabled Professionals, The Stables, 73 Pound Road, Banstead, Surrey or c/o REHAB, Tavistock House (South), Tavistock Square, London WC1H 9LB.

Centre on Environment for the Handicapped, 126 Albert Street, London NW1 7NE 01-267 6111.

DIG (Disablement Income Group), Attlee House, Toynbee Hall, 28 Commercial Street, London E1 6LR 01-247 2128.

Disability Alliance, 96 Portland Place, London W1N 4EX.

Disabled Drivers Association, Ashwelthorpe, Norwich NOR 89W.

Disabled Living Foundation, 364 Kensington High Street, London W14 8NS 01-602 2491.

Greater London Association for the Disabled, 1 Thorpe Close, London W10 5XL 01-960 5799.

National Association for the Education of the Partially Sighted, Hon. Sec: Mr R.J. Crosbie, Joseph Clarke School, Vincent Road, Highams Park, London E4 9PP.

National Bureau for Handicapped Students, c/o Middlesex Polytechnic, All Saints Site, White Hart Lane, London N17 8HR. 01-801 8549.

National Deaf Children's Society, 31 Gloucester Place, London W1H 4EA. 01-486 3251/2.

National Library for the Blind, 35 Great Smith Street, London SW1. 01-222 2725.

National Society for Mentally Handicapped Children, Pembridge Hall, 17 Pembridge Square, London W2 4EP. 01-229 8941.

National Study Group on Further and Higher Education for the Hearing Impaired, (examination arrangements and language) Mrs J. Sutton, Shirecliffe College, Standish Road, Sheffield 55 8XZ; (directory of courses) Mrs V. Hunter, North Notts College of Further Education, Carlton Road, Worksop, Nottingham S81 7HP.

(NB: a large stamped addressed envelope is requested when applying for examinations material; the directory costs 15p).

Nuffield Hearing and Speech Centre, Gray's Inn Road, London WC1. 01-837 8855.

Partially Sighted Society, Chairman: Mr G.H. Marshall, Exhall Grange School, Wheelwright Lane, Coventry.

Physically Handicapped Able-Bodied Association, 42 Devonshire Street, London W1N 1LN. 01-580 4053.

Royal Association for Disability and Rehabilitation, 25 Mortimer Street, London W1N 8AB. 01-637 5400.

Royal Association in Aid of the Deaf and Dumb, 7 Armstrong Road, London W3. 01-743 6187.

Royal National Institute for the Blind, 224 Great Portland Street, London W1N 6AA. 01-387 8033.

Royal National Institute for the Deaf, 105 Gower Street, London WC1. 01-387 8033.

Spastics Society, 12 Park Crescent, London W1N 4EQ. 01-636 5020.

Spinal Injuries Association, 126 Albert Street, London NW1 7NF. 01-267 6111.

Students Braille Library/The Students Tape Library, 224 Great Portland Street, London W1N 6AA.

REFERENCE

Chronically Sick and Disabled Persons Act, 1970 (Amended 1976), Chapter 44, HMSO.
Special Educational Needs, Report of the Committee of Enquiry into the Education of Handicapped Children and Young People, Cmnd. 7212, HMSO, 1978.
H.M. Warnock, *Meeting Special Educational Needs*, HMSO, 1978.

Access for the Handicapped Student, Centre on Environment for the Handicapped, 1976.
Access to University and Polytechnic Buildings, Royal Association for Disability and Rehabilitation.
An Educational Policy for Handicapped People, National Bureau for Handicapped Students, 1977.
Eileen Baranyay, *A lifetime of learning*, National Society for Mentally Handicapped Children, 1976.
Directory for the Disabled, Darnborough and Kinrade, 1977.
Disability Rights Handbook, 1978, Disability Alliance.
Educare, National Bureau for Handicapped Students.
Financial Assistance for Disabled Students, National Bureau for Handicapped Students/National Union of Students.
Further Education for Handicapped People 1978-79, Regional Advisory Council for the Organisation of Further Education in the East Midlands.
Selwyn Goldsmith, *Designing for the Disabled*, RIBA.
Handicapped School Leavers, National Children's Bureau Report, NFER, 1973.
Helping Hand, National Extension College, 1979.
P.M. Judd, "The Library and Information Needs of Visually Handicapped Students," *Journal of Librarianship*, 9, (2), April 1977, pp. 96-107.
Barbara MacMorland, *An ABC of Services and General Information for Disabled People*, Disablement Income Group, 1977.
Provision for the Disabled at Universities, University Grants Committee, (14 Park Crescent, London W1N 4DH; free).
The Disabled Student, National Union of Students.
Eda Topliss, *Provision for the Disabled*, Blackwell and Robertson, 1975.
Special Educational Needs, NATFHE, 1979.
University Buildings – Notes on Design Features. Royal Association for Disability and Rehabilitation.

INDEX

Because of space limitations the index is shorter than it might have been. There are no entries under personal names (apart from chairmen of committees) countries, or titles of publications and few entries under institutions of organizations. In addition, subheadings have been used sparingly and some entries under very specific topics have had to be omitted.

"App." indicates Appendix and "n" indicates footnote.

Organizations are normally entered under their full name unless (like NALGO) they are better known by their acronym. Some cross-references from initials have been provided for some organizations; others can be traced in Section **1.4** on pages 49-75.

The index is arranged alphabetically word by word, so that "car parking" precedes "careers". Hyphenated words are treated as one word.

References are to **SECTION NUMBERS**, not page numbers.

NOTES ON CONTRIBUTORS

JOHN C.N. BAILLIE, MA, DipFE, MBIM,

— has twenty years' teaching experience in five London colleges. He is now Principal of Southwark College. He is a further education teacher representative on the Inner London Education Authority; the National Chairman of the Further Education Teachers' Panel; a Council member of the National Bureau for Handicapped Students; and a Governor of the Centre on Educational Disadvantage.

KENNETH G.B. BAKEWELL, MA, FLA, MBIM,

— is a Principal Lecturer in the Department of Library and Information Studies, Liverpool Polytechnic. He is a Registered Indexer of the Society of Indexers and is Vice Chairman of that Society. He has compiled many indexes and written several books and articles on indexing.

PAUL BENNETT, MA,

— has worked in the Research Department of the General and Municipal Workers Union, and since 1972 has served as the Education Officer of the ATTI and subsequently NATFHE. He has written a number of articles on various education topics.

JEAN BOCOCK, BA,

— has lectured in politics and sociology at Kingston Polytechnic, Brunel University and Sheffield University. She joined the the ATTI as a Regional Official in 1974 and since 1976 has held the post of Assistant Secretary, Higher Education, NATFHE.

PETER DAWSON, BSc, DipEd,

— was a teacher for some years. A former vice president of the National Union of Students, he became a field officer of the National Union of Teachers in 1965. He was appointed Assistant Secretary of the ATTI in 1969, and served as the Negotiating Secretary of the ATTI and subsequently NATFHE until 1979 when he became General Secretary of NATFHE.

W.A.G. EASTON, MA, CEng, FIMechE, FRSA,

— has taught in further education for over thirty years. He is now Principal of Southgate College. He is a member of: Convocation of the Schools Council; the London and Home Counties Regional Advisory Council; the FE sub-committee of the Advisory Committee on the Supply and Education of Teachers; joint chairman of the Grading of Courses Sub-Committee of the Burnham FE Committee; and a long standing member of the Burnham FE Committee. He has contributed many articles to education journals, and has addressed many conferences on college management and organization.

D.B. EDWARDS, MSc,

— entered further education in 1946, retired in 1979 from the post of Principal of Rotherham College of Technology and is now a (part-time) professional adviser to the Yorkshire and Humberside Association of Education Authorities. He has served for many years on CGLI Committees, been a member of the National Advisory Committee on Education for Industry and Commerce, the Schools Council and two Industrial Training Boards. He was a member of the Haslegrave and Oakes Committees, and is now a member of the MSC Review Body on the Employment and Training Act 1973.

JEAN FINLAYSON,

— is an American trained journalist who has worked as a reporter and feature writer for newspapers and magazines in the USA and in England. She joined the staff of Coombe Lodge as Publications Editor in December 1977.

LYNTON GRAY, BA, MAEd, MSC, PGCE, AMBIM,

— taught for eight years in schools, was a senior lecturer in geography and subsequently educational technology at a college of education, and is currently Senior Lecturer in Education Management at the Anglian Regional Management Centre, North East London Polytechnic. He has written on the subjects of teaching materials for school teacher education, and management education. He is currently involved in the study of human resource development at a time of contracting career opportunities.

OSWALD DE HAESE, Lic,

— has a degree in Germanic Philology from the University of Ghent, is a licentiaat (qualified teacher), and has studied linguistics and language at universities in Cambridge, Reading, San Francisco, Antwerp and Noordwigkerhout. He is a former Fullbright Scholar. He teaches at the College of Education, Kortrijk, Belgium.

JACK HENDY, LLB, BSc (Econ),

— is a barrister and Member of the Industrial Tribunals (England and Wales). He is recently retired from the post of Principal Lecturer in Law, Ealing College of Higher Education, and is a past chairman of the Association of Law Teachers.

PETER C. KNIGHT, BA, MInstP, FRAS, DPhil,

— is a senior lecturer at Plymouth Polytechnic; he has been a school teacher and a Science Research Council administrator; was a member of the Oakes Committee (which reported in 1978 on the management of higher education in the maintained sector); and is a member of the Burnham FE Committee, the National Joint Council for Youth and Community Workers, and of the Council of Management of the Central Register and Clearing House.

PAULA LANNING, BSc (Econ),

— has been a training officer in an engineering company; has worked in the Research Department of the National Union of Public Employees; and as Research Officer, *Industrial Relations Law Reports*, and *Industrial Relations Review and Report.* She has been the Information Officer of the ATTI and subsequently NATFHE since 1974. She holds a specialist journalism qualification, has written widely on labour law and industrial relations, and has served on the NJC of Working Women's Organizations.

JACK MANSELL, MEd, CEng,

— entered further education in 1954 after experience in industry. He is currently Head of Engineering Technology at Paddington College, and is a member of various national committees, including the CGLI Policy Committee, Electricity Supply ITC and TEC Education Committee. He is a member of: the Further Education Curriculum Review and Development Unit, the Council for Educational Technology, Schools Council and NFER. He has lectured and written frequently on education and training, and carried out both in this country and abroad various curriculum evaluation, team teaching, and other feasibility studies. He chaired the FEU study group which produced *A Basis for Choice*, the Mansell Report.

KEITH SCRIBBINS, BSc (Soc), MA,

— has taught at colleges of further education in London and Worcester, joined the ATTI as a Regional Official in 1973 and was subsequently appointed to his current NATFHE post of Assistant Secretary, Salaries. He has recently concentrated on employment law, equal rights and the problems caused by teacher education reorganization. This latter area has involved him in representing college staff in most of the industrial tribunal cases arising from the Colleges of Education (Compensation) Regulations. He has published a number of articles on this topic, on the position of women in further education, and on employment law.

The Editor

IAN WAITT, BA, Ph.D,

— has taught in schools, been a senior lecturer in history at a college of education, and now lectures in education management at the Anglian Regional Management Centre, North East London Polytechnic. He is a member of the Council of the British and Foreign School Society, and a member of the Council of the National Bureau for Handicapped Students. He is a co-author and editor of an environmental studies book for schools, and has published articles on history, education and employment law.